PLACES
R·A·T·E·D
ALMANAC

PLACES
R·A·T·E·D
ALMANAC

Your Guide to Finding the Best Places to Live in North America

DAVID SAVAGEAU & RICHARD BOYER

Prentice Hall Travel
New York   London   Toronto   Sydney   Tokyo   Singapore

Prentice Hall General Reference
15 Columbus Circle
New York, NY 10023

Library of Congress Cataloging-in-Publication Data

Savageau, David.
    Places rated almanac : your guide to finding the best places to
live in America / David Savageau and Richard Boyer.
      p.   cm.
    Rev. ed. of: Places rated almanac / Richard Boyer & David
Savageau. All new ed. © 1989.
    ISBN 0-671-84947-6
    1. Quality of life—United States—Statistics. 2. Social
indicators—United States. 3. Metropolitan areas—United States—
Statistics. I. Boyer, Rick. II. Boyer, Rick. Places rated
almanac. III. Title.
HN60.S284 1993
307.76'4'0973—dc20   93-12340
                                                      CIP

Manufactured in the United States of America

10 9 8 7 6 5 4 3 2 1

Acknowledgments

This revision of *Places Rated Almanac* could not have been done without the insights and criticisms of hundreds of people in government and in private organizations in the United States and in Canada whom we've come to know over the years. Their affiliations and the data they have generously made available to us are cited throughout this book.

We are indebted, once more, to the people at Prentice Hall General Reference and Travel—particularly Leanne Coupe and Laura Giesman—for their energy and enthusiasm every step of the way.

Thanks also to: Thomas Nast, cartographer; Erin Nicholas Novakowski, Canadian researcher; Quality Education Data, of Denver, CO, for their invaluable private and public school figures; Right Choice, of Derry, NH, for their costs-of-living resources; and Karyl Savageau, American researcher.

Finally, special thanks are due Woods & Poole Economics, Inc., of Washington, DC, for their population, income, and employment forecasts. The use of this information, and the conclusions drawn from it, are solely the responsibility of the authors.

Contents

Introduction

If you could snap your fingers and suddenly find yourself living somewhere else, would you?

Forget for a moment the usual constraints. Family ties, friendships, a job, lack of cash, and a sentimental attachment to familiar turf can certainly jar you out of such fantasies. Let's put the question another way: What if there were a place somewhere in North America that suited you better than the one where you're living now, and you didn't know of it?

From time to time most people tell pollsters they would rather be somewhere else when asked whether they are satisfied with where they live. Most persons indeed change their address 11 times during their lives, but they do it by simply moving from one house to another within the same city. Each year, however, 8 million North Americans move to another state or province. They may count millions of differing reasons among them for relocating a long distance, but they do have one thing in common—the need for information.

Like its 1981, 1985, and 1989 predecessors, this edition of *Places Rated Almanac* is meant for people who are mulling over a relocation as well as for anyone who enjoys finding out about cities and towns and what they have to offer. As an almanac, it provides thousands of facts—found neither in standard guidebooks nor in chamber of commerce blandishments—about all 343 officially defined metropolitan areas where 75 percent of us live.

But *Places Rated Almanac* is more than a collection of interesting, odd, and useful information about metropolitan areas. It also rates and ranks these metro areas on 10 factors that greatly influence the quality of place: costs of living, job outlook, housing, transportation, education, health care, crime, the arts, recreation, and climate. *Places Rated Almanac* might be considered a self-help book with one difference: Instead of pointing the way toward inner peace or upward mobility as most such books do, it helps you decide whether geographical mobility might be the route to a more satisfying life. Where you live can affect your happiness and personal success; it just may be that your present location doesn't fit your needs and preferences. After all, given the extraordinary variety that North American cities offer, what are the odds that the place where you happen to live is the right one for you?

After using *Places Rated Almanac*, you may very well confirm your hunch that you've never had it so good. On the other hand, you may be in for a surprise. And if you're part of the discontented majority identified by pollsters, you may find yourself asking: What am I waiting for?

RATING PLACES: A CONTINENTAL PASTIME

"The tradition of hating New York started long before it began asking the rest of us to pay its bills while condescendingly viewing us as amusing rustics," Mike Royko wrote in a *Chicago Sun-Times* column a decade ago. "Actually, I like New York," he continued. "There are better reasons to hate cities like Cleveland or Indian-

1

Finding Your Way in the Chapters

Places Rated Almanac contains thousands of useful facts and many descriptive sections. It is organized so that readers can find specific items of interest. Each chapter has five parts:

- The **introductory** section gives basic information on the chapter's topic, interspersed with facts and figures to help you evaluate metro areas.
- **Scoring:** The system used to rate and rank the 343 metro areas for the chapter's topic is fully described, and several metro areas are selected as "scoring examples" to show why one place performs better than another in the ratings.
- **Rankings:** The 343 metro areas are listed in their rank order, from best to worst, along with their score. (Metro areas that are tied get the same rank and are listed in alphabetical order.)
- **Place Profiles:** Arranged alphabetically by metro area, these capsule comparisons cover all the elements used to rate the metro areas. These Place Profiles can be columns of information (like the recreation profiles) or page-wide charts (like the transportation profiles); the climate profiles have their own special format. All are designed to help you see differences among metro areas at a glance.
- **Et Cetera:** This section expands on the quality-of-life features mentioned in the introductory section. It also contains information on other topics ranging all the way from lists of metro-area professional sports championships, high school graduation requirements, and state and provincial holidays, to essays on traffic laws and tax bites.

The final chapter, "Putting It All Together," adds up the rankings to identify America's best all-around metro areas. Here, too, examples of using personal preferences to devise your own scoring system are given.

Postal Abbreviations

Places Rated uses standard U.S. Post Office and Canada Post abbreviations at the end of metro-area names. Here is a guide.

AB	Alberta	NB	New Brunswick
AK	Alaska	NC	North Carolina
AL	Alabama	ND	North Dakota
AR	Arkansas	NE	Nebraska
AZ	Arizona	NF	Newfoundland
BC	British Columbia	NH	New Hampshire
CA	California	NJ	New Jersey
CO	Colorado	NM	New Mexico
CT	Connecticut	NS	Nova Scotia
DC	District of Columbia	NV	Nevada
DE	Delaware	NY	New York
FL	Florida	OH	Ohio
GA	Georgia	OK	Oklahoma
HI	Hawaii	ON	Ontario
IA	Iowa	OR	Oregon
ID	Idaho	PA	Pennsylvania
IL	Illinois	PQ	Quebec
IN	Indiana	RI	Rhode Island
KS	Kansas	SC	South Carolina
KY	Kentucky	SD	South Dakota
LA	Louisiana	SK	Saskatchewan
MA	Massachusetts	TN	Tennessee
MB	Manitoba	TX	Texas
MD	Maryland	UT	Utah
ME	Maine	VA	Virginia
MI	Michigan	VT	Vermont
MN	Minnesota	WA	Washington
MO	Missouri	WI	Wisconsin
MS	Mississippi	WV	West Virginia
MT	Montana	WY	Wyoming

apolis or Detroit or Dallas. But I do dislike New Yorkers."

It may seem the utmost of brass, this business of judging places. Yet everyone does it, privately. Some suspect that culture in Omaha or Des Moines or Saskatoon is a contradiction. Others surmise that daily life in Miami consists of surviving drug-trade shoot-outs, that cold and windy Winnipeg is no place for the seasonally depressed, and that residents of Los Angeles spend most of their waking hours behind a steering wheel waiting for the Big One.

Judging places from best to worst with numbers may seem the highest effrontery of all. Ultimately, how can intangible things like friendliness and optimism be measured with statistics? Yet numeracy is almost as strong a North American character trait as literacy.

When it comes to choosing where to live, people have been digesting statistics for a long, long time.

To sell colonists on settling in Maryland, seventeenth-century promoters put together figures showing heavier livestock, more plentiful game, and lower mortality from foul air and Indian attacks than in neighboring Virginia.

California for Health, Wealth, and Residence, just one volume in a library of post–Civil War guides touting the West's superior quality of life, compiled data to show the climate along the southern Pacific coast to be the world's best. Not so, countered the Union Pacific Railroad's land office in 1871; settlers will find the most "genial and healthy" seasons in western Kansas.

In this century, the statistical nets were flung even wider. "There are plenty of Americans who regard Kansas as almost barbaric," noted H. L. Mencken in 1931, "just as there are other Americans who shudder whenever they think of Arkansas, Ohio, Indiana, Oklahoma, Texas, or California." Mencken wrote these words in his *American Mercury* magazine to introduce his formula for statistically measuring the progress of civilization in each of the states. He mixed the numbers of Boy Scouts and *Atlantic Monthly* subscribers with lynchings and pellagra cases, added a dash of *Who's Who* listings along with rates for divorce and murder, threw

Population Growth

Fastest Growing	Population Growth 1986-1993
Punta Gorda, FL	57.0%
Las Vegas, NV–AZ	48.6
Riverside-San Bernardino, CA	44.6
Yuma, AZ	42.9
Naples, FL	42.4
Fort Pierce–Port St. Lucie, FL	37.1
Fort Myers–Cape Coral, FL	36.6
Orlando, FL	34.7
Modesto, CA	31.6
West Palm Beach–Boca Raton, FL	28.9

No Growth	Population Loss 1986-1993
Casper, WY	−12.8%
Wheeling, WV–OH	−10.4
Enid, OK	−10.3
Steubenville–Weirton, OH–WV	−9.0
Lawton, OK	−8.2
Decatur, IL	−7.6
Shreveport–Bossier City, LA	−7.6
New Orleans, LA	−6.1
Anniston, AL	−6.1
Charleston, WV	−5.8

Source: Woods & Poole Economics, Inc., population forecasts.

Population Size

Smallest	1993 Population
Enid, OK	56,391
Casper, WY	61,817
Cheyenne, WY	73,569
Great Falls, MT	77,175
Victoria, TX	79,878
Rapid City, SD	82,818
Bismarck, ND	85,227
Pine Bluff, AR	85,436
Lawrence, KS	85,486
Dubuque, IA	86,734

Largest	1993 Population
Los Angeles–Long Beach, CA	9,046,571
New York, NY	8,607,521
Chicago, IL	6,985,302
Philadelphia, PA–NJ	4,978,037
Washington, DC–MD–VA–WV	4,466,545
Detroit, MI	4,292,807
Toronto, ON	4,077,472
Boston, MA	3,805,910
Houston, TX	3,566,711
Montreal, PQ	3,209,596

Source: Woods & Poole Economics, Inc., population forecasts.

in figures for rainfall and gasoline consumption, and found that, hands down, Mississippi was the worst American state.

METROPOLITAN AREAS

Places Rated Almanac, we believe, is more useful than any system that considers only states or provinces because broad-brush averages hide local realities. For persons who can live anywhere they wish, there may be more differences between the Texas metro areas of Houston and Amarillo than there are between the Lone Star State and Alberta, Canada.

Places Rated Almanac focuses on metropolitan areas, the smallest units of urban geography for which there is the largest amount of comparable data. From Abilene to Yuma; from huge Los Angeles–Long Beach (pop. 9,046,571) to tiny Enid (pop. 56,391); from foggy St. John's, NF, to sunny San Diego, CA, these 343 metro areas cover a lot of ground, indeed.

Here you'll find agricultural centers and fashion markets, college towns and mill towns and cow towns, bedroom communities, financial centers, resorts and retirement colonies, and cultural havens right next to ports of entry and industrial giants.

For more than 50 years, metropolitan areas have been defined by detailed government standards. Broadly speaking, an area qualifies as "metropolitan" by the following rules:

United States—any city with a population of at least 50,000, or an urbanized area (embracing one or more towns) of at least 50,000, located in a county or counties with a total population of at least 100,000 (75,000 in New England).

Canada—an urban area of at least 100,000 people located in the midst of surrounding urban and rural areas that have strong economic and social ties with the urban area as determined by the number of people commuting there to work.

In either case, the metro area's boundaries coincide with those of the surrounding county or counties (in Canada and in New England, metro areas are defined by towns and cities).

Most are within single states and provinces; 33 of them, however, cross state lines. Washington includes not just the District of Columbia, but 5 counties in Maryland, 11 counties and 7 independent cities in Virginia, and 2 counties in West Virginia. Memphis takes in 3 counties in Tennessee, another across the river in Arkansas, and another in Mississippi. Ottawa-Hull, the only Canadian metro area in more than one province, embraces cities and *villes* in Ontario and Quebec.

There are ample reasons for focusing on metro areas rather than on cities, counties, or states. Thanks to the four-lane highway, cities, counties, and states are less relevant to our daily personal geography. Commonly, we live in one community, commute to work in another, eat at the restaurants, shop at the stores, and take advantage of the recreation assets of all the towns around. We pay taxes or fees to water, sewer, park, and school districts that often cross city lines. And every so often we keep or throw out of office our local representa-

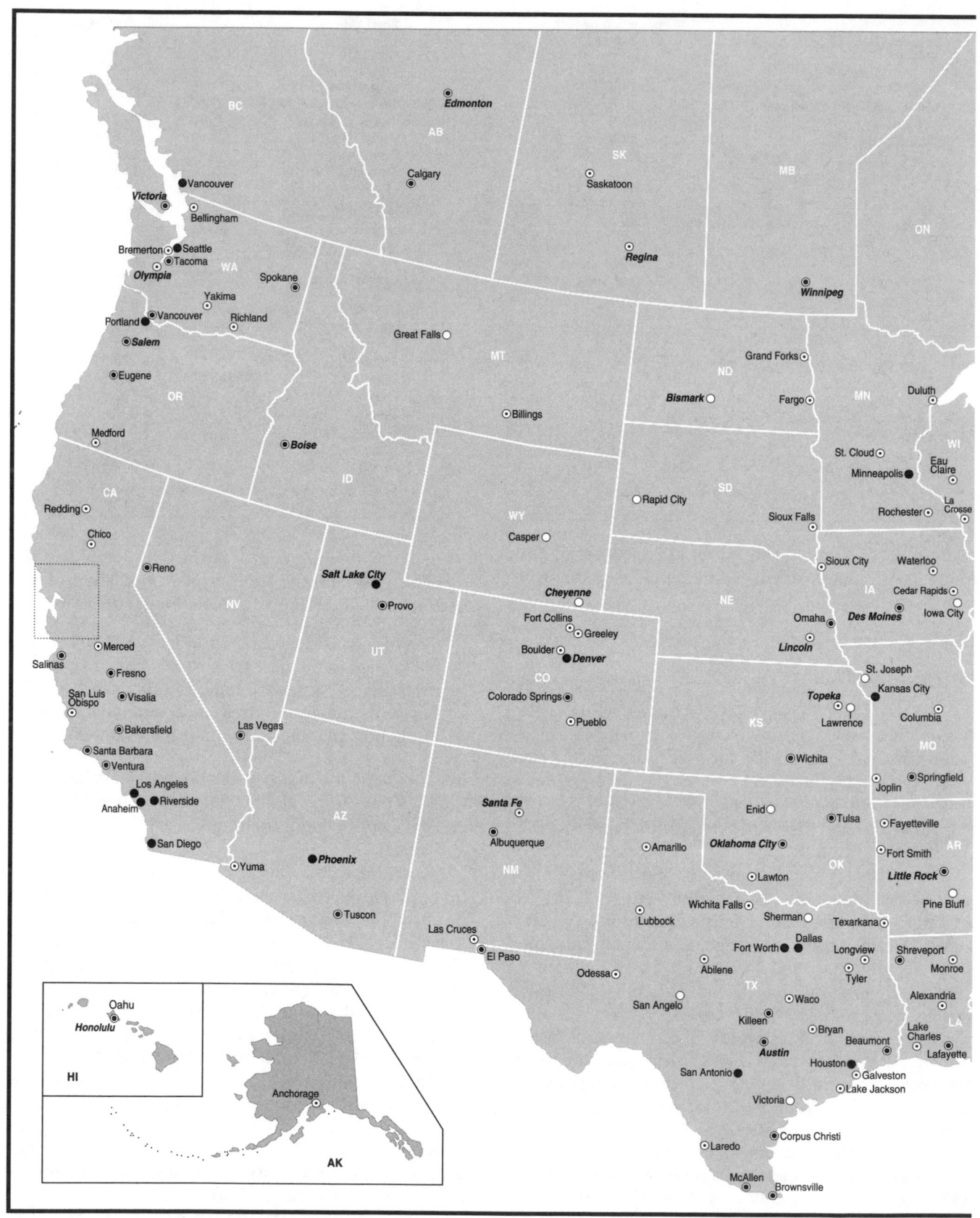

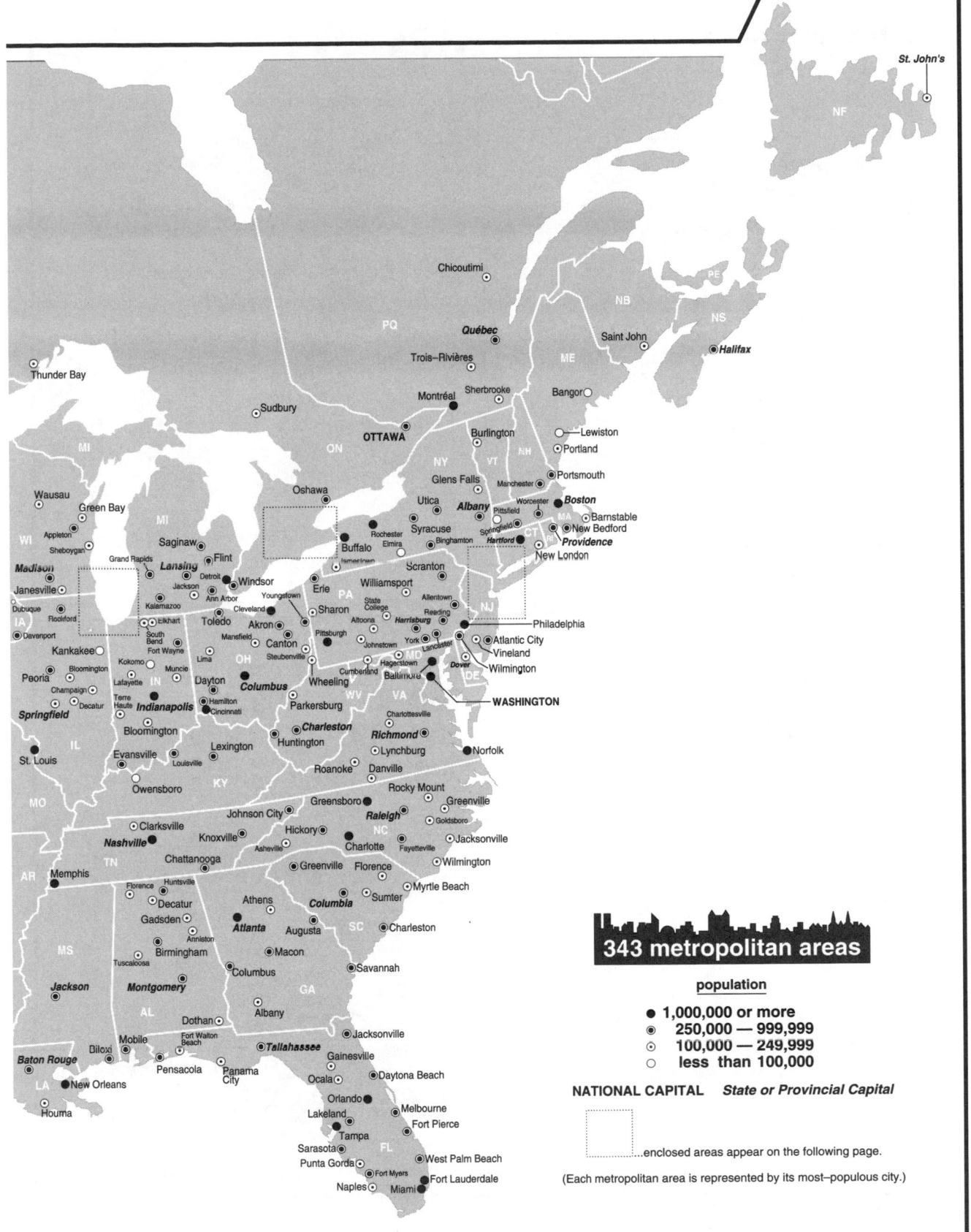

St. John's

NF

PE

Chicoutimi

NB

NS

Québec

Trois–Rivières

Halifax

Thunder Bay

Sudbury

Montréal

Sherbrooke

Saint John

Bangor

ME

Burlington

OTTAWA

Lewiston

Portland

ON

NY

VT

NH

Portsmouth

Wausau

Green Bay

Oshawa

Glens Falls

Manchester

MI

Utica

Albany

Worcester

Boston

Appleton

Rochester

Syracuse

Pittsfield

Barnstable

MA

Sheboygan

Saginaw

Flint

Buffalo

Elmira

Binghamton

Springfield

New Bedford

Madison

Grand Rapids

Lansing

Jamestown

Scranton

Hartford

Providence

New London

Janesville

Detroit

Windsor

Williamsport

Allentown

PA

CT

NJ

Dubuque

Jackson

Ann Arbor

Youngstown

Erie

State College

Reading

IA

Rockford

Kalamazoo

Cleveland

Sharon

Altoona

Harrisburg

Philadelphia

Davenport

Elkhart

Toledo

Akron

Mansfield

Pittsburgh

Johnstown

York

Lancaster

Atlantic City

Kankakee

South Bend

Canton

Steubenville

Cumberland

Hagerstown

Vineland

Dover

Wilmington

Kokomo

Lima

OH

Peoria

Bloomington

Muncie

Dayton

Wheeling

Baltimore

DE

Champaign

Lafayette

IN

Hamilton

Cincinnati

Parkersburg

MD

WASHINGTON

Decatur

Terre Haute

Indianapolis

WV

VA

Springfield

Bloomington

Charleston

Charlottesville

IL

Lexington

Huntington

Richmond

St. Louis

Evansville

Charleston

Lynchburg

Norfolk

Louisville

Roanoke

Danville

MO

KY

Owensboro

Rocky Mount

Greensboro

Greenville

Johnson City

NC

Clarksville

Hickory

Raleigh

Goldsboro

Knoxville

Asheville

Nashville

Charlotte

Fayetteville

Jacksonville

Chattanooga

TN

Greenville

Florence

Wilmington

AR

Memphis

Florence

Huntsville

Myrtle Beach

Decatur

Athens

Columbia

Sumter

Gadsden

Atlanta

Augusta

MS

Anniston

SC

Charleston

Birmingham

Macon

Tuscaloosa

Savannah

Jackson

Columbus

Montgomery

GA

AL

Dothan

Albany

Baton Rouge

Mobile

Fort Walton Beach

Tallahassee

Jacksonville

Biloxi

Pensacola

Panama City

Gainesville

LA

Baton Rouge

New Orleans

Ocala

Daytona Beach

Houma

Orlando

Melbourne

Lakeland

Fort Pierce

Tampa

Sarasota

FL

West Palm Beach

Punta Gorda

Fort Myers

Naples

Miami

Fort Lauderdale

343 metropolitan areas

population

● 1,000,000 or more

◉ 250,000 — 999,999

◎ 100,000 — 249,999

○ less than 100,000

NATIONAL CAPITAL *State or Provincial Capital*

................enclosed areas appear on the following page.

(Each metropolitan area is represented by its most–populous city.)

extracted areas
(from preceding pages)

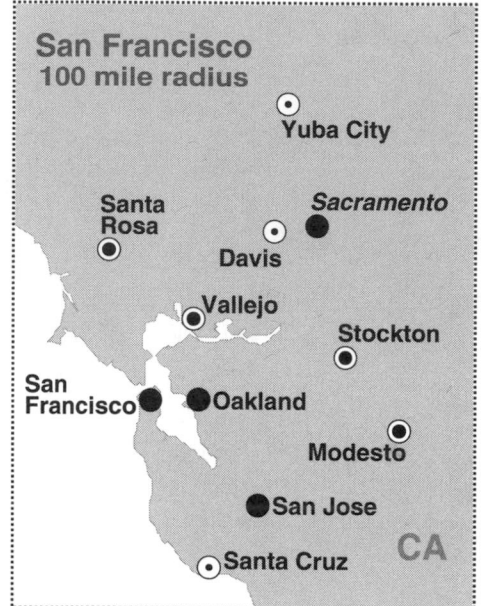

San Francisco
100 mile radius

Yuba City

Santa Rosa

Sacramento

Davis

Vallejo

Stockton

San Francisco

Oakland

Modesto

San Jose

Santa Cruz

CA

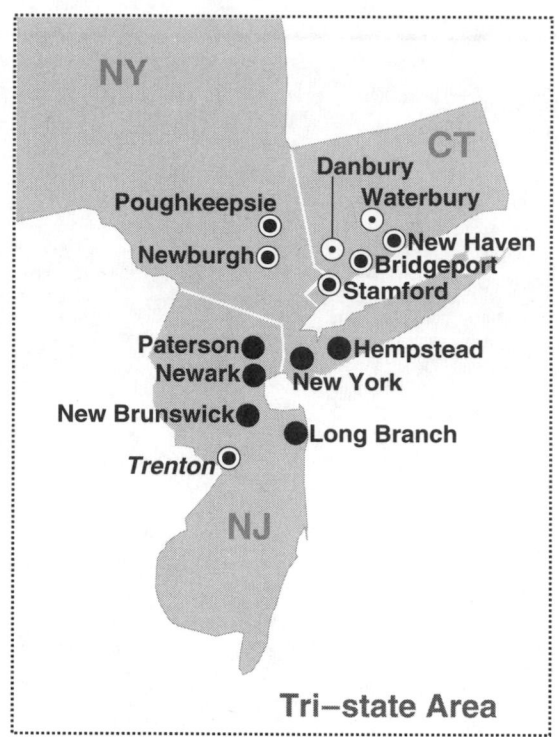

NY

CT

Danbury

Waterbury

Poughkeepsie

New Haven

Newburgh

Bridgeport

Stamford

Paterson

Hempstead

Newark

New York

New Brunswick

Trenton

Long Branch

NJ

Tri–state Area

population
- ● 1,000,000 or more
- ◉ 250,000 — 999,999
- ⊙ 100,000 — 249,999
- ○ less than 100,000

Lake Michigan

Milwaukee

WI

Racine

Kenosha

MI

Waukegan

Benton Harbor

Chicago

Gary

IN

IL

Southern Lake Michigan

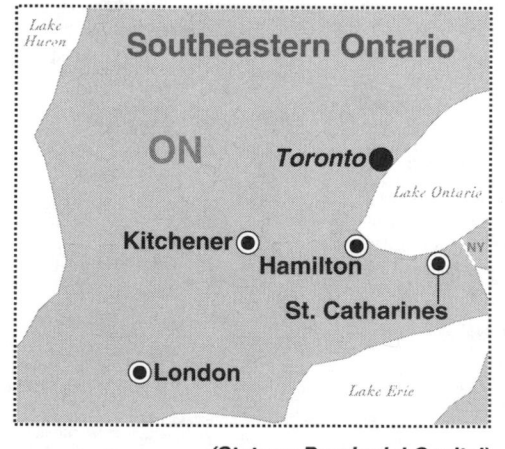

Lake Huron

Southeastern Ontario

ON

Toronto

Lake Ontario

Kitchener

Hamilton

NY

St. Catharines

London

Lake Erie

(Each metropolitan area is represented by its most–populous city.)

(State or Provincial Capital)

Thomas Nast, Cartographer

tive whose district seems to encompass everything in sight.

The perimeters of metro areas supersede the anachronistic political boundaries of incorporated areas and include not just the troubled and depressed older city cores but also the newer parts of suburbia with their sleek new malls, mirror-windowed office parks, low-rise factories, and choice neighborhoods.

Metropolitan Newark–Jersey City, for example, in-

cludes affluent Morris County; Buffalo–Niagara Falls includes quaint and tony Lewiston; Cleveland embraces Shaker Heights; and Boston, with its 147 cities and towns, takes in a wealthy fringe of high-tech industries.

The list on the following pages provides the county definitions of the metropolitan areas rated in this edition of *Places Rated Almanac*. The chances are good that you live in one of the official metropolitan areas profiled here.

343 Metropolitan Areas

Metro Areas and Component Counties	Population 1993	Population 1986	%Population Change, 1986–1993
Abilene, TX Taylor County	119,981	125,500	− 4.4
Akron, OH• Portage and Summit counties	666,046	644,800	+ 3.3
Albany, GA Dougherty and Lee counties	114,287	117,200	− 2.5
Albany–Schenectady–Troy, NY Albany, Montgomery, Rensselaer, Saratoga,Schenectady, and Schoharie counties	881,769	831,300	+ 6.1
Albuquerque, NM Bernalillo, Sandoval, and Valencia counties	645,721	561,900	+14.9
Alexandria, LA Rapides Parish	131,968	139,600	− 5.5
Allentown–Bethlehem–Easton, PA–NJ Warren County, NJ; Carbon, Lehigh, and Northampton counties, PA	699,936	656,800	+ 6.6
Altoona, PA Blair County	131,013	132,500	− 1.1
Amarillo, TX Potter and Randall counties	190,004	195,100	− 2.6
Anchorage, AK Anchorage Borough	242,189	235,000	+ 3.1
Ann Arbor, MI• Lenawee, Livingston, and Washtenaw counties	497,197	459,400	+ 8.2
Anniston, AL Calhoun County	116,309	123,800	− 6.1
Appleton–Oshkosh–Neenah, WI Calumet, Outagamie, and Winnebago counties	321,467	307,600	+ 4.5
Asheville, NC Buncombe and Madison counties	197,143	187,400	+ 5.2
Athens, GA Clarke, Madison, and Oconee counties	129,482	113,300	+14.3
Atlanta, GA Barrow, Bartow, Carroll, Cherokee, Clayton, Cobb, Coweta, De Kalb, Douglas, Fayette, Forsyth, Fulton, Gwinnett, Henry, Newton, Paulding, Pickens, Rockdale, Spalding, and Walton counties	3,174,100	2,671,400	+18.8
Atlantic City–Cape May, NJ• Atlantic and Cape May counties	329,962	297,400	+10.9
Augusta–Aiken, GA–SC Columbia and Richmond counties, GA; Aiken and Edgefield counties, SC	412,250	387,700	+ 6.3
Austin–San Marcos, TX Bastrop, Caldwell, Hays, Travis, and Williamson counties	918,977	792,000	+16.0
Bakersfield, CA Kern County	581,400	494,200	+17.6
Baltimore, MD• Anne Arundel, Baltimore, Carroll, Harford, Howard, and Queen Anne's counties; Baltimore city	2,472,186	2,279,900	+ 8.4
Bangor, ME Parts of Penobscot and Waldo counties	94,029	85,410	+10.1
Barnstable–Yarmouth, MA Barnstable County	190,908	170,600	+11.9
Baton Rouge, LA East Baton Rouge, Livingston, and West Baton Rouge parishes	483,798	421,100	+14.9
Beaumont–Port Arthur, TX Hardin, Jefferson, and Orange counties	367,468	375,800	− 2.2
Bellingham, WA Whatcom County	139,580	113,700	+22.8
Benton Harbor, MI Berrien County	164,431	163,600	+ 0.5
Billings, MT Yellowstone County	114,540	120,100	− 4.6
Biloxi–Gulfport–Pascagoula, MS Hancock, Harrison, and Jackson counties	319,589	332,400	− 3.9
Binghamton, NY Broome and Tioga counties	264,612	261,800	+ 1.1
Birmingham, AL Blount, Jefferson, St. Clair, and Shelby counties	855,161	843,500	+ 1.4
Bismarck, ND Burleigh and Morton counties	85,227	85,900	− 0.8
Bloomington, IN Monroe County	114,626	101,700	+12.7
Bloomington–Normal, IL McLean County	131,832	122,700	+ 7.4

• Identifies a metro area that is part of a Metropolitan Complex.

Metro Areas and Component Counties	Population 1993	Population 1986	%Population Change, 1986–1993	Metro Areas and Component Counties	Population 1993	Population 1986	%Population Change, 1986–1993
Boise City, ID Ada and Canyon counties	315,087	284,000	+10.9	**Chico-Paradise, CA** Butte County	189,423	166,700	+13.6
Boston, MA* Essex, Middlesex, Norfolk, Plymouth, and Suffolk counties	3,805,910	3,704,700	+ 2.7	**Chicoutimi-Jonquiere, PQ** 4 *villes* and 6 minor civil divisions	161,912	158,468	+ 2.2
Boulder–Longmont, CO* Boulder County	232,137	214,400	+ 8.3	**Cincinnati, OH-KY-IN*** Dearborn and Ohio counties, IN; Boone, Campbell, Gallatin, Grant, Kenton, and Pendleton counties, KY; Brown, Clermont, Hamilton, and Warren counties, OH	1,556,375	1,488,500	+ 4.6
Brazoria, TX* Brazoria County	205,796	188,700	+ 9.1				
Bremerton, WA* Kitsap County	199,729	169,200	+18.0				
Bridgeport, CT* Parts of Fairfield and New Haven counties	444,441	442,290	+ 0.5				
Brownsville–Harlingen– San Benito, TX Cameron County	269,203	257,300	+ 4.6	**Clarksville–Hopkinsville, TN-KY** Christian County, KY; Montgomery County, TN	174,331	154,400	+12.9
Bryan–College Station, TX Brazos County	130,704	120,800	+ 8.2	**Cleveland–Lorain– Elyria, OH*** Ashtabula, Cuyahoga, Geauga, Lake, Lorain, and Medina counties	2,209,946	2,222,100	− 0.5
Buffalo–Niagara Falls, NY* Erie and Niagara counties	1,202,029	1,181,600	+ 1.7				
Burlington, VT Parts of Chittendon, Franklin, and Grand Isle counties	144,285	134,160	+ 7.5	**Colorado Springs, CO** El Paso County	416,926	380,400	+ 9.6
Calgary, AB 2 cities, 2 towns, and 5 minor civil divisions	787,065	671,453	+17.2	**Columbia, MO** Boone County	118,483	106,500	+11.3
Canton–Massillon, OH Carroll and Stark counties	395,356	400,300	− 1.2	**Columbia, SC** Lexington and Richland counties	487,270	444,700	+ 9.6
Casper, WY Natrona County	61,817	70,900	−12.8	**Columbus, GA–AL** Russell County, AL; Chattahoochee, Harris, and Muscogee counties, GA	262,376	268,000	− 2.1
Cedar Rapids, IA Linn County	172,303	168,800	+ 2.1				
Central New Jersey, NJ* Hunterdon, Middlesex, and Somerset counties	1,070,976	950,100	+12.7	**Columbus, OH** Delaware, Fairfield, Franklin, Licking, Madison, and Pickaway counties, OH	1,416,504	1,268,300	+11.7
Champaign–Urbana, IL Champaign County	174,421	171,100	+ 1.9				
Charleston, WV Kanawha and Putnam counties	251,015	266,400	− 5.8	**Corpus Christi, TX** Nueces and San Patricio counties	361,280	363,300	− 0.6
Charleston– North Charleston, SC Berkeley, Charleston, and Dorchester counties	533,146	485,600	+ 9.8	**Cumberland, MD-WV** Allegany and Mineral counties	102,171	102,200	+ 0.0
Charlotte-Gastonia– Rock Hill, NC–SC Cabarrus, Gaston, Lincoln, Mecklenburg, Rowan, and Union counties, NC; York County, SC	1,259,693	1,065,400	+18.2	**Dallas, TX*** Collin, Dallas, Denton, Ellis, Henderson, Hunt, Kaufman, and Rockwall counties	2,850,369	2,522,900	+13.0
Charlottesville, VA Albemarle, Fluvanna, and Greene counties; Charlottesville city, VA	137,569	121,400	+13.3	**Danbury, CT*** Parts of Fairfield, Litchfield, and New Haven counties	189,516	186,810	+ 1.4
Chattanooga, TN–GA Catoosa, Dade, and Walker counties, GA; Hamilton County, TN	410,392	391,800	+ 4.7	**Danville, VA** Pittsylvania County and Danville city	108,856	110,300	− 1.3
				Davenport–Moline– Rock Island, IA–IL Scott County, IA; Henry and Rock Island counties, IL	353,846	371,300	− 4.7
Cheyenne, WY Laramie County	73,569	75,200	− 2.2	**Dayton–Springfield, OH** Clark, Greene, Miami, and Montgomery counties	955,708	933,500	+ 2.4
Chicago, IL* Cook, DuPage, Grundy, Kane, Kendall, McHenry, and Will counties	6,985,302	6,970,100	+ 0.2	**Daytona Beach, FL** Flagler and Volusia counties	435,637	339,100	+28.5
				Decatur, AL Lawrence and Morgan counties	136,945	130,300	+ 5.1
				Decatur, IL Macon County	117,119	126,700	− 7.6

* Identifies a metro area that is part of a Metropolitan Complex.

Metro Areas and Component Counties	Population 1993	Population 1986	%Population Change, 1986–1993	Metro Areas and Component Counties	Population 1993	Population 1986	%Population Change, 1986–1993
Denver, CO• Adams, Arapahoe, Denver, Douglas, and Jefferson counties	1,732,587	1,633,000	+ 6.1	**Fort Pierce– Port St. Lucie, FL** Martin and St. Lucie counties	282,012	205,700	+37.1
Des Moines, IA Dallas, Polk, and Warren counties	407,151	381,400	+ 6.8	**Fort Smith, AR–OK** Crawford and Sebastian counties, AR; Sequoyah County, OK	184,373	175,200	+ 5.2
Detroit, MI• Lapeer, Macomb, Monroe, Oakland, St. Clair, and Wayne counties	4,292,807	4,240,900	+ 1.2	**Fort Walton Beach, FL** Okaloosa County	150,792	141,300	+ 6.7
Dothan, AL Dale and Houston counties	135,808	129,900	+ 4.5	**Fort Wayne, IN** Adams, Allen, De Kalb, Huntington, Wells, and Whitley counties	472,115	446,300	+ 5.8
Dover, DE Kent County	111,866	105,200	+ 6.3	**Fort Worth–Arlington, TX•** Hood, Johnson, Parker, and Tarrant counties	1,473,304	1,281,800	+14.9
Dubuque, IA Dubuque County	86,734	91,100	− 4.8	**Fresno, CA** Fresno and Madera counties	830,447	665,500	+24.8
Duluth–Superior, MN–WI St. Louis County, MN; Douglas County, WI	237,939	243,500	− 2.3	**Gadsden, AL** Etowah County	100,052	102,300	− 2.2
Dutchess County, NY• Dutchess County	264,406	256,800	+ 3.0	**Gainesville, FL** Alachua County	197,378	176,000	+12.1
Eau Claire, WI Chippewa and Eau Claire counties	141,830	136,700	+ 3.8	**Galveston–Texas City, TX•** Galveston County	226,191	214,800	+ 5.3
Edmonton, AB 5 cities, 8 towns, and 22 minor civil divisions	866,283	774,026	+11.9	**Gary, IN•** Lake and Porter counties	607,947	614,800	− 1.1
El Paso, TX El Paso County	627,462	561,500	+11.7	**Glens Falls, NY** Warren and Washington counties	122,404	112,400	+ 8.9
Elkhart–Goshen, IN Elkhart County	161,143	146,400	+10.1	**Goldsboro, NC** Wayne County	106,523	97,900	+ 8.8
Elmira, NY Chemung County	95,813	90,500	+ 5.9	**Grand Forks, ND–MN** Polk County, MN; Grand Forks County, ND	103,673	102,800	+ 0.8
Enid, OK Garfield County	56,391	62,900	− 10.3	**Grand Rapids–Muskegon– Holland, MI** Allegan, Kent, Muskegon, and Ottawa counties	990,820	893,900	+10.8
Erie, PA Erie County	277,395	279,200	− 0.6	**Great Falls, MT** Cascade County	77,175	79,400	− 2.8
Eugene–Springfield, OR Lane County	292,447	263,200	+11.1	**Greeley, CO•** Weld County	133,233	135,000	− 1.3
Evansville–Henderson, IN–KY Posey, Vanderburgh, and Warrick counties, IN; Henderson County, KY	282,543	281,100	+ 0.5	**Green Bay, WI** Brown County	201,263	187,200	+ 7.5
Fargo–Moorhead, ND–MN Clay County, MN; Cass County, ND	156,539	145,300	+ 7.7	**Greensboro–Winston– Salem–High Point, NC** Alamance, Davidson, Davie, Forsyth, Guilford, Randolph, Stokes, and Yadkin counties	1,102,268	1,001,800	+10.0
Fayetteville, NC Cumberland County	276,344	258,500	+ 6.9	**Greenville, NC** Pitt County	119,883	98,000	+22.3
Fayetteville–Springdale– Rogers, AR Benton and Washington counties	228,335	197,000	+15.9	**Greenville–Spartanburg– Anderson, SC** Anderson, Cherokee, Greenville, Pickens, and Spartanburg counties	868,678	788,200	+10.2
Flint, MI• Genesee County	428,634	434,900	− 1.4	**Hagerstown, MD•** Washington County	124,919	114,100	+ 9.5
Florence, AL Colbert and Lauderdale counties	133,820	137,700	− 2.8	**Halifax, NS** 2 cities, 1 town, 2 minor civil divisions, and 5 census subdivisions	330,333	295,922	+11.6
Florence, SC Florence County	118,198	116,000	+ 1.9	**Hamilton, ON*** 3 cities, 4 towns, and 1 minor civil division	616,852	557,029	+10.7
Fort Collins–Loveland, CO Larimer County	199,131	174,600	+14.0	**Hamilton–Middletown, OH•** Butler County	296,157	271,500	+ 9.1
Fort Lauderdale, FL• Broward County	1,327,924	1,142,400	+16.2				
Fort Myers–Cape Coral, FL Lee County	381,263	279,100	+36.6				

Metro Areas and Component Counties	Population 1993	Population 1986	%Population Change, 1986–1993	Metro Areas and Component Counties	Population 1993	Population 1986	%Population Change, 1986–1993
Harrisburg–Lebanon–Carlisle, PA Cumberland, Dauphin, Lebanon, and Perry counties	609,056	577,300	+ 5.5	**Kankakee, IL•** Kankakee County	97,813	98,000	− 0.2
Hartford, CT Parts of Hartford, Litchfield, Middlesex, New London, Tolland, and Windham counties	1,171,430	1,106,620	+ 5.9	**Kansas City, MO–KS** Johnson, Leavenworth, Miami, and Wyandotte counties, KS; Cass, Clay, Clinton, Jackson, Lafayette, Platte, and Ray counties, MO	1,629,241	1,534,200	+ 6.2
Hickory–Morgantown, NC Alexander, Burke, Caldwell, and Catawba counties	302,150	288,000	+ 4.9	**Kenosha, WI•** Kenosha County	131,069	120,000	+ 9.2
Honolulu, HI Honolulu County	850,676	816,700	+ 4.2	**Killeen–Temple, TX** Bell and Coryell counties	257,120	234,600	+ 9.6
Houma, LA Lafourche and Terrebonne parishes	183,801	189,100	− 2.8	**Kitchener, ON*** 3 cities and 2 minor civil divisions	374,511	311,195	+20.3
Houston, TX• Chambers, Fort Bend, Harris, Liberty, Montgomery, and Waller counties	3,566,711	3,251,300	+ 9.7	**Knoxville, TN** Anderson, Blount, Knox, Loudon, Sevier, and Union counties	603,070	570,900	+ 5.6
Huntington–Ashland, WV–KY–OH Boyd and Greenup counties, KY; Lawrence County, OH; Cabell and Wayne counties, WV	289,820	302,800	− 4.3	**Kokomo, IN** Howard and Tipton counties	97,547	101,400	− 3.8
Huntsville, AL Limestone and Madison counties	310,879	285,500	+ 8.9	**La Crosse, WI–MN** Houston County, MN; La Crosse County, WI	119,335	113,100	+ 5.5
Indianapolis, IN Boone, Hamilton, Hancock, Hendricks, Johnson, Madison, Marion, Morgan, and Shelby counties	1,433,751	1,345,400	+ 6.6	**Lafayette, IN** Clinton and Tippecanoe counties	165,156	155,500	+ 6.2
Iowa City, IA Johnson County	99,975	85,300	+17.2	**Lafayette, LA** Acadia, Lafayette, St. Landry, and St. Martin parishes	351,277	366,000	− 4.0
Jackson, MI Jackson County	151,240	144,400	+ 4.7	**Lake Charles, LA** Calcasieu Parish	171,055	173,100	− 1.2
Jackson, MS Hinds, Madison, and Rankin counties	409,016	392,000	+ 4.3	**Lake County, IL•** Lake County	543,364	480,200	+13.2
Jacksonville, FL Clay, Duval, Nassau, and St. Johns counties	941,157	852,700	+10.4	**Lakeland–Winter Haven, FL** Polk County	426,920	377,200	+13.2
Jacksonville, NC Onslow County	153,427	126,600	+21.2	**Lancaster, PA** Lancaster County	439,586	393,500	+11.7
Jamestown, NY Chautauqua County	142,092	143,100	− 0.7	**Lansing–East Lansing, MI** Clinton, Eaton, and Ingham counties	443,151	424,700	+ 4.3
Janesville–Beloit, WI Rock County	140,385	137,800	+ 1.9	**Laredo, TX** Webb County	149,622	120,800	+23.9
Johnson City–Kingsport–Bristol, TN–VA Carter, Hawkins, Sullivan, Unicoi, and Washington counties, TN; Scott and Washington counties, VA; Bristol city, VA	441,827	443,400	− 0.4	**Las Cruces, NM** Dona Ana County	147,141	123,000	+19.6
Johnstown, PA Cambria and Somerset counties	242,419	254,100	− 4.6	**Las Vegas, NV–AZ** Mohave County, AZ; Clark and Nye counties, NV	983,313	661,800	+48.6
Joplin, MO Jasper and Newton counties	139,996	132,900	+ 5.3	**Lawrence, KS** Douglas County	85,486	72,600	+17.7
Kalamazoo–Battle Creek, MI Calhoun, Kalamazoo, and Van Buren counties	440,440	421,900	+ 4.4	**Lawton, OK** Comanche County	110,811	120,700	− 8.2
				Lewiston–Auburn, ME Parts of Androscoggin County	95,437	90,170	+ 5.8
				Lexington, KY Bourbon, Clark, Fayette, Jessamine, Madison, Scott, and Woodford counties	420,616	386,900	+ 8.7
				Lima, OH Allen and Auglaize counties	156,291	154,200	+ 1.4
				Lincoln, NE Lancaster County	223,124	206,100	+ 8.3

• Identifies a metro area that is part of a Metropolitan Complex.

Metro Areas and Component Counties	Population 1993	Population 1986	%Population Change, 1986–1993	Metro Areas and Component Counties	Population 1993	Population 1986	%Population Change, 1986–1993
Little Rock–North Little Rock, AR Faulkner, Lonoke, Pulaski, and Saline counties	525,818	505,600	+ 4.0	**Modesto, CA** Stanislaus County	416,794	316,600	+31.6
London, ON 2 cities, 1 town, and 9 minor civil divisions	397,210	342,302	+16.0	**Monmouth–Ocean, NJ•** Monmouth and Ocean counties	1,019,382	935,200	+ 9.0
Long Island, NY• Nassau and Suffolk counties	2,620,907	2,635,000	− 0.5	**Monroe, LA** Ouachita Parish	144,556	145,900	− 0.9
Longview–Marshall, TX Gregg, Harrison, and Upshur counties	195,622	202,600	− 3.4	**Montgomery, AL** Autauga, Elmore, and Montgomery counties	297,625	298,900	− 0.4
Los Angeles–Long Beach, CA• Los Angeles County	9,046,571	8,295,900	+ 9.0	**Montreal, PQ** 2 cities, 76 *villes,* and 27 minor civil divisions	3,209,596	2,921,357	+ 9.9
Louisville, KY–IN Clark, Floyd, Harrison, and Scott counties, IN; Bullitt, Jefferson, and Oldham counties, KY	969,910	959,100	+ 1.1	**Muncie, IN** Delaware County	121,162	120,900	+ 0.2
Lubbock, TX Lubbock County	228,584	224,700	+ 1.7	**Myrtle Beach, SC** Horry County	164,912	130,600	+26.3
Lynchburg, VA Amherst, Bedford, and Campbell counties; Bedford and Lynchburg cities	200,797	189,800	+ 5.8	**Naples, FL** Collier County	172,909	121,400	+42.4
Macon, GA Bibb, Houston, Jones, Peach, and Twiggs counties	295,634	292,300	+ 1.1	**Nashville, TN** Cheatham, Davidson, Dickson, Robertson, Rutherford, Sumner, Williamson, and Wilson counties	1,030,247	930,600	+10.7
Madison, WI Dane County	389,578	344,900	+13.0	**New Bedford–Fall River–Attleboro, MA•** Bristol County	513,963	484,900	+ 6.0
Manchester–Nashua, NH• Hillsborough County	348,039	314,300	+10.7	**New Haven–Meriden, CT•** Parts of Middlesex and New Haven counties	538,643	513,260	+ 4.9
Mansfield, OH Crawford and Richland counties	173,968	177,800	− 2.2	**New London–Norwich, CT–RI** Parts of Middlesex, New London, and Windham counties, CT; parts of Washington County, RI	211,279	210,840	+ 0.2
McAllen–Edinburg–Mission, TX Hidalgo County	419,484	365,900	+14.6	**New Orleans, LA** Jefferson, Orleans, Plaquemines, St. Bernard, St. Charles, St. James, St. John the Baptist, and St. Tammany parishes	1,299,325	1,383,500	− 6.1
Medford–Ashland, OR Jackson County	152,063	140,000	+ 8.6				
Melbourne–Titusville–Palm Bay, FL Brevard County	422,507	361,200	+17.0	**New York, NY•** Bronx, Kings, New York, Putnam, Queens, Richmond, Rockland, and Westchester counties	8,607,521	8,473,400	+ 1.6
Memphis, TN–AR–MS Crittenden County, AR; DeSoto County, MS; Fayette, Shelby, and Tipton counties, TN	1,042,869	985,300	+ 5.8				
Merced, CA Merced County	183,092	163,500	+12.0	**Newark–Jersey City, NJ•** Essex, Hudson, Morris, and Union counties	2,251,842	2,318,100	− 2.9
Miami, FL• Dade County	1,990,592	1,769,500	+12.5	**Norfolk–Virginia Beach–Newport News, VA–NC** Currituck County, NC; Gloucester, Isle of Wight, James City, Mathews, and York counties, VA; Chesapeake, Hampton, Newport News, Norfolk, Poquoson, Portsmouth, Suffolk, Virginia Beach, and Williamsburg cities, VA	1,479,845	1,355,500	+ 9.2
Milwaukee–Waukesha, WI• Milwaukee, Ozaukee, Washington, and Waukesha counties	1,448,922	1,379,700	+ 5.0				
Minneapolis–St. Paul, MN–WI Anoka, Carver, Chisago, Dakota, Hennepin, Isanti, Ramsey, Scott, Sherburne, Washington, and Wright counties, MN; Pierce and St. Croix counties, WI	2,638,367	2,363,100	+11.6				
				Northern New Jersey, NJ• Bergen, Passaic, and Sussex counties	1,410,098	1,421,500	− 0.8
Mobile, AL Baldwin and Mobile counties	492,903	470,000	+ 4.9	**Oakland, CA•** Alameda and Contra Costa counties	2,176,678	1,933,800	+12.6

Metro Areas and Component Counties	Population 1993	Population 1986	%Population Change, 1986–1993	Metro Areas and Component Counties	Population 1993	Population 1986	%Population Change, 1986–1993
Ocala, FL Marion County	214,601	171,000	+25.5	**Providence–Warwick– Cranston, RI** Bristol, Kent, Providence, and Washington counties	928,741	890,200	+ 4.3
Odessa–Midland, TX Ector and Midland counties	238,996	244,400	– 2.2	**Provo–Orem, UT** Utah County	299,084	240,500	+24.4
Oklahoma City, OK Canadian, Cleveland, Logan, McClain, Oklahoma, and Pottawatomie counties	969,425	983,000	– 1.4	**Pueblo, CO** Pueblo County	124,005	127,100	– 2.4
Olympia, WA• Thurston County	177,736	146,600	+21.2	**Punta Gorda, FL** Charlotte County	132,055	84,100	+57.0
Omaha, NE–IA Pottawattamie County, IA; Cass, Douglas, Sarpy, and Washington counties, NE	655,586	636,200	+ 3.0	**Quebec City, PQ** 20 *villes* and 25 minor civil divisions	662,463	603,267	+ 9.8
Orange County, CA• Orange County	2,620,077	2,166,800	+20.9	**Racine, WI•** Racine County	176,024	172,300	+ 2.2
Orange County, NY• Orange County	315,543	281,700	+12.0	**Raleigh–Durham– Chapel Hill, NC** Chatham, Durham, Franklin, Johnston, Orange, and Wake counties	924,328	764,500	+20.9
Orlando, FL Lake, Orange, Osceola, and Seminole counties	1,388,941	1,030,900	+34.7				
Oshawa, ON* 1 city and 2 towns	254,728	203,543	+25.1	**Rapid City, SD** Pennington County	82,818	76,100	+ 8.8
Ottawa–Hull, ON–PQ 5 cities and 5 *villes*, 1 town, and 12 minor civil divisions	961,495	819,263	+17.4	**Reading, PA** Berks County	338,627	321,000	+ 5.5
Owensboro, KY Daviess County	88,805	87,500	+ 1.5	**Redding, CA** Shasta County	156,171	133,100	+17.3
Panama City, FL Bay County	137,595	122,300	+12.5	**Regina, SK** 1 city, 4 towns, and 12 minor civil divisions	193,760	186,521	+ 3.9
Parkersburg–Marietta, WV– OH Washington County, OH; Wood County, WV	150,159	156,200	– 3.9	**Reno, NV** Washoe County	275,236	224,600	+22.5
Pensacola, FL Escambia and Santa Rosa counties	356,162	337,100	+ 5.7	**Richland–Kennewick– Pasco, WA** Benton and Franklin counties	155,596	149,500	+ 4.1
Peoria–Pekin, IL Peoria, Tazewell, and Woodford counties	340,663	340,400	+ 0.1	**Richmond–Petersburg, VA** Charles City, Chesterfield, Dinwiddie, Goochland, Hanover, Henrico, New Kent, Powhatan, and Prince George counties; Colonial Heights, Hopewell, Petersburg, and Richmond cities	911,134	810,200	+12.5
Philadelphia, PA–NJ• Burlington, Camden, Gloucester, and Salem counties, NJ; Bucks, Chester, Delaware, Montgomery, and Philadelphia counties, PA	4,978,037	4,891,200	+ 1.8				
Phoenix–Mesa, AZ Maricopa and Pinal counties	2,418,780	1,984,200	+21.9	**Riverside– San Bernardino, CA•** Riverside and San Bernardino counties	2,892,633	2,001,100	+44.6
Pine Bluff, AR Jefferson County	85,436	90,000	– 5.1				
Pittsburgh, PA Allegheny, Beaver, Butler, Fayette, Washington, and Westmoreland counties	2,407,603	2,467,300	– 2.4	**Roanoke, VA** Botetourt and Roanoke counties; Roanoke and Salem cities	229,168	224,800	+ 1.9
Pittsfield, MA Parts of Berkshire County	87,536	91,020	– 3.8	**Rochester, MN** Olmsted County	109,647	98,000	+11.9
Portland, ME Parts of Cumberland and York counties	226,296	210,700	+ 7.4	**Rochester, NY** Genesee, Livingston, Monroe, Ontario, Orleans, and Wayne counties	1,073,027	1,039,100	+ 3.3
Portland, OR• Clackamas, Columbia, Multnomah, Washington, and Yamhill counties	1,360,629	1,189,700	+14.4	**Rockford, IL** Boone, Ogle, and Winnebago counties	333,621	325,600	+ 2.5
				Rocky Mount, NC Edgecombe and Nash counties	139,773	130,200	+ 7.4
Portsmouth–Dover– Rochester, NH• Rockingham and Strafford counties	371,360	315,800	+17.6	**Sacramento, CA*** El Dorado, Placer, and Sacramento counties	1,436,232	1,165,400	+23.2

• Identifies a metro area that is part of a Metropolitan Complex.

Metro Areas and Component Counties	Population 1993	Population 1986	%Population Change, 1986–1993	Metro Areas and Component Counties	Population 1993	Population 1986	%Population Change, 1986–1993
Saginaw–Bay City–Midland, MI Bay, Midland, and Saginaw counties	404,137	403,600	+ 0.1	**Savannah, GA** Bryan, Chatham, and Effingham counties	262,415	252,900	+ 3.8
St. Catharines–Niagara, ON• 5 cities, 4 towns, and 1 minor civil division	373,070	343,258	+ 8.7	**Scranton–Wilkes-Barre–Hazelton, PA** Columbia, Lackawanna, Luzerne, and Wyoming counties	642,366	643,200	− 0.1
St. Cloud, MN Benton and Stearns counties	163,709	140,900	+16.2	**Seattle–Bellevue–Everett, WA•** Island, King, and Snohomish counties	2,178,199	1,800,700	+21.0
Saint John, NB 1 city, 3 towns, and 17 minor civil divisions	126,467	121,265	+ 4.3	**Sharon, PA** Mercer County	121,005	123,600	− 2.1
St. John's, NF 2 cities and 17 towns	175,842	161,901	+ 8.6	**Sheboygan, WI** Sheboygan County	104,862	102,700	+ 2.1
St. Joseph, MO Andrew and Buchanan counties	97,281	100,700	− 3.4	**Sherbrooke, PQ** 4 *villes* and 10 minor civil divisions	142,888	129,960	+ 9.9
St. Louis, MO–IL Clinton, Jersey, Madison, Monroe, and St. Clair counties, IL; Franklin, Jefferson, Lincoln, St. Charles, St. Louis, and Warren counties, MO; St. Louis city, MO	2,536,988	2,482,300	+ 2.2	**Sherman–Denison, TX** Grayson County	97,713	98,300	− 0.6
				Shreveport–Bossier City, LA Bossier, Caddo, and Webster parishes	379,354	410,700	− 7.6
Salem, OR• Marion and Polk counties	289,823	262,100	+10.6	**Sioux City, IA–NE** Woodbury County, IA; Dakota County, NE	115,870	115,900	+ 0.0
Salinas, CA Monterey County	366,487	339,700	+ 7.9	**Sioux Falls, SD** Lincoln and Minnehaha counties	142,131	137,100	+ 3.7
Salt Lake City–Ogden, UT Davis, Salt Lake, and Weber counties	1,130,989	1,041,400	+ 8.6	**South Bend, IN** St. Joseph County	249,804	241,400	+ 3.5
San Angelo, TX Tom Green County	99,902	98,000	+ 1.9	**Spokane, WA** Spokane County	366,507	356,900	+ 2.7
San Antonio, TX Bexar, Comal, Guadalupe, and Wilson counties	1,387,944	1,295,000	+ 7.2	**Springfield, IL** Menard and Sangamon counties	190,871	190,600	+ 0.1
San Diego, CA San Diego County	2,670,656	2,201,300	+21.3	**Springfield, MA** Parts of Franklin, Hampden, and Hampshire counties	595,915	571,840	+ 4.2
San Francisco, CA• Marin, San Francisco, and San Mateo counties	1,644,301	1,588,000	+ 3.5	**Springfield, MO** Christian, Greene, and Webster counties	279,271	247,900	+12.7
San Jose, CA• Santa Clara County	1,535,519	1,401,600	+ 9.6	**Stamford–Norwalk, CT•** Parts of Fairfield County	333,914	321,980	+ 3.7
San Luis Obispo–Atascadero–Paso Robles, CA San Luis Obispo County	233,337	196,700	+18.6	**State College, PA** Centre County	128,825	114,600	+12.4
Santa Barbara–Santa Maria–Lompoc, CA Santa Barbara County	377,361	339,400	+11.2	**Steubenville–Weirton, OH–WV** Jefferson County, OH; Brooke and Hancock counties, WV	140,913	154,800	− 9.0
Santa Cruz–Watsonville, CA• Santa Cruz County	250,545	218,500	+14.7	**Stockton–Lodi, CA** San Joaquin County	497,772	432,700	+15.0
Santa Fe, NM Los Alamos and Santa Fe counties	129,841	105,800	+22.7	**Sudbury, ON** 1 city, 5 towns, and 1 minor civil division	161,107	148,877	+ 8.2
Santa Rosa, CA• Sonoma County	432,055	343,600	+25.7	**Sumter, SC** Sumter County	105,103	95,000	+10.6
Sarasota–Bradenton, FL Manatee and Sarasota counties	542,530	424,700	+27.7	**Syracuse, NY** Cayuga, Madison, Onondaga, and Oswego counties	748,943	729,300	+ 2.7
Saskatoon, SK 1 city, 9 towns, and 11 minor civil divisions	213,766	200,665	+ 6.5	**Tacoma, WA•** Pierce County	600,441	533,300	+12.6

Metro Areas and Component Counties	Population 1993	Population 1986	%Population Change, 1986–1993	Metro Areas and Component Counties	Population 1993	Population 1986	%Population Change, 1986–1993
Tallahassee, FL Gadsden and Leon counties	257,920	218,000	+18.3	**Washington, DC–MD–VA–WV•** District of Columbia; Calvert, Charles, Frederick, Montgomery, and Prince George's counties, MD; Arlington, Clarke, Culpeper, Fairfax, Fauquier, King George, Loudoun, Prince William, Spotsylvania, Stafford, and Warren counties, VA; Alexandria, Fairfax, Falls Church, Fredericksburg, Manassas, and Manassas Park cities, VA; Berkeley and Jefferson counties, WV	4,466,545	3,819,100	+17.0
Tampa–St. Petersburg–Clearwater, FL Hernando, Hillsborough, Pasco, and Pinellas counties	2,261,075	1,914,200	+18.1				
Terre Haute, IN Clay, Vermillion, and Vigo counties	147,140	151,800	– 3.1				
Texarkana, TX–Texarkana, AR Miller County, AR; Bowie County, TX	121,407	119,800	+ 1.3				
Thunder Bay, ON 1 city and 7 minor civil divisions	125,311	122,217	+ 2.5				
Toledo, OH Fulton, Lucas, and Wood counties	618,422	611,200	+ 1.2	**Waterbury, CT** Parts of Litchfield and New Haven counties	210,930	195,580	+ 7.8
Topeka, KS Shawnee County	163,209	160,800	+ 1.5	**Waterloo–Cedar Falls, IA** Black Hawk County	124,454	127,600	– 2.5
Toronto, ON* 8 cities, 16 towns, and 4 minor civil divisions	4,077,472	3,431,981	+18.8	**Wausau, WI** Marathon County	118,469	112,500	+ 5.3
Trenton, NJ• Mercer County	328,084	320,800	+ 2.3	**West Palm Beach–Boca Raton, FL** Palm Beach County	973,630	755,600	+28.9
Trois–Rivieres, PQ 4 *villes* and 6 minor civil divisions	139,269	128,888	+ 8.1	**Wheeling, WV–OH** Belmont County, OH; Marshall and Ohio counties, WV	157,164	175,400	–10.4
Tucson, AZ Pima County	722,827	594,100	+21.7	**Wichita, KS** Butler, Harvey, and Sedgwick counties	500,032	469,900	+ 6.4
Tulsa, OK Creek, Osage, Rogers, Tulsa, and Wagoner counties	722,492	733,500	– 1.5	**Wichita Falls, TX** Archer and Wichita counties	130,980	135,000	– 3.0
Tuscaloosa, AL Tuscaloosa County	155,969	141,300	+10.4	**Williamsport, PA** Lycoming County	120,645	116,300	+ 3.7
Tyler, TX Smith County	156,886	152,100	+ 3.1	**Wilmington, NC** New Hanover County	127,828	114,100	+12.0
Utica–Rome, NY Herkimer and Oneida counties	315,567	315,400	+ 0.1	**Wilmington–Newark, DE–MD•** New Castle County, DE; Cecil County, MD	525,152	485,300	+ 8.2
Vallejo–Fairfield–Napa, CA* Napa and Solano counties	478,739	392,300	+22.0	**Windsor, ON•** 1 city, 3 towns, and 7 minor civil divisions	265,310	253,988	+ 4.5
Vancouver, BC 8 cities, 9 district municipalities, and 21 minor civil divisions	1,691,211	1,380,729	+22.5	**Winnipeg, MB** 1 city and 7 minor civil divisions	663,174	625,304	+ 6.1
Vancouver, WA• Clark County	263,439	211,300	+24.7	**Worcester–Fitchburg–Leominster, MA•** Worcester County	723,206	661,100	+ 9.4
Ventura, CA• Ventura County	729,050	611,000	+19.3	**Yakima, WA** Yakima County	192,775	183,200	+ 5.2
Victoria, BC 2 cities, 2 towns, 4 district municipalities, and 11 minor civil divisions	300,966	255,225	+17.9	**Yolo, CA•** Yolo County	150,044	126,000	+19.1
Victoria, TX Victoria County	79,878	76,000	+ 5.1	**York, PA** York County	351,248	326,600	+ 7.5
Vineland–Millville–Bridgeton, NJ• Cumberland County	138,669	135,300	+ 2.5	**Youngstown–Warren, OH** Columbiana, Mahoning, and Trumbull counties	604,473	620,200	– 2.5
Visalia–Tulare–Porterville, CA Tulare County	319,312	287,300	+11.1	**Yuba City, CA** Sutter and Yuba counties	124,286	114,200	+ 8.8
Waco, TX McLennan County	193,024	187,600	+ 2.9	**Yuma, AZ** Yuma County	124,026	86,800	+42.9

• Identifies a metro area that is part of a Metropolitan Complex

The list above includes American metro areas as defined by the U.S. Office of Management and Budget, and Canadian metro areas defined by Statistics Canada, as of January 1, 1993.

Decisions, Decisions

Some twenty years ago a group of futurists, academics, and government scientists got together at a hotel in northern Virginia for a conference sponsored by the U.S. Environmental Protection Agency. Their job was to discover just how to define "Quality of Life."

The players quickly split into three distinct groups over the issue. One group thought that defining quality of life for all people at all times wasn't just unfair, it was impossible and shouldn't be tried at all. A second group disagreed, maintaining that liveability could be quantified and defined—but shouldn't, because measuring a touchy thing like quality of life makes places unwilling competitors of one another and often leads to wrong conclusions. The third group held that judging local liveability could be done as long as you make clear what your statistical yardsticks are and go on to use them consistently.

Although the first and second positions may indeed be valid, *Places Rated Almanac* sides with the third.

Rating Places: One Way

This is a book of current statistics about North American metropolitan areas. Certainly it is a more objective source of information about urban liveability than the hearsay opinions that people share at a dinner party, a rest stop on the interstate, or an airport bar. Each of the 343 metro areas is rated by 10 factors that anyone thinking of moving would think were highly important.

- The **Costs of Living** chapter looks at household incomes and taxes, and it also measures the costs of such important items as housing, food, health care, and college tuition.
- The **Jobs** chapter weighs prospects for local employment growth in nine basic areas, including manufacturing, trade, services, finance, and government.
- **Housing** is compared in terms of prices for single homes, plus the taxes and utilities a would-be homeowner can expect to pay. Also noted: available housing alternatives in apartments, condos, and mobile homes.
- A metro area's **Crime** rating is determined by the average annual number of violent and property crimes per 100,000 people over the past five years.
- The supply of health-care facilities and practitioners, plus available special options, forms the basis for a metro area's **Health Care** rating.
- **Transportation** is rated by local commuting time, public transit, and the diverse intercity travel options by air, rail, and interstate highway.
- Each metro area's public school systems and private school alternatives, as well as their local colleges and universities, produce an **Education** rating.
- The chapter on **The Arts** compares cultural assets, among them museums and public libraries, opera companies and symphony orchestras.

- **Recreation** also rates assets, from good restaurants to public golf courses, zoos, professional sports, ocean coastlines, and national parks acreage.
- **Climate** is rated on mildness; that is, how close temperatures remain to 65 degrees Fahrenheit throughout the year.

Some readers may fault *Places Rated's* choice of criteria. Admittedly, its yardsticks for health care, public transportation, options for higher education, and performing arts amenities all favor big places over small ones. On the other hand, the methods for scoring safety from crime and high living costs favor smaller places over big ones. *Places Rated's* standards for climate and outdoor recreation assets are certainly not everyone's. But they have nothing to do with population size.

Here are gathered the most up-to-date figures for all 343 metro areas. In most instances, the information is as fresh as 1993. The sources, documented throughout this book, come from federal and state/provincial agencies and a growing number of private organizations.

This edition of *Places Rated Almanac* is as much a snapshot of a moving target as its predecessors. Metro areas are dynamic and just don't sit still for statistical portraits. An economic rebound in many Great Lakes metro areas continues to draw native sons and daughters back from Texas. Likewise, the deepest slump in California in decades is forcing thousands to emigrate to other, more promising areas. With so much in life that is unpredictable, you'd be wise to supplement *Places Rated Almanac* with your own independent verification.

Rating Places: Your Way

At the end of this book, in "Putting It All Together," costs of living, climate, housing, crime, health care, transportation, education, the arts, recreation, and jobs get equal weight when identifying metro areas with across-the-board strengths.

You may not agree with this system. You may give more weight to forecasted job growth than to a relative lack of crime or air pollution. For you, a place where living costs are least may be much more important than an ocean coastline, an abundance of medical specialists, or a busy performing arts calendar. To identify which factors are more important and which factors are less, you may want to take stock of your preferences.

YOUR PREFERENCE INVENTORY

The following Preference Inventory has 45 pairs of statements. For each pair, decide which statement is more important to you when judging a liveable place. Even if both statements are equally important or neither is important, select one anyway. If you can't decide quickly, pass up the item but return to it after you complete the rest of the inventory.

Don't worry about being consistent. The paired statements aren't repeated. There aren't any right or wrong answers, only those that are best for you. Although the inventory takes about 15 minutes to finish, there is no time limit. Before you start, you might want to photocopy the inventory and ask your spouse or a friend to take it independently. Comparing your preference inventory with another person's can be an interesting exercise.

Directions

For each numbered item, decide which of two statements is more important to you when choosing a place to live. Mark the box next to that statement. Be sure to make a choice for all items.

1. ☐ The cost of food and clothing,
   or
   ☐ Forecasted job growth.

2. ☐ The outlook for employment growth,
   or
   ☐ The annual number of auto thefts.

3. ☐ Boating, fishing, and swimming,
   or
   ☐ Annual percent of possible sunshine.

4. ☐ Number of robberies and assaults,
   or
   ☐ Supply of family medical practitioners.

5. ☐ Operas and symphony orchestras,
   or
   ☐ Movie theaters and good restaurants.

6. ☐ Variety of private high schools,
   or
   ☐ Nearby national parks and forests.

7. ☐ Typical health-care costs,

or

☐ Number of homicides.

8. ☐ Buses and commuter railroads,

or

☐ Alternatives to public schools.

9. ☐ Local supply of family doctors,

or

☐ Scheduled airline service.

10. ☐ Jobs in the service sector,

or

☐ Medical schools and teaching hospitals.

11. ☐ Airlines serving the area,

or

☐ Summer mildness and duration.

12. ☐ The cost of living,

or

☐ Local specialized medical care.

13. ☐ Forecasted growth of employment,

or

☐ Annual amount of rain and snow.

14. ☐ General hospitals and family doctors,

or

☐ Local community colleges.

15. ☐ Typical prices for homes,

or

☐ Supply of local public transit.

16. ☐ How mild the winters are,

or

☐ How old a typical home is.

17. ☐ Number of new jobs by 1998,

or

☐ Local colleges and universities.

18. ☐ Supply of medical specialists,

or

☐ How cold the winters are.

19. ☐ The cost of health care,

or

☐ New books added in local libraries.

20. ☐ Zoos and botanical gardens,

or

☐ Local multifamily housing.

21. ☐ Mix of white- and blue-collar jobs,

or

☐ The number of public golf courses.

22. ☐ Local auto thefts and burglaries,

or

☐ Local professional sports teams.

23. ☐ Local threat of unemployment,

or

☐ How long it takes to get to work.

24. ☐ Variety of performing arts,

or

☐ Annual amounts of rain and snow.

25. ☐ Public and private colleges,

or

☐ Annual number of freezing days.

26. ☐ Income tax and sales tax bites,

or

☐ Public school pupil/teacher ratio.

27. ☐ Job losses in manufacturing,

or

☐ Available apartments.

28. ☐ Local costs for utilities,

or

☐ Local college sports.

29. ☐ Incidence of street crime,

    or

    ☐ Condominium housing options.

30. ☐ Incidence of robberies in a year,

    or

    ☐ Local support of public schools.

31. ☐ Local repertory theater productions,

    or

    ☐ Apartments or houses for rent.

32. ☐ Intercity rail and air service,

    or

    ☐ New homes for sale.

33. ☐ Annual income and sales tax bite,

    or

    ☐ Rental housing options.

34. ☐ The mix of white- and blue-collar jobs,

    or

    ☐ Libraries and museums.

35. ☐ Alternatives to public schools,

    or

    ☐ Alternatives to buying a home.

36. ☐ Local household income and taxes,

    or

    ☐ Annual number of days over 90 degrees Fahrenheit.

37. ☐ Variety of private grade schools,

    or

    ☐ Dance companies and repertory theaters.

38. ☐ Supply of public transit,

    or

    ☐ Nearby national parks and forests.

39. ☐ Annual muggings per capita,

    or

    ☐ Annual number of clear and cloudy days.

40. ☐ Average daily commuting time,

    or

    ☐ Local performing arts calendar.

41. ☐ Number of burglaries annually,

    or

    ☐ Freeway traffic congestion.

42. ☐ Number of auto thefts in a year,

    or

    ☐ Museums and repertory theaters.

43. ☐ Supply of family doctors vs. specialists,

    or

    ☐ Age of the local housing stock.

44. ☐ Supply of specialized doctors,

    or

    ☐ Fine-arts broadcasting.

45. ☐ Specialized medical care,

    or

    ☐ Nearby water recreation.

Plotting Your Preference Profile

It is important that you make a choice for each of the 45 items. Have you left any unchecked? If not, you're ready to draw your Preference Profile.

First Step. Count all the marks you've made in the boxes next to the Costs of Living icon. Then enter the number of these statements at the top of your Preference Profile. In the same way, count the number of statements for each of the other icons. Enter their totals in their respective places at the top of your Preference Profile.

Second Step. Now plot your totals on the blank chart. Place a dot on the appropriate line for each of the numbers and connect the dots to form a line graph of your results (see the Sample Preference Profile).

Analyzing Your Preference Profile

Each of the factors in Your Preference Profile—the costs of living, climate, crime, housing, health care, transportation, education, the arts, recreation, and jobs—is not only a big concern when choosing a place to live; it also has a complete chapter in this book. The purpose of the Preference Inventory is to help you decide the relative importance of each of the chapters to you personally.

If your scores are high for one or two of these factors, you may want to give extra attention to the chapters devoted to them. Likewise, if your scores are low for any of the 10 factors, you may not need to give as much consideration to them as you would the ones with high scores. Bear in mind that the inventory orders your preferences in a hierarchy, that each of the factors has some importance to you, and that none should be completely ignored.

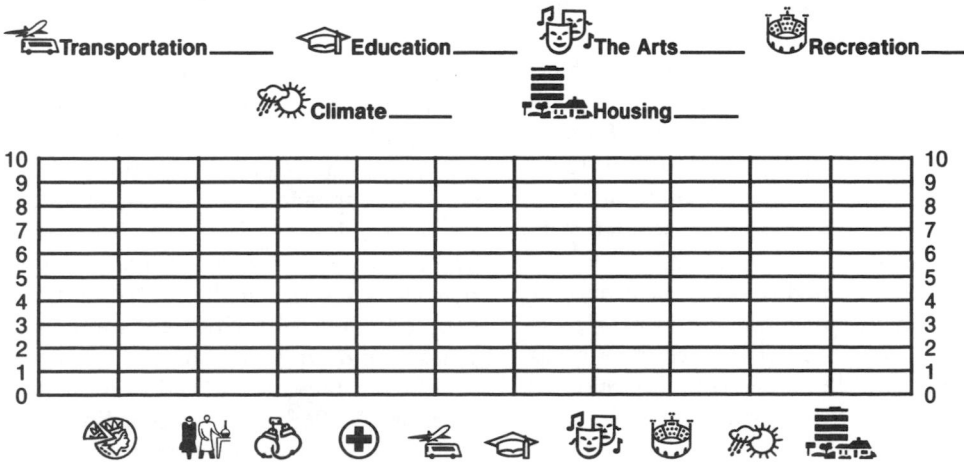

Sample Preference Profile

Costs of Living _7_   Jobs _5_   Crime _2_   Health Care _2_
Transportation _3_   Education _6_   The Arts _3_   Recreation _7_
Climate _6_   Housing _4_

Your Preference Profile

Costs of Living ___   Jobs ___   Crime ___   Health Care ___
Transportation ___   Education ___   The Arts ___   Recreation ___
Climate ___   Housing ___

Costs of Living

In the view of economists, we're all living resources looking for our highest valued use. We switch jobs readily if the money is right. We change careers, too, if the prospects are promising. And we may risk these changes even if it means packing up and moving far away.

We also flee living costs that have gotten so high we can't afford them. Metro areas attract people because of expanding job opportunities, but they also draw people because local costs of living are low enough to seem like bargains to many migrating people.

This is nothing new. For centuries, Americans have moved from rich places, where the benefits of high incomes are made empty by even higher costs of living, to low-income places, where cheap land and no taxes more than make up for the drawback of paltry incomes.

"Money's no problem," an accountant will tell you. "Lack of money . . . now *that's* a problem." As is the case for most people, your own short-term economic frets probably center on the price of hamburger, jeans, gasoline, or haircuts. Over the long run, your concerns may focus on tax bites and boosting your household's income at least to the level where it can provide basic day-to-day necessities.

SCRAPING BY ON $51,067 A YEAR

Do average household incomes in different parts of the continent indicate local living costs? For the most part, they do. According to economists at the Labor Department, two-thirds of the variation in personal incomes between Cincinnati and San Francisco, for example, reveals their different costs of living; the other third reflects their different employers, worker skills, and prevailing wages.

Households aren't always made up of families. According to the latest Census Bureau survey on living arrangements, one-quarter of all households are composed either of one person or of several people unrelated to one another (including millions of POSSLQs—Persons of Opposite Sex Sharing Living Quarters). There are 12 million single-parent households with at least one child present, and two million of them are headed by men. The rest of the households comprise married couples, some with children, some childless, and some whose children have scattered from the nest.

The average household income among 343 metro areas is $51,067 a year, according to estimates by the Washington, DC-based firm of Woods & Poole Econom-

Metro Area Household Incomes

The money coming to households isn't entirely from wages and salaries. It also includes interest from savings, dividends from stock holdings, government transfer payments, rents, and a multitude of other sources. If these typical incomes seem high, bear in mind that households now have more than one employed person in them.

Highest

Stamford-Norwalk, CT	$96,760
Long Island, NY	$88,415
Northern New Jersey, NJ	$84,416
Lake County, IL	$84,060
Central New Jersey, NJ	$81,411
San Francisco, CA	$80,087
Trenton, NJ	$78,772
San Jose, CA	$75,157
Honolulu, HI	$74,744
Newark-Jersey City, NJ	$73,817
Orange County, CA	$73,145
Anchorage, AK	$72,833
Monmouth-Ocean, NJ	$72,548
Washington, DC-MD-VA-WV	$72,535
Los Angeles-Long Beach, CA	$71,029

Lowest

McAllen-Edinburg-Mission, TX	$34,690
Las Cruces, NM	$35,339
Jacksonville, NC	$35,527
Bryan-College Station, TX	$36,152
Ocala, FL	$36,716
Laredo, TX	$36,720
Sumter, SC	$36,768
Yuma, AZ	$37,173
Myrtle Beach, SC	$37,401
Gadsden, AL	$37,504
Brownsville-Harlingen-San Benito, TX	$37,607
Bloomington, IN	$37,934
Goldsboro, NC	$37,980
Clarksville-Hopkinsville, TN-KY	$38,468
Florence, AL	$38,578

Source: Woods & Poole Economics, Inc., household income estimates, 1993.

---

ics, Inc., and *Places Rated*. These incomes range from $96,760 in Stamford, CT, to less than $35,000 in parts of Texas's historically poor Rio Grande valley.

TAXES: ONE OF LIFE'S CERTAINTIES

In a calendar year, mid-May marks the mythical Tax Freedom point on which we stop handing over all of our earnings to federal, state, and local tax collectors and start pocketing that money for ourselves. Looking at it another way, we spend two hours and 48 minutes of every eight-hour working day earning enough money to pay taxes, according to the District of Columbia-based Tax Foundation. That amounts to $28 a day for each employed person.

No matter where you live, Social Security taxes hit you with the same impact. So can federal personal income taxes. But state and local taxes vary tremendously. To determine the relative tax bite among metro areas, *Places Rated* focuses on the two most common levies: state personal income taxes and state sales taxes.

Based on a metro area's average household income, state incomes are estimated for a two-paycheck couple with two children, filing either a joint or a combined separate return (whichever would result in the smaller amount of taxes owed in each state), after taking typical exemptions and deductions. The taxes that a family pays throughout the year on retail purchases are also based on the household's average income, using Internal Revenue Service estimates.

As a percentage of average household incomes, Canadian provincial income and sales taxes take the biggest bites in North America. In the United States, state income and sales taxes are highest in the District of Columbia, Michigan, Minnesota, New York, Oregon, Utah, and Wisconsin. In Florida, New Mexico, Texas, and Wyoming, the bite is smallest. In Alaska and New Hampshire, there is no bite at all.

COSTS OF LIVING: SEVEN FACTORS

"It's a black hole," the *Wall Street Journal* commented on what is meant by *costs of living*. So what if the Consumer Price Index has gone up ninefold since World War II; what does all that have to do with the high price of getting by in San Francisco as opposed to Peoria?

Several years ago, a special committee appointed by the Department of Labor to look into better ways to measure cost-of-living variations among places threw in the towel. Given the infinite range of consumer tastes and household tactics for saving a dollar, the only way to pin down why life in one place was more expensive than in another was to focus on the weather's effect on clothing costs and household utility bills. Then look at taxes.

Taxes certainly do make a difference. But clothing and home energy bills? Not that much. According to one national retailer, the price difference between cotton and synthetic Sun Belt wardrobes and woolen and down-filled Frost Belt clothing amounts to about one percent of a household's budget. As for the comparative costs of keeping warm in Duluth and staying cool in Dallas, often the only difference is the season during which local residents pay most of their bill.

One firm that counsels transferred employees adopts an 80/20 rule. In its experience, 80 percent of the difference in living costs between where you've come from and where you're going comes down to two things: housing and taxes. The other 20 percent comes from prices for everything from a splint for a broken thumb to frozen orange juice, soap flakes, and a shampoo, trim, and blow-dry at a salon.

To measure what it costs to live in each metro area, *Places Rated* looks at cost indexes for houses, utilities, property taxes, groceries, health care, transportation, and college tuition. To produce an overall score, these indexes are weighted by their importance on household spending according to consumer surveys in various North American cities.

Paying off a mortgage based on local *house prices* is the biggest item in a household budget. It claims an average of 30 percent. Small wonder most newcomers start out renting; while it contributes nothing to net worth, renting permits a household to avoid much of cost-of-living differences among areas. Median, average, and up-market house prices, as well as apartment rents, are detailed later on in the Housing chapter.

Transportation, at 17 percent, is the next largest item. It covers everything from new cars to tires and gasoline, from auto body work to the fare you'd pay if you regularly took the bus.

Groceries—food at home, in home economists idiom —claims another 16 percent. The costs don't vary widely in the United States except in New York where not a leaf of cabbage reaches the supermarket except by truck, or in Anchorage and Honolulu where a great many packaged goods arrive by ship. The costs do vary widely between the United States and Canada. Not for nothing are American supermarkets in border towns from Maine to Washington full of shoppers who've driven hundreds of kilometers to save 30 percent or more on food.

At 7 percent, *health care* covers everything from over-the-counter cold remedies to teeth cleaning, and from an initial consultation with a doctor to a semi-private hospital room. Its importance on a household budget is on par with home heating and lighting. While Canadian households do not budget for physician treatment or hospitalization, they do pay for dental care and for some drugs. Indeed, about three out of every ten health-care dollars spent in that country come out of consumers' pockets.

Utilities cover everything from water and telephone to piped-in natural gas and electricity, and claim about 7 percent of a household's expenses. Utility bills around the continent vary widely for several reasons. Customer density, distance from oil and coal fuel sources, age of the power plant, and the type and size of equipment used in generating electricity all play a part in the charges to consumers.

Property taxes, on average, take a shade over 4 percent of the household's budget. Critics during the late 1970s likened them to a ransom homeowners paid to keep the house off the tax assessor's auction block. Using this analogy, homeowners in parts of Long Island, NY, buy their homes back every 20 years, since the effective tax rate (a tax on the home's full value) approaches 5 percent. Down in Mobile County, AL, on the other

---

Priced to Move: Using *Places Rated's* Scores

The Costs-of-Living scores are actually indexes against a mythical North American average of 10,000. They can be a useful starting point for figuring cost differences between any two metro areas.

From Lower to Higher. Suppose you are thinking of a job offer in a distant metro area with a higher costs-of-living score than the one where you live now. In the jargon of corporate recruiters, how much more after-tax income will you need in the new location to 'stay whole.' In other words, how much of an income boost will you need just to hang on to your current lifestyle?

A preliminary answer involves three steps: (1) determine the difference in *Places Rated* scores between your present location and the alternate, (2) divide that amount by your present location's score, (3) then multiply by 100. The answer is the approximate percent increase in income you'll need.

For example, the difference between Miami's score (11,292) and Tucson's score (10,010) is 1,282. When that difference is divided by Tucson's score and multiplied by 100, the result is 12.81. Moving from Tucson to Miami, therefore, would require about a 13% increase in compensation.

From Higher to Lower. The same formula applies if your move is in the opposite direction. How much of a cut in after-tax income can you handle without crimping your lifestyle?

The difference between Tucson's score (10,010) and Miami's score (11,292) is −1,282. When that figure is divided by Miami's score and multiplied by 100, the answer is 11.35. You can 'stay whole' relocating to Tucson from Miami as long as you're not facing a greater than 11 percent pay cut.

Several Caveats. Budgeting with a sharp pencil permits many a moderate income to live anywhere. Often, the costs-of-living differences between two areas come down to the individual household's shopping skills. Be aware, too, that prices are the most rapidly changing of criteria in *Places Rated Almanac.*

---

hand, the "ransom period" is 222 years because of an extremely low effective rate of 0.45 percent.

Locally, too, property taxes can vary enormously and can be madly confusing to homeowners. In California, two houses on the same block with identical prices and physical characteristics can have substantially different, yet legally impeccable, tax bills if one of them was sold before the approval of Proposition 13 and the other after. In Texas, a home's value can be assessed at different levels at different times of the year by different assessors.

SCORING: COSTS OF LIVING

For the same money, can you live equally well in Topeka, Toronto, or Tuscaloosa? Do costs of living really vary all that much among North American metro areas, or can skillful budgeting keep your head above water anywhere you choose to live?

To help you answer that question, *Places Rated* looks at seven factors that, aside from direct taxes and savings, account for most of a typical household's budget: (1) house price, (2) utilities, (3) property taxes, (4) college tuition, (5) food at home, (6) health care, and (7) transportation.

These items are each indexed against a metro average of 100. An index of 95 for health care, for example, means 5 percent less costly than the metro area average. An index of 110 for college tuition, for another example, means 10 percent more expensive than the metro area average.

Each indexed item is then weighted by its relative importance in a typical household's expenses. The house price index, for example, is weighted at 30 percent, the health care index at 7 percent, the food index at 16 percent.

Rankings: Costs of Living

To derive a score for costs of living, seven factors are indexed against the U.S. average of 100: (1) average house prices, (2) utilities, (3) property taxes, (4) college tuition, (5) food at home, (6) health care, and (7) transportation. These indexes are then weighted accord-

ing to their relative importance in a typical family's budget. The sum of these weighted indexes, rounded off, is the metro area's score. The higher the score, the more expensive the metro area. Places with tie scores get the same rank and are listed in alphabetical order.

Metro: Areas from Best to Worst

Places Rated Rank	Places Rated Score	Places Rated Rank	Places Rated Score	Places Rated Rank	Places Rated Score
1. Joplin, MO	7,325	21. Danville, VA	7,965	44. Biloxi–Gulfport–Pascagoula, MS	8,233
2. Enid, OK	7,429	22. Huntington–Ashland, WV–KY–OH	7,976	45. Wichita Falls, TX	8,241
3. Gadsden, AL	7,457	23. Lafayette, LA	8,012		
4. St. Joseph, MO	7,631	24. Abilene, TX	8,015	46. Oklahoma City, OK	8,249
5. McAllen–Edinburg–Mission, TX	7,634	25. Sumter, SC	8,027	47. Chattanooga, TN–GA	8,258
				48. Killeen–Temple, TX	8,289
6. Anniston, AL	7,637	26. Dothan, AL	8,040	49. Yakima, WA	8,311
7. Texarkana, TX–Texarkana, AR	7,669	27. Corpus Christi, TX	8,060	50. Tulsa, OK	8,314
8. Pine Bluff, AR	7,760	28. Florence, SC	8,063		
9. Florence, AL	7,818	29. Pueblo, CO	8,098	51. San Angelo, TX	8,324
10. Terre Haute, IN	7,832	30. Decatur, AL	8,130	52. Amarillo, TX	8,372
				53. Mansfield, OH	8,377
11. Fort Smith, AR–OK	7,835	31. Sherman–Denison, TX	8,138	54. Waco, TX	8,380
12. Wheeling, WV–OH	7,848	32. Shreveport–Bossier City, LA	8,142	55. Evansville–Henderson, IN–KY	8,385
13. Clarksville–Hopkinsville, TN–KY	7,869	32. South Bend, IN	8,142		
14. Parkersburg–Marietta, WV–OH	7,878	34. Lawton, OK	8,148	56. Waterloo–Cedar Falls, IA	8,403
15. Johnson City–Kingsport– Bristol, TN–VA	7,894	35. Steubenville–Weirton, OH–WV	8,149	57. Duluth–Superior, MN–WI	8,424
				58. Laredo, TX	8,439
16. Cumberland, MD–WV	7,911	36. Longview–Marshall, TX	8,160	59. Sharon, PA	8,446
17. Brownsville–Harlingen–San Benito, TX	7,927	37. Fayetteville–Springdale– Rogers, AR	8,185	60. Fort Wayne, IN	8,457
18. Owensboro, KY	7,950	38. Muncie, IN	8,199	61. Rocky Mount, NC	8,458
19. Houma, LA	7,955	39. Lake Charles, LA	8,200	62. Hickory–Morgantown, NC	8,464
20. Alexandria, LA	7,960	40. Sioux City, IA–NE	8,205	63. Charleston, WV	8,477
				64. Goldsboro, NC	8,483
		41. Casper, WY	8,206	64. Tuscaloosa, AL	8,483
		42. Beaumont–Port Arthur, TX	8,215		
		43. Monroe, LA	8,228	66. Elkhart–Goshen, IN	8,505

Places Rated Rank	Places Rated Score	Places Rated Rank	Places Rated Score	Places Rated Rank	Places Rated Score
67. Kokomo, IN	8,509	126. Omaha, NE–IA	9,149	182. Daytona Beach, FL	9,664
68. Columbus, GA–AL	8,539	127. Springfield, IL	9,158	183. Charlotte–Gastonia–Rock	
69. Greenville–Spartanburg–		128. Lexington, KY	9,162	Hill, NC–SC	9,727
Anderson, SC	8,545	129. Columbia, SC	9,173	184. Wilmington, NC	9,741
70. Albany, GA	8,546	130. Roanoke, VA	9,180	185. Bloomington–Normal, IL	9,763
71. Victoria, TX	8,560	131. Appleton–Oshkosh–Neenah,		186. Rockford, IL	9,790
72. Tyler, TX	8,561	WI	9,181	187. Hamilton–Middletown, OH	9,869
73. Youngstown–Warren, OH	8,575	132. Richland–Kennewick–Pasco,		188. Visalia–Tulare–Porterville,	
74. Grand Forks, ND–MN	8,577	WA	9,187	CA	9,883
75. Spokane, WA	8,581	132. Saginaw–Bay City–Midland,		189. Regina, SK	9,902
		MI	9,187	190. Kenosha, WI	9,914
76. Jacksonville, NC	8,586	134. Jamestown, NY	9,188		
77. Springfield, MO	8,588	135. Greensboro–Winston-Salem–		191. Vancouver, WA	9,954
78. Lubbock, TX	8,598	High Point, NC	9,194	192. Columbus, OH	9,961
79. Lynchburg, VA	8,613			193. Dover, DE	9,967
79. Montgomery, AL	8,613	136. Athens, GA	9,197	194. Tucson, AZ	10,010
		137. Asheville, NC	9,203	195. Punta Gorda, FL	10,014
81. Altoona, PA	8,616	138. Provo–Orem, UT	9,212		
82. Mobile, AL	8,631	139. Jackson, MI	9,215	195. Racine, WI	10,014
83. Topeka, KS	8,641	140. Lincoln, NE	9,230	197. Raleigh–Durham–Chapel	
84. Knoxville, TN	8,650			Hill, NC	10,019
85. Dubuque, IA	8,659	141. Des Moines, IA	9,239	198. Fort Worth–Arlington, TX	10,036
		141. Savannah, GA	9,239	199. Grand Rapids–Muskegon–	
86. Macon, GA	8,668	143. Brazoria, TX	9,251	Holland, MI	10,045
87. Janesville–Beloit, WI	8,672	144. Green Bay, WI	9,252	200. Colorado Springs, CO	10,065
88. Davenport–Moline–Rock		145. Huntsville, AL	9,258		
Island, IA–IL	8,681			201. St. Louis, MO–IL	10,073
89. Decatur, IL	8,710	146. Columbia, MO	9,259	202. Albuquerque, NM	10,089
90. Sioux Falls, SD	8,711	147. Memphis, TN–AR–MS	9,275	203. Cincinnati, OH–KY–IN	10,123
		148. Las Cruces, NM	9,276	204. Melbourne–Titusville–Palm	
91. Lima, OH	8,719	149. Greeley, CO	9,287	Bay, FL	10,144
92. Little Rock–North Little		150. San Antonio, TX	9,290	205. Olympia, WA	10,146
Rock, AR	8,729				
93. Fayetteville, NC	8,736	151. Sheboygan, WI	9,294	206. Austin–San Marcos, TX	10,158
94. Eau Claire, WI	8,751	152. Bloomington, IN	9,301	207. Champaign–Urbana, IL	10,162
94. Jackson, MS	8,751	153. Yuma, AZ	9,307	208. Houston, TX	10,236
		154. New Orleans, LA	9,313	209. Saskatoon, SK	10,258
96. Greenville, NC	8,763	155. Galveston–Texas City, TX	9,323	210. Lewiston–Auburn, ME	10,274
97. Johnstown, PA	8,766				
98. Odessa–Midland, TX	8,775	156. Tallahassee, FL	9,342	211. Trois-Rivieres, PQ	10,276
99. Wausau, WI	8,818	157. Kansas City, MO–KS	9,351	212. Atlanta, GA	10,294
100. Lawrence, KS	8,819	158. Charleston–North		213. Vineland–Millville–Bridgeton,	
		Charleston, SC	9,362	NJ	10,313
101. Pensacola, FL	8,820	159. Erie, PA	9,375	214. Lansing–East Lansing, MI	10,324
102. Cedar Rapids, IA	8,834	160. Salem, OR	9,429	215. Orlando, FL	10,326
103. Canton–Massillon, OH	8,840				
103. Rapid City, SD	8,840	161. Flint, MI	9,440	216. Rochester, MN	10,328
105. Lafayette, IN	8,865	162. Bryan–College Station, TX	9,452	217. Winnipeg, MB	10,332
		163. Kalamazoo–Battle Creek, MI	9,453	218. Fort Collins–Loveland, CO	10,360
106. Augusta–Aiken, GA–SC	8,869	164. Dayton–Springfield, OH	9,470	219. Medford–Ashland, OR	10,375
107. Birmingham, AL	8,878	165. Benton Harbor, MI	9,475	220. Iowa City, IA	10,377
108. Lakeland–Winter Haven, FL	8,885				
109. Ocala, FL	8,920	166. Gary, IN	9,486	220. Yuba City, CA	10,377
110. Louisville, KY–IN	8,922	167. Akron, OH	9,500	222. Fresno, CA	10,394
		168. Elmira, NY	9,502	223. Utica–Rome, NY	10,396
111. Bismarck, ND	8,926	169. Myrtle Beach, SC	9,506	224. Saint John, NB	10,417
112. Cheyenne, WY	8,928	170. Fort Walton Beach, FL	9,507	225. Bakersfield, CA	10,421
113. Great Falls, MT	8,930				
114. Panama City, FL	8,931	171. St. Cloud, MN	9,508	226. Las Vegas, NV–AZ	10,461
115. Baton Rouge, LA	8,933	172. Salt Lake City–Ogden, UT	9,514	227. Richmond–Petersburg, VA	10,475
		173. Nashville, TN	9,515	228. Binghamton, NY	10,526
116. El Paso, TX	8,945	174. Kankakee, IL	9,546	229. Chicoutimi–Jonquiere, PQ	10,540
117. Wichita, KS	8,958	175. Bangor, ME	9,594	230. Redding, CA	10,562
118. Boise City, ID	9,027				
119. Gainesville, FL	9,029	176. Toledo, OH	9,596	231. Merced, CA	10,571
120. Fargo–Moorhead, ND–MN	9,045	177. Jacksonville, FL	9,598	232. Phoenix–Mesa, AZ	10,612
		178. Eugene–Springfield, OR	9,628	233. State College, PA	10,625
121. Billings, MT	9,068	179. Scranton–Wilkes-Barre–		234. Norfolk–Virginia Beach–	
122. Peoria–Pekin, IL	9,091	Hazleton, PA	9,647	Newport News, VA–NC	10,637
123. Williamsport, PA	9,108	180. Hagerstown, MD	9,650	235. Sarasota–Bradenton, FL	10,658
124. Indianapolis, IN	9,136				
125. La Crosse, WI–MN	9,148	181. Tampa–St. Petersburg–		236. Fort Myers–Cape Coral, FL	10,661
		Clearwater, FL	9,654	237. Sherbrooke, PQ	10,707

Places Rated Rank	Places Rated Score
238. Bellingham, WA	10,717
239. Chico–Paradise, CA	10,724
240. Harrisburg–Lebanon–Carlisle, PA	10,743
241. Quebec City, PQ	10,748
242. Buffalo–Niagara Falls, NY	10,750
243. Tacoma, WA	10,761
244. Detroit, MI	10,786
245. Syracuse, NY	10,792
246. Fort Pierce–Port St. Lucie, FL	10,799
247. Milwaukee–Waukesha, WI	10,807
248. Denver, CO	10,817
249. Cleveland–Lorain–Elyria, OH	10,827
250. Dallas, TX	10,834
251. Madison, WI	10,853
252. Edmonton, AB	10,912
253. St. John's, NF	10,926
254. Bremerton, WA	11,036
255. York, PA	11,055
256. Charlottesville, VA	11,069
257. Minneapolis–St. Paul, MN–WI	11,099
258. Reading, PA	11,102
259. Portland, OR	11,142
260. Halifax, NS	11,174
261. Calgary, AB	11,208
262. Miami, FL	11,292
263. Windsor, ON	11,334
264. Glens Falls, NY	11,345
265. Lancaster, PA	11,361
266. Fort Lauderdale, FL	11,415
267. Baltimore, MD	11,433
268. Thunder Bay, ON	11,567
269. Pittsburgh, PA	11,631
270. St. Catharines–Niagara, ON	11,775
271. Rochester, NY	11,830
272. Modesto, CA	11,835
273. Boulder–Longmont, CO	11,894
274. Sudbury, ON	11,897
275. Montreal, PQ	11,902

Places Rated Rank	Places Rated Score
276. Allentown–Bethlehem–Easton, PA–NJ	11,925
277. Stockton–Lodi, CA	11,949
278. Reno, NV	12,008
279. Wilmington–Newark, DE–MD	12,014
280. Ann Arbor, MI	12,024
281. Albany–Schenectady–Troy, NY	12,109
282. West Palm Beach–Boca Raton, FL	12,112
283. London, ON	12,136
284. Santa Fe, NM	12,374
285. Kitchener, ON	12,391
286. Portland, ME	12,394
287. Ottawa–Hull, ON–PQ	12,613
288. Pittsfield, MA	12,647
289. Waterbury, CT	12,662
290. Hamilton, ON	12,675
291. Atlantic City–Cape May, NJ	12,741
292. Oshawa, ON	12,773
293. Bridgeport, CT	12,833
294. Burlington, VT	12,839
295. Springfield, MA	12,860
296. Chicago, IL	12,934
297. Riverside–San Bernardino, CA	13,058
298. Sacramento, CA	13,213
299. Anchorage, AK	13,214
300. Yolo, CA	13,324
301. Worcester–Fitchburg–Leominster, MA	13,442
302. Seattle–Bellevue–Everett, WA	13,509
303. New Bedford–Fall River–Attleboro, MA	13,558
304. Providence–Warwick–Cranston, RI	13,568
305. Danbury, CT	13,759
306. Naples, FL	13,789
307. Victoria, BC	13,836
308. Washington, DC–MD–VA–WV	14,004

Places Rated Rank	Places Rated Score
309. Vallejo–Fairfield–Napa, CA	14,043
310. Manchester–Nashua, NH	14,179
311. New London–Norwich, CT–RI	14,248
312. New Haven–Meriden, CT	14,332
313. Philadelphia, PA–NJ	14,507
314. Trenton, NJ	14,553
315. Orange County, NY	14,564
316. Portsmouth–Dover–Rochester, NH	14,565
317. Dutchess County, NY	14,893
318. Toronto, ON	15,139
319. Monmouth–Ocean, NJ	15,253
320. Hartford, CT	15,291
321. Lake County, IL	15,501
322. Vancouver, BC	15,688
323. Barnstable–Yarmouth, MA	16,086
324. Santa Rosa, CA	16,243
325. Central New Jersey, NJ	16,322
326. San Diego, CA	16,343
327. Salinas, CA	16,588
328. San Luis Obispo–Atascadero–Paso Robles, CA	16,702
329. Boston, MA	16,781
330. Stamford–Norwalk, CT	17,069
331. Newark–Jersey City, NJ	17,477
332. Oakland, CA	17,488
333. Northern New Jersey, NJ	18,333
334. Los Angeles–Long Beach, CA	18,350
335. Long Island, NY	18,393
336. Ventura, CA	18,478
337. Santa Barbara–Santa Maria–Lompoc, CA	18,672
338. Santa Cruz–Watsonville, CA	18,849
339. Orange County, CA	18,979
340. Honolulu, HI	19,194
341. San Jose, CA	20,493
342. New York, NY	20,513
343. San Francisco, CA	21,932

Place Profiles: Costs of Living

The following profiles detail metropolitan cost-of-living factors. These include the elements used to rank metro areas—three costs of homeownership and four other living costs indexed against the U.S. average of 100—as well as average household incomes and typical state/provincial tax bites. Income and tax figures are in American dollars.

The data are derived from these sources: Advisory Commission on Intergovernmental Relations, *Significant Features of Fiscal Federalism*, 1993; American Association of Realtors, *Existing Home Sales*, 1st quarter, 1993; American Chamber of Commerce Researchers Association, "Inter-City Cost of Living Index," 4th quarter, 1992, and 1st quarter, 1993; American Gas Association, *Gas Facts*, 1993; Canadian Real Estate Association, *MLS Resale Data*, April 1993; Commerce Clearing House, *Canadian Master Tax Guide* and *State Tax Guide*, 1989; District of

Columbia Department of Finance and Revenue, "Tax Rates and Tax Burdens: A Nationwide Comparison"; Royal LePage Real Estate Services, *Survey of Canadian House Prices*, winter 1993; Statistics Canada, *Consumer Prices and Price Indexes*, December 1992, "Inter-City Indexes of Retail Price Differentials," September 1992, and unpublished income estimates for subprovincial areas, 1993; U.S. Department of Energy, *Electric Sales and Revenue*, 1992; U.S. Department of Labor, Bureau of Labor Statistics, *CPI Detailed Report*, March 1993, and *Relative Importance of Components in the Consumer Price Index*, 1992; and Woods & Poole Economics, Inc., unpublished household income estimates.

A check mark (✓) preceding a metro area's name highlights it as one of the best 35 places for costs of living.

✓ Abilene, TX
Typical Household Income: $47,223
State and Local Taxes: $986
Housing Cost Indexes
  Average Price: 57
  Utilities: 82
  Property Taxes: 113
Other Living Cost Indexes
  College Tuition: 46
  Food at Home: 91
  Health Care: 91
  Transportation: 102
Places Rated Score: 8,015
Places Rated Rank: 24

Akron, OH
Typical Household Income: $52,151
State and Local Taxes: $3,231
Housing Cost Indexes
  Average Price: 80
  Utilities: 122
  Property Taxes: 119
Other Living Cost Indexes
  College Tuition: 148
  Food at Home: 96
  Health Care: 94
  Transportation: 99
Places Rated Score: 9,500
Places Rated Rank: 167

Albany, GA
Typical Household Income: $45,500
State and Local Taxes: $2,655
Housing Cost Indexes
  Average Price: 72
  Utilities: 96
  Property Taxes: 90
Other Living Cost Indexes
  College Tuition: 94
  Food at Home: 93
  Health Care: 85

Transportation: 96
Places Rated Score: 8,546
Places Rated Rank: 70

Albany–Schenectady–Troy, NY
Typical Household Income: $54,154
State and Local Taxes: $4,919
Housing Cost Indexes
  Average Price: 118
  Utilities: 108
  Property Taxes: 294
Other Living Cost Indexes
  College Tuition: 80
  Food at Home: 114
  Health Care: 101
  Transportation: 111
Places Rated Score: 12,109
Places Rated Rank: 281

Albuquerque, NM
Typical Household Income: $48,564
State and Local Taxes: $2,318
Housing Cost Indexes
  Average Price: 99
  Utilities: 113
  Property Taxes: 109
Other Living Cost Indexes
  College Tuition: 80
  Food at Home: 94
  Health Care: 114
  Transportation: 101
Places Rated Score: 10,089
Places Rated Rank: 202

✓ Alexandria, LA
Typical Household Income: $44,614
State and Local Taxes: $2,097
Housing Cost Indexes
  Average Price: 62
  Utilities: 79
  Property Taxes: 31

Other Living Cost Indexes
  College Tuition: 87
  Food at Home: 96
  Health Care: 94
  Transportation: 100
Places Rated Score: 7,960
Places Rated Rank: 20

Allentown–Bethlehem–Easton, PA–NJ
Typical Household Income: $56,800
State and Local Taxes: $5,022
Housing Cost Indexes
  Average Price: 122
  Utilities: 117
  Property Taxes: 191
Other Living Cost Indexes
  College Tuition: 216
  Food at Home: 112
  Health Care: 104
  Transportation: 100
Places Rated Score: 11,925
Places Rated Rank: 276

Altoona, PA
Typical Household Income: $42,567
State and Local Taxes: $3,763
Housing Cost Indexes
  Average Price: 50
  Utilities: 115
  Property Taxes: 125
Other Living Cost Indexes
  College Tuition: 216
  Food at Home: 97
  Health Care: 94
  Transportation: 100
Places Rated Score: 8,616
Places Rated Rank: 81

Amarillo, TX
Typical Household Income: $47,137

State and Local Taxes: $985
Housing Cost Indexes
Average Price: 65
Utilities: 80
Property Taxes: 129
Other Living Cost Indexes
College Tuition: 53
Food at Home: 100
Health Care: 84
Transportation: 96
Places Rated Score: 8,372
Places Rated Rank: 52

Anchorage, AK
Typical Household Income: $72,833
State and Local Taxes: None
Housing Cost Indexes
Average Price: 127
Utilities: 110
Property Taxes: 171
Other Living Cost Indexes
College Tuition: 70
Food at Home: 139
Health Care: 186
Transportation: 120
Places Rated Score: 13,214
Places Rated Rank: 299

Ann Arbor, MI
Typical Household Income: $62,165
State and Local Taxes: $4,099
Housing Cost Indexes
Average Price: 109
Utilities: 120
Property Taxes: 291
Other Living Cost Indexes
College Tuition: 168
Food at Home: 107
Health Care: 110
Transportation: 110
Places Rated Score: 12,024
Places Rated Rank: 280

✓ **Anniston, AL**
Typical Household Income: $39,776
State and Local Taxes: $2,151
Housing Cost Indexes
Average Price: 58
Utilities: 88
Property Taxes: 35
Other Living Cost Indexes
College Tuition: 73
Food at Home: 96
Health Care: 82
Transportation: 93
Places Rated Score: 7,637
Places Rated Rank: 6

Appleton-Oshkosh-Neenah, WI
Typical Household Income: $49,598
State and Local Taxes: $3,077
Housing Cost Indexes
Average Price: 74
Utilities: 105
Property Taxes: 165
Other Living Cost Indexes
College Tuition: 97
Food at Home: 96
Health Care: 93
Transportation: 95
Places Rated Score: 9,181
Places Rated Rank: 131

Asheville, NC
Typical Household Income: $43,827
State and Local Taxes: $2,674
Housing Cost Indexes

Average Price: 80
Utilities: 100
Property Taxes: 92
Other Living Cost Indexes
College Tuition: 57
Food at Home: 102
Health Care: 102
Transportation: 100
Places Rated Score: 9,203
Places Rated Rank: 137

Athens, GA
Typical Household Income: $40,586
State and Local Taxes: $2,368
Housing Cost Indexes
Average Price: 88
Utilities: 93
Property Taxes: 110
Other Living Cost Indexes
College Tuition: 110
Food at Home: 96
Health Care: 86
Transportation: 91
Places Rated Score: 9,197
Places Rated Rank: 136

Atlanta, GA
Typical Household Income: $56,098
State and Local Taxes: $3,273
Housing Cost Indexes
Average Price: 100
Utilities: 93
Property Taxes: 125
Other Living Cost Indexes
College Tuition: 92
Food at Home: 99
Health Care: 133
Transportation: 99
Places Rated Score: 10,294
Places Rated Rank: 212

Atlantic City-Cape May, NJ
Typical Household Income: $68,878
State and Local Taxes: $2,534
Housing Cost Indexes
Average Price: 137
Utilities: 127
Property Taxes: 275
Other Living Cost Indexes
College Tuition: 123
Food at Home: 103
Health Care: 100
Transportation: 109
Places Rated Score: 12,741
Places Rated Rank: 291

Augusta-Aiken, GA-SC
Typical Household Income: $48,794
State and Local Taxes: $2,847
Housing Cost Indexes
Average Price: 78
Utilities: 93
Property Taxes: 98
Other Living Cost Indexes
College Tuition: 90
Food at Home: 92
Health Care: 91
Transportation: 100
Places Rated Score: 8,869
Places Rated Rank: 106

Austin-San Marcos, TX
Typical Household Income: $46,426
State and Local Taxes: $970
Housing Cost Indexes
Average Price: 96
Utilities: 80
Property Taxes: 191

Other Living Cost Indexes
College Tuition: 54
Food at Home: 101
Health Care: 104
Transportation: 104
Places Rated Score: 10,158
Places Rated Rank: 206

Bakersfield, CA
Typical Household Income: $49,696
State and Local Taxes: $2,169
Housing Cost Indexes
Average Price: 99
Utilities: 93
Property Taxes: 102
Other Living Cost Indexes
College Tuition: 50
Food at Home: 109
Health Care: 124
Transportation: 112
Places Rated Score: 10,421
Places Rated Rank: 225

Baltimore, MD
Typical Household Income: $61,695
State and Local Taxes: $4,122
Housing Cost Indexes
Average Price: 128
Utilities: 96
Property Taxes: 160
Other Living Cost Indexes
College Tuition: 123
Food at Home: 105
Health Care: 103
Transportation: 99
Places Rated Score: 11,433
Places Rated Rank: 267

Bangor, ME
Typical Household Income: $46,599
State and Local Taxes: $2,500
Housing Cost Indexes
Average Price: 80
Utilities: 102
Property Taxes: 122
Other Living Cost Indexes
College Tuition: 132
Food at Home: 103
Health Care: 100
Transportation: 102
Places Rated Score: 9,594
Places Rated Rank: 175

Barnstable-Yarmouth, MA
Typical Household Income: $60,629
State and Local Taxes: $4,121
Housing Cost Indexes
Average Price: 203
Utilities: 132
Property Taxes: 305
Other Living Cost Indexes
College Tuition: 218
Food at Home: 108
Health Care: 125
Transportation: 121
Places Rated Score: 16,086
Places Rated Rank: 323

Baton Rouge, LA
Typical Household Income: $50,983
State and Local Taxes: $2,397
Housing Cost Indexes
Average Price: 80
Utilities: 82
Property Taxes: 40
Other Living Cost Indexes
College Tuition: 106

Food at Home: 103
Health Care: 98
Transportation: 102
Places Rated Score: 8,933
Places Rated Rank: 115

Beaumont–Port Arthur, TX
Typical Household Income: $51,184
State and Local Taxes: $1,069
Housing Cost Indexes
  Average Price: 53
  Utilities: 87
  Property Taxes: 106
Other Living Cost Indexes
  College Tuition: 53
  Food at Home: 99
  Health Care: 90
  Transportation: 110
Places Rated Score: 8,215
Places Rated Rank: 42

Bellingham, WA
Typical Household Income: $43,447
State and Local Taxes: $924
Housing Cost Indexes
  Average Price: 116
  Utilities: 84
  Property Taxes: 105
Other Living Cost Indexes
  College Tuition: 89
  Food at Home: 99
  Health Care: 141
  Transportation: 97
Places Rated Score: 10,717
Places Rated Rank: 238

Benton Harbor, MI
Typical Household Income: $46,045
State and Local Taxes: $3,036
Housing Cost Indexes
  Average Price: 67
  Utilities: 115
  Property Taxes: 179
Other Living Cost Indexes
  College Tuition: 125
  Food at Home: 111
  Health Care: 95
  Transportation: 96
Places Rated Score: 9,475
Places Rated Rank: 165

Billings, MT
Typical Household Income: $47,091
State and Local Taxes: $1,581
Housing Cost Indexes
  Average Price: 72
  Utilities: 91
  Property Taxes: 83
Other Living Cost Indexes
  College Tuition: 76
  Food at Home: 104
  Health Care: 104
  Transportation: 108
Places Rated Score: 9,068
Places Rated Rank: 121

Biloxi–Gulfport–Pascagoula, MS
Typical Household Income: $41,835
State and Local Taxes: $1,699
Housing Cost Indexes
  Average Price: 65
  Utilities: 78
  Property Taxes: 50
Other Living Cost Indexes
  College Tuition: 120
  Food at Home: 101
  Health Care: 92

Transportation: 96
Places Rated Score: 8,233
Places Rated Rank: 44

Binghamton, NY
Typical Household Income: $48,598
State and Local Taxes: $4,414
Housing Cost Indexes
  Average Price: 91
  Utilities: 118
  Property Taxes: 227
Other Living Cost Indexes
  College Tuition: 87
  Food at Home: 100
  Health Care: 93
  Transportation: 108
Places Rated Score: 10,526
Places Rated Rank: 228

Birmingham, AL
Typical Household Income: $49,945
State and Local Taxes: $2,702
Housing Cost Indexes
  Average Price: 80
  Utilities: 87
  Property Taxes: 48
Other Living Cost Indexes
  College Tuition: 105
  Food at Home: 97
  Health Care: 104
  Transportation: 100
Places Rated Score: 8,878
Places Rated Rank: 107

Bismarck, ND
Typical Household Income: $47,229
State and Local Taxes: $1,429
Housing Cost Indexes
  Average Price: 70
  Utilities: 108
  Property Taxes: 77
Other Living Cost Indexes
  College Tuition: 111
  Food at Home: 102
  Health Care: 99
  Transportation: 100
Places Rated Score: 8,926
Places Rated Rank: 111

Bloomington, IN
Typical Household Income: $37,934
State and Local Taxes: $1,892
Housing Cost Indexes
  Average Price: 82
  Utilities: 113
  Property Taxes: 97
Other Living Cost Indexes
  College Tuition: 122
  Food at Home: 98
  Health Care: 97
  Transportation: 94
Places Rated Score: 9,301
Places Rated Rank: 152

Bloomington–Normal, IL
Typical Household Income: $54,754
State and Local Taxes: $2,526
Housing Cost Indexes
  Average Price: 77
  Utilities: 136
  Property Taxes: 143
Other Living Cost Indexes
  College Tuition: 127
  Food at Home: 101
  Health Care: 92
  Transportation: 102
Places Rated Score: 9,763
Places Rated Rank: 185

Boise City, ID
Typical Household Income: $50,107
State and Local Taxes: $3,145
Housing Cost Indexes
  Average Price: 79
  Utilities: 77
  Property Taxes: 99
Other Living Cost Indexes
  College Tuition: 68
  Food at Home: 99
  Health Care: 112
  Transportation: 99
Places Rated Score: 9,027
Places Rated Rank: 118

Boston, MA
Typical Household Income: $68,411
State and Local Taxes: $4,650
Housing Cost Indexes
  Average Price: 219
  Utilities: 136
  Property Taxes: 328
Other Living Cost Indexes
  College Tuition: 133
  Food at Home: 115
  Health Care: 136
  Transportation: 120
Places Rated Score: 16,781
Places Rated Rank: 329

Boulder–Longmont, CO
Typical Household Income: $59,528
State and Local Taxes: $3,215
Housing Cost Indexes
  Average Price: 130
  Utilities: 94
  Property Taxes: 168
Other Living Cost Indexes
  College Tuition: 124
  Food at Home: 106
  Health Care: 123
  Transportation: 109
Places Rated Score: 11,894
Places Rated Rank: 273

Brazoria, TX
Typical Household Income: $55,176
State and Local Taxes: $1,153
Housing Cost Indexes
  Average Price: 71
  Utilities: 86
  Property Taxes: 141
Other Living Cost Indexes
  College Tuition: 51
  Food at Home: 99
  Health Care: 118
  Transportation: 110
Places Rated Score: 9,251
Places Rated Rank: 143

Bremerton, WA
Typical Household Income: $49,777
State and Local Taxes: $1,059
Housing Cost Indexes
  Average Price: 120
  Utilities: 82
  Property Taxes: 108
Other Living Cost Indexes
  College Tuition: 107
  Food at Home: 104
  Health Care: 129
  Transportation: 103
Places Rated Score: 11,036
Places Rated Rank: 254

Bridgeport, CT
Typical Household Income: $66,100
State and Local Taxes: $3,263

Housing Cost Indexes
  Average Price: 138
  Utilities: 130
  Property Taxes: 221
Other Living Cost Indexes
  College Tuition: 103
  Food at Home: 105
  Health Care: 113
  Transportation: 119
Places Rated Score: 12,833
Places Rated Rank: 293

✓ **Brownsville–Harlingen–San Benito, TX**
Typical Household Income: $37,607
State and Local Taxes: $786
Housing Cost Indexes
  Average Price: 51
  Utilities: 78
  Property Taxes: 101
Other Living Cost Indexes
  College Tuition: 63
  Food at Home: 97
  Health Care: 94
  Transportation: 104
Places Rated Score: 7,927
Places Rated Rank: 17

Bryan–College Station, TX
Typical Household Income: $36,152
State and Local Taxes: $755
Housing Cost Indexes
  Average Price: 80
  Utilities: 91
  Property Taxes: 161
Other Living Cost Indexes
  College Tuition: 58
  Food at Home: 98
  Health Care: 91
  Transportation: 107
Places Rated Score: 9,452
Places Rated Rank: 162

Buffalo–Niagara Falls, NY
Typical Household Income: $50,659
State and Local Taxes: $4,601
Housing Cost Indexes
  Average Price: 85
  Utilities: 108
  Property Taxes: 212
Other Living Cost Indexes
  College Tuition: 83
  Food at Home: 112
  Health Care: 111
  Transportation: 119
Places Rated Score: 10,750
Places Rated Rank: 242

Burlington, VT
Typical Household Income: $52,103
State and Local Taxes: $2,143
Housing Cost Indexes
  Average Price: 141
  Utilities: 117
  Property Taxes: 212
Other Living Cost Indexes
  College Tuition: 253
  Food at Home: 110
  Health Care: 114
  Transportation: 99
Places Rated Score: 12,839
Places Rated Rank: 294

Calgary, AB
Typical Household Income: $62,109
Provincial Taxes: $6,159
Housing Cost Indexes

Average Price: 109
  Utilities: 95
  Property Taxes: 136
Other Living Cost Indexes
  College Tuition: 60
  Food at Home: 153
  Health Care: 28
  Transportation: 121
Places Rated Score: 11,208
Places Rated Rank: 261

Canton–Massillon, OH
Typical Household Income: $48,059
State and Local Taxes: $2,977
Housing Cost Indexes
  Average Price: 67
  Utilities: 113
  Property Taxes: 100
Other Living Cost Indexes
  College Tuition: 148
  Food at Home: 92
  Health Care: 88
  Transportation: 103
Places Rated Score: 8,840
Places Rated Rank: 103

Casper, WY
Typical Household Income: $48,084
State and Local Taxes: $674
Housing Cost Indexes
  Average Price: 62
  Utilities: 89
  Property Taxes: 37
Other Living Cost Indexes
  College Tuition: 63
  Food at Home: 103
  Health Care: 102
  Transportation: 99
Places Rated Score: 8,206
Places Rated Rank: 41

Cedar Rapids, IA
Typical Household Income: $51,896
State and Local Taxes: $2,660
Housing Cost Indexes
  Average Price: 70
  Utilities: 123
  Property Taxes: 112
Other Living Cost Indexes
  College Tuition: 103
  Food at Home: 95
  Health Care: 93
  Transportation: 91
Places Rated Score: 8,834
Places Rated Rank: 102

Central New Jersey, NJ
Typical Household Income: $81,411
State and Local Taxes: $2,995
Housing Cost Indexes
  Average Price: 207
  Utilities: 126
  Property Taxes: 414
Other Living Cost Indexes
  College Tuition: 189
  Food at Home: 110
  Health Care: 115
  Transportation: 108
Places Rated Score: 16,322
Places Rated Rank: 325

Champaign–Urbana, IL
Typical Household Income: $48,711
State and Local Taxes: $2,247
Housing Cost Indexes
  Average Price: 83
  Utilities: 135
  Property Taxes: 154

Other Living Cost Indexes
  College Tuition: 163
  Food at Home: 100
  Health Care: 106
  Transportation: 101
Places Rated Score: 10,162
Places Rated Rank: 207

Charleston, WV
Typical Household Income: $45,101
State and Local Taxes: $2,375
Housing Cost Indexes
  Average Price: 68
  Utilities: 95
  Property Taxes: 34
Other Living Cost Indexes
  College Tuition: 79
  Food at Home: 96
  Health Care: 100
  Transportation: 106
Places Rated Score: 8,477
Places Rated Rank: 63

Charleston–North Charleston, SC
Typical Household Income: $46,195
State and Local Taxes: $2,676
Housing Cost Indexes
  Average Price: 95
  Utilities: 83
  Property Taxes: 87
Other Living Cost Indexes
  College Tuition: 130
  Food at Home: 94
  Health Care: 100
  Transportation: 90
Places Rated Score: 9,362
Places Rated Rank: 158

Charlotte–Gastonia–Rock Hill, NC–SC
Typical Household Income: $49,530
State and Local Taxes: $3,022
Housing Cost Indexes
  Average Price: 94
  Utilities: 95
  Property Taxes: 109
Other Living Cost Indexes
  College Tuition: 81
  Food at Home: 95
  Health Care: 118
  Transportation: 96
Places Rated Score: 9,727
Places Rated Rank: 183

Charlottesville, VA
Typical Household Income: $54,773
State and Local Taxes: $2,560
Housing Cost Indexes
  Average Price: 124
  Utilities: 103
  Property Taxes: 136
Other Living Cost Indexes
  College Tuition: 163
  Food at Home: 96
  Health Care: 96
  Transportation: 99
Places Rated Score: 11,069
Places Rated Rank: 256

Chattanooga, TN–GA
Typical Household Income: $47,276
State and Local Taxes: $1,190
Housing Cost Indexes
  Average Price: 74
  Utilities: 78
  Property Taxes: 79

Other Living Cost Indexes
  College Tuition: 82
  Food at Home: 94
  Health Care: 89
  Transportation: 87
Places Rated Score: 8,258
Places Rated Rank: 47

Cheyenne, WY
Typical Household Income: $47,143
State and Local Taxes: $660
Housing Cost Indexes
  Average Price: 79
  Utilities: 91
  Property Taxes: 48
Other Living Cost Indexes
  College Tuition: 63
  Food at Home: 101
  Health Care: 95
  Transportation: 106
Places Rated Score: 8,928
Places Rated Rank: 112

Chicago, IL
Typical Household Income: $66,300
State and Local Taxes: $3,059
Housing Cost Indexes
  Average Price: 137
  Utilities: 132
  Property Taxes: 253
Other Living Cost Indexes
  College Tuition: 139
  Food at Home: 102
  Health Care: 115
  Transportation: 116
Places Rated Score: 12,934
Places Rated Rank: 296

Chico-Paradise, CA
Typical Household Income: $42,406
State and Local Taxes: $1,851
Housing Cost Indexes
  Average Price: 113
  Utilities: 101
  Property Taxes: 116
Other Living Cost Indexes
  College Tuition: 50
  Food at Home: 105
  Health Care: 110
  Transportation: 106
Places Rated Score: 10,724
Places Rated Rank: 239

Chicoutimi-Jonquiere, PQ
Typical Household Income: $49,608
Provincial Taxes: $8,078
Housing Cost Indexes
  Average Price: 61
  Utilities: 124
  Property Taxes: 101
Other Living Cost Indexes
  College Tuition: 58
  Food at Home: 163
  Health Care: 28
  Transportation: 160
Places Rated Score: 10,540
Places Rated Rank: 229

Cincinnati, OH-KY-IN
Typical Household Income: $54,870
State and Local Taxes: $3,399
Housing Cost Indexes
  Average Price: 92
  Utilities: 112
  Property Taxes: 136
Other Living Cost Indexes
  College Tuition: 135

Food at Home: 96
Health Care: 95
Transportation: 108
Places Rated Score: 10,123
Places Rated Rank: 203

✓ **Clarksville-Hopkinsville, TN-KY**
Typical Household Income: $38,468
State and Local Taxes: $968
Housing Cost Indexes
  Average Price: 62
  Utilities: 75
  Property Taxes: 66
Other Living Cost Indexes
  College Tuition: 83
  Food at Home: 95
  Health Care: 81
  Transportation: 96
Places Rated Score: 7,869
Places Rated Rank: 13

Cleveland-Lorain-Elyria, OH
Typical Household Income: $56,848
State and Local Taxes: $3,522
Housing Cost Indexes
  Average Price: 94
  Utilities: 135
  Property Taxes: 141
Other Living Cost Indexes
  College Tuition: 158
  Food at Home: 104
  Health Care: 111
  Transportation: 111
Places Rated Score: 10,827
Places Rated Rank: 249

Colorado Springs, CO
Typical Household Income: $51,065
State and Local Taxes: $2,758
Housing Cost Indexes
  Average Price: 100
  Utilities: 86
  Property Taxes: 130
Other Living Cost Indexes
  College Tuition: 101
  Food at Home: 104
  Health Care: 95
  Transportation: 101
Places Rated Score: 10,065
Places Rated Rank: 200

Columbia, MO
Typical Household Income: $48,567
State and Local Taxes: $2,939
Housing Cost Indexes
  Average Price: 79
  Utilities: 103
  Property Taxes: 99
Other Living Cost Indexes
  College Tuition: 115
  Food at Home: 96
  Health Care: 106
  Transportation: 99
Places Rated Score: 9,259
Places Rated Rank: 146

Columbia, SC
Typical Household Income: $49,906
State and Local Taxes $2,891
Housing Cost Indexes
  Average Price: 91
  Utilities: 86
  Property Taxes: 84
Other Living Cost Indexes
  College Tuition: 141
  Food at Home: 94
  Health Care: 105

Transportation: 84
Places Rated Score: 9,173
Places Rated Rank: 129

Columbus, GA-AL
Typical Household Income: $43,811
State and Local Taxes: $2,556
Housing Cost Indexes
  Average Price: 70
  Utilities: 92
  Property Taxes: 87
Other Living Cost Indexes
  College Tuition: 78
  Food at Home: 97
  Health Care: 88
  Transportation: 99
Places Rated Score: 8,539
Places Rated Rank: 68

Columbus, OH
Typical Household Income: $51,630
State and Local Taxes: $3,199
Housing Cost Indexes
  Average Price: 91
  Utilities: 111
  Property Taxes: 137
Other Living Cost Indexes
  College Tuition: 129
  Food at Home: 99
  Health Care: 91
  Transportation: 102
Places Rated Score: 9,961
Places Rated Rank: 192

✓ **Corpus Christi, TX**
Typical Household Income: $48,790
State and Local Taxes: $1,019
Housing Cost Indexes
  Average Price: 66
  Utilities: 79
  Property Taxes: 131
Other Living Cost Indexes
  College Tuition: 50
  Food at Home: 93
  Health Care: 90
  Transportation: 83
Places Rated Score: 8,060
Places Rated Rank: 27

✓ **Cumberland, MD-WV**
Typical Household Income: $40,444
State and Local Taxes: $2,702
Housing Cost Indexes
  Average Price: 56
  Utilities: 89
  Property Taxes: 70
Other Living Cost Indexes
  College Tuition: 111
  Food at Home: 103
  Health Care: 91
  Transportation: 86
Places Rated Score: 7,911
Places Rated Rank: 16

Dallas, TX
Typical Household Income: $57,704
State and Local Taxes: $1,206
Housing Cost Indexes
  Average Price: 108
  Utilities: 89
  Property Taxes: 215
Other Living Cost Indexes
  College Tuition: 50
  Food at Home: 96
  Health Care: 115
  Transportation: 107
Places Rated Score: 10,834
Places Rated Rank: 250

Danbury, CT
Typical Household Income: $68,780
State and Local Taxes: $3,363
Housing Cost Indexes
  Average Price: 167
  Utilities: 123
  Property Taxes: 268
Other Living Cost Indexes
  College Tuition: 102
  Food at Home: 103
  Health Care: 113
  Transportation: 107
Places Rated Score: 13,759
Places Rated Rank: 305

✓ **Danville, VA**
Typical Household Income: $43,525
State and Local Taxes: $2,034
Housing Cost Indexes
  Average Price: 56
  Utilities: 89
  Property Taxes: 62
Other Living Cost Indexes
  College Tuition: 155
  Food at Home: 93
  Health Care: 93
  Transportation: 94
Places Rated Score: 7,965
Places Rated Rank: 21

Davenport-Moline-Rock Island, IA-IL
Typical Household Income: $50,443
State and Local Taxes: $2,585
Housing Cost Indexes
  Average Price: 59
  Utilities: 118
  Property Taxes: 95
Other Living Cost Indexes
  College Tuition: 103
  Food at Home: 101
  Health Care: 100
  Transportation: 100
Places Rated Score: 8,681
Places Rated Rank: 88

Dayton-Springfield, OH
Typical Household Income: $51,551
State and Local Taxes: $3,194
Housing Cost Indexes
  Average Price: 79
  Utilities: 120
  Property Taxes: 119
Other Living Cost Indexes
  College Tuition: 135
  Food at Home: 98
  Health Care: 92
  Transportation: 99
Places Rated Score: 9,470
Places Rated Rank: 164

Daytona Beach, FL
Typical Household Income: $41,421
State and Local Taxes: $743
Housing Cost Indexes
  Average Price: 89
  Utilities: 85
  Property Taxes: 142
Other Living Cost Indexes
  College Tuition: 73
  Food at Home: 96
  Health Care: 112
  Transportation: 101
Places Rated Score: 9,664
Places Rated Rank: 182

✓ **Decatur, AL**
Typical Household Income: $44,036
State and Local Taxes: $2,382
Housing Cost Indexes
  Average Price: 69
  Utilities: 74
  Property Taxes: 41
Other Living Cost Indexes
  College Tuition: 91
  Food at Home: 93
  Health Care: 89
  Transportation: 101
Places Rated Score: 8,130
Places Rated Rank: 30

Decatur, IL
Typical Household Income: $51,558
State and Local Taxes: $2,378
Housing Cost Indexes
  Average Price: 56
  Utilities: 141
  Property Taxes: 103
Other Living Cost Indexes
  College Tuition: 163
  Food at Home: 98
  Health Care: 88
  Transportation: 97
Places Rated Score: 8,710
Places Rated Rank: 89

Denver, CO
Typical Household Income: $58,114
State and Local Taxes: $3,139
Housing Cost Indexes
  Average Price: 107
  Utilities: 98
  Property Taxes: 139
Other Living Cost Indexes
  College Tuition: 97
  Food at Home: 100
  Health Care: 127
  Transportation: 109
Places Rated Score: 10,817
Places Rated Rank: 248

Des Moines, IA
Typical Household Income: $54,261
State and Local Taxes: $2,781
Housing Cost Indexes
  Average Price: 70
  Utilities: 111
  Property Taxes: 112
Other Living Cost Indexes
  College Tuition: 103
  Food at Home: 100
  Health Care: 100
  Transportation: 107
Places Rated Score: 9,239
Places Rated Rank: 141

Detroit, MI
Typical Household Income: $58,890
State and Local Taxes: $3,883
Housing Cost Indexes
  Average Price: 86
  Utilities: 120
  Property Taxes: 232
Other Living Cost Indexes
  College Tuition: 134
  Food at Home: 107
  Health Care: 103
  Transportation: 110
Places Rated Score: 10,786
Places Rated Rank: 244

✓ **Dothan, AL**
Typical Household Income: $42,643
State and Local Taxes: $2,307

Housing Cost Indexes
  Average Price: 64
  Utilities: 84
  Property Taxes: 38
Other Living Cost Indexes
  College Tuition: 78
  Food at Home: 99
  Health Care: 79
  Transportation: 101
Places Rated Score: 8,040
Places Rated Rank: 26

Dover, DE
Typical Household Income: $44,567
State and Local Taxes: $2,154
Housing Cost Indexes
  Average Price: 97
  Utilities: 110
  Property Taxes: 73
Other Living Cost Indexes
  College Tuition: 71
  Food at Home: 108
  Health Care: 105
  Transportation: 100
Places Rated Score: 9,967
Places Rated Rank: 193

Dubuque, IA
Typical Household Income: $48,865
State and Local Taxes: $2,504
Housing Cost Indexes
  Average Price: 63
  Utilities: 92
  Property Taxes: 100
Other Living Cost Indexes
  College Tuition: 103
  Food at Home: 103
  Health Care: 99
  Transportation: 101
Places Rated Score: 8,659
Places Rated Rank: 85

Duluth-Superior, MN-WI
Typical Household Income: $43,857
State and Local Taxes: $2,691
Housing Cost Indexes
  Average Price: 50
  Utilities: 100
  Property Taxes: 100
Other Living Cost Indexes
  College Tuition: 130
  Food at Home: 100
  Health Care: 101
  Transportation: 107
Places Rated Score: 8,424
Places Rated Rank: 57

Dutchess County, NY
Typical Household Income: $63,374
State and Local Taxes: $5,756
Housing Cost Indexes
  Average Price: 170
  Utilities: 125
  Property Taxes: 425
Other Living Cost Indexes
  College Tuition: 87
  Food at Home: 110
  Health Care: 112
  Transportation: 114
Places Rated Score: 14,893
Places Rated Rank: 317

Eau Claire, WI
Typical Household Income: $43,409
State and Local Taxes: $2,693
Housing Cost Indexes
  Average Price: 60

Utilities: 105
Property Taxes: 134
Other Living Cost Indexes
College Tuition: 101
Food at Home: 103
Health Care: 103
Transportation: 95
Places Rated Score: 8,751
Places Rated Rank: 94

Edmonton, AB
Typical Household Income: $55,726
Provincial Taxes: $5,147
Housing Cost Indexes
Average Price: 92
Utilities: 97
Property Taxes: 133
Other Living Cost Indexes
College Tuition: 63
Food at Home: 163
Health Care: 28
Transportation: 126
Places Rated Score: 10,912
Places Rated Rank: 252

El Paso, TX
Typical Household Income: $42,225
State and Local Taxes: $882
Housing Cost Indexes
Average Price: 71
Utilities: 86
Property Taxes: 142
Other Living Cost Indexes
College Tuition: 51
Food at Home: 94
Health Care: 93
Transportation: 110
Places Rated Score: 8,945
Places Rated Rank: 116

Elkhart–Goshen, IN
Typical Household Income: $47,738
State and Local Taxes: $2,382
Housing Cost Indexes
Average Price: 73
Utilities: 104
Property Taxes: 87
Other Living Cost Indexes
College Tuition: 100
Food at Home: 90
Health Care: 91
Transportation: 90
Places Rated Score: 8,505
Places Rated Rank: 66

Elmira, NY
Typical Household Income: $45,423
State and Local Taxes: $4,126
Housing Cost Indexes
Average Price: 65
Utilities: 118
Property Taxes: 162
Other Living Cost Indexes
College Tuition: 87
Food at Home: 108
Health Care: 117
Transportation: 102
Places Rated Score: 9,502
Places Rated Rank: 168

✓ **Enid, OK**
Typical Household Income: $44,392
State and Local Taxes: $2,511
Housing Cost Indexes
Average Price: 48
Utilities: 92
Property Taxes: 43

Other Living Cost Indexes
College Tuition: 75
Food at Home: 93
Health Care: 92
Transportation: 96
Places Rated Score: 7,429
Places Rated Rank: 2

Erie, PA
Typical Household Income: $48,381
State and Local Taxes: $4,277
Housing Cost Indexes
Average Price: 66
Utilities: 114
Property Taxes: 165
Other Living Cost Indexes
College Tuition: 165
Food at Home: 94
Health Care: 105
Transportation: 103
Places Rated Score: 9,375
Places Rated Rank: 159

Eugene–Springfield, OR
Typical Household Income: $43,095
State and Local Taxes: $1,572
Housing Cost Indexes
Average Price: 79
Utilities: 78
Property Taxes: 170
Other Living Cost Indexes
College Tuition: 108
Food at Home: 99
Health Care: 108
Transportation: 107
Places Rated Score: 9,628
Places Rated Rank: 178

Evansville–Henderson, IN–KY
Typical Household Income: $47,631
State and Local Taxes: $2,376
Housing Cost Indexes
Average Price: 66
Utilities: 107
Property Taxes: 79
Other Living Cost Indexes
College Tuition: 93
Food at Home: 95
Health Care: 85
Transportation: 95
Places Rated Score: 8,385
Places Rated Rank: 55

Fargo–Moorhead, ND–MN
Typical Household Income: $45,264
State and Local Taxes: $1,369
Housing Cost Indexes
Average Price: 74
Utilities: 99
Property Taxes: 82
Other Living Cost Indexes
College Tuition: 111
Food at Home: 104
Health Care: 98
Transportation: 99
Places Rated Score: 9,045
Places Rated Rank: 120

Fayetteville, NC
Typical Household Income: $41,447
State and Local Taxes: $2,529
Housing Cost Indexes
Average Price: 74
Utilities: 95
Property Taxes: 86
Other Living Cost Indexes
College Tuition: 54

Food at Home: 95
Health Care: 102
Transportation: 98
Places Rated Score: 8,736
Places Rated Rank: 93

Fayetteville–Springdale–Rogers, AR
Typical Household Income: $42,126
State and Local Taxes: $2,090
Housing Cost Indexes
Average Price: 69
Utilities: 78
Property Taxes: 77
Other Living Cost Indexes
College Tuition: 88
Food at Home: 94
Health Care: 84
Transportation: 94
Places Rated Score: 8,185
Places Rated Rank: 37

Flint, MI
Typical Household Income: $48,837
State and Local Taxes: $3,220
Housing Cost Indexes
Average Price: 60
Utilities: 116
Property Taxes: 161
Other Living Cost Indexes
College Tuition: 123
Food at Home: 107
Health Care: 100
Transportation: 112
Places Rated Score: 9,440
Places Rated Rank: 161

✓ **Florence, AL**
Typical Household Income: $38,578
State and Local Taxes: $2,087
Housing Cost Indexes
Average Price: 61
Utilities: 80
Property Taxes: 37
Other Living Cost Indexes
College Tuition: 67
Food at Home: 93
Health Care: 101
Transportation: 96
Places Rated Score: 7,818
Places Rated Rank: 9

✓ **Florence, SC**
Typical Household Income: $44,048
State and Local Taxes: $2,552
Housing Cost Indexes
Average Price: 69
Utilities: 87
Property Taxes: 63
Other Living Cost Indexes
College Tuition: 99
Food at Home: 95
Health Care: 84
Transportation: 86
Places Rated Score: 8,063
Places Rated Rank: 28

Fort Collins–Loveland, CO
Typical Household Income: $49,546
State and Local Taxes: $2,676
Housing Cost Indexes
Average Price: 101
Utilities: 85
Property Taxes: 131
Other Living Cost Indexes
College Tuition: 122
Food at Home: 104

Health Care: 113
Transportation: 103
Places Rated Score: 10,360
Places Rated Rank: 218

Fort Lauderdale, FL
Typical Household Income: $58,000
State and Local Taxes: $1,041
Housing Cost Indexes
Average Price: 124
Utilities: 83
Property Taxes: 198
Other Living Cost Indexes
College Tuition: 73
Food at Home: 97
Health Care: 125
Transportation: 106
Places Rated Score: 11,415
Places Rated Rank: 266

Fort Myers-Cape Coral, FL
Typical Household Income: $49,557
State and Local Taxes: $890
Housing Cost Indexes
Average Price: 116
Utilities: 83
Property Taxes: 186
Other Living Cost Indexes
College Tuition: 77
Food at Home: 98
Health Care: 93
Transportation: 98
Places Rated Score: 10,661
Places Rated Rank: 236

Fort Pierce-Port St. Lucie, FL
Typical Household Income: $46,986
State and Local Taxes: $843
Housing Cost Indexes
Average Price: 121
Utilities: 76
Property Taxes: 194
Other Living Cost Indexes
College Tuition: 74
Food at Home: 96
Health Care: 93
Transportation: 99
Places Rated Score: 10,799
Places Rated Rank: 246

✓ **Fort Smith, AR-OK**
Typical Household Income: $39,348
State and Local Taxes: $1,952
Housing Cost Indexes
Average Price: 57
Utilities: 86
Property Taxes: 63
Other Living Cost Indexes
College Tuition: 88
Food at Home: 95
Health Care: 93
Transportation: 94
Places Rated Score: 7,835
Places Rated Rank: 11

Fort Walton Beach, FL
Typical Household Income: $44,821
State and Local Taxes: $805
Housing Cost Indexes
Average Price: 90
Utilities: 75
Property Taxes: 144
Other Living Cost Indexes
College Tuition: 73
Food at Home: 95
Health Care: 103
Transportation: 100
Places Rated Score: 9,507
Places Rated Rank: 170

Fort Wayne, IN
Typical Household Income: $50,509
State and Local Taxes: $2,520
Housing Cost Indexes
Average Price: 69
Utilities: 105
Property Taxes: 82
Other Living Cost Indexes
College Tuition: 101
Food at Home: 94
Health Care: 82
Transportation: 95
Places Rated Score: 8,457
Places Rated Rank: 60

Fort Worth-Arlington, TX
Typical Household Income: $52,486
State and Local Taxes: $1,096
Housing Cost Indexes
Average Price: 90
Utilities: 89
Property Taxes: 179
Other Living Cost Indexes
College Tuition: 55
Food at Home: 104
Health Care: 108
Transportation: 104
Places Rated Score: 10,036
Places Rated Rank: 198

Fresno, CA
Typical Household Income: $52,046
State and Local Taxes: $2,272
Housing Cost Indexes
Average Price: 104
Utilities: 100
Property Taxes: 107
Other Living Cost Indexes
College Tuition: 51
Food at Home: 103
Health Care: 110
Transportation: 110
Places Rated Score: 10,394
Places Rated Rank: 222

✓ **Gadsden, AL**
Typical Household Income: $37,504
State and Local Taxes: $2,028
Housing Cost Indexes
Average Price: 52
Utilities: 87
Property Taxes: 31
Other Living Cost Indexes
College Tuition: 73
Food at Home: 96
Health Care: 94
Transportation: 92
Places Rated Score: 7,457
Places Rated Rank: 3

Gainesville, FL
Typical Household Income: $42,200
State and Local Taxes: $757
Housing Cost Indexes
Average Price: 80
Utilities: 69
Property Taxes: 128
Other Living Cost Indexes
College Tuition: 73
Food at Home: 98
Health Care: 98
Transportation: 99
Places Rated Score: 9,029
Places Rated Rank: 119

Galveston-Texas City, TX
Typical Household Income: $50,694
State and Local Taxes $1,059

Housing Cost Indexes
Average Price: 75
Utilities: 83
Property Taxes: 149
Other Living Cost Indexes
College Tuition: 57
Food at Home: 98
Health Care: 108
Transportation: 110
Places Rated Score: 9,323
Places Rated Rank: 155

Gary, IN
Typical Household Income: $49,409
State and Local Taxes: $2,465
Housing Cost Indexes
Average Price: 71
Utilities: 127
Property Taxes: 85
Other Living Cost Indexes
College Tuition: 101
Food at Home: 101
Health Care: 110
Transportation: 113
Places Rated Score: 9,486
Places Rated Rank: 166

Glens Falls, NY
Typical Household Income: $44,944
State and Local Taxes: $4,082
Housing Cost Indexes
Average Price: 101
Utilities: 110
Property Taxes: 252
Other Living Cost Indexes
College Tuition: 80
Food at Home: 115
Health Care: 120
Transportation: 104
Places Rated Score: 11,345
Places Rated Rank: 264

Goldsboro, NC
Typical Household Income: $37,980
State and Local Taxes: $2,317
Housing Cost Indexes
Average Price: 68
Utilities: 102
Property Taxes: 78
Other Living Cost Indexes
College Tuition: 60
Food at Home: 99
Health Care: 93
Transportation: 95
Places Rated Score: 8,483
Places Rated Rank: 64

Grand Forks, ND-MN
Typical Household Income: $44,942
State and Local Taxes: $1,359
Housing Cost Indexes
Average Price: 63
Utilities: 100
Property Taxes: 69
Other Living Cost Indexes
College Tuition: 112
Food at Home: 104
Health Care: 96
Transportation: 100
Places Rated Score: 8,577
Places Rated Rank: 74

Grand Rapids-Muskegon-Holland, MI
Typical Household Income: $52,007
State and Local Taxes: $3,429
Housing Cost Indexes
Average Price: 78

Utilities: 103
Property Taxes: 208
Other Living Cost Indexes
College Tuition: 117
Food at Home: 106
Health Care: 106
Transportation: 104
Places Rated Score: 10,045
Places Rated Rank: 199

Great Falls, MT
Typical Household Income: $46,750
State and Local Taxes: $1,569
Housing Cost Indexes
Average Price: 69
Utilities: 90
Property Taxes: 78
Other Living Cost Indexes
College Tuition: 76
Food at Home: 108
Health Care: 105
Transportation: 106
Places Rated Score: 8,930
Places Rated Rank: 113

Greeley, CO
Typical Household Income: $50,437
State and Local Taxes: $2,724
Housing Cost Indexes
Average Price: 80
Utilities: 95
Property Taxes: 104
Other Living Cost Indexes
College Tuition: 100
Food at Home: 101
Health Care: 106
Transportation: 99
Places Rated Score: 9,287
Places Rated Rank: 149

Green Bay, WI
Typical Household Income: $50,598
State and Local Taxes: $3,139
Housing Cost Indexes
Average Price: 73
Utilities: 105
Property Taxes: 165
Other Living Cost Indexes
College Tuition: 97
Food at Home: 96
Health Care: 96
Transportation: 98
Places Rated Score: 9,252
Places Rated Rank: 144

Greensboro-Winston-Salem-High Point, NC
Typical Household Income: $48,929
State and Local Taxes: $2,985
Housing Cost Indexes
Average Price: 89
Utilities: 100
Property Taxes: 102
Other Living Cost Indexes
College Tuition: 68
Food at Home: 90
Health Care: 93
Transportation: 96
Places Rated Score: 9,194
Places Rated Rank: 135

Greenville, NC
Typical Household Income: $40,965
State and Local Taxes: $2,499
Housing Cost Indexes
Average Price: 80
Utilities: 100
Property Taxes: 92

Other Living Cost Indexes
College Tuition: 60
Food at Home: 92
Health Care: 101
Transportation: 89
Places Rated Score: 8,763
Places Rated Rank: 96

Greenville-Spartanburg-Anderson, SC
Typical Household Income: $44,679
State and Local Taxes: $2,588
Housing Cost Indexes
Average Price: 73
Utilities: 87
Property Taxes: 67
Other Living Cost Indexes
College Tuition: 130
Food at Home: 97
Health Care: 92
Transportation: 92
Places Rated Score: 8,545
Places Rated Rank: 69

Hagerstown, MD
Typical Household Income: $47,681
State and Local Taxes: $3,186
Housing Cost Indexes
Average Price: 98
Utilities: 85
Property Taxes: 122
Other Living Cost Indexes
College Tuition: 110
Food at Home: 92
Health Care: 100
Transportation: 95
Places Rated Score: 9,650
Places Rated Rank: 180

Halifax, NS
Typical Household Income: $52,024
Provincial Taxes: $6,098
Housing Cost Indexes
Average Price: 86
Utilities: 111
Property Taxes: 116
Other Living Cost Indexes
College Tuition: 96
Food at Home: 159
Health Care: 28
Transportation: 148
Places Rated Score: 11,174
Places Rated Rank: 260

Hamilton, ON
Typical Household Income: $59,748
Provincial Taxes: $6,689
Housing Cost Indexes
Average Price: 127
Utilities: 110
Property Taxes: 191
Other Living Cost Indexes
College Tuition: 78
Food at Home: 158
Health Care: 28
Transportation: 134
Places Rated Score: 12,675
Places Rated Rank: 290

Hamilton-Middletown, OH
Typical Household Income: $49,185
State and Local Taxes: $3,047
Housing Cost Indexes
Average Price: 87
Utilities: 123
Property Taxes: 131
Other Living Cost Indexes
College Tuition: 181

Food at Home: 92
Health Care: 93
Transportation: 100
Places Rated Score: 9,869
Places Rated Rank: 187

Harrisburg-Lebanon-Carlisle, PA
Typical Household Income: $50,405
State and Local Taxes: $4,456
Housing Cost Indexes
Average Price: 87
Utilities: 120
Property Taxes: 219
Other Living Cost Indexes
College Tuition: 173
Food at Home: 97
Health Care: 99
Transportation: 116
Places Rated Score: 10,743
Places Rated Rank: 240

Hartford, CT
Typical Household Income: $69,989
State and Local Taxes: $2,311
Housing Cost Indexes
Average Price: 199
Utilities: 135
Property Taxes: 318
Other Living Cost Indexes
College Tuition: 103
Food at Home: 104
Health Care: 110
Transportation: 109
Places Rated Score: 15,291
Places Rated Rank: 320

Hickory-Morgantown, NC
Typical Household Income: $43,568
State and Local Taxes: $2,658
Housing Cost Indexes
Average Price: 71
Utilities: 102
Property Taxes: 81
Other Living Cost Indexes
College Tuition: 81
Food at Home: 93
Health Care: 87
Transportation: 95
Places Rated Score: 8,464
Places Rated Rank: 62

Honolulu, HI
Typical Household Income: $74,744
State and Local Taxes: $4,979
Housing Cost Indexes
Average Price: 327
Utilities: 97
Property Taxes: 124
Other Living Cost Indexes
College Tuition: 72
Food at Home: 125
Health Care: 115
Transportation: 120
Places Rated Score: 19,194
Places Rated Rank: 340

✓ **Houma, LA**
Typical Household Income: $43,749
State and Local Taxes: $2,057
Housing Cost Indexes
Average Price: 62
Utilities: 85
Property Taxes: 31
Other Living Cost Indexes
College Tuition: 88
Food at Home: 95
Health Care: 90
Transportation: 100
Places Rated Score: 7,955
Places Rated Rank: 19

Houston, TX
Typical Household Income: $56,795
State and Local Taxes: $1,187
Housing Cost Indexes
  Average Price: 88
  Utilities: 93
  Property Taxes: 176
Other Living Cost Indexes
  College Tuition: 51
  Food at Home: 99
  Health Care: 112
  Transportation: 118
Places Rated Score: 10,236
Places Rated Rank: 208

✓ **Huntington–Ashland, WV–KY–OH**
Typical Household Income: $40,764
State and Local Taxes: $2,147
Housing Cost Indexes
  Average Price: 57
  Utilities: 103
  Property Taxes: 28
Other Living Cost Indexes
  College Tuition: 88
  Food at Home: 93
  Health Care: 98
  Transportation: 102
Places Rated Score: 7,976
Places Rated Rank: 22

Huntsville, AL
Typical Household Income: $49,118
State and Local Taxes: $2,657
Housing Cost Indexes
  Average Price: 90
  Utilities: 81
  Property Taxes: 54
Other Living Cost Indexes
  College Tuition: 91
  Food at Home: 94
  Health Care: 95
  Transportation: 109
Places Rated Score: 9,258
Places Rated Rank: 145

Indianapolis, IN
Typical Household Income: $52,633
State and Local Taxes: $2,626
Housing Cost Indexes
  Average Price: 80
  Utilities: 100
  Property Taxes: 95
Other Living Cost Indexes
  College Tuition: 116
  Food at Home: 97
  Health Care: 97
  Transportation: 97
Places Rated Score: 9,136
Places Rated Rank: 124

Iowa City, IA
Typical Household Income: $48,250
State and Local Taxes: $2,473
Housing Cost Indexes
  Average Price: 95
  Utilities: 123
  Property Taxes: 152
Other Living Cost Indexes
  College Tuition: 103
  Food at Home: 100
  Health Care: 102
  Transportation: 104
Places Rated Score: 10,377
Places Rated Rank: 220

Jackson, MI
Typical Household Income: $45,276
State and Local Taxes: $2,985

Housing Cost Indexes
  Average Price: 59
  Utilities: 121
  Property Taxes: 157
Other Living Cost Indexes
  College Tuition: 168
  Food at Home: 101
  Health Care: 102
  Transportation: 102
Places Rated Score: 9,215
Places Rated Rank: 139

Jackson, MS
Typical Household Income: $47,577
State and Local Taxes: $1,932
Housing Cost Indexes
  Average Price: 74
  Utilities: 91
  Property Taxes: 57
Other Living Cost Indexes
  College Tuition: 95
  Food at Home: 101
  Health Care: 98
  Transportation: 99
Places Rated Score: 8,751
Places Rated Rank: 94

Jacksonville, FL
Typical Household Income: $50,836
State and Local Taxes: $913
Housing Cost Indexes
  Average Price: 87
  Utilities: 72
  Property Taxes: 139
Other Living Cost Indexes
  College Tuition: 73
  Food at Home: 100
  Health Care: 106
  Transportation: 106
Places Rated Score: 9,598
Places Rated Rank: 177

Jacksonville, NC
Typical Household Income: $35,527
State and Local Taxes: $2,167
Housing Cost Indexes
  Average Price: 73
  Utilities: 104
  Property Taxes: 84
Other Living Cost Indexes
  College Tuition: 65
  Food at Home: 95
  Health Care: 94
  Transportation: 92
Places Rated Score: 8,586
Places Rated Rank: 76

Jamestown, NY
Typical Household Income: $43,608
State and Local Taxes: $3,961
Housing Cost Indexes
  Average Price: 58
  Utilities: 110
  Property Taxes: 145
Other Living Cost Indexes
  College Tuition: 84
  Food at Home: 109
  Health Care: 110
  Transportation: 108
Places Rated Score: 9,188
Places Rated Rank: 134

Janesville–Beloit, WI
Typical Household Income: $46,187
State and Local Taxes: $2,865
Housing Cost Indexes
  Average Price: 60
  Utilities: 108

Property Taxes: 135
Other Living Cost Indexes
  College Tuition: 116
  Food at Home: 103
  Health Care: 99
  Transportation: 90
Places Rated Score: 8,672
Places Rated Rank: 87

✓ **Johnson City–Kingsport–Bristol, TN–VA**
Typical Household Income: $41,120
State and Local Taxes: $1,035
Housing Cost Indexes
  Average Price: 63
  Utilities: 79
  Property Taxes: 67
Other Living Cost Indexes
  College Tuition: 76
  Food at Home: 93
  Health Care: 83
  Transportation: 95
Places Rated Score: 7,894
Places Rated Rank: 15

Johnstown, PA
Typical Household Income: $42,529
State and Local Taxes: $3,760
Housing Cost Indexes
  Average Price: 50
  Utilities: 122
  Property Taxes: 125
Other Living Cost Indexes
  College Tuition: 235
  Food at Home: 97
  Health Care: 100
  Transportation: 100
Places Rated Score: 8,766
Places Rated Rank: 97

✓ **Joplin, MO**
Typical Household Income: $40,606
State and Local Taxes: $2,457
Housing Cost Indexes
  Average Price: 50
  Utilities: 86
  Property Taxes: 62
Other Living Cost Indexes
  College Tuition: 63
  Food at Home: 96
  Health Care: 88
  Transportation: 86
Places Rated Score: 7,325
Places Rated Rank: 1

Kalamazoo–Battle Creek, MI
Typical Household Income: $47,979
State and Local Taxes: $3,163
Housing Cost Indexes
  Average Price: 66
  Utilities: 114
  Property Taxes: 176
Other Living Cost Indexes
  College Tuition: 125
  Food at Home: 104
  Health Care: 102
  Transportation: 102
Places Rated Score: 9,453
Places Rated Rank: 163

Kankakee, IL
Typical Household Income: $51,749
State and Local Taxes: $2,387
Housing Cost Indexes
  Average Price: 64
  Utilities: 139
  Property Taxes: 119

Other Living Cost Indexes
College Tuition: 139
Food at Home: 101
Health Care: 105
Transportation: 112
Places Rated Score: 9,546
Places Rated Rank: 174

Kansas City, MO–KS
Typical Household Income: $56,286
State and Local Taxes: $3,406
Housing Cost Indexes
Average Price: 81
Utilities: 105
Property Taxes: 101
Other Living Cost Indexes
College Tuition: 112
Food at Home: 98
Health Care: 99
Transportation: 100
Places Rated Score: 9,351
Places Rated Rank: 157

Kenosha, WI
Typical Household Income: $52,491
State and Local Taxes: $3,256
Housing Cost Indexes
Average Price: 78
Utilities: 107
Property Taxes: 175
Other Living Cost Indexes
College Tuition: 98
Food at Home: 98
Health Care: 113
Transportation: 110
Places Rated Score: 9,914
Places Rated Rank: 190

Killeen–Temple, TX
Typical Household Income: $42,028
State and Local Taxes: $878
Housing Cost Indexes
Average Price: 65
Utilities: 86
Property Taxes: 131
Other Living Cost Indexes
College Tuition: 55
Food at Home: 95
Health Care: 91
Transportation: 90
Places Rated Score: 8,289
Places Rated Rank: 48

Kitchener, ON
Typical Household Income: $60,753
Provincial Taxes: $6,802
Housing Cost Indexes
Average Price: 122
Utilities: 114
Property Taxes: 156
Other Living Cost Indexes
College Tuition: 78
Food at Home: 160
Health Care: 28
Transportation: 134
Places Rated Score: 12,391
Places Rated Rank: 285

Knoxville, TN
Typical Household Income: $44,052
State and Local Taxes: $1,109
Housing Cost Indexes
Average Price: 76
Utilities: 79
Property Taxes: 84
Other Living Cost Indexes
College Tuition: 94
Food at Home: 96

Health Care: 95
Transportation: 95
Places Rated Score: 8,650
Places Rated Rank: 84

Kokomo, IN
Typical Household Income: $47,755
State and Local Taxes: $2,382
Housing Cost Indexes
Average Price: 61
Utilities: 116
Property Taxes: 73
Other Living Cost Indexes
College Tuition: 100
Food at Home: 98
Health Care: 95
Transportation: 99
Places Rated Score: 8,509
Places Rated Rank: 67

La Crosse, WI–MN
Typical Household Income: $45,768
State and Local Taxes: $2,839
Housing Cost Indexes
Average Price: 67
Utilities: 107
Property Taxes: 150
Other Living Cost Indexes
College Tuition: 102
Food at Home: 96
Health Care: 129
Transportation: 94
Places Rated Score: 9,148
Places Rated Rank: 125

Lafayette, IN
Typical Household Income: $44,068
State and Local Taxes: $2,199
Housing Cost Indexes
Average Price: 73
Utilities: 116
Property Taxes: 87
Other Living Cost Indexes
College Tuition: 118
Food at Home: 98
Health Care: 90
Transportation: 92
Places Rated Score: 8,865
Places Rated Rank: 105

✓ Lafayette, LA
Typical Household Income: $44,296
State and Local Taxes: $2,082
Housing Cost Indexes
Average Price: 63
Utilities: 83
Property Taxes: 31
Other Living Cost Indexes
College Tuition: 87
Food at Home: 96
Health Care: 90
Transportation: 101
Places Rated Score: 8,012
Places Rated Rank: 23

Lake Charles, LA
Typical Household Income: $46,575
State and Local Taxes: $2,189
Housing Cost Indexes
Average Price: 65
Utilities: 85
Property Taxes: 33
Other Living Cost Indexes
College Tuition: 89
Food at Home: 99
Health Care: 89
Transportation: 102
Places Rated Score: 8,200
Places Rated Rank: 39

Lake County, IL
Typical Household Income: $84,060
State and Local Taxes: $3,878
Housing Cost Indexes
Average Price: 191
Utilities: 144
Property Taxes: 354
Other Living Cost Indexes
College Tuition: 139
Food at Home: 102
Health Care: 110
Transportation: 118
Places Rated Score: 15,501
Places Rated Rank: 321

Lakeland–Winter Haven, FL
Typical Household Income: $42,871
State and Local Taxes: $769
Housing Cost Indexes
Average Price: 76
Utilities: 74
Property Taxes: 121
Other Living Cost Indexes
College Tuition: 73
Food at Home: 98
Health Care: 100
Transportation: 99
Places Rated Score: 8,885
Places Rated Rank: 108

Lancaster, PA
Typical Household Income: $55,290
State and Local Taxes: $4,888
Housing Cost Indexes
Average Price: 106
Utilities: 120
Property Taxes: 264
Other Living Cost Indexes
College Tuition: 145
Food at Home: 103
Health Care: 92
Transportation: 104
Places Rated Score: 11,361
Places Rated Rank: 265

Lansing–East Lansing, MI
Typical Household Income: $50,571
State and Local Taxes: $3,334
Housing Cost Indexes
Average Price: 77
Utilities: 112
Property Taxes: 206
Other Living Cost Indexes
College Tuition: 179
Food at Home: 103
Health Care: 112
Transportation: 109
Places Rated Score: 10,324
Places Rated Rank: 214

Laredo, TX
Typical Household Income: $36,720
State and Local Taxes: $767
Housing Cost Indexes
Average Price: 62
Utilities: 79
Property Taxes: 125
Other Living Cost Indexes
College Tuition: 38
Food at Home: 93
Health Care: 93
Transportation: 109
Places Rated Score: 8,439
Places Rated Rank: 58

Las Cruces, NM
Typical Household Income: $35,339
State and Local Taxes: $1,687
Housing Cost Indexes

Average Price: 81
Utilities: 104
Property Taxes: 89
Other Living Cost Indexes
College Tuition: 82
Food at Home: 94
Health Care: 94
Transportation: 110
Places Rated Score: 9,276
Places Rated Rank: 148

Las Vegas, NV–AZ
Typical Household Income: $49,228
State and Local Taxes: $931
Housing Cost Indexes
Average Price: 113
Utilities: 82
Property Taxes: 102
Other Living Cost Indexes
College Tuition: 76
Food at Home: 97
Health Care: 111
Transportation: 107
Places Rated Score: 10,461
Places Rated Rank: 226

Lawrence, KS
Typical Household Income: $40,687
State and Local Taxes: $1,690
Housing Cost Indexes
Average Price: 81
Utilities: 95
Property Taxes: 97
Other Living Cost Indexes
College Tuition: 86
Food at Home: 88
Health Care: 87
Transportation: 96
Places Rated Score: 8,819
Places Rated Rank: 100

✓ **Lawton, OK**
Typical Household Income: $40,577
State and Local Taxes: $2,295
Housing Cost Indexes
Average Price: 62
Utilities: 93
Property Taxes: 56
Other Living Cost Indexes
College Tuition: 57
Food at Home: 93
Health Care: 94
Transportation: 103
Places Rated Score: 8,148
Places Rated Rank: 34

Lewiston–Auburn, ME
Typical Household Income: $46,905
State and Local Taxes: $2,516
Housing Cost Indexes
Average Price: 99
Utilities: 87
Property Taxes: 150
Other Living Cost Indexes
College Tuition: 122
Food at Home: 103
Health Care: 100
Transportation: 103
Places Rated Score: 10,274
Places Rated Rank: 210

Lexington, KY
Typical Household Income: $47,509
State and Local Taxes: $3,741
Housing Cost Indexes
Average Price: 86
Utilities: 78
Property Taxes: 95

Other Living Cost Indexes
College Tuition: 85
Food at Home: 98
Health Care: 110
Transportation: 94
Places Rated Score: 9,162
Places Rated Rank: 128

Lima, OH
Typical Household Income: $48,226
State and Local Taxes: $2,988
Housing Cost Indexes
Average Price: 63
Utilities: 116
Property Taxes: 95
Other Living Cost Indexes
College Tuition: 124
Food at Home: 99
Health Care: 93
Transportation: 98
Places Rated Score: 8,719
Places Rated Rank: 91

Lincoln, NE
Typical Household Income: $49,601
State and Local Taxes: $2,416
Housing Cost Indexes
Average Price: 74
Utilities: 100
Property Taxes: 167
Other Living Cost Indexes
College Tuition: 105
Food at Home: 97
Health Care: 82
Transportation: 102
Places Rated Score: 9,230
Places Rated Rank: 140

Little Rock–North Little Rock, AR
Typical Household Income: $47,622
State and Local Taxes: $2,363
Housing Cost Indexes
Average Price: 74
Utilities: 105
Property Taxes: 82
Other Living Cost Indexes
College Tuition: 80
Food at Home: 96
Health Care: 88
Transportation: 98
Places Rated Score: 8,729
Places Rated Rank: 92

London, ON
Typical Household Income: $56,324
Provincial Taxes: $6,095
Housing Cost Indexes
Average Price: 117
Utilities: 115
Property Taxes: 155
Other Living Cost Indexes
College Tuition: 78
Food at Home: 157
Health Care: 28
Transportation: 134
Places Rated Score: 12,136
Places Rated Rank: 283

Long Island, NY
Typical Household Income: $88,415
State and Local Taxes: $9,506
Housing Cost Indexes
Average Price: 231
Utilities: 135
Property Taxes: 577
Other Living Cost Indexes
College Tuition: 83
Food at Home: 120

Health Care: 135
Transportation: 119
Places Rated Score: 18,393
Places Rated Rank: 335

Longview–Marshall, TX
Typical Household Income: $44,873
State and Local Taxes: $937
Housing Cost Indexes
Average Price: 60
Utilities: 87
Property Taxes: 120
Other Living Cost Indexes
College Tuition: 42
Food at Home: 96
Health Care: 83
Transportation: 99
Places Rated Score: 8,160
Places Rated Rank: 36

Los Angeles–Long Beach, CA
Typical Household Income: $71,029
State and Local Taxes $4,251
Housing Cost Indexes
Average Price: 282
Utilities: 89
Property Taxes: 291
Other Living Cost Indexes
College Tuition: 59
Food at Home: 112
Health Care: 143
Transportation: 122
Places Rated Score: 18,350
Places Rated Rank: 334

Louisville, KY–IN
Typical Household Income: $50,905
State and Local Taxes: $4,009
Housing Cost Indexes
Average Price: 75
Utilities: 97
Property Taxes: 86
Other Living Cost Indexes
College Tuition: 93
Food at Home: 98
Health Care: 99
Transportation: 99
Places Rated Score: 8,922
Places Rated Rank: 110

Lubbock, TX
Typical Household Income: $44,785
State and Local Taxes: $936
Housing Cost Indexes
Average Price: 66
Utilities: 92
Property Taxes: 131
Other Living Cost Indexes
College Tuition: 79
Food at Home: 97
Health Care: 91
Transportation: 97
Places Rated Score: 8,598
Places Rated Rank: 78

Lynchburg, VA
Typical Household Income: $47,132
State and Local Taxes: $2,202
Housing Cost Indexes
Average Price: 75
Utilities: 91
Property Taxes: 82
Other Living Cost Indexes
College Tuition: 150
Food at Home: 95
Health Care: 89
Transportation: 88
Places Rated Score: 8,613
Places Rated Rank: 79

Macon, GA
Typical Household Income: $48,931
State and Local Taxes: $2,855
Housing Cost Indexes
Average Price: 71
Utilities: 96
Property Taxes: 89
Other Living Cost Indexes
College Tuition: 88
Food at Home: 94
Health Care: 100
Transportation: 97
Places Rated Score: 8,668
Places Rated Rank: 86

Madison, WI
Typical Household Income: $53,757
State and Local Taxes: $3,335
Housing Cost Indexes
Average Price: 94
Utilities: 117
Property Taxes: 212
Other Living Cost Indexes
College Tuition: 116
Food at Home: 102
Health Care: 118
Transportation: 106
Places Rated Score: 10,853
Places Rated Rank: 251

Manchester–Nashua, NH
Typical Household Income: $67,289
State and Local Taxes: None
Housing Cost Indexes
Average Price: 158
Utilities: 128
Property Taxes: 380
Other Living Cost Indexes
College Tuition: 141
Food at Home: 103
Health Care: 116
Transportation: 108
Places Rated Score: 14,179
Places Rated Rank: 310

Mansfield, OH
Typical Household Income: $43,675
State and Local Taxes: $2,706
Housing Cost Indexes
Average Price: 57
Utilities: 124
Property Taxes: 86
Other Living Cost Indexes
College Tuition: 124
Food at Home: 100
Health Care: 95
Transportation: 89
Places Rated Score: 8,377
Places Rated Rank: 53

✓ McAllen–Edinburg–Mission, TX
Typical Household Income: $34,690
State and Local Taxes: $725
Housing Cost Indexes
Average Price: 47
Utilities: 79
Property Taxes: 95
Other Living Cost Indexes
College Tuition: 51
Food at Home: 97
Health Care: 93
Transportation: 98
Places Rated Score: 7,634
Places Rated Rank: 5

Medford–Ashland, OR
Typical Household Income: $42,447
State and Local Taxes: $1,548

Housing Cost Indexes
Average Price: 94
Utilities: 87
Property Taxes: 202
Other Living Cost Indexes
College Tuition: 100
Food at Home: 102
Health Care: 110
Transportation: 103
Places Rated Score: 10,375
Places Rated Rank: 219

Melbourne–Titusville–Palm Bay, FL
Typical Household Income: $47,408
State and Local Taxes: $851
Housing Cost Indexes
Average Price: 99
Utilities: 89
Property Taxes: 158
Other Living Cost Indexes
College Tuition: 74
Food at Home: 98
Health Care: 110
Transportation: 100
Places Rated Score: 10,144
Places Rated Rank: 204

Memphis, TN–AR–MS
Typical Household Income: $52,543
State and Local Taxes: $1,323
Housing Cost Indexes
Average Price: 83
Utilities: 79
Property Taxes: 89
Other Living Cost Indexes
College Tuition: 89
Food at Home: 100
Health Care: 98
Transportation: 107
Places Rated Score: 9,275
Places Rated Rank: 147

Merced, CA
Typical Household Income: $48,839
State and Local Taxes: $2,132
Housing Cost Indexes
Average Price: 108
Utilities: 103
Property Taxes: 111
Other Living Cost Indexes
College Tuition: 54
Food at Home: 103
Health Care: 108
Transportation: 109
Places Rated Score: 10,571
Places Rated Rank: 231

Miami, FL
Typical Household Income: $55,316
State and Local Taxes: $993
Housing Cost Indexes
Average Price: 118
Utilities: 83
Property Taxes: 188
Other Living Cost Indexes
College Tuition: 73
Food at Home: 102
Health Care: 125
Transportation: 109
Places Rated Score: 11,292
Places Rated Rank: 262

Milwaukee–Waukesha, WI
Typical Household Income: $55,757
State and Local Taxes: $3,459
Housing Cost Indexes
Average Price: 93
Utilities: 108

Property Taxes: 210
Other Living Cost Indexes
College Tuition: 119
Food at Home: 102
Health Care: 119
Transportation: 109
Places Rated Score: 10,807
Places Rated Rank: 247

Minneapolis–St. Paul, MN–WI
Typical Household Income: $61,029
State and Local Taxes: $3,744
Housing Cost Indexes
Average Price: 108
Utilities: 110
Property Taxes: 215
Other Living Cost Indexes
College Tuition: 135
Food at Home: 95
Health Care: 104
Transportation: 107
Places Rated Score: 11,099
Places Rated Rank: 257

Mobile, AL
Typical Household Income: $43,873
State and Local Taxes: $2,373
Housing Cost Indexes
Average Price: 70
Utilities: 88
Property Taxes: 42
Other Living Cost Indexes
College Tuition: 105
Food at Home: 99
Health Care: 92
Transportation: 109
Places Rated Score: 8,631
Places Rated Rank: 82

Modesto, CA
Typical Household Income: $46,010
State and Local Taxes: $2,008
Housing Cost Indexes
Average Price: 142
Utilities: 79
Property Taxes: 146
Other Living Cost Indexes
College Tuition: 50
Food at Home: 103
Health Care: 107
Transportation: 113
Places Rated Score: 11,835
Places Rated Rank: 272

Monmouth–Ocean, NJ
Typical Household Income: $72,548
State and Local Taxes: $2,669
Housing Cost Indexes
Average Price: 186
Utilities: 112
Property Taxes: 372
Other Living Cost Indexes
College Tuition: 189
Food at Home: 107
Health Care: 117
Transportation: 110
Places Rated Score: 15,253
Places Rated Rank: 319

Monroe, LA
Typical Household Income: $43,151
State and Local Taxes: $2,028
Housing Cost Indexes
Average Price: 65
Utilities: 81
Property Taxes: 32
Other Living Cost Indexes
College Tuition: 89

Food at Home: 99
Health Care: 95
Transportation: 104
Places Rated Score: 8,228
Places Rated Rank: 43

Montgomery, AL
Typical Household Income: $48,718
State and Local Taxes: $2,635
Housing Cost Indexes
  Average Price: 76
  Utilities: 88
  Property Taxes: 46
Other Living Cost Indexes
  College Tuition: 71
  Food at Home: 97
  Health Care: 94
  Transportation: 101
Places Rated Score: 8,613
Places Rated Rank: 79

Montreal, PQ
Typical Household Income: $50,607
Provincial Taxes: $8,224
Housing Cost Indexes
  Average Price: 96
  Utilities: 117
  Property Taxes: 163
Other Living Cost Indexes
  College Tuition: 59
  Food at Home: 161
  Health Care: 28
  Transportation: 155
Places Rated Score: 11,902
Places Rated Rank: 275

Muncie, IN
Typical Household Income: $42,549
State and Local Taxes: $2,123
Housing Cost Indexes
  Average Price: 52
  Utilities: 107
  Property Taxes: 62
Other Living Cost Indexes
  College Tuition: 116
  Food at Home: 97
  Health Care: 95
  Transportation: 106
Places Rated Score: 8,199
Places Rated Rank: 38

Myrtle Beach, SC
Typical Household Income: $37,401
State and Local Taxes: $2,167
Housing Cost Indexes
  Average Price: 96
  Utilities: 95
  Property Taxes: 88
Other Living Cost Indexes
  College Tuition: 106
  Food at Home: 94
  Health Care: 90
  Transportation: 97
Places Rated Score: 9,506
Places Rated Rank: 169

Naples, FL
Typical Household Income: $65,617
State and Local Taxes: $1,178
Housing Cost Indexes
  Average Price: 183
  Utilities: 83
  Property Taxes: 293
Other Living Cost Indexes
  College Tuition: 74
  Food at Home: 100
  Health Care: 99
  Transportation: 103
Places Rated Score: 13,789
Places Rated Rank: 306

Nashville, TN
Typical Household Income: $52,365
State and Local Taxes: $1,318
Housing Cost Indexes
  Average Price: 99
  Utilities: 77
  Property Taxes: 106
Other Living Cost Indexes
  College Tuition: 75
  Food at Home: 98
  Health Care: 86
  Transportation: 97
Places Rated Score: 9,515
Places Rated Rank: 173

New Bedford–Fall River–Attleboro, MA
Typical Household Income: $53,155
State and Local Taxes: $3,613
Housing Cost Indexes
  Average Price: 160
  Utilities: 115
  Property Taxes: 240
Other Living Cost Indexes
  College Tuition: 116
  Food at Home: 105
  Health Care: 120
  Transportation: 114
Places Rated Score: 13,558
Places Rated Rank: 303

New Haven–Meriden, CT
Typical Household Income: $65,474
State and Local Taxes: $3,742
Housing Cost Indexes
  Average Price: 177
  Utilities: 133
  Property Taxes: 284
Other Living Cost Indexes
  College Tuition: 99
  Food at Home: 103
  Health Care: 115
  Transportation: 109
Places Rated Score: 14,332
Places Rated Rank: 312

New London–Norwich, CT–RI
Typical Household Income: $57,783
State and Local Taxes: $2,667
Housing Cost Indexes
  Average Price: 181
  Utilities: 131
  Property Taxes: 289
Other Living Cost Indexes
  College Tuition: 103
  Food at Home: 101
  Health Care: 108
  Transportation: 102
Places Rated Score: 14,248
Places Rated Rank: 311

New Orleans, LA
Typical Household Income: $50,488
State and Local Taxes: $2,373
Housing Cost Indexes
  Average Price: 87
  Utilities: 99
  Property Taxes: 44
Other Living Cost Indexes
  College Tuition: 120
  Food at Home: 103
  Health Care: 84
  Transportation: 104
Places Rated Score: 9,313
Places Rated Rank: 154

New York, NY
Typical Household Income: $67,201
State and Local Taxes: $6,104

Housing Cost Indexes
  Average Price: 249
  Utilities: 137
  Property Taxes: 623
Other Living Cost Indexes
  College Tuition: 76
  Food at Home: 142
  Health Care: 204
  Transportation: 129
Places Rated Score: 20,513
Places Rated Rank: 342

Newark–Jersey City, NJ
Typical Household Income: $73,817
State and Local Taxes: $2,716
Housing Cost Indexes
  Average Price: 232
  Utilities: 127
  Property Taxes: 463
Other Living Cost Indexes
  College Tuition: 146
  Food at Home: 110
  Health Care: 116
  Transportation: 113
Places Rated Score: 17,477
Places Rated Rank: 331

Norfolk–Virginia Beach–Newport News, VA–NC
Typical Household Income: $51,376
State and Local Taxes: $2,401
Housing Cost Indexes
  Average Price: 107
  Utilities: 104
  Property Taxes: 118
Other Living Cost Indexes
  College Tuition: 140
  Food at Home: 101
  Health Care: 91
  Transportation: 111
Places Rated Score: 10,637
Places Rated Rank: 234

Northern New Jersey, NJ
Typical Household Income: $84,416
State and Local Taxes: $3,106
Housing Cost Indexes
  Average Price: 249
  Utilities: 125
  Property Taxes: 498
Other Living Cost Indexes
  College Tuition: 132
  Food at Home: 113
  Health Care: 118
  Transportation: 115
Places Rated Score: 18,333
Places Rated Rank: 333

Oakland, CA
Typical Household Income: $66,538
State and Local Taxes: $2,905
Housing Cost Indexes
  Average Price: 263
  Utilities: 110
  Property Taxes: 270
Other Living Cost Indexes
  College Tuition: 92
  Food at Home: 110
  Health Care: 118
  Transportation: 119
Places Rated Score: 17,488
Places Rated Rank: 332

Ocala, FL
Typical Household Income: $36,716
State and Local Taxes: $659
Housing Cost Indexes
  Average Price: 76
  Utilities: 81

Property Taxes: 121
Other Living Cost Indexes
College Tuition: 74
Food at Home: 102
Health Care: 92
Transportation: 98
Places Rated Score: 8,920
Places Rated Rank: 109

Odessa–Midland, TX
Typical Household Income: $48,564
State and Local Taxes: $1,015
Housing Cost Indexes
Average Price: 66
Utilities: 87
Property Taxes: 131
Other Living Cost Indexes
College Tuition: 64
Food at Home: 96
Health Care: 109
Transportation: 103
Places Rated Score: 8,775
Places Rated Rank: 98

Oklahoma City, OK
Typical Household Income: $46,056
State and Local Taxes: $2,605
Housing Cost Indexes
Average Price: 67
Utilities: 91
Property Taxes: 60
Other Living Cost Indexes
College Tuition: 75
Food at Home: 92
Health Care: 99
Transportation: 97
Places Rated Score: 8,249
Places Rated Rank: 46

Olympia, WA
Typical Household Income: $47,906
State and Local Taxes: $1,019
Housing Cost Indexes
Average Price: 97
Utilities: 86
Property Taxes: 88
Other Living Cost Indexes
College Tuition: 92
Food at Home: 105
Health Care: 137
Transportation: 101
Places Rated Score: 10,146
Places Rated Rank: 205

Omaha, NE–IA
Typical Household Income: $55,906
State and Local Taxes: $2,723
Housing Cost Indexes
Average Price: 70
Utilities: 99
Property Taxes: 160
Other Living Cost Indexes
College Tuition: 69
Food at Home: 96
Health Care: 98
Transportation: 105
Places Rated Score: 9,149
Places Rated Rank: 126

Orange County, CA
Typical Household Income: $73,145
State and Local Taxes: $4,378
Housing Cost Indexes
Average Price: 298
Utilities: 108
Property Taxes: 307
Other Living Cost Indexes
College Tuition: 72

Food at Home: 112
Health Care: 123
Transportation: 120
Places Rated Score: 18,979
Places Rated Rank: 339

Orange County, NY
Typical Household Income: $61,322
State and Local Taxes: $5,570
Housing Cost Indexes
Average Price: 162
Utilities: 135
Property Taxes: 404
Other Living Cost Indexes
College Tuition: 87
Food at Home: 111
Health Care: 118
Transportation: 110
Places Rated Score: 14,564
Places Rated Rank: 315

Orlando, FL
Typical Household Income: $48,537
State and Local Taxes: $871
Housing Cost Indexes
Average Price: 105
Utilities: 77
Property Taxes: 168
Other Living Cost Indexes
College Tuition: 74
Food at Home: 95
Health Care: 116
Transportation: 101
Places Rated Score: 10,326
Places Rated Rank: 215

Oshawa, ON
Typical Household Income: $63,512
Provincial Taxes: $7,397
Housing Cost Indexes
Average Price: 122
Utilities: 112
Property Taxes: 215
Other Living Cost Indexes
College Tuition: 78
Food at Home: 166
Health Care: 28
Transportation: 134
Places Rated Score: 12,773
Places Rated Rank: 292

Ottawa–Hull, ON–PQ
Typical Household Income: $63,176
Provincial Taxes: $7,357
Housing Cost Indexes
Average Price: 121
Utilities: 113
Property Taxes: 196
Other Living Cost Indexes
College Tuition: 76
Food at Home: 149
Health Care: 28
Transportation: 148
Places Rated Score: 12,613
Places Rated Rank: 287

✓ **Owensboro, KY**
Typical Household Income: $44,186
State and Local Taxes: $3,480
Housing Cost Indexes
Average Price: 60
Utilities: 79
Property Taxes: 67
Other Living Cost Indexes
College Tuition: 85
Food at Home: 104
Health Care: 90
Transportation: 89
Places Rated Score: 7,950
Places Rated Rank: 18

Panama City, FL
Typical Household Income: $41,364
State and Local Taxes: $742
Housing Cost Indexes
Average Price: 77
Utilities: 74
Property Taxes: 123
Other Living Cost Indexes
College Tuition: 73
Food at Home: 95
Health Care: 100
Transportation: 101
Places Rated Score: 8,931
Places Rated Rank: 114

✓ **Parkersburg–Marietta, WV–OH**
Typical Household Income: $43,368
State and Local Taxes $2,284
Housing Cost Indexes
Average Price: 60
Utilities: 101
Property Taxes: 30
Other Living Cost Indexes
College Tuition: 79
Food at Home: 96
Health Care: 99
Transportation: 91
Places Rated Score: 7,878
Places Rated Rank: 14

Pensacola, FL
Typical Household Income: $43,633
State and Local Taxes: $783
Housing Cost Indexes
Average Price: 74
Utilities: 75
Property Taxes: 119
Other Living Cost Indexes
College Tuition: 73
Food at Home: 96
Health Care: 101
Transportation: 100
Places Rated Score: 8,820
Places Rated Rank: 101

Peoria–Pekin, IL
Typical Household Income: $52,136
State and Local Taxes: $2,405
Housing Cost Indexes
Average Price: 62
Utilities: 124
Property Taxes: 114
Other Living Cost Indexes
College Tuition: 127
Food at Home: 106
Health Care: 92
Transportation: 104
Places Rated Score: 9,091
Places Rated Rank: 122

Philadelphia, PA–NJ
Typical Household Income: $63,701
State and Local Taxes: $5,632
Housing Cost Indexes
Average Price: 149
Utilities: 126
Property Taxes: 372
Other Living Cost Indexes
College Tuition: 206
Food at Home: 123
Health Care: 125
Transportation: 114
Places Rated Score: 14,507
Places Rated Rank: 313

Phoenix–Mesa, AZ
Typical Household Income: $50,740
State and Local Taxes: $2,085
Housing Cost Indexes

Average Price: 107
Utilities: 99
Property Taxes: 101
Other Living Cost Indexes
College Tuition: 81
Food at Home: 100
Health Care: 111
Transportation: 116
Places Rated Score: 10,612
Places Rated Rank: 232

✓ **Pine Bluff, AR**
Typical Household Income: $40,293
State and Local Taxes: $1,999
Housing Cost Indexes
Average Price: 52
Utilities: 102
Property Taxes: 58
Other Living Cost Indexes
College Tuition: 75
Food at Home: 93
Health Care: 88
Transportation: 98
Places Rated Score: 7,760
Places Rated Rank: 8

Pittsburgh, PA
Typical Household Income: $52,108
State and Local Taxes: $4,607
Housing Cost Indexes
Average Price: 92
Utilities: 132
Property Taxes: 230
Other Living Cost Indexes
College Tuition: 209
Food at Home: 109
Health Care: 120
Transportation: 119
Places Rated Score: 11,631
Places Rated Rank: 269

Pittsfield, MA
Typical Household Income: $55,800
State and Local Taxes: $3,793
Housing Cost Indexes
Average Price: 140
Utilities: 121
Property Taxes: 210
Other Living Cost Indexes
College Tuition: 178
Food at Home: 101
Health Care: 110
Transportation: 110
Places Rated Score: 12,647
Places Rated Rank: 288

Portland, ME
Typical Household Income: $57,821
State and Local Taxes: $3,102
Housing Cost Indexes
Average Price: 147
Utilities: 89
Property Taxes: 224
Other Living Cost Indexes
College Tuition: 122
Food at Home: 105
Health Care: 102
Transportation: 100
Places Rated Score: 12,394
Places Rated Rank: 286

Portland, OR
Typical Household Income: $53,763
State and Local Taxes: $1,961
Housing Cost Indexes
Average Price: 103
Utilities: 82
Property Taxes: 221

Other Living Cost Indexes
College Tuition: 110
Food at Home: 104
Health Care: 131
Transportation: 111
Places Rated Score: 11,142
Places Rated Rank: 259

Portsmouth–Dover–Rochester, NH
Typical Household Income: $61,354
State and Local Taxes: None
Housing Cost Indexes
Average Price: 165
Utilities: 124
Property Taxes: 397
Other Living Cost Indexes
College Tuition: 189
Food at Home: 103
Health Care: 115
Transportation: 107
Places Rated Score: 14,565
Places Rated Rank: 316

Providence–Warwick–Cranston, RI
Typical Household Income: $52,340
State and Local Taxes: $2,088
Housing Cost Indexes
Average Price: 157
Utilities: 113
Property Taxes: 275
Other Living Cost Indexes
College Tuition: 102
Food at Home: 106
Health Care: 117
Transportation: 113
Places Rated Score: 13,568
Places Rated Rank: 304

Provo–Orem, UT
Typical Household Income: $44,741
State and Local Taxes: $3,031
Housing Cost Indexes
Average Price: 85
Utilities: 86
Property Taxes: 98
Other Living Cost Indexes
College Tuition: 84
Food at Home: 97
Health Care: 107
Transportation: 95
Places Rated Score: 9,212
Places Rated Rank: 138

✓ **Pueblo, CO**
Typical Household Income: $44,230
State and Local Taxes: $2,389
Housing Cost Indexes
Average Price: 59
Utilities: 91
Property Taxes: 77
Other Living Cost Indexes
College Tuition: 88
Food at Home: 98
Health Care: 98
Transportation: 92
Places Rated Score: 8,098
Places Rated Rank: 29

Punta Gorda, FL
Typical Household Income: $40,273
State and Local Taxes: $723
Housing Cost Indexes
Average Price: 99
Utilities: 87
Property Taxes: 159
Other Living Cost Indexes
College Tuition: 72
Food at Home: 98

Health Care: 98
Transportation: 99
Places Rated Score: 10,014
Places Rated Rank: 195

Quebec City, PQ
Typical Household Income: $50,633
Provincial Taxes: $8,235
Housing Cost Indexes
Average Price: 73
Utilities: 119
Property Taxes: 89
Other Living Cost Indexes
College Tuition: 55
Food at Home: 160
Health Care: 28
Transportation: 158
Places Rated Score: 10,748
Places Rated Rank: 241

Racine, WI
Typical Household Income: $54,196
State and Local Taxes: $3,362
Housing Cost Indexes
Average Price: 78
Utilities: 107
Property Taxes: 175
Other Living Cost Indexes
College Tuition: 119
Food at Home: 101
Health Care: 112
Transportation: 110
Places Rated Score: 10,014
Places Rated Rank: 195

Raleigh–Durham–Chapel Hill, NC
Typical Household Income: $49,546
State and Local Taxes: $3,023
Housing Cost Indexes
Average Price: 110
Utilities: 99
Property Taxes: 111
Other Living Cost Indexes
College Tuition: 60
Food at Home: 92
Health Care: 96
Transportation: 95
Places Rated Score: 10,019
Places Rated Rank: 197

Rapid City, SD
Typical Household Income: $46,231
State and Local Taxes: $839
Housing Cost Indexes
Average Price: 66
Utilities: 107
Property Taxes: 83
Other Living Cost Indexes
College Tuition: 124
Food at Home: 105
Health Care: 93
Transportation: 99
Places Rated Score: 8,840
Places Rated Rank: 103

Reading, PA
Typical Household Income: $56,680
State and Local Taxes: $5,011
Housing Cost Indexes
Average Price: 94
Utilities: 121
Property Taxes: 235
Other Living Cost Indexes
College Tuition: 153
Food at Home: 103
Health Care: 119
Transportation: 106
Places Rated Score: 11,102
Places Rated Rank: 258

Redding, CA
Typical Household Income: $46,232
State and Local Taxes: $2,018
Housing Cost Indexes
Average Price: 109
Utilities: 77
Property Taxes: 113
Other Living Cost Indexes
College Tuition: 53
Food at Home: 105
Health Care: 105
Transportation: 116
Places Rated Score: 10,562
Places Rated Rank: 230

Regina, SK
Typical Household Income: $50,629
Provincial Taxes: $5,332
Housing Cost Indexes
Average Price: 61
Utilities: 107
Property Taxes: 140
Other Living Cost Indexes
College Tuition: 83
Food at Home: 166
Health Care: 28
Transportation: 121
Places Rated Score: 9,902
Places Rated Rank: 189

Reno, NV
Typical Household Income: $58,499
State and Local Taxes: $1,106
Housing Cost Indexes
Average Price: 144
Utilities: 103
Property Taxes: 130
Other Living Cost Indexes
College Tuition: 61
Food at Home: 105
Health Care: 122
Transportation: 103
Places Rated Score: 12,008
Places Rated Rank: 278

Richland–Kennewick–Pasco, WA
Typical Household Income: $50,710
State and Local Taxes: $1,079
Housing Cost Indexes
Average Price: 75
Utilities: 87
Property Taxes: 67
Other Living Cost Indexes
College Tuition: 95
Food at Home: 102
Health Care: 135
Transportation: 102
Places Rated Score: 9,187
Places Rated Rank: 132

Richmond–Petersburg, VA
Typical Household Income: $60,197
State and Local Taxes: $2,813
Housing Cost Indexes
Average Price: 100
Utilities: 105
Property Taxes: 110
Other Living Cost Indexes
College Tuition: 152
Food at Home: 101
Health Care: 106
Transportation: 110
Places Rated Score: 10,475
Places Rated Rank: 227

Riverside–San Bernardino, CA
Typical Household Income: $52,760
State and Local Taxes: $2,303

Housing Cost Indexes
Average Price: 161
Utilities: 104
Property Taxes: 166
Other Living Cost Indexes
College Tuition: 67
Food at Home: 105
Health Care: 117
Transportation: 117
Places Rated Score: 13,058
Places Rated Rank: 297

Roanoke, VA
Typical Household Income: $53,678
State and Local Taxes: $2,508
Housing Cost Indexes
Average Price: 83
Utilities: 91
Property Taxes: 91
Other Living Cost Indexes
College Tuition: 155
Food at Home: 93
Health Care: 91
Transportation: 99
Places Rated Score: 9,180
Places Rated Rank: 130

Rochester, MN
Typical Household Income: $61,954
State and Local Taxes: $4,230
Housing Cost Indexes
Average Price: 89
Utilities: 111
Property Taxes: 178
Other Living Cost Indexes
College Tuition: 108
Food at Home: 99
Health Care: 106
Transportation: 109
Places Rated Score: 10,328
Places Rated Rank: 216

Rochester, NY
Typical Household Income: $58,139
State and Local Taxes: $5,281
Housing Cost Indexes
Average Price: 102
Utilities: 123
Property Taxes: 254
Other Living Cost Indexes
College Tuition: 84
Food at Home: 115
Health Care: 114
Transportation: 122
Places Rated Score: 11,830
Places Rated Rank: 271

Rockford, IL
Typical Household Income: $51,911
State and Local Taxes: $2,395
Housing Cost Indexes
Average Price: 72
Utilities: 141
Property Taxes: 133
Other Living Cost Indexes
College Tuition: 139
Food at Home: 98
Health Care: 110
Transportation: 107
Places Rated Score: 9,790
Places Rated Rank: 186

Rocky Mount, NC
Typical Household Income: $43,229
State and Local Taxes: $2,637
Housing Cost Indexes
Average Price: 67
Utilities: 95

Property Taxes: 77
Other Living Cost Indexes
College Tuition: 60
Food at Home: 100
Health Care: 95
Transportation: 98
Places Rated Score: 8,458
Places Rated Rank: 61

Sacramento, CA
Typical Household Income: $54,026
State and Local Taxes: $2,358
Housing Cost Indexes
Average Price: 166
Utilities: 99
Property Taxes: 171
Other Living Cost Indexes
College Tuition: 49
Food at Home: 107
Health Care: 118
Transportation: 117
Places Rated Score: 13,213
Places Rated Rank: 298

Saginaw–Bay City–Midland, MI
Typical Household Income: $51,531
State and Local Taxes: $3,397
Housing Cost Indexes
Average Price: 60
Utilities: 117
Property Taxes: 161
Other Living Cost Indexes
College Tuition: 125
Food at Home: 103
Health Care: 100
Transportation: 103
Places Rated Score: 9,187
Places Rated Rank: 132

St. Catharines–Niagara, ON
Typical Household Income: $53,975
Provincial Taxes: $5,841
Housing Cost Indexes
Average Price: 109
Utilities: 109
Property Taxes: 150
Other Living Cost Indexes
College Tuition: 78
Food at Home: 157
Health Care: 28
Transportation: 134
Places Rated Score: 11,775
Places Rated Rank: 270

St. Cloud, MN
Typical Household Income: $44,960
State and Local Taxes: $2,758
Housing Cost Indexes
Average Price: 69
Utilities: 117
Property Taxes: 138
Other Living Cost Indexes
College Tuition: 108
Food at Home: 104
Health Care: 104
Transportation: 107
Places Rated Score: 9,508
Places Rated Rank: 171

Saint John, NB
Typical Household Income: $46,328
Provincial Taxes: $5,145
Housing Cost Indexes
Average Price: 69
Utilities: 114
Property Taxes: 92
Other Living Cost Indexes
College Tuition: 99

Food at Home: 163
Health Care: 28
Transportation: 142
Places Rated Score: 10,417
Places Rated Rank: 224

St. John's, NF
Typical Household Income: $53,779
Provincial Taxes: $7,110
Housing Cost Indexes
  Average Price: 78
  Utilities: 119
  Property Taxes: 78
Other Living Cost Indexes
  College Tuition: 68
  Food at Home: 166
  Health Care: 28
  Transportation: 154
Places Rated Score: 10,926
Places Rated Rank: 253

✓ **St. Joseph, MO**
Typical Household Income: $47,499
State and Local Taxes: $2,874
Housing Cost Indexes
  Average Price: 51
  Utilities: 96
  Property Taxes: 64
Other Living Cost Indexes
  College Tuition: 80
  Food at Home: 95
  Health Care: 98
  Transportation: 88
Places Rated Score: 7,631
Places Rated Rank: 4

St. Louis, MO-IL
Typical Household Income: $58,697
State and Local Taxes: $3,552
Housing Cost Indexes
  Average Price: 90
  Utilities: 120
  Property Taxes: 113
Other Living Cost Indexes
  College Tuition: 106
  Food at Home: 109
  Health Care: 100
  Transportation: 101
Places Rated Score: 10,073
Places Rated Rank: 201

Salem, OR
Typical Household Income: $47,543
State and Local Taxes: $1,734
Housing Cost Indexes
  Average Price: 72
  Utilities: 83
  Property Taxes: 155
Other Living Cost Indexes
  College Tuition: 100
  Food at Home: 94
  Health Care: 119
  Transportation: 112
Places Rated Score: 9,429
Places Rated Rank: 160

Salinas, CA
Typical Household Income: $62,064
State and Local Taxes: $3,714
Housing Cost Indexes
  Average Price: 252
  Utilities: 107
  Property Taxes: 260
Other Living Cost Indexes
  College Tuition: 53
  Food at Home: 106
  Health Care: 110

Transportation: 109
Places Rated Score: 16,588
Places Rated Rank: 327

Salt Lake City-Ogden, UT
Typical Household Income: $50,486
State and Local Taxes: $3,420
Housing Cost Indexes
  Average Price: 87
  Utilities: 88
  Property Taxes: 100
Other Living Cost Indexes
  College Tuition: 84
  Food at Home: 100
  Health Care: 102
  Transportation: 105
Places Rated Score: 9,514
Places Rated Rank: 172

San Angelo, TX
Typical Household Income: $46,632
State and Local Taxes: $974
Housing Cost Indexes
  Average Price: 61
  Utilities: 88
  Property Taxes: 122
Other Living Cost Indexes
  College Tuition: 46
  Food at Home: 97
  Health Care: 96
  Transportation: 97
Places Rated Score: 8,324
Places Rated Rank: 51

San Antonio, TX
Typical Household Income: $48,257
State and Local Taxes: $1,008
Housing Cost Indexes
  Average Price: 74
  Utilities: 81
  Property Taxes: 147
Other Living Cost Indexes
  College Tuition: 49
  Food at Home: 94
  Health Care: 104
  Transportation: 118
Places Rated Score: 9,290
Places Rated Rank: 150

San Diego, CA
Typical Household Income: $56,542
State and Local Taxes: $2,468
Housing Cost Indexes
  Average Price: 235
  Utilities: 123
  Property Taxes: 242
Other Living Cost Indexes
  College Tuition: 67
  Food at Home: 107
  Health Care: 125
  Transportation: 116
Places Rated Score: 16,343
Places Rated Rank: 326

San Francisco, CA
Typical Household Income: $80,087
State and Local Taxes: $4,793
Housing Cost Indexes
  Average Price: 372
  Utilities: 110
  Property Taxes: 384
Other Living Cost Indexes
  College Tuition: 56
  Food at Home: 110
  Health Care: 118
  Transportation: 120
Places Rated Score: 21,932
Places Rated Rank: 343

San Jose, CA
Typical Household Income: $75,157
State and Local Taxes: $4,498
Housing Cost Indexes
  Average Price: 340
  Utilities: 106
  Property Taxes: 350
Other Living Cost Indexes
  College Tuition: 54
  Food at Home: 108
  Health Care: 115
  Transportation: 120
Places Rated Score: 20,493
Places Rated Rank: 341

San Luis Obispo-Atascadero-Paso Robles, CA
Typical Household Income: $49,835
State and Local Taxes $2,175
Housing Cost Indexes
  Average Price: 251
  Utilities: 120
  Property Taxes: 259
Other Living Cost Indexes
  College Tuition: 56
  Food at Home: 108
  Health Care: 112
  Transportation: 108
Places Rated Score: 16,702
Places Rated Rank: 328

Santa Barbara-Santa Maria-Lompoc, CA
Typical Household Income: $64,354
State and Local Taxes: $3,851
Housing Cost Indexes
  Average Price: 295
  Utilities: 103
  Property Taxes: 304
Other Living Cost Indexes
  College Tuition: 91
  Food at Home: 109
  Health Care: 112
  Transportation: 118
Places Rated Score: 18,672
Places Rated Rank: 337

Santa Cruz-Watsonville, CA
Typical Household Income: $62,645
State and Local Taxes: $3,749
Housing Cost Indexes
  Average Price: 296
  Utilities: 107
  Property Taxes: 305
Other Living Cost Indexes
  College Tuition: 100
  Food at Home: 109
  Health Care: 120
  Transportation: 119
Places Rated Score: 18,849
Places Rated Rank: 338

Santa Fe, NM
Typical Household Income: $51,047
State and Local Taxes: $2,437
Housing Cost Indexes
  Average Price: 150
  Utilities: 114
  Property Taxes: 165
Other Living Cost Indexes
  College Tuition: 88
  Food at Home: 99
  Health Care: 104
  Transportation: 107
Places Rated Score: 12,374
Places Rated Rank: 284

Santa Rosa, CA
Typical Household Income: $61,392
State and Local Taxes: $3,674
Housing Cost Indexes
  Average Price: 240
  Utilities: 105
  Property Taxes: 247
Other Living Cost Indexes
  College Tuition: 51
  Food at Home: 107
  Health Care: 120
  Transportation: 113
Places Rated Score: 16,243
Places Rated Rank: 324

Sarasota-Bradenton, FL
Typical Household Income: $54,532
State and Local Taxes: $979
Housing Cost Indexes
  Average Price: 115
  Utilities: 81
  Property Taxes: 185
Other Living Cost Indexes
  College Tuition: 77
  Food at Home: 99
  Health Care: 95
  Transportation: 98
Places Rated Score: 10,658
Places Rated Rank: 235

Saskatoon, SK
Typical Household Income: $47,472
Provincial Taxes: $5,000
Housing Cost Indexes
  Average Price: 63
  Utilities: 114
  Property Taxes: 136
Other Living Cost Indexes
  College Tuition: 81
  Food at Home: 166
  Health Care: 28
  Transportation: 133
Places Rated Score: 10,258
Places Rated Rank: 209

Savannah, GA
Typical Household Income: $50,632
State and Local Taxes: $2,954
Housing Cost Indexes
  Average Price: 84
  Utilities: 103
  Property Taxes: 105
Other Living Cost Indexes
  College Tuition: 81
  Food at Home: 97
  Health Care: 93
  Transportation: 96
Places Rated Score: 9,239
Places Rated Rank: 141

Scranton-Wilkes-Barre-Hazleton, PA
Typical Household Income: $46,355
State and Local Taxes: $4,098
Housing Cost Indexes
  Average Price: 74
  Utilities: 118
  Property Taxes: 186
Other Living Cost Indexes
  College Tuition: 158
  Food at Home: 109
  Health Care: 92
  Transportation: 88
Places Rated Score: 9,647
Places Rated Rank: 179

Seattle-Bellevue-Everett, WA
Typical Household Income: $57,884
State and Local Taxes: $1,231
Housing Cost Indexes
  Average Price: 172
  Utilities: 77
  Property Taxes: 154
Other Living Cost Indexes
  College Tuition: 107
  Food at Home: 118
  Health Care: 133
  Transportation: 111
Places Rated Score: 13,509
Places Rated Rank: 302

Sharon, PA
Typical Household Income: $43,811
State and Local Taxes: $3,873
Housing Cost Indexes
  Average Price: 50
  Utilities: 114
  Property Taxes: 125
Other Living Cost Indexes
  College Tuition: 216
  Food at Home: 96
  Health Care: 89
  Transportation: 94
Places Rated Score: 8,446
Places Rated Rank: 59

Sheboygan, WI
Typical Household Income: $52,669
State and Local Taxes: $3,267
Housing Cost Indexes
  Average Price: 69
  Utilities: 108
  Property Taxes: 156
Other Living Cost Indexes
  College Tuition: 101
  Food at Home: 98
  Health Care: 105
  Transportation: 102
Places Rated Score: 9,294
Places Rated Rank: 151

Sherbrooke, PQ
Typical Household Income: $43,866
Provincial Taxes: $6,810
Housing Cost Indexes
  Average Price: 65
  Utilities: 118
  Property Taxes: 157
Other Living Cost Indexes
  College Tuition: 53
  Food at Home: 161
  Health Care: 28
  Transportation: 152
Places Rated Score: 10,707
Places Rated Rank: 237

✓ Sherman-Denison, TX
Typical Household Income: $46,476
State and Local Taxes: $971
Housing Cost Indexes
  Average Price: 57
  Utilities: 87
  Property Taxes: 114
Other Living Cost Indexes
  College Tuition: 50
  Food at Home: 95
  Health Care: 94
  Transportation: 99
Places Rated Score: 8,138
Places Rated Rank: 31

✓ Shreveport-Bossier City, LA
Typical Household Income: $46,531
State and Local Taxes: $2,187

Housing Cost Indexes
  Average Price: 67
  Utilities: 79
  Property Taxes: 33
Other Living Cost Indexes
  College Tuition: 81
  Food at Home: 98
  Health Care: 92
  Transportation: 100
Places Rated Score: 8,142
Places Rated Rank: 32

Sioux City, IA-NE
Typical Household Income: $49,810
State and Local Taxes: $2,553
Housing Cost Indexes
  Average Price: 51
  Utilities: 108
  Property Taxes: 81
Other Living Cost Indexes
  College Tuition: 101
  Food at Home: 101
  Health Care: 100
  Transportation: 99
Places Rated Score: 8,205
Places Rated Rank: 40

Sioux Falls, SD
Typical Household Income: $51,118
State and Local Taxes: $928
Housing Cost Indexes
  Average Price: 69
  Utilities: 102
  Property Taxes: 86
Other Living Cost Indexes
  College Tuition: 102
  Food at Home: 98
  Health Care: 97
  Transportation: 97
Places Rated Score: 8,711
Places Rated Rank: 90

✓ South Bend, IN
Typical Household Income: $48,817
State and Local Taxes: $2,436
Housing Cost Indexes
  Average Price: 64
  Utilities: 106
  Property Taxes: 76
Other Living Cost Indexes
  College Tuition: 100
  Food at Home: 90
  Health Care: 91
  Transportation: 90
Places Rated Score: 8,142
Places Rated Rank: 32

Spokane, WA
Typical Household Income: $46,466
State and Local Taxes: $988
Housing Cost Indexes
  Average Price: 71
  Utilities: 81
  Property Taxes: 64
Other Living Cost Indexes
  College Tuition: 89
  Food at Home: 95
  Health Care: 123
  Transportation: 94
Places Rated Score: 8,581
Places Rated Rank: 75

Springfield, IL
Typical Household Income: $55,258
State and Local Taxes: $2,549
Housing Cost Indexes
  Average Price: 73
  Utilities: 110

Property Taxes: 136
Other Living Cost Indexes
College Tuition: 101
Food at Home: 100
Health Care: 98
Transportation: 94
Places Rated Score: 9,158
Places Rated Rank: 127

Springfield, MA
Typical Household Income: $54,997
State and Local Taxes: $3,738
Housing Cost Indexes
Average Price: 146
Utilities: 119
Property Taxes: 219
Other Living Cost Indexes
College Tuition: 178
Food at Home: 102
Health Care: 112
Transportation: 106
Places Rated Score: 12,860
Places Rated Rank: 295

Springfield, MO
Typical Household Income: $45,172
State and Local Taxes: $2,733
Housing Cost Indexes
Average Price: 69
Utilities: 89
Property Taxes: 86
Other Living Cost Indexes
College Tuition: 79
Food at Home: 97
Health Care: 98
Transportation: 101
Places Rated Score: 8,588
Places Rated Rank: 77

Stamford–Norwalk, CT
Typical Household Income: $96,760
State and Local Taxes: $1,632
Housing Cost Indexes
Average Price: 239
Utilities: 131
Property Taxes: 382
Other Living Cost Indexes
College Tuition: 103
Food at Home: 105
Health Care: 113
Transportation: 110
Places Rated Score: 17,069
Places Rated Rank: 330

State College, PA
Typical Household Income: $45,533
State and Local Taxes: $4,026
Housing Cost Indexes
Average Price: 90
Utilities: 106
Property Taxes: 225
Other Living Cost Indexes
College Tuition: 223
Food at Home: 97
Health Care: 92
Transportation: 107
Places Rated Score: 10,625
Places Rated Rank: 233

✓ Steubenville–Weirton, OH–WV
Typical Household Income: $42,206
State and Local Taxes: $2,615
Housing Cost Indexes
Average Price: 50
Utilities: 114
Property Taxes: 76
Other Living Cost Indexes
College Tuition: 121

Food at Home: 100
Health Care: 93
Transportation: 97
Places Rated Score: 8,149
Places Rated Rank: 35

Stockton–Lodi, CA
Typical Household Income: $51,269
State and Local Taxes: $2,238
Housing Cost Indexes
Average Price: 142
Utilities: 103
Property Taxes: 146
Other Living Cost Indexes
College Tuition: 53
Food at Home: 103
Health Care: 111
Transportation: 107
Places Rated Score: 11,949
Places Rated Rank: 277

Sudbury, ON
Typical Household Income: $59,376
Provincial Taxes: $6,648
Housing Cost Indexes
Average Price: 98
Utilities: 124
Property Taxes: 154
Other Living Cost Indexes
College Tuition: 78
Food at Home: 166
Health Care: 28
Transportation: 144
Places Rated Score: 11,897
Places Rated Rank: 274

✓ Sumter, SC
Typical Household Income: $36,768
State and Local Taxes: $2,130
Housing Cost Indexes
Average Price: 66
Utilities: 69
Property Taxes: 61
Other Living Cost Indexes
College Tuition: 141
Food at Home: 96
Health Care: 69
Transportation: 97
Places Rated Score: 8,027
Places Rated Rank: 25

Syracuse, NY
Typical Household Income: $51,716
State and Local Taxes: $4,697
Housing Cost Indexes
Average Price: 89
Utilities: 109
Property Taxes: 223
Other Living Cost Indexes
College Tuition: 82
Food at Home: 115
Health Care: 108
Transportation: 109
Places Rated Score: 10,792
Places Rated Rank: 245

Tacoma, WA
Typical Household Income: $46,556
State and Local Taxes: $990
Housing Cost Indexes
Average Price: 104
Utilities: 77
Property Taxes: 93
Other Living Cost Indexes
College Tuition: 107
Food at Home: 111
Health Care: 157

Transportation: 107
Places Rated Score: 10,761
Places Rated Rank: 243

Tallahassee, FL
Typical Household Income: $43,879
State and Local Taxes: $788
Housing Cost Indexes
Average Price: 87
Utilities: 79
Property Taxes: 139
Other Living Cost Indexes
College Tuition: 72
Food at Home: 99
Health Care: 96
Transportation: 96
Places Rated Score: 9,342
Places Rated Rank: 156

Tampa–St. Petersburg–Clearwater, FL
Typical Household Income: $47,695
State and Local Taxes: $856
Housing Cost Indexes
Average Price: 93
Utilities: 83
Property Taxes: 148
Other Living Cost Indexes
College Tuition: 77
Food at Home: 98
Health Care: 92
Transportation: 99
Places Rated Score: 9,654
Places Rated Rank: 181

✓ Terre Haute, IN
Typical Household Income: $41,815
State and Local Taxes: $2,086
Housing Cost Indexes
Average Price: 48
Utilities: 114
Property Taxes: 57
Other Living Cost Indexes
College Tuition: 116
Food at Home: 94
Health Care: 92
Transportation: 98
Places Rated Score: 7,832
Places Rated Rank: 10

✓ Texarkana, TX–Texarkana, AR
Typical Household Income: $42,022
State and Local Taxes: $2,085
Housing Cost Indexes
Average Price: 56
Utilities: 81
Property Taxes: 62
Other Living Cost Indexes
College Tuition: 48
Food at Home: 94
Health Care: 94
Transportation: 95
Places Rated Score: 7,669
Places Rated Rank: 7

Thunder Bay, ON
Typical Household Income: $57,393
Provincial Taxes: $6,211
Housing Cost Indexes
Average Price: 92
Utilities: 124
Property Taxes: 118
Other Living Cost Indexes
College Tuition: 78
Food at Home: 169
Health Care: 28
Transportation: 144
Places Rated Score: 11,567
Places Rated Rank: 268

Toledo, OH
Typical Household Income: $51,398
State and Local Taxes: $3,184
Housing Cost Indexes
  Average Price: 75
  Utilities: 141
  Property Taxes: 112
Other Living Cost Indexes
  College Tuition: 146
  Food at Home: 101
  Health Care: 94
  Transportation: 101
Places Rated Score: 9,596
Places Rated Rank: 176

Topeka, KS
Typical Household Income: $54,568
State and Local Taxes: $2,267
Housing Cost Indexes
  Average Price: 67
  Utilities: 89
  Property Taxes: 93
Other Living Cost Indexes
  College Tuition: 129
  Food at Home: 98
  Health Care: 100
  Transportation: 97
Places Rated Score: 8,641
Places Rated Rank: 83

Toronto, ON
Typical Household Income: $66,003
Provincial Taxes: $7,686
Housing Cost Indexes
  Average Price: 181
  Utilities: 110
  Property Taxes: 261
Other Living Cost Indexes
  College Tuition: 78
  Food at Home: 167
  Health Care: 28
  Transportation: 134
Places Rated Score: 15,139
Places Rated Rank: 318

Trenton, NJ
Typical Household Income: $78,772
State and Local Taxes: $2,898
Housing Cost Indexes
  Average Price: 170
  Utilities: 130
  Property Taxes: 341
Other Living Cost Indexes
  College Tuition: 154
  Food at Home: 108
  Health Care: 112
  Transportation: 109
Places Rated Score: 14,553
Places Rated Rank: 314

Trois-Rivieres, PQ
Typical Household Income: $46,089
Provincial Taxes: $7,154
Housing Cost Indexes
  Average Price: 57
  Utilities: 120
  Property Taxes: 145
Other Living Cost Indexes
  College Tuition: 58
  Food at Home: 153
  Health Care: 28
  Transportation: 155
Places Rated Score: 10,276
Places Rated Rank: 211

Tucson, AZ
Typical Household Income: $42,988
State and Local Taxes: $1,766

Housing Cost Indexes
  Average Price: 97
  Utilities: 86
  Property Taxes: 109
Other Living Cost Indexes
  College Tuition: 81
  Food at Home: 103
  Health Care: 115
  Transportation: 102
Places Rated Score: 10,010
Places Rated Rank: 194

Tulsa, OK
Typical Household Income: $49,050
State and Local Taxes: $2,775
Housing Cost Indexes
  Average Price: 73
  Utilities: 92
  Property Taxes: 66
Other Living Cost Indexes
  College Tuition: 75
  Food at Home: 93
  Health Care: 89
  Transportation: 91
Places Rated Score: 8,314
Places Rated Rank: 50

Tuscaloosa, AL
Typical Household Income: $42,069
State and Local Taxes: $2,275
Housing Cost Indexes
  Average Price: 73
  Utilities: 88
  Property Taxes: 44
Other Living Cost Indexes
  College Tuition: 100
  Food at Home: 95
  Health Care: 91
  Transportation: 101
Places Rated Score: 8,483
Places Rated Rank: 64

Tyler, TX
Typical Household Income: $49,210
State and Local Taxes: $1,028
Housing Cost Indexes
  Average Price: 74
  Utilities: 88
  Property Taxes: 149
Other Living Cost Indexes
  College Tuition: 42
  Food at Home: 88
  Health Care: 87
  Transportation: 92
Places Rated Score: 8,561
Places Rated Rank: 72

Utica-Rome, NY
Typical Household Income: $45,754
State and Local Taxes: $4,156
Housing Cost Indexes
  Average Price: 80
  Utilities: 110
  Property Taxes: 201
Other Living Cost Indexes
  College Tuition: 83
  Food at Home: 113
  Health Care: 113
  Transportation: 110
Places Rated Score: 10,396
Places Rated Rank: 223

Vallejo-Fairfield-Napa, CA
Typical Household Income: $56,022
State and Local Taxes: $2,445
Housing Cost Indexes
  Average Price: 185
  Utilities: 106

Property Taxes: 191
Other Living Cost Indexes
  College Tuition: 72
  Food at Home: 105
  Health Care: 118
  Transportation: 115
Places Rated Score: 14,043
Places Rated Rank: 309

Vancouver, BC
Typical Household Income: $58,178
Provincial Taxes: $6,227
Housing Cost Indexes
  Average Price: 207
  Utilities: 102
  Property Taxes: 213
Other Living Cost Indexes
  College Tuition: 83
  Food at Home: 165
  Health Care: 28
  Transportation: 133
Places Rated Score: 15,688
Places Rated Rank: 322

Vancouver, WA
Typical Household Income: $46,082
State and Local Taxes $980
Housing Cost Indexes
  Average Price: 91
  Utilities: 85
  Property Taxes: 82
Other Living Cost Indexes
  College Tuition: 110
  Food at Home: 100
  Health Care: 130
  Transportation: 110
Places Rated Score: 9,954
Places Rated Rank: 191

Ventura, CA
Typical Household Income: $67,036
State and Local Taxes: $4,012
Housing Cost Indexes
  Average Price: 290
  Utilities: 102
  Property Taxes: 298
Other Living Cost Indexes
  College Tuition: 59
  Food at Home: 109
  Health Care: 125
  Transportation: 118
Places Rated Score: 18,478
Places Rated Rank: 336

Victoria, BC
Typical Household Income: $48,707
Provincial Taxes: $4,849
Housing Cost Indexes
  Average Price: 164
  Utilities: 100
  Property Taxes: 169
Other Living Cost Indexes
  College Tuition: 78
  Food at Home: 168
  Health Care: 28
  Transportation: 126
Places Rated Score: 13,836
Places Rated Rank: 307

Victoria, TX
Typical Household Income: $49,542
State and Local Taxes: $1,035
Housing Cost Indexes
  Average Price: 66
  Utilities: 81
  Property Taxes: 131
Other Living Cost Indexes
  College Tuition: 45

Food at Home: 96
Health Care: 89
Transportation: 105
Places Rated Score: 8,560
Places Rated Rank: 71

Vineland–Millville–Bridgeton, NJ
Typical Household Income: $55,018
State and Local Taxes: $2,024
Housing Cost Indexes
  Average Price: 85
  Utilities: 132
  Property Taxes: 171
Other Living Cost Indexes
  College Tuition: 123
  Food at Home: 103
  Health Care: 108
  Transportation: 102
Places Rated Score: 10,313
Places Rated Rank: 213

Visalia–Tulare–Porterville, CA
Typical Household Income: $49,003
State and Local Taxes: $2,139
Housing Cost Indexes
  Average Price: 92
  Utilities: 91
  Property Taxes: 94
Other Living Cost Indexes
  College Tuition: 51
  Food at Home: 108
  Health Care: 105
  Transportation: 110
Places Rated Score: 9,883
Places Rated Rank: 188

Waco, TX
Typical Household Income: $44,208
State and Local Taxes: $923
Housing Cost Indexes
  Average Price: 62
  Utilities: 87
  Property Taxes: 124
Other Living Cost Indexes
  College Tuition: 55
  Food at Home: 94
  Health Care: 92
  Transportation: 102
Places Rated Score: 8,380
Places Rated Rank: 54

Washington, DC–MD–VA–WV
Typical Household Income: $72,535
State and Local Taxes: $5,192
Housing Cost Indexes
  Average Price: 179
  Utilities: 99
  Property Taxes: 193
Other Living Cost Indexes
  College Tuition: 119
  Food at Home: 115
  Health Care: 116
  Transportation: 112
Places Rated Score: 14,004
Places Rated Rank: 308

Waterbury, CT
Typical Household Income: $61,256
State and Local Taxes: $1,033
Housing Cost Indexes
  Average Price: 144
  Utilities: 129
  Property Taxes: 231
Other Living Cost Indexes
  College Tuition: 102
  Food at Home: 103
  Health Care: 113

Transportation: 100
Places Rated Score: 12,662
Places Rated Rank: 289

Waterloo–Cedar Falls, IA
Typical Household Income: $47,430
State and Local Taxes: $2,431
Housing Cost Indexes
  Average Price: 53
  Utilities: 107
  Property Taxes: 85
Other Living Cost Indexes
  College Tuition: 103
  Food at Home: 98
  Health Care: 99
  Transportation: 106
Places Rated Score: 8,403
Places Rated Rank: 56

Wausau, WI
Typical Household Income: $48,432
State and Local Taxes: $3,004
Housing Cost Indexes
  Average Price: 64
  Utilities: 104
  Property Taxes: 143
Other Living Cost Indexes
  College Tuition: 101
  Food at Home: 98
  Health Care: 107
  Transportation: 93
Places Rated Score: 8,818
Places Rated Rank: 99

West Palm Beach–Boca Raton, FL
Typical Household Income: $61,937
State and Local Taxes: $1,112
Housing Cost Indexes
  Average Price: 144
  Utilities: 83
  Property Taxes: 231
Other Living Cost Indexes
  College Tuition: 74
  Food at Home: 95
  Health Care: 94
  Transportation: 111
Places Rated Score: 12,112
Places Rated Rank: 282

✓ **Wheeling, WV–OH**
Typical Household Income: $42,857
State and Local Taxes: $2,257
Housing Cost Indexes
  Average Price: 53
  Utilities: 104
  Property Taxes: 26
Other Living Cost Indexes
  College Tuition: 87
  Food at Home: 97
  Health Care: 97
  Transportation: 100
Places Rated Score: 7,848
Places Rated Rank: 12

Wichita, KS
Typical Household Income: $54,939
State and Local Taxes: $2,283
Housing Cost Indexes
  Average Price: 69
  Utilities: 112
  Property Taxes: 97
Other Living Cost Indexes
  College Tuition: 88
  Food at Home: 98
  Health Care: 103
  Transportation: 101
Places Rated Score: 8,958
Places Rated Rank: 117

Wichita Falls, TX
Typical Household Income: $49,261
State and Local Taxes: $1,029
Housing Cost Indexes
  Average Price: 58
  Utilities: 89
  Property Taxes: 115
Other Living Cost Indexes
  College Tuition: 66
  Food at Home: 96
  Health Care: 92
  Transportation: 100
Places Rated Score: 8,241
Places Rated Rank: 45

Williamsport, PA
Typical Household Income: $45,135
State and Local Taxes: $3,990
Housing Cost Indexes
  Average Price: 65
  Utilities: 121
  Property Taxes: 161
Other Living Cost Indexes
  College Tuition: 158
  Food at Home: 100
  Health Care: 96
  Transportation: 90
Places Rated Score: 9,108
Places Rated Rank: 123

Wilmington, NC
Typical Household Income: $45,418
State and Local Taxes: $3,826
Housing Cost Indexes
  Average Price: 96
  Utilities: 103
  Property Taxes: 110
Other Living Cost Indexes
  College Tuition: 65
  Food at Home: 98
  Health Care: 95
  Transportation: 98
Places Rated Score: 9,741
Places Rated Rank: 184

Wilmington–Newark, DE–MD
Typical Household Income: $62,712
State and Local Taxes: $2,195
Housing Cost Indexes
  Average Price: 135
  Utilities: 110
  Property Taxes: 101
Other Living Cost Indexes
  College Tuition: 172
  Food at Home: 117
  Health Care: 122
  Transportation: 99
Places Rated Score: 12,014
Places Rated Rank: 279

Windsor, ON
Typical Household Income: $55,071
Provincial Taxes: $5,960
Housing Cost Indexes
  Average Price: 92
  Utilities: 111
  Property Taxes: 181
Other Living Cost Indexes
  College Tuition: 78
  Food at Home: 156
  Health Care: 28
  Transportation: 134
Places Rated Score: 11,334
Places Rated Rank: 263

Winnipeg, MB
Typical Household Income: $48,958
Provincial Taxes: $5,312

Housing Cost Indexes
  Average Price: 69
  Utilities: 126
  Property Taxes: 173
Other Living Cost Indexes
  College Tuition: 75
  Food at Home: 152
  Health Care: 28
  Transportation: 126
Places Rated Score: 10,332
Places Rated Rank: 217

Worcester–Fitchburg–Leominster, MA
Typical Household Income: $56,517
State and Local Taxes: $3,842
Housing Cost Indexes
  Average Price: 162
  Utilities: 109
  Property Taxes: 243
Other Living Cost Indexes
  College Tuition: 103
  Food at Home: 105
  Health Care: 115
  Transportation: 109
Places Rated Score: 13,442
Places Rated Rank: 301

Yakima, WA
Typical Household Income: $49,201
State and Local Taxes: $1,047
Housing Cost Indexes
  Average Price: 66
  Utilities: 86
  Property Taxes: 59
Other Living Cost Indexes
  College Tuition: 89
  Food at Home: 94
  Health Care: 107

Transportation: 97
Places Rated Score: 8,311
Places Rated Rank: 49

Yolo, CA
Typical Household Income: $56,202
State and Local Taxes: $2,453
Housing Cost Indexes
  Average Price: 166
  Utilities: 98
  Property Taxes: 171
Other Living Cost Indexes
  College Tuition: 94
  Food at Home: 107
  Health Care: 118
  Transportation: 117
Places Rated Score: 13,324
Places Rated Rank: 300

York, PA
Typical Household Income: $55,683
State and Local Taxes: $4,923
Housing Cost Indexes
  Average Price: 92
  Utilities: 123
  Property Taxes: 230
Other Living Cost Indexes
  College Tuition: 216
  Food at Home: 100
  Health Care: 95
  Transportation: 114
Places Rated Score: 11,055
Places Rated Rank: 255

Youngstown–Warren, OH
Typical Household Income: $45,470
State and Local Taxes: $2,817
Housing Cost Indexes
  Average Price: 58

Utilities: 127
Property Taxes: 88
Other Living Cost Indexes
  College Tuition: 121
  Food at Home: 99
  Health Care: 85
  Transportation: 100
Places Rated Score: 8,575
Places Rated Rank: 73

Yuba City, CA
Typical Household Income: $46,004
State and Local Taxes: $2,008
Housing Cost Indexes
  Average Price: 98
  Utilities: 103
  Property Taxes: 101
Other Living Cost Indexes
  College Tuition: 50
  Food at Home: 104
  Health Care: 115
  Transportation: 116
Places Rated Score: 10,377
Places Rated Rank: 220

Yuma, AZ
Typical Household Income: $37,173
State and Local Taxes: $1,527
Housing Cost Indexes
  Average Price: 76
  Utilities: 104
  Property Taxes: 85
Other Living Cost Indexes
  College Tuition: 81
  Food at Home: 99
  Health Care: 104
  Transportation: 113
Places Rated Score: 9,307
Places Rated Rank: 153

Et Cetera

TAXES

Question: Where in North America can you find rock-bottom property taxes, no sales taxes, no taxes on any of your sources of income, no niggling nickel-and-dime fees for registering a car or taking out a license to catch largemouth bass, and no inheritance taxes for your heirs to pay?

Answer: Dream on. This ideal tax haven would have to combine the low property taxes of Louisiana, Alberta's absence of retail sales taxes, and South Dakota's forgiveness of taxes on personal income. Unfortunately, you just can't find all these terrific tax breaks in one place. Although federal income taxes take nearly the same bite whether you live in New Bedford, New Orleans, or New York, state taxes can differ dramatically around the country. Sales taxes, excise taxes, license taxes, income taxes, property taxes, death taxes, gift taxes, and head taxes are just some of the forms that

state taxes take. Depending on where you live, you may encounter all of them or only a few.

Property Taxes. Taxes on land and the buildings on it-whether they are homes, farms, industrial plants, or commercial buildings-are the biggest source of cash for local governments. They are imposed not by states but by the tens of thousands of cities, townships, counties, school districts, sanitary districts, hospital districts, and other assessing jurisdictions in the nation.

The states' role is to specify the maximum rate on the market value of the property, or a percentage of it, as the legal standard for local assessors to follow. The local assessor determines the value to be taxed. If you think the valuation is too high, you have a limited right of appeal. You can't escape property taxes in any state except Alaska (where you must be over 65 to take advantage of that break), but you can find significantly low rates in certain parts of the country. Nationally, the average bills on homes amount to 1.25 percent of their market value, whereas the average bills in Alabama, Arizona, Hawaii, Louisiana, New Mexico, and West Virginia are based on less than half that rate.

Sales Taxes. If people had a choice of raising income taxes or raising sales taxes, they would opt for the latter by a big margin according to recent polls. Sometimes called retail taxes or consumption taxes, sales taxes are collected at the retail level on the purchase of goods. After income taxes, they account for the second largest source of revenue for state governments.

Among the states, the average sales tax is 5 percent. Throughout Canada, the rate is much higher. If you're living in California, you're paying the America's highest state rate: 7.25 percent. If you're from Newfoundland, you're paying North America's highest rate: 12%. Canada also imposes a 7% value-added tax—the Goods and Services Tax, or GST–payable by consumers in addition to the province's sales tax.

Alaska has no statewide sales tax but local governments may levy the tax. Hawaii has a general excise tax; New Mexico a gross receipts tax. Alberta, Delaware, Montana, New Hampshire, and Oregon collect no sales taxes at all. To a four-person family, this could mean a savings of hundreds of dollars. But you can avoid paying almost that much in areas where such basics as food, medicine, and clothing are exempted.

Personal Income Taxes. When the first federal income tax went into effect in 1913, two states—Mississippi and Wisconsin—were already collecting income taxes on their own. It was only during the 1920s and 1930s that the majority of states began to raise cash by tapping personal incomes. Today, 41 states impose the tax; two (New Hampshire and Tennessee) apply it only to income from interest and dividends; and seven (Alaska, Florida, Nevada, South Dakota, Texas, Washington, and Wyoming) don't tax incomes at all.

THE HIGH COST OF COLLEGE

Some say that in the future white-collar workplace, only those who have college degrees will get the nod for new slots in management training, or even entry-level jobs behind the counter or in the mail room.

But coming up with four years of tuition and fees to help their children launch a career is breaking a lot of middle-income families. To go away to college and make it through in standard time, most students need at least two out of these three sources of money (aside from parental largesse): a scholarship, a student loan, and a part-time job.

The best way to cut costs at the very start is to do some sharp thinking when choosing a college. If you are planning on college, consider your options. You can:

- Live at home, enroll in a low-cost two-year college that offers courses good toward a bach-

elor's degree, and then transfer to a local four-year state college for your junior and senior years. This is the least expensive way to get a college education.

- Enroll in a public four-year college or university in your home state. The tuition will definitely be higher than that of a two-year college. And if you decide to live on campus, it will cost you $4,500 more per year than attending college while living at home.
- Enroll in a public college or university outside your home state. This will mean paying stiff tuition charges. But establishing legal residency could save you a significant amount. Tuitions in California public colleges, for example, are one-fifth what you'd pay in several northeastern states.
- Register at a private college or university. This is the most expensive option, even if you live at home.

PAYING FOR POWER

Aside from how old the power plant is and how far it is from oil and coal fuel sources, the biggest factors that play a part in charges to consumers are who owns the company, and how is the electricity generated.

The Energy Department's latest price comparison of electricity shows that, in general, publicly owned (municipal) electric power companies charge much lower rates than their larger, privately owned counterparts. Moreover, utilities that operate nuclear power plants tend to charge the consumer much higher rates than others.

Because of a lower demand for electricity, construction and regulatory delays, skyrocketing costs, and concerns about reactor safety after the Three Mile Island and Chernobyl incidents, the growth of nuclear power has halted. Utility planners are simply unwilling to take the risk of investing billions in a 12-14 year process of building a nuclear plant and then face the possibility of not being allowed to operate it.

During 1993, the billions of kilowatt hours produced by nuclear reactors counted for 16 percent of the total North American electrical output. Over half the electricity consumed in Connecticut, Maine, Nebraska, Ontario, and South Carolina is generated from nuclear power plants.

The following list shows the 32 states and 3 provinces in which nuclear power plants are found. The generating capacity, or power output, for a typical reactor is 1,000 megawatts (one million kilowatts) of electricity, or enough to supply the needs of a city of 600,000 people at any given moment. Each plant is either operating or under construction as of June, 1993. The date of operation—actual or planned—is also given for each unit along with its county location.

Alabama: 7,279 megawatts total capacity
Houston County: Farley #1 (1977), Farley #2 (1981). Jackson County: Bellefonte #1 (indefinite), Bellefonte #2 (indefinite). Morgan County: Browns Ferry #1 (1974), Browns Ferry #2 (1975), Browns Ferry #3 (1977).

Arkansas: 1,762 megawatts total capacity
Pope County: Arkansas Nuclear #1 (1974), Arkansas Nuclear #2 (1980).

Arizona: 3,810 megawatts total capacity
Maricopa County: Palo Verde #1 (1986), Palo Verde #2 (1986), Palo Verde #3 (1988).

California: 5,694 megawatts total capacity
San Diego County: San Onofre #2 (1983), San Onofre #3 (1984). San Luis Obispo County: Diablo Canyon #1 (1985), Diablo Canyon #2 (1986).

Connecticut: 3,262 megawatts total capacity
Middlesex County: Haddam Neck (1968). New London County: Millstone #1 (1970), Millstone #2 (1975), Millstone #3 (1986).

Florida: 3,856 megawatts total capacity
Citrus County: Crystal River #3 (1977). Dade County: Turkey Point #3 (1972), Turkey Point #4 (1973). St. Lucie County: St. Lucie #1 (1976), St. Lucie #2 (1983).

Georgia: 3,800 megawatts total capacity
Appling County: Hatch #1 (1975), Hatch #2 (1979). Burke County: Vogtle #1 (1987), Vogtle #2 (1989).

Iowa: 545 megawatts total capacity
Linn County: Duane Arnold (1975).

Illinois: 12,815 megawatts total capacity
Byron County: Byron #1 (1985), Byron #2 (1987). De Witt County: Clinton (1987). Grundy County: Dresden #2 (1970), Dresden #3 (1971). Lake County: Zion #1 (1973), Zion #2 (1974). La Salle County: La Salle #1 (1984), La Salle #2 (1984). Rock Island County: Quad Cities #1 (1972), Quad Cities #2 (1972). Will County: Braidwood #1 (1988), Braidwood #2 (1988).

Kansas: 1,150 megawatts total capacity
Coffee County: Wolf Creek (1985).

Louisiana: 2,044 megawatts total capacity
St. Charles Parish: Waterford #3 (1985). West Feliciana Parish: River Bend (1986).

Massachusetts: 545 megawatts total capacity
Plymouth County: Pilgrim (1972).

Maryland: 1,650 megawatts total capacity
Calvert County: Calvert Cliffs #1 (1975), Calvert Cliffs #2 (1977).

Maine: 825 megawatts total capacity
Lincoln County: Maine Yankee (1972).

Michigan: 4,078 megawatts total capacity
Berrien County: Cook #1 (1975), Cook #2 (1978). Charlevoix County: Big Rock Point (1965). Monroe County: Fermi #2 (1988). Van Buren County: Palisades (1971).

Minnesota: 1,605 megawatts total capacity
Goodhue County: Prairie Island #1 (1973), Prair-

Annual In-State Tuition Charges at Public Colleges and Universities

UNITED STATES	$2,171
Alabama	1,832
Alaska	1,589
Arizona	1,700
Arkansas	1,631
California	1,403
Colorado	2,207
Connecticut	2,660
Delaware	3,347
District of Columbia	764
Florida	1,538
Georgia	1,932
Hawaii	1,484
Idaho	1,367
Illinois	2,835
Indiana	2,377
Iowa	2,162
Kansas	1,804
Kentucky	1,661
Louisiana	2,060
Maine	2,602
Maryland	2,630
Massachusetts	2,967
Michigan	3,030
Minnesota	2,548
Mississippi	2,216
Missouri	1,993
Montana	1,786
Nebraska	1,831
Nevada	1,466
New Hampshire	3,577
New Jersey	3,289
New Mexico	1,620
New York	1,825
North Carolina	1,279
North Dakota	2,220
Ohio	3,015
Oklahoma	1,541
Oregon	2,192
Pennsylvania	3,911
Rhode Island	2,658
South Carolina	2,665
South Dakota	2,132
Tennessee	1,746
Texas	1,134
Utah	1,753
Vermont	4,706
Virginia	3,095
Washington	2,096
West Virginia	1,774
Wisconsin	2,244
Wyoming	1,320
CANADA	$1,647
Alberta	1,288
British Columbia	1,748
Manitoba	1,472
New Brunswick	1,932
Newfoundland	1,420
Nova Scotia	2,116
Ontario	1,628
Prince Edward Island	1,950
Quebec	1,214
Saskatchewan	1,702

Source: National Center for Education Statistics, unpublished data, 1993; Statistics Canada, *Tuition and living accomodation costs at Canadian universities,* 1992.

Costs are in American dollars. United States data are weighted averages; Canadian data are for undergraduate study at the largest university in each province.

Taxing the Necessities

You'll pay sales tax on groceries in . . .

Alabama	Louisiana	Tennessee
Arkansas	Mississippi	Utah
Georgia	Missouri	Virginia
Hawaii	New Mexico	West Virginia
Idaho	North Carolina	Wyoming
Illinois	South Carolina	
Kansas	South Dakota	

You'll pay sales tax on prescriptions in . . .

Illinois	New Mexico

You'll pay no sales tax on clothing in . . .

Connecticut	Nova Scotia
Massachusetts	Pennsylvania
Minnesota	Prince Edward Island
New Brunswick	Rhode Island
New Jersey	Saskatchewan

And no sales tax at all in . . .

Alaska
Alberta
Delaware
Montana
New Hampshire
Oregon

Source: Commerce Clearing House, *State Tax Guide,* 1993; *Canadian Master Tax Guide, 1993.*

North American Sales Tax Rates

UNITED STATES

Alabama	4
Arizona	5
Arkansas	4.5
California	7.25
Colorado	3
Connecticut *	6
District of Columbia	6
Florida	6
Georgia	4
Hawaii *	4
Idaho *	5
Illinois	6.25
Indiana *	5
Iowa	5
Kansas	4.9
Kentucky	6
Louisiana	4
Maine *	5
Maryland *	5
Massachusetts *	5
Michigan *	4
Minnesota	6.5
Mississippi *	7
Missouri	4.225
Nebraska	5
Nevada	6.5
New Jersey *	7
New Mexico	5
New York	4
North Carolina	4
North Dakota	5
Ohio	5
Oklahoma	4.5
Pennsylvania *	6
Rhode Island *	7
South Carolina	5
South Dakota	5
Tennessee	6
Texas	6.25
Utah	6
Vermont *	5
Virginia *	4.5
Washington	6.5
West Virginia *	6
Wisconsin	5
Wyoming	3

CANADA

British Columbia *	7
Manitoba *	7
New Brunswick *	11
Newfoundland *	12
Nova Scotia *	10
Ontario *	8
Prince Edward Island *	10
Quebec *	8
Saskatchewan *	9

Source: Commerce Clearing House, *Canadian Master Tax Guide,* 1993; *State Tax Guide,* 1993.

* Indicates a single tax rate throughout the state or province. All other states permit local additions to their base tax rates.

ie Island #2 (1974). Wright County: Monticello (1971). .

Missouri: 1,120 megawatts total capacity
Callaway County: Callaway (1984).

Mississippi: 1,250 megawatts total capacity
Claiborne County: Grand Gulf (1985).

North Carolina: 4,842 megawatts total capacity
Brunswick County: Brunswick #1 (1977), Brunswick #2 (1975). Mecklenburg County: McGuire #1 (1981), McGuire #2 (1984). Wake County: Harris (1987).

Nebraska: 1,246 megawatts total capacity
Namaha County: Cooper (1974). Washington County: Fort Calhoun (1973).

New Brunswick: 633 megawatts total capacity
Point Lepreau: Point Lepreau (1983).

New Hampshire: 650 megawatts total capacity
Rockingham County: Seabrook (1990).

New Jersey: 3,922 megawatts total capacity
Ocean County: Oyster Creek (1969). Salem County: Hope Creek (1986). Salem #1 (1977), Salem #2 (1981).

New York: 4,623 megawatts total capacity
Oswego County: Nine Mile Point #1 (1969), Nine Mile Point #2 (1988). Suffolk County: Fitzpatrick (1975). Wayne County: Ginna (1970). Westchester County: Indian Point #2 (1973), Indian Point #3 (1976).

Ohio: 3,270 megawatts total capacity
Lake County: Perry #1 (1987), Perry #2 (indefinite). Ottawa County: Davis-Besse (1977).

Ontario: 4,310 megawatts total capacity
Newcastle: Darlington A (1990), Darlington B

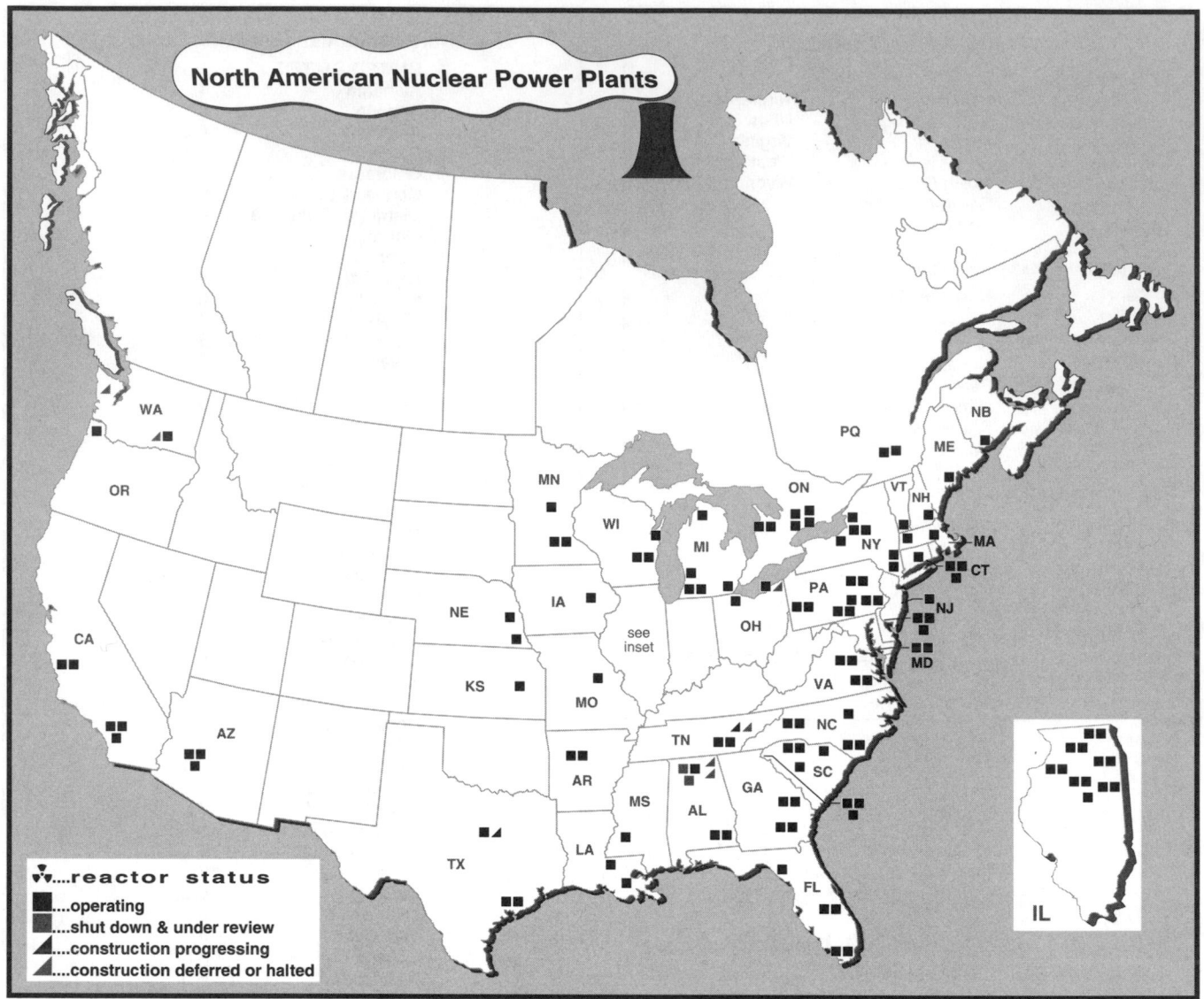

North American Nuclear Power Plants

reactor status
■ ....operating
▦ ....shut down & under review
◢ ....construction progressing
◤ ....construction deferred or halted

IL

Thomas Nast, Cartographer

(1992). Pickering: Pickering A (1972), Pickering B (1981). Tiverton: Bruce A (1971), Bruce B (1976).

Pennsylvania: 8,009 Total Capacity
Beaver County: Beaver Valley #1 (1976), Beaver Valley #2 (1987). Luzerne County: Susquehanna #1 (1983), Susquehanna #2 (1985). Montgomery County: Limerick #1 (1986), Limerick #2 (1990). York County: Peach Bottom #2 (1974), Peach Bottom #3 (1974).

Quebec: 638 megawatts total capacity
Becancour: Gentilly #2 (1983).

South Carolina: 6,435 megawatts total capacity
Darlington County: Robinson #2 (1971). Fairfield County: Summer (1984). Oconee County: Oconee #1 (1973), Oconee #2 (1973), Oconee #3 (1974). York County: Catawba (1986).

Tennessee: 4,650 megawatts total capacity
Hamilton County: Sequoyah #1 (1981), Sequoyah #2 (1982). Rhea County: Watts Bar #1 (indefi-

nite), Watts Bar #2 (indefinite).

Texas: 4,800 megawatts total capacity
Matagorda County: South Texas Project #1 (1988), South Texas Project #2 (1989). Somervell County: Comanche Peak #1 (1990), Comanche Peak #2 (1993).

Virginia: 3,414 megawatts total capacity
Louisa County: North Anna #1 (1978), North Anna #2 (1980). Surry County: Surry #1 (1972), Surry #2 (1973).

Vermont: 514 megawatts total capacity
Windham County: Vermont Yankee (1972).

Washington: 1,000 megawatts total capacity
Benton County: WPPSS #2 (1984).

Wisconsin: 1,505 megawatts total capacity
Kewaunee County: Kewaunee (1974). Manitowoc County: Point Beach #1 (1970), Point Beach #2 (1972).

State Individual Income Tax Rates

State	Tax Rates	Lowest Amount Under	Highest Amount Over
Alabama	2.0 to 5.0	$500	$3,000
Arizona	3.8 to 7.0	10,000	150,000
Arkansas	1.0 to 7.0	3,000	25,000
California	1.0 to 11.0	4,213	27,646
Colorado	3.0	Flat Rate	
Connecticut	4.5	Flat Rate	
Delaware	3.2 to 7.7	5,000	40,000
District of Columbia	6.0 to 9.5	10,000	20,000
Georgia	2.0 to 7.0	750	7,000
Hawaii	2.0 to 10.0	1,500	20,500
Idaho	2.0 to 8.2	1,000	20,000
Illinois	3.0	Flat Rate	
Indiana	3.4	Flat Rate	
Iowa	0.4 to 9.98	1,038	46,710
Kansas	3.5 to 6.45	27,500	27,500
Kentucky	2.0 to 6.0	3,000	8,000
Louisiana	2.0 to 6.0	10,000	50,000
Maine	2.1 to 9.89	4,050	16,200
Maryland	2.0 to 6.0	1,000	3,000
Massachusetts	5.95	Flat Rate	
Michigan	4.6	Flat Rate	
Minnesota	6.0 to 8.5	13,000	13,000
Mississippi	3.0 to 5.0	5,000	10,000
Missouri	1.5 to 6.0	1,000	9,000
Montana	2.0 to 11.0	1,600	55,000
Nebraska	2.37 to 6.92	1,800	27,000
New Jersey	2.0 to 7.0	20,000	50,000
New Mexico	2.4 to 8.5	5,200	64,000
New York	4.55 to 7.59	5,500	13,000
North Carolina	6.0 to 7.75	12,750	12,750
Ohio	0.74 to 7.5	5,000	100,000
Oklahoma	0.5 to 10.0	1,000	1,000
Oregon	5.0 to 9.0	2,000	5,000
Pennsylvania	2.8	Flat Rate	
Rhode Island *	27.5 to 29.75		
South Carolina	2.5 to 7.0	2,030	10,150
Utah	2.55 to 7.3	750	3,750
Vermont *	28.0 to 34.0		
Virginia	2.0 to 5.75	3,000	17,000
West Virginia	3.0 to 6.5	10,000	60,000
Wisconsin	4.9 to 6.93	7,500	15,000

Source: Commerce Clearing House, State Tax Guide, 1993.

Alaska, Nevada, New Hampshire, South Dakota, Tennessee, Texas, Washington, and Wyoming have no broad based income tax.

* Rhode Island and Vermont base their income taxes as a percentage of federal tax liability.

Jobs

In Newfoundland, Blue Star beer puts on a "Take this job and love it" contest with a job as first prize. The contest is halted after the provincial government, embarrassed by a 20 percent unemployment rate, threatens to suspend the brewery's license.

Along Florida's Gold Coast from Palm Beach down to Miami, joblessness is no joke, either, when 1,500 people at Jordan Marsh department stores, 700 Pratt & Whitney workers, 5,000 IBM employees, and thousands of construction workers hit by the building bust all get pink slips. Far to the west, the Los Angeles and Las Vegas job machines, to name two of many, choked up months ago and have been running roughly ever since.

Jobs will be the pervasive issue of the 1990s. Among all the mobility factors in *Places Rated*, it is the most important. For some, it is the *only* factor. While we will probably never again see any overheated boom towns in this century, many metro areas are expected to recover jobs lost during the latest recession and gain a good many more besides.

FORECASTING WHERE THE JOBS WILL BE

Economists who follow employment trends have an old joke: If you take each local planner's numbers for job growth in his or her area and add them all together, the total jobs forecasted would require that every man,

woman, and child hold down one day job and moonlight two others.

Fortunately, economists with a macro view have a better perspective. Although no one can predict the future with certainty, forecasting where jobs will be plentiful over the next few years isn't merely a matter of gazing into a crystal ball.

To start with, do people move to where the jobs are, or do jobs come to where the people are? Economists argue about this quite a bit, but most believe that jobs come to where the people are. In other words, any place that has a concentration of people and is also growing is by definition a job mecca.

But there's more to it than that. Some metro areas are saddled with sunset industries—shipbuilding, textiles, sawmills, and steel, for example—while others have sunrise industries—health care, higher education, and software. Most metro areas have varying mixes of both. Forecasting which ones will gain the jobs is as much a matter of determining the prospects for certain industries as it is predicting population shifts.

The great American job machine has churned out record numbers of jobs for decades and, apparently, the machine is showing significant wear and tear. Still, by the year 2000, no longer just a year in which science-fiction stories are set, more than 15 million new jobs could be added to the U.S. economy. Although projected employment increases are expected to occur at half the pace compared with the past, the growth in certain occupations will be quite healthy.

The biggest continuing trend is massive growth in service-oriented sectors and marked decline in goods-producing industries. In other words, opportunities for highly trained white-collar workers are growing rapidly, with the blue-collar shade of many metro areas fading to white.

BLUE-COLLAR BLUES . . .

Shortly after the end of World War II, white-collar jobs passed blue-collar jobs in numbers for the first time in the history of North America. White-collar workers as a group earn somewhat less than blue-collar workers because so many white-collar jobs are low-pay clerical and retail positions and so many blue-collar jobs are skilled occupations protected by union contracts. But white-collar jobs, though paying less, provide a ladder of opportunity that blue-collar jobs don't. And the work is steadier. One of the biggest union issues now is security against layoffs and plant closings rather than higher wages. Blue-collar workers are beginning to want what's best in the white-collar world, and they are willing to sacrifice higher wage demands.

The shrinking world of blue-collar work is divided into five basic industries. For the most part, job opportunities in four are expected to drop or merely hold steady to the year 2000.

Farming, Forestry, and Fishing

From Mississippi to Saskatchewan, the family farm is disappearing as mechanized agribusiness rounds up more acreage and concentrates on fewer crops. Despite some modest recovery from the agricultural production slump in the mid-1980s, exports will probably not regain the world dominance they once enjoyed. Still, some metro areas—those in California's Central Valley (Stockton, Merced, Bakersfield, Fresno) and in Canada's prairie provinces (Regina, Saskatoon, Winnipeg)—have large numbers of farming jobs.

One portion of the agricultural sector—the agricultural services (such as landscaping and lawn services)—has been growing rapidly, and the growth is expected to continue. Here is yet another indication of the shift toward a service economy.

Mining—A Hard Place

Jobs in mining, once a stable employer in the West, are in a deep hole and likely to remain there. Half of these jobs are in hard-hatted oil and natural gas production and high-tech oil field services, disaster industries for the Southwest and Rockies since 1986. The simple reason is that foreign oil is cheaper.

Metal mining isn't expected to recover any of the deep cuts experienced over the past decade, either. Exports of raw ores are expected to rise, but slow growth in basic steel as well as iron and steel foundries will limit increases in demand. And while coal is getting more important as alternative energy, the number of jobs in coal mines won't grow. Instead, new production methods will mean continued shrinking of employment.

Construction—Rebuilding Rather Than Building

Here's a footloose industry if there ever was one. Building contracts run out? Move on to another location. Why else do you think many itinerant general contractors have southwestern drawls? This industry, which thinks that half of North America must be rebuilt before the end of the century, is expected to provide most of the blue-collar jobs to 1998 and beyond. Whenever you see a place forecasted to gain a large number of blue-collar jobs, you'll be seeing hammers, bulldozers, bricks, and lumber.

Slow population growth and household formation, however, will slow home building in the 1990s; while little growth is likely for new single-family homes or house alterations and additions, this trend will be offset by declines in new apartment and condo construction. Nonresidential construction may recover from the over-supply of office and commercial space, but getting rid of the excess stock may take fifteen years in certain parts of the continent.

Manufacturing—Anything *but* Durable

Here is another job sector that's predicted to grow glacially or not at all. Smokestacks, low-rise buildings near rail tracks, even high-tech assembly work—we can tell it good-bye over time. Much of it is moving offshore or to third-world countries.

Although manufacturing will lose hundreds of thousands of jobs by the year 2000, output is expected almost to keep pace with total GNP growth. At the same time, the occupational composition of the remaining manufacturing jobs will change. In general, following the trend of the disappearing blue-collar job, manufacturing employment will shift from production and assembly-line jobs toward professional, managerial, and technical occupations. The shift is more pronounced in industries where imports play a significant role. In some of those cases, design and engineering are done domestically, but much of the actual assembly is performed overseas.

The computer manufacturing industry, as we all might have guessed, has been one of the fastest-growing industries during the past 25 years. The nature of work in this industry, however, is uncharacteristic of manufacturing industries. It employs a high concentration of scientific personnel and a relatively low concentration of production workers. Employment in computer manufacturing is expected to expand to 503,000 jobs in 2000, with even more of a shift at that time from production to research and development occupations.

The printing and publishing business is one of the

few manufacturing sectors to have registered consistent job gains in the past few years. Even during the recession, both output and employment increased steadily. And the introduction of electronic composition systems and other new technologies has not put a damper on this trend. As elsewhere, however, occupational shifts are occurring within the printing trades, from fewer typesetters and other craftspeople to more front-office personnel such as writers, editors, managers, and sales workers. Growth is expected to continue with vigor throughout the rest of the 1990s.

Transportation, Communications, and Public Utilities

This catchall industry classification embraces electric power generation, 18-wheel trucking, airline food and baggage handlers, cable television, and much more. In recent years, deregulation has boosted employment in the air transportation industry, as many smaller firms entered the market and price competition stimulated demand. But, in the long run, consolidation and takeovers are expected to dampen the rate of job growth.

Overall, employment in this group is expected to decrease in the next decade due to declining industry employment and technological changes. The railroad industry, for example, is expected to lose about 190,000 jobs. The number of water transportation workers is expected to decline by 8 percent. Greater efficiency in scheduling, marketing, and cost control in the trucking industry is expected to produce greater gains in output than in employment. The same goes for telephone workers; competition in the 1990s in that industry is expected to lead to an employment decline of about 121,000.

... AND A WHITE-COLLAR CHORUS

White-collar work, which corresponds roughly with service-oriented occupations, is divided into four basic industry categories. With some variations within categories, this is where the real action is expected to occur in the remaining years of the 20th century.

Trade

Retail jobs outnumber wholesale positions by five to one and are expected to gain by some 4.9 million over the next decade. Unfortunately, retail trade jobs (hamburger flipping, counter help, damage estimating, aisle sweeping, cashiering) aren't worth having if your cash needs are immediate and above average. These jobs do, however, provide rapid advancement to managerial slots, which are still lower-paid despite the title. Retail trade stores are the most ubiquitous establishments in North America, and heavy opportunity in this sector goes hand in hand with a local area that is swelling with people.

Industrial Winners and Losers

If you're searching for work or making a career change, it's important to think of *occupations* and *industries*. If you're a cartographer, you'll find a job in fewer industries than an accountant will. Below are expanding industries that may be attractive to persons with more generic occupations (like the accountant) and some that, for reasons of declining market or foreign competition, might be avoided.

Fastest Growing	Annual Rate
Residential care	4.5%
Data processing services	4.4
Management and public relations	3.9
Water and sanitation	3.3
Offices of health practitioners	3.1
Travel arrangement	3.0
Legal services	3.0
Nursing homes	2.9
Equipment rental and leasing	2.9
Accounting and auditing services	2.8

Fastest Declining	Annual Rate
Footwear	−4.3%
Ammunition and ordnance	−3.8
Luggage and handbags	−3.5
Tobacco manufacturers	−2.5
Agricultural chemicals	−2.5
Small arms and ammunition	−2.1
Guided missiles and space vehicles	−2.0
Household appliances	−1.9
Tires	−1.8
Clothing	−1.8

Source: U.S. Department of Labor, *Monthly Labor Review*, November 1991.

Finance, Insurance, and Real Estate

Referred to in regional developers' shorthand as FIRE, this is the purest of the white-collar industrial classifications. Here the compensation is greater than in the retail trade, and potentially greater by far than in any other industry. It is a briefcase and tie industry—an office-with-a-capital-O environment. It has both heavier government regulation than other industries and more unreported crime.

Banking, credit agencies, and investment offices—a big part of the FIRE industries—should enjoy substantial rates of business growth in the next decade, but not necessarily such growth in numbers of jobs. Consolidation and technological advances in automatic banking and other financial transactions will actually slow rates of employment gain. This doesn't mean no new jobs in these fields; there will be some growth—for example, 495,000 more in credit agencies and investment offices by the year 2000. But the rate of employment growth will be slower than in the past and will not match the growth in business output.

Similarly, greater efficiency in the insurance industry—computerized underwriting, for example—will mean that job gains will be limited for insurance carriers and for independent agents and brokers. Not no growth, but

Metro-Area Winners and Losers

Of the 20 metro areas forecasted to gain the most jobs between now and 1998, two are in Canada and seven are in regions of the United States that many pundits earlier predicted would decline throughout the rest of the century.

On the other hand, half of the metro areas showing a net loss in jobs over the next five years are in the Sun Belt. Many are stricken by the continuing slump in oil and gas production and by the closing of military installations.

Job Winners, 1993–1998

Metro Area	Total New Jobs
Washington, DC–MD–VA–WV	206,767
Orange County, CA	177,898
Atlanta, GA	168,300
Phoenix–Mesa, AZ	148,703
Los Angeles–Long Beach, CA	139,108
San Diego, CA	134,863
Toronto, ON	132,744
Tampa–St. Petersburg–Clearwater, FL	123,672
Orlando, FL	119,336
Philadelphia, PA–NJ	116,815
Riverside–San Bernardino, CA	110,695
Dallas, TX	110,363
Houston, TX	95,545
Chicago, IL	95,324
Seattle–Bellevue–Everett, WA	90,313
Vancouver, BC	88,113
Detroit, MI	86,601
Minneapolis–St. Paul, MN–WI	80,045
Baltimore, MD	73,730
Charlotte–Gastonia–Rock Hill, NC–SC	72,598

Job Losers, 1993–1998

Metro Area	Job loss
Lawton, OK	−2.67%
Great Falls, MT	−2.14
Houma, LA	−1.59
New York, NY	−0.91
Flint, MI	−0.68
Beaumont–Port Arthur, TX	−0.63
Enid, OK	−0.52
Jacksonville, NC	−0.44
Abilene, TX	−0.38
Grand Forks, ND–MN	−0.10
Amarillo, TX	−0.05

Source: Woods & Poole Economics, Inc., employment forecasts, 1993.

slower growth. Rapid projected growth in the real estate industry is expected to have a favorable impact on employment for brokers (increasing by 44 percent) and appraisers (increasing by 41 percent).

Service

Think of high-rise copper and glass office buildings and medical centers with piped-in music. Think of white smocks and clipboards and shaded college campuses. These are the most desirable kinds of developments— the kinds city fathers and mothers dream of. If the landscape is full of these buildings, you've got a well-educated work force, higher incomes, and a stable, service-oriented economy.

The service division includes careers in business, health, recreation, the professions, and education—an increasing proportion of which will require formal education and certification. Health and education, typically underwritten by government or third-party payers, lead the way in this division. It makes sense if you think about it; the numbers of educational staff are rising with the numbers of children of the baby-boom generation, and the health-care industry is growing as the population ages and needs more medical attention. Overall, this category has been and is projected to be the fastest-growing for new jobs, adding 10 million by the year 2000, for a total of more than 32 million payroll jobs.

The big story in services is, as expected, computer and data processing—systems design, programming, and software development. Another big story in business services, with a very large projected increase in employment, is the personnel supply business, especially the temporary help industry. No longer limited to placing office workers, temporary personnel service businesses are beginning to place workers from industrial, medical, managerial, engineering, and technical occupations as well. The employers like the lower fringe benefits and the access to added help during peak times, and the temporary workers like the flexibility, variety, and experience.

With the trend toward development of new service businesses, the demand is growing for research, management, and consulting services. Independent laboratories for research and development, market researchers, personnel training or management consultants, economic researchers, efficiency experts, lobbyists, and other business consultants will be in increasing demand.

In the professions, the legal services industry has been growing, taking a place among the top 10 fastest-growing employment industries. If you thought the legal profession was filled to capacity, think again. Increasing liability litigation, corporate mergers and acquisitions, high divorce levels, geographic expansion of law firms, a greater degree of legal specialization within firms, and an increase in litigation in general keep things moving.

In health care, too, important shifts are taking place. Cost-containment policies have halted the expansion of hospitals and hospital employment, with health-care delivery moving from the hospital to outpatient-care centers. Look for employment growth in the emergency-care clinics, surgicenters, and walk-in treatment centers that are popping up all around us.

Government

If you're considering a job in government, especially the federal government, you might reconsider. The federal government will definitely be shrinking because of military base closings and budgetary reductions. Total public employment is, however, projected to rise over the next decade, with almost all of the increase occurring among municipal workers such as teachers, firefighters, and police. On the other hand, count on a decline of jobs among clerical and administrative support workers.

For government jobs, though, some places—Austin, TX; Columbus, OH; the Lexington–Frankfort area in Kentucky; Toronto, ON; and Atlanta, GA—are in enviable positions. They are state or provincial capitals with large bureaucracies that face little unemployment threat. That they are all higher-education centers doesn't hurt, either.

SCORING: JOBS

If you're out of work or looking for better employment, would the raw odds of tracking down a job be better in Dallas, Denver, or Duluth? What about Honolulu, Houston, or Huntsville? To help you answer these questions, *Places Rated* compares the number of new jobs forecasted between now and 1998, as well as the rate of job growth during this period.

Each metro area starts with a base score of 2,000. The forecasted growth rate multiplied by the total number of new blue- and white-collar jobs is then added to the base score. The sum of these operations produces the *Places Rated* score.

Los Angeles–Long Beach, CA (#38)

Why does a sprawling, congested metro area on the edge of a desert, smack in the middle of a major earthquake hazard, far from adequate water and basic materials, keep growing? The answer is immigration from other countries, migration from other states, and the difficulty in leaving by disaffected residents who recently told the *Los Angeles Times* they'd move if only they could find a more promising spot.

Los Angeles–Long Beach, now the continent's largest metro area, recently was a blue-collar paradise. Besides the low-paying clothing, furniture, and food-processing industries, workers made good money in the area's many technology-based aerospace and electronics industries. That time is over; blue-collar employment is forecasted to grow here not at all.

The metro area's real strength lies in its emergence as a national and international banking and financial center. Many of the projected 138,770 new jobs in predominantly white-collar industries by 1998 will be created in the finance, insurance, and real estate fields.

When Los Angeles–Long Beach's rate of job growth (2.55 percent) is multiplied by its number of new jobs (139,000) and added to the base score of 2,000, the result is 5,547.

Casper, WY (#324)

Originally a small town along the Oregon–Mormon trail, Casper experienced its first boom when oil was discovered in the Salt Creek area a century ago, in 1889. But it was during the latter half of the 1970s that Wyoming's largest city saw its biggest boom, a period during which Casper was among the top 10 fastest-growing metro areas in the United States.

Unfortunately, this phenomenal growth came to an abrupt end in the early 1980s with the collapse of world prices for uranium, oil, and coal. Employment prospects in Casper to the year 1998 look unpromising. With a forecasted gain of fewer than 200 jobs, and a resulting growth rate of just 1.02 percent, Casper rates a score for jobs that is among the lowest of all 343 metro areas.

Pittsburgh, PA (#110)

Pittsburgh's boom years are behind it. For most of its history, nearby anthracite coal and an industrial base dominated by primary metals established the metro area as the country's Steel City, but because of the sharp decline in domestic steel production, the nickname no longer applies.

For all of its past troubles, Pittsburgh still has more promising job prospects than other metro areas such as Birmingham, AL, Corpus Chrisit, TX, and Pensacola, FL. How so?

Pittsburgh is still among the 25 largest metro areas in North America, and while it is forecasted to lose another 1,736 blue-collar jobs by 1995, it is also forecasted to gain more than 36,000 white-collar jobs. Multiplying its projected growth rate (2.75 percent) by its total number of new jobs (34,290) produces a score of 2,943, or 110th among 343 metro areas.

Rankings: Jobs

In ranking the 343 metro areas for near-term job growth, *Places Rated Almanac* uses two criteria: (1) the percent increase in new jobs by 1998, and (2) the number of new jobs created between now and that date. The product of these two criteria, rounded off, is the metro area's score. The higher the score, the more promising the metro area's job outlook. Places that are tied get the same rank and are listed in alphabetical order.

Metro Areas from Best to Worst

Places Rated Rank	Places Rated Score
1. Orange County, CA	23,028
2. Orlando, FL	20,223
3. Phoenix–Mesa, AZ	19,116
4. Atlanta, GA	16,777
5. Washington, DC–MD–VA–WV	16,288
6. Tampa–St. Petersburg–Clearwater, FL	15,060
7. San Diego, CA	14,772
8. Riverside–San Bernardino, CA	14,121
9. Toronto, ON	11,929
10. Vancouver, BC	11,455
11. Raleigh–Durham–Chapel Hill, NC	10,186
12. Las Vegas, NV–AZ	9,861
13. West Palm Beach–Boca Raton, FL	9,620
14. Dallas, TX	8,964
15. Charlotte–Gastonia–Rock Hill, NC–SC	8,853
16. Seattle–Bellevue–Everett, WA	7,970
17. Sacramento, CA	7,813
18. Fort Worth–Arlington, TX	7,613
19. Columbus, OH	7,239
20. Fort Lauderdale, FL	6,931
21. Philadelphia, PA–NJ	6,895
22. Sarasota–Bradenton, FL	6,668
23. Houston, TX	6,643
24. Greensboro–Winston-Salem–High Point, NC	6,622
25. Ventura, CA	6,617
26. Fort Myers–Cape Coral, FL	6,457
27. Oakland, CA	6,451
28. Portland, OR	6,321
29. Minneapolis–St. Paul, MN–WI	6,242
30. Indianapolis, IN	6,162
31. Greenville–Spartanburg–Anderson, SC	5,999
32. Tucson, AZ	5,973
33. Grand Rapids–Muskegon–Holland, MI	5,972
34. Cincinnati, OH–KY–IN	5,929
35. San Jose, CA	5,845
36. Baltimore, MD	5,745
37. Detroit, MI	5,559
38. Los Angeles–Long Beach, CA	5,547
39. Austin–San Marcos, TX	5,448
40. Nashville, TN	5,239
41. Central New Jersey, NJ	5,099
42. Lake County, IL	4,920
43. Portsmouth–Dover–Rochester, NH	4,758
44. Santa Rosa, CA	4,533
45. St. Louis, MO–IL	4,402
46. Providence–Warwick–Cranston, RI	4,327
47. Denver, CO	4,314
48. Rochester, NY	4,300
49. Miami, FL	4,291

Places Rated Rank	Places Rated Score
50. Chicago, IL	4,240
51. Memphis, TN–AR–MS	4,152
52. Long Island, NY	4,095
53. Daytona Beach, FL	4,061
54. Fort Wayne, IN	4,043
55. Naples, FL	3,961
56. Fort Pierce–Port St. Lucie, FL	3,960
57. Salt Lake City–Ogden, UT	3,952
58. Modesto, CA	3,950
59. Atlantic City–Cape May, NJ	3,941
60. Wilmington–Newark, DE–MD	3,931
61. Richmond–Petersburg, VA	3,872
62. Columbia, SC	3,843
63. Tallahassee, FL	3,770
64. Albuquerque, NM	3,768
64. Montreal, PQ	3,768
66. Milwaukee–Waukesha, WI	3,737
67. San Antonio, TX	3,734
68. El Paso, TX	3,636
69. Calgary, AB	3,606
70. Augusta–Aiken, GA–SC	3,566
71. San Francisco, CA	3,531
72. Fayetteville–Springdale–Rogers, AR	3,512
73. Greenville, NC	3,477
74. Bakersfield, CA	3,475
75. Huntsville, AL	3,474
76. Boston, MA	3,456
77. Fresno, CA	3,454
78. Monmouth–Ocean, NJ	3,440
79. Madison, WI	3,425
80. Portland, ME	3,422
81. Laredo, TX	3,412
82. Albany–Schenectady–Troy, NY	3,409
83. Hickory–Morgantown, NC	3,392
84. McAllen–Edinburg–Mission, TX	3,390
85. St. Cloud, MN	3,366
86. Lakeland–Winter Haven, FL	3,364
87. Lexington, KY	3,355
87. Ottawa–Hull, ON–PQ	3,355
89. Kansas City, MO–KS	3,352
90. Vancouver, WA	3,341
91. Jacksonville, FL	3,275
92. Santa Cruz–Watsonville, CA	3,216
93. Myrtle Beach, SC	3,199
94. Worcester–Fitchburg–Leominster, MA	3,189
95. Kitchener, ON	3,158
96. Norfolk–Virginia Beach–Newport News, VA–NC	3,154
97. Boise City, ID	3,151
98. Ocala, FL	3,137
99. Ann Arbor, MI	3,080
100. Lancaster, PA	3,077
101. Harrisburg–Lebanon–Carlisle, PA	3,069
102. Manchester–Nashua, NH	3,054

Places Rated Rank	Places Rated Score
103. Buffalo–Niagara Falls, NY	3,049
104. Knoxville, TN	3,034
105. Syracuse, NY	3,025
106. Melbourne–Titusville–Palm Bay, FL	2,987
107. Northern New Jersey, NJ	2,983
108. Elkhart–Goshen, IN	2,975
109. Pittsburgh, PA	2,943
110. Louisville, KY–IN	2,915
111. Allentown–Bethlehem–Easton, PA–NJ	2,904
112. San Luis Obispo–Atascadero–Paso Robles, CA	2,899
113. Lansing–East Lansing, MI	2,824
114. Santa Barbara–Santa Maria–Lompoc, CA	2,809
115. Reno, NV	2,804
116. Fort Smith, AR–OK	2,792
117. Chattanooga, TN–GA	2,789
117. Fort Collins–Loveland, CO	2,789
119. Salem, OR	2,787
120. Oshawa, ON	2,784
121. Dayton–Springfield, OH	2,783
122. Bryan–College Station, TX	2,777
123. Wichita, KS	2,767
124. Stockton–Lodi, CA	2,752
125. Anchorage, AK	2,749
126. Akron, OH	2,745
127. Colorado Springs, CO	2,742
127. Gainesville, FL	2,742
129. Edmonton, AB	2,737
130. Springfield, MO	2,719
131. Vallejo–Fairfield–Napa, CA	2,700
132. Provo–Orem, UT	2,697
133. Kalamazoo–Battle Creek, MI	2,683
134. Gary, IN	2,680
135. Dothan, AL	2,668
136. Punta Gorda, FL	2,666
137. London, ON	2,660
138. Burlington, VT	2,658
139. Victoria, BC	2,657
140. Rocky Mount, NC	2,652
141. York, PA	2,647
142. Boulder–Longmont, CO	2,644
143. Johnson City–Kingsport–Bristol, TN–VA	2,625
144. Little Rock–North Little Rock, AR	2,622
145. Rockford, IL	2,621
146. Wilmington, NC	2,620
147. Jackson, MS	2,601
148. Charleston–North Charleston, SC	2,581
149. Hartford, CT	2,570
150. Hagerstown, MD	2,563
151. Chico–Paradise, CA	2,555
152. Toledo, OH	2,527
153. Richland–Kennewick–Pasco, WA	2,525
153. Yolo, CA	2,525
155. Santa Fe, NM	2,518

Places Rated Rank	Places Rated Score	Places Rated Rank	Places Rated Score	Places Rated Rank	Places Rated Score
156. Salinas, CA	2,513	215. South Bend, IN	2,248	270. Pueblo, CO	2,082
157. Tulsa, OK	2,509			272. Goldsboro, NC	2,080
158. Eugene–Springfield, OR	2,491	216. Sheboygan, WI	2,246	273. Williamsport, PA	2,079
159. Appleton–Oshkosh–Neenah, WI	2,488	217. Lewiston–Auburn, ME	2,240	274. Lubbock, TX	2,077
		218. Greeley, CO	2,239	275. Muncie, IN	2,075
160. New Bedford–Fall River–Attleboro, MA	2,478	219. Athens, GA	2,231		
		220. Glens Falls, NY	2,230	275. New London–Norwich, CT–RI	2,075
161. Green Bay, WI	2,476			277. Mansfield, OH	2,074
162. Olympia, WA	2,475	221. Florence, SC	2,227	278. Decatur, IL	2,073
163. Springfield, MA	2,468	221. Rochester, MN	2,227	278. Windsor, ON	2,073
164. Brazoria, TX	2,463	223. Halifax, NS	2,220	280. St. Joseph, MO	2,070
164. Fort Walton Beach, FL	2,463	224. Honolulu, HI	2,219		
		225. Binghamton, NY	2,210	281. Kankakee, IL	2,065
166. Lincoln, NE	2,457			282. Sherbrooke, PQ	2,063
167. Barnstable–Yarmouth, MA	2,448	226. Reading, PA	2,208	283. Bismarck, ND	2,062
168. Redding, CA	2,447	226. State College, PA	2,208	284. Vineland–Millville–Bridgeton, NJ	2,059
169. Bloomington, IN	2,443	228. Tacoma, WA	2,207	284. Waterbury, CT	2,059
170. Tuscaloosa, AL	2,442	229. Evansville–Henderson, IN–KY	2,205		
		230. Savannah, GA	2,204	286. Wheeling, WV–OH	2,057
171. Cedar Rapids, IA	2,437			287. Fargo–Moorhead, ND–MN	2,056
172. Bangor, ME	2,434	231. Youngstown–Warren, OH	2,202	288. St. John's, NF	2,053
173. Asheville, NC	2,430	232. Iowa City, IA	2,201	288. Utica–Rome, NY	2,053
174. Birmingham, AL	2,429	233. Columbia, MO	2,200	290. Lake Charles, LA	2,052
175. Hamilton, ON	2,428	234. Lawrence, KS	2,199		
		234. Montgomery, AL	2,199	291. Sudbury, ON	2,051
176. Las Cruces, NM	2,413			292. Yuba City, CA	2,048
177. Bridgeport, CT	2,411	236. Roanoke, VA	2,198	293. Dover, DE	2,043
178. Mobile, AL	2,400	237. Dutchess County, NY	2,197	293. Kokomo, IN	2,043
179. Eau Claire, WI	2,399	238. Bremerton, WA	2,195	293. Saskatoon, SK	2,043
180. Wausau, WI	2,395	239. Topeka, KS	2,188		
		240. Saginaw–Bay City–Midland, MI	2,185	296. Sumter, SC	2,041
181. Champaign–Urbana, IL	2,388			296. Trois-Rivieres, PQ	2,041
182. Hamilton–Middletown, OH	2,386	241. Galveston–Texas City, TX	2,184	298. Gadsden, AL	2,034
183. Lynchburg, VA	2,374	242. Yakima, WA	2,181	298. Monroe, LA	2,034
184. Scranton–Wilkes-Barre–Hazelton, PA	2,369	243. Winnipeg, MB	2,178	300. Anniston, AL	2,032
185. Danbury, CT	2,361	244. Erie, PA	2,177		
		245. Lima, OH	2,160	301. Regina, SK	2,031
186. Stamford–Norwalk, CT	2,356			301. Texarkana, TX–Texarkana, AR	2,031
187. La Crosse, WI–MN	2,353	246. Janesville–Beloit, WI	2,158	303. Saint John, NB	2,030
188. Florence, AL	2,345	247. Brownsville–Harlingen–San Benito, TX	2,157	304. Terre Haute, IN	2,028
189. Benton Harbor, MI	2,339	247. Davenport–Moline–Rock Island, IA–IL	2,157	305. Jackson, MI	2,025
190. Panama City, FL	2,338	247. Springfield, IL	2,157		
		250. Bloomington–Normal, IL	2,154	306. Charleston, WV	2,023
190. Visalia–Tulare–Porterville, CA	2,338			307. Fayetteville, NC	2,022
192. Canton–Massillon, OH	2,334	251. Macon, GA	2,151	308. Danville, VA	2,020
193. Charlottesville, VA	2,333	252. Parkersburg–Marietta, WV–OH	2,146	309. Thunder Bay, ON	2,019
193. Quebec City, PQ	2,333	253. Spokane, WA	2,144	310. Cumberland, MD–WV	2,018
195. Medford–Ashland, OR	2,330	253. Sioux City, IA–NE	2,144		
		255. Longview–Marshall, TX	2,139	310. Duluth–Superior, MN–WI	2,018
196. Trenton, NJ	2,321			310. San Angelo, TX	2,018
197. Lafayette, IN	2,319	256. St. Catharines–Niagara, ON	2,138	310. Sharon, PA	2,018
198. Lafayette, LA	2,315	257. Dubuque, IA	2,137	314. Chicoutimi–Jonquiere, PQ	2,016
199. Bellingham, WA	2,313	258. Decatur, AL	2,130	314. Jamestown, NY	2,016
200. Des Moines, IA	2,312	259. Wichita Falls, TX	2,124		
		260. Johnstown, PA	2,121	314. Pine Bluff, AR	2,016
201. Orange County, NY	2,310			314. Waterloo–Cedar Falls, IA	2,016
202. Cleveland–Lorain–Elyria, OH	2,306			318. Rapid City, SD	2,012
203. Yuma, AZ	2,304	261. Huntington–Ashland, WV–KY–OH	2,120	319. Albany, GA	2,010
204. New Haven–Meriden, CT	2,302	262. Omaha, NE–IA	2,109	319. Killeen–Temple, TX	2,010
205. Pensacola, FL	2,298	263. Clarksville–Hopkinsville, TN–KY	2,100		
		263. Victoria, TX	2,100	321. Shreveport–Bossier City, LA	2,008
206. Corpus Christi, TX	2,287	265. Pittsfield, MA	2,093	322. Columbus, GA–AL	2,006
207. Oklahoma City, OK	2,280			323. Newark–Jersey City, NJ	2,005
208. Tyler, TX	2,279	265. Racine, WI	2,093	324. Casper, WY	2,004
209. Joplin, MO	2,278	267. Biloxi–Gulfport–Pascagoula, MS	2,088	325. Billings, MT	2,003
210. Merced, CA	2,272	267. Elmira, NY	2,088		
		269. Peoria–Pekin, IL	2,084	325. New Orleans, LA	2,003
211. Sioux Falls, SD	2,270	270. Owensboro, KY	2,082	327. Alexandria, LA	2,002
212. Sherman–Denison, TX	2,262			327. Waco, TX	2,002
213. Baton Rouge, LA	2,260			329. Altoona, PA	2,001
214. Odessa–Midland, TX	2,253			330. Abilene, TX	2,000

Places Rated Rank	Places Rated Score	Places Rated Rank	Places Rated Score	Places Rated Rank	Places Rated Score
330. Amarillo, TX	2,000	330. Steubenville–Weirton, OH–WV	2,000	340. Flint, MI	1,991
330. Cheyenne, WY	2,000	337. Jacksonville, NC	1,997	341. Great Falls, MT	1,984
330. Enid, OK	2,000	337. Lawton, OK	1,997	342. Houma, LA	1,981
330. Grand Forks, ND–MN	2,000	339. Beaumont–Port Arthur, TX	1,993	343. New York, NY	1,623
330. Kenosha, WI	2,000				

Place Profiles: Jobs

The following charts show forecasted job growth rates in each metro area, plus the number of new jobs created in predominantly blue-collar and in predominantly white-collar industries.

Included in the charts, under Cyclical Threat, is an arrow symbol indicating the metro area's vulnerability to recession based on too many blue-collar and military jobs. An arrow pointing downward indicates the cyclical unemployment threat is low; an upward-pointing arrow indicates it's high; a dash indicates an average unemployment threat.

Growth forecasts for U.S. metro areas are from July 1, 1993, to July 1, 1998; those for Canadian metro areas are from December 31, 1992, to December 31, 1997. Blue-collar industries include farming, forestry, fishing, mining, construction, manufacturing, and transportation and public utilities. White-collar industries include

trade, finance, insurance, real estate, services, and government other than military.

Military jobs are counted in determining growth rates, but are not counted in either blue- or white-collar job creation. Consequently, the growth rates for a small number of metro areas are negative while their figures for new jobs are positive, reflecting a net loss due to a forecasted drop in military employment over the period.

U.S. figures are derived from current employment forecasts from Woods & Poole Economics, Inc., of Washington, DC, and are used here with permission. Canadian forecasts are derived by Places Rated Partnership from *Labour Force Annual Averages, 1989–1993*.

A check mark (✓) in front of a metro area's name highlights it as one of the top 35 places for job growth between now and 1998.

	Growth	New Blue	New White	Cyclical Threat	Places Rated Score	Places Rated Rank
Abilene, TX	−0.38%	198	−295	▲	2,000	330
Akron, OH	4.67	3,797	12,149	▲	2,745	126
Albany, GA	1.16	−32	874	—	2,010	319
Albany–Schenectady–Troy, NY	5.31	2,461	24,081	▼	3,409	82
Albuquerque, NM	7.27	6,356	17,963	▼	3,768	64
Alexandria, LA	0.45	335	151	—	2,002	327
Allentown–Bethlehem–Easton, PA–NJ	5.03	913	17,051	▲	2,904	111
Altoona, PA	0.43	−311	616	▲	2,001	329
Amarillo, TX	−0.05	350	−359	—	2,000	330
Anchorage, AK	6.82	3,578	7,398	—	2,749	125
Ann Arbor, MI	6.15	4,834	12,719	—	3,080	99
Anniston, AL	1.78	661	1,112	▲	2,032	300
Appleton–Oshkosh–Neenah, WI	5.15	4,678	4,789	▲	2,488	159
Asheville, NC	6.14	1,896	5,102	▲	2,430	173
Athens, GA	5.70	955	3,093	—	2,231	219
✓ Atlanta, GA	8.78	44,060	124,240	—	16,777	4
Atlantic City–Cape May, NJ	9.39	2,573	18,101	▼	3,941	59
Augusta–Aiken, GA–SC	8.06	6,225	13,209	▲	3,566	70
Austin–San Marcos, TX	8.15	10,301	32,001	▼	5,448	39
Bakersfield, CA	7.56	7,458	12,050	▲	3,475	74
Baltimore, MD	5.08	9,975	63,755	▼	5,745	36
Bangor, ME	7.02	1,424	4,752	—	2,434	172
Barnstable–Yarmouth, MA	6.42	1,834	5,150	▼	2,448	167
Baton Rouge, LA	3.13	1,879	6,428	▼	2,260	213
Beaumont–Port Arthur, TX	−0.63	−2,299	1,240	▲	1,993	339
Bellingham, WA	6.60	963	3,784	▲	2,313	199
Benton Harbor, MI	6.43	1,080	4,188	▲	2,339	189
Billings, MT	0.60	−219	666	▼	2,003	325

	Growth	New Blue	New White	Cyclical Threat	Places Rated Score	Places Rated Rank
Biloxi–Gulfport–Pascagoula, MS	1.98	1,947	2,510	▲	2,088	267
Binghamton, NY	3.94	1,077	4,252	▲	2,210	225
Birmingham, AL	3.01	5,086	9,151	—	2,429	174
Bismarck, ND	3.47	316	1,477	▼	2,062	283
Bloomington, IN	8.21	1,660	3,733	▼	2,443	169
Bloomington–Normal, IL	4.32	1,012	2,552	▼	2,154	250
Boise City, ID	7.91	5,504	9,050	—	3,151	97
Boston, MA	2.41	–345	60,748	▼	3,456	76
Boulder–Longmont, CO	6.18	3,263	7,154	—	2,644	142
Brazoria, TX	7.48	2,187	3,998	▲	2,463	164
Bremerton, WA	4.55	645	3,642	▼	2,195	238
Bridgeport, CT	3.69	–2,134	13,282	▲	2,411	177
Brownsville–Harlingen–San Benito, TX	3.93	293	3,706	▼	2,157	247
Bryan–College Station, TX	10.80	627	6,569	▼	2,777	122
Buffalo–Niagara Falls, NY	4.07	410	25,358	—	3,049	103
Burlington, VT	8.22	2,215	5,788	—	2,658	138
Calgary, AB	6.66	5,050	19,066	—	3,606	69
Canton–Massillon, OH	4.09	2,030	6,129	▲	2,334	192
Casper, WY	1.02	–206	583	—	2,004	324
Cedar Rapids, IA	6.20	2,414	4,633	▲	2,437	171
Central New Jersey, NJ	6.91	3,087	41,765	▲	5,099	41
Champaign–Urbana, IL	5.60	1,674	5,257	▼	2,388	181
Charleston, WV	1.30	–683	2,477	▼	2,023	306
Charleston–North Charleston, SC	4.20	3,395	10,440	▲	2,581	148
✓ Charlotte–Gastonia–Rock Hill, NC–SC	9.44	21,751	50,847	▲	8,853	15
Charlottesville, VA	6.01	933	4,611	▼	2,333	193
Chattanooga, TN–GA	5.78	4,452	9,205	▲	2,789	117
Cheyenne, WY	0.33	–326	473	—	2,000	330
Chicago, IL	2.35	9,925	85,399	—	4,240	50
Chico–Paradise, CA	8.18	1,979	4,800	▼	2,555	151
Chicoutimi–Jonquiere, PQ	1.69	733	197	—	2,016	314
✓ Cincinnati, OH–KY–IN	6.53	14,614	45,553	—	5,929	34
Clarksville–Hopkinsville, TN–KY	3.02	1,046	2,275	▲	2,100	263
Cleveland–Lorain–Elyria, OH	1.56	4,515	15,114	—	2,306	202
Colorado Springs, CO	5.40	4,447	9,287	▲	2,742	127
Columbia, MO	4.96	721	3,319	▼	2,200	233
Columbia, SC	7.36	5,421	19,621	—	3,843	62
Columbus, GA–AL	0.28	370	1,617	▲	2,006	322
✓ Columbus, OH	7.76	8,416	59,098	▼	7,239	19
Corpus Christi, TX	3.95	395	6,873	—	2,287	206
Cumberland, MD–WV	1.95	–250	1,149	▲	2,018	310
✓ Dallas, TX	6.31	28,444	81,919	—	8,964	14
Danbury, CT	3.95	919	8,230	—	2,361	185
Danville, VA	1.93	411	642	▲	2,020	308
Davenport–Moline–Rock Island, IA–IL	2.80	–276	5,895	—	2,157	247
Dayton–Springfield, OH	3.78	4,491	16,232	▲	2,783	121
Daytona Beach, FL	10.63	4,663	14,721	▼	4,061	53
Decatur, AL	4.52	886	1,980	▲	2,130	258
Decatur, IL	3.31	695	1,525	▲	2,073	278
Denver, CO	4.43	11,327	40,919	▼	4,314	47
Des Moines, IA	3.31	1,740	7,676	▼	2,312	200
Detroit, MI	4.11	24,556	62,045	—	5,559	37
Dothan, AL	9.61	2,061	4,889	▲	2,668	135
Dover, DE	2.46	430	1,306	▲	2,043	293
Dubuque, IA	4.94	410	2,368	▲	2,137	257
Duluth–Superior, MN–WI	1.13	752	808	▼	2,018	310
Dutchess County, NY	3.76	604	4,641	▲	2,197	237
Eau Claire, WI	7.32	1,701	3,744	▲	2,399	179
Edmonton, AB	4.47	5,448	11,048	—	2,737	129
El Paso, TX	7.71	6,411	14,806	▲	3,636	68
Elkhart–Goshen, IN	9.33	6,439	4,012	▲	2,975	108
Elmira, NY	4.35	451	1,567	—	2,088	267
Enid, OK	–0.52	–252	214	▲	2,000	330
Erie, PA	3.48	856	4,239	▲	2,177	244
Eugene–Springfield, OR	5.62	2,352	6,391	—	2,491	158
Evansville–Henderson, IN–KY	3.56	1,321	4,449	▲	2,205	229
Fargo–Moorhead, ND–MN	2.39	701	1,648	▼	2,056	287
Fayetteville, NC	0.63	1,883	1,684	▲	2,022	307
Fayetteville–Springdale–Rogers, AR	10.83	6,604	7,355	▲	3,512	72
Flint, MI	–0.68	–2,152	883	▲	1,991	340
Florence, AL	7.43	1,777	2,870	▲	2,345	188
Florence, SC	5.73	279	3,678	▲	2,227	221

	Growth	New Blue	New White	Cyclical Threat	Places Rated Score	Places Rated Rank
Fort Collins–Loveland, CO	8.41	3,190	6,189	—	2,789	117
✓ Fort Lauderdale, FL	8.59	8,728	48,673	▼	6,931	20
✓ Fort Myers–Cape Coral, FL	15.17	6,360	23,020	▼	6,457	26
Fort Pierce–Port St. Lucie, FL	12.89	4,357	10,852	—	3,960	56
Fort Smith, AR–OK	8.91	3,874	5,010	▲	2,792	116
Fort Walton Beach, FL	7.56	1,716	4,408	▲	2,463	164
Fort Wayne, IN	8.60	8,966	14,793	▲	4,043	54
✓ Fort Worth–Arlington, TX	8.91	20,231	42,768	▲	7,613	18
Fresno, CA	6.16	9,045	14,555	▲	3,454	77
Gadsden, AL	2.89	369	815	▲	2,034	298
Gainesville, FL	7.98	1,112	8,186	▼	2,742	127
Galveston–Texas City, TX	4.41	590	3,587	—	2,184	241
Gary, IN	4.96	613	13,098	▲	2,680	134
Glens Falls, NY	6.15	1,257	2,480	▲	2,230	220
Goldsboro, NC	3.58	548	1,675	▲	2,080	272
Grand Forks, ND–MN	−0.10	−95	328	—	2,000	330
✓ Grand Rapids–Muskegon–Holland, MI	8.60	15,943	30,241	▲	5,972	33
Great Falls, MT	−2.14	−111	−646	—	1,984	341
Greeley, CO	5.83	2,176	1,924	▲	2,239	218
Green Bay, WI	6.27	3,072	4,518	▲	2,476	161
✓ Greensboro–Winston-Salem–High Point, NC	8.26	15,304	40,649	▲	6,622	24
Greenville, NC	15.26	2,040	7,638	—	3,477	73
✓ Greenville–Spartanburg–Anderson, SC	8.93	12,809	31,970	▲	5,999	31
Hagerstown, MD	9.15	912	5,243	▲	2,563	150
Halifax, NS	3.83	1,658	4,091	—	2,220	223
Hamilton, ON	3.84	4,696	6,447	—	2,428	175
Hamilton–Middletown, OH	5.79	902	5,769	▲	2,386	182
Harrisburg–Lebanon–Carlisle, PA	5.33	4,834	15,229	—	3,069	101
Hartford, CT	2.73	4,252	16,619	—	2,570	149
Hickory–Morgantown, NC	8.60	7,842	8,341	▲	3,392	83
Honolulu, HI	1.89	4,756	6,833	—	2,219	224
Houma, LA	−1.59	−412	−764	▲	1,981	342
✓ Houston, TX	4.86	16,034	79,511	—	6,643	23
Huntington–Ashland, WV–KY–OH	3.05	694	3,229	▲	2,120	261
Huntsville, AL	8.79	7,145	9,623	▲	3,474	75
✓ Indianapolis, IN	6.95	15,488	44,404	—	6,162	30
Iowa City, IA	5.55	754	2,864	▼	2,201	232
Jackson, MI	2.01	479	764	▲	2,025	305
Jackson, MS	5.08	4,666	7,163	▼	2,601	147
Jacksonville, FL	4.79	6,938	19,677	—	3,275	91
Jacksonville, NC	−0.44	302	355	▲	1,997	337
Jamestown, NY	1.48	260	791	▲	2,016	314
Janesville–Beloit, WI	4.85	372	2,889	▲	2,158	246
Johnson City–Kingsport–Bristol, TN–VA	5.20	3,744	8,270	▲	2,625	143
Johnstown, PA	3.40	866	2,697	▲	2,121	260
Joplin, MO	5.81	2,311	2,482	▲	2,278	209
Kalamazoo–Battle Creek, MI	5.50	3,684	8,734	▲	2,683	133
Kankakee, IL	3.74	274	1,459	—	2,065	281
Kansas City, MO–KS	3.65	9,707	27,346	—	3,352	89
Kenosha, WI	0.30	−859	1,006	▲	2,000	330
Killeen–Temple, TX	0.49	315	1,725	▲	2,010	319
Kitchener, ON	7.89	3,408	11,272	—	3,158	95
Knoxville, TN	5.74	1,946	16,071	—	3,034	104
Kokomo, IN	2.88	134	1,354	▲	2,043	293
La Crosse, WI–MN	7.10	1,056	3,912	—	2,353	187
Lafayette, IN	6.00	1,751	3,572	—	2,319	197
Lafayette, LA	4.28	2,229	5,136	▲	2,315	198
Lake Charles, LA	2.49	809	1,288	▲	2,052	290
Lake County, IL	9.66	8,436	21,793	▲	4,920	42
Lakeland–Winter Haven, FL	8.14	4,041	12,719	▲	3,364	86
Lancaster, PA	6.72	5,756	10,270	▲	3,077	100
Lansing–East Lansing, MI	5.86	916	13,140	▼	2,824	113
Laredo, TX	16.15	1,974	6,771	—	3,412	81
Las Cruces, NM	8.49	1,343	3,527	▼	2,413	176
✓ Las Vegas, NV–AZ	12.22	14,342	49,989	▼	9,861	12
Lawrence, KS	6.50	785	2,274	▼	2,199	234
Lawton, OK	−2.67	324	−219	▲	1,997	337
Lewiston–Auburn, ME	6.59	315	3,323	▲	2,240	217
Lexington, KY	7.18	7,008	11,862	▲	3,355	87
Lima, OH	4.27	1,344	2,402	▼	2,160	245
Lincoln, NE	5.46	2,465	5,901	▼	2,457	166
Little Rock–North Little Rock, AR	4.40	3,174	10,970	—	2,622	144

	Growth	New Blue	New White	Cyclical Threat	Places Rated Score	Places Rated Rank
London, ON	6.34	2,243	8,162	—	2,660	137
Long Island, NY	3.88	6,135	47,856	▼	4,095	52
Longview–Marshall, TX	3.82	1,480	2,162	▲	2,139	255
Los Angeles–Long Beach, CA	2.55	338	138,770	—	5,547	38
Louisville, KY–IN	3.98	2,974	20,000	—	2,915	110
Lubbock, TX	2.39	134	3,106	▼	2,077	274
Lynchburg, VA	5.79	1,461	4,996	▲	2,374	183
Macon, GA	2.98	1,782	3,271	—	2,151	251
Madison, WI	7.29	4,945	14,607	▼	3,425	79
Manchester–Nashua, NH	6.88	1,184	14,140	▲	3,054	102
Mansfield, OH	2.88	702	1,858	▲	2,074	277
McAllen–Edinburg–Mission, TX	10.02	3,386	10,488	—	3,390	84
Medford–Ashland, OR	6.70	1,772	3,147	—	2,330	195
Melbourne–Titusville–Palm Bay, FL	6.90	4,102	10,207	—	2,987	106
Memphis, TN–AR–MS	5.85	14,861	21,920	—	4,152	51
Merced, CA	5.96	2,200	2,364	▲	2,272	210
Miami, FL	4.55	6,483	43,867	▼	4,291	49
Milwaukee–Waukesha, WI	4.49	7,366	31,331	—	3,737	66
✓ Minneapolis–St. Paul, MN–WI	5.30	25,056	54,989	—	6,242	29
Mobile, AL	4.15	2,195	7,450	—	2,400	178
Modesto, CA	10.90	7,285	10,605	▲	3,950	58
Monmouth–Ocean, NJ	5.64	3,275	22,264	▼	3,440	78
Monroe, LA	2.17	461	1,107	▼	2,034	298
Montgomery, AL	3.44	2,101	3,677	—	2,199	234
Montreal, PQ	3.58	21,652	27,722	—	3,768	64
Muncie, IN	3.51	345	1,805	—	2,075	275
Myrtle Beach, SC	11.29	869	9,755	▼	3,199	93
Naples, FL	13.82	3,999	10,190	—	3,961	55
Nashville, TN	7.05	12,820	33,124	—	5,239	40
New Bedford–Fall River–Attleboro, MA	4.49	214	10,436	▲	2,478	160
New Haven–Meriden, CT	3.95	623	7,019	—	2,302	204
New London–Norwich, CT–RI	2.01	941	2,809	▲	2,075	275
New Orleans, LA	0.19	−933	2,399	▼	2,003	325
New York, NY	−0.91	−39,046	−2,380	▼	1,623	343
Newark–Jersey City, NJ	0.18	−13,159	16,094	—	2,005	323
Norfolk–Virginia Beach–Newport News, VA–NC	3.57	9,874	22,446	▲	3,154	96
Northern New Jersey, NJ	3.46	−356	28,770	—	2,983	107
✓ Oakland, CA	6.22	19,433	52,127	—	6,451	27
Ocala, FL	11.51	3,305	6,570	—	3,137	98
Odessa–Midland, TX	4.54	760	4,820	▲	2,253	214
Oklahoma City, OK	2.26	2,578	9,827	▼	2,280	207
Olympia, WA	7.44	1,201	5,187	▼	2,475	162
Omaha, NE–IA	1.50	1,519	5,726	▼	2,109	262
✓ Orange County, CA	11.82	35,503	142,395	—	23,028	1
Orange County, NY	4.72	878	5,691	—	2,310	201
✓ Orlando, FL	15.27	21,815	97,521	—	20,223	2
Oshawa, ON	8.68	1,989	7,041	—	2,784	120
Ottawa–Hull, ON–PQ	5.55	4,358	20,057	—	3,355	87
Owensboro, KY	4.23	296	1,631	▲	2,082	270
Panama City, FL	6.83	584	4,364	▼	2,338	190
Parkersburg–Marietta, WV–OH	4.34	646	2,713	▲	2,146	252
Pensacola, FL	4.02	1,206	6,204	—	2,298	205
Peoria–Pekin, IL	2.14	456	3,451	▲	2,084	269
✓ Philadelphia, PA–NJ	4.19	15,774	101,041	—	6,895	21
✓ Phoenix–Mesa, AZ	11.51	33,298	115,405	▼	19,116	3
Pine Bluff, AR	1.99	446	368	▲	2,016	314
Pittsburgh, PA	2.75	−1,763	36,053	▼	2,943	109
Pittsfield, MA	3.39	828	1,901	—	2,093	265
Portland, ME	8.62	2,872	13,625	▼	3,422	80
✓ Portland, OR	7.12	18,439	42,248	—	6,321	28
Portsmouth–Dover–Rochester, NH	11.78	4,625	18,785	—	4,758	43
Providence–Warwick–Cranston, RI	6.84	6,013	28,004	—	4,327	46
Provo–Orem, UT	7.54	1,169	8,076	▼	2,697	132
Pueblo, CO	3.74	521	1,660	▼	2,082	270
Punta Gorda, FL	12.70	1,450	3,793	▼	2,666	136
Quebec City, PQ	3.41	3,322	6,445	—	2,333	193
Racine, WI	3.31	1,105	1,708	▲	2,093	265
✓ Raleigh–Durham–Chapel Hill, NC	11.92	16,337	52,338	—	10,186	11
Rapid City, SD	1.32	506	378	▲	2,012	318
Reading, PA	3.33	1,662	4,572	▲	2,208	226
Redding, CA	7.99	1,872	3,717	—	2,447	168
Regina, SK	1.87	1,032	609	—	2,031	201

	Growth	New Blue	New White	Cyclical Threat	Places Rated Score	Places Rated Rank
Reno, NV	6.72	2,037	9,928	▼	2,804	115
Richland–Kennewick–Pasco, WA	7.95	3,412	3,197	▲	2,525	153
Richmond–Petersburg, VA	5.51	10,251	23,721	—	3,872	61
✓ Riverside–San Bernardino, CA	10.95	35,734	74,961	—	14,121	8
Roanoke, VA	3.46	1,097	4,619	—	2,198	236
Rochester, MN	5.14	1,222	3,191	—	2,227	221
Rochester, NY	6.19	9,175	27,983	▲	4,300	48
Rockford, IL	5.85	3,055	7,553	▲	2,621	145
Rocky Mount, NC	9.04	3,695	3,513	▲	2,652	140
✓ Sacramento, CA	8.83	18,066	47,761	▼	7,813	17
Saginaw–Bay City–Midland, MI	3.07	1,210	4,828	▲	2,185	240
St. Catharines–Niagara, ON	3.11	2,285	2,162	—	2,138	256
St. Cloud, MN	11.88	2,992	8,506	▲	3,366	85
Saint John, NB	2.34	931	355	—	2,030	303
St. John's, NF	2.78	660	1,261	—	2,053	288
St. Joseph, MO	3.52	1,295	687	▲	2,070	280
St. Louis, MO–IL	4.01	15,638	44,270	—	4,402	45
Salem, OR	7.25	3,707	7,149	—	2,787	119
Salinas, CA	4.69	6,687	4,242	▲	2,513	156
Salt Lake City–Ogden, UT	5.66	7,018	27,476	▼	3,952	57
San Angelo, TX	1.83	171	789	▲	2,018	310
San Antonio, TX	4.99	4,225	30,516	▼	3,734	67
✓ San Diego, CA	9.47	40,786	94,077	▲	14,772	7
San Francisco, CA	3.46	1,800	42,456	▼	3,531	71
✓ San Jose, CA	6.28	25,567	35,656	▲	5,845	35
San Luis Obispo–Atascadero–Paso Robles, CA	9.15	2,758	7,063	—	2,899	112
Santa Barbara–Santa Maria–Lompoc, CA	6.10	3,340	9,922	—	2,809	114
Santa Cruz–Watsonville, CA	9.82	3,539	8,842	—	3,216	92
Santa Fe, NM	8.08	1,143	5,268	▼	2,518	155
Santa Rosa, CA	10.84	9,004	14,360	—	4,533	44
✓ Sarasota–Bradenton, FL	12.99	7,709	28,225	▼	6,668	22
Saskatoon, SK	2.26	873	1,030	—	2,043	293
Savannah, GA	3.49	2,601	3,250	▲	2,204	230
Scranton–Wilkes-Barre–Hazelton, PA	3.38	2,230	8,686	▲	2,369	184
✓ Seattle–Bellevue–Everett, WA	6.61	32,791	57,522	▲	7,970	16
Sharon, PA	1.81	−310	1,321	▲	2,018	310
Sheboygan, WI	6.39	2,161	1,694	▲	2,246	216
Sherbrooke, PQ	3.39	651	1,214	—	2,063	282
Sherman–Denison, TX	7.36	736	2,823	▲	2,262	212
Shreveport–Bossier City, LA	0.60	−42	1,387	▲	2,008	321
Sioux City, IA–NE	4.36	1,551	1,744	▲	2,144	253
Sioux Falls, SD	5.20	1,123	4,066	—	2,270	211
South Bend, IN	4.27	546	5,268	—	2,248	215
Spokane, WA	2.65	2,242	3,191	—	2,144	253
Springfield, IL	3.48	−188	4,692	▼	2,157	247
Springfield, MA	3.82	2,414	9,827	—	2,468	163
Springfield, MO	6.38	2,761	8,516	—	2,719	130
Stamford–Norwalk, CT	3.69	−316	9,962	—	2,356	186
State College, PA	5.33	1,237	2,668	▼	2,208	226
Steubenville–Weirton, OH–WV	0.01	−348	389	▲	2,000	330
Stockton–Lodi, CA	5.99	4,793	7,754	▲	2,752	124
Sudbury, ON	2.80	925	897	—	2,051	291
Sumter, SC	2.67	760	778	▲	2,041	296
Syracuse, NY	5.07	6,017	14,202	—	3,025	105
Tacoma, WA	2.39	1,254	7,395	—	2,207	228
Tallahassee, FL	10.65	2,210	14,408	▼	3,770	63
✓ Tampa–St. Petersburg–Clearwater, FL	10.56	21,722	101,950	▼	15,060	6
Terre Haute, IN	1.91	435	1,010	▲	2,028	304
Texarkana, TX–Texarkana, AR	2.30	96	1,264	—	2,031	301
Thunder Bay, ON	1.83	828	233	—	2,019	309
Toledo, OH	3.94	1,083	12,300	—	2,527	152
Topeka, KS	4.11	355	4,224	▼	2,188	239
✓ Toronto, ON	7.48	27,278	105,466	—	11,929	9
Trenton, NJ	3.79	1,100	7,371	▼	2,321	196
Trois-Rivieres, PQ	2.88	734	704	—	2,041	296
✓ Tucson, AZ	10.75	6,372	30,587	▼	5,973	32
Tulsa, OK	3.56	4,512	9,787	▲	2,509	157
Tuscaloosa, AL	7.64	2,405	3,384	▲	2,442	170
Tyler, TX	5.70	727	4,171	—	2,279	208
Utica–Rome, NY	1.79	187	2,748	—	2,053	288
Vallejo–Fairfield–Napa, CA	5.82	4,206	7,825	—	2,700	131
✓ Vancouver, BC	10.73	12,852	75,261	—	11,455	10

	Growth	New Blue	New White	Cyclical Threat	Places Rated Score	Places Rated Rank
Vancouver, WA	11.33	3,963	7,873	▲	3,341	90
✓ Ventura, CA	12.01	11,804	26,635	▲	6,617	25
Victoria, BC	7.25	1,366	7,695	—	2,657	139
Victoria, TX	5.12	9	1,947	—	2,100	263
Vineland–Millville–Bridgeton, NJ	2.88	481	1,555	▲	2,059	284
Visalia–Tulare–Porterville, CA	4.95	3,978	2,842	▲	2,338	190
Waco, TX	0.40	773	−367	—	2,002	327
✓ Washington, DC–MD–VA–WV	6.91	44,349	162,418	▼	16,288	5
Waterbury, CT	3.95	277	1,225	—	2,059	284
Waterloo–Cedar Falls, IA	1.43	−645	1,743	—	2,016	314
Wausau, WI	7.69	2,685	2,448	▲	2,395	180
✓ West Palm Beach–Boca Raton, FL	12.33	11,282	50,520	▼	9,620	13
Wheeling, WV–OH	2.77	−403	2,466	—	2,057	286
Wichita, KS	4.91	5,462	10,152	▲	2,767	123
Wichita Falls, TX	3.64	712	2,696	▲	2,124	259
Williamsport, PA	3.57	776	1,428	▲	2,079	273
Wilmington, NC	8.80	1,518	5,527	—	2,620	146
Wilmington–Newark, DE–MD	7.77	4,558	20,297	▲	3,931	60
Windsor, ON	2.51	2,185	707	—	2,073	278
Winnipeg, MB	2.45	4,108	3,176	—	2,178	243
Worcester–Fitchburg–Leominster, MA	5.89	2,910	17,282	▲	3,189	94
Yakima, WA	4.30	1,842	2,376	▲	2,181	242
Yolo, CA	8.02	2,325	4,215	—	2,525	153
York, PA	5.91	3,352	7,601	▲	2,647	141
Youngstown–Warren, OH	2.69	−1,776	9,302	▲	2,202	231
Yuba City, CA	2.78	822	922	▲	2,048	292
Yuma, AZ	7.64	1,921	2,059	▲	2,304	203

Et Cetera

LIFE IN A BOOM TOWN

If you could live anywhere you choose, would you choose a boom town? There are practically none in North America at this writing. But if there were, the advantages would include rising personal incomes ensuring real estate appreciation; expanding personal employment opportunities; improved infrastructures; somewhat lower violent crime; increasing amenities; and high-quality health care and education.

The disadvantages of living in a boom town include rising costs of living; increased property crime rates; environmental pollution; and, maybe worst of all, noticeable loss of personal discretionary time.

But if you stay in a no-growth area, you face possible job loss, depreciating value of real estate, boarded-up businesses, and backwater schools and health care. Any advantages? Try declining living costs, increased personal time, and lower crime rates.

Employment opportunities are the single most important factor behind geographic mobility. Joblessness or underemployment can push a settled person to become a mobile one. Consider, for example, that in 1980 you moved from withering Chicago or Detroit to booming Los Angeles. Now it's 1993 and you're thinking about your next move. Who would have guessed during the 1980 job boom that California would now be grabbing the ropes, or that the Great Lakes states would be making a comeback?

The past decade has seen some surprising shifts in regional economic growth. So the big question remains: Will a move to Anaheim or San Jose or Raleigh really solve your jobless or underemployment problem? If there is any trend to be spotted from the past, it is that boom times and slumps aren't permanent in any metro area.

LEGAL HOLIDAYS

Properly speaking, the United States has no national holidays. A day off on Independence Day, Thanksgiving, or Christmas comes by the grace of local state legislatures rather than presidential proclamations or acts of Congress from Washington.

The only thing "national" about the U.S. holiday calendar is the 10 days off given to everyone who works for the federal government: Christmas, Independence Day, Labor Day, New Year's Day, Thanksgiving, and five Mondays—Columbus Day, Memorial Day, Veterans Day, Washington's Birthday, and Martin Luther King

Day. The first four holiday Mondays were approved in 1968 to create predictable long weekends. The fifth, approved in 1986, honors Martin Luther King, Jr., on the third Monday of January.

Most states observe federal legal holidays, and, depending on where you are, they commemorate 72 local ones as well. The Civil War era produced more events and heroes to honor with days off than any other period in American history. However, they aren't all celebrated nationwide. Just as no former secessionist state takes notice of Lincoln's birthday, so none of the Union states honors Robert E. Lee's birthday. Memorial Day, a date originally created to mourn those who died for the Union cause, isn't observed in Alabama, Mississippi, or South Carolina. Those states, as well as Florida, Georgia, Kentucky, and Louisiana, celebrate Confederate Memorial Day instead.

In contrast, the Canadian provinces celebrate 10 national holidays in harmony with the terms of Canada's *Holidays Act*. Four days—Christmas, Labor Day, New Year's Day, and Remembrance Day (formerly Armistice Day, as was the U.S.'s Veterans Day)—may be said to be North American holidays since they are celebrated on the same date for the same reason throughout the United States. Again, depending on where you are in Canada, some 15 local holidays are observed as well.

A North American List of Days

JANUARY

Fixed Dates

January 1, *New Year's Day*: All states and Canadian provinces
January 8, *Battle of New Orleans Day*: Louisiana
January 15, *Martin Luther King Day*: United States, except New Hampshire
January 19, *Robert E. Lee's Birthday*: Arkansas, Florida, Kentucky, Louisiana, and South Carolina; *Confederate Heroes Day*: Texas
January 30, *Franklin D. Roosevelt's Birthday*: Kentucky

Movable Feasts

Third Monday, *Robert E. Lee's Birthday*: Alabama and Mississippi; *Lee–Jackson–King Day*: Virginia

FEBRUARY

Fixed Dates

February 12, *Lincoln's Birthday*: Alaska, California, Colorado, Connecticut, Florida, Illinois, Indiana, Iowa, Kansas, Kentucky, Maryland, Missouri, Montana, New Jersey, New Mexico, New York, Utah, Vermont, Washington, and West Virginia
February 15, *Susan B. Anthony's* Birthday: Florida and Minnesota
February 19, *Robert E. Lee Day*: Kentucky

Movable Feasts

First Monday, *Lincoln's Birthday*: Delaware and Oregon
Second Monday, *Lincoln Day*: Arizona
Third Monday, *Washington's Birthday*: All states; *Alberta Family Day*: Alberta
Tuesday before Ash Wednesday, *Mardi Gras*: Alabama, Florida (some counties), and Louisiana (some parishes)

MARCH

Fixed Dates

March 2, *Texas Independence Day*: Texas
March 17, *Evacuation Day*: Massachusetts (Suffolk County only)

Fastest-Growing Jobs to 2000
(numbers in thousands)

Occupation	Numerical Change
Salespersons, retail	887
Registered nurses	767
Cashiers	685
General office clerks	670
Nursing aides, orderlies, and attendants	552
Food counter, fountain, and related workers	550
Waiters and waitresses	449
Teachers, secondary school	437
Receptionists and information clerks	422
Systems analysts and computer scientists	366
Food preparation workers	365
Child-care workers	353
Gardeners and groundskeepers, except farm	348
Accountants and auditors	340
Computer programmers	317
Teachers, elementary	313
Guards	298
Teacher aides and educational assistants	278
Licensed practical nurses	269
Home health aides	263
Clerical supervisors and managers	263
Cooks, restaurant	257
Maintenance repairers, general utility	251

Source: U.S. Department of Labor, *Monthly Labor Review*, November 1991. Listed above are occupations expected to grow by a quarter-million or more by the year 2000.

Turn-of-the-Century Job Winners

Occupation	Percent Change
Home health aides	91.7%
Systems analysts and computer scientists	78.9
Computer programmers	56.1
Child-care workers	48.8
Receptionists and information clerks	46.9
Registered nurses	44.4
Nursing aides, orderlies, and attendants	43.4
Licensed practical nurses	41.9
Cooks, restaurant	41.8
Gardeners and groundskeepers, except farm	39.8
Lawyers	35.1
Accountants and auditors	34.5
Teacher aides and educational assistants	34.4
Teachers, secondary school	34.2
Food counter, fountain, and related workers	34.2
Guards	33.7
Cooks, short order and fast food	33.0
Food preparation workers	31.6
Cashiers	26.0
Truck drivers, light and heavy	26.1
Waiters and waitresses	25.7

Source: U.S. Department of Labor, *Monthly Labor Review*, November 1991. Listed above are jobs expected to grow at 25 percent or more by the year 2000.

March 20, *Youth Day*: Oklahoma
March 25, *Maryland Day*: Maryland
March 26, *Prince Jonah Kuhio Kalanianaole Day*: Hawaii

Movable Feasts

First Monday, *Casimir Pulaski's Birthday*: Illinois
First Tuesday, *Town Meeting Day*: Vermont
Second Monday, *Commonwealth Day*: Newfoundland
Nearest Monday to March 17, *St. Patrick's Day*: Newfoundland
Last Monday, *Seward's Day*: Alaska

APRIL

Fixed Dates

April 2, *Pascua Florida Day*: Florida
April 3, *Arbor Day*: Arizona
April 13, *Thomas Jefferson's Birthday*: Alabama and Oklahoma
April 21, *San Jacinto Day*: Texas
April 22, *Arbor Day*: Nebraska; *Oklahoma Day*: Oklahoma
April 26, *Confederate Memorial Day*: Florida and Georgia

Movable Feasts

Two days before Easter, *Good Friday*: Delaware, Florida, Hawaii, Indiana, Louisiana, Maryland, New Jersey, North Dakota, Pennsylvania, Tennessee, Wisconsin, and all Canadian provinces
One day after Easter, *Easter Monday*: North Carolina and all Canadian provinces
Third Monday, *Patriots' Day*: Maine and Massachusetts
Nearest Monday to April 23, *St. George's Day*: Newfoundland
Fourth Monday, *Fast Day*: New Hampshire
Last Monday, *Confederate Memorial Day*: Alabama and Mississippi

MAY

Fixed Dates

May 1, *Bird Day*: Oklahoma
May 4, *Rhode Island Independence Day*: Rhode Island
May 8, *Truman Day*: Missouri
May 10, *Confederate Memorial Day*: South Carolina
May 11, *Minnesota Day*: Minnesota
May 20, *Mecklenburg Independence Day*: North Carolina
May 25, *Memorial Day*: New Mexico, South Dakota, and Vermont
May 30, *Memorial Day*: Delaware, Illinois, Maryland, and New Hampshire

Movable Feasts

First Tuesday after first Monday, *Primary Election Day*: Indiana
First Monday before May 25, *Victoria Day and the Sovereign's Birthday*: All Canadian provinces
Last Monday, *Memorial Day*: All states except Alabama, Mississippi, and South Carolina, and those celebrating on May 25 or 30

JUNE

Fixed Dates

June 3, *Confederate Memorial Day*: Kentucky and Louisiana; *Jefferson Davis's Birthday*: Florida and South Carolina
June 9, *Senior Citizens Day*: Oklahoma
June 11, *King Kamehameha I Day*: Hawaii
June 14, *Flag Day*: Pennsylvania
June 15, *Separation Day*: Delaware
June 17, *Bunker Hill Day*: Massachusetts (Suffolk County only)
June 19, *Emancipation Day*: Texas
June 20, *West Virginia Day*: West Virginia
June 24, *Quebec Day*: Quebec

Movable Feasts

First Monday, *Jefferson Davis's Birthday*: Alabama and Mississippi
Nearest Monday to June 24, *Discovery Day*: Newfoundland

JULY

Fixed Dates

July 1, *Canada Day*: All Canadian provinces
July 4, *Independence Day*: All states
July 24, *Pioneer Day*: Utah

Movable Feasts

Nearest Monday to July 12, *Orangemen's Day*: Newfoundland

AUGUST

Fixed Dates

August 16, *Bennington Battle Day*: Vermont
August 27, *Lyndon Johnson's Birthday*: Texas
August 30, *Huey Long Day*: Louisiana

Movable Feasts

First Monday, *British Columbia Day*: British Columbia; *Civic Holiday*: Manitoba, Ontario, and Saskatchewan; *Colorado Day*: Colorado; *Heritage Day*: Alberta; *New Brunswick Day*: New Brunswick
Second Monday, *Victory Day*: Rhode Island
Third Friday, *Admission Day*: Hawaii

SEPTEMBER

Fixed Dates

September 9, *Admission Day*: California
September 12, *Defenders' Day*: Maryland
September 16, *Cherokee Strip Day*: Oklahoma

Movable Feasts

First Monday, *Labor Day*: All states and Canadian provinces
First Tuesday, *Primary Election Day*: Wisconsin
Second Tuesday, *Primary Election Day*: Wyoming
First Saturday after full moon, *Indian Day*: Oklahoma

OCTOBER

Fixed Dates

October 10, *Leif Erickson Day*: Minnesota; *Oklahoma Historical Day*: Oklahoma
October 12, *Columbus Day*: Maryland
October 18, *Alaska Day*: Alaska
October 31, *Nevada Day*: Nevada

Movable Feasts

Second Monday, *Columbus Day*: All states except Alaska, Iowa, Maryland, Michigan, Mississippi, Nevada, North Carolina, North Dakota, Oregon, South Carolina, and Washington
Thanksgiving Day: All Canadian provinces
Fourth Monday, *Veterans Day*: Arkansas, Montana, North Carolina, and Utah

NOVEMBER

Fixed Dates

November 1, *All Saints' Day*: Louisiana
November 4, *Will Rogers Day*: Oklahoma
November 11, *Veterans Day*: All States except those celebrating in October; *Remembrance Day*: All Canadian provinces
Week of November 16, *Oklahoma Heritage Week*: Oklahoma
November 29, *Nellie Tayloe Ross's Birthday*: Wyoming

Movable Feasts

First Tuesday after first Monday, *Election Day*: Arkansas, California, Colorado, District of Columbia, Delaware, Florida, Hawaii, Idaho, Illinois, Kentucky, Louisiana, Maryland, Missouri, Montana, New Jersey, New York, Oklahoma, Pennsylvania, Rhode Island, South Carolina, Tennessee, Texas, Virginia, West Virginia, Wisconsin, and Wyoming

DECEMBER

Fixed Dates

December 7, *Delaware Day*: Delaware
December 10, *Wyoming Day*: Wyoming
December 25, *Christmas Day*: All states and Canadian provinces
December 26, *Boxing Day*: All Canadian provinces

Housing

In a new, upscale California development, owners who paid close to half a million dollars for their homes are looking to lynch the builder who auctioned the development's unsold homes for hundreds of thousands less.

In Boston, some sellers not only had to bring lawyers to the sale's closing but they had to bring cash to make up the difference between what they got for the house and what they owed the bank.

In Toronto, buyers who bought unbuilt condominiums sued the developer, not because their units weren't finished long after the date agreed upon but because they wanted to be excused from a deal where their future address was now worth half what it was when they signed up to purchase.

Scattered reports from the burst North American real estate bubble, these are. Experts now forecast that houses will probably never again be outstanding investments, but they sure will make nice shelters.

Most of us change our address several times during our lives. The usual options are an apartment, a single home, a condominium, or a mobile home. The choices often fall within common life stages and income levels. Here are several possibilities:

- You are eighteen to twenty-one, carefully looking at a college or graduate school in Big Ten country. Unless you take a room in a dormitory, the odds are you'll rent an apartment. Small metro areas dominated by a major university tend to have an oversupply of buildings with five or more rental units.

- You are twenty to twenty-five, single, with a minimum of responsibilities, diligently working at your first job but willing to change employers and move anywhere for a better opportunity. If moving in with Mom and Dad is not your preference, you could take the common tack of renting a studio or one-bedroom apartment; your commitment lasts only as long as the term of the lease.

- You are twenty-five to thirty-five, married, with two small children and an offer for a better job in a distant and unfamiliar metro area. Renting a house for a year or so may give you an opportunity to become thoroughly acquainted with the new area before you invest in a home of your own. You might also consider buying an inexpensive condominium that can easily be resold or rented once you find a house and neighborhood that are right for you.

- You are thirty-five to forty-five, married, with children, and have recently taken a promotion in another city with a fat relocation bonus and corresponding pay increase. If you're selling a home, the odds are you'll trade up for a larger house in the suburbs.

- You are well into your sixth decade, your children have scattered like tumbleweeds in the wind, and you have an ark of a home that you plan to sell. Your options are wider than those of other age groups; you can rent an apartment or buy a smaller home, condo, or mobile home in town or in another metro area, perhaps one with a milder climate and a lower cost of living.

TYPICAL HOUSING CHOICES

If you're thinking of moving to a metro area hundreds of miles distant, it would help to know what kinds of local shelter choices are available, what the average costs would be for renting, and—because two-thirds of us eventually end up buying a single-family home—what are the average homeowner costs you'll encounter there.

Single Houses

Step through the front door of the typical home, and you'll find yourself in a detached structure that was built after 1970 and has a single-level, 1,600-square-foot floor plan enclosing five rooms (three bedrooms, one bath, a complete kitchen), no basement, and an insulated attic and storm windows to conserve heat from its gas-fired, warm-air furnace. This house is kept cool during hot spells by a central air-conditioning unit. It is also connected to city water and sewerage lines.

So much for composites. Among the millions of single houses in the United States and Canada, a buyer can choose from many building styles—Cape Cods and Cape Anns, mountain A-frames, cabins of peeled pine log, desert adobes, Greek revivals, American and Dutch colonials, Puget Sounds, catslides, exotic glass solaria, futuristic earth berms, Victorians, plantation cottages, and especially among the newer suburban homes, the ubiquitous executive split-levels and California bungalows.

Among metro areas, the portion of single homes you'll actually find among all the other options—apartments, condos, rental duplexes and triplexes, and mobile homes—varies considerably from nearly 9 of 10 housing units in Barnstable–Yarmouth, MA, to less than 2 of 5 in New York.

Condominiums

Condominium was nothing more than an obscure Latin word before a new legal concept for owning real estate was imported from Puerto Rico to North America in 1960. Under the arrangement, you could own outright an apartment, town house, or single house in a multiple-unit development. You could also sell, lease, bequeath, and furnish that legally described cube of air space independent of other unit owners.

Moreover, you owned the elevators, heating plant, streets, parking spaces, garden landscaping, tennis

---

Newer Homes in Metro Areas

At least a quarter of all single homes in the following metro areas were built since 1985.

	Percent Built, 1985 or later
Las Vegas, NV–AZ	29%
Myrtle Beach, SC	29
Naples, FL	29
Riverside–San Bernardino, CA	29
Orlando, FL	28
Punta Gorda, FL	28
Fort Pierce–Port St. Lucie, FL	27
Atlanta, GA	25
Daytona Beach, FL	25
Fort Myers–Cape Coral, FL	25
Melbourne–Titusville–Palm Bay, FL	25
Ocala, FL	25
Oshawa, ON	25
Panama City, FL	25
Raleigh–Durham–Chapel Hill, NC	25

Source: U.S. Bureau of the Census, *1990 Census of Population and Housing* and C-40 *Building Permits*, annual to January 1993; Statistics Canada, *Profile of Census Metropolitan Areas*, 1992.

---

courts, swimming pool, lights, and walkways in common with the rest of the development's residents.

Throughout most of the 1970s, condominiums were heavily promoted to "newlywed or nearly dead" buyers, as some brokers called them. Indeed, young couples and singles making their way out of the rental market and retired couples who wanted to unload a large house for a smaller one were major reasons for the number of condominium units growing from zero to millions today.

If you've been reluctantly tearing rental payments from your checkbook and are weighing the purchase of a home for the first time, you might consider a condominium as a compromise between apartment living and the tax advantages of owning a single-family home. With a condominium, you have freedom from house and yard maintenance, a ready-made social life, and the common recreation facilities. You also receive the tax advantages of ownership, often at a lower cost than buying a house would entail.

On the minus side, some condo owners complain of ticky-tacky construction, parking problems, thin party walls, and living cheek by jowl with renters and other unfamiliar neighbors. In many markets, profitable resales are impossible because poorly developed suburban condos and frequent builders' auctions have created a large supply of unsold units.

Condos can be high-rise (vertical) or low-rise (horizontal), depending on local zoning laws and available land. You'll find residential condominiums in metro areas where land is scarce and where the prices of single detached homes are out of reach for people looking to buy a first home. This form of real estate is most common in the resort-and-vacation metro areas.

Mobile Homes in Metro Areas

A popular Sun Belt housing style, *manufactured housing*—as the mobile home industry prefers to call it—shelters one of 16 people in the United States, far fewer in Canada.

	Portion of Occupied Housing
Yuma, AZ	38%
Ocala, FL	31
Lakeland–Winter Haven, FL	27
Jacksonville, NC	26
Las Cruces, NM	25
Dover, DE	21
Goldsboro, NC	21
Myrtle Beach, SC	21
Sumter, SC	21

Source: U.S. Bureau of the Census, *1990 Census of Population and Housing.*

Mobile Homes

As you struggle to scrape up the down payment for a suburban ranch or a town house close to work, you may already have the $30,000 needed to buy an average mobile home outright.

The major advantage of a mobile home is price. It takes a contractor's crew several months to build a typical three-bedroom house, whereas a mobile home takes 80 to 100 hours. Moreover, the per-square-foot cost of manufacturing a mobile home is less than half that of a site-built home.

This doesn't mean that mobile homes lack quality. Since World War II, when many defense workers were housed in 300-square-foot sheet-metal boxes with ersatz cooking facilities and no plumbing, mobile homes have gradually shaken their reputation for tackiness. Mobile homes now are at least 14 feet wide. Seventy-foot-long Double Wides can enclose three bedrooms, two baths, a living room, dining room, kitchen, and closets. New mobile homes are usually sold complete: appliances, furniture, draperies, lamps, and carpeting are all included in the price, as are built-in plumbing, heating, air conditioning, and electrical systems.

The value of a mobile home, however, may depreciate in many areas where conventional homes increase in value. Arbitrary evictions from mobile home parks are not uncommon in many states, nor are restrictive zoning laws that confine this kind of housing to the urban/rural fringe.

The only time the mobile home is actually mobile is when it leaves the factory and is towed by a truck in one or more sections to a concrete foundation, whether on the owner's acreage or at one of 24,000 trailer parks in the country. When it arrives, the wheels, axle, and towing tongue are removed, and all that still resembles a trailer is the I-beamed chassis, which quickly becomes hidden structural reinforcement once the unit is winched onto the foundation and plumbed. After that, the mobile home becomes more or less permanent; no more than 3 percent of them are ever moved again.

Half of all new mobile homes are trucked to just eight states: California, Florida, Georgia, Louisiana, North Carolina, Oklahoma, South Carolina, and Texas. You're more likely to find permissive zoning regulations and a wider choice of mobile home parks in smaller metro areas of the Sun Belt. You're less likely to find them in Canada, the northern states, and in large metro areas where the high cost of residential land offsets any economic benefits of owning a mobile home.

Renting an Apartment

It happens. One day you're out with a real estate broker scouting for a condo and you spot an immaculate, stately old building near downtown with flowers in front and no sign but one: APARTMENT FOR RENT. The next day you're a tenant.

Looking for digs close to work, with reasonable rent, tenants similar to yourself, a pleasant landlord, off-street parking, ambience, and all the other items on your checklist might turn out to be a quest that stops when the lease is signed but starts up again on the lease's anniversary. Still, for most newcomers to a metro area, renting is the main style of housing tenure.

As a renter you remain flexible, since you need not stay in an apartment beyond the term of the lease should your income slump or your job take you to another part of the country. You don't need to come up with a down payment; taxes, insurance, repairs, and sometimes utilities are the landlord's headaches.

Renting is also cheaper. Rents haven't gone up as fast as the costs of ownership. What's more, vacancy rates are predicted to climb as more and more renters buy in the current depressed housing market. In some areas overbuilt with apartments, landlords are scrounging for

Apartments in Metro Areas

Apartment life isn't just a New York cliché. A form of housing tenure in older, densely populated areas as well as resorts, the lifestyle is common from Montreal to Honolulu and Vancouver to Miami.

	Percent of Occupied Housing
Montreal, PQ	58%
New York, NY	58
Sherbrooke, PQ	46
Quebec City, PQ	44
Fort Lauderdale, FL	43
Miami, FL	40
Honolulu, HI	37
Naples, FL	37
Vancouver, BC	34
Los Angeles–Long Beach, CA	33
West Palm Beach–Boca Raton, FL	33
San Francisco, CA	32
Victoria, BC	31
Washington, DC–MD–VA–WV	31
Houston, TX	30

Source: U.S. Bureau of the Census, *1990 Census of Population and Housing;* Statistics Canada, *Profile of Census Metropolitan Areas,* 1992.

Older Homes in Metro Areas

At least two out of five homes in the following metro areas are more than 50 years old.

	Percent Built, 1940 or earlier
Jamestown, NY	50%
Scranton–Wilkes-Barre–Hazleton, PA	48
Utica–Rome, NY	44
Altoona, PA	43
Boston, MA	41
Wheeling, WV–OH	41
Williamsport, PA	41
Elmira, NY	40
Johnstown, PA	40
New Bedford–Fall River–Attleboro, MA	40

Source: U.S. Bureau of the Census, *1990 Census of Population and Housing* and C-40 *Building Permits*, annual to January 1993; Statistics Canada, *Profile of Census Metropolitan Areas*, 1992.

Older Isn't Always Cheaper

Most people live in homes built years ago that were bought, lived in, and sold by a succession of owners. We all confirm the "filtering theory" of housing, which states that houses filter down from high-income first owners to middle-income buyers to lower-income owners. To put it another way, many high-income families live in newer homes, and most lower-income households occupy older homes.

So what else is new? Just that when the weekend real estate sections of the *Boston Globe*, *Washington Post*, *Toronto Globe and Mail*, or *San Francisco Chronicle* list residential landmarks in historic neighborhoods on the market for $500,000 or more, you're looking at the exceptions to this theory. Nowhere is this more apparent than in Connecticut's Fairfield County. Stamford and Norwalk homes carry some of the biggest price tags in the country, and most of them were built long before World War II.

Nevertheless, the filtering theory holds true for most North American metro areas; the older the housing, the lower the price.

---

tenants and offering month-to-month arrangements or leases with several months of free rent.

There is a downside. You miss out on ownership benefits such as growing equity, property appreciation, and tax deductions for mortgage interest, while being subject to condo conversion or arbitrary rent hikes in times of low vacancy rates.

Many of us think that apartments are available only in blocks of large, high-rise tower complexes near a large metro area's central business district. In fact, only one out of 50 apartments is in a building of 13 stories or more, and only one out of 10 is in a building higher than 3 stories. Moreover, apartments make up as large a part of occupied housing in smaller metro areas dominated by state universities as they do in metro areas that are much larger in population.

WHAT A DIFFERENCE AGE MAKES

Anyone watching the speed at which houses can be put up on pricey lots in suburbia or in cheap-jack developments near the industrial fringe might well agree with old-timers who watched large, balloon-framed homes built with a good deal of craftsmanship years ago. "They don't build them the way they used to," some of them might mutter.

No, they don't. Scuff over the sawdust and around the empty nail kegs, the stacked Sheetrock, and the crated fiberglass shower stall in a newly framed ranch in a suburban housing development and you might wonder why the contractor is asking a bundle for something he's putting up so quickly.

Wraparound porches are rarely found. A porch is now merely a recessed space at the entrance of a house. The 10-foot interior ceilings common before World War II have been replaced with the 8-foot standard. The kind of formal stairway with well-turned balusters and waxed

rails that Andy Hardy used to slide down are no longer necessary—most new homes are built on a single level. Milled red oak fascias and moldings have become too expensive for common use; walls are envelopes of ⅜-inch gypsum board nailed to studs rather that the old "mud jobs" of plaster on lath; and solid six-panel doors have lost out to hollow-core flush doors of hemlock veneer.

On the other hand, copper and polyvinyl chloride water pipes have replaced galvanized iron plumbing with lead joints; knob and tube wiring has surrendered to safer electrical circuitry; cast-iron radiators no longer interfere with furniture arrangement; pressure-treated wood has eliminated termite and dry-rot risks; and the seasonal problem of cellar flooding arises less often because there aren't many cellars being excavated. Indeed, as much as 20 percent of a new home's price tag is due to vastly superior building materials.

One useful indication of the quality of a metro area's housing stock is the percent of homes put up before World War II (defined here as "old") and the portion built since 1985 (defined here as "new"). Although an older house isn't necessarily on the verge of tumbling down, age can signal functional obsolescence and looming maintenance headaches. Clapboards do need scraping and repainting every three years, clogged sewer drains must be snaked, furnaces do wear out, and storm windows must be retrofitted. These tasks can mean both dollars and difficulties.

Expensive Housing . . . Despite the Bust

For all the decline in Pacific Coast property values since the real estate market peaked in 1990, average prices still top a quarter-million dollars in nine metro areas.

	Average House Price
San Francisco, CA	$353,400
San Jose, CA	$322,500
Honolulu, HI	$310,100
Orange County, CA	$282,800
Santa Cruz–Watsonville, CA	$280,800
Santa Barbara–Santa Maria–Lompoc, CA	$280,100
Ventura, CA	$275,000
Los Angeles–Long Beach, CA	$268,000

Source: Places Rated Partnership estimates.

BUYING THAT SINGLE-FAMILY HOME

Despite the number of choices for shelter, the single-family house is still the most common (87 percent of home-owner units are single-family homes) and the most popular (two-thirds of us eventually buy a single-family home).

Where are the best markets for prospective buyers? You might guess that a consequence of the continent's west-by-south population shift would be dramatically inflated home prices in the same direction. But some of the highest prices are found in places where homes have always been expensive: Anchorage, Honolulu, New York City and its suburbs in Connecticut and New Jersey, the District of Columbia and its environs, and since 1975, California metro areas.

We may never again experience the explosive 178-percent inflation in prices seen during the 1970s, or the 151-percent increase over the following decade. However, the inflation doesn't mean that solid, quality-built houses can't be found for less than $150,000. They can, in smaller metro areas of Alabama, Indiana, Missouri, Saskatchewan, and Texas.

SCORING: HOUSING

On the average, is shelter more expensive in Danbury, Dayton, or Duluth? To help you answer these questions, *Places Rated* tallies typical annual mortgage payments on an average-priced house. The single house is the kind of residence most commonly bought by North Americans; that's why we use it here as the basis for judging home-owning costs.

Each metro area starts with a base score of zero. Points are added for each dollar of annual mortgage payments, based on a 15-year, 8-percent loan on the average price of a house with a 20-percent down payment. The lower the score, the higher the rank.

SCORING EXAMPLES

Hawaii's capital, a rebounding Rocky Mountain metro area, and a small metro area in southwest Missouri illustrate the housing scoring method.

Honolulu, HI (#341)

Although sky-high shelter costs don't always indicate quality housing, they do indicate the pitch of local supply and demand in desirable locations. Nowhere is this truer than in Honolulu.

During the later half of the 1980s, Japanese seeking second homes quickly ran up housing prices. Stories of investors cruising residential neighborhoods to make attractive, on-the-spot offers to home owners who answered their doorbells are true.

The economy in Japan has slumped badly, and its wealthier citizens aren't snapping up Hawaiian homes any longer. For all that, prices in Honolulu remain high. Here the annual mortgage payment on a home with a $310,000 average price tag is $28,262, a figure that also represents Honolulu's housing score.

Denver, CO (#254)

At a particularly low period in the mid-1980s energy bust, residential multiple-listing catalogues in the five county metro Denver market looked like thick telephone books. Tens of thousands of foreclosed homes were offered for sale by their new, reluctant owners, the banks.

Eight years later, with a cyclical return to a flusher economy, the housing market here has turned so dramatically that one national personal finance magazine named the area as the most promising for continued appreciation throughout the 1990s. As in other parts of the country, the market has been helped by years of pent-up demand from first-time buyers. The average home price now exceeds $100,000, with annual mortgage payments amounting to $9,237, Denver's housing score.

Joplin, MO (#5)

In contrast, one of the lowest mortgage totals on a typical home is found some 700 miles east in Joplin, a city in Missouri's Ozark corner. Unlike Denver and Honolulu, a goodly portion of homes here were built before World War II. Unlike larger metro areas, too, there is no market for condominium's here. Most residences are owner-occupied single houses, an indication of the area's affordability.

These homes range from nineteenth-century farmhouses in rural sections to Victorian homes in town and newer brick-and-frame bilevels and ranches out along U.S. 71. Unlike pricey Honolulu metro area, too, Joplin's $47,300 average home price is well within the incomes of residents. Annual mortgage payments total $4,314, Joplin's housing score.

Rankings: Housing

One factor is used to rank metro areas for housing: the annual payments on a 15-year, 8-percent mortgage on an average-priced home after making a 20-percent down payment. The lower the score, the higher the rank. Places that are tied get the same rank and are listed in alphabetical order.

Metro Areas from Least to Most Expensive

Places Rated Rank	Places Rated Score	Places Rated Rank	Places Rated Score	Places Rated Rank	Places Rated Score
1. McAllen–Edinburg–Mission, TX	4,102	40. Owensboro, KY	5,194	84. Topeka, KS	5,758
2. Terre Haute, IN	4,116	42. Flint, MI	5,195	85. La Crosse, WI–MN	5,762
3. Enid, OK	4,139	43. Florence, AL	5,273		
4. Johnstown, PA	4,312	44. Regina, SK	5,276	86. Shreveport–Bossier City, LA	5,767
5. Joplin, MO	4,314	45. San Angelo, TX	5,283	87. Rocky Mount, NC	5,780
				88. Benton Harbor, MI	5,781
6. Duluth–Superior, MN–WI	4,321	46. Chicoutimi–Jonquiere, PQ	5,285	89. Oklahoma City, OK	5,784
7. Altoona, PA	4,329	47. Kokomo, IN	5,313	90. Canton–Massillon, OH	5,785
8. Sharon, PA	4,336	48. Clarksville–Hopkinsville, TN–KY	5,348		
9. Steubenville–Weirton, OH–WV	4,367	49. Peoria–Pekin, IL	5,350	91. Goldsboro, NC	5,904
10. Brownsville–Harlingen–San Benito, TX	4,372	50. Waco, TX	5,367	92. Charleston, WV	5,906
				93. Great Falls, MT	5,925
				94. Springfield, MO	5,931
11. Sioux City, IA–NE	4,374	51. Houma, LA	5,368	95. Sioux Falls, SD	5,934
12. St. Joseph, MO	4,434	52. Alexandria, LA	5,375		
13. Muncie, IN	4,501	53. Casper, WY	5,388	96. Fort Wayne, IN	5,935
14. Pine Bluff, AR	4,523	54. Laredo, TX	5,396	97. Saint John's, NF	5,946
15. Gadsden, AL	4,530	55. Lawton, OK	5,399	98. Florence, SC	5,955
				99. Decatur, AL	5,957
16. Wheeling, WV–OH	4,542	56. Dubuque, IA	5,414	100. Winnipeg, MB	5,978
17. Beaumont–Port Arthur, TX	4,597	57. Lafayette, LA	5,433		
18. Waterloo–Cedar Falls, IA	4,621	58. Grand Forks, ND–MN	5,448	101. St. Cloud, MN	5,979
19. Decatur, IL	4,821	59. Johnson City–Kingsport–Bristol, TN–VA	5,456	102. Fayetteville–Springdale–Rogers, AR	5,994
20. Texarkana, TX–Texarkana, AR	4,844	60. Lima, OH	5,458	103. Sheboygan, WI	6,003
				104. Wichita, KS	6,007
21. Cumberland, MD–WV	4,855	61. Saskatoon, SK	5,464	105. Mobile, AL	6,015
22. Danville, VA	4,869	62. Wausau, WI	5,503		
23. Huntington–Ashland, WV–KY–OH	4,894	63. South Bend, IN	5,513	106. Columbus, GA–AL	6,047
24. Abilene, TX	4,906	64. Dothan, AL	5,544	107. Bismarck, ND	6,053
25. Trois-Rivieres, PQ	4,916	65. Kankakee, IL	5,570	108. Cedar Rapids, IA	6,065
				109. Des Moines, IA	6,080
26. Fort Smith, AR–OK	4,930	66. Williamsport, PA	5,582	110. Omaha, NE–IA	6,089
27. Sherman–Denison, TX	4,949	67. Amarillo, TX	5,586		
28. Mansfield, OH	4,950	68. Elmira, NY	5,603	111. Hickory–Morgantown, NC	6,110
29. Wichita Falls, TX	4,991	69. Monroe, LA	5,616	112. Brazoria, TX	6,111
30. Jamestown, NY	5,023	70. Lake Charles, LA	5,640	113. El Paso, TX	6,131
				114. Gary, IN	6,151
31. Youngstown–Warren, OH	5,053	71. Biloxi–Gulfport–Pascagoula, MS	5,648	115. Macon, GA	6,164
32. Anniston, AL	5,056	72. Sherbrooke, PQ	5,650		
33. Jackson, MI	5,069	73. Killeen–Temple, TX	5,664	116. Spokane, WA	6,171
34. Davenport–Moline–Rock Island, IA–IL	5,132	74. Victoria, TX	5,670	117. Louisville, KY–IN	6,197
35. Pueblo, CO	5,134	75. Kalamazoo–Battle Creek, MI	5,672	118. Albany, GA	6,208
		75. Lubbock, TX	5,672	119. Salem, OR	6,226
36. Parkersburg–Marietta, WV–OH	5,159			120. Rockford, IL	6,230
37. Eau Claire, WI	5,164	77. Corpus Christi, TX	5,677		
38. Saginaw–Bay City–Midland, MI	5,187	78. Odessa–Midland, TX	5,678	121. Billings, MT	6,268
39. Janesville–Beloit, WI	5,191	79. Sumter, SC	5,699	122. Quebec City, PQ	6,281
40. Longview–Marshall, TX	5,194	80. Yakima, WA	5,706	123. Jacksonville, NC	6,295
				124. Elkhart–Goshen, IN	6,301
		81. Erie, PA	5,707	125. Tuscaloosa, AL	6,316
		82. Evansville–Henderson, IN–KY	5,714		
		83. Rapid City, SD	5,725	126. Tulsa, OK	6,321
				127. Greenville–Spartanburg–Anderson, SC	6,329

Places Rated Rank	Places Rated Score	Places Rated Rank	Places Rated Score	Places Rated Rank	Places Rated Score
128. Lafayette, IN	6,343	185. Provo–Orem, UT	7,393	240. Punta Gorda, FL	8,589
129. Green Bay, WI	6,344			241. Bakersfield, CA	8,590
130. Springfield, IL	6,356	186. Lexington, KY	7,430	242. Richmond–Petersburg, VA	8,612
		187. Halifax, NS	7,438	243. Colorado Springs, CO	8,622
131. Appleton–Oshkosh–Neenah, WI	6,359	188. Detroit, MI	7,478	244. Atlanta, GA	8,676
132. Lincoln, NE	6,362	189. Tallahassee, FL	7,510		
133. Little Rock–North Little Rock, AR	6,368	190. Salt Lake City–Ogden, UT	7,534	245. Fort Collins–Loveland, CO	8,693
134. San Antonio, TX	6,373			246. Glens Falls, NY	8,712
135. Chattanooga, TN–GA	6,389	191. Jacksonville, FL	7,535	247. Rochester, NY	8,780
		192. Hamilton–Middletown, OH	7,539	249. Tacoma, WA	8,963
136. Pensacola, FL	6,417	193. New Orleans, LA	7,552	250. Fresno, CA	8,977
137. Scranton–Wilkes-Barre–Hazleton, PA	6,421	194. Harrisburg–Lebanon–Carlisle, PA	7,568		
138. Tyler, TX	6,427	195. Athens, GA	7,594	251. Orlando, FL	9,093
139. Fargo–Moorhead, ND–MN	6,433			252. Lancaster, PA	9,140
139. Jackson, MS	6,433	196. Houston, TX	7,625	253. Phoenix–Mesa, AZ	9,218
		197. Greensboro–Winston-Salem–High Point, NC	7,666	254. Denver, CO	9,237
141. Fayetteville, NC	6,444	198. Daytona Beach, FL	7,689	255. Norfolk–Virginia Beach–Newport News, VA–NC	9,269
142. Galveston–Texas City, TX	6,456	199. Rochester, MN	7,712		
143. Richland–Kennewick–Pasco, WA	6,460	200. Syracuse, NY	7,721	256. Dallas, TX	9,315
144. Toledo, OH	6,461			257. Minneapolis–St. Paul, MN–WI	9,316
145. Lynchburg, VA	6,482	201. Fort Worth–Arlington, TX	7,750	258. Merced, CA	9,349
		202. Fort Walton Beach, FL	7,775	259. Ann Arbor, MI	9,404
146. Yuma, AZ	6,541	203. State College, PA	7,776	260. St. Catharines–Niagara, ON	9,405
147. Ocala, FL	6,542	204. Huntsville, AL	7,791		
148. Lakeland–Winter Haven, FL	6,543	205. Cleveland–Lorain–Elyria, OH	7,798	261. Calgary, AB	9,442
149. Montgomery, AL	6,571			262. Redding, CA	9,467
150. Knoxville, TN	6,587	205. St. Louis, MO–IL	7,810	263. Raleigh–Durham–Chapel Hill, NC	9,541
		206. Cincinnati, OH–KY–IN	7,858	264. Chico–Paradise, CA	9,756
151. Lansing–East Lansing, MI	6,645	207. Binghamton, NY	7,863	265. Las Vegas, NV–AZ	9,818
152. Panama City, FL	6,666	208. Portland, OR	7,841		
153. Bloomington–Normal, IL	6,694	208. Columbia, SC	7,873	266. Sarasota–Bradenton, FL	9,986
154. St. John, NB	6,705			267. Fort Myers–Cape Coral, FL	10,030
155. Grand Rapids–Muskegon–Holland, MI	6,728	209. Columbus, OH	7,893	268. Bellingham, WA	10,069
		210. Vancouver, WA	7,897	269. London, ON	10,085
156. Kenosha, WI	6,743	211. Visalia–Tulare–Porterville, CA	7,915	270. Miami, FL	10,164
157. Racine, WI	6,744	212. Thunder Bay, ON	7,921		
158. Augusta–Aiken, GA–SC	6,761	213. York, PA	7,943	271. Albany–Schenectady–Troy, NY	10,177
159. Boise City, ID	6,837			272. Bremerton, WA	10,418
160. Dayton–Springfield, OH	6,839	214. Pittsburgh, PA	7,956	273. Fort Pierce–Port St. Lucie, FL	10,468
		215. Windsor, ON	7,964	274. Ottawa–Hull, ON–PQ	10,489
161. Columbia, MO	6,855	216. Edmonton, AB	7,991	275. Allentown–Bethlehem–Easton, PA–NJ	10,560
162. Eugene–Springfield, OR	6,859	217. Tampa–St. Petersburg–Clearwater, FL	8,010		
163. Cheyenne, WY	6,867	218. Milwaukee–Waukesha, WI	8,079	276. Oshawa, ON	10,572
164. Akron, OH	6,878			277. Kitchener, ON	10,573
165. Indianapolis, IN	6,889	219. Medford–Ashland, OR	8,126	278. Charlottesville, VA	10,705
		220. Reading, PA	8,145	279. Fort Lauderdale, FL	10,718
166. Greeley, CO	6,892	222. Madison, WI	8,164	280. Anchorage, AK	10,967
167. Greenville, NC	6,911	223. Charlotte–Gastonia–Rock Hill, NC–SC	8,171		
168. Birmingham, AL	6,916	224. Charleston–North Charleston, SC	8,205	281. Hamilton, ON	11,012
169. Asheville, NC	6,939			282. Baltimore, MD	11,082
170. Bangor, ME	6,944	225. Iowa City, IA	8,211	283. Boulder–Longmont, CO	11,202
		226. Myrtle Beach, SC	8,270	284. Wilmington–Newark, DE–MD	11,662
170. Gainesville, FL	6,944	227. Austin–San Marcos, TX	8,277	285. Chicago, IL	11,818
170. Utica–Rome, NY	6,944	228. Montreal, PQ	8,289		
173. Bryan–College Station, TX	6,945	229. Wilmington, NC	8,298	286. Atlantic City–Cape May, NJ	11,878
174. Baton Rouge, LA	6,956			287. Bridgeport, CT	11,957
175. Las Cruces, NM	6,969	230. Dover, DE	8,390	288. Pittsfield, MA	12,087
		231. Olympia, WA	8,418	289. Burlington, VT	12,237
176. Kansas City, MO–KS	7,003	232. Tucson, AZ	8,424	290. Stockton–Lodi, CA	12,290
177. Lawrence, KS	7,037	233. Hagerstown, MD	8,434		
178. Bloomington, IN	7,057	234. Sudbury, ON	8,463	291. Modesto, CA	12,302
179. Roanoke, VA	7,175			292. West Palm Beach–Boca Raton, FL	12,479
180. Champaign–Urbana, IL	7,178	235. Yuba City, CA	8,495	293. Waterbury, CT	12,485
		236. Nashville, TN	8,545	294. Reno, NV	12,488
181. Memphis, TN–AR–MS	7,205	237. Lewiston–Auburn, ME	8,555	295. Springfield, MA	12,636
182. Savannah, GA	7,285	238. Albuquerque, NM	8,561		
183. Buffalo–Niagara Falls, NY	7,322	238. Melbourne–Titusville–Palm Bay, FL	8,561		
184. Vineland–Millville–Bridgeton, NJ	7,376				

Places Rated Rank	Places Rated Score	Places Rated Rank	Places Rated Score	Places Rated Rank	Places Rated Score
296. Portland, ME	12,749	311. Trenton, NJ	14,743	328. San Diego, CA	20,322
297. Philadelphia, PA–NJ	10,790	312. Seattle–Bellevue–Everett, WA	14,843	329. Stamford–Norwalk, CT	20,642
298. Santa Fe, NM	12,987	313. New Haven–Meriden, CT	15,329	330. Santa Rosa, CA	20,729
299. Providence–Warwick–Cranston, RI	13,588	314. Washington, DC–MD–VA–WV	15,466	331. Northern New Jersey, NJ	21,539
300. Manchester–Nashua, NH	13,692	315. New London–Norwich, CT–RI	15,638	332. New York, NY	21,561
301. New Bedford–Fall River–Attleboro, MA	13,813	316. Toronto, ON	15,673	333. San Luis Obispo–Atascadero–Paso Robles, CA	21,719
302. Riverside–San Bernardino, CA	13,923	317. Naples, FL	15,830	334. Salinas, CA	21,801
303. Orange County, NY	13,985	318. Vallejo–Fairfield–Napa, CA	16,000	335. Oakland, CA	22,707
304. Worcester–Fitchburg–Leominster, MA	14,039	319. Monmouth–Ocean, NJ	16,107	336. Los Angeles–Long Beach, CA	24,421
305. Victoria, BC	14,193	320. Lake County, IL	16,545	337. Ventura, CA	25,063
306. Portsmouth–Dover–Rochester, NH	14,305	321. Hartford, CT	17,202	338. Santa Barbara–Santa Maria–Lompoc, CA	25,525
307. Sacramento, CA	14,324	322. Barnstable–Yarmouth, MA	17,593	339. Santa Cruz–Watsonville, CA	25,594
308. Yolo, CA	14,351	323. Vancouver, BC	17,881	340. Orange County, CA	25,772
309. Danbury, CT	14,463	324. Central New Jersey, NJ	17,914	341. Honolulu, HI	28,262
310. Dutchess County, NY	14,696	325. Boston, MA	18,903	342. San Jose, CA	29,395
		326. Long Island, NY	19,951	343. San Francisco, CA	32,211
		327. Newark–Jersey City, NJ	20,044		

Place Profiles: Housing

The following pages summarize housing features in each metro area. Figures under the first heading, **Local Choices,** show the mix of single houses, condominiums, mobile homes, and apartments (defined here as a rented housing unit in a building with three or more rental units). The sums of these percentages (which are rounded) aren't always 100; the balance represents renter-occupied duplexes and row houses.

Data under the second heading, **Apartments,** show the portion of apartments that are in complexes of 50 units or more in U.S. metro areas, or are in high-rise buildings of five or more stories in Canadian metro areas. Under that figure is the average rent, in American dollars, for a one-bedroom apartment.

The third heading, **Houses,** details the portion of detached homes built between January 1985 and January 1993 (defined here as "new") and the portion of homes built before World War II (defined here as "old"). Included under this heading, too, is the dominant form of energy used for heating and cooking.

Under the fourth heading, **Prices,** are figures for owner-occupied homes at three intervals. *Median* is the point at which half the homes are cheaper and half more expensive. *Average,* a higher figure than median, is the total value of owner-occupied homes divided by the number of homes. *Upper Tenth* is the price of homes weighted at the top 10 percent of the market. All figures are in American dollars.

Data are derived from these sources: American Association of Realtors, *Existing Home Sales,* 1990–1993; Canadian Real Estate Association, *MLS Resale Data,* 1990–1993; Royal LePage Real Estate Services, *Survey of Canadian House Prices,* Winter 1993; Statistics Canada, *Profile of Census Metropolitan Areas,* 1992; U.S. Department of Commerce, Bureau of the Census, *1990 Census of Population and Housing;* U.S Department of Labor, Bureau of Labor Statistics, *Consumer Price Index,* monthly from April 1990 to January 1993.

A check (✓) preceding a metro area's name identifies it as one of North America's best 35 places for homeowning costs.

Metro Area	Local Choices	Apartments	Houses	Prices	Places Rated Score	Places Rated Rank
✓ Abilene, TX	73% houses 13% apartments 1% condos 6% mobile homes	29% complexes One bedroom: $450/month	7% new 9% old Utilities: Gas/Electric	Median: $44,800 Average: $53,800 Upper Tenth: $82,900	4,906	24
Akron, OH	72% houses 15% apartments 3% condos 3% mobile homes	34% complexes One bedroom: $520/month	9% new 23% old Utilities: Gas/Electric	Median: $62,300 Average: $75,500 Upper Tenth: $114,500	6,878	164
Albany, GA	62% houses 13% apartments 1% condos 9% mobile homes	9% complexes One bedroom: $465/month	11% new 4% old Utilities: Total Electric	Median: $58,400 Average: $68,100 Upper Tenth: $110,400	6,208	118
Albany–Schenectady–Troy, NY	56% houses 18% apartments 1% condos 5% mobile homes	20% complexes One bedroom: $575/month	11% new 37% old Utilities: Gas/Electric	Median: $99,800 Average: $111,700 Upper Tenth: $194,800	10,177	271
Albuquerque, NM	65% houses 19% apartments 2% condos 9% mobile homes	41% complexes One bedroom: $525/month	17% new 5% old Utilities: Gas/Electric	Median: $82,000 Average: $93,900 Upper Tenth: $157,100	8,561	238
Alexandria, LA	72% houses 9% apartments 1% condos 11% mobile homes	21% complexes One bedroom: $450/month	10% new 9% old Utilities: Gas/Electric	Median: $50,900 Average: $59,000 Upper Tenth: $96,600	5,375	52
Allentown–Bethlehem–Easton, PA–NJ	74% houses 14% apartments 1% condos 3% mobile homes	21% complexes One bedroom: $585/month	11% new 34% old Utilities: Oil/Electric	Median: $102,900 Average: $115,900 Upper Tenth: $199,800	10,560	275
✓ Altoona, PA	74% houses 10% apartments 7% mobile homes	23% complexes One bedroom: $400/month	6% new 43% old Utilities: Gas/Electric	Median: $40,700 Average: $47,500 Upper Tenth: $76,900	4,329	7
Amarillo, TX	72% houses 13% apartments 1% condos 7% mobile homes	50% complexes One bedroom: $450/month	7% new 9% old Utilities: Gas/Electric	Median: $51,900 Average: $61,300 Upper Tenth: $97,100	5,586	67
Anchorage, AK	52% houses 25% apartments 10% condos 7% mobile homes	23% complexes One bedroom: $610/month	11% new 1% old Utilities: Gas/Electric	Median: $109,800 Average: $120,300 Upper Tenth: $218,100	10,967	280
Ann Arbor, MI	67% houses 21% apartments 4% condos 5% mobile homes	25% complexes One bedroom: $650/month	14% new 19% old Utilities: Gas/Electric	Median: $87,700 Average: $103,200 Upper Tenth: $164,600	9,404	259
✓ Anniston, AL	73% houses 8% apartments 14% mobile homes	17% complexes One bedroom: $400/month	12% new 10% old Utilities: Gas/Electric	Median: $51,300 Average: $55,500 Upper Tenth: $103,000	5,056	32
Appleton–Oshkosh–Neenah, WI	72% houses 13% apartments 1% condos 3% mobile homes	26% complexes One bedroom: $480/month	13% new 26% old Utilities: Gas/Electric	Median: $61,900 Average: $69,800 Upper Tenth: $120,100	6,359	131
Asheville, NC	67% houses 10% apartments 3% condos 17% mobile homes	22% complexes One bedroom: $495/month	16% new 17% old Utilities: Oil/Electric	Median: $63,400 Average: $76,100 Upper Tenth: $117,300	6,939	169
Athens, GA	55% houses 20% apartments 4% condos 13% mobile homes	30% complexes One bedroom: $490/month	20% new 9% old Utilities: Gas/Electric	Median: $70,300 Average: $83,300 Upper Tenth: $131,300	7,594	195
Atlanta, GA	64% houses 22% apartments 5% condos 5% mobile homes	20% complexes One bedroom: $650/month	25% new 6% old Utilities: Gas/Electric	Median: $86,400 Average: $95,200 Upper Tenth: $152,300	8,676	244
Atlantic City–Cape May, NJ	60% houses 10% apartments 10% condos 3% mobile homes	30% complexes One bedroom: $670/month	15% new 19% old Utilities: Gas/Electric	Median: $107,500 Average: $130,300 Upper Tenth: $197,600	11,878	286
Augusta–Aiken, GA–SC	67% houses 13% apartments 2% condos 13% mobile homes	12% complexes One bedroom: $510/month	21% new 8% old Utilities: Gas/Electric	Median: $63,400 Average: $74,200 Upper Tenth: $119,500	6,761	158

Metro Area	Local Choices	Apartments	Houses	Prices	Places Rated Score	Places Rated Rank
Austin–San Marcos, TX	59% houses 24% apartments 4% condos 6% mobile homes	45% complexes One bedroom: $520/month	18% new 5% old Utilities: Gas/Electric	Median: $74,800 Average: $90,800 Upper Tenth: $137,300	8,277	227
Bakersfield, CA	67% houses 15% apartments 3% condos 12% mobile homes	24% complexes One bedroom: $535/month	17% new 7% old Utilities: Gas/Electric	Median: $82,400 Average: $94,300 Upper Tenth: $158,000	8,590	241
Baltimore, MD	72% houses 18% apartments 4% condos 1% mobile homes	21% complexes One bedroom: $625/month	12% new 20% old Utilities: Gas/Electric	Median: $101,000 Average: $121,600 Upper Tenth: $186,500	11,082	282
Bangor, ME	60% houses 16% apartments 13% mobile homes	9% complexes One bedroom: $520/month	11% new 32% old Utilities: Oil/Electric	Median: $68,900 Average: $76,200 Upper Tenth: $135,800	6,944	170
Barnstable–Yarmouth, MA	85% houses 5% apartments 6% condos 1% mobile homes	21% complexes One bedroom: $675/month	18% new 15% old Utilities: Oil/Electric	Median: $162,500 Average: $193,000 Upper Tenth: $303,100	17,593	322
Baton Rouge, LA	66% houses 18% apartments 3% condos 8% mobile homes	36% complexes One bedroom: $475/month	10% new 5% old Utilities: Gas/Electric	Median: $66,700 Average: $76,300 Upper Tenth: $127,900	6,956	174
✓ Beaumont–Port Arthur, TX	75% houses 11% apartments 1% condos 9% mobile homes	39% complexes One bedroom: $470/month	6% new 10% old Utilities: Gas/Electric	Median: $42,400 Average: $50,400 Upper Tenth: $79,000	4,597	17
Bellingham, WA	67% houses 14% apartments 3% condos 12% mobile homes	32% complexes One bedroom: $535/month	16% new 20% old Utilities: Total Electric	Median: $90,400 Average: $110,500 Upper Tenth: $165,200	10,069	268
Benton Harbor, MI	76% houses 10% apartments 1% condos 6% mobile homes	27% complexes One bedroom: $480/month	7% new 24% old Utilities: Gas/Electric	Median: $52,700 Average: $63,400 Upper Tenth: $97,300	5,781	88
Billings, MT	65% houses 13% apartments 2% condos 12% mobile homes	19% complexes One bedroom: $425/month	8% new 11% old Utilities: Gas/Electric	Median: $62,700 Average: $68,800 Upper Tenth: $124,400	6,268	121
Biloxi–Gulfport–Pascagoula, MS	70% houses 12% apartments 2% condos 10% mobile homes	25% complexes One bedroom: $465/month	12% new 6% old Utilities: Total Electric	Median: $52,500 Average: $62,000 Upper Tenth: $98,300	5,648	71
Binghamton, NY	60% houses 15% apartments 8% mobile homes	15% complexes One bedroom: $490/month	8% new 36% old Utilities: Gas/Electric	Median: $77,700 Average: $86,300 Upper Tenth: $152,600	7,863	207
Birmingham, AL	70% houses 17% apartments 2% condos 8% mobile homes	24% complexes One bedroom: $500/month	14% new 11% old Utilities: Gas/Electric	Median: $60,700 Average: $75,900 Upper Tenth: $109,200	6,916	168
Bismarck, ND	59% houses 19% apartments 4% condos 13% mobile homes	22% complexes One bedroom: $430/month	8% new 13% old Utilities: Gas/Electric	Median: $62,600 Average $66,400 Upper Tenth: $127,800	6,053	107
Bloomington, IN	55% houses 29% apartments 5% condos 9% mobile homes	30% complexes One bedroom: $510/month	15% new 13% old Utilities: Gas/Electric	Median: $66,600 Average: $77,400 Upper Tenth: $126,200	7,057	178
Bloomington–Normal, IL	64% houses 22% apartments 3% condos 7% mobile homes	15% complexes One bedroom: $485/month	14% new 24% old Utilities: Gas/Electric	Median: $65,400 Average: $73,400 Upper Tenth: $127,300	6,694	153
Boise City, ID	72% houses 11% apartments 2% condos 11% mobile homes	24% complexes One bedroom: $500/month	15% new 10% old Utilities: Gas/Electric	Median: $65,400 Average: $75,000 Upper Tenth: $125,200	6,837	159
Boston, MA	49% houses 27% apartments 8% condos 1% mobile homes	32% complexes One bedroom: $775/month	8% new 41% old Utilities: Oil/Electric	Median: $179,600 Average: $207,400 Upper Tenth: $342,000	18,903	325

Metro Area	Local Choices	Apartments	Houses	Prices	Places Rated Score	Places Rated Rank
Boulder–Longmont, CO	66% houses 22% apartments 9% condos 4% mobile homes	39% complexes One bedroom: $600/month	16% new 9% old Utilities: Gas/Electric	Median: $102,300 Average: $122,900 Upper Tenth: $189,200	11,202	283
Brazoria, TX	67% houses 13% apartments 1% condos 14% mobile homes	43% complexes One bedroom: $500/month	14% new 3% old Utilities: Gas/Electric	Median: $61,200 Average: $67,000 Upper Tenth: $121,600	6,111	112
Bremerton, WA	69% houses 14% apartments 2% condos 10% mobile homes	26% complexes One bedroom: $540/month	16% new 12% old Utilities: Total Electric	Median: $89,100 Average: $114,300 Upper Tenth: $157,600	10,418	272
Bridgeport, CT	56% houses 23% apartments 10% condos	29% complexes One bedroom: $600/month	9% new 28% old Utilities: Oil/Electric	Median: $121,700 Average: $131,200 Upper Tenth: $245,100	11,957	287
✓ Brownsville–Harlingen–San Benito, TX	64% houses 12% apartments 6% condos 13% mobile homes	32% complexes One bedroom: $450/month	14% new 6% old Utilities: Total Electric	Median: $38,100 Average: $48,000 Upper Tenth: $68,200	4,372	10
Bryan–College Station, TX	49% houses 31% apartments 3% condos 8% mobile homes	27% complexes One bedroom: $510/month	11% new 4% old Utilities: Total Electric	Median: $66,800 Average: $76,200 Upper Tenth: $128,400	6,945	173
Buffalo–Niagara Falls, NY	57% houses 15% apartments 1% condos 2% mobile homes	19% complexes One bedroom: $500/month	6% new 37% old Utilities: Gas/Electric	Median: $71,400 Average: $80,300 Upper Tenth: $138,800	7,322	183
Burlington, VT	60% houses 19% apartments 10% condos 5% mobile homes	16% complexes One bedroom: $590/month	15% new 25% old Utilities: Oil/Electric	Median: $117,300 Average: $134,300 Upper Tenth: $224,900	12,237	289
Calgary, AB	64% houses 23% apartments 3% condos 1% mobile homes	31% high rise One bedroom: $580/month	14% new 7% old Utilities: Gas/Electric	Median: n.a. Average: $103,600 Upper Tenth: $220,000	9,442	261
Canton–Massillon, OH	74% houses 12% apartments 1% condos 4% mobile homes	19% complexes One bedroom: $460/month	6% new 26% old Utilities: Gas/Electric	Median: $56,900 Average: $63,500 Upper Tenth: $111,300	5,785	90
Casper, WY	70% houses 11% apartments 1% condos 12% mobile homes	37% complexes One bedroom: $375/month	2% new 12% old Utilities: Gas/Electric	Median: $52,300 Average: $59,100 Upper Tenth: $101,300	5,388	53
Cedar Rapids, IA	71% houses 17% apartments 2% condos 5% mobile homes	24% complexes One bedroom: $480/month	8% new 24% old Utilities: Gas/Electric	Median: $58,200 Average: $66,600 Upper Tenth: $111,600	6,065	108
Central New Jersey, NJ	68% houses 18% apartments 12% condos 1% mobile homes	27% complexes One bedroom: $800/month	17% new 16% old Utilities: Gas/Electric	Median: $177,400 Average: $196,600 Upper Tenth: $349,000	17,914	324
Champaign–Urbana, IL	58% houses 26% apartments 4% condos 7% mobile homes	28% complexes One bedroom: $510/month	11% new 15% old Utilities: Gas/Electric	Median: $67,500 Average: $78,800 Upper Tenth: $127,500	7,178	180
Charleston, WV	71% houses 11% apartments 2% condos 11% mobile homes	24% complexes One bedroom: $450/month	8% new 17% old Utilities: Gas/Electric	Median: $56,800 Average: $64,800 Upper Tenth: $109,200	5,906	92
Charleston–North Charleston, SC	61% houses 16% apartments 5% condos 13% mobile homes	11% complexes One bedroom: $550/month	21% new 7% old Utilities: Total Electric	Median: $72,100 Average: $90,000 Upper Tenth: $129,900	8,205	224
Charlotte–Gastonia–Rock Hill, NC–SC	68% houses 15% apartments 4% condos 10% mobile homes	16% complexes One bedroom: $565/month	19% new 8% old Utilities: Total Electric	Median: $73,100 Average: $89,700 Upper Tenth: $133,200	8,171	223
Charlottesville, VA	68% houses 18% apartments 3% condos 5% mobile homes	26% complexes One bedroom: $575/month	17% new 14% old Utilities: Total Electric	Median: $96,400 Average: $117,500 Upper Tenth: $176,500	10,705	278

Metro Area	Local Choices	Apartments	Houses	Prices	Places Rated Score	Places Rated Rank
Chattanooga, TN–GA	68% houses 13% apartments 1% condos 8% mobile homes	29% complexes One bedroom: $500/month	15% new 12% old Utilities: Total Electric	Median: $58,500 Average: $70,100 Upper Tenth: $108,400	6,389	135
Cheyenne, WY	68% houses 13% apartments 2% condos 12% mobile homes	17% complexes One bedroom: $460/month	9% new 15% old Utilities: Gas/Electric	Median: $69,200 Average: $75,400 Upper Tenth: $138,100	6,867	163
Chicago, IL	50% houses 28% apartments 8% condos 1% mobile homes	37% complexes One bedroom: $665/month	8% new 27% old Utilities: Gas/Electric	Median: $105,800 Average: $129,700 Upper Tenth: $192,900	11,818	285
Chico–Paradise, CA	61% houses 16% apartments 2% condos 18% mobile homes	25% complexes One bedroom: $530/month	15% new 10% old Utilities: Gas/Electric	Median: $94,000 Average: $107,100 Upper Tenth: $180,900	9,756	264
Chicoutimi–Jonquiere, PQ	55% houses 25% apartments 1% mobile homes	3% high rise One bedroom: $400/month	13% new 14% old Utilities: Total Electric	Median: n.a. Average: $58,000 Upper Tenth: $80,000	5,285	46
Cincinnati, OH–KY–IN	62% houses 23% apartments 3% condos 4% mobile homes	22% complexes One bedroom: $500/month	11% new 25% old Utilities: Gas/Electric	Median: $69,700 Average: $86,200 Upper Tenth: $126,300	7,858	206
Clarksville–Hopkinsville, TN–KY	69% houses 15% apartments 1% condos 10% mobile homes	11% complexes One bedroom: $470/month	19% new 8% old Utilities: Total Electric	Median: $52,800 Average: $58,700 Upper Tenth: $103,600	5,348	48
Cleveland–Lorain–Elyria, OH	67% houses 18% apartments 4% condos 2% mobile homes	44% complexes One bedroom: $540/month	6% new 27% old Utilities: Gas/Electric	Median: $80,600 Average: $89,400 Upper Tenth: $143,000	8,147	221
Colorado Springs, CO	66% houses 20% apartments 5% condos 5% mobile homes	39% complexes One bedroom: $490/month	15% new 8% old Utilities: Gas/Electric	Median: $81,300 Average: $94,600 Upper Tenth: $153,900	8,622	243
Columbia, MO	56% houses 22% apartments 3% condos 11% mobile homes	18% complexes One bedroom: $465/month	18% new 8% old Utilities: Gas/Electric	Median: $65,400 Average: $75,200 Upper Tenth: $124,900	6,855	161
Columbia, SC	64% houses 16% apartments 4% condos 11% mobile homes	20% complexes One bedroom: $540/month	17% new 6% old Utilities: Total Electric	Median: $72,300 Average: $86,400 Upper Tenth: $134,200	7,873	208
Columbus, GA–AL	65% houses 19% apartments 2% condos 8% mobile homes	17% complexes One bedroom: $490/month	13% new 9% old Utilities: Gas/Electric	Median: $56,300 Average: $66,400 Upper Tenth: $105,500	6,047	106
Columbus, OH	65% houses 23% apartments 4% condos 3% mobile homes	20% complexes One bedroom: $530/month	14% new 17% old Utilities: Gas/Electric	Median: $72,300 Average: $86,600 Upper Tenth: $134,000	7,893	209
Corpus Christi, TX	69% houses 17% apartments 4% condos 5% mobile homes	30% complexes One bedroom: $485/month	10% new 6% old Utilities: Gas/Electric	Median: $52,300 Average: $62,300 Upper Tenth: $97,300	5,677	77
✓ Cumberland, MD–WV	75% houses 10% apartments 7% mobile homes	26% complexes One bedroom: $410/month	7% new 36% old Utilities: Gas/Electric	Median: $46,700 Average: $53,300 Upper Tenth: $89,700	4,855	21
Dallas, TX	60% houses 27% apartments 4% condos 4% mobile homes	39% complexes One bedroom: $575/month	17% new 5% old Utilities: Gas/Electric	Median: $80,800 Average: $102,200 Upper Tenth: $144,300	9,315	256
Danbury, CT	56% houses 23% apartments 10% condos	29% complexes One bedroom: $675/month	9% new 28% old Utilities: Oil/Electric	Median: $146,200 Average: $158,700 Upper Tenth: $292,700	14,463	309
✓ Danville, VA	72% houses 10% apartments 1% condos 13% mobile homes	13% complexes One bedroom: $400/month	10% new 17% old Utilities: Gas/Electric	Median: $47,400 Average: $53,400 Upper Tenth: $92,000	4,869	22

Metro Area	Local Choices	Apartments	Houses	Prices	Places Rated Score	Places Rated Rank
✓ Davenport–Moline–Rock Island, IA–IL	73% houses 14% apartments 2% condos 4% mobile homes	26% complexes One bedroom: $440/month	4% new 28% old Utilities: Gas/Electric	Median: $49,100 Average: $56,300 Upper Tenth: $94,000	5,132	34
Dayton–Springfield, OH	73% houses 17% apartments 3% condos 2% mobile homes	20% complexes One bedroom: $515/month	8% new 20% old Utilities: Gas/Electric	Median: $64,500 Average: $75,000 Upper Tenth: $122,200	6,839	160
Daytona Beach, FL	65% houses 11% apartments 9% condos 12% mobile homes	28% complexes One bedroom: $585/month	25% new 4% old Utilities: Total Electric	Median: $71,400 Average: $84,400 Upper Tenth: $133,600	7,689	198
Decatur, AL	71% houses 10% apartments 1% condos 14% mobile homes	19% complexes One bedroom: $475/month	20% new 7% old Utilities: Total Electric	Median: $57,500 Average: $65,400 Upper Tenth: $110,800	5,957	99
✓ Decatur, IL	77% houses 13% apartments 1% condos 5% mobile homes	28% complexes One bedroom: $450/month	4% new 25% old Utilities: Gas/Electric	Median: $45,100 Average: $52,900 Upper Tenth: $84,800	4,821	19
Denver, CO	65% houses 22% apartments 10% condos 2% mobile homes	47% complexes One bedroom: $530/month	11% new 10% old Utilities: Gas/Electric	Median: $87,300 Average: $101,400 Upper Tenth: $165,500	9,237	254
Des Moines, IA	69% houses 19% apartments 2% condos 4% mobile homes	44% complexes One bedroom: $540/month	12% new 23% old Utilities: Gas/Electric	Median: $58,600 Average: $66,700 Upper Tenth: $112,800	6,080	109
Detroit, MI	72% houses 15% apartments 4% condos 3% mobile homes	35% complexes One bedroom: $585/month	9% new 17% old Utilities: Gas/Electric	Median: $66,900 Average: $82,100 Upper Tenth: $121,900	7,478	188
Dothan, AL	70% houses 11% apartments 15% mobile homes	13% complexes One bedroom: $435/month	15% new 6% old Utilities: Total Electric	Median: $51,100 Average: $60,800 Upper Tenth: $95,100	5,544	64
Dover, DE	64% houses 11% apartments 1% condos 21% mobile homes	19% complexes One bedroom: $560/month	18% new 12% old Utilities: Oil/Electric	Median: $81,000 Average: $92,100 Upper Tenth: $156,100	8,390	230
Dubuque, IA	70% houses 15% apartments 1% condos 5% mobile homes	15% complexes One bedroom: $410/month	6% new 36% old Utilities: Gas/Electric	Median: $53,400 Average: $59,400 Upper Tenth: $104,700	5,414	56
✓ Duluth–Superior, MN–WI	73% houses 13% apartments 6% mobile homes	44% complexes One bedroom: $430/month	5% new 38% old Utilities: Oil/Electric	Median: $41,000 Average: $47,400 Upper Tenth: $78,000	4,321	6
Dutchess County, NY	66% houses 17% apartments 5% condos 5% mobile homes	17% complexes One bedroom: $725/month	12% new 23% old Utilities: Oil/Electric	Median: $149,200 Average: $161,300 Upper Tenth: $299,700	14,696	310
Eau Claire, WI	70% houses 13% apartments 1% condos 6% mobile homes	23% complexes One bedroom: $430/month	10% new 27% old Utilities: Oil/Electric	Median: $50,200 Average: $56,700 Upper Tenth: $97,200	5,164	37
Edmonton, AB	61% houses 26% apartments 4% condos 2% mobile homes	25% high rise One bedroom: $520/month	10% new 6% old Utilities: Gas/Electric	Median: n.a. Average: $87,700 Upper Tenth: $140,300	7,991	216
El Paso, TX	66% houses 22% apartments 2% condos 6% mobile homes	37% complexes One bedroom: $470/month	12% new 7% old Utilities: Gas/Electric	Median: $56,700 Average: $67,300 Upper Tenth: $105,800	6,131	113
Elkhart–Goshen, IN	72% houses 13% apartments 1% condos 8% mobile homes	23% complexes One bedroom: $510/month	15% new 23% old Utilities: Gas/Electric	Median: $62,100 Average: $69,100 Upper Tenth: $121,700	6,301	124
Elmira, NY	66% houses 13% apartments 6% mobile homes	14% complexes One bedroom: $470/month	4% new 40% old Utilities: Gas/Electric	Median: $53,100 Average: $61,500 Upper Tenth: $100,900	5,603	68

Metro Area	Local Choices	Apartments	Houses	Prices	Places Rated Score	Places Rated Rank
✓ Enid, OK	83% houses 6% apartments 1% condos 4% mobile homes	34% complexes One bedroom: $430/month	3% new 21% old Utilities: Gas/Electric	Median: $37,800 Average: $45,400 Upper Tenth: $69,900	4,139	3
Erie, PA	65% houses 13% apartments 1% condos 7% mobile homes	24% complexes One bedroom: $450/month	8% new 32% old Utilities: Gas/Electric	Median: $53,600 Average: $62,600 Upper Tenth: $101,200	5,707	81
Eugene–Springfield, OR	67% houses 15% apartments 2% condos 12% mobile homes	34% complexes One bedroom: $540/month	7% new 10% old Utilities: Total Electric	Median: $65,500 Average: $75,300 Upper Tenth: $125,100	6,859	162
Evansville–Henderson, IN–KY	71% houses 15% apartments 1% condos 6% mobile homes	23% complexes One bedroom: $450/month	10% new 21% old Utilities: Gas/Electric	Median: $54,000 Average: $62,700 Upper Tenth: $102,400	5,714	82
Fargo–Moorhead, ND–MN	56% houses 30% apartments 4% condos 5% mobile homes	39% complexes One bedroom: $460/month	13% new 17% old Utilities: Total Electric	Median: $64,500 Average: $70,600 Upper Tenth: $128,200	6,433	139
Fayetteville, NC	68% houses 13% apartments 2% condos 14% mobile homes	6% complexes One bedroom: $525/month	18% new 4% old Utilities: Total Electric	Median: $62,900 Average: $70,700 Upper Tenth: $122,300	6,444	141
Fayetteville–Springdale–Rogers, AR	71% houses 12% apartments 1% condos 10% mobile homes	17% complexes One bedroom: $445/month	19% new 9% old Utilities: Gas/Electric	Median: $57,300 Average: $65,800 Upper Tenth: $109,600	5,994	102
Flint, MI	74% houses 13% apartments 1% condos 7% mobile homes	30% complexes One bedroom: $510/month	7% new 16% old Utilities: Gas/Electric	Median: $50,000 Average: $57,000 Upper Tenth: $96,100	5,195	42
Florence, AL	77% houses 8% apartments 9% mobile homes	20% complexes One bedroom: $400/month	10% new 9% old Utilities: Total Electric	Median: $49,500 Average: $57,900 Upper Tenth: $93,300	5,273	43
Florence, SC	67% houses 8% apartments 1% condos 19% mobile homes	14% complexes One bedroom: $500/month	17% new 7% old Utilities: Total Electric	Median: $54,600 Average: $65,300 Upper Tenth: $101,300	5,955	98
Fort Collins–Loveland, CO	68% houses 17% apartments 5% condos 7% mobile homes	24% complexes One bedroom: $510/month	17% new 9% old Utilities: Gas/Electric	Median: $84,000 Average: $95,400 Upper Tenth: $162,000	8,693	245
Fort Lauderdale, FL	44% houses 19% apartments 33% condos 5% mobile homes	43% complexes One bedroom: $700/month	17% new 1% old Utilities: Total Electric	Median: $91,300 Average: $117,600 Upper Tenth: $161,100	10,718	279
Fort Myers–Cape Coral, FL	52% houses 10% apartments 19% condos 17% mobile homes	27% complexes One bedroom: $620/month	25% new 2% old Utilities: Total Electric	Median: $83,700 Average: $110,100 Upper Tenth: $145,800	10,030	267
Fort Pierce–Port St. Lucie, FL	59% houses 6% apartments 18% condos 15% mobile homes	15% complexes One bedroom: $600/month	27% new 2% old Utilities: Total Electric	Median: $88,700 Average: $114,900 Upper Tenth: $156,000	10,468	273
✓ Fort Smith, AR–OK	72% houses 11% apartments 10% mobile homes	25% complexes One bedroom: $395/month	14% new 10% old Utilities: Gas/Electric	Median: $45,800 Average: $54,100 Upper Tenth: $85,700	4,930	26
Fort Walton Beach, FL	66% houses 11% apartments 11% condos 10% mobile homes	21% complexes One bedroom: $530/month	23% new 1% old Utilities: Total Electric	Median: $70,200 Average: $85,300 Upper Tenth: $128,800	7,775	202
Fort Wayne, IN	74% houses 13% apartments 1% condos 6% mobile homes	26% complexes One bedroom: $490/month	11% new 25% old Utilities: Gas/Electric	Median: $56,700 Average: $65,100 Upper Tenth: $108,400	5,935	96
Fort Worth–Arlington, TX	65% houses 21% apartments 2% condos 6% mobile homes	29% complexes One bedroom: $540/month	18% new 5% old Utilities: Total Electric	Median: $71,400 Average: $85,000 Upper Tenth: $132,900	7,750	201

Metro Area	Local Choices	Apartments	Houses	Prices	Places Rated Score	Places Rated Rank
Fresno, CA	67% houses 21% apartments 3% condos 6% mobile homes	32% complexes One bedroom: $550/month	17% new 8% old Utilities: Gas/Electric	Median: $83,200 Average: $98,500 Upper Tenth: $155,500	8,977	250
✓ Gadsden, AL	77% houses 8% apartments 10% mobile homes	21% complexes One bedroom: $420/month	9% new 12% old Utilities: Gas/Electric	Median: $42,400 Average: $49,700 Upper Tenth: $79,800	4,530	15
Gainesville, FL	52% houses 27% apartments 6% condos 13% mobile homes	27% complexes One bedroom: $520/month	18% new 4% old Utilities: Total Electric	Median: $65,500 Average: $76,200 Upper Tenth: $124,000	6,944	170
Galveston–Texas City, TX	70% houses 16% apartments 2% condos 6% mobile homes	42% complexes One bedroom: $520/month	12% new 10% old Utilities: Gas/Electric	Median: $59,300 Average: $70,800 Upper Tenth: $110,100	6,456	142
Gary, IN	72% houses 15% apartments 1% condos 3% mobile homes	27% complexes One bedroom: $525/month	7% new 17% old Utilities: Gas/Electric	Median: $57,400 Average: $67,500 Upper Tenth: $107,800	6,151	114
Glens Falls, NY	71% houses 9% apartments 1% condos 8% mobile homes	15% complexes One bedroom: $550/month	14% new 37% old Utilities: Oil/Electric	Median: $81,400 Average: $95,600 Upper Tenth: $153,000	8,712	246
Goldsboro, NC	66% houses 8% apartments 21% mobile homes	3% complexes One bedroom: $435/month	14% new 10% old Utilities: Total Electric	Median: $58,500 Average: $64,800 Upper Tenth: $115,100	5,904	91
Grand Forks, ND–MN	60% houses 24% apartments 3% condos 7% mobile homes	42% complexes One bedroom: $450/month	8% new 23% old Utilities: Total Electric	Median: $56,200 Average: $59,800 Upper Tenth: $114,400	5,448	58
Grand Rapids–Muskegon–Holland, MI	71% houses 13% apartments 3% condos 7% mobile homes	27% complexes One bedroom: $530/month	15% new 21% old Utilities: Gas/Electric	Median: $64,500 Average: $73,800 Upper Tenth: $123,700	6,728	155
Great Falls, MT	66% houses 16% apartments 2% condos 10% mobile homes	25% complexes One bedroom: $410/month	4% new 19% old Utilities: Gas/Electric	Median: $60,000 Average: $65,000 Upper Tenth: $120,300	5,925	93
Greeley, CO	64% houses 16% apartments 3% condos 13% mobile homes	24% complexes One bedroom: $445/month	9% new 18% old Utilities: Gas/Electric	Median: $67,500 Average: $75,600 Upper Tenth: $131,600	6,892	166
Green Bay, WI	68% houses 18% apartments 1% condos 2% mobile homes	27% complexes One bedroom: $475/month	15% new 17% old Utilities: Gas/Electric	Median: $62,200 Average: $69,600 Upper Tenth: $121,400	6,344	129
Greensboro–Winston-Salem–High Point, NC	69% houses 14% apartments 3% condos 10% mobile homes	14% complexes One bedroom: $520/month	17% new 10% old Utilities: Total Electric	Median: $70,800 Average: $84,100 Upper Tenth: $132,000	7,666	197
Greenville, NC	58% houses 15% apartments 4% condos 17% mobile homes	16% complexes One bedroom: $450/month	21% new 7% old Utilities: Total Electric	Median: $64,500 Average: $75,800 Upper Tenth: $121,200	6,911	167
Greenville–Spartanburg–Anderson, SC	69% houses 11% apartments 2% condos 14% mobile homes	21% complexes One bedroom: $500/month	15% new 10% old Utilities: Total Electric	Median: $58,700 Average: $69,400 Upper Tenth: $109,800	6,329	127
Hagerstown, MD	70% houses 16% apartments 2% condos 5% mobile homes	17% complexes One bedroom: $460/month	13% new 28% old Utilities: Oil/Electric	Median: $82,700 Average: $92,500 Upper Tenth: $161,500	8,434	233
Halifax, NS	56% houses 32% apartments 2% condos 3% mobile homes	27% high rise One bedroom: $600/month	17% new 16% old Utilities: Oil/Electric	Median: n.a. Average: $81,600 Upper Tenth: $248,000	7,438	187
Hamilton, ON	63% houses 26% apartments 4% condos	63% high rise One bedroom: $560/month	12% new 20% old Utilities: Gas/Electric	Median: n.a. Average: $120,800 Upper Tenth: $216,000	11,012	281

Metro Area	Local Choices	Apartments	Houses	Prices	Places Rated Score	Places Rated Rank
Hamilton–Middletown, OH	71% houses 16% apartments 5% condos 5% mobile homes	20% complexes One bedroom: $520/month	14% new 16% old Utilities: Gas/Electric	Median: $72,500 Average: $82,700 Upper Tenth: $139,400	7,539	192
Harrisburg–Lebanon–Carlisle, PA	71% houses 15% apartments 2% condos 6% mobile homes	22% complexes One bedroom: $520/month	12% new 27% old Utilities: Oil/Electric	Median: $75,200 Average: $83,000 Upper Tenth: $148,400	7,568	194
Hartford, CT	61% houses 23% apartments 10% condos 1% mobile homes	28% complexes One bedroom: $700/month	9% new 23% old Utilities: Oil/Electric	Median: $168,600 Average: $188,800 Upper Tenth: $328,900	17,202	321
Hickory–Morgantown, NC	69% houses 7% apartments 1% condos 18% mobile homes	9% complexes One bedroom: $475/month	17% new 9% old Utilities: Total Electric	Median: $56,600 Average: $67,000 Upper Tenth: $105,800	6,110	111
Honolulu, HI	55% houses 26% apartments 24% condos	51% complexes One bedroom: $820/month	8% new 6% old Utilities: Total Electric	Median: $281,500 Average: $310,100 Upper Tenth: $556,600	28,262	341
Houma, LA	70% houses 7% apartments 18% mobile homes	22% complexes One bedroom: $430/month	9% new 8% old Utilities: Gas/Electric	Median: $52,200 Average: $58,900 Upper Tenth: $101,200	5,368	51
Houston, TX	60% houses 25% apartments 6% condos 4% mobile homes	51% complexes One bedroom: $520/month	8% new 4% old Utilities: Gas/Electric	Median: $63,200 Average: $83,700 Upper Tenth: $109,600	7,625	196
✓ Huntington–Ashland, WV–KY–OH	73% houses 10% apartments 11% mobile homes	20% complexes One bedroom: $410/month	7% new 21% old Utilities: Gas/Electric	Median: $47,200 Average: $53,700 Upper Tenth: $90,900	4,894	23
Huntsville, AL	68% houses 17% apartments 8% mobile homes	17% complexes One bedroom: $520/month	23% new 4% old Utilities: Total Electric	Median: $73,400 Average: $85,500 Upper Tenth: $138,800	7,791	204
Indianapolis, IN	69% houses 20% apartments 3% condos 4% mobile homes	21% complexes One bedroom: $530/month	13% new 19% old Utilities: Gas/Electric	Median: $64,600 Average: $75,600 Upper Tenth: $121,800	6,889	165
Iowa City, IA	52% houses 32% apartments 4% condos 7% mobile homes	25% complexes One bedroom: $510/month	12% new 19% old Utilities: Gas/Electric	Median: $76,600 Average: $90,100 Upper Tenth: $143,800	8,211	225
✓ Jackson, MI	74% houses 11% apartments 1% condos 8% mobile homes	29% complexes One bedroom: $520/month	8% new 29% old Utilities: Gas/Electric	Median: $47,600 Average: $55,600 Upper Tenth: $89,800	5,069	33
Jackson, MS	69% houses 16% apartments 1% condos 8% mobile homes	26% complexes One bedroom: $525/month	16% new 6% old Utilities: Gas/Electric	Median: $59,500 Average: $70,600 Upper Tenth: $111,000	6,433	140
Jacksonville, FL	62% houses 18% apartments 5% condos 11% mobile homes	28% complexes One bedroom: $560/month	21% new 6% old Utilities: Total Electric	Median: $67,900 Average: $82,700 Upper Tenth: $124,400	7,535	191
Jacksonville, NC	61% houses 8% apartments 2% condos 26% mobile homes	8% complexes One bedroom: $490/month	22% new 3% old Utilities: Total Electric	Median: $62,200 Average: $69,100 Upper Tenth: $122,100	6,295	123
✓ Jamestown, NY	65% houses 10% apartments 1% condos 7% mobile homes	18% complexes One bedroom: $425/month	5% new 50% old Utilities: Gas/Electric	Median: $47,600 Average: $55,100 Upper Tenth: $90,400	5,023	30
Janesville–Beloit, WI	74% houses 11% apartments 1% condos 3% mobile homes	29% complexes One bedroom: $460/month	7% new 30% old Utilities: Gas/Electric	Median: $52,500 Average: $57,000 Upper Tenth: $105,100	5,191	39
Johnson City–Kingsport–Bristol, TN–VA	72% houses 10% apartments 1% condos 13% mobile homes	15% complexes One bedroom: $400/month	12% new 13% old Utilities: Total Electric	Median: $52,200 Average: $59,900 Upper Tenth: $99,900	5,456	59

Metro Area	Local Choices	Apartments	Houses	Prices	Places Rated Score	Places Rated Rank
✓ Johnstown, PA	75% houses 8% apartments 1% condos 8% mobile homes	26% complexes One bedroom: $400/month	5% new 40% old Utilities: Gas/Electric	Median: $40,600 Average: $47,300 Upper Tenth: $76,800	4,312	4
✓ Joplin, MO	79% houses 7% apartments 9% mobile homes	15% complexes One bedroom: $400/month	10% new 26% old Utilities: Gas/Electric	Median: $39,500 Average: $47,300 Upper Tenth: $73,200	4,314	5
Kalamazoo–Battle Creek, MI	69% houses 16% apartments 2% condos 7% mobile homes	33% complexes One bedroom: $515/month	9% new 24% old Utilities: Gas/Electric	Median: $53,600 Average: $62,200 Upper Tenth: $101,700	5,672	75
Kankakee, IL	72% houses 12% apartments 7% mobile homes	16% complexes One bedroom: $450/month	6% new 24% old Utilities: Gas/Electric	Median: $54,300 Average: $61,100 Upper Tenth: $105,500	5,570	65
Kansas City, MO–KS	72% houses 18% apartments 2% condos 3% mobile homes	27% complexes One bedroom: $550/month	15% new 16% old Utilities: Gas/Electric	Median: $66,400 Average: $76,800 Upper Tenth: $126,300	7,003	176
Kenosha, WI	68% houses 15% apartments 1% condos 3% mobile homes	31% complexes One bedroom: $500/month	11% new 26% old Utilities: Gas/Electric	Median: $64,600 Average: $74,000 Upper Tenth: $123,800	6,743	156
Killeen–Temple, TX	63% houses 18% apartments 1% condos 8% mobile homes	26% complexes One bedroom: $465/month	17% new 5% old Utilities: Total Electric	Median: $56,800 Average: $62,100 Upper Tenth: $113,000	5,664	73
Kitchener, ON	62% houses 27% apartments 3% condos	36% high rise One bedroom: $520/month	19% new 15% old Utilities: Gas/Electric	Median: n.a. Average: $116,000 Upper Tenth: $212,000	10,573	277
Knoxville, TN	70% houses 15% apartments 2% condos 9% mobile homes	27% complexes One bedroom: $460/month	14% new 10% old Utilities: Total Electric	Median: $60,800 Average: $72,300 Upper Tenth: $113,300	6,587	150
Kokomo, IN	78% houses 11% apartments 1% condos 6% mobile homes	19% complexes One bedroom: $435/month	6% new 27% old Utilities: Gas/Electric	Median: $51,300 Average: $58,300 Upper Tenth: $98,900	5,313	47
La Crosse, WI–MN	65% houses 16% apartments 1% condos 6% mobile homes	30% complexes One bedroom: $445/month	11% new 26% old Utilities: Gas/Electric	Median: $57,100 Average: $63,200 Upper Tenth: $112,400	5,762	85
Lafayette, IN	64% houses 23% apartments 2% condos 5% mobile homes	22% complexes One bedroom: $485/month	12% new 24% old Utilities: Gas/Electric	Median: $59,700 Average: $69,600 Upper Tenth: $112,800	6,343	128
Lafayette, LA	70% houses 11% apartments 2% condos 13% mobile homes	30% complexes One bedroom: $410/month	8% new 8% old Utilities: Gas/Electric	Median: $51,100 Average: $59,600 Upper Tenth: $96,500	5,433	57
Lake Charles, LA	70% houses 9% apartments 1% condos 15% mobile homes	25% complexes One bedroom: $465/month	8% new 7% old Utilities: Gas/Electric	Median: $54,300 Average: $61,900 Upper Tenth: $104,400	5,640	70
Lake County, IL	75% houses 15% apartments 7% condos 2% mobile homes	31% complexes One bedroom: $670/month	21% new 12% old Utilities: Gas/Electric	Median: $136,100 Average: $181,500 Upper Tenth: $235,100	16,545	320
Lakeland–Winter Haven, FL	56% houses 8% apartments 3% condos 27% mobile homes	23% complexes One bedroom: $500/month	19% new 6% old Utilities: Total Electric	Median: $60,700 Average: $71,800 Upper Tenth: $113,500	6,543	148
Lancaster, PA	73% houses 14% apartments 1% condos 5% mobile homes	15% complexes One bedroom: $550/month	16% new 29% old Utilities: Oil/Electric	Median: $89,300 Average: $100,300 Upper Tenth: $173,800	9,140	252
Lansing–East Lansing, MI	68% houses 20% apartments 3% condos 5% mobile homes	30% complexes One bedroom: $530/month	11% new 21% old Utilities: Gas/Electric	Median: $63,900 Average: $72,900 Upper Tenth: $122,800	6,645	151

Metro Area	Local Choices	Apartments	Houses	Prices	Places Rated Score	Places Rated Rank
Laredo, TX	72% houses 12% apartments 3% condos 10% mobile homes	45% complexes One bedroom: $475/month	22% new 8% old Utilities: Gas/Electric	Median: $48,800 Average: $59,200 Upper Tenth: $89,600	5,396	54
Las Cruces, NM	57% houses 13% apartments 1% condos 25% mobile homes	30% complexes One bedroom: $475/month	21% new 7% old Utilities: Gas/Electric	Median: $66,900 Average: $76,500 Upper Tenth: $128,300	6,969	175
Las Vegas, NV–AZ	48% houses 28% apartments 7% condos 15% mobile homes	22% complexes One bedroom: $625/month	29% new 1% old Utilities: Total Electric	Median: $90,500 Average: $107,700 Upper Tenth: $168,500	9,818	265
Lawrence, KS	58% houses 27% apartments 3% condos 6% mobile homes	29% complexes One bedroom: $515/month	21% new 17% old Utilities: Gas/Electric	Median: $67,500 Average: $77,200 Upper Tenth: $129,500	7,037	177
Lawton, OK	74% houses 11% apartments 1% condos 6% mobile homes	19% complexes One bedroom: $460/month	9% new 7% old Utilities: Gas/Electric	Median: $53,500 Average: $59,200 Upper Tenth: $105,400	5,399	55
Lewiston–Auburn, ME	50% houses 24% apartments 1% condos 9% mobile homes	14% complexes One bedroom: $520/month	11% new 39% old Utilities: Oil/Electric	Median: $86,400 Average: $93,900 Upper Tenth: $172,800	8,555	237
Lexington, KY	63% houses 22% apartments 3% condos 5% mobile homes	25% complexes One bedroom: $500/month	16% new 13% old Utilities: Gas/Electric	Median: $67,600 Average: $81,500 Upper Tenth: $124,700	7,430	186
Lima, OH	76% houses 10% apartments 1% condos 6% mobile homes	26% complexes One bedroom: $450/month	7% new 29% old Utilities: Gas/Electric	Median: $54,000 Average: $59,900 Upper Tenth: $106,100	5,458	60
Lincoln, NE	66% houses 22% apartments 3% condos 3% mobile homes	28% complexes One bedroom: $475/month	11% new 21% old Utilities: Gas/Electric	Median: $61,800 Average: $69,800 Upper Tenth: $119,700	6,362	132
Little Rock–North Little Rock, AR	67% houses 14% apartments 1% condos 11% mobile homes	32% complexes One bedroom: $520/month	15% new 7% old Utilities: Gas/Electric	Median: $59,400 Average: $69,900 Upper Tenth: $111,500	6,368	133
London, ON	59% houses 28% apartments 2% condos	55% high rise One bedroom: $600/month	16% new 20% old Utilities: Gas/Electric	Median: n.a. Average: $110,700 Upper Tenth: $256,000	10,085	269
Long Island, NY	82% houses 7% apartments 4% condos 1% mobile homes	40% complexes One bedroom: $870/month	6% new 16% old Utilities: Oil/Electric	Median: $186,900 Average: $218,900 Upper Tenth: $352,200	19,951	326
Longview–Marshall, TX	70% houses 10% apartments 1% condos 13% mobile homes	27% complexes One bedroom: $435/month	9% new 9% old Utilities: Gas/Electric	Median: $50,800 Average: $57,000 Upper Tenth: $98,900	5,194	40
Los Angeles–Long Beach, CA	55% houses 33% apartments 8% condos 2% mobile homes	39% complexes One bedroom: $780/month	11% new 13% old Utilities: Gas/Electric	Median: $223,800 Average: $268,000 Upper Tenth: $414,900	24,421	336
Louisville, KY–IN	69% houses 20% apartments 3% condos 4% mobile homes	21% complexes One bedroom: $475/month	9% new 17% old Utilities: Gas/Electric	Median: $56,100 Average: $68,000 Upper Tenth: $103,100	6,197	117
Lubbock, TX	67% houses 17% apartments 1% condos 5% mobile homes	54% complexes One bedroom: $485/month	9% new 4% old Utilities: Gas/Electric	Median: $53,700 Average: $62,200 Upper Tenth: $102,000	5,672	75
Lynchburg, VA	71% houses 10% apartments 2% condos 12% mobile homes	16% complexes One bedroom: $490/month	15% new 13% old Utilities: Total Electric	Median: $62,200 Average: $71,100 Upper Tenth: $119,400	6,482	145
Macon, GA	67% houses 14% apartments 1% condos 9% mobile homes	14% complexes One bedroom: $490/month	17% new 8% old Utilities: Gas/Electric	Median: $58,500 Average: $67,600 Upper Tenth: $111,300	6,164	115

Metro Area	Local Choices	Apartments	Houses	Prices	Places Rated Score	Places Rated Rank
Madison, WI	58% houses 31% apartments 3% condos 2% mobile homes	37% complexes One bedroom: $575/month	14% new 19% old Utilities: Gas/Electric	Median: $77,900 Average: $89,600 Upper Tenth: $148,800	8,164	222
Manchester–Nashua, NH	58% houses 22% apartments 9% condos 2% mobile homes	32% complexes One bedroom: $675/month	18% new 25% old Utilities: Oil/Electric	Median: $137,100 Average: $150,200 Upper Tenth: $272,300	13,692	300
✓ Mansfield, OH	74% houses 11% apartments 5% mobile homes	9% complexes One bedroom: $430/month	5% new 27% old Utilities: Gas/Electric	Median: $49,200 Average: $54,300 Upper Tenth: $97,100	4,950	28
✓ McAllen–Edinburg–Mission, TX	64% houses 9% apartments 2% condos 19% mobile homes	23% complexes One bedroom: $460/month	20% new 4% old Utilities: Total Electric	Median: $35,600 Average: $45,000 Upper Tenth: $63,600	4,102	1
Medford–Ashland, OR	66% houses 11% apartments 1% condos 17% mobile homes	24% complexes One bedroom: $510/month	15% new 12% old Utilities: Total Electric	Median: $74,800 Average: $89,200 Upper Tenth: $139,100	8,126	219
Melbourne–Titusville–Palm Bay, FL	62% houses 14% apartments 12% condos 12% mobile homes	31% complexes One bedroom: $575/month	25% new 1% old Utilities: Total Electric	Median: $74,600 Average: $93,900 Upper Tenth: $133,600	8,561	238
Memphis, TN–AR–MS	68% houses 20% apartments 3% condos 3% mobile homes	23% complexes One bedroom: $520/month	15% new 8% old Utilities: Gas/Electric	Median: $64,000 Average: $79,100 Upper Tenth: $116,000	7,205	181
Merced, CA	72% houses 15% apartments 1% condos 7% mobile homes	16% complexes One bedroom: $540/month	18% new 8% old Utilities: Gas/Electric	Median: $90,100 Average: $102,600 Upper Tenth: $173,400	9,349	258
Miami, FL	50% houses 28% apartments 20% condos 2% mobile homes	57% complexes One bedroom: $670/month	12% new 5% old Utilities: Total Electric	Median: $86,000 Average: $111,500 Upper Tenth: $151,100	10,164	270
Milwaukee–Waukesha, WI	57% houses 22% apartments 3% condos 1% mobile homes	39% complexes One bedroom: $565/month	8% new 27% old Utilities: Gas/Electric	Median: $77,000 Average: $88,700 Upper Tenth: $146,900	8,079	218
Minneapolis–St. Paul, MN–WI	66% houses 22% apartments 5% condos 2% mobile homes	58% complexes One bedroom: $610/month	17% new 20% old Utilities: Gas/Electric	Median: $87,900 Average: $102,200 Upper Tenth: $166,500	9,316	257
Mobile, AL	70% houses 12% apartments 4% condos 10% mobile homes	22% complexes One bedroom: $465/month	12% new 7% old Utilities: Gas/Electric	Median: $55,200 Average: $66,000 Upper Tenth: $102,400	6,015	105
Modesto, CA	74% houses 14% apartments 3% condos 7% mobile homes	40% complexes One bedroom: $575/month	23% new 8% old Utilities: Gas/Electric	Median: $123,000 Average: $135,000 Upper Tenth: $243,900	12,302	291
Monmouth–Ocean, NJ	77% houses 10% apartments 10% condos 2% mobile homes	33% complexes One bedroom: $750/month	15% new 13% old Utilities: Gas/Electric	Median: $152,700 Average: $176,700 Upper Tenth: $290,300	16,107	319
Monroe, LA	70% houses 14% apartments 1% condos 10% mobile homes	23% complexes One bedroom: $450/month	10% new 7% old Utilities: Gas/Electric	Median: $52,300 Average: $61,600 Upper Tenth: $98,100	5,616	69
Montgomery, AL	71% houses 14% apartments 1% condos 9% mobile homes	20% complexes One bedroom: $500/month	14% new 9% old Utilities: Gas/Electric	Median: $60,600 Average: $72,100 Upper Tenth: $112,800	6,571	149
Montreal, PQ	35% houses 58% apartments 2% condos	14% high rise One bedroom: $600/month	13% new 16% old Utilities: Total Electric	Median: n.a. Average: $91,000 Upper Tenth: $236,000	8,289	228
✓ Muncie, IN	73% houses 13% apartments 1% condos 6% mobile homes	15% complexes One bedroom: $450/month	6% new 25% old Utilities: Gas/Electric	Median: $41,800 Average: $49,400 Upper Tenth: $78,200	4,501	13

Metro Area	Local Choices	Apartments	Houses	Prices	Places Rated Score	Places Rated Rank
Myrtle Beach, SC	45% houses 8% apartments 21% condos 21% mobile homes	8% complexes One bedroom: $515/month	9% new 3% old Utilities: Total Electric	Median: $75,500 Average: $90,700 Upper Tenth: $139,600	8,270	226
Naples, FL	43% houses 10% apartments 37% condos 11% mobile homes	23% complexes One bedroom: $685/month	29% new 1% old Utilities: Total Electric	Median: $121,400 Average: $173,700 Upper Tenth: $201,500	15,830	317
Nashville, TN	65% houses 19% apartments 5% condos 5% mobile homes	31% complexes One bedroom: $540/month	22% new 8% old Utilities: Total Electric	Median: $78,900 Average: $93,800 Upper Tenth: $147,000	8,545	236
New Bedford–Fall River–Attleboro, MA	51% houses 27% apartments 4% condos 2% mobile homes	15% complexes One bedroom: $600/month	11% new 40% old Utilities: Gas/Electric	Median: $141,200 Average: $151,600 Upper Tenth: $285,400	13,813	301
New Haven–Meriden, CT	56% houses 23% apartments 10% condos	29% complexes One bedroom: $675/month	9% new 28% old Utilities: Oil/Electric	Median: $146,700 Average: $168,200 Upper Tenth: $284,000	15,329	313
New London–Norwich, CT–RI	65% houses 16% apartments 4% condos 3% mobile homes	18% complexes One bedroom: $685/month	10% new 30% old Utilities: Oil/Electric	Median: $148,900 Average: $171,600 Upper Tenth: $128,900	15,638	315
New Orleans, LA	63% houses 18% apartments 2% condos 4% mobile homes	32% complexes One bedroom: $525/month	8% new 16% old Utilities: Gas/Electric	Median: $69,400 Average: $82,900 Upper Tenth: $280,900	7,552	193
New York, NY	20% houses 53% apartments 8% condos	68% complexes One bedroom: $725/month	4% new 39% old Utilities: Oil/Electric	Median: $215,600 Average: $236,600 Upper Tenth: $427,700	21,561	332
Newark–Jersey City, NJ	41% houses 33% apartments 5% condos	38% complexes One bedroom: $720/month	5% new 35% old Utilities: Gas/Electric	Median: $194,300 Average: $219,900 Upper Tenth: $375,900	20,044	327
Norfolk–Virginia Beach–Newport News, VA–NC	67% houses 21% apartments 4% condos 4% mobile homes	16% complexes One bedroom: $585/month	20% new 7% old Utilities: Total Electric	Median: $86,800 Average: $101,700 Upper Tenth: $163,500	9,269	255
Northern New Jersey, NJ	57% houses 19% apartments 6% condos	35% complexes One bedroom: $780/month	6% new 27% old Utilities: Gas/Electric	Median: $207,400 Average: $236,300 Upper Tenth: $399,100	21,539	331
Oakland, CA	64% houses 24% apartments 8% condos 2% mobile homes	40% complexes One bedroom: $750/month	13% new 16% old Utilities: Gas/Electric	Median: $221,700 Average: $249,200 Upper Tenth: $431,200	22,707	335
Ocala, FL	58% houses 7% apartments 3% condos 31% mobile homes	13% complexes One bedroom: $510/month	25% new 3% old Utilities: Total Electric	Median: $61,800 Average: $71,800 Upper Tenth: $117,100	6,542	147
Odessa–Midland, TX	65% houses 16% apartments 2% condos 11% mobile homes	43% complexes One bedroom: $400/month	6% new 2% old Utilities: Gas/Electric	Median: $52,600 Average: $62,300 Upper Tenth: $98,300	5,678	78
Oklahoma City, OK	71% houses 15% apartments 2% condos 5% mobile homes	30% complexes One bedroom: $465/month	9% new 9% old Utilities: Gas/Electric	Median: $53,600 Average: $63,500 Upper Tenth: $100,100	5,784	89
Olympia, WA	64% houses 14% apartments 1% condos 15% mobile homes	27% complexes One bedroom: $560/month	19% new 9% old Utilities: Total Electric	Median: $79,800 Average: $92,400 Upper Tenth: $151,600	8,418	231
Omaha, NE–IA	71% houses 20% apartments 1% condos 3% mobile homes	32% complexes One bedroom: $515/month	10% new 22% old Utilities: Gas/Electric	Median: $58,200 Average: $66,800 Upper Tenth: $111,300	6,089	110
Orange County, CA	61% houses 25% apartments 16% condos 4% mobile homes	38% complexes One bedroom: $885/month	14% new 3% old Utilities: Gas/Electric	Median: $250,300 Average: $282,800 Upper Tenth: $484,900	25,772	340

Metro Area	Local Choices	Apartments	Houses	Prices	Places Rated Score	Places Rated Rank
Orange County, NY	66% houses 15% apartments 5% condos 4% mobile homes	13% complexes One bedroom: $700/month	15% new 28% old Utilities: Gas/Electric	Median: $141,200 Average: $153,500 Upper Tenth: $282,300	13,985	303
Orlando, FL	61% houses 18% apartments 7% condos 12% mobile homes	26% complexes One bedroom: $620/month	28% new 3% old Utilities: Total Electric	Median: $81,600 Average: $99,800 Upper Tenth: $149,000	9,093	251
Oshawa, ON	73% houses 18% apartments 3% condos	45% high rise One bedroom: $600/month	25% new 12% old Utilities: Gas/Electric	Median: n.a. Average: $116,000 Upper Tenth: $188,000	10,572	276
Ottawa–Hull, ON–PQ	51% houses 32% apartments 6% condos	50% high rise One bedroom: $620/month	18% new 12% old Utilities: Gas/Electric	Median: n.a. Average: $115,100 Upper Tenth: $240,000	10,489	274
Owensboro, KY	73% houses 14% apartments 1% condos 6% mobile homes	19% complexes One bedroom: $400/month	10% new 12% old Utilities: Gas/Electric	Median: $47,600 Average: $57,000 Upper Tenth: $88,200	5,194	40
Panama City, FL	57% houses 9% apartments 10% condos 17% mobile homes	10% complexes One bedroom: $475/month	25% new 3% old Utilities: Total Electric	Median: $61,000 Average: $73,100 Upper Tenth: $113,000	6,666	152
Parkersburg–Marietta, WV–OH	75% houses 9% apartments 10% mobile homes	21% complexes One bedroom: $425/month	7% new 24% old Utilities: Gas/Electric	Median: $50,500 Average: $56,600 Upper Tenth: $98,400	5,159	36
Pensacola, FL	69% houses 11% apartments 5% condos 11% mobile homes	22% complexes One bedroom: $520/month	18% new 5% old Utilities: Total Electric	Median: $59,100 Average: $70,400 Upper Tenth: $110,000	6,417	136
Peoria–Pekin, IL	77% houses 14% apartments 1% condos 3% mobile homes	28% complexes One bedroom: $470/month	4% new 22% old Utilities: Gas/Electric	Median: $49,300 Average: $58,700 Upper Tenth: $91,700	5,350	49
Philadelphia, PA–NJ	72% houses 16% apartments 4% condos 1% mobile homes	39% complexes One bedroom: $675/month	9% new 31% old Utilities: Gas/Electric	Median: $117,600 Average: $141,100 Upper Tenth: $225,000	12,859	297
Phoenix–Mesa, AZ	60% houses 20% apartments 8% condos 11% mobile homes	48% complexes One bedroom: $585/month	22% new 2% old Utilities: Total Electric	Median: $83,600 Average: $101,200 Upper Tenth: $153,800	9,218	253
✓ Pine Bluff, AR	75% houses 9% apartments 11% mobile homes	30% complexes One bedroom: $430/month	8% new 8% old Utilities: Gas/Electric	Median: $43,100 Average: $49,600 Upper Tenth: $82,300	4,523	14
Pittsburgh, PA	72% houses 14% apartments 2% condos 4% mobile homes	33% complexes One bedroom: $515/month	6% new 33% old Utilities: Gas/Electric	Median: $78,200 Average: $87,300 Upper Tenth: $139,700	7,956	214
Pittsfield, MA	61% houses 17% apartments 2% condos 3% mobile homes	16% complexes One bedroom: $560/month	8% new 45% old Utilities: Oil/Electric	Median: $114,500 Average: $132,600 Upper Tenth: $217,600	12,087	288
Portland, ME	64% houses 19% apartments 4% condos 4% mobile homes	22% complexes One bedroom: $625/month	13% new 33% old Utilities: Oil/Electric	Median: $117,800 Average: $139,900 Upper Tenth: $219,700	12,749	296
Portland, OR	67% houses 21% apartments 3% condos 5% mobile homes	37% complexes One bedroom: $570/month	12% new 20% old Utilities: Total Electric	Median: $79,500 Average: $97,700 Upper Tenth: $156,300	8,904	248
Portsmouth–Dover–Rochester, NH	63% houses 15% apartments 7% condos 9% mobile homes	27% complexes One bedroom: $645/month	20% new 21% old Utilities: Oil/Electric	Median: $141,200 Average: $157,000 Upper Tenth: $277,100	14,305	306
Providence–Warwick–Cranston, RI	55% houses 24% apartments 3% condos 1% mobile homes	25% complexes One bedroom: $615/month	10% new 34% old Utilities: Oil/Electric	Median: $131,200 Average: $149,100 Upper Tenth: $253,000	13,588	299

Metro Area	Local Choices	Apartments	Houses	Prices	Places Rated Score	Places Rated Rank
Provo–Orem, UT	67% houses 19% apartments 4% condos 4% mobile homes	26% complexes One bedroom: $435/month	14% new 12% old Utilities: Gas/Electric	Median: $69,900 Average: $81,100 Upper Tenth: $132,600	7,393	185
✓ Pueblo, CO	75% houses 13% apartments 1% condos 7% mobile homes	40% complexes One bedroom: $425/month	6% new 23% old Utilities: Gas/Electric	Median: $50,600 Average: $56,300 Upper Tenth: $99,200	5,134	35
Punta Gorda, FL	66% houses 5% apartments 12% condos 16% mobile homes	33% complexes One bedroom: $640/month	28% new 1% old Utilities: Total Electric	Median: $76,400 Average: $94,200 Upper Tenth: $138,700	8,589	240
Quebec City, PQ	47% houses 44% apartments 2% condos 1% mobile homes	11% high rise One bedroom: $720/month	18% new 15% old Utilities: Total Electric	Median: n.a. Average: $68,900 Upper Tenth: $168,000	6,281	122
Racine, WI	68% houses 14% apartments 2% condos 1% mobile homes	32% complexes One bedroom: $475/month	7% new 29% old Utilities: Gas/Electric	Median: $63,500 Average: $74,000 Upper Tenth: $120,100	6,744	157
Raleigh–Durham–Chapel Hill, NC	62% houses 20% apartments 5% condos 10% mobile homes	15% complexes One bedroom: $575/month	25% new 8% old Utilities: Total Electric	Median: $88,400 Average: $104,700 Upper Tenth: $165,200	9,541	263
Rapid City, SD	63% houses 14% apartments 2% condos 16% mobile homes	41% complexes One bedroom: $480/month	12% new 9% old Utilities: Gas/Electric	Median: $56,400 Average: $62,800 Upper Tenth: $110,500	5,725	83
Reading, PA	76% houses 12% apartments 2% condos 4% mobile homes	20% complexes One bedroom: $530/month	11% new 39% old Utilities: Oil/Electric	Median: $80,900 Average: $89,400 Upper Tenth: $159,500	8,145	220
Redding, CA	65% houses 13% apartments 1% condos 19% mobile homes	20% complexes One bedroom: $540/month	20% new 5% old Utilities: Gas/Electric	Median: $91,000 Average: $103,900 Upper Tenth: $174,800	9,467	262
Regina, SK	72% houses 22% apartments 2% condos 1% mobile homes	22% high rise One bedroom: $440/month	8% new 13% old Utilities: Gas/Electric	Median: n.a. Average: $57,900 Upper Tenth: $180,000	5,276	44
Reno, NV	53% houses 26% apartments 9% condos 11% mobile homes	33% complexes One bedroom: $600/month	20% new 4% old Utilities: Gas/Electric	Median: $110,900 Average: $137,000 Upper Tenth: $201,200	12,488	294
Richland–Kennewick–Pasco, WA	61% houses 17% apartments 2% condos 13% mobile homes	33% complexes One bedroom: $450/month	6% new 4% old Utilities: Total Electric	Median: $64,000 Average: $70,900 Upper Tenth: $125,900	6,460	143
Richmond–Petersburg, VA	71% houses 19% apartments 3% condos 2% mobile homes	18% complexes One bedroom: $600/month	17% new 12% old Utilities: Total Electric	Median: $78,400 Average: $94,500 Upper Tenth: $144,600	8,612	242
Riverside–San Bernardino, CA	68% houses 15% apartments 6% condos 11% mobile homes	31% complexes One bedroom: $660/month	29% new 4% old Utilities: Gas/Electric	Median: $133,100 Average: $152,800 Upper Tenth: $254,600	13,923	302
Roanoke, VA	71% houses 17% apartments 2% condos 3% mobile homes	14% complexes One bedroom: $465/month	11% new 15% old Utilities: Gas/Electric	Median: $67,600 Average: $78,700 Upper Tenth: $127,900	7,175	179
Rochester, MN	68% houses 18% apartments 5% condos 6% mobile homes	36% complexes One bedroom: $535/month	16% new 15% old Utilities: Gas/Electric	Median: $72,100 Average: $84,600 Upper Tenth: $135,600	7,712	199
Rochester, NY	67% houses 17% apartments 2% condos 4% mobile homes	21% complexes One bedroom: $560/month	9% new 34% old Utilities: Gas/Electric	Median: $84,600 Average: $96,300 Upper Tenth: $162,900	8,780	247
Rockford, IL	71% houses 14% apartments 1% condos 3% mobile homes	27% complexes One bedroom: $490/month	10% new 23% old Utilities: Gas/Electric	Median: $60,200 Average: $68,400 Upper Tenth: $116,100	6,230	120

Metro Area	Local Choices	Apartments	Houses	Prices	Places Rated Score	Places Rated Rank
Rocky Mount, NC	68% houses 10% apartments 1% condos 15% mobile homes	7% complexes One bedroom: $470/month	16% new 12% old Utilities: Total Electric	Median: $55,900 Average: $63,400 Upper Tenth: $107,900	5,780	87
Sacramento, CA	70% houses 19% apartments 4% condos 5% mobile homes	39% complexes One bedroom: $625/month	19% new 6% old Utilities: Gas/Electric	Median: $137,300 Average: $157,200 Upper Tenth: $263,200	14,324	307
Saginaw–Bay City–Midland, MI	76% houses 11% apartments 1% condos 6% mobile homes	26% complexes One bedroom: $480/month	6% new 23% old Utilities: Gas/Electric	Median: $49,100 Average: $56,900 Upper Tenth: $93,200	5,187	38
St. Catharines–Niagara, ON	76% houses 17% apartments 1% condos 1% mobile homes	32% high rise One bedroom: $520/month	12% new 24% old Utilities: Gas/Electric	Median: n.a. Average: $103,200 Upper Tenth: $240,000	9,405	260
St. Cloud, MN	68% houses 19% apartments 1% condos 6% mobile homes	49% complexes One bedroom: $500/month	17% new 19% old Utilities: Gas/Electric	Median: $61,200 Average: $65,600 Upper Tenth: $123,800	5,979	101
Saint John, NB	57% houses 27% apartments 1% condos 4% mobile homes	12% high rise One bedroom: $560/month	10% new 27% old Utilities: Total Electric	Median: n.a. Average: $65,300 Upper Tenth: $184,000	5,946	97
St. John's, NF	64% houses 13% apartments	5% high rise One bedroom: $680/month	18% new 15% old Utilities: Oil/Electric	Median: n.a. Average: $73,600 Upper Tenth: $212,800	6,705	154
✓ St. Joseph, MO	74% houses 11% apartments 1% condos 6% mobile homes	20% complexes One bedroom: $410/month	6% new 37% old Utilities: Gas/Electric	Median: $40,900 Average: $48,700 Upper Tenth: $76,100	4,434	12
St. Louis, MO–IL	67% houses 17% apartments 3% condos 5% mobile homes	22% complexes One bedroom: $525/month	12% new 21% old Utilities: Gas/Electric	Median: $70,500 Average: $85,700 Upper Tenth: $129,300	7,810	205
Salem, OR	68% houses 16% apartments 1% condos 10% mobile homes	26% complexes One bedroom: $500/month	11% new 12% old Utilities: Total Electric	Median: $60,700 Average: $68,300 Upper Tenth: $117,900	6,226	119
Salinas, CA	67% houses 21% apartments 5% condos 5% mobile homes	27% complexes One bedroom: $750/month	15% new 9% old Utilities: Gas/Electric	Median: $196,300 Average: $239,200 Upper Tenth: $359,500	21,801	334
Salt Lake City–Ogden, UT	69% houses 18% apartments 6% condos 3% mobile homes	32% complexes One bedroom: $470/month	14% new 11% old Utilities: Gas/Electric	Median: $70,700 Average: $82,700 Upper Tenth: $133,300	7,534	190
San Angelo, TX	72% houses 16% apartments 2% condos 6% mobile homes	48% complexes One bedroom: $465/month	9% new 9% old Utilities: Gas/Electric	Median: $49,700 Average: $58,000 Upper Tenth: $93,900	5,283	45
San Antonio, TX	67% houses 20% apartments 3% condos 5% mobile homes	33% complexes One bedroom: $500/month	13% new 8% old Utilities: Gas/Electric	Median: $56,500 Average: $69,900 Upper Tenth: $102,400	6,373	134
San Diego, CA	58% houses 27% apartments 12% condos 5% mobile homes	38% complexes One bedroom: $720/month	19% new 5% old Utilities: Gas/Electric	Median: $186,200 Average: $223,000 Upper Tenth: $345,200	20,322	328
San Francisco, CA	50% houses 34% apartments 7% condos 1% mobile homes	36% complexes One bedroom: $855/month	5% new 32% old Utilities: Gas/Electric	Median: $329,800 Average: $353,400 Upper Tenth: $667,700	32,211	343
San Jose, CA	65% houses 24% apartments 10% condos 4% mobile homes	42% complexes One bedroom: $875/month	10% new 6% old Utilities: Gas/Electric	Median: $287,700 Average: $322,500 Upper Tenth: $560,900	29,395	342
San Luis Obispo–Atascadero–Paso Robles, CA	68% houses 14% apartments 4% condos 12% mobile homes	23% complexes One bedroom: $660/month	21% new 7% old Utilities: Gas/Electric	Median: $213,200 Average: $238,300 Upper Tenth: $416,600	21,719	333

Metro Area	Local Choices	Apartments	Houses	Prices	Places Rated Score	Places Rated Rank
Santa Barbara–Santa Maria–Lompoc, CA	63% houses 22% apartments 7% condos 6% mobile homes	27% complexes One bedroom: $800/month	13% new 10% old Utilities: Gas/Electric	Median: $249,200 Average: $280,100 Upper Tenth: $484,700	25,525	338
Santa Cruz–Watsonville, CA	72% houses 13% apartments 7% condos 7% mobile homes	26% complexes One bedroom: $785/month	10% new 14% old Utilities: Gas/Electric	Median: $255,400 Average: $280,800 Upper Tenth: $505,900	25,594	339
Santa Fe, NM	66% houses 12% apartments 4% condos 14% mobile homes	35% complexes One bedroom: $615/month	18% new 9% old Utilities: Gas/Electric	Median: $107,300 Average: $142,500 Upper Tenth: $185,800	12,987	298
Santa Rosa, CA	74% houses 13% apartments 5% condos 7% mobile homes	33% complexes One bedroom: $720/month	19% new 11% old Utilities: Gas/Electric	Median: $200,600 Average: $227,500 Upper Tenth: $387,400	20,729	330
Sarasota–Bradenton, FL	55% houses 9% apartments 20% condos 17% mobile homes	32% complexes One bedroom: $625/month	17% new 3% old Utilities: Total Electric	Median: $84,000 Average: $109,600 Upper Tenth: $147,000	9,986	266
Saskatoon, SK	45% houses 46% apartments 1% condos 1% mobile homes	20% high rise One bedroom: $360/month	9% new 12% old Utilities: Gas/Electric	Median: n.a. Average: $59,900 Upper Tenth: $152,000	5,464	61
Savannah, GA	63% houses 16% apartments 2% condos 10% mobile homes	17% complexes One bedroom: $540/month	18% new 12% old Utilities: Gas/Electric	Median: $62,700 Average: $79,900 Upper Tenth: $111,400	7,285	182
Scranton–Wilkes-Barre–Hazleton, PA	68% houses 13% apartments 5% mobile homes	22% complexes One bedroom: $465/month	6% new 48% old Utilities: Gas/Electric	Median: $60,000 Average: $70,500 Upper Tenth: $112,800	6,421	137
Seattle–Bellevue–Everett, WA	62% houses 25% apartments 5% condos 5% mobile homes	40% complexes One bedroom: $630/month	16% new 15% old Utilities: Total Electric	Median: $135,800 Average: $162,900 Upper Tenth: $251,400	14,843	312
✓ Sharon, PA	74% houses 10% apartments 9% mobile homes	24% complexes One bedroom: $435/month	5% new 33% old Utilities: Gas/Electric	Median: $41,800 Average: $47,600 Upper Tenth: $80,400	4,336	8
Sheboygan, WI	67% houses 10% apartments 1% condos 3% mobile homes	28% complexes One bedroom: $475/month	8% new 39% old Utilities: Gas/Electric	Median: $59,200 Average: $65,900 Upper Tenth: $116,000	6,003	103
Sherbrooke, PQ	45% houses 46% apartments 1% condos 1% mobile homes	6% high rise One bedroom: $480/month	17% new 9% old Utilities: Total Electric	Median: n.a. Average: $63,600 Upper Tenth: $119,000	5,650	72
✓ Sherman–Denison, TX	74% houses 9% apartments 10% mobile homes	32% complexes One bedroom: $515/month	11% new 14% old Utilities: Gas/Electric	Median: $45,500 Average: $54,300 Upper Tenth: $84,500	4,949	27
Shreveport–Bossier City, LA	71% houses 13% apartments 2% condos 9% mobile homes	25% complexes One bedroom: $480/month	9% new 8% old Utilities: Gas/Electric	Median: $54,200 Average: $63,300 Upper Tenth: $102,300	5,767	86
✓ Sioux City, IA–NE	74% houses 13% apartments 1% condos 6% mobile homes	28% complexes One bedroom: $425/month	5% new 39% old Utilities: Gas/Electric	Median: $40,900 Average: $48,000 Upper Tenth: $76,900	4,374	11
Sioux Falls, SD	66% houses 21% apartments 1% condos 6% mobile homes	32% complexes One bedroom: $475/month	13% new 21% old Utilities: Gas/Electric	Median: $57,100 Average: $65,100 Upper Tenth: $109,800	5,934	95
South Bend, IN	77% houses 14% apartments 2% condos 2% mobile homes	26% complexes One bedroom: $525/month	10% new 25% old Utilities: Gas/Electric	Median: $50,200 Average: $60,500 Upper Tenth: $92,600	5,513	63
Spokane, WA	69% houses 16% apartments 1% condos 7% mobile homes	38% complexes One bedroom: $440/month	8% new 21% old Utilities: Total Electric	Median: $58,600 Average: $67,700 Upper Tenth: $111,500	6,171	116

Metro Area	Local Choices	Apartments	Houses	Prices	Places Rated Score	Places Rated Rank
Springfield, IL	70% houses 14% apartments 2% condos 7% mobile homes	23% complexes One bedroom: $475/month	10% new 23% old Utilities: Gas/Electric	Median: $59,800 Average: $69,700 Upper Tenth: $113,100	6,356	130
Springfield, MA	75% houses 12% apartments 7% mobile homes	24% complexes One bedroom: $615/month	7% new 33% old Utilities: Oil/Electric	Median: $125,200 Average: $138,700 Upper Tenth: $246,400	12,636	295
Springfield, MO	75% houses 23% apartments 7% mobile homes	37% complexes One bedroom: $440/month	19% new 14% old Utilities: Gas/Electric	Median: $56,700 Average: $65,100 Upper Tenth: $108,400	5,931	94
Stamford–Norwalk, CT	56% houses 23% apartments 10% condos	17% complexes One bedroom: $700/month	9% new 28% old Utilities: Oil/Electric	Median: $195,200 Average: $226,500 Upper Tenth: $370,400	20,642	329
State College, PA	59% houses 23% apartments 4% condos 9% mobile homes	47% complexes One bedroom: $580/month	14% new 21% old Utilities: Oil/Electric	Median: $74,900 Average: $85,300 Upper Tenth: $144,200	7,776	203
✓ Steubenville–Weirton, OH–WV	77% houses 8% apartments 8% mobile homes	25% complexes One bedroom: $410/month	3% new 29% old Utilities: Gas/Electric	Median: $43,300 Average: $47,900 Upper Tenth: $85,300	4,367	9
Stockton–Lodi, CA	70% houses 18% apartments 4% condos 5% mobile homes	35% complexes One bedroom: $590/month	15% new 10% old Utilities: Gas/Electric	Median: $120,500 Average: $134,900 Upper Tenth: $235,100	12,290	290
Sudbury, ON	67% houses 23% apartments 1% condos 1% mobile homes	25% high rise One bedroom: $520/month	14% new 14% old Utilities: Gas/Electric	Median: n.a. Average: $92,900 Upper Tenth: $184,000	8,463	234
Sumter, SC	67% houses 7% apartments 1% condos 21% mobile homes	16% complexes One bedroom: $480/month	18% new 6% old Utilities: Total Electric	Median: $56,400 Average: $62,500 Upper Tenth: $110,900	5,699	79
Syracuse, NY	63% houses 18% apartments 1% condos 6% mobile homes	25% complexes One bedroom: $530/month	10% new 34% old Utilities: Gas/Electric	Median: $75,500 Average: $84,700 Upper Tenth: $147,100	7,721	200
Tacoma, WA	65% houses 19% apartments 1% condos 9% mobile homes	32% complexes One bedroom: $535/month	15% new 15% old Utilities: Total Electric	Median: $82,300 Average: $98,300 Upper Tenth: $152,800	8,963	249
Tallahassee, FL	57% houses 20% apartments 2% condos 14% mobile homes	32% complexes One bedroom: $550/month	23% new 4% old Utilities: Total Electric	Median: $69,000 Average: $82,400 Upper Tenth: $128,100	7,510	189
Tampa–St. Petersburg–Clearwater, FL	57% houses 15% apartments 11% condos 14% mobile homes	29% complexes One bedroom: $565/month	16% new 4% old Utilities: Total Electric	Median: $70,700 Average: $87,900 Upper Tenth: $127,700	8,010	217
✓ Terre Haute, IN	75% houses 10% apartments 1% condos 8% mobile homes	23% complexes One bedroom: $420/month	6% new 38% old Utilities: Gas/Electric	Median: $37,600 Average: $45,200 Upper Tenth: $69,500	4,116	2
✓ Texarkana, TX–Texarkana, AR	72% houses 9% apartments 12% mobile homes	25% complexes One bedroom: $564/month	12% new 9% old Utilities: Gas/Electric	Median: $45,800 Average: $53,200 Upper Tenth: $86,800	4,844	20
Thunder Bay, ON	73% houses 20% apartments 1% condos 1% mobile homes	23% high rise One bedroom: $500/month	9% new 26% old Utilities: Gas/Electric	Median: n.a. Average: $86,900 Upper Tenth: $248,000	7,921	212
Toledo, OH	68% houses 17% apartments 2% condos 5% mobile homes	29% complexes One bedroom: $515/month	7% new 28% old Utilities: Gas/Electric	Median: $59,200 Average: $70,900 Upper Tenth: $109,700	6,461	144
Topeka, KS	72% houses 16% apartments 3% condos 4% mobile homes	43% complexes One bedroom: $515/month	10% new 19% old Utilities: Gas/Electric	Median: $55,300 Average: $63,200 Upper Tenth: $106,100	5,758	84

Metro Area	Local Choices	Apartments	Houses	Prices	Places Rated Score	Places Rated Rank
Toronto, ON	54% houses 38 apartments 7 condos	71% high rise One bedroom: $680/month	17% new 16% old Utilities: Gas/Electric	Median: n.a. Average: $172,000 Upper Tenth: $275,200	15,673	316
Trenton, NJ	69% houses 19% apartments 7% condos	31% complexes One bedroom: $715/month	11% new 28% old Utilities: Gas/Electric	Median: $136,700 Average: $161,800 Upper Tenth: $255,600	14,743	311
✓ Trois-Rivieres, PQ	50% houses 37% apartments 1% condos	5% high rise One bedroom: $520/month	16% new 18% old Utilities: Total Electric	Median: n.a. Average: $53,900 Upper Tenth: $88,000	4,916	25
Tucson, AZ	58% houses 20% apartments 5% condos 13% mobile homes	54% complexes One bedroom: $520/month	17% new 4% old Utilities: Gas/Electric	Median: $76,500 Average: $92,400 Upper Tenth: $140,900	8,424	232
Tulsa, OK	70% houses 16% apartments 2% condos 7% mobile homes	31% complexes One bedroom: $460/month	9% new 10% old Utilities: Gas/Electric	Median: $58,200 Average: $69,400 Upper Tenth: $108,200	6,321	126
Tuscaloosa, AL	62% houses 21% apartments 1% condos 11% mobile homes	29% complexes One bedroom: $450/month	16% new 6% old Utilities: Gas/Electric	Median: $61,300 Average: $69,300 Upper Tenth: $118,700	6,316	125
Tyler, TX	71% houses 13% apartments 1% condos 10% mobile homes	42% complexes One bedroom: $490/month	11% new 7% old Utilities: Gas/Electric	Median: $59,300 Average: $70,500 Upper Tenth: $110,500	6,427	138
Utica–Rome, NY	58% houses 15% apartments 8% mobile homes	25% complexes One bedroom: $480/month	7% new 44% old Utilities: Gas/Electric	Median: $68,400 Average: $76,200 Upper Tenth: $134,000	6,944	170
Vallejo–Fairfield–Napa, CA	72% houses 17% apartments 4% condos 5% mobile homes	26% complexes One bedroom: $700/month	22% new 9% old Utilities: Gas/Electric	Median: $156,000 Average: $175,600 Upper Tenth: $303,100	16,000	318
Vancouver, BC	52% houses 34% apartments 6% condos 1% mobile homes	24% high rise One bedroom: $740/month	17% new 13% old Utilities: Gas/Electric	Median: n.a. Average: $196,200 Upper Tenth: $360,000	17,881	323
Vancouver, WA	69% houses 15% apartments 2% condos 8% mobile homes	32% complexes One bedroom: $550/month	17% new 9% old Utilities: Total Electric	Median: $74,000 Average: $86,600 Upper Tenth: $139,500	7,897	210
Ventura, CA	73% houses 15% apartments 12% condos 5% mobile homes	32% complexes One bedroom: $820/month	15% new 4% old Utilities: Gas/Electric	Median: $243,500 Average: $275,000 Upper Tenth: $471,900	25,063	337
Victoria, BC	57% houses 31% apartments 6% condos 2% mobile homes	14% high rise One bedroom: $600/month	16% new 18% old Utilities: Gas/Electric	Median: n.a. Average: $155,800 Upper Tenth: $288,000	14,193	305
Victoria, TX	72% houses 14% apartments 8% mobile homes	31% complexes One bedroom: $460/month	8% new 7% old Utilities: Total Electric	Median: $54,300 Average: $62,200 Upper Tenth: $104,000	5,670	74
Vineland–Millville–Bridgeton, NJ	71% houses 14% apartments 1% condos 6% mobile homes	29% complexes One bedroom: $600/month	7% new 26% old Utilities: Oil/Electric	Median: $73,600 Average: $80,900 Upper Tenth: $145,800	7,376	184
Visalia–Tulare–Porterville, CA	75% houses 11% apartments 1% condos 10% mobile homes	20% complexes One bedroom: $510/month	17% new 9% old Utilities: Gas/Electric	Median: $73,400 Average: $86,800 Upper Tenth: $137,300	7,915	211
Waco, TX	69% houses 17% apartments 2% condos 5% mobile homes	35% complexes One bedroom: $460/month	10% new 10% old Utilities: Gas/Electric	Median: $49,200 Average: $58,900 Upper Tenth: $91,200	5,367	50
Washington, DC–MD–VA–WV	64% houses 25% apartments 10% condos 1% mobile homes	38% complexes One bedroom: $780/month	16% new 12% old Utilities: Gas/Electric	Median: $157,800 Average: $169,700 Upper Tenth: $271,500	15,466	314

Metro Area	Local Choices	Apartments	Houses	Prices	Places Rated Score	Places Rated Rank
Waterbury, CT	56% houses 23% apartments 10% condos	30% complexes One bedroom: $550/month	9% new 28% old Utilities: Oil/Electric	Median: $118,700 Average: $137,000 Upper Tenth: $226,100	12,485	293
✓ Waterloo–Cedar Falls, IA	75% houses 15% apartments 1% condos 2% mobile homes	24% complexes One bedroom: $420/month	2% new 25% old Utilities: Gas/Electric	Median: $44,000 Average: $50,700 Upper Tenth: $83,900	4,621	18
Wausau, WI	75% houses 9% apartments 1% condos 5% mobile homes	19% complexes One bedroom: $465/month	9% new 27% old Utilities: Gas/Electric	Median: $54,600 Average: $60,400 Upper Tenth: $107,600	5,503	62
West Palm Beach–Boca Raton, FL	49% houses 13% apartments 35% condos 5% mobile homes	33% complexes One bedroom: $700/month	22% new 2% old Utilities: Total Electric	Median: $98,100 Average: $136,900 Upper Tenth: $165,100	12,479	292
✓ Wheeling, WV–OH	72% houses 10% apartments 1% condos 7% mobile homes	29% complexes One bedroom: $400/month	3% new 41% old Utilities: Gas/Electric	Median: $43,800 Average: $49,800 Upper Tenth: $84,400	4,542	16
Wichita, KS	71% houses 15% apartments 2% condos 6% mobile homes	32% complexes One bedroom: $500/month	9% new 15% old Utilities: Gas/Electric	Median: $56,700 Average: $65,900 Upper Tenth: $107,400	6,007	104
✓ Wichita Falls, TX	76% houses 11% apartments 1% condos 6% mobile homes	29% complexes One bedroom: $465/month	5% new 15% old Utilities: Gas/Electric	Median: $45,700 Average: $54,800 Upper Tenth: $84,600	4,991	29
Williamsport, PA	71% houses 11% apartments 9% mobile homes	16% complexes One bedroom: $445/month	8% new 41% old Utilities: Oil/Electric	Median: $54,100 Average: $61,300 Upper Tenth: $104,500	5,582	66
Wilmington, NC	62% houses 14% apartments 8% condos 9% mobile homes	12% complexes One bedroom: $550/month	19% new 9% old Utilities: Total Electric	Median: $71,400 Average: $91,000 Upper Tenth: $126,800	8,298	229
Wilmington–Newark, DE–MD	72% houses 17% apartments 3% condos 4% mobile homes	23% complexes One bedroom: $630/month	15% new 15% old Utilities: Oil/Electric	Median: $108,500 Average: $128,000 Upper Tenth: $203,300	11,662	284
Windsor, ON	71% houses 20% apartments 2% condos 1% mobile homes	48% high rise One bedroom: $600/month	8% new 27% old Utilities: Gas/Electric	Median: n.a. Average: $87,400 Upper Tenth: $232,000	7,964	215
Winnipeg, MB	65% houses 29% apartments 2% condos	43% high rise One bedroom: $480/month	9% new 20% old Utilities: Gas/Electric	Median: n.a. Average: $65,600 Upper Tenth: $156,800	5,978	100
Worcester–Fitchburg–Leominster, MA	56% houses 25% apartments 4% condos 1% mobile homes	19% complexes One bedroom: $640/month	13% new 37% old Utilities: Oil/Electric	Median: $139,600 Average: $154,000 Upper Tenth: $275,700	14,039	304
Yakima, WA	70% houses 11% apartments 1% condos 13% mobile homes	25% complexes One bedroom: $450/month	8% new 15% old Utilities: Total Electric	Median: $54,900 Average: $62,600 Upper Tenth: $105,500	5,706	80
Yolo, CA	60% houses 27% apartments 3% condos 7% mobile homes	44% complexes One bedroom: $615/month	16% new 7% old Utilities: Gas/Electric	Median: $137,400 Average: $157,500 Upper Tenth: $263,200	14,351	308
York, PA	74% houses 11% apartments 1% condos 8% mobile homes	14% complexes One bedroom: $515/month	14% new 27% old Utilities: Gas/Electric	Median: $79,400 Average: $87,200 Upper Tenth: $157,400	7,943	213
✓ Youngstown–Warren, OH	76% houses 11% apartments 1% condos 5% mobile homes	24% complexes One bedroom: $450/month	5% new 27% old Utilities: Gas/Electric	Median: $48,700 Average: $55,500 Upper Tenth: $93,700	5,053	31

Metro Area	Local Choices	Apartments	Houses	Prices	Places Rated Score	Places Rated Rank
Yuba City, CA	67% houses 17% apartments 2% condos 11% mobile homes	36% complexes One bedroom: $480/month	16% new 8% old Utilities: Gas/Electric	Median: $81,900 Average: $93,200 Upper Tenth: $157,700	8,495	235
Yuma, AZ	45% houses 11% apartments 4% condos 38% mobile homes	32% complexes One bedroom: $535/month	22% new 3% old Utilities: Total Electric	Median: $63,700 Average: $71,800 Upper Tenth: $123,600	6,541	146

Et Cetera

HOME FEATURES

Each year, the Federal Housing Authority (FHA) reports on characteristics of single-family homes whose mortgages it insures. Here's a United States geography of eight selected features.

Stories. The use of the word "story" to refer to flights of buildings may have originated with tiers of stained-glass or painted windows that described a special event. The common definition today is the space between the floor and the ceiling, roof, or the floor above, in the case of a multistory home. It has nothing to do with the height of a house; a house that appears from the outside to be two stories may actually be a single-story with a cathedral ceiling. More than 85 percent of new houses have only one story. Older homes with more than one story predominate in Connecticut, Maine, Maryland, Massachusetts, New Jersey, New York, Pennsylvania, and Wisconsin.

Construction and Exterior. In frame construction, the wood frame supports the floors and roof; in masonry construction, the exterior masonry wall serves as the support. Except in Texas, masonry construction using local stone has virtually disappeared in new houses. Concrete block construction, however, is a common technique in Arizona (40 percent of new homes have it) and Florida (85 percent), where the exterior is either spray-painted or stuccoed. Everywhere else, the majority of new houses are of frame construction. Aluminum siding is the preferred exterior in Maryland and Ohio; wood is the choice in Georgia and Washington. The majority (86 percent) of all homes being built with brick exteriors in the United States are in the southern states. Exteriors of brick or stucco are preferred in California and Nevada.

Basements. The basement is an area of full-story height below the first floor that is not meant for year-round living. Only a third of new houses have basements, because they are expensive to excavate. In six states, however, two out of three new houses come with some kind of basement, reflecting a pattern of locating the furnace below grade and a preference for extra living space. These states are Illinois, Iowa, Michigan, Minnesota, New York, and Pennsylvania. Most new houses without basements either have a crawl space (an unfinished, accessible space below the first floor that is usually less than full-story height) or are simply resting on a concrete slab poured on the ground. In the United States, crawl spaces are preferred only in the Pacific Northwest and the Carolinas. Concrete slab footings support almost all new houses in the Sun Belt states of Arizona, Arkansas, Georgia, Louisiana, Mississippi, Oklahoma, and Texas.

Bathrooms. Bathrooms are either full (a tub or shower stall, a sink, and a toilet) or half (just a sink and a toilet). All new houses have at least one full bathroom. You'll find the majority of new homes with both a full bathroom and a half-bathroom only in the states of Alabama, Arkansas, Georgia, Louisiana, Maryland, Mississippi, New Jersey, Oklahoma, South Carolina, and Tennessee.

Fireplaces. Flueless imitation fireplaces, like dinettes and rumpus rooms, are memories of the 1950s. Half of all new American homes now are built with working fireplaces and chimneys. Unfortunately, many fireplaces in these new homes aren't used, because of smoke problems caused by short chimneys. For a good fireplace draft, the chimney cap should be at least 20 feet above the hearth. Homes with two fireplaces can be found more frequently in the northern timber states of Idaho, Minnesota, Montana, Oregon, and Washington, and also in North Carolina and Pennsylvania.

Enclosed Porches. A porch is a covered addition or recessed space at the entrance of a home. These Main Street lookouts have disappeared from new home markets. You'll find an enclosed porch attached to one out of every 12 older homes in this country. In Connecticut, Iowa, Maine, Massachusetts, New Jersey, and New York, more than one fifth of older homes have them.

Garages and Carports. Garages, as everyone knows, are completely enclosed shelters for automobiles; carports are roofed shelters that aren't completely enclosed. Detached garages are a feature of older homes and were typically built behind the home, invisible from the street. Attached two-car garages, which became a popular feature on new homes during the 1950s, now are a standard feature on half of all newly built homes. Today, 6 out of 10 houses, new and old, have garages; just one in 10 has a carport. Only in Arizona, Hawaii, Louisiana, and Mississippi is this pattern reversed.

Swimming Pools. You won't find new tract houses anywhere with in-ground swimming pools. Builders have learned that few buyers shop for shelter and a swimming pool at the same time. Moreover, local ordinances can require expensive liability insurance and a four-foot-high fence around the pool's perimeter to prevent accidents. Among older homes, fewer than 2 percent have in-ground pools. You'll find at least twice that portion in Arizona California, Florida, Nevada, and, surprisingly, Maine, Massachusetts, and New York.

HOW MUCH HOUSE CAN YOU AFFORD?

One way of figuring how much house you can afford is to use the 20/25 lending requirements set by the Federal National Mortgage Association, a major purchaser of mortgages in the secondary mortgage market. According to this rule, a family making a 20 percent down payment can finance the rest as long as no more than 25 percent of their gross income (income before taxes) covers the annual principal and interest.

For example, at a typical 1993 mortgage rate of 8 percent, a family would need a gross income of $45,000 to handle the $950 monthly principal and interest payments on a 15-year, $100,000 home loan.

That's one way of looking at it. A far simpler way is to recall the long-standing rule of thumb handed down from parents to children, which states that if you buy a house that costs much more than two and a half times your gross income, you're headed for trouble. For example, if your gross annual income is $40,000, the price range of houses to shop for is $80,000 to $100,00; if your

income is $60,000, you can afford a house costing between $120,000 and $150,000.

Based on either of these rules, can a typical family afford a typical home? Unfortunately, no. Just under half can qualify to buy a median-priced home in the region where they live, using a conventional mortgage with a 5 percent down payment. Indeed, just 1 in 10 renters can afford that median-priced home.

A RENTER'S MISCELLANY

The kind of apartment building you choose to live in makes a difference in your monthly costs. Rents for a typical four-room, 850-square-foot unit are much higher in high-rise elevator buildings than in walk-ups or elevator buildings of three stories or fewer, according to the latest Institute of Real Estate Management survey. The least expensive kind of building is the garden apartment, defined by the institute as a group of low-rise apartment buildings on a large landscaped lot under one manager.

You'll find that the annual turnover rate, defined as newly occupied apartments as a percent of all the apartments in the building in a year's time, also varies by the kind of building. High-rise elevator buildings have the lowest turnover rate, whereas the turnover rate in walk-ups and elevator buildings of three or fewer stories is twice this. The kind of apartment building with the most transient population is the garden apartment, in which 54 percent of tenants moved in within the previous 12 months.

Renters' Rights

In many states with large renter populations, laws concerning landlord/tenant relations give rights to the landlord while imposing obligations on the tenant.

Twenty states, however, have passed landlord-tenant laws based on the Uniform Residential Landlord and Tenant Act (1972), a model law drawn up by the National Conference of Commissioners on Uniform State Laws. These states are Alaska, Arizona, Connecticut, Florida, Hawaii, Iowa, Kansas, Kentucky, Michigan, Mississippi, Montana, Nebraska, New Mexico, Oklahoma, Oregon, Rhode Island, South Carolina, Tennessee, Virginia, and Washington.

This law defines rights and obligations of both parties to a lease on an apartment or house, and it also specifies the way disputes can be resolved. Among its provisions are the following:

- If your dispute with a landlord leads you to complain to the local housing board, to join a tenants' group, or to sue your landlord, the landlord cannot retaliate by cutting services, raising your rent, or evicting you.
- If the landlord doesn't make needed repairs, and the cost of the repairs is no more than $100 or half the rent (whichever is greater), you may

make the repairs and deduct the expense from your monthly rent.

- After you vacate the apartment or house, any money you've deposited as security must be returned. If there are any deductions from the deposit for damages or other reasons, these deductions must be itemized.
- If your landlord doesn't live up to the lease's terms, you can recover damages in small claims court.

The Rule of 156

One useful way of determining the rent for a house is to divide its market value by 156. This rule of 156 was developed by the city of San Francisco as a way of specifying the fair value of an apartment being converted into a condo for a tenant who had been renting it. As the landlord might put it, the price equals 156 times your monthly rent, take it or leave it.

What the rule implies in reverse is that landlords can expect a 156-month (or 13-year) payback on houses they rent. Using this rule plus the median prices of houses given in the Place Profiles, it isn't difficult to figure roughly what it would cost you to rent a house in a given metro area, assuming that the landlord has realistic expectations for the rate of return on property.

In Miami, the rent would be $550; in San Francisco, $1,800; in Chicago, $675. The rule of 156 may seem unfair to landlords, since there is only an 8 percent return from which maintenance and taxes must be paid. Bear in mind, however, that landlords do not buy houses for the rental income they may bring; rather, they buy them for their market appreciation and rent them during the interim merely to cover expenses.

A CONDO MISCELLANY

Almost 1 of every 25 housing units in North America is a condominium. Since 1980, their number has increased six times as fast as any other type of housing.

Except for seasonal resorts, condos are virtually absent from rural areas. Nor are they found in equal proportion in every region. Nearly 2 out of 5 condos are in the southern states, 1 of 4 in the western states; the northeast and midwest each account for 1 of 8, and Canada 1 of 12. In fact, three Florida metro areas— Miami, Fort Lauderdale, Tampa-St. Petersburg—and Orange County, CA, together have 1 in 10 of all the condos on the continent.

Protection for Condo Buyers

During the 1960s and 1970s, condo buyers had little legal protection when they signed a purchase agreement. Over the past ten years, eleven states have passed comprehensive laws to deal with condominium owner-

---

Condos in the Metro Areas

The condominium form of home ownership is more American than Canadian. The Canadian metro area with the highest portion of housing as condominiums is Toronto with 7%

	Portion of Occupied Housing
Naples, FL	37%
West Palm Beach-Boca Raton, FL	35
Fort Lauderdale, FL	33
Honolulu, HI	24
Myrtle Beach, SC	21
Sarasota-Bradenton, FL	20
Miami, FL	20
Fort Myers-Cape Coral, FL	19
Fort Pierce-Port St. Lucie, FL	18
Orange County, CA	16

Source: U.S. Bureau of the Census, *1990 Census of Population and Housing*; Statistics Canada, *Profile of Census Metropolitan Areas*, 1992.

---

ship based on the Uniform Condominium Act (1980), drawn up by the National Conference of Commissioners on Uniform State Laws. These states are Maine, Minnesota, Missouri, Nebraska, New Hampshire, New Mexico, North Carolina, Pennsylvania, Rhode Island, Virginia, and Washington.

The Uniform Condominium Act covers owners' associations, developers' activities, eminent domain, separate titles and taxation, and safeguards for condo buyers. It stipulates, among other things, that

- The developer must provide you with a Public Offering Statement, accurately and fully disclosing a schedule for finishing construction, the total number of units, the bylaws of the owners' association, copies of any contracts or leases that you have to sign, a current balance sheet and projected one-year budget for the owners' association, and a statement of the monthly common assessments you'll have to pay.
- After signing a purchase agreement, you are given 15 days to cool off, after which you can either cancel the agreement without penalty or accept conveyance of the property.
- If you buy a condominium without first being given a Public Offering Statement, you're entitled to receive from the developer an amount equal to 10 percent of the sales price of the unit you bought. The developer and real estate agent must guarantee that the unit you are buying is free from defective materials, is built to sound engineering and construction standards, and conforms to local codes.

Transportation

If you travel often enough, you might take for granted expressway networks, airline routes, and passenger rails that lace up the continent's different points. But spreading out a map would show you certain metro areas to be hubs with highway, rail, and air-route spokes, while others appear as lesser intersections, removed from the mainstream of intercity travel.

Population size has something to do with an area's transportation assets, but so do the accidents of geography. There are 27 metro areas bigger than Denver, but because the Mile-High City is plunked down at the edge of the Rocky Mountains halfway between Chicago and Southern California, and midway from Houston to Seattle, only four other airports in North America are busier than Denver International.

Intercity travel is only part of the picture. Some metro areas have efficient public transit fleets relied on by hundreds of thousands of commuters each working day. In other metro areas, aging diesel buses with optimistic schedules lurch along routes that rarely reach any neighborhoods but those close to downtown. Still other metro areas have no public transit at all.

GETTING AROUND TOWN

If you are moving to Atlanta, might your family get by without a second car if MARTA's routes reach your new neighborhood? If you are being transferred to company headquarters in downtown Cleveland, will it be more convenient to carpool or ride the RTA rails if you settle in Shaker Heights? How much time will you expect to spend each day getting to and from work? Becoming familiar with the local transportation features of a particular metro area will help you answer some of these questions.

The Commuting Life

Every weekday morning, in cities and towns all over, traffic trickles out of suburban streets, flows into arterial roads, and floods freeways to capacity with people bound for work. According to transportation experts, the morning rush hour lasts 118 minutes, between 7:01 and 8:59. Most workers travel by automobile, alone; one out of 5 belongs to a car pool; and one out of 15 opts for public transit.

The evening rush hour lasts longer, 150 minutes,

from 4:30 to 7:00. There are more traffic delays at this time than in the morning when people so purposefully leave home and arrive at work in the shortest possible time. In the evening, many commuters stop for a drink, go shopping, run errands, or just dawdle. After all, one can't be fired for being late for supper. In fact, traffic experts say, even if you head straight home, the evening trip not only seems longer than the trip to work but actually is—20 percent longer.

How much time do metro-area workers spend going to and from the job each day? To allow for the longer trip home in the evening, *Places Rated* multiplies the average journey-to-work figure by 2.2 to estimate the round-trip time in each of the metro areas.

Daily commuting time increases with city size. Workers in Bismarck, ND, for instance, putting in 220 working days a year, spend about 100 hours commuting. Workers residing on Staten Island spend 325 hours taking the ferry to and from their Manhattan jobs. The contrast between Bismarck and Staten Island, then, is more than one between a prairie state capital and a section of the continent's largest city. Based on commuting time alone, Bismarckers have more free time than Staten Islanders, the equivalent of six 40-hour weeks each year.

Public Mass Transit

One reason for the long commute in big cities is the often exhausting job of making linked transit trips to get to work. The average duration of an *unlinked* transit trip—a direct route, with no transfers—is about 15 minutes. But many big-city commuters have to make linked trips—driving to a park-and-ride or kiss-and-ride lot; boarding a train, ferry, or bus; and sometimes switching again before finally getting to work.

Still, in larger cities where the tab for daily parking in a downtown garage nears $20, where rush-hour traffic approaches grid-lock, where distances are long and time always seems short, public transit really counts. In many a large city—Houston and Phoenix, for example—daily driving over long distances is a way of life unrelieved by rapid public transit; taking the bus is the only alternative. In other places such as Atlanta, Toronto, Washington, and San Francisco, large local bus fleets are complemented by rapid transit rail systems.

Depending on where they want to go, New York City commuters can choose from bus, heavy rail, light rail, commuter railroad, ferryboat, and even aerial tramway service. New York straphangers may not always enjoy their subway ride to work, but few among the jostled riders aboard a rocking, grimy IRT car would ever envy a Houston driver who has missed his or her exit on the Southwest Freeway at rush hour.

By bus. In most cities, public transit and "the bus" are synonymous. Unlike rapid rail and trolley networks, a bus system requires no expensive construction, and routes can be easily changed to meet demand.

Each of the continent's 1,500 transit systems with fixed-route service puts motor buses on the street, but these systems vary in size and type of operation. Several large systems—CTA (Chicago), TTC (Toronto), WMATA (Washington, DC), and NYCTA (New York), for example—operate thousands of GMC, Orion, and Flyer buses around the clock with less than one minute between buses on the heaviest routes during morning and evening rush hours. At the other extreme are the one- and two-bus "shoppers' specials" that run loops in the central business district of smaller metro areas.

By rail. Although buses can meet the demand for public transit nearly everywhere, rail lines are more efficient in carrying large numbers of rush-hour commuters in the major cities. Several kinds of rail service are available in the big metro areas, from rapid rail to trolley car to commuter train.

Rapid rail lines. Owing to their exclusive rights-of-way, these are unaffected by traffic jams. Their trains and trams not only carry thousands of people but carry them quickly. The average speed of buses during peak rush hour, nationwide, is 12 miles per hour. Rapid rail systems average more than 20 miles per hour. There are two types of rapid rail lines in use today in 24 metro areas: heavy rail, which accounts for 2.5 billion passenger trips in a year, and light rail, which accounts for 150 million passenger trips. Both are electrically powered, and both may be found in the same city.

Heavy rail systems—known locally as subways, elevated railways, or ELS—have high-level platform sta-

---

Getting to Work and Back

Longest Commute

1. New York, NY	75.8 minutes
2. Long Island, NY	64.6
3. Washington, DC–MD–VA–WV	63.0
4. Chicago, IL	61.5
5. Riverside–San Bernardino, CA	59.3
6. Orange County, NY	58.5
7. Monmouth–Ocean, NJ	58.3
8. Oakland, CA	57.5
9. Houston, TX	56.9
10. Vallejo–Fairfield–Napa, CA	56.8

Shortest Commute

1. Bismarck, ND	27.1
2. Grand Forks, ND–MN	27.4
3. Cheyenne, WY	29.5
4. Dubuque, IA	30.1
5. Fargo–Moorhead, ND–MN	30.7
6. Enid, OK	30.8
7. Great Falls, MT	30.9
8. Sheboygan, WI	31.5
9. Rochester, MN	31.6
10. Waterloo–Cedar Falls, IA	31.9

Source: Derived from U.S. Bureau of the Census, *1990 Census of Population and Housing.*

tions. The cars are individually powered through the third rail, and are hitched together to form longer trains during rush hours. New York City's heavy rail system, composed of two separate networks, is the world's largest, with 6,248 cars traveling more than 450 miles of track; Philadelphia also has two systems. As of January 1993, 15 metro areas have heavy rail systems.

Light rail cars. Powered by overhead electrical wires, these travel at half the speed of heavy rail cars. Because their tracks are laid aboveground, they are less expensive to build and therefore are the fastest-growing form of mass transit.

Trolley coaches. Trolleys are streetcar-type railways that travel on city streets with semiprivate or exclusive rights-of-way. They are a less efficient form of travel than rapid rail since the trams are at the mercy of automobile traffic and, in some cities, must stop for streetlights. Another disadvantage is that their routes cannot be altered. These systems have been largely replaced by bus; in fact, only nine metro areas in North America have trolley coach operations.

Commuter railroads. Trains have been an important form of transportation from more distant suburbs to the central part of major cities since the nineteenth century. Using both locomotive-hauled and self-propelled passenger cars, this service is marked by multitrip tickets, station-to-station fares, railroad employment practices, and usually only one or two stations in the central business district.

Twenty-four commuter railroads in 15 metro areas ferry nearly 1.5 million commuters to and from work. The largest commuter railroad network, made up of seven firms, is found in New York and uses 1,650 cars to move 525,000 riders in a typical weekday. In Chicago, the next largest commuter railroad center, nine carriers operating 850 cars transport 300,000 workers in a typical day.

Light Rail: The Desire Named Streetcar

Twenty-one metro areas have light rail systems . . .

Atlanta, GA	Philadelphia, PA–NJ
Baltimore, MD	Pittsburgh, PA
Boston, MA	Portland, OR
Buffalo–Niagara Falls, NY	Sacramento, CA
Chicago, IL	San Diego, CA
Cleveland, OH	San Francisco, CA
Edmonton, AB	San Jose, CA,
Los Angeles, CA	Seattle–Bellevue–Everett, WA
Miami, FL	Toronto, ON
Newark–Jersey City, NJ	Vancouver, BC
New Orleans, LA	

And in 11 others, light rail lines are proposed, planned, or already under construction . . .

Dallas, TX	Oklahoma City, OK
Denver, CO	Phoenix–Mesa, AZ
Detroit, MI	St. Louis, MO–IL
Honolulu, HI	Salt Lake City–Ogden, UT
Indianapolis, IN	Tampa–St. Petersburg–
Minneapolis–	Clearwater, FL
St. Paul, MN–WI	

The Busiest Intercity Rail Routes

AMTRAK, Northeast Corridor*

	Annual Passengers
1. Metroliners, Boston–New York–Washington	1,921,642
2. New York–Philadelphia	1,861,746
3. Atlantic City	422,338
4. Philadelphia–Harrisburg	330,619

AMTRAK, Short Distance

1. Los Angeles–San Diego	1,724,321
2. New York–Albany–Niagara Falls	1,036,721
3. Oakland–Bakersfield	465,425
4. Chicago–Detroit–Toledo	390,145
5. Chicago–Milwaukee	315,440

AMTRAK, Long Distance

1. New York–Florida	913,000
2. Chicago–Oakland–Los Angeles	725,064
3. Los Angeles–Seattle	583,462
4. Chicago–Seattle–Portland	462,675

VIA, The Corridor (Quebec City–Windsor)

1. Montreal–Toronto	904,209
2. Toronto–Windsor	607,461
3. Toronto–Ottawa	516,205

Sources: AMTRAK, VIA Rail Canada.

*Another 6 million passengers a year travel various AMTRAK routes along the Northeast Corridor not listed here.

The Busiest North American Two-Way Air Routes

City Pairs	**Annual Passengers**
1. Los Angeles–New York	2,900,000
2. Los Angeles–San Francisco	2,850,000
3. Boston–New York	2,470,000
4. New York–Washington	2,450,000
5. Miami–New York	2,340,000
6. Chicago–New York	2,320,000
7. Dallas/Fort Worth–Houston	2,140,000
8. Honolulu–Kahului, Maui	2,120,000
9. New York–San Francisco	2,020,000
10. New York–Orlando	1,700,000
11. New York–San Juan, PR	1,640,000
12. Honolulu–Lihue, Kauai	1,630,000
13. Los Angeles–Phoenix	1,540,000
14. Fort Lauderdale–New York	1,530,000
15. Montreal–Toronto	1,500,000

Sources: Air Transport Association of America, *Annual Report,* 1993; Statistics Canada, Aviation Statistics Centre, *Aviation Bulletin,* 1992.

INTERCITY TRAVEL

"You can't get there from here" is the punch line of the old joke about the lost city sharper who asked directions of a bemused farmer. The line has little meaning in today's metropolitan areas, given the networks of well-traveled highways, railroads, and airways that connect these places.

Or does it? Obviously, you can't ramp on to the Interstate or board AMTRAK if your destination is Anchorage or Honolulu. For that matter, you can't get to

Bloomington, Brazoria, or Bremerton by the same means. When it comes to intercity travel options, some metro areas are better off than others.

National Highways

When President Franklin Roosevelt idly penciled three east-west and five north-south lines on a U.S. map back in 1938 as part of a proposed national highway system, he probably had no idea that his drawing would be so important in determining whether many rural towns would grow and many others would decline. He was thinking of a 34,000-mile network of multilane toll roads.

Although the concept of collecting tolls was soon dropped by the Bureau of Public Roads, the basic routes on his map foresaw the Interstate Highway System, a river of economic life to cities and towns along the way and possibly a cause of stagnation for those that were bypassed.

The interstate system is now an almost complete 42,500-mile road network, at least four traffic lanes wide, linking together nearly every American city with a population of more than 50,000. Even though interstate routes account for only 1 percent of all road and street mileage in the United States, they carry 25 percent of all the traffic. One in six U.S. metro areas isn't on the interstate network; in Canada, half of the metro areas aren't on that country's counterpart, the 4,800-mile Trans-Canada Highway.

Boarding Pass, Please

It's getting to be an old saying in the South that when you die and are enroute to heaven or hell, you'll have to make connections in Atlanta. Atlanta's airport, Hartsfield International, is the world's second busiest.

Like other airports that are reached by scheduled airlines, Hartsfield is a twentieth-century urban landmark in the same way the railroad station was a sign of the times in the late nineteenth century. Most of the 276 airports served by major airlines in the United States and Canada are quiet, even desolate places. But some, like Hartsfield, resemble self-contained cities, and last year 47 of these airports in the continent's large hubs handled 70 percent of the nearly 700 million people who boarded domestic flights. The busiest, Chicago's O'Hare International Airport, boards more passengers than the 200 smallest airports combined.

Riding the Rails

Sixty years ago, 8 out of 10 people who had to get from one North American city to another did it aboard a train. There were 20,000 different ones from which to choose, if you didn't care where you were going. The Twentieth Century Limited, El Capitan, Blue Streak—each had a unique, trademarked name. They still do—Desert Wind, Sunset Limited, Empire Builder, Texas Eagle, Bonaventure, Canadian—but today there are just 280 of

---

Decoding the Interstate System

The numbers in the middle of the red, white, and blue, shield-shaped signs along the interstate system were developed in 1957 by the American Association of State Highway Transportation officials. There are 34 odd-numbered routes running north and south, and 27 even-numbered routes running east and west. The lowest-numbered routes are in the West and the South; I-5, for example, lies along the nation's West Coast and I-10 runs along the southern border.

In cities, these one- or two-digit numbers don't change as long as they are part of the major traffic stream. Beltways around the city, on the other hand, carry three numbers: the main route number with an even-numbered prefix. For example, I-495, an 88 mile-long route around Boston, and I-287, a 94-mile long loop skirting New York City, are the two longest beltways in the interstate system. If a main route carries an odd-numbered prefix (such as I-195 in Miami or I-780 in San Francisco), the route is a spur that connects with the main route at only one end.

Three-digit route numbers are never used twice in the same state. In New York, I-90 runs through Schenectady, Syracuse, Rochester, and Buffalo, and the beltways off this main route in those cities are numbered, respectively, I-890, I-690, I-490, and I-290. This rule isn't carried across state lines, however. Two cities on I-10 but in different states, Houston and New Orleans, have the identical beltway number of I-610.

---

them. Over the years, their share of the commercial passenger traffic has dwindled to 7 percent.

If passenger trains are ever to rise again, the renaissance will be caused not by high gasoline prices and spot fuel shortages but by intolerable congestion on intercity highways. Railroads have a priceless asset: existing tracks and rights-of-way into the continent's population centers.

The National Railroad Passenger Corporation, a profit-making body, was created by Congress to subsidize the passenger business of its member railroads. Better known as AMTRAK, it started operation in 1971. Today it carries virtually all of the 25 million passengers who board U.S. intercity trains each year. VIA, Canada's intercity rail counterpart, also carries nearly all of that country's train passengers.

The passenger rails don't reach everywhere, however. Although AMTRAK's and VIA's timetables boast stops at hundreds of cities and towns from Halifax, NS, to San Diego, CA, 157 of the 343 metro areas aren't on the route system. The metro areas bypassed include such large places as Calgary, Tulsa, Louisville, and Des Moines.

By far the biggest markets for train service are in the U.S. northeast corridor and the St. Lawrence corridor in

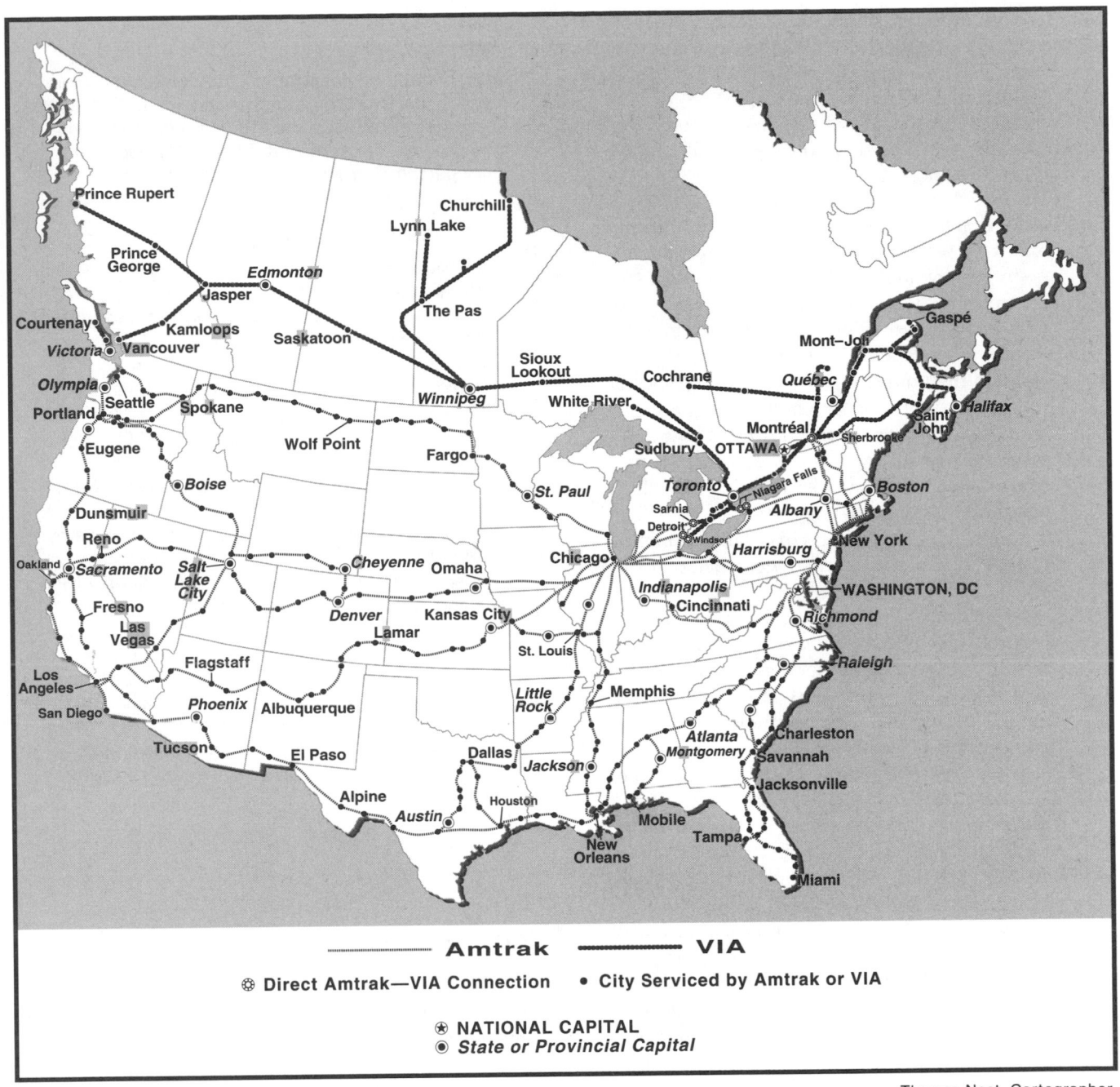

Amtrak ——— VIA

⊛ Direct Amtrak—VIA Connection   • City Serviced by Amtrak or VIA

⊛ NATIONAL CAPITAL
◉ State or Provincial Capital

Thomas Nast, Cartographer

Canada. But the fastest-growing markets are on the West Coast, particularly for the two-hour-and-forty-minute run between Los Angeles and San Diego and for the six-hour San Francisco–Bakersfield route.

SCORING: TRANSPORTATION

When it comes to rating the transportation in a metro area, good measurements must include how long it takes to commute to work, how many people can use the local transit system, and what the travel options are for getting to another city. Would a shopper in Syracuse or San Angelo have a better chance of finding a seat on a bus? Which metro-area airport—Calgary's or Denver's —has more daily departures per local population?

Places Rated considers three intercity indicators— national highways, major scheduled airline flights, and passenger train departures—and two local ones—mass transit and daily commuting time. To arrive at a score for each metro area, these five criteria are compared with the metro-area averages.

In judging air service, some further adjustments were made in rating the 75 metro areas that are part of Metropolitan Complexes (see the Appendix for a list of MCs and component metro areas). Because major airports tend to serve a wide geographical area and accommodate large numbers of travelers, *Places Rated* considers the air service assets of MC component metro areas to be shared equally by all members of the MC, no matter which metro area has the airport.

Each metro area starts with a base score of zero, to which points are added according to the following indicators:

1. *Daily commute.* The time spent commuting to and from work is almost entirely unproductive —and unavoidable. To rate each place for commuting time, the metro-area average of 42.2 minutes is divided by the average minutes local workers spend in daily commuting. The result is then multiplied by 1,000. The shorter the commuting time, the more points a metro area will receive. Workers in Houston, for instance, spend an average of 56.9 minutes commuting, which works out to 742 points, compared with an average time of only 29.5 minutes in Cheyenne. This daily commute results in a score nearly twice that of Houston's.

2. *Mass transit.* Based on local transit agency reports, the annual mileage the transit fleet rolls up in scheduled service in each metro area is divided by the population served and multiplied by 100. The maximum number of points for this factor is 3,000.

3. *National highways.* An average of 1.496 main, numbered U.S. Interstate or Trans-Canada routes reach 270 metro areas. To rate metro areas, the number of routes in the metro area is divided by this average and multiplied by 1,000, with a ceiling of 2,000 points.

4. *Airline flights.* For the 248 metro areas with airports having passenger service aboard major scheduled airlines, the average number of residents per departing flight each week is 1,727. To rate each metro area, this average is divided by the local ratio of residents to departure, then multiplied by 1,000. (In the case of MC component metro areas, the ratio of residents per departure is arrived at by dividing the total number of departures in the MC by the total MC population. Each member metro area receives the same number of points.) The maximum score for each metro area is 1,500 points.

5. *AMTRAK or VIA train departures.* The average number of residents per train departure each week in the 186 metro areas served by national passenger railroads is 16,849. To arrive at a score for each metro area, this average is divided by the local number of residents per weekly train departure, then multiplied by 1,000, with a ceiling of 1,000 points.

Some Days . . .

You'll stand the best chance of dodging airport jams if you fly on Thursday afternoon and Saturday night. The worst travel days used to be Friday and Sunday. Now they are Tuesday and Wednesday because more people take advantage of special fares requiring midweek travel.

. . . You're Better Off in Large Hubs

The Federal Aviation Administration (FAA) rates each metro area for its share of airline service:

A metro area is a . . .	if passengers leaving its airport(s) total . . .
large hub	1% or more
medium hub	0.25% to 0.99%
small hub	0.05% to 0.24%
nonhub	less than 0.05%
	of all U.S. airline passengers in a year.

There's one big advantage to living in a large hub besides having a wider choice of carriers with more frequent nonstop flights to more destinations. Flying between large hubs is cheaper.

The cost of an airline ticket into and out of Bismarck, ND (a nonhub), or Charleston, WV (a small hub), helps subsidize the same airline's small profit from a New York vacationer's air travel to Miami or a Los Angeles conventioneer's trip to Chicago. When airlines skirmish with bargain fares between large hubs, travelers in the smaller hubs end up paying part of the tab.

SCORING EXAMPLES

The largest metro area in Canada and a small one in northwest Alabama illuminate the scoring method for transportation.

Toronto, ON (#30)

This Ontario lakeshore area's pluses are its public transit and intercity travel connections rather than being a location on a national highway or having a bearable commuting time.

After the NYCTA in New York, North America's largest transit system is the TTC/GO Transit network in metropolitan Toronto. Accounting for hundreds of Orion and Flyer buses, Bombardier and Hawker-Siddley subway cars, plus the CP and CN suburban trains, this system has the highest ridership on the continent. In a year, these transit fleets and those of Oakville, Mississauga, and other suburban areas together roll up nearly 200 million miles in revenue service. That alone is good for a maximum 3,000 points.

The size and location of Greater Toronto Area (GTA,

it's locally called) mean that it has, in Pearson International, one of the continent's largest airline hubs. The GTA is also Canada's largest passenger rail hub. These factors contribute another 1,766 points to Toronto's score.

Florence, AL (#343)

In contrast, Florence, in Alabama's Shoals region, has no published-schedule, fixed-route transit. While commuter aircraft serve nearby Muscle Shoals airport, making nonstop flights on major airlines means driving 50 miles east to Huntsville International.

Passenger trains departed here years ago and no interstate runs nearby (though a proposed route between Memphis and Atlanta may include the Shoals along the way). The area is growing, and the equally growing rush-hour congestion contributes to Florence's 44.5 minutes of commuting time. That figure is the sole basis for the area's score, 948, lowest among the metro areas.

Rankings: Transportation

Determining a score for transportation means looking at a metro area's ability to meet the transportation needs of residents, using the following criteria: (1) daily commute, (2) public transportation, (3) national highways, (4) air service, and (5) passenger rail service.

Places that are tied get the same rank and are listed in alphabetical order.

Metro Areas from Best to Worst

Places Rated Rank	Places Rated Score	Places Rated Rank	Places Rated Score	Places Rated Rank	Places Rated Score
1. Chicago, IL	7,429	27. San Diego, CA	5,655	49. Kansas City, MO–KS	5,081
2. Newark–Jersey City, NJ	7,342	28. Albany–Schenectady–Troy, NY	5,627	49. Vancouver, WA	5,081
3. New York, NY	7,148	29. Gary, IN	5,620	50. Bellingham, WA	5,025
4. Boston, MA	7,042	30. Toronto, ON	5,610	50. Regina, SK	5,025
5. Atlanta, GA	6,967			52. Nashville, TN	5,017
6. Champaign–Urbana, IL	6,853	31. Reno, NV	5,534	53. Dallas, TX	5,014
7. Salt Lake City–Ogden, UT	6,973	32. San Antonio, TX	5,500	54. Burlington, VT	5,006
8. Ottawa–Hull, ON–PQ	6,751	33. Eugene–Springfield, OR	5,482		
9. Baltimore, MD	6,672	34. Edmonton, AB	5,422	55. Hartford, CT	4,996
10. Washington, DC–MD–VA–WV	6,546	35. Halifax, NS	5,418	56. Indianapolis, IN	4,961
				57. Greensboro–Winston-Salem–High Point, NC	4,957
11. Syracuse, NY	6,290	36. Davenport–Moline–Rock Island, IA–IL	5,412	58. Dayton–Springfield, OH	4,939
12. Calgary, AB	6,173	37. Bloomington–Normal, IL	5,411	59. Salem, OR	4,936
13. Montreal, PQ	6,081	38. Thunder Bay, ON	5,403		
14. Winnipeg, MB	5,983	39. Quebec City, PQ	5,397	60. Saskatoon, SK	4,925
15. Kitchener, ON	5,956	40. Cleveland–Lorain–Elyria, OH	5,340	61. Albuquerque, NM	4,918
				62. Minneapolis–St. Paul, MN–WI	4,880
15. Seattle–Bellevue–Everett, WA	5,956	41. Raleigh–Durham–Chapel Hill, NC	5,331	63. Springfield, IL	4,874
17. Vancouver, BC	5,947	42. Milwaukee–Waukesha, WI	5,310	64. Olympia, WA	4,869
18. Portland, OR	5,937	43. Philadelphia, PA–NJ	5,237		
19. Spokane, WA	5,896	44. Charlotte–Gastonia–Rock Hill, NC–SC	5,210	65. Vallejo–Fairfield–Napa, CA	4,836
20. St. Louis, MO–IL	5,824	45. Cincinnati, OH–KY–IN	5,203	66. Billings, MT	4,802
				67. Santa Cruz–Watsonville, CA	4,769
21. San Francisco, CA	5,821			68. Sherbrooke, PQ	4,765
22. St. Catharines–Niagara, ON	5,794	46. Harrisburg–Lebanon–Carlisle, PA	5,170	69. Toledo, OH	4,740
23. Denver, CO	5,737	47. Tacoma, WA	5,161		
24. Pittsburgh, PA	5,729	48. Hamilton, ON	5,113	70. Columbia, SC	4,732
25. Richmond–Petersburg, VA	5,727			71. Madison, WI	4,726
26. Richland–Kennewick–Pasco, WA	5,695			72. Honolulu, HI	4,714

Places Rated Rank	Places Rated Score	Places Rated Rank	Places Rated Score	Places Rated Rank	Places Rated Score
73. Detroit, MI	4,705	129. Redding, CA	4,085	186. Anchorage, AK	3,515
74. Lafayette, IN	4,693	130. Hagerstown, MD	4,083	187. Sacramento, CA	3,512
				188. Topeka, KS	3,509
75. Providence–Warwick–Cranston, RI	4,687	131. Charleston, WV	4,082	189. Benton Harbor, MI	3,478
76. Charleston–North Charleston, SC	4,669	132. Greeley, CO	4,067	190. St. John's, NF	3,473
77. London, ON	4,668	133. El Paso, TX	4,047		
78. Memphis, TN–AR–MS	4,660	134. Tampa–St. Petersburg–Clearwater, FL	4,042	191. Youngstown–Warren, OH	3,468
79. Medford–Ashland, OR	4,655	135. Fort Lauderdale, FL	4,040	192. Yuma, AZ	3,451
				193. Wichita, KS	3,432
80. Grand Forks, ND–MN	4,640	136. Lansing–East Lansing, MI	4,036	194. Tulsa, OK	3,425
81. Jacksonville, FL	4,617	137. Worcester–Fitchburg–Leominster, MA	4,034	195. Bremerton, WA	3,417
82. Sioux Falls, SD	4,615	138. Central New Jersey, NJ	4,024		
83. Windsor, ON	4,597	139. Des Moines, IA	4,007	196. Fayetteville, NC	3,405
84. Erie, PA	4,583	140. Atlantic City–Cape May, NJ	4,001	197. San Luis Obispo–Atascadero–Paso Robles, CA	3,403
85. New Haven–Meriden, CT	4,568	140. Trenton, NJ	4,001	197. Stockton–Lodi, CA	3,403
86. La Crosse, WI–MN	4,560	142. Amarillo, TX	3,997	199. Appleton–Oshkosh–Neenah, WI	3,376
87. Oakland, CA	4,551	143. Bangor, ME	3,990	200. Sheboygan, WI	3,375
88. Birmingham, AL	4,534	144. Salinas, CA	3,968		
88. Savannah, GA	4,534	145. Pittsfield, MA	3,948	201. Cumberland, MD–WV	3,369
90. South Bend, IN	4,521	146. Saginaw–Bay City–Midland, MI	3,906	202. Grand Rapids–Muskegon–Holland, MI	3,320
91. Houston, TX	4,497	147. Green Bay, WI	3,904	203. Scranton–Wilkes-Barre–Hazleton, PA	3,312
92. Kalamazoo–Battle Creek, MI	4,495	148. Lubbock, TX	3,895	204. Sioux City, IA–NE	3,281
93. San Jose, CA	4,462	149. Cheyenne, WY	3,894	205. Brownsville–Harlingen–San Benito, TX	3,275
95. Boise City, ID	4,442	150. Mobile, AL	3,892		
96. Yolo, CA	4,417	151. Omaha, NE–IA	3,887	206. Lynchburg, VA	3,273
97. Ann Arbor, MI	4,410	152. Montgomery, AL	3,879	207. Roanoke, VA	3,268
98. Daytona Beach, FL	4,398	153. Jackson, MS	3,858	208. West Palm Beach–Boca Raton, FL	3,254
99. Little Rock–North Little Rock, AR	4,392	154. Springfield, MA	3,849	209. Modesto, CA	3,244
100. Santa Barbara–Santa Maria–Lompoc, CA	4,375	155. Hamilton–Middletown, OH	3,821	210. New London–Norwich, CT–RI	3,227
101. New Bedford–Fall River–Attleboro, MA	4,351	156. Las Vegas, NV–AZ	3,817	211. Colorado Springs, CO	3,226
102. Miami, FL	4,328	157. St. Cloud, MN	3,789	212. Baton Rouge, LA	3,214
103. Orlando, FL	4,313	158. Kenosha, WI	3,777	213. Santa Rosa, CA	3,193
104. Rochester, NY	4,311	159. Yakima, WA	3,774	214. Lakeland–Winter Haven, FL	3,189
105. Oshawa, ON	4,308	159. Fort Wayne, IN	3,774	215. Chattanooga, TN–GA	3,167
106. Tucson, AZ	4,295	161. Columbus, OH	3,758	216. Macon, GA	3,118
107. Riverside–San Bernardino, CA	4,284	162. Portland, ME	3,751	217. Jackson, MI	3,096
108. Phoenix–Mesa, AZ	4,269	163. Duluth–Superior, MN–WI	3,746	218. Corpus Christi, TX	3,090
109. New Orleans, LA	4,263	164. Dutchess County, NY	3,729	219. Johnstown, PA	3,079
110. Sudbury, ON	4,233	165. Bismarck, ND	3,725	220. Glens Falls, NY	3,076
111. Stamford–Norwalk, CT	4,225	166. Asheville, NC	3,719	221. Rapid City, SD	3,072
112. Louisville, KY–IN	4,221	167. Utica–Rome, NY	3,703	222. Bakersfield, CA	3,051
113. Racine, WI	4,220	168. Peoria–Pekin, IL	3,684	222. Lake County, IL	3,051
114. Los Angeles–Long Beach, CA	4,211	169. Wilmington–Newark, DE–MD	3,683	224. Decatur, IL	3,049
115. Lincoln, NE	4,196	170. Boulder–Longmont, CO	3,664	225. Waco, TX	3,038
116. Gainesville, FL	4,187	171. Orange County, CA	3,657	226. Rocky Mount, NC	2,988
117. Great Falls, MT	4,185	172. Galveston–Texas City, TX	3,655	227. Manchester–Nashua, NH	2,977
118. Fargo–Moorhead, ND–MN	4,166	173. Tuscaloosa, AL	3,653	228. Chico–Paradise, CA	2,972
119. Victoria, BC	4,160	174. Fort Myers–Cape Coral, FL	3,639	229. Rockford, IL	2,964
120. Cedar Rapids, IA	4,159	175. Tallahassee, FL	3,635	230. Ventura, CA	2,961
121. Kankakee, IL	4,156	176. Bridgeport, CT	3,614	231. Janesville–Beloit, WI	2,953
122. Flint, MI	4,150	177. Binghamton, NY	3,608	232. Altoona, PA	2,943
123. Austin–San Marcos, TX	4,148	178. Rochester, MN	3,591	232. Knoxville, TN	2,943
124. Buffalo–Niagara Falls, NY	4,140	179. Shreveport–Bossier City, LA	3,589	232. Odessa–Midland, TX	2,943
125. Oklahoma City, OK	4,118	180. Lexington, KY	3,587	235. Norfolk–Virginia Beach–Newport News, VA–NC	2,932
126. Fort Worth–Arlington, TX	4,109	181. Greenville–Spartanburg–Anderson, SC	3,558		
127. Akron, OH	4,100	182. Iowa City, IA	3,553	236. Myrtle Beach, SC	2,920
128. Charlottesville, VA	4,088	183. Elmira, NY	3,549		
		184. Florence, SC	3,533		
		185. Springfield, MO	3,517		

Places Rated Rank	Places Rated Score	Places Rated Rank	Places Rated Score	Places Rated Rank	Places Rated Score
237. Monroe, LA	2,916	272. Columbus, GA–AL	2,416	308. Tyler, TX	1,962
238. Sarasota–Bradenton, FL	2,904	273. Danbury, CT	2,414	309. Bloomington, IN	1,912
238. Wilmington, NC	2,904	274. Allentown–Bethlehem–Easton, PA–NJ	2,410	310. Fort Smith, AR–OK	1,854
240. Elkhart–Goshen, IN	2,860	275. Reading, PA	2,395		
241. State College, PA	2,839			311. Joplin, MO	1,821
242. Huntington–Ashland, WV–KY–OH	2,825	276. Lafayette, LA	2,387	312. Sumter, SC	1,805
243. Las Cruces, NM	2,809	277. St. Joseph, MO	2,352	313. Athens, GA	1,801
243. Lawrence, KS	2,809	278. Greenville, NC	2,349	314. Santa Fe, NM	1,773
245. Killeen–Temple, TX	2,787	279. Chicoutimi–Jonquiere, PQ	2,347	315. Fort Walton Beach, FL	1,758
		280. Terre Haute, IN	2,326		
246. Lancaster, PA	2,767			316. Naples, FL	1,723
247. Pensacola, FL	2,764	281. Merced, CA	2,311	317. McAllen–Edinburg–Mission, TX	1,721
248. Evansville–Henderson, IN–KY	2,759	282. Waterloo–Cedar Falls, IA	2,301	318. Punta Gorda, FL	1,687
249. Casper, WY	2,749	283. Sharon, PA	2,277	319. Gadsden, AL	1,661
250. Anniston, AL	2,723	284. Northern New Jersey, NJ	2,273	320. Albany, GA	1,623
		284. Parkersburg–Marietta, WV–OH	2,273		
251. Longview–Marshall, TX	2,702			321. Fort Pierce–Port St. Lucie, FL	1,610
251. Texarkana, TX–Texarkana, AR	2,702	286. Dubuque, IA	2,264	322. Owensboro, KY	1,594
253. Muncie, IN	2,696	287. Alexandria, LA	2,261	323. Decatur, AL	1,566
254. Huntsville, AL	2,694	288. Wichita Falls, TX	2,257	324. Pine Bluff, AR	1,541
255. Portsmouth–Dover–Rochester, NH	2,655	289. Augusta–Aiken, GA–SC	2,231	325. San Angelo, TX	1,527
		290. Columbia, MO	2,216		
256. Orange County, NY	2,648			326. Fayetteville–Springdale–Rogers, AR	1,504
257. Johnson City–Kingsport–Bristol, TN–VA	2,640	291. Lima, OH	2,214	327. Long Island, NY	1,483
258. Fresno, CA	2,638	292. Waterbury, CT	2,205	328. Visalia–Tulare–Porterville, CA	1,439
259. Provo–Orem, UT	2,632	293. Vineland–Millville–Bridgeton, NJ	2,199	329. Barnstable–Yarmouth, MA	1,430
260. Ocala, FL	2,612	294. Williamsport, PA	2,179	330. Houma, LA	1,377
		295. Brazoria, TX	2,174		
261. Beaumont–Port Arthur, TX	2,606			331. Enid, OK	1,370
262. Pueblo, CO	2,604	296. Biloxi–Gulfport–Pascagoula, MS	2,140	332. Steubenville–Weirton, OH–WV	1,358
263. Bryan–College Station, TX	2,569	297. Clarksville–Hopkinsville, TN–KY	2,139	333. Monmouth–Ocean, NJ	1,315
264. Wheeling, WV–OH	2,557	298. Mansfield, OH	2,135	334. Jamestown, NY	1,307
265. Eau Claire, WI	2,537	299. Lewiston–Auburn, ME	2,134	334. Trois-Rivieres, PQ	1,307
		300. Fort Collins–Loveland, CO	2,119		
266. Laredo, TX	2,508			336. Lawton, OK	1,287
267. Lake Charles, LA	2,506	301. Wausau, WI	2,116	337. Jacksonville, NC	1,260
268. Saint John, NB	2,473	302. Canton–Massillon, OH	2,100	338. Dothan, AL	1,194
269. Melbourne–Titusville–Palm Bay, FL	2,465	303. Hickory–Morgantown, NC	2,084	339. Dover, DE	1,172
270. Danville, VA	2,458	304. Sherman–Denison, TX	2,045	340. Kokomo, IN	1,163
		305. York, PA	2,036		
271. Abilene, TX	2,430			341. Goldsboro, NC	1,128
		306. Panama City, FL	1,987	342. Victoria, TX	1,019
		307. Yuba City, CA	1,972	343. Florence, AL	948

Place Profiles: Transportation

The following pages detail local commuting time, mass transit, and intercity travel assets in each metro area.

Sources for the information include American Public Transit Association, *Transit Fact Book*, 1992; Canadian Urban Transit Association, *Canadian Transit Fact Book*,

1992; Community Transportation Association of America, *Directory of UMTA-Funded Rural and Specialized Transit Systems*, 1990; Jane's Information Group, *Jane's Urban Transport Systems*, 1992; National Railroad Passenger Corporation, *AMTRAK's America*, 1993, and AMTRAK

Timetable, 1993; Official Airline Guides, Inc., *Travel Planner*, Spring 1993; Statistics Canada, Aviation Statistics Center, *Aviation Bulletins*, 1992; U.S. Department of Commerce, Bureau of the Census, 1990 Census of Population; U.S. Department of Transportation, Federal Aviation Administration, *Airport Activity Statistics of Certificated Route Air Carriers*, 1992; Federal Highway Administration, unpublished "Interstate System Log and Finder List," 1993; and Federal Transit Administration, *Section 15 Report*, 1993.

The first entry, **Daily Commute**, is the time workers spend getting to and from the job, regardless of the mode of transportation. These times are 1990 U.S. Census journey-to-work data multiplied by 2.2 to represent a round-trip whose return half takes slightly longer than the first half. Figures for Canadian metro areas are *Places Rated* estimates.

A major part of a metro area's freeways are also heavily traveled routes of the country's **National Highways.** These routes are intercity travel assets, too. Accordingly, each main route in the system that reaches the metro area is listed.

Under the heading **Public Transportation** is the name of the local transit agency (or the name of the largest agency if there is more than one) and the number of mass transit vehicles from all local agencies on the street at rush hour.

The first item under the heading **Scheduled Domestic Air Service** is the FAA's hub classification for the metro area: large hub, medium hub, small hub, or nonhub. Hub classifications for Canadian airports are derived from their share in total North American pas-senger enplanements. In the 20 Metropolitan Complexes, the core metro area is usually designated as a large hub, and other member metro areas are classified as part of that hub. The entry for Greeley, CO, for example, reads "Part of Denver hub."

The airport's name comes next, followed by the airport's three-letter international identifier enclosed in parentheses. All airports, including those that *Places Rated* scores as part of the air service shared by members of a Metropolitan Complex, are listed under the metro area in which they are located. Also noted are the number of major scheduled airlines that serve the airport and their total number of flights departing weekly.

In three exceptions, airports are listed under two metro areas and credited to both. One involves Dallas–Fort Worth Regional, situated in both Dallas, TX, and Fort Worth, TX; the other two are airports located in one metro area but roughly equidistant from both metro areas: Akron–Canton Regional, located in Akron, OH, but also close to Canton, OH, and Bradley International of Hartford, CT, about 20 minutes away from both downtown Hartford, CT, and Springfield, MA.

For metro areas that neither have airports nor share them, the location of the nearest airport is given along with its distance and direction.

Finally, under **Passenger Rail**, figures for AMTRAK and VIA service are the number of scheduled passenger trains departing from the metro area in a typical week.

A check (✓) preceding a metro area's name highlights it as one of the top 35 places for transportation assets.

Metro Area	Daily Commute	National Highways	Public Transportation	Scheduled Domestic Air Service	Passenger Rail	Places Rated Score	Places Rated Rank
Abilene, TX	32.3 minutes	I-20	Abilene TS 10 city buses	Nonhub Abilene Regional (ABI) 1 airline, 6 flights/week	—	2,430	271
Akron, OH	44.6 minutes	I-76 I-77	Metropolitan RTA 129 city buses	Part of Cleveland hub Akron–Canton Regional (CAK) 6 airlines, 102 flights/week	14 trains/week	4,100	127
Albany, GA	36.5 minutes	—	Albany TS 13 city buses	Nonhub Southwest Georgia Regional (ABY) Commuter service only	—	1,623	320
✓ Albany–Schenectady–Troy, NY	43.9 minutes	I-87 I-88 I-90	Capital District TA 196 city buses	Small hub Albany County (ALB) 10 airlines, 262 flights/week	129 trains/week	5,627	28
Albuquerque, NM	43.2 minutes	I-25 I-40	SUNTRAN 106 city buses	Medium hub Albuquerque International (ABQ) 10 airlines, 629 flights/week	14 trains/week	4,918	61
Alexandria, LA	43.6 minutes	I-49	Alexandria TS 10 city buses	Nonhub Alexandria Esler Regional (ESF) Commuter service only	—	2,261	287
Allentown–Bethlehem–Easton, PA–NJ	44.8 minutes	I-78	LANTA 55 city buses	Small hub Allentown–Bethlehem–Easton (ABE) 8 airlines, 157 flights/week	—	2,410	274

Metro Area	Daily Commute	National Highways	Public Transportation	Scheduled Domestic Air Service	Passenger Rail	Places Rated Score	Places Rated Rank
Altoona, PA	35.0 minutes	—	AMTRAN 24 city buses	Nonhub Altoona–Blair County (AOO) Commuter service only	28 trains/week	2,943	232
Amarillo, TX	37.1 minutes	I-27 I-40	Amarillo TS 14 city buses	Small hub Amarillo Air Terminal (AMA) 6 airlines, 116 flights/week	—	3,997	142
Anchorage, AK	39.2 minutes	—	Anchorage TS 45 city buses	Medium hub Anchorage International (ANC) 9 airlines, 650 flights/week	—	3,515	186
Ann Arbor, MI	46.8 minutes	I-94	Ann Arbor TA 53 city buses	Part of Detroit hub	35 trains/week	4,410	97
Anniston, AL	40.0 minutes	I-20	—	Nearest airport: Birmingham, AL, 65 mi W	14 trains/week	2,723	250
Appleton–Oshkosh–Neenah, WI	33.8 minutes	—	Valley Transit/Oshkosh TS 50 city buses	Nonhub Outagamie County (ATW) 2 airlines, 92 flights/week Wittman Regional (OSH) 1 airline, 19 flights/week	—	3,376	199
Asheville, NC	41.1 minutes	I-26 I-40	Asheville TA 18 city buses	Small hub Asheville Regional (AVL) 4 airlines, 77 flights/week	—	3,719	165
Athens, GA	37.8 minutes	—	Athens TS 14 city buses	Nonhub Athens–Ben Epps (AHN) Commuter service only	—	1,801	313
✓ Atlanta, GA	55.8 minutes	I-20 I-75 I-85	MARTA 581 city buses 138 rapid railcars	Large hub Hartsfield–Atlanta International (ATL) 15 airlines, 3,957 flights/week	14 trains/week	6,967	5
Atlantic City–Cape May, NJ	42.8 minutes	—	NJTC 65 city buses	Part of Philadelphia hub Atlantic City International (ACY) 5 airlines, 38 flights/week	22 trains/week	4,001	140
Augusta–Aiken, GA–SC	47.1 minutes	I-20	Augusta TD 27 city buses	Nonhub Bush Field (AGS) 3 airlines, 66 flights/week	—	2,231	289
Austin–San Marcos, TX	46.3 minutes	I-35	Capital MTA 258 city buses	Medium hub Robert Mueller Municipal (AUS) 10 airlines, 625 flights/week	14 trains/week	4,148	123
Bakersfield, CA	42.2 minutes	—	Golden Empire TD 52 city buses	Nonhub Meadows Field (BFL) 6 airlines, 100 flights/week	42 trains/week	3,051	222
✓ Baltimore, MD	55.9 minutes	I-70 I-83 I-95 I-97	Baltimore MTA 792 city buses 60 rapid rail cars 1 commuter railroad	Part of Washington, DC, hub Baltimore–Washington International (BWI) 15 airlines, 1,286 flights/week	497 trains/week	6,672	9
Bangor, ME	32.0 minutes	I-95	The Bus 10 city buses	Nonhub Bangor International (BGR) 10 airlines, 71 flights/week	—	3,990	143
Barnstable–Yarmouth, MA	41.4 minutes	—	Cape Cod RTA 20 city buses	Nonhub Barnstable County (HYA) Commuter service only	—	1,430	329
Baton Rouge, LA	48.9 minutes	I-10 I-12	Cap Trans 37 city buses	Small hub Ryan Field (BTR) 7 airlines, 162 flights/week	—	3,214	212
Beaumont–Port Arthur, TX	42.5 minutes	I-10	Transit 18 city buses	Nonhub Jefferson County (BPT) Commuter service only	6 trains/week	2,606	261
Bellingham, WA	36.1 minutes	I-5	Muni Transit 20 city buses	Nonhub Bellingham International (BLI) 5 airlines, 123 flights/week	—	5,025	50
Benton Harbor, MI	37.0 minutes	I-94 I-96	—	Nearest airport: South Bend, IN, 33 mi SE	63 trains/week	3,478	189
Billings, MT	34.1 minutes	I-90 I-94	Metro Transit 16 city buses	Small hub Logan Field (BIL) 9 airlines, 177 flights/week	—	4,802	66
Biloxi–Gulfport–Pascagoula, MS	44.5 minutes	I-10	MS Coast 24 city buses	Nonhub Gulfport–Biloxi Regional (GPT) 1 airline, 14 flights/week	—	2,140	296
Binghamton, NY	37.2 minutes	I-81 I-88	Broome County DPT 36 city buses	Nonhub Broome County (BGM) 3 airlines, 61 flights/week	—	3,608	177

Metro Area	Daily Commute	National Highways	Public Transportation	Scheduled Domestic Air Service	Passenger Rail	Places Rated Score	Places Rated Rank
Birmingham, AL	49.4 minutes	I-20 I-59 I-65	MAX 101 city buses	Small hub Birmingham Municipal (BHM) 9 airlines, 363 flights/week	21 trains/week	4,534	88
Bismarck, ND	27.1 minutes	I-94	—	Nonhub Bismarck Municipal (BIS) 4 airlines, 73 flights/week	—	3,725	165
Bloomington, IN	37.8 minutes	—	Bloomington PTC 14 city buses	Nearest airport: Indianapolis, IN, 47 mi N	—	1,912	309
Bloomington–Normal, IL	33.9 minutes	I-39 I-55 I-74	B-N PTS 14 city buses	Nonhub Bloomington–Normal (BMI) 3 airlines, 35 flights/week	47 trains/week	5,411	37
Boise City, ID	36.6 minutes	I-84	Boise Urban Stages 19 city buses	Small hub Boise Air Terminal (BOI) 9 airlines, 387 flights/week	14 trains/week	4,442	95
✓ Boston, MA	51.8 minutes	I-90 I-93 I-95	MBTA 1,408 city buses 320 rapid rail cars 25 trolley coaches 2 commuter railroads 2 ferries	Large hub Logan International (BOS) 17 airlines, 2,098 flights/week	120 trains/week	7,042	4
Boulder–Longmont, CO	43.1 minutes	I-25	RTD 34 city buses	Part of Denver hub	—	3,664	170
Brazoria, TX	51.5 minutes	—	—	Part of Houston hub	—	2,174	295
Bremerton, WA	51.5 minutes	—	Kitsap Transit 60 city buses	Part of Seattle hub Bremerton National (PWT) Commuter service only	—	3,417	195
Bridgeport, CT	44.7 minutes	I-95	GBTD 50 city buses	Part of New York hub	112 trains/week	3,614	176
Brownsville–Harlingen–San Benito, TX	36.5 minutes	—	BUS and Valley TS 30 city buses	Small hub Rio Grande Valley International (HRL) 3 airlines, 129 flights/week	—	3,275	205
Bryan–College Station, TX	32.3 minutes	—	Brazos Valley TA 7 city buses	Nonhub Easterwood Field (CLL) Commuter service only	14 trains/week	2,569	263
Buffalo–Niagara Falls, NY	41.9 minutes	I-90	Niagara Frontier 335 city buses 23 rapid rail	Medium hub Greater Buffalo International (BUF) 10 airlines, 545 flights/week	50 trains/week	4,140	124
Burlington, VT	37.0 minutes	I-89	Chittenden County TA 24 city buses	Small hub Burlington International (BTV) 4 airlines, 127 flights/week	14 trains/week	5,006	55
✓ Calgary, AB	42.0 minutes	TC	Calgary Transit 408 city buses 83 rapid rail cars	Large hub Calgary International (YYC) 7 airlines, 1,163 flights/week	—	6,173	12
Canton–Massillon, OH	41.3 minutes	I-77	Canton RTA 32 city buses	Part of Cleveland hub Akron–Canton Regional (CAK) 6 airlines, 102 flights/week	—	2,100	302
Casper, WY	32.6 minutes	I-25	—	Nonhub Casper Air Terminal (CPR) 4 airlines, 28 flights/week	—	2,749	249
Cedar Rapids, IA	34.1 minutes	I-80	City Bus Department 34 city buses	Small hub Cedar Rapids Municipal (CID) 8 airlines, 167 flights/week	—	4,159	120
Central New Jersey, NJ	56.6 minutes	I-78 I-80	NJTC 150 city buses	Part of New York hub	38 trains/week	4,024	138
✓ Champaign–Urbana, IL	31.9 minutes	I-57 I-72 I-74	Champaign–Urbana MTD 50 city buses	Nonhub University of Illinois–Willard (CMI) 4 airlines, 102 flights/week	28 trains/week	6,853	6
Charleston, WV	42.9 minutes	I-64 I-77 I-79	Kanawha Valley RTA 41 city buses	Nonhub Yeager Field (CRW) 3 airlines, 89 flights/week	6 trains/week	4,669	76
Charleston–North Charleston, SC	48.5 minutes	I-26	SC E&G Co 35 city buses	Small hub Charleston–International (CHS) 11 airlines, 220 flights/week	21 trains/week	4,082	131
Charlotte–Gastonia–Rock Hill, NC–SC	46.7 minutes	I-77 I-85	Charlotte TS 141 city buses	Large hub Douglas International (CLT) 11 airlines, 2,479 flights/week	28 trains/week	5,210	44

Metro Area	Daily Commute	National Highways	Public Transportation	Scheduled Domestic Air Service	Passenger Rail	Places Rated Score	Places Rated Rank
Charlottesville, VA	40.9 minutes	I-64	Charlottesville TS 11 city buses	Nonhub Charlottesville–Albemarle (CHO) 2 airlines, 58 flights/week	20 trains/week	4,088	128
Chattanooga, TN–GA	46.6 minutes	I-24 I-75	Area RTA 40 city buses 2 cable inclines	Nonhub Lovell Field (CHA) 5 airlines, 80 flights/week	—	3,167	215
Cheyenne, WY	29.5 minutes	I-25 I-80	—	Nonhub Cheyenne Municipal (CYS) 4 airlines, 5 flights/week	14 trains/week	3,894	149
✓ Chicago, IL	61.5 minutes	I-55 I-57 I-80 I-88 I-90 I-94	CTA 2,325 city buses 924 rapid rail cars 4 commuter railroads	Large hub Chicago Midway (MDW) 8 airlines, 1,037 flights/week O'Hare International (ORD) 16 airlines, 6,326 flights/week	286 trains/week	7,429	1
Chico–Paradise, CA	36.5 minutes	—	Chico TS 8 city buses	Nonhub Chico Municipal (CIC) 1 airline, 32 flights/week	14 trains/week	2,972	228
Chicoutimi–Jonquiere, PQ	36.5 minutes	—	CITS 30 city buses	Nearest airport: Bagotville, PQ, 11 mi NW	3 trains/week	2,347	279
Cincinnati, OH–KY–IN	48.9 minutes	I-71 I-74 I-75	SORTA 429 city buses	Large hub Greater Cincinnati (CVG) 11 airlines, 1,338 flights/week	6 trains/week	5,203	46
Clarksville–Hopkinsville, TN–KY	40.6 minutes	I-24	Clarksville TS 7 city buses	Nearest airport: Nashville, 50 mi SE	—	2,139	297
Cleveland–Lorain–Elyria, OH	48.1 minutes	I-71 I-77 I-80 I-90	RTA 657 city buses 68 rapid rail cars	Medium hub Hopkins International (CLE) 14 airlines, 1,250 flights/week	28 trains/week	5,340	40
Colorado Springs, CO	39.8 minutes	I-25	CST 38 city buses	Small hub Colorado Springs Municipal (COS) 8 airlines, 234 flights/week	—	3,226	211
Columbia, MO	35.6 minutes	I-70	Columbia Area TS 15 city buses	Nonhub Columbia Regional (COU) Commuter service only	—	2,216	290
Columbia, SC	44.4 minutes	I-20 I-26 I-77	SC E&G Co 35 city buses	Small hub Columbia Metropolitan (CAE) 8 airlines, 210 flights/week	14 trains/week	4,732	70
Columbus, GA–AL	38.6 minutes	I-185 I-71	METRA 24 city buses	Nonhub Columbus Metropolitan (CSG) 1 airline, 19 flights/week	—	2,416	272
Columbus, OH	45.6 minutes	I-70	COTA 264 city buses	Medium hub Port Columbus International (CMH) 13 airlines, 569 flights/week	—	3,758	161
Corpus Christi, TX	41.4 minutes	I-37	Corpus Christi RTA 53 city buses	Small hub Corpus Christi International (CRP) 4 airlines, 136 flights/week	—	3,090	218
Cumberland, MD–WV	40.5 minutes	I-68	Allegany County TA 10 city buses	Nonhub Municipal (CBE) Commuter service only	14 trains/week	3,369	201
Dallas, TX	52.9 minutes	I-20 I-30 I-35E I-45	DART 517 city buses	Large hub Dallas–Fort Worth International (DFW) 19 airlines, 5,166 flights/week Dallas Love Field (DAL) 3 airlines, 790 flights/week	21 trains/week	5,014	53
Danbury, CT	55.0 minutes	I-84	Hart Lines 11 city buses	Part of New York hub	—	2,414	273
Danville, VA	41.1 minutes	—	Danville TS 6 city buses	Nonhub Danville Regional (DAN) Commuter service only	14 trains/week	2,458	270
Davenport–Moline–Rock Island, IA–IL	37.2 minutes	I-74 I-80 I-88	County MTD 68 city buses	Small hub Quad-City (MLI) 6 airlines, 150 flights/week	14 trains/week	5,412	36
Dayton–Springfield, OH	42.1 minutes	I-70 I-75	Miami Valley RTA 162 city buses 26 trolley coaches	Medium hub Cox–Dayton International (DAY) 8 airlines, 687 flights/week	—	4,939	58
Daytona Beach, FL	45.0 minutes	I-4 I-95	Volusia TA 30 city buses	Small hub Daytona Beach Regional (DAB) 6 airlines, 116 flights/week	28 trains/week	4,398	98

Metro Area	Daily Commute	National Highways	Public Transportation	Scheduled Domestic Air Service	Passenger Rail	Places Rated Score	Places Rated Rank
Decatur, AL	47.0 minutes	I-65	—	Nearest airport: Huntsville, AL, 12 mi NE	—	1,566	323
Decatur, IL	35.4 minutes	I-72	DPTS 17 city buses	Nonhub Decatur Municipal (DEC) 2 airlines, 36 flights/week	—	3,049	224
✓ Denver, CO	48.1 minutes	I-25 I-70 I-76	RTD 540 city buses	Large hub Stapleton International (DEN) 17 airlines, 2,911 flights/week	21 trains/week	5,737	23
Des Moines, IA	38.0 minutes	I-35 I-80	MTA 67 city buses	Small hub Des Moines International (DSM) 10 airlines, 246 flights/week	—	4,007	139
Detroit, MI	50.9 minutes	I-75 I-94 I-96	Detroit DOT/SEMTA 700 city buses 2 commuter railroads	Large hub Detroit City (DET) 2 airlines, 101 flights/week Detroit Metro–Wayne County (DTW) 17 airlines, 2,539 flights/week	49 trains/week	4,705	73
Dothan, AL	37.0 minutes	—	SE Alabama Transit 4 city buses	Nonhub Municipal (DHN) Commuter service only	—	1,194	338
Dover, DE	42.2 minutes	—	Delaware TA 6 city buses	Nearest airport: Philadelphia, PA, 60 mi NE	—	1,172	339
Dubuque, IA	30.1 minutes	—	KeyLine 21 city buses	Nonhub Dubuque Regional (DBQ) 2 airlines, 11 flights/week	—	2,264	286
Duluth–Superior, MN–WI	37.0 minutes	I-35	Duluth TA 71 city buses	Nonhub Duluth International (DLH) 4 airlines, 46 flights/week	—	3,746	163
Dutchess County, NY	52.8 minutes	I-97	Dutchess County Loop 22 city buses	Part of New York hub Dutchess County (POU) Commuter service only	136 trains/week	3,729	164
Eau Claire, WI	33.5 minutes	I-94	Transit System 12 city buses	Nonhub Eau Claire County (EAU) Commuter service only	—	2,537	265
✓ Edmonton, AB	45.6 minutes	—	Edmonton Transit 604 city buses 37 rapid rail cars 100 trolley coaches	Large hub Edmonton International (YEG) 6 airlines, 512 flights/week Edmonton Municipal (YXD) 6 airlines, 168 flights/week	6 trains/week	5,422	34
El Paso, TX	43.1 minutes	I-10	Sun Metro 95 city buses	Medium hub El Paso International (ELP) 7 airlines, 536 flights/week	6 trains/week	4,047	133
Elkhart–Goshen, IN	35.4 minutes	I-80	—	Nearest airport: South Bend, IN, 22 mi W	42 trains/week	2,860	240
Elmira, NY	36.3 minutes	—	Chemung County TS 19 city buses	Nonhub Elmira–Corning Regional (ELM) 1 airline, 37 flights/week	—	3,549	183
Enid, OK	30.8 minutes	—	—	Nearest airport: Oklahoma City, 95 mi N	—	1,370	331
Erie, PA	35.6 minutes	I-79 I-90	Erie MTA 51 city buses	Nonhub Erie International (ERI) 1 airline, 56 flights/week	14 trains/week	4,583	84
✓ Eugene–Springfield, OR	38.1 minutes	I-5	Lane County MTD 62 city buses	Small hub Mahlon Sweet Field (EUG) 5 airlines, 216 flights/week	14 trains/week	5,482	33
Evansville–Henderson, IN–KY	39.1 minutes	I-64	Evansville TS/HART 23 city buses	Nonhub Evansville Dress Regional (EVV) 4 airlines, 76 flights/week	—	2,759	248
Fargo–Moorhead, ND–MN	30.7 minutes	I-29	MAT/Moorhead CMT 18 city buses	Nonhub Hector International (FAR) 3 airlines, 52 flights/week	14 trains/week	4,166	118
Fayetteville, NC	38.3 minutes	I-95	Area Transit 12 city buses	Nonhub Fayetteville–Grannis Field (FAY) 3 airlines, 66 flights/week	21 trains/week	3,405	196
Fayetteville–Springdale–Rogers, AR	36.5 minutes	—	ATA 9 city buses	Nonhub Drake Field (FYV) 1 airline, 20 flights/week	—	1,504	326
Flint, MI	44.9 minutes	I-69 I-75	MTA 41 city buses	Part of Detroit hub Bishop International (FNT) 3 airlines, 34 flights/week	14 trains/week	4,150	122

Metro Area	Daily Commute	National Highways	Public Transportation	Scheduled Domestic Air Service	Passenger Rail	Places Rated Score	Places Rated Rank
Florence, AL	44.5 minutes	—	—	Nonhub Muscle Shoals (MSL) Commuter service only	—	948	343
Florence, SC	40.9 minutes	I-20 I-95	Pee Dee RTA 6 city buses	Nonhub Florence Regional (FLO) Commuter service only	21 trains/week	3,533	184
Fort Collins–Loveland, CO	39.6 minutes	I-25	TransFort 10 city buses	Nearest airport: Denver, CO, 64 mi S	—	2,119	300
Fort Lauderdale, FL	49.5 minutes	I-95	Broward County MTD 178 city buses 1 commuter railroad	Part of Miami hub Fort Lauderdale–Hollywood International (FLL) 15 airlines, 778 flights/week	28 trains/week	4,040	135
Fort Myers–Cape Coral, FL	45.3 minutes	I-75	Lee County Transit 26 city buses	Medium hub Southwest Florida Regional (RSW) 11 airlines, 397 flights/week	—	3,639	174
Fort Pierce–Port St. Lucie, FL	44.8 minutes	I-95	—	Nearest airport: West Palm Beach, 40 mi S	—	1,610	321
Fort Smith, AR–OK	41.3 minutes	I-40	—	Nonhub Fort Smith Regional (FSM) 1 airline, 17 flights/week	—	1,854	310
Fort Walton Beach, FL	38.7 minutes	I-10	—	Nonhub Okaloosa County (VPS) Commuter service only	—	1,758	315
Fort Wayne, IN	40.9 minutes	I-69	PTC 54 city buses	Nonhub Baer Field (FWA) 8 airlines, 145 flights/week	28 trains/week	3,774	159
Fort Worth–Arlington, TX	49.7 minutes	I-20 I-35W	The T 105 city buses	Part of Dallas hub Dallas–Fort Worth International (DFW) 19 airlines, 5,166 flights/week	14 trains/week	4,109	126
Fresno, CA	41.2 minutes	—	—	Small hub Fresno Air Terminal (FAT) 7 airlines, 360 flights/week	42 trains/week	2,638	258
Gadsden, AL	42.5 minutes	I-59	—	Nearest airport: Birmingham, AL, 50 mi SW	—	1,661	319
Gainesville, FL	39.8 minutes	I-75	RTS 32 city buses	Nonhub Gainesville Regional (GNV) 3 airlines, 39 flights/week	14 trains/week	4,187	116
Galveston–Texas City, TX	51.3 minutes	I-45	Island TS 12 city buses 1 ferry	Part of Houston hub	—	3,655	172
✓ Gary, IN	51.2 minutes	I-65 I-80 I-90 I-94	Gary PTC/TS 42 city buses 1 commuter railroad	Part of Chicago hub	125 trains/week	5,620	29
Glens Falls, NY	41.3 minutes	I-87	Glens Falls TS 7 city buses	Nearest airport: Albany, NY, 47 mi S	14 trains/week	3,076	220
Goldsboro, NC	37.4 minutes	—	—	Nearest airport: Raleigh, NC, 60 mi NW	—	1,128	341
Grand Forks, ND–MN	27.4 minutes	I-29	City Bus 12 city buses	Nonhub Grand Forks International (GFK) 4 airlines, 53 flights/week	14 trains/week	4,640	80
Grand Rapids–Muskegon–Holland, MI	39.2 minutes	I-96	GRATA/MATS 80 city buses	Small hub Kent County International (GRR) 7 airlines, 238 flights/week Muskegon County (MKG) 1 airline, 9 flights/week	14 trains/week	3,321	202
Great Falls, MT	30.8 minutes	I-15	Great Falls TD 13 city buses	Small hub Great Falls International (GTF) 8 airlines, 190 flights/week	—	4,185	117
Greeley, CO	39.2 minutes	—	The Bus 10 city buses	Part of Denver hub	14 trains/week	4,067	132
Green Bay, WI	34.1 minutes	I-43	Green Bay TS 26 city buses	Nonhub Austin–Straubel International (GRB) 4 airlines, 143 flights/week	—	3,904	147
Greensboro–Winston-Salem–High Point, NC	40.6 minutes	I-40 I-85	Triad 70 city buses	Small hub Piedmont Triad International (GSO) 8 airlines, 411 flights/week Smith Reynolds (INT) Commuter service only	28 trains/week	4,957	57

Metro Area	Daily Commute	National Highways	Public Transportation	Scheduled Domestic Air Service	Passenger Rail	Places Rated Score	Places Rated Rank
Greenville, NC	38.1 minutes	—	Greenville Area TD 6 city buses	Nonhub Pitt–Greenville (PGV) 1 airline, 31 flights/week	—	2,349	278
Greenville–Spartanburg–Anderson, SC	40.2 minutes	I-26 I-85	Greenville TA 22 city buses	Small hub Greenville–Spartanburg (GSP) 8 airlines, 190 flights/week	14 trains/week	3,557	181
Hagerstown, MD	47.1 minutes	I-70 I-81	Wash County TC 11 city buses	Part of Washington, DC, hub	—	4,083	130
✓ Halifax, NS	35.0 minutes	—	METRO TRANSIT 144 city buses 1 ferry	Medium hub Halifax International (YHZ) 3 airlines, 416 flights/week Civic (YHM) Commuter service only	6 trains/week	5,418	35
Hamilton, ON	41.7 minutes	—	Street Railway 304 city buses 51 trolley coaches	Part of Toronto hub	—	5,113	48
Hamilton–Middletown, OH	44.9 minutes	I-75	City Lines 15 city buses	Part of Cincinnati hub	6 trains/week	3,821	155
Harrisburg–Lebanon–Carlisle, PA	41.7 minutes	I-76 I-81 I-93	CAT 59 city buses	Small hub Harrisburg International (MDT) 7 airlines, 219 flights/week	105 trains/week	5,170	46
Hartford, CT	44.4 minutes	I-84 I-91	Conn Transit 200 city buses	Medium hub Bradley International (BDL) 14 airlines, 587 flights/week	126 trains/week	4,996	54
Hickory–Morgantown, NC	38.9 minutes	I-40	Piedmont Wagon 4 city buses	Nonhub Hickory Regional (HKY) Commuter service only	—	2,084	303
Honolulu, HI	52.8 minutes	I-1	The Bus 408 city buses	Large hub Honolulu International (HNL) 13 airlines, 1,684 flights/week	—	4,714	72
Houma, LA	51.0 minutes	—	—	Nearest airport: New Orleans, LA, 55 mi NE	6 trains/week	1,377	330
Houston, TX	56.8 minutes	I-10 I-45	MTA 793 city buses	Large hub Ellington Field (EFD) 2 airlines, 17 flights/week William P. Hobby (HOU) 15 airlines, 1,135 flights/week Houston Intercontinental (IAH) 13 airlines, 1,929 flights/week	13 trains/week	4,497	91
Huntington–Ashland, WV–KY–OH	41.7 minutes	I-64	Tri-State TA 28 city buses	Nonhub Tri-State–Ferguson Field (HTS) 3 airlines, 53 flights/week	6 trains/week	2,825	242
Huntsville, AL	43.4 minutes	I-65	City of Huntsville 4 city buses	Small hub Huntsville International (HSV) 10 airlines, 179 flights/week	—	2,694	254
Indianapolis, IN	46.8 minutes	I-65 I-69 I-70 I-74	Indianapolis METRO 173 city buses	Medium hub Indianapolis International (IND) 13 airlines, 1,015 flights/week	13 trains/week	4,961	56
Iowa City, IA	34.5 minutes	I-80	ICT/CAMBUS 32 city buses	Nearest airport: Cedar Rapids, IA, 22 mi NW	—	3,553	181
Jackson, MI	43.8 minutes	I-94	Jackson TA 8 city buses	Nearest airport: Lansing, MI, 38 mi N	35 trains/week	3,096	217
Jackson, MS	43.8 minutes	I-20 I-55	JATRAN 34 city buses	Small hub Allen C. Thompsen Field (JAN) 6 airlines, 152 flights/week	14 trains/week	3,858	153
Jacksonville, FL	48.4 minutes	I-10 I-95	JTA 134 city buses	Medium hub Jacksonville International (10X) 12 airlines, 389 flights/week	49 trains/week	4,617	81
Jacksonville, NC	40.9 minutes	—	—	Nonhub Albert J. Ellis (OAJ) 1 airline, 20 flights/week	—	1,260	337
Jamestown, NY	32.3 minutes	—	—	Nonhub Chautauqua County (JHW) Commuter service only	—	1,307	334
Janesville–Beloit, WI	38.3 minutes	I-90	Transit System 25 city buses	Nearest airport: Rockford, IL 40 mi SW	—	2,953	231

Metro Area	Daily Commute	National Highways	Public Transportation	Scheduled Domestic Air Service	Passenger Rail	Places Rated Score	Places Rated Rank
Johnson City–Kingsport–Bristol, TN–VA	41.9 minutes	I-81	Tri-City TS 12 city buses	Nonhub Tri-City Regional (TRI) 3 airlines, 66 flights/week	—	2,640	257
Johnstown, PA	39.2 minutes	—	Cambria County TA 20 city buses	Nonhub Johnstown–Cambria County (JST) Commuter service only	28 trains/week	3,079	219
Joplin, MO	36.6 minutes	I-44	—	Nonhub Joplin Regional (JLN) Commuter service only	—	1,821	311
Kalamazoo–Battle Creek, MI	38.4 minutes	I-94	Metro TS 45 city buses	Nonhub Kalamazoo–Battle Creek International (AZO) 5 airlines, 105 flights/week	63 trains/week	4,495	92
Kankakee, IL	42.7 minutes	I-57	—	Part of Chicago hub	28 trains/week	4,156	121
Kansas City, MO–KS	46.0 minutes	I-29 I-35 I-70	KCATA 266 city buses	Medium hub Kansas City International (MCI) 16 airlines, 1,005 flights/week	42 trains/week	5,081	49
Kenosha, WI	46.6 minutes	I-94	Transit Comm 27 city buses	Part of Chicago hub	—	3,777	158
Killeen–Temple, TX	35.1 minutes	I-35	—	Nonhub Municipal (ILE) Commuter service only	14 trains/week	2,787	245
✓ Kitchener, ON	39.0 minutes	—	Kitchener–Cambridge TS 116 city buses	Part of Toronto hub	28 trains/week	5,956	15
Knoxville, TN	45.8 minutes	I-40 I-75	Knoxville TA 54 city buses	Small hub McGhee Tyson (TYS) 9 airlines, 215 flights/week	—	2,943	232
Kokomo, IN	36.3 minutes	—	—	Nearest airport: Indianapolis, IN, 58 mi S	—	1,163	340
La Crosse, WI–MN	32.8 minutes	I-90	MTU 14 city buses	Nonhub La Crosse Municipal (LSE) 4 airlines, 55 flights/week	14 trains/week	4,560	86
Lafayette, LA	44.7 minutes	I-10 I-49	COLT 12 city buses	Nonhub Lafayette Regional (LFT) 1 airline, 22 flights/week	6 trains/week	2,387	276
Lafayette, IN	35.1 minutes	I-65	PTC 35 city buses	Nonhub Purdue University (LAF) 1 airline, 8 flights/week	20 trains/week	4,693	74
Lake Charles, LA	40.9 minutes	I-10	Lake Charles TS 6 city buses	Nonhub Lake Charles Regional (LCH) Commuter service only	6 trains/week	2,506	267
Lake County, IL	56.1 minutes	I-94	Transit 5 city buses	Part of Chicago hub	—	3,051	222
Lakeland–Winter Haven, FL	44.4 minutes	I-4	MTD 15 city buses	Nearest airport: Tampa, FL, 35 mi SW	56 trains/week	3,189	214
Lancaster, PA	38.5 minutes	—	Red Rose TA 30 city buses	Nonhub Lancaster Municipal (LNS) Commuter service only	119 trains/week	2,767	246
Lansing–East Lansing, MI	40.6 minutes	I-69 I-96	Capital Area TA 52 city buses	Nonhub Capital City (LAN) 5 airlines, 105 flights/week	14 trains/week	4,036	136
Laredo, TX	37.6 minutes	I-35	Muni TS 21 city buses	Nonhub Laredo International (LRD) Commuter service only	—	2,508	266
Las Cruces, NM	40.7 minutes	I-10 I-25	Roadrunner Transit 8 city buses	Nearest airport: El Paso, TX, 44 mi SE	—	2,809	243
Las Vegas, NV–AZ	44.1 minutes	I-15	Las Vegas RTC 32 city buses	Large hub McCarran International (LAS) 12 airlines, 1,863 flights/week	28 trains/week	3,817	156
Lawrence, KS	37.0 minutes	I-70	—	Nearest airport: Kansas City, MO, 35 mi NE	7 trains/week	2,809	243
Lawton, OK	32.8 minutes	—	—	Nonhub Lawton Municipal (LAW) Commuter service only	—	1,287	336
Lewiston–Auburn, ME	33.9 minutes	I-95	Lewiston–Auburn TC 10 city buses	Nearest airport: Portland, ME, 35 mi S	—	2,134	299

Metro Area	Daily Commute	National Highways	Public Transportation	Scheduled Domestic Air Service	Passenger Rail	Places Rated Score	Places Rated Rank
Lexington, KY	39.8 minutes	I-64 I-75	Lexington TA 36 city buses	Small hub Blue Grass Field (LEX) 4 airlines, 162 flights/week	—	3,587	180
Lima, OH	35.5 minutes	I-75	Allen County RTA 8 city buses	Nearest airport: Dayton, OH, 60 mi S	—	2,214	291
Lincoln, NE	34.5 minutes	I-80	Lincoln TS 43 city buses	Nonhub Lincoln Municipal (LNK) 7 airlines, 78 flights/week	14 trains/week	4,196	115
Little Rock–North Little Rock, AR	42.7 minutes	I-30 I-40	Metroplan 48 city buses	Small hub Adams Field (LIT) 9 airlines, 308 flights/week	14 trains/week	4,392	99
London, ON	38.0 minutes	—	London Transit 157 city buses	Large hub London Municipal (YXU) Commuter service only	147 trains/week	4,668	77
Long Island, NY	64.6 minutes	—	Suffolk Transit 133 city buses 1 commuter railroad	Part of New York hub Long Island MacArthur (ISP) 6 airlines, 142 flights/week	—	1,483	327
Longview–Marshall, TX	40.8 minutes	I-20	—	Nonhub Gregg County (GGG) Commuter service only	14 trains/week	2,702	251
Los Angeles–Long Beach, CA	56.8 minutes	I-5	SCRTD 2,468 city buses 33 rapid rail 1 commuter railroad	Large hub Hollywood–Burbank (BUR) 8 airlines, 576 flights/week Long Beach–Daugherty Field (LGB) 6 airlines, 227 flights/week Los Angeles International (LAX) 22 airlines, 3,818 flights/week	116 trains/week	4,211	114
Louisville, KY–IN	46.0 minutes	I-64 I-65	TA River City 244 city buses	Small hub Standiford Field (SDF) 13 airlines, 508 flights/week	—	4,221	112
Lubbock, TX	35.0 minutes	I-27	CTM 27 city buses	Small hub Lubbock International (LBB) 5 airlines, 203 flights/week	—	3,895	148
Lynchburg, VA	41.6 minutes	—	Lynchburg TC 20 city buses	Nonhub Lynchburg Regional–Glenn Field (LYH) 1 airline, 32 flights/week	14 trains/week	3,273	206
Macon, GA	40.6 minutes	I-16 I-75	Macon–Bibb County TA 22 city buses	Nonhub Middle Georgia Regional (MCN) 1 airline, 13 flights/week	—	3,118	216
Madison, WI	38.5 minutes	I-90 I-94	Metro 155 city buses	Small hub Truax Field (MSN) 10 airlines, 168 flights/week	—	4,726	71
Manchester–Nashua, NH	48.2 minutes	I-93	Manchester TA 24 city buses	Part of Boston hub Manchester Municipal (MHT) 4 airlines, 149 flights/week	—	2,977	227
Mansfield, OH	36.8 minutes	I-71	Richland County Tran 14 city buses	Nearest airport: Columbus, OH, 67 mi SW	—	2,135	298
McAllen–Edinburg–Mission, TX	38.5 minutes	—	Valley Transit 25 city buses	Small hub Miller International (MFE) 2 airlines, 61 flights/week	—	1,721	317
Medford–Ashland, OR	34.8 minutes	I-5	Rogue Valley TD 19 city buses	Nonhub Medford–Jackson County (MFR) 4 airlines, 151 flights/week	—	4,655	79
Melbourne–Titusville–Palm Bay, FL	44.4 minutes	I-95	Space Coast AT 35 city buses	Small hub Melbourne Regional (MLB) 5 airlines, 96 flights/week	—	2,465	269
Memphis, TN–AR–MS	47.2 minutes	I-40 I-55	MATA 163 city buses	Medium hub Memphis International (MEM) 9 airlines, 1,707 flights/week	14 trains/week	4,660	78
Merced, CA	35.9 minutes	—	Merced TS 2 city buses	Nearest airport: Modesto, CA, 40 mi N	42 trains/week	2,311	281
Miami, FL	53.5 minutes	I-95	Metro Dade TA 501 city buses 82 rapid rail cars 1 commuter railroad	Large hub Miami International (MIA) 19 airlines, 1,968 flights/week	14 trains/week	4,328	102
Milwaukee–Waukesha, WI	43.3 minutes	I-43 I-94	Milwaukee County TS 480 city buses	Medium hub General Mitchell International (MKE) 16 airlines, 724 flights/week	62 trains/week	5,310	42

Metro Area	Daily Commute	National Highways	Public Transportation	Scheduled Domestic Air Service	Passenger Rail	Places Rated Score	Places Rated Rank
Minneapolis–St. Paul, MN–WI	45.0 minutes	I-35 I-94	MTC 869 city buses	Large hub Minneapolis–St. Paul International (MSP) 13 airlines, 2,224 flights/week	14 trains/week	4,880	62
Mobile, AL	47.3 minutes	I-10 I-65	MTA 37 city buses	Small hub Bates Field (MOB) 9 airlines, 189 flights/week	14 trains/week	3,892	150
Modesto, CA	47.7 minutes	I-5	Intracity Transit 24 city buses	Nonhub Modesto–Sham Field (MOD) 1 airline, 38 flights/week	42 trains/week	3,244	209
Monmouth–Ocean, NJ	58.3 minutes	—	NJTS 150 city buses	Part of New York hub	—	1,315	333
Monroe, LA	39.8 minutes	I-20	Monroe TS 15 city buses	Nonhub Monroe Regional (MLU) 2 airlines, 49 flights/week	—	2,916	237
Montgomery, AL	42.1 minutes	I-65 I-85	Montgomery Area TS 31 city buses	Nonhub Dannelly Field (MGM) 3 airlines, 50 flights/week	14 trains/week	3,879	152
✓ Montreal, PQ	48.7 minutes	TC	STCUM/STRSM 2,023 city buses 759 rapid rail cars	Large hub Dorval International (YUL) 8 airlines, 1,222 flights/week Mirabel International (YMX) 8 airlines, 306 flights/week	135 trains/week	6,082	13
Muncie, IN	38.3 minutes	I-69	Indiana TS 17 city buses	Nearest airport: Indianapolis, IN, 70 mi SW	—	2,696	253
Myrtle Beach, SC	40.3 minutes	—	Coastal RPTA 17 city buses	Small hub Myrtle Beach AFB (MYR) 3 airlines, 69 flights/week	—	2,920	236
Naples, FL	40.0 minutes	I-75	—	Nearest airport: Fort Myers, FL, 28 mi N	—	1,723	316
Nashville, TN	48.6 minutes	I-24 I-40 I-65	MTA 113 city buses	Medium hub Nashville Metropolitan (BNA) 12 airlines, 1,262 flights/week	—	5,017	52
New Bedford–Fall River–Attleboro, MA	45.1 minutes	I-95	SERTA 97 city buses	Part of Boston hub	—	4,351	101
New Haven–Meriden, CT	42.9 minutes	I-91 I-95	Conn Transit 85 city buses	Part of New York hub Tweed–New Haven (HVN) 2 airlines, 32 flights/week	258 trains/week	4,568	85
New London–Norwich, CT–RI	40.3 minutes	I-95	SEAT 21 city buses	Nearest airport: Hartford, CT, 60 mi NW	140 trains/week	3,227	210
New Orleans, LA	52.5 minutes	I-10	NORTA 446 city buses 22 rapid rail cars 1 ferry	Medium hub New Orleans–Moisant International (MSY) 12 airlines, 818 flights/week	24 trains/week	4,263	109
✓ New York, NY	75.8 minutes	I-78 I-87 I-95	NYCTA 3,355 city buses 6,248 rapid rail cars 3 commuter railroads 2 ferries	Large hub Kennedy International (JFK) 14 airlines, 1,299 flights/week La Guardia (LGA) 13 airlines, 2,316 flights/week Westchester County (HPN) 3 airlines, 101 flights/week	543 trains/week	7,148	3
✓ Newark–Jersey City, NJ	56.2 minutes	I-78 I-80 I-95	NJTC 1,249 city buses 112 rapid rail cars 2 commuter railroads	Part of New York hub Newark International (EWR) 16 airlines, 2,460 flights/week	546 trains/week	7,342	2
Norfolk–Virginia Beach–Newport News, VA–NC	45.6 minutes	I-64	Tidewater TDC 211 city buses 1 ferry	Nonhub Newport News–Williamsburg International (PHF) 2 airlines, 54 flights/week Norfolk International (ORF) 13 airlines, 459 flights/week	14 trains/week	2,932	235
Northern New Jersey, NJ	54.9 minutes	I-80	NJTC 65 city buses	Part of New York hub	—	2,273	284
Oakland, CA	57.5 minutes	I-80	Alameda–Contra Costa 706 city buses 388 rapid rail cars	Part of San Francisco hub Buchanan Field (CCR) 1 airline, 4 flights/week Metropolitan Oakland International (OAK) 9 airlines, 956 flights/week	70 trains/week	4,551	87
Ocala, FL	44.7 minutes	I-75	—	Nearest airport: Gainesville, FL, 40 mi N	14 trains/week	2,612	260

Metro Area	Daily Commute	National Highways	Public Transportation	Scheduled Domestic Air Service	Passenger Rail	Places Rated Score	Places Rated Rank
Odessa–Midland, TX	36.5 minutes	I-20	—	Small hub Midland International (MAF) 4 airlines, 152 flights/week	—	2,943	232
Oklahoma City, OK	43.4 minutes	I-35 I-40 I-44	Central PTA 69 city buses	Medium hub Will Rogers World (OKC) 11 airlines, 492 flights/week	—	4,118	125
Olympia, WA	44.0 minutes	I-5	Intercity Transit 41 city buses	Part of Seattle hub	—	4,869	64
Omaha, NE–IA	38.8 minutes	I-80	MAT 133 city buses	Small hub Eppley Airfield (OMA) 12 airlines, 371 flights/week	14 trains/week	3,887	151
Orange County, CA	54.6 minutes	I-5	Orange County TD 388 city buses	Part of Los Angeles hub John Wayne–Orange County (SNA) 11 airlines, 692 flights/week	136 trains/week	3,657	171
Orange County, NY	58.5 minutes	I-84 I-87	—	Part of New York hub Stewart International (SWF) 6 airlines, 162 flights/week	—	2,648	256
Orlando, FL	49.2 minutes	I-4	Tri-County Comm Rail 84 city buses 1 commuter railroad	Large hub Orlando International (MCO) 14 airlines, 1,666 flights/week	49 trains/week	4,313	103
Oshawa, ON	35.1 minutes	—	Oshawa Transit 38 city buses	Part of Toronto hub	52 trains/week	4,308	105
✓ Ottawa–Hull, ON–PQ	44.3 minutes	TC	OC Transpo 686 city buses	Medium hub Ottawa International (YOW) 6 airlines, 618 flights/week	71 trains/week	6,751	8
Owensboro, KY	37.0 minutes	—	Owensboro TS 7 city buses	Nonhub Owensboro–Daviess County (OWB) Commuter service only	—	1,594	322
Panama City, FL	37.8 minutes	I-10	—	Nonhub Panama City–Bay County (PFN) 1 airline, 16 flights/week	—	1,987	306
Parkersburg–Marietta, WV–OH	38.8 minutes	I-77	Mid-Ohio Valley TA 7 city buses	Nonhub Wood County Airport–Wilson Field (PKB) Commuter service only	—	2,273	284
Pensacola, FL	42.8 minutes	I-10	Escambia County TS 18 city buses	Small hub Pensacola Regional (PNS) 5 airlines, 153 flights/week	—	2,764	247
Peoria–Pekin, IL	38.9 minutes	I-74	Peoria MTD 38 city buses	Small hub Greater Peoria Regional (PIA) 8 airlines, 113 flights/week	14 trains/week	3,685	168
Philadelphia, PA–NJ	53.2 minutes	I-76 I-95	SEPTA 1,118 city buses 540 rapid rail cars 61 trolley coaches 1 commuter railroad	Large hub Philadelphia International (PHL) 17 airlines, 1,742 flights/week	659 trains/week	5,237	43
Phoenix–Mesa, AZ	49.0 minutes	I-10 I-17	Phoenix TS 286 city buses	Large hub Sky Harbor International (PHX) 15 airlines, 2,785 flights/week	6 trains/week	4,269	108
Pine Bluff, AR	40.0 minutes	—	City Bus Company 7 city buses	Nearest airport: Little Rock, AR, 45 mi NW	—	1,541	324
✓ Pittsburgh, PA	49.8 minutes	I-76 I-79	PAT 779 city buses 45 rapid rail cars 2 cable inclines	Large hub Greater Pittsburgh International (PIT) 15 airlines, 2,421 flights/week Westmoreland County (LBE) Commuter service only	42 trains/week	5,729	24
Pittsfield, MA	33.2 minutes	—	BRTA 14 city buses	Nearest airport: Albany, NY, 45 mi NW	14 trains/week	3,948	145
Portland, ME	37.6 minutes	I-95	PTD 16 city buses 1 ferry	Small hub Portland International Jetport (PWM) 5 airlines, 171 flights/week	—	3,751	162
✓ Portland, OR	46.3 minutes	I-5 I-80	TRI-MET 430 city buses 23 rapid rail cars	Medium hub Portland International (PDX) 15 airlines, 1,608 flights/week	42 trains/week	5,936	18
Portsmouth–Dover–Rochester, NH	51.7 minutes	I-95	COAST 14 city buses	Part of Boston hub	—	2,655	255

Metro Area	Daily Commute	National Highways	Public Transportation	Scheduled Domestic Air Service	Passenger Rail	Places Rated Score	Places Rated Rank
Providence– Warwick– Cranston, RI	41.9 minutes	I-84 I-95	RIPTA 187 city buses	Small hub Green State (PVD) 9 airlines, 312 flights/week	154 trains/week	4,687	75
Provo–Orem, UT	35.9 minutes	I-15	—	Nearest airport: Salt Lake City, UT, 50 mi N	14 trains/week	2,632	259
Pueblo, CO	36.7 minutes	I-25	Pueblo TC 11 city buses	Nonhub Pueblo Memorial (PUB) 5 airlines, 28 flights/week	—	2,604	262
Punta Gorda, FL	41.4 minutes	I-75	—	Nearest airport: Fort Myers, FL, 29 mi SE	—	1,687	318
Quebec City, PQ	37.2 minutes	TC	CTCUQ 393 city buses	Small hub Quebec Municipal (YQB) 3 airlines, 44 flights/week	21 trains/week	5,397	39
Racine, WI	39.8 minutes	I-94	Belle Urban System 33 city buses	Part of Milwaukee hub	96 trains/week	4,220	113
Raleigh–Durham– Chapel Hill, NC	43.3 minutes	I-40 I-85	Raleigh Transit 88 city buses	Large hub Raleigh–Durham International (RDU) 11 airlines, 1,214 flights/week	35 trains/week	5,331	41
Rapid City, SD	35.0 minutes	I-40	—	Nonhub Rapid City Regional (RAP) 7 airlines, 56 flights/week	—	3,072	221
Reading, PA	40.0 minutes	I-76	BARTA 42 city buses	Nonhub Reading Regional–Spaatz Field (RDG) Commuter service only	—	2,395	275
Redding, CA	36.5 minutes	I-5	Redding Area Bus 8 city buses	Nonhub Redding Municipal (RDD) 1 airline, 57 flights/week	14 trains/week	4,085	129
Regina, SK	34.8 minutes	TC	Regina TS 87 city buses	Small hub Regina Municipal (YQR) 2 airlines, 167 flights/week	—	5,025	51
✓ Reno, NV	37.0 minutes	I-80	Citifare 49 city buses	Medium hub Cannon International (RNO) 9 airlines, 466 flights/week	14 trains/week	5,534	31
✓ Richland– Kennewick–Pasco, WA	41.0 minutes	I-82	Ben Franklin 41 city buses	Small hub Tri-Cities (PSC) 4 airlines, 229 flights/week	14 trains/week	5,695	26
✓ Richmond– Petersburg, VA	46.9 minutes	I-64 I-85 I-95	GRTC 172 city buses	Small hub Richard E. Byrd Flying Field (RIC) 6 airlines, 361 flights/week	105 trains/week	5,727	25
Riverside– San Bernardino, CA	59.3 minutes	I-10	OMNITRANS 139 city buses	Part of Los Angeles hub Ontario International (ONT) 14 airlines, 837 flights/week Palm Springs Municipal (PSP) 8 airlines, 183 flights/week	34 trains/week	4,284	107
Roanoke, VA	39.3 minutes	I-81	Roanoke TC 31 city buses	Nonhub Roanoke–Woodrum Field (ROA) 3 airlines, 125 flights/week	—	3,268	207
Rochester, MN	31.5 minutes	I-90	Rochester Transit 17 city buses	Nonhub Rochester Municipal (RST) 4 airlines, 57 flights/week	—	3,591	178
Rochester, NY	42.5 minutes	I-90	Rochester RTS 187 city buses	Small hub Greater Rochester International (ROC) 9 airlines, 458 flights/week	64 trains/week	4,311	104
Rockford, IL	39.4 minutes	I-39 I-90	Rockford TS 33 city buses	Nonhub Greater Rockford (RFD) 6 airlines, 17 flights/week	—	2,964	229
Rocky Mount, NC	38.7 minutes	I-95	Rocky Mount TS 4 city buses	Nonhub Rocky Mount–Wilson (RWI) Commuter service only	49 trains/week	2,988	226
Sacramento, CA	47.3 minutes	I-5 I-80	RTD 158 city buses 23 rapid rail cars	Medium hub Sacramento Metropolitan (SMF) 10 airlines, 193 flights/week Lake Tahoe (TVL) 1 airline, 5 flights/week	28 trains/week	3,512	187
Saginaw–Bay City– Midland, MI	40.7 minutes	I-75	Tri-Cities Bay Metro 63 city buses	Small hub Tri-City International (MBS) 4 airlines, 75 flights/week	—	3,906	146

Metro Area	Daily Commute	National Highways	Public Transportation	Scheduled Domestic Air Service	Passenger Rail	Places Rated Score	Places Rated Rank
✓ St. Catharines–Niagara, ON	37.0 minutes	—	SC Transit 62 city buses	nearest airport Buffalo 60 mi SE	28 trains/week	5,794	22
St. Cloud, MN	33.4 minutes	I-94	MTC 15 city buses	Nearest airport: Minneapolis, MN, 68 mi SE	14 trains/week	3,789	157
Saint John, NB	36.0 minutes	—	Saint John TC 31 city buses	Nonhub Municipal (YSJ) 2 airlines, 40 flights/week	—	2,473	268
St. John's, NF	32.0 minutes	TC	St. John's TC 59 city buses	Nonhub St. John's (YYT) 3 airlines, 119 flights/week	—	3,473	190
St. Joseph, MO	38.1 minutes	I-29	Express 11 city buses	Nearest airport: Kansas City, MO, 30 mi SE	—	2,352	277
✓ St. Louis, MO–IL	49.9 minutes	I-44 I-55 I-64 I-70	Bi-State 575 city buses	Large hub Lambert–St. Louis International (STL) 13 airlines, 3,079 flights/week	84 trains/week	5,824	20
Salem, OR	41.4 minutes	I-5	MTD 40 city buses	Part of Portland hub McNary Field (SLE) 2 airlines, 12 flights/week	14 trains/week	4,936	59
Salinas, CA	38.3 minutes	—	Salinas Transit 40 city buses	Nonhub Monterey Peninsula (MRY) 3 airlines, 102 flights/week	14 trains/week	3,968	144
✓ Salt Lake City–Ogden, UT	42.2 minutes	I-15 I-80 I-84	UTA 359 city buses	Large hub Salt Lake City International (SLC) 14 airlines, 1,469 flights/week	35 trains/week	6,793	7
San Angelo, TX	33.9 minutes	—	Antran 5 city buses	Nonhub Mathis Field (SJT) Commuter service only	—	1,527	325
✓ San Antonio, TX	47.2 minutes	I-10 I-35 I-37	VIA Metro Tr 499 city buses	Medium hub San Antonio International (SAT) 14 airlines, 728 flights/week	13 trains/week	5,500	32
✓ San Diego, CA	46.4 minutes	I-5 I-8 I-15	San Diego TS 607 city buses 45 rapid rail cars 1 commuter railroad	Large hub San Diego International–Lindbergh (SAN) 12 airlines, 1,337 flights/week	112 trains/week	5,655	27
✓ San Francisco, CA	54.9 minutes	I-80	MUNI/BART 847 city buses 488 rapid rail cars 262 trolley coaches 2 ferries 1 commuter railroad	Large hub San Francisco International (SFO) 16 airlines, 3,227 flights/week	—	5,821	21
San Jose, CA	49.9 minutes	I-80	Santa Clara County TS 415 city buses 10 rapid rail cars	Part of San Francisco hub San Jose International (SJC) 11 airlines, 884 flights/week	14 trains/week	4,462	93
San Luis Obispo–Atascadero–Paso Robles, CA	38.7 minutes	—	SLO County TA 15 city buses	Nonhub McChesney Field (SBP) 1 airline, 20 flights/week	14 trains/week	3,403	197
Santa Barbara–Santa Maria–Lompoc, CA	37.4 minutes	—	MTD 60 city buses	Nonhub Santa Barbara Municipal (SBA) 4 airlines, 155 flights/week	28 trains/week	4,375	100
Santa Cruz–Watsonville, CA	51.0 minutes	—	MTD 75 city buses	Part of San Francisco hub	—	4,769	67
Santa Fe, NM	38.2 minutes	I-25	—	Nonhub Los Alamos (LAM) Commuter service only	—	1,773	314
Santa Rosa, CA	50.4 minutes	—	Sonoma County TA 44 city buses	Part of San Francisco hub Sonoma County (STS) 1 airline, 58 flights/week	—	3,193	213
Sarasota–Bradenton, FL	40.0 minutes	I-75	County Area Transit 117 city buses	Small hub Sarasota–Bradenton (SRQ) 8 airlines, 260 flights/week	—	2,904	238
Saskatoon, SK	34.0 minutes	—	Saskatoon Transit 99 city buses	Small hub Saskatoon Municipal (YXE) 2 airlines, 145 flights/week	6 trains/week	4,925	60
Savannah, GA	45.1 minutes	I-16 I-95	Savannah TA 48 city buses	Small hub Savannah International (SAV) 6 airlines, 177 flights/week	35 trains/week	4,534	88

Metro Area	Daily Commute	National Highways	Public Transportation	Scheduled Domestic Air Service	Passenger Rail	Places Rated Score	Places Rated Rank
Scranton–Wilkes-Barre–Hazleton, PA	38.3 minutes	I-81 I-84	Scranton County TA 72 city buses	Nonhub Wilkes-Barre–Scranton International (AVP) 3 airlines, 82 flights/week	—	3,312	203
✓ Seattle–Bellevue–Everett, WA	51.6 minutes	I-5 I-90	METRO 1,034 city buses 109 trolley coaches 21 ferry	Large hub Seattle–Tacoma International (SEA) 18 airlines, 2,731 flights/week Boeing Field–King County (BFI) Commuter service only	56 trains/week	5,956	15
Sharon, PA	36.1 minutes	I-80	Shenango Valley TS 6 city buses	Nearest airport: Youngstown, OH, 10 mi W	—	2,277	283
Sheboygan, WI	31.5 minutes	I-43	Transit 29 city buses	Nearest airport: Green Bay, WI, 67 mi N	—	3,375	200
Sherbrooke, PQ	31.7 minutes	—	CMTS 50 city buses	Nearest airport: Montreal, 100 mi W	6 trains/week	4,765	68
Sherman-Denison, TX	44.0 minutes	I-35	Denison TS 6 city buses	Nearest airport: Dallas, TX, 65 mi SW	—	2,045	304
Shreveport–Bossier City, LA	42.1 minutes	I-20 I-49	Area TS 36 city buses	Small hub Shreveport Regional (SHV) 7 airlines, 127 flights/week	—	3,589	179
Sioux City, IA–NE	32.3 minutes	I-29	Sioux City TS 22 city buses	Nonhub Sioux Gateway (SUX) 5 airlines, 42 flights/week	—	3,280	204
Sioux Falls, SD	32.5 minutes	I-29 I-90	SFTS 23 city buses	Small hub Joe Foss Field (FSD) 6 airlines, 123 flights/week	—	4,615	82
South Bend, IN	38.9 minutes	I-80	South Bend PTC 44 city buses	Small hub Michiana Regional (SBN) 7 airlines, 155 flights/week	28 trains/week	4,521	90
✓ Spokane, WA	39.6 minutes	I-90	STA 111 city buses	Small hub Spokane International (GEG) 10 airlines, 587 flights/week	21 trains/week	5,896	19
Springfield, IL	38.2 minutes	I-55 I-72	MTD 33 city buses	Nonhub Capital (SPI) 6 airlines, 75 flights/week	41 trains/week	4,874	63
Springfield, MA	39.8 minutes	I-90 I-91	Springfield TS/Pioneer Valley 95 city buses	Medium hub Bradley International (BDL) 14 airlines, 587 flights/week	91 trains/week	3,849	154
Springfield, MO	41.4 minutes	I-44	City Utility 23 city buses	Small hub Springfield Regional (SGF) 5 airlines, 77 flights/week	—	3,517	185
Stamford–Norwalk, CT	53.2 minutes	I-95	CT Transit 41 city buses	Part of New York hub	180 trains/week	4,225	111
State College, PA	36.3 minutes	—	CATA 26 city buses	Nonhub State College Air Depot (UNV) 1 airline, 35 flights/week	—	2,839	241
Steubenville–Weirton, OH–WV	41.5 minutes	—	Steel Valley Transit 8 city buses	Nearest airport: Pittsburgh, PA, 33 mi NE	—	1,358	332
Stockton–Lodi, CA	46.6 minutes	I-5	MTD 48 city buses	Nonhub Stockton Metropolitan (SCK) 1 airline, 38 flights/week	42 trains/week	3,403	198
Sudbury, ON	30.7 minutes	TC	Sudbury Transit 39 city buses	Nonhub Sudbury Municipal (YSB) Commuter service only	3 trains/week	4,233	110
Sumter, SC	37.4 minutes	—	Santee Wateree RTA 20 city buses	Nearest airport: Columbia, SC, 43 mi W	—	1,805	312
✓ Syracuse, NY	41.0 minutes	I-81 I-90	CNY Centro 162 city buses	Small hub Hancock International (SYR) 10 airlines, 545 flights/week	56 trains/week	6,290	11
Tacoma, WA	51.0 minutes	I-5	Pierce County TS 138 city buses 1 ferry	Part of Seattle hub	42 trains/week	5,161	47
Tallahassee, FL	41.1 minutes	I-10	Taltran 40 city buses	Small hub Tallahassee Regional (TLH) 4 airlines, 148 flights/week	—	3,635	175

Metro Area	Daily Commute	National Highways	Public Transportation	Scheduled Domestic Air Service	Passenger Rail	Places Rated Score	Places Rated Rank
Tampa–St. Petersburg– Clearwater, FL	46.8 minutes	I-4 I-75	HART/Suncoast 259 city buses	Large hub St. Petersburg–Clearwater International (PIE) 3 airlines, 4 flights/week Tampa International (TPA) 12 airlines, 1,103 flights/week	28 trains/week	4,042	134
Terre Haute, IN	40.5 minutes	I-70	Transit Utility 13 city buses	Nonhub Hulman Regional (HUF) 2 airlines, 5 flights/week	—	2,326	280
Texarkana, TX– Texarkana, AR	40.8 minutes	I-30	—	Nearest airport: Shreveport, LA, 74 mi S	14 trains/week	2,702	251
Thunder Bay, ON	31.5 minutes	TC	TB Transit 43 city buses	Nonhub Thunder Bay (YQT) 2 airlines, 95 flights/week	—	5,403	38
Toledo, OH	40.0 minutes	I-75 I-80	RTA 179 city buses	Nonhub Toledo Express (TOL) 7 airlines, 100 flights/week	35 trains/week	4,740	69
Topeka, KS	36.5 minutes	I-70	MTA 22 city buses	Nonhub Forbes Field (FOE) 1 airline, 10 flights/week	14 trains/week	3,509	188
✓ Toronto, ON	50.0 minutes	—	Toronto TC/GO Transit 2,277 city buses 139 trolley coaches 662 rapid rail cars 1 commuter railroad	Large hub Pearson International (YYZ) 9 airlines, 3,333 flights/week Toronto Island (YTZ) Commuter service only	161 trains/week	5,610	30
Trenton, NJ	47.3 minutes	I-95	—	Part of New York hub Mercer County (TTN) 1 airline, 3 flights/week	382 trains/week	4,001	140
Trois–Rivieres, PQ	32.3 minutes	—	—	Nearest airport: Quebec City, PQ, 80 mi NE	—	1,307	334
Tucson, AZ	45.3 minutes	I-10 I-19	MTS 145 city buses	Medium hub Tucson International (TUS) 11 airlines, 371 flights/week	6 trains/week	4,295	106
Tulsa, OK	42.3 minutes	I-44	Metro Tulsa TA 67 city buses	Medium hub Tulsa International (TUL) 10 airlines, 501 flights/week	—	3,425	194
Tuscaloosa, AL	39.8 minutes	I-20 I-59	Tuscaloosa TA 6 city buses	Nonhub Municipal (TCL) Commuter service only	14 trains/week	3,653	173
Tyler, TX	42.2 minutes	I-20	Tyler Transit 6 city buses	Nonhub Tyler Pounds Field (TYR) Commuter service only	—	1,962	308
Utica–Rome, NY	37.4 minutes	I-90	Utica TA 40 city buses	Nonhub Oneida County (UCA) 1 airline, 19 flights/week	62 trains/week	3,704	167
Vallejo–Fairfield– Napa, CA	56.8 minutes	I-80	Transit 53 city buses 1 ferry	Part of San Francisco hub	14 trains/week	4,836	65
✓ Vancouver, BC	55.0 minutes	TC	BC Transit 643 city buses 296 trolley coaches 114 rapid rail cars 1 ferry	Large hub Vancouver International (YVR) 8 airlines, 1,426 flights/week Coal Harbour (CXH) Commuter service only	3 trains/week	5,948	17
Vancouver, WA	45.1 minutes	I-5	C-Tran 61 city buses	Part of Portland hub	56 trains/week	5,081	49
Ventura, CA	52.8 minutes	—	Coast Area Transit 30 city buses	Part of Los Angeles hub Ventura County (OXR) 1 airline, 44 flights/week	42 trains/week	2,961	230
Victoria, BC	35.0 minutes	TC	BC Transit 130 city buses	Nonhub Victoria International (YWJ) 2 airlines, 10 flights/week Inner Harbor (YWH) Commuter service only	7 trains/week	4,160	119
Victoria, TX	41.4 minutes	—	—	Nearest airport: Corpus Christi, TX, 60 mi S	—	1,019	342
Vineland–Millville– Bridgeton, NJ	42.2 minutes	—	NJTC 24 city buses	Part of Philadelphia hub	—	2,199	293
Visalia–Tulare– Porterville, CA	37.8 minutes	—	Visalia City Coach 7 city buses	Nearest airport: Fresno, CA, 45 mi NW	—	1,439	328

Metro Area	Daily Commute	National Highways	Public Transportation	Scheduled Domestic Air Service	Passenger Rail	Places Rated Score	Places Rated Rank
Waco, TX	37.2 minutes	I-35	Transit System 12 city buses	Nonhub Waco Regional (ACT) Commuter service only	14 trains/week	3,038	225
✓ Washington, DC–MD–VA–WV	63.0 minutes	I-66 I-95	WMATA 1,598 city buses 478 rapid rail cars 2 commuter railroads	Large hub Washington National (DCA) 14 airlines, 1,738 flights/week Dulles International (IAD) 13 airlines, 1,791 flights/week	492 trains/week	6,546	10
Waterbury, CT	41.3 minutes	I-84	Northeast Transp Co 33 city buses	Nearest airport: New Haven, CT, 30 mi SE	—	2,205	292
Waterloo–Cedar Falls, IA	31.5 minutes	—	Black Hawk Cnty 15 city buses	Nonhub Waterloo Municipal (ALO) 4 airlines, 31 flights/week	—	2,301	282
Wausau, WI	33.4 minutes	—	Area TS 20 city buses	Nonhub Central Wisconsin (CWA) Commuter service only	—	2,116	301
West Palm Beach–Boca Raton, FL	44.7 minutes	I-95	Florida Transit 76 city buses	Medium hub Palm Beach International (PBI) 13 airlines, 485 flights/week	28 trains/week	3,254	208
Wheeling, WV–OH	42.4 minutes	I-70	Ohio Valley RTA 16 city buses	Nearest airport: Pittsburgh, PA, 50 mi NE	—	2,557	264
Wichita, KS	38.7 minutes	I-35	Metropolitan TA 44 city buses	Small hub Wichita Mid-Continent (ICT) 10 airlines, 248 flights/week	7 trains/week	3,432	193
Wichita Falls, TX	33.2 minutes	I-44	Wichita Falls TS 6 city buses	Nonhub Wichita Falls Municipal (SPS) Commuter service only	—	2,257	288
Williamsport, PA	35.6 minutes	—	Bu of Trans 14 city buses	Nonhub Williamsport–Lycoming County (IPT) Commuter service only	—	2,179	294
Wilmington–Newark, DE–MD	44.8 minutes	I-95	DART 87 city buses	Part of Philadelphia hub	457 trains/week	3,683	169
Wilmington, NC	39.2 minutes	I-40	Wilmington TA 9 city buses	Nonhub New Hanover International (ILM) 2 airlines, 54 flights/week	—	2,904	238
Windsor, ON	36.5 minutes	—	Windsor Transit 91 city buses	Nonhub Windsor International (YQG) Commuter service only	45 trains/week	4,597	83
✓ Winnipeg, MB	41.2 minutes	TC	WTS 445 city buses	Medium hub Winnipeg International (YWG) 9 airlines, 532 flights/week	9 trains/week	5,983	14
Worcester–Fitchburg–Leominster, MA	46.2 minutes	I-90	RTA 74 city buses	Part of Boston hub Worcester Municipal (ORH) 1 airline, 34 flights/week	42 trains/week	4,034	137
Yakima, WA	34.8 minutes	I-82	Transit Fund 16 city buses	Nonhub Yakima Air Terminal (YKM) 4 airlines, 140 flights/week	—	3,774	159
Yolo, CA	38.1 minutes	I-5	Yolobus 12 city buses	Part of Sacramento hub	28 trains/week	4,417	96
York, PA	43.3 minutes	I-83	Area TA 15 city buses	Nearest airport: Harrisburg, PA 20 mi NE	—	2,036	305
Youngstown–Warren, OH	41.2 minutes	I-76	Western Reserve TS 38 city buses	Nonhub Youngstown Municipal (YNG) 2 airlines, 18 flights/week	28 trains/week	3,468	191
Yuba City, CA	43.4 minutes	—	—	Nearest airport: Sacramento, CA, 35 mi SE	14 trains/week	1,972	307
Yuma, AZ	34.5 minutes	I-8	Yuma Bus Company 4 city buses	Nonhub Yuma International (YUM) 1 airline, 37 flights/week	6 trains/week	3,451	192

Et Cetera

FERRYBOATS, CABLE CARS, MONORAILS, AERIAL TRAMS, AND INCLINES

Besides the ubiquitous bus and the different rail systems in larger cities, North American transit systems operate other types of vehicles. Although these modes have little impact on total mass transit, they are by far the most fun to watch and ride, undeniably adding to a city's flavor.

San Francisco has the nation's only **cable car** system. In operation since the nineteenth century, the MUNI's 41 cars and the 26 cars in New Orlean's trolley system are the only transit properties in the National Register of Historic Places. New York operates the only public **aerial tram,** between Roosevelt Island and Manhattan. **Automated guideways,** the newest public transit mode, are electric vehicles running over fixed guideways without operators or other crewpersons. You can catch one in Detroit, MI, Miami, FL, Morgantown, WV, and Tampa, FL.

The largest transit vehicles are **ferryboats,** which range in size up to 380 feet and can carry as many as 2,500 commuters per trip. Public ferryboat systems, which provide frequent "bridge" service over a fixed route and on a published schedule between two or more points, are part of the mass-transit mix in 13 metro areas:

Boston, MA	Massachusetts Bay Transit Authority
Erie, PA	Erie Metropolitan Transit Authority
Galveston, TX	Texas Department of Transportation
Halifax, NS	METRO
New Orleans, LA	Mississippi River Bridge Authority
New York, NY	City of New York—Staten Island Ferry
Norfolk, VA	Tidewater Transportation District
Portland, ME	Casco Bay Transit District
San Francisco, CA	Golden Gate Bridge Transportation
Seattle, WA	Washington State Ferries
Tacoma, WA	Pierce County Ferry
Vallejo, CA	Vallejo TS
Vancouver, BC	BC Transit

Four metro areas operate cog or cable incline cars that traverse steep hills:

> Chattanooga, TN–GA: Lookout Mountain
> Dubuque, IA: Fourth Street Elevator
> Johnstown, PA: Johnstown-Westmont Incline
> Pittsburgh, PA: Monongahela and Duquesne Heights

WHERE'S THE BUS (OR TRAM, OR STREETCAR)?

If you've got the fare and you know where your transit stops and where it's going, on a darkening and cold winter afternoon the quality of public transportation ultimately comes down to how long you have to stand around waiting for it. Basing our calculations on the assumption that all the vehicles of a transit system are in service and spaced evenly over each mile of their routes, *Places Rated* ranks the 35 largest such systems according to their waiting times (see table below).

In the second column of the table are detailed the different modes of transportation in the system. *Route miles* means the number of miles over which a system's fleet travels in service. If a bus or tram travels in only one direction within the right-of-way, each mile is counted once. If a vehicle travels in both directions, each mile is counted twice. For example, a mile of single track over which street cars operate in two directions represents 2 route miles.

Fleet age is simply the average number of years a transit system's collection of vehicles has been in service. The oldest fleets in the United States are the San Francisco Municipal Railway's historic cable cars (91 years old) and the charming street cars (66 years old) operated by the New Orleans Public Service Company. The transit vehicle with the shortest active life is the ever-present diesel-powered bus. By the time these roarers are finally scrapped—after an average of nine years on the street—their odometers may register more than 300,000 miles.

But just because a vehicle is old doesn't necessarily mean it's slow. The *average speed* (the average number of miles traveled per hour including frequent stops for passengers) is governed by local congestion on the roads. Seattle's METRO buses are more than twice as old as the Dallas Transit System's fleet, but they still move faster over their routes.

Headway is the distance between vehicles if they are spaced evenly over each mile of route; if you just miss a CTA bus in Chicago, for example, the next one should be only 1.18 miles behind. *Waiting time,* finally, represents the average amount of time you should have to wait for a ride given the number of vehicles in the system, their average speed, and their headway.

The transit systems are presented in order of their average waiting time for all modes of transportation, from shortest to longest. This average is a weighted average and is derived in the following way, using the NYCTA system as an example: The waiting time of

5.96 minutes for buses is multiplied by the number of buses (4,573) and then added to the product of the waiting time for rapid rail cars (0.57 minutes) and the number of cars (6,263). This sum (30,825) is then divided by the total number of transit vehicles within the system (10,836), which results in an average waiting time of 2.84 minutes, second best in this ranking.

Not all the figures for numbers of vehicles jibe with those presented in the Place Profiles. This is because the figures in the profiles are for the entire metro area —which might encompass more than one network —whereas the numbers in this table are for individual transit systems.

CONTRADICTORY RULES OF THE ROAD

Driving across political boundaries can mean a brush with contradictory traffic codes. Here are examples, with one caveat. The information comes from the American Automobile Association's latest *Digest of Motor Laws*, but it may not reflect recent changes in the law.

Speed Limits. There are two kinds of speed limits— absolute and prima facie, a legal phrase meaning "at first view." If the speed limit of 55 is absolute, going 56 means breaking the law. If the speed limit of 55 is prima facie, however, going 56 or even 60 is merely apparent evidence of unreasonable and imprudent speed. Drivers may escape a fine if they can convince the traffic court that their speed was reasonable and safe in light of the highway's condition, traffic, and visibility. In all Canadian provinces but Newfoundland and Nova Scotia, speed limits are absolute. States where all or some speed limits are prima facie are

Arizona	Massachusetts
Connecticut	New Hampshire
District of Columbia	New Jersey
Hawaii	New York
Idaho	Oregon
Indiana	Rhode Island
Louisiana	South Dakota
Maryland	Utah

Right and Left Turn on Red. In 1947, California became the first state to permit drivers to turn right on a red signal after a complete stop. The last was Massachusetts, in 1980. New York City now is the only major jurisdiction that prohibits the turn. According to the Federal Highway Administration, fewer accidents occur when drivers turn right on a red light than when they turn right on a green light. Furthermore, the rule saves each drive an average of 14 seconds at a turn, cuts gasoline consumption and exhaust emissions, and allows intersections to handle more traffic.

In the past five years, most states have enacted statutes permitting left turns on a red signal, but only after a complete stop and only from a one-way street into another one-way street. The practice remains prohibited everywhere in Canada except Alberta, British Columbia, and Ontario. Nine states and DC also prohibit turning left on red:

Connecticut	New Jersey
District of Columbia	North Carolina
Maryland	Rhode Island
Mississippi	Vermont
Missouri	Wisconsin

The state of New York permits a left turn on red everywhere except New York City. Tennessee permits the turn when so marked by each city.

Studded Tires. Most states and provinces allow drivers to mount studded snow tires on their automobiles for better traction during an icy winter. Because the carbide-tipped studs damage road surfaces, these jurisdictions prohibit their use:

Alabama	Minnesota
Georgia	Mississippi
Hawaii	New Mexico
Illinois	Ontario
Louisiana	Texas
Maryland (except certain counties)	Utah
Michigan	Wisconsin

Glass Tinting. Tinted automobile window glass is a frequently chosen factory option. Over the past 10 years, however, aftermarket application of black and gunmetal-gray plastic sheeting to the inside of the windshield has become extremely popular. Because it interferes with night vision, it is restricted in varying degrees everywhere except Newfoundland.

Audio Headsets. The issue here is whether the ears are as necessary for safe driving as the eyes. When you don't hear an ambulance siren, a ticket for failing to yield the right-of-way to an emergency vehicle is the likely consequence. But when you can't hear a train whistle or the air horn of an oncoming 18-wheeler, the result could be far more serious. Accordingly, these jurisdictions prohibit the driver from wearing an audio headset:

Alaska	Minnesota
California	Ohio
Colorado	Pennsylvania
Florida	Quebec
Georgia	Rhode Island
Illinois	Virginia
Maryland	Washington
Massachusetts	

Motorcycle Helmets. The mileage fatality rate (deaths per 100 million miles) for motorcycle travel is five times that for auto travel, and the major cause is head injuries. Consequently, many states and all Canadian provinces require motorcycle riders to wear helmets. Motorcyclists have challenged the law, but state courts have generally upheld it because it affects the biker's right to receive insurance compensation for injuries. These states, however, do not require protective headgear of any kind for motorcyclists and passengers:

Colorado	Illinois
Connecticut	Iowa

Mandatory Annual Safety Inspections. All states and provinces require regular safety inspection or emissions testing of automobiles to rid the highways of dangerous vehicles with bald tires, wobbly suspensions, smoky exhausts, and defective brakes and lights.

Mandatory Seat Belt Use. Because automobile accidents are the leading cause of death among young children, all states and provinces now require the use of special vehicle restraints for children who are less than preschool age. Most jurisdictions also require the use of seat belts by the driver and all front-seat passengers. These states do not:

Kentucky	New Hampshire
Maine	North Dakota
Massachusetts	South Dakota
Nebraska	West Virginia

Radar Detectors. All states and provinces use radar in their speed enforcement programs, and all but eight —Connecticut, Manitoba, Newfoundland, Ontario, Prince Edward Island, Quebec, and Virginia—plus the District of Columbia permit drivers to install radar detectors for advance warning.

DRIVER LICENSING

When you settle in a new state or province, you have to surrender your old driver's license and get a new one. The time permitted to do this ranges from "immediately" in 12 states and New Brunswick, to 30 days in 16 jurisdictions, and up to 6 months in British Columbia and Vermont. New Hampshire allows you as much time as your former state gives newcomers. Hawaii lets you keep your license until it expires.

Required Tests

For a new resident with a valid driver's license from a former state, the requirement for getting a license from the new jurisdiction varies considerably. In Connecticut, Massachusetts, and New Hampshire, a vision test is required, but all other tests may be waived. Florida, Montana, Saskatchewan, and Washington require you to get behind the wheel with a license examiner for a road test; in 28 other states, a road test may be waived or required at the discretion of the examiner.

Problem Drivers

If your license has been revoked, you won't get a new one simply by moving to another state. Every license application is checked with the National Driver Registry, a federal data file of persons whose license to drive has been denied or withdrawn. Moreover, 30 states belong to the National Driver License Compact, an agreement among states to share information on drivers who accumulate tickets in one jurisdiction and try to escape control in another. All provinces are members of the Canadian Driver License Compact; traffic offense information covering eight categories is exchanged among the jurisdictions.

Obtaining a Driver's License After Relocating: A Guide for Persons with a Current License from Their Former Jurisdiction

		Examinations Required				
	Time Limit	Rules of the Road	Signs and Signals	Vision	Road Test	NDR Compact
Alabama	30 days	●	●	●		●
Alaska	90 days	●	●	●		●
Alberta	3 months					●
Arizona	immediately	●	●	●	○	●
Arkansas	immediately	●	●	●		●
British Columbia	6 months	○	●	●	○	
California	10 days	●	●	●		●
Colorado	30 days	●	●	●	○	●
Connecticut	60 days	○	○	●	○	
Delaware	60 days	●	●	●	○	●

Examinations Required

	Time Limit	Rules of the Road	Signs and Signals	Vision	Road Test	NDR Compact
District of Columbia	immediately	●	●	●		●
Florida	30 days	○	○	●	●	●
Georgia	30 days	●	●	●		●
Hawaii	*	●	●	●	○	●
Idaho	90 days	●	●	●		●
Illinois	90 days	●	●	●		●
Indiana	60 days	●	●	●		●
Iowa	immediately	●	●	●		●
Kansas	90 days	●	●	●		●
Kentucky	immediately	○	○	○		
Louisiana	90 days			●	○	●
Maine	30 days	●	○	●	○	●
Manitoba	3 months			●		
Maryland	30 days	○	○	●	○	●
Massachusetts	immediately	●		●		
Michigan	immediately	●	●	●		
Minnesota	60 days	●	●	●	○	●
Mississippi	60 days	●	●	●		●
Missouri	immediately	●	●	●	○	●
Montana	90 days	○	○	●	●	●
Nebraska	30 days	●	●	●	○	●
Nevada	45 days	●	●	●	○	●
New Brunswick	immediately					
New Hampshire	60 days	○		●		●
New Jersey	60 days	●		●	○	●
New Mexico	30 days	●		●		●
New York	30 days	○	○	○		●
Newfoundland	3 months	●	●	●		
North Carolina	30 days	●	●	●	○	
North Dakota	60 days	●	●	●	○	●
Nova Scotia	90 days	●	●	●	○	
Ohio	30 days	●	●	●	○	●
Oklahoma	immediately	●	●	●	○	●
Ontario	60 days			●		●
Oregon	immediately	●	●	●	○	●
Pennsylvania	60 days	●	●	●	○	
Prince Edward Island	120 days					
Quebec	90 days	●	●	●		
Rhode Island	30 days	●	●	●		●
Saskatchewan	90 days				●	
South Carolina	90 days	●	●	●	○	●
South Dakota	90 days	●	●	●	○	●
Tennessee	30 days	○	○	●	○	●
Texas	30 days	●	●	●	○	
Utah	60 days	●	●	●		●
Vermont	6 months	●	●	●	○	●
Virginia	30 days	○	○	●		●
Washington	30 days	●	●	●	●	●
West Virginia	immediately	●	●	●		●
Wisconsin	immediately	●	●	●	○	●
Wyoming	120 days	●	●	●	○	●

Source: U.S. Federal Highway Administration, *Driver License Administration Requirements and Fees*, 1992.

* In Hawaii, a driver's license from any state or province is valid until its expiration if the driver is over 18.

● Required.

○ May be required or waived at the discretion of the examiner.

FINDING YOUR WAY ON THE INTERSTATE

By staying with a combination of interstate routes, it is possible for you to drive from one metro area in the United States to almost any other without stopping for a traffic light.

Five of the routes are more than 2,000 miles long. The longest, I-90, stretches 3,082 miles between downtown Boston and Seattle's waterfront. The next longest routes are I-80 (2,907 miles, from San Francisco to Hackensack, New Jersey), I-10 (2,460 miles along the nation's southern border, from Los Angeles to Jacksonville, Florida), I-40 (2,461 miles, from Barstow, California, to Smithfield, North Carolina), and I-70 (2,175 miles from Cove Fort, Utah, to Baltimore). Three of these routes, I-10, I-80, and I-90, cross the country from coast to coast, and I-40 nearly makes it.

Seven interstate routes span the nation in a north-south direction: I-5 (1,382 miles, from San Diego to Bellingham, Washington), I-15 (1,437 miles, from San Diego to the Montana–Canada border), I-35 (1,568 miles, from suburban New Orleans to Chicago), I-65 (888 miles, from Mobile, Alabama, to Gary–Hammond, Indiana), I-75 (1,787 miles, from Naples, Florida, to the Michigan–Canada border), and I-95 (1,894 miles, from the city of Miami to the Maine–Canada border).

The Interstate System: A Route Log and Finder List

Route	Total Mileage	Mileage by State		Selected Cities Served
4	132.06	Florida	132.06	Daytona Beach, Lakeland, Orlando, Tampa, Winter Haven
5	1,382.05	California	797.01	Anaheim, Los Angeles, Redding, Sacramento, San Diego, Santa Ana, Stockton
		Oregon	308.41	Eugene, Medford, Portland, Salem
		Washington	276.63	Bellingham, Olympia, Seattle, Tacoma, Vancouver
8	348.32	California	170.00	El Centro, San Diego
		Arizona	178.32	Casa Grande, Yuma
10	2,459.96	California	242.50	Los Angeles, Riverside, San Bernardino
		Arizona	391.94	Phoenix, Tucson
		New Mexico	164.28	Deming, Las Cruces
		Texas	880.60	Beaumont, El Paso, Houston, San Antonio
		Louisiana	274.42	Baton Rouge, Lafayette, Lake Charles, New Orleans
		Mississippi	77.10	Biloxi, Gulfport, Pascagoula
		Alabama	66.30	Mobile
		Florida	362.82	Jacksonville, Pensacola, Tallahassee
12	85.59	Louisiana	85.59	Baton Rouge
15	1,436.85	California	287.30	Riverside, San Bernardino, San Diego
		Nevada	123.77	Las Vegas
		Arizona	29.37	—
		Utah	405.49	Brigham City, Ogden, Orem, Provo, St. George, Salt Lake City
		Idaho	195.87	Blackfoot, Idaho Falls, Pocatello
		Montana	395.05	Butte, Great Falls, Helena, Sweetgrass
16	165.41	Georgia	165.41	Macon, Savannah
17	145.24	Arizona	145.24	Flagstaff, Phoenix
19	63.35	Arizona	63.35	Nogales, Tucson
20	1,538.31	Texas	635.98	Abilene, Arlington, Dallas, Fort Worth, Longview, Marshall, Midland, Odessa, Tyler
		Louisiana	189.87	Monroe, Shreveport
		Mississippi	154.50	Jackson, Meridian, Vicksburg
		Alabama	214.70	Anniston, Birmingham, Tuscaloosa
		Georgia	201.75	Atlanta, Augusta
		South Carolina	141.51	Columbia, Florence
24	316.52	Illinois	38.73	Metropolis
		Kentucky	93.37	Hopkinsville, Paducah
		Tennessee	180.30	Chattanooga, Clarksville, Nashville
		Georgia	4.12	—

Route	Total Mileage	Mileage by State		Selected Cities Served
25	1,062.52	New Mexico	462.68	Albuquerque, Las Cruces, Santa Fe
		Colorado	298.94	Colorado Springs, Denver, Fort Collins, Longmont, Pueblo
		Wyoming	300.90	Casper, Cheyenne
26	260.90	North Carolina	39.95	Asheville, Hendersonville
		South Carolina	220.95	Charleston, Columbia, Spartanburg
27	124.38	Texas	124.38	Amarillo, Lubbock
29	752.26	Missouri	130.30	Kansas City, St. Joseph
		Iowa	151.81	Council Bluffs, Sioux City
		South Dakota	252.65	Sioux Falls
		North Dakota	217.50	Fargo, Grand Forks
30	366.71	Texas	223.63	Dallas, Fort Worth, Texarkana
		Arkansas	143.08	Little Rock, Texarkana
35	1,568.27	Texas	503.83	Arlington, Austin, Dallas, Fort Worth, Laredo, San Antonio, Temple, Waco
		Oklahoma	235.96	Norman, Oklahoma City
		Kansas	235.52	Kansas City, Lawrence, Topeka, Wichita
		Missouri	114.80	Kansas City
		Iowa	218.47	Ames, Des Moines
		Minnesota	259.69	Albert Lea, Duluth, Minneapolis, St. Paul
37	143.06	Texas	143.06	Corpus Christi, San Antonio
39	131.03	Illinois	131.03	Bloomington, Rockford
40	2,460.68	California	154.60	Barstow, Needles
		Arizona	359.23	Flagstaff, Kingman
		New Mexico	371.37	Albuquerque, Gallup, Tucumcari
		Texas	177.00	Amarillo
		Oklahoma	331.03	Clinton, Oklahoma City
		Arkansas	284.80	Fort Smith, Little Rock
		Tennessee	455.25	Jackson, Knoxville, Memphis, Nashville
		North Carolina	327.40	Asheville, Burlington, Durham, Greensboro, Hickory, Raleigh, Winston-Salem
43	182.58	Wisconsin	182.58	Green Bay, Milwaukee, Sheboygan
44	634.03	Texas	14.70	Wichita Falls
		Oklahoma	328.53	Oklahoma City, Tulsa
		Missouri	290.80	Joplin, St. Louis, Springfield
45	284.99	Texas	284.99	Dallas, Galveston, Houston, Texas City
49	206.57	Louisiana	206.57	Alexandria, Lafayette, Nachitoches, Opelousas, Shreveport
55	943.69	Louisiana	65.81	Hammond, La Place
		Mississippi	289.70	Grenada, Jackson, McComb
		Tennessee	12.20	Memphis
		Arkansas	72.22	Blytheville, West Memphis
		Missouri	209.40	Cape Girardeau, St. Louis
		Illinois	294.36	Bloomington, Chicago, East St. Louis, Joliet, Springfield
57	380.57	Missouri	22.00	Charleston, Sikeston
		Illinois	358.57	Champaign, Chicago, Kankakee, Rantoul, Urbana
59	444.02	Louisiana	11.48	New Orleans, Slidell
		Mississippi	171.20	Hattiesburg, Laurel, Meridian
		Alabama	241.40	Birmingham, Gadsden, Tuscaloosa
		Georgia	19.94	—
64	944.19	Missouri	14.70	St. Louis
		Illinois	128.12	Belleville, East St. Louis
		Indiana	124.04	Evansville, New Albany
		Kentucky	191.55	Frankfort, Lexington, Louisville
		West Virginia	186.86	Charleston, Huntington, White Sulphur Springs
		Virginia	298.92	Charlottesville, Newport News, Norfolk, Richmond

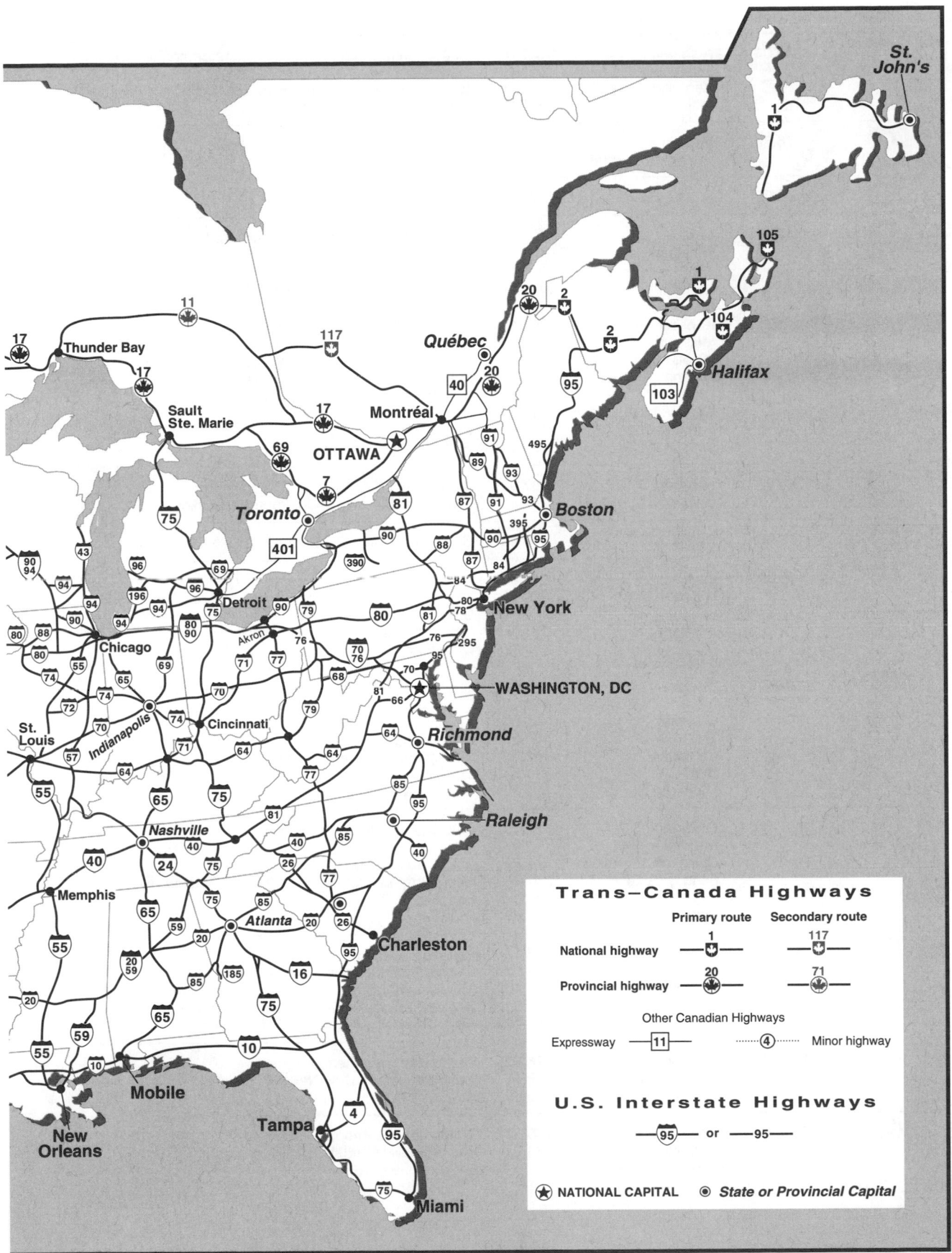

Thomas Nast, Cartographer

Route	Total Mileage	Mileage by State		Selected Cities Served
65	888.08	Alabama	367.00	Birmingham, Decatur, Mobile, Montgomery
		Tennessee	121.40	Nashville
		Kentucky	137.60	Bowling Green, Elizabethtown, Louisville
		Indiana	262.08	Gary, Indianapolis, Lafayette
66	76.37	Virginia	75.26	Arlington, Fairfax, Falls Church, Front Royal, Vienna
		District of Columbia	1.11	Washington, DC
68	72.00	West Virginia	72.00	Morgantown
69	356.19	Indiana	157.79	Anderson, Fort Wayne, Indianapolis, Muncie
		Michigan	198.40	Battle Creek, Flint, Lansing
70	2,175.46	Utah	230.77	Cove Fort, Green River, Richfield
		Colorado	450.30	Denver, Grand Junction
		Kansas	424.17	Kansas City, Lawrence, Topeka
		Missouri	251.60	Columbia, Kansas City, St. Louis
		Illinois	160.25	East St. Louis, Effingham, Vandalia
		Indiana	156.27	Indianapolis, Richmond, Terre Haute
		Ohio	225.69	Columbus, Dayton, Springfield, Zanesville
		West Virginia	14.45	Wheeling
		Pennsylvania	168.73	Pittsburgh
		Maryland	93.23	Baltimore, Hagerstown
71	345.58	Kentucky	97.92	Covington, Louisville
		Ohio	247.66	Cincinnati, Cleveland, Columbus, Mansfield
72	78.66	Illinois	78.66	Champaign, Decatur, Springfield
74	416.89	Iowa	5.39	Davenport
		Illinois	220.18	Bloomington, Champaign, Moline, Peoria, Rock Island, Urbana
		Indiana	171.87	Crawfordsville, Indianapolis, Shelbyville
		Ohio	19.45	Cincinnati
75	1,786.99	Florida	472.06	Bradenton, Fort Myers, Gainesville, Lakeland, Naples, Ocala, St. Petersburg, Sarasota, Tampa
		Georgia	355.00	Atlanta, Macon, Valdosta
		Tennessee	161.60	Chattanooga, Knoxville
		Kentucky	191.60	Covington, Lexington, Richmond
		Ohio	211.53	Cincinnati, Dayton, Lima, Middletown, Toledo
		Michigan	395.20	Bay City, Detroit, Flint, Saginaw
76	618.49	Colorado	184.14	Denver, Fort Morgan, Sterling
		Nebraska	2.48	—
		Ohio	77.82	Akron, Youngstown
		Pennsylvania	351.25	Harrisburg, Lancaster, Philadelphia, Pittsburgh, Reading
		New Jersey	2.80	Camden
77	598.25	South Carolina	75.17	Columbia, Rock Hill
		North Carolina	105.37	Charlotte, Mooresville, Statesville
		Virginia	67.40	Bluefield, Wytheville
		West Virginia	187.21	Beckley, Bluefield, Charleston, Parkersburg
		Ohio	163.10	Akron, Canton, Cleveland, Marietta
78	145.34	Pennsylvania	76.69	Allentown, Bethlehem, Easton
		New Jersey	68.15	Irvington, Jersey City, Newark, Plainfield
		New York	0.50	New York City
79	344.25	West Virginia	160.52	Charleston, Fairmont, Morgantown
		Pennsylvania	183.73	Erie, Meadville, Pittsburgh, Washington

Route	Total Mileage	Mileage by State		Selected Cities Served
80	2,906.75	California	202.20	Davis, Fairfield, Oakland, Sacramento, San Francisco, Vallejo,
		Nevada	410.67	Elko, Reno, Sparks, Winnemucca
		Utah	197.58	Salt Lake City
		Wyoming	402.86	Cheyenne, Evanston, Laramie, Rawlings, Rock Springs
		Nebraska	455.31	Grand Island, Kearney, Lincoln, Omaha
		Iowa	306.55	Davenport, Des Moines, Iowa City
		Illinois	163.52	Chicago, Joliet, Moline, Rock Island
		Indiana	151.65	Elkhart, Gary, Hammond, Mishawaka, South Bend
		Ohio	237.07	Cleveland, Elyria, Toledo, Warren, Youngstown
		Pennsylvania	311.24	Du Bois, Milton, Sharon, Stroudsburg
		New Jersey	68.10	Bergen–Passaic
81	855.07	Tennessee	75.30	Bristol, Johnson City, Kingsport, Knoxville
		Virginia	324.01	Bristol, Roanoke
		West Virginia	26.00	Martinsburg
		Maryland	11.96	Hagerstown
		Pennsylvania	233.70	Harrisburg, Scranton, Wilkes-Barre
		New York	184.10	Binghamton, Syracuse
82	142.99	Washington	132.20	Kennewick, Pasco, Richland, Yakima
		Oregon	10.79	Hermiston
83	84.11	Maryland	34.05	Baltimore
		Pennsylvania	50.06	Harrisburg, York
84	995.62	Oregon	375.15	Baker, Pendleton, Portland
		Idaho	275.36	Boise, Twin Falls
		Utah	117.18	Ogden
		Pennsylvania	49.75	Scranton
		New York	71.60	Orange County
		Connecticut	98.52	Bristol, Danbury, Hartford, New Britain, Waterbury
		Massachusetts	8.06	—
85	667.11	Alabama	80.00	Auburn, Montgomery, Opelika
		Georgia	178.94	Atlanta
		South Carolina	106.13	Anderson, Greenville, Spartanburg
		North Carolina	233.40	Burlington, Charlotte, Durham, Gastonia, Greensboro, High Point
		Virginia	68.64	Petersburg
86	63.18	Idaho	63.18	American Falls, Pocatello
87	333.20	New York	333.20	Albany, Glens Falls, New York City, Orange County, Poughkeepsie, Troy
88	173.09	Illinois	173.09	Chicago, Moline
89	191.32	New Hampshire	60.93	Concord, Lebanon
		Vermont	130.39	Burlington, Montpelier
90	3,081.87	Washington	297.01	Seattle, Spokane
		Idaho	73.73	Coeur d'Alene, Kellogg
		Montana	549.98	Billings, Bozeman, Butte, Missoula
		Wyoming	208.79	Buffalo, Sheridan
		South Dakota	412.84	Rapid City, Sioux Falls
		Minnesota	275.70	Albert Lea, Austin, Rochester
		Wisconsin	187.17	Beloit, Janesville, La Crosse, Madison
		Illinois	108.05	Chicago, Elgin, Rockford
		Indiana	156.90	Elkhart, Gary, Hammond, Mishawaka, South Bend
		Ohio	244.13	Cleveland, Elyria, Lorain, Toledo
		Pennsylvania	46.60	Erie
		New York	386.77	Albany, Buffalo, Rochester, Rome, Schenectady, Syracuse, Troy, Utica
		Massachusetts	134.20	Boston, Pittsfield, Springfield, Worcester

Route	Total Mileage	Mileage by State		Selected Cities Served
91	290.52	Connecticut	57.98	Hartford, Meriden, New Haven
		Massachusetts	54.92	Springfield
		Vermont	177.62	Brattleboro, St. Johnsbury
93	188.91	Massachusetts	46.00	Boston, Lawrence, Lowell
		New Hampshire	131.85	Concord, Manchester
		Vermont	11.06	St. Johnsbury
94	1,606.71	Montana	247.91	Billings, Glendive, Miles City
		North Dakota	352.50	Bismarck, Fargo
		Minnesota	259.49	Minneapolis, Moorhead, St. Cloud, St. Paul
		Wisconsin	348.11	Eau Claire, Kenosha, Madison, Milwaukee, Racine
		Illinois	77.37	Chicago, Lake County
		Indiana	45.73	Gary, Hammond, Michigan City, Portage
		Michigan	275.60	Ann Arbor, Battle Creek, Benton Harbor, Detroit, Jackson, Kalamazoo
95	1,894.02	Florida	382.40	Boca Raton, Daytona Beach, Fort Lauderdale, Fort Pierce, Hialeah, Hollywood, Jacksonville, Melbourne, Miami, Palm Beach, Pompano Beach
		Georgia	111.69	Brunswick, Savannah
		South Carolina	198.76	Florence
		North Carolina	181.39	Fayetteville
		Virginia	174.52	Arlington, Petersburg, Richmond
		District of Columbia	0.12	Washington, DC
		Maryland	108.83	Baltimore
		Delaware	23.43	Wilmington
		Pennsylvania	51.95	Philadelphia
		New Jersey	79.08	Elizabeth, Newark, Trenton
		New York	23.35	New York City
		Connecticut	111.57	Bridgeport, Milford, New Haven, New London, Norwalk, Stamford
		Rhode Island	43.31	Cranston, Pawtucket, Providence, Warwick
		Massachusetts	89.60	Attleboro, Boston
		New Hampshire	16.13	Portsmouth
		Maine	297.89	Augusta, Bangor, Portland
96	192.70	Michigan	192.70	Detroit, Grand Rapids, Lansing, Muskegon
97	17.88	Maryland	17.88	Annapolis, Baltimore

Source: U.S. Department of Transportation, *Interstate System Route Log and Finder List,* undated.

Education

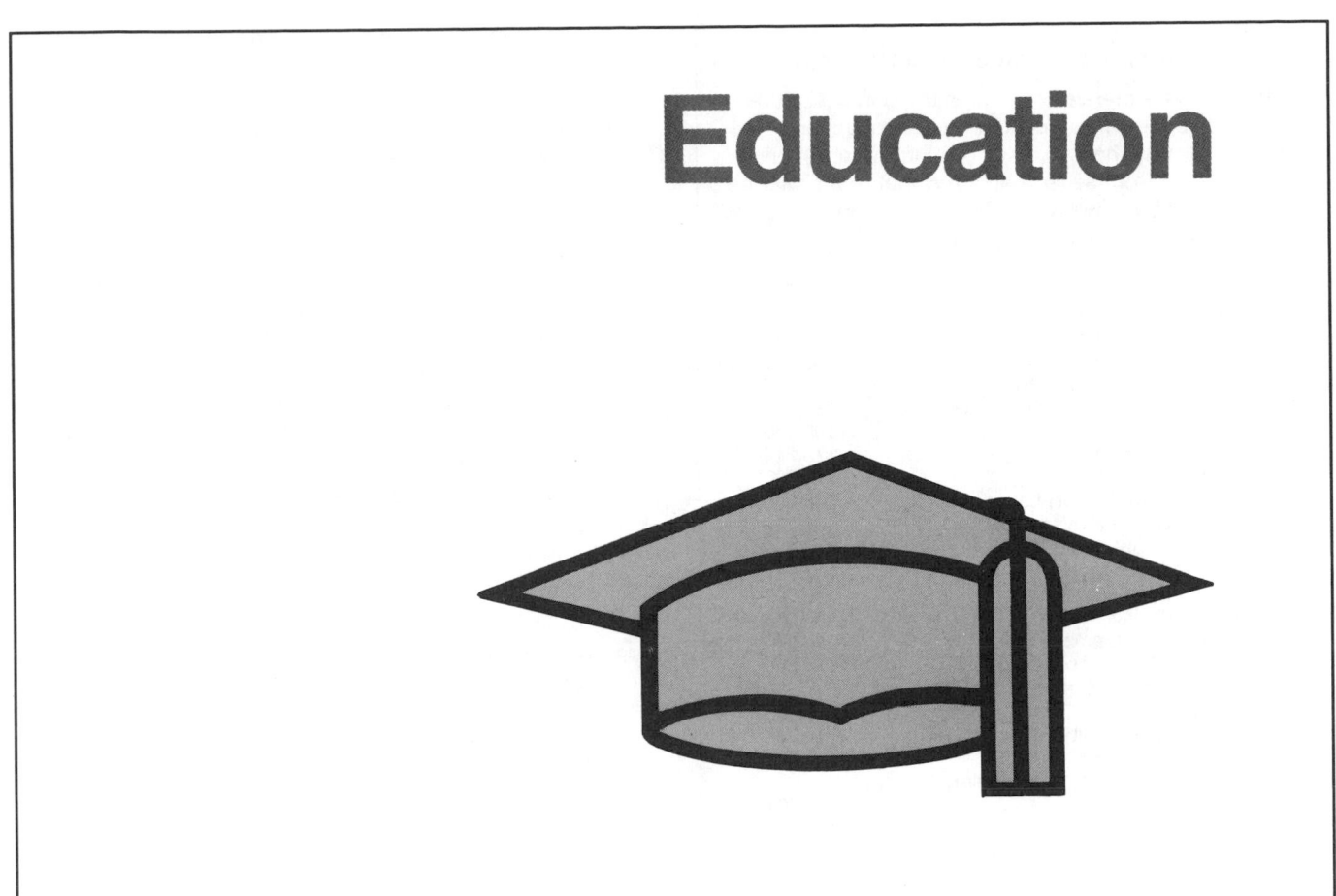

Nine months of the year, 3 of every 10 persons either work in an educational institution or learn in one. Keeping the enterprise going is the biggest item on city budgets. Whether the results are worth all the money spent is sometimes an excuse for teachers, administrators, parents, politicians, and taxpayers to shout at each other.

Education will never be the sacred cow it once was. The scores of high school students on most standardized tests are lower today than they were 30 years ago. Among high school seniors, nearly 40 percent can't draw inferences from written material, only one-fifth can write a persuasive essay, and only one-third can solve a math problem requiring several steps.

Parents and teachers blame each other. Although the public trusts teachers more than they do politicians, journalists, or business people, teachers don't get high marks. For their part, teachers are even stingier graders; most parents, they say, are too tired and uninterested to get involved in their child's schooling.

PUBLIC K-12

The quality of the public schools usually tips the balance when a relocating family weighs a neighborhood's good and bad points. Often their choice is influenced by a real estate agent's hearsay that the schools are great or ought to be because the local tax rate is high. Are there ways to compare districts and schools more objectively? Definitely.

Shopping for a District

A sign of the times: In some of Long Island's 131 school districts, local cops check the addresses of children and discover interlopers who live beyond the district's boundaries taking up seats in local schools. Parents had registered their kids under the addresses of relatives or friends to meet residency requirements.

Moving into an unfamiliar area means stepping into a thicket of school districts, each with its own politics, funding, philosophy, standards, curricula, and results. Since your taxes support the district, you'll want to find

North America's Largest School Districts

In the 1930s, America was fragmented into 128,000 school districts. After decades of consolidation, there are fewer than 16,000 (1,000 in Canada). They range in size from several hundred that don't operate schools (but bus children to other districts) to the giant ones listed below.

Unit	Pupils Enrolled
1. New York City Community	973,263
2. Los Angeles Unified	610,210
3. Chicago Public Schools	409,731
4. Dade County (Miami, FL)	304,287
5. Houston Independent School District	191,330
6. Philadelphia City Schools	190,000
7. Hawaii Public Schools	173,244
8. Detroit Public Schools	171,000
9. Broward County (Fort Lauderdale, FL)	168,086
10. Clark County (Las Vegas, NV)	136,204
11. Fairfax County (Fairfax, VA)	136,000
12. Dallas Independent	133,722
13. Hillsborough County (Tampa, FL)	128,962
14. San Diego Unified	126,000
15. Duval County (Jacksonville, FL)	115,000
16. Baltimore City School District	112,866
17. Prince George's County (Upper Marlboro, MD)	111,002
18. Montgomery County (Rockville, MD)	110,267
19. Orange County (Orlando, FL)	109,474
20. Palm Beach County (West Palm Beach, FL)	108,904
21. Memphis City Schools	106,756
22. Metropolitan (Toronto) Separate School Board	103,000
23. Milwaukee School District	100,832
24. Commission des Ecoles Catholiques (Montreal, PQ)	99,591
25. Jefferson County (KY) Public Schools	96,250
26. Pinellas County (Largo, FL)	93,415
27. Peel Board of Education (Mississauga, ON)	91,410
28. Baltimore County School District (Towson, MD)	90,844
29. District of Columbia Schools	89,043
30. Albuquerque School District	84,257
31. Jefferson County (CO) Schools	79,244
32. Orleans Parish Schools (New Orleans, LA)	78,813
33. Charlotte–Mecklenburg (Charlotte, NC)	78,358
34. Granite School District (Salt Lake City, UT)	77,608
35. De Kalb County (Decatur, GA)	76,574
36. Cleveland City Schools	76,481
37. Cobb County Schools (Marietta, GA)	75,897
38. Long Beach (CA) Unified	75,000
39. Virginia Beach (VA) City Schools	74,221
40. Scarborough (ON) Board of Education	73,630

Source: Quality Education Data, unpublished records, 1993.

and objectives are explicit and under constant examination and review, then a district takes its mission seriously.

- The classroom teachers in the district should have not only a standard certificate but also (in 50 percent of the cases or better) at least a master's degree or equivalent in the subject they teach.
- A district's holding power—that is, the percentage of its ninth-grade pupils who stay in school and finish—should be at least 90 percent. If 95 percent of a district's enrollment is in average daily attendance, that's a good indication of how closely parents and schools keep tabs on children.
- Beware of the professional revolving door. A high number of eligible teachers not getting tenure might mean that the district has tough standards; but it could also be a sign that the district cuts costs by hiring beginners and then refusing them tenure at the end of their probationary period. Under this scheme, it is possible for a child to progress from kindergarten through high school and have inexperienced, unfamiliar teachers each year.

Shopping for a School

Outside Washington, DC, parents bring lawn chairs, paperbacks, and blankets *days* before the Prince George's County school district throws open a window to register children in choice magnet schools on a first-come, first-serve basis.

Moving into a good school district won't necessarily mean that you'll find quality education in all of its schools. Get a district map of neighborhood boundaries for the schools as well as a list of Parent-Teacher Association (PTA) contacts. Talking with a local parent will save you time. Then make an appointment with the school's principal or the head guidance counselor to obtain specific information.

- A good high school should have one guidance counselor for every 200 students, and it should have at least one full-time career counselor.
- Classroom size in high school should average no more than 30 students. The size of the senior class shouldn't be less than 300 to 500 students. If the enrollment is much smaller than that, many worthwhile specialized courses won't be offered.
- A quality high school should offer four years of English, three years of mathematics, three years of science, three years of social studies, two years of foreign languages; second-year courses in biology, astronomy, chemistry, and physics;

out their differences with a consumer's eye. Visit the district principal or superintendent's office and consider several factors:

- A good district can give you a written philosophy or a statement of educational objectives approved within the last five years by the state board of education. If educational philosophy

Catholic Private Schools in Metro Areas

Whatever the reason—religious content, cultural tradition, dress codes, discipline, a more rigorous education—at least one out of seven children in the following metro areas attends a Catholic private school.

		Children in Catholic Private Schools
1.	Dubuque, IA	35.5%
2.	Kankakee, IL	22.1
3.	New Orleans, LA	19.5
4.	Owensboro, KY	17.9
5.	Philadelphia, PA–NJ	17.8
6.	Cincinnati, OH–KY–IN	15.5
7.	Scranton–Wilkes-Barre–Hazleton, PA	15.3
8.	Toledo, OH	14.9
9.	St. Louis, MO–IL	14.8
10.	Northern New Jersey, NJ	14.6
11.	Cleveland–Lorain–Elyria, OH	14.5
12.	St. Cloud, MN	14.2
13.	Green Bay, WI	14.0

Source: Derived from Quality Education Data, unpublished records, 1993.

The percent of children attending Catholic schools in many Canadian metro areas is much higher than the list above. These are *public* schools, however, operating under separate Catholic school boards.

Non-Catholic Private Schools in Metro Areas

While more than half of all private school pupils in the United States are in Catholic parochial systems, two out of three private schools are non-Catholic. Many are operated as religious schools by groups such as the Evangelical Lutheran Church, the Seventh-Day Adventist Board of Education, and the National Society for Hebrew Day Schools. Many others are nonsectarian. Below are metro areas where at least one child in 10 attends a non-Catholic private school.

		Children in Non-Catholic Private Schools
1.	Charlottesville, VA	14.1%
2.	West Palm Beach–Boca Raton, FL	11.8
3.	Chattanooga, TN–GA	11.7
4.	Jackson, MS	11.6
5.	Lancaster, PA	11.4
6.	Columbus, GA–AL	11.4
7.	Tallahassee, FL	11.3
8.	Stamford–Norwalk, CT	11.1
9.	Macon, GA	10.8
10.	Montgomery, AL	10.8
11.	Wilmington–Newark, DE–MD	10.8
12.	Honolulu, HI	10.7
13.	Grand Rapids–Muskegon–Holland, MI	10.2

Source: Derived from Quality Education Data, unpublished records, 1993.

college-preparatory courses in the humanities; at least one year of computer literacy; and Advanced Placement (AP) courses for college credit.

- Because one-fifth of all four-year public colleges must accept every high school graduate within the state, regardless of program followed or grades earned, it is no longer noteworthy that most of a high school's graduating seniors go on to college. The question to ask is: Which colleges are accepting them—top schools with tough admissions standards, or open-admission institutions with no requirements but that the check be good and the diploma in hand?

- Don't cross a high school off your list if it doesn't measure up on all of these points. A school can have all but one or two and still be a good one. Relocation experts advise clients that the stability of a town is reflected best in its schools. If the high school is good, chances are that the schools at the lower levels will also be good.

In choosing an elementary school or a junior high, again ask questions of principals and other parents.

- Class size in elementary schools should average no more than 20 pupils. Reading should be emphasized over all other subjects, but writing,

Grand High Schools

Small schools may have beneficial effects on student participation, attendance, satisfaction, and achievement. However, the prevailing view since the 1960s has been that large schools, such as the ones listed below, could offer more comprehensive curricula and a wider variety of programs at lower cost.

United States	Students
Sachem North HS (Ronkonkoma, NY)	5,542
Braddock HS (Miami, FL)	4,990
John F. Kennedy HS (Bronx, NY)	4,838
Dewitt Clinton HS (Bronx, NY)	4,694
Franklin K. Lane HS (Brooklyn, NY)	4,497
Brooklyn Tech (Brooklyn, NY)	4,378
Newtown HS (Elmhurst, NY)	4,256
Elizabeth HS (Elizabeth, NJ)	4,233
Belmont Senior HS (Los Angeles, CA)	4,182
Independence HS (San Jose, CA)	4,136

Canada	Students
Fredericton HS (Fredericton, NB)	2,896
Beal Secondary School (London, ON)	2,735
Polyvalente Nicholas (Gatineau, PQ)	2,600
Ecole Jean Baptiste (Repentigy, PQ)	2,500
Lord Beaverbrook HS (Calgary, AB)	2,400

Source: Quality Education Data, unpublished records, 1993.

Grand Campuses: North America's Fifteen Largest Universities

Some 15 million persons attend baccalaureate and graduate-level institutions in the United States and Canada. In both countries, slightly more men than women enroll, and in both countries, slightly more women than men graduate. Below are the continent's largest universities.

University	Students
University of Minnesota	58,815
Ohio State University	52,895
University of Texas	50,245
University of Toronto	50,130
Michigan State University	44,423
Arizona State University	43,550
University of Wisconsin	43,364
Université de Montreal	41,690
Texas A&M University	40,492
Pennsylvania State University	37,718
University of Illinois	37,481
Purdue University	37,459
University of Arizona	36,676
University of Michigan	36,474
Université du Quebec	36,353

Source: U.S. Department of Education, *Directory of Postsecondary Institutions*, 1992; Statistics Canada, *Universities: Enrollment and Degrees*, 1992.

problem solving in math, hands-on work in science, and the social studies curriculum should get their due.

- In elementary schools, there should be a full-time librarian and a classroom-size library. There should also be one large room or auditorium for school meetings, arts performances, and special guest presentations.
- In junior high schools—grades 7, 8, and 9—there should be special provision for both bright students and slow learners.

PRIVATE SCHOOL ALTERNATIVES

One statistic about elementary and secondary education in the United States since 1930 is the nearly 100-percent growth in the number of private schools, in contrast to the 75-percent decline in the number of public schools. This isn't to say that the public schools are collapsing; most of the schools that have closed are rural, one-room buildings. But it does show that private schools are a thriving alternative.

Today, one out of nine school-age children attends a private or parochial school. In spite of the decline in school enrollments in recent years, private schools held on to more of their enrollment than did public schools, losing only 6 percent as compared with 11 percent for public schools.

Recent research from the Department of Education shows that students in private high schools take more courses than their public school counterparts and that they take these courses in smaller classes. Critics of public education point out that because private institutions forgo the smorgasbord of electives that public schools offer their students, graduates of private high schools have tougher basic courses on their transcripts and are better prepared for college study. (In fact, private school pupils generally score higher on the Scholastic Aptitude Tests (SATs) than students in public schools.)

COLLEGES AND UNIVERSITIES

Educators like to say that schooling leads to just three outcomes: more schooling, employment, or unemployment. When high school graduates go on to college or find jobs, the public education system is successful; if they do neither, the system is considered a flop.

In fact, nearly half of metro-area high school graduates eventually go to college, and 6 out of 10 of these begin their freshman year at an institution within 50 miles of home.

More Than an Education

Everywhere from Abilene to Yuma, chamber of commerce promotional brochures tout local colleges and universities more frequently than other urban assets. And with good reason. Among the 20 million students taking college courses in North America, 15 million are studying in metro areas. For 21 million other people, the typical location for their evening or

North America's Largest Community Colleges

About one in four people going on to college after high school attends a community college. Almost all institutions are publicly supported. Many of the largest ones below have several campuses.

College	Students
Miami–Dade (FL) Community College	47,330
Northern Virginia Community College	34,539
Houston Community College System	32,536
St. Louis (MO) Community College System	31,847
Macomb Community College (Warren, MI)	31,670
Durham College (Oshawa, ON)	25,000
College of Du Page (Glen Ellyn, IL)	28,037
Oakland Community College (Bloomfield Hills, MI)	27,504
Tarrant County Junior College (Fort Worth, TX)	27,109
Pima Community College (Tucson, AZ)	26,747
El Camino College (Torrance, CA)	25,789
Orange Coast College (Costa Mesa, CA)	24,468
City College of San Francisco	24,408
Broward (FL) Community College	23,547
Austin (TX) Community College	23,067

Source: U.S. Department of Education, *Directory of Postsecondary Institutions*, 1992; Statistics Canada, *Universities: Enrollment and Degrees*, 1992.

weekend continuing education course is a local college classroom.

Colleges and universities contribute other things besides education. In smaller metro areas, a worthy theater where a touring group of professional players can stage *Playboy of the Western World* or an auditorium where an orchestra and choral group can perform *The Messiah* can only be found at the local college campus.

Colleges and universities are stable white-collar employers, too. In Iowa City, IA, Lawrence, KS, and Tuscaloosa, AL, they are the major employers.

Finally, there is the connection between research-oriented universities and healthy economies. Two historic examples are Stanford University's impetus to the growth of Silicon Valley high-tech enterprises in San Jose and Bay Area environs, and MIT's faculty and alumni who started electronics firms along Route 128 outside of Boston.

SCORING: EDUCATION

To profile a metro area's academic features, *Places Rated* details the local mix of public and private schools and public and private colleges and universities.

Places Rated's tack for scoring, however, is based only on the variety of higher education options that meet the needs of residents: low-cost night and weekend continuing education courses for people who work, full-time graduate courses in the professions, courses leading to occupational certification in two-year colleges, and the traditional bachelor's degree curriculum offered in a college or university.

Counting colleges and universities reveals which metro areas are enriched and which aren't. But a clearer picture can be made by totaling up the number of students in the area's two-year schools and in its baccalaureate and graduate-level institutions.

Like ratings in the arts and transportation, ratings in education get better with population size. There are exceptions, though. One hundred and five metro areas are larger than Ann Arbor, MI, but only 28 are ranked higher in education. Likewise, Raleigh-Durham, NC, Vancouver, BC, and Central New Jersey are ranked much higher than their population size indicates.

Each metro area begins with a base score of zero, to which points are added according to the following indicators:

1. Enrollment, **two-year**. A metro area's number of students enrolled in two-year colleges is divided by 100, and the result is added to the score.
2. Enrollment, **private baccalaureate and beyond**. A metro area's number of students enrolled in private colleges and universities with baccalaureate and graduate programs is divided by 75, and the result is added to the score.
3. Enrollment, **public baccalaureate and beyond**. A metro area's number of students enrolled in public colleges and universities with baccalaureate and graduate programs is divided by 50, and the result is added to the score.
4. **MC access.** Each of the 75 metro areas that is part of a Metropolitan Complex (MC) is eligible for bonus points based on shared educational assets: public four-year and graduate-level institutions. A place gets a bonus of 10 percent of the points accumulated by *adjacent* places in the MC for these resources.

In the Dallas–Fort Worth metropolitan complex, for example, Fort Worth–Arlington gets 88 access points based on Dallas's public four-year and graduate-level institutions. Likewise, Dallas gets a 48-point bonus because the University of Texas's Arlington campus lies within adjacent Fort Worth–Arlington.

SCORING EXAMPLES

A sprawling West Coast suburban area and a Southern state capital illustrate the education scoring method.

Orange County, CA (#11)

Embracing affluent Newport Beach and Irvine all the way through middle-class Anaheim to run-down Santa Ana, Orange County—south of Los Angeles—might be called North America's largest suburb.

Here you can find all three types of Calfornia's master-planned higher educational institutions: a branch of the prestigious University of California (at Irvine), a campus of the Cal State system (at Fullerton), and eight two-year colleges taking in nearly 10 percent of everyone enrolled in the California Community College system.

By themselves, those assets are good for 2,042 points. But Orange County, adjacent to Los Angeles and San Bernardino–Riverside, is part of a metropolitan complex. That factor contributes another 427 points to its score.

Raleigh–Durham–Chapel Hill, NC (#27)

While Durhams' public school system was recently rated the state's worst, the metro area is lucky, not just for being the seat of state government but for being the home of three nationally known universities: Duke, North Carolina State, and the University of North Carolina.

Locally called the Triangle, Raleigh–Durham–Chapel Hill is an example of a small place doing better than many larger ones. There are 64 metro areas more populous than here, but only 26 that rank better in higher education options. With six two-year colleges enrolling 13,647 students (136 points), five private four-year and graduate-level institutions enrolling 17,216 students (230 points), plus NC State, NC Central, and UNC (all public, good for another 136 points), the Triangle's score is 1,483.

Rankings: Education

The following criteria are used to rate a metro area for higher education opportunities available to residents: (1) the number of students enrolled in community or two-year colleges, (2) the number of students enrolled in *private* four-year and graduate-level institutions, and (3) the number of students enrolled in *public* four-year and graduate-level institutions. Places with tie scores get the same rank and are listed alphabetically.

Metro Areas from Best to Worst

Places Rated Rank	Places Rated Score	Places Rated Rank	Places Rated Score	Places Rated Rank	Places Rated Score
1. Los Angeles–Long Beach, CA	6,728	30. Riverside–San Bernardino, CA	1,451	57. Kitchener, ON	879
2. New York, NY	6,648			58. Edmonton, AB	876
3. Chicago, IL	5,276			59. Kansas City, MO–KS	873
4. Boston, MA	4,176	31. Seattle–Bellevue–Everett, WA	1,447	60. Dayton–Springfield, OH	867
5. Montreal, PQ	3,896	32. Albany–Schenectady–Troy, NY	1,359		
		33. Central New Jersey, NJ	1,245	61. Lexington, KY	860
6. Washington, DC–MD–VA–WV	3,764	34. Miami, FL	1,216	62. New Orleans, LA	848
7. Philadelphia, PA–NJ	3,333	35. Cleveland–Lorain–Elyria, OH	1,206	63. Champaign–Urbana, IL	834
8. Dallas, TX	2,675			64. Greensboro–Winston-Salem–High Point, NC	825
9. Detroit, MI	2,638	36. Tampa–St. Petersburg–Clearwater, FL	1,194	65. Bryan–College Station, TX	810
10. Toronto, ON	2,517	37. Denver, CO	1,184		
		38. Ottawa–Hull, ON–PQ	1,180	66. Tallahassee, FL	791
11. Orange County, CA	2,469	39. Oklahoma City, OK	1,164	67. San Antonio, TX	789
12. San Diego, CA	2,335	40. Buffalo–Niagara Falls, NY	1,160	68. Gainesville, FL	783
13. Minneapolis–St. Paul, MN–WI	2,212			69. Providence–Warwick–Cranston, RI	781
14. Newark–Jersey City, NJ	2,064	41. Lansing–East Lansing, MI	1,153	70. Nashville, TN	770
15. Baltimore, MD	2,045	42. Milwaukee–Waukesha, WI	1,122		
		43. Cincinnati, OH–KY–IN	1,120	71. Lafayette, IN	766
16. Long Island, NY	2,037	44. Akron, OH	1,117	72. Louisville , KY–IN	764
17. Oakland, CA	1,921	44. Fort Worth–Arlington, TX	1,117	73. Kalamazoo–Battle Creek, MI	755
18. Vancouver, BC	1,895			74. State College, PA	754
19. Phoenix–Mesa, AZ	1,894	46. Madison, WI	1,114	75. Syracuse, NY	751
20. San Jose, CA	1,854	47. Norfolk–Virginia Beach–Newport News, VA	1,108	76. Hartford, CT	747
21. St. Louis, MO–IL	1,813	48. Sacramento, CA	1,054	77. Indianapolis, IN	739
22. Austin–San Marcos, TX	1,730	49. Springfield, MA	1,027	78. Winnipeg, MB	737
23. San Francisco, CA	1,723	50. Tucson, AZ	1,001	79. Charlotte–Gastonia–Rock Hill, NC	734
24. Pittsburgh, PA	1,696			80. Orlando, FL	732
25. Atlanta, GA	1,692	51. Portland, OR	944		
		51. Toledo, OH	944	81. Hamilton, ON	720
26. Houston, TX	1,497	53. Quebec City, PQ	934	82. Baton Rouge, LA	713
27. Raleigh–Durham–Chapel Hill, NC	1,483	54. Northern New Jersey, NJ	933	83. Bloomington, IN	697
28. Columbus, OH	1,478	55. Rochester, NY	898	84. Worcester–Fitchburg–Leominster, MA	696
29. Ann Arbor, MI	1,461	56. Salt Lake City–Ogden, UT	881	85. Honolulu, HI	695

Places Rated Rank	Places Rated Score	Places Rated Rank	Places Rated Score	Places Rated Rank	Places Rated Score
86. London, ON	684	141. Fargo–Moorhead, ND–MN	403	196. Grand Forks, ND	259
87. Wilmington–Newark, DE–MD	682	142. Fort Lauderdale, FL	400	196. Waco, TX	259
88. Montgomery, AL	666	143. Huntsville, AL	399	198. Trois-Rivieres, PQ	253
89. Monmouth–Ocean, NJ	661	144. Chico–Paradise, CA	396	199. Eau Claire, WI	252
90. Memphis, TN	659	144. Santa Rosa, CA	396	200. Bakersfield, CA	250
91. Grand Rapids–Muskegon–Holland, MI	649	146. Greeley, CO	387	201. Colorado Springs, CO	245
92. Calgary, AB	647	146. Spokane, WA	387	202. McAllen–Edinburg–Mission, TX	242
93. Greenville–Spartanburg–Anderson, SC	644	148. St. Cloud, MN–WI	384	203. Reading, PA	241
94. Columbia, SC	643	149. Greenville, NC	377	204. Kenosha, WI	240
95. Scranton–Wilkes-Barre–Hazleton, PA	623	150. St. John's, NF	374	205. Salem, OR	237
95. Ventura, CA	623	151. Stamford–Norwalk, CT	370	206. La Crosse, WI	231
97. Trenton, NJ	621	152. Harrisburg–Lebanon–Carlisle, PA	364	207. Lancaster, PA	228
98. Knoxville, TN	617	153. Lake County, IL	354	208. Stockton–Lodi, CA	227
99. Omaha, NE–IA	606	154. Jackson, MS	352	209. Augusta–Aiken, GA–SC	225
100. Fresno, CA	598	155. Manchester–Nashua, NH	350	210. Davenport–Moline–Rock Island, IA–IL	224
101. Iowa City, IA	593	156. Vallejo–Fairfield–Napa, CA	342	211. Chicoutimi–Jonquiere, PQ	221
102. New Haven–Meriden, CT	589	157. Anchorage, AK	338	212. Vineland–Millville–Bridgeton, NJ	213
103. Saskatoon, SK	587	158. Allentown–Bethlehem–Easton, PA–NJ	336	213. Bellingham, WA	211
104. Santa Barbara–Santa Maria–Lompoc, CA	582	159. South Bend, IN	334	213. Modesto, CA	211
105. Albuquerque, NM	581	160. Youngstown–Warren, OH	330	213. Monroe, LA	211
106. Boulder–Longmont, CO	576	161. Mobile, AL	329	216. Dutchess County, NY	208
107. Lincoln, NE	554	162. Lafayette, LA	328	216. Peoria–Pekin, IL	208
108. Columbia, MO	552	163. Charleston–North Charleston, SC	326	218. Kankakee, IL	199
109. Lawrence, KS	550	164. Daytona Beach, FL	322	219. Sudbury, ON	197
110. Athens, GA	549	165. Portland, ME	319	219. Utica–Rome, NY	197
111. Birmingham, AL	546	166. Duluth–Superior, MN–WI	316	221. Evansville–Henderson, IN–KY	190
112. Halifax, NS	539	167. New Bedford–Fall River–Attleboro, MA	315	221. Green Bay, WI	190
113. Lubbock, TX	531	168. Lynchburg, VA	314	223. Amarillo, TX	178
114. Provo–Orem, UT	507	169. Reno, NV	313	224. Corpus Christi, TX	177
115. Orange County, NY	493	170. Johnson City–Kingsport–Bristol, TN–VA	310	224. Wilmington, NC	177
116. Las Vegas, NV	491	171. Huntington–Ashland, WV–KY	309	226. Galveston–Texas City, TX	174
117. Bloomington–Normal, IL	487	171. Tulsa, OK	309	227. Anniston, AL	170
118. Gary, IN	485	173. Binghamton, NY	307	228. Tyler, TX	167
119. El Paso, TX	480	173. Las Cruces, NM	307	229. Charleston, WV	163
120. West Palm Beach–Boca Raton, FL	477	175. Regina, SK	305	230. Springfield, IL	161
121. Yolo, CA	476	176. Fayetteville–Springdale–Rogers, AR	303	231. Thunder Bay, ON	156
122. Hamilton–Middletown, OH	465	176. Tacoma, WA	303	232. Lake Charles, LA	151
123. Springfield, MO	461	178. Bangor, ME	301	233. Fort Pierce–Port St. Lucie, FL	148
124. Charlottesville, VA	460	179. Fort Wayne, IN	298	233. Macon, GA	148
125. Atlantic City–Cape May, NJ	459	180. Burlington, VT	297	235. Clarksville–Hopkinsville, TN–KY	145
126. Eugene–Springfield, OR	455	180. Erie, PA	297	236. Fayetteville, NC	143
127. Tuscaloosa, AL	450	182. Terre Haute, IN	290	237. Brazoria, TX	140
128. Oshawa, ON	446	183. Victoria, BC	289	237. Joplin, MO	140
129. Windsor, ON	442	184. St. Catharines–Niagara, ON	283	239. Jamestown, NY	139
130. Jacksonville, FL	440	185. Boise City, ID	281	240. Houma, LA	137
131. Danbury, CT	437	185. Des Moines, IA	281	240. Savannah, GA	137
132. Santa Cruz–Watsonville, CA	426	187. Chattanooga, TN–GA	280	242. Wheeling, WV–OH	135
132. Sherbrooke, PQ	426	188. Appleton–Oshkosh–Neenah, WI	275	243. Redding, CA	134
134. Flint, MI	425	188. Melbourne–Titusville–Palm Bay, FL	275	243. Shreveport–Bossier City, LA	134
135. Wichita, KS	421	190. Beaumont–Port Arthur, TX	273	245. Cumberland, MD–WV	133
136. Little Rock–North Little Rock, AR	420	191. Pensacola, FL	272	246. Topeka, KS	131
137. Portsmouth–Dover–Rochester, NH	416	192. Waterloo–Cedar Falls, IA	271	247. Cedar Rapids, IA	130
138. Fort Collins–Loveland, CO	415	193. Richmond–Petersburg, VA	269	247. Florence, AL	130
139. Muncie, IN	413	193. Saginaw–Bay City–Midland, MI	269	249. Bremerton, WA	129
140. San Luis Obispo–Atascadero–Paso Robles, CA	406	195. Bridgeport, CT	262	249. Columbus, GA	129
				249. San Angelo, TX	129
				252. Asheville, NC	128
				252. Lakeland–Winter Haven, FL	128

Places Rated Rank	Places Rated Score	Places Rated Rank	Places Rated Score	Places Rated Rank	Places Rated Score
254. Odessa–Midland, TX	125	285. Benton Harbor, MI	73	312. Yuma, CA	47
254. Salinas, CA	125				
		285. Laredo, TX	73	316. Mansfield, OH	46
256. Hagerstown, MD	124	287. Fort Walton Beach, FL	72	316. Yakima, WA	46
257. Olympia, WA	117	287. Longview–Marshall, TX	72	318. Sioux Falls, SD	44
258. Lawton, OK	116	289. Parkersburg–Marietta,		319. Rapid City, SD	43
259. Brownsville–Harlingen–San		OH–WV	71	320. Cheyenne, WY	40
Benito, TX	114	289. Pine Bluff, AR	71		
260. Canton–Massillon, OH	111			320. Janesville–Beloit, WI	40
		291. Merced, CA	69	320. Owensboro, KY	40
260. Pueblo, CO	111	292. Albany, GA	65	320. Sumter, SC	40
262. Roanoke, VA	106	292. Texarkana, TX–Texarkana,		324. Steubenville–Weirton,	
263. York, PA	105	AR	65	OH–WV	39
264. Hickory–Morgantown, NC	104	294. Sharon, PA	64	325. Casper, WY	38
264. Medford–Ashland, OR	104	294. Decatur, IL	64		
				325. Wausau, WI	38
266. Abilene, TX	103	296. Ocala, FL	62	327. Alexandria, LA	37
266. Wichita Falls, TX	103	297. Panama City, FL	60	327. Jacksonville, NC	37
268. Visalia–Tulare–Porterville,		297. Rochester, MN	60	329. Vancouver, WA	36
CA	102	297. Santa Fe, NM	60	330. Biloxi–Gulfport–Pascagoula,	
269. Johnstown, PA	100	300. Dubuque, IA	59	MS	35
270. Myrtle Beach, SC	99				
		301. Barnstable–Yarmouth, MA	58	330. Goldsboro, NC	35
270. Rockford, IL	99	302. Lima, OH	57	332. Glens Falls, NY	33
272. Florence, SC	97	302. Williamsport, PA	57	333. Pittsfield, MA	32
272. New London–Norwich, CT	97	304. Richland–Kennewick–Pasco,		334. Lewiston–Auburn, NY	28
274. Killeen–Temple, TX	93	WA	56	335. Elmira, NY	26
275. Billings, MT	91	305. Victoria, TX	55		
				336. Saint John, NB	25
276. Fort Myers–Cape Coral, FL	87	306. Altoona, PA	52	337. Sheboygan, WI	24
276. Sarasota–Bradenton, FL	87	307. Racine, WI	50	338. Elkhart–Goshen, IN	18
278. Dover, DE	86	307. Sherman–Denison, TX	50	339. Great Falls, MT	16
279. Jackson, MI	85	309. Fort Smith, AR–OK	49	340. Yuba City, CA	15
279. St. Joseph, MO	85	309. Gadsden, AL	49		
				341. Enid, OK	13
281. Kokomo, IN	82	309. Rocky Mount, NC	49	342. Naples, FL	0
282. Waterbury, CT	81	312. Bismarck, ND	47	342. Punta Gorda, FL	0
283. Dothan, AL	80	312. Danville, VA	47		
284. Decatur, AL	75	312. Sioux City, IA–NE	47		

Place Profiles: Education

The following pages detail four facets of local education: (1) public schools, (2) private schools, (3) two-year colleges, and (4) colleges and universities offering baccalaureate and advanced degrees.

In parentheses next to the heading **Public K–12** is the percent of children attending public schools. Underneath is the number of districts, the number of schools, and their total enrollment.

In parentheses next to the heading **Private School Options** is the percent of children attending private schools (in Canada, nonfunded schools). Underneath are the number of local Catholic schools and pupils and the number of Other, that is, non-Catholic private schools and pupils.

Under the heading **Colleges and Universities** are (1) the number of community or two-year colleges and their total enrollment, and (2) the names and enrollments of local institutions granting at least bachelor's or advanced degrees. A • indicates a public-controlled institution in the United States. In Canada, degree-granting institutions get their charters from the province, or are affiliated with institutions that do. They essentially are publicly-supported.

Figures for American and Canadian public and private schools come from Quality Education Data, Inc., Denver, CO, and from Places Rated Partnership survey, 1992–1993.

Figures for American colleges and universities are derived from Volume 1 of the U.S. Department of Education's *Directory of Postsecondary Institutions*, 1992. Similar data for Canadian higher education institutions come from the Association of Canadian Community Colleges, *ACCC Directory of Canadian Colleges and Institutes*, 1992; the Association of Universities and Colleges of Canada, *Directory of Canadian Universities*, 1992; and Statistics Canada's *Universities: Enrollment and Degrees*, 1992, and *Community Colleges and Related Institutions*, 1992.

A check mark (✓) preceding the metro area's name identifies it as one of *Places Rated Almanac's* top 35 places for education.

Abilene, TX
Public K–12 (98.0%)
    5 districts, 46 schools
        25,591 pupils
Private School Options (2.0%)
    4 Other, 535 pupils
Colleges and Universities
    Baccalaureate and beyond:
        Abilene Christian University (4,186)
        Hardin–Simmons University (1,863)
        McMurry University (1,706)
Places Rated Score: 103
Places Rated Rank: 266

Akron, OH
Public K–12 (88.8%)
    35 districts, 203 schools
        103,201 pupils
Private School Options (11.2%)
    29 Catholic, 9,429 pupils
    16 Other, 3,525 pupils
Colleges and Universities
    Baccalaureate and beyond:
        Hiram College (1,338)
        • Kent State University (23,746)
        • NE Ohio College of Medicine (402)
        • University of Akron (28,967)
MC Access: Cleveland–Akron, OH
Places Rated Score: 1,117
Places Rated Rank: 44

Albany, GA
Public K–12 (94.0%)
    3 districts, 36 schools
        22,999 pupils
Private School Options (6.0%)
    1 Catholic, 463 pupils
    5 Other, 996 pupils
Colleges and Universities
    Two-year: 1 campus; 1,929 students
    Baccalaureate and beyond:
        • Albany State College (2,306)
Places Rated Score: 65
Places Rated Rank: 292

✓ Albany–Schenectady–Troy, NY
Public K–12 (88.3%)
    59 districts, 237 schools
        127,802 pupils
Private School Options (11.7%)
    49 Catholic, 11,839 pupils
    37 Other, 5,146 pupils
Colleges and Universities
    Two-year: 5 campuses; 16,006 students
    Baccalaureate and beyond:
        Albany College of Pharmacy (667)
        Albany Law School (831)
        Albany Medical College (621)
        College of St. Rose (3,483)
        Rensselaer Polytechnic (6,604)
        Russell Sage College (4,107)
        Siena College (3,438)
        Skidmore College (2,604)
        • SUNY College, Cobleskill (2,769)

        • SUNY Empire State College (7,229)
        • SUNY, Albany (16,628)
        Union College (2,922)
Places Rated Score: 1,359
Places Rated Rank: 32

Albuquerque, NM
Public K–12 (91.5%)
    7 districts, 160 schools
        100,088 pupils
Private School Options (8.5%)
    16 Catholic, 4,194 pupils
    26 Other, 5,103 pupils
Colleges and Universities
    Two-year: 2 campuses; 8,853 students
    Baccalaureate and beyond:
        • University of New Mexico (24,645)
Places Rated Score: 581
Places Rated Rank: 105

Alexandria, LA
Public K–12 (89.9%)
    2 districts, 59 schools
        23,980 pupils
Private School Options (10.1%)
    5 Catholic, 1,730 pupils
    9 Other, 955 pupils
Colleges and Universities
    Two-year: 1 campus; 2,283 students
    Baccalaureate and beyond:
        Louisiana College (1,042)
Places Rated Score: 37
Places Rated Rank: 327

Allentown–Bethlehem–Easton, PA–NJ
Public K–12 (87.3%)
    53 districts, 196 schools
        98,485 pupils
Private School Options (12.7%)
    42 Catholic, 11,273 pupils
    26 Other, 3,101 pupils
Colleges and Universities
    Two-year: 4 campuses; 10,267 students
    Baccalaureate and beyond:
        College of St. Francis De Sales (1,791)
        Cedar Crest College (962)
        Centenary College (820)
        Lafayette College (2,303)
        Lehigh University (6,610)
        Moravian College (1,785)
        Muhlenberg College (2,076)
        • Penn State University (783)
Places Rated Score: 336
Places Rated Rank: 158

Altoona, PA
Public K–12 (87.5%)
    7 districts, 36 schools
        20,446 pupils
Private School Options (12.5%)
    13 Catholic, 2,184 pupils
    9 Other, 730 pupils
Colleges and Universities

Baccalaureate and beyond:
    • Penn State University (2,615)
Places Rated Score: 52
Places Rated Rank: 306

Amarillo, TX
Public K–12 (94.7%)
    6 districts, 64 schools
        36,222 pupils
Private School Options (5.3%)
    5 Catholic, 618 pupils
    10 Other, 1,428 pupils
Colleges and Universities
    Two-year: 2 campuses; 6,347 students
    Baccalaureate and beyond:
        • West Texas State University (5,718)
Places Rated Score: 178
Places Rated Rank: 223

Anchorage, AK
Public K–12 (94.6%)
    2 districts, 79 schools
        42,403 pupils
Private School Options (5.4%)
    1 Catholic, 123 pupils
    15 Other, 2,281 pupils
Colleges and Universities
    Baccalaureate and beyond:
        Alaska Pacific University (1,437)
        • University of Alaska (15,942)
Places Rated Score: 338
Places Rated Rank: 157

✓ Ann Arbor, MI
Public K–12 (92.3%)
    30 districts, 162 schools
        75,641 pupils
Private School Options (7.7%)
    12 Catholic, 2,468 pupils
    26 Other, 3,798 pupils
Colleges and Universities
    Two-year: 1 campus; 10,117 students
    Baccalaureate and beyond:
        Adrian College (1,207)
        Cleary College (1,073)
        Concordia College (595)
        • Eastern Michigan University (23,288)
        Siena Heights College (1,617)
        • University of Michigan (36,474)
MC Access: Detroit–Ann Arbor–Flint, MI–ON
Places Rated Score: 1,461
Places Rated Rank: 29

Anniston, AL
Public K–12 (92.7%)
    5 districts, 34 schools
        21,359 pupils
Private School Options (7.3%)
    1 Catholic, 155 pupils
    4 Other, 1,528 pupils
Colleges and Universities
    Two-year: 1 campus; 504 students
    Baccalaureate and beyond:

• Jacksonville State University (8,260)
Places Rated Score: 170
Places Rated Rank: 227

Appleton–Oshkosh–Neenah, WI
Public K–12 (83.2%)
    20 districts, 113 schools
        51,748 pupils
Private School Options (16.8%)
    35 Catholic, 7,025 pupils
    25 Other, 3,446 pupils
Colleges and Universities
    Two-year: 1 campus; 3,479 students
    Baccalaureate and beyond:
        Lawrence University (1,202)
        • University of Wisconsin (11,209)
Places Rated Score: 275
Places Rated Rank: 188

Asheville, NC
Public K–12 (93.9%)
    3 districts, 52 schools
        29,998 pupils
Private School Options (6.1%)
    1 Catholic, 260 pupils
    10 Other, 1,676 pupils
Colleges and Universities
    Two-year: 1 campus; 3,200 students
    Baccalaureate and beyond:
        Mars Hill College (1,344)
        Montreat–Anderson College (414)
        • University of North Carolina (3,265)
        Warren Wilson College (557)
Places Rated Score: 128
Places Rated Rank: 252

Athens, GA
Public K–12 (89.9%)
    5 districts, 28 schools
        17,886 pupils
Private School Options (10.1%)
    1 Catholic, 363 pupils
    5 Other, 1,655 pupils
Colleges and Universities
    Baccalaureate and beyond:
        • University of Georgia (27,448)
Places Rated Score: 549
Places Rated Rank: 110

✓ Atlanta, GA
Public K–12 (93.1%)
    39 districts, 742 schools
        521,425 pupils
Private School Options (6.9%)
    13 Catholic, 5,028 pupils
    167 Other, 33,742 pupils
Colleges and Universities
    Two-year: 8 campuses; 21,769 students
    Baccalaureate and beyond:
        Agnes Scott College (591)
        Clark Atlanta University (1,023)
        • Clayton State College (3,863)
        Columbia Theological Seminary (541)
        Emory University (9,398)
        • Georgia Inst. of Technology (12,090)
        • Georgia State University (23,004)
        • Kennesaw State College (9,117)
        Life College (1,588)
        Morehouse College (2,606)
        Morris Brown College (1,995)
        Oglethorpe University (1,075)
        • Southern College of Technology
          (4,009)
        Spelman College (1,742)
        • West Georgia College (7,247)
Places Rated Score: 1,692
Places Rated Rank: 25

Atlantic City–Cape May, NJ
Public K–12 (85.7%)
    44 districts, 105 schools
        44,780 pupils
Private School Options (14.3%)
    20 Catholic, 5,674 pupils
    10 Other, 1,813 pupils
Colleges and Universities
    Two-year: 1 campus; 4,848 students
    Baccalaureate and beyond:
        • Glassboro State College (9,364)
        • Stockton State College (5,286)
MC Access: Philadelphia–Wilmington–
    Atlantic City, PA–NJ–DE–MD
Places Rated Score: 459
Places Rated Rank: 125

Augusta–Aiken, GA–SC
Public K–12 (92.1%)
    5 districts, 118 schools
        77,849 pupils
Private School Options (7.9%)
    5 Catholic, 1,581 pupils
    33 Other, 5,123 pupils
Colleges and Universities
    Two-year: 1 campus; 1,485 students
    Baccalaureate and beyond:
        • Augusta College (5,201)
        • Medical College of Georgia (2,386)
        Paine College (580)
        • University of South Carolina (2,532)
Places Rated Score: 225
Places Rated Rank: 209

✓ Austin–San Marcos, TX
Public K–12 (95.2%)
    33 districts, 244 schools
        157,816 pupils
Private School Options (4.8%)
    10 Catholic, 1,953 pupils
    32 Other, 6,052 pupils
Colleges and Universities
    Two-year: 1 campus; 23,067 students
    Baccalaureate and beyond:
        Concordia Lutheran College (603)
        Huston–Tillotson College (695)
        • SW Texas State University (20,800)
        Southwestern University (1,239)
        St. Edward's University (2,964)
        • University of Texas (50,245)
Places Rated Score: 1,730
Places Rated Rank: 22

Bakersfield, CA
Public K–12 (95.7%)
    52 districts, 223 schools
        123,624 pupils
Private School Options (4.3%)
    7 Catholic, 1,864 pupils
    28 Other, 3,724 pupils
Colleges and Universities
    Two-year: 3 campus; 15,246 students
    Baccalaureate and beyond:
        • California State College (4,890)
Places Rated Score: 250
Places Rated Rank: 200

✓ Baltimore, MD
Public K–12 (86.2%)
    8 districts, 590 schools
        363,907 pupils
Private School Options (13.8%)
    87 Catholic, 29,802 pupils
    161 Other, 28,488 pupils
Colleges and Universities
    Two-year: 9 campuses; 54,117 students
    Baccalaureate and beyond:

College of Notre Dame (2,674)
• Coppin State College (2,229)
Goucher College (958)
Johns Hopkins University (12,984)
Loyola College (6,133)
Maryland Inst. College of Art (1,279)
• Morgan State University (4,399)
• Towson State University (14,958)
• United States Naval Academy (4,452)
• University of Baltimore (5,522)
• University of Maryland (9,740)
• University of Maryland Professional
  (4,683)
Villa Julie College (1,459)
Western Maryland College (2,073)
MC Access: Washington–Baltimore,
    DC–MD–VA–WV
Places Rated Score: 2,045
Places Rated Rank: 15

Bangor, ME
Public K–12 (92.0%)
    20 districts, 46 schools
        14,898 pupils
Private School Options (8.0%)
    2 Catholic, 356 pupils
    9 Other, 940 pupils
Colleges and Universities
    Two-year: 1 campus; 1,348
    Baccalaureate and beyond:
        Husson College (1,817)
        • University of Maine (13,076)
Places Rated Score: 301
Places Rated Rank: 178

Barnstable–Yarmouth, MA
Public K–12 (95.8%)
    19 districts, 54 schools
        27,274 pupils
Private School Options (4.2%)
    10 Other, 1,195 pupils
Colleges and Universities
    Two-year: 1 campus; 4,496 students
    Baccalaureate and beyond:
        • Massachusetts Maritime Academy
          (628)
Places Rated Score: 58
Places Rated Rank: 301

Baton Rouge, LA
Public K–12 (81.0%)
    5 districts, 153 schools
        79,038 pupils
Private School Options (19.0%)
    21 Catholic, 10,289 pupils
    35 Other, 8,297 pupils
Colleges and Universities
    Baccalaureate and beyond:
        Jimmy Swaggart Bible College (487)
        • Louisiana State University (26,750)
        • Southern University (8,564)
Places Rated Score: 713
Places Rated Rank: 82

Beaumont–Port Arthur, TX
Public K–12 (93.3%)
    17 districts, 125 schools
        72,551 pupils
Private School Options (6.7%)
    8 Catholic, 2,532 pupils
    13 Other, 2,701 pupils
Colleges and Universities
    Two-year: 2 campuses; 3,219 students
    Baccalaureate and beyond:
        • Lamar University (12,041)
Places Rated Score: 273
Places Rated Rank: 190

Bellingham, WA
Public K–12 (91.3%)
  7 districts, 45 schools
    21,014 pupils
Private School Options (8.7%)
  1 Catholic, 267 pupils
  10 Other, 1,744 pupils
Colleges and Universities
  Two-year: 1 campus; 2,420 students
  Baccalaureate and beyond:
    • Western Washington University
      (9,322)
Places Rated Score: 211
Places Rated Rank: 213

Benton Harbor, MI
Public K–12 (87.0%)
  17 districts, 84 schools
    30,661 pupils
Private School Options (13.0%)
  5 Catholic, 1,238 pupils
  24 Other, 3,328 pupils
Colleges and Universities
  Two-year: 1 campus; 3,338 students
  Baccalaureate and beyond:
    Andrews University (2,998)
Places Rated Score: 73
Places Rated Rank: 285

Billings, MT
Public K–12 (96.3%)
  18 districts, 57 schools
    22,806 pupils
Private School Options (3.7%)
  1 Catholic, 341 pupils
  6 Other, 527 pupils
Colleges and Universities
  Baccalaureate and beyond:
    • Eastern Montana College (4,055)
    Rocky Mountain College (759)
Places Rated Score: 91
Places Rated Rank: 275

Biloxi–Gulfport–Pascagoula, MS
Public K–12 (92.0%)
  11 districts, 104 schools
    58,219 pupils
Private School Options (8.0%)
  17 Catholic, 4,320 pupils
  8 Other, 742 pupils
Colleges and Universities
  Two-year: 1 campus; 3,450 students
Places Rated Score: 35
Places Rated Rank: 330

Binghamton, NY
Public K–12 (93.0%)
  19 districts, 78 schools
    43,589 pupils
Private School Options (7.0%)
  13 Catholic, 2,209 pupils
  10 Other, 1,089 pupils
Colleges and Universities
  Two-year: 1 campus; 6,312 students
  Baccalaureate and beyond:
    • State University of New York (12,218)
Places Rated Score: 307
Places Rated Rank: 173

Birmingham, AL
Public K–12 (92.0%)
  15 districts, 241 schools
    143,804 pupils
Private School Options (8.0%)
  16 Catholic, 3,665 pupils
  46 Other, 8,768 pupils
Colleges and Universities

Two-year: 3 campuses; 9,678 students
Baccalaureate and beyond:
  Birmingham Southern College (1,937)
  Miles College (616)
  Samford University (4,159)
  • University of Alabama (14,692)
  • University of Montevallo (3,175)
Places Rated Score: 546
Places Rated Rank: 111

Bismarck, ND
Public K–12 (90.4%)
  27 districts, 54 schools
    16,315 pupils
Private School Options (9.6%)
  6 Catholic, 1,428 pupils
  4 Other, 301 pupils
Colleges and Universities
  Two-year: 2 campuses; 2,779 students
  Baccalaureate and beyond:
    University of Mary (1,341)
Places Rated Score: 47
Places Rated Rank: 312

Bloomington, IN
Public K–12 (93.6%)
  3 districts, 23 schools
    13,223 pupils
Private School Options (6.4%)
  1 Catholic, 380 pupils
  8 Other, 524 pupils
Colleges and Universities
  Baccalaureate and beyond:
    • Indiana University (34,863)
Places Rated Score: 697
Places Rated Rank: 83

Bloomington–Normal, IL
Public K–12 (92.0%)
  13 districts, 54 schools
    20,326 pupils
Private School Options (8.0%)
  5 Catholic, 1,074 pupils
  5 Other, 699 pupils
Colleges and Universities
  Baccalaureate and beyond:
    • Illinois State University (23,107)
    Illinois Wesleyan University (1,749)
Places Rated Score: 487
Places Rated Rank: 117

Boise City, ID
Public K–12 (94.8%)
  12 districts, 110 schools
    60,772 pupils
Private School Options (5.2%)
  6 Catholic, 1,643 pupils
  12 Other, 1,662 pupils
Colleges and Universities
  Baccalaureate and beyond:
    • Boise State University (12,508)
    College of Idaho (1,130)
    NW Nazarene College (1,120)
Places Rated Score: 281
Places Rated Rank: 185

✓ Boston, MA
Public K–12 (84.6%)
  185 districts, 1,012 schools
    722,617 pupils
Private School Options (15.4%)
  181 Catholic, 53,076 pupils
  292 Other, 36,549 pupils
Colleges and Universities
  Two-year: 18 campuses; 52,044 students
  Baccalaureate and beyond:
    Andover Newton Seminary (459)

Atlantic Union College (805)
Babson College (3,000)
Bentley College (7,253)
Berklee College of Music (2,803)
Boston Architectural Center (1,115)
Boston College (14,446)
Boston Conservatory (410)
Boston University (28,529)
Bradford College (419)
Brandeis University (3,811)
• Bridgewater State College (8,911)
Cambridge College (556)
Curry College (1,201)
Eastern Nazarene College (912)
Emerson College (2,688)
Emmanuel College (964)
Endicott College (980)
• Framingham State College (5,979)
Gordon College (1,216)
Gordon–Conwell Seminary (761)
Harvard University (24,509)
Lesley College (4,747)
• Massachusetts College of Art (2,029)
Massachusetts College of Pharmacy
  (1,142)
Massachusetts Institute of Technology
  (9,536)
Merrimack College (3,733)
Mount Ida College (1,794)
New England Conservatory of Music
  (732)
New England School of Law (1,194)
Northeastern University (32,809)
Pine Manor College (599)
Radcliffe College (2,692)
Regis College (1,079)
• Salem State College (10,115)
School of the Museum of Fine Arts
  (746)
Simmons College (2,856)
Suffolk University (5,246)
Tufts University (7,938)
• University of Lowell (14,622)
• University of Massachusetts (13,813)
Wellesley College (2,323)
Wentworth Institiute of Technology
  (4,021)
Wheaton College (1,214)
Wheelock College (1,725)
MC Access: Boston–New
  Bedford–Nashua, MA–NH
Places Rated Score: 4,176
Places Rated Rank: 4

Boulder–Longmont, CO
Public K–12 (95.4%)
  4 districts, 77 schools
    38,732 pupils
Private School Options (4.6%)
  3 Catholic, 633 pupils
  10 Other, 1,236 pupils
Colleges and Universities
  Baccalaureate and beyond:
    • University of Colorado (24,589)
MC Access: Denver–Boulder–Greeley,
  CO
Places Rated Score: 576
Places Rated Rank: 106

Brazoria, TX
Public K–12 (97.9%)
  8 districts, 59 schools
    43,219 pupils
Private School Options (2.1%)
  1 Catholic, 347 pupils
  3 Other, 575 pupils
Colleges and Universities

Two-year: 2 campuses; 7,465 students
MC Access: Houston–Galveston–
Brazoria, TX
Places Rated Score: 140
Places Rated Rank: 237

Bremerton, WA
Public K–12 (97.1%)
6 districts, 58 schools
37,707 pupils
Private School Options (2.9%)
1 Catholic, 187 pupils
11 Other, 933 pupils
Colleges and Universities
Two-year: 1 campus; 6,287 students
MC Access: Seattle–Tacoma–Bremerton,
WA
Places Rated Score: 129
Places Rated Rank: 249

Bridgeport, CT
Public K–12 (84.4%)
18 districts, 130 schools,
61,592 pupils
Private School Options (15.6%)
30 Catholic, 9,605 pupils
13 Other, 1,746 pupils
Colleges and Universities
Two-year: 1 campus; 2,568 students
Baccalaureate and beyond:
Bridgeport Engineering Institute (473)
Fairfield University (4,895)
Sacred Heart University (4,194)
University of Bridgeport (5,258)
MC Access: New York–Northern New
Jersey–Long Island, NY–NJ–CT
Places Rated Score: 262
Places Rated Rank: 195

**Brownsville–Harlingen–San Benito,
TX**
Public K–12 (95.0%)
11 districts, 103 schools
74,658 pupils
Private School Options (5.0%)
5 Catholic, 1,776 pupils
12 Other, 2,138 pupils
Colleges and Universities
Two-year: 2 campuses; 8,481 students
Baccalaureate and beyond:
• University of Texas–Pan American
(1,476)
Places Rated Score: 114
Places Rated Rank: 259

Bryan–College Station, TX
Public Schools
2 districts, 25 schools
18,211 pupils
Private School Options (3.9%)
1 Catholic, 361 pupils
6 Other, 825 pupils
Colleges and Universities
Baccalaureate and beyond:
• Texas A&M University (40,492)
Places Rated Score: 810
Places Rated Rank: 65

Buffalo–Niagara Falls, NY
Public Schools (83.0%)
41 districts, 293 schools
173,908 pupils
Private School Options (17.0%)
102 Catholic, 28,815 pupils
39 Other, 6,799 pupils
Colleges and Universities
Two-year: 7 campuses; 20,173 students
Baccalaureate and beyond:

Canisius College (4,685)
D'Youville College (1,258)
Daemen College (1,699)
Medaille College (1,021)
Niagara University (3,137)
• SUNY College at Buffalo (12,570)
• State University of New York (27,406)
MC Access: Buffalo–St.
Catharines–Niagara, NY–ON
Places Rated Score: 1,160
Places Rated Rank: 40

Burlington, VT
Public Schools (93.0%)
38 districts, 60 schools,
23,563 pupils
Private School Options (7.0%)
5 Catholic, 1,407 pupils
6 Other, 357 pupils
Colleges and Universities
Two-year: 1 campus; 1,997 students
Baccalaureate and beyond:
St. Michael's College (2,447)
Trinity College (1,108)
• University of Vermont (11,338)
Places Rated Score: 297
Places Rated Rank: 180

Calgary, AB
Public Instruction (96.9%)
300 schools, 141,385 pupils
Private School Options (3.1%)
22 Other, 4,406 pupils
Colleges and Universities
Community: 4 campuses; 21,000
students
Baccalaureate and beyond:
University of Calgary (21,843)
Places Rated Score: 647
Places Rated Rank: 92

Canton–Massillon, OH
Public Schools (91.1%)
25 districts, 140 schools
68,487 pupils
Private School Options (8.9%)
17 Catholic, 5,141 pupils
10 Other, 1,570 pupils
Colleges and Universities
Two-year: 2 campuses; 5,384 students
Baccalaureate and beyond:
Malone College (1,449)
Mount Union College (1,367)
Walsh College (1,444)
Places Rated Score: 111
Places Rated Rank: 260

Casper, WY
Public K–12 (97.1%)
2 districts, 38 schools
13,121 pupils
Private School Options (2.9%)
1 Catholic, 298 pupils
2 Other, 100 pupils
Colleges and Universities
Two-year: 1 campus; 3,798 students
Places Rated Score: 38
Places Rated Rank: 325

Cedar Rapids, IA
Public K–12 (89.5%)
12 districts, 64 schools
29,612 pupils
Private School Options (10.5%)
9 Catholic, 2,843 pupils
6 Other, 619 pupils
Colleges and Universities
Two-year: 1 campus; 7,741 students

Baccalaureate and beyond:
Coe College (1,217)
Cornell College (1,147)
Mount Mercy College (1,591)
Places Rated Score: 130
Places Rated Rank: 247

✓ **Central New Jersey, NJ**
Public K–12 (86.4%)
76 districts, 295 schools
134,826 pupils
Private School Options (13.6%)
50 Catholic, 14,873 pupils
37 Other, 6,406 pupils
Colleges and Universities
Two-year: 2 campuses; 16,358 students
Baccalaureate and beyond:
• Rutgers University (33,020)
MC Access: New York–Northern New
Jersey–Long Island, NY–NJ–CT
Places Rated Score: 1,245
Places Rated Rank: 33

Champaign–Urbana, IL
Public K–12 (93.2%)
19 districts, 59 schools
23,913 pupils
Private School Options (6.8%)
4 Catholic, 1,051 pupils
7 Other, 697 pupils
Colleges and Universities
Two-year: 1 campus; 8,483 students
Baccalaureate and beyond:
• University of Illinois (37,481)
Places Rated Score: 834
Places Rated Rank: 63

Charleston, WV
Public K–12 (94.2%)
3 districts, 104 schools
42,393 pupils
Private School Options (5.8%)
5 Catholic, 1,188 pupils
14 Other, 1,434 pupils
Colleges and Universities
Baccalaureate and beyond:
University of Charleston (1,610)
• UWV Graduate Studies (2,458)
• West Virginia State College (4,635)
Places Rated Score: 163
Places Rated Rank: 229

Charleston–North Charleston, SC
Public K–12 (90.2%)
5 districts, 135 schools
90,236 pupils
Private School Options (9.8%)
7 Catholic, 2,675 pupils
57 Other, 7,152 pupils
Colleges and Universities
Two-year: 2 campuses; 6,094 students
Baccalaureate and beyond:
Charleston Southern University (1,926)
• The Citadel (3,628)
• College of Charleston (6,205)
• Medical University of South Carolina
(2,118)
Places Rated Score: 326
Places Rated Rank: 163

**Charlotte–Gastonia–Rock Hill,
NC–SC**
Public K–12 (93.0%)
12 districts, 307 schools
191,097 pupils
Private School Options (7.0%)
8 Catholic, 3,061 pupils
41 Other, 11,332 pupils

Colleges and Universities
Two-year: 5 campuses; 23,158 students
Baccalaureate and beyond:
Belmont Abbey College (1,029)
Catawba College (1,044)
Davidson College (1,428)
Johnson C. Smith University (1,310)
Livingstone College (580)
Queens College (1,573)
• University of North Carolina (13,451)
Wingate College (1,709)
• Winthrop College (5,351)
Places Rated Score: 734
Places Rated Rank: 79

Charlottesville, VA
Public K–12 (85.9%)
4 districts, 43 schools
18,654 pupils
Private School Options (14.1%)
20 Other, 3,063 pupils
Colleges and Universities
Two-year: 1 campus; 4,245 students
Baccalaureate and beyond:
• University of Virginia (20,879)
Places Rated Score: 460
Places Rated Rank: 124

Chattanooga, TN–GA
Public K–12 (86.7%)
6 districts, 117 schools
64,071 pupils
Private School Options (13.3%)
3 Catholic, 1,191 pupils
41 Other, 8,644 pupils
Colleges and Universities
Two-year: 2 campuses; 8,437 students
Baccalaureate and beyond:
Covenant College (580)
Southern College of Seventh-Day
Adventists (1,526)
Tennessee Temple University (1,215)
• University of Tennessee (7,564)
Places Rated Score: 280
Places Rated Rank: 187

Cheyenne, WY
Public K–12 (97.0%)
3 districts, 38 schools
14,286 pupils
Private School Options (3.0%)
1 Catholic, 250 pupils
4 Other, 193 pupils
Colleges and Universities
Two-year: 1 campus; 4,026 students
Places Rated Score: 40
Places Rated Rank: 320

✓ Chicago, IL
Public K–12 (82.3%)
319 districts, 1,825 schools
1,055,484 pupils
Private School Options (17.7%)
449 Catholic, 174,036 pupils
320 Other, 52,734 pupils
Colleges and Universities
Two-year: 26 campuses; 214,170 students
Baccalaureate and beyond:
Chicago College of Osteopathic
Medicine (441)
• Chicago State University (6,032)
College of St. Francis (3,947)
Columbia College (6,498)
Concordia University (1,233)
Depaul University (15,387)
Elmhurst College (3,007)
• Governors State University (5,314)

Illinois Benedictine College (2,570)
Illinois College of Optometry (583)
Illinois Institute of Technology (6,300)
John Marshall Law School (1,272)
Judson College (522)
Lewis University (3,500)
Loyola University (14,292)
Lutheran School of Theology (401)
McCormick Theological Seminary (585)
Moody Bible Institute (1,507)
Mundelein College (1,102)
National College of Chiropractic (749)
National-Louis University (7,218)
North Central College (2,542)
North Park Theological Seminary
(1,097)
• Northeastern Illinois University
(10,293)
• Northern Illinois University (24,443)
Northwestern University (16,807)
Roosevelt University (6,437)
Rosary College (1,749)
Rush University (1,122)
St. Xavier College (2,636)
Scholl College of Podiatric (428)
School of Art Institute of Chicago
(2,077)
Trinity Christian College (534)
University of Chicago (10,680)
• University of Illinois (24,050)
Wheaton College (2,548)
MC Access: Chicago–Gary–Kenosha,
IL–IN–WI
Places Rated Score: 5,276
Places Rated Rank: 3

Chico–Paradise, CA
Public K–12 (94.4%)
17 districts, 65 schools
30,383 pupils
Private School Options (5.6%)
3 Catholic, 593 pupils
13 Other, 1,223 pupils
Colleges and Universities
Two-year: 1 campus; 7,928 students
Baccalaureate and beyond:
• Cal State University (15,847)
Places Rated Score: 396
Places Rated Rank: 144

Chicoutimi–Jonquiere, PQ
Public Instruction
3 districts, 64 schools
7,874 pupils
Colleges and Universities
Community: 2 campuses; 7,391 students
Baccalaureate and beyond:
Université du Quebec (7,372)
Places Rated Score: 221
Places Rated Rank: 211

Cincinnati, OH–KY–IN
Public K–12 (82.3%)
81 districts, 434 schools
240,471 pupils
Private School Options (17.7%)
129 Catholic, 45,402 pupils
42 Other, 6,379 pupils
Colleges and Universities
Two-year: 4 campuses; 8,609 students
Baccalaureate and beyond:
Cincinnati Bible College (815)
College of Mount St. Joseph (2,566)
• N Kentucky University (10,322)
Thomas More College (1,125)
Union Institute (1,226)
• University of Cincinnati (30,787)

Xavier University (6,477)
MC Access: Cincinnati–Hamilton,
OH–KY–IN
Places Rated Score: 1,120
Places Rated Rank: 43

Clarksville–Hopkinsville, TN–KY
Public K–12 (96.4%)
2 districts, 40 schools
26,226 pupils
Private School Options (3.6%)
1 Catholic, 160 pupils
6 Other, 807 pupils
Colleges and Universities
Two-year: 1 campus; 1,876 students
Baccalaureate and beyond:
• Austin Peay State University (6,292)
Places Rated Score: 145
Places Rated Rank: 235

✓ Cleveland–Lorain–Elyria, OH
Public K–12 (81.9%)
97 districts, 615 schools
328,400 pupils
Private School Options (18.1%)
159 Catholic, 58,225 pupils
71 Other, 14,559 pupils
Colleges and Universities
Two-year: 5 campuses; 38,923 students
Baccalaureate and beyond:
Baldwin-Wallace College (4,718)
Case Western Reserve University
(7,500)
• Cleveland State University (18,534)
Dyke College (1,261)
John Carroll University (4,423)
Lake Erie College (835)
Notre Dame College (827)
Oberlin College (3,024)
Ursuline College (1,547)
MC Access: Cleveland–Akron, OH
Places Rated Score: 1,206
Places Rated Rank: 35

Colorado Springs, CO
Public K–12 (94.7%)
16 districts, 144 schools
73,860 pupils
Private School Options (5.3%)
4 Catholic, 986 pupils
17 Other, 3,178 pupils
Colleges and Universities
Two-year: 2 campuses; 8,150 students
Baccalaureate and beyond:
Colorado College (1,901)
• U.S. Air Force Academy (1,640)
• University of Colorado (5,124)
Places Rated Score: 245
Places Rated Rank: 201

Columbia, MO
Public K–12 (94.0%)
6 districts, 36 schools
17,211 pupils
Private School Options (6.0%)
1 Catholic, 465 pupils
9 Other, 643 pupils
Colleges and Universities
Baccalaureate and beyond:
Columbia College (3,736)
Stephens College (1,166)
• University of Missouri (24,344)
Places Rated Score: 552
Places Rated Rank: 108

Columbia, SC
Public K–12 (92.3%)

8 districts, 121 schools
82,094 pupils
Private School Options (7.7%)
4 Catholic, 936 pupils
56 Other, 5,925 pupils
Colleges and Universities
Two-year: 1 campus; 6,082 students
Baccalaureate and beyond:
Benedict College (1,448)
Columbia Bible College (929)
Columbia College (1,213)
• University of South Carolina (26,435)
Places Rated Score: 643
Places Rated Rank: 94

Columbus, GA–AL
Public K–12 (86.0%)
6 districts, 74 schools
42,471 pupils
Private School Options (14.0%)
6 Catholic, 1,265 pupils
23 Other, 5,625 pupils
Colleges and Universities
Two-year: 2 campuses; 5,086 students
Baccalaureate and beyond:
• Columbus College (3,890)
Places Rated Score: 129
Places Rated Rank: 249

✓ Columbus, OH
Public K–12 (91.2%)
66 districts, 458 schools
223,376 pupils
Private School Options (8.8%)
45 Catholic, 13,901 pupils
43 Other, 7,542 pupils
Colleges and Universities
Two-year: 2 campuses; 12,639 students
Baccalaureate and beyond:
Capital University (3,008)
Columbus College of Art and Design
(1,585)
Denison University (2,043)
Franklin University (3,946)
Ohio Dominican College (1,257)
• Ohio State University (54,477)
• Ohio University (1,843)
Ohio Wesleyan University (1,961)
Otterbein College (2,287)
Places Rated Score: 1,478
Places Rated Rank: 28

Corpus Christi, TX
Public K–12 (93.7%)
20 districts, 137 schools
79,300 pupils
Private School Options (6.3%)
16 Catholic, 3,293 pupils
15 Other, 1,995 pupils
Colleges and Universities
Two-year: 1 campus; 10,283 students
Baccalaureate and beyond:
• Corpus Christi State University
(3,725)
Places Rated Score: 177
Places Rated Rank: 224

Cumberland, MD–WV
Public K–12 (94.0%)
2 districts, 39 schools
15,800 pupils
Private School Options (6.0%)
4 Catholic, 703 pupils
4 Other, 305 pupils
Colleges and Universities
Two-year: 2 campuses; 3,680 students
Baccalaureate and beyond:

• Frostburg State University (4,786)
Places Rated Score: 133
Places Rated Rank: 245

✓ Dallas, TX
Public K–12 (93.3%)
80 districts, 789 schools
488,934 pupils
Private School Options (6.7%)
31 Catholic, 10,813 pupils
112 Other, 24,471 pupils
Colleges and Universities
Two-year: 9 campuses; 65,885 students
Baccalaureate and beyond:
Amber University (1,355)
Baylor College of Dentistry (454)
Dallas Baptist University (2,269)
Dallas Theological Seminary (1,200)
• East Texas State University (7,811)
Parker College of Chiropractic (496)
Southern Methodist University (8,924)
Southwestern Assemblies of God
College (701)
• Texas Woman's University (9,412)
University of Dallas (2,816)
• University of North Texas (26,523)
• University of Texas (8,101)
• University of Texas Medical Center
(1,479)
MC Access: Dallas–Fort Worth, TX
Places Rated Score: 2,675
Places Rated Rank: 8

Danbury, CT
Public K–12 (88.5%)
10 districts, 53 schools,
28,927 pupils
Private School Options (11.5%)
9 Catholic, 2,499 pupils
9 Other, 1,259 pupils
Colleges and Universities
Baccalaureate and beyond:
• Western Connecticut State University
(6,293)
MC Access: New York–Northern New
Jersey–Long Island, NY–NJ–CT
Places Rated Score: 437
Places Rated Rank: 131

Danville, VA
Public K–12 (93.4%)
2 districts, 36 schools
17,802 pupils
Private School Options (6.6%)
1 Catholic, 240 pupils
6 Other, 1,014 pupils
Colleges and Universities
Two-year: 1 campus; 3,055 students
Baccalaureate and beyond:
Averett College (1,216)
Places Rated Score: 47
Places Rated Rank: 312

Davenport–Moline–Rock Island, IA–IL
Public K–12 (89.7%)
26 districts, 142 schools
62,344 pupils
Private School Options (10.3%)
23 Catholic, 5,433 pupils
10 Other, 1,741 pupils
Colleges and Universities
Two-year: 3 campuses; 11,575 students
Baccalaureate and beyond:
Augustana College (2,267)
Marycrest College (2,239)
Palmer College of Chiropractic (1,328)

St. Ambrose University (2,278)
Places Rated Score: 224
Places Rated Rank: 210

Dayton–Springfield, OH
Public K–12 (89.0%)
52 districts, 287 schools
153,200 pupils
Private School Options (11.0%)
32 Catholic, 12,815 pupils
32 Other, 6,202 pupils
Colleges and Universities
Two-year: 4 campuses; 23,193 students
Baccalaureate and beyond:
• Air Force Institute of Technology (687)
Antioch University (554)
Cedarville College (1,943)
• Central State University (2,549)
University of Dayton (11,326)
Wilberforce University (779)
Wittenberg University (2,361)
• Wright State University (16,516)
Places Rated Score: 867
Places Rated Rank: 60

Daytona Beach, FL
Public K–12 (93.3%)
4 districts, 64 schools
55,248 pupils
Private School Options (6.7%)
6 Catholic, 1,588 pupils
21 Other, 2,402 pupils
Colleges and Universities
Two-year: 4 campuses; 23,193 students
Baccalaureate and beyond:
Bethune Cookman College (2,145)
Embry-Riddle University (11,215)
Stetson University (3,092)
Places Rated Score: 322
Places Rated Rank: 164

Decatur, AL
Public K–12 (96.2%)
4 districts, 52 schools
25,010 pupils
Private School Options (3.8%)
1 Catholic, 207 pupils
7 Other, 671 pupils
Colleges and Universities
Two-year: 1 campus; 7,544 students
Places Rated Score: 75
Places Rated Rank: 284

Decatur, IL
Public K–12 (89.4%)
10 districts, 57 schools
21,105 pupils
Private School Options (10.6%)
5 Catholic, 1,119 pupils
7 Other, 1,374 pupils
Colleges and Universities
Two-year: 1 campus; 3,888 students
Baccalaureate and beyond:
Millikin University (1,805)
Places Rated Score: 64
Places Rated Rank: 294

Denver, CO
Public K–12 (92.1%)
19 districts, 476 schools
299,723 pupils
Private School Options (7.9%)
38 Catholic, 11,724 pupils
95 Other, 13,887 pupils
Colleges and Universities
Two-year: 5 campus; 31,937 students
Baccalaureate and beyond:

Colorado Christian University (781)
- Colorado School of Mines (2,669)
Denver Conservative Baptist Seminary (512)
- Metropolitan State College (16,840)
Regis University (4,894)
- University of Colorado (9,520)
- University of Colorado Health Sciences (1,495)
University of Denver (7,150)
MC Access: Denver–Boulder–Greeley, CO
Places Rated Score: 1,184
Places Rated Rank: 37

Des Moines, IA
Public K–12 (92.5%)
23 districts, 151 schools
68,156 pupils
Private School Options (7.5%)
13 Catholic, 4,144 pupils
10 Other, 1,387 pupils
Colleges and Universities
Two-year: 3 campuses; 11,544 students
Baccalaureate and beyond:
Drake University (7,778)
Grand View College (1,407)
Simpson College (1,737)
University of Osteopathic Medicine (1,236)
Places Rated Score: 281
Places Rated Rank: 185

✓ Detroit, MI
Public K–12 (88.3%)
110 districts, 1263 schools
689,312 pupils
Private School Options (11.7%)
179 Catholic, 58,367 pupils
170 Other, 32,792 pupils
Colleges and Universities
Two-year: 9 campuses; 104,844 students
Baccalaureate and beyond:
Center for Creative Studies (1,075)
Detroit College of Business (3,480)
Detroit College of Law (727)
Lawrence Institute of Technology (5,509)
Madonna College (3,925)
Marygrove College (1,079)
Mercy College of Detroit (2,218)
- Oakland University (12,385)
University of Detroit (5,832)
- University of Michigan (7,617)
Walsh College of Business Administration (2,996)
- Wayne State University (32,477)
MC Access: Detroit–Ann Arbor–Flint, MI–ON
Places Rated Score: 2,638
Places Rated Rank: 9

Dothan, AL
Public K–12 (93.4%)
5 districts, 44 schools
23,570 pupils
Private School Options (6.6%)
12 Other, 1,654 pupils
Colleges and Universities
Two-year: 2 campuses; 4,335 students
Baccalaureate and beyond:
- Troy State University (1,833)
Places Rated Score: 80
Places Rated Rank: 283

Dover, DE
Public K–12 (97.0%)

6 districts, 40 schools
22,464 pupils
Private School Options (3.0%)
13 Other, 683 pupils
Colleges and Universities
Two-year: 1 campus; 1,749 students
Baccalaureate and beyond:
- Delaware State College (2,603)
Wesley College (1,249)
Places Rated Score: 86
Places Rated Rank: 278

Dubuque, IA
Public K–12 (64.5%)
2 districts, 25 schools
12,353 pupils
Private School Options (35.5%)
20 Catholic, 6,804 pupils
Colleges and Universities
Baccalaureate and beyond:
Clarke College (854)
Loras College (1,984)
University of Dubuque (1,084)
Places Rated Score: 59
Places Rated Rank: 300

Duluth–Superior, MN–WI
Public K–12 (94.6%)
23 districts, 95 schools
40,176 pupils
Private School Options (5.4%)
8 Catholic, 1,468 pupils
8 Other, 816 pupils
Colleges and Universities
Two-year: 3 campuses; 4,128 students
Baccalaureate and beyond:
College of St. Scholastica (1,901)
- University of Minnesota (10,020)
- University of Wisconsin (2,437)
Places Rated Score: 316
Places Rated Rank: 166

Dutchess County, NY
Public K–12 (88.5%)
15 districts, 70 schools
39,469 pupils
Private School Options (11.5%)
13 Catholic, 3,061 pupils
22 Other, 2,087 pupils
Colleges and Universities
Two-year: 2 campuses; 8,558 students
Baccalaureate and beyond:
Bard College (1,079)
Marist College (5,069)
Vassar College (2,461)
MC Access: New York–Northern New Jersey–Long Island, NY–NJ–CT
Places Rated Score: 208
Places Rated Rank: 216

Eau Claire, WI
Public K–12 (87.7%)
12 districts, 55 schools
23,325 pupils
Private School Options (12.3%)
17 Catholic, 2,538 pupils
11 Other, 721 pupils
Colleges and Universities
Two-year: 1 campus; 3,159 students
Baccalaureate and beyond:
- University of Wisconsin (11,038)
Places Rated Score: 252
Places Rated Rank: 199

Edmonton, AB
Public Instruction (96.1%)
355 schools, 145,319 pupils

Private School Options (3.8%)
28 Catholic and Other, 5,884 pupils
Colleges and Universities
Community: 5 campuses; 25,803 students
Baccalaureate and beyond:
Concordia College (1,100)
The King's College (316)
University of Alberta (29,500)
Places Rated Score: 876
Places Rated Rank: 58

El Paso, TX
Public K–12 (95.7%)
10 districts, 165 schools
140,324 pupils
Private School Options (4.3%)
16 Catholic, 4,550 pupils
11 Other, 1,751 pupils
Colleges and Universities
Two-year: 1 campus; 16,566 students
Baccalaureate and beyond:
- University of Texas (15,707)
Places Rated Score: 480
Places Rated Rank: 119

Elkhart–Goshen, IN
Public K–12 (92.3%)
9 districts, 56 schools
27,670 pupils
Private School Options (7.7%)
3 Catholic, 624 pupils
20 Other, 1,688 pupils
Colleges and Universities
Baccalaureate and beyond:
Goshen College (1,152)
Places Rated Score: 18
Places Rated Rank: 338

Elmira, NY
Public K–12 (91.1%)
4 districts, 22 schools
14,345 pupils
Private School Options (8.9%)
5 Catholic, 1,099 pupils
4 Other, 304 pupils
Colleges and Universities
Baccalaureate and beyond:
Elmira College (1,955)
Places Rated Score: 26
Places Rated Rank: 335

Enid, OK
Public K–12 (4.5%)
11 districts, 35 schools
10,590 pupils
Private School Options (95.5%)
6 Other, 505 pupils
Colleges and Universities
Baccalaureate and beyond:
Phillips University (1,005)
Places Rated Score: 13
Places Rated Rank: 341

Erie, PA
Public K–12 (96.5%)
16 districts, 79 schools
42,752 pupils
Private School Options (3.5%)
29 Catholic, 9,237 pupils
14 Other, 1,546 pupils
Colleges and Universities
Baccalaureate and beyond:
- Edinboro University (7,466)
Gannon University (4,680)
Mercyhurst College (2,110)
- Penn State University (2,838)

Places Rated Score: 297
Places Rated Rank: 180

Eugene–Springfield, OR
Public K–12 (95.7%)
17 districts, 119 schools
46,960 pupils
Private School Options (4.3%)
3 Catholic, 824 pupils
14 Other, 1,288 pupils
Colleges and Universities
Two-year: 1 campus; 7,970 students
Baccalaureate and beyond:
• University of Oregon (18,565)
Places Rated Score: 455
Places Rated Rank: 126

Evansville–Henderson, IN–KY
Public K–12 (86.4%)
7 districts, 79 schools
44,302 pupils
Private School Options (13.6%)
20 Catholic, 5,202 pupils
13 Other, 1,795 pupils
Colleges and Universities
Two-year: 2 campuses; 3,333 students
Baccalaureate and beyond:
University of Evansville (3,175)
• University of Southern Indiana (5,713)
Places Rated Score: 190
Places Rated Rank: 221

Fargo–Moorhead, ND–MN
Public K–12 (93.4%)
22 districts, 62 schools
26,621 pupils
Private School Options (6.6%)
6 Catholic, 1,208 pupils
5 Other, 667 pupils
Colleges and Universities
Baccalaureate and beyond:
Concordia College (2,884)
• Moorhead State University (8,793)
• North Dakota State University (9,432)
Places Rated Score: 403
Places Rated Rank: 141

Fayetteville, NC
Public K–12 (96.1%)
2 districts, 67 schools
43,843 pupils
Private School Options (3.9%)
2 Catholic, 406 pupils
7 Other, 1,372 pupils
Colleges and Universities
Two-year: 1 campus; 6,342 students
Baccalaureate and beyond:
• Fayetteville State University (3,034)
Methodist College (1,447)
Places Rated Score: 143
Places Rated Rank: 236

Fayetteville–Springdale–Rogers, AR
Public K–12 (96.1%)
17 districts, 76 schools
38,441 pupils
Private School Options (3.9%)
2 Catholic, 275 pupils
10 Other, 1,273 pupils
Colleges and Universities
Baccalaureate and beyond:
John Brown University (1,087)
• University of Arkansas (14,433)
Places Rated Score: 303
Places Rated Rank: 176

Flint, MI
Public K–12 (92.7%)
22 districts, 151 schools
82,181 pupils
Private School Options (7.3%)
13 Catholic, 4,135 pupils
14 Other, 2,311 pupils
Colleges and Universities
Two-year: 1 campus; 10,469
Baccalaureate and beyond:
Baker College of Flint (3,233)
GMI Engineering and Management
Institute (3,149)
• University of Michigan (6,506)
MC Access: Detroit–Ann Arbor–Flint, MI–ON
Places Rated Score: 425
Places Rated Rank: 134

Florence, AL
Public K–12 (97.5%)
6 districts, 51 schools
22,433 pupils
Private School Options (2.5%)
1 Catholic, 222 pupils
4 Other, 351 pupils
Colleges and Universities
Two-year: 1 campus; 1,695 students
Baccalaureate and beyond:
• University of North Alabama (5,581)
Places Rated Score: 130
Places Rated Rank: 247

Florence, SC
Public K–12 (90.9%)
5 districts, 38 schools
23,592 pupils
Private School Options (9.1%)
1 Catholic, 177 pupils
16 Other, 2,499 pupils
Colleges and Universities
Two-year: 1 campus; 1,875 students
Baccalaureate and beyond:
• Francis Marion College (3,929)
Places Rated Score: 97
Places Rated Rank: 272

Fort Collins–Loveland, CO
Public K–12 (95.1%)
4 districts, 69 schools
33,595 pupils
Private School Options (4.9%)
2 Catholic, 343 pupils
11 Other, 1,374 pupils
Colleges and Universities
Baccalaureate and beyond:
• Colorado State University (19,994)
National Technological University
(1,137)
Places Rated Score: 415
Places Rated Rank: 138

Fort Lauderdale, FL
Public K–12 (85.9%)
2 districts, 197 schools
168,086 pupils
Private School Options (14.1%)
21 Catholic, 9,450 pupils
94 Other, 18,117 pupils
Colleges and Universities
Two-year: 1 campus; 23,547 students
Baccalaureate and beyond:
Nova University (9,320)
MC Access: Miami–Fort Lauderdale, FL
Places Rated Score: 400
Places Rated Rank: 142

Fort Myers–Cape Coral, FL
Public K–12 (90.8%)
2 districts, 55 schools
43,386 pupils
Private School Options (9.2%)
3 Catholic, 1,376 pupils
20 Other, 3,030 pupils
Colleges and Universities
Two-year: 1 campus; 8,695 students
Places Rated Score: 87
Places Rated Rank: 276

Fort Pierce–Port St. Lucie, FL
Public K–12 (93.3%)
4 districts, 49 schools
35,637 pupils
Private School Options (6.7%)
1 Catholic, 301 pupils
17 Other, 2,265 pupils
Colleges and Universities
Two-year: 1 campus; 14,570 students
Places Rated Score: 148
Places Rated Rank: 233

Fort Smith, AR–OK
Public K–12 (97.0%)
26 districts, 83 schools
33,955 pupils
Private School Options (3.0%)
3 Catholic, 696 pupils
7 Other, 355 pupils
Colleges and Universities
Two-year: 1 campus; 4,911 students
Places Rated Score: 49
Places Rated Rank: 309

Fort Walton Beach, FL
Public K–12 (96.3%)
2 districts, 36 schools
26,270 pupils
Private School Options (3.7%)
1 Catholic, 360 pupils
4 Other, 653 pupils
Colleges and Universities
Two-year: 1 campus; 7,236 students
Places Rated Score: 72
Places Rated Rank: 287

Fort Wayne, IN
Public K–12 (83.8%)
20 districts, 142 schools
78,093 pupils
Private School Options (16.2%)
21 Catholic, 6,379 pupils
51 Other, 8,663 pupils
Colleges and Universities
Two-year: 1 campus; 2,905 students
Baccalaureate and beyond:
Huntington College (594)
• Indiana University–Purdue University
(11,435)
St. Francis College (916)
Places Rated Score: 298
Places Rated Rank: 179

Fort Worth–Arlington, TX
Public K–12 (93.2%)
38 districts, 379 schools
254,159 pupils
Private School Options (6.8%)
12 Catholic, 3,913 pupils
58 Other, 14,566 pupils
Colleges and Universities
Two-year: 2 campuses; 29,149 students
Baccalaureate and beyond:
Southwestern Adventist College (758)

SW Baptist Theological Seminary (3,500)
Texas Christian University (6,725)
Texas Wesleyan University (1,561)
• University of Texas (23,871)
MC Access: Dallas–Fort Worth, TX
Places Rated Score: 1,117
Places Rated Rank: 44

Fresno, CA
Public K–12 (96.6%)
51 districts, 296 schools
172,056 pupils
Private School Options (3.4%)
9 Catholic, 2,747 pupils
31 Other, 3,306 pupils
Colleges and Universities
Two-year: 4 campuses; 20,524 students
Baccalaureate and beyond:
• Cal State University (18,222)
Fresno Pacific College (1,282)
Places Rated Score: 598
Places Rated Rank: 100

Gadsden, AL
Public K–12 (96.1%)
3 districts, 40 schools
17,876 pupils
Private School Options (3.9%)
1 Catholic, 183 pupils
3 Other, 535 pupils
Colleges and Universities
Two-year: 1 campus; 4,912 students
Places Rated Score: 49
Places Rated Rank: 309

Gainesville, FL
Public K–12 (92.2%)
2 districts, 39 schools
26,877 pupils
Private School Options (7.8%)
1 Catholic, 339 pupils
22 Other, 1,926 pupils
Colleges and Universities
Two-year: 1 campus; 10,140 students
Baccalaureate and beyond:
• University of Florida (34,098)
Places Rated Score: 783
Places Rated Rank: 68

Galveston–Texas City, TX
Public K–12 (96.9%)
9 districts, 78 schools
61,349 pupils
Private School Options (3.1%)
5 Catholic, 1,299 pupils
5 Other, 695 pupils
Colleges and Universities
Two-year: 2 campuses; 5,705 students
Baccalaureate and beyond:
• Texas A&M University (935)
• University of Texas Medical (1,676)
MC Access: Houston–Galveston–Brazoria, TX
Places Rated Score: 174
Places Rated Rank: 226

Gary, IN
Public K–12 (89.0%)
29 districts, 203 schools
112,110 pupils
Private School Options (11.0%)
31 Catholic, 9,208 pupils
24 Other, 4,648 pupils
Colleges and Universities
Two-year: 2 campuses 2,745 students
Baccalaureate and beyond:

Calumet College of St. Joseph (1,000)
• Indiana University NW (4,891)
• Purdue University (7,790)
Valparaiso University (3,782)
MC Access: Chicago–Gary–Kenosha, IL–IN–WI
Places Rated Score: 485
Places Rated Rank: 118

Glens Falls, NY
Public K–12 (99.1%)
21 districts, 48 schools
21,493 pupils
Private School Options (0.9%)
5 Other, 206 pupils
Colleges and Universities
Two-year: 1 campus; 3,267 students
Places Rated Score: 33
Places Rated Rank: 332

Goldsboro, NC
Public K–12 (95.9%)
1 district, 26 schools
18,500 pupils
Private School Options (4.1%)
1 Catholic, 238 pupils
3 Other, 550 pupils
Colleges and Universities
Two-year: 1 campus; 2,177 students
Baccalaureate and beyond:
Mount Olive College (996)
Places Rated Score: 35
Places Rated Rank: 330

Grand Forks, ND–MN
Public K–12 (93.9%)
18 districts, 50 schools
18,232 pupils
Private School Options (6.1%)
7 Catholic, 975 pupils
5 Other, 217 pupils
Colleges and Universities
Two-year: 1 campus; 1,288 students
Baccalaureate and beyond:
• University of North Dakota (12,281)
Places Rated Score: 259
Places Rated Rank: 196

Grand Rapids–Muskegon–Holland, MI
Public K–12 (85.0%)
54 districts, 368 schools
172,949 pupils
Private School Options (15.0%)
40 Catholic, 9,581 pupils
70 Other, 20,842 pupils
Colleges and Universities
Two-year: 2 campuses; 16,597 students
Baccalaureate and beyond:
Aquinas College (2,633)
Baker College of Muskegon (1,779)
Calvin College (4,305)
Davenport College (3,869)
Grand Rapids Baptist College (902)
• Grand Valley State University (10,914)
Hope College (2,770)
Jordan College (2,140)
Kendall College of Art and Design (742)
Places Rated Score: 649
Places Rated Rank: 91

Great Falls, MT
Public K–12 (95.7%)
10 districts, 33 schools
14,406 pupils
Private School Options (4.3%)

2 Catholic, 400 pupils
5 Other, 245 pupils
Colleges and Universities
Baccalaureate and beyond:
College of Great Falls (1,164)
Places Rated Score: 16
Places Rated Rank: 339

Greeley, CO
Public K–12 (97.9%)
13 districts, 61 schools
24,071 pupils
Private School Options (2.1%)
6 Other, 521 pupils
Colleges and Universities
Two-year: 1 campus; 8,018 students
Baccalaureate and beyond:
• University of Northern Colorado (9,842)
MC Access: Denver–Boulder–Greeley, CO
Places Rated Score: 387
Places Rated Rank: 146

Green Bay, WI
Public K–12 (82.0%)
10 districts, 62 schools
33,404 pupils
Private School Options (18.0%)
21 Catholic, 5,716 pupils
17 Other, 1,636 pupils
Colleges and Universities
Two-year: 1 campus; 5,816 students
Baccalaureate and beyond:
St. Norbert College (1,938)
• University of Wisconsin (5,221)
Places Rated Score: 190
Places Rated Rank: 221

Greensboro–Winston-Salem–High Point, NC
Public K–12 (93.4%)
14 districts, 278 schools
163,283 pupils
Private School Options (6.6%)
7 Catholic, 1,686 pupils
43 Other, 9,820 pupils
Colleges and Universities
Two-year: 5 campuses; 16,597 students
Baccalaureate and beyond:
Bennett College (572)
Elon College (3,368)
Greensboro College (1,891)
Guilford College (1,682)
High Point College (2,023)
• North Carolina A&T State University (6,658)
• North Carolina School of the Arts (507)
Salem College (855)
• University of North Carolina (11,584)
Wake Forest University (5,360)
• Winston-Salem State University (2,576)
Places Rated Score: 825
Places Rated Rank: 64

Greenville, NC
Public K–12 (94.2%)
1 district, 31 schools
17,365 pupils
Private School Options (5.8%)
2 Catholic, 442 pupils
3 Other, 628 pupils
Colleges and Universities
Two-year: 1 campus; 3,810 students
Baccalaureate and beyond:

- East Carolina University (16,954)
Places Rated Score: 377
Places Rated Rank: 149

Greenville–Spartanburg–Anderson, SC
Public K–12 (92.7%)
   18 districts, 259 schools
      147,364 pupils
Private School Options (7.3%)
   5 Catholic, 947 pupils
   93 Other, 10,223 pupils
Colleges and Universities
   Two-year: 6 campuses; 12,740 students
   Baccalaureate and beyond:
      Bob Jones University (4,390)
      Central Wesleyan College (679)
      • Clemson University (14,794)
      Converse College (1,251)
      Furman University (3,205)
      Limestone College (921)
      • University of South Carolina (3,265)
      Wofford College (1,118)
Places Rated Score: 644
Places Rated Rank: 93

Hagerstown, MD
Public K–12 (90.3%)
   1 district, 44 schools
      18,282 pupils
Private School Options (9.7%)
   2 Catholic, 475 pupils
   10 Other, 1,478 pupils
Colleges and Universities
   Two-year: 1 campus; 3,164 students
MC Access: Washington–Baltimore, DC–MD–VA–WV
Places Rated Score: 124
Places Rated Rank: 256

Halifax, NS
Public Instruction
   3 school boards, 89 schools
      40,848 pupils
Colleges and Universities
   Community: 5 campuses; 8,608 students
   Baccalaureate and beyond:
      Dalhousie University (10,324)
      Mount St. Vincent University (3,520)
      St. Mary's University (6,798)
      Technical University of Nova Scotia (1,141)
      University of King's College (725)
Places Rated Score: 539
Places Rated Rank: 112

Hamilton, ON
Public Instruction
   156 public, 71,968 pupils (69.2%)
   71 Catholic, 32,018 pupils (30.8%)
Colleges and Universities
   Community: 1 campus; 13,300 students
   Baccalaureate and beyond:
      McMaster University (16,423)
MC Access: Toronto–Ontario Shore, ON
Places Rated Score: 720
Places Rated Rank: 81

Hamilton–Middletown, OH
Public K–12 (90.5%)
   13 districts, 77 schools
      50,077 pupils
Private School Options (9.5%)
   10 Catholic, 3,928 pupils
   8 Other, 1,359 pupils
Colleges and Universities
   Two-year: 1 campus; 1,972 students

Baccalaureate and beyond:
   • Miami University (18,143)
MC Access: Cincinnati–Hamilton, OH–KY–IN
Places Rated Score: 465
Places Rated Rank: 122

Harrisburg–Lebanon–Carlisle, PA
Public K–12 (89.3%)
   34 districts, 194 schools
      93,616 pupils
Private School Options (10.7%)
   16 Catholic, 5,571 pupils
   48 Other, 5,671 pupils
Colleges and Universities
   Two-year: 2 campuses; 7,465 students
   Baccalaureate and beyond:
      Dickinson College (2,029)
      Dickinson School of Law (588)
      Lebanon Valley College (1,333)
      Messiah College (2,270)
      • Penn State University (3,276)
      • Shippensburg University (6,529)
Places Rated Score: 364
Places Rated Rank: 152

Hartford, CT
Public K–12 (88.6%)
   56 districts, 307 schools,
      150,583 pupils
Private School Options (11.4%)
   44 Catholic, 11,494 pupils
   44 Other, 7,885 pupils
Colleges and Universities
   Two-year: 7 campuses; 19,599 students
   Baccalaureate and beyond:
      • Central Connecticut State (14,436)
      • Charter Oak College (940)
      Hartford Graduate Center (2,410)
      St. Joseph College (1,638)
      Trinity College (2,131)
      • University of Connecticut Health Center (492)
      University of Hartford (7,498)
      Wesleyan University (3,452)
Places Rated Score: 747
Places Rated Rank: 76

Hickory–Morgantown, NC
Public K–12 (97.9%)
   6 districts, 89 schools
      49,243 pupils
Private School Options (2.1%)
   8 Other, 1,040 pupils
Colleges and Universities
   Two-year: 3 campuses; 8,141 students
   Baccalaureate and beyond:
      Lenoir–Rhyne College (1,676)
Places Rated Score: 104
Places Rated Rank: 264

Honolulu, HI
Public K–12 (83.5%)
   1 districts, 251 schools
      173,244 pupils
Private School Options (16.5%)
   41 Catholic, 12,091 pupils
   71 Other, 22,179 pupils
Colleges and Universities
   Two-year: 4 campuses; 17,160 students
   Baccalaureate and beyond:
      Brigham Young University (2,043)
      Chaminade University (2,912)
      Hawaii Loa College (593)
      Hawaii Pacific University (4,962)
      • University of Hawaii (18,546)
Places Rated Score: 695
Places Rated Rank: 85

Houma, LA
Public K–12 (87.7%)
   3 districts, 77 schools
      36,865 pupils
Private School Options (12.3%)
   12 Catholic, 4,906 pupils
   2 Other, 280 pupils
Colleges and Universities
   Baccalaureate and beyond:
      • Nicholls State University (6,840)
Places Rated Score: 137
Places Rated Rank: 240

✓ Houston, TX
Public K–12 (94.4%)
   46 districts, 817 schools
      668,666 pupils
Private School Options (5.6%)
   44 Catholic, 12,853 pupils
   131 Other, 26,699 pupils
Colleges and Universities
   Two-year: 7 campuses; 68,751 students
   Baccalaureate and beyond:
      Baylor College of Medicine (981)
      Houston Baptist University (2,395)
      • Prairie View A&M (5,812)
      Rice University (4,216)
      South Texas College of Law (1,329)
      • Texas Southern University (9,499)
      • University of Houston (45,450)
      University of St. Thomas (1,884)
      • University of Texas Health Science Center (2,894)
MC Access: Houston–Galveston–Brazoria, TX
Places Rated Score: 1,497
Places Rated Rank: 26

Huntington–Ashland, WV–KY–OH
Public K–12 (96.6%)
   20 districts, 145 schools
      50,573 pupils
Private School Options (3.4%)
   6 Catholic, 944 pupils
   8 Other, 836 pupils
Colleges and Universities
   Two-year: 1 campus; 2,769 students
   Baccalaureate and beyond:
      Kentucky Christian College (532)
      • Marshall University (12,574)
      • Ohio University (1,481)
Places Rated Score: 309
Places Rated Rank: 171

Huntsville, AL
Public K–12 (92.7%)
   4 districts, 80 schools
      49,609 pupils
Private School Options (7.3%)
   2 Catholic, 510 pupils
   17 Other, 3,393 pupils
Colleges and Universities
   Two-year: 2 campuses; 8,221 students
   Baccalaureate and beyond:
      • Alabama A&M (4,501)
      • Athens State College (2,417)
      Oakwood College (1,224)
      • University of Alabama (8,082)
Places Rated Score: 399
Places Rated Rank: 143

Indianapolis, IN
Public K–12 (89.4%)
   57 districts, 400 schools
      231,360 pupils
Private School Options (10.6%)
   44 Catholic, 13,995 pupils

90 Other, 13,516 pupils
Colleges and Universities
Two-year: 1 campus; 4,442 students
Baccalaureate and beyond:
Anderson University (1,939)
Butler University (4,052)
Franklin College (885)
• Indiana University–Purdue University (26,649)
Marian College (1,215)
University of Indianapolis (3,355)
Places Rated Score: 739
Places Rated Rank: 77

Iowa City, IA
Public K–12 (91.9%)
4 districts, 25 schools
11,302 pupils
Private School Options (8.1%)
2 Catholic, 760 pupils
3 Other, 232 pupils
Colleges and Universities
Baccalaureate and beyond:
• University of Iowa (29,674)
Places Rated Score: 593
Places Rated Rank: 101

Jackson, MI
Public K–12 (88.2%)
13 districts, 56 schools
23,398 pupils
Private School Options (11.8%)
8 Catholic, 2,378 pupils
5 Other, 757 pupils
Colleges and Universities
Two-year: 1 campus; 6,450 students
Baccalaureate and beyond:
Spring Arbor College (1,542)
Places Rated Score: 85
Places Rated Rank: 279

Jackson, MS
Public K–12 (86.4%)
9 districts, 114 schools
70,693 pupils
Private School Options (13.6%)
8 Catholic, 1,629 pupils
26 Other, 9,533 pupils
Colleges and Universities
Two-year: 1 campus; 8,107 students
Baccalaureate and beyond:
Belhaven College (721)
• Jackson State University (7,152)
Millsaps College (1,443)
Mississippi College (3,601)
Tougaloo College (948)
• University of Mississippi Medical Center (1,502)
Places Rated Score: 352
Places Rated Rank: 154

Jacksonville, FL
Public K–12 (89.2%)
8 districts, 209 schools
160,309 pupils
Private School Options (10.8%)
17 Catholic, 5,431 pupils
69 Other, 13,907 pupils
Colleges and Universities
Two-year: 1 campus; 21,381 students
Baccalaureate and beyond:
Edward Waters College (643)
Flagler College (1,204)
Jacksonville University (2,439)
Jones College Jacksonville (1,115)
• University of North Florida (7,723)
Places Rated Score: 440
Places Rated Rank: 130

Jacksonville, NC
Public K–12 (96.1%)
2 districts, 28 schools
17,836 pupils
Private School Options (3.9%)
1 Catholic, 413 pupils
2 Other, 311 pupils
Colleges and Universities
Two-year: 1 campus; 3,696 students
Places Rated Score: 37
Places Rated Rank: 327

Jamestown, NY
Public K–12 (95.8%)
19 districts, 56 schools
25,369 pupils
Private School Options (4.2%)
3 Catholic, 604 pupils
8 Other, 503 pupils
Colleges and Universities
Two-year: 1 campus; 4,229 students
Baccalaureate and beyond:
• SUNY College, Fredonia (4,851)
Places Rated Score: 139
Places Rated Rank: 239

Janesville–Beloit, WI
Public K–12 (92.1%)
10 districts, 56 schools
25,875 pupils
Private School Options (7.9%)
7 Catholic, 1,300 pupils
11 Other, 915 pupils
Colleges and Universities
Two-year: 1 campus; 2,420 students
Baccalaureate and beyond:
Beloit College (1,181)
Places Rated Score: 40
Places Rated Rank: 320

Johnson City–Kingsport–Bristol, TN–VA
Public K–12 (97.6%)
14 districts, 155 schools
69,716 pupils
Private School Options (2.4%)
3 Catholic, 527 pupils
13 Other, 1,162 pupils
Colleges and Universities
Two-year: 2 campuses; 4,411 students
Baccalaureate and beyond:
• East Tennessee State University (11,411)
Emory and Henry College (853)
King College (585)
Milligan College (760)
Virginia Intermont College (521)
Places Rated Score: 310
Places Rated Rank: 170

Johnstown, PA
Public K–12 (87.4%)
27 districts, 80 schools
36,448 pupils
Private School Options (12.6%)
21 Catholic, 4,593 pupils
12 Other, 676 pupils
Colleges and Universities
Two-year: 1 campus; 1,176 students
Baccalaureate and beyond:
St. Francis College (1,757)
• University of Pittsburgh (3,242)
Places Rated Score: 100
Places Rated Rank: 269

Joplin, MO
Public K–12 (95.4%)

12 districts, 62 schools
24,418 pupils
Private School Options (4.6%)
4 Catholic, 443 pupils
6 Other, 746 pupils
Colleges and Universities
Two-year: 1 campus; 1,531 students
Baccalaureate and beyond:
• Missouri Southern State College (5,901)
Ozark Christian College (535)
Places Rated Score: 140
Places Rated Rank: 237

Kalamazoo–Battle Creek, MI
Public K–12 (92.5%)
35 districts, 189 schools
74,157 pupils
Private School Options (7.5%)
10 Catholic, 2,611 pupils
22 Other, 3,409 pupils
Colleges and Universities
Two-year: 2 campuses; 16,449 students
Baccalaureate and beyond:
Albion College (1,639)
Davenport College (1,189)
Kalamazoo College (1,270)
Nazareth College (681)
• Western Michigan University (26,315)
Places Rated Score: 755
Places Rated Rank: 73

Kankakee, IL
Public K–12 (74.8%)
14 districts, 44 schools
17,372 pupils
Private School Options (25.2%)
6 Catholic, 5,132 pupils
5 Other, 713 pupils
Colleges and Universities
Two-year: 1 campus; 3,456 students
Baccalaureate and beyond:
Olivet Nazarene University (1,818)
MC Access: Chicago–Gary–Kenosha, IL–IN–WI
Places Rated Score: 199
Places Rated Rank: 218

Kansas City, MO–KS
Public K–12 (89.4%)
74 districts, 561 schools
271,741 pupils
Private School Options (10.6%)
64 Catholic, 19,909 pupils
72 Other, 12,285 pupils
Colleges and Universities
Two-year: 7 campuses; 36,158 students
Baccalaureate and beyond:
Avila College (1,307)
Kansas City Art Institute (562)
Mid-America Nazarene College (1,189)
Park College (6,065)
Rockhurst College (2,814)
St. Mary College (1,029)
University of Health Sciences (522)
• University of Kansas Medical Center (2,453)
• University of Missouri (11,430)
William Jewell College (1,968)
Places Rated Score: 873
Places Rated Rank: 59

Kenosha, WI
Public K–12 (83.7%)
13 districts, 44 schools
20,484 pupils
Private School Options (16.3%)

14 Catholic, 2,772 pupils
8 Other, 1,228 pupils
Colleges and Universities
Two-year: 1 campus; 9,470 students
Baccalaureate and beyond:
Carthage College (2,002)
• University of Wisconsin (5,172)
MC Access: Chicago–Gary–Kenosha,
IL–IN–WI
Places Rated Score: 240
Places Rated Rank: 204

Killeen–Temple, TX
Public K–12 (98.5%)
14 districts, 94 schools
51,121 pupils
Private School Options (1.5%)
2 Catholic, 262 pupils
5 Other, 492 pupils
Colleges and Universities
Two-year: 2 campuses; 8,269 students
Baccalaureate and beyond:
University of Central Texas (602)
Places Rated Score: 93
Places Rated Rank: 274

Kitchener, ON
Public Instruction
1 district, 90 schools
45,690 pupils
Private School Options
46 Catholic, 18,887 pupils
Colleges and Universities
Community: 1 campus; 4,500 students
Baccalaureate and beyond:
University of Waterloo (21,880)
Wilfrid Laurier University (8,363)
MC Access: Toronto–Ontario Shore, ON
Places Rated Score: 879
Places Rated Rank: 57

Knoxville, TN
Public K–12 (95.9%)
12 districts, 178 schools
95,229 pupils
Private School Options (4.1%)
4 Catholic, 1,129 pupils
18 Other, 2,934 pupils
Colleges and Universities
Two-year: 1 campus; 4,702 students
Baccalaureate and beyond:
Carson-Newman College (2,002)
Knoxville College (1,225)
Maryville College (856)
• University of Tennessee (25,512)
Places Rated Score: 617
Places Rated Rank: 98

Kokomo, IN
Public K–12 (93.8%)
9 districts, 36 schools
17,115 pupils
Private School Options (6.2%)
3 Catholic, 426 pupils
7 Other, 700 pupils
Colleges and Universities
Two-year: 1 campus; 1,914 students
Baccalaureate and beyond:
• Indiana University (3,142)
Places Rated Score: 82
Places Rated Rank: 281

La Crosse, WI–MN
Public K–12 (81.9%)
10 districts, 40 schools
17,933 pupils
Private School Options (18.1%)

11 Catholic, 2,532 pupils
13 Other, 1,433 pupils
Colleges and Universities
Two-year: 1 campus; 3,073 students
Baccalaureate and beyond:
• University of Wisconsin (9,242)
Viterbo College (1,183)
Places Rated Score: 231
Places Rated Rank: 206

Lafayette, IN
Public K–12 (92.9%)
10 districts, 46 schools
23,398 pupils
Private School Options (7.1%)
4 Catholic, 854 pupils
8 Other, 935 pupils
Colleges and Universities
Two-year: 1 campus; 1,708 students
Baccalaureate and beyond:
• Purdue University (37,459)
Places Rated Score: 766
Places Rated Rank: 71

Lafayette, LA
Public K–12 (84.6%)
7 districts, 128 schools
67,383 pupils
Private School Options (15.4%)
27 Catholic, 9,723 pupils
19 Other, 2,583 pupils
Colleges and Universities
Two-year: 1 campus; 1,847 students
Baccalaureate and beyond:
• University of SW Louisiana (15,461)
Places Rated Score: 328
Places Rated Rank: 162

Lake Charles, LA
Public K–12 (91.8%)
2 districts, 60 schools
33,844 pupils
Private School Options (8.2%)
8 Catholic, 2,572 pupils
4 Other, 443 pupils
Colleges and Universities
Baccalaureate and beyond:
• McNeese State University (7,547)
Places Rated Score: 151
Places Rated Rank: 232

Lake County, IL
Public K–12 (89.6%)
53 districts, 180 schools
93,827 pupils
Private School Options (10.4%)
21 Catholic, 7,452 pupils
21 Other, 3,421 pupils
Colleges and Universities
Two-year: 1 campus; 12,757 students
Baccalaureate and beyond:
Barat College (701)
Lake Forest College (1,126)
Lake Forest Graduate School of
Management (528)
Trinity College (769)
Trinity Evangelical Divinity School
(1,262)
University of Health Sciences (892)
MC Access: Chicago–Gary–Kenosha,
IL–IN–WI
Places Rated Score: 354
Places Rated Rank: 153

Lakeland–Winter Haven, FL
Public K–12 (94.2%)
2 districts, 104 schools

68,039 pupils
Private School Options (5.8%)
3 Catholic, 790 pupils
22 Other, 3,398 pupils
Colleges and Universities
Two-year: 1 campus; 6,712 students
Baccalaureate and beyond:
Florida Southern College (2,691)
Southeastern College Assemblies of
God (1,130)
Places Rated Score: 128
Places Rated Rank: 252

Lancaster, PA
Public K–12 (84.1%)
18 districts, 128 schools
61,648 pupils
Private School Options (15.9%)
11 Catholic, 3,263 pupils
92 Other, 8,391 pupils
Colleges and Universities
Two-year: 1 campus; 836 students
Baccalaureate and beyond:
Elizabethtown College (1,908)
Franklin and Marshall College (2,305)
• Millersville University (7,791)
Places Rated Score: 228
Places Rated Rank: 207

Lansing–East Lansing, MI
Public K–12 (92.8%)
30 districts, 170 schools
76,266 pupils
Private School Options (7.2%)
14 Catholic, 3,782 pupils
18 Other, 2,127 pupils
Colleges and Universities
Two-year: 1 campus; 21,716 students
Baccalaureate and beyond:
Davenport College (1,144)
• Michigan State University (44,423)
Olivet College (766)
Thomas M. Cooley Law School (1,498)
Places Rated Score: 1,153
Places Rated Rank: 41

Laredo, TX
Public K–12 (93.7%)
4 districts, 47 schools
37,766 pupils
Private School Options (6.3%)
6 Catholic, 2,182 pupils
2 Other, 365 pupils
Colleges and Universities
Two-year: 1 campus; 4,982 students
Baccalaureate and beyond:
• Laredo State University (1,143)
Places Rated Score: 73
Places Rated Rank: 285

Las Cruces, NM
Public K–12 (96.9%)
3 districts, 50 schools
32,704 pupils
Private School Options (3.1%)
2 Catholic, 342 pupils
4 Other, 693 pupils
Colleges and Universities
Two-year: 1 campus; 2,289 students
Baccalaureate and beyond:
• New Mexico State University (14,212)
Places Rated Score: 307
Places Rated Rank: 173

Las Vegas, NV–AZ
Public K–12 (95.8%)
17 districts, 220 schools
156,656 pupils

Private School Options (4.2%)
9 Catholic, 3,129 pupils
32 Other, 3,680 pupils
Colleges and Universities
Two-year: 2 campuses; 16,771 students
Baccalaureate and beyond:
• University of Nevada (16,163)
Places Rated Score: 491
Places Rated Rank: 116

Lawrence, KS
Public K-12 (96.9%)
4 districts, 29 schools
11,054 pupils
Private School Options (3.1%)
1 Catholic, 277 pupils
1 Other, 79 pupils
Colleges and Universities
Two-year: 1 campus; 827 students
Baccalaureate and beyond:
Baker University (1,121)
• University of Kansas (26,320)
Places Rated Score: 550
Places Rated Rank: 109

Lawton, OK
Public K-12 (98.4%)
15 districts, 65 schools
22,614 pupils
Private School Options (1.6%)
1 Catholic, 164 pupils
2 Other, 212 pupils
Colleges and Universities
Baccalaureate and beyond:
• Cameron University (5,777)
Places Rated Score: 116
Places Rated Rank: 258

Lewiston-Auburn, ME
Public K-12 (90.2%)
15 districts, 43 schools,
17,123 pupils
Private School Options (9.8%)
4 Catholic, 1,102 pupils
6 Other, 764 pupils
Colleges and Universities
Two-year: 2 campuses; 781 students
Baccalaureate and beyond:
Bates College (1,522)
Places Rated Score: 28
Places Rated Rank: 334

Lexington, KY
Public K-12 (91.8%)
10 districts, 127 schools
64,802 pupils
Private School Options (8.2%)
9 Catholic, 2,149 pupils
18 Other, 3,640 pupils
Colleges and Universities
Two-year: 1 campus; 3,923 students
Baccalaureate and beyond:
Asbury College (1,077)
Asbury Theological Seminary (694)
Berea College (1,550)
• Eastern Kentucky University (14,210)
Georgetown College (1,562)
Midway College (524)
Transylvania University (1,076)
• University of Kentucky (22,407)
Places Rated Score: 860
Places Rated Rank: 61

Lima, OH
Public K-12 (89.0%)
20 districts, 65 schools
28,143 pupils

Private School Options (11.0%)
8 Catholic, 2,964 pupils
3 Other, 524 pupils
Colleges and Universities
Two-year: 1 campus; 2,269 students
Baccalaureate and beyond:
Bluffton College (623)
• Ohio State University (1,313)
Places Rated Score: 57
Places Rated Rank: 302

Lincoln, NE
Public K-12 (88.0%)
13 districts, 67 schools
31,474 pupils
Private School Options (12.0%)
10 Catholic, 3,147 pupils
11 Other, 1,152 pupils
Colleges and Universities
Two-year: 1 campus; 4,670 students
Baccalaureate and beyond:
Nebraska Wesleyan University (1,579)
Union College (609)
• University of Nebraska (23,926)
Places Rated Score: 554
Places Rated Rank: 107

Little Rock-North Little Rock, AR
Public K-12 (87.6%)
19 districts, 171 schools
89,046 pupils
Private School Options (12.4%)
17 Catholic, 4,912 pupils
37 Other, 7,655 pupils
Colleges and Universities
Two-year: 1 campus; 91 students
Baccalaureate and beyond:
Hendrix College (1,028)
Philander Smith College (622)
• University of Arkansas (10,740)
• University of Arkansas Medical (l,356)
• University of Central Arkansas (7,477)
Places Rated Score: 420
Places Rated Rank: 136

London, ON
Public Instruction
2 districts, 91 schools
51,972 pupils
Private School Options
34 Catholic, 14,439 pupils
Colleges and Universities
Community: 1 campus; 11,500 students
Baccalaureate and beyond:
Brescia College (820)
Huron College (811)
King's College (1,929)
University of Western Ontario (24,885)
Places Rated Score: 684
Places Rated Rank: 86

✓ **Long Island, NY**
Public K-12 (86.9%)
131 districts, 659 schools
396,256 pupils
Private School Options (13.1%)
93 Catholic, 38,173 pupils
102 Other, 21,451 pupils
Colleges and Universities
Two-year: 4 campuses; 39,365 students
Baccalaureate and beyond:
Adelphi University (8,739)
Dowling College (4,206)
Hofstra University (12,317)
Long Island University (10,715)
Molloy College (1,531)
New York Chiropractic College (745)

New York Institute of Technology
(9,937)
St. Joseph's College, Suffolk (1,918)
• SUNY College, Farmingdale (10,880)
• SUNY College, Old Westbury (4,057)
• SUNY, Stony Brook (17,012)
United States Merchant Marine
Academy (878)
MC Access: New York-Northern New
Jersey-Long Island, NY-NJ-CT
Places Rated Score: 2,037
Places Rated Rank: 16

Longview-Marshall, TX
Public K-12 (96.9%)
21 districts, 91 schools
41,747 pupils
Private School Options (3.1%)
2 Catholic, 337 pupils
8 Other, 1,012 pupils
Colleges and Universities
Two-year: 1 campus; 4,599 students
Baccalaureate and beyond:
East Texas Baptist University (809)
Letourneau University (765)
Places Rated Score: 72
Places Rated Rank: 287

✓ **Los Angeles-Long Beach, CA**
Public K-12 (90.2%)
94 districts, 1,968 schools
1,994,725 pupils
Private School Options (9.8%)
259 Catholic, 93,969 pupils
662 Other, 121,806 pupils
Colleges and Universities
Two-year: 24 campuses; 271,158 students
Baccalaureate and beyond:
Art Center College of Design (1,292)
Azusa Pacific University (2,917)
Biola University (2,566)
California Institute of Arts (955)
California Institute of Technology
(1,823)
California School of Professional
Psychology (508)
• Cal State, Dominguez Hills (8,124)
• Cal State, Long Beach (30,665)
• Cal State, Los Angeles (18,472)
• Cal State, Northridge (28,604)
• Cal State Polytechnic (18,507)
Claremont Graduate School (1,648)
Claremont McKenna College (851)
Fuller Theological Seminary (2,120)
Harvey Mudd College (604)
Los Angeles College of Chiropractic
(1,003)
Loyola Marymount University (6,440)
Master's College (868)
Mount St. Mary's College (1,200)
Northrop University (928)
Occidental College (1,697)
Otis Art Institute (751)
Pacific Oaks College (522)
Pepperdine University (7,193)
Pitzer College (821)
Pomona College (1,393)
Scripps College (617)
Southwestern University School of Law
(1,064)
• University of California (34,993)
University of Laverne (5,376)
University of Southern California
(29,657)
University of West Los Angeles (691)
West Coast University (1,338)
Whittier College (1,720)
Woodbury University (946)

MC Access: Los Angeles–Riverside–
Orange County, CA
Places Rated Score: 6,728
Places Rated Rank: 1

Louisville, KY–IN
Public K–12 (83.3%)
18 districts, 253 schools
148,712 pupils
Private School Options (16.7%)
79 Catholic, 23,022 pupils
38 Other, 6,713 pupils
Colleges and Universities
Two-year: 2 campuses; 10,433 students
Baccalaureate and beyond:
Bellarmine College (3,724)
• Indiana University SE (5,452)
Southern Baptist Theological Seminary
(2,344)
Spalding University (1,112)
• University of Louisville (22,555)
Places Rated Score: 764
Places Rated Rank: 72

Lubbock, TX
Public K–12 (95.1%)
9 districts, 85 schools
42,477 pupils
Private School Options (4.9%)
3 Catholic, 441 pupils
7 Other, 1,740 pupils
Colleges and Universities
Baccalaureate and beyond:
Lubbock Christian University (1,015)
• Texas Tech University (26,027)
Places Rated Score: 531
Places Rated Rank: 113

Lynchburg, VA
Public K–12 (92.5%)
4 districts, 65 schools
30,859 pupils
Private School Options (7.5%)
2 Catholic, 384 pupils
7 Other, 2,111 pupils
Colleges and Universities
Two-year: 1 campus; 4,121 students
Baccalaureate and beyond:
Liberty University (16,607)
Lynchburg College (2,559)
Randolph-Macon Woman's College
(738)
Sweet Briar College (579)
Places Rated Score: 314
Places Rated Rank: 168

Macon, GA
Public K–12 (86.9%)
8 districts, 80 schools
50,304 pupils
Private School Options (13.1%)
4 Catholic, 1,332 pupils
21 Other, 6,255 pupils
Colleges and Universities
Two-year: 2 campuses; 4,930 students
Baccalaureate and beyond:
• Fort Valley State College (2,097)
Mercer University (3,725)
Wesleyan College (498)
Places Rated Score: 148
Places Rated Rank: 233

Madison, WI
Public K–12 (91.2%)
17 districts, 115 schools
53,052 pupils
Private School Options (8.8%)

15 Catholic, 3,318 pupils
18 Other, 1,802 pupils
Colleges and Universities
Two-year: 2 campuses; 23,049 students
Baccalaureate and beyond:
Edgewood College (1,222)
• University of Wisconsin (43,364)
Places Rated Score: 1,114
Places Rated Rank: 46

Manchester–Nashua, NH
Public K–12 (87.1%)
40 districts, 100 schools
54,407 pupils
Private School Options (12.9%)
27 Catholic, 5,297 pupils
20 Other, 2,740 pupils
Colleges and Universities
Two-year: 2 campuses; 3,121 students
Baccalaureate and beyond:
Daniel Webster College (1,044)
Magdalen College (45)
New Hampshire College (6,521)
Notre Dame College (1,087)
Rivier College (2,602)
St. Anselm College (1,949)
• University of New Hampshire (1,564)
MC Access: Boston–New
Bedford–Nashua, MA–NH
Places Rated Score: 350
Places Rated Rank: 155

Mansfield, OH
Public K–12 (90.4%)
21 districts, 79 schools
31,437 pupils
Private School Options (9.6%)
9 Catholic, 1,797 pupils
9 Other, 1,537 pupils
Colleges and Universities
Two-year: 1 campus; 1,924 students
Baccalaureate and beyond:
• Ohio State University (1,336)
Places Rated Score: 46
Places Rated Rank: 316

McAllen–Edinburg–Mission, TX
Public K–12 (98.1%)
16 districts, 155 schools
116,415 pupils
Private School Options (1.9%)
1 Catholic, 488 pupils
12 Other, 1,711 pupils
Colleges and Universities
Baccalaureate and beyond:
• University of Texas–Pan American
(12,082)
Places Rated Score: 242
Places Rated Rank: 202

Medford–Ashland, OR
Public K–12 (95.6%)
11 districts, 55 schools
25,674 pupils
Private School Options (4.4%)
2 Catholic, 357 pupils
7 Other, 822 pupils
Colleges and Universities
Baccalaureate and beyond:
• Southern Oregon State College
(5,196)
Places Rated Score: 104
Places Rated Rank: 264

Melbourne–Titusville–Palm Bay, FL
Public K–12 (92.2%)
3 districts, 72 schools

59,545 pupils
Private School Options (7.8%)
8 Catholic, 2,353 pupils
19 Other, 2,694 pupils
Colleges and Universities
Two-year: 1 campus; 19,248 students
Baccalaureate and beyond:
Florida Institute of Technology (6,199)
Places Rated Score: 275
Places Rated Rank: 188

Memphis, TN–AR–MS
Public K–12 (88.0%)
12 districts, 268 schools
187,352 pupils
Private School Options (12.0%)
21 Catholic, 6,970 pupils
64 Other, 18,561 pupils
Colleges and Universities
Two-year: 2 campuses; 13,068 students
Baccalaureate and beyond:
Christian Brothers University (1,774)
Le Moyne–Owen College (1,279)
Rhodes College (1,386)
• University of Memphis (20,605)
• University of Tennessee (1,747)
Places Rated Score: 659
Places Rated Rank: 90

Merced, CA
Public K–12 (96.1%)
23 districts, 80 schools
41,919 pupils
Private School Options (3.9%)
4 Catholic, 1,050 pupils
10 Other, 650 pupils
Colleges and Universities
Two-year: 1 campus; 6,854 students
Places Rated Score: 69
Places Rated Rank: 291

✓ Miami, FL
Public K–12 (85.1%)
2 districts, 295 schools
304,287 pupils
Private School Options (14.9%)
40 Catholic, 20,266 pupils
173 Other, 32,925 pupils
Colleges and Universities
Two-year: 1 campus; 47,330 students
Baccalaureate and beyond:
Barry University (5,900)
• Florida International University
(20,222)
Florida Memorial College (2,150)
St. Thomas University (2,518)
University of Miami (13,790)
MC Access: Miami–Fort Lauderdale, FL
Places Rated Score: 1,216
Places Rated Rank: 34

Milwaukee–Waukesha, WI
Public K–12 (81.2%)
55 districts, 411 schools
231,082 pupils
Private School Options (18.8%)
113 Catholic, 30,960 pupils
133 Other, 22,676 pupils
Colleges and Universities
Two-year: 2 campuses; 25,472 students
Baccalaureate and beyond:
Alverno College (2,310)
Cardinal Stritch College (3,376)
Carroll College (2,169)
Concordia University (1,363)
Marquette University (12,025)
Medical College of Wisconsin (849)

Milwaukee School of Engineering
(2,767)
Mount Mary College (1,420)
• University of Wisconsin (25,212)
MC Access: Milwaukee–Racine, WI
Places Rated Score: 1,122
Places Rated Rank: 42

✓ Minneapolis–St. Paul, MN–WI
Public K–12 (89.5%)
89 districts, 654 schools
428,201 pupils
Private School Options (10.5%)
117 Catholic, 31,712 pupils
137 Other, 18,746 pupils
Colleges and Universities
Two-year: 10 campuses; 41,193 students
Baccalaureate and beyond:
Augsburg College (2,931)
Bethel College (1,832)
College of St. Catherine (2,625)
Concordia College (1,128)
Hamline University (2,444)
Luther NW Seminary (755)
Macalester College (1,855)
• Metropolitan State University (6,602)
Minneapolis College of Art and Design
(741)
North Central Bible College (1,110)
Northwestern College (1,033)
Northwestern College of Chiropractic
(527)
St. Paul Bible College (526)
• University of Minnesota (58,815)
University of St. Thomas (9,120)
• University of Wisconsin (5,544)
William Mitchell College of Law (1,109)
Places Rated Score: 2,212
Places Rated Rank: 13

Mobile, AL
Public K–12 (85.5%)
2 districts, 123 schools
85,155 pupils
Private School Options (14.5%)
15 Catholic, 5,335 pupils
32 Other, 9,151 pupils
Colleges and Universities
Two-year: 6 campuses; 6,774 students
Baccalaureate and beyond:
Mobile College (1,190)
Spring Hill College (1,174)
• University of South Alabama (11,329)
Places Rated Score: 329
Places Rated Rank: 161

Modesto, CA
Public K–12 (95.9%)
30 districts, 124 schools
80,332 pupils
Private School Options (4.1%)
4 Catholic, 1,111 pupils
20 Other, 2,352 pupils
Colleges and Universities
Two-year: 1 campus; 11,300 students
Baccalaureate and beyond:
• Cal State University (4,910)
Places Rated Score: 211
Places Rated Rank: 213

Monmouth–Ocean, NJ
Public K–12 (87.6%)
83 districts, 270 schools
145,005 pupils
Private School Options (12.4%)
30 Catholic, 14,224 pupils
36 Other, 6,347 pupils

Colleges and Universities
Two-year: 2 campuses; 18,060 students
Baccalaureate and beyond:
Beth Medrash Govoha (1,304)
Georgian Court College (2,151)
Monmouth College (4,273)
MC Access: New York–Northern New
Jersey–Long Island, NY–NJ–CT
Places Rated Score: 661
Places Rated Rank: 89

Monroe, LA
Public K–12 (90.8%)
4 districts, 59 schools
27,632 pupils
Private School Options (9.2%)
5 Catholic, 962 pupils
6 Other, 1,822 pupils
Colleges and Universities
Baccalaureate and beyond:
• NE Louisiana University (10,560)
Places Rated Score: 211
Places Rated Rank: 213

Montgomery, AL
Public K–12 (86.8%)
4 districts, 81 schools
51,795 pupils
Private School Options (13.2%)
6 Catholic, 1,404 pupils
23 Other, 6,454 pupils
Colleges and Universities
Two-year: 3 campuses; 38,411 students
Baccalaureate and beyond:
• Alabama State University (4,456)
• Auburn University (5,997)
Huntingdon College (838)
• Troy State University (2,833)
Places Rated Score: 666
Places Rated Rank: 88

✓ Montreal, PQ
Public Instruction
27 districts, 903 schools
314,857 pupils
Colleges and Universities
Community: 17 campuses; 92,267
students
Baccalaureate and beyond:
Concordia University (25,812)
Ecole de Technologie Superieure
(1,601)
Ecole des Hautes Etudes
Commerciales (9,764)
Ecole Polytechnique (5,244)
McGill University (28,129)
Université de Montreal (41,690)
Université du Quebec (36,353)
Places Rated Score: 3,896
Places Rated Rank: 5

Muncie, IN
Public K–12 (94.6%)
9 districts, 40 schools
17,796 pupils
Private School Options (5.4%)
2 Catholic, 530 pupils
5 Other, 495 pupils
Colleges and Universities
Two-year: 1 campus; 1,848 students
Baccalaureate and beyond:
• Ball State University (19,724)
Places Rated Score: 413
Places Rated Rank: 139

Myrtle Beach, SC
Public K–12 (96.1%)

1 district, 37 schools
24,677 pupils
Private School Options (3.9%)
1 Catholic, 234 pupils
8 Other, 766 pupils
Colleges and Universities
Two-year: 1 campus; 1,661 students
Baccalaureate and beyond:
• University of South Carolina (4,135)
Places Rated Score: 99
Places Rated Rank: 270

Naples, FL
Public K–12 (95.4%)
2 districts, 29 schools
24,019 pupils
Private School Options (4.6%)
3 Catholic, 633 pupils
6 Other, 520 pupils
Places Rated Score: 0
Places Rated Rank: 342

Nashville, TN
Public K–12 (88.2%)
11 districts, 272 schools
156,713 pupils
Private School Options (11.8%)
13 Catholic, 4,211 pupils
54 Other, 16,784 pupils
Colleges and Universities
Two-year: 4 campuses; 9,739 students
Baccalaureate and beyond:
Belmont College (2,681)
Cumberland University (632)
David Lipscomb University (2,518)
Fisk University (896)
• Middle Tennessee State University
(14,136)
• Tennessee State University (7,362)
Trevecca Nazarene College (1,761)
Vanderbilt University (8,996)
Places Rated Score: 770
Places Rated Rank: 70

New Bedford–Fall River–Attleboro, MA
Public K–12 (88.2%)
29 districts, 164 schools
76,260 pupils
Private School Options (11.8%)
29 Catholic, 8,440 pupils
17 Other, 1,720 pupils
Colleges and Universities
Two-year: 1 campus; 5,020 students
Baccalaureate and beyond:
• SE Massachusetts University (7,696)
MC Access: Boston–New
Bedford–Nashua, MA–NH
Places Rated Score: 315
Places Rated Rank: 167

New Haven–Meriden, CT
Public K–12 (87.5%)
19 districts, 153 schools,
72,171 pupils
Private School Options (12.5%)
24 Catholic, 5,619 pupils
24 Other, 4,737 pupils
Colleges and Universities
Two-year: 2 campuses; 4,320 students
Baccalaureate and beyond:
Albertus Magnus College (707)
Quinnipiac College (3,126)
• S Connecticut State (13,182)
University of New Haven (6,360)
Yale University (10,975)

MC Access: New York–Northern New
Jersey–Long Island, NY–NJ–CT
Places Rated Score: 589
Places Rated Rank: 102

New London–Norwich, CT–RI
Public K–12 (87.7%)
  19 districts, 80 schools,
    29,912 pupils
Private School Options (12.3%)
  6 Catholic, 1,202 pupils
  10 Other, 3,001 pupils
Colleges and Universities
  Two-year: 3 campuses; 5,220 students
  Baccalaureate and beyond:
    Connecticut College (2,017)
    • United States Coast Guard Academy
      (878)
Places Rated Score: 97
Places Rated Rank: 272

New Orleans, LA
Public K–12 (74.1%)
  10 districts, 314 schools
    200,107 pupils
Private School Options (25.9%)
  108 Catholic, 52,599 pupils
  66 Other, 17,447 pupils
Colleges and Universities
  Two-year: 2 campuses; 10,113 students
  Baccalaureate and beyond:
    Dillard University (1,562)
    • Louisiana State University Medical
      Center (2,470)
    Loyola University (5,618)
    New Orleans Baptist Seminary (1,361)
    Our Lady of Holy Cross College (1,239)
    • Southern University (3,534)
    Tulane University (10,791)
    • University of New Orleans (15,559)
    Xavier University (2,906)
Places Rated Score: 848
Places Rated Rank: 62

✓ New York, NY
Public K–12 (78.1%)
  66 districts, 1319 schools
    1,132,108 pupils
Private School Options (21.9%)
  451 Catholic, 184,001 pupils
  488 Other, 133,054 pupils
Colleges and Universities
  Two-year: 18 campuses; 76,434 students
  Baccalaureate and beyond:
    Bank Street College of Education (687)
    Barnard College (2,121)
    Beth Jacob Hebrew Teachers College
      (539)
    Brooklyn Law School (1,414)
    College for Human Service (802)
    College of Aeronautics (1,243)
    College of Insurance (655)
    College of Mount St. Vincent (1,047)
    College of New Rochelle (5,138)
    Columbia University (17,532)
    Concordia College (547)
    Cooper Union (1,024)
    Cornell University Medical College
      (598)
    • CUNY Bernard Baruch College
      (16,467)
    • CUNY Brooklyn College (16,298)
    • CUNY City College (13,563)
    • CUNY College of Staten Island
      (11,386)
    • CUNY Graduate School (4,013)
    • CUNY Hunter College (19,894)

• CUNY John Jay College (8,127)
• CUNY Lehman College (9,851)
• CUNY Medgar Evers College (2,713)
• CUNY New York City Technical
  College (11,065)
• CUNY Queens College (17,708)
• CUNY York College (5,229)
Dominican College of Blauvelt (1,479)
• Fashion Institute of Technology
  (11,798)
Fordham University (13,124)
Iona College (7,489)
Juilliard School (1,035)
King's College (506)
Long Island University (5,737)
Manhattan College (3,835)
Manhattan School of Music (838)
Manhattanville College (1,528)
Mannes College of Music (539)
Marymount College (1,173)
Marymount Manhattan College (1,222)
Mercy College (5,107)
Mount Sinai School of Medicine (511)
New School for Social Research (6,186)
New York Institute of Technology
  (2,807)
New York Law School (1,246)
New York Medical College (1,257)
New York School of Interior Design
  (609)
New York University (31,083)
Nyack College (889)
Pace University (17,870)
Polytechnic University (3,783)
Pratt Institute (3,510)
St. Francis College (1,785)
St. John's University (18,969)
St. Joseph's College (821)
St. Thomas Aquinas College (2,141)
Sarah Lawrence College (1,178)
• SUNY College, Purchase (4,393)
• SUNY Health Science Center,
  Brooklyn (1,640)
• SUNY Maritime College (790)
Teachers College at Columbia
  University (4,139)
Wagner College (1,654)
Yeshiva University (4,604)
MC Access: New York–Northern New
  Jersey–Long Island, NY–NJ–CT
Places Rated Score: 6,648
Places Rated Rank: 2

✓ Newark–Jersey City, NJ
Public K–12 (82.6%)
  103 districts, 625 schools
    305,653 pupils
Private School Options (17.4%)
  171 Catholic, 50,850 pupils
  76 Other, 13,613 pupils
Colleges and Universities
  Two-year: 4 campuses; 26,677 students
  Baccalaureate and beyond:
    Bloomfield College (1,606)
    Caldwell College (1,069)
    College of St. Elizabeth (1,073)
    Drew University (2,303)
    • Kean College of New Jersey (12,885)
    • Montclair State College (13,123)
    • New Jersey Institute of Technology
      (7,801)
    • Rutgers University (9,483)
    St. Peter's College (3,380)
    Seton Hall University (9,723)
    • University of Medicine and Dentistry
      of NJ (2,995)
    Upsala College (1,208)

MC Access: New York–Northern New
Jersey–Long Island, NY–NJ–CT
Places Rated Score: 2,064
Places Rated Rank: 14

Norfolk–Virginia Beach–Newport News, VA–NC
Public K–12 (92.2%)
  16 districts, 349 schools
    254,163 pupils
Private School Options (7.8%)
  14 Catholic, 4,180 pupils
  99 Other, 17,374 pupils
Colleges and Universities
  Two-year: 3 campuses; 27,523 students
  Baccalaureate and beyond:
    • Christopher Newport College (4,832)
    • College of William and Mary (7,542)
    Hampton University (5,342)
    • Norfolk State University (8,288)
    • Old Dominion University (16,239)
    Virginia Wesleyan College (1,280)
Places Rated Score: 1,108
Places Rated Rank: 47

Northern New Jersey, NJ
Public K–12 (80.9%)
  123 districts, 427 schools
    184,974 pupils
Private School Options (19.1%)
  111 Catholic, 33,339 pupils
  61 Other, 10,407 pupils
Colleges and Universities
  Two-year: 4 campuses; 17,642 students
  Baccalaureate and beyond:
    Fairleigh Dickinson University (4,259)
    Felician College (690)
    • Ramapo College (4,291)
    • William Paterson College (9,282)
MC Access: New York–Northern New
  Jersey–Long Island, NY–NJ–CT
Places Rated Score: 933
Places Rated Rank: 54

✓ Oakland, CA
Public K–12 (87.7%)
  44 districts, 540 schools
    311,568 pupils
Private School Options (12.3%)
  64 Catholic, 21,167 pupils
  162 Other, 22,651 pupils
Colleges and Universities
  Two-year: 13 campuses; 83,380 students
  Baccalaureate and beyond:
    California College of Arts and Crafts
      (1,057)
    Cal School of Profressional Psychology
      (512)
    • Cal State University (12,171)
    Holy Names College (717)
    Mills College (1,038)
    St. Mary's College of California (3,757)
    • University of California (29,674)
MC Access: San Francisco–Oakland–San
  Jose, CA
Places Rated Score: 1,921
Places Rated Rank: 17

Ocala, FL
Public K–12 (92.6%)
  2 districts, 40 schools
    30,034 pupils
Private School Options (7.4%)
  1 Catholic, 338 pupils
  15 Other, 2,054 pupils
Colleges and Universities

Two-year: 1 campus; 6,246 students
Places Rated Score: 62
Places Rated Rank: 296

Odessa–Midland, TX
Public K–12 (95.1%)
  4 districts, 76 schools
    49,249 pupils
Private School Options (4.9%)
  2 Catholic, 507 pupils
  11 Other, 2,043 pupils
Colleges and Universities
  Two-year: 2 campuses; 8,254 students
  Baccalaureate and beyond:
    • University of Texas Permian Basin
      (2,111)
Places Rated Score: 125
Places Rated Rank: 254

Oklahoma City, OK
Public K–12 (94.4%)
  72 districts, 371 schools
    177,518 pupils
Private School Options (5.6%)
  15 Catholic, 3,685 pupils
  28 Other, 6,892 pupils
Colleges and Universities
  Two-year: 5 campuses; 22,890 students
  Baccalaureate and beyond:
    • Central State University (14,269)
    • Langston University (2,308)
    Oklahoma Baptist University (1,847)
    Oklahoma Christian University of
      Science and Arts (1,617)
    Oklahoma City University (2,957)
    SW College of Christian Ministries
      (1,499)
    • University of Oklahoma (22,225)
    • University of Oklahoma Health
      Science Center (2,459)
Places Rated Score: 1,164
Places Rated Rank: 39

Olympia, WA
Public K–12 (97.3%)
  10 districts, 64 schools
    33,050 pupils
Private School Options (2.7%)
  1 Catholic, 228 pupils
  12 Other, 675 pupils
Colleges and Universities
  Two-year: 1 campus; 3,870 students
  Baccalaureate and beyond:
    • Evergreen State College (3,238)
    St. Martin's College (1,010)
MC Access: Seattle–Tacoma–Bremerton,
  WA
Places Rated Score: 117
Places Rated Rank: 257

Omaha, NE–IA
Public K–12 (86.1%)
  44 districts, 248 schools
    111,857 pupils
Private School Options (13.9%)
  47 Catholic, 15,356 pupils
  25 Other, 2,659 pupils
Colleges and Universities
  Two-year: 2 campuses; 10,596 students
  Baccalaureate and beyond:
    Bellevue College (1,956)
    College of St. Mary (1,127)
    Creighton University (6,068)
    • University of Nebraska (15,475)

  • University of Nebraska Medical
    Center (2,405)
Places Rated Score: 606
Places Rated Rank: 99

✓ Orange County, CA
Public K–12 (89.6%)
  32 districts, 520 schools
    379,649 pupils
Private School Options (10.4%)
  42 Catholic, 17,628 pupils
  169 Other, 26,210 pupils
Colleges and Universities
  Two-year: 8 campuses; 123,925 students
  Baccalaureate and beyond:
    • Cal State University (23,588)
    Chapman College (2,200)
    Chapman College Academic Centers
      (5,579)
    Christ College (569)
    Pacific Christian College (518)
    Southern California College (889)
    • University of California (15,074)
MC Access: Los Angeles–Riverside–
  Orange County, CA
Places Rated Score: 2,469
Places Rated Rank: 11

Orange County, NY
Public K–12 (88.6%)
  18 districts, 88 schools
    52,964 pupils
Private School Options (11.4%)
  14 Catholic, 3,128 pupils
  13 Other, 3,675 pupils
Colleges and Universities
  Two-year: 1 campus; 5,356 students
  Baccalaureate and beyond:
    Mount St. Mary College (1,281)
    • United States Military Academy
      (4,236)
MC Access: New York–Northern New
  Jersey–Long Island, NY–NJ–CT
Places Rated Score: 493
Places Rated Rank: 115

Orlando, FL
Public K–12 (91.7%)
  8 districts, 249 schools
    203,015 pupils
Private School Options (8.3%)
  13 Catholic, 5,295 pupils
  74 Other, 13,150 pupils
Colleges and Universities
  Two-year: 3 campuses; 26,261 students
  Baccalaureate and beyond:
    Orlando College (838)
    Rollins College (3,574)
    • University of Central Florida (20,345)
Places Rated Score: 732
Places Rated Rank: 80

Oshawa, ON
Public K–12
  1 district, 57 schools
    28,137 pupils
Private School Options
  24 Catholic, 10,339 pupils
Colleges and Universities
  Community: 1 campus; 25,000 students
MC Access: Toronto–Ontario Shore, ON
Places Rated Score: 446
Places Rated Rank: 128

Ottawa–Hull, ON–PQ
Public Instruction

6 districts, 210 schools
  98,782 pupils
Private School Options
  87 Catholic, 30,688 pupils
Colleges and Universities
  Community: 4 campuses; 18,825
    students
  Baccalaureate and beyond:
    Carleton University (19,621)
    Université du Quebec (5,444)
    Université Saint-Paul (843)
    University of Ottawa (23,679)
Places Rated Score: 1,180
Places Rated Rank: 38

Owensboro, KY
Public K–12 (80.9%)
  2 districts, 30 schools
    13,994 pupils
Private School Options (19.1%)
  11 Catholic, 3,090 pupils
  3 Other, 208 pupils
Colleges and Universities
  Two-year: 1 campus; 2,116 students
  Baccalaureate and beyond:
    Brescia College (689)
    Kentucky Wesleyan College (716)
Places Rated Score: 40
Places Rated Rank: 320

Panama City, FL
Public K–12 (93.9%)
  2 districts, 32 schools
    22,679 pupils
Private School Options (6.1%)
  1 Catholic, 235 pupils
  7 Other, 1,226 pupils
Colleges and Universities
  Two-year: 1 campus; 5,966 students
Places Rated Score: 60
Places Rated Rank: 297

Parkersburg–Marietta, WV–OH
Public K–12 (96.2%)
  12 districts, 68 schools
    26,055 pupils
Private School Options (3.8%)
  4 Catholic, 703 pupils
  5 Other, 337 pupils
Colleges and Universities
  Two-year: 2 campuses; 4,967 students
  Baccalaureate and beyond:
    Marietta College (1,365)
Places Rated Score: 71
Places Rated Rank: 289

Pensacola, FL
Public K–12 (90.8%)
  4 districts, 94 schools
    58,842 pupils
Private School Options (9.2%)
  7 Catholic, 1,597 pupils
  19 Other, 4,353 pupils
Colleges and Universities
  Two-year: 1 campus; 11,485 students
  Baccalaureate and beyond:
    • University of West Florida (7,728)
Places Rated Score: 272
Places Rated Rank: 191

Peoria–Pekin, IL
Public K–12 (87.0%)
  51 districts, 157 schools
    58,050 pupils
Private School Options (13.0%)
  16 Catholic, 4,739 pupils
  41 Other, 3,963 pupils

Colleges and Universities
Two-year: 1 campus; 12,465 students
Baccalaureate and beyond:
Bradley University (5,658)
Places Rated Score: 208
Places Rated Rank: 216

✓ Philadelphia, PA–NJ
Public K–12 (75.9%)
204 districts, 1130 schools
656,024 pupils
Private School Options (24.1%)
375 Catholic, 153,969 pupils
318 Other, 54,837 pupils
Colleges and Universities
Two-year: 15 campuses; 67,764 students
Baccalaureate and beyond:
Beaver College (2,293)
Bryn Mawr College (1,839)
Cabrini College (1,375)
Chestnut Hill College (1,144)
• Cheyney University (1,641)
Delaware Valley College of Science
and Agriculture (1,615)
Drexel University (11,959)
Eastern College (1,155)
Gratz College (539)
Gwynedd-Mercy College (1,913)
Hahnemann University (2,011)
Haverford College (1,159)
Holy Family College (1,827)
Immaculata College (2,181)
La Salle University (6,478)
• Lincoln University (1,304)
Medical College of PA (563)
Moore College of Art and Design (678)
Neumann College (1,093)
Penn College of Optometry (623)
• Penn State University (6,335)
Philadelphia College of Bible (582)
Philadelphia College of Osteopathic
Medicine (813)
Philadelphia College of Pharmacy
(1,643)
Philadelphia College of Textiles (3,373)
Rosemont College (615)
• Rutgers University (5,337)
St. Joseph's University (6,170)
Spring Garden College (1,084)
Swarthmore College (1,304)
• Temple University (32,713)
Thomas Jefferson University (2,316)
University of Pennsylvania (22,016)
University of the Arts (1,420)
Ursinus College (2,373)
Valley Forge Christian College (529)
Villanova University (11,388)
• West Chester University (11,815)
Widener University (6,307)
MC Access: Philadelphia–Wilmington–
Atlantic City, PA–NJ–DE–MD
Places Rated Score: 3,333
Places Rated Rank: 7

✓ Phoenix–Mesa, AZ
Public K–12 (93.1%)
80 districts, 521 schools
396,065 pupils
Private School Options (6.9%)
29 Catholic, 10,085 pupils
145 Other, 19,465 pupils
Colleges and Universities
Two-year: 9 campuses; 91,306 students
Baccalaureate and beyond:
American School of International.
Management (1,340)

• Arizona State University (43,550)
Grand Canyon University (1,842)
Ottawa University (1,894)
Western International University (2,784)
Places Rated Score: 1,894
Places Rated Rank: 19

Pine Bluff, AR
Public K–12 (98.0%)
7 districts, 37 schools
16,871 pupils
Private School Options (2.0%)
3 Other, 345 pupils
Colleges and Universities
Baccalaureate and beyond:
• University of Arkansas (3,531)
Places Rated Score: 71
Places Rated Rank: 289

✓ Pittsburgh, PA
Public K–12 (84.9%)
122 districts, 634 schools
324,043 pupils
Private School Options (15.1%)
171 Catholic, 43,130 pupils
123 Other, 14,395 pupils
Colleges and Universities
Two-year: 6 campuses; 29,874 students
Baccalaureate and beyond:
• California University (6,748)
Carlow College (1,044)
Carnegie Mellon University (7,090)
Chatham College (659)
Duquesne University (6,901)
Geneva College (1,330)
La Roche College (1,868)
• Penn State University (4,866)
Point Park College (2,870)
Robert Morris College (5,371)
St. Vincent College (1,180)
Seton Hill College (976)
• Slippery Rock University (7,484)
• University of Pittsburgh (29,925)
Washington and Jefferson College
(1,388)
Places Rated Score: 1,696
Places Rated Rank: 24

Pittsfield, MA
Public K–12 (88.2%)
18 districts, 48 schools,
18,073 pupils
Private School Options (11.8%)
6 Catholic, 1,568 pupils
9 Other, 855 pupils
Colleges and Universities
Two-year: 1 campus; 3,159 students
Places Rated Score: 32
Places Rated Rank: 333

Portland, ME
Public K–12 (91.9%)
14 districts, 85 schools
30,412 pupils
Private School Options (8.1%)
6 Catholic, 1,148 pupils
11 Other, 1,534 pupils
Colleges and Universities
Two-year: 1 campus; 1,920 students
Baccalaureate and beyond:
Portland School of Art (307)
St. Joseph's College (5,754)
• University of Southern Maine (10,545)
Westbrook College (575)
Places Rated Score: 319
Places Rated Rank: 165

Portland, OR
Public K–12 (92.7%)
74 districts, 415 schools
218,959 pupils
Private School Options (7.3%)
34 Catholic, 7,871 pupils
72 Other, 9,428 pupils
Colleges and Universities
Two-year: 3 campuses; 35,529 students
Baccalaureate and beyond:
Concordia College (555)
George Fox College (940)
Lewis and Clark College (3,418)
Linfield College (2,164)
Marylhurst College (1,031)
Multnomah School of Bible (659)
• Oregon Health Science University
(1,317)
Pacific University (1,456)
• Portland State University (16,750)
Reed College (1,348)
University of Portland (2,417)
W Conservative Baptist Seminary (619)
MC Access: Portland–Salem–Vancouver,
OR–WA
Places Rated Score: 944
Places Rated Rank: 51

Portsmouth–Dover–Rochester, NH
Public K–12 (85.9%)
60 districts, 103 schools
45,855 pupils
Private School Options (14.1%)
9 Catholic, 2,367 pupils
17 Other, 5,153 pupils
Colleges and Universities
Two-year: 3 campuses; 1,185 students
Baccalaureate and beyond:
• School for Lifelong Learning (1,499)
• University of New Hampshire (12,984)
MC Access: Boston–New Bedford–
Nashua, MA–NH
Places Rated Score: 416
Places Rated Rank: 137

Providence–Warwick–Cranston, RI
Public K–12 (85.8%)
31 districts, 279 schools
126,919 pupils
Private School Options (14.2%)
60 Catholic, 15,991 pupils
32 Other, 5,021 pupils
Colleges and Universities
Two-year: 1 campus; 15,400 students
Baccalaureate and beyond:
Brown University (7,643)
Bryant College of Business
Administration (5,495)
Johnson and Wales University (7,085)
New England Institute of Technology
(1,966)
Providence College (5,755)
• Rhode Island College (8,950)
Rhode Island School of Design (1,900)
Roger Williams College (3,730)
• University of Rhode Island (16,254)
Places Rated Score: 781
Places Rated Rank: 69

Provo–Orem, UT
Public K–12 (99.2%)
3 districts, 92 schools
69,639 pupils
Private School Options (0.8%)
5 Other, 546 pupils
Colleges and Universities
Two-year: 1 campus; 7,758 students

Baccalaureate and beyond:
  Brigham Young University (32,213)
Places Rated Score: 507
Places Rated Rank: 114

Pueblo, CO
Public K–12 (95.3%)
  3 districts, 47 schools
    22,645 pupils
Private School Options (4.7%)
  2 Catholic, 290 pupils
  7 Other, 833 pupils
Colleges and Universities
  Two-year: 1 campus; 2,956 students
  Baccalaureate and beyond:
    • University of Southern Colorado
      (4,084)
Places Rated Score: 111
Places Rated Rank: 260

Punta Gorda, FL
Public K–12 (95.4%)
  2 districts, 21 schools
    14,500 pupils
Private School Options (4.6%)
  1 Catholic, 220 pupils
  4 Other, 479 pupils
Places Rated Score: 0
Places Rated Rank: 342

Quebec City, PQ
Public Instruction
  3 districts, 242 schools
    44,872 pupils
Colleges and Universities
  Community: 5 campuses; 19,878
    students
  Baccalaureate and beyond:
    Université Laval (35,816)
Places Rated Score: 934
Places Rated Rank: 53

Racine, WI
Public K–12 (85.4%)
  13 districts, 53 schools
    28,598 pupils
Private School Options (14.6%)
  12 Catholic, 2,728 pupils
  19 Other, 2,147 pupils
MC Access: Milwaukee–Racine, WI
Places Rated Score: 50
Places Rated Rank: 307

✓ Raleigh–Durham–Chapel Hill, NC
Public K–12 (94.1%)
  9 districts, 203 schools
    135,915 pupils
Private School Options (5.9%)
  10 Catholic, 1,847 pupils
  27 Other, 6,611 pupils
Colleges and Universities
  Two-year: 6 campuses; 13,647 students
  Baccalaureate and beyond:
    Duke University (10,848)
    Meredith College (2,206)
    • North Carolina Central University
      (5,343)
    • North Carolina State University
      (26,870)
    St. Augustine's College (1,885)
    Shaw University (1,620)
    SE Baptist Seminary (657)
    • University of North Carolina (23,619)
Places Rated Score: 1,483
Places Rated Rank: 27

Rapid City, SD
Public K–12 (93.1%)
  5 districts, 45 schools
    18,586 pupils
Private School Options (6.9%)
  2 Catholic, 548 pupils
  10 Other, 821 pupils
Colleges and Universities
  Baccalaureate and beyond:
    • South Dakota School of Mines and
      Technology (2,156)
Places Rated Score: 43
Places Rated Rank: 319

Reading, PA
Public K–12 (89.3%)
  19 districts, 121 schools
    53,837 pupils
Private School Options (10.7%)
  14 Catholic, 3,844 pupils
  31 Other, 2,634 pupils
Colleges and Universities
  Two-year: 1 campus; 2,075 students
  Baccalaureate and beyond:
    Albright College (1,791)
    Alvernia College (1,099)
    • Kutztown University (7,609)
    • Penn State University (1,489)
Places Rated Score: 241
Places Rated Rank: 203

Redding, CA
Public K–12 (92.9%)
  27 districts, 73 schools
    27,783 pupils
Private School Options (7.1%)
  3 Catholic, 640 pupils
  15 Other, 1,489 pupils
Colleges and Universities
  Two-year: 1 campus; 13,000 students
Places Rated Score: 134
Places Rated Rank: 243

Regina, SK
Public Instruction
  3 public divisions, 76 schools
    27,105 pupils (74.9%)
  1 Roman Catholic division, 28 schools
    8,416 pupils (23.2%)
Private School Options
  5 Other, 628 pupils (1.7%)
Colleges and Universities
  Community: 1 campus; 9,000 students
  Baccalaureate and beyond:
    Campion College (860)
    Canadian Theological College (146)
    Luther College (667)
    Saskatchewan Indian College (425)
    University of Regina (8,644)
Places Rated Score: 305
Places Rated Rank: 175

Reno, NV
Public K–12 (95.3%)
  1 districts, 72 schools
    41,600 pupils
Private School Options (4.7%)
  6 Catholic, 1,129 pupils
  11 Other, 932 pupils
Colleges and Universities
  Two-year: 1 campus; 9,131 students
  Baccalaureate and beyond:
    • University of Nevada (10,922)
Places Rated Score: 313
Places Rated Rank: 169

Richland–Kennewick–Pasco, WA
Public K–12 (94.2%)
  10 districts, 62 schools
    33,144 pupils
Private School Options (5.8%)
  4 Catholic, 1,020 pupils
  9 Other, 1,026 pupils
Colleges and Universities
  Two-year: 1 campus; 5,602 students
Places Rated Score: 56
Places Rated Rank: 304

Richmond–Petersburg, VA
Public K–12 (93.9%)
  14 districts, 230 schools
    144,863 pupils
Private School Options (6.1%)
  13 Catholic, 2,834 pupils
  41 Other, 6,497 pupils
Colleges and Universities
  Two-year: 3 campuses; 17,239
  Baccalaureate and beyond:
    Randolph-Macon College (1,118)
    • Virginia State University (4,073)
Places Rated Score: 269
Places Rated Rank: 193

✓ Riverside–San Bernardino, CA
Public K–12 (94.3%)
  61 districts, 702 schools
    534,829 pupils
Private School Options (5.7%)
  34 Catholic, 9,177 pupils
  159 Other, 23,303 pupils
Colleges and Universities
  Two-year: 10 campuses; 62,737 students
  Baccalaureate and beyond:
    California Baptist College (673)
    • Cal State University (10,248)
    Loma Linda University (4,349)
    • University of California (7,774)
    University of Redlands (2,947)
MC Access: Los Angeles–Riverside–
Orange County, CA
Places Rated Score: 1,451
Places Rated Rank: 30

Roanoke, VA
Public K–12 (94.1%)
  4 districts, 72 schools
    33,808 pupils
Private School Options (5.9%)
  2 Catholic, 348 pupils
  9 Other, 1,784 pupils
Colleges and Universities
  Two-year: 2 campuses; 6,873 students
  Baccalaureate and beyond:
    Hollins College (1,108)
    Roanoke College (1,696)
Places Rated Score: 106
Places Rated Rank: 262

Rochester, MN
Public K–12 (89.0%)
  6 districts, 32 schools
    19,441 pupils
Private School Options (11.0%)
  4 Catholic, 1,623 pupils
  7 Other, 774 pupils
Colleges and Universities
  Two-year: 2 campuses; 4,210 students
  Baccalaureate and beyond:
    Mayo Graduate School of Medicine
      (1,092)
Places Rated Score: 60
Places Rated Rank: 297

Rochester, NY
Public K–12 (88.9%)
65 districts, 298 schools
172,107 pupils
Private School Options (11.1%)
59 Catholic, 16,132 pupils
42 Other, 5,218 pupils
Colleges and Universities
Two-year: 3 campuses; 19,933 students
Baccalaureate and beyond:
Hobart William Smith Colleges (1,899)
Nazareth College of Rochester (2,882)
Roberts Wesleyan College (871)
Rochester Institute of Technology
(12,527)
St. John Fisher College (2,529)
• SUNY College, Brockport (9,222)
• SUNY College, Geneseo (5,373)
University of Rochester (9,321)
Places Rated Score: 898
Places Rated Rank: 55

Rockford, IL
Public K–12 (87.2%)
28 districts, 124 schools
56,915 pupils
Private School Options (12.8%)
11 Catholic, 3,628 pupils
23 Other, 4,757 pupils
Colleges and Universities
Two-year: 1 campus; 7,957 students
Baccalaureate and beyond:
Rockford College (1,472)
Places Rated Score: 99
Places Rated Rank: 270

Rocky Mount, NC
Public K–12 (94.0%)
3 districts, 40 schools
24,631 pupils
Private School Options (6.0%)
1 Catholic, 238 pupils
8 Other, 1,340 pupils
Colleges and Universities
Two-year: 2 campuses; 2,955 students
Baccalaureate and beyond:
North Carolina Wesleyan College
(1,485)
Places Rated Score: 49
Places Rated Rank: 309

Sacramento, CA
Public K–12 (92.4%)
56 districts, 440 schools
240,056 pupils
Private School Options (7.6%)
28 Catholic, 9,785 pupils
77 Other, 9,991 pupils
Colleges and Universities
Two-year: 7 campuses; 54,610 students
Baccalaureate and beyond:
• Cal State University (23,337)
MC Access: Sacramento–Yolo, CA
Places Rated Score: 1,054
Places Rated Rank: 48

Saginaw–Bay City–Midland, MI
Public K–12 (86.1%)
24 districts, 157 schools
69,669 pupils
Private School Options (13.9%)
24 Catholic, 4,942 pupils
41 Other, 6,269 pupils
Colleges and Universities
Two-year: 2 campuses; 12,813
Baccalaureate and beyond:

Northwood Institute (1,724)
• Saginaw Valley State University
(5,899)
Places Rated Score: 269
Places Rated Rank: 193

St. Catharines–Niagara, ON
Public Instruction
4 districts, 128 schools
40,259 pupils
Private School Options
60 Catholic, 20,264 pupils
Colleges and Universities
Community: 1 campus; 4,000 students
Baccalaureate and beyond:
Brock University (8,152)
MC Access: Buffalo–St.
Catharines–Niagara, NY–ON
Places Rated Score: 283
Places Rated Rank: 184

St. Cloud, MN
Public K–12 (84.8%)
16 districts, 55 schools
28,515 pupils
Private School Options (15.2%)
25 Catholic, 4,780 pupils
4 Other, 335 pupils
Colleges and Universities
Baccalaureate and beyond:
College of St. Benedict (1,960)
• St. Cloud State University (16,551)
St. John's University (2,003)
Places Rated Score: 384
Places Rated Rank: 148

Saint John, NB
Public Instruction
1 district, 60 schools
14,732 pupils
Private School Options
47 Catholic, 20,680 pupils
4 Other, 222 pupils
Colleges and Universities
Baccalaureate and beyond:
Mount Allison University (1,268)
Places Rated Score: 25
Places Rated Rank: 336

St. John's, NF
Public Education
1 integrated board, 28 schools
11,427 pupils (36.6%)
1 Roman Catholic board, 42 schools
19,441 (62.3%)
Private School Options
8 Other, 314 pupils (1.1%)
Colleges and Universities
Community: 2 campuses; 9,000 students
Baccalaureate and beyond:
Memorial University of Newfoundland
(14,196)
Places Rated Score: 374
Places Rated Rank: 150

St. Joseph, MO
Public K–12 (92.5%)
7 districts, 45 schools
17,027 pupils
Private School Options (7.5%)
5 Catholic, 1,140 pupils
2 Other, 235 pupils
Colleges and Universities
Baccalaureate and beyond:
• Missouri Western State College
(4,255)
Places Rated Score: 85
Places Rated Rank: 279

✓ St. Louis, MO–IL
Public K–12 (79.8%)
125 districts, 736 schools
375,299 pupils
Private School Options (20.2%)
229 Catholic, 69,551 pupils
142 Other, 25,414 pupils
Colleges and Universities
Two-year: 9 campuses; 64,975 students
Baccalaureate and beyond:
Fontbonne College (1,108)
• Harris-Stowe State College (1,771)
Lindenwood College (2,037)
Logan College of Chiropractic (768)
Maryville College, St. Louis (3,143)
McKendree College (1,098)
Missouri Baptist College (1,032)
Parks College of St. Louis University
(1,139)
Principia College (632)
St. Louis College of Pharmacy (791)
St. Louis University (12,391)
• Southern Illinois University (11,320)
• University of Missouri (14,635)
Washington University (11,556)
Webster University (8,317)
Places Rated Score: 1,813
Places Rated Rank: 21

Salem, OR
Public K–12 (93.1%)
39 districts, 116 schools
48,962 pupils
Private School Options (6.9%)
8 Catholic, 1,398 pupils
26 Other, 2,253 pupils
Colleges and Universities
Two-year: 1 campus; 8,800 students
Baccalaureate and beyond:
• Western Oregon State College
(3,856)
Willamette University (2,225)
MC Access: Portland–Salem–Vancouver,
OR–WA
Places Rated Score: 237
Places Rated Rank: 205

Salinas, CA
Public K–12 (92.9%)
27 districts, 112 schools
59,881 pupils
Private School Options (7.1%)
8 Catholic, 2,589 pupils
14 Other, 2,007 pupils
Colleges and Universities
Two-year: 2 campuses; 7,960 students
Baccalaureate and beyond:
Monterey Institute of International
Studies (638)
• Naval Postgraduate School (1,864)
Places Rated Score: 125
Places Rated Rank: 254

Salt Lake City–Ogden, UT
Public K–12 (97.9%)
10 districts, 345 schools
269,240 pupils
Private School Options (2.1%)
10 Catholic, 3,105 pupils
15 Other, 2,638 pupils
Colleges and Universities
Two-year: 2 campuses; 11,766 students
Baccalaureate and beyond:
• University of Utah (23,883)
• Weber State University (12,970)
Westminster College (1,951)
Places Rated Score: 881
Places Rated Rank: 56

San Angelo, TX
Public K–12 (98.1%)
  7 districts, 39 schools
    19,411 pupils
Private School Options (1.9%)
  1 Catholic, 164 pupils
  2 Other, 204 pupils
Colleges and Universities
  Baccalaureate and beyond:
    • Angelo State University (6,469)
Places Rated Score: 129
Places Rated Rank: 249

San Antonio, TX
Public K–12 (92.5%)
  26 districts, 387 schools
    264,452 pupils
Private School Options (7.5%)
  43 Catholic, 12,288 pupils
  45 Other, 9,000 pupils
Colleges and Universities
  Two-year: 3 campuses; 29,257 students
  Baccalaureate and beyond:
    Incarnate Word College (2,429)
    Our Lady of the Lake University (2,381)
    St. Mary's University (3,883)
    Texas Lutheran College (1,293)
    Trinity University (2,573)
    • University of Texas (14,031)
    • University of Texas Health Science
      (2,362)
Places Rated Score: 789
Places Rated Rank: 67

✓ San Diego, CA
Public K–12 (92.3%)
  45 districts, 530 schools
    407,276 pupils
Private School Options (7.7%)
  46 Catholic, 13,820 pupils
  147 Other, 20,195 pupils
Colleges and Universities
  Two-year: 9 campuses; 101,678 students
  Baccalaureate and beyond:
    • Cal State University (650)
    California Western School of Law (840)
    National University (10,136)
    Point Loma Nazarene College (2,221)
    • San Diego State University (33,406)
    • University of California (16,700)
    University of San Diego (5,921)
    U.S. International University (2,615)
Places Rated Score: 2,335
Places Rated Rank: 12

✓ San Francisco, CA
Public K–12 (78.8%)
  48 districts, 361 schools
    167,452 pupils
Private School Options (21.2%)
  82 Catholic, 28,110 pupils
  142 Other, 16,871 pupils
Colleges and Universities
  Two-year: 7 campuses; 64,343 students
  Baccalaureate and beyond:
    California Institute of Integral Studies
      (509)
    College of Notre Dame (1,117)
    Dominican College of San Rafael (657)
    Golden Gate Baptist Seminary (651)
    Golden Gate University (8,030)
    Menlo College (536)
    New College of California (702)
    San Francisco Art Institute (756)
    • San Francisco State University
      (25,656)

    San Francisco Theological Seminary
      (614)
    • University of California, Hastings
      College of Law (1,367)
    • University of California (3,711)
    University of San Francisco (6,394)
MC Access: San Francisco–Oakland–San
  Jose, CA
Places Rated Score: 1,723
Places Rated Rank: 23

✓ San Jose, CA
Public K–12 (89.2%)
  37 districts, 360 schools
    227,690 pupils
Private School Options (10.8%)
  35 Catholic, 13,477 pupils
  100 Other, 14,053 pupils
Colleges and Universities
  Two-year: 8 campuses; 80,402 students
  Baccalaureate and beyond:
    Palmer College of Chiropractic, West
      (529)
    • San Jose State University (27,650)
    Santa Clara University (7,892)
    Stanford University (14,723)
MC Access: San Francisco–Oakland–San
  Jose, CA
Places Rated Score: 1,854
Places Rated Rank: 20

San Luis Obispo–Atascadero–Paso Robles, CA
Public K–12 (93.0%)
  15 districts, 69 schools
    31,307 pupils
Private School Options (7.0%)
  4 Catholic, 1,050 pupils
  14 Other, 1,316 pupils
Colleges and Universities
  Two-year: 1 campus; 7,127 students
  Baccalaureate and beyond:
    • California Polytechnic (16,721)
Places Rated Score: 406
Places Rated Rank: 140

Santa Barbara–Santa Maria–Lompoc, CA
Public K–12 (90.3%)
  26 districts, 112 schools
    52,843 pupils
Private School Options (9.7%)
  10 Catholic, 2,573 pupils
  25 Other, 3,132 pupils
Colleges and Universities
  Two-year: 2 campuses; 19,006 students
  Baccalaureate and beyond:
    Fielding Institute (688)
    • University of California (18,193)
    Westmont College (1,256)
Places Rated Score: 582
Places Rated Rank: 104

Santa Cruz–Watsonville, CA
Public K–12 (90.9%)
  12 districts, 66 schools
    34,734 pupils
Private School Options (9.1%)
  3 Catholic, 554 pupils
  16 Other, 2,932 pupils
Colleges and Universities
  Two-year: 1 campus; 12,075 students
  Baccalaureate and beyond:
    • University of California (9,137)
MC Access: San Francisco–Oakland–San
  Jose, CA
Places Rated Score: 426
Places Rated Rank: 132

Santa Fe, NM
Public K–12 (88.8%)
  3 districts, 36 schools
    16,799 pupils
Private School Options (11.2%)
  5 Catholic, 1,035 pupils
  10 Other, 1,080 pupils
Colleges and Universities
  Two-year: 3 campuses; 3,795 students
  Baccalaureate and beyond:
    College of Santa Fe (1,214)
Places Rated Score: 60
Places Rated Rank: 297

Santa Rosa, CA
Public K–12 (93.4%)
  41 districts, 132 schools
    61,900 pupils
Private School Options (6.6%)
  7 Catholic, 2,035 pupils
  20 Other, 2,365 pupils
Colleges and Universities
  Two-year: 2 campuses; 20,609 students
  Baccalaureate and beyond:
    • Sonoma State University (6,441)
MC Access: San Francisco–Oakland–San
  Jose, CA
Places Rated Score: 396
Places Rated Rank: 144

Sarasota–Bradenton, FL
Public K–12 (90.1%)
  4 districts, 74 schools
    54,270 pupils
Private School Options (9.9%)
  5 Catholic, 1,681 pupils
  30 Other, 4,297 pupils
Colleges and Universities
  Two-year: 1 campus; 7,874 students
  Baccalaureate and beyond:
    Ringling School of Art and Design (508)
Places Rated Score: 87
Places Rated Rank: 276

Saskatoon, SK
Public Instruction
  4 public divisions, 72 schools
    29,935 pupils (70.4%)
  1 Roman Catholic division, 36 schools,
    12,094 pupils (28.4%)
Private School Options
  8 Other, 444 pupils (1.2%)
Colleges and Universities
  Community: 3 campuses; 20,928
    students
  Baccalaureate and beyond:
    St. Thomas More College (1,003)
    University of Saskatchewan (17,631)
Places Rated Score: 587
Places Rated Rank: 103

Savannah, GA
Public K–12 (86.4%)
  4 districts, 63 schools
    45,489 pupils
Private School Options (13.6%)
  7 Catholic, 2,411 pupils
  16 Other, 4,766 pupils
Colleges and Universities
  Baccalaureate and beyond:
    • Armstrong State College (3,702)
    Savannah College of Art and Design
      (1,663)
    • Savannah State College (2,043)
Places Rated Score: 137
Places Rated Rank: 240

Scranton-Wilkes-Barre-Hazleton, PA
Public K-12 (82.0%)
35 districts, 162 schools
82,696 pupils
Private School Options (18.0%)
60 Catholic, 15,395 pupils
28 Other, 2,796 pupils
Colleges and Universities
Two-year: 4 campuses; 8,752 students
Baccalaureate and beyond:
Baptist Bible College (672)
• Bloomsburg University (7,143)
College Misericordia (1,349)
• East Stroudsburg University (5,359)
King's College (2,323)
Marywood College (3,058)
• Penn State University (3,505)
University of Scranton (5,111)
Wilkes University (3,651)
Places Rated Score: 623
Places Rated Rank: 95

✓ Seattle-Bellevue-Everett, WA
Public K-12 (90.1%)
37 districts, 554 schools
305,739 pupils
Private School Options (9.9%)
45 Catholic, 14,191 pupils
139 Other, 19,229 pupils
Colleges and Universities
Two-year: 10 campuses; 60,184 students
Baccalaureate and beyond:
City University (3,055)
Cornish College of the Arts (556)
NW College, Assemblies of God (695)
Seattle Pacific University (3,435)
Seattle University (4,469)
• University of Washington (33,238)
MC Access: Seattle-Tacoma-Bremerton, WA
Places Rated Score: 1,447
Places Rated Rank: 31

Sharon, PA
Public K-12 (91.0%)
14 districts, 44 schools
19,046 pupils
Private School Options (9.0%)
5 Catholic, 1,446 pupils
7 Other, 437 pupils
Colleges and Universities
Baccalaureate and beyond:
Grove City College (2,125)
• Penn State University (1,196)
Thiel College (918)
Places Rated Score: 64
Places Rated Rank: 294

Sheboygan, WI
Public K-12 (84.4%)
10 districts, 51 schools
18,784 pupils
Private School Options (15.6%)
8 Catholic, 1,546 pupils
16 Other, 1,937 pupils
Colleges and Universities
Baccalaureate and beyond:
Lakeland College (1,766)
Places Rated Score: 24
Places Rated Rank: 337

Sherbrooke, PQ
Public Instruction
2 districts, 62 schools
5,396 pupils
Colleges and Universities
Community: 2 campuses; 9,434 students
Baccalaureate and beyond:
Bishop's University (2,443)
Université de Sherbrooke (16,581)
Places Rated Score: 426
Places Rated Rank: 132

Sherman-Denison, TX
Public K-12 (97.1%)
13 districts, 47 schools
17,837 pupils
Private School Options (2.9%)
1 Catholic, 133 pupils
5 Other, 392 pupils
Colleges and Universities
Two-year: 1 campus; 3,410 students
Baccalaureate and beyond:
Austin College (1,227)
Places Rated Score: 50
Places Rated Rank: 307

Shreveport-Bossier City, LA
Public K-12 (93.6%)
4 districts, 135 schools
76,111 pupils
Private School Options (6.4%)
6 Catholic, 1,859 pupils
20 Other, 3,321 pupils
Colleges and Universities
Two-year: 2 campuses; 3,634 students
Baccalaureate and beyond:
Centenary College of Louisiana (1,123)
• Louisiana State University (4,110)
Places Rated Score: 134
Places Rated Rank: 243

Sioux City, IA-NE
Public K-12 (86.5%)
12 districts, 54 schools
20,333 pupils
Private School Options (13.5%)
7 Catholic, 2,814 pupils
2 Other, 367 pupils
Colleges and Universities
Two-year: 1 campus; 1,555 students
Baccalaureate and beyond:
Briar Cliff College (1,106)
Morningside College (1,277)
Places Rated Score: 47
Places Rated Rank: 312

Sioux Falls, SD
Public K-12 (87.7%)
12 districts, 67 schools
25,177 pupils
Private School Options (12.3%)
8 Catholic, 2,224 pupils
15 Other, 1,319 pupils
Colleges and Universities
Two-year: 1 campus; 202 students
Baccalaureate and beyond:
Augustana College (1,998)
Sioux Falls College (962)
Places Rated Score: 44
Places Rated Rank: 318

South Bend, IN
Public K-12 (83.4%)
7 districts, 63 schools
38,481 pupils
Private School Options (16.6%)
18 Catholic, 5,506 pupils
14 Other, 2,130 pupils
Colleges and Universities
Two-year: 3 campuses; 3,237 students
Baccalaureate and beyond:
Bethel College (552)
• Indiana University (6,891)
St. Mary's College (1,758)
University of Notre Dame (9,952)
Places Rated Score: 334
Places Rated Rank: 159

Spokane, WA
Public K-12 (92.9%)
15 districts, 129 schools
66,214 pupils
Private School Options (7.1%)
13 Catholic, 2,476 pupils
24 Other, 2,594 pupils
Colleges and Universities
Two-year: 2 campuses; 15,337 students
Baccalaureate and beyond:
• Eastern Washington University (8,095)
Gonzaga University (3,599)
Whitworth College (1,788)
Places Rated Score: 387
Places Rated Rank: 146

Springfield, IL
Public K-12 (82.2%)
18 districts, 81 schools
29,432 pupils
Private School Options (17.8%)
13 Catholic, 4,330 pupils
18 Other, 2,065 pupils
Colleges and Universities
Two-year: 2 campuses; 8,187 students
Baccalaureate and beyond:
• Sangamon State University (3,971)
Places Rated Score: 161
Places Rated Rank: 230

Springfield, MA
Public K-12 (86.0%)
38 districts, 187 schools
84,702 pupils
Private School Options (14.0%)
29 Catholic, 9,729 pupils
39 Other, 4,116 pupils
Colleges and Universities
Two-year: 3 campuses; 11,596 students
Baccalaureate and beyond:
American International College (1,945)
Amherst College (1,578)
College of Our Lady of the Elms (1,161)
Hampshire College (1,333)
Mount Holyoke College (1,988)
St. Hyacinth College and Seminary (25)
Smith College (2,983)
Springfield College (3,444)
• University of Massachusetts (27,298)
Western New England College (5,265)
• Westfield State College (5,130)
Places Rated Score: 1,027
Places Rated Rank: 49

Springfield, MO
Public K-12 (96.3%)
20 districts, 102 schools
44,527 pupils
Private School Options (3.7%)
5 Catholic, 932 pupils
7 Other, 766 pupils
Colleges and Universities
Baccalaureate and beyond:
Baptist Bible College (812)
Central Bible College (964)
Drury College (3,319)
Evangel College (1,525)
• SW Missouri State University (18,427)
Places Rated Score: 461
Places Rated Rank: 123

Stamford–Norwalk, CT
Public K–12 (82.8%)
9 districts, 76 schools,
41,684 pupils
Private School Options (17.2%)
14 Catholic, 3,067 pupils
26 Other, 5,613 pupils
Colleges and Universities
Two-year: 2 campuses; 4,640 students
MC Access: New York–Northern New
Jersey–Long Island, NY–NJ–CT
Places Rated Score: 370
Places Rated Rank: 151

State College, PA
Public K–12 (91.9%)
6 districts, 33 schools
12,850 pupils
Private School Options (8.1%)
2 Catholic, 419 pupils
10 Other, 709 pupils
Colleges and Universities
Baccalaureate and beyond:
• Penn State University (37,718)
Places Rated Score: 754
Places Rated Rank: 74

Steubenville–Weirton, OH–WV
Public K–12 (90.4%)
10 districts, 62 schools
22,833 pupils
Private School Options (9.6%)
13 Catholic, 2,338 pupils
1 Other, 76 pupils
Colleges and Universities
Two-year: 1 campus; 1,528 students
Baccalaureate and beyond:
Franciscan University of Steubenville
(1,523)
Places Rated Score: 39
Places Rated Rank: 324

Stockton–Lodi, CA
Public K–12 (93.3%)
19 districts, 158 schools
94,301 pupils
Private School Options (6.7%)
10 Catholic, 2,974 pupils
28 Other, 3,791 pupils
Colleges and Universities
Two-year: 1 campus; 14,792 students
Baccalaureate and beyond:
University of the Pacific (5,435)
Places Rated Score: 227
Places Rated Rank: 208

Sudbury, ON
Public Instruction
2 districts, 28 schools
11,615 pupils
Private School Options
32 Catholic, 9,291 pupils
Colleges and Universities
Community: 1 campus; 6,000 students
Baccalaureate and beyond:
Laurentian University (6,854)
Places Rated Score: 197
Places Rated Rank: 219

Sumter, SC
Public K–12 (89.6%)
2 districts, 27 schools
18,806 pupils
Private School Options (10.4%)
3 Catholic, 650 pupils
6 Other, 1,533 pupils

Colleges and Universities
Two-year: 2 campuses; 3,004 students
Baccalaureate and beyond:
Morris College (774)
Places Rated Score: 40
Places Rated Rank: 320

Syracuse, NY
Public K–12 (93.0%)
48 districts, 219 schools
124,602 pupils
Private School Options (7.0%)
35 Catholic, 7,086 pupils
25 Other, 2,339 pupils
Colleges and Universities
Two-year: 4 campuses; 14,128 students
Baccalaureate and beyond:
Cazenovia College (1,054)
Colgate University (2,716)
Le Moyne College (2,336)
• SUNY College, Oswego (8,839)
• SUNY College of Environmental
Science and Forestry (1,452)
• SUNY Health Science Center,
Syracuse (1,051)
Syracuse University (22,196)
Places Rated Score: 751
Places Rated Rank: 75

Tacoma, WA
Public K–12 (94.1%)
15 districts, 203 schools
111,108 pupils
Private School Options (5.9%)
7 Catholic, 2,691 pupils
22 Other, 4,279 pupils
Colleges and Universities
Two-year: 2 campuses; 12,934 students
Baccalaureate and beyond:
Pacific Lutheran University (3,855)
University of Puget Sound (4,208)
MC Access: Seattle–Tacoma–Bremerton,
WA
Places Rated Score: 303
Places Rated Rank: 176

Tallahassee, FL
Public K–12 (87.3%)
4 districts, 54 schools
35,345 pupils
Private School Options (12.7%)
1 Catholic, 553 pupils
23 Other, 4,567 pupils
Colleges and Universities
Two-year: 1 campus; 8,183 students
Baccalaureate and beyond:
• Florida A&M University (7,460)
• Florida State University (27,975)
Places Rated Score: 791
Places Rated Rank: 66

Tampa–St. Petersburg–Clearwater, FL
Public K–12 (88.0%)
8 districts, 370 schools
271,275 pupils
Private School Options (12.0%)
44 Catholic, 12,351 pupils
132 Other, 24,641 pupils
Colleges and Universities
Two-year: 4 campuses; 42,426 students
Baccalaureate and beyond:
Eckerd College (1,323)
St. Leo College (6,071)
• University of South Florida (31,566)
University of Tampa (2,476)
Places Rated Score: 1,194
Places Rated Rank: 36

Terre Haute, IN
Public K–12 (95.2%)
6 districts, 49 schools
24,198 pupils
Private School Options (4.8%)
4 Catholic, 473 pupils
10 Other, 748 pupils
Colleges and Universities
Two-year: 1 campus; 1,835 students
Baccalaureate and beyond:
• Indiana State University (12,005)
Rose-Hulman Institute of Technology
(1,446)
St. Mary-of-the-Woods College (906)
Places Rated Score: 290
Places Rated Rank: 182

Texarkana, TX–Texarkana, AR
Public K–12 (97.9%)
56 districts, 17 schools
24,642 pupils
Private School Options (2.1%)
4 Other, 510 pupils
Colleges and Universities
Two-year: 1 campus; 3,814 students
Baccalaureate and beyond:
• East Texas State University (1,337)
Places Rated Score: 65
Places Rated Rank: 292

Thunder Bay, ON
Public Instruction
6 districts, 43 schools
15,264 pupils
Private School Options
24 Catholic, 8,066 pupils
Colleges and Universities
Community: 1 campus; 3,700 students
Baccalaureate and beyond:
Lakehead University (5,952)
Places Rated Score: 156
Places Rated Rank: 231

Toledo, OH
Public K–12 (82.4%)
33 districts, 185 schools
94,724 pupils
Private School Options (17.6%)
50 Catholic, 17,133 pupils
13 Other, 3,059 pupils
Colleges and Universities
Two-year: 1 campus; 6,603 students
Baccalaureate and beyond:
• Bowling Green State University
(18,584)
Lourdes College (886)
• Medical College of Ohio (800)
• University of Toledo (23,928)
Places Rated Score: 944
Places Rated Rank: 51

Topeka, KS
Public K–12 (91.3%)
6 districts, 69 schools
27,320 pupils
Private School Options (8.7%)
7 Catholic, 2,042 pupils
5 Other, 567 pupils
Colleges and Universities
Baccalaureate and beyond:
• Washburn University (6,574)
Places Rated Score: 131
Places Rated Rank: 246

✓ Toronto, ON
Public Instruction

32 districts, 1,111 schools
519,446 pupils
Private School Options
149 Catholic, 88,331 pupils
Colleges and Universities
Community: 6 campuses; 46,100 students
Baccalaureate and beyond:
Ryerson Polytechnical Institute (18,592)
University of Toronto (50,130)
York University (29,388)
MC Access: Toronto–Ontario Shore, ON
Places Rated Score: 2,517
Places Rated Rank: 10

Trenton, NJ
Public K–12 (76.9%)
12 districts, 92 schools
44,465 pupils
Private School Options (23.1%)
26 Catholic, 7,936 pupils
29 Other, 5,435 pupils
Colleges and Universities
Two-year: 1 campus; 8,814 students
Baccalaureate and beyond:
Princeton Theological Seminary (784)
Princeton University (6,466)
Rider College (5,509)
• Thomas A. Edison State College (7,202)
• Trenton State College (7,386)
MC Access: New York–Northern New Jersey–Long Island, NY–NJ–CT
Places Rated Score: 621
Places Rated Rank: 97

Trois-Rivieres, PQ
Public Instruction
2 districts, 60 schools
4,640 pupils
Colleges and Universities
Community: 1 campus; 4,500 students
Baccalaureate and beyond:
Université du Quebec (10,414)
Places Rated Score: 253
Places Rated Rank: 198

Tucson, AZ
Public K–12 (91.0%)
18 districts, 188 schools
108,804 pupils
Private School Options (9.0%)
13 Catholic, 4,193 pupils
59 Other, 6,529 pupils
Colleges and Universities
Two-year: 1 campus; 26,747 students
Baccalaureate and beyond:
• University of Arizona (36,676)
Places Rated Score: 1,001
Places Rated Rank: 50

Tulsa, OK
Public K–12 (94.8%)
64 districts, 283 schools
129,022 pupils
Private School Options (5.2%)
12 Catholic, 3,994 pupils
18 Other, 3,139 pupils
Colleges and Universities
Two-year: 2 campuses; 19,833 students
Baccalaureate and beyond:
Oral Roberts University (3,550)
University of Tulsa (4,344)
Places Rated Score: 309
Places Rated Rank: 171

Tuscaloosa, AL
Public K–12 (95.3%)
2 districts, 46 schools
25,200 pupils
Private School Options (4.7%)
1 Catholic, 258 pupils
5 Other, 983 pupils
Colleges and Universities
Two-year: 2 campuses; 4,415 students
Baccalaureate and beyond:
Stillman College (774)
• University of Alabama (19,765)
Places Rated Score: 450
Places Rated Rank: 127

Tyler, TX
Public K–12 (95.3%)
8 districts, 52 schools
28,811 pupils
Private School Options (4.7%)
3 Catholic, 571 pupils
7 Other, 849 pupils
Colleges and Universities
Two-year: 1 campus; 7,953 students
Baccalaureate and beyond:
• University of Texas (4,103)
Places Rated Score: 167
Places Rated Rank: 228

Utica–Rome, NY
Public K–12 (92.8%)
29 districts, 101 schools
52,472 pupils
Private School Options (7.2%)
18 Catholic, 3,515 pupils
8 Other, 527 pupils
Colleges and Universities
Two-year: 3 campuses; 9,025 students
Baccalaureate and beyond:
Hamilton College (1,661)
• SUNY Institute of Technology (2,510)
Utica College (2,584)
Places Rated Score: 197
Places Rated Rank: 219

Vallejo–Fairfield–Napa, CA
Public K–12 (91.5%)
15 districts, 143 schools
78,838 pupils
Private School Options (8.5%)
11 Catholic, 3,641 pupils
28 Other, 3,636 pupils
Colleges and Universities
Two-year: 2 campuses; 15,358 students
Baccalaureate and beyond:
Pacific Union College (1,678)
MC Access: San Francisco–Oakland–San Jose, CA
Places Rated Score: 342
Places Rated Rank: 156

✓ **Vancouver, BC**
Public Instruction (91.7%)
553 schools, 236,989 pupils
Private School Options (8.3%)
33 Catholic, 8,138 pupils
78 Other, 13,366 pupils
Colleges and Universities
Community: 9 campuses; 49,763 students
Baccalaureate and beyond:
NW Baptist Theological College (103)
Open Learning Agency (21,000)
Simon Fraser University (15,579)
Trinity Western University (1,351)
University of British Columbia (27,993)
Vancouver School of Theology (102)
Places Rated Score: 1,895
Places Rated Rank: 18

Vancouver, WA
Public K–12 (96.4%)
10 districts, 91 schools
49,667 pupils
Private School Options (3.6%)
2 Catholic, 453 pupils
12 Other, 1,426 pupils
Colleges and Universities
Two-year: 1 campus; 7,470 students
MC Access: Portland–Salem–Vancouver, OR–WA
Places Rated Score: 36
Places Rated Rank: 329

Ventura, CA
Public K–12 (89.7%)
22 districts, 191 schools
115,318 pupils
Private School Options (10.3%)
14 Catholic, 4,876 pupils
56 Other, 8,394 pupils
Colleges and Universities
Two-year: 3 campuses; 30,371 students
Baccalaureate and beyond:
California Lutheran University (2,879)
MC Access: Los Angeles–Riverside–Orange County, CA
Places Rated Score: 623
Places Rated Rank: 95

Victoria, BC
Public Instruction (90.8%)
106 schools, 37,830 pupils
Private School Options (9.2%)
27 Catholic and Other, 3,811 pupils
Colleges and Universities
Community: 2 campuses; 1,612 students
Baccalaureate and beyond:
Camosun College (1,572)
Royal Roads Military College (275)
University of Victoria (13,363)
Places Rated Score: 289
Places Rated Rank: 183

Victoria, TX
Public K–12 (87.8%)
5 districts, 28 schools
15,098 pupils
Private School Options (12.2%)
4 Catholic, 1,499 pupils
6 Other, 591 pupils
Colleges and Universities
Two-year: 1 campus; 3,172 students
Baccalaureate and beyond:
• University of Houston (1,175)
Places Rated Score: 55
Places Rated Rank: 305

Vineland–Millville–Bridgeton, NJ
Public K–12 (89.0%)
17 districts, 56 schools
24,449 pupils
Private School Options (11.0%)
6 Catholic, 1,666 pupils
8 Other, 1,355 pupils
Colleges and Universities
Two-year: 1 campus; 2,415 students
MC Access: Philadelphia–Wilmington–Atlantic City, PA–NJ–DE–MD
Places Rated Score: 213
Places Rated Rank: 212

Visalia–Tulare–Porterville, CA
Public K–12 (97.3%)
51 districts, 145 schools
73,541 pupils
Private School Options (2.7%)

3 Catholic, 676 pupils
11 Other, 1,341 pupils
Colleges and Universities
Two-year: 2 campuses; 10,173 students
Places Rated Score: 102
Places Rated Rank: 268

Waco, TX
Public K–12 (94.0%)
20 districts, 73 schools
35,185 pupils
Private School Options (6.0%)
4 Catholic, 894 pupils
7 Other, 1,351 pupils
Colleges and Universities
Two-year: 2 campuses; 9,492 students
Baccalaureate and beyond:
Baylor University (11,774)
Paul Quinn College (517)
Places Rated Score: 259
Places Rated Rank: 196

✓ **Washington, DC–MD–VA–WV**
Public K–12 (89.7%)
28 districts, 1,088 schools
680,490 pupils
Private School Options (10.3%)
71 Catholic, 22,440 pupils
368 Other, 55,967 pupils
Colleges and Universities
Two-year: 8 campuses; 78,997 students
Baccalaureate and beyond:
American University (11,122)
• Bowie State University (3,748)
Capitol College (723)
Catholic University of America (6,693)
Columbia Union College (1,131)
• Defense Intelligence College (570)
Gallaudet University (2,298)
• George Mason University (19,747)
George Washington University (18,949)
Georgetown University (11,497)
Hood College (1,960)
Howard University (11,222)
• Mary Washington College (3,533)
Marymount University (2,934)
Mount St. Mary's College (1,801)
Mount Vernon College (552)
• Shepherd College (3,597)
Southeastern University (744)
Trinity College (1,123)
• Uniformed Services University of
Health Sciences (793)
• University of Maryland (50,439)
• University of the District of Columbia
(11,869)
MC Access: Washington–Baltimore,
DC–MD–VA–WV
Places Rated Score: 3,764
Places Rated Rank: 6

Waterbury, CT
Public K–12 (84.0%)
9 districts, 67 schools,
32,162 pupils
Private School Options (16.0%)
14 Catholic, 4,849 pupils
8 Other, 1,281 pupils
Colleges and Universities
Two-year: 2 campuses; 5,545 students
Baccalaureate and beyond:
Teikyo Post University (1,883)
Places Rated Score: 81
Places Rated Rank: 282

Waterloo–Cedar Falls, IA
Public K–12 (83.0%)

6 districts, 39 schools
18,440 pupils
Private School Options (17.0%)
9 Catholic, 3,027 pupils
3 Other, 750 pupils
Colleges and Universities
Two-year: 1 campus; 2,052 students
Baccalaureate and beyond:
• University of Northern Iowa (12,509)
Wartburg College (1,456)
Places Rated Score: 271
Places Rated Rank: 192

Wausau, WI
Public K–12 (85.0%)
9 districts, 44 schools
18,441 pupils
Private School Options (15.0%)
13 Catholic, 2,305 pupils
10 Other, 941 pupils
Colleges and Universities
Two-year: 1 campus; 3,809 students
Places Rated Score: 38
Places Rated Rank: 325

West Palm Beach–Boca Raton, FL
Public K–12 (83.3%)
2 districts, 120 schools
108,904 pupils
Private School Options (16.7%)
18 Catholic, 6,309 pupils
70 Other, 15,450 pupils
Colleges and Universities
Two year: 1 campus; 21,191 students
Baccalaureate and beyond:
College of Boca Raton (1,164)
• Florida Atlantic University (11,459)
Palm Beach Atlantic College (1,426)
Places Rated Score: 477
Places Rated Rank: 120

Wheeling, WV–OH
Public K–12 (84.7%)
13 districts, 66 schools
22,915 pupils
Private School Options (15.3%)
16 Catholic, 3,259 pupils
9 Other, 868 pupils
Colleges and Universities
Two-year: 2 campuses; 4,505 students
Baccalaureate and beyond:
• Ohio University (1,117)
• West Liberty State College (2,467)
Wheeling Jesuit College (1,375)
Places Rated Score: 135
Places Rated Rank: 242

Wichita, KS
Public K–12 (90.5%)
29 districts, 213 schools
86,712 pupils
Private School Options (9.5%)
21 Catholic, 6,723 pupils
16 Other, 2,379 pupils
Colleges and Universities
Two-year: 2 campuses; 4,917 students
Baccalaureate and beyond:
Bethel College (609)
Friends University (1,286)
Kansas Newman College (851)
• Wichita State University (16,765)
Places Rated Score: 421
Places Rated Rank: 135

Wichita Falls, TX
Public K–12 (96.4%)
10 districts, 51 schools
23,504 pupils

Private School Options (3.6%)
1 Catholic, 410 pupils
5 Other, 478 pupils
Colleges and Universities
Baccalaureate and beyond:
• Midwestern State University (5,164)
Places Rated Score: 103
Places Rated Rank: 266

Williamsport, PA
Public K–12 (94.4%)
9 districts, 40 schools
19,765 pupils
Private School Options (5.6%)
5 Catholic, 879 pupils
5 Other, 296 pupils
Colleges and Universities
Two-year: 1 campus; 4,114 students
Baccalaureate and beyond:
Lycoming College (1,191)
Places Rated Score: 57
Places Rated Rank: 302

Wilmington, NC
Public K–12 (92.4%)
1 district, 30 schools
18,771 pupils
Private School Options (7.6%)
2 Catholic, 259 pupils
9 Other, 1,293 pupils
Colleges and Universities
Two-year: 1 campus; 2,622 students
Baccalaureate and beyond:
• University of North Carolina (7,525)
Places Rated Score: 177
Places Rated Rank: 224

Wilmington–Newark, DE–MD
Public K–12 (75.3%)
7 districts, 126 schools
70,066 pupils
Private School Options (24.7%)
30 Catholic, 12,909 pupils
56 Other, 10,045 pupils
Colleges and Universities
Two-year: 3 campuses; 8,351 students
Baccalaureate and beyond:
Goldey Beacom College (1,920)
• University of Delaware (20,477)
Widener University (1,130)
Widener University School of Law
(1,528)
Wilmington College (1,698)
MC Access: Philadelphia–Wilmington–
Atlantic City, PA–NJ–DE–MD
Places Rated Score: 682
Places Rated Rank: 87

Windsor, ON
Public Instruction
3 districts, 60 schools
25,057 pupils
Private School Options
61 Catholic, 24,167 pupils
Colleges and Universities
Community: 1 campus; 4,000 students
Baccalaureate and beyond:
University of Windsor (14,871)
MC Access: Detroit–Ann Arbor–Flint,
MI–ON
Places Rated Score: 442
Places Rated Rank: 129

Winnipeg, MB
Public Instruction (92.8%)
10 school divisions, 256 schools
106,476 pupils

Private School Options (7.2%)
  41 Catholic and Other, 8,230 pupils
Colleges and Universities
  Community: 2 campuses; 11,000
    students
  Baccalaureate and beyond:
    Canadian Mennonite Bible College
      (165)
    Canadian Nazarene College (137)
    Mennonite Brethren College of Arts
      (141)
    University of Manitoba (23,826)
    University of Winnipeg (7,050)
Places Rated Score: 737
Places Rated Rank: 78

Worcester–Fitchburg–Leominster, MA
Public K–12 (87.7%)
  65 districts, 251 schools
    101,880 pupils
Private School Options (12.3%)
  29 Catholic, 9,029 pupils
  43 Other, 5,256 pupils
Colleges and Universities
  Two-year: 4 campuses; 9,773 students
  Baccalaureate and beyond:
    Anna Maria College (1,393)
    Assumption College (3,100)
    Clark University (3,353)
    College of the Holy Cross (2,711)
    • Fitchburg State College (6,961)
    Nichols College (1,987)
    • University of Massachusetts Medical
      School (552)
    Worcester Polytechnic (3,970)
    • Worcester State College (5,836)
MC Access: Boston–New Bedford–
  Nashua, MA–NH
Places Rated Score: 696
Places Rated Rank: 84

Yakima, WA
Public K–12 (96.2%)
  16 districts, 76 schools
    40,051 pupils
Private School Options (3.8%)
  2 Catholic, 472 pupils
  12 Other, 1,091 pupils
Colleges and Universities
  Two-year: 1 campus; 3,880 students
  Baccalaureate and beyond:
    Heritage College (540)
Places Rated Score: 46
Places Rated Rank: 316

Yolo, CA
Public K–12 (93.1%)
  7 districts, 50 schools
    21,737 pupils
Private School Options (6.9%)
  4 Catholic, 946 pupils
  4 Other, 676 pupils
Colleges and Universities
  Two-year: 1 campus; 165 students
  Baccalaureate and beyond:
    • University of California (21,388)
MC Access: Sacramento–Yolo, CA
Places Rated Score: 476
Places Rated Rank: 121

York, PA
Public K–12 (93.6%)
  16 districts, 97 schools
    48,426 pupils
Private School Options (6.4%)
  3 Catholic, 851 pupils
  22 Other, 2,444 pupils
Colleges and Universities
  Baccalaureate and beyond:
    Gettysburg College (1,995)
    • Penn State University (1,946)
    York College (4,954)
Places Rated Score: 105
Places Rated Rank: 263

Youngstown–Warren, OH
Public K–12 (90.2%)
  55 districts, 228 schools
    99,820 pupils
Private School Options (9.8%)
  35 Catholic, 9,408 pupils
  9 Other, 1,461 pupils
Colleges and Universities
  Two-year: 3 campuses; 3,262 students
  Baccalaureate and beyond:
    • Youngstown State University (14,864)
Places Rated Score: 330
Places Rated Rank: 160

Yuba City, CA
Public K–12 (95.8%)
  20 districts, 70 schools
    25,763 pupils
Private School Options (4.2%)
  2 Catholic, 354 pupils
  8 Other, 776 pupils
Colleges and Universities
  Two-year: 1 campus; 1,461 students
Places Rated Score: 15
Places Rated Rank: 340

Yuma, AZ
Public K–12 (97.1%)
  11 districts, 34 schools
    23,618 pupils
Private School Options (2.9%)
  2 Catholic, 415 pupils
  4 Other, 290 pupils
Colleges and Universities
  Two-year: 1 campus; 4,661 students
Places Rated Score: 47
Places Rated Rank: 312

Et Cetera

CONTINUING EDUCATION: A GROWING TREND

More and more, education is seen as a lifelong experience rather than one that ends abruptly upon graduation from high school or college. There are reasons for this: Workers in technical industries need retraining, professionals need state of the art courses for recertification, and others pursue personal and vocational interests. Today, there are more than twice as many adults enrolled in part-time education as there are full-time college students.

One measure of the importance of continuing education is the way states have responded to demands that professionals such as dentists, doctors, lawyers, nurses, psychologists and social workers be certified as competent. Mandatory continuing education is found in most states as a condition for renewing a license to practice in many of these professions. Connecticut and New York are the only exceptions.

HIGH SCHOOL DROPOUT RATES

The dropout rate has improved in the United States but has gone up in Canada over the latest five year period. Secondary school in Quebec, for example, begins at Grade 7. For every hundred pupils who start, only 64 leave with a diploma. Of the 36 dropouts, 24 are girls. Worse, by the time they're in their late 20s, few have returned to complete secondary school.

The United States and Canada both report similar causes: not getting along with teachers, lack of interest, getting a full-time job, and pregnancy among girls.

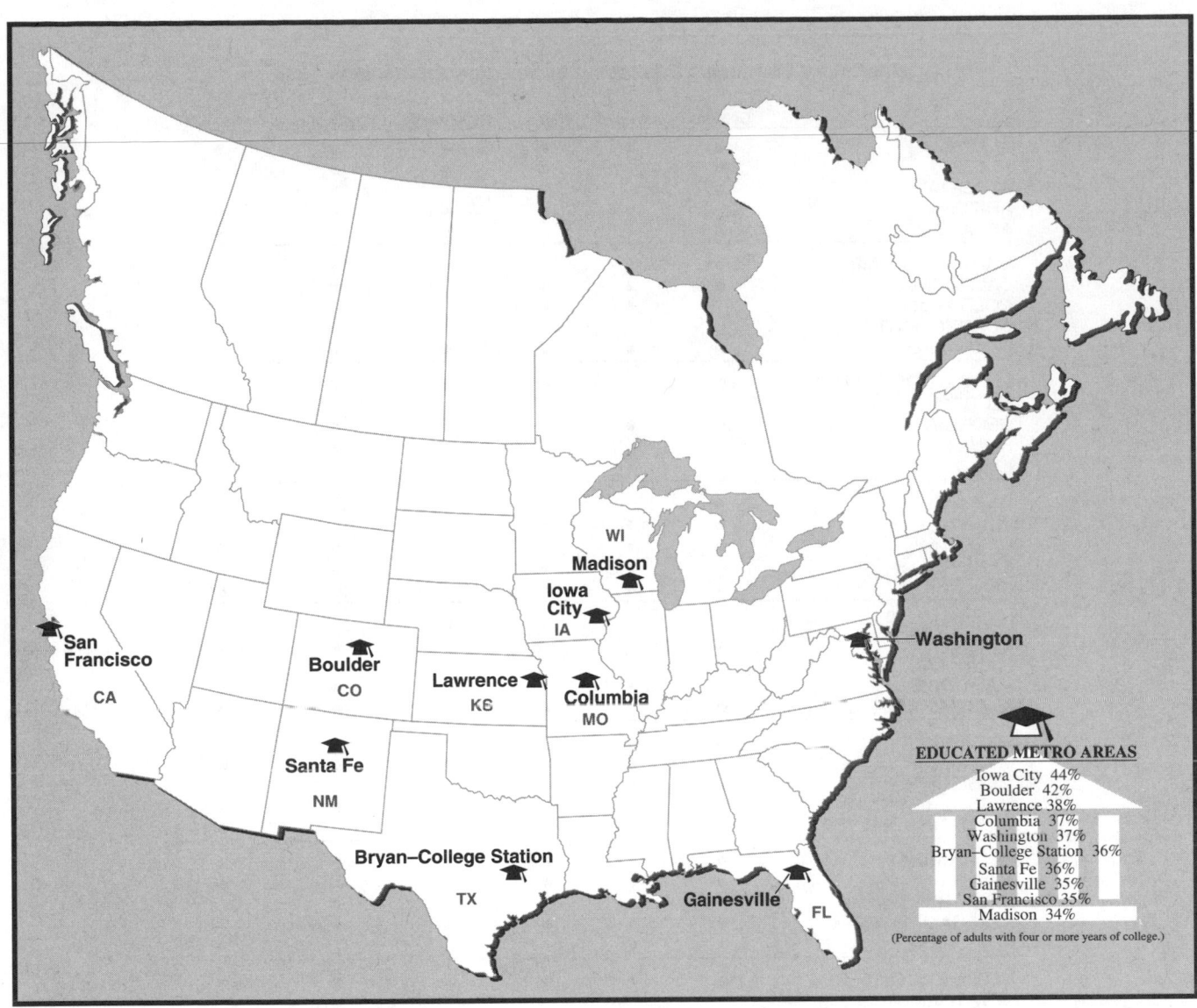

EDUCATED METRO AREAS

Iowa City 44%
Boulder 42%
Lawrence 38%
Columbia 37%
Washington 37%
Bryan–College Station 36%
Santa Fe 36%
Gainesville 35%
San Francisco 35%
Madison 34%

(Percentage of adults with four or more years of college.)

Thomas Nast, Cartographer

SOLVING THE SAT PUZZLE . . . OR TRYING

After 17 years of unbroken decline, the average scores of students on the Scholastic Aptitude Tests (SAT), given by the College Entrance Examination Board, bottomed out in 1980 and started slowly upward in 1982. At the current rate of recovery, however, math scores won't match their 1963 high until the year 2000 and verbal scores not until well into the next century.

Two researchers pointed out that SAT scores started declining 18 years after the 1945 atomic bomb tests and began rising 18 years after the United States suspended all but underground atomic testing in 1963. The steepest drops in scores occurred in states nearest the bomb detonations, especially Nevada and Utah; smaller declines occurred in the northeastern and southeastern states that were far from the proving grounds. According to these researchers, those who blame the drop in SAT scores on television viewing, the Vietnam War, the child-spacing effect, changes in the number and mix of students taking the test, and poorer performance of schools are overlooking the effects of atomic fallout on the cognitive abilities of children.

But in Texas two other scholars of SAT trends have a

Mandatory Continuing Education for Selected Professions 1993

	Dentists	Lawyers	Nurses	Psychology	Physicians	Social Work
ALABAMA	•	•	•	•	•	•
ALASKA	•		•	•	•	•
ALBERTA	•				•	
ARIZONA		•	•	•	•	•
ARKANSAS		•		E	E	•
BRITISH COLUMBIA	•				•	
CALIFORNIA	•	•	•		•	
COLORADO		•	•			
CONNECTICUT						
DELAWARE	•	•	•			•
DISTRICT OF COLUMBIA	•		•	•	•	•
FLORIDA	•	•	•	•	•	•
GEORGIA	•	•		•	•	•
HAWAII					•	
IDAHO		•		•		
ILLINOIS	•					•
INDIANA	•	•				
IOWA	•	•	•	•	•	•
KANSAS	•	•	•	•	•	•
KENTUCKY	•	•	•		E	E
LOUISIANA		•	•	•		•
MAINE	•			•	•	•
MANITOBA	•					
MARYLAND	•	•		•	•	•
MASSACHUSETTS	•		•	•	•	•
MICHIGAN	•	•	E	•	•	
MINNESOTA	•	•	•	E	•	•
MISSISSIPPI		•	•			
MISSOURI		•			•	E
MONTANA		•				•
NEBRASKA	•		•		E	•
NEVADA	•	•	•	•	•	•
NEW BRUNSWICK	•				•	
NEW HAMPSHIRE	•	•	•	•	•	
NEW JERSEY	•	•				•
NEW MEXICO	•	•	•	•	•	•
NEW YORK						
NEWFOUNDLAND	•			E		
NORTH CAROLINA		•		•		•
NORTH DAKOTA	•	•				•
NOVA SCOTIA						
OHIO	•	•	•		•	•
OKLAHOMA	•	•		•		•
ONTARIO					•	
OREGON	•	•	•	•		•
PENNSYLVANIA		•		•		E
PRINCE EDWARD ISLAND						
QUEBEC	•				•	
RHODE ISLAND	•			•	•	
SASKATCHEWAN	•				•	
SOUTH CAROLINA		•		•		•
SOUTH DAKOTA	•					•
TENNESSEE	•	•				
TEXAS		•	•	E		•
UTAH		•		•		
VERMONT		•		•		
VIRGINIA		•				
WASHINGTON		•		•	•	E
WEST VIRGINIA	E	•		•		•
WISCONSIN		•		•	•	•
WYOMING	•	•		E		•

Source: Louis Phillips and Associates, Athens, GA; Places Rated Partnership Survey, 1993
• - continuing education required
E - enabling legislation passed but not implemented.

SAT Scores by State

State	SATs Raw Score	Taking Test
Alabama	991	8%
Alaska	920	41
Arizona	932	26
Arkansas	1005	6
California	897	47
Colorado	959	29
Connecticut	897	81
Delaware	892	61
District of Columbia	840	71
Florida	882	48
Georgia	844	62
Hawaii	883	55
Idaho	968	18
Illinois	1006	16
Indiana	865	57
Iowa	1093	5
Kansas	1039	10
Kentucky	993	11
Louisiana	994	9
Maine	879	64
Maryland	904	64
Massachusetts	896	79
Michigan	980	11
Minnesota	1023	12
Mississippi	997	4
Missouri	1002	12
Montana	982	22
Nebraska	1024	10
Nevada	919	25
New Hampshire	921	75
New Jersey	886	74
New Mexico	996	12
New York	881	75
North Carolina	844	57
North Dakota	1073	6
Ohio	946	22
Oklahoma	997	9
Oregon	922	54
Pennsylvania	876	67
Rhode Island	880	67
South Carolina	832	58
South Dakota	1047	5
Tennessee	1015	12
Texas	874	44
Utah	1031	5
Vermont	890	68
Virginia	890	60
Washington	913	49
West Virginia	926	17
Wisconsin	1023	11
Wyoming	980	13

Source: College Entrance Examination Board, 1993.

North American Drop-Out Rates

State or Province	Rate *
Alabama	12.6%
Alaska	9.6
Alberta	36.8
Arizona	14.3
Arkansas	10.9
British Columbia	35.4
California	14.3
Colorado	9.6
Connecticut	9.2
Delaware	11.2
District of Columbia	19.1
Florida	14.2
Georgia	14.1
Hawaii	7.0
Idaho	9.6
Illinois	10.4
Indiana	11.4
Iowa	6.5
Kansas	8.4
Kentucky	13.0
Louisiana	11.9
Maine	8.4
Manitoba	28.6
Maryland	11.0
Massachusetts	9.5
Michigan	9.9
Minnesota	6.1
Mississippi	11.7
Missouri	11.2
Montana	7.1
Nebraska	6.6
Nevada	14.9
New Brunswick	20.8
New Hampshire	9.9
New Jersey	9.3
New Mexico	10.8
New York	10.1
Newfoundland	30.9
North Carolina	13.2
North Dakota	4.3
Nova Scotia	34.7
Ohio	8.8
Oklahoma	9.9
Ontario	36.3
Oregon	11.0
Pennsylvania	9.4
Quebec	37.1
Rhode Island	12.9
Saskatchewan	23.0
South Carolina	11.9
South Dakota	7.1
Tennessee	13.6
Texas	12.5
Utah	7.9
Vermont	8.7
Virginia	10.4
Washington	10.2
West Virginia	10.6
Wisconsin	6.9
Wyoming	6.3

* U.S. figures are for 1992 and include persons between 16 and 19 who don't go to school and haven't graduated; Canadian figures are for 1989, the latest available, and include people who would be attending any of four years of secondary school but aren't.

Source: U.S. Department of Education, 1992; Statistics Canada, 1992

different theory. The states that have the records of the highest scores, they claim, are not those that spend the most money for education, nor those with a long tradition of quality public education, but those with the coldest winters: Average scores from cold-weather states are consistently higher than scores from warm-weather states. They offer two explanations for the link between cold weather and high SAT scores: (1) research on thermal conditions and human behavior suggests that cool room temperatures reduce mistakes on tests, and 2) long winters force children to remain inside after school and on weekends, thereby favoring family interaction, which is critical for pupil achievement.

Nonsense, another researcher points out. If one were to rank the states by their average total SATS, one would be ranking the states by the percent of college-bound seniors who actually took the test. When the percentage is low, students taking the test are among the highest achievers; more students in the test-taking pool usually means more students of average ability.

CERTIFYING PUPILS . . .

In the late 1970s, parents became convinced that teachers were neglecting the primary subjects, particularly reading, writing, and mathematics. Moreover, it wasn't possible to tell from a report card just how well a child was doing in relation to other children. Students were being promoted from grade to grade regardless of accomplishment. The result: Elementary pupils and even high school graduates who couldn't read a newspaper, write an intelligent sentence, address a postcard, or balance a checkbook.

This concern about students being ill-prepared for adulthood led to a movement among taxpayers for accountability, or the holding of school districts responsible for teaching basic skills. One form of accountability is mandatory competency testing, an exam taken by each pupil to certify whether he or she can actually read, write, and solve mathematical problems.

Forty states employ competency tests mainly to identify students who need "remediation," a term that means tutoring or retaking a course. Twenty-two states, however, use the test to certify pupils for grade promotion in elementary school or for high school graduation.

. . . AND TESTING THE TEACHERS

Pupils in public schools aren't the only ones encountering competency tests. To identify candidates who have neither an aptitude for teaching nor skill in an academic discipline, 20 states require new teachers to take a competency test before they get their first license. Some of these states administer the test before the candidate enters a teacher-training program, while other states test the candidate after the training sequence but before the license is awarded.

That's not the end of teacher accountability. Thirty-nine states require teachers to renew their licenses, or become recertified, by taking continuing education courses. The renewal period is usually every three to five years, though some states allow longer periods based on the candidate's successful teaching experience. Thirty-four of these states will issue no lifetime licenses. Five states—Indiana, Michigan, Rhode Island, Texas, and Washington—have periodic renewal leading to life certificates, which are increasingly being linked to advanced professional training.

Teacher Testing

State	Effective	Test *
Alabama	1981	State
Arizona	1980	State
Arkansas	1983	NTE
California	1982	CBEST
Colorado	1983	CBEST
Connecticut	1985	State
Delaware	1983	PPST
Florida	1980	State
Georgia	1979	State
Hawaii	1986	NTE
Idaho	1988	NTE
Illinois	1988	State
Indiana	1985	NTE
Kentucky	1985	NTE
Louisiana	1979	NTE
Maine	1988	NTE
Maryland	1986	NTE
Mississippi	1977	NTE
Montana	1986	NTE
New Hampshire	1985	NTE
New Jersey	1985	NTE
New Mexico	1983	NTE
New York	1984	NTE
North Carolina	1981	NTE
Ohio	1987	NTE
Oklahoma	1982	State
Oregon	1985	CBEST
Pennsylvania	1987	State
Rhode Island	1986	NTE
South Carolina	1982	NTE
South Dakota	1986	NTE
Tennessee	1981	NTE
Texas	1985	State
Virginia	1981	NTE
West Virginia	1985	State

*Tests administered are either developed by the state or are the National Teach Examination (NTE), the California Basic Education Skills Test (CBEST) or the Pre-Professional Skills Test (PPST).

Source: U.S. Department of Education, *Digest of Education Statistics*, 1992.

High School Courses Required for Graduation

	Tracks	Foreign Language	English	Math	Science	Social Studies	Physical Education	Electives
Alabama	2	2	4	3	3	4	1.5	4
Alaska			4	2	2	3	1	9
Arizona			4	2	2	2.5	1	9.5
Arkansas			4	3	2	3	1	7
California	2	2	3	3	2	3	2	1
Connecticut			4	3	2	3	1	6
Delaware			4	2	2	3	1.5	6.5
District of Columbia		1	4	3	2	3	1	
Florida	2	2	4	2	2	2	1.5	9
Georgia	2	2	4	3	3	3	1	4
Hawaii			4	2	2	4	1.5	6
Idaho			4	2	2	2	1.5	6
Illinois		1	4	2	1	2	4.5	2.25
Indiana	2	3	4	4	4	3	1	4-5
Kansas			4	2	2	3	1	9
Kentucky	2		5	6	6	2	1	7
Louisiana	2	3.5	4	2	2	3	1	4.5
Maine			4	2	2	2	1.5	3.5
Maryland			4	3	2	3	1	5
Minnesota			4	1	1	3	1.5	9.5
Mississippi			4	2	2	2		8
Missouri	2		4	3	3	3	1	8
Montana			4	2	1	1.5	1	10.5
Nevada			4	2	2	2	2.5	8.5
New Hampshire			4	2	2	2.5	1.25	4
New Jersey			4	3	2	3	4	4
New Mexico	2		4	3	2	3	1	9
New York	2		4	2	2	4	0.5	0-2
North Carolina	2	2	4	3	3	3	1	4
North Dakota			4	2	2	3	1	5
Ohio			3	2	1	2	1	9
Oklahoma	2	2	4	3	2	2		4
Oregon		1	3	2	2	3.5	2	8
Pennsylvania			4	3	3	3	1	5
Rhode Island	2	2	4	2	2	3		6
South Carolina			4	3	2	3		7
South Dakota			4	2	2	3.5	2	8
Tennessee	2	2	4	3	3	3	1.5	2
Texas	2	2	4	3	3	2.5	1.5	3
Utah			3	2	2	3	2	9
Vermont			4	3	3	4	1.5	
Virginia	2	3	4	3	3	3	2	4
Washington			3	2	2	2.5	2	5.5
West Virginia			4	2	2	3	2	7
Alberta	2		3	2	2	3	1	10
British Columbia	2		3	2	2	2	1	11
Manitoba	2		5	2	2	2	1	8
New Brunswick	2		4	3	2	2	2	10
Newfoundland			3	2	2	2	2	10
Nova Scotia	2	3	3	1	1	2		8
Ontario	2	4	4	2	2	3	1	14
Prince Edward Island		1	3	2	2	2		8
Quebec	2	3	3	3	2	3	1	
Saskatchewan			6	2	1	2	2	11

Source: Council of Ministers of Education, Canada, *Secondary Education in Canada: A Student Transfer Guide,* 1991; U.S. Department of Education, *Digest of Education Statistics,* 1992.

Compulsory Education

Most laws requiring school attendance until a specified age were passed near the beginning of the century and haven't changed much in the decades since. The span of compulsory attendance ranges from eight years in Mississippi to 13 in Arkansas and Virginia.

From 7 to 16	From 6 to 16	From 7 to 17	From 6 to 18	From 5 to 18
Alabama	Alberta	DC	Hawaii	Arkansas
Alaska	British Columbia	Louisiana	New Mexico	Delaware (5-15)
Arizona (8-16)	California	Maine	Ohio	South Carolina (5-17*)
Colorado	Florida	Nevada	Utah	Virginia
Connecticut	Kentucky	Oklahoma (7-18)	Washington (8-18)	
Georgia	Maryland	Oregon (7-18)	Wisconsin	
Idaho	Massachusetts	Pennsylvania (8-17)		
Illinois	Michigan	Tennessee		
Indiana +	Mississippi (6-14)	Texas		
Iowa	Newfoundland			
Kansas	New Hampshire			
Manitoba	New Jersey			
Minnesota	New York			
Missouri	Nova Scotia			
Montana (or 8th grade)	Ontario			
Nebraska	Quebec			
New Brunswick	Rhode Island			
North Carolina	West Virginia			
North Dakota				
Prince Edward Island				
Saskatchewan				
South Dakota				
Vermont				
Wyoming				

* Parent may waive kindergarten

+ Parent must sign until 18

Source: U.S. Department of Education, *Digest of Education Statistics,* 1992; Statistics Canada, *A Statistical Portrait of Elementary and Secondary Education in Canada,* 1992.

Health Care

America, land of plenty, land of high technology, isn't the world's healthiest nation. We lag behind Canada in life expectancy* and in infant mortality, for instance, while Canada in turn lags behind other developed countries such as Sweden and Japan.

Millions of Americans are uninsured and lack access to the full range of health services they may need. Indeed, almost one-third of all American children aren't covered by any health insurance. In spite of our abundance of physicians and their advanced training and technical support, the basic problem is an unfair distribution of medical care.

WHAT THE NUMBERS SAY

Americans continue to get healthier. Judging by two universal measures of population health, infant mortality and life expectancy, the United States is healthier now than it was just a few years ago. Why are life expectancy and infant mortality such commonly accepted indicators of a nation's health? First, because these data can be found in almost every developed nation in the form of birth and death certificates.

Second, the quality of postpartum and infant care available in a nation (or state or town) generally reflects the quality of other important health services as well. As

for life expectancy, it remains a very broad but meaningful indicator of a nation's ability to provide sanitary food and drinking water, proper immunization and disease screening, and professional medical attention throughout life.

In 1990, infant mortality in America had dropped to its lowest level ever, with data showing 10 deaths per 1,000 live births (compared to 7 per 1,000 live births in Canada). At the same time, life expectancy for children born in 1990 had risen to 75.8 years (77.0 in Canada). This represents an increase of nearly 3 years since 1978, and a gain of 30 years since 1900.

TWO SYSTEMS—INSURANCE, ACCESS, AND THE REST

Unfortunately, not all Americans share equally in these statistical gains, and the inequality contributes to the poor U.S. health ranking compared with other countries. Black/white. Rich/poor. Urban/rural. Insured/uninsured. Profit/nonprofit. Short-term/long-term care. Consumer/provider. These are the poles of a health-care system that is a business enterprise. To get at the real essence of the system, one needs to look at the providers—the doctors and the hospitals.

Physician Classifications

The American Medical Association classifies a physician as a general practitioner, medical specialist, surgeon, or other specialist by 35 specialties in which the physician reports spending the largest number of his or her professional hours.

General Practitioners

General Practice
Family Practice

Medical Specialists

Allergy
Cardiovascular Diseases
Dermatology
Gastroenterology
Internal Medicine
Pediatric Allergy
Pediatric Cardiology
Pediatrics
Pulmonary Diseases

Surgical Specialists

General Surgery
Neurological Surgery
Obstetrics and Gynecology
Ophthalmology
Orthopedic Surgery
Otolaryngology
Plastic Surgery
Colon and Rectal Surgery
Thoracic Surgery
Urology

Other Specialists

Aerospace Medicine
Anesthesiology
Child Psychiatry
Diagnostic Radiology
Forensic Pathology
General Preventive Medicine
Neurology
Occupational Medicine
Pathology
Physical Medicine and Rehabilitation
Psychiatry
Public Health
Radiology
Therapeutic Radiology

PHYSICIANS AND THEIR SPECIALTIES

Not every doctor is listed in the yellow pages. Some are hospital administrators, medical school professors, journalists, lawyers, or researchers for pharmaceutical companies. Others work for government public-health services or Department of Defense service branches. Still others are in residency training or are full-time members of hospital staffs. When it comes to the number of physicians per capita, what really counts is the number of doctors who maintain offices and see patients. It's surprising how many of them don't.

Whether in the United States or in Canada, depending on how office-based or fee-for-service physicians spend their professional hours, they can be classified into three groups:

General Practitioners are physicians who treat diseases and injuries, provide preventive care, give routine checkups, prescribe drugs, and perform some surgery. They also refer patients to medical specialists. General practitioners use all accepted methods of medical care.

Medical Specialists focus on specific medical disciplines, such as cardiology, allergy, gastroenterology, and dermatology. Medical specialists (and general practitioners) are likely to give attention to surgical and nonsurgical approaches to treatment. If they decide that surgery is the method of treatment, they refer their patients to surgeons.

Surgical Specialists operate on a regular basis several times a week. In the United States the letters F.A.C.S. (Fellow of the American College of Surgeons) after the surgeon's name indicate that he or she has passed an evaluation of surgical training and skills as well as ethical fitness.

Where Physicians Cluster—One Measure of Health Care

Where doctors end up practicing is partly determined by sentiment, their perceptions of local quality of life, or both. But mainly it's a matter of economics. The physician has invested three to seven years in graduate medical education and frequently has to start out with a monstrous loan to repay.

Some begin work on a hospital staff, develop a practice, then open an office. Others are taken into someone else's practice as a partner or as one of a group of physicians. Still others buy practices from doctors who are preparing to retire. By whatever means they launch themselves professionally, new physicians who wish to specialize are concerned primarily with a place's population size.

Many physicians want to practice near a major hospital and also want to live in a city large enough to provide them with the amenities their incomes allow. In general, larger, more affluent places—Boston, New York, San Francisco, and Toronto, for example—have a greater proportion of health-care facilities, medical specialists, high-tech equipment, and exotic procedures.

On the other hand, small American metro areas tend to have more general and family practitioners than specialists. The common explanation is that the smaller metro areas don't have enough patients to support a large number of specialists. A doctor who wants to see 30 to 40 patients a day needs to be a generalist.

Another pattern is for expensive, complex procedures to be available only in major metro areas or in areas with medical schools and veterans' hospitals. In Utica, NY, for example, no one performs open-heart surgery. A patient has to go to Syracuse—about 50 miles away—for that. Surgeons, too, tend to cluster in metro areas with medical schools, veterans' hospitals, and ancillary medical centers.

A countertrend in physician clustering is developing, however. Some newly graduated specialists are leaving the big cities, where things are so competitive that they can't find jobs and where it's simply too expensive for them to set up their own practices. They choose, instead, to go to smaller metro areas—often the towns in which they grew up—to establish a practice and to penetrate the existing referral network of doctors.

Another phenomenon north of the border is the active and successful recruitment of Canadian physicians by American headhunters whose seminars detail the intricacies of emigration and setting up a practice in underserved areas in the United States.

HOSPITALS

The word *health* can also mean its opposite, illness. A hospital is not really a health-care institution; its business is to take care of sick people. The truly healthy need little health care except for an occasional shot or checkup; the unhealthy need a lot more.

Not all hospitals handle typical illnesses and emergencies. Many of them exclusively treat chronic diseases or alcohol and drug addiction, or they may be burn centers, psychiatric hospitals, or rehabilitation hospitals. When rating a metro area for its health care, *Places Rated* counts only general hospitals accredited for acute care by the Joint Commission on Accreditation of Hospitals (JCAH) or, in Canada, similar institutions certified by the Canadian Council for Health Facilities Accreditation (CCHFA).

The number of accredited acute-care hospitals and their inpatient beds varies among places. Although the number of hospital beds isn't as valuable an indicator as it was before advances in medicine and pharmacology shortened a hospital stay, it is still a reliable gauge of relative health-care supply.

Hospital Services

Each year, the American Hospital Association (AHA) surveys its thousands of member hospitals, enumerating which of 80 AHA-defined services each institution provides. The number of services a hospital offers is one index of the level of care you may receive there and certainly of the level of technology and specialization in that hospital.

Some of the AHA-defined services (a postoperative recovery room, a blood bank, an intensive-care unit, for example) are basic. Others (a radioactive implant department, a department that provides X-ray radiation therapy, a histopathology laboratory, or a department with organ transplant capabilities), however, are highly specialized. Of course, it really depends on one's situation; if a woman is of child-bearing years, access to genetic counseling services, an obstetrics unit, a neonatal intensive-care unit, and a pediatric inpatient unit may be extremely important.

Quality Care—What's a Consumer to Do?

Many hospitals, pressured by public and private cost-containment efforts, have had to slash services and staff. At the same time, hospitals remain critically short of

Hospital Services

The American Hospital Association (AHA) classifies
hospital services into 80 categories.

General inpatient care for AIDS/ARC
AIDS/ARC unit
Specialized outpatient program for AIDS/ARC
Alcohol/drug abuse or dependency inpatient unit
Alcohol/drug abuse or dependency outpatient unit
Arthritis treatment center
Birthing room/LDRP room
Burn-care unit
Cardiac catheterization laboratory
Open-heart surgery
Cardiac intensive-care unit
Angioplasty
Chronic obstructive pulmonary disease services
Emergency department
Trauma center (certified)
Extracorporeal shock wave lithotripter
Fitness center
Genetic counseling/screening services
Adult day-care program
Alzheimer's diagnostic/assessment services
Comprehensive geriatric assessment
Emergency response (geriatric)
Geriatric acute-care unit
Geriatric clinics
Respite care
Senior membership program
Patient education
Community health promotion
Worksite health promotion
Hemodialysis
Home health services
Hospice
Medical surgical or other intensive-care unit
Histopathology laboratory
Blood bank
Neonatal intensive-care unit
Obstetrics unit
Occupational health services
Organized outpatient services
Pediatric acute inpatient unit

Psychiatric child/adolescent services
Psychiatric consultation/liaison services
Psychiatric education services
Psychiatric emergency services
Psychiatric geriatric services
Psychiatric inpatient services
Psychiatric outpatient services
Psychiatric partial hospitalization program
Megavoltage radiation therapy
Radioactive implants
Therapeutic radioisotope facility
X-ray radiation therapy
CT scanner
Diagnostic radioisotope facility
Magnetic resonance imaging
Ultrasound
Rehabilitation inpatient unit
Rehabilitation outpatient services
Reproductive health services
Skilled nursing or other long-term-care facility
Single photon emission computerized tomography (SPECT)
Organized social work services
Outpatient social work services
Emergency department social work services
Sports medicine clinic/services
Patient representative services
Volunteer services department
Outpatient surgery services
Organ/tissue transplant
Orthopedic surgery
Occupational therapy services
Physical therapy services
Recreational therapy services
Respiratory therapy services
Speech therapy services
Women's health center/services
Health sciences library
Cardiac rehabilitation program
Noninvasive cardiac assessment services

Source: American Hospital Association, *Guide to the Health Care Field*, 1993.

---

qualified nurses. No wonder the quality of care is such a concern today. Since it's just about impossible to measure quality of care in any statistical way, how do we judge the skills of a doctor or hospital? Accreditation, with certain caveats, is one way.

Hospital Accreditation

JCAH is the private nonprofit body that investigates and certifies hospitals. The JCAH certification determines which hospitals are eligible for federal funds or state licensure. The commission came under question recently, however, when federal investigations found that 156 JCAH-accredited hospitals in 30 states had serious deficiencies in at least one area of operation. Texas, the state with the most hospitals on this list, had 50 hospitals that were accredited but were found to be deficient in some area by federal standards. At least two hospitals in New York continued to operate under the JCAH-accredited

designation for two years after the JCAH had investigated them and found them deficient.

Since JCAH assessments have been kept confidential, consumers have no way of knowing how to interpret this discrepancy between JCAH findings and those of federal investigators. In other words, a patient could only find out whether or not a hospital was accredited—a questionable indicator of quality, considering the extent of deficiencies found over the past few years.

However, starting in 1989, the JCAH has made public the names of hospitals that provide "risky" or marginal care—400 hospitals, by some estimates. Such hospitals will in the future be given a probationary or conditional accreditation, an indication to patients or physicians that serious problems were found. Although stopping short of making actual inspection reports public, the new JCAH rating will give consumers somewhat more to go on.

A hospital has incentives to qualify for accreditation. It makes it easier to recruit doctors and operate residency programs, and it reduces malpractice liability. Now that accreditation status is becoming a more public matter, it may also become a useful tool for attracting patients—the consumers of health care.

SCORING: HEALTH CARE

What is being judged in this chapter is health care in each metro area, not how sick the resident population is. Moreover, *Places Rated* doesn't assess the quality of health care but its supply. As for the expense of health care to the consumer, see the Costs of Living chapter.

Keeping these distinctions in mind will help the reader avoid assuming that a low score in this chapter means either (1) that the people in a given place are unhealthy and don't live very long, or (2) that if one were to relocate to this place, basic health care—including even such complex emergency surgery as a coronary bypass—would be unavailable or inferior. *Both of these conclusions are incorrect.* A low score or rank in this chapter does indicate, however, that the emphasis in that metro area is probably on basic health care and that the latest techniques and equipment, and personnel trained to implement them, are more likely to be found elsewhere.

Affluent, big-city metro areas generally score higher in the rankings than the smaller, poorer metro areas. This doesn't mean that a person cannot receive excellent medical care in a rural clinic or, conversely, experience medical care that is bad enough to be life-threatening in even the finest of big-city hospitals. The quality of medical and nursing care most people receive depends on a number of factors, including the patient's ability to pay, blind chance, and human error.

Each metro area starts with a base score of zero, to which points are added according to the following criteria:

In the Office-Based (in Canada, Fee-for-Service) Physicians category, access to the major professional groups of physicians is given a rating of AA, A, B, or C (AA indicating the best access and C the least) as follows:

1. *General/Family Practitioners.*

A metro area gets a rating of:	if, for every 100,000 people, General Practitioners number:
AA	50 or more
A	between 40 and 49
B	between 30 and 39
C	fewer than 30

2. *Medical Specialists.*

A metro area gets a rating of:	if, for every 100,000 people, Medical Specialists number:
AA	55 or more
A	between 42 and 54
B	between 32 and 41
C	fewer than 32

3. *Surgical Specialists.*

A metro area gets a rating of:	if, for every 100,000 people, Surgical Specialists number:
AA	47 or more
A	40 to 46
B	33 to 39
C	fewer than 33

Metro areas are awarded one point for each physician per 100,000 people, regardless of the access rating. Asheville, NC, for instance, has 65 general practitioners, 99 medical specialists, and 54 surgeons, good for 218 points.

As stated earlier, just as not all MDs see patients, not all hospitals handle typical illnesses and emergencies. In the Short-Term General Hospitals category, *Places Rated* counts only hospitals classified by the AHA or the CHA as acute-care facilities whose patients stay fewer than 30 days.

1. Accredited General Hospital Beds. In U.S. metro areas, 91 percent of short-term general hospitals are accredited by the JCAH. In Canadian metro areas, 94 percent are accredited by the CCHFA. While the lack of accreditation doesn't necessarily mean a facility is substandard, the presence of such accreditation means the hospital has passed rigorous and periodic reviews.

While the number of hospital beds is dropping throughout North America because of cost-containment policies and the shift to outpatient services, it still is an indicator of health-care supply. Accordingly, 1 point for each accredited general hospital bed per 10,000 population is added to a metro area's score.

2. Physician Residency Programs. One-third of short-term general hospitals in the United States and half of Canada's general hospitals have approved physician training programs. Hospitals with no teaching programs aren't necessarily lagging in quality, but facilities with such programs tend to be larger urban institutions where the interaction between students and faculty encourages the development and use of the latest techniques, equipment, and therapy. Accordingly, each metro area hospital with approved residency programs earns 10 points.

3. MC Access. Each of the 75 metro areas that is part of a Metropolitan Complex (MC) is eligible for bonus points based on shared hospitals with physician teaching programs. A place gets a bonus of 10 percent of the points accumulated by adjacent places in the MC for these shared amenities.

SCORING EXAMPLE

A midcontinent metro area with a medium-size population and a middling health-care ranking illustrates the scoring method.

Peoria–Pekin, IL (#156)

Aside from keeping people well, there is one more reason why health care is important in this tri-county area in downstate Illinois: It employs nearly one out of five people. If the United States were to move to a Canadian-style system with fewer but fuller hospitals, the area stands to lose many jobs.

All five hospitals here are accredited by the JCAH and four offer an extensive menu of services. The two hospitals that train doctors—St. Francis and Methodist —crowd Peoria's skyline on both sides of I-74. "If you're going to have a heart attack, this is the communi- ty to have it in," says Dr. James Ward, president of Peoria's Medical Society. Most physicians specialize, but the number who are in general or family practice is outstanding.

The 157 physicians per 100,000 people here are good for 157 points. Add to that number the 46 accredited hospital beds per 10,000 people, plus 20 points for St. Francis's and Methodist's residency programs, and the total score is 223.

Rankings: Health Care

Five criteria are used to rate the supply of health care in a metro area: (1) general/family practitioners per 100,000 population, (2) medical specialists per 100,000 popula- tion, (3) surgical specialists per 100,000 population, (4) short-term, general hospital beds per 10,000 population, and (5) hospitals approved for physician residency pro- grams by the AMA or Association of Canadian Teaching Hospitals. Metro areas that are part of Metropolitan Complexes (MCs) also earn bonus points for teaching hospitals shared within the MC. Places that receive tie scores get the same rank and are listed alphabetically.

Metro Areas from Best to Worst

Places Rated Rank	Places Rated Score	Places Rated Rank	Places Rated Score	Places Rated Rank	Places Rated Score
1. Rochester, MN	880	31. Birmingham, AL	319	61. Hamilton, ON	286
2. New York, NY	819	32. Ann Arbor, MI	318	62. Indianapolis, IN	284
3. Philadelphia, PA–NJ	557	32. La Crosse, WI–MN	318	63. Houston, TX	283
4. Chicago, IL	554	34. Cleveland–Lorain–Elyria, OH	317	64. Richmond–Petersburg, VA	282
5. Iowa City, IA	518	35. Central New Jersey, NJ	316	64. Springfield, IL	282
6. Los Angeles–Long Beach, CA	494	35. New Orleans, LA	316	66. Cincinnati, OH–KY–IN	281
7. Boston, MA	477	35. Stamford–Norwalk, CT	316	66. Orange County, CA	281
8. San Francisco, CA	463	38. Little Rock–North Little Rock, AR	315	66. San Diego, CA	281
9. Newark–Jersey City, NJ	458	38. Madison, WI	315	66. Winnipeg, MB	281
10. Washington, DC–MD–VA–WV	428	38. Miami, FL	315	70. Bismarck, ND	280
11. Long Island, NY	427	41. Portland, OR	314	71. Nashville, TN	279
12. Columbia, MO	419	41. Pittsburgh, PA	314	72. Danbury, CT	278
13. Montreal, PQ	406	43. Baltimore, MD	313	73. Portland, ME	277
14. Charlottesville, VA	399	43. Denver, CO	313	74. Calgary, AB	276
15. Halifax, NS	398	45. Omaha, NE–IA	311	74. Fargo–Moorhead, ND–MN	276
16. Vancouver, BC	390	46. Kansas City, MO–KS	310	74. Toledo, OH	276
17. St. John's NF	388	46. Sherbrooke, PQ	310	74. Tucson, AZ	276
18. Gainesville, FL	382	48. Edmonton, AB	309	78. Burlington, VT	275
19. Quebec City, PQ	375	48. Greenville, NC	309	78. Dayton–Springfield, OH	275
20. London, ON	362	50. Milwaukee–Waukesha, WI	308	80. Louisville, KY–IN	274
21. Toronto, ON	350	51. Jackson, MS	307	80. Shreveport–Bossier City, LA	274
22. Saskatoon, SK	348	52. Bridgeport, CT	306	80. Spokane, WA	274
23. Ottawa–Hull, ON–PQ	337	53. New Haven–Meriden, CT	302	83. Memphis, TN–AR–MS	273
23. Sioux Falls, SD	337	54. Asheville, NC	298	83. Regina, SK	273
25. Detroit, MI	334	55. Minneapolis–St. Paul, MN–WI	297	85. Alexandria, LA	266
25. Lexington, KY	334	56. Oakland, CA	295	85. San Antonio, TX	266
27. Northern New Jersey, NJ	332	57. Lubbock, TX	294	87. Albuquerque, NM	265
28. Raleigh–Durham–Chapel Hill, NC	329	58. Victoria, BC	289	87. Honolulu, HI	265
29. Roanoke, VA	321	59. Augusta–Aiken, GA–SC	288	89. Scranton–Wilkes-Barre–Hazleton, PA	264
30. Seattle–Bellevue–Everett, WA	320	60. Trenton, NJ	287	89. Worcester–Fitchburg–Leominster, MA	264

Places Rated Rank	Places Rated Score
91. Amarillo, TX	263
91. St. Louis, MO–IL	263
93. Atlanta, GA	261
93. Buffalo–Niagara Falls, NY	261
93. Hartford, CT	261
96. Eau Claire, WI	260
96. Galveston–Texas City, TX	260
96. Great Falls, MT	260
99. Victoria, TX	259
100. Oklahoma City, OK	258
101. San Jose, CA	257
102. Pittsfield, MA	256
103. Albany–Schenectady–Troy, NY	255
103. Charleston–North Charleston, SC	255
103. Cheyenne, WY	255
106. Phoenix–Mesa, AZ	253
107. Charleston, WV	251
107. Reno, NV	251
109. Billings, MT	250
110. Duluth–Superior, MN–WI	249
110. Evansville–Henderson, IN–KY	249
110. Johnson City–Kingsport–Bristol, TN–VA	249
110. Wichita, KS	249
114. Tyler, TX	248
115. Monmouth–Ocean, NJ	246
116. Springfield, MO	245
117. Wilmington, NC	244
118. Tampa–St. Petersburg–Clearwater, FL	243
118. Wheeling, WV–OH	243
120. Champaign–Urbana, IL	241
120. Killeen–Temple, TX	241
120. Salt Lake City–Ogden, UT	241
120. Wilmington–Newark, DE–MD	241
124. Pueblo, CO	240
125. Des Moines, IA	239
125. Santa Fe, NM	239
127. Lincoln, NE	238
128. Trois-Rivieres, PQ	237
128. Topeka, KS	237
130. Santa Rosa, CA	236
130. Columbus, OH	236
130. Enid, OK	236
130. Saint John, NB	236
134. Allentown–Bethlehem–Easton, PA–NJ	235
134. Rochester, NY	235
136. Dallas, TX	234
136. Santa Barbara–Santa Maria–Lompoc, CA	234
136. Williamsport, PA	234
139. Lake County, IL	233
139. Syracuse, NY	233
141. Gary, IN	232
141. Grand Forks, ND–MN	232
141. Waterloo–Cedar Falls, IA	232
144. Fort Lauderdale, FL	231
144. Providence–Warwick–Cranston, RI	231
146. Fort Smith, AR–OK	230
146. Riverside–San Bernardino, CA	230
148. Harrisburg–Lebanon–Carlisle, PA	227
149. Elmira, NY	226
150. Sioux City, IA–NE	225
150. Waterbury, CT	225
152. Jacksonville, FL	224
152. Manchester–Nashua, NH	224
152. Monroe, LA	224
155. Florence, SC	223
155. Knoxville, TN	223
155. Peoria–Pekin, IL	223
158. Akron, OH	222
158. Boulder–Longmont, CO	222
158. Columbia, SC	222
158. Rapid City, SD	222
158. Rockford, IL	222
163. Wichita Falls, TX	221
164. Lewiston–Auburn, ME	220
165. Erie, PA	218
165. Huntington–Ashland, WV–KY–OH	218
167. Bangor, ME	217
168. Cedar Rapids, IA	216
169. Sarasota–Bradenton, FL	215
170. Biloxi–Gulfport–Pascagoula, MS	214
170. Pensacola, FL	214
172. Fort Wayne, IN	213
173. Dutchess County, NY	212
173. Thunder Bay, ON	212
173. West Palm Beach–Boca Raton, FL	212
176. Kankakee, IL	211
176. Saginaw–Bay City–Midland, MI	211
176. Tacoma, WA	211
176. Texarkana, TX–Texarkana, AR	211
176. Tulsa, OK	211
181. Chicoutimi–Jonquiere, PQ	210
181. Sacramento, CA	210
183. Montgomery, AL	209
183. Vallejo–Fairfield–Napa, CA	209
185. Dubuque, IA	208
186. Olympia, WA	207
186. Pine Bluff, AR	207
186. Ventura, CA	207
189. Santa Cruz–Watsonville, CA	206
190. Casper, WY	205
190. Chattanooga, TN–GA	205
190. Kalamazoo–Battle Creek, MI	205
190. Lake Charles, LA	205
190. South Bend, IN	205
195. Boise City, ID	204
195. Decatur, IL	204
195. Flint, MI	204
195. Orange County, NY	204
195. Redding, CA	204
195. Sherman–Denison, TX	204
195. Windsor, ON	204
202. Medford–Ashland, OR	203
203. Savannah, GA	202
204. Altoona, PA	201
204. Tallahassee, FL	201
206. Appleton–Oshkosh–Neenah, WI	200
207. Columbus, GA–AL	199
207. Eugene–Springfield, OR	199
207. Greensboro–Winston-Salem–High Point, NC	199
210. Cumberland, MD–WV	198
211. Chico–Paradise, CA	197
211. Corpus Christi, TX	197
213. Baton Rouge, LA	196
213. Dothan, AL	196
213. Fort Collins–Loveland, CO	196
216. San Angelo, TX	195
217. Fayetteville–Springdale–Rogers, AR	194
218. Macon, GA	193
218. Mobile, AL	193
218. Muncie, IN	193
218. Vineland–Millville–Bridgeton, NJ	193
222. Atlantic City–Cape May, NJ	192
222. Owensboro, KY	192
224. Greenville–Spartanburg–Anderson, SC	191
224. San Luis Obispo–Atascadero–Paso Robles, CA	191
224. St. Cloud, MN	191
224. Tuscaloosa, AL	191
228. Beaumont–Port Arthur, TX	190
229. Florence, AL	189
229. Lansing–East Lansing, MI	189
229. Reading, PA	189
232. Davenport–Moline–Rock Island, IA–IL	187
233. Grand Rapids–Muskegon–Holland, MI	186
233. Orlando, FL	186
233. St. Joseph, MO	186
233. Yolo, CA	186
237. Albany, GA	185
237. Binghamton, NY	185
237. Springfield, MA	185
237. Waco, TX	185
241. Canton–Massillon, OH	183
242. Youngstown–Warren, OH	182
243. Barnstable–Yarmouth, MA	181
243. Lynchburg, VA	181
245. Terre Haute, IN	180
246. Athens, GA	179
246. Naples, FL	179
248. Gadsden, AL	177
248. Glens Falls, NY	177
250. Fort Worth–Arlington, TX	176
250. Johnstown, PA	176
250. Modesto, CA	176
250. New London–Norwich, CT–RI	176
254. Punta Gorda, FL	175
255. Abilene, TX	174

Places Rated Rank	Places Rated Score	Places Rated Rank	Places Rated Score	Places Rated Rank	Places Rated Score
255. Bellingham, WA	174	284. Fort Myers–Cape Coral, FL	160	316. Richland–Kennewick–Pasco, WA	143
255. St. Catharines–Niagara, ON	174	284. Kenosha, WI	160	318. Las Vegas, NV–AZ	138
258. Colorado Springs, CO	173	284. Panama City, FL	160	319. Mansfield, OH	137
258. Green Bay, WI	173	289. Janesville–Beloit, WI	159	320. Hamilton–Middletown, OH	136
258. Huntsville, AL	173	290. Daytona Beach, FL	158		
				320. New Bedford–Fall River– Attleboro, MA	136
258. Lafayette, IN	173	291. Joplin, MO	157	320. Rocky Mount, NC	136
258. Lancaster, PA	173	291. Salem, OR	157	323. Las Cruces, NM	134
263. Salinas, CA	171	293. Fort Walton Beach, FL	156	324. Lawrence, KS	132
263. Sharon, PA	171	294. Hickory–Morgantown, NC	154	324. Steubenville–Weirton, OH–WV	132
263. Wausau, WI	171	295. Lawton, OK	153		
				326. Houma, LA	130
266. Portsmouth–Dover–Rochester, NH	170	296. Danville, VA	152	327. Bakersfield, CA	128
267. Lafayette, LA	169	296. Elkhart–Goshen, IN	152	328. Ocala, FL	127
268. Austin–San Marcos, TX	168	296. Hagerstown, MD	152	329. Vancouver, WA	126
268. Fresno, CA	168	296. Lakeland–Winter Haven, FL	152	330. Visalia–Tulare–Porterville, CA	125
270. Greeley, CO	167	296. York, PA	152		
				331. Merced, CA	123
270. Sudbury, ON	167	301. Myrtle Beach, SC	151	332. Provo–Orem, UT	122
272. Lima, OH	166	302. Yuba City, CA	150	333. Brownsville–Harlingen–San Benito, TX	119
272. Norfolk–Virginia Beach– Newport News, VA–NC	166	303. Melbourne–Titusville–Palm Bay, FL	149	333. Jackson, MI	119
274. Bloomington–Normal, IL	165	303. Stockton–Lodi, CA	149	333. Yuma, AZ	119
274. Kitchener, ON	165	305. Fayetteville, NC	148		
				336. Goldsboro, NC	115
274. Racine, WI	165	305. Fort Pierce–Port St. Lucie, FL	148	337. Clarksville–Hopkinsville, TN–KY	109
277. Anniston, AL	164	305. Sheboygan, WI	148	337. McAllen–Edinburg–Mission, TX	109
278. Benton Harbor, MI	163	308. Anchorage, AK	147		
278. Charlotte–Gastonia–Rock Hill, NC–SC	163	309. Bryan–College Station, TX	145	339. Sumter, SC	105
280. Bloomington, IN	162	309. Oshawa, ON	145	340. Dover, DE	103
		309. State College, PA	145		
280. Utica–Rome, NY	162	312. Jamestown, NY	144	341. Laredo, TX	96
282. Kokomo, IN	161	312. Odessa–Midland, TX	144	342. Brazoria, TX	92
282. Parkersburg–Marietta, WV–OH	161	312. Yakima, WA	144	343. Jacksonville, NC	76
284. Bremerton, WA	160	316. Decatur, AL	143		
284. El Paso, TX	160	316. Longview–Marshall, TX	143		

Place Profiles: Health Care

In the following pages, selected health-care assets for the 343 metro areas are detailed.

Under the heading **Office-Based Physicians** (In Canada, **Fee-for-Service Physicians**) are groupings by professional activity of local doctors who maintain offices and treat patients.

U.S. metro-area figures for Medical Specialists are totals for AMA "Medical Specialists" and for AMA "Other Specialists," but do not include diagnostic radiologists, forensic pathologists, pathologists, radiologists, and radiologic oncologists, to ensure comparability with Canadian figures.

The access rating for each professional group (AA, A, B, or C) is shown in the right-hand column. Anchorage figures are imputed from Alaska totals; Sherbrooke figures are imputed from Quebec totals. For five New England metro areas, no figures are available; in these cases, summary figures for their surrounding counties are used in place of cities and towns.

To the right of the heading **Short-Term General**

Hospitals is the number of acute-care hospitals and their total number of beds. Under this heading are the number of facilities accredited by the JCAH or the CCHFA, the number approved for physician residency training by the AMA, and, except for Canadian metro areas, the number grouped by range of services offered. A single star (∗) indicates 1–4 services, two stars (∗∗) indicate 5–14 services, three stars (∗∗∗) mean 15–24 services, and four stars (∗∗∗∗) indicate 25 or more services.

The information is derived from these sources: American Hospital Association, *Guide to the Health Care Field*, 1993; Canadian Hospital Association, *Canadian Hospital Directory*, 1993; Health and Welfare Canada, Health Information Division, National Physician Database, 1993; and U.S. Department of Health and Human Services, Bureau of Health-Care Professions, Area Resource File, September 1992.

A check (✔) in front of a metro area's name highlights it as one of the top 35 places for health care.

Rating

Rating

Abilene, TX
Office-Based Physicians
General/Family Practitioners: 53   A
Medical Specialists: 75   A
Surgical Specialists: 56   A
Short-Term General Hospitals: 3 (491 beds)
Services: 1 ★, 2 ★★★★
JCAH Accredited: 2
Places Rated Score: 174   Places Rated Rank: 255

Akron, OH
Office-Based Physicians
General/Family Practitioners: 233   B
Medical Specialists: 381   B
Surgical Specialists: 243   B
Short-Term General Hospitals: 6 (2,105 beds)
Services: 6 ★★★★
JCAH Accredited: 5
AMA Residency: 5
MC Access: Cleveland–Akron, OH
Places Rated Score: 222   Places Rated Rank: 158

Albany, GA
Office-Based Physicians
General/Family Practitioners: 22   C
Medical Specialists: 70   A
Surgical Specialists: 53   A
Short-Term General Hospitals: 2 (638 beds)
Services: 2 ★★★★
JCAH Accredited: 2
Places Rated Score: 185   Places Rated Rank: 237

Albany–Schenectady–Troy, NY
Office-Based Physicians
General/Family Practitioners: 277   B
Medical Specialists: 738   AA
Surgical Specialists: 403   A
Short-Term General Hospitals: 14 (3,571 beds)
Services: 1 ★★, 2 ★★★, 11 ★★★★
JCAH Accredited: 14
AMA Residency: 5
Places Rated Score: 255   Places Rated Rank: 103

Albuquerque, NM
Office-Based Physicians
General/Family Practitioners: 261   A
Medical Specialists: 541   AA
Surgical Specialists: 295   A
Short-Term General Hospitals: 13 (2,339 beds)
Services: 2 ★★, 3 ★★★, 8 ★★★★
JCAH Accredited: 11
AMA Residency: 5
Places Rated Score: 265   Places Rated Rank: 87

Alexandria, LA
Office-Based Physicians
General/Family Practitioners: 42   B
Medical Specialists: 84   A
Surgical Specialists: 74   A
Short-Term General Hospitals: 5 (1,247 beds)
Services: 2 ★★★, 3 ★★★★
JCAH Accredited: 3
AMA Residency: 2
Places Rated Score: 266   Places Rated Rank: 85

Allentown–Bethlehem–Easton, PA–NJ
Office-Based Physicians
General/Family Practitioners: 272   B
Medical Specialists: 427   A
Surgical Specialists: 311   A
Short-Term General Hospitals: 10 (2,650 beds)
Services: 1 ★★★, 9 ★★★★
JCAH Accredited: 9
AMA Residency: 5
Places Rated Score: 235   Places Rated Rank: 134

Altoona, PA
Office-Based Physicians
General/Family Practitioners: 61   A
Medical Specialists: 71   B
Surgical Specialists: 43   C
Short-Term General Hospitals: 5 (741 beds)
Services: 3 ★★★, 2 ★★★★
JCAH Accredited: 5
AMA Residency: 1
Places Rated Score: 201   Places Rated Rank: 204

Amarillo, TX
Office-Based Physicians
General/Family Practitioners: 67   B
Medical Specialists: 132   A
Surgical Specialists: 97   AA
Short-Term General Hospitals: 6 (1,233 beds)
Services: 2 ★★★, 4 ★★★★
JCAH Accredited: 5
AMA Residency: 4
Places Rated Score: 263   Places Rated Rank: 91

Anchorage, AK
Office-Based Physicians
General/Family Practitioners: 130   AA
Medical Specialists: 76   C
Surgical Specialists: 75   C
Short-Term General Hospitals: 4 (760 beds)
Services: 1 ★★★, 3 ★★★★
JCAH Accredited: 3
Places Rated Score: 147   Places Rated Rank: 308

✓ Ann Arbor, MI
Office-Based Physicians
General/Family Practitioners: 167   B
Medical Specialists: 631   AA
Surgical Specialists: 233   A
Short-Term General Hospitals: 11 (2,513 beds)
Services: 1 ★★, 1 ★★★, 9 ★★★★
JCAH Accredited: 11
AMA Residency: 4
MC Access: Detroit–Ann Arbor–Flint, MI
Places Rated Score: 318   Places Rated Rank: 32

Anniston, AL
Office-Based Physicians
General/Family Practitioners: 41   B
Medical Specialists: 40   C
Surgical Specialists: 39   C
Short-Term General Hospitals: 5 (584 beds)
Services: 1 ★, 2 ★★, 1 ★★★, 1 ★★★★
JCAH Accredited: 3
AMA Residency: 1
Places Rated Score: 164   Places Rated Rank: 277

Appleton–Oshkosh–Neenah, WI
Office-Based Physicians
General/Family Practitioners: 151   A
Medical Specialists: 166   B
Surgical Specialists: 109   C
Short-Term General Hospitals: 7 (1,117 beds)
Services: 1 ★★★, 6 ★★★★
JCAH Accredited: 6
AMA Residency: 3
Places Rated Score: 200   Places Rated Rank: 206

Asheville, NC
Office-Based Physicians
General/Family Practitioners: 125   AA
Medical Specialists: 191   AA
Surgical Specialists: 104   AA
Short-Term General Hospitals: 3 (1,167 beds)
Services: 3 ★★★★
JCAH Accredited: 3
AMA Residency: 2
Places Rated Score: 298   Places Rated Rank: 54

Rating   Rating

Athens, GA
Office-Based Physicians
General/Family Practitioners: 42   B
Medical Specialists: 76   A
Surgical Specialists: 61   A
Short-Term General Hospitals: 2 (485 beds)
Services: 2 ★★★★
JCAH Accredited: 2
Places Rated Score: 179   Places Rated Rank: 246

Atlanta, GA
Office-Based Physicians
General/Family Practitioners: 698   B
Medical Specialists: 2,507   AA
Surgical Specialists: 1,428   A
Short-Term General Hospitals: 44 (10,968 beds)
Services: 5 ★, 3 ★★, 11 ★★★, 25 ★★★★
JCAH Accredited: 41
AMA Residency: 8
Places Rated Score: 261   Places Rated Rank: 93

Atlantic City-Cape May, NJ
Office-Based Physicians
General/Family Practitioners: 66   C
Medical Specialists: 178   B
Surgical Specialists: 121   B
Short-Term General Hospitals: 4 (1,113 beds)
Services: 2 ★★★, 2 ★★★★
JCAH Accredited: 4
AMA Residency: 1
MC Access: Philadelphia-Wilmington-Atlantic City,
PA-NJ-DE-MD
Places Rated Score: 192   Places Rated Rank: 222

Augusta-Aiken, GA-SC
Office-Based Physicians
General/Family Practitioners: 110   C
Medical Specialists: 333   AA
Surgical Specialists: 204   AA
Short-Term General Hospitals: 8 (3,454 beds)
Services: 1 ★★★, 7 ★★★★
JCAH Accredited: 8
AMA Residency: 4
Places Rated Score: 288   Places Rated Rank: 59

Austin-San Marcos, TX
Office-Based Physicians
General/Family Practitioners: 347   A
Medical Specialists: 521   A
Surgical Specialists: 317   B
Short-Term General Hospitals: 12 (1,688 beds)
Services: 3 ★★, 3 ★★★, 6 ★★★★
JCAH Accredited: 9
AMA Residency: 1
Places Rated Score: 168   Places Rated Rank: 268

Bakersfield, CA
Office-Based Physicians
General/Family Practitioners: 140   C
Medical Specialists: 238   C
Surgical Specialists: 146   C
Short-Term General Hospitals: 11 (1,244 beds)
Services: 1 ★, 5 ★★, 5 ★★★★
JCAH Accredited: 6
AMA Residency: 1
Places Rated Score: 128   Places Rated Rank: 327

Baltimore, MD
Office-Based Physicians
General/Family Practitioners: 361   C
Medical Specialists: 1,080   A
Surgical Specialists: 535   C
Short-Term General Hospitals: 26 (8,364 beds)
Services: 1 ★, 3 ★★★, 22 ★★★★
JCAH Accredited: 26

AMA Residency: 14
MC Access: Washington-Baltimore,
DC-MD-VA-WV
Places Rated Score: 313   Places Rated Rank: 43

Bangor, ME
Office-Based Physicians
General/Family Practitioners: 58   B
Medical Specialists: 98   A
Surgical Specialists: 54   B
Short-Term General Hospitals: 4 (599 beds)
Services: 1 ★★★, 3 ★★★★
JCAH Accredited: 4
AMA Residency: 1
Places Rated Score: 217   Places Rated Rank: 167

Barnstable-Yarmouth, MA
Office-Based Physicians
General/Family Practitioners: 62   B
Medical Specialists: 151   AA
Surgical Specialists: 68   B
Short-Term General Hospitals: 2 (385 beds)
Services: 1 ★★★, 1 ★★★★
JCAH Accredited: 2
AMA Residency: 1
Places Rated Score: 181   Places Rated Rank: 243

Baton Rouge, LA
Office-Based Physicians
General/Family Practitioners: 172   B
Medical Specialists: 317   A
Surgical Specialists: 232   A
Short-Term General Hospitals: 5 (1,561 beds)
Services: 1 ★★★, 4 ★★★★
JCAH Accredited: 5
AMA Residency: 1
Places Rated Score: 196   Places Rated Rank: 213

Beaumont-Port Arthur, TX
Office-Based Physicians
General/Family Practitioners: 145   A
Medical Specialists: 182   B
Surgical Specialists: 131   B
Short-Term General Hospitals: 9 (1,947 beds)
Services: 1 ★★, 2 ★★★, 6 ★★★★
JCAH Accredited: 7
AMA Residency: 1
Places Rated Score: 190   Places Rated Rank: 228

Bellingham, WA
Office-Based Physicians
General/Family Practitioners: 75   AA
Medical Specialists: 82   A
Surgical Specialists: 46   B
Short-Term General Hospitals: 1 (211 beds)
Services: 1 ★★★★
JCAH Accredited: 1
Places Rated Score: 174   Places Rated Rank: 255

Benton Harbor, MI
Office-Based Physicians
General/Family Practitioners: 59   B
Medical Specialists: 75   B
Surgical Specialists: 54   C
Short-Term General Hospitals: 4 (765 beds)
Services: 1 ★★, 1 ★★★, 2 ★★★★
JCAH Accredited: 4
Places Rated Score: 163   Places Rated Rank: 278

Billings, MT
Office-Based Physicians
General/Family Practitioners: 35   C
Medical Specialists: 115   AA
Surgical Specialists: 78   AA
Short-Term General Hospitals: 2 (560 beds)

Rating   Rating

Services: 2 ★★★★
JCAH Accredited: 2
Places Rated Score: 250   Places Rated Rank: 109

Biloxi–Gulfport–Pascagoula, MS
Office-Based Physicians
  General/Family Practitioners: 83   C
  Medical Specialists: 158   B
  Surgical Specialists: 128   B
Short-Term General Hospitals: 9 (2,431 beds)
  Services: 4 ★★★, 5 ★★★★
  JCAH Accredited: 9
  AMA Residency: 2
Places Rated Score: 214   Places Rated Rank: 170

Binghamton, NY
Office-Based Physicians
  General/Family Practitioners: 85   B
  Medical Specialists: 171   A
  Surgical Specialists: 116   A
Short-Term General Hospitals: 2 (899 beds)
  Services: 2 ★★★★
  JCAH Accredited: 2
  AMA Residency: 1
Places Rated Score: 185   Places Rated Rank: 237

✓ Birmingham, AL
Office-Based Physicians
  General/Family Practitioners: 258   C
  Medical Specialists: 813   AA
  Surgical Specialists: 479   AA
Short-Term General Hospitals: 16 (4,689 beds)
  Services: 1 ★, 3 ★★, 2 ★★★, 10 ★★★★
  JCAH Accredited: 13
  AMA Residency: 8
Places Rated Score: 319   Places Rated Rank: 31

Bismarck, ND
Office-Based Physicians
  General/Family Practitioners: 30   B
  Medical Specialists: 80   AA
  Surgical Specialists: 54   AA
Short-Term General Hospitals: 3 (547 beds)
  Services: 1 ★★★, 2 ★★★★
  JCAH Accredited: 3
  AMA Residency: 2
Places Rated Score: 280   Places Rated Rank: 70

Bloomington, IN
Office-Based Physicians
  General/Family Practitioners: 46   A
  Medical Specialists: 65   B
  Surgical Specialists: 38   C
Short-Term General Hospitals: 1 (285 beds)
  Services: 1 ★★★★
  JCAH Accredited: 1
Places Rated Score: 162   Places Rated Rank: 280

Bloomington–Normal, IL
Office-Based Physicians
  General/Family Practitioners: 44   B
  Medical Specialists: 63   B
  Surgical Specialists: 46   B
Short-Term General Hospitals: 2 (617 beds)
  Services: 2 ★★★★
  JCAH Accredited: 2
Places Rated Score: 165   Places Rated Rank: 274

Boise City, ID
Office-Based Physicians
  General/Family Practitioners: 144   A
  Medical Specialists: 153   B
  Surgical Specialists: 128   A
Short-Term General Hospitals: 5 (944 beds)

Services: 5 ★★★★
JCAH Accredited: 5
AMA Residency: 3
Places Rated Score: 204   Places Rated Rank: 195

✓ Boston, MA
Office-Based Physicians
  General/Family Practitioners: 674   C
  Medical Specialists: 4,668   AA
  Surgical Specialists: 1,961   AA
Short-Term General Hospitals: 58 (14,452 beds)
  Services: 2 ★, 4 ★★★, 52 ★★★★★
  JCAH Accredited: 48
  AMA Residency: 24
MC Access: Boston–New Bedford–Nashua, MA–NH
Places Rated Score: 477   Places Rated Rank: 7

Boulder–Longmont, CO
Office-Based Physicians
  General/Family Practitioners: 161   AA
  Medical Specialists: 187   AA
  Surgical Specialists: 88   B
Short-Term General Hospitals: 3 (395 beds)
  Services: 3 ★★★★
  JCAH Accredited: 2
MC Access: Denver–Boulder–Greeley, CO
Places Rated Score: 222   Places Rated Rank: 158

Brazoria, TX
Office-Based Physicians
  General/Family Practitioners: 65   B
  Medical Specialists: 41   C
  Surgical Specialists: 24   C
Short-Term General Hospitals: 4 (314 beds)
  Services: 1 ★★, 2 ★★★, 1 ★★★★
  JCAH Accredited: 4
MC Access: Houston–Galveston–Brazoria, TX
Places Rated Score: 92   Places Rated Rank: 342

Bremerton, WA
Office-Based Physicians
  General/Family Practitioners: 92   A
  Medical Specialists: 90   B
  Surgical Specialists: 46   C
Short-Term General Hospitals: 2 (377 beds)
  Services: 2 ★★★★
  JCAH Accredited: 2
  AMA Residency: 1
MC Access: Seattle–Tacoma–Bremerton, WA
Places Rated Score: 160   Places Rated Rank: 284

Bridgeport, CT
Office-Based Physicians
  General/Family Practitioners: 210   C
  Medical Specialists: 660   AA
  Surgical Specialists: 482   AA
Short-Term General Hospitals: 8 (2,430 beds)
  JCAH Accredited: 8
  AMA Residency: 7
  Services: 8 ★★★★
MC Access: New York–Northern New Jersey–Long
  Island, NY–NJ–CT
Places Rated Score: 306   Places Rated Rank: 52

Brownsville–Harlingen–San Benito, TX
Office-Based Physicians
  General/Family Practitioners: 60   C
  Medical Specialists: 99   C
  Surgical Specialists: 74   C
Short-Term General Hospitals: 5 (803 beds)
  Services: 2 ★★, 1 ★★★, 2 ★★★★
  JCAH Accredited: 5
Places Rated Score: 119   Places Rated Rank: 333

Rating   Rating

Bryan–College Station, TX
Office-Based Physicians
General/Family Practitioners: 48   B
Medical Specialists: 64   B
Surgical Specialists: 39   C
Short-Term General Hospitals: 2 (279 beds)
Services: 2 ★★★★
JCAH Accredited: 2
Places Rated Score: 145   Places Rated Rank: 309

Buffalo–Niagara Falls, NY
Office-Based Physicians
General/Family Practitioners: 320   C
Medical Specialists: 851   A
Surgical Specialists: 550   A
Short-Term General Hospitals: 17 (5,623 beds)
Services: 1 ★, 2 ★★★, 14 ★★★★
JCAH Accredited: 15
AMA Residency: 7
Places Rated Score: 261   Places Rated Rank: 93

Burlington, VT
Office-Based Physicians
General/Family Practitioners: 83   A
Medical Specialists: 191   AA
Surgical Specialists: 99   AA
Short-Term General Hospitals: 3 (644 beds)
Services: 1 ★★★, 2 ★★★★
JCAH Accredited: 3
AMA Residency: 2
Places Rated Score: 275   Places Rated Rank: 78

Calgary, AB
Fee-for-Service Physicians
General/Family Practitioners: 646   AA
Medical Specialists: 410   B
Surgical Specialists: 213   C
Short-Term General Hospitals: 7 (3,173 beds)
CCHFA Accredited: 6
Residency Program: 6
Places Rated Score: 276   Places Rated Rank: 74

Canton–Massillon, OH
Office-Based Physicians
General/Family Practitioners: 140   B
Medical Specialists: 221   B
Surgical Specialists: 129   C
Short-Term General Hospitals: 5 (1,536 beds)
Services: 5 ★★★★
JCAH Accredited: 4
AMA Residency: 2
Places Rated Score: 183   Places Rated Rank: 241

Casper, WY
Office-Based Physicians
General/Family Practitioners: 27   A
Medical Specialists: 42   A
Surgical Specialists: 28   A
Short-Term General Hospitals: 1 (225 beds)
Services: 1 ★★★★
JCAH Accredited: 1
AMA Residency: 1
Places Rated Score: 205   Places Rated Rank: 190

Cedar Rapids, IA
Office-Based Physicians
General/Family Practitioners: 95   AA
Medical Specialists: 86   B
Surgical Specialists: 59   C
Short-Term General Hospitals: 2 (919 beds)
Services: 2 ★★★★
JCAH Accredited: 2
AMA Residency: 2
Places Rated Score: 216   Places Rated Rank: 168

✓ Central New Jersey, NJ
Office-Based Physicians
General/Family Practitioners: 332   B
Medical Specialists: 896   AA
Surgical Specialists: 405   B
Short-Term General Hospitals: 8 (2,430 beds)
Services: 1 ★★★, 7 ★★★★
JCAH Accredited: 7
AMA Residency: 6
MC Access: New York–Northern New Jersey–Long
Island, NY–NJ–CT
Places Rated Score: 316   Places Rated Rank: 35

Champaign–Urbana, IL
Office-Based Physicians
General/Family Practitioners: 90   AA
Medical Specialists: 142   AA
Surgical Specialists: 76   A
Short-Term General Hospitals: 3 (923 beds)
Services: 3 ★★★★
JCAH Accredited: 2
AMA Residency: 1
Places Rated Score: 241   Places Rated Rank: 120

Charleston, WV
Office-Based Physicians
General/Family Practitioners: 130   AA
Medical Specialists: 167   A
Surgical Specialists: 140   AA
Short-Term General Hospitals: 5 (1,423 beds)
Services: 1 ★, 1 ★★★, 3 ★★★★
JCAH Accredited: 4
AMA Residency: 2
Places Rated Score: 251   Places Rated Rank: 107

Charleston–North Charleston, SC
Office-Based Physicians
General/Family Practitioners: 205   A
Medical Specialists: 389   A
Surgical Specialists: 228   A
Short-Term General Hospitals: 9 (2,285 beds)
Services: 1 ★, 1 ★★★, 7 ★★★★
JCAH Accredited: 7
AMA Residency: 5
Places Rated Score: 255   Places Rated Rank: 103

Charlotte–Gastonia–Rock Hill, NC–SC
Office-Based Physicians
General/Family Practitioners: 351   C
Medical Specialists: 638   B
Surgical Specialists: 468   B
Short-Term General Hospitals: 12 (3,478 beds)
Services: 1 ★, 2 ★★, 2 ★★★, 7 ★★★★
JCAH Accredited: 11
AMA Residency: 1
Places Rated Score: 163   Places Rated Rank: 278

✓ Charlottesville, VA
Office-Based Physicians
General/Family Practitioners: 72   AA
Medical Specialists: 258   AA
Surgical Specialists: 99   AA
Short-Term General Hospitals: 2 (851 beds)
Services: 2 ★★★★
JCAH Accredited: 2
AMA Residency: 1
Places Rated Score: 399   Places Rated Rank: 14

Chattanooga, TN–GA
Office-Based Physicians
General/Family Practitioners: 107   C
Medical Specialists: 305   A
Surgical Specialists: 186   A

Rating   Rating

Short-Term General Hospitals: 10 (1,853 beds)
  Services: 1 ★, 1 ★★, 2 ★★★, 6 ★★★★
  JCAH Accredited: 8
  AMA Residency: 1
Places Rated Score: 205   Places Rated Rank: 190

Cheyenne, WY
Office-Based Physicians
  General/Family Practitioners: 48   AA
  Medical Specialists: 43   B
  Surgical Specialists: 40   AA
Short-Term General Hospitals: 4 (407 beds)
  Services: 4 ★★★★
  JCAH Accredited: 3
  AMA Residency: 2
Places Rated Score: 255   Places Rated Rank: 103

✓ Chicago, IL
Office-Based Physicians
  General/Family Practitioners: 2,337   B
  Medical Specialists: 5,842   AA
  Surgical Specialists: 2,853   B
Short-Term General Hospitals: 85 (27,949 beds)
  Services: 7 ★, 1 ★★, 7 ★★★, 70 ★★★★
  JCAH Accredited: 81
  AMA Residency: 35
MC Access: Chicago–Gary–Kenosha, IL–IN–WI
Places Rated Score: 554   Places Rated Rank: 4

Chico–Paradise, CA
Office-Based Physicians
  General/Family Practitioners: 100   AA
  Medical Specialists: 108   B
  Surgical Specialists: 94   AA
Short-Term General Hospitals: 5 (595 beds)
  Services: 1 ★, 1 ★★★, 3 ★★★★
  JCAH Accredited: 4
Places Rated Score: 197   Places Rated Rank: 211

Chicoutimi–Jonquiere, PQ
Fee-for-Service Physicians
  General/Family Practitioners: 127   AA
  Medical Specialists: 61   C
  Surgical Specialists: 45   C
Short-Term General Hospitals: 2 (856 beds)
  CCHFA Accredited: 2
  Residency Program: 1
Places Rated Score: 210   Places Rated Rank: 181

Cincinnati, OH–KY–IN
Office-Based Physicians
  General/Family Practitioners: 585   B
  Medical Specialists: 1,242   AA
  Surgical Specialists: 666   A
Short-Term General Hospitals: 19 (5,905 beds)
  Services: 1 ★★, 1 ★★★, 17 ★★★★
  JCAH Accredited: 17
  AMA Residency: 8
MC Access: Cincinnati–Hamilton, OH–KY–IN
Places Rated Score: 281   Places Rated Rank: 66

Clarksville–Hopkinsville, TN–KY
Office-Based Physicians
  General/Family Practitioners: 33   C
  Medical Specialists: 56   C
  Surgical Specialists: 44   C
Short-Term General Hospitals: 3 (539 beds)
  Services: 1 ★★★, 2 ★★★★
  JCAH Accredited: 3
Places Rated Score: 109   Places Rated Rank: 337

✓ Cleveland–Lorain–Elyria, OH
Office-Based Physicians
  General/Family Practitioners: 516   C

Medical Specialists: 2,006   AA
Surgical Specialists: 1,064   A
Short-Term General Hospitals: 39 (10,941 beds)
  Services: 2 ★★, 7 ★★★, 30 ★★★★
  JCAH Accredited: 37
  AMA Residency: 10
MC Access: Cleveland–Akron, OH
Places Rated Score: 317   Places Rated Rank: 34

Colorado Springs, CO
Office-Based Physicians
  General/Family Practitioners: 92   C
  Medical Specialists: 241   A
  Surgical Specialists: 152   B
Short-Term General Hospitals: 4 (1,271 beds)
  Services: 4 ★★★★
  JCAH Accredited: 4
  AMA Residency: 2
Places Rated Score: 173   Places Rated Rank: 258

✓ Columbia, MO
Office-Based Physicians
  General/Family Practitioners: 57   AA
  Medical Specialists: 160   AA
  Surgical Specialists: 93   AA
Short-Term General Hospitals: 4 (1,345 beds)
  Services: 4 ★★★★
  JCAH Accredited: 4
  AMA Residency: 3
Places Rated Score: 419   Places Rated Rank: 12

Columbia, SC
Office-Based Physicians
  General/Family Practitioners: 186   A
  Medical Specialists: 319   A
  Surgical Specialists: 221   A
Short-Term General Hospitals: 6 (2,042 beds)
  Services: 6 ★★★★
  JCAH Accredited: 6
  AMA Residency: 2
Places Rated Score: 222   Places Rated Rank: 158

Columbus, GA–AL
Office-Based Physicians
  General/Family Practitioners: 94   B
  Medical Specialists: 118   B
  Surgical Specialists: 110   A
Short-Term General Hospitals: 5 (1,452 beds)
  Services: 1 ★★★, 4 ★★★★
  JCAH Accredited: 5
  AMA Residency: 2
Places Rated Score: 199   Places Rated Rank: 207

Columbus, OH
Office-Based Physicians
  General/Family Practitioners: 539   A
  Medical Specialists: 894   A
  Surgical Specialists: 511   B
Short-Term General Hospitals: 12 (4,398 beds)
  Services: 1 ★★★, 11 ★★★★
  JCAH Accredited: 12
  AMA Residency: 6
Places Rated Score: 236   Places Rated Rank: 130

Corpus Christi, TX
Office-Based Physicians
  General/Family Practitioners: 154   A
  Medical Specialists: 212   A
  Surgical Specialists: 160   A
Short-Term General Hospitals: 8 (1,306 beds)
  Services: 1 ★, 4 ★★★, 3 ★★★★
  JCAH Accredited: 7
  AMA Residency: 1
Places Rated Score: 197   Places Rated Rank: 211

Rating   Rating

Cumberland, MD–WV
Office-Based Physicians
    General/Family Practitioners: 34   **B**
    Medical Specialists: 70   **A**
    Surgical Specialists: 42   **B**
Short-Term General Hospitals: 4 (552 beds)
    Services: 2 ★★, 2 ★★★★
    JCAH Accredited: 4
Places Rated Score: 198   Places Rated Rank: 210

Dallas, TX
Office-Based Physicians
    General/Family Practitioners: 775   **C**
    Medical Specialists: 1,803   **A**
    Surgical Specialists: 1,154   **A**
Short-Term General Hospitals: 43 (8,898 beds)
    Services: 1 ★, 4 ★★, 15 ★★★, 23 ★★★★
    JCAH Accredited: 35
    AMA Residency: 6
MC Access: Dallas–Fort Worth, TX
Places Rated Score: 234   Places Rated Rank: 136

Danbury, CT
Office-Based Physicians
    General/Family Practitioners: 131   **C**
    Medical Specialists: 659   **AA**
    Surgical Specialists: 459   **AA**
Short-Term General Hospitals: 2 (543 beds)
    Services: 1 ★★★, 1 ★★★★
    JCAH Accredited: 2
    AMA Residency: 1
MC Access: New York–Northern New Jersey–Long
  Island, NY–NJ–CT
Places Rated Score: 278   Places Rated Rank: 72

Danville, VA
Office-Based Physicians
    General/Family Practitioners: 22   **C**
    Medical Specialists: 52   **B**
    Surgical Specialists: 41   **B**
Short-Term General Hospitals: 1 (391 beds)
    Services: 1 ★★★★
    JCAH Accredited: 1
    AMA Residency: 1
Places Rated Score: 152   Places Rated Rank: 296

Davenport–Moline–Rock Island, IA–IL
Office-Based Physicians
    General/Family Practitioners: 147   **A**
    Medical Specialists: 154   **C**
    Surgical Specialists: 127   **B**
Short-Term General Hospitals: 8 (1,583 beds)
    Services: 2 ★★★, 6 ★★★★
    JCAH Accredited: 8
    AMA Residency: 2
Places Rated Score: 187   Places Rated Rank: 232

Dayton–Springfield, OH
Office-Based Physicians
    General/Family Practitioners: 433   **A**
    Medical Specialists: 524   **B**
    Surgical Specialists: 338   **B**
Short-Term General Hospitals: 12 (5,647 beds)
    Services: 12 ★★★★
    JCAH Accredited: 11
    AMA Residency: 8
Places Rated Score: 275   Places Rated Rank: 78

Daytona Beach, FL
Office-Based Physicians
    General/Family Practitioners: 153   **B**
    Medical Specialists: 169   **C**
    Surgical Specialists: 139   **C**
Short-Term General Hospitals: 8 (1,439 beds)

    Services: 2 ★★★, 6 ★★★★
    JCAH Accredited: 7
    AMA Residency: 1
Places Rated Score: 158   Places Rated Rank: 290

Decatur, AL
Office-Based Physicians
    General/Family Practitioners: 56   **A**
    Medical Specialists: 45   **C**
    Surgical Specialists: 37   **C**
Short-Term General Hospitals: 4 (522 beds)
    Services: 2 ★, 1 ★★, 1 ★★★★
    JCAH Accredited: 4
Places Rated Score: 143   Places Rated Rank: 316

Decatur, IL
Office-Based Physicians
    General/Family Practitioners: 39   **B**
    Medical Specialists: 67   **B**
    Surgical Specialists: 37   **C**
Short-Term General Hospitals: 2 (725 beds)
    Services: 2 ★★★★
    JCAH Accredited: 2
    AMA Residency: 2
Places Rated Score: 204   Places Rated Rank: 195

Denver, CO
Office-Based Physicians
    General/Family Practitioners: 626   **B**
    Medical Specialists: 1,514   **AA**
    Surgical Specialists: 771   **A**
Short-Term General Hospitals: 17 (5,579 beds)
    Services: 1 ★, 1 ★★★, 15 ★★★★
    JCAH Accredited: 15
    AMA Residency: 10
MC Access: Denver–Boulder–Greeley, CO
Places Rated Score: 313   Places Rated Rank: 43

Des Moines, IA
Office-Based Physicians
    General/Family Practitioners: 142   **B**
    Medical Specialists: 228   **B**
    Surgical Specialists: 147   **B**
Short-Term General Hospitals: 8 (2,355 beds)
    Services: 1 ★★★, 7 ★★★★
    JCAH Accredited: 7
    AMA Residency: 5
Places Rated Score: 239   Places Rated Rank: 125

✓ Detroit, MI
Office-Based Physicians
    General/Family Practitioners: 767   **C**
    Medical Specialists: 2,851   **A**
    Surgical Specialists: 1,557   **B**
Short-Term General Hospitals: 53 (15,176 beds)
    Services: 3 ★, 2 ★★, 4 ★★★, 44 ★★★★
    JCAH Accredited: 45
    AMA Residency: 17
MC Access: Detroit–Ann Arbor–Flint, MI
Places Rated Score: 334   Places Rated Rank: 25

Dothan, AL
Office-Based Physicians
    General/Family Practitioners: 38   **C**
    Medical Specialists: 80   **A**
    Surgical Specialists: 68   **AA**
Short-Term General Hospitals: 4 (728 beds)
    Services: 1 ★, 3 ★★★★
    JCAH Accredited: 3
Places Rated Score: 196   Places Rated Rank: 213

Dover, DE
Office-Based Physicians
    General/Family Practitioners: 20   **C**
    Medical Specialists: 40   **C**
    Surgical Specialists: 32   **C**

Rating

Rating

Short-Term General Hospitals: 2 (224 beds)
    Services: 1 ★★★, 1 ★★★★
    JCAH Accredited: 1
Places Rated Score: 103   Places Rated Rank: 340

Dubuque, IA
Office-Based Physicians
    General/Family Practitioners: 10   C
    Medical Specialists: 66   A
    Surgical Specialists: 48   AA
Short-Term General Hospitals: 2 (558 beds)
    Services: 2 ★★★★
    JCAH Accredited: 2
Places Rated Score: 208   Places Rated Rank: 185

Duluth–Superior, MN–WI
Office-Based Physicians
    General/Family Practitioners: 161   AA
    Medical Specialists: 144   A
    Surgical Specialists: 98   B
Short-Term General Hospitals: 10 (1,445 beds)
    Services: 1 ★★, 2 ★★★, 7 ★★★★
    JCAH Accredited: 6
    AMA Residency: 2
Places Rated Score: 249   Places Rated Rank: 110

Dutchess County, NY
Office-Based Physicians
    General/Family Practitioners: 61   C
    Medical Specialists: 220   AA
    Surgical Specialists: 114   A
Short-Term General Hospitals: 4 (1,048 beds)
    Services: 4 ★★★★
    JCAH Accredited: 4
    AMA Residency: 2
MC Access: New York–Northern New Jersey–Long
    Island, NY–NJ–CT
Places Rated Score: 212   Places Rated Rank: 173

Eau Claire, WI
Office-Based Physicians
    General/Family Practitioners: 111   AA
    Medical Specialists: 77   B
    Surgical Specialists: 57   B
Short-Term General Hospitals: 5 (874 beds)
    Services: 5 ★★★★
    JCAH Accredited: 5
    AMA Residency: 2
Places Rated Score: 260   Places Rated Rank: 96

Edmonton, AB
Fee-for-Service Physicians
    General/Family Practitioners: 849   AA
    Medical Specialists: 486   B
    Surgical Specialists: 249   C
Short-Term General Hospitals: 12 (4,011 beds)
    CCHFA Accredited: 12
    Residency Program: 7
Places Rated Score: 309   Places Rated Rank: 48

El Paso, TX
Office-Based Physicians
    General/Family Practitioners: 129   C
    Medical Specialists: 265   C
    Surgical Specialists: 177   C
Short-Term General Hospitals: 8 (2,124 beds)
    Services: 1 ★, 2 ★★, 5 ★★★★
    JCAH Accredited: 7
    AMA Residency: 3
Places Rated Score: 160   Places Rated Rank: 284

Elkhart–Goshen, IN
Office-Based Physicians
    General/Family Practitioners: 72   A
    Medical Specialists: 58   C
    Surgical Specialists: 41   C

Short-Term General Hospitals: 2 (527 beds)
    Services: 1 ★, 1 ★★★★
    JCAH Accredited: 2
    AMA Residency: 1
Places Rated Score: 152   Places Rated Rank: 296

Elmira, NY
Office-Based Physicians
    General/Family Practitioners: 29   C
    Medical Specialists: 83   AA
    Surgical Specialists: 49   AA
Short-Term General Hospitals: 2 (542 beds)
    Services: 2 ★★★★
    JCAH Accredited: 2
Places Rated Score: 226   Places Rated Rank: 149

Enid, OK
Office-Based Physicians
    General/Family Practitioners: 27   A
    Medical Specialists: 32   B
    Surgical Specialists: 26   A
Short-Term General Hospitals: 3 (371 beds)
    Services: 1 ★★★, 2 ★★★★
    JCAH Accredited: 2
    AMA Residency: 2
Places Rated Score: 236   Places Rated Rank: 130

Erie, PA
Office-Based Physicians
    General/Family Practitioners: 118   A
    Medical Specialists: 147   B
    Surgical Specialists: 125   A
Short-Term General Hospitals: 7 (1,566 beds)
    Services: 2 ★★★, 5 ★★★★
    JCAH Accredited: 5
    AMA Residency: 2
Places Rated Score: 218   Places Rated Rank: 165

Eugene–Springfield, OR
Office-Based Physicians
    General/Family Practitioners: 171   AA
    Medical Specialists: 208   A
    Surgical Specialists: 116   B
Short-Term General Hospitals: 5 (698 beds)
    Services: 1 ★, 1 ★★, 1 ★★★, 2 ★★★★
    JCAH Accredited: 3
Places Rated Score: 199   Places Rated Rank: 207

Evansville–Henderson, IN–KY
Office-Based Physicians
    General/Family Practitioners: 178   AA
    Medical Specialists: 172   A
    Surgical Specialists: 119   A
Short-Term General Hospitals: 5 (1,723 beds)
    Services: 1 ★★★, 4 ★★★★
    JCAH Accredited: 5
    AMA Residency: 2
Places Rated Score: 249   Places Rated Rank: 110

Fargo–Moorhead, ND–MN
Office-Based Physicians
    General/Family Practitioners: 62   A
    Medical Specialists: 151   AA
    Surgical Specialists: 84   AA
Short-Term General Hospitals: 4 (816 beds)
    Services: 4 ★★★★
    JCAH Accredited: 3
    AMA Residency: 3
Places Rated Score: 276   Places Rated Rank: 74

Fayetteville, NC
Office-Based Physicians
    General/Family Practitioners: 69   C
    Medical Specialists: 88   C
    Surgical Specialists: 75   C

Rating

Short-Term General Hospitals: 4 (1,211 beds)
  Services: 4 ★★★★
  JCAH Accredited: 4
  AMA Residency: 2
Places Rated Score: 148   Places Rated Rank: 305

Fayetteville–Springdale–Rogers, AR
Office-Based Physicians
  General/Family Practitioners: 118   **AA**
  Medical Specialists: 96   **B**
  Surgical Specialists: 72   **C**
Short-Term General Hospitals: 8 (1,103 beds)
  Services: 1 ★, 1 ★★, 3 ★★★, 3 ★★★★
  JCAH Accredited: 6
  AMA Residency: 1
Places Rated Score: 194   Places Rated Rank: 217

Flint, MI
Office-Based Physicians
  General/Family Practitioners: 177   **A**
  Medical Specialists: 202   **B**
  Surgical Specialists: 118   **C**
Short-Term General Hospitals: 6 (1,789 beds)
  Services: 2 ★★, 4 ★★★★
  JCAH Accredited: 5
  AMA Residency: 3
MC Access: Detroit–Ann Arbor–Flint, MI
Places Rated Score: 204   Places Rated Rank: 195

Florence, AL
Office-Based Physicians
  General/Family Practitioners: 29   **C**
  Medical Specialists: 69   **B**
  Surgical Specialists: 61   **A**
Short-Term General Hospitals: 4 (904 beds)
  Services: 1 ★, 2 ★★★, 1 ★★★★
  JCAH Accredited: 4
Places Rated Score: 189   Places Rated Rank: 229

Florence, SC
Office-Based Physicians
  General/Family Practitioners: 47   **A**
  Medical Specialists: 71   **A**
  Surgical Specialists: 59   **AA**
Short-Term General Hospitals: 4 (689 beds)
  Services: 1 ★★★, 3 ★★★★
  JCAH Accredited: 3
  AMA Residency: 1
Places Rated Score: 223   Places Rated Rank: 155

Fort Collins–Loveland, CO
Office-Based Physicians
  General/Family Practitioners: 151   **AA**
  Medical Specialists: 86   **B**
  Surgical Specialists: 72   **B**
Short-Term General Hospitals: 3 (407 beds)
  Services: 3 ★★★★
  JCAH Accredited: 3
  AMA Residency: 1
Places Rated Score: 196   Places Rated Rank: 213

Fort Lauderdale, FL
Office-Based Physicians
  General/Family Practitioners: 371   **C**
  Medical Specialists: 1,077   **AA**
  Surgical Specialists: 601   **A**
Short-Term General Hospitals: 20 (5,626 beds)
  Services: 2 ★, 3 ★★★, 15 ★★★★
  JCAH Accredited: 20
  AMA Residency: 2
MC Access: Miami–Fort Lauderdale, FL
Places Rated Score: 231   Places Rated Rank: 144

Rating

Fort Myers–Cape Coral, FL
Office-Based Physicians
  General/Family Practitioners: 111   **B**
  Medical Specialists: 194   **B**
  Surgical Specialists: 125   **B**
Short-Term General Hospitals: 4 (1,202 beds)
  Services: 1 ★★★, 3 ★★★★
  JCAH Accredited: 4
Places Rated Score: 160   Places Rated Rank: 284

Fort Pierce–Port St. Lucie, FL
Office-Based Physicians
  General/Family Practitioners: 64   **C**
  Medical Specialists: 147   **B**
  Surgical Specialists: 103   **B**
Short-Term General Hospitals: 3 (661 beds)
  Services: 3 ★★★★
  JCAH Accredited: 3
Places Rated Score: 148   Places Rated Rank: 305

Fort Smith, AR–OK
Office-Based Physicians
  General/Family Practitioners: 103   **AA**
  Medical Specialists: 101   **B**
  Surgical Specialists: 72   **B**
Short-Term General Hospitals: 4 (970 beds)
  Services: 2 ★, 2 ★★★★
  JCAH Accredited: 3
  AMA Residency: 2
Places Rated Score: 230   Places Rated Rank: 146

Fort Walton Beach, FL
Office-Based Physicians
  General/Family Practitioners: 44   **C**
  Medical Specialists: 57   **C**
  Surgical Specialists: 49   **C**
Short-Term General Hospitals: 5 (627 beds)
  Services: 1 ★, 2 ★★★, 2 ★★★★
  JCAH Accredited: 4
  AMA Residency: 1
Places Rated Score: 156   Places Rated Rank: 293

Fort Wayne, IN
Office-Based Physicians
  General/Family Practitioners: 264   **AA**
  Medical Specialists: 208   **B**
  Surgical Specialists: 169   **B**
Short-Term General Hospitals: 10 (2,022 beds)
  Services: 1 ★★★, 9 ★★★★
  JCAH Accredited: 8
  AMA Residency: 3
Places Rated Score: 213   Places Rated Rank: 172

Fort Worth–Arlington, TX
Office-Based Physicians
  General/Family Practitioners: 471   **B**
  Medical Specialists: 630   **B**
  Surgical Specialists: 451   **C**
Short-Term General Hospitals: 22 (3,820 beds)
  Services: 1 ★, 2 ★★, 4 ★★★, 15 ★★★★
  JCAH Accredited: 17
  AMA Residency: 3
MC Access: Dallas–Fort Worth, TX
Places Rated Score: 176   Places Rated Rank: 250

Fresno, CA
Office-Based Physicians
  General/Family Practitioners: 291   **B**
  Medical Specialists: 426   **B**
  Surgical Specialists: 242   **C**
Short-Term General Hospitals: 12 (1,775 beds)
  Services: 1 ★, 4 ★★, 2 ★★★, 5 ★★★★
  JCAH Accredited: 9
  AMA Residency: 2
Places Rated Score: 168   Places Rated Rank: 268

Rating

Rating

Gadsden, AL
Office-Based Physicians
General/Family Practitioners: 42   A
Medical Specialists: 49   B
Surgical Specialists: 35   B
Short-Term General Hospitals: 2 (503 beds)
Services: 2 ★★★★
JCAH Accredited: 2
Places Rated Score: 177   Places Rated Rank: 248

✓ Gainesville, FL
Office-Based Physicians
General/Family Practitioners: 82   A
Medical Specialists: 241   AA
Surgical Specialists: 142   AA
Short-Term General Hospitals: 4 (1,706 beds)
Services: 4 ★★★★
JCAH Accredited: 4
AMA Residency: 4
Places Rated Score: 382   Places Rated Rank: 18

Galveston–Texas City, TX
Office-Based Physicians
General/Family Practitioners: 90   A
Medical Specialists: 183   AA
Surgical Specialists: 103   A
Short-Term General Hospitals: 5 (1,542 beds)
Services: 2 ★★★, 3 ★★★★
JCAH Accredited: 5
AMA Residency: 1
MC Access: Houston–Galveston–Brazoria, TX
Places Rated Score: 260   Places Rated Rank: 96

Gary, IN
Office-Based Physicians
General/Family Practitioners: 258   A
Medical Specialists: 301   B
Surgical Specialists: 232   B
Short-Term General Hospitals: 7 (2,785 beds)
Services: 7 ★★★★
JCAH Accredited: 6
AMA Residency: 2
MC Access: Chicago–Gary–Kenosha, IL–IN–WI
Places Rated Score: 232   Places Rated Rank: 141

Glens Falls, NY
Office-Based Physicians
General/Family Practitioners: 44   B
Medical Specialists: 62   B
Surgical Specialists: 50   A
Short-Term General Hospitals: 2 (553 beds)
Services: 2 ★★★★
JCAH Accredited: 2
Places Rated Score: 177   Places Rated Rank: 248

Goldsboro, NC
Office-Based Physicians
General/Family Practitioners: 32   C
Medical Specialists: 33   C
Surgical Specialists: 27   C
Short-Term General Hospitals: 2 (292 beds)
Services: 1 ★, 1 ★★★★
JCAH Accredited: 1
Places Rated Score: 115   Places Rated Rank: 336

Grand Forks, ND–MN
Office-Based Physicians
General/Family Practitioners: 63   AA
Medical Specialists: 55   B
Surgical Specialists: 41   B
Short-Term General Hospitals: 5 (709 beds)
Services: 3 ★★★, 2 ★★★★
JCAH Accredited: 2
AMA Residency: 1
Places Rated Score: 232   Places Rated Rank: 141

Grand Rapids–Muskegon–Holland, MI
Office-Based Physicians
General/Family Practitioners: 307   B
Medical Specialists: 454   B
Surgical Specialists: 327   C
Short-Term General Hospitals: 13 (3,007 beds)
Services: 3 ★★★, 10 ★★★★
JCAH Accredited: 11
AMA Residency: 4
Places Rated Score: 186   Places Rated Rank: 233

Great Falls, MT
Office-Based Physicians
General/Family Practitioners: 29   B
Medical Specialists: 67   AA
Surgical Specialists: 43   AA
Short-Term General Hospitals: 2 (624 beds)
Services: 2 ★★★★
JCAH Accredited: 2
Places Rated Score: 260   Places Rated Rank: 96

Greeley, CO
Office-Based Physicians
General/Family Practitioners: 66   AA
Medical Specialists: 53   C
Surgical Specialists: 47   B
Short-Term General Hospitals: 1 (281 beds)
Services: 1 ★★★★
JCAH Accredited: 1
AMA Residency: 1
MC Access: Denver–Boulder–Greeley, CO
Places Rated Score: 167   Places Rated Rank: 270

Green Bay, WI
Office-Based Physicians
General/Family Practitioners: 57   C
Medical Specialists: 121   A
Surgical Specialists: 85   A
Short-Term General Hospitals: 3 (768 beds)
Services: 3 ★★★★
JCAH Accredited: 3
Places Rated Score: 173   Places Rated Rank: 258

Greensboro–Winston-Salem–High Point, NC
Office-Based Physicians
General/Family Practitioners: 372   B
Medical Specialists: 708   A
Surgical Specialists: 448   A
Short-Term General Hospitals: 15 (3,659 beds)
Services: 2 ★★, 5 ★★★, 8 ★★★★
JCAH Accredited: 14
AMA Residency: 2
Places Rated Score: 199   Places Rated Rank: 207

Greenville, NC
Office-Based Physicians
General/Family Practitioners: 90   AA
Medical Specialists: 122   AA
Surgical Specialists: 60   AA
Short-Term General Hospitals: 1 (566 beds)
Services: 1 ★★★★
JCAH Accredited: 1
AMA Residency: 1
Places Rated Score: 309   Places Rated Rank: 48

Greenville–Spartanburg–Anderson, SC
Office-Based Physicians
General/Family Practitioners: 468   AA
Medical Specialists: 390   B
Surgical Specialists: 308   B
Short-Term General Hospitals: 12 (2,692 beds)
Services: 1 ★★, 5 ★★★, 6 ★★★★
JCAH Accredited: 9
AMA Residency: 2
Places Rated Score: 191   Places Rated Rank: 224

Rating   Rating

Hagerstown, MD
Office-Based Physicians
General/Family Practitioners: 36   C
Medical Specialists: 57   B
Surgical Specialists: 44   B
Short-Term General Hospitals: 1 (312 beds)
Services: 1 ★★★★
JCAH Accredited: 1
MC Access: Washington–Baltimore,
DC–MD–VA–WV
Places Rated Score: 152   Places Rated Rank: 296

✓ Halifax, NS
Fee-for-Service Physicians
General/Family Practitioners: 490   AA
Medical Specialists: 331   AA
Surgical Specialists: 159   AA
Short-Term General Hospitals: 6 (2,047 beds)
CCHFA Accredited: 6
Residency Program: 5
Places Rated Score: 398   Places Rated Rank: 15

Hamilton, ON
Fee-for-Service Physicians
General/Family Practitioners: 560   AA
Medical Specialists: 422   A
Surgical Specialists: 186   C
Short-Term General Hospitals: 6 (2,322 beds)
CCHFA Accredited: 5
Residency Program: 4
MC Access: Toronto–Ontario Shore, ON
Places Rated Score: 286   Places Rated Rank: 61

Hamilton–Middletown, OH
Office-Based Physicians
General/Family Practitioners: 99   B
Medical Specialists: 108   C
Surgical Specialists: 78   C
Short-Term General Hospitals: 4 (892 beds)
Services: 1 ★★★, 3 ★★★★
JCAH Accredited: 4
MC Access: Cincinnati–Hamilton, OH–KY–IN
Places Rated Score: 136   Places Rated Rank: 320

Harrisburg–Lebanon–Carlisle, PA
Office-Based Physicians
General/Family Practitioners: 260   A
Medical Specialists: 388   A
Surgical Specialists: 239   B
Short-Term General Hospitals: 9 (2,213 beds)
Services: 1 ★★★, 8 ★★★★
JCAH Accredited: 8
AMA Residency: 4
Places Rated Score: 227   Places Rated Rank: 148

Hartford, CT
Office-Based Physicians
General/Family Practitioners: 278   C
Medical Specialists: 1,113   AA
Surgical Specialists: 553   A
Short-Term General Hospitals: 11 (3,290 beds)
Services: 1 ★, 10 ★★★★
JCAH Accredited: 11
AMA Residency: 6
Places Rated Score: 261   Places Rated Rank: 93

Hickory–Morgantown, NC
Office-Based Physicians
General/Family Practitioners: 150   AA
Medical Specialists: 112   C
Surgical Specialists: 101   C
Short-Term General Hospitals: 6 (894 beds)
Services: 1 ★, 5 ★★★★
JCAH Accredited: 6
Places Rated Score: 154   Places Rated Rank: 294

Honolulu, HI
Office-Based Physicians
General/Family Practitioners: 207   C
Medical Specialists: 854   AA
Surgical Specialists: 420   AA
Short-Term General Hospitals: 10 (2,411 beds)
Services: 2 ★, 8 ★★★★
JCAH Accredited: 9
AMA Residency: 6
Places Rated Score: 265   Places Rated Rank: 87

Houma, LA
Office-Based Physicians
General/Family Practitioners: 47   C
Medical Specialists: 46   C
Surgical Specialists: 63   C
Short-Term General Hospitals: 5 (630 beds)
Services: 3 ★★★, 2 ★★★★
JCAH Accredited: 5
AMA Residency: 1
Places Rated Score: 130   Places Rated Rank: 326

Houston, TX
Office-Based Physicians
General/Family Practitioners: 1,180   B
Medical Specialists: 2,506   A
Surgical Specialists: 1,438   A
Short-Term General Hospitals: 48 (13,329 beds)
Services: 2 ★, 3 ★★, 13 ★★★, 30 ★★★★
JCAH Accredited: 46
AMA Residency: 9
MC Access: Houston–Galveston–Brazoria, TX
Places Rated Score: 283   Places Rated Rank: 63

Huntington–Ashland, WV–KY–OH
Office-Based Physicians
General/Family Practitioners: 121   A
Medical Specialists: 166   B
Surgical Specialists: 106   B
Short-Term General Hospitals: 6 (1,485 beds)
Services: 1 ★, 5 ★★★★
JCAH Accredited: 6
AMA Residency: 3
Places Rated Score: 218   Places Rated Rank: 165

Huntsville, AL
Office-Based Physicians
General/Family Practitioners: 120   A
Medical Specialists: 151   B
Surgical Specialists: 102   C
Short-Term General Hospitals: 6 (1,099 beds)
Services: 1 ★, 3 ★★★, 2 ★★★★
JCAH Accredited: 6
AMA Residency: 1
Places Rated Score: 173   Places Rated Rank: 258

Indianapolis, IN
Office-Based Physicians
General/Family Practitioners: 754   AA
Medical Specialists: 1,026   A
Surgical Specialists: 567   B
Short-Term General Hospitals: 21 (6,324 beds)
Services: 1 ★, 3 ★★★, 17 ★★★★
JCAH Accredited: 19
AMA Residency: 7
Places Rated Score: 284   Places Rated Rank: 62

✓ Iowa City, IA
Office-Based Physicians
General/Family Practitioners: 61   AA
Medical Specialists: 172   AA
Surgical Specialists: 102   AA
Short-Term General Hospitals: 3 (1,397 beds)
Services: 3 ★★★★

Rating

Rating

JCAH Accredited: 3
AMA Residency: 3
Places Rated Score: 518   Places Rated Rank: 5

Jackson, MI
Office-Based Physicians
  General/Family Practitioners: 35   C
  Medical Specialists: 49   C
  Surgical Specialists: 36   C
Short-Term General Hospitals: 3 (589 beds)
  Services: 1 ★★★, 2 ★★★★
  JCAH Accredited: 2
Places Rated Score: 119   Places Rated Rank: 333

Jackson, MS
Office-Based Physicians
  General/Family Practitioners: 182   A
  Medical Specialists: 362   AA
  Surgical Specialists: 227   AA
Short-Term General Hospitals: 10 (2,930 beds)
  Services: 1 ★, 1 ★★, 1 ★★★, 7 ★★★★
  JCAH Accredited: 8
  AMA Residency: 4
Places Rated Score: 307   Places Rated Rank: 51

Jacksonville, FL
Office-Based Physicians
  General/Family Practitioners: 342   B
  Medical Specialists: 615   A
  Surgical Specialists: 401   A
Short-Term General Hospitals: 15 (3,191 beds)
  Services: 1 ★★, 3 ★★★, 11 ★★★★
  JCAH Accredited: 15
  AMA Residency: 4
Places Rated Score: 224   Places Rated Rank: 152

Jacksonville, NC
Office-Based Physicians
  General/Family Practitioners: 28   C
  Medical Specialists: 33   C
  Surgical Specialists: 27   C
Short-Term General Hospitals: 2 (269 beds)
  Services: 1 ★★★, 1 ★★★★
  JCAH Accredited: 2
Places Rated Score: 76   Places Rated Rank: 343

Jamestown, NY
Office-Based Physicians
  General/Family Practitioners: 40   C
  Medical Specialists: 57   C
  Surgical Specialists: 50   B
Short-Term General Hospitals: 4 (581 beds)
  Services: 1 ★★, 1 ★★★, 2 ★★★★
  JCAH Accredited: 3
Places Rated Score: 144   Places Rated Rank: 312

Janesville–Beloit, WI
Office-Based Physicians
  General/Family Practitioners: 34   C
  Medical Specialists: 76   B
  Surgical Specialists: 48   C
Short-Term General Hospitals: 3 (495 beds)
  Services: 3 ★★★★
  JCAH Accredited: 3
  AMA Residency: 1
Places Rated Score: 159   Places Rated Rank: 289

Johnson City–Kingsport–Bristol, TN–VA
Office-Based Physicians
  General/Family Practitioners: 218   AA
  Medical Specialists: 273   A
  Surgical Specialists: 187   A
Short-Term General Hospitals: 10 (2,369 beds)
  Services: 3 ★★★, 7 ★★★★
  JCAH Accredited: 9
  AMA Residency: 4
Places Rated Score: 249   Places Rated Rank: 110

Johnstown, PA
Office-Based Physicians
  General/Family Practitioners: 111   A
  Medical Specialists: 102   C
  Surgical Specialists: 77   C
Short-Term General Hospitals: 7 (1,112 beds)
  Services: 3 ★★★, 4 ★★★★
  JCAH Accredited: 7
  AMA Residency: 1
Places Rated Score: 176   Places Rated Rank: 250

Joplin, MO
Office-Based Physicians
  General/Family Practitioners: 42   B
  Medical Specialists: 50   C
  Surgical Specialists: 49   B
Short-Term General Hospitals: 5 (739 beds)
  Services: 1 ★★, 1 ★★★, 3 ★★★★
  JCAH Accredited: 2
Places Rated Score: 157   Places Rated Rank: 291

Kalamazoo–Battle Creek, MI
Office-Based Physicians
  General/Family Practitioners: 188   A
  Medical Specialists: 279   A
  Surgical Specialists: 170   B
Short-Term General Hospitals: 7 (1,605 beds)
  Services: 1 ★★★, 6 ★★★★
  JCAH Accredited: 7
  AMA Residency: 2
Places Rated Score: 205   Places Rated Rank: 190

Kankakee, IL
Office-Based Physicians
  General/Family Practitioners: 40   A
  Medical Specialists: 47   B
  Surgical Specialists: 28   C
Short-Term General Hospitals: 2 (558 beds)
  Services: 2 ★★★★
  JCAH Accredited: 2
MC Access: Chicago–Gary–Kenosha, IL–IN–WI
Places Rated Score: 211   Places Rated Rank: 176

Kansas City, MO–KS
Office-Based Physicians
  General/Family Practitioners: 568   B
  Medical Specialists: 1,198   A
  Surgical Specialists: 669   A
Short-Term General Hospitals: 36 (7,488 beds)
  Services: 1 ★, 3 ★★★, 32 ★★★★
  JCAH Accredited: 28
  AMA Residency: 11
Places Rated Score: 310   Places Rated Rank: 46

Kenosha, WI
Office-Based Physicians
  General/Family Practitioners: 35   C
  Medical Specialists: 51   C
  Surgical Specialists: 27   C
Short-Term General Hospitals: 2 (336 beds)
  Services: 2 ★★★★
  JCAH Accredited: 2
  AMA Residency: 1
MC Access: Chicago–Gary–Kenosha, IL–IN–WI
Places Rated Score: 160   Places Rated Rank: 284

Killeen–Temple, TX
Office-Based Physicians
  General/Family Practitioners: 82   B
  Medical Specialists: 186   A
  Surgical Specialists: 84   C
Short-Term General Hospitals: 6 (1,888 beds)
  Services: 1 ★★★, 5 ★★★★
  JCAH Accredited: 6
  AMA Residency: 3
Places Rated Score: 241   Places Rated Rank: 120

Rating   Rating

Kitchener, ON
Fee-for-Service Physicians
   General/Family Practitioners: 257   **AA**
   Medical Specialists: 93   **C**
   Surgical Specialists: 73   **C**
Short-Term General Hospitals: 3 (983 beds)
   CCHFA Accredited: 3
MC Access: Toronto–Ontario Shore, ON
Places Rated Score: 165   Places Rated Rank: 274

Knoxville, TN
Office-Based Physicians
   General/Family Practitioners: 277   **A**
   Medical Specialists: 482   **AA**
   Surgical Specialists: 283   **AA**
Short-Term General Hospitals: 10 (2,399 beds)
   Services: 2 ★★, 1 ★★★, 7 ★★★★
   JCAH Accredited: 9
   AMA Residency: 1
Places Rated Score: 223   Places Rated Rank: 155

Kokomo, IN
Office-Based Physicians
   General/Family Practitioners: 54   **AA**
   Medical Specialists: 29   **C**
   Surgical Specialists: 25   **C**
Short-Term General Hospitals: 3 (486 beds)
   Services: 3 ★★★★
   JCAH Accredited: 3
Places Rated Score: 161   Places Rated Rank: 282

✓ La Crosse, WI–MN
Office-Based Physicians
   General/Family Practitioners: 55   **A**
   Medical Specialists: 154   **AA**
   Surgical Specialists: 68   **AA**
Short-Term General Hospitals: 3 (714 beds)
   Services: 1 ★★★, 2 ★★★★
   JCAH Accredited: 2
   AMA Residency: 2
Places Rated Score: 318   Places Rated Rank: 32

Lafayette, IN
Office-Based Physicians
   General/Family Practitioners: 56   **B**
   Medical Specialists: 101   **A**
   Surgical Specialists: 57   **B**
Short-Term General Hospitals: 3 (672 beds)
   Services: 3 ★★★★
   JCAH Accredited: 3
Places Rated Score: 173   Places Rated Rank: 258

Lafayette, LA
Office-Based Physicians
   General/Family Practitioners: 125   **B**
   Medical Specialists: 153   **C**
   Surgical Specialists: 137   **B**
Short-Term General Hospitals: 11 (1,358 beds)
   Services: 2 ★★, 4 ★★★, 5 ★★★★
   JCAH Accredited: 10
   AMA Residency: 1
Places Rated Score: 169   Places Rated Rank: 267

Lake Charles, LA
Office-Based Physicians
   General/Family Practitioners: 78   **A**
   Medical Specialists: 74   **C**
   Surgical Specialists: 75   **A**
Short-Term General Hospitals: 6 (849 beds)
   Services: 1 ★★, 3 ★★★, 2 ★★★★
   JCAH Accredited: 5
   AMA Residency: 2
Places Rated Score: 205   Places Rated Rank: 190

Lake County, IL
Office-Based Physicians
   General/Family Practitioners: 145   **C**
   Medical Specialists: 444   **AA**
   Surgical Specialists: 223   **A**
Short-Term General Hospitals: 8 (1,637 beds)
   Services: 1 ★, 7 ★★★★
   JCAH Accredited: 8
   AMA Residency: 1
MC Access: Chicago–Gary–Kenosha, IL–IN–WI
Places Rated Score: 233   Places Rated Rank: 139

Lakeland–Winter Haven, FL
Office-Based Physicians
   General/Family Practitioners: 100   **C**
   Medical Specialists: 236   **B**
   Surgical Specialists: 152   **B**
Short-Term General Hospitals: 7 (1,338 beds)
   Services: 1 ★, 2 ★★, 2 ★★★, 2 ★★★★
   JCAH Accredited: 7
Places Rated Score: 152   Places Rated Rank: 296

Lancaster, PA
Office-Based Physicians
   General/Family Practitioners: 296   **AA**
   Medical Specialists: 163   **C**
   Surgical Specialists: 107   **C**
Short-Term General Hospitals: 5 (1,278 beds)
   Services: 5 ★★★★
   JCAH Accredited: 4
   AMA Residency: 1
Places Rated Score: 173   Places Rated Rank: 258

Lansing–East Lansing, MI
Office-Based Physicians
   General/Family Practitioners: 162   **B**
   Medical Specialists: 245   **B**
   Surgical Specialists: 121   **C**
Short-Term General Hospitals: 7 (1,627 beds)
   Services: 2 ★★★, 5 ★★★★
   JCAH Accredited: 6
   AMA Residency: 3
Places Rated Score: 189   Places Rated Rank: 229

Laredo, TX
Office-Based Physicians
   General/Family Practitioners: 29   **C**
   Medical Specialists: 44   **C**
   Surgical Specialists: 21   **C**
Short-Term General Hospitals: 2 (383 beds)
   Services: 2 ★★★
   JCAH Accredited: 2
Places Rated Score: 96   Places Rated Rank: 341

Las Cruces, NM
Office-Based Physicians
   General/Family Practitioners: 56   **A**
   Medical Specialists: 62   **B**
   Surgical Specialists: 41   **C**
Short-Term General Hospitals: 1 (240 beds)
   Services: 1 ★★★★
   JCAH Accredited: 1
Places Rated Score: 134   Places Rated Rank: 323

Las Vegas, NV–AZ
Office-Based Physicians
   General/Family Practitioners: 214   **C**
   Medical Specialists: 426   **B**
   Surgical Specialists: 264   **C**
Short-Term General Hospitals: 12 (2,171 beds)
   Services: 1 ★, 3 ★★★, 8 ★★★★
   JCAH Accredited: 9
   AMA Residency: 1
Places Rated Score: 138   Places Rated Rank: 318

Rating

Lawrence, KS
Office-Based Physicians
  General/Family Practitioners: 36 — A
  Medical Specialists: 33 — C
  Surgical Specialists: 23 — C
Short-Term General Hospitals: 1 (165 beds)
  Services: 1 ★★★★
  JCAH Accredited: 1
Places Rated Score: 132   Places Rated Rank: 324

Lawton, OK
Office-Based Physicians
  General/Family Practitioners: 35 — B
  Medical Specialists: 42 — C
  Surgical Specialists: 37 — C
Short-Term General Hospitals: 4 (557 beds)
  Services: 1 ★, 1 ★★, 2 ★★★★
  JCAH Accredited: 4
Places Rated Score: 153   Places Rated Rank: 295

Lewiston–Auburn, ME
Office-Based Physicians
  General/Family Practitioners: 48 — A
  Medical Specialists: 64 — A
  Surgical Specialists: 50 — A
Short-Term General Hospitals: 3 (537 beds)
  Services: 3 ★★★★
  JCAH Accredited: 3
  AMA Residency: 1
Places Rated Score: 220   Places Rated Rank: 164

✓ Lexington, KY
Office-Based Physicians
  General/Family Practitioners: 228 — AA
  Medical Specialists: 445 — AA
  Surgical Specialists: 237 — AA
Short-Term General Hospitals: 12 (2,942 beds)
  Services: 1 ★, 5 ★★★, 6 ★★★★
  JCAH Accredited: 12
  AMA Residency: 4
Places Rated Score: 334   Places Rated Rank: 25

Lima, OH
Office-Based Physicians
  General/Family Practitioners: 94 — AA
  Medical Specialists: 53 — C
  Surgical Specialists: 45 — C
Short-Term General Hospitals: 4 (651 beds)
  Services: 1 ★★, 3 ★★★★
  JCAH Accredited: 3
Places Rated Score: 166   Places Rated Rank: 272

Lincoln, NE
Office-Based Physicians
  General/Family Practitioners: 108 — AA
  Medical Specialists: 133 — A
  Surgical Specialists: 95 — A
Short-Term General Hospitals: 4 (915 beds)
  Services: 4 ★★★★
  JCAH Accredited: 4
  AMA Residency: 4
Places Rated Score: 238   Places Rated Rank: 127

Little Rock–North Little Rock, AR
Office-Based Physicians
  General/Family Practitioners: 292 — AA
  Medical Specialists: 448 — AA
  Surgical Specialists: 301 — AA
Short-Term General Hospitals: 11 (3,778 beds)
  Services: 3 ★★★, 8 ★★★★
  JCAH Accredited: 10
  AMA Residency: 4
Places Rated Score: 315   Places Rated Rank: 38

Rating

✓ London, ON
Fee-for-Service Physicians
  General/Family Practitioners: 504 — AA
  Medical Specialists: 393 — AA
  Surgical Specialists: 153 — B
Short-Term General Hospitals: 4 (1,845 beds)
  CCHFA Accredited: 4
  Residency Program: 3
Places Rated Score: 362   Places Rated Rank: 20

✓ Long Island, NY
Office-Based Physicians
  General/Family Practitioners: 799 — C
  Medical Specialists: 3,296 — AA
  Surgical Specialists: 1,547 — AA
Short-Term General Hospitals: 27 (9,616 beds)
  Services: 1 ★, 1 ★★, 25 ★★★★
  JCAH Accredited: 26
  AMA Residency: 12
MC Access: New York–Northern New Jersey–Long
  Island, NY–NJ–CT
Places Rated Score: 427   Places Rated Rank: 11

Longview–Marshall, TX
Office-Based Physicians
  General/Family Practitioners: 87 — A
  Medical Specialists: 75 — C
  Surgical Specialists: 61 — C
Short-Term General Hospitals: 6 (551 beds)
  Services: 1 ★★, 3 ★★★, 2 ★★★★
  JCAH Accredited: 5
Places Rated Score: 143   Places Rated Rank: 316

✓ Los Angeles–Long Beach, CA
Office-Based Physicians
  General/Family Practitioners: 3,281 — B
  Medical Specialists: 8,314 — AA
  Surgical Specialists: 4,304 — A
Short-Term General Hospitals: 124 (30,374 beds)
  Services: 27 ★, 6 ★★, 22 ★★★, 69 ★★★★
  JCAH Accredited: 120
  AMA Residency: 27
MC Access: Los Angeles–Riverside–Orange
  County, CA
Places Rated Score: 494   Places Rated Rank: 6

Louisville, KY–IN
Office-Based Physicians
  General/Family Practitioners: 455 — A
  Medical Specialists: 843 — AA
  Surgical Specialists: 436 — A
Short-Term General Hospitals: 17 (4,408 beds)
  Services: 1 ★, 5 ★★★, 11 ★★★★
  JCAH Accredited: 16
  AMA Residency: 5
Places Rated Score: 274   Places Rated Rank: 80

Lubbock, TX
Office-Based Physicians
  General/Family Practitioners: 120 — AA
  Medical Specialists: 188 — AA
  Surgical Specialists: 126 — AA
Short-Term General Hospitals: 7 (1,588 beds)
  Services: 1 ★, 2 ★★★, 4 ★★★★
  JCAH Accredited: 6
  AMA Residency: 3
Places Rated Score: 294   Places Rated Rank: 57

Lynchburg, VA
Office-Based Physicians
  General/Family Practitioners: 105 — AA
  Medical Specialists: 90 — B
  Surgical Specialists: 70 — B
Short-Term General Hospitals: 3 (900 beds)

Rating

Rating

Services: 1 ★★★, 2 ★★★★
JCAH Accredited: 2
Places Rated Score: 181   Places Rated Rank: 243

Macon, GA
Office-Based Physicians
   General/Family Practitioners: 96   **B**
   Medical Specialists: 172   **B**
   Surgical Specialists: 136   **A**
Short-Term General Hospitals: 8 (1,298 beds)
   Services: 5 ★★★, 3 ★★★★
   JCAH Accredited: 8
   AMA Residency: 1
Places Rated Score: 193   Places Rated Rank: 218

Madison, WI
Office-Based Physicians
   General/Family Practitioners: 219   **AA**
   Medical Specialists: 451   **AA**
   Surgical Specialists: 188   **AA**
Short-Term General Hospitals: 5 (1,608 beds)
   Services: 5 ★★★★
   JCAH Accredited: 5
   AMA Residency: 4
Places Rated Score: 315   Places Rated Rank: 38

Manchester–Nashua, NH
Office-Based Physicians
   General/Family Practitioners: 108   **B**
   Medical Specialists: 258   **A**
   Surgical Specialists: 150   **A**
Short-Term General Hospitals: 6 (1,273 beds)
   Services: 6 ★★★★
   JCAH Accredited: 6
   AMA Residency: 1
MC Access: Boston–New Bedford–Nashua,
   MA–NH
Places Rated Score: 224   Places Rated Rank: 152

Mansfield, OH
Office-Based Physicians
   General/Family Practitioners: 56   **B**
   Medical Specialists: 70   **C**
   Surgical Specialists: 48   **C**
Short-Term General Hospitals: 6 (645 beds)
   Services: 5 ★★★, 1 ★★★★
   JCAH Accredited: 5
Places Rated Score: 137   Places Rated Rank: 319

McAllen–Edinburg–Mission, TX
Office-Based Physicians
   General/Family Practitioners: 145   **B**
   Medical Specialists: 88   **C**
   Surgical Specialists: 68   **C**
Short-Term General Hospitals: 5 (864 beds)
   Services: 2 ★★★, 3 ★★★★
   JCAH Accredited: 5
   AMA Residency: 1
Places Rated Score: 109   Places Rated Rank: 337

Medford–Ashland, OR
Office-Based Physicians
   General/Family Practitioners: 73   **A**
   Medical Specialists: 104   **A**
   Surgical Specialists: 70   **A**
Short-Term General Hospitals: 3 (519 beds)
   Services: 3 ★★★★
   JCAH Accredited: 3
Places Rated Score: 203   Places Rated Rank: 202

Melbourne–Titusville–Palm Bay, FL
Office-Based Physicians
   General/Family Practitioners: 131   **B**
   Medical Specialists: 238   **B**
   Surgical Specialists: 132   **C**
Short-Term General Hospitals: 5 (981 beds)

Services: 1 ★★★, 4 ★★★★
JCAH Accredited: 4
Places Rated Score: 149   Places Rated Rank: 303

Memphis, TN–AR–MS
Office-Based Physicians
   General/Family Practitioners: 285   **C**
   Medical Specialists: 771   **A**
   Surgical Specialists: 501   **A**
Short-Term General Hospitals: 15 (6,127 beds)
   Services: 1 ★★, 5 ★★★, 9 ★★★★
   JCAH Accredited: 12
   AMA Residency: 6
Places Rated Score: 273   Places Rated Rank: 83

Merced, CA
Office-Based Physicians
   General/Family Practitioners: 71   **B**
   Medical Specialists: 56   **C**
   Surgical Specialists: 40   **C**
Short-Term General Hospitals: 6 (362 beds)
   Services: 2 ★, 3 ★★★, 1 ★★★★
   JCAH Accredited: 4
   AMA Residency: 1
Places Rated Score: 123   Places Rated Rank: 331

Miami, FL
Office-Based Physicians
   General/Family Practitioners: 944   **A**
   Medical Specialists: 2,123   **AA**
   Surgical Specialists: 1,119   **AA**
Short-Term General Hospitals: 29 (9,347 beds)
   Services: 5 ★, 1 ★★, 4 ★★★, 19 ★★★★
   JCAH Accredited: 27
   AMA Residency: 5
MC Access: Miami–Fort Lauderdale, FL
Places Rated Score: 315   Places Rated Rank: 38

Milwaukee–Waukesha, WI
Office-Based Physicians
   General/Family Practitioners: 511   **B**
   Medical Specialists: 1,278   **AA**
   Surgical Specialists: 639   **A**
Short-Term General Hospitals: 21 (5,530 beds)
   Services: 1 ★, 2 ★★★, 18 ★★★★
   JCAH Accredited: 19
   AMA Residency: 10
MC Access: Milwaukee–Racine, WI
Places Rated Score: 308   Places Rated Rank: 50

Minneapolis–St. Paul, MN–WI
Office-Based Physicians
   General/Family Practitioners: 1,688   **AA**
   Medical Specialists: 1,926   **AA**
   Surgical Specialists: 1,002   **B**
Short-Term General Hospitals: 30 (8,458 beds)
   Services: 1 ★, 1 ★★, 4 ★★★, 24 ★★★★
   JCAH Accredited: 23
   AMA Residency: 9
Places Rated Score: 297   Places Rated Rank: 55

Mobile, AL
Office-Based Physicians
   General/Family Practitioners: 148   **B**
   Medical Specialists: 306   **A**
   Surgical Specialists: 220   **A**
Short-Term General Hospitals: 9 (2,073 beds)
   Services: 1 ★★, 2 ★★★, 6 ★★★★
   JCAH Accredited: 8
   AMA Residency: 1
Places Rated Score: 193   Places Rated Rank: 218

Modesto, CA
Office-Based Physicians
   General/Family Practitioners: 180   **A**
   Medical Specialists: 202   **B**

Rating   Rating

Surgical Specialists: 122   C   Medical Specialists: 106   A
Short-Term General Hospitals: 7 (1,244 beds)   Surgical Specialists: 64   A
  Services: 1 **, 3 ***, 3 ****   Short-Term General Hospitals: 1 (436 beds)
  JCAH Accredited: 5   Services: 1 ****
  AMA Residency: 1   JCAH Accredited: 1
Places Rated Score: 176   Places Rated Rank: 250   Places Rated Score: 179   Places Rated Rank: 246

Monmouth–Ocean, NJ
Office-Based Physicians   ### Nashville, TN
  General/Family Practitioners: 167   C   Office-Based Physicians
  Medical Specialists: 730   A   General/Family Practitioners: 262   C
  Surgical Specialists: 424   A   Medical Specialists: 847   AA
Short-Term General Hospitals: 10 (3,259 beds)   Surgical Specialists: 541   AA
  Services: 1 ***, 9 ****   Short-Term General Hospitals: 22 (5,291 beds)
  JCAH Accredited: 10   Services: 2 *, 2 ***, 18 ****
  AMA Residency: 2   JCAH Accredited: 21
MC Access: New York–Northern New Jersey–Long   AMA Residency: 6
  Island, NY–NJ–CT   Places Rated Score: 279   Places Rated Rank: 71
Places Rated Score: 246   Places Rated Rank: 115

                                                           ### New Bedford–Fall River–Attleboro, MA
Monroe, LA   Office-Based Physicians
Office-Based Physicians   General/Family Practitioners: 80   C
  General/Family Practitioners: 58   A   Medical Specialists: 215   C
  Medical Specialists: 77   B   Surgical Specialists: 140   C
  Surgical Specialists: 65   A   Short-Term General Hospitals: 5 (1,316 beds)
Short-Term General Hospitals: 5 (1,060 beds)   Services: 5 ****
  Services: 1 *, 1 ***, 3 ****   JCAH Accredited: 5
  JCAH Accredited: 4   MC Access: Boston–New Bedford–Nashua,
  AMA Residency: 1   MA–NH
Places Rated Score: 224   Places Rated Rank: 152   Places Rated Score: 136   Places Rated Rank: 320

Montgomery, AL   ### New Haven–Meriden, CT
Office-Based Physicians   Office-Based Physicians
  General/Family Practitioners: 104   B   General/Family Practitioners: 131   C
  Medical Specialists: 168   B   Medical Specialists: 659   AA
  Surgical Specialists: 134   A   Surgical Specialists: 459   AA
Short-Term General Hospitals: 9 (1,481 beds)   Short-Term General Hospitals: 9 (3,265 beds)
  Services: 1 *, 4 ***, 4 ****   JCAH Accredited: 9
  JCAH Accredited: 9   AMA Residency: 6
  AMA Residency: 2   Services: 1 ***, 8 ****
Places Rated Score: 209   Places Rated Rank: 183   MC Access: New York–Northern New Jersey–Long
                                                             Island, NY–NJ–CT
✓ Montreal, PQ   Places Rated Score: 302   Places Rated Rank: 53
Fee-for-Service Physicians
  General/Family Practitioners: 2,713   AA   ### New London–Norwich, CT–RI
  Medical Specialists: 2,252   A   Office-Based Physicians
  Surgical Specialists: 1,061   C   General/Family Practitioners: 71   C
Short-Term General Hospitals: 40 (12,676 beds)   Medical Specialists: 179   A
  CCHFA Accredited: 31   Surgical Specialists: 111   A
  Residency Program: 17   Short-Term General Hospitals: 3 (526 beds)
Places Rated Score: 406   Places Rated Rank: 13   Services: 3 ****
                                                             JCAH Accredited: 3
Muncie, IN   AMA Residency: 1
Office-Based Physicians   Places Rated Score: 176   Places Rated Rank: 250
  General/Family Practitioners: 53   A
  Medical Specialists: 74   A   ### ✓ New Orleans, LA
  Surgical Specialists: 39   C   Office-Based Physicians
Short-Term General Hospitals: 1 (542 beds)   General/Family Practitioners: 306   C
  Services: 1 ****   Medical Specialists: 1,294   AA
  JCAH Accredited: 1   Surgical Specialists: 796   AA
  AMA Residency: 1   Short-Term General Hospitals: 30 (6,392 beds)
Places Rated Score: 193   Places Rated Rank: 218   Services: 5 *, 1 **, 2 ***, 22 ****
                                                             JCAH Accredited: 25
Myrtle Beach, SC   AMA Residency: 8
Office-Based Physicians   Places Rated Score: 316   Places Rated Rank: 35
  General/Family Practitioners: 64   A
  Medical Specialists: 59   C   ### ✓ New York, NY
  Surgical Specialists: 48   C   Office-Based Physicians
Short-Term General Hospitals: 4 (541 beds)   General/Family Practitioners: 1,475   C
  Services: 1 *, 2 ***, 1 ****   Medical Specialists: 10,366   AA
  JCAH Accredited: 3   Surgical Specialists: 4,149   A
Places Rated Score: 151   Places Rated Rank: 301   Short-Term General Hospitals: 79 (40,017 beds)
                                                             Services: 4 *, 9 ***, 66 ****
Naples, FL   JCAH Accredited: 77
Office-Based Physicians   AMA Residency: 54
  General/Family Practitioners: 64   A   MC Access: New York–Northern New Jersey–Long
                                                             Island, NY–NJ–CT
                                                           Places Rated Score: 819   Places Rated Rank: 2

Rating   Rating

✓ Newark–Jersey City, NJ
Office-Based Physicians
  General/Family Practitioners: 424   C
  Medical Specialists: 2,296   AA
  Surgical Specialists: 1,173   AA
Short-Term General Hospitals: 33 (11,310 beds)
  Services: 2 ★★★, 31 ★★★★
  JCAH Accredited: 32
  AMA Residency: 17
MC Access: New York–Northern New Jersey–Long
  Island, NY–NJ–CT
Places Rated Score: 458   Places Rated Rank: 9

Norfolk–Virginia Beach–Newport News, VA–NC
Office-Based Physicians
  General/Family Practitioners: 416   A
  Medical Specialists: 577   B
  Surgical Specialists: 327   C
Short-Term General Hospitals: 11 (2,544 beds)
  Services: 1 ★, 1 ★★★, 9 ★★★★
  JCAH Accredited: 11
  AMA Residency: 2
Places Rated Score: 166   Places Rated Rank: 272

✓ Northern New Jersey, NJ
Office-Based Physicians
  General/Family Practitioners: 281   C
  Medical Specialists: 1,590   AA
  Surgical Specialists: 795   AA
Short-Term General Hospitals: 14 (4,441 beds)
  Services: 14 ★★★★
  JCAH Accredited: 14
  AMA Residency: 4
MC Access: New York–Northern New Jersey–Long
  Island, NY–NJ–CT
Places Rated Score: 332   Places Rated Rank: 27

Oakland, CA
Office-Based Physicians
  General/Family Practitioners: 680   B
  Medical Specialists: 2,037   AA
  Surgical Specialists: 910   A
Short-Term General Hospitals: 30 (5,503 beds)
  Services: 8 ★, 2 ★★★, 20 ★★★★
  JCAH Accredited: 27
  AMA Residency: 8
MC Access: San Francisco–Oakland–San Jose, CA
Places Rated Score: 295   Places Rated Rank: 56

Ocala, FL
Office-Based Physicians
  General/Family Practitioners: 54   C
  Medical Specialists: 92   B
  Surgical Specialists: 62   C
Short-Term General Hospitals: 2 (432 beds)
  Services: 1 ★★★, 1 ★★★★
  JCAH Accredited: 2
Places Rated Score: 127   Places Rated Rank: 328

Odessa–Midland, TX
Office-Based Physicians
  General/Family Practitioners: 61   C
  Medical Specialists: 107   B
  Surgical Specialists: 82   B
Short-Term General Hospitals: 3 (554 beds)
  Services: 1 ★★★, 2 ★★★★
  JCAH Accredited: 2
  AMA Residency: 1
Places Rated Score: 144   Places Rated Rank: 312

Oklahoma City, OK
Office-Based Physicians
  General/Family Practitioners: 387   A
  Medical Specialists: 684   A
  Surgical Specialists: 407   A

Short-Term General Hospitals: 20 (4,288 beds)
  Services: 1 ★, 5 ★★★, 14 ★★★★
  JCAH Accredited: 17
  AMA Residency: 6
Places Rated Score: 258   Places Rated Rank: 100

Olympia, WA
Office-Based Physicians
  General/Family Practitioners: 100   AA
  Medical Specialists: 109   A
  Surgical Specialists: 62   B
Short-Term General Hospitals: 2 (463 beds)
  Services: 2 ★★★★
  JCAH Accredited: 2
  AMA Residency: 1
MC Access: Seattle–Tacoma–Bremerton, WA
Places Rated Score: 207   Places Rated Rank: 186

Omaha, NE–IA
Office-Based Physicians
  General/Family Practitioners: 361   AA
  Medical Specialists: 499   A
  Surgical Specialists: 319   A
Short-Term General Hospitals: 12 (3,732 beds)
  Services: 2 ★★★, 10 ★★★★
  JCAH Accredited: 12
  AMA Residency: 7
Places Rated Score: 311   Places Rated Rank: 45

Orange County, CA
Office-Based Physicians
  General/Family Practitioners: 1,174   A
  Medical Specialists: 2,227   AA
  Surgical Specialists: 1,247   AA
Short-Term General Hospitals: 35 (6,300 beds)
  Services: 6 ★, 2 ★★, 6 ★★★, 21 ★★★★
  JCAH Accredited: 33
  AMA Residency: 3
MC Access: Los Angeles–Riverside–Orange
  County, CA
Places Rated Score: 281   Places Rated Rank: 66

Orange County, NY
Office-Based Physicians
  General/Family Practitioners: 43   C
  Medical Specialists: 183   B
  Surgical Specialists: 118   B
Short-Term General Hospitals: 7 (1,081 beds)
  Services: 3 ★★★, 4 ★★★★
  JCAH Accredited: 7
MC Access: New York–Northern New Jersey–Long
  Island, NY–NJ–CT
Places Rated Score: 204   Places Rated Rank: 195

Orlando, FL
Office-Based Physicians
  General/Family Practitioners: 435   B
  Medical Specialists: 700   B
  Surgical Specialists: 504   B
Short-Term General Hospitals: 16 (4,454 beds)
  Services: 1 ★, 1 ★★, 3 ★★★, 11 ★★★★
  JCAH Accredited: 16
  AMA Residency: 2
Places Rated Score: 186   Places Rated Rank: 233

Oshawa, ON
Fee-for-Service Physicians
  General/Family Practitioners: 146   AA
  Medical Specialists: 59   C
  Surgical Specialists: 48   C
Short-Term General Hospitals: 2 (761 beds)
  CCHFA Accredited: 2
MC Access: Toronto–Ontario Shore, ON
Places Rated Score: 145   Places Rated Rank: 309

Rating   Rating

✓ **Ottawa–Hull, ON–PQ**
Fee-for-Service Physicians
   General/Family Practitioners: 934   **AA**
   Medical Specialists: 688   **A**
   Surgical Specialists: 292   **C**
Short-Term General Hospitals: 11 (3,449 beds)
   CCHFA Accredited: 11
   Residency Program: 8
Places Rated Score: 337   Places Rated Rank: 23

Owensboro, KY
Office-Based Physicians
   General/Family Practitioners: 24   **C**
   Medical Specialists: 51   **B**
   Surgical Specialists: 44   **AA**
Short-Term General Hospitals: 2 (494 beds)
   Services: 1 ★★★, 1 ★★★★
   JCAH Accredited: 2
Places Rated Score: 192   Places Rated Rank: 222

Panama City, FL
Office-Based Physicians
   General/Family Practitioners: 38   **C**
   Medical Specialists: 66   **B**
   Surgical Specialists: 51   **B**
Short-Term General Hospitals: 3 (521 beds)
   Services: 3 ★★★★
   JCAH Accredited: 2
Places Rated Score: 160   Places Rated Rank: 284

Parkersburg–Marietta, WV–OH
Office-Based Physicians
   General/Family Practitioners: 57   **B**
   Medical Specialists: 50   **C**
   Surgical Specialists: 51   **C**
Short-Term General Hospitals: 4 (832 beds)
   Services: 4 ★★★★
   JCAH Accredited: 3
Places Rated Score: 161   Places Rated Rank: 282

Pensacola, FL
Office-Based Physicians
   General/Family Practitioners: 136   **B**
   Medical Specialists: 205   **B**
   Surgical Specialists: 149   **A**
Short-Term General Hospitals: 8 (1,858 beds)
   Services: 1 ★, 1 ★★, 2 ★★★, 4 ★★★★
   JCAH Accredited: 7
   AMA Residency: 2
Places Rated Score: 214   Places Rated Rank: 170

Peoria–Pekin, IL
Office-Based Physicians
   General/Family Practitioners: 182   **AA**
   Medical Specialists: 232   **A**
   Surgical Specialists: 119   **B**
Short-Term General Hospitals: 5 (1,558 beds)
   Services: 1 ★, 4 ★★★★
   JCAH Accredited: 5
   AMA Residency: 2
Places Rated Score: 223   Places Rated Rank: 155

✓ **Philadelphia, PA–NJ**
Office-Based Physicians
   General/Family Practitioners: 1,500   **C**
   Medical Specialists: 4,788   **AA**
   Surgical Specialists: 2,269   **A**
Short-Term General Hospitals: 74 (19,715 beds)
   Services: 7 ★, 8 ★★★, 59 ★★★★
   JCAH Accredited: 64
   AMA Residency: 34
MC Access: Philadelphia–Wilmington–Atlantic City,
   PA–NJ–DE–MD
Places Rated Score: 557   Places Rated Rank: 3

Phoenix–Mesa, AZ
Office-Based Physicians
   General/Family Practitioners: 872   **B**
   Medical Specialists: 1,591   **A**
   Surgical Specialists: 972   **A**
Short-Term General Hospitals: 33 (7,140 beds)
   Services: 3 ★, 3 ★★★, 27 ★★★★
   JCAH Accredited: 31
   AMA Residency: 7
Places Rated Score: 253   Places Rated Rank: 106

Pine Bluff, AR
Office-Based Physicians
   General/Family Practitioners: 43   **AA**
   Medical Specialists: 38   **C**
   Surgical Specialists: 40   **A**
Short-Term General Hospitals: 1 (475 beds)
   Services: 1 ★★★★
   JCAH Accredited: 1
   AMA Residency: 1
Places Rated Score: 207   Places Rated Rank: 186

Pittsburgh, PA
Office-Based Physicians
   General/Family Practitioners: 818   **B**
   Medical Specialists: 1,817   **AA**
   Surgical Specialists: 1,011   **A**
Short-Term General Hospitals: 40 (11,933 beds)
   Services: 1 ★, 1 ★★★, 38 ★★★★
   JCAH Accredited: 38
   AMA Residency: 11
Places Rated Score: 314   Places Rated Rank: 41

Pittsfield, MA
Office-Based Physicians
   General/Family Practitioners: 44   **B**
   Medical Specialists: 136   **AA**
   Surgical Specialists: 64   **A**
Short-Term General Hospitals: 4 (618 beds)
   Services: 4 ★★★★
   JCAH Accredited: 4
   AMA Residency: 1
Places Rated Score: 256   Places Rated Rank: 102

Portland, ME
Office-Based Physicians
   General/Family Practitioners: 108   **A**
   Medical Specialists: 257   **AA**
   Surgical Specialists: 136   **AA**
Short-Term General Hospitals: 7 (1,144 beds)
   Services: 1 ★★, 1 ★★★, 5 ★★★★
   JCAH Accredited: 5
   AMA Residency: 2
Places Rated Score: 277   Places Rated Rank: 73

Portland, OR
Office-Based Physicians
   General/Family Practitioners: 472   **B**
   Medical Specialists: 1,278   **AA**
   Surgical Specialists: 705   **AA**
Short-Term General Hospitals: 21 (4,275 beds)
   Services: 1 ★, 2 ★★★, 18 ★★★★
   JCAH Accredited: 19
   AMA Residency: 9
MC Access: Portland–Salem–Vancouver, OR–WA
Places Rated Score: 314   Places Rated Rank: 41

Portsmouth–Dover–Rochester, NH
Office-Based Physicians
   General/Family Practitioners: 123   **B**
   Medical Specialists: 207   **B**
   Surgical Specialists: 115   **C**
Short-Term General Hospitals: 5 (678 beds)
   Services: 5 ★★★★
   JCAH Accredited: 5

Rating

Rating

MC Access: Boston–New Bedford–Nashua,
MA–NH
Places Rated Score: 170   Places Rated Rank: 266

Providence–Warwick–Cranston, RI
Office-Based Physicians
General/Family Practitioners: 169   C
Medical Specialists: 771   AA
Surgical Specialists: 418   A
Short-Term General Hospitals: 11 (3,044 beds)
Services: 1 ★★★, 10 ★★★★
JCAH Accredited: 10
AMA Residency: 5
Places Rated Score: 231   Places Rated Rank: 144

Provo–Orem, UT
Office-Based Physicians
General/Family Practitioners: 90   B
Medical Specialists: 98   C
Surgical Specialists: 82   C
Short-Term General Hospitals: 4 (574 beds)
Services: 4 ★★★★
JCAH Accredited: 3
Places Rated Score: 122   Places Rated Rank: 332

Pueblo, CO
Office-Based Physicians
General/Family Practitioners: 71   AA
Medical Specialists: 95   A
Surgical Specialists: 63   AA
Short-Term General Hospitals: 2 (541 beds)
Services: 2 ★★★★
JCAH Accredited: 2
AMA Residency: 1
Places Rated Score: 240   Places Rated Rank: 124

Punta Gorda, FL
Office-Based Physicians
General/Family Practitioners: 27   C
Medical Specialists: 70   A
Surgical Specialists: 41   B
Short-Term General Hospitals: 3 (674 beds)
Services: 1 ★★★, 2 ★★★★
JCAH Accredited: 3
Places Rated Score: 175   Places Rated Rank: 254

✓ Quebec City, PQ
Fee-for-Service Physicians
General/Family Practitioners: 658   AA
Medical Specialists: 537   AA
Surgical Specialists: 291   A
Short-Term General Hospitals: 12 (4,374 beds)
CCHFA Accredited: 11
Residency Program: 7
Places Rated Score: 375   Places Rated Rank: 19

Racine, WI
Office-Based Physicians
General/Family Practitioners: 57   B
Medical Specialists: 95   B
Surgical Specialists: 65   B
Short-Term General Hospitals: 3 (543 beds)
Services: 3 ★★★★
JCAH Accredited: 3
MC Access: Milwaukee–Racine, WI
Places Rated Score: 165   Places Rated Rank: 274

✓ Raleigh–Durham–Chapel Hill, NC
Office-Based Physicians
General/Family Practitioners: 471   AA
Medical Specialists: 1,090   AA
Surgical Specialists: 526   AA
Short-Term General Hospitals: 10 (3,844 beds)
Services: 2 ★, 8 ★★★★
JCAH Accredited: 9
AMA Residency: 6
Places Rated Score: 329   Places Rated Rank: 28

Rapid City, SD
Office-Based Physicians
General/Family Practitioners: 39   A
Medical Specialists: 63   A
Surgical Specialists: 46   AA
Short-Term General Hospitals: 2 (329 beds)
Services: 1 ★★★, 1 ★★★★
JCAH Accredited: 2
Places Rated Score: 222   Places Rated Rank: 158

Reading, PA
Office-Based Physicians
General/Family Practitioners: 170   AA
Medical Specialists: 180   B
Surgical Specialists: 123   B
Short-Term General Hospitals: 3 (972 beds)
Services: 3 ★★★★
JCAH Accredited: 3
AMA Residency: 2
Places Rated Score: 189   Places Rated Rank: 229

Redding, CA
Office-Based Physicians
General/Family Practitioners: 95   AA
Medical Specialists: 85   B
Surgical Specialists: 62   A
Short-Term General Hospitals: 3 (455 beds)
Services: 1 ★★, 2 ★★★★
JCAH Accredited: 2
AMA Residency: 1
Places Rated Score: 204   Places Rated Rank: 195

Regina, SK
Fee-for-Service Physicians
General/Family Practitioners: 217   AA
Medical Specialists: 74   C
Surgical Specialists: 71   B
Short-Term General Hospitals: 3 (1,029 beds)
CCHFA Accredited: 3
Residency Program: 3
Places Rated Score: 273   Places Rated Rank: 83

Reno, NV
Office-Based Physicians
General/Family Practitioners: 105   A
Medical Specialists: 224   AA
Surgical Specialists: 152   AA
Short-Term General Hospitals: 4 (1,173 beds)
Services: 4 ★★★★
JCAH Accredited: 4
AMA Residency: 2
Places Rated Score: 251   Places Rated Rank: 107

Richland–Kennewick–Pasco, WA
Office-Based Physicians
General/Family Practitioners: 72   A
Medical Specialists: 61   C
Surgical Specialists: 45   C
Short-Term General Hospitals: 4 (385 beds)
Services: 1 ★★★, 3 ★★★★
JCAH Accredited: 3
Places Rated Score: 143   Places Rated Rank: 316

Richmond–Petersburg, VA
Office-Based Physicians
General/Family Practitioners: 404   A
Medical Specialists: 765   AA
Surgical Specialists: 398   A
Short-Term General Hospitals: 15 (4,610 beds)
Services: 2 ★, 1 ★★★, 12 ★★★★
JCAH Accredited: 15
AMA Residency: 5
Places Rated Score: 282   Places Rated Rank: 64

Riverside–San Bernardino, CA
Office-Based Physicians
General/Family Practitioners: 793   C

Rating

Rating

Medical Specialists: 1,255 **B**
Surgical Specialists: 753 **C**
Short-Term General Hospitals: 37 (6,313 beds)
    Services: 5 ★, 4 ★★, 11 ★★★, 17 ★★★★
    JCAH Accredited: 34
    AMA Residency: 7
MC Access: Los Angeles–Riverside–Orange
    County, CA
Places Rated Score: 230   Places Rated Rank: 146

✓ Roanoke, VA
Office-Based Physicians
    General/Family Practitioners: 110 **A**
    Medical Specialists: 202 **AA**
    Surgical Specialists: 148 **AA**
Short-Term General Hospitals: 4 (1,962 beds)
    Services: 4 ★★★★
    JCAH Accredited: 4
    AMA Residency: 3
Places Rated Score: 321   Places Rated Rank: 29

✓ Rochester, MN
Office-Based Physicians
    General/Family Practitioners: 62 **AA**
    Medical Specialists: 536 **AA**
    Surgical Specialists: 168 **AA**
Short-Term General Hospitals: 3 (1,541 beds)
    Services: 1 ★★, 2 ★★★★
    JCAH Accredited: 3
    AMA Residency: 2
Places Rated Score: 880   Places Rated Rank: 1

Rochester, NY
Office-Based Physicians
    General/Family Practitioners: 250 **C**
    Medical Specialists: 905 **AA**
    Surgical Specialists: 451 **A**
Short-Term General Hospitals: 16 (3,620 beds)
    Services: 1 ★★, 3 ★★★, 12 ★★★★
    JCAH Accredited: 16
    AMA Residency: 5
Places Rated Score: 235   Places Rated Rank: 134

Rockford, IL
Office-Based Physicians
    General/Family Practitioners: 169 **AA**
    Medical Specialists: 221 **A**
    Surgical Specialists: 128 **B**
Short-Term General Hospitals: 6 (1,152 beds)
    Services: 2 ★, 1 ★★★, 3 ★★★★
    JCAH Accredited: 6
    AMA Residency: 3
Places Rated Score: 222   Places Rated Rank: 158

Rocky Mount, NC
Office-Based Physicians
    General/Family Practitioners: 40 **C**
    Medical Specialists: 56 **C**
    Surgical Specialists: 41 **C**
Short-Term General Hospitals: 3 (459 beds)
    Services: 1 ★, 2 ★★★★
    JCAH Accredited: 3
Places Rated Score: 136   Places Rated Rank: 320

Sacramento, CA
Office-Based Physicians
    General/Family Practitioners: 593 **A**
    Medical Specialists: 1,046 **A**
    Surgical Specialists: 596 **A**
Short-Term General Hospitals: 15 (3,383 beds)
    Services: 1 ★, 2 ★★★, 12 ★★★★
    JCAH Accredited: 15
    AMA Residency: 2
MC Access: Sacramento–Yolo, CA
Places Rated Score: 210   Places Rated Rank: 181

Saginaw–Bay City–Midland, MI
Office-Based Physicians
    General/Family Practitioners: 196 **A**
    Medical Specialists: 193 **B**
    Surgical Specialists: 120 **C**
Short-Term General Hospitals: 6 (1,744 beds)
    Services: 6 ★★★★
    JCAH Accredited: 6
    AMA Residency: 4
Places Rated Score: 211   Places Rated Rank: 176

St. Catharines–Niagara, ON
Fee-for-Service Physicians
    General/Family Practitioners: 266 **AA**
    Medical Specialists: 88 **C**
    Surgical Specialists: 87 **C**
Short-Term General Hospitals: 7 (1,533 beds)
    CCHFA Accredited: 7
    Residency Program: 1
Places Rated Score: 174   Places Rated Rank: 255

St. Cloud, MN
Office-Based Physicians
    General/Family Practitioners: 82 **AA**
    Medical Specialists: 71 **B**
    Surgical Specialists: 57 **B**
Short-Term General Hospitals: 5 (660 beds)
    Services: 2 ★★, 2 ★★★, 1 ★★★★
    JCAH Accredited: 2
    AMA Residency: 1
Places Rated Score: 191   Places Rated Rank: 224

Saint John, NB
Fee-for-Service Physicians
    General/Family Practitioners: 110 **AA**
    Medical Specialists: 59 **B**
    Surgical Specialists: 44 **B**
Short-Term General Hospitals: 2 (776 beds)
    CCHFA Accredited: 2
    Residency Program: 2
Places Rated Score: 236   Places Rated Rank: 130

✓ St. John's, NF
Fee-for-Service Physicians
    General/Family Practitioners: 200 **AA**
    Medical Specialists: 145 **AA**
    Surgical Specialists: 69 **A**
Short-Term General Hospitals: 4 (1,206 beds)
    CCHFA Accredited: 4
    Residency Program: 4
Places Rated Score: 388   Places Rated Rank: 17

St. Joseph, MO
Office-Based Physicians
    General/Family Practitioners: 37 **B**
    Medical Specialists: 52 **B**
    Surgical Specialists: 34 **C**
Short-Term General Hospitals: 1 (580 beds)
    Services: 1 ★★★★
    JCAH Accredited: 1
Places Rated Score: 186   Places Rated Rank: 233

St. Louis, MO–IL
Office-Based Physicians
    General/Family Practitioners: 319 **C**
    Medical Specialists: 784 **C**
    Surgical Specialists: 422 **C**
Short-Term General Hospitals: 41 (12,620 beds)
    Services: 1 ★★, 3 ★★★, 37 ★★★★
    JCAH Accredited: 37
    AMA Residency: 14
Places Rated Score: 263   Places Rated Rank: 91

Salem, OR
Office-Based Physicians
    General/Family Practitioners: 142 **AA**

Rating

Rating

Medical Specialists: 129 — **B**
Surgical Specialists: 88 — **C**
Short-Term General Hospitals: 4 (533 beds)
  Services: 1 ★, 1 ★★★, 2 ★★★★
  JCAH Accredited: 4
MC Access: Portland–Salem–Vancouver, OR–WA
Places Rated Score: 157 — Places Rated Rank: 291

Salinas, CA
Office-Based Physicians
  General/Family Practitioners: 160 — **A**
  Medical Specialists: 177 — **B**
  Surgical Specialists: 126 — **B**
Short-Term General Hospitals: 5 (763 beds)
  Services: 1 ★★, 1 ★★★, 3 ★★★★
  JCAH Accredited: 5
  AMA Residency: 2
Places Rated Score: 171 — Places Rated Rank: 263

Salt Lake City–Ogden, UT
Office-Based Physicians
  General/Family Practitioners: 361 — **C**
  Medical Specialists: 927 — **A**
  Surgical Specialists: 554 — **A**
Short-Term General Hospitals: 14 (3,143 beds)
  Services: 3 ★★★, 11 ★★★★
  JCAH Accredited: 12
  AMA Residency: 5
Places Rated Score: 241 — Places Rated Rank: 120

San Angelo, TX
Office-Based Physicians
  General/Family Practitioners: 20 — **C**
  Medical Specialists: 73 — **A**
  Surgical Specialists: 51 — **AA**
Short-Term General Hospitals: 3 (486 beds)
  Services: 3 ★★★★
  JCAH Accredited: 3
Places Rated Score: 195 — Places Rated Rank: 216

San Antonio, TX
Office-Based Physicians
  General/Family Practitioners: 496 — **B**
  Medical Specialists: 935 — **A**
  Surgical Specialists: 560 — **A**
Short-Term General Hospitals: 19 (6,339 beds)
  Services: 1 ★, 1 ★★, 4 ★★★, 13 ★★★★
  JCAH Accredited: 16
  AMA Residency: 7
Places Rated Score: 266 — Places Rated Rank: 85

San Diego, CA
Office-Based Physicians
  General/Family Practitioners: 1,071 — **A**
  Medical Specialists: 2,137 — **AA**
  Surgical Specialists: 1,140 — **A**
Short-Term General Hospitals: 27 (7,302 beds)
  Services: 3 ★, 3 ★★★, 21 ★★★★
  JCAH Accredited: 27
  AMA Residency: 8
Places Rated Score: 281 — Places Rated Rank: 66

✓ San Francisco, CA
Office-Based Physicians
  General/Family Practitioners: 549 — **B**
  Medical Specialists: 2,827 — **AA**
  Surgical Specialists: 1,165 — **AA**
Short-Term General Hospitals: 22 (6,068 beds)
  Services: 3 ★, 3 ★★★, 16 ★★★★
  JCAH Accredited: 21
  AMA Residency: 13
MC Access: San Francisco–Oakland–San Jose, CA
Places Rated Score: 463 — Places Rated Rank: 8

San Jose, CA
Office-Based Physicians
  General/Family Practitioners: 476 — **B**
  Medical Specialists: 1,452 — **AA**
  Surgical Specialists: 795 — **AA**
Short-Term General Hospitals: 13 (3,425 beds)
  Services: 3 ★, 2 ★★★, 8 ★★★★
  JCAH Accredited: 10
  AMA Residency: 3
MC Access: San Francisco–Oakland–San Jose, CA
Places Rated Score: 257 — Places Rated Rank: 101

San Luis Obispo–Atascadero–Paso Robles, CA
Office-Based Physicians
  General/Family Practitioners: 116 — **AA**
  Medical Specialists: 156 — **A**
  Surgical Specialists: 97 — **A**
Short-Term General Hospitals: 5 (504 beds)
  Services: 1 ★★★, 4 ★★★★
  JCAH Accredited: 5
Places Rated Score: 191 — Places Rated Rank: 224

Santa Barbara–Santa Maria–Lompoc, CA
Office-Based Physicians
  General/Family Practitioners: 157 — **A**
  Medical Specialists: 364 — **AA**
  Surgical Specialists: 202 — **AA**
Short-Term General Hospitals: 8 (1,066 beds)
  Services: 1 ★★, 3 ★★★, 4 ★★★★
  JCAH Accredited: 8
  AMA Residency: 1
Places Rated Score: 234 — Places Rated Rank: 136

Santa Cruz–Watsonville, CA
Office-Based Physicians
  General/Family Practitioners: 131 — **AA**
  Medical Specialists: 171 — **A**
  Surgical Specialists: 98 — **A**
Short-Term General Hospitals: 2 (392 beds)
  Services: 1 ★, 1 ★★★★
  JCAH Accredited: 2
MC Access: San Francisco-Oakland-San Jose, CA
Places Rated Score: 206 — Places Rated Rank: 189

Santa Fe, NM
Office-Based Physicians
  General/Family Practitioners: 79 — **AA**
  Medical Specialists: 113 — **AA**
  Surgical Specialists: 59 — **AA**
Short-Term General Hospitals: 3 (318 beds)
  Services: 2 ★★★, 1 ★★★★
  JCAH Accredited: 2
Places Rated Score: 239 — Places Rated Rank: 125

Santa Rosa, CA
Office-Based Physicians
  General/Family Practitioners: 300 — **AA**
  Medical Specialists: 282 — **A**
  Surgical Specialists: 179 — **A**
Short-Term General Hospitals: 7 (743 beds)
  Services: 2 ★, 1 ★★★, 4 ★★★★
  JCAH Accredited: 7
  AMA Residency: 1
MC Access: San Francisco-Oakland-San Jose, CA
Places Rated Score: 236 — Places Rated Rank: 130

Sarasota-Bradenton, FL
Office-Based Physicians
  General/Family Practitioners: 207 — **A**
  Medical Specialists: 391 — **A**
  Surgical Specialists: 254 — **AA**
Short-Term General Hospitals: 6 (2,204 beds)
  Services: 1 ★★★, 5 ★★★★
  JCAH Accredited: 6
Places Rated Score: 215 — Places Rated Rank: 169

Rating   Rating

✓ Saskatoon, SK
Fee-for-Service Physicians
- General/Family Practitioners: 284   **AA**
- Medical Specialists: 161   **A**
- Surgical Specialists: 94   **A**

Short-Term General Hospitals: 3 (1,185 beds)
- CCHFA Accredited: 3
- Residency Program: 3

Places Rated Score: 348   Places Rated Rank: 22

Savannah, GA
Office-Based Physicians
- General/Family Practitioners: 86   **B**
- Medical Specialists: 165   **A**
- Surgical Specialists: 128   **A**

Short-Term General Hospitals: 4 (1,174 beds)
- Services: 1 ★★★, 3 ★★★★
- JCAH Accredited: 4
- AMA Residency: 1

Places Rated Score: 202   Places Rated Rank: 203

Scranton–Wilkes-Barre–Hazleton, PA
Office-Based Physicians
- General/Family Practitioners: 312   **A**
- Medical Specialists: 383   **B**
- Surgical Specialists: 245   **B**

Short-Term General Hospitals: 17 (3,653 beds)
- Services: 1 ★, 1 ★★, 2 ★★★, 13 ★★★★
- JCAH Accredited: 15
- AMA Residency: 6

Places Rated Score: 264   Places Rated Rank: 89

✓ Seattle–Bellevue–Everett, WA
Office-Based Physicians
- General/Family Practitioners: 1,384   **AA**
- Medical Specialists: 1,960   **AA**
- Surgical Specialists: 956   **A**

Short-Term General Hospitals: 26 (5,118 beds)
- Services: 1 ★★, 2 ★★★, 23 ★★★★
- JCAH Accredited: 22
- AMA Residency: 8

MC Access: Seattle–Tacoma–Bremerton, WA

Places Rated Score: 320   Places Rated Rank: 30

Sharon, PA
Office-Based Physicians
- General/Family Practitioners: 44   **B**
- Medical Specialists: 48   **C**
- Surgical Specialists: 48   **B**

Short-Term General Hospitals: 4 (666 beds)
- Services: 1 ★★★, 3 ★★★★
- JCAH Accredited: 3

Places Rated Score: 171   Places Rated Rank: 263

Sheboygan, WI
Office-Based Physicians
- General/Family Practitioners: 39   **B**
- Medical Specialists: 41   **C**
- Surgical Specialists: 34   **C**

Short-Term General Hospitals: 3 (397 beds)
- Services: 3 ★★★★
- JCAH Accredited: 3

Places Rated Score: 148   Places Rated Rank: 305

Sherbrooke, PQ
Fee-for-Service Physicians
- General/Family Practitioners: 130   **AA**
- Medical Specialists: 79   **B**
- Surgical Specialists: 42   **C**

Short-Term General Hospitals: 4 (1,193 beds)
- CCHFA Accredited: 4
- Residency Program: 4

Places Rated Score: 310   Places Rated Rank: 46

Sherman–Denison, TX
Office-Based Physicians
- General/Family Practitioners: 29   **C**
- Medical Specialists: 68   **A**
- Surgical Specialists: 42   **A**

Short-Term General Hospitals: 3 (562 beds)
- Services: 1 ★★★, 2 ★★★★
- JCAH Accredited: 3

Places Rated Score: 204   Places Rated Rank: 195

Shreveport–Bossier City, LA
Office-Based Physicians
- General/Family Practitioners: 116   **C**
- Medical Specialists: 313   **AA**
- Surgical Specialists: 223   **AA**

Short-Term General Hospitals: 14 (2,675 beds)
- Services: 4 ★, 1 ★★, 4 ★★★, 5 ★★★★
- JCAH Accredited: 12
- AMA Residency: 3

Places Rated Score: 274   Places Rated Rank: 80

Sioux City, IA–NE
Office-Based Physicians
- General/Family Practitioners: 51   **A**
- Medical Specialists: 57   **B**
- Surgical Specialists: 48   **B**

Short-Term General Hospitals: 2 (807 beds)
- Services: 2 ★★★★
- JCAH Accredited: 2
- AMA Residency: 2

Places Rated Score: 225   Places Rated Rank: 150

✓ Sioux Falls, SD
Office-Based Physicians
- General/Family Practitioners: 130   **AA**
- Medical Specialists: 115   **AA**
- Surgical Specialists: 65   **A**

Short-Term General Hospitals: 5 (1,201 beds)
- Services: 1 ★★, 1 ★★★, 3 ★★★★
- JCAH Accredited: 3
- AMA Residency: 3

Places Rated Score: 337   Places Rated Rank: 23

South Bend, IN
Office-Based Physicians
- General/Family Practitioners: 151   **AA**
- Medical Specialists: 137   **B**
- Surgical Specialists: 83   **C**

Short-Term General Hospitals: 3 (879 beds)
- Services: 3 ★★★★
- JCAH Accredited: 2
- AMA Residency: 2

Places Rated Score: 205   Places Rated Rank: 190

Spokane, WA
Office-Based Physicians
- General/Family Practitioners: 250   **AA**
- Medical Specialists: 287   **A**
- Surgical Specialists: 192   **AA**

Short-Term General Hospitals: 7 (1,545 beds)
- Services: 1 ★★★, 6 ★★★★
- JCAH Accredited: 7
- AMA Residency: 3

Places Rated Score: 274   Places Rated Rank: 80

Springfield, IL
Office-Based Physicians
- General/Family Practitioners: 70   **B**
- Medical Specialists: 180   **AA**
- Surgical Specialists: 113   **AA**

Short-Term General Hospitals: 3 (1,351 beds)
- Services: 3 ★★★★
- JCAH Accredited: 3
- AMA Residency: 2

Places Rated Score: 282   Places Rated Rank: 64

Rating

Rating

Springfield, MA
Office-Based Physicians
   General/Family Practitioners: 165   C
   Medical Specialists: 460   A
   Surgical Specialists: 239   B
Short-Term General Hospitals: 9 (1,898 beds)
   Services: 1 ★★★, 8 ★★★★
   JCAH Accredited: 9
   AMA Residency: 1
Places Rated Score: 185   Places Rated Rank: 237

Springfield, MO
Office-Based Physicians
   General/Family Practitioners: 75   C
   Medical Specialists: 222   AA
   Surgical Specialists: 147   AA
Short-Term General Hospitals: 4 (1,877 beds)
   Services: 4 ★★★★
   JCAH Accredited: 3
   AMA Residency: 1
Places Rated Score: 245   Places Rated Rank: 116

✓ Stamford–Norwalk, CT
Office-Based Physicians
   General/Family Practitioners: 210   C
   Medical Specialists: 660   AA
   Surgical Specialists: 482   AA
Short-Term General Hospitals: 6 (1,315 beds)
   Services: 2 ★★, 1 ★★★, 3 ★★★★
   JCAH Accredited: 6
   AMA Residency: 4
MC Access: New York–Northern New Jersey–Long
Island, NY–NJ–CT
Places Rated Score: 316   Places Rated Rank: 35

State College, PA
Office-Based Physicians
   General/Family Practitioners: 61   A
   Medical Specialists: 58   B
   Surgical Specialists: 32   C
Short-Term General Hospitals: 2 (298 beds)
   Services: 1 ★★★, 1 ★★★★
   JCAH Accredited: 2
Places Rated Score: 145   Places Rated Rank: 309

Steubenville–Weirton, OH–WV
Office-Based Physicians
   General/Family Practitioners: 38   C
   Medical Specialists: 50   C
   Surgical Specialists: 33   C
Short-Term General Hospitals: 4 (666 beds)
   Services: 1 ★★, 3 ★★★★
   JCAH Accredited: 3
Places Rated Score: 132   Places Rated Rank: 324

Stockton–Lodi, CA
Office-Based Physicians
   General/Family Practitioners: 197   A
   Medical Specialists: 222   B
   Surgical Specialists: 152   C
Short-Term General Hospitals: 7 (1,023 beds)
   Services: 1 ★, 6 ★★★★
   JCAH Accredited: 6
   AMA Residency: 1
Places Rated Score: 149   Places Rated Rank: 303

Sudbury, ON
Fee-for-Service Physicians
   General/Family Practitioners: 115   AA
   Medical Specialists: 57   C
   Surgical Specialists: 53   B
Short-Term General Hospitals: 3 (857 beds)
   CCHFA Accredited: 3
   Residency Program: 2
Places Rated Score: 167   Places Rated Rank: 270

Sumter, SC
Office-Based Physicians
   General/Family Practitioners: 23   C
   Medical Specialists: 34   C
   Surgical Specialists: 26   C
Short-Term General Hospitals: 2 (254 beds)
   Services: 1 ★, 1 ★★★★
   JCAH Accredited: 2
Places Rated Score: 105   Places Rated Rank: 339

Syracuse, NY
Office-Based Physicians
   General/Family Practitioners: 255   B
   Medical Specialists: 508   A
   Surgical Specialists: 320   A
Short-Term General Hospitals: 10 (2,781 beds)
   Services: 2 ★★★, 8 ★★★★
   JCAH Accredited: 10
   AMA Residency: 5
Places Rated Score: 233   Places Rated Rank: 139

Tacoma, WA
Office-Based Physicians
   General/Family Practitioners: 294   AA
   Medical Specialists: 315   B
   Surgical Specialists: 191   C
Short-Term General Hospitals: 9 (2,117 beds)
   Services: 2 ★, 1 ★★★, 6 ★★★★
   JCAH Accredited: 8
   AMA Residency: 3
MC Access: Seattle–Tacoma–Bremerton, WA
Places Rated Score: 211   Places Rated Rank: 176

Tallahassee, FL
Office-Based Physicians
   General/Family Practitioners: 139   AA
   Medical Specialists: 136   B
   Surgical Specialists: 98   B
Short-Term General Hospitals: 3 (807 beds)
   Services: 1 ★★★, 2 ★★★★
   JCAH Accredited: 3
   AMA Residency: 1
Places Rated Score: 201   Places Rated Rank: 204

Tampa–St. Petersburg–Clearwater, FL
Office-Based Physicians
   General/Family Practitioners: 672   B
   Medical Specialists: 1,530   A
   Surgical Specialists: 869   A
Short-Term General Hospitals: 37 (9,954 beds)
   Services: 4 ★, 1 ★★, 10 ★★★, 22 ★★★★
   JCAH Accredited: 33
   AMA Residency: 5
Places Rated Score: 243   Places Rated Rank: 118

Terre Haute, IN
Office-Based Physicians
   General/Family Practitioners: 62   A
   Medical Specialists: 64   C
   Surgical Specialists: 54   B
Short-Term General Hospitals: 4 (705 beds)
   Services: 1 ★★★, 3 ★★★★
   JCAH Accredited: 4
   AMA Residency: 1
Places Rated Score: 180   Places Rated Rank: 245

Texarkana, TX–Texarkana, AR
Office-Based Physicians
   General/Family Practitioners: 49   A
   Medical Specialists: 70   B
   Surgical Specialists: 62   AA
Short-Term General Hospitals: 4 (730 beds)
   Services: 1 ★, 1 ★★★, 2 ★★★★
   JCAH Accredited: 3
Places Rated Score: 211   Places Rated Rank: 176

Thunder Bay, ON
Fee-for-Service Physicians
   General/Family Practitioners: 117   AA
   Medical Specialists: 39   C
   Surgical Specialists: 29   C
Short-Term General Hospitals: 3 (655 beds)
   CCHFA Accredited: 3
   Residency Program: 1
Places Rated Score: 212   Places Rated Rank: 173

Toledo, OH
Office-Based Physicians
   General/Family Practitioners: 327   AA
   Medical Specialists: 441   A
   Surgical Specialists: 298   A
Short-Term General Hospitals: 11 (3,254 beds)
   Services: 1 ★★★, 10 ★★★★
   JCAH Accredited: 10
   AMA Residency: 5
Places Rated Score: 276   Places Rated Rank: 74

Topeka, KS
Office-Based Physicians
   General/Family Practitioners: 48   C
   Medical Specialists: 168   AA
   Surgical Specialists: 80   A
Short-Term General Hospitals: 2 (700 beds)
   Services: 2 ★★★★
   JCAH Accredited: 2
   AMA Residency: 1
Places Rated Score: 237   Places Rated Rank: 128

✓ Toronto, ON
Fee-for-Service Physicians
   General/Family Practitioners: 4,190   AA
   Medical Specialists: 2,180   B
   Surgical Specialists: 989   C
Short-Term General Hospitals: 35 (12,314 beds)
   CCHFA Accredited: 34
   Residency Program: 12
MC Access: Toronto–Ontario Shore, ON
Places Rated Score: 350   Places Rated Rank: 21

Trenton, NJ
Office-Based Physicians
   General/Family Practitioners: 67   C
   Medical Specialists: 392   AA
   Surgical Specialists: 199   AA
Short-Term General Hospitals: 5 (1,608 beds)
   Services: 5 ★★★★
   JCAH Accredited: 5
   AMA Residency: 3
MC Access: New York–Northern New Jersey–Long
   Island, NY–NJ–CT
Places Rated Score: 287   Places Rated Rank: 60

Trois–Rivieres, PQ
Fee-for-Service Physicians
   General/Family Practitioners: 109   AA
   Medical Specialists: 50   C
   Surgical Specialists: 47   B
Short-Term General Hospitals: 3 (846 beds)
   CCHFA Accredited: 3
   Residency Program: 2
Places Rated Score: 237   Places Rated Rank: 128

Tucson, AZ
Office-Based Physicians
   General/Family Practitioners: 216   B
   Medical Specialists: 677   AA
   Surgical Specialists: 324   A
Short-Term General Hospitals: 11 (2,408 beds)
   Services: 1 ★, 1 ★★, 1 ★★★, 8 ★★★★
   JCAH Accredited: 11
   AMA Residency: 6
Places Rated Score: 276   Places Rated Rank: 74

Tulsa, OK
Office-Based Physicians
   General/Family Practitioners: 244   B
   Medical Specialists: 473   A
   Surgical Specialists: 275   B
Short-Term General Hospitals: 15 (2,948 beds)
   Services: 4 ★, 3 ★★, 2 ★★★, 6 ★★★★
   JCAH Accredited: 10
   AMA Residency: 3
Places Rated Score: 211   Places Rated Rank: 176

Tuscaloosa, AL
Office-Based Physicians
   General/Family Practitioners: 46   C
   Medical Specialists: 97   A
   Surgical Specialists: 60   B
Short-Term General Hospitals: 3 (724 beds)
   Services: 1 ★, 1 ★★★, 1 ★★★★
   JCAH Accredited: 3
   AMA Residency: 1
Places Rated Score: 191   Places Rated Rank: 224

Tyler, TX
Office-Based Physicians
   General/Family Practitioners: 53   B
   Medical Specialists: 137   AA
   Surgical Specialists: 90   AA
Short-Term General Hospitals: 4 (667 beds)
   Services: 1 ★★, 1 ★★★, 2 ★★★★
   JCAH Accredited: 3
   AMA Residency: 2
Places Rated Score: 248   Places Rated Rank: 114

Utica–Rome, NY
Office-Based Physicians
   General/Family Practitioners: 111   B
   Medical Specialists: 143   B
   Surgical Specialists: 117   B
Short-Term General Hospitals: 7 (1,087 beds)
   Services: 3 ★★★, 4 ★★★★
   JCAH Accredited: 5
   AMA Residency: 1
Places Rated Score: 162   Places Rated Rank: 280

Vallejo–Fairfield–Napa, CA
Office-Based Physicians
   General/Family Practitioners: 176   B
   Medical Specialists: 299   A
   Surgical Specialists: 151   C
Short-Term General Hospitals: 9 (1,808 beds)
   Services: 1 ★, 1 ★★★, 7 ★★★★
   JCAH Accredited: 7
   AMA Residency: 1
MC Access: San Francisco–Oakland–San Jose, CA
Places Rated Score: 209   Places Rated Rank: 183

✓ Vancouver, BC
Fee-for-Service Physicians
   General/Family Practitioners: 1,856   AA
   Medical Specialists: 940   A
   Surgical Specialists: 528   C
Short-Term General Hospitals: 21 (9,338 beds)
   CCHFA Accredited: 21
   Residency Program: 12
Places Rated Score: 390   Places Rated Rank: 16

Vancouver, WA
Office-Based Physicians
   General/Family Practitioners: 81   B
   Medical Specialists: 102   C
   Surgical Specialists: 69   C
Short-Term General Hospitals: 1 (290 beds)
   Services: 1 ★★★★
   JCAH Accredited: 1
MC Access: Portland–Salem–Vancouver, OR–WA
Places Rated Score: 126   Places Rated Rank: 329

Rating

Rating

Ventura, CA
Office-Based Physicians
General/Family Practitioners: 321   A
Medical Specialists: 430   A
Surgical Specialists: 256   B
Short-Term General Hospitals: 8 (1,427 beds)
Services: 2 ★★★, 6 ★★★★
JCAH Accredited: 8
AMA Residency: 1
MC Access: Los Angeles–Riverside–Orange
County, CA
Places Rated Score: 207   Places Rated Rank: 186

Victoria, BC
Fee-for-Service Physicians
General/Family Practitioners: 382   AA
Medical Specialists: 151   B
Surgical Specialists: 95   C
Short-Term General Hospitals: 2 (1,914 beds)
CCHFA Accredited: 2
Places Rated Score: 289   Places Rated Rank: 58

Victoria, TX
Office-Based Physicians
General/Family Practitioners: 45   AA
Medical Specialists: 59   A
Surgical Specialists: 39   AA
Short-Term General Hospitals: 3 (531 beds)
Services: 3 ★★★★
JCAH Accredited: 3
Places Rated Score: 259   Places Rated Rank: 99

Vineland–Millville–Bridgeton, NJ
Office-Based Physicians
General/Family Practitioners: 45   B
Medical Specialists: 70   B
Surgical Specialists: 44   C
Short-Term General Hospitals: 2 (553 beds)
Services: 2 ★★★★
JCAH Accredited: 1
MC Access: Philadelphia–Wilmington–Atlantic City,
PA–NJ–DE–MD
Places Rated Score: 193   Places Rated Rank: 218

Visalia–Tulare–Porterville, CA
Office-Based Physicians
General/Family Practitioners: 131   A
Medical Specialists: 126   C
Surgical Specialists: 71   C
Short-Term General Hospitals: 7 (648 beds)
Services: 1 ★, 2 ★★, 1 ★★★, 3 ★★★★
JCAH Accredited: 7
Places Rated Score: 125   Places Rated Rank: 330

Waco, TX
Office-Based Physicians
General/Family Practitioners: 91   A
Medical Specialists: 96   B
Surgical Specialists: 72   B
Short-Term General Hospitals: 3 (541 beds)
Services: 1 ★★★, 2 ★★★★
JCAH Accredited: 3
AMA Residency: 2
Places Rated Score: 185   Places Rated Rank: 237

✓ Washington, DC–MD–VA–WV
Office-Based Physicians
General/Family Practitioners: 1,225   C
Medical Specialists: 4,742   AA
Surgical Specialists: 2,166   AA
Short-Term General Hospitals: 45 (13,821 beds)
Services: 1 ★, 4 ★★★, 40 ★★★★
JCAH Accredited: 45
AMA Residency: 19

MC Access: Washington–Baltimore,
DC–MD–VA–WV
Places Rated Score: 428   Places Rated Rank: 10

Waterbury, CT
Office-Based Physicians
General/Family Practitioners: 131   C
Medical Specialists: 655   AA
Surgical Specialists: 459   AA
Short-Term General Hospitals: 2 (618 beds)
Services: 2 ★★★★
JCAH Accredited: 2
AMA Residency: 2
Places Rated Score: 225   Places Rated Rank: 150

Waterloo–Cedar Falls, IA
Office-Based Physicians
General/Family Practitioners: 79   AA
Medical Specialists: 67   B
Surgical Specialists: 51   B
Short-Term General Hospitals: 3 (657 beds)
Services: 3 ★★★★
JCAH Accredited: 3
AMA Residency: 2
Places Rated Score: 232   Places Rated Rank: 141

Wausau, WI
Office-Based Physicians
General/Family Practitioners: 64   AA
Medical Specialists: 55   B
Surgical Specialists: 42   B
Short-Term General Hospitals: 1 (253 beds)
Services: 1 ★★★★
JCAH Accredited: 1
AMA Residency: 1
Places Rated Score: 171   Places Rated Rank: 263

West Palm Beach–Boca Raton, FL
Office-Based Physicians
General/Family Practitioners: 274   B
Medical Specialists: 787   AA
Surgical Specialists: 480   AA
Short-Term General Hospitals: 15 (3,311 beds)
Services: 4 ★★★, 11 ★★★★
JCAH Accredited: 15
Places Rated Score: 212   Places Rated Rank: 173

Wheeling, WV–OH
Office-Based Physicians
General/Family Practitioners: 81   AA
Medical Specialists: 89   B
Surgical Specialists: 75   A
Short-Term General Hospitals: 6 (1,085 beds)
Services: 6 ★★★★
JCAH Accredited: 6
AMA Residency: 2
Places Rated Score: 243   Places Rated Rank: 118

Wichita, KS
Office-Based Physicians
General/Family Practitioners: 256   AA
Medical Specialists: 319   A
Surgical Specialists: 192   B
Short-Term General Hospitals: 10 (2,544 beds)
Services: 1 ★, 2 ★★★, 7 ★★★★
JCAH Accredited: 8
AMA Residency: 4
Places Rated Score: 249   Places Rated Rank: 110

Wichita Falls, TX
Office-Based Physicians
General/Family Practitioners: 69   AA
Medical Specialists: 77   B
Surgical Specialists: 60   A

Rating

Rating

Short-Term General Hospitals: 4 (567 beds)
   Services: 1 ⋆⋆, 1 ⋆⋆⋆, 2 ⋆⋆⋆⋆
   JCAH Accredited: 3
   AMA Residency: 2
Places Rated Score: 221   Places Rated Rank: 163

Williamsport, PA
Office-Based Physicians
   General/Family Practitioners: 78   AA
   Medical Specialists: 70   B
   Surgical Specialists: 51   A
Short-Term General Hospitals: 4 (675 beds)
   Services: 1 ⋆⋆⋆, 3 ⋆⋆⋆⋆
   JCAH Accredited: 4
   AMA Residency: 1
Places Rated Score: 234   Places Rated Rank: 136

Wilmington, NC
Office-Based Physicians
   General/Family Practitioners: 20   C
   Medical Specialists: 122   AA
   Surgical Specialists: 87   AA
Short-Term General Hospitals: 2 (558 beds)
   Services: 2 ⋆⋆⋆⋆
   JCAH Accredited: 2
   AMA Residency: 1
Places Rated Score: 244   Places Rated Rank: 117

Wilmington–Newark, DE–MD
Office-Based Physicians
   General/Family Practitioners: 178   B
   Medical Specialists: 367   A
   Surgical Specialists: 190   B
Short-Term General Hospitals: 5 (1,755 beds)
   Services: 5 ⋆⋆⋆⋆
   JCAH Accredited: 4
   AMA Residency: 3
MC Access: Philadelphia–Wilmington–Atlantic City,
   PA–NJ–DE–MD
Places Rated Score: 241   Places Rated Rank: 120

Windsor, ON
Fee-for-Service Physicians
   General/Family Practitioners: 187   AA
   Medical Specialists: 75   C
   Surgical Specialists: 81   C
Short-Term General Hospitals: 4 (1,385 beds)
   CCHFA Accredited: 4
   Residency Program: 2
Places Rated Score: 204   Places Rated Rank: 195

Winnipeg, MB
Fee-for-Service Physicians
   General/Family Practitioners: 634   AA
   Medical Specialists: 500   A
   Surgical Specialists: 237   B
Short-Term General Hospitals: 7 (3,261 beds)
   CCHFA Accredited: 7
   Residency Program: 2
Places Rated Score: 281   Places Rated Rank: 66

Worcester–Fitchburg–Leominster, MA
Office-Based Physicians
   General/Family Practitioners: 238   B
   Medical Specialists: 598   AA
   Surgical Specialists: 267   B
Short-Term General Hospitals: 13 (2,489 beds)
   Services: 1 ⋆, 1 ⋆⋆⋆, 11 ⋆⋆⋆⋆
   JCAH Accredited: 13
   AMA Residency: 5
MC Access: Boston–New Bedford–Nashua,
   MA–NH
Places Rated Score: 264   Places Rated Rank: 89

Yakima, WA
Office-Based Physicians
   General/Family Practitioners: 68   B
   Medical Specialists: 85   B
   Surgical Specialists: 66   C
Short-Term General Hospitals: 5 (532 beds)
   Services: 1 ⋆, 1 ⋆⋆⋆, 3 ⋆⋆⋆⋆
   JCAH Accredited: 3
Places Rated Score: 144   Places Rated Rank: 312

Yolo, CA
Office-Based Physicians
   General/Family Practitioners: 73   AA
   Medical Specialists: 106   A
   Surgical Specialists: 54   B
Short-Term General Hospitals: 3 (286 beds)
   Services: 2 ⋆⋆⋆, 1 ⋆⋆⋆⋆
   JCAH Accredited: 3
MC Access: Sacramento–Yolo, CA
Places Rated Score: 186   Places Rated Rank: 233

York, PA
Office-Based Physicians
   General/Family Practitioners: 175   AA
   Medical Specialists: 140   C
   Surgical Specialists: 83   C
Short-Term General Hospitals: 3 (863 beds)
   Services: 1 ⋆⋆⋆, 2 ⋆⋆⋆⋆
   JCAH Accredited: 2
   AMA Residency: 1
Places Rated Score: 152   Places Rated Rank: 296

Youngstown–Warren, OH
Office-Based Physicians
   General/Family Practitioners: 132   C
   Medical Specialists: 304   B
   Surgical Specialists: 204   C
Short-Term General Hospitals: 10 (2,763 beds)
   Services: 1 ⋆⋆, 9 ⋆⋆⋆⋆
   JCAH Accredited: 6
   AMA Residency: 3
Places Rated Score: 182   Places Rated Rank: 242

Yuba City, CA
Office-Based Physicians
   General/Family Practitioners: 45   B
   Medical Specialists: 66   B
   Surgical Specialists: 46   B
Short-Term General Hospitals: 3 (272 beds)
   Services: 1 ⋆, 2 ⋆⋆⋆
   JCAH Accredited: 2
Places Rated Score: 150   Places Rated Rank: 302

Yuma, AZ
Office-Based Physicians
   General/Family Practitioners: 35   C
   Medical Specialists: 50   C
   Surgical Specialists: 31   C
Short-Term General Hospitals: 3 (287 beds)
   Services: 1 ⋆⋆, 1 ⋆⋆⋆, 1 ⋆⋆⋆⋆
   JCAH Accredited: 2
Places Rated Score: 119   Places Rated Rank: 333

Et Cetera

HEALTH CARE IN CANADA

Canada's taxpayer-financed, comprehensive health insurance system had much opposition when *medicare*, as it's popularly called, came into play nearly three decades ago. Business and industry predicted failure because if it were to be managed by government, doctors saw it as a threat to their livelihoods and some made plans to move south. Today, most Canadian doctors rate the system as "good to excellent," and business has been brought round because the cost is spread across society on the basis of ability to pay.

How It Works

Canada's health insurance system covers all medically necessary hospital and physician services for everyone. When Canadians need medical care, they make an appointment with the doctor of their choice, pull out the health insurance card issued to them by their province, and ask for treatment. Patients contend with no flurry of forms to fill out; there aren't any. Nor are there deductibles, co-payments, or dollar limits on coverage.

There are forms the physician fills out, but the paperwork is swift and simple. He or she bills the province on a fee-for-service basis under a published schedule negotiated each year by peers in their own medical association and the provincial government.

Almost all hospitals are nonprofit institutions operated by municipalities, religious, or voluntary organizations. The hospital's board and its administrators grapple with tight budgets, but they control spending decisions as long as they don't overspend a figure they negotiate every year with the provincial ministry of health.

Canadians do have to spend their own money on dental care, eyeglasses, and some drugs. About three out of every ten dollars spent on health care comes out of pocket. There are private insurers, but they may not offer coverage that duplicates government programs, only supplemental benefits. Their customers include retired Canadians who winter in Florida, Texas, and the American Southwest.

Money Matters

In 1991, Canada spent $2,100 and the United States spent $2,800 on health care per capita. American administrative costs make up most of the $700 difference. Under the Canadian system, there are no marketing expenses, no staff to estimate risk and decide who should be denied or offered coverage. Neither doctors nor hospitals have to verify coverage or complete onerous paperwork required by multiple private insurance firms or resolve double-billing problems. Also, Canadian doctors pay relatively low premiums to the nonprofit Medical Protective Association for malpractice insurance.

Problems

For all the attention Canada's health-care system gets in the debate over reform, it isn't likely that the United States will copy the Canadian system. "America, with the world's most expensive health-care system," one expert noted, "has little to learn from a neighbor with the world's *second* most expensive system."

Canada is working out its *own* health-care crisis. As popular as it is with consumers, the system has become a monster to fund. Nearly a third of provincial budgets go to health care, the money coming from general revenues, high sales taxes, and high employer-paid payroll taxes. Two provinces, Alberta and British Columbia, collect premiums from residents.

Critics, many of them Canadian physicians, also point to crowded hospitals, limited availability of new medical technology, long waiting lists even for lifesaving surgeries, and a reliance on rationing for the system to function.

HEALTHY LIFE/LONGER LIFE

Do you subscribe to the theory of when your time is up, you go? Then you may be surprised at current thinking. Experts now conclude that it's less likely to be a stray bullet or virus that kills you than the way you lead your life.

The most common causes of death at the turn of the century—typhoid fever, cholera, tuberculosis, smallpox, gastroenteritis, and nephritis—have been practically eliminated by scientific advances and improved sanitation. Today, more than 70 percent of the two million Americans who die each year are victims of heart disease, cancer, stroke, cirrhosis of the liver, bronchitis, asthma, and emphysema—the so-called lifestyle diseases that may be aggravated by such behavior as overeating, heavy drinking, smoking, and lack of exercise. To see how your daily habits measure up, take a look at the table "How Healthy Is Your Lifestyle?" The creators of this table warn that some risk factors are more important than others. Thus, an entirely accurate picture of your health may not emerge from practicing self-analysis. However, they add, changing your habits so that you qualify for the low-risk ratings will result in a longer life. The following are some suggestions—certainly not new,

How Healthy Is Your Lifestyle?

Risk Category	No Risk	Slight Risk	Substantial Risk	Heavy Risk	Dangerous Risk
Smoking	No smoking or stopped for at least 10 years	Less than 10 cigarettes, 5 pipes or cigars a day	Half pack a day	1 pack a day	2 or more packs a day
Alcohol	Nondrinker	Stopped drinker	6 drinks per week	More than 6 drinks per week	More than 2 drinks per day
Trimness	Lean	Slightly plump	Moderately obese	Considerably obese	Grossly obese
Physical activity	Walk more than 2 miles a day or climb 20 or more flights of stairs a day	Walk 1.5–2 miles a day or climb 15–20 flights of stairs a day	Walk only 0.5 to 1.5 miles a day or climb only 5–15 flights of stairs a day	Walk only 2–5 blocks a day or climb 2–4 flights of stairs a day	Walk less than 2 blocks a day or climb less than 2 flights of stairs a day
Prescription drugs	With doctor's consent, following orders carefully	Take medication daily without side effects	Take medication when needed with few side effects	Use sleeping and nerve pills regularly without doctor's supervision	Without doctor's consent, mix with other drugs or alcohol
Nonprescription drugs	Use occasionally only for short periods. Label warnings heeded				Continuing use, drinking or driving despite label warnings
Alcohol and driving —boats, cars, motor- cycles, snowmobiles	Never drink. Drive only with safety aids—seat belt, helmet, life jacket	Never drive after drinking without safety aids	Drive after 2 drinks with safety aids	Drive after 2 drinks without safety aids	Drive after more than 2 drinks without safety aids
Motor vehicle safety	Always wear seat belt	Wear seat belt more than half of the time	Wear seat belt as a driver half of the time	Wear seat belt as a passenger half of the time	Wear seat belt less than half of the time
Water safety— swimming and boating	Qualified expert	Know how to swim and the safety rules	Know how to swim and may swim after 1 drink or nerve drug	Do not know how to swim but use life jacket half of the time	Do not know how to swim; never use life jacket
Blood cholesterol	Less than 180	180–220	220–280	280–320	320 and up
Blood pressure	120/80 or less	120/80–140/90	140/90–160/100	160/100–180/105	Above 180/105
Blood sugar	Less than 120 two hours after a meal of syrup and pancakes	Between 110 and 130 two hours after meals; checked each 3 months	Blood sugar more than 150 without diet control	Blood sugar more than 150 without diet control, doctor's care	Diabetes without doctor's care at less than 45 years of age
FOR WOMEN ONLY					
Breast check for lumps	Monthly self-exam and yearly check by physician	Monthly self-exam but no doctor exam	Self-exam 2–3 times a year but no doctor's exam	1 time a year by a doctor	Never
Pap smear	Every year	Every 3 years	Every 4 years	Never	Never; nonmenstrual bleeding

Source: Methodist Hospital of Indianapolis, Inc. Prepared by Pamela Hall under the supervision of Drs. Lewis C. Robbins and Jack H. Hall, developers of the Health Hazard Appraisal System. Used by permission.

but still as healthful as the first time you heard them—that can help you reduce your health risks. If you haven't yet paid heed to the wisdom of these suggestions, perhaps this will nudge you into a healthier style of living.

Stop smoking and drink only in moderation. Cigarette smokers run twice the risk that nonsmokers do of death from coronary disease. Smoking also contributes to stroke, lung cancer, emphysema, and bronchitis. Likewise, an excess of alcohol can be dangerous, increasing chances of developing cirrhosis of the liver (this condition is found six times as frequently among alcoholics as among nonalcoholics) and cardiovascular problems. Drinking, too, combined with driving multiplies the risk of dying in an automobile accident; at least half of such accidents in the United States involve drunk drivers.

Eat a balanced diet and watch your weight. Six of the ten leading causes of death have been linked to diet: heart attack, stroke, atherosclerosis, cancer, cirrhosis of the liver, and diabetes. Reducing your intake of refined flour and sugar, salt (which in excess contributes to high blood pressure), and saturated fats (which have been implicated as factors in heart disease and stroke) while choosing from a range of meat, poultry, fish, fruits, vegetables, and fiber foods (which have been shown to prevent colon cancer) is highly recommended. A balanced diet can also help you to lose extra weight, which puts added stress on the heart and organs, aggravating disease conditions.

Get regular exercise. Exercise, now seen almost as a miracle drug, can help you maintain proper weight, keep your body in good operating condition, and relieve stress (which contributes to ulcers and high blood pressure). It helps prevent premature aging and degeneration of bone (osteoporosis), muscles, and joints. The use-it-or-lose-it maxim definitely applies here.

Get regular medical care. Be sure to consult your doctor regularly and have whatever checkups or tests he or she recommends, such as a Pap smear, blood pressure, or blood cholesterol tests.

Health-Care Reform

While overhauling the U.S. health-care system continues to preoccupy policymakers in Washington, six states have already undertaken their own reforms.

Florida—Legislation providing universal coverage beginning in 1995 is on the governor's desk. Included in the plan is a standard benefits package and a system of community health purchasing agents.

Hawaii—The state will begin its third decade of requiring employers to provide health insurance to all workers who put in more than 20 hours per week. In 1988, Hawaii also established the first state health insurance program to provide low-cost insurance to low-income people.

Massachusetts—Legislation passed to require employers to either provide insurance to workers or pay into a state fund that would purchase insurance becomes effective in 1995.

Minnesota—Legislation passed to offer subsidized insurance to low-income, uninsured families became effective in January 1992.

Oregon—By 1995, employers not offering health insurance to workers will be taxed and their employees will be placed in a state-run plan. Medicaid will cover all persons below the official poverty line, but fewer services would be covered.

Vermont—Reform legislation to form a universal access system with global budgets for hospitals and physician services and a centralized health planning agency was passed in 1992.

FINDING THE RIGHT DOCTOR

Not all doctors are created equal. The doctor you select and the hospital in which you're treated may be more important in determining the outcome of your illness than the disease you have. When you're selecting a surgeon, for example, you need to know how often the surgeon has done your kind of surgery (more is better) and what the outcome has been. Compare the records of several surgeons to get a sense of what a "good" track record is. Don't forget to trust your intuitions about doctors. How comfortable do you feel with the doctor? Your gut feeling could be the deciding factor.

The American Medical Association is the U.S. licensing body for physicians, but individual states vary in their licensing requirements. Highly populated states like New York and California have large staffs in their state licensing departments that can perform more thorough investigations of complaints against doctors. On the other hand, less densely populated states such as Idaho do not have the same investigative resources. But licensing boards alone cannot track down all the bad doctors. Medical schools, where students first enter the doctor track; licensing boards; national, state, and local professional societies; and hospitals (where most doc-

tors have staff privileges) must work together in order to assure that patients are treated by competent, licensed professionals.

The Health Care Financing Administration, which reimburses doctors and hospitals that treat Medicare and Medicaid patients, also has plans to help consumers in their selection of doctors. It will soon begin a long-term project of rating doctors by how well their patients do—as indicated by mortality rates and speed of recovery, for example.

In the meantime, consider the following suggestions. Chances are good that you'll have to choose a new physician at some point; even if you don't move, your doctor might. Finding a replacement for the person in whom you may have put a lot of trust isn't always easy. Give some thought to the kind of doctor you are most comfortable with. Do you want to place complete faith in your physician? Or do you have questions about your treatment? Do you like a cooperative arrangement in which you and your doctor work as a team? It's very important to most people that they have a doctor who will listen to their complaints, worries, and concerns, rather than one who may make patients feel that they're questioning the doctor's authority.

If you're planning to move, you might ask your present doctor if he or she knows anything about doctors in your destination. Or you may get names from the nearest hospital at the new location, from friends you make, from medical societies, and from new neighbors. Given the competition for insured patients, don't be surprised to receive mail from hospitals touting their services and the quality of physicians on their referral network.

When you have decided whom you want to contact call that doctor's office, saying that you are a prospective patient, and ask to speak to the doctor briefly. You may have to agree to call back, but making connection with a professional voice is an important step. If you can't arrange this, if the doctor is "too busy," you probably ought to go to the next name on your list.

When you do make contact, tell the doctor enough about yourself so that he or she has a good idea of who you are and what your problems may be. If the doctor sounds "right" to you, you could ask about fees and emergencies. Or you may wish to save some of these questions for a personal visit. It is important to establish through the initial phone call or visit that you and the doctor will be at ease with each other.

Evaluate the doctor's attitude. If he or she doesn't want to bother with you now, you will probably get that don't-bother-me treatment sooner or later when dealing with specific problems. Make sure that:

- You can openly discuss your feelings and personal concerns about sexual and emotional problems.
- The doctor isn't vague, impatient, or unwilling to answer all your questions about the causes and treatment of your physical problems.

- The doctor takes a thorough history on you and asks about past physical and emotional problems, family medical history, medication you are taking, and other matters affecting your health.
- The doctor doesn't automatically prescribe drugs rather than deal with real causes of your medical problems.
- The doctor has an associate to whom you can turn should your doctor retire or die.

Talk with the doctor about the transfer of your medical records. Some doctors like to have them, especially if there is any specific medical problem or chronic condition. Other doctors prefer to develop new records.

Even if you feel fine, arrange to have a physical or at least a quick checkup. Should an emergency occur, the doctor will have basic information about you and some knowledge of your needs, and you will avoid the stress of trying to work with a doctor who has to learn about you in an emergency.

Crime

In Duluth, MN, domestic violence on the farm and outside pushers developing a base for their illegal pharmaceutical trade are common items in the local news. Down I-35 in the Twin Cities, stories of convenience-store stickups and drug-related drive-by killings aren't uncommon either. If you were passing through either metro area and learned of these crimes, you might wonder whether you were any safer on the prairie than you'd be in East Los Angeles or the Bronx.

In fact, neither Duluth nor Minneapolis–St. Paul have crime rates anywhere near the metro-area average. The raw odds of your being a crime victim in either place are much below what they would be elsewhere. Indeed, among the metro areas profiled in *Places Rated Almanac*, reporters working the police beat in some have so few violent crime stories to write up that a reader of the paper may wonder whether anything interesting goes on there at all. In other metro areas, day-to-day existence seems just plain dangerous.

If you decide to live in Johnstown, PA, the raw odds of your being a crime victim in a year's residence are 60 to 1. Should you choose Miami, FL, on the other hand, the odds increase to 8 to 1. One could say that life in rapidly growing southern Florida is more than 7 times as dangerous as it is in Pennsylvania's lagging, postindustrial Conemaugh River Valley.

But quoting raw odds distorts the local crime picture. Violence isn't uniformly distributed throughout a metro area's neighborhoods; veteran cops tell you that most murders and robberies occur within the same few square miles or even blocks. Moreover, if you're young, white, female, and earn enough money, your chances of meeting up with crime are much less than those of an older, poor male. So why a chapter on crime if a combination of factors such as age, sex, race, income, and a wise selection of neighborhood can statistically remove you from danger?

The simple answer is that you are a different kind of crime victim whenever you have to trim back shrubbery along your home's foundation to restrict a thief's potential hiding places, or get rid of the mailbox and install a mail slot in your front door, or press down your car's door locks when driving down a darkened avenue, or keep feeling for your wallet at street festivals, or use only empty elevators, or stay indoors evenings more than you really care to. In some metro areas such tactics are advised, in others they are merely prudent, and in still others they may not be necessary at all.

CRIME RISK: SEVERAL CONNECTIONS

Why some metro areas are safer than others provokes arguments among citizens, politicians, police, and social scientists. For all of the debate, experts recognize several factors.

Population size is closely tied to crime rates. Metro areas with lower crime rates—Grand Forks, ND, or Wausau, WI, for example—have smaller populations. Metro areas with the highest rates—Los Angeles–Long Beach, CA, or New York, NY, are two extreme examples—have large, overcrowded populations. There are exceptions, to be sure. Toronto's crime rate is as low as that of Great Falls, MT. Tallahassee's crime rate is as high as New York's.

Climate, too, has a striking connection with lawbreaking. Police respond to more disturbance calls on

Florida's Defense

In 1931, while researching his famous piece "The Worst American State," H. L. Mencken found the best source for data on causes of death was the life insurance industry and that, when it came to murder, Florida had the highest rate.

After six decades, not much is different. Most metro areas in Florida rank near the bottom in personal safety. Of all the states, Florida has the highest rates for violent crime and for property crime. The state is the setting for Elmore Leonard and John D. MacDonald's best-selling crime fiction, and its largest city, Miami, was the tropical backdrop for a bloody Friday-night television series in the early 1980s.

This isn't entirely fair. Local crime rates are figured per 100,000 residents. But the state draws millions of four-season visitors. A truer way to measure crime rates, notes Florida's Department of Law Enforcement, would be to add a place's average daily number of tourists to its number of year-round residents, *then* determine the rate. The results would produce dramatically lower crime rates and improve the Sunshine State's national image.

the day after summer temperatures are highest than on any other days of the year. The numbers of burglaries, vandalisms, and rapes increase with ambient temperature up to 85 degrees Fahrenheit. Indeed, in the Sun Belt and in the Frost Belt, cops and criminals are busiest throughout July and August when all crimes except robbery are the likeliest to happen. Since people spend more time outdoors during these months, they are more exposed. Homes, too, are more unprotected during this time of year because they are left with open windows and unlocked doors. Robbery is the cold-weather exception. It is highest in December when shoppers and retail stores doing brisk holiday business make tempting targets.

Time of day and the *photoperiod*, or length of the day, are two other factors. After sundown is the time most cars are stolen, most persons and businesses are robbed, most persons are assaulted, and most thefts are committed. Burglaries, purse-snatchings and pocket-pickings, on the other hand, happen more often during daylight hours. Indeed, some police dispatchers contend that the number of daylight minutes is a predictor of the kind of 911 calls they handle.

Even local *traffic* plays a role. The ease with which a criminal can drive off down the street, escape onto an arterial road, and disappear among commuters on the Interstate is an encouragement. Neighborhoods near Houston's I-610 Beltway urged the city to turn their streets into cul-de-sacs, and in Elizabeth City, NJ, cops stationed barricades at the corner of Madison Avenue and Fanny Street to stop neighboring Newark lawbreakers from fleeing into their jurisdiction.

Age and sex figure into the equation, too. Some 45 million persons in North America have arrest records for misdeeds other than traffic violations. The proportion of suspects who are male is much higher than their proportion in the general population. Half the persons picked up by police for violent and property crimes are under 20 years of age and four-fifths are male. None of this should be taken to mean that persons hold up convenience stores, boost Chevrolet Camaros, or duke it out in disco parking lots *because* they are young and male, but these characteristics are associated with other factors in crime.

The *economy* also plays a role. In most metro areas, each time the unemployment rate goes up the police make more arrests. But joblessness and loss of income won't automatically make a place unsafe. Metro areas in the Ohio Valley, in the Northern Plains, and in Atlantic Canada suffer job losses during business slumps but continue to experience low crime rates. More affluent areas, given similar sets of circumstances, aren't nearly as safe as they seem: Rich offenders are arrested less often than poor ones, especially on suspicion. Once arrested, they are convicted with less frequency. This is especially true in juvenile cases involving thefts and break-ins.

Transience affects crime rates. A warning sign for crooks is a stable neighborhood where people know one another and look out for one another's safety and property no matter how many police cruise the area. High neighborhood turnover leading to more and more strangers living next to each other leads to higher crime rates. Moreover, resort areas that draw transients—Las Vegas, NV–AZ; Orlando, FL; or Atlantic City–Cape May, NJ, for instance—also have serious crime problems. When visitors are added to the year-round residents, the higher population betters the odds that victim and crook will meet.

Police strength, too, is linked to the local crime rate. Most metro areas have between 1 and 3 sworn uniformed officers for every 1,000 residents. In Manhattan, there are 1,300 police officers per square mile; in sparsely populated parts of Alaska and the Canadian Yukon and Northwest Territories, there are none. It's natural to think personal safety in a metro area rises or falls in proportion to the size of the local police force, but it just isn't so. Police enforce traffic codes, investigate accidents, find lost children, and calm down fighting spouses. They battle crime, too, but most of what they do is after the fact. They respond to complaints; they interview victims and fill out reports; they follow up on tips; and they collar suspects and bring them to book. A large number of police per capita, however, is usually an indication of a high-crime area rather than an area where crime is being foiled.

Other factors related to criminal activity include the practices of local prosecutors, judges, juries, and parole boards; the attitudes of the community toward crime; and the willingness of ordinary citizens to report crime.

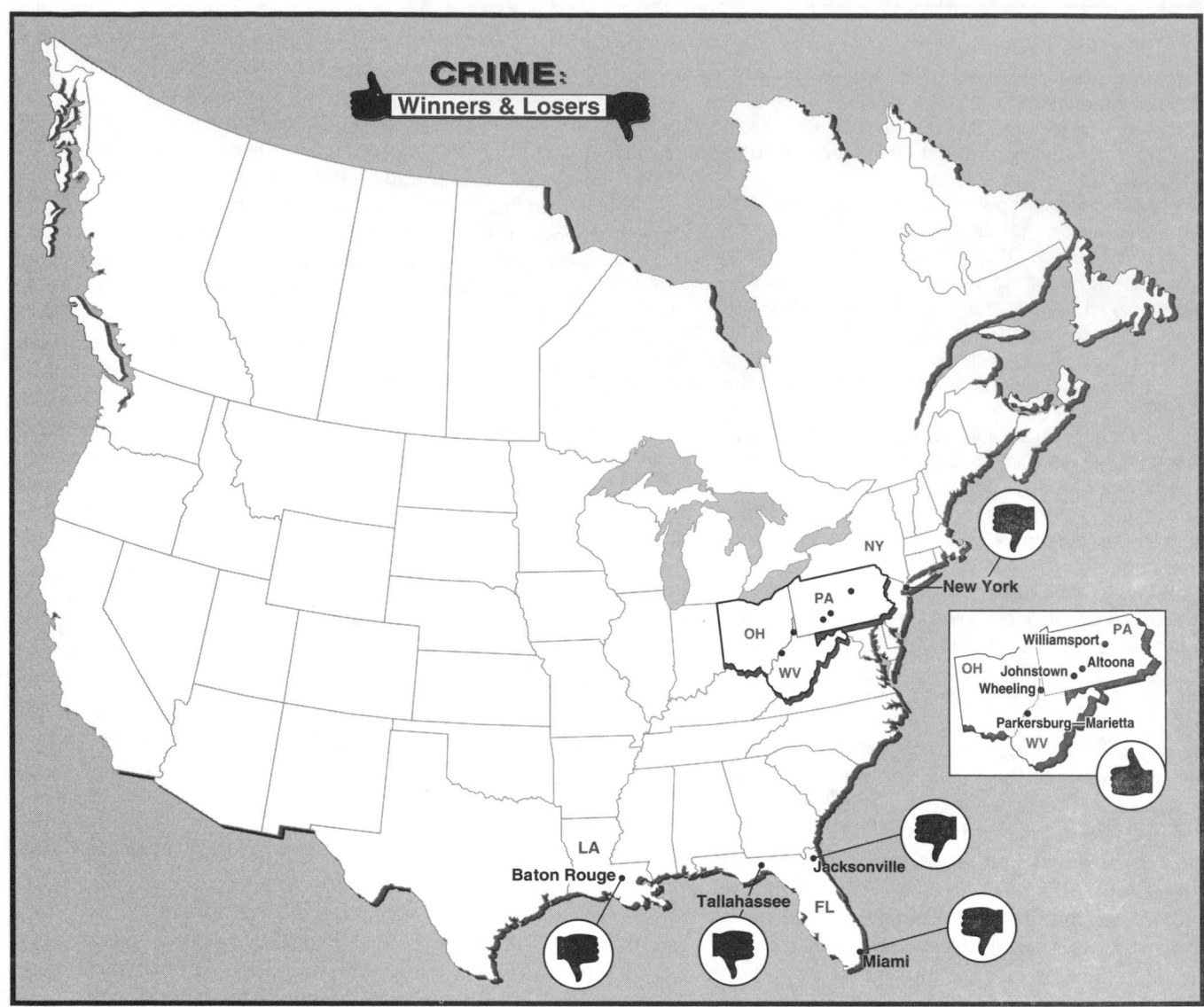

CRIME: Winners & Losers

Thomas Nast, Cartographer

CRIME INDEXES

Each year, the Federal Bureau of Investigation in Washington and the Canadian Centre for Justice Statistics in Ottawa report crime figures from police departments in their respective countries. Eight crimes make up a Crime Index for measuring local wrongdoing. Four are *violent* crimes; the other four are *property* crimes.

Violent Crime

Murder is the most reported of all crimes and has the highest rate of charges being laid. Incidence is at an all-time high in both the United States and Canada, though Canada's rate is less than a fourth that of its more violent southern neighbor.

Half of all victims knew their killers, perhaps even sat across from them at the breakfast table the morning of the crime. Victims and killers are becoming less connected, however, because of random violence. Based on the number of unsolved killings each year and an increase in slayings involving strangers, the FBI estimates at least 25 serial killers are on the loose in the United States.

Rape, too, frequently involves acquainted victims and aggressors. It is the most underreported of crimes and has the highest proportion of "unfounded" complaints. Except in Illinois and all Canadian jurisdictions, rape victims are always female by current crime reporting standards.

Robbery is the violent crime that most often involves more than one criminal, and is the one violent crime committed less out of anger than as a way of making a living. It differs from common theft because it involves force or threat, thereby placing the victim in fear.

Assault is simply an attempt, successful or not, to injure another person. Its rate is highest in August and lowest in February, higher in Canada's West and America's West than in other parts of these countries, and higher in areas with resort or military economies.

Property Crime

Most *burglaries*, jailed pros say, are planned for hours and pulled off in minutes. The typical target is the home or apartment. Nearly half of the incidents involve walking in rather than breaking in. The typical time is between 9:00 and 11:00 A.M. or between 1:00 and 3:00 P.M. when you're least likely to be inside.

Larceny–theft, after drunk driving, is the most common crime in North America. Walking off with an unattended garden hose is one example; shoplifting a Russian sable coat is another. In almost all of the cases, the victim never sees the offender.

Auto theft, it's been said, is a victimless crime because you get over your loss with a check from the insurance company. The North American auto-theft capitals—Miami, FL, and Vancouver, BC—are at opposite ends of the continent. Each area has seen an increase in persons arrested who had recently arrived from California and New York, where auto insurance fraud is an underground art.

Because victims often believe it futile to file complaints, many crimes aren't always reported and this affects the

accuracy of the Crime Index. Even if a complaint is filed, the investigating officer's definition of the crime may affect the numbers. Purse-snatching, for instance, is either a robbery or a larceny depending on the jurisdiction. Likewise, a slap in the face is either an aggravated or simple assault depending on motive.

Moreover, some police departments have either padded the figures to oust a judge considered soft on crime or to persuade the city council to increase the department's budget, or they fudged the number of crimes to create an image of effective law enforcement.

It's important to distinguish between the *incidence* of crime and the crime *rate*. Incidence is simply how many crimes are reported in a given place. The more people living in a place, the greater the crime incidence will be. In Quebec City, PQ, police investigate some 500 aggravated assaults a year. South of Chicago, police in Kankakee handle a similar number each year. From these figures, you might think that Quebec's capital is as dangerous as Kankakee. But 565,000 people live in Quebec City and its environs, while just 97,000 live in Kankakee.

A truer measure of safety is the crime rate—the number of crimes per 100,000 people. Quebec City's assault rate is 100. Kankakee's rate is 542, or more than five times that of Quebec City.

SCORING: CRIME

The one crime cops file the most reports on is theft: a stolen bike, a necklace missing from a jewelry retailer's display case, hubcaps gone from a used-car lot. Yet these heists are counted as heavily as homicides to determine metropolitan crime rates. When it comes to comparing places, this method doesn't realistically show relative danger.

The realistic way to judge metro areas for personal safety is simple: For each place, *Places Rated* averages the rates for violent and property crimes for the latest five-year period, but since property crimes are much less serious than crimes against people, they are given one-tenth the weight of violent crimes. [Note, (1) although forcible rape is a violent crime, figures for forcible rape aren't included in the scoring because comparable data aren't reported for Canada and for Illinois, and (2) although arson has been considered a property crime since 1979, arson figures aren't included in the scoring because they are unavailable for many metro areas.] Each place starts with a base score of zero and points are added according to these indicators:

1. *Violent crime rate.* The rates for murder, robbery, and aggravated assault are added together.
2. *Property crime rate.* The rates for burglary, larceny-theft, and motor vehicle theft are totaled, and the result is divided by 10.

The sum of a place's violent crime rate and one-tenth of its property crime rate, rounded off, represents the score (the higher the score, the more dangerous the metro area).

SCORING EXAMPLES

Two national capitals and the unofficial Latin-American capital on the U.S. mainland illustrate the scoring method for crime.

Ottawa–Hull, ON–PQ (#132)

Despite a sober population of civil servants and a summer landscape of tulips, statues, and leafy public spaces tended by the National Capital Commission, Ottawa's coarse lumberjack heritage arises each time a fight breaks out at a Rough Riders game in Landsdowne Park. The cops are busy across the river in Quebec, too, because neighboring Hull draws thousands of young people nightly to a lower legal drinking age and pubs that close later than in Ontario.

Like other Canadian metro areas, Ottawa–Hull has a rate of violent crimes (218) well below average in spite of the rowdiness. On the other hand, the property crime rate (5,732) here is well above average—the primary reason for the area's middling rank in personal safety.

Washington, DC–MD–VA–WV (#216)

In contrast to Ottawa–Hull, the U.S. capital and its surrounding Maryland and Virginia suburbs earns a crime score of 1,028, the sum of its violent crime rate (549) and one-tenth its property crime rate (4,790). With just 15 percent of the population, the District of Columbia accounts for 7 out of 10 murders and half the robberies and aggravated assaults in the entire area. Disappointed at not being able to stop the drive-by killings and close down the open-air drug markets, Washington's police chief recently resigned.

Miami, FL (#343)

Greater Miami has a crime score of 2,821, the sum of its violent crime rate (1,721) and one-tenth its property crime rate (10,934). Beset by rapid population growth and caught in the crosscurrents of the drug trade, this area is truly a North American crime capital. Even the American Society of Criminology decided against holding its convention here because of the city's dubious reputation.

In a typical year some 250,000 violent and property crimes are reported to the Metro-Dade police and their fellow officers in Hialeah, Miami, Miami Beach, and

---

Safe vs. More Dangerous Places

If you look at the crime rates for places detailed in the Place Profiles later in this chapter, one thing stands out. Whether you're talking of crimes of violence (which account for just 10 percent of all lawbreaking) or property crime, larger Sunbelt resorts suffer more from criminal activity than smaller places in the frostbelt.

Violent Crime in the Metro Areas

Safest	Violent Crime Rate
Bismarck, ND	45
State College, PA	57
Parkersburg–Marietta, WV–OH	59
Fargo–Moorhead, ND–MN	61
Eau Claire, WI	67

Dangerous	Violent Crime Rate
Jacksonville, FL	1,064
Tallahassee, FL	1,192
Los Angeles–Long Beach, CA	1,273
New York, NY	1,592
Miami, FL	1,727

Source: FBI, unpublished reports, 1988, 1989, 1990, 1991, and 1992.

The violent crime rate is the sum of rates for murder, robbery, and aggravated assault. The metro area average is 408.

Property Crime in the Metro Areas

Safest	Property Crime Rate
Johnstown, PA	1,478
Wheeling, WV–OH	1,874
Steubenville–Weirton, OH–WV	1,965
Sharon, PA	2,065
Scranton–Wilkes-Barre–Hazleton, PA	2,275

Dangerous	Property Crime Rate
Atlantic City–Cape May, NJ	9,354
Dallas, TX	9,442
San Antonio, TX	9,980
Miami, FL	10,934
Baton Rouge, LA	11,394

Source: FBI, unpublished reports, 1988, 1989, 1990, 1991, and 1992.

The property crime rate is the sum of rates for burglary, larceny–theft, and motor-vehicle theft. The metro-area average is 5,721.

Opa-Locka. Lawbreaking is so startlingly high in this vacation area that a standard item in hotel and rental car packets is a bulletin on guerrilla tactics for avoiding crime.

Rankings: Crime

In ranking 343 metro areas for relative safety, *Places Rated* uses two criteria: (1) the violent crime rate and (2) the property crime rate divided by 10. The sum of these rates, rounded off, is the metro area's score. The higher the score, the more dangerous the metro area. Places with tie scores get the same rank and are listed in alphabetical order.

Metro Areas from Best to Worst

Places Rated Rank	Places Rated Score
1. Johnstown, PA	284
2. Wheeling, WV–OH	303
3. Parkersburg–Marietta, WV–OH	308
4. Williamsport, PA	329
5. Altoona, PA	341
6. Scranton–Wilkes-Barre–Hazleton, PA	359
7. Sharon, PA	365
8. Danville, VA	380
9. Lancaster, PA	385
10. Danbury, CT	387
11. Utica–Rome, NY	392
12. Wausau, WI	403
13. Binghamton, NY	410
14. Cumberland, MD–WV	415
15. Portsmouth–Dover–Rochester, NH	416
15. State College, PA	416
17. Allentown–Bethlehem–Easton, PA–NJ	428
17. Eau Claire, WI	428
19. Appleton–Oshkosh–Neenah, WI	429
20. Bismarck, ND	430
21. Steubenville–Weirton, OH–WV	438
22. Punta Gorda, FL	445
23. Hagerstown, MD	447
23. Rochester, MN	447
25. Grand Forks, ND–MN	460
26. La Crosse, WI–MN	461
27. Fargo–Moorhead, ND–MN	467
27. Worcester–Fitchburg–Leominster, MA	467
29. Jamestown, NY	471
30. Johnson City–Kingsport–Bristol, TN–VA	476
31. York, PA	480
32. Provo–Orem, UT	483
33. Huntington–Ashland, WV–KY–OH	485
34. Sheboygan, WI	487
35. Fayetteville–Springdale–Rogers, AR	495
36. Owensboro, KY	496
36. Saint John, NB	496
38. Duluth–Superior, MN–WI	497
39. Bangor, ME	505
40. Lafayette, IN	509
41. Florence, AL	521
42. Chicoutimi–Jonquiere, PQ	524
43. Green Bay, WI	528
44. Central New Jersey, NJ	531
45. Lewiston–Auburn, ME	539
46. Sioux Falls, SD	540
47. St. John's, NF	542
48. Glens Falls, NY	543
48. Muncie, IN	543
50. Harrisburg–Lebanon–Carlisle, PA	544
51. Pittsburgh, PA	550
52. Lynchburg, VA	551
53. Erie, PA	561
53. Monmouth–Ocean, NJ	561
55. Manchester–Nashua, NH	565
56. Kokomo, IN	570
57. Long Island, NY	572
57. New London–Norwich, CT–RI	572
59. Charleston, WV	575
60. Decatur, AL	578
60. Reading, PA	578
62. Fort Walton Beach, FL	580
63. Cheyenne, WY	586
64. San Luis Obispo–Atascadero–Paso Robles, CA	588
65. Billings, MT	593
66. Syracuse, NY	594
67. Bloomington, IN	595
68. Lake County, IL	598
69. Kitchener, ON	601
70. Bremerton, WA	602
71. Bloomington–Normal, IL	608
72. Charlottesville, VA	609
72. Oshawa, ON	609
74. Kenosha, WI	610
75. Joplin, MO	611
76. Olympia, WA	612
77. Dubuque, IA	615
78. Albany–Schenectady–Troy, NY	616
78. Dutchess County, NY	616
80. Vancouver, WA	618
81. Houma, LA	619
82. Brazoria, TX	621
83. Trois-Rivieres, PQ	624
84. Elmira, NY	633
85. Youngstown–Warren, OH	646
86. Pittsfield, MA	649
87. Janesville–Beloit, WI	661
88. Boise City, ID	662
89. Fort Collins–Loveland, CO	663
90. Hickory–Morgantown, NC	669
90. Sherbrooke, PQ	669
92. Northern New Jersey, NJ	677
93. St. Catharines–Niagara, ON	682
94. Jacksonville, NC	683
94. Orange County, NY	683
96. Bellingham, WA	685
97. Ventura, CA	687
98. Asheville, NC	689
98. Madison, WI	689
100. Stamford–Norwalk, CT	703
101. Elkhart–Goshen, IN	704
102. Cedar Rapids, IA	712
102. Rochester, NY	712
104. Fort Smith, AR–OK	720
105. Medford–Ashland, OR	722
106. Waterloo–Cedar Falls, IA	723
107. Fort Myers–Cape Coral, FL	725
107. Santa Rosa, CA	725
109. Roanoke, VA	727
110. Santa Fe, NM	732
111. Toronto, ON	733
112. Killeen–Temple, TX	745
113. Springfield, MO	753
114. Canton–Massillon, OH	755
115. Fort Wayne, IN	756
116. Honolulu, HI	757
116. Quebec City, PQ	757
118. St. Cloud, MN	758
118. Windsor, ON	758
120. Sudbury, ON	764
121. Dover, DE	767
122. Hamilton, ON	770
123. Knoxville, TN	772
124. Portland, ME	775
125. Boulder–Longmont, CO	777
126. Lafayette, LA	778
127. Louisville, KY–IN	780
128. Great Falls, MT	781
129. Merced, CA	783
130. Eugene–Springfield, OR	785
131. Cincinnati, OH–KY–IN	788
132. Ottawa–Hull, ON–PQ	791
132. Rapid City, SD	791
134. Burlington, VT	800
135. Peoria–Pekin, IL	801
136. Cleveland–Lorain–Elyria, OH	803
137. Santa Barbara–Santa Maria–Lompoc, CA	804
138. Chico–Paradise, CA	805
139. Davenport–Moline–Rock Island, IA–IL	806
140. Providence–Warwick–Cranston, RI	807
140. San Jose, CA	807
142. Columbia, MO	813
143. Terre Haute, IN	823
144. Richland–Kennewick–Pasco, WA	834
145. Iowa City, IA	835
146. Evansville–Henderson, IN–KY	837
146. Hamilton–Middletown, OH	837
146. London, ON	837
146. Minneapolis–St. Paul, MN–WI	837
150. Ann Arbor, MI	838
151. Wilmington–Newark, DE–MD	843
152. Huntsville, AL	845
153. Biloxi–Gulfport–Pascagoula, MS	847
154. Casper, WY	856
155. Greeley, CO	857
156. Milwaukee–Waukesha, WI	863
157. Grand Rapids–Muskegon–Holland, MI	868
158. Salem, OR	869
159. Lawton, OK	871
160. Goldsboro, NC	873
161. Omaha, NE–IA	876
162. St. Joseph, MO	877
163. Racine, WI	881
164. Colorado Springs, CO	882
164. Greenville, NC	882
166. Waterbury, CT	886
167. Salt Lake City–Ogden, UT	889
168. Redding, CA	895
169. Montgomery, AL	900

Places Rated Rank	Places Rated Score
170. Santa Cruz–Watsonville, CA	904
171. Philadelphia, PA–NJ	909
171. Spokane, WA	909
173. Columbus, GA–AL	912
173. Hartford, CT	912
175. Raleigh–Durham–Chapel Hill, NC	916
176. Calgary, AB	920
177. Champaign–Urbana, IL	921
177. Lawrence, KS	921
177. Rocky Mount, NC	921
180. Richmond–Petersburg, VA	926
181. Las Cruces, NM	927
182. Orange County, CA	929
183. Anchorage, AK	934
184. Greensboro–Winston–Salem–High Point, NC	936
185. Indianapolis, IN	937
186. New Bedford–Fall River–Attleboro, MA	938
187. Decatur, IL	940
188. Lansing–East Lansing, MI	941
189. Buffalo–Niagara Falls, NY	945
190. Alexandria, LA	946
191. South Bend, IN	947
192. Salinas, CA	949
193. McAllen–Edinburg–Mission, TX	950
194. Sioux City, IA–NE	953
195. Barnstable–Yarmouth, MA	954
196. Norfolk–Virginia Beach–Newport News, VA–NC	960
196. Springfield, IL	960
198. Gadsden, AL	964
199. Athens, GA	971
200. Lexington, KY	976
201. Dayton–Springfield, OH	980
202. Victoria, BC	981
203. Enid, OK	990
204. Lincoln, NE	993
205. Abilene, TX	994
206. Anniston, AL	995
207. Longview–Marshall, TX	996
208. Des Moines, IA	1,002
209. Wichita, KS	1,003
210. Montreal, PQ	1,004
211. Macon, GA	1,008
212. San Angelo, TX	1,012
213. Mansfield, OH	1,016
214. Augusta–Aiken, GA–SC	1,024
215. Washington, DC–MD–VA–WV	1,028
216. Saginaw–Bay City–Midland, MI	1,038
217. Sherman–Denison, TX	1,040
218. Thunder Bay, ON	1,045
219. Panama City, FL	1,046
220. Visalia–Tulare–Porterville, CA	1,047
221. Boston, MA	1,051
222. Saskatoon, SK	1,052
223. Amarillo, TX	1,057
224. Yolo, CA	1,059
225. Bridgeport, CT	1,060
226. Gary, IN	1,062
227. Clarksville–Hopkinsville, TN–KY	1,073
228. Dothan, AL	1,078
229. Lubbock, TX	1,081
230. Denver, CO	1,082
230. Springfield, MA	1,082
232. Columbus, OH	1,084
233. Bryan–College Station, TX	1,099
234. Trenton, NJ	1,101
235. Akron, OH	1,102
235. Brownsville–Harlingen–San Benito, TX	1,102
235. Vallejo–Fairfield–Napa, CA	1,102
238. Toledo, OH	1,105
239. Reno, NV	1,106
240. Nashville, TN	1,111
240. Seattle–Bellevue–Everett, WA	1,111
242. Jackson, MI	1,113
243. Texarkana, TX–Texarkana, AR	1,114
244. Winnipeg, MB	1,116
245. Chattanooga, TN–GA	1,120
246. Tyler, TX	1,131
247. Jackson, MS	1,133
248. Tulsa, OK	1,137
249. Naples, FL	1,138
250. Las Vegas, NV–AZ	1,139
251. Lima, OH	1,140
252. Rockford, IL	1,141
253. St. Louis, MO–IL	1,150
254. Kankakee, IL	1,151
254. Savannah, GA	1,151
256. Greenville–Spartanburg–Anderson, SC	1,152
257. Fort Pierce–Port St. Lucie, FL	1,154
258. Melbourne–Titusville–Palm Bay, FL	1,159
259. Vineland–Millville–Bridgeton, NJ	1,163
260. Austin–San Marcos, TX	1,165
260. Monroe, LA	1,165
262. New Haven–Meriden, CT	1,166
263. Victoria, TX	1,170
264. Charleston–North Charleston, SC	1,175
265. Halifax, NS	1,179
266. Galveston–Texas City, TX	1,181
267. Sacramento, CA	1,184
268. Kalamazoo–Battle Creek, MI	1,186
269. Yuba City, CA	1,189
270. Modesto, CA	1,205
271. Odessa–Midland, TX	1,211
272. Tuscaloosa, AL	1,214
273. Birmingham, AL	1,221
274. Lake Charles, LA	1,224
274. Oklahoma City, OK	1,224
276. Florence, SC	1,233
277. Edmonton, AB	1,236
277. Topeka, KS	1,236
279. Yakima, WA	1,237
280. Corpus Christi, TX	1,254
281. Phoenix–Mesa, AZ	1,259
282. Bakersfield, CA	1,261
283. Vancouver, BC	1,263
284. Pine Bluff, AR	1,265
285. San Diego, CA	1,266
286. Daytona Beach, FL	1,268
287. Sarasota–Bradenton, FL	1,276
288. San Francisco, CA	1,284
289. Tacoma, WA	1,287
290. Regina, SK	1,289
291. Beaumont–Port Arthur, TX	1,291
292. Portland, OR	1,294
293. Sumter, SC	1,295
294. Pensacola, FL	1,308
295. Benton Harbor, MI	1,321
296. Oakland, CA	1,322
297. Wilmington, NC	1,323
298. Detroit, MI	1,331
299. Tucson, AZ	1,335
300. Laredo, TX	1,336
301. Stockton–Lodi, CA	1,337
302. Wichita Falls, TX	1,345
303. Waco, TX	1,350
304. Myrtle Beach, SC	1,381
305. Kansas City, MO–KS	1,384
306. Albany, GA	1,386
307. Memphis, TN–AR–MS	1,401
308. Ocala, FL	1,405
309. Newark–Jersey City, NJ	1,406
310. San Antonio, TX	1,412
311. Columbia, SC	1,415
311. Houston, TX	1,415
313. Shreveport–Bossier City, LA	1,417
314. Baltimore, MD	1,430
315. Fresno, CA	1,455
316. Pueblo, CO	1,457
317. Orlando, FL	1,473
318. Atlanta, GA	1,474
319. Charlotte–Gastonia–Rock Hill, NC–SC	1,477
320. Albuquerque, NM	1,478
321. Riverside–San Bernardino, CA	1,498
322. Fort Lauderdale, FL	1,505
323. Yuma, AZ	1,506
324. El Paso, TX	1,514
325. Mobile, AL	1,524
326. Flint, MI	1,533
327. Little Rock–North Little Rock, AR	1,540
328. Fort Worth–Arlington, TX	1,545
329. Atlantic City–Cape May, NJ	1,552
330. Chicago, IL	1,566
331. Lakeland–Winter Haven, FL	1,631
332. Tampa–St. Petersburg–Clearwater, FL	1,657
333. Fayetteville, NC	1,667
334. New Orleans, LA	1,686
335. West Palm Beach–Boca Raton, FL	1,694
336. Gainesville, FL	1,743
337. Los Angeles–Long Beach, CA	1,838
338. Dallas, TX	1,841
339. Jacksonville, FL	1,861
340. Baton Rouge, LA	2,030
341. Tallahassee, FL	2,083
342. New York, NY	2,264
343. Miami, FL	2,821

Place Profiles: Crime

The Place Profiles show each metro area's average annual rates for seven serious crimes: murder, rape, robbery, assault, burglary, larceny–theft, and motor vehicle theft for the latest five years for which data are available. These rates are divided into violent and property categories, and a total rate for each of these categories is also given.

Note: Although figures for rape are shown for most metro areas, they aren't included in the scoring because comparable data are unavailable for Canadian and Illinois jurisdictions.

Figures for the United States are derived from the FBI's *Crime in the United States*, 1988, 1989, 1990, 1991, and 1992, and from the Bureau's unpublished "Crime by County" reports for each of these years. For metro areas not included in either of these sources, figures are derived from state Uniform Crime Reporting programs.

Canadian figures are derived from the Centre for Justice Statistics unpublished "Table 3" reports for 1987, 1988, 1989, 1990, and 1991.

The next-to-the-last column indicates the crime trend over the previous five years: 112 metro areas have an arrow pointing upward, meaning their *Places Rated* crime rates during this period are up; 110 metro areas have a dash, meaning their crime rates are essentially unchanged; and 121 metro areas have an arrow pointing downward, meaning their crime rates have dropped.

A check mark (✓) next to a metro area's name highlights it as one of the top 35 places for safety from crime.

Metro Area	Murder	Rape	Robbery	Assault	VIOLENT	Burglary	Theft	Auto Theft	PROPERTY	SCORE	TREND	RANK
Metro Area Average	5.2	41.3	119.3	283.9	408	1,365	3,485	420	5,721	—	▼	—
Abilene, TX	6.1	54.5	124.2	364.5	495	1,861	2,917	216	4,994	994	—	205
Akron, OH	6.1	53.3	178.0	366.2	550	1,216	3,808	494	5,518	1,102	—	235
Albany, GA	13.3	70.0	304.0	315.0	632	2,887	4,281	373	7,541	1,386	▼	306
Albany–Schenectady–Troy, NY	3.9	25.3	64.2	186.4	255	938	2,503	176	3,617	616	—	78
Albuquerque, NM	8.3	48.8	160.3	599.9	769	2,242	4,376	480	7,098	1,478	—	320
Alexandria, LA	6.4	38.4	70.9	359.2	437	1,383	3,447	265	5,095	946	▲	190
✓ Allentown–Bethlehem–Easton, PA–NJ	2.4	17.5	41.9	95.7	140	631	2,056	197	2,884	428	—	17
✓ Altoona, PA	0.9	27.0	26.3	82.3	110	681	1,492	141	2,314	341	—	5
Amarillo, TX	8.3	42.2	109.0	260.0	377	1,739	4,756	303	6,798	1,057	—	223
Anchorage, AK	5.2	80.8	127.3	264.2	397	904	3,889	578	5,371	934	—	183
Ann Arbor, MI	2.0	67.1	80.1	260.8	343	971	3,650	325	4,946	838	▼	150
Anniston, AL	7.0	30.5	105.5	511.2	624	1,112	2,393	211	3,716	995	▼	206
✓ Appleton–Oshkosh–Neenah, WI	1.1	9.8	9.8	65.6	77	596	2,840	89	3,525	429	—	19
Asheville, NC	5.3	30.0	81.9	146.3	234	1,433	2,807	311	4,551	689	▲	98
Athens, GA	7.1	46.8	146.1	243.0	396	1,801	3,561	386	5,748	971	▲	199
Atlanta, GA	10.8	57.9	314.5	403.5	729	1,868	4,620	962	7,450	1,474	—	318
Atlantic City–Cape May, NJ	5.8	65.2	227.1	383.4	616	1,710	7,196	448	9,354	1,552	—	329
Augusta–Aiken, GA–SC	12.3	42.4	197.7	279.0	489	1,864	3,025	464	5,353	1,024	▲	214
Austin–San Marcos, TX	5.9	54.7	139.2	217.6	363	2,041	5,499	487	8,027	1,165	—	260
Bakersfield, CA	8.7	48.5	172.6	482.6	664	1,807	3,662	504	5,973	1,261	▼	282
Baltimore, MD	11.4	45.3	386.4	481.2	879	1,323	3,466	721	5,510	1,430	—	314
Bangor, ME	4.2	17.5	19.3	47.9	71	738	3,442	159	4,339	505	▼	39
Barnstable–Yarmouth, MA	1.9	26.9	31.4	428.1	461	1,569	3,041	317	4,927	954	▼	195
Baton Rouge, LA	10.3	37.5	177.4	702.9	891	5,732	5,006	656	11,394	2,030	▲	340
Beaumont–Port Arthur, TX	8.7	61.5	218.6	422.8	650	2,142	3,801	462	6,405	1,291	▲	291
Bellingham, WA	2.6	51.8	32.5	133.3	168	1,107	3,780	274	5,161	685	—	96
Benton Harbor, MI	5.7	110.8	103.2	592.9	702	1,650	4,243	294	6,187	1,321	—	295

Metro Area	Murder	Rape	Robbery	Assault	VIOLENT	Burglary	Theft	Auto Theft	PROPERTY	SCORE	TREND	RANK
Metro Area Average	5.2	41.3	119.3	283.9	408	1,365	3,485	420	5,721	—	▼	—
Billings, MT	4.7	23.9	36.7	28.0	69	1,040	3,908	292	5,240	593	▼	65
Biloxi–Gulfport–Pascagoula, MS	4.9	66.3	83.0	265.5	353	1,954	2,660	322	4,936	847	—	153
✓ Binghamton, NY	2.1	18.2	22.6	84.8	110	565	2,313	129	3,007	410	▲	13
Birmingham, AL	15.2	47.6	227.9	450.4	694	1,515	3,080	677	5,272	1,221	▲	273
✓ Bismarck, ND	2.1	9.0	5.9	37.5	46	531	3,154	157	3,842	430	▼	20
Bloomington, IN	1.0	19.8	17.3	205.4	224	713	2,762	236	3,711	595	▼	67
Bloomington–Normal, IL	1.4	0.0	30.4	147.6	179	1,039	3,123	124	4,286	608	▼	71
Boise City, ID	2.1	30.2	23.2	183.2	209	1,113	3,219	207	4,539	662	▼	88
Boston, MA	4.1	31.4	211.6	380.5	596	960	2,472	1,115	4,547	1,051	—	221
Boulder–Longmont, CO	1.5	37.6	28.2	177.5	207	1,108	4,364	229	5,701	777	▼	125
Brazoria, TX	3.5	29.3	36.1	201.5	241	949	2,542	310	3,801	621	▲	82
Bremerton, WA	3.1	65.0	41.0	146.7	191	955	2,908	245	4,108	602	—	70
Bridgeport, CT	9.5	25.0	306.6	214.2	530	1,406	2,585	1,304	5,295	1,060	▲	225
Brownsville–Harlingen–San Benito, TX	10.0	31.3	81.9	368.4	460	1,953	3,794	669	6,416	1,102	▼	235
Bryan–College Station, TX	4.5	52.2	81.4	303.5	389	1,917	4,807	370	7,094	1,099	—	233
Buffalo–Niagara Falls, NY	3.6	37.1	177.8	326.1	508	1,175	2,705	490	4,370	945	▲	189
Burlington, VT	2.6	38.6	25.4	61.9	90	1,595	5,200	310	7,105	800	▼	134
Calgary, AB	2.2	0.0	92.8	177.6	273	1,453	4,540	476	6,469	920	▲	176
Canton–Massillon, OH	3.2	34.1	148.9	206.2	358	1,043	2,607	312	3,962	755	▲	114
Casper, WY	3.2	29.7	23.0	308.8	335	1,315	3,660	232	5,207	856	—	154
Cedar Rapids, IA	1.4	9.0	41.4	134.4	177	1,057	4,055	235	5,347	712	▼	102
Central New Jersey, NJ	1.5	16.9	61.1	119.4	182	703	2,338	448	3,489	531	—	44
Champaign–Urbana, IL	2.4	0.0	105.7	291.1	399	1,199	3,775	240	5,214	921	▼	177
Charleston, WV	6.5	32.4	82.1	115.0	204	907	2,532	273	3,712	575	▲	59
Charleston–North Charleston, SC	6.8	56.2	131.5	483.3	622	1,442	3,661	426	5,529	1,175	▲	264
Charlotte–Gastonia–Rock Hill, NC–SC	9.9	47.0	235.8	577.1	823	2,003	4,164	379	6,546	1,477	▲	319
Charlottesville, VA	4.2	30.3	55.3	152.9	212	752	3,015	194	3,961	609	▼	72
Chattanooga, TN–GA	7.6	49.4	165.6	451.8	625	1,472	2,859	623	4,954	1,120	▲	245
Cheyenne, WY	2.2	29.9	23.1	119.9	145	548	3,724	140	4,412	586	—	63
Chicago, IL	10.7	0.0	456.7	531.3	999	1,222	3,553	902	5,677	1,566	—	330
Chico–Paradise, CA	4.6	39.3	45.9	265.7	316	1,473	3,022	395	4,890	805	▼	138
Chicoutimi–Jonquiere, PQ	1.4	0.0	48.9	92.2	143	1,387	2,147	282	3,816	524	▼	42
Cincinnati, OH–KY–IN	4.0	45.4	123.5	223.2	351	934	3,192	246	4,372	788	—	131
Clarksville–Hopkinsville, TN–KY	6.5	39.8	59.6	628.2	694	1,041	2,541	201	3,783	1,073	▲	227
Cleveland–Lorain–Elyria, OH	7.6	55.3	209.9	180.2	398	1,012	2,261	781	4,054	803	—	136
Colorado Springs, CO	3.6	56.7	72.1	199.7	275	1,444	4,202	417	6,063	882	▼	164
Columbia, MO	2.0	20.9	55.1	251.0	308	941	3,954	158	5,053	813	—	142
Columbia, SC	7.9	66.0	212.3	598.7	819	1,515	3,862	580	5,957	1,415	—	311
Columbus, GA–AL	8.9	41.0	149.6	261.4	420	1,308	3,303	314	4,925	912	▲	173
Columbus, OH	6.6	60.8	238.2	232.6	477	1,582	3,866	615	6,063	1,084	—	232
Corpus Christi, TX	7.3	59.5	125.3	319.4	452	2,235	5,389	398	8,022	1,254	—	280
✓ Cumberland, MD–WV	1.4	19.8	14.2	162.1	178	566	1,722	85	2,373	415	▲	14
Dallas, TX	15.8	71.6	373.4	507.8	897	2,500	5,643	1,299	9,442	1,841	—	338
✓ Danbury, CT	1.2	16.5	32.5	56.2	90	687	2,037	246	2,970	387	▲	10
✓ Danville, VA	8.0	20.1	32.0	93.1	133	506	1,846	116	2,468	380	▲	8

Metro Area	Murder	Rape	Robbery	Assault	VIOLENT	Burglary	Theft	Auto Theft	PROPERTY	SCORE	TREND	RANK
Metro Area Average	5.2	41.3	119.3	283.9	408	1,365	3,485	420	5,721	—	▼	—
Davenport–Moline–Rock Island, IA–IL	1.4	14.5	67.8	289.3	359	1,005	3,320	154	4,479	806	▲	139
Dayton–Springfield, OH	6.1	63.8	193.1	264.4	464	1,113	3,514	536	5,163	980	▼	201
Daytona Beach, FL	5.8	52.8	187.4	439.7	633	2,076	3,879	397	6,352	1,268	▼	286
Decatur, AL	3.3	16.2	50.5	188.1	242	883	2,296	186	3,365	578	▼	60
Decatur, IL	6.1	0.0	116.9	291.3	414	1,367	3,734	154	5,255	940	▼	187
Denver, CO	5.1	46.7	118.7	343.6	467	1,524	4,012	610	6,146	1,082	▼	230
Des Moines, IA	3.6	26.2	81.3	285.0	370	1,176	4,870	279	6,325	1,002	▼	208
Detroit, MI	13.6	66.0	304.6	394.1	712	1,400	3,585	1,205	6,190	1,331	▼	298
Dothan, AL	6.7	30.6	68.0	512.0	587	1,112	3,633	165	4,910	1,078	▲	228
Dover, DE	3.8	97.3	85.4	271.1	360	805	3,057	207	4,069	767	—	121
Dubuque, IA	0.2	6.8	12.1	276.9	289	593	2,535	131	3,259	615	—	77
Duluth–Superior, MN–WI	1.4	31.6	21.3	87.4	110	882	2,752	238	3,872	497	—	38
Dutchess County, NY	3.1	16.1	79.5	223.2	306	718	2,220	167	3,105	616	▲	78
✓ Eau Claire, WI	1.2	6.1	7.8	57.6	67	654	2,836	123	3,613	428	▲	17
Edmonton, AB	2.9	0.0	140.4	188.4	332	2,127	6,268	648	9,043	1,236	—	277
El Paso, TX	6.2	47.2	177.8	495.4	679	1,945	5,548	856	8,349	1,514	▲	324
Elkhart–Goshen, IN	2.5	35.6	52.5	195.1	250	912	3,412	216	4,540	704	▲	101
Elmira, NY	1.9	24.6	43.7	172.5	218	777	3,245	127	4,149	633	▼	84
Enid, OK	2.8	49.5	53.3	359.2	415	1,704	3,866	177	5,747	990	—	203
Erie, PA	1.9	37.6	100.3	137.0	239	794	2,213	210	3,217	561	—	53
Eugene–Springfield, OR	2.3	45.0	73.7	135.9	212	1,373	4,042	318	5,733	785	▼	130
Evansville–Henderson, IN–KY	4.9	27.4	58.7	343.9	408	967	3,074	254	4,295	837	▲	146
✓ Fargo–Moorhead, ND–MN	0.1	33.8	13.8	46.9	61	573	3,293	196	4,062	467	▼	27
Fayetteville, NC	14.1	78.5	237.0	559.5	811	2,760	5,207	601	8,568	1,667	▲	333
✓ Fayetteville–Springdale–Rogers, AR	4.6	21.7	16.8	94.4	116	956	2,595	237	3,788	495	—	35
Flint, MI	11.7	82.9	245.9	591.9	850	1,983	4,059	795	6,837	1,533	▼	326
Florence, AL	3.0	14.2	32.0	185.8	221	723	2,113	161	2,997	521	—	41
Florence, SC	10.6	63.2	135.0	591.1	737	1,607	3,033	320	4,960	1,233	▲	276
Fort Collins–Loveland, CO	2.0	34.5	13.5	197.3	213	817	3,519	165	4,501	663	▼	89
Fort Lauderdale, FL	6.8	37.7	306.7	420.3	734	1,975	4,885	850	7,710	1,505	—	322
Fort Myers–Cape Coral, FL	5.3	22.5	151.7	109.6	267	1,510	2,564	509	4,583	725	—	107
Fort Pierce–Port St. Lucie, FL	8.3	48.2	146.4	389.8	545	1,994	3,664	440	6,098	1,154	▼	257
Fort Smith, AR–OK	4.0	36.4	45.6	240.6	290	1,162	2,841	296	4,299	720	▼	104
Fort Walton Beach, FL	1.5	19.4	50.6	187.2	239	875	2,356	176	3,407	580	—	62
Fort Wayne, IN	4.0	30.3	114.3	138.5	257	1,021	3,525	444	4,990	756	—	115
Fort Worth–Arlington, TX	10.2	58.7	238.7	389.2	638	2,362	5,483	1,228	9,073	1,545	▼	328
Fresno, CA	9.4	61.0	228.1	513.6	751	1,930	3,993	1,118	7,041	1,455	—	315
Gadsden, AL	7.5	34.6	86.0	462.7	556	1,032	2,741	300	4,073	964	▲	198
Gainesville, FL	15.2	60.6	226.7	666.1	908	2,528	5,385	434	8,347	1,743	—	336
Galveston–Texas City, TX	10.2	60.7	192.2	278.0	480	1,909	4,496	605	7,010	1,181	—	266
Gary, IN	10.8	38.0	144.2	440.5	596	1,027	2,622	1,018	4,667	1,062	▲	226
Glens Falls, NY	2.1	19.2	11.7	239.2	253	709	2,080	111	2,900	543	▲	48
Goldsboro, NC	9.1	19.4	111.0	320.3	440	1,412	2,675	238	4,325	873	▲	160
✓ Grand Forks, ND–MN	1.4	22.5	10.1	59.8	71	554	3,167	165	3,886	460	—	25
Grand Rapids–Muskegon–Holland, MI	3.1	78.5	88.4	306.0	398	1,060	3,334	307	4,701	868	▼	157
Great Falls, MT	3.6	55.1	29.4	92.3	125	914	5,329	309	6,552	781	—	128

Metro Area	Murder	Rape	Robbery	Assault	VIOLENT	Burglary	Theft	Auto Theft	PROPERTY	SCORE	TREND	RANK
Metro Area Average	5.2	41.3	119.3	283.9	408	1,365	3,485	420	5,721	—	▼	—
Greeley, CO	2.2	41.1	31.1	258.5	292	1,270	4,157	227	5,654	857	▼	155
Green Bay, WI	1.3	16.6	14.1	126.3	142	546	3,176	137	3,859	528	—	43
Greensboro–Winston–Salem–High Point, NC	6.7	35.3	127.9	324.0	459	1,447	3,058	271	4,776	936	—	184
Greenville, NC	7.2	35.4	112.6	290.0	410	1,606	2,883	236	4,725	882	—	164
Greenville–Spartanburg–Anderson, SC	7.3	45.2	116.5	524.6	648	1,412	3,302	320	5,034	1,152	▲	256
✓ Hagerstown, MD	3.2	17.1	37.6	166.5	207	627	1,619	149	2,395	447	▼	23
Halifax, NS	2.1	0.0	109.6	218.8	331	1,878	6,265	343	8,486	1,179	—	265
Hamilton, ON	1.9	0.0	62.5	173.9	238	1,288	3,638	393	5,319	770	—	122
Hamilton–Middletown, OH	3.5	37.1	87.3	263.2	354	1,103	3,456	275	4,834	837	—	146
Harrisburg–Lebanon–Carlisle, PA	3.1	27.0	84.6	172.4	260	575	2,053	208	2,836	544	—	50
Hartford, CT	3.6	31.6	178.9	242.7	425	1,239	3,056	568	4,863	912	—	173
Hickory–Morgantown, NC	7.5	20.3	53.6	256.6	318	1,092	2,223	199	3,514	669	▲	90
Honolulu, HI	3.2	37.2	80.4	98.9	183	1,171	4,185	392	5,748	757	—	116
Houma, LA	6.2	28.6	59.6	272.6	338	855	1,835	114	2,804	619	▼	81
Houston, TX	15.7	52.5	340.4	326.1	682	2,139	3,718	1,472	7,329	1,415	—	311
✓ Huntington–Ashland, WV–KY–OH	3.3	30.0	59.4	115.2	178	820	2,090	163	3,073	485	—	33
Huntsville, AL	6.5	32.8	80.6	222.1	309	984	4,118	260	5,362	845	▲	152
Indianapolis, IN	6.2	56.7	139.3	311.9	457	1,251	2,990	559	4,800	937	—	185
Iowa City, IA	0.5	50.6	19.6	322.8	343	953	3,788	180	4,921	835	—	145
Jackson, MI	6.4	105.1	79.7	603.4	690	989	2,998	251	4,238	1,113	▼	242
Jackson, MS	14.4	60.9	223.9	195.0	433	2,486	3,792	716	6,994	1,133	▼	247
Jacksonville, FL	14.6	87.1	400.4	648.8	1064	2,425	4,841	705	7,971	1,861	▼	339
Jacksonville, NC	3.4	28.8	69.8	210.3	284	1,180	2,637	174	3,991	683	▼	94
✓ Jamestown, NY	1.0	13.1	24.1	82.7	108	771	2,783	82	3,636	471	—	29
Janesville–Beloit, WI	1.4	20.0	42.4	122.5	166	955	3,796	200	4,951	661	▼	87
✓ Johnson City–Kingsport–Bristol, TN–VA	3.6	20.2	27.7	144.1	175	806	2,010	194	3,010	476	▲	30
✓ Johnstown, PA	0.9	14.0	20.5	114.6	136	462	906	110	1,478	284	—	1
Joplin, MO	2.1	20.4	34.7	129.2	166	982	3,244	225	4,451	611	—	75
Kalamazoo–Battle Creek, MI	6.2	78.2	132.6	462.2	601	1,489	4,071	289	5,849	1,186	—	268
Kankakee, IL	8.6	0.0	169.8	436.5	615	1,508	3,498	353	5,359	1,151	—	254
Kansas City, MO–KS	10.0	54.7	287.7	455.3	753	1,657	3,795	862	6,314	1,384	—	305
Kenosha, WI	2.6	43.6	66.7	60.5	130	1,043	3,464	297	4,804	610	▼	74
Killeen–Temple, TX	7.7	71.4	59.6	218.6	286	1,310	3,064	215	4,589	745	—	112
Kitchener, ON	1.3	0.0	37.8	99.8	139	1,102	3,274	246	4,622	601	—	69
Knoxville, TN	6.4	29.5	97.7	261.8	366	1,383	2,191	483	4,057	772	▲	123
Kokomo, IN	1.4	19.9	34.5	198.3	234	709	2,453	192	3,354	570	▲	56
✓ La Crosse, WI–MN	0.5	18.6	10.3	68.0	79	361	3,327	135	3,823	461	—	26
Lafayette, IN	1.7	21.7	18.0	97.2	117	690	3,063	170	3,923	509	▼	40
Lafayette, LA	6.5	33.4	90.1	325.3	422	959	2,441	157	3,557	778	▲	126
Lake Charles, LA	7.2	56.3	104.4	526.5	638	1,586	4,010	258	5,854	1,224	▲	274
Lake County, IL	2.1	0.0	65.6	133.9	202	744	3,006	216	3,966	598	▼	68
Lakeland–Winter Haven, FL	5.3	33.1	227.8	533.7	767	2,572	5,355	715	8,642	1,631	—	331
✓ Lancaster, PA	2.1	18.4	43.3	78.0	123	577	1,869	167	2,613	385	—	9
Lansing–East Lansing, MI	3.1	87.9	95.3	329.1	428	1,064	3,717	351	5,132	941	▼	188
Laredo, TX	10.1	10.3	102.5	443.7	556	1,807	5,302	687	7,796	1,336	▲	300
Las Cruces, NM	5.0	48.4	60.5	239.8	305	1,944	3,899	377	6,220	927	—	181

Metro Area	Murder	Rape	Robbery	Assault	VIOLENT	Burglary	Theft	Auto Theft	PROPERTY	SCORE	TREND	RANK
Metro Area Average	5.2	41.3	119.3	283.9	408	1,365	3,485	420	5,721	—	▼	—
Las Vegas, NV–AZ	9.2	61.5	258.6	252.4	520	1,680	3,778	732	6,190	1,139	▼	250
Lawrence, KS	2.3	34.5	41.6	225.2	269	1,369	4,927	227	6,523	921	▼	177
Lawton, OK	4.5	51.2	77.2	345.4	427	1,461	2,734	247	4,442	871	▼	159
Lewiston–Auburn, ME	2.9	20.5	45.2	74.0	122	1,062	2,902	203	4,167	539	▼	45
Lexington, KY	4.8	46.6	101.1	370.2	476	1,113	3,604	278	4,995	976	▲	200
Lima, OH	3.9	42.7	97.8	571.4	673	1,180	3,254	233	4,667	1,140	▼	251
Lincoln, NE	1.3	39.7	39.9	291.8	333	1,153	5,232	217	6,602	993	▲	204
Little Rock–North Little Rock, AR	11.1	75.5	235.3	572.4	819	1,903	4,788	517	7,208	1,540	▲	327
London, ON	0.7	0.0	46.9	193.3	241	1,385	4,298	274	5,957	837	—	146
Long Island, NY	2.3	11.2	95.0	114.8	212	784	2,242	576	3,602	572	—	57
Longview–Marshall, TX	8.3	61.8	87.1	362.8	458	1,609	3,418	346	5,373	996	▲	207
Los Angeles–Long Beach, CA	14.8	46.9	522.0	736.2	1273	1,401	2,877	1,374	5,652	1,838	—	337
Louisville, KY–IN	5.3	34.3	139.2	203.6	348	1,112	2,856	353	4,321	780	▼	127
Lubbock, TX	7.1	69.8	108.1	249.2	364	2,062	4,744	362	7,168	1,081	▼	229
Lynchburg, VA	6.6	27.3	47.6	210.8	265	550	2,181	131	2,862	551	▲	52
Macon, GA	10.5	43.1	128.3	266.0	405	1,608	4,016	412	6,036	1,008	▲	211
Madison, WI	1.5	22.7	61.2	131.4	194	911	3,763	273	4,947	689	▲	98
Manchester–Nashua, NH	2.4	21.9	48.0	52.3	103	1,151	3,117	350	4,618	565	▲	55
Mansfield, OH	1.5	35.1	85.1	495.0	582	1,181	2,946	213	4,340	1,016	▲	213
McAllen–Edinburg–Mission, TX	5.6	22.8	48.6	289.6	344	1,810	3,713	536	6,059	950	—	193
Medford–Ashland, OR	2.5	43.4	38.0	209.8	250	995	3,466	253	4,714	722	—	105
Melbourne–Titusville–Palm Bay, FL	3.7	34.4	125.1	407.1	536	1,684	4,202	349	6,235	1,159	—	258
Memphis, TN–AR–MS	16.0	100.2	370.7	353.2	740	2,086	3,047	1,478	6,611	1,401	▼	307
Merced, CA	4.1	34.9	72.4	277.4	354	1,270	2,695	326	4,291	783	▼	129
Miami, FL	15.6	61.3	846.1	865.4	1727	2,830	6,266	1,838	10,934	2,821	—	343
Milwaukee–Waukesha, WI	7.6	37.4	197.7	133.1	338	959	3,497	786	5,242	863	▼	156
Minneapolis–St. Paul, MN–WI	3.0	47.5	130.2	185.7	319	1,151	3,531	495	5,177	837	▼	146
Mobile, AL	9.4	42.4	179.2	788.2	977	2,037	3,112	318	5,467	1,524	—	325
Modesto, CA	4.6	46.3	109.6	485.7	600	1,664	3,878	507	6,049	1,205	—	270
Monmouth–Ocean, NJ	1.5	23.2	49.7	149.8	201	767	2,595	239	3,601	561	▼	53
Monroe, LA	5.0	47.8	71.8	542.8	620	1,444	3,811	203	5,458	1,165	—	260
Montgomery, AL	10.3	37.0	120.2	270.1	401	1,381	3,324	291	4,996	900	▲	169
Montreal, PQ	2.7	0.0	252.4	122.7	378	1,997	3,415	845	6,257	1,004	—	210
Muncie, IN	5.3	33.1	60.6	127.8	194	1,079	2,158	258	3,495	543	—	48
Myrtle Beach, SC	8.6	50.6	130.6	433.9	573	2,308	5,292	483	8,083	1,381	—	304
Naples, FL	6.7	79.0	119.1	452.1	578	1,754	3,504	342	5,600	1,138	—	249
Nashville, TN	8.2	64.0	189.2	415.4	613	1,401	3,137	440	4,978	1,111	▼	240
New Bedford–Fall River–Attleboro, MA	2.1	29.9	118.0	335.2	455	1,375	2,454	993	4,822	938	▲	186
New Haven–Meriden, CT	5.6	35.3	257.9	316.4	580	1,511	3,433	917	5,861	1,166	▲	262
New London–Norwich, CT–RI	2.2	27.9	50.1	176.4	229	891	2,301	243	3,435	572	—	57
New Orleans, LA	22.0	52.2	457.0	488.1	967	1,891	4,150	1,144	7,185	1,686	▲	334
New York, NY	19.6	39.8	903.0	669.0	1592	1,518	3,646	1,562	6,726	2,264	—	342
Newark–Jersey City, NJ	7.4	41.4	436.6	363.2	807	1,219	2,832	1,938	5,989	1,406	—	309
Norfolk–Virginia Beach–Newport News, VA–NC	9.6	45.1	183.5	199.6	393	1,173	4,036	463	5,672	960	▲	196
Northern New Jersey, NJ	2.3	14.9	134.4	154.1	291	722	2,500	636	3,858	677	—	92

Metro Area	Murder	Rape	Robbery	Assault	VIOLENT	Burglary	Theft	Auto Theft	PROPERTY	SCORE	TREND	RANK
Metro Area Average	5.2	41.3	119.3	283.9	408	1,365	3,485	420	5,721	—	▼	—
Oakland, CA	10.1	50.8	275.0	386.7	672	1,547	4,132	824	6,503	1,322	▼	296
Ocala, FL	7.0	55.5	211.8	564.2	783	2,098	3,772	352	6,222	1,405	—	308
Odessa–Midland, TX	7.8	62.3	89.7	307.6	405	2,220	5,462	374	8,056	1,211	▲	271
Oklahoma City, OK	6.9	59.9	150.4	312.0	469	2,217	4,480	851	7,548	1,224	▼	274
Olympia, WA	2.1	57.7	29.4	126.0	158	1,103	3,226	220	4,549	612	—	76
Omaha, NE–IA	3.7	38.8	91.8	305.4	401	1,038	3,405	306	4,749	876	▼	161
Orange County, CA	4.8	27.0	162.4	223.9	391	1,293	3,279	810	5,382	929	—	182
Orange County, NY	3.6	24.0	90.3	239.9	334	923	2,361	212	3,496	683	▼	94
Orlando, FL	4.7	45.7	215.5	559.2	779	2,186	4,154	594	6,934	1,473	—	317
Oshawa, ON	1.4	0.0	40.5	153.0	195	1,034	2,810	292	4,136	609	▼	72
Ottawa–Hull, ON–PQ	1.6	0.0	99.3	117.1	218	1,507	3,813	412	5,732	791	—	132
Owensboro, KY	2.0	30.3	32.6	101.7	136	857	2,594	145	3,596	496	▲	36
Panama City, FL	6.6	55.8	65.7	384.0	456	1,423	4,183	291	5,897	1,046	▲	219
✓ Parkersburg–Marietta, WV–OH	1.3	22.2	18.6	39.4	59	652	1,704	135	2,491	308	—	3
Pensacola, FL	4.6	51.5	155.1	475.0	635	1,963	4,359	413	6,735	1,308	—	294
Peoria–Pekin, IL	3.9	0.0	88.0	294.5	386	1,117	2,867	157	4,141	801	—	135
Philadelphia, PA–NJ	9.3	34.1	252.8	250.9	513	912	2,288	759	3,959	909	—	171
Phoenix–Mesa, AZ	7.1	40.5	150.9	362.1	520	1,825	4,714	850	7,389	1,259	—	281
Pine Bluff, AR	10.4	79.1	171.2	560.4	742	1,916	2,965	344	5,225	1,265	▲	284
Pittsburgh, PA	2.3	27.0	113.9	157.6	274	692	1,479	594	2,765	550	—	51
Pittsfield, MA	1.6	18.4	37.8	318.9	358	1,026	1,636	249	2,911	649	▲	86
Portland, ME	2.8	26.3	49.9	155.2	208	1,273	4,039	355	5,667	775	▼	124
Portland, OR	4.3	54.9	228.2	374.9	607	1,780	4,289	792	6,861	1,294	▼	292
✓ Portsmouth–Dover–Rochester, NH	1.9	25.7	19.2	77.9	99	601	2,299	272	3,172	416	▼	15
Providence–Warwick–Cranston, RI	3.7	28.1	98.8	215.2	318	1,298	2,679	915	4,892	807	▼	140
✓ Provo–Orem, UT	0.5	29.0	9.4	80.6	91	523	3,260	145	3,928	483	▼	32
Pueblo, CO	5.5	72.1	95.1	794.4	895	1,412	3,918	293	5,623	1,457	▲	316
✓ Punta Gorda, FL	2.6	13.9	33.7	78.7	115	1,025	2,085	193	3,303	445	▼	22
Quebec City, PQ	1.5	0.0	128.1	80.8	210	1,924	3,121	424	5,469	757	—	116
Racine, WI	4.1	38.3	151.2	200.6	356	1,287	3,584	383	5,254	881	—	163
Raleigh–Durham–Chapel Hill, NC	6.8	32.4	112.1	275.8	395	1,605	3,302	308	5,215	916	▲	175
Rapid City, SD	2.5	94.8	39.7	222.3	265	877	4,148	239	5,264	791	▼	132
Reading, PA	3.0	20.1	108.0	158.3	269	856	1,966	262	3,084	578	▲	60
Redding, CA	4.2	53.6	60.5	346.0	411	1,452	3,010	378	4,840	895	▼	168
Regina, SK	2.5	0.0	93.4	264.6	361	2,901	5,943	444	9,288	1,289	▼	290
Reno, NV	5.4	95.4	170.5	314.8	491	1,388	4,336	427	6,151	1,106	—	239
Richland–Kennewick–Pasco, WA	4.5	57.7	51.4	195.3	251	1,548	4,039	243	5,830	834	—	144
Richmond–Petersburg, VA	13.5	40.8	163.8	233.9	411	1,129	3,594	427	5,150	926	▲	180
Riverside–San Bernardino, CA	8.2	42.7	194.2	643.3	846	2,125	3,464	935	6,524	1,498	▼	321
Roanoke, VA	5.9	23.1	93.0	142.9	242	948	3,716	189	4,853	727	▲	109
✓ Rochester, MN	1.8	17.0	16.9	59.6	78	738	2,797	153	3,688	447	▲	23
Rochester, NY	5.3	28.3	110.2	131.3	247	961	3,409	278	4,648	712	—	102
Rockford, IL	5.4	0.2	178.3	347.0	531	1,666	4,047	393	6,106	1,141	▼	252
Rocky Mount, NC	13.1	30.9	117.3	278.0	408	1,636	3,250	235	5,121	921	—	177
Sacramento, CA	6.7	44.0	204.2	339.4	550	1,630	3,724	979	6,333	1,184	▼	267

Metro Area	Murder	Rape	Robbery	Assault	VIOLENT	Burglary	Theft	Auto Theft	PROPERTY	SCORE	TREND	RANK
Metro Area Average	**5.2**	**41.3**	**119.3**	**283.9**	**408**	**1,365**	**3,485**	**420**	**5,721**	**—**	**▼**	**—**
Saginaw–Bay City–Midland, MI	6.5	89.9	115.8	437.7	560	1,156	3,393	231	4,780	1,038	▲	216
St. Catharines–Niagara, ON	1.9	0.0	35.5	136.5	174	1,461	3,288	333	5,082	682	▼	93
St. Cloud, MN	1.9	23.1	8.5	256.8	267	2,321	2,420	166	4,907	758	▼	118
Saint John, NB	1.9	0.0	32.0	83.2	117	922	2,508	363	3,793	496	—	36
St. John's, NF	0.6	0.0	14.4	115.7	131	1,052	2,858	200	4,110	542	▲	47
St. Joseph, MO	2.4	24.0	36.5	356.9	396	1,175	3,390	246	4,811	877	—	162
St. Louis, MO–IL	10.3	25.0	209.9	437.4	658	1,291	3,052	585	4,928	1,150	▲	253
Salem, OR	3.1	46.1	93.6	166.5	263	1,377	4,308	372	6,057	869	▼	158
Salinas, CA	5.1	41.6	108.3	387.3	501	1,105	3,079	298	4,482	949	▼	192
Salt Lake City–Ogden, UT	2.8	37.8	65.4	172.3	241	1,096	5,108	285	6,489	889	—	167
San Angelo, TX	5.2	42.4	40.6	369.4	415	1,623	4,151	192	5,966	1,012	▲	212
San Antonio, TX	12.4	53.8	198.7	203.3	414	2,567	6,191	1,222	9,980	1,412	—	310
San Diego, CA	7.4	35.4	210.3	414.7	632	1,442	3,383	1,511	6,336	1,266	—	285
San Francisco, CA	6.7	38.8	347.4	362.5	717	1,063	3,740	873	5,676	1,284	—	288
San Jose, CA	3.5	43.3	88.0	279.3	371	820	3,098	439	4,357	807	▼	140
San Luis Obispo–Atascadero–Paso Robles, CA	1.9	35.9	34.2	205.4	242	850	2,423	190	3,463	588	▼	64
Santa Barbara–Santa Maria–Lompoc, CA	3.2	38.2	71.5	279.2	354	1,112	3,110	279	4,501	804	—	137
Santa Cruz–Watsonville, CA	4.2	37.3	83.4	267.5	355	1,332	3,793	366	5,491	904	▼	170
Santa Fe, NM	6.9	18.5	42.5	371.8	421	1,135	1,781	191	3,107	732	—	110
Santa Rosa, CA	3.7	40.1	59.1	227.1	290	1,198	2,828	328	4,354	725	▼	107
Sarasota–Bradenton, FL	4.6	45.2	162.8	436.0	603	1,994	4,342	385	6,721	1,276	—	287
Saskatoon, SK	2.0	0.0	74.8	191.0	268	1,866	5,529	451	7,846	1,052	▼	222
Savannah, GA	12.6	54.0	251.1	243.4	507	1,711	4,288	442	6,441	1,151	—	254
✓ Scranton–Wilkes-Barre–Hazleton, PA	2.2	68.3	23.0	106.3	132	476	1,125	674	2,275	359	▼	6
Seattle–Bellevue–Everett, WA	3.5	64.7	154.8	244.2	403	1,664	4,812	611	7,087	1,111	▼	240
✓ Sharon, PA	2.1	13.5	33.0	123.6	159	479	1,412	174	2,065	365	—	7
✓ Sheboygan, WI	0.6	11.4	14.2	105.0	120	616	2,943	109	3,668	487	▲	34
Sherbrooke, PQ	0.7	0.0	59.4	100.2	160	2,051	2,674	365	5,090	669	▲	90
Sherman–Denison, TX	6.8	29.6	94.4	254.4	356	1,950	4,506	387	6,843	1,040	▼	217
Shreveport–Bossier City, LA	14.1	49.4	206.5	438.7	659	2,086	5,124	370	7,580	1,417	—	313
Sioux City, IA–NE	1.6	36.6	62.0	266.0	330	1,698	4,258	276	6,232	953	▼	194
Sioux Falls, SD	2.2	49.1	27.7	126.4	156	781	2,904	148	3,833	540	▲	46
South Bend, IN	6.6	56.8	131.6	143.8	282	1,737	4,554	357	6,648	947	▼	191
Spokane, WA	2.6	40.0	94.7	184.3	282	1,789	4,150	335	6,274	909	—	171
Springfield, IL	3.8	0.0	112.5	347.7	464	1,388	3,369	200	4,957	960	—	196
Springfield, MA	2.6	47.9	162.3	463.2	628	1,314	2,439	783	4,536	1,082	▲	230
Springfield, MO	2.1	28.0	55.2	151.0	208	1,271	3,954	225	5,450	753	—	113
Stamford–Norwalk, CT	3.5	12.6	115.7	111.8	231	1,097	2,998	624	4,719	703	▼	100
✓ State College, PA	0.7	26.0	11.1	45.0	57	606	2,898	89	3,593	416	—	16
✓ Steubenville–Weirton, OH–WV	1.0	10.9	26.2	214.7	242	629	1,190	146	1,965	438	▲	21
Stockton–Lodi, CA	11.4	52.7	263.9	319.1	594	1,999	4,588	841	7,428	1,337	▲	301
Sudbury, ON	2.2	0.0	51.9	131.6	186	1,868	3,122	790	5,780	764	▲	120
Sumter, SC	9.4	46.4	115.1	711.0	836	1,440	2,849	303	4,592	1,295	▲	293
Syracuse, NY	2.2	25.7	71.0	138.5	212	980	2,685	155	3,820	594	—	66

Metro Area	Murder	Rape	Robbery	Assault	VIOLENT	Burglary	Theft	Auto Theft	PROPERTY	SCORE	TREND	RANK
Metro Area Average	5.2	41.3	119.3	283.9	408	1,365	3,485	420	5,721	—	▼	—
Tacoma, WA	7.0	96.0	215.1	386.2	608	1,901	4,386	500	6,787	1,287	—	289
Tallahassee, FL	7.4	77.7	296.9	888.2	1193	2,743	5,553	608	8,904	2,083	▲	341
Tampa–St. Petersburg– Clearwater, FL	6.7	51.0	283.4	650.2	940	1,979	4,500	692	7,171	1,657	—	332
Terre Haute, IN	5.8	43.4	51.5	293.0	350	1,322	2,946	457	4,725	823	▼	143
Texarkana, TX–Texarkana, AR	8.6	49.1	140.8	293.6	443	1,865	4,525	323	6,713	1,114	—	243
Thunder Bay, ON	1.2	0.0	58.7	338.4	398	1,566	4,462	438	6,466	1,045	▼	218
Toledo, OH	5.4	76.3	244.8	219.6	470	1,358	4,179	815	6,352	1,105	▲	238
Topeka, KS	5.7	45.6	140.5	393.9	540	2,049	4,619	288	6,956	1,236	▲	277
Toronto, ON	1.7	0.0	106.0	175.5	283	985	3,216	298	4,499	733	—	111
Trenton, NJ	5.2	41.2	231.7	297.8	535	1,317	3,179	1,166	5,662	1,101	▼	234
Trois–Rivieres, PQ	1.4	0.0	67.9	97.8	167	1,424	2,763	377	4,564	624	▲	83
Tucson, AZ	5.8	60.1	124.6	376.1	507	1,610	6,144	526	8,280	1,335	▼	299
Tulsa, OK	6.5	56.2	166.5	386.8	560	1,728	3,033	1,007	5,768	1,137	▲	248
Tuscaloosa, AL	5.2	36.4	111.7	525.6	643	1,388	4,015	314	5,717	1,214	▼	272
Tyler, TX	8.6	65.0	99.4	294.6	403	2,018	4,831	436	7,285	1,131	—	246
✓ Utica–Rome, NY	2.1	16.5	42.0	69.0	113	759	1,906	128	2,793	392	—	11
Vallejo–Fairfield–Napa, CA	5.3	42.3	148.7	425.5	580	1,230	3,470	529	5,229	1,102	▼	235
Vancouver, BC	2.5	0.0	163.2	207.6	373	2,333	5,824	740	8,897	1,263	—	283
Vancouver, WA	2.8	45.2	52.7	119.1	175	1,238	2,857	343	4,438	618	▼	80
Ventura, CA	3.0	31.0	93.8	232.6	329	995	2,221	356	3,572	687	▼	97
Victoria, BC	1.5	0.0	82.4	186.6	271	1,540	5,231	330	7,101	981	—	202
Victoria, TX	6.7	34.0	78.6	481.7	567	1,836	3,947	249	6,032	1,170	—	263
Vineland–Millville–Bridgeton, NJ	4.5	59.6	192.0	423.4	620	1,485	3,520	422	5,427	1,163	▲	259
Visalia–Tulare–Porterville, CA	7.4	37.1	98.5	437.7	544	1,537	3,126	373	5,036	1,047	▼	220
Waco, TX	11.6	61.7	162.6	380.5	555	2,593	4,887	471	7,951	1,350	—	303
Washington, DC–MD–VA–WV	12.9	32.2	258.5	277.6	549	967	3,140	683	4,790	1,028	—	215
Waterbury, CT	3.9	22.8	146.9	158.9	310	1,596	3,442	724	5,762	886	▲	166
Waterloo–Cedar Falls, IA	3.0	23.0	65.6	165.1	234	1,405	3,339	152	4,896	723	—	106
✓ Wausau, WI	0.1	7.6	6.5	81.0	88	487	2,547	116	3,150	403	▼	12
West Palm Beach–Boca Raton, FL	8.9	44.3	301.9	505.9	817	2,785	5,114	875	8,774	1,694	▼	335
✓ Wheeling, WV–OH	2.9	12.8	34.4	78.1	115	578	1,133	163	1,874	303	▲	2
Wichita, KS	4.2	66.4	175.9	202.7	383	1,608	4,143	452	6,203	1,003	—	209
Wichita Falls, TX	9.4	61.8	191.9	326.3	528	2,375	5,322	481	8,178	1,345	▲	302
✓ Williamsport, PA	0.0	17.0	23.0	76.6	100	570	1,612	116	2,298	329	—	4
Wilmington, NC	3.8	47.6	163.6	351.3	519	2,366	5,281	397	8,044	1,323	—	297
Wilmington–Newark, DE–MD	4.1	64.2	131.6	249.5	385	1,023	3,130	421	4,574	843	▼	151
Windsor, ON	2.0	0.0	60.3	136.0	198	1,386	3,910	298	5,594	758	—	118
Winnipeg, MB	2.3	0.0	148.4	228.6	379	2,065	4,840	460	7,365	1,116	▼	244
✓ Worcester–Fitchburg– Leominster, MA	1.0	24.6	36.9	187.2	225	712	1,427	275	2,414	467	▼	27
Yakima, WA	6.9	65.1	104.3	327.0	438	2,322	5,274	387	7,983	1,237	▲	279
Yolo, CA	6.4	43.2	80.9	320.5	408	1,407	4,613	495	6,515	1,059	▼	224
✓ York, PA	2.6	19.4	95.9	77.7	176	592	2,303	144	3,039	480	▲	31
Youngstown–Warren, OH	4.2	29.3	100.7	199.0	304	1,047	1,968	406	3,421	646	▼	85
Yuba City, CA	9.3	38.7	63.3	588.5	661	1,528	3,372	381	5,281	1,189	▼	269
Yuma, AZ	4.7	52.8	105.8	556.9	667	1,655	6,204	524	8,383	1,506	▼	323

Et Cetera

DRUNK DRIVING

Drunk driving is the most common single cause of arrest in the United States, and the penalties for the crime have gotten more serious. Most states and all provinces in Canada mandate license suspensions for first offenses, and license revocations and jail terms for repeat offenses. Three other ways of controlling the drunk driver come by means of legislation.

Blood-Alcohol Exceptions. The American Medical Association (AMA) says that anyone with a blood-alcohol level of 0.05 percent is too drunk to drive. Most state law uses the 0.10-percent baseline, or twice the AMA standard. The Canadian provinces and five states, including California with the highest number of drunk-driving arrests on the continent, have lowered the illegal per se blood-alcohol level to 0.08 percent.

Dram Shop Laws allow the last person and establishment to serve a drink to an intoxicated patron to be held responsible for the patron's actions immediately afterward. Victims of drunk drivers may sue not just the driver but also the bar owner, bar tender, or party host who served the driver.

Happy Hour Prohibitions, a new form of server responsibility law, mean that drinking establishments cannot encourage excessive or immoderate consumption. Fifteen states and Ontario have passed such laws that prohibit bars from advertising Happy Hour, selling two drinks for the price of one, or changing their prices at any time during the day.

HANDGUNS

Handgun control isn't a subject to be lightly entered into in conversation unless you have the time and are ready for a prolonged discussion.

Canada's 1992 gun control law, C-17, passed after the mass-murder of 14 young women on a Montreal campus, requires would-be buyers of rifles and shotguns to obtain a Firearms Acquisition Certificate (FAC), wait 28 days for background checks, and then undergo mandatory training in firearms use. All handguns are restricted weapons, available only to collectors and gun-club members after rigorous background checks.

In the United States, the controversy continues. Changes in regulations occur frequently from state to state and even within municipalities.

The National Rifle Association, the fiercest defender of gun enthusiasts, attempts to keep its members informed of regulation changes with a regular publication of state-by-state gun purchase-and-carrying laws, but even this comes with a disclaimer warning of the constant changes. The variations in different states' restrictions can be immense, reflecting how well those who vehemently defend their weapons and those who would take them away have done their jobs in state legislatures.

In Georgia and South Carolina, for example, there are few constraints. You can walk into a store, buy a pistol, and walk out. There's not even a record of the sale. In Illinois, on the other hand, a prospective gun buyer has to apply for a permit, then wait 30 days for a check of criminal records. A gun must then be registered and the sale is reported. However, carrying a weapon, either openly or concealed, is unlawful in the state.

In Chicago, the same rules apply, but only to old guns. No new guns may be brought into the city since a recent law change. In the suburbs of Evanston, Oak Park, and Morton Grove, there are no handguns at all; they're prohibited.

Most of the states fall somewhere between these extremes, but the penalties for not knowing the law or for violating the law can be severe. Massachusetts, for example, has a law requiring a mandatory one-year jail term for anyone caught with an unlicensed gun.

CRIME CLOCK

one CRIME INDEX OFFENSE every 1 second

one VIOLENT CRIME every 15 seconds
- one MURDER every 21 minutes
- one FORCIBLE RAPE every 5 minutes
- one ROBBERY every 44 seconds
- one AGGRAVATED ASSAULT every 26 seconds

one PROPERTY CRIME every 2 seconds
- one BURGLARY every 9 seconds
- one LARCENY-THEFT every 4 seconds
- one MOTOR VEHICLE THEFT every 18 seconds

DUI Inhibitors
(Driving Under the Influence)

	Blood Alcohol*	Dram Shop Law	No Happy Hour
Alabama		•	
Alaska		•	
Alberta	0.08		
Arizona		•	•
Arkansas			
British Columbia	0.08		
California	0.08	•	
Colorado		•	
Connecticut		•	
Delaware			
District of Columbia			
Florida		•	
Georgia		•	
Hawaii		•	
Idaho		•	
Illinois		•	•
Indiana		•	•
Iowa		•	
Kansas			•
Kentucky		•	
Louisiana		•	
Maine	0.08	•	
Manitoba	0.08		
Maryland			
Massachusetts		•	•
Michigan		•	
Minnesota		•	
Mississippi		•	
Missouri		•	•
Montana		•	
Nebraska			•
Nevada			
New Brunswick	0.08		
New Hampshire		•	
New Jersey		•	•
New Mexico		•	•
New York		•	
Newfoundland	0.08		
North Carolina		•	
North Dakota		•	
Nova Scotia	0.08		
Ohio		•	
Oklahoma		•	
Ontario	0.08		•
Oregon	0.08	•	
Pennsylvania		•	•
Prince Edward Island	0.08		
Quebec	0.08		
Rhode Island		•	•
Saskatchewan	0.08		
South Carolina		•	
South Dakota		•	
Tennessee		•	•
Texas		•	•
Utah	0.08	•	•
Vermont	0.08	•	•
Virginia	0.08		
Washington		•	
West Virginia		•	
Wisconsin		•	
Wyoming		•	

Source: Transport Canada, 1993; U.S. Department of Transportation, 1993.
* Most states use the 0.10-percent blood alcohol baseline.

CAPITAL PUNISHMENT

In 1972, the U.S. Supreme Court struck down on Eighth Amendment grounds (forbidding cruel and unusual punishment) laws that permitted wide discretion in the application of the death penalty. In 1976, the court also struck down mandatory use of the death penalty for specified crimes but upheld laws that permitted executions after consideration of aggravating and mitigating circumstances. That same year, Canada abolished the death penalty entirely.

While the justice of capital punishment continues to be debated in state houses and courts throughout the United States, one thing is clear: Execution doesn't follow soon after a guilty verdict. In the 37 states with death penalty laws, half of the 2,600 convicted inmates have been on Death Row more than 3 years. Several recent executions have taken place 15 years after sentencing.

Supporters of capital punishment cite the huge financial burden that the delays cost and point to the demographics of Death Row: All inmates are convicted murderers, two out of three have at least one prior felony conviction, nearly 10 percent have a prior murder conviction, and 40 percent were on bail, probation, or parole at the time of the murder.

The most compelling arguments against capital punishment are that it is barbaric and irreversible, that mistakes have and will be made, and that in many areas adequate legal defenses aren't provided. Moreover, a life sentence would cost a state one-third of the millions it spends seeing a typical death conviction through the extensive appeals process.

Death Penalty Differences

Fourteen states and Canada have abandoned or avoided the death penalty in the modern age. Implementation in the 37 states that have it on their statutes is far from consistent.

Twenty states have executed convicted murderers in the years since capital punishment was reinstated. Among some 2,600 persons sentenced, fewer than 180 have been executed. Three out of five executions have taken place in Georgia, Florida, Louisiana, and Texas. New Hampshire, South Dakota, and Wyoming have capital punishment statutes but have never imposed sentences.

Methods of execution vary. Idaho and Utah offer the choice of receiving a lethal injection or facing a firing squad, the latter method a relic of nineteenth-century Mormonism requiring murderers to atone for their crime by having their blood spilled on the ground. Lethal injections and electrocution are the most common execution methods. Delaware and New Hampshire prescribe hanging as the only acceptable method.

NATIONAL AND REGIONAL CRIME RATES

With one-fourth the murder rate, one-third the robbery rate, and less than half the aggravated assault rate of the

State Restrictions on Purchase and Carrying of Handguns

State	Law	Wait	Coverage	Carrying Prohibited* Concealed	Open
Alabama	waiting period	2 days	handguns		
Alaska				•	
Arizona				•	
Arkansas				•	•
California	waiting period	15 days	all firearms	•	
Colorado				•	
Connecticut	waiting period	14 days	all firearms		
Delaware	telephone check	3 days	all firearms	•	
District of Columbia				•	•
Florida	telephone check	3 days	all firearms		
Georgia					
Hawaii	permit to purchase	15 days	all firearms		
Idaho				•	
Illinois	permit to purchase	30 days	all firearms	•	•
Indiana	waiting period	7 days	handguns		
Iowa	permit to purchase	3 days	handguns		
Kansas				•	
Kentucky				•	
Louisiana				•	
Maine				•	
Maryland	waiting period	7 days	handguns		
Massachusetts	permit to purchase	40 days	all firearms		
Michigan	permit to purchase		handguns		
Minnesota	permit to purchase	14 days	handguns		
Mississippi				•	
Missouri	permit to purchase	7 days	handguns	•	
Montana				•	
Nebraska	permit to purchase	2 days	handguns	•	
Nevada				•	
New Hampshire				•	
New Jersey	permit to purchase	30 days	all firearms		
New Mexico				•	
New York	permit to purchase	180 days	handguns	•	
North Carolina	permit to purchase	30 days	handguns	•	
North Dakota				•	•
Ohio				•	
Oklahoma				•	•
Oregon	waiting period	15 days	handguns	•	
Pennsylvania	waiting period	2 days	handguns		
Rhode Island	waiting period	7 days	all firearms		
South Carolina					
South Dakota	waiting period	2 days	handguns	•	•
Tennessee	waiting period	15 days	handguns	•	•
Texas				•	•
Utah				•	•
Vermont				•	•
Virginia	telephone check	2 days	all firearms	•	
Washington	waiting period	5 days	handguns		
West Virginia				•	
Wisconsin	telephone check	5 days	handguns	•	
Wyoming				•	

Source: Handgun Control, Inc., 1993; National Rifle Association, 1993

State firearms laws are subject to change. State and local statutes and ordinances, as well as local police, should be consulted for full text and meaning of statutory provisions.

* Most states that do not prohibit carrying handguns nevertheless require a license to carry them openly or concealed.

United States, Canada is a much less violent country than its southern neighbor. For all that, there are more burglaries in Canada per capita and a nearly identical rate for theft.

Although criminal activity varies from place to place and from year to year, regional patterns haven't changed much in decades. The murder rate in the West South Central states, where the frequency of people killing one another has traditionally been the country's highest, is nearly nine times that of Canada's Atlantic provinces. Armed robbery, a big-city crime, is highest in the Mid-Atlantic states, lowest again in the Atlantic provinces.

Criminologists recognize the geographic pattern of crime-ridden places immediately. The continent's more dangerous places are located on the East Coast south of Delaware Bay. This area is growing, and the resulting conditions of strangers living close together are strongly associated with crime.

There are other reasons for high crime in this area. Professional crooks travel to where the living is easy and the pickings bountiful; they don't stay in the industrial towns of the North but head South to warm weather and popular resorts. This is one factor behind Miami's decades-old crime image.

Finally, most of the more dangerous places are hot much of the year. Knowing what we do about climate's influence on crime, it isn't surprising that large southern cities going through a steamy summer are America's most violent. Persons bidding farewell to Cedar Rapids, Milwaukee, Pittsburgh, or Syracuse to make their new homes in Palm Beach, Orlando, Phoenix, or Las Vegas may need time not only for acclimatizing to warm weather, but also for getting used to crime's share in the local evening news.

Neighborhood Crime Watches

It is not uncommon to see a crime in progress without recognizing it as such. Here are some situations that might be observed in any neighborhood. These are situations a trained police officer would investigate if he or she were making the observation.

Situations Involving Vehicles

Situation	Possible Significance
Moving vehicles, especially if moving slowly without lights, following an aimless or repetitive course	Casing for a place to rob or burglarize; drug pusher, sex offender, or vandal
Parked, occupied vehicle, especially at an unusual hour	Lookout for burglary in progress (sometimes two people masquerading as lovers)
Vehicle parked in neighbor's drive being loaded with valuables, even if the vehicle looks legitimate, i.e., moving van or commercial van	Burglary or larceny in progress
Abandoned vehicle with or without license plate	Stolen or abandoned after being used in a crime
Persons loitering around parked cars	Burglary of vehicle contents, theft of accessories, vandalism
Persons detaching accessories and mechanical parts	Theft or vandalism
Apparent business transactions from a vehicle near school, park, or quiet residential neighborhood	Drug sales
Persons being forced into vehicle	Kidnapping, rape, robbery
Objects thrown from a moving vehicle	Disposal of contraband

Situations Involving Property

Situation	Possible Significance
Property in homes, garages, or storage areas, especially if several items of the same kind such as TVs and bicycles	Storage of stolen property

Situations Involving Property

Situation	Possible Significance
Property in vehicles, especially meaningful at night or if property is household goods, appliances, unmounted tape decks, stereo equipment	Stolen property, burglary in progress
Property being removed from a house or building; meaningful if residents are at work, on vacation, or are known to be absent	Burglary or larceny in progress
Open doors, broken doors or windows, or other signs of a forced entry	Burglary in progress or the scene of a recent burglary

Situations Involving Persons

Situation	Possible Significance
Door-to-door solicitors—especially significant if one goes to the back of the house and one stays in front. Can be men or women, clean-cut and well dressed	Casing for burglary, burglary in progress, soliciting violation
Waiting in front of a house	Lookout for burglary in progress
Forced entry or entry through window	Burglary, vandalism, theft
Persons shortcutting through yards	Fleeing the scene of a crime
Persons running, especially if carrying items of value	Fleeing the scene of a crime
Person carrying property, especially if property isn't boxed or wrapped	Offender leaving the scene of a burglary, robbery, or larceny
High volume of human traffic in and out of residence	Drug sales, vice activities, "fence" operation

States with Death Penalties and Their Methods of Execution

Lethal Injection	Electrocution	Lethal Gas	Hanging	Firing Squad
Arkansas *	Alabama	Arizona	Delaware	Idaho *
Colorado	Arkansas *	California	Montana *	Utah *
Delaware *	Connecticut	Maryland	New Hampshire	
Idaho *	Florida	Mississippi *		
Illinois	Georgia	North Carolina *		
Louisiana	Indiana	Wyoming *		
Mississippi *	Kentucky			
Missouri	Nebraska			
Montana *	Ohio			
Nevada	South Carolina			
New Jersey	Tennessee			
New Mexico	Virginia			
North Carolina *				
Oklahoma				
Oregon				
Pennsylvania				
South Dakota				
Texas				
Utah *				
Washington				
Wyoming *				

Source: NAACP Legal Defense and Educational Fund, 1993

* Authorizes two methods of execution

Regional Crime Rates

Region	Murder	Rape	Robbery	Assault	Burglary	Larceny-Theft	Motor Vehicle Theft
U.S. Average	9.8	42.3	272.7	433.3	1,252.0	3,228.8	659.0
New England: Connecticut, Maine, Massachusetts, New Hampshire, Rhode Island, Vermont	4.1	30.1	159.1	338.3	1,102.9	2,599.8	716.2
Mid-Atlantic: New Jersey, New York, Pennsylvania	9.9	28.5	419.0	371.8	977.8	2,597.7	822.5
Great Lakes: Illinois, Indiana, Michigan, Ohio, Wisconsin	8.9	50.2	262.6	382.6	1,056.0	3,151.3	570.0
Plains: Iowa, Kansas, Minnesota, Missouri, Nebraska, North Dakota, South Dakota	5.4	34.0	129.4	287.8	990.6	2,918.4	356.2
South Atlantic: Delaware, District of Columbia, Florida, Georgia, Maryland, North Carolina, South Carolina, Virginia, West Virginia	11.4	43.7	285.6	510.3	1,508.3	3,665.2	560.8
East South Central: Alabama, Kentucky, Mississippi, Tennessee	10.4	40.8	149.1	430.5	1,196.2	2,464.7	395.1
West South Central: Arkansas, Louisiana, Oklahoma, Texas	14.2	50.4	253.7	487.6	1,653.0	3,871.2	788.2
Mountain: Arizona, Colorado, Idaho, Montana, Nevada, New Mexico, Utah, Wyoming	6.5	44.3	122.1	370.7	1,246.6	3,843.4	491.3
Pacific: Alaska, California, Hawaii, Oregon, Washington	10.7	47.2	345.4	542.0	1,350.7	3,409.5	896.0
Canadian Average	2.5	n.a.	98.1	186.2	1,331.7	3,226.1	382.7
Atlantic: New Brunswick, Newfoundland, Nova Scotia, Prince Edward Island	1.6	n.a.	20.7	107.0	814.2	1,121.7	173.1
East: Ontario, Quebec	2.4	n.a.	112.9	155.8	1,255.1	2,773.3	384.1
West: Alberta, British Columbia, Manitoba, Saskatchewan	2.9	n.a.	90.2	257.1	1,636.8	3,265.4	437.3

Source: FBI, *Crime in the United States,* 1992; Statistics Canada, *Canadian Crime Statistics,* 1992.

The Arts

Most people would exchange any worn-out city for a serene place that's safer, cheaper, and less crowded. The escape to a smaller place is a sustaining dream for big-city residents, according to opinion polls.

You might even pack up and make your *own* break if the chance arrives in the form of a job transfer, a midlife change, or retirement. You may be pleased to discover that towns with courthouse squares, angle parking, and streets actually named Main still exist. You might write home that you'd finally found a sense of cohesion, of continuity and tradition, of community spirit and neighborliness that you thought had vanished. You're happier than you've been in years.

For about four months.

Because in your headlong rush to abandon the aggravations of big-city life, you abandoned the classic marble art museum you barely glanced at in passing twice each day in the crush of commuter traffic.

You left behind a library system with a generous budget not just for books, but for software, videos, compact-disc recordings, and fascinating lectures and exhibits.

You also turned your back on the local newspaper's arts section, the local public television station's earnest fund-raising auctions, and your yearly subscription to the repertory theatre's season.

Of all the factors that coalesce into quality of life, the one called the arts inevitably improves with the size of the city. The likelihood of professional sports teams, zoological gardens, and amusement parks being found anywhere improves with population size, too. Many of the most valuable recreation assets—lakes, hiking trails, forests, campgrounds—are found far from cities; indeed, they *must* be far from cities. The arts alone are big-city phenomena.

Places Rated's top two metro areas for the arts are New York and Los Angeles. This isn't to say that culture cannot be found in smaller metro areas. Although it is safe to assume that the larger a metro area is, the more artistic and cultural amenities it will possess, there are interesting exceptions.

TUNING IN TO CONCERT RADIO

While album rock, oldies, and country dominate FM radio formats, nearly 8 of every 100 hours of FM listening in New York and Toronto is classical music. Metropolitan audiences can tune in to music aired around the clock by 434 concert- or classical-format radio stations. Fifty-one of these stations with the biggest share of the fine-arts audience (CFMX-FM in Toronto or WCRB-FM in Boston, for example) are commercial

232

Classical-Format Radio: The Top Markets

Five Stations	Four Stations
Boston, MA	Chicago, IL
Indianapolis, IN	San Francisco, CA
New York, NY	Toronto, ON
Washington, DC–MD–VA–WV	Vancouver, BC

Source: Broadcasting and Cable Market Place, 1993; Concert Music Broadcasters Association, Directory, 1993.

Touring Artist Bookings: The Top Markets

Metro Area	Dates
New York, NY	2,581
Los Angeles–Long Beach, CA	1,874
Washington, DC–MD–VA–WV	1,500
Chicago, IL	774
Phoenix–Mesa, AZ	612
Oakland, CA	588
Boston, MA	569
Tampa–St. Petersburg–Clearwater, FL	550
Philadelphia, PA–NJ	492
Toronto, ON	488
Long Island, NY	484
St. Louis, MO–IL	455
Hartford, CT	428
Ann Arbor, MI	422
Cleveland–Lorain–Elyria, OH	415

Source: Derived from Musical America: International Directory of the Performing Arts, 1993.

---

operations, but most belong to the American Public Broadcasting System or the CBC in Canada. The cities of license for nearly all are within 219 metro areas; 44 metro areas have two stations, and 22 have three or more.

THE LIVELY ARTS CALENDAR

The cultural side of urban life might be divided into two categories: possessions and performances. Collected art on museum walls and books on a public library's shelves belong in the first group. The lively arts—symphony, opera, dance, and theatre—belong in the second.

Despite the competition, the audience's increasingly precious leisure time, the economic recession, and the drop in government arts funding, the lively arts continue to endure. This isn't the case everywhere, however.

In recent years, the Nashville Symphony filed for bankruptcy, the Oklahoma and New Orleans symphonies closed for good, and Montreal's, Toronto's, and Vancouver's orchestras went on life-support. Most professional theatres are operating in the red; major ballet companies have merged—Cleveland's with San Jose's, Cincinnati's with New Orleans'—to cut costs and, ultimately, to survive.

For all their troubles, the lively arts still outdraw professional sports. Unlike professional football or major league baseball, however, resident symphony orchestras, opera companies, professional theatre, and dance companies are urban assets that are all the more exceptional in a metro area because they are endangered.

Touring Artists Bookings

Long before the Empire Brass, Harlem Spiritual Ensemble, or Borealis Wind Quintet comes to town for a date at the local performing arts center, they are booked by a college or nonprofit community concert association.

Filling the concert halls with classical artists, big business for agents and presenters in former times, is getting tougher and less fun. In spite of 1990s marketing twists like rush-hour recitals, park concerts, tie-ins with art exhibits, celebrity narrators, and free kids admission, younger audiences are demanding more popular entertainment.

Opera

Opera fans boast that their passion embraces the greatest of the performing arts, since it combines a love for orchestral and vocal music, theatre, and dance. The first grand opera performed in this country was Rossini's *The Barber of Seville*, at New York's Park Theatre in 1825. To this day, New York remains America's operatic capital, though the art form has been diffused throughout the continent. From 650 performing groups 15 years ago, opera has expanded to nearly 1,000 professional and amateur groups, reaching an audience of 20 million during the 1990–91 season.

Some of these performing groups are college and university workshops, others local clubs and choruses. But 148 are companies with annual budgets topping $250,000. Full-scale opera productions using professional orchestras and bringing the world's leading singers to the stage aren't cheap tickets, and most metro areas haven't the resources or the audiences to support this singular form of the lively arts.

Operatic Chestnuts

Ten operas accounted for nearly one-third of all performances during the 1990–1991 season. By number of productions, they were

Madame Butterfly, 22	*The Magic Flute,* 12
Don Giovanni, 18	*Carmen,* 11
Die Fledermaus, 13	*Barber of Seville,* 8
Rigoletto, 13	*Tales of Hoffman,* 8
La Traviata, 12	*Faust,* 8

Source: Opera America.

Ballet

New York is the center for great dance as it is a center for so much more in the performing arts. America's top companies are here, including the New York City Ballet, the American Ballet Theatre, the Joffrey Ballet, the Alvin Ailey American Dance Theatre, the Martha Graham Company, the Merce Cunningham Dance Company, the Paul Tayler Dance Company, and the Dance Theatre of Harlem.

In the 1960s, Rudolf Nureyev heralded a boom in ballet when he jumped the fence from Russia to the West. He showed how athletic dance could be, and suddenly it was socially acceptable for teenage boys to join dance classes. The growth decade for dance was the 1970s, when touring New York dance troupes spread the gospel to new audiences. The charisma of another Russian émigré, Mikhail Baryshnikov, later the artistic director of the American Ballet Theatre, helped consolidate the popularity of dance.

America has a number of well-established dance companies. The New York City Ballet is 40 years old, and the Pennsylvania Ballet is 25. Unlikely as it may seem, the ballet company of Dayton, OH, is older than both, at half a century.

Symphony Orchestras

"The greatest instrument ever invented," Andre Previn once called the symphony. Of course, it is really a collection of many different instruments and musicians. The original definition—"to sound together," from the Greek—is just vague enough to embrace all the ensembles playing some type of symphonic music today in America.

In all, there are some 1,500 groups, ranging in size and experience from youths playing before captive audiences of parents to accomplished and well-paid professionals working under the baton of Kurt Masur at the New York Philharmonic. Orchestras are far from uncommon in metro areas: 275 metro areas claim at least one. Forty-six of these places support four or more orchestras, and 12 metro areas support eight or more.

Professional Theatre

Long known as the "fabulous invalid," theatre continues to hold its own despite perennial predictions of its demise. In *Huckleberry Finn*, Mark Twain described two scamsters who arrive in a small Arkansas town and tout a theatrical production pompously titled the "Royal Nonesuch." The performance consisted of an actor, wearing bright body paint but nothing else, streaking across the stage to the delight and outrage of the audience.

The history of American theatre is a blend of the grand and comic. Its many forms have encompassed Shakespeare, vaudeville, and Broadway musicals, and its first challenge came with silent movies at the century's turn, when the number of legitimate theatres fell from 1,500 to 500. In the 1920s, a resurgence took place on Broadway, which opened more than 400 new theatres in less than a decade. In the 1950s, Off-Broadway grew in response to overcommercialized mainstream theatre.

Broadway was once the center of American theatre. It alone established what was successful and sent these hits on the road to the provinces. New York still has the greatest concentration of theatres. Yet a number of regional theatres are now recognized for their vigor and innovation, including the Arena Stage in Washington, DC, the Guthrie in Minneapolis, MN, and the Trinity Rep in Providence, RI.

On another level are the fringe theatre groups across the continent, surviving on a shoestring, or disappearing only to be replaced by others. Some of the productions undoubtedly make Twain's "Royal Nonesuch" seem like great theatre. Yet the appeal of small theatre is that you may be happily surprised by its spunk and sense of craft. It's worth quoting the self-description of Germinal Stage Denver, a group that calls itself "the runt stepchild of regional theatres, a mom-and-pop store of Thespis, a vestige of the little theatre movement masquerading as an institution. In 13 years, we've gone through several periods of artistic coherence, but these days we're just trying to do the best plays we can, as well as we can, without talking too much about it."

ART MUSEUMS AND GALLERIES

In ancient Greece, it wasn't just the devoutly religious who visited temples; uninvited tourists also stole in to admire the statues and paintings. In Revolutionary France, artists had their daily exclusive run of the Louvre in order to copy the great works of the past. But on infrequent public days, the peasants, prostitutes, soldiers, and common laborers came in great numbers. To this day, going to an art museum has something of the democratic, the sacred, and the carnival to it.

The first great North American art museums were founded in Montreal in 1860, and in Boston and New York 10 years later. New York now has more art museums than any other city on the continent, and the Metropolitan Museum, with some four million visitors a year, is its most popular tourist attraction.

To qualify for inclusion in *Places Rated*, the American Association of Museums' requirements are as solid as any: "an organized and permanent nonprofit institution, essentially educational or aesthetic in purpose, with professional staff, which owns and utilizes tangible objects, cares for them, and exhibits them to the public on some regular schedule."

THE PUBLIC LIBRARY: SOMETHING FOR EVERYONE

Every metro area, no matter how small, poor, or isolated, has a network of public libraries. More than any of the different arts institutions mentioned above, libraries

Art Museums: 10 Top Metro Areas

Metro Area	Museums
New York, NY	52
Los Angeles–Long Beach, CA	33
Washington, DC–MD–VA–WV	30
Toronto, ON	29
Philadelphia, PA–NJ	25
Boston, MA	25
Chicago, IL	19
Montreal, PQ	17
San Francisco, CA	17
Vancouver, BC	13

Source: American Association of Museums, *Official Museum Directory;* Canadian Museums Association, *Canadian Museums.*

Public Library Acquisitions

Long Island, NY	461
Saskatoon, SK	384
Cleveland–Lorain–Elyria, OH	378
Halifax, NS	366
Stamford–Norwalk, CT	334
Orange County, NY	306
Regina, SK	300
South Bend, IN	282
Columbus, OH	280
London, ON	279

Source: Places Rated Partnership survey, 1992–1993; Statistics Canada, *Public Libraries,* 1993.

are vital centers and ultimate cultural resources for everyone.

Again, New York. Within the five boroughs and suburban Putnam, Rockland, and Westchester counties are five library systems acquiring 2 million books each year to add to the 30 million already housed in 282 libraries. Immense as these amenities are, that's one new book for every five people. Other metro areas do better; small ones in the inner South and in Texas do a lot worse.

What Are the Arts, Anyway?

"We know what culture is," a Sharon, PA, newspaper editor wrote in 1985. "We find it in our refrigerators every week." Although people can't get together on a single definition, or even on one element that culture shares, it's possible to name certain things about art that seem to ring true. For example, the following two lists draw a distinction that most would recognize:

Definitely Art	Possibly Art
anything by Shakespeare	comic books
ballet	folk music, blues, jazz
Chicago Symphony Orchestra	grunge bands
Greek sculpture	pop star Phil Collins
paintings	rap music
Placido Domingo	subway graffiti
poet Dylan Thomas	tap dancing
stained glass	Woody Allen

Places Rated doesn't make choices from the right-hand list on what precisely constitutes art. Instead, it focuses on the categories in the first list, those which most agree have artistic or cultural merit. Whether any of the items in the second list are art is moot; most are controversial or dubious because they haven't withstood the test of time.

SCORING: THE ARTS

Institutions that people usually associate with the arts number not just hundreds but thousands throughout the continent. The American Association of Museums' *Official Museum Directory,* for example, catalogues more than 6,000 American museums, many very specialized, many others small and existing only to make money or to serve as a tax shelter for their proprietors.

The amenities that really count can be filtered out from the dross and used to measure the arts. Start by focusing on nonprofit institutions. Then rely on ratings and classifications devised by appropriate associations or accrediting bodies such as the Concert Music Broadcasters Association and the American Association of Museums.

It can still be argued that it is impossible to rank metro areas in the arts with total fairness. Nevertheless, one can focus on certain amenities and illustrate their supply among metro areas. Accordingly, each metro area starts with a base score of zero, to which points are added according to the following indicators:

1. **Lively Arts Calendar.** For each performance of a touring fine arts musical group and local resident ensemble—whether a symphony orchestra, an opera company, a dance company, or a professional theatre—the metro area receives one point.
2. **Art Museums and Galleries.** Among the nearly 8,000 museums in North America, 1,034 are classified as nonprofit "Art Museums and Galleries," or "Civic Art and Cultural Centers," and are located within metro areas. Each contributes 50 points toward a metro area's score.

   Metropolitan Los Angeles's 7 university, 24 private, and 2 civic art museums and galleries, for example, account for 1,650 points of the metro area's total 5,115 points.
3. **Public Libraries.** The points awarded for libraries are the number of new books all public libraries within the metro area add each year

per 1,000 residents. The 282 public libraries in New York, for example, cumulatively acquire 1,830,221 new books, according to the New York State Library's latest annual report. That works out to 213 new books for every 1,000 people, good for 213 points.

4. **MC Access.** Each of the 75 metro areas that is part of a Metropolitan Complex is eligible for bonus points based on shared amenities: 10 percent of the points accumulated by adjacent places in the MC for these amenities.

In the Buffalo–St. Catharines–Niagara metropolitan complex, for example, St. Catharines–Niagara gets 76 access points based on Buffalo–Niagara Falls' total score. Likewise, Buffalo–Niagara Falls gets a 46 point bonus thanks to the St. Catharines–Niagara area's similar amenities.

SCORING EXAMPLES

The largest metro area between Chicago and the Pacific Ocean and a small southwest state capital illustrate the scoring method for the Arts.

Minneapolis–St. Paul, MN–WI (#18)

Some 400 miles northwest of Chicago and 1,600 miles east of Seattle, the Twin Cities are an example of the cultural isolation/proximity principle: large cities that are isolated or in the geographic center of a region gain a monopoly on the arts.

While each city is the butt of the other's jokes, Minneapolis and St. Paul are both arts capitals. Both support a major symphony (orchestras with annual budgets over $7 million), where New York has just one. The renowned Guthrie is starting its fourth decade of repertory drama. The Minnesota Opera continues its tradition of producing new or lesser-known operas in English.

Between them, these cities count 1,168 fine-arts performance dates, 6 art museums good for 300 points, and 192 points for new public library books, producing a score of 1,660.

Santa Fe, NM (#110)

One of the oldest settlements in North America, Santa Fe has a reputation as a cultural center dating back to the

---

New York, New York

"New York, New York, it's a wonderful town!" says the song from *On the Town*. Certainly the Big Apple is less wonderful for its violent crime, gridlock traffic, shabby subways, and appalling living costs. Yet the lyrics hold true as applied to the arts; for many reasons, New York is the culture capital of North America. Consider these assets:

Museums: Metropolitan New York has no fewer than 52 art museums, including 7 of world renown.
Concert radio: Five FM radio stations, airing a total of 500 hours per week, compete fiercely for a share of the limited classical music market.
Symphony orchestras: Greater New York has 48 orchestras, including one major orchestra (the Philharmonic), 3 regional orchestras, and 4 metropolitan orchestras.
Professional theatres: The actual number is unknown when one considers not only Broadway but off-Broadway and off-off-Broadway as well. The Big Apple does have 46 professional theatres with budgets that have also been in business more than five years.
Dance companies: Among all companies in North America with annual budgets over $250,000, one in six is headquartered here.

1920s when craftspeople and artists in a small arts colony began displaying their work in the city's central plaza. Back then, too, D. H. Lawrence and other writers came here and to the surrounding Sangre de Cristo Mountains and nearby Taos for quiet stimulation.

Santa Fe's international renown is due to a summer opera season in which one or more new works get their world premieres in an open-air theatre built into a mountainside. Those performances, plus touring artist bookings and local symphony and theatre dates, contribute 128 points to Santa Fe's score. Art museums kick in 250 points, and library acquisitions another 123, producing a total score of 501.

Rankings: The Arts

Eight amenities are used to derive a metro area's score for the arts: (1) concert or classical-format radio stations; (2) touring artists bookings at local campus and civic auditoriums; (3) resident symphony orchestras; (4) resident opera companies; (5) resident ballet companies; (6) resident professional theatres; (7) nonprofit art museums and galleries; (8) and public libraries. Metro areas also earn bonus points for shared amenities if they are part of metropolitan complexes (MCs).

Metro Areas from Best to Worst

Places Rated Rank	Places Rated Score	Places Rated Rank	Places Rated Score	Places Rated Rank	Places Rated Score
1. New York, NY	9,681	41. Norfolk–Virginia Beach–Newport News, VA–NC	1,040	78. Santa Cruz–Watsonville, CA	682
2. Los Angeles–Long Beach, CA	4,977	42. Raleigh–Durham–Chapel Hill, NC	1,036	78. Winnipeg, MB	682
3. Washington, DC–MD–VA–WV	4,250	43. Indianapolis, IN	1,033	80. Jamestown, NY	674
4. Chicago, IL	3,231	44. Hamilton, ON	1,018	81. Omaha, NE–IA	661
5. Toronto, ON	3,138	45. Saskatoon, SK	1,002	81. Portsmouth–Dover–Rochester, NH	661
6. San Francisco, CA	2,877	46. Calgary, AB	995	83. Vallejo–Fairfield–Napa, CA	646
7. Boston, MA	2,819	47. Denver, CO	958	84. Tucson, AZ	639
8. Philadelphia, PA–NJ	2,733	48. West Palm Beach–Boca Raton, FL	950	85. Lake County, IL	633
9. Long Island, NY	2,370	49. Miami, FL	945	86. Sacramento, CA	620
10. Newark–Jersey City, NJ	2,098	50. Ann Arbor, MI	944	87. Bridgeport, CT	612
11. Montreal, PQ	2,072	51. Kitchener, ON	931	88. Knoxville, TN	597
12. Oakland, CA	2,032	52. Columbus, OH	916	88. Portland, OR	597
13. Baltimore, MD	1,961	53. Albany–Schenectady–Troy, NY	895	90. Greenville–Spartanburg–Anderson, SC	594
14. Stamford–Norwalk, CT	1,870	54. Salt Lake City–Ogden, UT	892	91. San Antonio, TX	589
15. Cleveland–Lorain–Elyria, OH	1,795	55. Fort Lauderdale, FL	876	92. Atlantic City–Cape May, NJ	581
16. Central New Jersey, NJ	1,744	56. Cincinnati, OH–KY–IN	854	93. Santa Rosa, CA	579
17. San Jose, CA	1,685	57. Orlando, FL	837	94. Trenton, NJ	574
18. Minneapolis–St. Paul, MN–WI	1,660	58. Halifax, NS	826	95. Austin–San Marcos, TX	560
19. Orange County, CA	1,591	59. Gary, IN	818	96. Providence–Warwick–Cranston, RI	559
20. Hartford, CT	1,567	60. Oklahoma City, OK	808	97. London, ON	539
21. Phoenix–Mesa, AZ	1,541	61. Ventura, CA	804	98. Madison, WI	527
22. Northern New Jersey, NJ	1,538	62. Akron, OH	789	98. Youngstown–Warren, OH	527
23. St. Louis, MO–IL	1,529	63. Charlotte–Gastonia–Rock Hill, NC–SC	776	100. Quebec City, PQ	525
24. Seattle–Bellevue–Everett, WA	1,506	64. Buffalo–Niagara Falls, NY	764	100. Tacoma, WA	525
25. Detroit, MI	1,500	65. Rochester, NY	763	102. Louisville, KY–IN	521
26. Atlanta, GA	1,452	66. Albuquerque, NM	758	103. Victoria, BC	520
27. Monmouth–Ocean, NJ	1,384	67. Greensboro–Winston-Salem–High Point, NC	755	104. Allentown–Bethlehem–Easton, PA–NJ	514
28. Orange County, NY	1,372	68. Honolulu, HI	754	104. Toledo, OH	514
29. Riverside–San Bernardino, CA	1,362	69. Regina, SK	728	106. Edmonton, AB	512
30. Tampa–St. Petersburg–Clearwater, FL	1,336	70. Worcester–Fitchburg–Leominster, MA	725	106. Jacksonville, FL	512
31. Danbury, CT	1,334	71. Manchester–Nashua, NH	722	108. South Bend, IN	506
32. Ottawa–Hull, ON–PQ	1,316	72. Wilmington–Newark, DE–MD	718	109. Dutchess County, NY	503
33. San Diego, CA	1,304	73. Kansas City, MO–KS	714	110. Santa Fe, NM	501
34. Vancouver, BC	1,270	74. Fort Worth–Arlington, TX	712	111. New Bedford–Fall River–Attleboro, MA	492
35. Milwaukee–Waukesha, WI	1,248	75. Nashville, TN	707	112. Oshawa, ON	491
36. Pittsburgh, PA	1,244	76. New Haven–Meriden, CT	705	113. St. Catharines–Niagara, ON	458
37. Houston, TX	1,156	77. Richmond–Petersburg, VA	690	114. Boulder–Longmont, CO	456
38. Dayton–Springfield, OH	1,101			115. Las Vegas, NV–AZ	454
39. Dallas, TX	1,083			115. Windsor, ON	454
40. Syracuse, NY	1,049			117. Springfield, MA	452

Places Rated Rank	Places Rated Score
118. Vineland–Millville–Bridgeton, NJ	451
119. Barnstable–Yarmouth, MA	449
120. Scranton–Wilkes-Barre–Hazleton, PA	448
121. Santa Barbara–Santa Maria–Lompoc, CA	439
122. Grand Rapids–Muskegon–Holland, MI	436
122. Hamilton–Middletown, OH	436
124. Tulsa, OK	434
125. Sarasota–Bradenton, FL	429
126. Portland, ME	428
127. Kankakee, IL	427
128. Colorado Springs, CO	423
129. Lincoln, NE	421
130. Charleston–North Charleston, SC	420
130. Kalamazoo–Battle Creek, MI	420
132. Trois-Rivieres, PQ	419
133. Memphis, TN–AR–MS	416
134. Wichita, KS	413
135. Fort Myers–Cape Coral, FL	409
136. Bellingham, WA	408
137. Hagerstown, MD	402
137. Pittsfield, MA	402
139. Birmingham, AL	399
140. Burlington, VT	391
140. Utica–Rome, NY	391
142. New Orleans, LA	390
143. Eugene–Springfield, OR	386
144. Gainesville, FL	384
145. Thunder Bay, ON	369
146. Naples, FL	366
147. Boise City, ID	364
148. New London–Norwich, CT–RI	362
149. Lafayette, IN	355
150. Charlottesville, VA	353
151. Des Moines, IA	352
152. Huntsville, AL	346
153. Salem, OR	345
154. Lansing–East Lansing, MI	343
154. Pensacola, FL	343
156. Canton–Massillon, OH	342
157. Waterloo–Cedar Falls, IA	339
158. Chattanooga, TN–GA	337
159. Lexington, KY	329
159. Wheeling, WV–OH	329
161. Champaign–Urbana, IL	326
162. Roanoke, VA	323
163. Spokane, WA	319
164. Columbia, SC	315
165. Charleston, WV	314
165. Duluth–Superior, MN–WI	314
165. Evansville–Henderson, IN–KY	314
165. Racine, WI	314
169. Anchorage, AK	309
170. Rockford, IL	308
171. Bremerton, WA	303
172. Cedar Rapids, IA	300
172. Peoria–Pekin, IL	300

Places Rated Rank	Places Rated Score
174. Baton Rouge, LA	299
175. Beaumont–Port Arthur, TX	298
176. Flint, MI	296
177. Olympia, WA	295
178. Mansfield, OH	290
179. Greeley, CO	287
180. Daytona Beach, FL	286
181. Appleton–Oshkosh–Neenah, WI	284
181. Davenport–Moline–Rock Island, IA–IL	284
183. Little Rock–North Little Rock, AR	283
184. Pueblo, CO	281
184. Binghamton, NY	281
184. Harrisburg–Lebanon–Carlisle, PA	281
187. Lubbock, TX	278
188. Springfield, IL	277
189. Glens Falls, NY	276
189. St. John's, NF	276
191. Johnson City–Kingsport–Bristol, TN–VA	273
192. Topeka, KS	271
193. Fargo–Moorhead, ND–MN	266
193. Green Bay, WI	266
195. Jackson, MS	265
195. La Crosse, WI–MN	265
195. Yolo, CA	265
198. Fort Collins–Loveland, CO	262
199. Sudbury, ON	260
200. Parkersburg–Marietta, WV–OH	258
201. Salinas, CA	257
202. Terre Haute, IN	256
203. Sheboygan, WI	255
204. Iowa City, IA	254
205. Columbia, MO	253
205. Fayetteville, NC	253
207. Melbourne–Titusville–Palm Bay, FL	248
208. Bangor, ME	247
208. Decatur, IL	247
210. St. Cloud, MN	246
211. Athens, GA	245
212. Bloomington–Normal, IL	244
213. Medford–Ashland, OR	243
213. Saginaw–Bay City–Midland, MI	243
215. Janesville–Beloit, WI	241
216. Vancouver, WA	240
217. St. Joseph, MO	239
218. Bloomington, IN	238
218. Kokomo, IN	238
220. Elmira, NY	237
221. Reading, PA	236
222. Galveston–Texas City, TX	235
222. Mobile, AL	235
224. Lancaster, PA	233
225. State College, PA	231
226. Saint John, NB	230
227. Lima, OH	229
228. Shreveport–Bossier City, LA	226

Places Rated Rank	Places Rated Score
229. Lawrence, KS	225
229. Lynchburg, VA	225
231. Kenosha, WI	222
232. Albany, GA	221
233. Hickory–Morgantown, NC	219
234. Dubuque, IA	213
235. Huntington–Ashland, WV–KY–OH	212
235. Yakima, WA	212
237. Augusta–Aiken, GA–SC	206
237. Chicoutimi–Jonquiere, PQ	206
239. Lafayette, LA	203
240. Brazoria, TX	201
240. Florence, AL	201
240. San Luis Obispo–Atascadero–Paso Robles, CA	201
243. Wausau, WI	199
244. Rapid City, SD	198
244. Reno, NV	198
246. Muncie, IN	197
247. Savannah, GA	195
248. Fort Wayne, IN	193
249. Montgomery, AL	192
249. Springfield, MO	192
249. Tallahassee, FL	192
252. Macon, GA	191
253. Lewiston–Auburn, ME	190
254. Benton Harbor, MI	189
254. Fresno, CA	189
256. Amarillo, TX	188
256. Asheville, NC	188
256. Elkhart–Goshen, IN	188
256. Rocky Mount, NC	188
260. Monroe, LA	186
260. Sioux Falls, SD	186
262. Sherbrooke, PQ	185
263. Corpus Christi, TX	184
264. Erie, PA	183
264. Gadsden, AL	183
266. Johnstown, PA	182
266. Sioux City, IA–NE	182
266. Wilmington, NC	182
269. Wichita Falls, TX	180
270. Waterbury, CT	177
271. Eau Claire, WI	170
271. Stockton–Lodi, CA	170
273. El Paso, TX	169
274. Jackson, MI	167
274. Steubenville–Weirton, OH–WV	167
276. Cheyenne, WY	164
277. Danville, VA	161
277. Enid, OK	161
279. Billings, MT	159
280. San Angelo, TX	158
281. Yuma, AZ	155
282. Bakersfield, CA	152
283. Greenville, NC	151
283. Joplin, MO	151
285. Lakeland–Winter Haven, FL	147
286. Decatur, AL	145

Places Rated Rank	Places Rated Score	Places Rated Rank	Places Rated Score	Places Rated Rank	Places Rated Score
286. Great Falls, MT	145	305. Ocala, FL	118	322. Sherman–Denison, TX	93
288. Grand Forks, ND–MN	143			325. McAllen–Edinburg–Mission,	
289. Provo–Orem, UT	142	306. Abilene, TX	116	TX	91
290. Clarksville–Hopkinsville,		307. Goldsboro, NC	114		
TN–KY	140	308. Bismarck, ND	113	326. Victoria, TX	80
		308. Pine Bluff, AR	113	327. Panama City, FL	77
291. Altoona, PA	138	310. Tuscaloosa, AL	110	328. York, PA	76
291. Fort Pierce–Port St. Lucie,				329. Rochester, MN	75
FL	138	311. Fort Smith, AR–OK	109	330. Casper, WY	74
291. Richland–Kennewick–Pasco,		311. Texarkana, TX–Texarkana,			
WA	138	AR	109	331. Fort Walton Beach, FL	73
294. Columbus, GA–AL	136	313. Longview–Marshall, TX	105	332. Anniston, AL	72
294. Florence, SC	136	313. Waco, TX	105	332. Visalia–Tulare–Porterville,	
		315. Lake Charles, LA	104	CA	72
294. Las Cruces, NM	136			334. Cumberland, MD–WV	71
297. Odessa–Midland, TX	134	316. Merced, CA	101	334. Redding, CA	71
298. Owensboro, KY	133	316. Sumter, SC	101		
298. Williamsport, PA	133	318. Tyler, TX	100	336. Jacksonville, NC	63
300. Alexandria, LA	132	319. Dover, DE	98	337. Lawton, OK	56
		320. Biloxi–Gulfport–Pascagoula,		338. Sharon, PA	54
301. Modesto, CA	131	MS	97	338. Yuba City, CA	54
302. Bryan–College Station, TX	124			340. Killeen–Temple, TX	52
303. Fayetteville–Springdale–		321. Myrtle Beach, SC	94		
Rogers, AR	121	322. Brownsville–Harlingen–San		341. Houma, LA	49
304. Dothan, AL	120	Benito, TX	93	342. Punta Gorda, FL	48
		322. Chico–Paradise, CA	93	343. Laredo, TX	46

Place Profiles: The Arts

The profiles that follow are divided into four headings and show cultural and artistic features in each metro area.

Under the first heading, **Concert Radio,** are concert radio stations whose city of license is within the metro area. Concert radio stations are stations with part or all of their programming dedicated to a classical music format. For powerful radio and television stations, programming may also be received in nearby metro areas. In these instances, the media market defined by Arbitron Ratings Service is listed for the metro area that receives fine arts broadcasting from another area.

The **Lively Arts Calendar** heading encompasses the total number of touring artist bookings at local campus and civic auditoriums and the names of resident symphony orchestras, opera companies, professional theatres, and ballet companies.

Under the heading **Art Museums and Galleries** is the number of nonprofit institutions whose main function is exhibiting art to the public. Museums listed are either accredited by the American Association of Museums or are institutions with three or more curators, a publication program, and a research library.

The **Public Libraries** heading shows the total number of public library buildings within the metro area, including central-city, suburban, and rural branches, along with figures on the size of their collections and the number of new books acquired during their latest fiscal year (estimated, in many instances, from each library's reported book budget).

The information is derived from these sources: American Association of Museums, *Official Museum Directory,* 1992; American Library Association, *American Library Directory, 1992–1993,* 1992; American Symphony Orchestra League, *Symphony* magazine, January–February 1993, and *Orchestra and Business Directory,* 1993; Association of Canadian Orchestras, *Directory of Canadian Orchestras,* 1993; Canadian Museums Association, *Official Directory of Canadian Museums,* 1992; Concert Music Broadcasters Association, *Directory of Concert Music Stations,* 1993; Conseil Quebecois de Theatre, *Repertoire Theatral de Quebec,* 1990; Musical America, *International Directory of the Performing Arts,* 1993; Opera America, *Profile,* 1992; Opera Canada Publications, *Opera Canada* magazine, 1992–1993; Places Rated Partnership, Survey of State Library Association Annual Reports, 1992–1993; Professional Association of Canadian Theatres, *The Theatre Listing, 1992/93,* 1993; Reed Reference Publishing Company, *Broadcasting and Cable Market Place,* 1993; Statistics Canada, *Performing Arts,* 1993, and *Public Libraries,* 1992; Theatre Communications Group, *Profile 19,* 1992; and the University/Resident Theatre Association, *Directory,* 1993.

A check mark (✓) in front of the metro area's name highlights it as one of the top 35 places for the arts.

Abilene, TX
Concert Radio
   KACU-FM
Lively Arts Calendar
   Touring Artists Bookings, 4 dates
   Resident Ensembles, 16 dates
      Abilene Opera
      Abilene Philharmonic
Public Libraries
   2 branches, 289,016 volumes
   11,463 books added/year
Places Rated Score: 116
Places Rated Rank: 306

Akron, OH
Concert Radio
   WKSU-FM
Lively Arts Calendar
   Touring Artists Bookings, 63 dates
   Resident Ensembles, 98 dates
      Akron Symphony
      Ohio Ballet
      Porthouse Theatre Company
Art Museums and Galleries, 4
   Akron Art Museum
Public Libraries
   31 branches, 2,073,360 volumes
   158,751 books added/year
MC Access: Cleveland–Akron, OH
Places Rated Score: 789
Places Rated Rank: 62

Albany, GA
Concert Radio
   WUNV-FM
Lively Arts Calendar
   Touring Artists Bookings, 19 dates
   Resident Ensemble, 18 dates
      Albany Symphony
Art Museums and Galleries, 1
Public Libraries
   6 branches, 217,285 volumes
   15,260 books added/year
Places Rated Score: 221
Places Rated Rank: 232

Albany–Schenectady–Troy, NY
Concert Radio
   WAMC-FM, WCAN-FM, WMHT-FM
Lively Arts Calendar
   Touring Artists Bookings, 320 dates
   Resident Ensembles, 126 dates
      Albany Symphony
      Albany–Berkshire Ballet
      Capital Philharmonic
      Capital Repertory Company
      Music Company Orchestra
      Schenectady Symphony
Art Museums and Galleries, 6
   Albany Institute of History and Art
Public Libraries
   69 branches, 2,487,387 volumes
   131,529 books added/year
Places Rated Score: 895
Places Rated Rank: 53

Albuquerque, NM
Concert Radio
   KHFM-FM
Lively Arts Calendar
   Touring Artists Bookings, 28 dates
   Resident Ensembles, 416 dates
      Albuquerque Civic Light Opera
      Chamber Orchestra of Albuquerque
      New Mexico Symphony
      New Mexico Repertory Theatre
      Opera Southwest
      Southwest Ballet
Art Museums and Galleries, 4

Public Libraries
   23 branches, 1,012,844 volumes
   73,679 books added/year
Places Rated Score: 758
Places Rated Rank: 66

Alexandria, LA
Concert Radio
   KLSA-FM
Lively Arts Calendar
   Resident Ensemble, 8 dates
      Rapides Symphony
Art Museums and Galleries, 1
   Alexandria Museum, Visual Art Center
Public Libraries
   11 branches, 285,525 volumes
   9,807 books added/year
Places Rated Score: 132
Places Rated Rank: 300

Allentown–Bethlehem–Easton, PA–NJ
Concert Radio
   In Philadelphia media market
Lively Arts Calendar
   Touring Artists Bookings, 121 dates
   Resident Ensembles, 160 dates
      Allentown Symphony
      Lehigh Valley Chamber Orchestra
      Pennsylvania Stage Company
      The Pennsylvania Sinfonia
      Touchstone Theatre
Art Museums and Galleries, 3
   Allentown Art Museum
Public Libraries
   31 branches, 1,332,910 volumes
   58,258 books added/year
Places Rated Score: 514
Places Rated Rank: 104

Altoona, PA
Lively Arts Calendar
   Touring Artists Bookings, 6 dates
   Resident Ensemble, 7 dates
      Altoona Symphony
Art Museums and Galleries, 1
Public Libraries
   9 branches, 387,613 volumes
   9,777 books added/year
Places Rated Score: 138
Places Rated Rank: 291

Amarillo, TX
Lively Arts Calendar
   Resident Ensembles, 59 dates
      Amarillo Symphony
      Lone Star Ballet
Art Museum and Gallery
   Amarillo Art Center
Public Libraries
   5 branches, 543,063 volumes
   15,021 books added/year
Places Rated Score: 188
Places Rated Rank: 256

Anchorage, AK
Concert Radio
   KLEF-FM, KSKA-FM
Lively Arts Calendar
   Touring Artists Bookings, 35 dates
   Resident Ensembles, 30 dates
      Alaska Stage Company
      Anchorage Opera
      Anchorage Symphony
Art Museums and Galleries, 2
   Anchorage Museum of History and Art
Public Libraries
   5 branches, 379,720 volumes
   34,884 books added/year

Places Rated Score: 309
Places Rated Rank: 169

Ann Arbor, MI
Concert Radio
   WUOM-FM
Lively Arts Calendar
   Touring Artists Bookings, 422 dates
   Resident Ensembles, 76 dates
      Adrian Symphony
      Ann Arbor Chamber Orchestra
      Ann Arbor Symphony
      Comic Opera Guild
      Opera! Lenawee
Art Museums and Galleries, 4
   University of Michigan Museum of Art
Public Libraries
   31 branches, 1,164,809 volumes
   53,848 books added/year
MC Access: Detroit–Ann Arbor–Flint, MI
Places Rated Score: 944
Places Rated Rank: 50

Anniston, AL
Lively Arts Calendar
   Touring Artists Bookings, 5 dates
   Resident Ensemble, 8 dates
      AC Theatre
Public Libraries
   6 branches, 254,010 volumes
   6,887 books added/year
Places Rated Score: 72
Places Rated Rank: 332

Appleton–Oshkosh–Neenah, WI
Concert Radio
   In Green Bay media market
Lively Arts Calendar
   Touring Artists Bookings, 19 dates
   Resident Ensembles, 10 dates
      Fox Valley Symphony
      Oshkosh Symphony
Art Museums and Galleries, 2
   Bergstrom–Mahler Museum
   Paine Art Center
Public Libraries
   17 branches, 995,500 volumes
   49,726 books added/year
Places Rated Score: 284
Places Rated Rank: 181

Asheville, NC
Concert Radio
   WCQS-FM
Lively Arts Calendar
   Touring Artists Bookings, 16 dates
   Resident Ensemble, 15 dates
      Asheville Symphony
Art Museums and Galleries, 1
   Pack Place Art Museum
Public Libraries
   13 branches, 355,121 volumes
   21,026 books added/year
Places Rated Score: 188
Places Rated Rank: 256

Athens, GA
Concert Radio
   WUGA-FM
Lively Arts Calendar
   Touring Artists Bookings, 6 dates
   Resident Ensemble, 16 dates
      University of Georgia Theatre
Art Museums and Galleries, 2
   Georgia Museum of Art, University of
      Georgia
Public Libraries
   10 branches, 260,380 volumes
   15,931 books added/year

Places Rated Score: 245
Places Rated Rank: 211

✓ Atlanta, GA
Concert Radio
WABE-FM, WGKA-AM
Lively Arts Calendar
Touring Artists Bookings, 335 dates
Symphony Orchestras, 290 dates
Atlanta Community Orchestra
Atlanta Pops Orchestra
Atlanta Symphony
Cobb Symphony
De Kalb Symphony
Sandy Springs Chamber Orchestra
Opera Company, 9 dates
Atlanta Opera
Ballet Company, 55 dates
Atlanta Ballet
Professional Theatres, 179 dates
Academy Theatre
Actor's Express
Alliance Theatre Company
Horizon Theatre Company
Jomandi Productions
Seven Stages
Theatre Emory
Theatre in the Square
Theatrical Outfit
Art Museums and Galleries, 9
High Museum of Art
Public Libraries
118 branches, 4,541,812 volumes
426,466 books added/year
Places Rated Score: 1,452
Places Rated Rank: 26

Atlantic City–Cape May, NJ
Concert Radio
In Philadelphia media market
Lively Arts Calendar
Touring Artists Bookings, 50 dates
Resident Ensemble, 16 dates
South Jersey Regional Theatre
Art Museums and Galleries, 1
Public Libraries
25 branches, 1,146,914 volumes
66,243 books added/year
MC Access:
Philadelphia–Wilmington–Atlantic City,
PA–NJ–DE–MD
Places Rated Score: 581
Places Rated Rank: 92

Augusta–Aiken, GA–SC
Concert Radio
WACG-FM
Lively Arts Calendar
Touring Artists Bookings, 14 dates
Resident Ensembles, 73 dates
Augusta Ballet
Augusta Opera
Augusta Symphony
Art Museums and Galleries, 1
Public Libraries
25 branches, 618,197 volumes
28,557 books added/year
Places Rated Score: 206
Places Rated Rank: 237

Austin–San Marcos, TX
Concert Radio
KMFA-FM
Lively Arts Calendar
Touring Artists Bookings, 51 dates
Resident Ensembles, 182 dates
Austin Civic Orchestra

Austin Lyric Opera
Austin Symphony
Ballet Austin
Live Oak Theatre
University of Texas Theatre
Zachary Scott Theatre Center
Art Museums and Galleries, 5
Archer Huntington Art Gallery
Public Libraries
39 branches, 1,348,046 volumes
71,197 books added/year
Places Rated Score: 560
Places Rated Rank: 95

Bakersfield, CA
Concert Radio
KIWI-FM, KPRX-FM
Lively Arts Calendar
Touring Artists Bookings, 16 dates
Resident Ensemble, 50 dates
Bakersfield Symphony
Art Museums and Galleries, 1
Public Libraries
21 branches, 960,000 volumes
20,780 books added/year
Places Rated Score: 152
Places Rated Rank: 282

✓ Baltimore, MD
Concert Radio
WBJC-FM, WHFC-FM, WJHU-FM
Lively Arts Calendar
Touring Artists Bookings, 371 dates
Symphony Orchestras, 279 dates
Annapolis Symphony
Baltimore Chamber Orchestra
Baltimore Symphony
Gettysburg Symphony
Hopkins Symphony
Peabody Conservatory Symphony
Susquehanna Symphony
Opera Companies, 77 dates
Annapolis Opera
Baltimore Opera
Baltimore Opera Touring Theatre
Ballet Companies, 72 dates
Ballet Theatre of Annapolis
The Maryland Ballet
Professional Theatres, 84 dates
Baltimore Theatre Project
Center Stage
Art Museums and Galleries, 8
Baltimore Museum of Art
Walters Art Gallery
Public Libraries
102 branches, 5,744,646 volumes
600,738 books added/year
MC Access: Washington–Baltimore,
DC–MD–VA–WV
Places Rated Score: 1,961
Places Rated Rank: 13

Bangor, ME
Lively Arts Calendar
Touring Artists Bookings, 50 dates
Resident Ensemble, 20 dates
Bangor Symphony
Art Museums and Galleries, 1
Public Libraries
9 branches, 669,746 volumes
11,973 books added/year
Places Rated Score: 247
Places Rated Rank: 208

Barnstable–Yarmouth, MA
Concert Radio
WFCC-FM, WOMR-FM

Lively Arts Calendar
Touring Artists Bookings, 15 dates
Resident Ensembles: 74 dates
Cape Cod Symphony
College Light Opera
Art Museums and Galleries, 3
Public Libraries
34 branches, 983,146 volumes
39,008 books added/year
Places Rated Score: 449
Places Rated Rank: 119

Baton Rouge, LA
Concert Radio
WRKF-FM
Lively Arts Calendar
Touring Artists Bookings, 4 dates
Resident Ensembles, 38 dates
Baton Rouge Ballet Theatre
Baton Rouge Opera
Baton Rouge Symphony
Art Museums and Galleries, 2
Louisiana Arts and Science Center
Public Libraries
21 branches, 911,238 volumes
76,067 books added/year
Places Rated Score: 299
Places Rated Rank: 174

Beaumont–Port Arthur, TX
Concert Radio
KVLU-FM
Lively Arts Calendar
Touring Artists Bookings, 27 dates
Resident Ensemble, 3 dates
Beaumont Civic Opera
Art Museums and Galleries, 4
Public Libraries
15 branches, 826,539 volumes
25,105 books added/year
Places Rated Score: 298
Places Rated Rank: 175

Bellingham, WA
Concert Radio
KZAZ-FM
Lively Arts Calendar
Touring Artists Bookings, 27 dates
Resident Ensemble, 5 dates
Whatcom Symphony
Art Museums and Galleries, 4
Whatcom Museum of History and Art
Public Libraries
13 branches, 390,399 volumes
24,574 books added/year
Places Rated Score: 408
Places Rated Rank: 136

Benton Harbor, MI
Concert Radio
WAUS-FM
Lively Arts Calendar
Resident Ensemble, 10 dates
Southwest Michigan Symphony
Art Museum and Gallery
Krasl Art Center
Public Libraries
14 branches, 665,131 volumes
21,153 books added/year
Places Rated Score: 189
Places Rated Rank: 254

Billings, MT
Concert Radio
KEMC-FM
Lively Arts Calendar
Touring Artists Bookings, 30 dates

Resident Ensemble, 10 dates
  Billings Symphony
Art Museums and Galleries, 1
  Yellowstone Art Center
Public Libraries
  3 branches, 279,954 volumes
  7,930 books added/year
Places Rated Score: 159
Places Rated Rank: 279

Biloxi–Gulfport–Pascagoula, MS
Concert Radio
  WMAH-FM
Lively Arts Calendar
  Touring Artists Bookings, 4 dates
  Resident Ensembles, 7 dates
    Gulf Coast Opera Theatre
    Gulf Coast Symphony
Public Libraries
  22 branches, 539,145 volumes
  27,395 books added/year
Places Rated Score: 97
Places Rated Rank: 320

Binghamton, NY
Concert Radio
  WSKG-FM
Lively Arts Calendar
  Resident Ensembles, 44 dates
    BC Pops
    Binghamton Symphony
    Tri-Cities Opera
Art Museums and Galleries, 2
  Roberson Museum and Science Center
Public Libraries
  21 branches, 859,880 volumes
  36,217 books added/year
Places Rated Score: 281
Places Rated Rank: 184

Birmingham, AL
Concert Radio
  WBHM-FM
Lively Arts Calendar
  Touring Artists Bookings, 18 dates
  Resident Ensembles, 167 dates
    Alabama Symphony
    Ballet South
    Birmingham Children's Theatre
    Birmingham Opera Theater
    Red Mountain Chamber Orchestra
    Sunbelt Sinfonia
Art Museums and Galleries, 2
  Birmingham Museum of Art
Public Libraries
  59 branches, 1,963,388 volumes
  97,196 books added/year
Places Rated Score: 399
Places Rated Rank: 139

Bismarck, ND
Concert Radio
  KCND-FM
Lively Arts Calendar
  Resident Ensemble, 12 dates
    Bismarck-Mandan Symphony
Public Libraries
  2 branches, 244,179 volumes
  8,581 books added/year
Places Rated Score: 113
Places Rated Rank: 308

Bloomington, IN
Concert Radio
  WFIU-FM
Lively Arts Calendar
  Touring Artists Bookings, 20 dates

Resident Ensembles, 26 dates
  Bloomington Symphony
  Indiana University Theatre
Art Museums and Galleries, 1
  Indiana University Art Museum
Public Libraries
  2 branches, 183,666 volumes
  16,302 books added/year
Places Rated Score: 238
Places Rated Rank: 218

Bloomington–Normal, IL
Concert Radio
  WGLT-FM
Lively Arts Calendar
  Touring Artists Bookings, 15 dates
  Resident Ensembles, 26 dates
    Bloomington–Normal Symphony
    ISU Theatre
Art Museums and Galleries, 1
Public Libraries
  13 branches, 361,619 volumes
  20,162 books added/year
Places Rated Score: 244
Places Rated Rank: 212

Boise City, ID
Concert Radio
  KBSU-FM
Lively Arts Calendar
  Touring Artists Bookings, 128 dates
  Resident Ensembles, 63 dates
    American Festival Ballet
    Boise Opera
    Boise Philharmonic
    Idaho Shakespeare Festival
Art Museums and Galleries, 2
Public Libraries
  18 branches, 570,770 volumes
  22,931 books added/year
Places Rated Score: 364
Places Rated Rank: 147

✓ Boston, MA
Concert Radio
  WBOQ-FM, WBUR-FM, WCRB-FM,
  WGBH-FM, WHRB-FM
Lively Arts Calendar
  Touring Artists Bookings, 569 dates
  Symphony Orchestras, 299 dates
    Boston Baroque
    Boston Classical Orchestra
    Boston Philharmonic
    Boston Symphony
    Boston Symphony Chamber Players
    Brockton Symphony
    Cape Ann Symphony
    Civic Symphony of Boston
    Concord Orchestra
    Handel and Haydn Society
    Indian Hill Symphony
    Jamaica Plain Symphony
    Melrose Symphony
    New Arts Symphony
    New England Philharmonic
    Newton Symphony
    Plymouth Philharmonic
    Pro Arte Chamber Orchestra
    Sinfo Nova Orchestra
    Symphony by the Sea
    Symphony Pro Musica
    Tri-Town Symphony
    Waltham Philharmonic
  Opera Companies, 55 dates
    Boston Lyric Opera
    Boston Opera
    Longwood Opera
    Opera Company of Boston

Ballet Companies, 143 dates
  Boston Ballet
  Boston Ballet II
Professional Theatres, 124 dates
  American Repertory Theatre
  Gloucester Stage Company
  Huntington Theatre Company
  Merrimack Repertory Theatre
  New Repertory Theatre
Art Museums and Galleries, 25
  Busch–Reisinger Museum
  De Cordova Museum and Sculpture Park
  Fogg Art Museum
  Museum of Fine Arts
Public Libraries
  240 branches, 18,235,725 volumes
  875,052 books added/year
MC Access: Boston–New
  Bedford–Nashua, MA–NH
Places Rated Score: 2,819
Places Rated Rank: 7

Boulder–Longmont, CO
Concert Radio
  In Denver media market
Lively Arts Calendar
  Touring Artists Bookings, 15 dates
  Resident Ensembles, 88 dates
    Boulder Philharmonic
    Colorado Music Festival Orchestra
    Colorado Shakespeare Festival
    Longmont Symphony
Art Museums and Galleries, 2
Public Libraries
  9 branches, 503,668 volumes
  33,955 books added/year
MC Access: Denver–Boulder–Greeley,
  CO
Places Rated Score: 456
Places Rated Rank: 114

Brazoria, TX
Concert Radio
  In Houston media market
Lively Arts Calendar
  Resident Ensemble, 6 dates
    Brazosport Symphony
Public Libraries
  11 branches, 318,259 volumes
  16,758 books added/year
MC Access: Houston–Galveston–
  Brazoria, TX
Places Rated Score: 201
Places Rated Rank: 240

Bremerton, WA
Concert Radio
  In Seattle–Tacoma media market
Lively Arts Calendar
  Resident Ensemble, 7 dates
    Bremerton Symphony
Public Libraries
  10 branches, 381,407 volumes
  23,149 books added/year
MC Access: Seattle–Tacoma–Bremerton,
  WA
Places Rated Score: 303
Places Rated Rank: 171

Bridgeport, CT
Lively Arts Calendar
  Touring Artists Bookings, 45 dates
  Resident Ensemble, 8 dates
    Greater Bridgeport Symphony
Art Museums and Galleries, 4
Public Libraries
  21 branches, 1,623,893 volumes
  78,050 books added/year

MC Access: New York–Northern New
  Jersey–Long Island, NY–NJ–CT
Places Rated Score: 612
Places Rated Rank: 87

**Brownsville–Harlingen–San Benito,
  TX**
Concert Radio
  KMBH-FM
Lively Arts Calendar
  Touring Artists Bookings, 3 dates
Art Museums and Galleries, 1
Public Libraries
  8 branches, 319,964 volumes
  10,848 books added/year
Places Rated Score: 93
Places Rated Rank: 322

Bryan–College Station, TX
Concert Radio
  KAMU-FM
Lively Arts Calendar
  Touring Artists Bookings, 19 dates
  Resident Ensemble, 5 dates
    Brazos Valley Symphony
5 Art Museums and Galleries, 1
Public Libraries
  2 branches, 159,441 volumes
  6,592 books added/year
Places Rated Score: 124
Places Rated Rank: 302

Buffalo–Niagara Falls, NY
Concert Radio
  WNED-FM
Lively Arts Calendar
  Touring Artists Bookings, 83 dates
  Resident Ensembles, 178 dates
    Amherst Symphony
    Arts Nova Chamber Orchestra
    Buffalo Philharmonic
    Cheektowaga Symphony
    Empire State Ballet
    Greater Buffalo Opera
    Orchard Park Symphony
    Studio Arena Theatre
Art Museums and Galleries, 3
  Albright–Knox Art Gallery
Public Libraries
  66 branches, 4,640,649 volumes
  140,275 books added/year
Places Rated Score: 764
Places Rated Rank: 64

Burlington, VT
Lively Arts Calendar
  Touring Artists Bookings, 29 dates
  Resident Ensemble, 124 dates
    Vermont Symphony
Art Museums and Galleries, 3
Public Libraries
  19 branches, 338,508 volumes
  12,532 books added/year
Places Rated Score: 391
Places Rated Rank: 140

Calgary, AB
Concert Radio
  CBR-AM
Lively Arts Calendar
  Touring Artists Bookings, 244 dates
  Resident Ensembles, 237 dates
    Alberta Ballet
    Alberta Theatre Projects
    Calgary Opera
    Calgary Philharmonic
    Lunchbox Theatre
    One Yellow Rabbit Theatre

    Pleiades Mystery Theatre
    Pumphouse Theatres Society
    Quest Theatre
    Theatre Calgary
Art Museums and Galleries, 6
  Glenbow–Alberta Institute
Public Libraries
  16 branches, 1,335,937 volumes
  173,257 books added/year
Places Rated Score: 995
Places Rated Rank: 46

Canton–Massillon, OH
Concert Radio
  In Cleveland media market
Lively Arts Calendar
  Touring Artists Bookings, 1 date
  Resident Ensembles, 65 dates
    Canton Ballet
    Canton Symphony
Art Museums and Galleries, 1
  Canton Art Institute
Public Libraries
  20 branches, 1,281,345 volumes
  89,280 books added/year
Places Rated Score: 342
Places Rated Rank: 156

Casper, WY
Lively Arts Calendar
  Touring Artists Bookings, 6 dates
  Resident Ensemble, 6 dates
    Casper Symphony
Public Libraries
  2 branches, 148,860 volumes
  3,806 books added/year
Places Rated Score: 74
Places Rated Rank: 330

Cedar Rapids, IA
Lively Arts Calendar
  Touring Artists Bookings, 24 dates
  Resident Ensemble, 28 dates
    Cedar Rapids Symphony
Art Museums and Galleries, 2
  Cedar Rapids Museum of Art
Public Libraries
  12 branches, 419,117 volumes
  25,491 books added/year
Places Rated Score: 300
Places Rated Rank: 172

✓ **Central New Jersey, NJ**
Concert Radio
  In New York media market
Lively Arts Calendar
  Touring Artists Bookings, 196 dates
  Resident Ensembles, 133 dates
    American Repertory Ballet
    Brunswick Symphony
    Chamber Symphony of New Jersey
    Crossroads Theatre Company
    George Street Playhouse
    Philharmonic Orchestra of New Jersey
    Rutgers University Theatre
Art Museums and Galleries, 3
Public Libraries
  64 branches, 3,453,458 volumes
  219,385 books added/year
MC Access: New York–Northern New
  Jersey–Long Island, NY–NJ–CT
Places Rated Score: 1,744
Places Rated Rank: 16

Champaign–Urbana, IL
Concert Radio
  WILL-FM
Lively Arts Calendar
  Touring Artists Bookings, 72 dates

  Resident Ensembles, 33 dates
    Champaign–Urbana Symphony
    Sinfonia da Camera
    University of Illinois Theatre
Art Museums and Galleries, 1
  Krannert Art Museum
Public Libraries
  11 branches, 582,459 volumes
  29,826 books added/year
Places Rated Score: 326
Places Rated Rank: 161

Charleston, WV
Concert Radio
  WVPN-FM
Lively Arts Calendar
  Touring Artists Bookings, 61 dates
  Resident Ensembles, 46 dates
    Charleston Ballet
    Lilliput Orchestra
    West Virginia Symphony
Art Museums and Galleries, 2
Public Libraries
  16 branches, 620,664 volumes
  26,742 books added/year
Places Rated Score: 314
Places Rated Rank: 165

Charleston–North Charleston, SC
Concert Radio
  WJYQ-FM, WSCI-FM
Lively Arts Calendar
  Touring Artists Bookings, 8 dates
  Resident Ensembles, 126 dates
    Charleston Ballet Theatre
    Charleston Symphony
    Chopstick Theatre
    USC Theatre
Art Museums and Galleries, 4
Public Libraries
  18 branches, 656,856 volumes
  45,920 books added/year
Places Rated Score: 420
Places Rated Rank: 130

**Charlotte–Gastonia–Rock Hill,
  NC–SC**
Concert Radio
  WDAV-FM, WNSC-FM, WSGE-FM
Lively Arts Calendar
  Touring Artists Bookings, 206 dates
  Resident Ensembles, 263 dates
    Charlotte City Ballet
    Charlotte Philharmonic
    Charlotte Symphony
    Opera Carolina
    Salisbury Symphony
Art Museums and Galleries, 4
Public Libraries
  41 branches, 2,180,963 volumes
  135,322 books added/year
Places Rated Score: 776
Places Rated Rank: 63

Charlottesville, VA
Concert Radio
  In Richmond media market
Lively Arts Calendar
  Touring Artists Bookings, 56 dates
  Resident Ensembles, 37 dates
    Ash Lawn–Highland Opera
    Charlottesville Symphony
Art Museums and Galleries, 2
Public Libraries
  8 branches, 305,488 volumes
  22,043 books added/year
Places Rated Score: 353
Places Rated Rank: 150

Chattanooga, TN–GA
Concert Radio
WSMC-FM
Lively Arts Calendar
Touring Artists Bookings, 35 dates
Resident Ensembles, 82 dates
Ballet Tennessee
Chattanooga Opera
Chattanooga Symphony
Art Museums and Galleries, 3
Hunter Museum of Art
Public Libraries
10 branches, 508,525 volumes
28,692 books added/year
Places Rated Score: 337
Places Rated Rank: 158

Cheyenne, WY
Lively Arts Calendar
Touring Artists Bookings, 10 dates
Resident Ensemble, 7 dates
Cheyenne Symphony
Art Museums and Galleries, 1
Wyoming State Museum
Public Libraries
3 branches, 139,326 volumes
7,128 books added/year
Places Rated Score: 164
Places Rated Rank: 276

✓ Chicago, IL
Concert Radio
WFMT-FM, WMWA-FM, WNIB-FM,
WNIU-FM
Lively Arts Calendar
Touring Artists Bookings, 774 dates
Symphony Orchestras, 529 dates
Chicago Bar Symphony
Chicago Chamber Orchestra
Chicago Philharmonia
Chicago Sinfonietta
Chicago Symphonic Wind Ensemble
Chicago Symphony
Civic Orchestra of Chicago
Classical Symphony
Concerts Symphoniques
Downers Grove Orchestra
Du Page Symphony
Elgin Symphony
Fox River Valley Symphony
Grant Park Symphony
Hinsdale Chamber Orchestra
Illinois Philharmonic
Music of the Baroque
New Philharmonic
Northbrook Symphony
Orchestra Chinese Music Society
River Cities Philharmonic
Skokie Valley Symphony
Southwest Symphony
Symphony of Oak Park and River
Forest
Valley Civic Orchestra
West Suburban Symphony
Wheaton Symphony
Opera Companies, 172 dates
Chamber Opera Chicago
Chicago Opera Repertory Theatre
Chicago Opera Theater
Du Page Opera Theatre
Hungarian Opera Workshop
Light Opera Works
Lincoln Opera
Lyric Opera of Chicago
Opera Factory
Ballet Company, 60 dates
Ballet Chicago
Professional Theatres, 452 dates

Bailiwick Repertory
Body Politic Theatre
Center Theater
Child's Play Touring Theatre
City Lit Theatre Company
Court Theatre
Free Street Theater
Goodman Theatre
Illinois Theatre Center National Jewish
Theater
New Tuners Theatre
NIU Stage Company
Northlight Theatre
Organic Theater Company
Pegasus Players
Remains Theatre
Shakespeare Repertory
Stage Left Theatre
Steppenwolf Theatre Company
Victory Gardens Theater
Wisdom Bridge Theatre
Art Museums and Galleries, 19
Art Institute of Chicago
Museum of Contemporary Art
Public Libraries
271 branches, 18,632,998 volumes
1,273,942 books added/year
MC Access: Chicago–Gary–Kenosha,
IL–IN–WI
Places Rated Score: 3,231
Places Rated Rank: 4

Chico–Paradise, CA
Concert Radio
KHCO-FM
Lively Arts Calendar
Touring Artists Bookings, 60 dates
Resident Ensembles, 13 dates
Chico Symphony
Paradise Symphony
Public Libraries
4 branches, 247,915 volumes
3,719 books added/year
Places Rated Score: 93
Places Rated Rank: 322

Chicoutimi–Jonquiere, PQ
Lively Arts Calendar
Resident Ensembles, 35 dates
La Rubrique Theatre
Orchestre Symphonique du
Saguenay-Lac-St-Jean
Art Museums and Galleries, 2
Public Libraries
4 branches, 164,977 volumes
11,529 books added/year
Places Rated Score: 206
Places Rated Rank: 237

Cincinnati, OH–KY–IN
Concert Radio
WCIN-FM, WGUC-FM
Lively Arts Calendar
Touring Artists Bookings, 59 dates
Resident Ensembles, 309 dates
ArtReach Touring Theatre
Cincinnati Chamber Orchestra
Cincinnati Opera
Cincinnati Symphony
Cincinnati–Knoxville–New Orleans City
Ballet
Conservatory of Music Opera
Ensemble Theatre
Playhouse in the Park
Art Museums and Galleries, 4
Cincinnati Art Museum
Public Libraries
71 branches, 5,477,773 volumes
389,329 books added/year

MC Access: Cincinnati–Hamilton,
OH–KY–IN
Places Rated Score: 854
Places Rated Rank: 56

Clarksville–Hopkinsville, TN–KY
Concert Radio
In Nashville media market
Lively Arts Calendar
Touring Artists Bookings, 4 dates
Art Museums and Galleries, 1
Public Libraries
3 branches, 214,076 volumes
14,965 books added/year
Places Rated Score: 140
Places Rated Rank: 290

✓ Cleveland–Lorain–Elyria, OH
Concert Radio
WCLV-FM
Lively Arts Calendar
Touring Artists Bookings, 415 dates
Symphony Orchestras, 240 dates
Cleveland Orchestra
Cleveland Philharmonic
Lakeland Civic Orchestra
Ohio Chamber Orchestra
Shaker Symphony
Trinity Chamber Orchestra
Opera Companies, 89 dates
Cleveland Opera
Lyric Opera Cleveland
Ballet Companies, 93 dates
Cleveland–San Jose Ballet
North Coast Ballet Theatre
Professional Theatres, 68 dates
Cleveland Play House
Cleveland Public Theatre
Great Lakes Theatre Festival
Art Museums and Galleries, 9
Cleveland Museum of Art
Public Libraries
119 branches, 8,894,007 volumes
835,628 books added/year
MC Access: Cleveland–Akron, OH
Places Rated Score: 1,795
Places Rated Rank: 15

Colorado Springs, CO
Concert Radio
KCME-FM
Lively Arts Calendar
Touring Artists Bookings, 27 dates
Resident Ensembles, 94 dates
Colorado Opera Festival
Colorado Springs Symphony
Theatreworks Colorado
Art Museums and Galleries, 3
Colorado Springs Fine Arts Center
Public Libraries
13 branches, 823,386 volumes
63,408 books added/year
Places Rated Score: 423
Places Rated Rank: 128

Columbia, MO
Concert Radio
KBIA-FM
Lively Arts Calendar
Touring Artists Bookings, 15 dates
Resident Ensemble, 23 dates
Missouri Symphony Society
Art Museums and Galleries, 2
University of Missouri Museum of Art
Public Libraries
3 branches, 315,563 volumes
13,576 books added/year
Places Rated Score: 253
Places Rated Rank: 205

Columbia, SC
Concert Radio
   WLTR-FM
Lively Arts Calendar
   Touring Artists Bookings, 13 dates
   Resident Ensembles, 50 dates
      Carolina Ballet
      Columbia City Ballet
      South Carolina Philharmonic
      Southeastern Regional Opera
      Trustus
Art Museums and Galleries, 2
   Museum of Art and Science
Public Libraries
   17 branches, 787,113 volumes
   74,241 books added/year
Places Rated Score: 315
Places Rated Rank: 164

Columbus, GA–AL
Concert Radio
   WTJB-FM
Lively Arts Calendar
   Resident Ensemble, 30 dates
      Columbus Symphony
Art Museum and Gallery
   The Columbus Museum
Public Libraries
   10 branches, 526,253 volumes
   14,626 books added/year
Places Rated Score: 136
Places Rated Rank: 294

Columbus, OH
Concert Radio
   WOSU-FM
Lively Arts Calendar
   Touring Artists Bookings, 139 dates
   Resident Ensembles, 197 dates
      Central Ohio Symphony
      Columbus Symphony
      Opera Columbus
      OSU Theatre Company
      Players Theatre
      Pro Musica Chamber Orchestra
      Westerville Civic Symphony
Art Museums and Galleries, 6
   Columbus Museum of Art
Public Libraries
   51 branches, 3,639,280 volumes
   396,242 books added/year
Places Rated Score: 916
Places Rated Rank: 52

Corpus Christi, TX
Concert Radio
   KEDT-FM
Lively Arts Calendar
   Touring Artists Bookings, 23 dates
   Resident Ensembles, 32 dates
      Corpus Christi Ballet
      Corpus Christi Symphony
Art Museums and Galleries, 1
   Art Museum South Texas
Public Libraries
   13 branches, 466,917 volumes
   28,478 books added/year
Places Rated Score: 184
Places Rated Rank: 263

Cumberland, MD–WV
Concert Radio
   WFWM-FM
Lively Arts Calendar
   Touring Artists Bookings, 4 dates
Public Libraries
   9 branches, 219,328 volumes

6,881 books added/year
Places Rated Score: 71
Places Rated Rank: 334

✓ Dallas, TX
Concert Radio
   KNTU-FM, WRR-FM
Lively Arts Calendar
   Touring Artists Bookings, 246 dates
   Symphony Orchestras, 413 dates
      AIMS Festival Orchestra in Graz
      Chamber Symphony of the Metrocrest
      Dallas Bach Orchestra
      Dallas Chamber Orchestra
      Dallas Symphony
      Dallas Wind Symphony
      Garland Symphony
      Irving Symphony
      Las Colinas Symphony
      Plano Chamber Orchestra
      Richardson Symphony
   Opera Companies, 41 dates
      Dallas Opera
      Lyric Opera of Dallas
   Professional Theatres, 84 dates
      Addison Center Theatre
      Dallas Theatre Center
      SMU Theatre
      Undermain Theatre
Art Museums and Galleries, 3
   Dallas Museum of Art
Public Libraries
   81 branches, 5,519,063 volumes
   250,739 books added/year
MC Access: Dallas–Fort Worth, TX
Places Rated Score: 1,083
Places Rated Rank: 39

✓ Danbury, CT
Lively Arts Calendar
   Touring Artists Bookings, 12 dates
   Resident Ensemble, 5 dates
      Ridgefield Symphony
Art Museums and Galleries, 1
Public Libraries
   13 branches, 627,965 volumes
   41,996 books added/year
MC Access: New York–Northern New
   Jersey–Long Island, NY–NJ–CT
Places Rated Score: 1,334
Places Rated Rank: 31

Danville, VA
Concert Radio
   In Roanoke media market
Lively Arts Calendar
   Touring Artists Bookings, 10 dates
Art Museums and Galleries, 1
Public Libraries
   6 branches, 182,242 volumes
   10,991 books added/year
Places Rated Score: 161
Places Rated Rank: 277

Davenport–Moline–Rock Island, IA–IL
Concert Radio
   WVIK-FM
Lively Arts Calendar
   Touring Artists Bookings, 39 dates
   Resident Ensembles, 27 dates
      Augustana Symphony
      Quad City Symphony
Art Museums and Galleries, 2
   Davenport Museum of Art
Public Libraries
   34 branches, 1,108,061 volumes

41,614 books added/year
Places Rated Score: 284
Places Rated Rank: 181

Dayton–Springfield, OH
Concert Radio
   WDPR-FM
Lively Arts Calendar
   Touring Artists Bookings, 86 dates
   Resident Ensembles, 562 dates
      Dayton Ballet
      Dayton Opera
      Dayton Philharmonic
      Ohio Lyric Theatre
      Springfield Symphony
Art Museums and Galleries, 4
   Dayton Art Institute
Public Libraries
   43 branches, 3,077,978 volumes
   241,416 books added/year
Places Rated Score: 1,101
Places Rated Rank: 38

Daytona Beach, FL
Concert Radio
   In Orlando media market
Lively Arts Calendar
   Touring Artists Bookings, 83 dates
   Resident Ensemble, 8 dates
      Seaside Music Theater
Art Museums and Galleries, 2
Public Libraries
   16 branches, 669,807 volumes
   41,423 books added/year
Places Rated Score: 286
Places Rated Rank: 180

Decatur, AL
Concert Radio
   In Huntsville media market
Lively Arts Calendar
   Touring Artists Bookings, 20 dates
Art Museums and Galleries, 1
Public Libraries
   6 branches, 123,044 volumes
   10,238 books added/year
Places Rated Score: 145
Places Rated Rank: 286

Decatur, IL
Concert Radio
   In Springfield media market
Lively Arts Calendar
   Touring Artists Bookings, 16 dates
   Resident Ensemble, 10 dates
      Millikin–Decatur Civic Symphony
Art Museums and Galleries, 1
Public Libraries
   9 branches, 314,435 volumes
   19,982 books added/year
Places Rated Score: 247
Places Rated Rank: 208

Denver, CO
Concert Radio
   KCFR-FM, KPOF-AM, KVOD-FM
Lively Arts Calendar
   Touring Artists Bookings, 215 dates
   Resident Ensembles, 280 dates
      Arapahoe Philharmonic
      Central City Opera House
      Colorado Ballet
      Colorado Symphony
      Denver Center Theatre Company
      Denver Chamber Orchestra
      Germinal Stage
      Jefferson Symphony
      Opera Colorado

Art Museums and Galleries, 5
  Denver Art Museum
Public Libraries
  60 branches, 4,187,206 volumes
  281,327 books added/year
MC Access: Denver–Boulder–Greeley,
  CO
Places Rated Score: 958
Places Rated Rank: 47

Des Moines, IA
Lively Arts Calendar
  Touring Artists Bookings, 25 dates
  Resident Ensembles, 82 dates
    Ballet Iowa
    Des Moines Community Orchestra
    Des Moines Metro Opera
    Des Moines Symphony
Art Museums and Galleries, 3
Public Libraries
  33 branches, 1,113,464 volumes
  38,561 books added/year
Places Rated Score: 352
Places Rated Rank: 151

✓ **Detroit, MI**
Concert Radio
  WQRS-FM
Lively Arts Calendar
  Touring Artists Bookings, 218 dates
  Symphony Orchestras, 478 dates
    Allen Park Symphony
    Birmingham–Bloomfield Symphony
    Dearborn Symphony
    Detroit Symphony
    Grosse Pointe Symphony
    Lake St. Clair Symphony
    Livonia Symphony
    Michigan Chamber Orchestra
    National Sinfonietta
    New American Chamber Orchestra
    Pontiac–Oakland Symphony
    Warren Symphony
  Opera Company, 32 dates
    Michigan Opera Theatre
  Professional Theatres, 144 dates
    Actors Alliance Theatre Company
    Attic Theatre
    Detroit Repertory Theatre
    Hilberry Theatre
    Meadow Brook Theatre
    Theatre Grottesco
    Wayne State Repertory Theatre
Art Museums and Galleries, 8
  Cranbrook Academy of Art Museum
  Detroit Institute of Arts
  Henry Ford Museum
Public Libraries
  161 branches, 9,170,134 volumes
  430,070 books added/year
MC Access: Detroit–Ann Arbor–Flint, MI
Places Rated Score: 1,500
Places Rated Rank: 25

Dothan, AL
Concert Radio
  WRWA-FM
Art Museums and Galleries, 1
Public Libraries
  9 branches, 242,507 volumes
  9,537 books added/year
Places Rated Score: 120
Places Rated Rank: 304

Dover, DE
Concert Radio
  In Philadelphia media market

Lively Arts Calendar
  Touring Artists Bookings, 7 dates
Public Libraries
  5 branches, 137,212 volumes
  10,205 books added/year
Places Rated Score: 98
Places Rated Rank: 319

Dubuque, IA
Lively Arts Calendar
  Touring Artists Bookings, 26 dates
  Resident Ensemble, 23 dates
    Dubuque Symphony
Art Museums and Galleries, 1
Public Libraries
  6 branches, 285,283 volumes
  9,856 books added/year
Places Rated Score: 213
Places Rated Rank: 234

Duluth–Superior, MN–WI
Concert Radio
  WHSA-FM, WIRR-FM, WSCD-FM
Lively Arts Calendar
  Touring Artists Bookings, 39 dates
  Resident Ensembles, 65 dates
    Duluth Ballet
    Duluth–Superior Symphony
Art Museums and Galleries, 1
Public Libraries
  22 branches, 923,667 volumes
  37,961 books added/year
Places Rated Score: 314
Places Rated Rank: 165

Dutchess County, NY
Concert Radio
  WRHV-FM
Lively Arts Calendar
  Touring Artists Bookings, 180 dates
  Resident Ensemble, 22 dates
    Hudson Valley Philharmonic
Art Museums and Galleries, 2
Public Libraries
  25 branches, 585,174 volumes
  42,526 books added/year
Places Rated Score: 503
Places Rated Rank: 109

Eau Claire, WI
Concert Radio
  In La Crosse media market
Lively Arts Calendar
  Touring Artists Bookings, 15 dates
  Resident Ensemble, 4 dates
    Chippewa Valley Symphony
Public Libraries
  10 branches, 407,477 volumes
  20,908 books added/year
Places Rated Score: 170
Places Rated Rank: 271

Edmonton, AB
Concert Radio
  CHQT-AM
Lively Arts Calendar
  Touring Artists Bookings, 130 dates
  Resident Ensembles, 84 dates
    Catalyst Theatre
    Chinook Theatre Society
    Edmonton Fringe Theatre Event
    Edmonton Opera
    Edmonton Symphony
    Nexus Theatre
    Northern Light Theatre
    Stage Polaris
    The Phoenix Theatre

    Theatre Network Society
    Workshop West Theatre
Art Museums and Galleries, 4
  The Edmonton Art Gallery
Public Libraries
  17 branches, 1,244,256 volumes
  88,704 books added/year
Places Rated Score: 512
Places Rated Rank: 106

El Paso, TX
Concert Radio
  KTEP-FM
Lively Arts Calendar
  Touring Artists Bookings, 3 dates
  Resident Ensembles, 47 dates
    Ballet of the Americas
    El Paso Philharmonic Strings
    El Paso Symphony
Art Museums and Galleries, 1
  El Paso Museum of Art
Public Libraries
  11 branches, 925,287 volumes
  43,228 books added/year
Places Rated Score: 169
Places Rated Rank: 273

Elkhart–Goshen, IN
Concert Radio
  WGCS-FM
Lively Arts Calendar
  Touring Artists Bookings, 4 dates
  Resident Ensemble, 6 dates
    Elkhart County Symphony
Public Libraries
  8 branches, 395,683 volumes
  28,688 books added/year
Places Rated Score: 188
Places Rated Rank: 256

Elmira, NY
Lively Arts Calendar
  Touring Artists Bookings, 56 dates
  Resident Ensemble, 7 dates
    Elmira Symphony
Art Museums and Galleries, 1
  Arnot Art Museum
Public Libraries
  6 branches, 326,556 volumes
  11,924 books added/year
Places Rated Score: 237
Places Rated Rank: 220

Enid, OK
Concert Radio
  In Oklahoma City media market
Lively Arts Calendar
  Touring Artists Bookings, 20 dates
  Resident Ensemble, 15 dates
    Enid–Phillips Symphony
Art Museums and Galleries, 1
Public Libraries
  1 branch, 90,797 volumes
  4,282 books added/year
Places Rated Score: 161
Places Rated Rank: 277

Erie, PA
Lively Arts Calendar
  Touring Artists Bookings, 54 dates
  Resident Ensemble, 16 dates
    Erie Philharmonic
Art Museums and Galleries, 1
Public Libraries
  14 branches, 678,359 volumes
  17,488 books added/year
Places Rated Score: 183
Places Rated Rank: 264

Eugene–Springfield, OR
Concert Radio
  KWAX-FM
Lively Arts Calendar
  Touring Artists Bookings, 237 dates
  Resident Ensembles, 39 dates
    Eugene Opera
    Eugene Symphony
    Oregon Mozart Players
Art Museums and Galleries, 1
Public Libraries
  7 branches, 446,915 volumes
  17,598 books added/year
Places Rated Score: 386
Places Rated Rank: 143

Evansville–Henderson, IN–KY
Concert Radio
  WINN-FM
Lively Arts Calendar
  Touring Artists Bookings, 32 dates
  Resident Ensemble, 24 dates
    Evansville Philharmonic
Art Museums and Galleries, 2
Public Libraries
  18 branches, 1,108,498 volumes
  44,714 books added/year
Places Rated Score: 314
Places Rated Rank: 165

Fargo–Moorhead, ND–MN
Concert Radio
  KCCM-FM
Lively Arts Calendar
  Touring Artists Bookings, 17 dates
  Resident Ensembles, 16 dates
    Fargo–Moorhead Civic Opera
    Fargo–Moorhead Symphony
Art Museums and Galleries, 2
Public Libraries
  7 branches, 483,653 volumes
  19,218 books added/year
Places Rated Score: 266
Places Rated Rank: 193

Fayetteville, NC
Concert Radio
  In Raleigh–Durham media market
Lively Arts Calendar
  Resident Ensemble, 5 dates
    Fayetteville Symphony
Art Museums and Galleries, 2
Public Libraries
  8 branches, 378,108 volumes
  40,811 books added/year
Places Rated Score: 253
Places Rated Rank: 205

Fayetteville–Springdale–Rogers, AR
Concert Radio
  KUAF-FM
Lively Arts Calendar
  Touring Artists Bookings, 38 dates
  Resident Ensemble, 20 dates
    North Arkansas Symphony
Public Libraries
  10 branches, 271,551 volumes
  14,456 books added/year
Places Rated Score: 121
Places Rated Rank: 303

Flint, MI
Concert Radio
  WFBE-FM, WFUM-FM
Lively Arts Calendar
  Touring Artists Bookings, 5 dates

Resident Ensemble, 6 dates
    Flint Symphony
Art Museums and Galleries, 1
    Flint Institute of Arts
Public Libraries
  20 branches, 1,066,707 volumes
  41,863 books added/year
MC Access: Detroit–Ann Arbor–Flint, MI
Places Rated Score: 296
Places Rated Rank: 176

Florence, AL
Concert Radio
  WQPR-FM
Lively Arts Calendar
  Touring Artists Bookings, 4 dates
Art Museums and Galleries, 3
Public Libraries
  10 branches, 203,550 volumes
  6,253 books added/year
Places Rated Score: 201
Places Rated Rank: 240

Florence, SC
Lively Arts Calendar
  Touring Artists Bookings, 8 dates
  Resident Ensemble, 5 dates
    Florence Symphony
Art Museums and Galleries, 1
Public Libraries
  7 branches, 167,590 volumes
  8,642 books added/year
Places Rated Score: 136
Places Rated Rank: 294

Fort Collins–Loveland, CO
Concert Radio
  KCSU-FM
Lively Arts Calendar
  Touring Artists Bookings, 55 dates
  Resident Ensemble, 15 dates
    Fort Collins Symphony
Art Museums and Galleries, 2
Public Libraries
  6 branches, 368,753 volumes
  18,239 books added/year
Places Rated Score: 262
Places Rated Rank: 198

Fort Lauderdale, FL
Lively Arts Calendar
  Touring Artists Bookings, 385 dates
  Resident Ensembles, 184 dates
    Florida Philharmonic
    Fort Lauderdale Opera
    Sinfonia Virtuosi
Art Museums and Galleries, 1
Public Libraries
  32 branches, 2,006,324 volumes
  225,810 books added/year
MC Access: Miami–Fort Lauderdale, FL
Places Rated Score: 876
Places Rated Rank: 55

Fort Myers–Cape Coral, FL
Concert Radio
  WSFO-FM, WWCL-AM
Lively Arts Calendar
  Touring Artists Bookings, 190 dates
  Resident Ensemble, 17 dates
    Southwest Florida Symphony
Art Museums and Galleries, 1
Public Libraries
  10 branches, 437,712 volumes
  57,898 books added/year
Places Rated Score: 409
Places Rated Rank: 135

Fort Pierce–Port St. Lucie, FL
Concert Radio
  WQCS-FM
Lively Arts Calendar
  Touring Artists Bookings, 16 dates
Public Libraries
  7 branches, 300,311 volumes
  34,451 books added/year
Places Rated Score: 138
Places Rated Rank: 291

Fort Smith, AR–OK
Lively Arts Calendar
  Touring Artists Bookings, 5 dates
  Resident Ensemble, 5 dates
    Fort Smith Symphony
Art Museums and Galleries, 1
Public Libraries
  7 branches, 185,584 volumes
  9,066 books added/year
Places Rated Score: 109
Places Rated Rank: 311

Fort Walton Beach, FL
Concert Radio
  In Mobile media market
Lively Arts Calendar
  Touring Artists Bookings, 5 dates
  Resident Ensembles, 34 dates
    Northwest Florida Ballet
    Okaloosa Symphony
Public Libraries
  6 branches, 154,590 volumes
  5,197 books added/year
Places Rated Score: 73
Places Rated Rank: 331

Fort Wayne, IN
Concert Radio
  WBNI-FM
Lively Arts Calendar
  Touring Artists Bookings, 39 dates
  Resident Ensembles, 64 dates
    Fort Wayne Ballet
    Fort Wayne Philharmonic
Art Museums and Galleries, 1
Public Libraries
  31 branches, 2,668,999 volumes
  18,735 books added/year
Places Rated Score: 193
Places Rated Rank: 248

Fort Worth–Arlington, TX
Concert Radio
  KTCU-FM
Lively Arts Calendar
  Touring Artists Bookings, 39 dates
  Resident Ensembles, 302 dates
    Ballet Concerto
    Fort Worth Ballet
    Fort Worth Civic Orchestra
    Fort Worth Opera
    Fort Worth Symphony
    Stage West
Art Museums and Galleries, 4
    Amon Carter Museum
    Fort Worth Art Museum
    Kimbell Art Museum
Public Libraries
  38 branches, 3,235,286 volumes
  100,661 books added/year
MC Access: Dallas–Fort Worth, TX
Places Rated Score: 712
Places Rated Rank: 74

Fresno, CA
Concert Radio
  KVPR-FM

Lively Arts Calendar
Touring Artists Bookings, 63 dates
Resident Ensembles, 31 dates
Fresno Ballet
Fresno Philharmonic
Art Museums and Galleries, 1
Fresno Art Museum
Public Libraries
17 branches, 1,380,581 volumes
37,332 books added/year
Places Rated Score: 189
Places Rated Rank: 254

Gadsden, AL
Concert Radio
WSGN-FM
Lively Arts Calendar
Touring Artists Bookings, 6 dates
Art Museums and Galleries, 2
Public Libraries
7 branches, 228,389 volumes
7,752 books added/year
Places Rated Score: 183
Places Rated Rank: 264

Gainesville, FL
Concert Radio
WUFT-FM
Lively Arts Calendar
Touring Artists Bookings, 25 dates
Resident Ensembles, 74 dates
Gainesville Chamber Orchestra
Hippodrome State Theatre
University of Florida Theatre
Art Museums and Galleries, 3
University of Florida Gallery
Public Libraries
6 branches, (1) volumes
26,594 books added/year
Places Rated Score: 384
Places Rated Rank: 144

Galveston–Texas City, TX
Concert Radio
In Houston media market
Lively Arts Calendar
Touring Artists Bookings, 20 dates
Resident Ensemble, 6 dates
Galveston Symphony
Public Libraries
8 branches, 852,373 volumes
21,574 books added/year
MC Access: Houston–Galveston–
Brazoria, TX
Places Rated Score: 235
Places Rated Rank: 222

Gary, IN
Concert Radio
In Chicago media market
Lively Arts Calendar
Touring Artists Bookings, 210 dates
Resident Ensemble, 15 dates
Northwest Indiana Symphony
Art Museums and Galleries, 2
Public Libraries
41 branches, 2,211,803 volumes
110,315 books added/year
MC Access: Chicago–Gary–Kenosha,
IL–IN–WI
Places Rated Score: 818
Places Rated Rank: 59

Glens Falls, NY
Concert Radio
In Albany media market
Lively Arts Calendar
Resident Ensembles, 29 dates

Glens Falls Symphony
Lake George Opera Festival
Art Museums and Galleries, 3
Public Libraries
18 branches, 325,911 volumes
11,917 books added/year
Places Rated Score: 276
Places Rated Rank: 189

Goldsboro, NC
Concert Radio
In Raleigh–Durham media market
Art Museums and Galleries, 1
Public Libraries
7 branches, 92,010 volumes
6,833 books added/year
Places Rated Score: 114
Places Rated Rank: 307

Grand Forks, ND–MN
Concert Radio
KFJM-FM
Lively Arts Calendar
Touring Artists Bookings, 19 dates
Resident Ensemble, 7 dates
Greater Grand Forks Symphony, 7
Art Museums and Galleries, 1
Public Libraries
4 branches, 170,994 volumes
6,928 books added/year
Places Rated Score: 143
Places Rated Rank: 288

**Grand Rapids–Muskegon–Holland,
MI**
Concert Radio
WVGR-FM
Lively Arts Calendar
Touring Artists Bookings, 74 dates
Resident Ensembles, 114 dates
Grand Rapids Ballet
Grand Rapids Symphony
Opera Grand Rapids
West Shore Symphony
Art Museums and Galleries, 3
Grand Rapids Art Museum
Public Libraries
62 branches, 2,401,211 volumes
97,025 books added/year
Places Rated Score: 436
Places Rated Rank: 122

Great Falls, MT
Concert Radio
KGPR-FM
Lively Arts Calendar
Resident Ensemble,
Great Falls Symphony
Art Museums and Galleries, 2
C. M. Russell Museum
Public Libraries
3 branches, 185,250 volumes
2,721 books added/year
Places Rated Score: 145
Places Rated Rank: 286

Greeley, CO
Concert Radio
In Denver media market
Lively Arts Calendar
Touring Artists Bookings, 25 dates
Resident Ensemble, 14 dates
Greeley Philharmonic
Public Libraries
11 branches, 383,034 volumes
16,329 books added/year
MC Access: Denver–Boulder–Greeley,
CO

Places Rated Score: 287
Places Rated Rank: 179

Green Bay, WI
Concert Radio
WPNE-FM
Lively Arts Calendar
Touring Artists Bookings, 79 dates
Resident Ensembles, 20 dates
Green Bay Symphony
Pamiro Opera
Sebastian Chamber Orchestra
Art Museums and Galleries, 1
Public Libraries
9 branches, 335,719 volumes
23,534 books added/year
Places Rated Score: 266
Places Rated Rank: 193

**Greensboro–Winston-Salem–High
Point, NC**
Concert Radio
WFDD-FM
Lively Arts Calendar
Touring Artists Bookings, 146 dates
Resident Ensembles, 147 dates
Eastern Philharmonic
Greensboro Symphony
Greensboro Opera
Philharmonia of Greensboro
Piedmont Opera Theatre
Winston-Salem Symphony
Art Museums and Galleries, 7
Public Libraries
40 branches, 1,938,584 volumes
123,577 books added/year
Places Rated Score: 755
Places Rated Rank: 67

Greenville, NC
Lively Arts Calendar
Touring Artists Bookings, 24 dates
Art Museums and Galleries, 1
Public Libraries
4 branches, 184,239 volumes
9,205 books added/year
Places Rated Score: 151
Places Rated Rank: 283

**Greenville–Spartanburg–Anderson,
SC**
Concert Radio
WEPR-FM, WMUU-FM
Lively Arts Calendar
Touring Artists Bookings, 109 dates
Resident Ensembles, 36 dates
Anderson Symphony
Greenville Symphony
Spartanburg Symphony
Art Museums and Galleries, 7
Greenville County Museum of Art
Public Libraries
34 branches, 1,409,155 volumes
85,617 books added/year
Places Rated Score: 594
Places Rated Rank: 90

Hagerstown, MD
Lively Arts Calendar
Touring Artists Bookings, 90 dates
Resident Ensemble, 16 dates
Maryland Symphony
Art Museums and Galleries, 1
Washington County Museum of Fine Arts
Public Libraries
7 branches, 216,234 volumes
11,641 books added/year

MC Access: Washington–Baltimore,
DC–MD–VA–WV
Places Rated Score: 402
Places Rated Rank: 137

Halifax, NS
Concert Radio
CKDU-FM
Lively Arts Calendar
Touring Artists Bookings, 10 dates
Resident Ensembles, 107 dates
Atlantic Fringe Festival
Chebucto Symphony
Neptune Theatre
Scotia Chamber Players
Symphony Nova Scotia
Art Museums and Galleries, 7
Art Gallery of Nova Scotia
Public Libraries
16 branches, 853,391 volumes
120,894 books added/year
Places Rated Score: 826
Places Rated Rank: 58

Hamilton, ON
Concert Radio
CFMU-FM, CING-FM
Lively Arts Calendar
Touring Artists Bookings, 35 dates
Resident Ensembles, 116 dates
Hamilton Philharmonic
Opera Hamilton
Sir Ernest String Ensemble
Symphony Hamilton
Te Deum Orchestra
Theatre Aquarius
Theatre Erebus
Art Museums and Galleries, 7
Art Gallery of Hamilton
Public Libraries
31 branches, 1,350,217 volumes
103,729 books added/year
MC Access: Toronto–Ontario Shore, ON
Places Rated Score: 1,018
Places Rated Rank: 44

Hamilton–Middletown, OH
Concert Radio
In Cincinnati media market
Lively Arts Calendar
Touring Artists Bookings, 22 dates
Resident Ensembles, 12 dates
Middletown Symphony
Sorg Opera
Art Museums and Galleries, 1
Public Libraries
11 branches, 870,701 volumes
79,872 books added/year
MC Access: Cincinnati–Hamilton,
OH–KY–IN
Places Rated Score: 436
Places Rated Rank: 122

Harrisburg–Lebanon–Carlisle, PA
Concert Radio
WITF-FM, WWKL-FM
Lively Arts Calendar
Touring Artists Bookings, 123 dates
Resident Ensembles, 36 dates
Gretna Theatre Productions
Harrisburg Civic Opera
Open Stage of Harrisburg
Art Museums and Galleries, 1
Public Libraries
31 branches, 845,130 volumes
43,760 books added/year
Places Rated Score: 281
Places Rated Rank: 184

✓ Hartford, CT
Lively Arts Calendar
Touring Artists Bookings, 428 dates
Resident Ensembles, 587 dates
Company One Theatre
Connecticut Opera
Goodspeed Opera House
Hartford Ballet
Hartford Stage Company
Hartford Symphony
Hartt Symphony
New Britain Symphony
Opera Theater of Connecticut
Art Museums and Galleries, 8
Wadsworth Athenaeum
Public Libraries
84 branches, 4,079,183 volumes
177,008 books added/year
Places Rated Score: 1,567
Places Rated Rank: 20

Hickory–Morgantown, NC
Concert Radio
In Charlotte media market
Lively Arts Calendar
Touring Artists Bookings, 9 dates
Resident Ensemble, 8 dates
Western Piedmont Symphony
Art Museums and Galleries, 2
Hickory Museum of Art
Public Libraries
13 branches, 450,625 volumes
30,816 books added/year
Places Rated Score: 219
Places Rated Rank: 233

Honolulu, HI
Concert Radio
KHPR-FM
Lively Arts Calendar
Touring Artists Bookings, 101 dates
Resident Ensembles, 250 dates
Hawaii Opera Theatre
Hawaii State Ballet
Honolulu Symphony
Honolulu Theatre for Youth
Art Museums and Galleries, 4
Honolulu Academy of Arts
Public Libraries
48 branches, 2,391,704 volumes
172,522 books added/year
Places Rated Score: 754
Places Rated Rank: 68

Houma, LA
Concert Radio
In New Orleans media market
Public Libraries
16 branches, 305,626 volumes
8,932 books added/year
Places Rated Score: 49
Places Rated Rank: 341

Houston, TX
Concert Radio
KRTS-FM, KUHF-FM
Lively Arts Calendar
Touring Artists Bookings, 348 dates
Resident Ensembles, 511 dates
A.D. Players
Alley Theatre
Clear Lake Symphony
Houston Ballet
Houston Grand Opera
Houston Symphony
Main Street Theatre
Stages Repertory Theatre
Symphony North of Houston

Texas Opera Theater
Art Museums and Galleries, 4
Contemporary Arts Museum
Museum of Fine Arts
Public Libraries
81 branches, 6,907,371 volumes
270,555 books added/year
MC Access: Houston–Galveston–
Brazoria, TX
Places Rated Score: 1,156
Places Rated Rank: 37

Huntington–Ashland, WV–KY–OH
Concert Radio
WOUL-FM, WVWV-FM
Lively Arts Calendar
Touring Artists Bookings, 52 dates
Resident Ensemble, 8 dates
Huntington Chamber Orchestra
Art Museums and Galleries, 1
Huntington Museum of Art
Public Libraries
20 branches, 595,212 volumes
29,577 books added/year
Places Rated Score: 212
Places Rated Rank: 235

Huntsville, AL
Concert Radio
WLRH-FM
Lively Arts Calendar
Touring Artists Bookings, 131 dates
Resident Ensembles, 24 dates
Huntsville Opera Theater
Huntsville Symphony
Art Museums and Galleries, 2
Huntsville Museum of Art
Public Libraries
9 branches, 357,581 volumes
28,179 books added/year
Places Rated Score: 346
Places Rated Rank: 152

Indianapolis, IN
Concert Radio
WAJC-FM, WFYI-FM,
WICR-FM, WSYW-AM, WSYW-FM
Lively Arts Calendar
Touring Artists Bookings, 141 dates
Resident Ensembles, 408 dates
Anderson Symphony
Carmel Symphony
Indiana Opera Theatre
Indiana Repertory Theatre
Indianapolis Ballet Theatre
Indianapolis Chamber Orchestra
Indianapolis Opera
Indianapolis Symphony
Philharmonic Orchestra, Indianapolis
Art Museums and Galleries, 6
Indianapolis Museum of Art
Public Libraries
56 branches, 3,391,492 volumes
263,815 books added/year
Places Rated Score: 1,033
Places Rated Rank: 43

Iowa City, IA
Concert Radio
KSUI-FM
Lively Arts Calendar
Touring Artists Bookings, 40 dates
Resident Ensemble, 16 dates
University of Iowa Theatre
Art Museums and Galleries, 1
University of Iowa Museum of Art
Public Libraries
5 branches, 245,288 volumes

14,770 books added/year
Places Rated Score: 254
Places Rated Rank: 204

Jackson, MI
Concert Radio
In Lansing media market
Lively Arts Calendar
Touring Artists Bookings, 36 dates
Resident Ensemble, 12 dates
Jackson Symphony
Public Libraries
13 branches, 222,545 volumes
18,058 books added/year
Places Rated Score: 167
Places Rated Rank: 274

Jackson, MS
Concert Radio
WMPN-FM
Lively Arts Calendar
Touring Artists Bookings, 14 dates
Resident Ensembles, 119 dates
Ballet Mississippi
Jackson Symphony
Mississippi Opera
Mississippi Symphony
New Stage Theatre
Art Museums and Galleries, 1
Public Libraries
38 branches, 959,122 volumes
33,490 books added/year
Places Rated Score: 265
Places Rated Rank: 195

Jacksonville, FL
Concert Radio
WJCT-FM, WJGC-AM
Lively Arts Calendar
Touring Artists Bookings, 75 dates
Resident Ensembles, 185 dates
Jacksonville Symphony
The Florida Ballet
Art Museums and Galleries, 3
Cummer Gallery of Art
Jacksonville Art Museum
Public Libraries
24 branches, 2,104,398 volumes
95,710 books added/year
Places Rated Score: 512
Places Rated Rank: 106

Jacksonville, NC
Concert Radio
In Greenville media market
Lively Arts Calendar
Touring Artists Bookings, 14 dates
Public Libraries
5 branches, 103,537 volumes
7,551 books added/year
Places Rated Score: 63
Places Rated Rank: 336

Jamestown, NY
Concert Radio
In Buffalo media market
Lively Arts Calendar
Touring Artists Bookings, 355 dates
Resident Ensembles, 50 dates
Chautauqua Festival Orchestra
Chautauqua Opera
Chautauqua Symphony
Fredonia Chamber Players
Art Museums and Galleries, 1
Public Libraries
24 branches, 728,812 volumes
31,128 books added/year
Places Rated Score: 674
Places Rated Rank: 80

Janesville–Beloit, WI
Concert Radio
In Madison media market
Lively Arts Calendar
Touring Artists Bookings, 5 dates
Resident Ensemble, 14 dates
Beloit–Janesville Symphony
Art Museums and Galleries, 1
Public Libraries
7 branches, 398,514 volumes
24,089 books added/year
Places Rated Score: 241
Places Rated Rank: 215

Johnson City–Kingsport–Bristol, TN–VA
Concert Radio
WCSK-FM, WETS-FM
Lively Arts Calendar
Touring Artists Bookings, 17 dates
Resident Ensembles, 71 dates
Barter Theatre
Johnson City Symphony
Kingsport Symphony
Road Company
Art Museums and Galleries, 2
Carroll Reece Museum
Public Libraries
31 branches, 765,789 volumes
37,761 books added/year
Places Rated Score: 273
Places Rated Rank: 191

Johnstown, PA
Lively Arts Calendar
Touring Artists Bookings, 16 dates
Resident Ensemble, 20 dates
Johnstown Symphony
Art Museums and Galleries, 2
Johnstown Art Museum
Public Libraries
19 branches, 472,687 volumes
11,087 books added/year
Places Rated Score: 182
Places Rated Rank: 266

Joplin, MO
Concert Radio
KXMS-FM
Art Museums and Galleries, 2
Crowder College–Longwell Museum
Public Libraries
9 branches, 284,319 volumes
7,171 books added/year
Places Rated Score: 151
Places Rated Rank: 283

Kalamazoo–Battle Creek, MI
Concert Radio
WMUK-FM
Lively Arts Calendar
Touring Artists Bookings, 14 dates
Resident Ensemble, 26 dates
Battle Creek Symphony
Art Museums and Galleries, 5
Kalamazoo Institute of Arts
Public Libraries
34 branches, 1,252,107 volumes
57,084 books added/year
Places Rated Score: 420
Places Rated Rank: 130

Kankakee, IL
Concert Radio
In Chicago media market
Lively Arts Calendar
Touring Artists Bookings, 5 dates
Resident Ensemble, 9 dates
Kankakee Valley Symphony

Public Libraries
6 branches, 171,961 volumes
9,842 books added/year
MC Access: Chicago–Gary–Kenosha, IL–IN–WI
Places Rated Score: 427
Places Rated Rank: 127

Kansas City, MO–KS
Concert Radio
KCUR-FM, KSTR-FM, KXTR-FM
Lively Arts Calendar
Touring Artists Bookings, 119 dates
Resident Ensembles, 235 dates
Coterie Theatre
Independence Symphony
Kansas City Chamber Orchestra
Kansas City Civic Orchestra
Kansas City Symphony
Liberty Symphony
Lyric Opera of Kansas City
Missouri Repertory Theatre
Northland Symphony
Philharmonia of Greater Kansas City
State Ballet of Missouri
Unicorn Theatre
Art Museums and Galleries, 3
Nelson–Atkins Museum of Art
Public Libraries
68 branches, 4,189,386 volumes
342,688 books added/year
Places Rated Score: 714
Places Rated Rank: 73

Kenosha, WI
Concert Radio
WGTD-FM
Lively Arts Calendar
Touring Artists Bookings, 13 dates
Resident Ensemble, 4 dates
Kenosha Symphony
Art Museums and Galleries, 1
Kenosha Public Museum
Public Libraries
6 branches, 235,860 volumes
16,391 books added/year
MC Access: Chicago–Gary–Kenosha, IL–IN–WI
Places Rated Score: 222
Places Rated Rank: 231

Killeen–Temple, TX
Concert Radio
In Waco media market
Lively Arts Calendar
Touring Artists Bookings, 18 dates
Public Libraries
9 branches, 291,524 volumes
8,617 books added/year
Places Rated Score: 52
Places Rated Rank: 340

Kitchener, ON
Concert Radio
CFCA-FM, CKWR-FM
Lively Arts Calendar
Touring Artists Bookings, 267 dates
Resident Ensembles, 104 dates
Kitchener–Waterloo Chamber Orchestra
Kitchener–Waterloo Symphony
Art Museums and Galleries, 6
Kitchener–Waterloo Art Gallery
Public Libraries
19 branches, 803,482 volumes
62,551 books added/year
MC Access: Toronto–Ontario Shore, ON
Places Rated Score: 931
Places Rated Rank: 51

Knoxville, TN
Concert Radio
 WUOT-FM
Lively Arts Calendar
 Touring Artists Bookings, 50 dates
 Resident Ensembles, 291 dates
  Cincinnati–Knoxville–New Orleans City
   Ballet
  Clarence Brown Theatre Company
  Knoxville Opera
  Knoxville Symphony
  Oak Ridge Symphony Orchestra
Art Museums and Galleries, 3
 Knoxville Museum of Art
Public Libraries
 29 branches, 1,179,358 volumes
 64,097 books added/year
Places Rated Score: 597
Places Rated Rank: 88

Kokomo, IN
Concert Radio
 In Indianapolis media market
Lively Arts Calendar
 Resident Ensemble, 8 dates
  Kokomo Symphony
Public Libraries
 7 branches, 319,992 volumes
 22,416 books added/year
Places Rated Score: 238
Places Rated Rank: 218

La Crosse, WI–MN
Concert Radio
 WHLA-FM
Lively Arts Calendar
 Touring Artists Bookings, 23 dates
 Resident Ensemble, 6 dates
  La Crosse Symphony
Art Museums and Galleries, 1
 Pump House Regional Center for the Arts
Public Libraries
 12 branches, 478,126 volumes
 22,239 books added/year
Places Rated Score: 265
Places Rated Rank: 195

Lafayette, IN
Concert Radio
 WBAA-AM
Lively Arts Calendar
 Touring Artists Bookings, 15 dates
 Resident Ensembles, 32 dates
  Lafayette Symphony
  Purdue University Theatre
Art Museums and Galleries, 2
 Greater Lafayette Museum of Art
Public Libraries
 9 branches, 353,341 volumes
 34,319 books added/year
Places Rated Score: 355
Places Rated Rank: 149

Lafayette, LA
Concert Radio
 KRVS-FM
Lively Arts Calendar
 Touring Artists Bookings, 75 dates
 Resident Ensemble, 4 dates
  Acadiana Symphony
Art Museums and Galleries, 1
Public Libraries
 22 branches, 546,131 volumes
 26,114 books added/year
Places Rated Score: 203
Places Rated Rank: 239

Lake Charles, LA
Lively Arts Calendar
 Resident Ensemble, 8 dates
  Lake Charles Symphony
Public Libraries
 13 branches, 272,615 volumes
 16,353 books added/year
Places Rated Score: 104
Places Rated Rank: 315

Lake County, IL
Concert Radio
 WNIZ-FM
Lively Arts Calendar
 Touring Artists Bookings, 32 dates
 Resident Ensembles, 44 dates
  Lake Forest Symphony
  Sinfonetta Americana
  Waukegan Symphony
  Zion Chamber Orchestra
Public Libraries
 20 branches, 1,728,421 volumes
 122,959 books added/year
MC Access: Chicago–Gary–Kenosha,
 IL–IN–WI
Places Rated Score: 633
Places Rated Rank: 85

Lakeland–Winter Haven, FL
Concert Radio
 In Tampa media market
Lively Arts Calendar
 Touring Artists Bookings, 55 dates
 Resident Ensemble, 7 dates
  Imperial Symphony
Art Museums and Galleries, 1
 Polk Museum of Art
Public Libraries
 7 branches, 388,295 volumes
 15,097 books added/year
Places Rated Score: 147
Places Rated Rank: 285

Lancaster, PA
Concert Radio
 In Harrisburg media market
Lively Arts Calendar
 Touring Artists Bookings, 19 dates
 Resident Ensembles, 79 dates
  Actor's Company of Pennsylvania
  Fulton Opera House
  Independent Eye
  Lancaster Opera
  Lancaster Symphony
Art Museums and Galleries, 2
Public Libraries
 15 branches, 514,254 volumes
 15,184 books added/year
Places Rated Score: 233
Places Rated Rank: 224

Lansing–East Lansing, MI
Concert Radio
 WKAR-FM
Lively Arts Calendar
 Touring Artists Bookings, 55 dates
 Resident Ensembles, 95 dates
  BoarsHead: Michigan Public Theatre
  Greater Lansing Symphony
  MSU Theatre
  Opera Company of Mid-Michigan
Art Museums and Galleries, 2
 Kresge Art Museum
Public Libraries
 30 branches, 1,001,386 volumes
 41,157 books added/year
Places Rated Score: 343
Places Rated Rank: 154

Laredo, TX
Lively Arts Calendar
 Resident Ensemble,
  Laredo Philharmonic, 17 dates
Public Libraries
 1 branch, 69,321 volumes
 4,394 books added/year
Places Rated Score: 46
Places Rated Rank: 343

Las Cruces, NM
Concert Radio
 KRWG-FM
Lively Arts Calendar
 Touring Artists Bookings, 12 dates
 Resident Ensemble, 12 dates
  Las Cruces Symphony, 12
Art Museums and Galleries, 1
Public Libraries
 2 branches, 136,043 volumes
 9,137 books added/year
Places Rated Score: 136
Places Rated Rank: 294

Las Vegas, NV–AZ
Concert Radio
 KNPR-FM, KTPH-FM
Lively Arts Calendar
 Touring Artists Bookings, 132 dates
 Resident Ensembles, 70 dates
  Las Vegas Civic Symphony
  Nevada Dance Theatre
  Nevada Opera Theatre
  Nevada Symphony
Art Museums and Galleries, 3
 Las Vegas Art Museum
Public Libraries
 39 branches, 1,124,303 volumes
 100,204 books added/year
Places Rated Score: 454
Places Rated Rank: 115

Lawrence, KS
Concert Radio
 KANU-FM
Lively Arts Calendar
 Touring Artists Bookings, 26 dates
Art Museums and Galleries, 1
 University of Kansas, Spencer Gallery
Public Libraries
 3 branches, 211,333 volumes
 12,772 books added/year
Places Rated Score: 225
Places Rated Rank: 229

Lawton, OK
Concert Radio
 In Wichita Falls media market
Lively Arts Calendar
 Resident Ensemble, 12 dates
  Lawton Philharmonic
Public Libraries
 1 branch, 123,173 volumes
 4,898 books added/year
Places Rated Score: 56
Places Rated Rank: 337

Lewiston–Auburn, ME
Lively Arts Calendar
 Touring Artists Bookings, 25 dates
 Resident Ensemble, 53 dates
  Portland Symphony
Public Libraries
 8 branches, 266,383 volumes
 10,662 books added/year
Places Rated Score: 190
Places Rated Rank: 253

Lexington, KY
Concert Radio
WEKU-FM, WUKY-FM
Lively Arts Calendar
Touring Artists Bookings, 66 dates
Resident Ensemble, 90 dates
Lexington Philharmonic
Art Museums and Galleries, 1
Public Libraries
13 branches, 753,139 volumes
51,685 books added/year
Places Rated Score: 329
Places Rated Rank: 159

Lima, OH
Concert Radio
WGLE-FM
Lively Arts Calendar
Touring Artists Bookings, 24 dates
Resident Ensemble, 15 dates
Lima Symphony
Public Libraries
15 branches, 511,797 volumes
29,723 books added/year
Places Rated Score: 229
Places Rated Rank: 227

Lincoln, NE
Concert Radio
KUCV-FM
Lively Arts Calendar
Touring Artists Bookings, 73 dates
Resident Ensembles, 74 dates
Lincoln Symphony
Nebraska Chamber Orchestra
Nebraska Jazz Orchestra
Nebraska Repertory Theatre
University of Nebraska Theatre
Art Museums and Galleries, 3
University of Nebraska, Sheldon Gallery
Public Libraries
7 branches, 534,840 volumes
27,714 books added/year
Places Rated Score: 421
Places Rated Rank: 129

Little Rock–North Little Rock, AR
Concert Radio
KLRE-FM, KUAR-FM
Lively Arts Calendar
Touring Artists Bookings, 17 dates
Resident Ensembles, 132 dates
Arkansas Repertory Theatre
Arkansas Symphony
Arts Center Children's Theatre
Ballet Arkansas
Opera Theatre at Wildwood
Art Museums and Galleries, 1
Arkansas Arts Center
Public Libraries
15 branches, 847,316 volumes
44,384 books added/year
Places Rated Score: 283
Places Rated Rank: 183

London, ON
Concert Radio
CBBL-FM, CIXX-FM
Lively Arts Calendar
Resident Ensembles, 113 dates
Fanshawe Community Orchestra
Orchestra London Canada
The Grand Theatre
Art Museums and Galleries, 3
London Regional Art Gallery
Public Libraries
36 branches, 1,196,594 volumes

110,852 books added/year
Places Rated Score: 539
Places Rated Rank: 97

✓ Long Island, NY
Concert Radio
WPBX-FM, WRHU-FM, WUSB-FM
Lively Arts Calendar
Touring Artists Bookings, 484 dates
Resident Ensembles, 111 dates
Arena Players Repertory Theatre
Eglevsky Ballet
Forest Hills Symphony of Queens
Long Island Philharmonic
Massapequa Philharmonic
Nassau Symphony
National Grand Opera
New York Virtuosi Chamber Symphony
Queens Festival Orchestra
Sound Symphony
Stony Brook Symphony
Art Museums and Galleries, 8
Fine Arts Museum of Long Island
Parrish Art Museum
Public Libraries
129 branches, 12,896,023 volumes
1,209,208 books added/year
MC Access: New York–Northern New
Jersey–Long Island, NY–NJ–CT
Places Rated Score: 2,370
Places Rated Rank: 9

Longview–Marshall, TX
Lively Arts Calendar
Touring Artists Bookings, 7 dates
Resident Ensembles, 8 dates
Longview Symphony
Marshall Symphony
Art Museums and Galleries, 1
Longview Museum and Arts Center
Public Libraries
5 branches, 326,797 volumes
7,874 books added/year
Places Rated Score: 105
Places Rated Rank: 313

✓ Los Angeles–Long Beach, CA
Concert Radio
KCSN-FM, KKGO-FM, KUSC-FM
Lively Arts Calendar
Touring Artists Bookings, 1,874 dates
Symphony Orchestras, 435 dates
Antelope Valley Symphony
Beach Cities Symphony
Beverly Hills Symphony
Brentwood Westwood Symphony
Carson Dominguez Hills Symphony
Chamber Orchestra of the South Bay
Claremont Chamber Orchestra
Claremont Symphony
Glendale Symphony
Hollywood Bowl Orchestra
Japan America Symphony, Los
Angeles
Long Beach Symphony
Los Angeles Baroque Orchestra
Los Angeles Chamber Orchestra
Los Angeles Doctors Symphony
Los Angeles Mozart Orchestra
Los Angeles Performing Arts Orchestra
Los Angeles Philharmonic
Los Angeles Solo Repertory Orchestra
Los Angeles Symphonic Jazz
Orchestra
Marina Del Rey Westchester Symphony
Palisades Symphony
Pasadena Symphony
San Fernando Valley Symphony

Santa Monica Symphony
Opera Companies, 122 dates
Casa Italiana Opera
Guild Opera
Long Beach Civic Light Opera
Long Beach Opera
Los Angeles Music Center Opera
Opera A La Carte
Santa Cecilia Opera
Ballet Companies, 116 dates
Ballet Folklorico De Mexico
Los Angeles Chamber Ballet
Los Angeles Classical Ballet
Professional Theatres, 440 dates
Bilingual Foundation of the Arts
California Repertory Theatre
CAST Theatre
Colony Studio Theatre
East West Players
L.A. Theatre Works
Los Angeles Theatre Center
Mark Taper Forum
Odyssey Theatre Ensemble
Santa Monica Playhouse
Stages Trilingual Theatre
Theatre Forty
Theatre West
USC Theatre
West Coast Ensemble
Art Museums and Galleries, 33
California State University at Long Beach
Art Museum
Hebrew Union College Skirball Museum
J. Paul Getty Museum
Long Beach Museum of Art
Los Angeles County Museum of Art
Wight Art Gallery, UCLA
Public Libraries
222 branches, 16,552,724 volumes
1,134,240 books added/year
MC Access: Los Angeles–Riverside–
Orange County, CA
Places Rated Score: 4,977
Places Rated Rank: 2

Louisville, KY–IN
Concert Radio
WFPK-FM, WUOL-FM
Lively Arts Calendar
Touring Artists Bookings, 95 dates
Resident Ensembles, 278 dates
Actors Theatre
Kentucky Opera
Kentucky Shakespeare Festival
Louisville Ballet
Stage One: Children's Theatre
The Louisville Orchestra
Art Museums and Galleries, 1
J. B. Speed Art Museum
Public Libraries
29 branches, 1,429,613 volumes
94,894 books added/year
Places Rated Score: 521
Places Rated Rank: 102

Lubbock, TX
Concert Radio
KOHM-FM
Lively Arts Calendar
Touring Artists Bookings, 220 dates
Resident Ensemble, 5 dates
Lubbock Symphony
Public Libraries
5 branches, 382,293 volumes
12,099 books added/year
Places Rated Score: 278
Places Rated Rank: 187

Lynchburg, VA
Concert Radio
In Roanoke media market
Lively Arts Calendar
Touring Artists Bookings, 6 dates
Resident Ensemble, 5 dates
Lynchburg Symphony
Art Museums and Galleries, 2
Maier Museum of Art
Public Libraries
12 branches, 367,699 volumes
22,840 books added/year
Places Rated Score: 225
Places Rated Rank: 229

Macon, GA
Lively Arts Calendar
Touring Artists Bookings, 35 dates
Resident Ensemble, 13 dates
Macon Symphony
Art Museums and Galleries, 1
Museum of Arts and Sciences
Public Libraries
20 branches, 573,092 volumes
27,458 books added/year
Places Rated Score: 191
Places Rated Rank: 252

Madison, WI
Concert Radio
WERN-FM
Lively Arts Calendar
Touring Artists Bookings, 97 dates
Resident Ensembles, 111 dates
Madison Opera
Madison Repertory Theatre
Madison Symphony
University of Wisconsin Theatre
Wisconsin Chamber Orchestra
Art Museums and Galleries, 3
Elvehjem Museum of Art
Madison Art Center
Public Libraries
25 branches, 1,126,584 volumes
65,919 books added/year
Places Rated Score: 527
Places Rated Rank: 98

Manchester–Nashua, NH
Concert Radio
In Boston media market
Lively Arts Calendar
Touring Artists Bookings, 36 dates
Resident Ensembles, 180 dates
American Stage Festival
Nashua Symphony
New England Marionette Opera
New Hampshire Philharmonic
Peterborough Players
Art Museums and Galleries, 2
Currier Gallery of Art
Public Libraries
33 branches, 1,095,534 volumes
48,197 books added/year
MC Access: Boston–New
Bedford–Nashua, MA–NH
Places Rated Score: 722
Places Rated Rank: 71

Mansfield, OH
Concert Radio
WOSV-FM
Lively Arts Calendar
Touring Artists Bookings, 4 dates
Resident Ensemble, 20 dates
Mansfield Symphony
Art Museums and Galleries, 1
Mansfield Art Center

Public Libraries
12 branches, 523,315 volumes
37,608 books added/year
Places Rated Score: 290
Places Rated Rank: 178

McAllen–Edinburg–Mission, TX
Lively Arts Calendar
Touring Artists Bookings, 4 dates
Resident Ensembles, 40 dates
Ballet Fiesta Mexicana
Valley Symphony
Art Museums and Galleries, 4
Public Libraries
10 branches, 456,893 volumes
19,537 books added/year
Places Rated Score: 91
Places Rated Rank: 325

Medford–Ashland, OR
Concert Radio
KSMF-FM, KSOR-FM
Lively Arts Calendar
Touring Artists Bookings, 5 dates
Resident Ensembles, 91 dates
Oregon Shakespeare Festival
Rogue Opera
Rogue Valley Symphony
Art Museums and Galleries, 1
Public Libraries
15 branches, 322,181 volumes
14,806 books added/year
Places Rated Score: 243
Places Rated Rank: 213

Melbourne–Titusville–Palm Bay, FL
Concert Radio
In Orlando media market
Lively Arts Calendar
Touring Artists Bookings, 52 dates
Resident Ensembles, 29 dates
Brevard Symphony
Florida Space Coast Philharmonic
Art Museums and Galleries, 1
Brevard Art Center and Museum
Public Libraries
13 branches, 768,470 volumes
49,526 books added/year
Places Rated Score: 248
Places Rated Rank: 207

Memphis, TN–AR–MS
Concert Radio
WKNO-FM
Lively Arts Calendar
Touring Artists Bookings, 9 dates
Resident Ensembles, 201 dates
Memphis Concert Ballet
Memphis Symphony
Opera Memphis
Playhouse on the Square
Southern Opera Theatre
Art Museums and Galleries, 2
Dixon Gallery
Public Libraries
46 branches, 1,964,124 volumes
110,403 books added/year
Places Rated Score: 416
Places Rated Rank: 133

Merced, CA
Concert Radio
In Fresno media market
Lively Arts Calendar
Resident Ensemble, 6 dates
Merced Symphony
Art Museums and Galleries, 1

Public Libraries
1 branch, 339,023 volumes
8,181 books added/year
Places Rated Score: 101
Places Rated Rank: 316

Miami, FL
Concert Radio
WTMI-FM
Lively Arts Calendar
Touring Artists Bookings, 117 dates
Resident Ensembles, 270 dates
Ballet Concerto Miami
Ballet Spectacular
Greater Miami Opera
Miami City Ballet
Miami Chamber Symphony
New World Symphony
North Miami Beach Opera
North Miami Beach Symphony
Art Museums and Galleries, 7
Lowe Art Museum, University of Miami
Public Libraries
35 branches, 3,116,776 volumes
256,109 books added/year
MC Access: Miami–Fort Lauderdale, FL
Places Rated Score: 945
Places Rated Rank: 49

✓ **Milwaukee–Waukesha, WI**
Concert Radio
WFME-FM, WFMR-FM, WHAD-FM
Lively Arts Calendar
Touring Artists Bookings, 180 dates
Symphony Orchestras, 244 dates
Milwaukee Chamber Orchestra
Milwaukee Symphony
Music Under the Stars Orchestra
Waukesha Symphony
Opera Companies, 157 dates
Florentine Opera
Milwaukee Opera
Skylight Opera Theatre
Ballet Companies, 59 dates
Bauer Contemporary Ballet
Milwaukee Ballet
Professional Theatres, 140 dates
First Stage Milwaukee
Milwaukee Chamber Theatre
Milwaukee Public Theatre
Milwaukee Repertory Theatre
Theatre X
Art Museums and Galleries, 6
Milwaukee Art Museum
Public Libraries
52 branches, 4,699,837 volumes
215,355 books added/year
MC Access: Milwaukee–Racine, WI
Places Rated Score: 1,248
Places Rated Rank: 35

✓ **Minneapolis–St. Paul, MN–WI**
Concert Radio
KNOW-FM, KSJN-FM, KUOM-AM
Lively Arts Calendar
Touring Artists Bookings, 348 dates
Symphony Orchestras, 479 dates
Bloomington Symphony
Civic Orchestra of Minneapolis
Lakewood Orchestra
Metropolitan Symphony
Minneapolis Chamber Symphony
Minnesota Orchestra
Minnetonka Symphony
Saint Paul Chamber Orchestra
Opera Companies, 93 dates
Minnesota Opera
Minnesota Opera on Tour

North Star Opera
Professional Theatres, 264 dates
  Children's Theatre Company
  Cricket Theatre
  Great American History Theatre
  Guthrie Theatre
  Illusion Theatre
  Mixed Blood Theatre Company
  Park Square Theatre Company
  Penumbra Theatre Company
  Playwright's Center
  Red Eye Collaboration
  Theatre de la Jeune Lune
  University of Minnesota Theatre
Art Museums and Galleries, 6
  Minneapolis Institute of Arts
  Minnesota Museum of Art
  Walker Art Center
Public Libraries
  131 branches, 6,182,400 volumes
  465,493 books added/year
Places Rated Score: 1,660
Places Rated Rank: 18

Mobile, AL
Concert Radio
  WHIL-FM
Lively Arts Calendar
  Touring Artists Bookings, 48 dates
  Resident Ensemble, 5 dates
    Mobile Opera
Art Museums and Galleries, 2
  Eastern Shore Art Center
Public Libraries
  20 branches, 687,431 volumes
  40,192 books added/year
Places Rated Score: 235
Places Rated Rank: 222

Modesto, CA
Concert Radio
  KADV-FM
Lively Arts Calendar
  Resident Ensemble, 20 dates
    Modesto Symphony
Art Museums and Galleries, 1
  Oakdale Museum
Public Libraries
  3 branches, 607,321 volumes
  25,595 books added/year
Places Rated Score: 131
Places Rated Rank: 301

✓ Monmouth-Ocean, NJ
Concert Radio
  WSLT-FM
Lively Arts Calendar
  Touring Artists Bookings, 142 dates
  Resident Ensembles, 29 dates
    Garden State Philharmonic Symphony
    Metro Lyric Opera
    Monmouth Symphony
    New Jersey State Orchestra
    Paradise Chamber Orchestra
Art Museums and Galleries, 1
Public Libraries
  56 branches, 2,907,298 volumes
  184,238 books added/year
MC Access: New York–Northern New
  Jersey–Long Island, NY–NJ–CT
Places Rated Score: 1,384
Places Rated Rank: 27

Monroe, LA
Concert Radio
  KEDM-FM
Lively Arts Calendar
  Touring Artists Bookings, 11 dates

Art Museums and Galleries, 1
Public Libraries
  5 branches, 191,947 volumes
  18,099 books added/year
Places Rated Score: 186
Places Rated Rank: 260

Montgomery, AL
Lively Arts Calendar
  Touring Artists Bookings, 5 dates
  Resident Ensembles, 70 dates
    Alabama Shakespeare Festival
    Montgomery Ballet
    Montgomery Symphony
Art Museums and Galleries, 1
Public Libraries
  20 branches, 391,544 volumes
  19,836 books added/year
Places Rated Score: 192
Places Rated Rank: 249

✓ Montreal, PQ
Concert Radio
  CITE-FM, CJAD-AM
Lively Arts Calendar
  Touring Artists Bookings, 305 dates
  Symphony Orchestras, 300 dates
    McGill Chamber Orchestra
    Montreal Chamber Orchestra
    Musici de Montreal
    Orchestre Metropolitain
    Orchestre Symphonique de Laval
    Orchestre Symphonique de Montreal
  Opera Company, 36 dates
    l'Opera de Montreal
  Ballet Companies, 200 dates
    Les Ballets Jazz de Montreal
    Les Grands Ballets Canadiens
  Professional Theatres:
    Beton Blues
    Black Theatre Workshop
    Carbone 14
    Centaur Theatre Company
    Festival Theatre des Ameriques
    Groupe de la Veilee
    Momentum
    Nouveau Theatre Experimental
    Nouvelle Compagnie Theatrale
    Playwrights' Workshop
    Productions Chocolat Show
    Theatre d'Aujourd'hui
    Theatre de Campagnie Carrousel
    Theatre de la Ligue Nationale
      d'Improvisation
    Theatre de la Manufacture
    Theatre de Quat'sous
    Theatre du Cafe de la Place
    Theatre du Nouveau Monde
    Theatre du Rideau Vert
    Theatre du Vieux-Terrebonne
    Theatre Experimental des Femmes
    Theatre Ubu
    Theatre Zoopsie
Art Museums and Galleries, 17
  Musee d'Art Contemporain
  Musee Des Beaux-Arts De Montreal
Public Libraries
  196 branches, 6,788,011 volumes
  483,708 books added/year
Places Rated Score: 2,072
Places Rated Rank: 11

Muncie, IN
Concert Radio
  WBST-FM
Lively Arts Calendar
  Touring Artists Bookings, 25 dates
  Resident Ensemble, 8 dates

    Muncie Symphony
Art Museums and Galleries, 1
  Ball State University Museum of Art
Public Libraries
  6 branches, 243,089 volumes
  13,838 books added/year
Places Rated Score: 197
Places Rated Rank: 246

Myrtle Beach, SC
Concert Radio
  In Florence media market
Lively Arts Calendar
  Touring Artists Bookings, 5 dates
  Resident Ensemble, 5 dates
    Long Bay Symphony
Art Museums and Galleries, 5
Public Libraries
  6 branches, 218,405 volumes
  13,774 books added/year
Places Rated Score: 94
Places Rated Rank: 321

Naples, FL
Concert Radio
  In Fort Myers media market
Lively Arts Calendar
  Touring Artists Bookings, 104 dates
  Resident Ensemble, 130 dates
    Naples Philharmonic
Public Libraries
  6 branches, 209,616 volumes
  22,890 books added/year
Places Rated Score: 366
Places Rated Rank: 146

Nashville, TN
Concert Radio
  WPLN-FM
Lively Arts Calendar
  Touring Artists Bookings, 216 dates
  Resident Ensembles, 244 dates
    Nashville Ballet
    Nashville Opera
    Nashville Symphony
    Tennessee Opera Theatre
    Tennessee Repertory Theatre
Art Museums and Galleries, 4
  Fisk University Museum of Art
  Vanderbilt Fine Arts Gallery
Public Libraries
  37 branches, 1,340,042 volumes
  48,588 books added/year
Places Rated Score: 707
Places Rated Rank: 75

New Bedford-Fall River-Attleboro, MA
Concert Radio
  In Providence media market
Lively Arts Calendar
  Touring Artists Bookings, 70 dates
  Resident Ensembles, 10 dates
    Greater Fall River Symphony
    New Bedford Symphony
Art Museums and Galleries, 1
Public Libraries
  31 branches, 1,606,514 volumes
  45,089 books added/year
MC Access: Boston–New
  Bedford–Nashua, MA–NH
Places Rated Score: 492
Places Rated Rank: 111

New Haven-Meriden, CT
Lively Arts Calendar
  Touring Artists Bookings, 128 dates

Resident Ensembles, 250 dates
American Sinfonietta
Connecticut Chamber Orchestra
Hamden Symphony
Long Wharf Theatre
Meriden Symphony
New Haven Symphony
Orchestra New England
Shubert New Haven Opera
Wallingford Symphony
Yale Philharmonia Orchestra
Yale Repertory Theatre
Art Museums and Galleries, 3
Yale University Art Gallery
Public Libraries
24 branches, 1,692,752 volumes
67,280 books added/year
MC Access: New York–Northern New
Jersey–Long Island, NY–NJ–CT
Places Rated Score: 705
Places Rated Rank: 76

New London–Norwich, CT–RI
Lively Arts Calendar
Touring Artists Bookings, 66 dates
Resident Ensemble, 6 dates
Eastern Connecticut Symphony
Art Museums and Galleries, 3
Lyman Allyn Art Museum
Public Libraries
17 branches, 634,026 volumes
29,574 books added/year
Places Rated Score: 362
Places Rated Rank: 148

New Orleans, LA
Concert Radio
WTUL-FM, WWNO-FM
Lively Arts Calendar
Touring Artists Bookings, 120 dates
Resident Ensembles, 128 dates
Cincinnati–Knoxville–New Orleans City
Ballet
Jefferson Symphony
Louisiana Philharmonic
New Orleans Opera
Art Museums and Galleries, 1
New Orleans Museum of Art
Public Libraries
53 branches, 2,435,942 volumes
120,169 books added/year
Places Rated Score: 390
Places Rated Rank: 142

✓ New York, NY
Concert Radio
WKCR-FM, WNCN-FM, WNYC-FM,
WQXR-AM, WQXR-FM
Lively Arts Calendar
Touring Artists Bookings, 2,581 dates
Symphony Orchestras, 1,035 dates
American Composers Orchestra
American Jazz Orchestra
American Symphony
Atlantic Sinfonietta
Bloomingdale Chamber Orchestra
Bronx Arts Ensemble Orchestra
Bronx Symphony
Brooklyn Neighborhood Chamber
Orchestra
Brooklyn Philharmonic
Clarion Music Society
Concordia: A Chamber Symphony
Cosmopolitan Symphony
Empire State Pops Orchestra
Goliard Chamber Orchestra
Greenwich Village Orchestra
Hunter Symphony

Juilliard Orchestra
Julius Grossman Orchestra
Jupiter Symphony
Manhattan Symphony
Mozart Festival Orchestra
New Orchestra of Westchester
New Repertory Ensemble
New York Chamber Orchestra
New York Chamber Symphony of the
92nd Street Y
New York City Symphony
New York Doctors' Orchestral Society
New York Orchestral Society
New York Philharmonic
New York Pops Orchestra
New York Pro Arte Chamber Orchestra
New York Sinfonia Orchestra
Opera Orchestra of New York
Orchestra of St. Luke's
Orpheus Chamber Orchestra
Philharmonia Virtuosi
Queens Symphony
Queensborough Orchestra
Rockaway-Five Towns Symphony
Society
Staten Island Symphony
Symphony for United Nations
The Boston Group
The Little Orchestra Society of New
York
The Riverside Symphony
Washington Square Chamber
Orchestra
West End Symphony
Westchester Conservatory Orchestra
Westchester Symphony
Opera Companies, 1,008 dates
After Dinner Opera
Amato Opera Theatre
American Chamber Opera
American International Lyric Theatre
Apollo Opera
Bel Canto
Bronx Opera
Brooklyn Lyric Opera
Il Piccolo Teatro Dell' Opera
Juilliard Opera Center
l'Opera Français de New York
La Gran Scena Opera
Liederkranz Opera Theatre
Magic Circle Chamber Opera
Manhattan Opera
Marcel Achille Opera
Measured Breaths Theatre
Metropolitan Opera
Music Theatre Group
New Rochelle Opera
New York City Opera
New York City Opera National
New York Gilbert and Sullivan Players
New York Grand Opera
Opera at the Academy
Opera Ebony
Opera Northeast
Opera Orchestra of New York
Operaworks
PALA Opera
Queens Opera
Regina Opera
Rockland Opera
Theatre Rococo
Village Light Opera
Ballet Companies, 695 dates
American Ballet Theatre
Ballet Manhattan
Balletmet
Feld Ballets

New York City Ballet
The Joffrey Ballet
Professional Theatres, 1,008 dates
Acting Company
American Place Theatre
Circle Repertory Company
Classic Stage Company
Coney Island USA
Emeline Theatre
Ensemble Studio Theatre
HOME for Contemporary Theatre
INTAR Hispanic Arts Center
Irondale Ensemble Project
Jean Cocteau Repertory Theatre
Lincoln Center Theatre
Love Creek Productions
Mabou Mines
Manhattan Class Company
Manhattan Theatre Club
Mettawee River Company
Music-Theatre Group
New Dramatists
New Federal Theatre
New York Shakespeare Festival
New York Theatre Workshop
Ontological-Hysteric Theatre
Open Eye: New Stagings
Pan Asian Repertory Theatre
Penguin Repertory Company
Ping Chong and Company
Playwrights Horizons
Quaigh Theatre
Repertorio Espanol
Roundabout Theatre Company
Second Stage Theatre
Shaliko Company
Sidewalks Theatre
Street Theatre
TADA!
Talking Band
Thalia Spanish Theatre
Theatre by the Blind
Theatre for a New Audience
Theatre for the New City
Theatreworks-USA
Vineyard Theatre
Women's Project and Productions
Wooster Group
Young Playwrights Festival
Art Museums and Galleries, 52
American Craft Museum
Brooklyn Museum
Frick Collection
Metropolitan Museum of Art
Museum of Modern Art
Pierpont Morgan Library and Art Museum
Solomon R. Guggenheim Museum
Public Libraries
282 branches, 29,907,685 volumes
1,830,221 books added/year
MC Access: New York–Northern New
Jersey–Long Island, NY–NJ–CT
Places Rated Score: 9,681
Places Rated Rank: 1

✓ Newark–Jersey City, NJ
Concert Radio
WWNJ-FM
Lively Arts Calendar
Touring Artists Bookings, 262 dates
Symphony Orchestras, 218 dates
Colonial Symphony
Hudson Chamber Symphony
Livingston Symphony
Masterwork Orchestra
Metropolitan Orchestra
New Jersey Symphony

New Philharmonic of New Jersey
Nutley Symphony Society
Plainfield Symphony
South Orange Symphony
Summit Symphony
Westfield Symphony
Opera Companies, 26 dates
   Community Opera
   Lubo Opera
   New Jersey State Opera
   Opera At Florham
Ballet Companies, 195 dates
   Garden State Ballet
   New Jersey Ballet
Professional Theatres, 36 dates
   Growing Stage Theatre
   New Jersey Shakespeare Festival
Art Museums and Galleries, 3
   Hoboken Museum of Art
Public Libraries
   124 branches, 9,368,610 volumes
   399,458 books added/year
MC Access: New York–Northern New
   Jersey–Long Island, NY–NJ–CT
Places Rated Score: 2,098
Places Rated Rank: 10

Norfolk–Virginia Beach–Newport News, VA–NC
Concert Radio
   WFOS-FM
Lively Arts Calendar
   Touring Artists Bookings, 131 dates
   Resident Ensembles: 215 dates
      Virginia Beach Pops
      Virginia Beach Symphony
      Virginia Opera
      Virginia Stage Company
      Virginia Symphony
      Williamsburg Symphonia
Art Museums and Galleries, 11
   Chrysler Museum
Public Libraries
   43 branches, 2,981,591 volumes
   212,668 books added/year
Places Rated Score: 1,040
Places Rated Rank: 41

✓ Northern New Jersey, NJ
Concert Radio
   In New York media market
Lively Arts Calendar
   Touring Artists Bookings, 127 dates
   Resident Ensembles, 38 dates
      Ars Musica Orchestra
      Bergen Philharmonic
      Irine Fokine Ballet
      Ridgewood Gilbert and Sullivan Opera
      Wayne Chamber Orchestra
Art Museums and Galleries, 3
   African Art Museum
   Hiram Blauvelt Art Museum
Public Libraries
   99 branches, 5,393,646 volumes
   285,494 books added/year
MC Access: New York–Northern New
   Jersey–Long Island, NY–NJ–CT
Places Rated Score: 1,538
Places Rated Rank: 22

✓ Oakland, CA
Concert Radio
   KSMC-FM
Lively Arts Calendar 976 total
   Touring Artists Bookings, 588 dates
   Symphony Orchestras
      Berkeley Symphony
      Berkeley University Symphony

California Chamber Orchestra
California Symphony
Diablo Symphony
Diablo Valley Philharmonic
Livermore Amador Symphony
Oakland East Bay Symphony
Philharmonic Society of
   Fremont–Newark
Prometheus Symphony
San Francisco Chamber Orchestra
Opera Companies
   Berkeley Opera
   Oakland Opera
Ballet Companies
   Berkeley Ballet Theater
   Oakland Ballet
Professional Theatres
   Berkeley Repertory Theatre
   California Shakespeare Festival
   CitiArts Theatre
   Oakland Ensemble Theatre
Art Museums and Galleries, 11
   Oakland Museum
   University of California Art Museum
Public Libraries
   54 branches, 4,282,438 volumes
   274,431 books added/year
MC Access: San Francisco–Oakland–San
   Jose, CA
Places Rated Score: 2,032
Places Rated Rank: 12

Ocala, FL
Concert Radio
   In Orlando media market
Art Museums and Galleries, 1
   Appleton Museum of Art
Public Libraries
   10 branches, 141,498 volumes
   14,607 books added/year
Places Rated Score: 118
Places Rated Rank: 305

Odessa–Midland, TX
Lively Arts Calendar
   Resident Ensemble, 35 dates
      Midland–Odessa Symphony
Art Museums and Galleries, 1
   Art Institute for the Permian Basin
Public Libraries
   3 branches, 371,022 volumes
   11,650 books added/year
Places Rated Score: 134
Places Rated Rank: 297

Oklahoma City, OK
Concert Radio
   KCSC-FM, KGOU-FM, KROU-FM
Lively Arts Calendar
   Touring Artists Bookings, 21 dates
   Resident Ensembles, 251 dates
      Ballet Oklahoma
      Cimarron Circuit Opera
      Lyric Theatre of Oklahoma
      Oklahoma City Philharmonic
      Oklahoma Festival Ballet
Art Museums and Galleries, 9
   Oklahoma City Art Museum
Public Libraries
   24 branches, 1,331,095 volumes
   83,745 books added/year
Places Rated Score: 808
Places Rated Rank: 60

Olympia, WA
Concert Radio
   In Seattle media market
Lively Arts Calendar
   Touring Artists Bookings, 28 dates

Resident Ensemble, 5 dates
   Olympia Symphony
Art Museums and Galleries, 2
Public Libraries
   5 branches, 349,967 volumes
   21,419 books added/year
MC Access: Seattle–Tacoma–Bremerton,
   WA
Places Rated Score: 295
Places Rated Rank: 177

Omaha, NE–IA
Concert Radio
   KIOS-FM, KIWR-FM, KVNO-FM
Lively Arts Calendar
   Touring Artists Bookings, 6 dates
   Resident Ensembles, 505 dates
      Ballet Omaha
      Circle Theatre
      Emmy Gifford Children's Theatre
      Nebraska Theatre Caravan
      Omaha Magic Theatre
      Omaha Symphony
      Omaha Symphony Chamber Orchestra
      Opera Omaha
Art Museums and Galleries, 1
   Joslyn Art Museum
Public Libraries
   32 branches, 1,228,654 volumes
   65,623 books added/year
Places Rated Score: 661
Places Rated Rank: 81

✓ Orange County, CA
Concert Radio
   In Los Angeles media market
Lively Arts Calendar
   Touring Artists Bookings, 202 dates
   Symphony Orchestras, 153 dates
      Capistrano Valley Symphony
      Chapman Symphony
      Cypress Pops Orchestra
      Mozart Camerata
      Orange County Symphony
      Pacific Symphony
      Saddleback Chamber Players
      South Coast Symphony
   Opera Companies, 62 dates
      Fullerton Civic Light Opera
      Opera Pacific
   Professional Theatres, 124 dates
      Grove Shakespeare Festival
      Laguna Playhouse
      South Coast Repertory Theatre
      University of California Theatre
Art Museums and Galleries, 7
   Laguna Art Museum
Public Libraries
   50 branches, 4,335,586 volumes
   380,088 books added/year
MC Access: Los Angeles–Riverside–
   Orange County, CA
Places Rated Score: 1,591
Places Rated Rank: 19

✓ Orange County, NY
Concert Radio
   In New York media market
Lively Arts Calendar
   Touring Artists Bookings, 50 dates
Art Museums and Galleries, 1
Public Libraries
   22 branches, 747,803 volumes
   96,628 books added/year
MC Access: New York–Northern New
   Jersey–Long Island, NY–NJ–CT
Places Rated Score: 1,372
Places Rated Rank: 28

Orlando, FL
Concert Radio
  WMFE-FM, WPRK-FM, WUCF-FM
Lively Arts Calendar
  Touring Artists Bookings, 27 dates
  Resident Ensembles, 224 dates
    Florida Symphony
    Orlando Opera
    Southern Ballet Theatre
Art Museums and Galleries, 8
  Charles H. Morse Museum of American
    Art
  Orlando Museum of Art
Public Libraries
  20 branches, 2,136,409 volumes
  257,801 books added/year
Places Rated Score: 837
Places Rated Rank: 57

Oshawa, ON
Concert Radio
  CKQT-FM
Lively Arts Calendar
  Resident Ensemble, 6 dates
    Oshawa Symphony
Art Museums and Galleries, 2
Public Libraries
  6 branches, 458,684 volumes
  21,651 books added/year
MC Access: Toronto-Ontario Shore, ON
Places Rated Score: 491
Places Rated Rank: 112

✓ Ottawa-Hull, ON-PQ
Concert Radio
  CFMO-FM, CKCU-FM
Lively Arts Calendar
  Touring Artists Bookings, 278 dates
  Resident Ensembles, 285 dates
    Great Canadian Theatre Company
    Groupe Derives Urbaines
    National Arts Centre Orchestra
    Nepean Symphony
    Odyssey Theatre
    Opera Lyra Ottawa
    Ottawa Ballet
    Ottawa Symphony
    Theatre de L'Ile
Art Museums and Galleries, 11
  Canadian Museum of Contemporary
    Photography
  National Gallery of Canada
Public Libraries
  84 branches, 2,065,216 volumes
  156,739 books added/year
Places Rated Score: 1,316
Places Rated Rank: 32

Owensboro, KY
Concert Radio
  WKWC-FM
Lively Arts Calendar
  Touring Artists Bookings, 5 dates
  Resident Ensemble, 15 dates
    Owensboro Symphony
Art Museums and Galleries, 1
Public Libraries
  1 branch, 127,225 volumes
  5,590 books added/year
Places Rated Score: 133
Places Rated Rank: 298

Panama City, FL
Concert Radio
  WKGC-FM
Lively Arts Calendar
  Touring Artists Bookings, 15 dates

Public Libraries
  11 branches, 143,956 volumes
  8,571 books added/year
Places Rated Score: 77
Places Rated Rank: 327

Parkersburg-Marietta, WV-OH
Concert Radio
  WMRT-FM
Lively Arts Calendar
  Touring Artists Bookings, 4 dates
  Resident Ensemble, 100 dates
    Parkersburg-Wheeling Ballet
Art Museums and Galleries, 1
Public Libraries
  8 branches, 231,697 volumes
  15,643 books added/year
Places Rated Score: 258
Places Rated Rank: 200

Pensacola, FL
Concert Radio
  WUWF-FM
Lively Arts Calendar
  Touring Artists Bookings, 148 dates
  Resident Ensemble, 9 dates
    Pensacola Symphony
Art Museums and Galleries, 3
  Pensacola Museum of Art
Public Libraries
  5 branches, 266,305 volumes
  12,782 books added/year
Places Rated Score: 343
Places Rated Rank: 154

Peoria-Pekin, IL
Concert Radio
  WCBU-FM
Lively Arts Calendar
  Touring Artists Bookings, 100 dates
  Resident Ensembles, 31 dates
    Peoria Ballet
    Peoria Civic Opera
    Peoria Symphony
Art Museums and Galleries, 1
  Lakeview Museum of Arts and Sciences
Public Libraries
  36 branches, 1,460,278 volumes
  40,707 books added/year
Places Rated Score: 300
Places Rated Rank: 172

✓ Philadelphia, PA-NJ
Concert Radio
  WFLN-FM, WHYY-FM
Lively Arts Calendar
  Touring Artists Bookings, 492 dates
  Symphony Orchestras, 467 dates
    Academy Chamber Orchestra
    Ambler Symphony
    Concerto Soloists Chamber Orchestra
    Delaware Valley Philharmonic
    Haddonfield Symphony
    Harrisburg Symphony
    Haverford-Bryn Mawr Symphony
    Kennett Symphony
    Lansdowne Symphony
    Philadelphia Chamber Players
    Philadelphia Doctors' Symphony
    Philadelphia Orchestra
    Pottstown Symphony
    South Jersey Symphony
    Warminster Symphony
    West Jersey Chamber Symphony
  Opera Companies, 27 dates
    Little Lyric Opera Theatre
    Opera Company of Philadelphia
    Pennsylvania Opera Theater

  Ballet Companies, 100 dates
    Pennsylvania Ballet
    The National Ballet of New Jersey
  Professional Theatres, 180 dates
    Arden Theatre Company
    Cheltenham Center for the Arts
    Festival Theatre for New Plays
    Novel Stages
    People's Theatre Company
    Philadelphia Drama Guild
    Philadelphia Theatre Company
    Riverside Theatre
    Society Hill Playhouse
    Temple University Theatre
    Wilma Theatre
Art Museums and Galleries, 25
  La Salle University Art Museum
  Pennsylvania Academy of Fine Arts
  Philadelphia Museum of Art
Public Libraries
  216 branches, 11,681,582 volumes
  646,950 books added/year
MC Access: Philadelphia-Wilmington-
  Atlantic City, PA-NJ-DE-MD
Places Rated Score: 2,733
Places Rated Rank: 8

✓ Phoenix-Mesa, AZ
Concert Radio
  KONC-FM
Lively Arts Calendar
  Touring Artists Bookings, 612 dates
  Resident Ensembles, 201 dates
    Actors Theatre of Phoenix
    Arizona Opera
    Arizona Theatre Company
    Ballet Arizona
    Childsplay
    Fine Arts Orchestra
    Mesa Symphony
    Metro Pops Orchestra
    Phoenix Symphony
    Scottsdale Symphony
    Sun Cities Symphony
Art Museums and Galleries, 10
  Heard Museum
  Phoenix Art Museum
Public Libraries
  51 branches, 4,243,180 volumes
  358,547 books added/year
Places Rated Score: 1,541
Places Rated Rank: 21

Pine Bluff, AR
Concert Radio
  In Little Rock media market
Lively Arts Calendar
  Resident Ensemble, 2 dates
    Pine Bluff Symphony
Art Museums and Galleries, 1
  Arts and Science Center for Southeast
    Arkansas
Public Libraries
  3 branches, 153,160 volumes
  5,239 books added/year
Places Rated Score: 113
Places Rated Rank: 308

Pittsburgh, PA
Concert Radio
  WQED-FM, WWCS-AM
Lively Arts Calendar
  Touring Artists Bookings, 158 dates
  Symphony Orchestras, 385 dates
    American Waterways Wind Orchestra
    Carnegie-Mellon Philharmonic
    Edgewood Symphony

McKeesport Symphony
Orchestra Nova
Pittsburgh Civic Orchestra
Pittsburgh Symphony
River City Brass Band
Westmoreland Symphony
Opera Companies, 89 dates
Civic Light Opera
Opera Theater of Pittsburgh
Pittsburgh Opera Theater
Ballet Company, 72 dates
Pittsburgh Ballet Theatre
Professional Theatres, 68 dates
City Theatre Company
Pittsburgh Public Theatre
Three Rivers Shakespeare Festival
Art Museums and Galleries, 8
Carnegie
Frick Art Museum
Westmoreland Museum of Art
Public Libraries
124 branches, 5,206,033 volumes
173,912 books added/year
Places Rated Score: 1,244
Places Rated Rank: 36

Pittsfield, MA
Lively Arts Calendar
Touring Artists Bookings, 58 dates
Resident Ensembles, 54 dates
Berkshire Festival Theatre
Berkshire Opera
Berkshire Public Theatre
Art Museums and Galleries, 3
Norman Rockwell Museum at Stockbridge
Public Libraries
10 branches, 457,911 volumes
12,229 books added/year
Places Rated Score: 402
Places Rated Rank: 137

Portland, ME
Lively Arts Calendar
Touring Artists Bookings, 36 dates
Resident Ensemble, 24 dates
Portland Stage Company
Art Museums and Galleries, 5
Portland Museum of Art
Public Libraries
21 branches, 662,743 volumes
23,031 books added/year
Places Rated Score: 428
Places Rated Rank: 126

Portland, OR
Concert Radio
KBPS-AM, KBPS-FM
Lively Arts Calendar
Touring Artists Bookings, 28 dates
Resident Ensembles, 227 dates
Maryhurst Symphony
Oregon Ballet Theatre
Oregon Stage Company
Oregon Symphony
Portland Opera
Portland Repertory Theatre
Art Museums and Galleries, 3
Portland Art Museum
Public Libraries
50 branches, 2,437,946 volumes
196,754 books added/year
MC Access: Portland–Salem–Vancouver,
OR–WA
Places Rated Score: 597
Places Rated Rank: 88

Portsmouth–Dover–Rochester, NH
Concert Radio
In Boston media market

Lively Arts Calendar
Touring Artists Bookings, 67 dates
Resident Ensembles, 31 dates
New Hampshire Symphony
Sea Coast Repertory Company
Art Museums and Galleries, 2
Art Gallery University of New Hampshire
Public Libraries
54 branches, 1,075,093 volumes
55,279 books added/year
MC Access: Boston–New
Bedford–Nashua, MA–NH
Places Rated Score: 661
Places Rated Rank: 81

Providence–Warwick–Cranston, RI
Concert Radio
WLKW-AM
Lively Arts Calendar
Touring Artists Bookings, 33 dates
Resident Ensembles, 102 dates
American Ballet
Festival Ballet
Rhode Island Civic Orchestra
Rhode Island Philharmonic
State Ballet of Rhode Island
Trinity Repertory Theatre
Art Museums and Galleries, 6
Museum of Art, Rhode Island School of
Design
Warwick Museum
Public Libraries
59 branches, 2,895,466 volumes
107,218 books added/year
Places Rated Score: 559
Places Rated Rank: 96

Provo–Orem, UT
Concert Radio
KBYU-FM
Lively Arts Calendar
Touring Artists Bookings, 16 dates
Resident Ensemble, 10 dates
Utah Valley Symphony
Art Museums and Galleries, 1
Public Libraries
9 branches, 486,767 volumes
19,869 books added/year
Places Rated Score: 142
Places Rated Rank: 289

Pueblo, CO
Concert Radio
In Colorado Springs media market
Lively Arts Calendar
Touring Artists Bookings, 38 dates
Resident Ensemble, 6 dates
Pueblo Symphony
Art Museums and Galleries, 2
Public Libraries
3 branches, 326,330 volumes
16,991 books added/year
Places Rated Score: 281
Places Rated Rank: 184

Punta Gorda, FL
Concert Radio
In Fort Myers media market
Lively Arts Calendar
Touring Artists Bookings, 15 dates
Public Libraries
6 branches, 130,707 volumes
6,309 books added/year
Places Rated Score: 48
Places Rated Rank: 342

Quebec City, PQ
Concert Radio
CBV-FM, CKIA-FM, CKRL-FM

Lively Arts Calendar
Touring Artists Bookings, 15 dates
Resident Ensembles, 158 dates
Opera de Quebec
Orchestre Symphonique de Quebec
Theatre de la Bordee
Theatre de la Commune
Theatre du Bois de Coulonge
Theatre Niveau Parking
Theatre Repere
Art Museums and Galleries, 5
Musee du Quebec
Public Libraries
11 branches, 1,119,949 volumes
80,965 books added/year
Places Rated Score: 525
Places Rated Rank: 100

Racine, WI
Concert Radio
In Milwaukee media market
Lively Arts Calendar
Resident Ensemble, 11 dates
Racine Symphony
Art Museums and Galleries, 1
Charles A. Wurstum Museum of Fine Arts
Public Libraries
5 branches, 336,485 volumes
22,983 books added/year
MC Access: Milwaukee–Racine, WI
Places Rated Score: 314
Places Rated Rank: 165

Raleigh–Durham–Chapel Hill, NC
Concert Radio
WCPE-FM, WUNC-FM
Lively Arts Calendar
Touring Artists Bookings, 258 dates
Resident Ensembles, 319 dates
National Opera
North Carolina Symphony
PlayMakers Repertory Company
Raleigh Symphony
The Durham Symphony
Triangle Opera Theater
Art Museums and Galleries, 7
Ackland Art Museum
Duke University Museum of Art
North Carolina Museum of Art
Public Libraries
33 branches, 1,351,727 volumes
100,746 books added/year
Places Rated Score: 1,036
Places Rated Rank: 42

Rapid City, SD
Concert Radio
KBHE-FM
Lively Arts Calendar
Touring Artists Bookings, 30 dates
Resident Ensemble, 6 dates
Black Hills Symphony
Art Museums and Galleries, 2
Dahl Fine Arts Center
Public Libraries
3 branches, 150,731 volumes
5,170 books added/year
Places Rated Score: 198
Places Rated Rank: 244

Reading, PA
Concert Radio
In Philadelphia media market
Lively Arts Calendar
Touring Artists Bookings, 73 dates
Resident Ensembles, 21 dates
Berks Grand Opera
Reading Symphony

Art Museums and Galleries, 2
Reading Public Museum and Art Gallery
Public Libraries
17 branches, 438,853 volumes
14,355 books added/year
Places Rated Score: 236
Places Rated Rank: 221

Redding, CA
Concert Radio
In Chico media market
Lively Arts Calendar
Touring Artists Bookings, 13 dates
Resident Ensemble, 4 dates
Shasta Symphony
Art Museums and Galleries, 1
Redding Museum of Art and History
Public Libraries
3 branches, 234,709 volumes
634 books added/year
Places Rated Score: 71
Places Rated Rank: 334

Regina, SK
Lively Arts Calendar
Touring Artists Bookings, 142 dates
Resident Ensembles, 183 dates
Globe Theatre
Regina Symphony
Art Museums and Galleries, 5
Dunlop Art Gallery
Public Libraries
10 branches, 745,127 volumes
58,096 books added/year
Places Rated Score: 728
Places Rated Rank: 69

Reno, NV
Concert Radio
KUNR-FM
Lively Arts Calendar
Touring Artists Bookings, 4 dates
Resident Ensembles, 48 dates
Nevada Opera
Reno Chamber Orchestra
Reno Philharmonic
Sierra Community Orchestra
Art Museums and Galleries, 1
Public Libraries
7 branches, 430,000 volumes
26,526 books added/year
Places Rated Score: 198
Places Rated Rank: 244

Richland-Kennewick-Pasco, WA
Concert Radio
KFAE-FM
Lively Arts Calendar
Resident Ensemble, 5 dates
Mid-Columbia Symphony
Public Libraries
11 branches, 379,303 volumes
20,739 books added/year
Places Rated Score: 138
Places Rated Rank: 291

Richmond-Petersburg, VA
Concert Radio
WCVE-FM
Lively Arts Calendar
Touring Artists Bookings, 41 dates
Resident Ensembles, 362 dates
Concert Ballet of Virginia
Richmond Philharmonic
Richmond Symphony
State Ballet of Virginia
Theatre IV
Theatre Virginia

Art Museums and Galleries, 3
Virginia Museum of Fine Arts
Public Libraries
39 branches, 2,357,918 volumes
125,027 books added/year
Places Rated Score: 690
Places Rated Rank: 77

✓ Riverside-San Bernardino, CA
Concert Radio
KPSC-FM, KPSL-AM
Lively Arts Calendar
Touring Artists Bookings, 261 dates
Resident Ensembles, 90 dates
Inland Empire Symphony
Redlands Symphony
Riverside Ballet Theatre
Riverside County Philharmonic
Riverside Opera
San Bernardino Civic Light Opera
West Coast Opera Theatre
Art Museums and Galleries, 7
California Museum of Photography
Palm Springs Desert Museum
Riverside Art Museum
Public Libraries
70 branches, 3,170,115 volumes
235,791 books added/year
MC Access: Los Angeles-Riverside-
Orange County, CA
Places Rated Score: 1,362
Places Rated Rank: 29

Roanoke, VA
Concert Radio
WVTF-FM
Lively Arts Calendar
Touring Artists Bookings, 9 dates
Resident Ensembles, 63 dates
Mill Mountain Theatre
Opera Roanoke
Roanoke Symphony
Art Museums and Galleries, 2
Roanoke Museum of Fine Arts
Public Libraries
17 branches, 727,028 volumes
34,598 books added/year
Places Rated Score: 323
Places Rated Rank: 162

Rochester, MN
Concert Radio
KLSE-FM
Lively Arts Calendar
Touring Artists Bookings, 3 dates
Resident Ensemble, 13 dates
Rochester Symphony
Art Museums and Galleries, 1
Public Libraries
3 branches, 34,735 volumes
1,016 books added/year
Places Rated Score: 75
Places Rated Rank: 329

Rochester, NY
Concert Radio
WRUR-FM, WXXI-FM
Lively Arts Calendar
Touring Artists Bookings, 145 dates
Resident Ensembles, 246 dates
Eastman Philharmonia
GeVa Theatre
Opera Theatre of Rochester
Penfield Symphony
Rochester Chamber Orchestra
Rochester Philharmonic
Art Museums and Galleries, 4

University of Rochester Memorial Art
Gallery
Public Libraries
83 branches, 3,856,374 volumes
185,041 books added/year
Places Rated Score: 763
Places Rated Rank: 65

Rockford, IL
Lively Arts Calendar
Touring Artists Bookings, 45 dates
Resident Ensembles, 44 dates
New American Theater
Rockford Symphony
Art Museums and Galleries, 2
Rockford Art Museum
Public Libraries
21 branches, 946,501 volumes
39,584 books added/year
Places Rated Score: 308
Places Rated Rank: 170

Rocky Mount, NC
Concert Radio
In Raleigh-Durham media market
Lively Arts Calendar
Resident Ensemble, 5 dates
Tar River Orchestral Society
Art Museums and Galleries, 2
Public Libraries
3 branches, 216,027 volumes
11,495 books added/year
Places Rated Score: 188
Places Rated Rank: 256

Sacramento, CA
Concert Radio
KSAC-AM, KXPR-FM
Lively Arts Calendar
Touring Artists Bookings, 88 dates
Resident Ensembles, 311 dates
Camellia Symphony
Fantasy Theatre
Phares Theatre Ballet
Sacramento Ballet
Sacramento Opera
Sacramento Symphony
Sacramento Theatre Company
Art Museums and Galleries, 2
Crocker Art Museum
Public Libraries
36 branches, 2,320,588 volumes
142,986 books added/year
MC Access: Sacramento-Yolo, CA
Places Rated Score: 620
Places Rated Rank: 86

Saginaw-Bay City-Midland, MI
Concert Radio
WUCX-FM
Lively Arts Calendar
Touring Artists Bookings, 16 dates
Resident Ensembles, 39 dates
Midland Symphony
Northwood Orchestra
Saginaw Symphony
Art Museums and Galleries, 1
Saginaw Art Museum
Public Libraries
22 branches, 1,098,959 volumes
55,936 books added/year
Places Rated Score: 243
Places Rated Rank: 213

St. Catharines-Niagara, ON
Lively Arts Calendar
Touring Artists Bookings, 30 dates

Resident Ensembles, 76 dates
Niagara Symphony
Shaw Festival
Theatre Beyond Words
Art Museums and Galleries, 2
Public Libraries
22 branches, 1,129,414 volumes
78,001 books added/year
MC Access: Toronto–Ontario Shore, ON
Places Rated Score: 458
Places Rated Rank: 113

St. Cloud, MN
Concert Radio
KSJR-FM
Lively Arts Calendar
Touring Artists Bookings, 28 dates
Resident Ensembles, 10 dates
Quite Light Opera
St. Cloud Symphony
Art Museums and Galleries, 1
Public Libraries
30 branches, 569,538 volumes
25,831 books added/year
Places Rated Score: 246
Places Rated Rank: 210

Saint John, NB
Concert Radio
CBN-FM
Lively Arts Calendar
Resident Ensemble, 25 dates
Symphony New Brunswick
Art Museums and Galleries, 3
New Brunswick Museum
Public Libraries
9 branches, 362,494 volumes
6,938 books added/year
Places Rated Score: 230
Places Rated Rank: 226

St. John's, NF
Concert Radio
CHMR-FM
Lively Arts Calendar
Touring Artists Bookings, 112 dates
Resident Ensembles, 152 dates
Newfoundland Symphony
RCA Theatre
Rising Tide Theatre
Art Museums and Galleries, 1
Public Libraries
28 branches, 299,188 volumes
13,199 books added/year
Places Rated Score: 276
Places Rated Rank: 189

St. Joseph, MO
Concert Radio
In Kansas City media market
Lively Arts Calendar
Touring Artists Bookings, 12 dates
Resident Ensembles, 8 dates
Missouri Western Philharmonia
St. Joseph Symphony
Art Museum and Gallery
Albrecht–Kemper Museum of Art
Public Libraries
5 branches, 347,175 volumes
16,404 books added/year
Places Rated Score: 239
Places Rated Rank: 217

✓ St. Louis, MO–IL
Concert Radio
KFUO-FM, KWMU-FM
Lively Arts Calendar

Touring Artists Bookings, 455 dates
Resident Ensembles, 452 dates
Alton Symphony
Black Repertory Company
Brentwood Symphony
Gateway Festival Orchestra
Kirkwood Symphony
Metro Theatre Company
Opera Theatre of St. Louis
Repertory Theatre of St. Louis
St. Louis Ballet
St. Louis Philharmonic
St. Louis String Ensemble
St. Louis Symphony
Theatre Factory
Art Museums and Galleries, 10
Laumeier Sculpture Park and Museum
Saint Louis Art Museum
Public Libraries
104 branches, 7,471,893 volumes
309,286 books added/year
Places Rated Score: 1,529
Places Rated Rank: 23

Salem, OR
Concert Radio
In Portland media market
Lively Arts Calendar
Touring Artists Bookings, 9 dates
Resident Ensemble, 140 dates
Eugene Ballet
Art Museums and Galleries, 1
Public Libraries
12 branches, 495,683 volumes
26,301 books added/year
MC Access: Portland–Salem–Vancouver, OR–WA
Places Rated Score: 345
Places Rated Rank: 153

Salinas, CA
Concert Radio
KBOQ-FM
Lively Arts Calendar
Touring Artists Bookings, 36 dates
Resident Ensembles, 35 dates
Hidden Valley Opera Ensemble
Monterey Bay Chamber Orchestra
Monterey County Symphony
Art Museums and Galleries, 1
Pacific Grove Art Center
Public Libraries
13 branches, 1,213,270 volumes
49,839 books added/year
Places Rated Score: 257
Places Rated Rank: 201

Salt Lake City–Ogden, UT
Concert Radio
KUER-FM
Lively Arts Calendar
Touring Artists Bookings, 359 dates
Resident Ensembles, 204 dates
Ballet West
Pioneer Theatre Company
Rocky Mountain Symphony
Salt Lake Acting Company
Salt Lake Opera Theatre
Utah Opera
Wasatch Community Symphony
Art Museums and Galleries, 4
Utah Museum of Fine Arts
Public Libraries
31 branches, 2,217,668 volumes
145,348 books added/year
Places Rated Score: 892
Places Rated Rank: 54

San Angelo, TX
Lively Arts Calendar
Touring Artists Bookings, 4 dates
Resident Ensemble, 12 dates
San Angelo Symphony
Art Museums and Galleries, 1
San Angelo Museum of Fine Arts
Public Libraries
3 branches, 231,215 volumes
9,146 books added/year
Places Rated Score: 158
Places Rated Rank: 280

San Antonio, TX
Concert Radio
KPAC-FM, KRTU-FM
Lively Arts Calendar
Touring Artists Bookings, 200 dates
Resident Ensembles, 110 dates
Mid-Texas Symphony
San Antonio Symphony
Art Museums and Galleries, 4
San Antonio Museum of Art
Public Libraries
29 branches, 2,686,325 volumes
109,377 books added/year
Places Rated Score: 589
Places Rated Rank: 91

✓ San Diego, CA
Concert Radio
KFSD-FM
Lively Arts Calendar
Touring Artists Bookings, 395 dates
Resident Ensembles, 519 dates
Blackfriars Theatre
California Ballet
East County Jewish Community Symphony
La Jolla Playhouse
La Jolla Symphony
Lamb's Players Theatre
North Coast Symphony
Old Globe Theatre
San Diego Chamber Orchestra
San Diego Civic Light Opera
San Diego Comic Opera
San Diego Opera
San Diego Repertory Theatre
San Diego Symphony
Art Museums and Galleries, 6
San Diego Museum of Art
Public Libraries
66 branches, 3,593,208 volumes
240,766 books added/year
Places Rated Score: 1,304
Places Rated Rank: 33

✓ San Francisco, CA
Concert Radio
KDFC-AM, KDFC-FM, KKHI-AM, KKHI-FM
Lively Arts Calendar
Touring Artists Bookings, 249 dates
Symphony Orchestras, 334 dates
ARTEA Chamber Orchestra
Conservatory of Music Orchestra
Marin Symphony
Peninsula Symphony
Philharmonia Baroque Orchestra
Redwood Symphony
San Francisco Chamber Symphony
San Francisco Symphony
The Wonen's Philharmonic
Opera Companies, 379 dates
Marin Opera
Marin–Sonoma Civic Light Opera
Opera Center Singers

Pocket Opera
San Francisco Opera
San Francisco Opera Center
Western Opera Theater
Ballet Companies, 332 dates
  Khadra
  Lines Contemporary Ballet
  Marin Ballet
  Peninsula Ballet Theatre
  San Francisco Ballet
  Ballet Celeste-International
  Theatre Ballet of San Francisco
Professional Theatres, 188 dates
  A Traveling Jewish Theatre
  Amazing Stage
  American Conservatory Theatre
  Eureka Theatre Company
  Magic Theatre
  Marin Theatre Company
  New Conservatory Children's Theatre
  San Francisco Shakespeare Festival
  Theatre Rhinoceros
Art Museums and Galleries, 17
Asian Art Museum of San Francisco
Cartoon Art Museum
Fine Arts Museums of San Francisco
Friends of Photography Ansel Adams
  Center
San Francisco Museum of Modern Art
Public Libraries
58 branches, 4,942,985 volumes
273,054 books added/year
MC Access: San Francisco–Oakland–San
  Jose, CA
Places Rated Score: 2,877
Places Rated Rank: 6

✓ **San Jose, CA**
Concert Radio
In San Francisco media market
Lively Arts Calendar
Touring Artists Bookings, 389 dates
Resident Ensembles, 393 dates
  California Theatre Center
  Nova Vista Symphony
  Opera San Jose
  San Jose Civic Light Opera
  San Jose Repertory Theatre
  San Jose Symphony
  Santa Clara Ballet
  South Valley Symphony
  Stanford Symphony
  TheatreWorks
  West Bay Opera
Art Museums and Galleries, 7
San Jose Museum of Art
Public Libraries
37 branches, 3,319,678 volumes
266,929 books added/year
MC Access: San Francisco–Oakland–San
  Jose, CA
Places Rated Score: 1,685
Places Rated Rank: 17

**San Luis Obispo–Atascadero–Paso
  Robles, CA**
Concert Radio
KCBX-FM
Lively Arts Calendar
Touring Artists Bookings, 47 dates
Resident Ensemble, 10 dates
  San Luis Obispo County Symphony
Art Museums and Galleries, 1
Public Libraries
7 branches, 341,355 volumes
21,876 books added/year
Places Rated Score: 201
Places Rated Rank: 240

**Santa Barbara–Santa
  Maria–Lompoc, CA**
Concert Radio
KDB-FM, KFAC-FM
Lively Arts Calendar
Touring Artists Bookings, 77 dates
Resident Ensembles, 68 dates
  Music Academy of the West Summer
    Festival
  PCPA Theatrefest
  Santa Barbara Symphony
  West Coast Symphony
Art Museums and Galleries, 4
San Fernando Mission
Public Libraries
10 branches, 575,854 volumes
35,603 books added/year
Places Rated Score: 439
Places Rated Rank: 121

Santa Cruz–Watsonville, CA
Concert Radio
KUSP-FM
Lively Arts Calendar
Touring Artists Bookings, 78 dates
Resident Ensembles, 24 dates
  Santa Cruz County Symphony
  Shakespeare Santa Cruz
Art Museums and Galleries, 2
Art Museum Santa Cruz County
Public Libraries
8 branches, 458,940 volumes
24,861 books added/year
MC Access: San Francisco–Oakland–San
  Jose, CA
Places Rated Score: 682
Places Rated Rank: 78

Santa Fe, NM
Concert Radio
In Albuquerque media market
Lively Arts Calendar
Touring Artists Bookings, 44 dates
Resident Ensembles, 84 dates
  New Mexico Repertory Theatre
  Orchestra of Santa Fe
  Santa Fe Opera
  Santa Fe Symphony
Art Museums and Galleries, 5
Governor's Gallery
Santuario De Nuestra Senora De
  Guadalupe
Public Libraries
6 branches, 333,181 volumes
16,016 books added/year
Places Rated Score: 501
Places Rated Rank: 110

Santa Rosa, CA
Concert Radio
In San Francisco media market
Lively Arts Calendar
Touring Artists Bookings, 16 dates
Resident Ensembles, 75 dates
  Redwood Empire Ballet
  Rohnert Park Symphony
  Santa Rosa Symphony
Art Museums and Galleries, 3
Public Libraries
9 branches, 563,351 volumes
38,213 books added/year
MC Access: San Francisco–Oakland–San
  Jose, CA
Places Rated Score: 579
Places Rated Rank: 93

Sarasota–Bradenton, FL
Concert Radio
WSPB-AM

Lively Arts Calendar
Touring Artists Bookings, 107 dates
Resident Ensembles, 145 dates
  Asolo Center for Performing Arts
  Florida West Coast Symphony
  Florida Studio Theatre
  Sarasota Ballet of Florida
  Sarasota Manatee Community
    Orchestra
  Sarasota Opera
  Venice Symphony
Art Museums and Galleries, 2
Ringling Museum of Art
Public Libraries
7 branches, 523,183 volumes
41,774 books added/year
Places Rated Score: 429
Places Rated Rank: 125

Saskatoon, SK
Concert Radio
CFMC-FM
Lively Arts Calendar
Touring Artists Bookings, 5 dates
Resident Ensembles, 63 dates
  Nightcap Theatre
  Persephone Theatre
  Saskatoon Opera
  Saskatoon Symphony
  25th Street Theatre
Art Museums and Galleries, 11
Mendel Art Gallery
Public Libraries
45 branches, 846,390 volumes
96,568 books added/year
Places Rated Score: 1,002
Places Rated Rank: 45

Savannah, GA
Concert Radio
WSVH-FM
Lively Arts Calendar
Touring Artists Bookings, 5 dates
Resident Ensemble, 45 dates
  Savannah Symphony
Art Museums and Galleries, 1
Public Libraries
19 branches, 512,693 volumes
24,997 books added/year
Places Rated Score: 195
Places Rated Rank: 247

**Scranton–Wilkes-Barre–Hazelton,
  PA**
Concert Radio
WVIA-FM
Lively Arts Calendar
Touring Artists Bookings, 145 dates
Resident Ensembles, 147 dates
  Ballet Theatre Pennsylvania
  Bloomsburg Theatre Ensemble
  Northeastern Pennsylvania
    Philharmonic
Art Museums and Galleries, 2
Everhart Museum
Public Libraries
33 branches, 1,068,661 volumes
35,785 books added/year
Places Rated Score: 448
Places Rated Rank: 120

✓ **Seattle–Bellevue–Everett, WA**
Concert Radio
KING-FM, KUOW-FM
Lively Arts Calendar
Touring Artists Bookings, 241 dates
Symphony Orchestras, 183 dates
  Bellevue Philharmonic

Cascade Symphony
Everett Symphony
Northwest Chamber Orchestra
Orchestra Seattle
Seattle Symphony
Opera Companies, 66 dates
Civic Light Opera
Seattle Opera
Ballet Companies, 110 dates
Olympic Ballet Theatre
Pacific Northwest Ballet
Professional Theatres, 264 dates
A Contemporary Theatre
Bathhouse Theatre
Empty Space Theatre
Intiman Theatre Company
New City Theatre and Art Center
Seattle Children's Theatre
Seattle Group Theatre
Seattle Repertory Theatre
Taproot Theatre Company
University of Washington Theatre
Art Museums and Galleries, 7
Bellevue Art Museum
Henry Art Gallery
Public Libraries
117 branches, 5,308,403 volumes
472,802 books added/year
MC Access: Seattle–Tacoma–Bremerton,
WA
Places Rated Score: 1,506
Places Rated Rank: 24

Sharon, PA
Concert Radio
WSAJ-FM
Lively Arts Calendar
Touring Artists Bookings, 2 dates
Resident Ensembles, 17 dates
Greenville Symphony
Romanenko Chamber Players
Public Libraries
5 branches, 168,999 volumes
4,224 books added/year
Places Rated Score: 54
Places Rated Rank: 338

Sheboygan, WI
Concert Radio
In Milwaukee media market
Lively Arts Calendar
Touring Artists Bookings, 15 dates
Resident Ensemble, 6 dates
Sheboygan Symphony
Art Museums and Galleries, 1
John M. Kohler Arts Center
Public Libraries
8 branches, 425,047 volumes
19,259 books added/year
Places Rated Score: 255
Places Rated Rank: 203

Sherbrooke, PQ
Lively Arts Calendar
Touring Artists Bookings, 25 dates
Resident Ensembles, 42 dates
Orchestre Symphonique de Sherbrooke
Theatre du Sang Neuf
Art Museums and Galleries, 2
Public Libraries
3 branches, 248,774 volumes
12,093 books added/year
Places Rated Score: 185
Places Rated Rank: 262

Sherman–Denison, TX
Concert Radio
In Dallas media market

Lively Arts Calendar
Touring Artists Bookings, 37 dates
Resident Ensemble, 5 dates
Sherman Symphony
Public Libraries
6 branches, 255,535 volumes
4,993 books added/year
Places Rated Score: 93
Places Rated Rank: 322

Shreveport–Bossier City, LA
Concert Radio
KDAW-FM
Lively Arts Calendar
Touring Artists Bookings, 42 dates
Resident Ensembles, 45 dates
Shreveport Opera
Shreveport Symphony
Art Museums and Galleries, 1
Public Libraries
35 branches, 643,170 volumes
33,751 books added/year
Places Rated Score: 226
Places Rated Rank: 228

Sioux City, IA–NE
Concert Radio
KWIT-FM
Lively Arts Calendar
Touring Artists Bookings, 4 dates
Resident Ensemble, 12 dates
Sioux City Symphony
Art Museums and Galleries, 1
Public Libraries
9 branches, 321,178 volumes
13,486 books added/year
Places Rated Score: 182
Places Rated Rank: 266

Sioux Falls, SD
Concert Radio
KCSD-FM, KRSD-FM
Lively Arts Calendar
Resident Ensemble, 8 dates
South Dakota Symphony
Art Museums and Galleries, 1
Civic Fine Arts Center
Public Libraries
15 branches, 360,576 volumes
18,243 books added/year
Places Rated Score: 186
Places Rated Rank: 260

South Bend, IN
Concert Radio
WSND-FM
Lively Arts Calendar
Touring Artists Bookings, 54 dates
Resident Ensemble, 20 dates
South Bend Symphony
Art Museums and Galleries, 3
Snite Museum, University of Notre Dame
Public Libraries
12 branches, 655,178 volumes
70,459 books added/year
Places Rated Score: 506
Places Rated Rank: 108

Spokane, WA
Concert Radio
KSVY-AM, KSVY-FM
Lively Arts Calendar
Touring Artists Bookings, 6 dates
Resident Ensembles, 59 dates
Interplayers Ensemble
Spokane Symphony
Art Museums and Galleries, 2
Public Libraries
13 branches, 940,754 volumes

56,360 books added/year
Places Rated Score: 319
Places Rated Rank: 163

Springfield, IL
Concert Radio
WSSU-FM
Lively Arts Calendar
Touring Artists Bookings, 30 dates
Resident Ensembles, 42 dates
Illinois Chamber Orchestra
Springfield Ballet
Springfield Symphony
Art Museums and Galleries, 2
Public Libraries
12 branches, 457,297 volumes
20,059 books added/year
Places Rated Score: 277
Places Rated Rank: 188

Springfield, MA
Concert Radio
In Worcester media market
Lively Arts Calendar
Touring Artists Bookings, 49 dates
Resident Ensembles, 59 dates
Commonwealth Opera
Springfield Symphony
Art Museums and Galleries, 4
Jasper Rand Art Museum
Public Libraries
43 branches, 2,167,285 volumes
81,852 books added/year
Places Rated Score: 452
Places Rated Rank: 117

Springfield, MO
Concert Radio
KSMU-FM
Lively Arts Calendar
Touring Artists Bookings, 18
Resident Ensembles, 53 dates
Springfield Ballet
Springfield Regional Opera
Springfield Symphony
Art Museums and Galleries, 1
Public Libraries
8 branches, 485,534 volumes
19,847 books added/year
Places Rated Score: 192
Places Rated Rank: 249

✓ Stamford–Norwalk, CT
Lively Arts Calendar
Touring Artists Bookings, 246 dates
Resident Ensembles, 154 dates
Boston Post Road Stage
Connecticut Ballet Theatre
Connecticut Grand Opera
Connecticut Philharmonic
Greenwich Symphony
New England Lyric Operetta
Norwalk Symphony
Stamford Chamber Orchestra
Stamford Symphony
Stamford Theatre Works
Symphony on the Sound
Art Museums and Galleries, 3
Public Libraries
17 branches, 1,593,757 volumes
111,665 books added/year
MC Access: New York–Northern New
Jersey–Long Island, NY–NJ–CT
Places Rated Score: 1,870
Places Rated Rank: 14

State College, PA
Concert Radio
WPSU-FM

Lively Arts Calendar
  Touring Artists Bookings, 30 dates
  Resident Ensembles, 33 dates
    Nittany Valley Symphony
    Penn State Philharmonic
    PSU Theatre Company
Art Museums and Galleries, 2
  Palmer Museum of Art, Penn State
    University
Public Libraries
  4 branches, 197,460 volumes
  8,701 books added/year
Places Rated Score: 231
Places Rated Rank: 225

Steubenville–Weirton, OH–WV
Concert Radio
  In Wheeling media market
Lively Arts Calendar
  Touring Artists Bookings, 16 dates
Public Libraries
  13 branches, 329,790 volumes
  21,272 books added/year
Places Rated Score: 167
Places Rated Rank: 274

Stockton–Lodi, CA
Concert Radio
  KUOP-FM
Lively Arts Calendar
  Touring Artists Bookings, 8 dates
  Resident Ensembles, 24 dates
    Stockton Opera
    Stockton Symphony
Art Museums and Galleries, 1
Public Libraries
  11 branches, 929,876 volumes
  43,873 books added/year
Places Rated Score: 170
Places Rated Rank: 271

Sudbury, ON
Lively Arts Calendar
  Resident Ensembles, 71 dates
    Sudbury Symphony
    Sudbury Theatre
Art Museums and Galleries, 1
Public Libraries
  13 branches, 333,943 volumes
  22,504 books added/year
Places Rated Score: 260
Places Rated Rank: 199

Sumter, SC
Concert Radio
  WRJA-FM
Lively Arts Calendar
  Touring Artists Bookings, 7 dates
Art Museums and Galleries, 1
Public Libraries
  1 branch, 108,791 volumes
  4,636 books added/year
Places Rated Score: 101
Places Rated Rank: 316

Syracuse, NY
Concert Radio
  WCNY-FM, WVOA-FM
Lively Arts Calendar
  Touring Artists Bookings, 145 dates
  Resident Ensembles, 334 dates
    Auburn Chamber Orchestra
    Merry-Go-Round Playhouse
    Onondaga Civic Symphony
    Syracuse Opera
    Syracuse Stage
    Syracuse Symphony
Art Museums and Galleries, 8

Everson Museum of Art
  Picker Art Gallery
Public Libraries
  57 branches, 1,759,485 volumes
  127,205 books added/year
Places Rated Score: 1,049
Places Rated Rank: 40

Tacoma, WA
Concert Radio
  In Seattle media market
Lively Arts Calendar
  Touring Artists Bookings, 47 dates
  Resident Ensembles, 66 dates
    Balletacoma
    Tacoma Actors Guild
    Tacoma Opera
    Tacoma Symphony
Art Museums and Galleries, 2
  Tacoma Art Museum
Public Libraries
  28 branches, 1,895,104 volumes
  93,889 books added/year
MC Access: Seattle–Tacoma–Bremerton,
  WA
Places Rated Score: 525
Places Rated Rank: 100

Tallahassee, FL
Concert Radio
  WFSQ-FM
Lively Arts Calendar
  Touring Artists Bookings, 51 dates
  Resident Ensembles, 21 dates
    Florida State University Theatre
    Tallahassee Symphony
Art Museums and Galleries, 1
Public Libraries
  6 branches, 269,034 volumes
  17,927 books added/year
Places Rated Score: 192
Places Rated Rank: 249

✓ **Tampa–St. Petersburg–Clearwater,
FL**
Concert Radio
  WUSE-FM
Lively Arts Calendar
  Touring Artists Bookings, 550 dates
  Resident Ensembles, 252 dates
    American Stage
    Florida Lyric Opera Theatre
    Riverside Theatre
    Spanish Lyric Theatre
    Tampa Bay Opera
    The Florida Orchestra
Art Museums and Galleries, 9
  Salvador Dali Museum
  Scarfone Gallery, University of Tampa
Public Libraries
  50 branches, 2,805,594 volumes
  189,175 books added/year
Places Rated Score: 1,336
Places Rated Rank: 30

Terre Haute, IN
Concert Radio
  WISU-FM
Lively Arts Calendar
  Touring Artists Bookings, 12 dates
  Resident Ensemble, 16 dates
    Terre Haute Symphony
Art Museums and Galleries, 2
Public Libraries
  14 branches, 416,299 volumes
  18,766 books added/year
Places Rated Score: 256
Places Rated Rank: 202

Texarkana, TX–Texarkana, AR
Concert Radio
  KTXK-FM
Lively Arts Calendar
  Touring Artists Bookings, 25 dates
Public Libraries
  3 branches, 168,636 volumes
  10,142 books added/year
Places Rated Score: 109
Places Rated Rank: 311

Thunder Bay, ON
Lively Arts Calendar
  Touring Artists Bookings, 25 dates
  Resident Ensembles, 82 dates
    Magnus Theatre Company Northwest
    Thunder Bay Symphony
Art Museums and Galleries, 1
Public Libraries
  5 branches, 338,203 volumes
  29,789 books added/year
Places Rated Score: 369
Places Rated Rank: 145

Toledo, OH
Concert Radio
  WGTE-FM
Lively Arts Calendar
  Touring Artists Bookings, 83 dates
  Resident Ensembles, 117 dates
    Bowling Green Philharmonia
    Toledo Opera
    Toledo Symphony
Art Museums and Galleries, 1
Public Libraries
  38 branches, 2,483,274 volumes
  163,564 books added/year
Places Rated Score: 514
Places Rated Rank: 104

Topeka, KS
Lively Arts Calendar
  Touring Artists Bookings, 11 dates
  Resident Ensemble, 6 dates
    Topeka Symphony
Art Museums and Galleries, 1
  Gallery of Fine Arts, Topeka Public
    Library
Public Libraries
  3 branches, 371,413 volumes
  33,241 books added/year
Places Rated Score: 271
Places Rated Rank: 192

✓ **Toronto, ON**
Concert Radio
  CBL-FM, CFNY-FM,
  CFRB-AM, CJRT-FM
Lively Arts Calendar
  Touring Artists Bookings, 488 dates
  Symphony Orchestras, 373 dates
    Brampton Symphony
    Cathedral Bluffs Symphony
    Chamber Players of Toronto
    Chinese Philharmonic
    CJRT Radio Orchestra
    East York Symphony
    Esprit Orchestra
    Etobicoke Philharmonic
    Hart House Orchestra
    Mississauga Symphony
    North York Concert Orchestra
    North York Symphony
    Oakville Symphony
    Pro Arte Orchestra
    Royal Conservatory Orchestra
    Scarborough Philharmonic

Tafelmusik Baroque Orchestra
The Toronto Symphony
Toronto Philharmonic
Toronto Sinfonietta
York Symphony
Opera Companies, 98 dates
  Canadian Opera
  Opera Atelier
  Opera in Concert
  Toronto Operetta Theatre
Ballet Company, 162 dates
  National Ballet of Canada
Professional Theatres, 727 dates
  Crow's Theatre
  Cullen Theatre
  Equity Showcase Theatre
  Factory Theatre
  Inner Stage Theatre
  Leah Posluns Theatre
  Mime Company Limited
  Necessary Angel Theatre
  Nightwood Theatre
  Shakespeare in Action
  Solar Stage
  Tapestry Musical Theatre
  Tarragon Theatre
  The Canadian Stage Company
  The Fringe of Toronto Festival
  Theatre Columbus
  Theatre Direct Canada
  Theatre Français de Toronto
  Theatre Passe Muraille
  Theatre Plus
  Theatre Smith-Gilmour
Art Museums and Galleries, 29
  Art Gallery of Ontario
  Royal Ontario Museum
Public Libraries
  152 branches, 9,825,830 volumes
  876,341 books added/year
MC Access: Toronto–Ontario Shore, ON
Places Rated Score: 3,138
Places Rated Rank: 5

Trenton, NJ
Concert Radio
  WPRB-FM, WWFM-FM
Lively Arts Calendar
  Touring Artists Bookings, 132 dates
  Resident Ensembles, 114 dates
    Atlantic Contemporary Ballet Theatre
    Chamber Symphony of Princeton
    Greater Trenton Symphony
    McCarter Theatre Center
    Opera Festival of New Jersey
    Ridgewood Symphony
Art Museums and Galleries, 1
  Art Museum, Princeton University
Public Libraries
  18 branches, 1,288,599 volumes
  68,774 books added/year
MC Access: New York–Northern New
  Jersey–Long Island, NY–NJ–CT
Places Rated Score: 574
Places Rated Rank: 94

Trois-Rivieres, PQ
Concert Radio
  CBF-FM
Lively Arts Calendar
  Resident Ensemble, 25 dates
    Orchestra Symphonique
Art Museums and Galleries, 3
Public Libraries
  4 branches, 598,072 volumes
  33,974 books added/year
Places Rated Score: 419
Places Rated Rank: 132

Tucson, AZ
Concert Radio
  KUAT-FM
Lively Arts Calendar
  Touring Artists Bookings, 104 dates
  Resident Ensembles, 103 dates
    Arizona Opera
    Civic Orchestra of Tucson
    Invisible Theatre Company
    Tucson Symphony
    University of Arizona Theatre
Art Museums and Galleries, 6
  Tucson Museum of Art
Public Libraries
  15 branches, 1,071,000 volumes
  95,084 books added/year
Places Rated Score: 639
Places Rated Rank: 84

Tulsa, OK
Concert Radio
  KCMA-FM
Lively Arts Calendar
  Touring Artists Bookings, 65 dates
  Resident Ensembles, 191 dates
    American Theatre Company
    Oklahoma Sinfonia–Tulsa Pops
    Tulsa Ballet Theatre
    Tulsa Opera
    Tulsa Philharmonic
Art Museums and Galleries, 1
  Philbrook Museum of Art
Public Libraries
  36 branches, 1,156,625 volumes
  92,724 books added/year
Places Rated Score: 434
Places Rated Rank: 124

Tuscaloosa, AL
Concert Radio
  WUAL-FM
Lively Arts Calendar
  Touring Artists Bookings, 12 dates
  Resident Ensembles, 29 dates
    Tuscaloosa Symphony
    University of Alabama Theatre
Art Museums and Galleries, 1
Public Libraries
  3 branches, 162,864 volumes
  3,031 books added/year
Places Rated Score: 110
Places Rated Rank: 310

Tyler, TX
Lively Arts Calendar
  Touring Artists Bookings, 9 dates
  Resident Ensemble, 10 dates
    East Texas Symphony
Art Museums and Galleries, 1
Public Libraries
  2 branches, 125,774 volumes
  4,940 books added/year
Places Rated Score: 100
Places Rated Rank: 318

Utica–Rome, NY
Concert Radio
  WUNY-FM
Lively Arts Calendar
  Touring Artists Bookings, 100 dates
  Resident Ensemble, 5 dates
    Utica Symphony
Art Museums and Galleries, 3
  Munson–Williams–Proctor Institute
Public Libraries
  37 branches, 978,279 volumes
  42,940 books added/year
Places Rated Score: 391
Places Rated Rank: 140

Vallejo–Fairfield–Napa, CA
Concert Radio
  In San Francisco media market
Lively Arts Calendar
  Touring Artists Bookings, 26 dates
  Resident Ensembles, 26 dates
    Napa Valley Symphony
    Vallejo Symphony
Art Museums and Galleries, 1
Public Libraries
  10 branches, 936,796 volumes
  46,271 books added/year
MC Access: San Francisco–Oakland–San
  Jose, CA
Places Rated Score: 646
Places Rated Rank: 83

✓ **Vancouver, BC**
Concert Radio
  CFRO-FM, CHQM-FM,
  CITR-FM, CJVB-AM
Lively Arts Calendar
  Touring Artists Bookings, 132 dates
  Symphony Orchestras, 153 dates
    Richmond Community Orchestra
    Vancouver Philharmonic
    Vancouver Symphony
  Opera Companies, 44 dates
    Canada Opera Piccola
    Vancouver Opera
  Ballet Company, 70 dates
    Ballet British Columbia
  Professional Theatres, 235 dates
    Arena Theatre Company
    Arts Club Theatre
    Back Alley Theatre
    Carousel Theatre Company
    New Play Centre
    Richmond Gateway Theatre
    Tamahnous Theatre
    Touchstone Theatre
    Vancouver Playhouse
Art Museums and Galleries, 13
  Vancouver Art Gallery
Public Libraries
  44 branches, 2,720,749 volumes
  221,754 books added/year
Places Rated Score: 1,270
Places Rated Rank: 34

Vancouver, WA
Art Museums and Galleries, 1
  Index Gallery
Public Libraries
  11 branches, 486,456 volumes
  35,699 books added/year
MC Access: Portland–Salem–Vancouver,
  OR–WA
Places Rated Score: 240
Places Rated Rank: 216

Ventura, CA
Concert Radio
  KCPB-FM
Lively Arts Calendar
  Touring Artists Bookings, 80 dates
  Resident Ensembles, 21 dates
    Conejo Symphony
    Ventura County Symphony
Art Museums and Galleries, 2
  Carnegie Art Museum
Public Libraries
  14 branches, 1,287,968 volumes
  92,459 books added/year
MC Access: Los Angeles–Riverside–
  Orange County, CA
Places Rated Score: 804
Places Rated Rank: 61

Victoria, BC
Concert Radio
CFMS-FM, CFVU-FM
Lively Arts Calendar
Resident Ensembles, 159 dates
Intrepid Theatre Company
Kaleidoscope Theatre
Pacific Opera Victoria
The Belfry Theatre
The New Bastion Theatre Company
Victoria Symphony
Art Museums and Galleries, 4
Art Gallery of Greater Victoria
Public Libraries
9 branches, 610,810 volumes
49,707 books added/year
Places Rated Score: 520
Places Rated Rank: 103

Victoria, TX
Lively Arts Calendar
Touring Artists Bookings, 8 dates
Resident Ensemble, 5 dates
Victoria Symphony
Public Libraries
1 branch, 131,516 volumes
5,365 books added/year
Places Rated Score: 80
Places Rated Rank: 326

Vineland–Millville–Bridgeton, NJ
Concert Radio
In Philadelphia media market
Lively Arts Calendar
Resident Ensemble, 12 dates
Bridgeton Symphony
Public Libraries
6 branches, 431,296 volumes
13,627 books added/year
MC Access: Philadelphia–Wilmington–Atlantic City, PA–NJ–DE–MD
Places Rated Score: 451
Places Rated Rank: 118

Visalia–Tulare–Porterville, CA
Concert Radio
In Fresno media market
Lively Arts Calendar
Touring Artists Bookings, 12 dates
Resident Ensemble, 13 dates
Tulare County Symphony
Public Libraries
5 branches, 581,012 volumes
15,109 books added/year
Places Rated Score: 72
Places Rated Rank: 332

Waco, TX
Concert Radio
KWBU-FM
Lively Arts Calendar
Touring Artists Bookings, 11 dates
Resident Ensemble, 8 dates
Waco Symphony
Art Museums and Galleries, 1
Public Libraries
7 branches, 358,531 volumes
6,931 books added/year
Places Rated Score: 105
Places Rated Rank: 313

✓ Washington, DC–MD–VA–WV
Concert Radio
WETA-FM, WGMS-AM,
WGMS-FM, WGTS-FM, WVEP-FM
Lively Arts Calendar
Touring Artists Bookings, 1,500 dates
Symphony Orchestras, 383 dates
Alexandria Symphony

Amadeus Orchestra
American Chamber Orchestra
Arlington Symphony
Fairfax Symphony
Georgetown Symphony
Jewish Community Center Symphony
McLean Orchestra
Mid-Atlantic Chamber Orchestra
Millbrook Orchestra
Mount Vernon Chamber Orchestra
National Chamber Orchestra
National Gallery Orchestra
National Symphony
Prince George's Philharmonic
Prince William Symphony
Theater Chamber Players of Kennedy
Center
United States Air Force Symphony
Virginia Chamber Orchestra
Washington Chamber Symphony
Washington Philharmonic
Opera Companies, 213 dates
National Lyric Opera
Opera Americana
Opera Theatre of Northern Virginia
Potomac Valley Opera
Summer Opera Theatre
Washington Concert Opera
Washington Opera
Washington Savoyards
Wolf Trap Opera
Ballet Company, 70 dates
The Washington Ballet
Professional Theatres, 260 dates
Arena Stage
Ford's Theatre
GALA Hispanic Theatre
Living Stage Theatre Company
Potomac Theatre Project
Round House Theatre
Shakespeare Theatre at Folger
Source Theatre Company
Studio Theatre
Theatre of the First Amendment
Woolly Mammoth Theatre Company
Art Museums and Galleries, 30
Corcoran Gallery of Art
Freer Gallery of Art
Hirshhorn Museum and Sculpture Garden
National Gallery of Art
National Museum of African Art
National Museum of American Art
National Portrait Gallery
Phillips Collection
Wilderness Society's Ansel Adams
Collection
Public Libraries
148 branches, 9,600,621 volumes
765,552 books added/year
MC Access: Washington–Baltimore, DC–MD–VA–WV
Places Rated Score: 4,250
Places Rated Rank: 3

Waterbury, CT
Lively Arts Calendar
Resident Ensemble, 5 dates
Waterbury Symphony
Public Libraries
12 branches, 468,853 volumes
22,581 books added/year
Places Rated Score: 177
Places Rated Rank: 270

Waterloo–Cedar Falls, IA
Concert Radio
KHKE-FM

Lively Arts Calendar
Touring Artists Bookings, 8 dates
Resident Ensemble, 22 dates
Waterloo–Cedar Falls Symphony
Art Museums and Galleries, 4
Hearst Center for the Arts
Waterloo Museum of Art
Public Libraries
7 branches, 325,061 volumes
13,577 books added/year
Places Rated Score: 339
Places Rated Rank: 157

Wausau, WI
Concert Radio
WHRM-FM
Lively Arts Calendar
Touring Artists Bookings, 45 dates
Resident Ensemble, 5 dates
Wisconsin Valley Musicians
Art Museums and Galleries, 1
Leigh Yawkey Woodson Art Museum
Public Libraries
11 branches, 244,046 volumes
11,693 books added/year
Places Rated Score: 199
Places Rated Rank: 243

West Palm Beach–Boca Raton, FL
Concert Radio
WXEL-FM
Lively Arts Calendar
Touring Artists Bookings, 374 dates
Resident Ensembles, 194 dates
Ballet Florida
Caldwell Theatre Company
Florida Symphonic Pops
Gilbert and Sullivan Light Opera
Greater Palm Beach Symphony
Harid Philharmonia
Palm Beach Opera
Piccolo Opera
Theatre Club of the Palm Beaches
Art Museums and Galleries, 5
Hibel Museum of Art
Norton Gallery and School of Art
Public Libraries
13 branches, 959,979 volumes
128,210 books added/year
Places Rated Score: 950
Places Rated Rank: 48

Wheeling, WV–OH
Concert Radio
WVNP-FM
Lively Arts Calendar
Touring Artists Bookings, 121 dates
Resident Ensemble, 20 dates
Wheeling Symphony
Public Libraries
17 branches, 506,428 volumes
29,576 books added/year
Places Rated Score: 329
Places Rated Rank: 159

Wichita, KS
Concert Radio
KMUW-FM, KSOF-FM
Lively Arts Calendar
Touring Artists Bookings, 10 dates
Resident Ensemble, 60 dates
Wichita Symphony
Art Museums and Galleries, 5
Coutts Memorial Museum of Art
Wichita Art Museum
Public Libraries
36 branches, 1,047,398 volumes

46,310 books added/year
Places Rated Score: 413
Places Rated Rank: 134

Wichita Falls, TX
Lively Arts Calendar
    Touring Artists Bookings, 6 dates
    Resident Ensemble, 8 dates
        Wichita Falls Symphony
Art Museums and Galleries, 2
    Archer County Museum
Public Libraries
    5 branches, 197,878 volumes
    8,597 books added/year
Places Rated Score: 180
Places Rated Rank: 269

Williamsport, PA
Concert Radio
    In Wilkes-Barre media market
Lively Arts Calendar
    Touring Artists Bookings, 39 dates
    Resident Ensemble, 6 dates
        Williamsport Symphony
Public Libraries
    6 branches, 200,363 volumes
    10,569 books added/year
Places Rated Score: 133
Places Rated Rank: 298

Wilmington, NC
Concert Radio
    WHQR-FM
Lively Arts Calendar
    Touring Artists Bookings, 29 dates
    Resident Ensemble, 5 dates
        Wilmington Symphony
Art Museums and Galleries, 1
    St. John's Museum of Art
Public Libraries
    4 branches, 234,366 volumes
    12,564 books added/year
Places Rated Score: 182
Places Rated Rank: 266

Wilmington–Newark, DE–MD
Concert Radio
    In Philadelphia media market
Lively Arts Calendar
    Touring Artists Bookings, 106 dates
    Resident Ensembles, 88 dates
        Delaware Symphony
        Delaware Theatre Company
        Opera Delaware
Art Museums and Galleries, 3
    Delaware Art Museum
Public Libraries
    19 branches, 891,894 volumes
    51,648 books added/year
MC Access: Philadelphia–Wilmington–
    Atlantic City, PA–NJ–DE–MD
Places Rated Score: 718
Places Rated Rank: 72

Windsor, ON
Concert Radio
    CBE-FM, CBE-AM
Lively Arts Calendar

Touring Artists Bookings, 12 dates
Resident Ensemble, 32 dates
    Windsor Symphony
Art Museums and Galleries, 1
Public Libraries
    26 branches, 917,640 volumes
    59,192 books added/year
MC Access: Detroit–Ann Arbor–Flint, MI
Places Rated Score: 454
Places Rated Rank: 115

Winnipeg, MB
Concert Radio
    CBW-AM, CBW-FM
Lively Arts Calendar
    Touring Artists Bookings, 20 dates
    Resident Ensembles, 273 dates
        Manitoba Chamber Orchestra
        Manitoba Opera
        Manitoba Theatre
        Manitoba Theatre for Young People
        Prairie Theatre Exchange
        Royal Winnipeg Ballet
        Winnipeg Fringe Festival
        Winnipeg Symphony
Art Museums and Galleries, 5
    Winnipeg Art Gallery
Public Libraries
    23 branches, 1,310,165 volumes
    108,774 books added/year
Places Rated Score: 682
Places Rated Rank: 78

Worcester–Fitchburg–Leominster, MA
Concert Radio
    WICN-FM
Lively Arts Calendar
    Touring Artists Bookings, 52 dates
    Resident Ensembles, 44 dates
        Foothills Theatre Company
        Salisbury Lyric Opera
        Thayer Symphony
Art Museums and Galleries, 4
    Worcester Art Museum
Public Libraries
    70 branches, 2,433,891 volumes
    110,487 books added/year
MC Access: Boston–New
    Bedford–Nashua, MA–NH
Places Rated Score: 725
Places Rated Rank: 70

Yakima, WA
Lively Arts Calendar
    Touring Artists Bookings, 24 dates
    Resident Ensemble, 7 dates
        Yakima Symphony
Art Museums and Galleries, 1
Public Libraries
    21 branches, 333,476 volumes
    25,171 books added/year
Places Rated Score: 212
Places Rated Rank: 235

Yolo, CA
Concert Radio
    In Sacramento media market

Lively Arts Calendar
    Touring Artists Bookings, 23 dates
Art Museums and Galleries, 2
    Richard Nelson Gallery
Public Libraries
    3 branches, 318,204 volumes
    12,381 books added/year
MC Access: Sacramento–Yolo, CA
Places Rated Score: 265
Places Rated Rank: 195

York, PA
Concert Radio
    In Harrisburg media market
Lively Arts Calendar
    Touring Artists Bookings, 22 dates
    Resident Ensemble, 10 dates
        York Symphony
Public Libraries
    15 branches, 300,883 volumes
    15,525 books added/year
Places Rated Score: 76
Places Rated Rank: 328

Youngstown–Warren, OH
Concert Radio
    WYSU-FM
Lively Arts Calendar
    Touring Artists Bookings, 146 dates
    Resident Ensembles, 75 dates
        Ballet Western Reserve
        Warren Chamber Orchestra
        Youngstown Symphony
Art Museums and Galleries, 2
    Butler Institute of American Art
Public Libraries
    40 branches, 1,560,725 volumes
    124,418 books added/year
Places Rated Score: 527
Places Rated Rank: 98

Yuba City, CA
Concert Radio
    In Sacramento media market
Lively Arts Calendar
    Touring Artists Bookings, 9 dates
Public Libraries
    2 branches, 253,746 volumes
    5,641 books added/year
Places Rated Score: 54
Places Rated Rank: 338

Yuma, AZ
Concert Radio
    KAWC-FM
Lively Arts Calendar
    Touring Artists Bookings, 20 dates
    Resident Ensemble, 5 dates
        Yuma Community Orchestra
Art Museums and Galleries, 1
    Yuma Fine Arts Association
Public Libraries
    6 branches, 166,901 volumes
    9,974 books added/year
Places Rated Score: 155
Places Rated Rank: 281

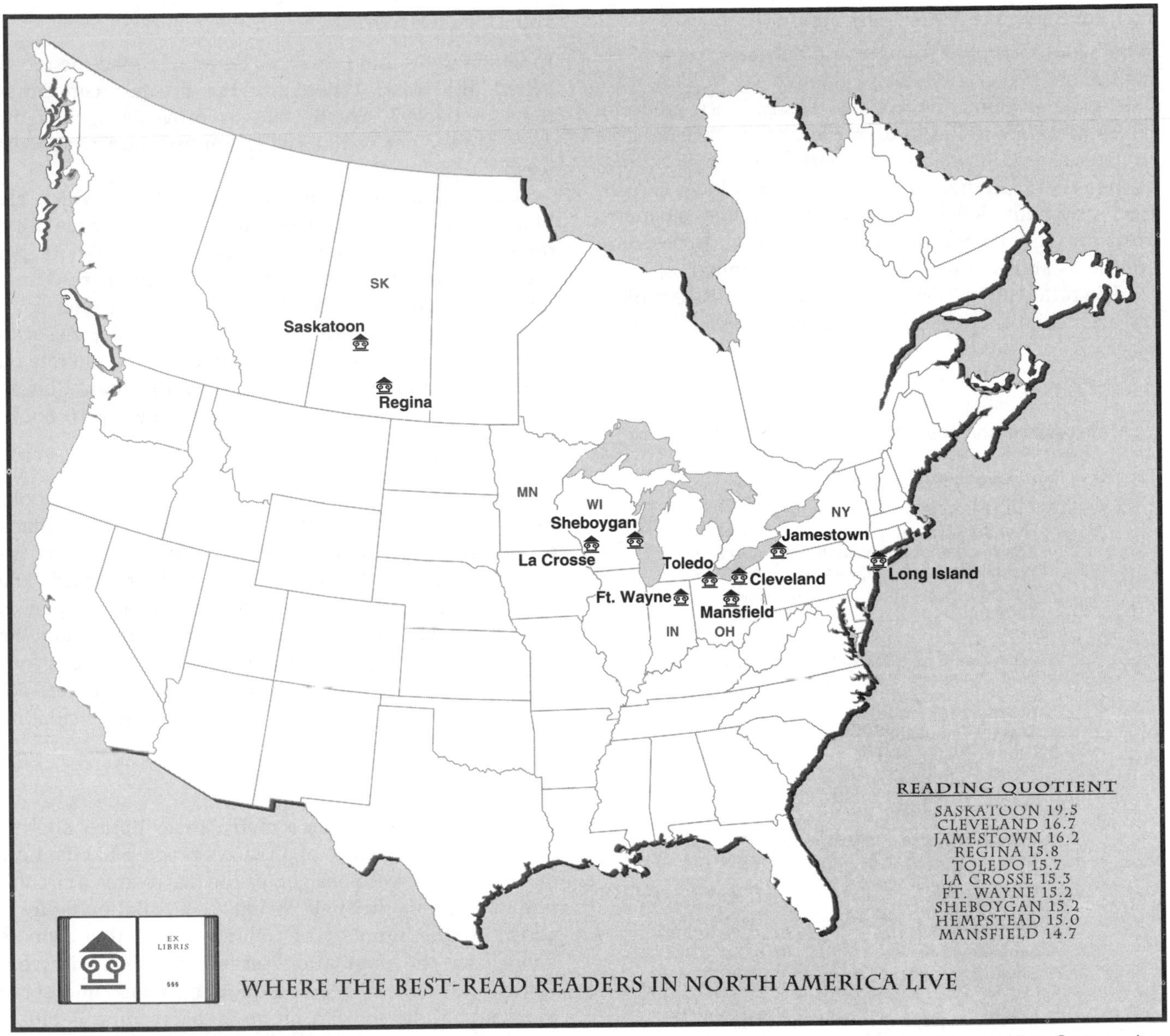

SK

Saskatoon

Regina

MN

WI
Sheboygan

La Crosse

Toledo

Ft. Wayne

Mansfield

IN

OH

NY

Jamestown

Cleveland

Long Island

READING QUOTIENT

SASKATOON 19.5
CLEVELAND 16.7
JAMESTOWN 16.2
REGINA 15.8
TOLEDO 15.7
LA CROSSE 15.3
FT. WAYNE 15.2
SHEBOYGAN 15.2
HEMPSTEAD 15.0
MANSFIELD 14.7

EX
LIBRIS

$$$

WHERE THE BEST-READ READERS IN NORTH AMERICA LIVE

Copyright © 1993 by Places Rated Partnership

Thomas Nast, Cartographer

Et Cetera

THE DAVID AND GOLIATH PROPOSITION

Show you the biggest metro areas and you'll be shown the best places to live for the arts: New York, Los Angeles, Washington, Boston, Toronto, and San Francisco. The consistent relationship between a metro area's size and its arts facilities might make you think that such places as Bangor, ME, and Bismarck, ND—both with populations under 100,000 and ranking 247th and 308th, respectively, in the arts—must resign themselves to being cultural underdogs. But think again.

Pick on Someone Your Own Size

What would happen if Bangor and Bismarck, remembering the old playground cliché, were to say to New York, "Go pick on someone your own size"? By grouping metro areas according to their populations, we are able to explore which ones have a large supply of cultural assets relative to their size and which might be considered artistically deficient. *Places Rated* divides the metro areas into four competitive population groups, based on criteria established by the federal government.

The following lists show how the metro areas rank in the arts when they are measured against similarly sized places:

Metro Areas and the Arts: Some Size Comparisons

Largest (Population over 1,000,000)

Best	Score
New York, NY	9,681
Los Angeles–Long Beach, CA	4,977
Washington, DC–MD–VA–WV	4,250
Chicago, IL	3,231
Toronto, ON	3,138

Medium-Size (Population 250,000 to 1,000,000)

Best	Score
Stamford–Norwalk, CT	1,870
Orange County, NY	1,372
Ottawa–Hull, ON–PQ	1,316
Dayton–Springfield, OH	1,101
Syracuse, NY	1,049

Small (Population 100,000 to 250,000)

Best	Score
Danbury, CT	1,334
Saskatoon, SK	1,002
Regina, SK	728
Jamestown, NY	674
South Bend, IN	506

Smallest (Population under 100,000)

Best	Score
Kankakee, IL	427
Pittsfield, MA	402
Iowa City, IA	254
Bangor, ME	247
St. Joseph, MO	239

HITTING THE BOOKS

In which states and provinces do people read the most? Where the least? Where are the greatest concentrations of books? Which state or province spends the most money per capita on its libraries and which the least?

Circulation rate is one way to find out which are North America's readingest areas. Library circulation rates—that is, the annual number of checkouts per resident—indicate both how much people read and how successful local libraries are in serving their communities. According to the American Library Association's *Directory*, the annual per capita circulation rate on the continent ranges from a low of fewer than 2 books per person in Mississippi to a high of nearly 10 books per person in Iowa.

Do circulation rates reflect the availability of library volumes, or does the number of public library books reveal the importance that people in an area attach to collecting and disseminating knowledge? It is interesting to note that the two states that provide the greatest number of public library volumes per person —Maine and New Hampshire—are also among the states with the highest circulation rates, whereas four out of five states with the fewest library volumes per capita are among those with the lowest circulation rates.

The Reading Quotient

The number of books on a metro area's library shelves tells only half the story of a place's reading habits; how much *use* those volumes get, or the metro area's circulation rate, is the other half. When the circulation figure is added to the number of volumes, and that sum is divided by the population served, the result is what *Places Rated* calls the reading quotient, which may serve as a rough indicator of a metro area's reading habits.

The metro area average is 7.7. In metro areas that have reading quotients of 3.0 or less, reading as expressed in visits to the library is not a pastime. But metro areas with reading quotients above 15.0 are places where libraries are used and used often.

Recreation

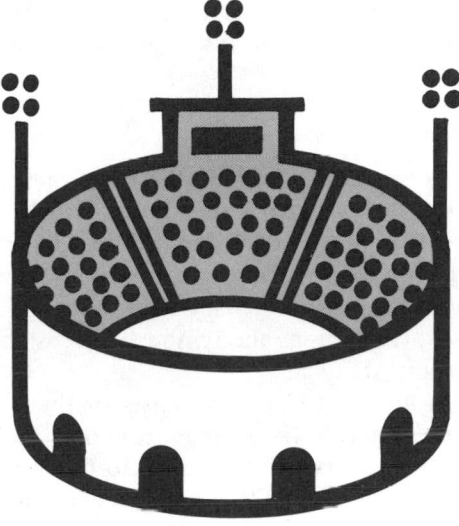

After "Where's that?" the thing people most often wonder about an unfamiliar place is, "Is there anything to do there?" Wherever they are, people want to make the most of leisure. Consider the billions spent each year on everything from video rentals, insulated jogging clothes, season tickets at the ballpark, European vacations, and down-filled sleeping bags to graphite fishing rods.

Not everyone can take advantage of *all* the opportunities for recreation. An Aspen ski trip or a Hilton Head golf weekend costs too much for most people. Even a backpacking trip in a national park with cheap camping fees might be out of the question for the dollars and time it takes to get there and back.

Fortunately, there are many other things to do that are inexpensive and nearby. Movies, golf, and good restaurants are available almost anywhere; in fact, people living in smaller metro areas usually have better access to these than residents of bigger ones. On the other hand, zoos, family theme parks, professional sports, and racetracks enhance life in larger places. For more and more people, convenient outdoor recreation in a national forest or on a wild and scenic river is a lucky geographical circumstance; the protected outdoors is a part of the landscape just as developed urban land is. *Places Rated* looks at each of these kinds of recreation in determining the best places to play.

COMMON DENOMINATORS

For scuba diving, the coasts of Florida, California, and Hawaii are best bets. For skiing on powdery snow, British Columbia and Colorado are better suited than most other areas. Weather and winds turn still other areas into premier places for hang gliding. But there are certain kinds of recreation that you can find everywhere: dining out at a quality restaurant, a round of weekend golf, or movie-going at a downtown picture palace or multiplex cinema at a suburban mall.

Counting Stars: Good Restaurants

If you're among the one in 10 who gets out at least once a week for dinner, you may as well go to a worthwhile eatery instead of a portion-controlled Casa House de la Maison where distantly prepared frozen packages of beef Wellington and veal cordon bleu are microwaved, dished up, and menued at 10 times what the restaurant paid for them.

The 10 Best Metro Areas for Dining Out

Metro Area	Quality Stars	Residents per Star
1. Santa Fe, NM	80	1,623
2. Barnstable–Yarmouth, MA	115	1,660
3. Naples, FL	66	2,619
4. Pittsfield, MA	28	3,126
5. Salinas, CA	106	3,457
6. Sarasota–Bradenton, FL	109	4,977
7. Billings, MT	22	5,206
8. Glens Falls, NY	18	6,800
9. Dutchess County, NY	38	6,958
10. San Francisco, CA	235	6,997

Source: Derived from *Mobile Travel Guide* (7 vols.), 1993, and Woods & Poole Economics, Inc., population forecasts.

To determine the best metro areas in America for eating out, *Places Rated* uses the *Mobil Travel Guide,* which rates restaurants across the continent. The ratings are derived from two sources: an extensive review of consumer comments, and the inspection reports of field representatives who dine anonymously at establishments throughout the year.

Restaurants are judged on the basis of their food, service, and ambience. Ratings range from one star for a "good, better than average" restaurant to five stars for "one of the country's best." Only a very few restaurants receive five stars in any given year; there were just nine top-rated restaurants in 1993.

Places Rated gauges access to good restaurants by dividing the resident population by the total number of quality stars awarded by *Mobil Travel Guide* to metro-area restaurants. Four one-star restaurants and one three-star restaurant, for example, would yield seven quality stars. Though Santa Fe has just 38 rated restaurants—not an overwhelming number when compared with the 322 found in New York, the most of any metro area—it can boast one quality star for every 1,623 residents, the best ratio among the metro areas.

Access to Public Golf

Metro Area	Public Holes
Ann Arbor, MI	504
Barnstable–Yarmouth, MA	315
Benton Harbor, MI	171
Canton–Massillon, OH	414
Fort Walton Beach, FL	216
Glens Falls, NY	135
Jackson, MI	270
Jamestown, NY	153
Kankakee, IL	126
Kenosha, WI	144
Myrtle Beach, SC	891
Sarasota–Bradenton, FL	639
Sheboygan, WI	108

Source: Derived from National Golf Foundation, unpublished data, and Woods & Poole Economics, Inc., population forecasts.

Listed above are metro areas with fewer than 1,000 residents per public golf hole.

Counting Holes: Golf Courses

Certainly golf is a common denominator; the game is played in every metro area, even in Anchorage, AK. When it comes to finding a local golf course on an idle, sunny weekend, there are three options: the private equity course, typically part of a country club open only to members and guests; daily-fee operations open to all players; and city-built and operated courses, again open to everyone.

If you're a golfer who can afford to join a private country club with an 18-hole course, your dues buy one big advantage: you belong to the fortunate 14 percent of golfers who don't have to wait to tee off at a crowded municipal or daily-fee course.

On the other hand, if you're one of nearly 25 million North American golfers who've played a round at a local municipal or daily-fee course, only 6 out of every 10 of the continent's 16,234 courses are open to you. This may be changing; thanks to hard times, membership waiting periods have shortened and initiation fees have plunged at many clubs. However, because access to public golf is still an excellent reflection of recreation opportunities in metro areas, *Places Rated* counts the number of local municipal and daily-fee holes per capita.

Counting Screens: The Movies

In 1948, John Huston won two academy awards—best director and best screenplay—for *The Treasure of Sierra Madre.* His father, Walter, was named best supporting actor for his portrayal of the old prospector in the same film. Jane Wyman won an Oscar for her role in *Johnny Belinda; Hamlet* was best picture, and its star, Lawrence Olivier, best actor.

The 1940s were a time when moviegoing was the thing to do any evening. Popcorn was regularly swept up from the aisles between shows, the next John Wayne or Spencer Tracy film was announced on a large easel in the lobby, usherettes took you to your seat with a red-lensed flashlight, and you always got a Movietone or Warner Pathe newsreel with the show. There were nearly 20,000 movie houses back then. Never again would there be so many.

Places Rated divides the local population by the number of commercial four-wall (as opposed to the fast-disappearing drive-in) theater screens to figure access to movies. Most are in multiplex cinemas run by chain exhibitors like Famous Players, United Artists, Cinemark, or Cineplex Odeon. But the single-screen or twin Bijou or Roxy kind of neighborhood theater is still alive in smaller metro areas.

CROWD PLEASERS

At different times of the year in Los Angeles–Long Beach, CA, you can visit the animals at the Los Angeles Zoo; join the crowds at Six Flags Magic Mountain and the Universal Studios tour; bet on the horses at Hollywood Park or Santa Anita; or take in professional baseball, football, basketball, and hockey, as well as NCAA Division I competition.

The Nine Best Metro Areas for Moviegoing

1. Lewiston–Auburn, ME   3,078
2. Dubuque, IA   3,771
3. Burlington, VT   3,899
4. Barnstable–Yarmouth, MA   4,338
5. Lawrence, KS   4,499
6. Champaign–Urbana, IL   4,590
7. Waterloo–Cedar Falls, IA   4,609
8. Lima, OH   4,736
9. Fargo–Morehead, ND–MN   4,891

Source: Derived from North American Theater Owners *Encyclopedia of Exhibition,* 1993; *Film Canada Yearbook,* 1993; *Motion Picture Almanac,* 1993, and Woods & Poole Economics, Inc., population forecasts.

Listed above are metro areas with fewer than 5,000 people per movie screen.

Few metro areas have as varied a supply of crowd pleasers as Los Angeles–Long Beach, but some of these opportunities are common in many of the larger metro areas. From Disneyland in Anaheim, CA, to New York's Bronx Zoo, these attractions offer Americans interesting ways to spend their leisure time.

Seeing the Animals: Zoos and Aquariums

The two best metro areas for seeing the animals are Chicago and San Diego. Each has not one but two of the continent's top-ranked zoological parks. Altogether, 112 metro areas have at least one zoo accredited by the American Association of Zoological Parks and Aquariums (AAZPA) or the Canadian counterpart, the CAZPA.

The idea that zoos enhance people's lives is a European one flourishing in America's Midwest. Besides Chicago's two great zoos, the Cincinnati, Cleveland, Detroit, Milwaukee, and St. Louis zoological parks are among the best in the United States. It is not coincidental that the working-class citizens of these cities can trace their roots to European countries—particularly Germany—that also have great zoos.

"Postage-stamp collecting" is the name that zookeepers give to the assembling of colorful animal specimens without regard to whether the animals fit and thrive in a zoo's limited space. This was once a sure way of drawing more patrons and carving out a reputation as an outstanding institution. Today, professionally run zoos have fewer species on exhibit but more specimens of each. The standard phylogenetic exhibits (grouping African lions with Bengal tigers, timber wolves with hyenas) have been replaced with ecological displays (wildlife in desert or mountain environments) and behavioral exhibits (hibernation, burrowing, nocturnalism) that group specimens more creatively and openly.

This isn't to say that zoos no longer maintain large, diverse collections, for the best zoos are those with the biggest animal populations. But today the benchmark of a zoo's quality isn't simply how many animals it can keep or breed; just as important is how creatively and naturally the animals are exhibited.

Aquariums are far less common than zoos; just 16 of

The Most Popular Zoos and Aquariums

Twenty-eight North American zoos and aquariums are visited by at least one million people each year. Most are city- or society-owned; several are tourist destinations in their own right.

Zoo	Annual Visitors
Sea World of Florida Orlando, FL	4,000,000
Lincoln Park Zoological Gardens Chicago, IL	4,000,000
San Diego Zoo San Diego, CA	3,400,000
Sea World of California San Diego, CA	3,000,000
National Zoological Park Washington, DC	3,000,000
Busch Gardens Tampa, FL	3,000,000
St. Louis Zoological Park St. Louis, MO	2,800,000
John G. Shedd Aquarium Chicago, IL	2,186,075
Chicago Zoological Park Brookfield, IL	2,000,000
New York Zoological Park Bronx, NY	2,000,000
Los Angeles Zoo Los Angeles, CA	1,800,000
Monterey Bay Aquarium Monterey, CA	1,700,000
National Aquarium Baltimore, MD	1,500,000
Marine World Africa USA Vallejo, CA	1,454,000
Milwaukee Zoological Gardens Milwaukee, WI	1,400,000
Houston Zoological Gardens Houston, TX	1,300,000
San Diego Wild Animal Park Escondido, CA	1,300,000
Philadelphia Zoological Gardens Philadelphia, PA	1,300,000
New England Aquarium Boston, MA	1,300,000
Metropolitan Toronto Zoo Scarborough, ON	1,300,000
Denver Zoological Gardens Denver, CO	1,300,000
Cincinnati Zoo Cincinnati, OH	1,287,000
Stanley Park Zoological Gardens Vancouver, BC	1,200,000
Minnesota Zoological Gardens Apple Valley, MN	1,164,000
San Francisco Zoological Gardens San Francisco, CA	1,000,000
Sea World of Texas San Antonio, TX	1,000,000
Metro Washington Park Zoo Portland, OR	1,000,000
Sea World of Ohio Aurora, OH	1,000,000

Source: American and Canadian Associations of Zoological Parks and Aquariums, 1993.

the 343 metro areas have one and most of these are in areas with ocean coastlines. Unlike the great zoological parks, which are run municipally or by societies, some of the best aquariums (including Boston's New England Aquarium) are owned and operated for profit by private firms.

Family Theme Parks

The person who started it all was Walter Elias Disney; his creation was Disneyland. Because he ignored a waterfront location and games of chance and skill, the amusement park pros predicted he'd go broke when his 180-acre park opened in Anaheim, CA, in 1954. Disney's purpose was to use his famous cartoon characters and feature films as themes to structure a family-centered park more carefully than such parks as Chicago's Riverview or Ocean Park in Santa Monica, places avoided by families because of their tawdry, carny atmosphere.

That he succeeded is obvious; today, Disneyland and Walt Disney World in Florida—which includes the Magic Kingdom, opened in 1971, Epcot Center, opened in 1982, and MGM Studios Tour, opened in 1989— together attract more than 30 million people a year.

Two vacation states—California and Florida—have 10 of the top 25 theme parks, attracting more than half of the country's annual 75 million theme-park visitors. In these states, some theme park owners have chosen their locations strategically. The Orlando metro area, for example, is home not only to Walt Disney World, and Universal Studios Florida, but Sea World of Florida, which located there to take advantage of Disney World's draw. In Southern California, Knott's Berry Farm, a traditional roadside attraction since 1920, converted to theme-park format and joined Sea World of California and Six Flags Magic Mountain in trying to capitalize on Disneyland's crowds.

Pari-Mutuel Betting

The biggest spectator sport in North America is pari-mutuel racing at the track. Based on a system in which the players who bet on the first-, second-, and third-place finishers share the total amount of money bet, pari-mutuel racing draws nearly 100 million people each year. One hundred twenty metro areas offer pari-mutuel betting.

Thoroughbred racing dominates the North American racing scene. There are 5,695 days of racing at the 65 thoroughbred tracks, exclusive of county fairs. Ak-Sar-Ben (Nebraska spelled backward), is a 77-day, nonprofit civic meet held near downtown Omaha that attracts nearly a million race goers. In the Los Angeles–Long Beach metro area, Santa Anita Park's two-part season draws close to three million spectators. Aqueduct's three-part season is one of the longest in thoroughbred racing, and although attendance has fallen over the years, the track draws almost as many fans as do the New York Yankees across town in the Bronx.

Standardbred horses are entered in harness racing; jockeys ride behind the horses in small, two-wheeled carts. Harness racing competes with thoroughbred racing for the race goer's wager in 15 states and in Canada. Its annual following at the track is a good deal smaller than that of thoroughbred racing (44 million versus 18 million race goers). However, in Delaware, upstate New York, Michigan, and the Chicago environs, pacing and trotting races attract more bettors and a greater cash total in bets than their thoroughbred competition, and in Canada they outdraw thoroughbred races two to one.

The country cousin of the more citified and patrician thoroughbred contests, quarter-horse racing usually takes place at state and county fairs. It gets its name from the wide-open quarter-mile sprint the horses run on the track. Fourteen states permit betting on quarter-horse races, usually on mixed programs with thoroughbred races. The sport is more popular in the West and Northwest than in any other region.

Dog racing evolved from the early sport of coursing, in which two greyhounds were released together in pursuit of a hare. Modern greyhound racing stems from a 1904 coursing contest held in South Dakota. Its sponsor, Owen Patrick Smith, developed a strong distaste for the killing of hares and spent the next 15 years adapting a mechanical lure to the inside rail of an oval track. The lure now resembles a rabbit and moves around the track on an electric rail. Since greyhounds chase by sight rather than scent, it has proven to be effective.

Rooting for the Home Team

A frequent topic of discussion on talk shows, in bars, and at work is where the "good" sports towns are. The question is usually argued from two perspectives: whether a town has winners or whether fans turn out to root for the teams. These two trends are often linked; over the regular seasons, the clubs with the best attendance usually have had some of the best records.

Another way to find the best sports towns is to measure the access that a metro area's fans have to regular-season games. "Game seats per capita" is an elementary measurement used most often in professional sports franchising and marketing, especially at expansion time. This figure is found by multiplying the number of home games played by all the teams in a metro area (for example, 81 baseball; 41 basketball; 8 football) by the combined seating capacity of the teams' playing arenas and then dividing that number by the metro area's population.

Professional Sports. In arriving at a figure for game seats per capita at professional sporting events, *Places Rated* surveyed each of the 159 metro areas with major-league or minor-league teams in any of four sports: baseball, basketball, football, and hockey. For example, the number of regular-season football games played by the Indianapolis Colts multiplied by the Hoosier Dome's capacity is 480,000. The same calculations yield a figure of 1,037,000 for NBA Pacers basketball and Ice minor-league hockey games played in Market Square Arena, and 995,918 for Indians Triple-A baseball games played at Bush Stadium. The sum of these four figures divided by Indianapolis's metro area population is 2.15, or more than two game seats for everyone in the eight-county metro area. Other metro areas have better averages, and in each of them the presence of a baseball team, with its large stadium and long playing season, makes a good deal of difference.

Collegiate Sports. Among the biggest crowd pleasers around are varsity teams fielded by colleges and universities. The cream of those is generally found among the teams classified Division I (split into Divisions I-A and I-AA for football only) by the National Collegiate Athletic Association (NCAA). Eligibility for this division is based on the quality of a school's typical opponent, or "schedule strength," and game attendance figures.

Nearly 37 million fans attend the 3,353 regular season games played by the 667 colleges and universities with varsity football. Although the 191 Division I-A and I-AA teams play only one third of these games, they draw 83 percent of the attendance. Basketball is even more widely available. More than 32 million fans come out for the 16,596 regular season and tournament games played by the 1,277 schools that had men's varsity basketball teams. The 290 NCAA Division I teams play one-quarter of these games, yet they account for 65 percent of total attendance.

Division I and Canadian Inter-University Athletic Union (CIAU) football, basketball, and hockey are on view in 178 of the 343 metro areas, from the Aces of the University of Evansville to the Zips of the University of Akron. Using game seats per capita as the criterion, the best metro area for college football and basketball is Lawrence, KS. The number of University of Kansas Jayhawks games played at home multiplied by the seating capacities of Memorial Stadium (football) and Allen Fieldhouse (basketball) yields a figure of 465,498, or almost seven game seats for everyone in town and in surrounding Douglas County.

OUTDOOR RECREATION ASSETS

To many people, recreation is not something that takes place within four walls or in the middle of a crowded city. Instead, it means turning to the open spaces for fishing, boating, swimming, hiking, running, picnicking, or getting away from it all. Just as some metro areas have more to offer in urban recreation, others undeniably are richer in access to the great outdoors.

Coastlines and Inland Water

Sooners boast that Oklahoma has so many impounded lakes of every size that if you were to tip the state to the south a bit, the water would flow out and flood Texas for

Baseball's Odyssey

Which major-league baseball team is descended from the old Beaneaters? It's not the Boston Red Sox; in fact, it's not even an American League team. It's the Atlanta Braves.

This is just one of many odd and intriguing changes major-league baseball teams have undergone since 1876, when eight professional clubs joined forces to form the National League. Twenty-five years later, in 1901, the American League began play, also with eight teams. Since that time, many of the teams have changed names and moved form one city to another, and the leagues have expanded the number of franchises. The list below shows which of today's American League (AL) and National League (NL) teams have moved to another city and/or changed their name since their founding date.*

Atlanta Braves (NL)—*1876*, began as Boston Red Caps; *1883*, renamed Beaneaters; *1907*, renamed Doves; *1909*, renamed Pilgrims; *1936*, renamed Bees; *1941*, renamed Braves; *1953*, moved to Milwaukee and renamed Milwaukee Braves; *1966*, moved to Atlanta and renamed Atlanta Braves.

Baltimore Orioles (AL)—*1901*, began as Milwaukee Brewers; *1902*, moved to St. Louis and renamed St. Louis Browns; *1954*, moved to Baltimore and renamed Baltimore Orioles.

Boston Red Sox (AL)—*1901*, began as Somersets; *1905*, renamed Puritans; *1907*, renamed Red Sox.

California Angels (AL)—*1901*, began as Bronchos; *1902*, renamed Blues; *1905*, renamed Naps; *1912*, renamed Molly McGuires; *1914*, renamed Indians.

Houston Astros (NL)—*1962*, began as Houston Colt .45's; *1964*, renamed Astros.

Los Angeles Dodgers (NL)—*1962*, began as Brooklyn Bridegrooms; *1898*, renamed Superbas; *1911*, renamed Dodgers; *1958*, moved to Los Angeles and renamed Los Angeles Dodgers.

Milwaukee Brewers (AL)—*1969*, began as Seattle Pilots; *1970*, moved to Milwaukee and renamed Milwaukee Brewers.

Minnesota Twins (AL)—*1901*, began as Washington Senators; *1960*, moved to Minneapolis-St. Paul and renamed Minnesota Twins.

New York Yankees (AL)—*1901*, began as Baltimore Orioles; *1903*, moved to New York and renamed New York Highlanders; *1912*, renamed Yankees.

Oakland A's (AL)—*1901*, began as Philadelphia Athletics; *1955*, moved to Kansas City and renamed Kansas City Athletics; *1968*, moved to Oakland and renamed Oakland Athletics; *1974*, renamed Oakland A's.

Pittsburgh Pirates (NL)—*1887*, began as Alleghenys; *1890*, renamed Innocents; *1891*, renamed Pirates.

San Francisco Giants (NL)—*1879*, began as Troy (NY) Trojans; *1883*, moved to New York City and renamed New York Gothams; *1886*, renamed Giants; *1958*, moved to San Francisco and renamed San Francisco Giants.

Texas Rangers (AL)—*1961*, began as Washington Senators; *1971*, moved to Arlington and renamed Texas Rangers.

*The Cincinnati Reds (NL, 1876), Philadelphia Phillies (NL, 1883), St. Louis Cardinals (NL, 1892), Chicago White Sox (AL, 1901), Detroit Tigers (AL, 1901), New York Mets (NL, 1962), Kansas City Royals (AL, 1969), Montreal Expos (NL, 1969), San Diego Padres (NL, 1969), Seattle Mariners (AL, 1977), Toronto Blue Jays (AL, 1977), Colorado Rockies (NL, 1993), and Florida Marlins (NL, 1993) have neither changed their name nor moved.

Hockey's Odyssey

The National Hockey League was formed by five team owners in the Windsor Hotel, in Montreal, back in 1917.

Calgary Flames—*1972*, began as Atlanta Flames; *1980*, moved to Calgary and renamed Calgary Flames.

Detroit Red Wings—*1926*, began as Cougars; *1929*, renamed Falcons; *1932*, renamed Red Wings.

Edmonton Oilers—*1972*, began as Alberta Oilers of the World Hockey Association; *1973*, renamed Edmonton Oilers; *1979*, joined NHL.

Hartford Whalers—*1972*, began as New England Whalers (Boston) of the World Hockey Association; *1977*, moved to Hartford; *1979*, joined NHL.

Toronto Maple Leafs—*1917*, began as Arenas; *1919*, changed name to St. Patricks; *1926*, changed name to Maple Leafs.

New Jersey Devils—*1974*, began as Kansas City Scouts; *1976*, moved to Denver and renamed Colorado Rockies; *1982*, moved to East Rutherford and renamed New Jersey Devils.

*The Anaheim Mighty Ducks (1993), Boston Bruins (1924), Buffalo Sabres (1970), Chicago Black Hawks (1926), Los Angeles Kings (1967), Minnesota North Stars (1967), Montreal Canadiens (1917), New York Islanders (1972), New York Rangers (1926), Philadelphia Flyers (1967), Pittsburgh Penguins (1967), Quebec Nordiques (1979), St. Louis Blues (1967), San Jose Sharks (1990), South Florida Panthers (1993), Vancouver Canucks (1970), Washington Capitals (1974), and Winnipeg Jets (1979) have neither changed their name nor moved.

In contrast to the National Forest System, the National Park System is meant expressly for recreation. The founding of Yellowstone National Park in 1872 marked the beginning of the oldest and now the largest national park system in the world. It comprises 354 national

Football's Odyssey

The first NFL franchise in Cleveland belonged not to the Browns but to the Rams, who played such opponents as the Brooklyn Dodgers, Chicago Cardinals, and Pittsburgh Pirates back in the 1930s.

Organized professional football began to take shape in 1922 with the establishment of the National Football League, although the early teams seem ragtag compared to today's juggernauts. Through a series of splits and mergers with other leagues over the years, the NFL has remained the dominant pro football organization, and presently consists of 28 teams. The list below recaps the moves and name changes of today's NFL teams since their founding date.*

Detroit Lions—*1930*, began as the Portsmouth (OH) Spartans; *1934*, moved to Detroit and renamed Detroit Lions.

Indianapolis Colts—*1952*, defunct Dallas Texans of the All-America Football Conference moved to Baltimore, renamed Baltimore Colts, and joined the NFL; *1983*, moved to Indianapolis and renamed Indianapolis Colts.

Kansas City Chiefs—*1959*, began as Dallas Texans of the American Football League; *1963*, moved to Kansas City and renamed Kansas City Chiefs; *1970*, joined NFL.

Los Angeles Raiders—*1959*, began as Oakland Raiders of the American Football League; *1970*, joined NFL; *1982*, moved to Los Angeles and renamed Los Angeles Raiders.

Los Angeles Rams—*1937*, began as Cleveland Rams; *1946*, moved to Los Angeles and renamed Los Angeles Rams.

New England Patriots—*1959*, began as Boston Patriots of the American Football League; *1970*, joined NFL; *1971*, renamed New England Patriots.

New York Jets—*1959*, began as New York Titans of the American Football League; *1963*, renamed New York Jets; *1970*, joined NFL.

Phoenix Cardinals—*1913*, began as Racine Avenue (Chicago) Cardinals; *1922*, renamed Chicago Cardinals; *1960*, moved to St. Louis and renamed St. Louis Cardinals; *1988*, moved to Phoenix and renamed Phoenix Cardinals.

San Diego Chargers—*1959*, franchised as Los Angeles Chargers of the American Football League; *1961*, moved to San Diego and renamed San Diego Chargers; *1970* joined NFL.

Washington Redskins—*1932*, began as Boston Braves; *1933*, renamed Boston Redskins; *1937*, moved to Washington and renamed Washington Redskins.

*The Chicago Bears (1922), Green Bay Packers (1922), New York Giants (1925), Philadelphia Eagles (1933), Pittsburgh Steelers (1933), Dallas Cowboys (1960), Minnesota Vikings (1960), Atlanta Falcons (1965), New Orleans Saints (1966), Seattle Seahawks (1974), and Tampa Bay Buccaneers (1974) began as NFL teams and have neither moved nor changed their team name.

The Cleveland Browns (1946) and San Francisco 49ers (1946) are former All-American Football Conference teams that joined the NFL in 1949.

The Buffalo Bills (1959), Denver Broncos (1959), Houston Oilers (1959), Miami Dolphins (1965), and Cincinnati Bengals (1967) are former American Football League franchises that merged with the NFL in 1970.

a good while. And Maryland crabbers point out to newcomers that the true length of estuarine shore reached by the Chesapeake Bay's tide would total more than 8,000 miles if all the bends and kinks were straightened out.

Four of every five North Americans today are congregated together in metro areas within 100 miles of an ocean or Great Lakes coastline; in less than 10 years, the U.S. Department of the Interior predicts that three of every four Americans will live within 50 miles of a coastline. Ocean or Great Lakes coastlines form part of the peripheries of 121 metro areas and 100 percent of another, Honolulu.

National Forests, Parks, and Wildlife Refuges

Some of the most popular outdoor activities—driving for pleasure, walking, picnicking, sight-seeing, bird watching, nature walking, and fishing—would probably be even more enjoyable in the country's splendid system of national forests, parks, and wildlife refuges.

There are 156 national forests and 19 national grasslands on 191 million acres in the United States. The main purpose of the National Forest System is silviculture: growing wood, harvesting it carefully, and preserving naturally beautiful areas. Within the forest system are more than a quarter of a million miles of roads, built not only for loggers but for everyone. They lead to a wide variety of recreation outlets: ski resorts, marinas, fishing lakes and streams, hiking trails, and campgrounds.

parks, preserves, monuments, memorials, battlefields, seashores, riverways, and trails that together cover some 80 million acres.

Whereas the National Park System acts to keep irreplaceable geographical and historical treasures in the public domain, the national wildlife refuges protect native flora and fauna from people. There are 452 of these remarkable sanctuaries throughout the country, embracing more than 89 million acres. Most of them are open to the public for a variety of wildlife activities, particularly photography and nature observation. In certain refuges at irregular times, fishing and hunting are permitted, depending on the size of the wild populations. Although the majority of the nation's wildlife refuges are located in open, sometimes remote country, they aren't exclusively a rural amenity. Several can be found within metropolitan areas, such as the Nisqually National Wildlife Refuge in Olympia, WA, and San Pablo Bay National Wildlife Refuge in the California metro area of Santa Rosa–Petaluma.

SCORING: RECREATION

Is there more to do in Houston than in Dallas? How do the California rivals—Los Angeles and San Francisco—compare for recreation? Or Jacksonville and Tampa–St. Petersburg? To answer these questions, *Places Rated* examines three categories: Common Denominators (golf, quality restaurants, and movies), Crowd Pleasers (zoos, aquariums, theme parks, pari-mutuel betting, and professional and collegiate sports), and Outdoor Recreation Assets (miles of coastline, and acreage in federal and state or provincial parks).

In the categories of Common Denominators and Crowd Pleasers, metro areas are awarded points not for their number of facilities but rather for the availability of these facilities to residents. Access to these different events is given a rating of AA, A, B, or C (AA indicating the best access and C the worst), and those ratings mean a certain number of points for the metro area: 400 for an AA rating, 300 for A, 200 for B, and 100 for C. The exceptions to this rule—zoos, aquariums, and family theme parks below—are explained in the next column.

Each metro area starts with a base score of zero, to which points are added according to the following criteria:

1. *Good restaurants.*

A metro area gets a rating of:	If there is one quality star for every:
AA	15,000 or fewer people
A	15,001 to 25,000 people
B	25,001 to 40,000 people
C	40,001 or more people

2. *Golf courses.*

A metro area gets a rating of:	If there is one hole for every:
AA	1,750 or fewer people
A	1,751 to 2,500 people
B	2,501 to 4,000 people
C	4,001 or more people

3. *Movie theaters.*

A metro area gets a rating of:	If there is one screen for every:
AA	9,000 or fewer people
A	9,001 to 11,500 people
B	11,501 to 16,000 people
C	16,001 or more people

4. *Zoos.*

A metro area gets a rating of:	If the annual operating budget for its zoo(s):
AA	exceeds $10 M
A	is between $2 and $9.9 M
B	is between $.75 and $1.99 M
C	is less than $749,999

5. *Aquariums.* Sixteen metro areas receive an A rating for having an aquarium certified by the American or Canadian Associations of Zoological Parks and Aquariums.

6. *Family theme parks.*

A metro area gets a rating of:	If the annual open days for all the parks total:
AA	more than 365
A	between 125 and 364
B	between 100 and 125
C	less than 99

7. *Pari-mutuel betting.*

A metro area gets a rating of:	If there is one racing day for every:
AA	1,750 or fewer people
A	1,751 to 4,000 people
B	4,501 to 7,500 people
C	7,501 or more people

8. *Professional sports.*

A metro area gets a rating of:	If local major- and minor-league teams provide:
AA	2 or more game seats per capita
A	1.35 to 1.99 game seats per capita
B	1 to 1.34 game seats per capita
C	.99 or fewer game seats per capita

9. *College football, basketball, and hockey.*

A metro area gets a rating of:	If NCAA-I or CIAU teams provide:
AA	1 or more game seats per capita
A	.30 to .99 game seats per capita
B	.15 to .29 game seats per capita
C	.15 or fewer game seats per capita

10. *Coastlines.* Each mile of general coastline, whether on the ocean or on the Great Lakes, gets 10 points. For example, the 55 miles of Pacific coastline west of San Diego earn the California metro area 550 points.

11. *Public recreation land.* The percent of a metro area's total acreage set aside for national forests, parks, wildlife refuges, and state parks is multiplied by 50. Seattle has more than 2,704,640 total acres, 36.37 percent of which composes the Mount Baker and Snoqualmie national forests (981,515 acres) and 10 state parks (4,534 acres), giving the Washington metro area 1,819 points.

12. *MC Access.* The 75 metro areas that are part of Metropolitan Complexes (MCs) are eligible

for bonus points based on the total number of points amassed for Crowd Pleasers by the other metro areas in the MC.

To maintain relative parity among the three major recreation categories—Common Denominators, Crowd Pleasers, and Outdoor Recreation Assets—a ceiling of 2,000 points is applied to the total for outdoor assets (items 10 and 11).

RANKINGS: Recreation

Twelve criteria are used to rate a metro area's supply of recreation assets: (1) public golf, (2) good restaurants, (3) movie theater screens, (4) zoos, (5) aquariums, (6) family theme parks, (7) pari-mutuel betting attractions, (8) professional sports, (9) collegiate sports, (10) miles of ocean or Great Lakes coastline, (11) national forests, national parks, and national wildlife refuges, and (12) state or provincial parks. The 75 metro areas that are part of Metropolitan Complexes (MCs) also earn points for shared assets found in other metro areas within the metropolitan complex. Metro areas that receive tie scores get the same rank and are listed alphabetically.

Places Rated Rank	Places Rated Score
1. Miami, FL	3,940
2. Los Angeles–Long Beach, CA	3,857
3. San Diego, CA	3,800
4. Fort Collins–Loveland, CO	3,700
5. San Francisco, CA	3,697
6. Seattle–Bellevue–Everett, WA	3,620
7. Naples, FL	3,600
8. Eugene–Springfield, OR	3,500
8. Quebec City, PQ	3,500
10. Tucson, AZ	3,253
11. Bellingham, WA	3,200
11. Santa Barbara–Santa Maria–Lompoc, CA	3,200
13. Vancouver, BC	3,154
14. Boulder–Longmont, CO	3,148
15. Salinas, CA	3,105
16. Houston, TX	3,030
17. Orange County, CA	3,004
18. Knoxville, TN	2,932
19. Charleston–North Charleston, SC	2,913
20. Orlando, FL	2,906
21. Phoenix–Mesa, AZ	2,877
22. Portland, OR	2,851
23. Provo–Orem, UT	2,804
24. Sacramento, CA	2,802
25. Ocala, FL	2,788
26. Honolulu, HI	2,787
27. Barnstable–Yarmouth, MA	2,781
27. Rapid City, SD	2,781
29. Norfolk–Virginia Beach–Newport News, VA–NC	2,764
30. Baltimore, MD	2,748
31. Rochester, NY	2,737
32. Fresno, CA	2,664
33. Jacksonville, FL	2,642
33. Las Vegas, NV–AZ	2,642
35. Ventura, CA	2,630

Places Rated Rank	Places Rated Score
36. Tampa–St. Petersburg–Clearwater, FL	2,624
37. Salt Lake City–Ogden, UT	2,618
38. Anchorage, AK	2,600
39. Albuquerque, NM	2,566
40. Tallahassee, FL	2,542
41. Atlantic City–Cape May, NJ	2,523
42. Cleveland–Lorain–Elyria, OH	2,508
43. Duluth–Superior, MN–WI	2,501
44. Biloxi–Gulfport–Pascagoula, MS	2,500
45. Tacoma, WA	2,498
46. Sarasota–Bradenton, FL	2,478
47. Daytona Beach, FL	2,477
48. Yuma, AZ	2,469
49. New Orleans, LA	2,402
50. West Palm Beach–Boca Raton, FL	2,401
51. Visalia–Tulare–Porterville, CA	2,400
52. Brownsville–Harlingen–San Benito, TX	2,397
53. Redding, CA	2,392
54. Fort Myers–Cape Coral, FL	2,358
55. Myrtle Beach, SC	2,352
56. Fort Pierce–Port St. Lucie, FL	2,343
57. Yakima, WA	2,321
58. Akron, OH	2,304
59. Melbourne–Titusville–Palm Bay, FL	2,295
60. Santa Fe, NM	2,294
61. Denver, CO	2,293
62. Monmouth–Ocean, NJ	2,284
63. Boston, MA	2,278
64. Cincinnati, OH–KY–IN	2,277
64. Long Island, NY	2,277
66. Minneapolis–St. Paul, MN–WI	2,273

Places Rated Rank	Places Rated Score
67. Colorado Springs, CO	2,270
68. Portsmouth–Dover–Rochester, NH	2,260
69. Chicago, IL	2,252
70. Santa Cruz–Watsonville, CA	2,235
71. Omaha, NE–IA	2,229
72. Buffalo–Niagara Falls, NY	2,218
73. Syracuse, NY	2,173
74. Medford–Ashland, OR	2,165
75. Mobile, AL	2,161
76. Toronto, ON	2,157
77. New York, NY	2,125
78. Milwaukee–Waukesha, WI	2,107
78. Waterloo–Cedar Falls, IA	2,107
80. Oklahoma City, OK	2,104
81. Philadelphia, PA–NJ	2,402
82. Detroit, MI	2,096
83. Fort Worth–Arlington, TX	2,071
84. Lynchburg, VA	2,066
85. Reno, NV	2,035
86. Las Cruces, NM	2,026
86. Roanoke, VA	2,026
88. Edmonton, AB	2,018
89. Des Moines, IA	2,013
90. Dover, DE	2,011
91. Kansas City, MO–KS	2,007
92. St. Catharines–Niagara, ON	1,978
93. San Luis Obispo–Atascadero–Paso Robles, CA	1,976
94. Riverside–San Bernardino, CA	1,972
95. Toledo, OH	1,956
96. Jamestown, NY	1,955
97. Hickory–Morgantown, NC	1,954
98. Columbus, OH	1,949
99. Victoria, BC	1,947
100. Saginaw–Bay City–Midland, MI	1,941

Places Rated Rank	Places Rated Score	Places Rated Rank	Places Rated Score	Places Rated Rank	Places Rated Score
101. St. Louis, MO–IL	1,936	156. Harrisburg–Lebanon–Carlisle, PA	1,536	210. New London–Norwich, CT–RI	1,281
102. Tulsa, OK	1,907	157. Providence–Warwick–Cranston, RI	1,530		
103. St. John's, NF	1,898	158. Springfield, MO	1,526	211. Portland, ME	1,280
104. Wilmington, NC	1,870	159. Burlington, VT	1,525	212. Trenton, NJ	1,278
105. Great Falls, MT	1,857	160. Bloomington, IN	1,524	213. Orange County, NY	1,259
				214. Columbus, GA–AL	1,250
105. Washington, DC–MD–VA–WV	1,857	161. Birmingham, AL	1,520	215. Benton Harbor, MI	1,248
106. Atlanta, GA	1,822	162. San Antonio, TX	1,509		
107. Windsor, ON	1,821	163. Lake Charles, LA	1,508	216. Jackson, MI	1,243
108. Peoria–Pekin, IL	1,814	164. Punta Gorda, FL	1,504	217. Charlotte–Gastonia–Rock Hill, NC–SC	1,225
109. Wichita Falls, KS	1,811	165. Bangor, ME	1,500	217. Lawrence, KS	1,225
				219. Dubuque, IA	1,224
110. Grand Rapids–Muskegon–Holland, MI	1,787	166. Johnson City–Kingsport–Bristol, TN–VA	1,493	220. Gary, IN	1,218
111. Salem, OR	1,784	167. Houma, LA	1,490		
112. Kitchener, ON	1,777	168. Lincoln, NE	1,486	221. Allentown–Bethlehem–Easton, PA–NJ	1,211
113. Northern New Jersey, NJ	1,774	169. Ann Arbor, MI	1,480	222. Sioux Falls, SD	1,210
114. Panama City, FL	1,753	170. Fort Walton Beach, FL	1,478	223. Wheeling, WV–OH	1,209
				224. Baton Rouge, LA	1,207
115. Erie, PA	1,751	171. Decatur, AL	1,475	225. Fort Wayne, IN	1,203
116. Fort Lauderdale, FL	1,773	172. New Bedford–Fall River–Attleboro, MA	1,460		
116. Asheville, NC	1,733	173. Lakeland–Winter Haven, FL	1,458	225. Jackson, MS	1,203
116. Greensboro–Winston-Salem–High Point, NC	1,733	174. Macon, GA	1,455	227. Pittsfield, MA	1,200
119. Calgary, AB	1,728	175. Memphis, TN–AR–MS	1,450	227. Rochester, MN	1,200
				227. Wichita Falls, TX	1,200
120. Savannah, GA	1,713	176. Hamilton, ON	1,440	230. El Paso, TX	1,190
121. Green Bay, WI	1,711	177. Boise City, ID	1,430		
122. Thunder Bay, ON	1,710	177. San Jose, CA	1,430	231. Chico–Paradise, CA	1,173
123. La Crosse, WI–MN	1,701	177. State College, PA	1,430	232. Tuscaloosa, AL	1,171
124. Madison, WI	1,706	180. Albany–Schenectady–Troy, NY	1,427	233. Cumberland, MD–WV	1,168
				234. Montreal, PQ	1,166
125. Wilmington–Newark, DE–MD	1,688	181. Vallejo–Fairfield–Napa, CA	1,422	235. Greenville–Spartanburg–Anderson, SC	1,063
126. Chattanooga, TN–GA	1,680	182. Sheboygan, WI	1,407	236. Shreveport–Bossier City, LA	1,145
127. Kenosha, WI	1,679	183. Huntington–Ashland, WV–KY–OH	1,402		
128. Kalamazoo–Battle Creek, MI	1,664	184. Champaign–Urbana, IL	1,400	237. New Haven–Meriden, CT	1,143
129. Spokane, WA	1,663	184. Sioux City, IA–NE	1,400	237. Saskatoon, SK	1,143
				239. Bremerton, WA	1,139
130. Oakland, CA	1,659	184. Springfield, IL	1,400	240. Lawton, OK	1,131
130. Sudbury, ON	1,659	184. Waco, TX	1,400	241. Richmond–Petersburg, VA	1,130
132. Pensacola, FL	1,656	188. Saint John, NB	1,371		
134. Fort Smith, AR–OK	1,640	189. Columbia, MO	1,338	242. Dayton–Springfield, OH	1,129
135. Lake County, IL	1,639	189. Dallas, TX	1,338	242. Lima, OH	1,129
				242. Springfield, MA	1,129
136. Gainesville, FL	1,636	191. Glens Falls, NY	1,327	245. Rockford, IL	1,128
137. Utica–Rome, NY	1,618	192. Raleigh–Durham–Chapel Hill, NC	1,322	246. Iowa City, IA	1,124
138. Nashville, TN	1,617	192. Evansville–Henderson, IN–KY	1,322		
139. Elmira, NY	1,615	194. Winnipeg, MB	1,318	247. Ottawa–Hull, ON–PQ	1,117
140. Fayetteville–Springdale–Rogers, AR	1,612	195. Bloomington–Normal, IL	1,309	248. Huntsville, AL	1,116
				249. Lansing–East Lansing, MI	1,112
141. Austin–San Marcos, TX	1,611	196. Cedar Rapids, IA	1,307	250. Pueblo, CO	1,107
142. Columbia, SC	1,610	196. Lafayette, LA	1,307	251. Regina, SK	1,106
143. Davenport–Moline–Rock Island, IA–IL	1,608	198. Dutchess County, NY	1,304		
144. Appleton–Oshkosh–Neenah, WI	1,606	199. Athens, GA	1,303	252. Binghamton, NY	1,103
145. Charlottesville, VA	1,604	199. Lubbock, TX	1,303	253. Billings, MT	1,102
				254. Amarillo, TX	1,101
146. Indianapolis, IN	1,603	201. Alexandria, LA	1,300	255. Montgomery, AL	1,100
147. Hagerstown, MD	1,601	201. Bryan–College Station, TX	1,300	255. St. Cloud, MN	1,100
147. Lexington, KY	1,601	201. Charleston, WV	1,300		
147. Louisville, KY–IN	1,601	201. Lafayette, IN	1,300	255. Terre Haute, IN	1,100
150. Pittsburgh, PA	1,594	201. London, ON	1,300	255. Topeka, KS	1,100
				255. Trois-Rivieres, PQ	1,000
151. Santa Rosa, CA	1,587	201. Monroe, LA	1,300	260. Stamford–Norwalk, CT	1,084
152. South Bend, IN	1,566	201. Muncie, IN	1,300	261. Reading, PA	1,082
153. Halifax, NS	1,561	208. Galveston–Texas City, TX	1,298		
154. Little Rock–North Little Rock, AR	1,550	209. Parkersburg–Marietta, WV–OH	1,289	262. Flint, MI	1,080
155. Beaumont–Port Arthur, TX	1,540			263. Bismarck, ND	1,059
				263. Brazoria, TX	1,059
				265. Florence, AL	1,039
				266. Clarksville–Hopkinsville, TN–KY	1,006

Places Rated Rank	Places Rated Score	Places Rated Rank	Places Rated Score	Places Rated Rank	Places Rated Score
267. Owensboro, KY	1,005	292. Worcester–Fitchburg–Leominster, MA	904	319. Decatur, IL	704
268. Fargo–Moorhead, ND–MN	1,003	293. Grand Forks, ND–MN	903	320. Gadsden, AL	700
269. Stockton–Lodi, CA	1,002	294. Joplin, MO	901	321. McAllen–Edinburg–Mission, TX	688
269. Anniston, AL	1,002	295. Greenville, NC	900		
271. Enid, OK	1,000	296. Bakersfield, CA	896	322. Scranton–Wilkes-Barre–Hazleton, PA	660
271. Janesville–Beloit, WI	1,000	297. Corpus Christi, TX	870	323. York, PA	649
271. Kokomo, IN	1,000	298. Youngstown–Warren, OH	836	324. Central New Jersey, NJ	637
271. Odessa–Midland, TX	1,000	299. Sumter, SC	823	325. Eau Claire, WI	610
271. San Angelo, TX	1,000	300. Danbury, CT	810	326. Goldsboro, NC	609
276. Johnstown, PA	987	301. Mansfield, OH	809		
				327. Dothan, AL	604
277. Hartford, CT	986	302. Tyler, TX	808	328. Vancouver, WA	590
278. Steubenville–Weirton, OH–WV	969	303. Wausau, WI	805	329. Olympia, WA	562
279. Hamilton–Middletown, OH	967	304. Lancaster, PA	802	330. Modesto, CA	548
280. Greeley, CO	950	305. St. Joseph, MO	801	331. Merced, CA	547
281. Vineland–Millville–Bridgeton, NJ	930	306. Albany, GA	800		
				332. Waterbury, CT	506
282. Richland–Kennewick–Pasco, WA	921	306. Elkhart–Goshen, IN	800	333. Sherman–Denison, TX	504
		306. Fayetteville, NC	800	334. Longview–Marshall, TX	502
283. Kankakee, IL	920	306. Victoria, TX	800	335. Pine Bluff, AR	500
284. Yuba City, CA	917	310. Sherbrooke, PQ	773	336. Oshawa, ON	448
285. Sharon, PA	916	311. Chicoutimi–Jonquiere, PQ	733		
286. Manchester–Nashua, NH	915			337. Williamsport, PA	414
		312. Altoona, PA	724	338. Yolo, CA	370
287. Lewiston–Auburn, ME	912	313. Augusta–Aiken, GA–SC	723	339. Killeen–Temple, TX	301
288. Casper, WY	911	314. Newark–Jersey City, NJ	720	340. Rocky Mount, NC	300
289. Racine, WI	910	315. Bridgeport, CT	707	340. Texarkana, TX–Texarkana, AR	300
290. Jacksonville, NC	909	315. Florence, SC	707		
291. Canton–Massillon, OH	906			342. Laredo, TX	201
		317. Cheyenne, WY	706	343. Danville, VA	200
		318. Abilene, TX	705		

Place Profiles: Recreation

The following profiles are a selective catalogue of recreation features in each metro area.

Common Denominators are options for recreation available everywhere. The *Golf courses* entry shows the number of private, daily-fee, and municipal courses and their total regulation holes; *Good restaurants* tells how many restaurants at each quality level are in a metro area ("4 **" means, for example, that the place has four two-star restaurants); *Movie theaters* shows the number of independently owned theaters and chain-exhibitor theaters and their total screens. The access rating for each item is shown in the right-hand column.

Crowd Pleasers lists local zoos, aquariums, theme parks, and pari-mutuel betting attractions. Also included are the days per year that theme parks and pari-mutuel tracks are open, along with their access rating.

Under the heading *Professional Sports,* the names of major- and minor-league baseball, basketball, football, and hockey teams are given along with the total game seats per capita and access rating.

Local colleges and universities that field NCAA Division I or CIAU teams in football, basketball, and ice hockey are also listed with separate total game seats per capita and access rating. If the school doesn't participate in all of these sports, the team's name is followed by one or two letters—(B) or (F) or (H)—for the sport it plays.

Outdoor Recreation Assets counts the metro area's number of miles of ocean or Great Lakes coastline and the acreage for all protected land located there.

Lengths of ocean and Great Lakes coastlines for American metro areas are estimated from state totals measured by the National Oceanic and Atmospheric Administration. Similar measurements for Canadian metro areas are estimated from National Atlas provincial totals.

American protected lands include all national forest, park, and wildlife refuge acres, plus all state park units located within metro-area counties; Canadian protected lands include all federal parks, natural areas and wildlife areas, plus all provincial parks and natural areas located within metro-area census divisions.

A number of abbreviations are used in this section:

NF National Forest	NM National Monument
NP National Park	NWA National Wildlife Area
NHP National Historic Park	NWR National Wildlife Refuge
NRA National Recreation Area	PP Provincial Park
NHS National Historic Site	SNA State Natural Area
NSR National Scenic River	SP State Park
NMP National Military Park	PNA Provincial Natural Area
NS National Seashore	SRA State Recreation Area
SF State Forest	MBS Migratory Bird Sanctuary

Information comes from these sources: American Association of Zoological Parks and Aquariums, *Zoological Parks and Aquariums in the Americas*, 1993; American Baseball League, unpublished data, 1993; American Greyhound Track Operators Association, *Directory*, 1993; American Hockey League, *Media Guide*, 1992; Baseball America, *Directory*, 1993; Brown Publishing Company, *National Speedway Directory*, 1993; Canadian Association of Zoological Parks and Aquariums, *Zoos, Aquariums, and Game Farms*, 1993; Canadian Inter-University Athletic Union, *Directory*, 1993; Continental Basketball Association, unpublished data, 1993; Environment Canada, unpublished national conservation area data, 1993; *Film Canada Yearbook*, 1993; International Hockey League, *Media Guide*, 1992; National Association of Collegiate Directors of Athletics, *The 1992–93*

National Directory of College Athletics, 1993; National Association of Professional Baseball Leagues, unpublished data, 1988; National Association of Theater Owners, *Encyclopedia of Exhibition*, 1993; National Basketball Association, unpublished data, 1992; National Collegiate Athletic Association, *National Collegiate Championships*, 1992, *NCAA Basketball*, 1992, and *NCAA Football*, 1993; National Football League, unpublished data, 1992; National Golf Foundation, unpublished data, 1993; National Hockey League, unpublished data, 1992; National League of Professional Baseball Teams, unpublished data, 1992; Prentice Hall Press, *Mobil Travel Guide*, 1989; Quigley Publishing Company, *Motion Picture Almanac*, 1993; Thoroughbred Racing Associations of North America, Inc., *Directory and Record Book*, 1993; U.S. Department of Agriculture, Forest Service, *Land Areas of the National Forest System*, 1992; U.S. Department of Commerce: Bureau of the Census, unpublished "Coastal Counties of the United States," and unpublished area measurements, 1990; National Oceanic and Atmospheric Administration, *The Coastline of the United States*, 1975; U.S. Department of the Interior: Fish and Wildlife Service, unpublished master deed listing, 1993, and National Park Service, *Index to the National Park System and Related Areas*, 1993, and unpublished master deed listing, 1993; and U.S. Trotting Association, *Trotting and Pacing Guide*, 1992.

A check mark (✓) preceding a metro area's name highlights it as one of the top 35 places for recreation.

Abilene, TX
Common Denominators

	Rating
Golf courses: 3 private (54 holes), 1 daily fee (9 holes), 1 municipal (18 holes)	C
Movie theaters: 2 chain (16 screens), 2 independent (3 screens)	AA

Crowd Pleasers

Aquariums and Zoos:	B
Abilene Zoo (249 species, 1,180 specimens)	

Outdoor Recreation Assets
State Recreation Area
Abilene SRA, 621 acres

Places Rated Score: 705   Places Rated Rank: 318

Akron, OH
Common Denominators

Golf courses: 13 private (216 holes), 26 daily fee (423 holes), 3 municipal (54 holes)	AA
Good restaurants: 3 ★, 3 ★★, 3 ★★★	B
Movie theaters: 6 chain (37 screens), 6 independent (7 screens)	B

Crowd Pleasers

Aquariums and Zoos:	AA
Akron Zoological Park (93 species, 238 specimens)	
Sea World of Ohio (374 species, 2,513 specimens)	
Family Theme Parks:	C
Geauga Lake (108 days)	
Professional Sports: 2.47 game seats per capita	AA
Cavaliers (NBA Basketball)	
NCAA Division I: 0.71 game seats per capita	A
Kent State University Golden Flashes	
University of Akron Zips (F, B)	

Outdoor Recreation Assets
Federal Protected Area
Cuyahoga Valley NRA, 14,146 acres
State Recreation Areas
Eagle Creek SNA, 441 acres
Portage Lakes SP, 2,443 acres
West Branch SP, 5,352 acres
MC Access: Cleveland–Akron, OH

Places Rated Score: 2,304   Places Rated Rank: 58

Albany, GA
Common Denominators

Golf courses: 3 private (45 holes), 1 daily fee (9 holes), 1 municipal (18 holes)	C
Good restaurants: 1 ★★	C
Movie theaters: 2 chain (12 screens)	A

Crowd Pleasers

Professional Sports: 2.45 game seats per capita	A
Polecats (Class A Baseball)	

Places Rated Score: 800   Places Rated Rank: 306

Albany–Schenectady–Troy, NY
Common Denominators

Golf courses: 18 private (279 holes), 20 daily fee (279 holes), 7 municipal (117 holes)	A
Good restaurants: 2 ★, 10 ★★, 5 ★★★	A
Movie theaters: 18 chain (84 screens), 5 independent (9 screens)	A

Crowd Pleasers

Pari-mutuel Betting:	B
Saratoga Raceway (mixed meetings, 215 days)	
Professional Sports: 1.33 game seats per capita	B
Colonie Yankees (Class AA Baseball)	
Islanders (AHL Hockey)	

Rating

Patroons (CBA Basketball)
NCAA Division I: 0.09 game seats per capita   **C**
  Rensselaer Polytechnic Institute Engineers (H)
  Siena College Saints (B)
Outdoor Recreation Assets
  Federal Protected Area
    Saratoga NHP, 2,848 acres
  State Recreation Areas
    Cherry Plain SP, 175 acres
    Grafton Lakes SP, 2,357 acres
    Peebles Island SP, 142 acres
    Thompson's Lake SP, 152 acres
Places Rated Score: 1,427   Places Rated Rank: 180

Albuquerque, NM
Common Denominators
  Golf courses: 8 private (126 holes), 6 daily fee (90   **B**
  holes), 6 municipal (81 holes)
  Good restaurants: 8 *, 19 **, 6 ***   **AA**
  Movie theaters: 7 chain (51 screens), 3   **A**
  independent (6 screens)
Crowd Pleasers
  Aquariums and Zoos: **A**
    Rio Grande Zoological Park (274 species, 1,137
    specimens)
  Pari-mutuel Betting: **B**
    The Downs (thoroughbred, 90 days)
  Professional Sports: 1.14 game seats per capita   **B**
    Dukes (Triple A Baseball)
  NCAA Division I: 0.51 game seats per capita   **A**
    University of New Mexico Lobos (F, B)
Outdoor Recreation Assets
  Federal Protected Areas
    Bandelier NM, 25,428 acres
    Cibola NF, 136,765 acres
    Santa Fe NF, 338,997 acres
  State Recreation Areas
    Coronado SP, 218 acres
    Rio Grande Nature Center SP, 170 acres
    Senator Willie M. Chavez SP, 107 acres
Places Rated Score: 2,566   Places Rated Rank: 39

Alexandria, LA
Common Denominators
  Golf courses: 3 private (45 holes), 2 daily fee (18   **C**
  holes)
  Good restaurants: 1 **   **C**
  Movie theaters: 3 chain (20 screens), 1   **AA**
  independent (1 screen)
Crowd Pleasers
  Aquariums and Zoos: **C**
    Alexandria Zoo (120 species, 565 specimens)
Outdoor Recreation Assets
  Federal Protected Area
    Kisatchee NF, 101,667 acres
Places Rated Score: 1,300   Places Rated Rank: 201

Allentown–Bethlehem–Easton, PA–NJ
Common Denominators
  Golf courses: 12 private (207 holes), 13 daily fee   **B**
  (189 holes), 2 municipal (36 holes)
  Good restaurants: 1 **, 1 ***, 1 ****   **C**
  Movie theaters: 10 chain (37 screens), 7   **B**
  independent (7 screens)
Crowd Pleasers
  Family Theme Parks: **B**
    Dorney Park and Wildwater Kingdom (102 days)
  NCAA Division I: 0.30 game seats per capita   **A**
    Lafayette College Leopards (F, B)
    Lehigh University Engineers (F, B)
Outdoor Recreation Assets
  Federal Protected Areas
    Appalachian Trail, 2,485 acres
    Delaware Water Gap NRA, 10,319 acres

Rating

  State Recreation Areas
    Hickory Run SP, 15,500 acres
    Lehigh Gorge SP, 3,390 acres
Places Rated Score: 1,211   Places Rated Rank: 221

Altoona, PA
Common Denominators
  Golf courses: 1 private (18 holes), 5 daily fee (72   **A**
  holes)
  Good restaurants: 1 *, 1 ***   **B**
  Movie theaters: 3 chain (9 screens)   **B**
Outdoor Recreation Assets
  Federal Protected Area
    Allegheny Portage Railroad NHS, 627 acres
  State Recreation Area
    Canoe Creek SP, 959 acres
Places Rated Score: 724   Places Rated Rank: 312

Amarillo, TX
Common Denominators
  Golf courses: 4 private (54 holes), 5 daily fee (72   **A**
  holes), 2 municipal (36 holes)
  Good restaurants: 1 *, 3 **   **B**
  Movie theaters: 7 chain (26 screens), 1   **AA**
  independent (1 screen)
Outdoor Recreation Assets
  Federal Protected Areas
    Alibates Flint Quarries NM, 1,079 acres
    Buffalo Lake NWR, 7,664 acres
    Lake Meredith NRA, 23,379 acres
Places Rated Score: 1,101   Places Rated Rank: 254

Anchorage, AK
Common Denominators
  Golf courses: 1 daily fee (18 holes), 1 municipal (18   **C**
  holes)
  Movie theaters: 6 chain (31 screens), 1   **AA**
  independent (1 screen)
Crowd Pleasers
  Aquariums and Zoos: **C**
    The Alaska Zoo (47 species, 102 specimens)
Outdoor Recreation Assets
  Pacific Coastline: 90 miles
  Federal Protected Area
    Chugach NF, 274,290 acres
Places Rated Score: 2,600   Places Rated Rank: 38

Ann Arbor, MI
Common Denominators
  Golf courses: 12 private (198 holes), 27 daily fee   **AA**
  (414 holes), 5 municipal (90 holes)
  Good restaurants: 2 *, 5 **, 2 ***   **B**
  Movie theaters: 7 chain (40 screens), 3   **A**
  independent (5 screens)
Crowd Pleasers
  NCAA Division I: 1.72 game seats per capita   **AA**
    Eastern Michigan University Eagles (F, B)
    University of Michigan Wolverines
Outdoor Recreation Assets
  State Recreation Areas
    Brighton SRA, 4,915 acres
    Lake Hudson SRA, 2,747 acres
    Pinckney SRA, 3,480 acres
    W. J. Hayes SP, 609 acres
MC Access: Detroit–Ann Arbor–Flint, MI
Places Rated Score: 1,480   Places Rated Rank: 169

Anniston, AL
Common Denominators
  Golf courses: 2 private (36 holes), 3 daily fee (54   **A**
  holes), 1 municipal (9 holes)
  Good restaurants: 1 **   **C**
  Movie theaters: 2 chain (12 screens)   **A**

	Rating

Outdoor Recreation Assets
  Federal Protected Area
    Talladega NF, 23,543 acres
Places Rated Score: 1,002   Places Rated Rank: 269

Appleton–Oshkosh–Neenah, WI
Common Denominators
  Golf courses: 6 private (99 holes), 14 daily fee (216   **AA**
  holes), 2 municipal (36 holes)
  Good restaurants: 1 *, 4 **, 1 ***   **B**
  Movie theaters: 7 chain (33 screens), 2   **AA**
  independent (3 screens)
Crowd Pleasers
  Pari-mutuel Betting: **AA**
    Fox Valley Greyhound Park (greyhound, 347 days)
  Professional Sports: 0.94 game seats per capita   **B**
    Foxes (Class A Baseball)
Outdoor Recreation Assets
  State Recreation Area
    High Cliff SP, 1,145 acres
Places Rated Score: 1,606   Places Rated Rank: 144

Asheville, NC
Common Denominators
  Golf courses: 5 private (90 holes), 3 daily fee (45   **A**
  holes), 2 municipal (36 holes)
  Good restaurants: 2 *, 4 **, 1 ***   **A**
  Movie theaters: 7 chain (13 screens), 1   **B**
  independent (1 screen)
Crowd Pleasers
  Professional Sports: 1.24 game seats per capita   **B**
    Tourists (Class A Baseball)
  NCAA Division I: 0.13 game seats per capita   **C**
    University of North Carolina, Asheville Bulldogs (B)
Outdoor Recreation Assets
  Federal Protected Areas
    Appalachian Trail, 250 acres
    Blue Ridge Parkway, 5,493 acres
    Pisgah NF, 83,773 acres
Places Rated Score: 1,733   Places Rated Rank: 116

Athens, GA
Common Denominators
  Golf courses: 3 private (45 holes), 5 daily fee (90   **AA**
  holes)
  Good restaurants: 1 **   **C**
  Movie theaters: 2 chain (13 screens), 1   **AA**
  independent (2 screens)
Crowd Pleasers
  NCAA Division I: 4.11 game seats per capita   **AA**
    University of Georgia Bulldogs (F, B)
Outdoor Recreation Assets
  Federal Protected Area
    Oconee NF, 157 acres
  State Recreation Area
    Watson Mill Bridge SP, 100 acres
Places Rated Score: 1,303   Places Rated Rank: 199

Atlanta, GA
Common Denominators
  Golf courses: 53 private (891 holes), 36 daily fee   **C**
  (585 holes), 10 municipal (171 holes)
  Good restaurants: 12 *, 27 **, 25 ***, 5 ****   **A**
  Movie theaters: 63 chain (374 screens), 7   **AA**
  independent (11 screens)
Crowd Pleasers
  Aquariums and Zoos: **A**
    Zoo Atlanta (245 species, 924 specimens)
  Family Theme Parks: **A**
    Six Flags Over Georgia (130 days)
    White Water and American Adventures (119 days)
  Professional Sports: 1.89 game seats per capita   **A**
    Braves (NL Baseball)
    Falcons (NFL Football)
    Hawks (NBA Basketball)

NCAA Division I: 0.12 game seats per capita   **C**
    Georgia Institute of Technology Yellow Jackets
    (F, B)
    Georgia State University Panthers (B)
Outdoor Recreation Assets
  Federal Protected Areas
    Chattahoochee River NRA, 4,015 acres
    Kennesaw Mountain NBP, 2,880 acres
  State Recreation Areas
    Fort Yargo SP, 1,850 acres
    Hard Labor Creek SP, 3,005 acres
    Panola Mountain SP, 617 acres
    Red Top Mountain SP, 1,950 acres
Places Rated Score: 1,822   Places Rated Rank: 106

Atlantic City–Cape May, NJ
Common Denominators
  Golf courses: 6 private (108 holes), 8 daily fee (135   **A**
  holes), 1 municipal (9 holes)
  Good restaurants: 1 *, 15 **, 3 ***   **AA**
  Movie theaters: 13 chain (54 screens), 1   **AA**
  independent (1 screen)
Crowd Pleasers
  Aquariums and Zoos: **B**
    Cape May County Park Zoo (135 species, 369
    specimens)
  Pari-mutuel Betting: **B**
    Atlantic City Race Course (thoroughbred, 69
    days)
Outdoor Recreation Assets
  Atlantic Coastline: 67 miles
  Federal Protected Areas
    Cape May NWR, 2,587 acres
    Edwin B. Forsythe NWR, 19,939 acres
  State Recreation Area
    Corson's Inlet SP, 341 acres
  MC Access: Philadelphia–Wilmington–Atlantic City,
    PA–NJ–DE–MD
Places Rated Score: 2,523   Places Rated Rank: 41

Augusta–Aiken, GA–SC
Common Denominators
  Golf courses: 12 private (198 holes), 8 daily fee   **B**
  (126 holes), 1 municipal (18 holes)
  Good restaurants: 2 **, 1 ***   **C**
  Movie theaters: 8 chain (29 screens), 2   **B**
  independent (2 screens)
Crowd Pleasers
  Professional Sports: 0.61 game seats per capita   **C**
    Pirates (Class A Baseball)
Outdoor Recreation Assets
  Federal Protected Area
    Sumter NF, 31,142 acres
  State Recreation Areas
    Mistletoe SP, 1,920 acres
    Redcliffe SP, 350 acres
Places Rated Score: 723   Places Rated Rank: 313

Austin–San Marcos, TX
Common Denominators
  Golf courses: 15 private (261 holes), 12 daily fee   **B**
  (189 holes), 9 municipal (126 holes)
  Good restaurants: 5 *, 6 **, 4 ***   **B**
  Movie theaters: 21 chain (133 screens), 3   **AA**
  independent (4 screens)
Crowd Pleasers
  Family Theme Parks: **AA**
    Aquarena Springs (365 days)
  Pari-mutuel Betting: **C**
    Manor Downs (mixed meetings, 92 days)
  NCAA Division I: 0.74 game seats per capita   **A**
    Southwest Texas State University Bobcats (F, B)
    University of Texas Longhorns (F, B)
Outdoor Recreation Assets

	Rating

State Recreation Areas
Buescher SP, 1,017 acres
Lake Bastrop SRA, 785 acres
Places Rated Score: 1,611   Places Rated Rank: 141

Bakersfield, CA
Common Denominators
Golf courses: 7 private (117 holes), 7 daily fee (108 — **B**
holes), 7 municipal (117 holes)
Good restaurants: 4 *, 1 ** — **C**
Movie theaters: 5 chain (20 screens) — **C**
Crowd Pleasers
Professional Sports: 0.39 game seats per capita — **C**
Dodgers (Class A Baseball)
Outdoor Recreation Assets
Federal Protected Areas
Bitter Creek NWR, 13,535 acres
Kern NWR, 10,618 acres
Los Padres NF, 64,803 acres
Sequoia NF, 312,029 acres
State Recreation Areas
Fort Tejon SHP, 205 acres
Red Rock Canyon SP, 10,343 acres
Places Rated Score: 896   Places Rated Rank: 296

✓ Baltimore, MD
Common Denominators
Golf courses: 32 private (522 holes), 8 daily fee — **C**
(126 holes), 5 municipal (81 holes)
Good restaurants: 11 *, 29 **, 17 *** — **A**
Movie theaters: 30 chain (147 screens), 6 — **B**
independent (13 screens)
Crowd Pleasers
Aquariums and Zoos: — **AA**
Baltimore Zoo (234 species, 1,500 specimens)
National Aquarium
Pari-mutuel Betting: — **C**
Pimlico (thoroughbred, 106 days)
Professional Sports: 1.77 game seats per capita — **A**
Orioles (AL Baseball)
NCAA Division I: 0.21 game seats per capita — **B**
Coppin State College Eagles (B)
Loyola College Greyhounds (B)
Morgan State University Bears (F, B)
Towson State University Tigers (F, B)
United States Naval Academy Midshipmen (F, B)
University of Maryland, Baltimore County
Retrievers (B)
Outdoor Recreation Assets
Chesapeake Bay Coastline: 96 miles
Federal Protected Area
National Capital Parks, 432 acres
State Recreation Areas
Gunpowder Falls SP, 1,903 acres
Hart-Miller Island SP, 244 acres
Patapsco Valley SP, 6,578 acres
Rocks SP, 855 acres
MC Access: Washington-Baltimore,
DC-MD-VA-WV
Places Rated Score: 2,748   Places Rated Rank: 30

Bangor, ME
Common Denominators
Golf courses: 5 daily fee (63 holes), 2 municipal (27 — **AA**
holes)
Good restaurants: 1 *, 5 ** — **AA**
Movie theaters: 1 chain (10 screens) — **A**
Crowd Pleasers
NCAA Division I: 1.61 game seats per capita — **AA**
University of Maine Black Bears
Places Rated Score: 1,500   Places Rated Rank: 165

✓ Barnstable-Yarmouth, MA
Common Denominators
Golf courses: 12 private (207 holes), 13 daily fee — **AA**
(207 holes), 6 municipal (108 holes)

	Rating

Good restaurants: 26 *, 26 **, 11 ***, 1 **** — **AA**
Movie theaters: 8 chain (44 screens) — **AA**
Crowd Pleasers
Aquariums and Zoos: — **A**
Aquarium of Cape Cod
Outdoor Recreation Assets
Atlantic Coastline: 110 miles
Federal Protected Areas
Cape Cod NS, 27,379 acres
Monomoy NWR, 2,702 acres
State Recreation Areas
Hawksnest SP, 218 acres
Nickerson SP, 1,779 acres
Scusset Beach State Reservation, 380 acres
Shawne-Crowell SF, 2,756 acres
South Cape Beach SP, 790 acres
Washburn Island SNA, 355 acres
Places Rated Score: 2,781   Places Rated Rank: 27

Baton Rouge, LA
Common Denominators
Golf courses: 8 private (126 holes), 3 daily fee (54 — **B**
holes), 5 municipal (72 holes)
Good restaurants: 3 *, 5 **, 2 *** — **B**
Movie theaters: 5 chain (33 screens), 2 — **B**
independent (3 screens)
Crowd Pleasers
Aquariums and Zoos: — **B**
Greater Baton Rouge Zoo (226 species, 880
specimens)
NCAA Division I: 1.53 game seats per capita — **AA**
Louisiana State University Fighting Tigers (F, B)
Southern University, Baton Rouge Jaguars (F, B)
Outdoor Recreation Assets
State Recreation Area
Tickfaw SP, 1,169 acres
Places Rated Score: 1,207 .   Places Rated Rank: 224

Beaumont-Port Arthur, TX
Common Denominators
Golf courses: 8 private (135 holes), 4 daily fee (63 — **B**
holes), 2 municipal (36 holes)
Good restaurants: 2 *, 2 ** — **C**
Movie theaters: 9 chain (29 screens), 2 — **A**
independent (3 screens)
Crowd Pleasers
NCAA Division I: 0.29 game seats per capita — **B**
Lamar University, Beaumont Cardinals (B)
Outdoor Recreation Assets
Gulf Coastline: 32 miles
Federal Protected Areas
Big Thicket NP, 47,374 acres
McFaddin NWR, 41,682 acres
Texas Point NWR, 8,952 acres
State Recreation Area
Village Creek SP, 942 acres
Places Rated Score: 1,540   Places Rated Rank: 155

✓ Bellingham, WA
Common Denominators
Golf courses: 3 private (36 holes), 6 daily fee (81 — **AA**
holes), 1 municipal (18 holes)
Good restaurants: 3 **, 1 *** — **A**
Movie theaters: 2 chain (9 screens) — **B**
Crowd Pleasers
Family Theme Parks: — **C**
Wild 'n' Wet Water Park (87 days)
Professional Sports: 1.10 game seats per capita — **B**
Mariners (Class A Baseball)
Outdoor Recreation Assets
Pacific Coastline: 30 miles
Federal Protected Areas
Mt. Baker NF, 452,736 acres
North Cascades NP, 281,690 acres
Ross Lake NRA, 107,067 acres

	Rating

State Recreation Area
   Birch Bay SP, 193 acres
Places Rated Score: 3,200   Places Rated Rank: 11

Benton Harbor, MI
Common Denominators

	Rating
Golf courses: 5 private (81 holes), 9 daily fee (153 holes), 2 municipal (18 holes)	AA
Good restaurants: 1 **, 1 ***	B
Movie theaters: 1 chain (5 screens)	C

Crowd Pleasers

	Rating
Family Theme Parks: Deer Forest (92 days)	C

Outdoor Recreation Assets
   Lake Michigan Coastline: 44 miles
   State Recreation Area
      Grand Mere SP, 982 acres
Places Rated Score: 1,248   Places Rated Rank: 215

Billings, MT
Common Denominators

	Rating
Golf courses: 5 private (81 holes), 2 daily fee (27 holes)	C
Good restaurants: 4 *, 6 **, 2 ***	AA
Movie theaters: 4 chain (21 screens), 1 independent (1 screen)	AA

Crowd Pleasers

	Rating
Pari-mutuel Betting: Metra Park (thoroughbred, 23 days)	B

Outdoor Recreation Assets
   State Recreation Area
      Lake Elmo SP, 123 acres
Places Rated Score: 1,102   Places Rated Rank: 253

Biloxi–Gulfport–Pascagoula, MS
Common Denominators

	Rating
Golf courses: 6 private (90 holes), 13 daily fee (216 holes), 1 municipal (18 holes)	AA
Good restaurants: 5 *, 4 **, 2 ***	A
Movie theaters: 6 chain (21 screens), 5 independent (18 screens)	AA

Outdoor Recreation Assets
   Gulf Coastline: 30 miles
   Federal Protected Areas
      DeSoto NF, 81,311 acres
      Grand Bay NWR, 2,901 acres
      Gulf Islands NS, 69,937 acres
      Mississippi Sandhill Crane NWR, 17,909 acres
   State Recreation Area
      Buccaneer SP, 393 acres
Places Rated Score: 2,500   Places Rated Rank: 44

Binghamton, NY
Common Denominators

	Rating
Golf courses: 4 private (63 holes), 12 daily fee (180 holes), 3 municipal (54 holes)	AA
Good restaurants: 1 *, 3 **, 1 ***	B
Movie theaters: 8 chain (11 screens), 3 independent (4 screens)	C

Crowd Pleasers

	Rating
Aquariums and Zoos: Ross Park Zoo (59 species, 151 specimens)	C

Professional Sports: 1.95 game seats per capita
   Mets (Class AA Baseball)
   Rangers (AHL Hockey)
	A

Outdoor Recreation Assets
   State Recreation Area
      Chenango Valley SP, 1,071 acres
Places Rated Score: 1,103   Places Rated Rank: 252

Birmingham, AL
Common Denominators

	Rating
Golf courses: 23 private (387 holes), 7 daily fee (108 holes), 9 municipal (153 holes)	B
Good restaurants: 3 *, 10 **, 4 ***	A
Movie theaters: 10 chain (86 screens), 2 independent (2 screens)	A

Crowd Pleasers

	Rating
Aquariums and Zoos: Birmingham Zoo (223 species, 793 specimens)	A

Professional Sports: 1.05 game seats per capita
   Bandits (CBA Basketball)
   Barons (Class AA Baseball)
	B

NCAA Division I: 0.28 game seats per capita
   Samford University Bulldogs (F, B)
   University of Alabama, Birmingham Blazers (B)
	B

Outdoor Recreation Assets
   Federal Protected Area
      Watercress Darter NWR, 7 acres
   State Recreation Area
      Rickwood Caverns SP, 380 acres
Places Rated Score: 1,520   Places Rated Rank: 161

Bismarck, ND
Common Denominators

	Rating
Golf courses: 1 private (18 holes), 4 municipal (45 holes)	A
Good restaurants: 2 **	A
Movie theaters: 3 independent (5 screens)	C

Crowd Pleasers

	Rating
Aquariums and Zoos: Dakota Zoo (104 species, 511 specimens)	C

Outdoor Recreation Assets
   Federal Protected Areas
      Florence Lake NWR, 1,468 acres
      Long Lake NWR, 10,330 acres
Places Rated Score: 1,059   Places Rated Rank: 263

Bloomington, IN
Common Denominators

	Rating
Golf courses: 1 private (18 holes), 2 daily fee (36 holes), 1 municipal (18 holes)	A
Good restaurants: 1 *, 3 **	A
Movie theaters: 5 chain (17 screens)	AA

Crowd Pleasers

	Rating
NCAA Division I: 3.81 game seats per capita Indiana University Hoosiers (F, B)	AA

Outdoor Recreation Assets
   Federal Protected Area
      Hoosier NF, 18,840 acres
Places Rated Score: 1,524   Places Rated Rank: 160

Bloomington–Normal, IL
Common Denominators

	Rating
Golf courses: 3 private (45 holes), 4 daily fee (36 holes), 3 municipal (54 holes)	AA
Movie theaters: 5 chain (22 screens)	AA

Crowd Pleasers

	Rating
Aquariums and Zoos: Miller Park Zoo (86 species, 242 specimens)	C
NCAA Division I: 1.37 game seats per capita Illinois State University Redbirds (F, B)	AA

Outdoor Recreation Assets
   State Recreation Area
      Funk's Grove SP, 202 acres
Places Rated Score: 1,309   Places Rated Rank: 195

Boise City, ID
Common Denominators

	Rating
Golf courses: 4 private (63 holes), 5 daily fee (81 holes), 4 municipal (54 holes)	A
Good restaurants: 1 *	C
Movie theaters: 5 chain (13 screens), 3 independent (6 screens)	C

Crowd Pleasers

	Rating
Family Theme Parks: Wild Waters (107 days)	B
Pari-mutuel Betting: Les Bois Park (thoroughbred, 49 days)	B
Professional Sports: 1.00 game seats per capita Hawks (Class A Baseball)	B
NCAA Division I: 0.75 game seats per capita Boise State University Broncos (F, B)	A

Rating

Outdoor Recreation Assets
  Federal Protected Areas
    Boise NF, 4,220 acres
    Deer Flat NWR, 1,243 acres
  State Recreation Area
    Lucky Peak SP, 247 acres
Places Rated Score: 1,430   **Places Rated Rank: 177**

Boston, MA
Common Denominators
  Golf courses: 65 private (963 holes), 50 daily fee   **B**
    (738 holes), 22 municipal (324 holes)
  Good restaurants: 14 *, 43 **, 23 ***, 1 ****   **A**
  Movie theaters: 56 chain (249 screens), 19   **B**
    independent (30 screens)
Crowd Pleasers
  Aquariums and Zoos: **AA**
    Metro Parks Zoos (257 species, 1,576 specimens)
    New England Aquarium
  Pari-mutuel Betting: **B**
    Foxboro Raceway (mixed meetings, 159 days)
    Suffolk Downs (thoroughbred, 200 days)
    Wonderland Park (greyhound, 365 days)
  Professional Sports: 1.33 game seats per capita   **B**
    Bruins (NHL Hockey)
    Celtics (NBA Basketball)
    New England Patriots (NFL Football)
    Red Sox (AL Baseball)
  NCAA Division I: 0.24 game seats per capita   **B**
    Boston College Eagles
    Boston University Terriers
    Harvard University Crimson
    Merrimack College Warriors (H)
    Northeastern University Huskies
    University of Lowell Chiefs (H)
Outdoor Recreation Assets
  Atlantic Coastline: 41 miles
  Federal Protected Areas
    Great Meadows NWR, 3,063 acres
    Massasoit NWR, 184 acres
    Minute Man NHP, 665 acres
    Parker River NWR, 4,663 acres
  State Recreation Areas
    Ames Nowell SP, 600 acres
    Ashland SP, 470 acres
    Billerica SF, 168 acres
    Boston Harbor Islands SP, 195 acres
    Boxford SF, 780 acres
    Bradley Palmer SP, 721 acres
    Bristol Blake SP, 200 acres
    Callahan SP, 425 acres
    Cochituate SP, 1,126 acres
    F. Gilbert Hills SP, 810 acres
    Franklin SF, 843 acres
    Georgetown-Rowley SF, 1,112 acres
    Great Brook Farm SP, 934 acres
    Harold Parker SF, 3,000 acres
    Hopkinton SP, 1,450 acres
    J. Harry Rich SF, 508 acres
    Lowell-Dracut-Tyngsboro SF, 1,000 acres
    Marlboro-Sudbury SF, 300 acres
    Maudslay SP, 450 acres
    Myles Standish SF, 15,000 acres
    Pearl Hill SP, 1,000 acres
    Salisbury Beach State Reservation, 520 acres
    Squannacook River SNA, 300 acres
    Townsend SF, 2,500 acres
    Walden Pond SR, 411 acres
    Warren Manning SF, 380 acres
    Whitehall SP, 877 acres
    Willard Brook SF, 2,380 acres
    Willowdale SF, 2,400 acres
    Wompatuck SP, 2,877 acres
    Wrentham SF, 1,064 acres
MC Access: Boston-New Bedford-Nashua, MA-NH
Places Rated Score: 2,278   **Places Rated Rank: 63**

Rating

✓ Boulder-Longmont, CO
Common Denominators
  Golf courses: 2 private (36 holes), 3 daily fee (54   **A**
    holes), 3 municipal (45 holes)
  Good restaurants: 6 **, 3 ***, 1 ****   **AA**
  Movie theaters: 6 chain (17 screens), 2   **B**
    independent (2 screens)
Crowd Pleasers
  NCAA Division I: 1.58 game seats per capita   **AA**
    University of Colorado Golden Buffaloes (F, B)
Outdoor Recreation Assets
  Federal Protected Areas
    Rocky Mountain NP, 27,253 acres
    Roosevelt NF, 136,994 acres
MC Access: Denver-Boulder-Greeley, CO
Places Rated Score: 3,148   **Places Rated Rank: 14**

Brazoria, TX
Common Denominators
  Golf courses: 2 private (36 holes), 6 daily fee (72   **A**
    holes), 1 municipal (18 holes)
  Movie theaters: 2 chain (9 screens), 1 independent   **C**
    (2 screens)
Outdoor Recreation Assets
  Gulf Coastline: 35 miles
  Federal Protected Areas
    Brazoria NWR, 12,096 acres
    San Bernard NWR, 21,782 acres
  State Recreation Area
    Bryan Beach SRA, 878 acres
MC Access: Houston-Galveston-Brazoria, TX
Places Rated Score: 1,059   **Places Rated Rank: 263**

Bremerton, WA
Common Denominators
  Golf courses: 2 private (27 holes), 3 daily fee (45   **B**
    holes), 1 municipal (18 holes)
  Good restaurants: 2 *, 1 ***   **B**
  Movie theaters: 4 chain (20 screens), 1   **A**
    independent (2 screens)
Outdoor Recreation Assets
  Puget Sound Coastline: 30 miles
  State Recreation Areas
    Fay-Bainbridge SP, 17 acres
    Kitsap Memorial SP, 58 acres
MC Access: Seattle-Tacoma-Bremerton, WA
Places Rated Score: 1,139   **Places Rated Rank: 239**

Bridgeport, CT
Common Denominators
  Golf courses: 7 private (126 holes), 2 daily fee (27   **B**
    holes), 6 municipal (90 holes)
  Good restaurants: 4 *, 1 **   **C**
  Movie theaters: 6 chain (21 screens), 2   **C**
    independent (2 screens)
Crowd Pleasers
  NCAA Division I: 0.09 game seats per capita   **C**
    Fairfield University Stags (B, H)
Outdoor Recreation Assets
  Long Island Sound Coastline: 17 miles
  State Recreation Areas
    Indian Well SP, 153 acres
    Osbornedale SP, 350 acres
    Southford Falls SP, 120 acres
**MC Access: New York-Northern New Jersey-Long
  Island, NY-NJ-CT**
Places Rated Score: 707   **Places Rated Rank: 315**

Brownsville-Harlingen-San Benito, TX
Common Denominators
  Golf courses: 5 private (81 holes), 4 daily fee (72   **B**
    holes), 2 municipal (27 holes)
  Good restaurants: 4 *, 5 **, 1 ***   **A**
  Movie theaters: 8 chain (39 screens), 2   **AA**
    independent (2 screens)

	Rating
Crowd Pleasers	
Aquariums and Zoos:	A
Gladys Porter Zoo (449 species, 1,902 specimens)	
Pari-mutuel Betting:	AA
Valley Greyhound Park (greyhound, 156 days)	

Outdoor Recreation Assets
Gulf Coastline: 31 miles
Federal Protected Areas
Laguna Atascosa NWR, 44,922 acres
Lower Rio Grande Valley NWR, 9,788 acres
State Recreation Area
Arroyo Colorado SRA, 687 acres
Places Rated Score: 2,397   Places Rated Rank: 52

Bryan–College Station, TX
Common Denominators

	Rating
Golf courses: 1 private (18 holes), 1 daily fee (18 holes), 1 municipal (18 holes)	B
Good restaurants: 2 *, 2 **	A
Movie theaters: 5 chain (18 screens), 1 independent (1 screen)	AA
Crowd Pleasers	
NCAA Division I: 3.33 game seats per capita	AA
Texas A&M University Aggies (F, B)	

Places Rated Score: 1,300   Places Rated Rank: 201

Buffalo–Niagara Falls, NY
Common Denominators

	Rating
Golf courses: 16 private (279 holes), 15 daily fee (234 holes), 15 municipal (234 holes)	B
Good restaurants: 5 *, 6 **, 7 ***	B
Movie theaters: 14 chain (83 screens), 12 independent (22 screens)	A
Crowd Pleasers	
Aquariums and Zoos:	A
Aquarium of Niagara Falls USA	
Buffalo Zoological Gardens (212 species, 1,377 specimens)	
Family Theme Parks:	C
Fantasy Island (80 days)	
Pari-mutuel Betting:	C
Buffalo Raceway (harness, 146 days)	
Professional Sports: 2.43 game seats per capita	AA
Bills (NFL Football)	
Bisons (Triple A Baseball)	
Rapids (Class A Baseball)	
Sabres (NHL Hockey)	
NCAA Division I: 0.15 game seats per capita	B
Canisius College Golden Griffins (B, H)	
Niagara University Purple Eagles (B)	
SUNY at Buffalo Bulls (B)	

Outdoor Recreation Assets
Lake Erie Coastline: 29 miles
State Recreation Areas
Beaver Island SP, 952 acres
Buckhorn Island SP, 895 acres
Earl W. Brydges Artpark, 197 acres
Fort Niagara SP, 504 acres
Golden Hill SP, 510 acres
Niagara Reservation SP, 435 acres
Reservoir SP, 132 acres
Wilson–Tuscarora SP, 390 acres
MC Access: Buffalo–St. Catharines–Niagara, NY–ON
Places Rated Score: 2,218   Places Rated Rank: 72

Burlington, VT
Common Denominators

	Rating
Golf courses: 1 private (18 holes), 8 daily fee (126 holes)	AA
Good restaurants: 1 *, 3 **, 3 ***	AA
Movie theaters: 7 chain (30 screens), 2 independent (7 screens)	AA
Crowd Pleasers	
NCAA Division I: 0.39 game seats per capita	A
University of Vermont Catamounts (B, H)	

Outdoor Recreation Assets
State Recreation Areas
Burton Island SP, 253 acres
Grand Isle SP, 226 acres
Lake Carmi SP, 482 acres
North Hero SP, 399 acres
Underhill SP, 150 acres
Woods Island SP, 125 acres
Places Rated Score: 1,525   Places Rated Rank: 159

Calgary, AB
Common Denominators

	Rating
Golf courses: 8 private (144 holes), 8 daily fee (135 holes), 7 municipal (99 holes)	B
Good restaurants: 4 **, 7 ***	B
Movie theaters: 16 chain (69 screens), 1 independent (1 screen)	A
Crowd Pleasers	
Aquariums and Zoos:	A
Calgary Zoo (309 species, 1,313 specimens)	
Pari-mutuel Betting:	B
Stampede Park (mixed meetings, 83 days)	
Professional Sports: 1.91 game seats per capita	A
Cannons (Triple A Baseball)	
Flames (NHL Hockey)	
Stampeders (CFL Football)	
CIAU: 0.26 game seats per capita	B
University of Calgary Dinosaurs	

Outdoor Recreation Assets
Federal Protected Area
Inglewood MBS, 395 acres
Provincial Recreation Areas
Brag Creek PP, 301 acres
Fish Creek PP, 1,804 acres
Places Rated Score: 1,728   Places Rated Rank: 119

Canton–Massillon, OH
Common Denominators

	Rating
Golf courses: 6 private (108 holes), 25 daily fee (414 holes)	AA
Good restaurants: 1 **, 2 ***	C
Movie theaters: 2 chain (16 screens), 4 independent (10 screens)	B
Crowd Pleasers	
Professional Sports: 1.02 game seats per capita	B
Indians (Class AA Baseball)	

Outdoor Recreation Assets
State Recreation Area
Jackson Bog SNA, 6 acres
Places Rated Score: 906   Places Rated Rank: 291

Casper, WY
Common Denominators

	Rating
Golf courses: 2 private (36 holes), 1 daily fee (9 holes), 1 municipal (18 holes)	A
Good restaurants: 2 **, 1 ***	AA
Movie theaters: 1 chain (4 screens)	B

Outdoor Recreation Assets
Federal Protected Areas
Medicine Bow NF, 5,615 acres
Pathfinder NWR, 1,535 acres
State Recreation Area
Wilkins SP, 319 acres
Places Rated Score: 911   Places Rated Rank: 288

Cedar Rapids, IA
Common Denominators

	Rating
Golf courses: 3 private (45 holes), 4 daily fee (45 holes), 4 municipal (63 holes)	AA
Good restaurants: 1 *	C
Movie theaters: 7 chain (29 screens), 2 independent (2 screens)	AA
Crowd Pleasers	
Professional Sports: 2.44 game seats per capita	AA
Reds (Class A Baseball)	

	Rating

Outdoor Recreation Assets
State Recreation Area
Palisades–Kepler SP, 603 acres
Places Rated Score: 1,307   Places Rated Rank: 196

Central New Jersey, NJ
Common Denominators

	Rating
Golf courses: 20 private (351 holes), 3 daily fee (45 holes), 6 municipal (108 holes)	C
Good restaurants: 2 *, 9 **, 2 ***	C
Movie theaters: 11 chain (45 screens), 6 independent (11 screens)	C

Crowd Pleasers

NCAA Division I: 0.14 game seats per capita	C

Rutgers University, New Brunswick Scarlet Knights (F, B)
Outdoor Recreation Assets
Federal Protected Area
Morristown NHP, 188 acres
State Recreation Areas
D and R Canal SP, 630 acres
Pigeon Swamp SP, 1,063 acres
Spruce Run SRA, 1,910 acres
MC Access: New York–Northern New Jersey–Long Island, NY–NJ–CT
Places Rated Score: 637   Places Rated Rank: 324

Champaign–Urbana, IL
Common Denominators

	Rating
Golf courses: 4 private (72 holes), 2 daily fee (36 holes), 2 municipal (36 holes)	A
Good restaurants: 1 *, 4 **	A
Movie theaters: 8 chain (38 screens)	AA

Crowd Pleasers

NCAA Division I: 2.90 game seats per capita	AA

University of Illinois Illini (F, B)
Places Rated Score: 1,400   Places Rated Rank: 184

Charleston, WV
Common Denominators

	Rating
Golf courses: 4 private (72 holes), 1 daily fee (18 holes), 3 municipal (45 holes)	B
Good restaurants: 3 **, 2 ***	A
Movie theaters: 2 chain (12 screens), 1 independent (1 screen)	C

Crowd Pleasers

Pari-mutuel Betting:	AA

Tri–State Greyhound Park (greyhound, 310 days)

Professional Sports: 1.81 game seats per capita	A

Wheelers (Class A Baseball)
Places Rated Score: 1,300   Places Rated Rank: 201

✓ Charleston–North Charleston, SC
Common Denominators

	Rating
Golf courses: 11 private (189 holes), 15 daily fee (252 holes), 2 municipal (36 holes)	A
Good restaurants: 1 *, 15 **, 7 ***	AA
Movie theaters: 10 chain (52 screens)	A

Crowd Pleasers

Professional Sports: 0.79 game seats per capita	C

Rainbows (Class A Baseball)

NCAA Division I: 0.43 game seats per capita	A

Charleston Southern University Buccaneers (B)
College of Charleston Cougars (B)
The Citadel Bulldogs (F, B)
Outdoor Recreation Assets
Atlantic Coastline: 75 miles
Federal Protected Areas
Cape Romain NWR, 34,049 acres
Fort Sumter NM, 194 acres
Francis Marion NF, 248,973 acres
State Recreation Areas
Drayton Hall SP, 550 acres
Hampton Plantation SP, 322 acres
Old Santee Canal SP, 224 acres
Places Rated Score: 2,913   Places Rated Rank: 19

Charlotte–Gastonia–Rock Hill, NC–SC
Common Denominators

	Rating
Golf courses: 24 private (423 holes), 23 daily fee (378 holes), 5 municipal (72 holes)	B
Good restaurants: 3 *, 4 **, 5 ***	C
Movie theaters: 25 chain (128 screens), 6 independent (9 screens)	A

Crowd Pleasers

Family Theme Parks:	C

Carowinds (98 days)

Professional Sports: 1.84 game seats per capita	A

Hornets (NBA Basketball)
Ice Hockey (ECHL Hockey)
Rangers (Class A Baseball)

NCAA Division I: 0.28 game seats per capita	B

Davidson College Wildcats (B)
University of North Carolina, Charlotte 49ers (B)
Winthrop College Eagles (B)
Outdoor Recreation Assets
Federal Protected Area
Kings Mountain NMP, 2,529 acres
State Recreation Area
Crowder's Mountain, 2,364 acres
Places Rated Score: 1,225   Places Rated Rank: 217

Charlottesville, VA
Common Denominators

	Rating
Golf courses: 5 private (72 holes), 1 daily fee (18 holes), 2 municipal (18 holes)	B
Good restaurants: 1 *, 3 **, 2 ***	AA
Movie theaters: 5 chain (16 screens), 2 independent (3 screens)	AA

Crowd Pleasers

NCAA Division I: 2.12 game seats per capita	AA

University of Virginia Cavaliers (F, B)
Outdoor Recreation Assets
Federal Protected Areas
Appalachian Trail, 928 acres
Shenandoah NP, 29,800 acres
Places Rated Score: 1,604   Places Rated Rank: 145

Chattanooga, TN–GA
Common Denominators

	Rating
Golf courses: 9 private (144 holes), 7 daily fee (99 holes), 3 municipal (45 holes)	B
Good restaurants: 2 **, 2 ***	C
Movie theaters: 9 chain (46 screens)	AA

Crowd Pleasers

Aquariums and Zoos:	A

Tennessee Aquarium

Professional Sports: 1.28 game seats per capita	B

Lookouts (Class AA Baseball)

NCAA Division I: 0.41 game seats per capita	A

University of Tennessee, Chattanooga Moccasins (F, B)
Outdoor Recreation Assets
Federal Protected Areas
Chattahoochee NF, 18,780 acres
Chickamauga and Chattanooga NMP, 8,085 acres
State Recreation Areas
Cloudland Canyon SP, 2,120 acres
Harrison Bay SRA, 1,199 acres
Places Rated Score: 1,680   Places Rated Rank: 126

Cheyenne, WY
Common Denominators

	Rating
Golf courses: 2 private (36 holes), 2 municipal (27 holes)	B
Good restaurants: 1 **	B
Movie theaters: 3 chain (8 screens)	A

Places Rated Score: 706   Places Rated Rank: 317

Chicago, IL
Common Denominators

	Rating
Golf courses: 68 private (1179 holes), 68 daily fee (1134 holes), 69 municipal (1053 holes)	B

	Rating
Good restaurants: 71 *, 92 **, 42 ***, 8 ****	A
Movie theaters: 80 chain (367 screens), 34 independent (39 screens)	C

Crowd Pleasers
	Rating
Aquariums and Zoos:	AA

Brookfield Zoo (419 species, 2,516 specimens)
John G. Shedd Aquarium
Lincoln Park Zoo (337 species, 1,592 specimens)

Family Theme Parks:	A

Racing Rapids Action Park (92 days)
Three Worlds of Santa's Village (106 days)

Pari-mutuel Betting:	C

Balmoral Park (harness, 150 days)
Hawthorne Race Course (thoroughbred, 124 days)
Maywood Park (harness, 143 days)
Sportsman's Park (mixed meetings, 195 days)

Professional Sports: 1.37 game seats per capita	A

Bears (NFL Football)
Blackhawks (NHL Hockey)
Bulls (NBA Basketball)
Cubs (NL Baseball)
K. C. Cougars (Class A Baseball)
White Sox (AL Baseball)

NCAA Division I: 0.12 game seats per capita	C

Chicago State University Cougars (B)
De Paul University Blue Demons (B)
Loyola University of Chicago Ramblers (B)
Northeastern Illinois University Golden Eagles (B)
Northern Illinois University Huskies (F, B)
Northwestern University Wildcats (F, B)
University of Illinois, Chicago Flames (B, H)

Outdoor Recreation Assets
Lake Michigan Coastline: 33 miles
State Recreation Areas
McHenry Dam and Lake Defiance SP, 1,690 acres
Shabbona SP, 1,546 acres
MC Access: Chicago–Gary–Kenosha, IL–IN–WI
Places Rated Score: 2,252   Places Rated Rank: 69

Chico–Paradise, CA
Common Denominators
Golf courses: 2 private (36 holes), 2 daily fee (18 holes), 2 municipal (36 holes)	B
Good restaurants: 1 **	C
Movie theaters: 3 chain (5 screens), 2 independent (2 screens)	C

Outdoor Recreation Assets
Federal Protected Areas
Lassen NF, 51,178 acres
Plumas NF, 82,299 acres
State Recreation Area
Bidwell Mansion SHP, 5 acres
Places Rated Score: 1,173   Places Rated Rank: 231

Chicoutimi–Jonquiere, PQ
Common Denominators
Golf courses: 2 daily fee (36 holes), 1 municipal (9 holes)	B
Movie theaters: 1 chain (3 screens), 2 independent (3 screens)	C

Crowd Pleasers
Pari-mutuel Betting:	AA

Hippodrome Saquenay (harness, 250 days)
Outdoor Recreation Assets
Provincial Recreation Area
Saquenay PP, 70,078 acres
Places Rated Score: 733   Places Rated Rank: 311

Cincinnati, OH–KY–IN
Common Denominators
Golf courses: 30 private (486 holes), 20 daily fee (315 holes), 24 municipal (378 holes)	A
Good restaurants: 12 *, 24 **, 10 ***, 1 ****	A
Movie theaters: 22 chain (92 screens), 5 independent (5 screens)	C

Crowd Pleasers
	Rating
Aquariums and Zoos:	A

Cincinnati Zoo (715 species, 11,613 specimens)

Family Theme Parks:	A

Kings Island (92 days)
The Beach Waterpark (92 days)

Pari-mutuel Betting:	A

Lebanon Raceway (harness, 130 days)
River Downs (thoroughbred, 152 days)
Turfway Park (thoroughbred, 110 days)

Professional Sports: 3.29 game seats per capita	AA

Bengals (NFL Football)
Cyclones (ECHL Hockey)
Reds (NL Baseball)

NCAA Division I: 0.19 game seats per capita	B

University of Cincinnati Bearcats (F, B)
Xavier University Musketeers (B)

Outdoor Recreation Assets
State Recreation Areas
Big Bone Lick SP, 525 acres
Caesar Creek SP, 7,941 acres
Little Miami SP, 136 acres
MC Access: Cincinnati–Hamilton, OH–KY–IN
Places Rated Score: 2,277   Places Rated Rank: 64

Clarksville–Hopkinsville, TN–KY
Common Denominators
Golf courses: 3 private (54 holes), 2 daily fee (27 holes), 5 municipal (63 holes)	A
Movie theaters: 4 chain (22 screens)	AA

Crowd Pleasers
NCAA Division I: 0.80 game seats per capita	A

Austin Peay State University Governors (F, B)
Outdoor Recreation Assets
State Recreation Area
Dunbar Cave SNA, 110 acres
Places Rated Score: 1,006   Places Rated Rank: 266

Cleveland–Lorain–Elyria, OH
Common Denominators
Golf courses: 33 private (585 holes), 71 daily fee (1125 holes), 18 municipal (315 holes)	AA
Good restaurants: 5 *, 24 **, 7 ***	B
Movie theaters: 26 chain (138 screens), 16 independent (23 screens)	B

Crowd Pleasers
Aquariums and Zoos:	A

Metroparks Zoo (467 species, 3,817 specimens)

Pari-mutuel Betting:	B

Northfield Park (harness, 210 days)
Thistledown (thoroughbred, 186 days)

Professional Sports: 3.02 game seats per capita	AA

Browns (NFL Football)
Indians (AL Baseball)

NCAA Division I: 0.01 game seats per capita	C

Cleveland State University Vikings (B)
Outdoor Recreation Assets
Lake Erie Coastline: 56 miles
Federal Protected Area
Cuyahoga Valley NRA, 2,398 acres
State Recreation Areas
Findley SP, 838 acres
Headlands Beach SP, 125 acres
Mentor Marsh SNA, 644 acres
Pymatuning SP, 3,500 acres
MC Access: Cleveland–Akron, OH
Places Rated Score: 2,508   Places Rated Rank: 42

Colorado Springs, CO
Common Denominators
Golf courses: 12 private (216 holes), 3 daily fee (45 holes), 3 municipal (45 holes)	C
Good restaurants: 3 *, 9 **, 1 ***, 1 ****	AA
Movie theaters: 9 chain (41 screens), 1 independent (1 screen)	A

Rating

Crowd Pleasers
Aquariums and Zoos: **A**
  Cheyenne Mountain Zoological Park (139 species, 508 specimens)
Pari-mutuel Betting: **A**
  Rocky Mountain Greyhound Park (greyhound, 180 days)
Professional Sports: 1.01 game seats per capita   **B**
  Sky Sox (Triple A Baseball)
NCAA Division I: 0.97 game seats per capita   **A**
  Colorado College Tigers (H)
  United States Air Force Academy Falcons
Outdoor Recreation Assets
Federal Protected Area
  Pike NF, 100,701 acres

Places Rated Score: 2,270   Places Rated Rank: 67

Columbia, MO
Common Denominators
  Golf courses: 4 private (54 holes), 1 daily fee (18   **A**
  holes), 2 municipal (36 holes)
  Good restaurants: 2 **   **B**
  Movie theaters: 5 chain (14 screens)   **AA**
Crowd Pleasers
  NCAA Division I: 3.72 game seats per capita   **AA**
  University of Missouri Tigers (F, B)
Outdoor Recreation Assets
  State Recreation Area
  Finger Lakes SP, 1,131 acres

Places Rated Score: 1,338   Places Rated Rank: 189

Columbia, SC
Common Denominators
  Golf courses: 10 private (171 holes), 10 daily fee   **B**
  (171 holes), 1 municipal (18 holes)
  Good restaurants: 4 **, 2 ***   **B**
  Movie theaters: 11 chain (60 screens), 1   **AA**
  independent (1 screen)
Crowd Pleasers
Aquariums and Zoos: **A**
  Riverbanks Zoological Park (483 species, 2,250 specimens)
Professional Sports: 0.86 game seats per capita   **C**
  Mets (Class A Baseball)
NCAA Division I: 0.99 game seats per capita   **A**
  University of South Carolina Gamecocks (F, B)
Outdoor Recreation Assets
Federal Protected Area
  Congaree Swamp NM, 19,064 acres

Places Rated Score: 1,610   Places Rated Rank: 142

Columbus, GA-AL
Common Denominators
  Golf courses: 5 private (81 holes), 4 daily fee (63   **A**
  holes), 3 municipal (45 holes)
  Good restaurants: 3 *, 1 **, 2 ***   **A**
  Movie theaters: 5 chain (23 screens), 1   **A**
  independent (1 screen)
Crowd Pleasers
Professional Sports: 1.60 game seats per capita   **A**
  Redstixx (Class A Baseball)
Outdoor Recreation Assets
State Recreation Area
  F. D. Roosevelt SP, 10,000 acres

Places Rated Score: 1,250   Places Rated Rank: 214

Columbus, OH
Common Denominators
  Golf courses: 27 private (441 holes), 35 daily fee   **A**
  (495 holes), 9 municipal (144 holes)
  Good restaurants: 10 *, 18 **, 7 ***   **A**
  Movie theaters: 24 chain (134 screens), 6   **A**
  independent (12 screens)
Crowd Pleasers
Aquariums and Zoos: **A**
  Columbus Zoological Park (624 species, 6,267 specimens)

Pari-mutuel Betting: **B**
  Beulah Park (thoroughbred, 148 days)
  Scioto Downs (harness, 121 days)
Professional Sports: 1.08 game seats per capita   **B**
  Chill (ECHL Hockey)
  Clippers (Triple A Baseball)
  Horizon (CBA Basketball)
NCAA Division I: 0.40 game seats per capita   **A**
  Ohio State University Buckeyes
Outdoor Recreation Assets
State Recreation Areas
  A. W. Marion SP, 308 acres
  Buckeye Lake SP, 785 acres
  Delaware SP, 7,411 acres
  Stage's Pond SNA, 178 acres

Places Rated Score: 1,949   Places Rated Rank: 98

Corpus Christi, TX
Common Denominators
  Golf courses: 7 private (117 holes), 1 daily fee (18   **C**
  holes), 3 municipal (54 holes)
  Movie theaters: 5 chain (25 screens), 1   **B**
  independent (1 screen)
Crowd Pleasers
Pari-mutuel Betting: **A**
  Corpus Christi Greyhound Track (greyhound, 157 days)
Outdoor Recreation Assets
  Gulf Coastline: 25 miles
  State Recreation Area
  Lake Corpus Christi SRA, 288 acres

Places Rated Score: 870   Places Rated Rank: 297

Cumberland, MD-WV
Common Denominators
  Golf courses: 2 private (36 holes), 5 daily fee (63   **AA**
  holes)
  Good restaurants: 1 *, 1 **, 2 ***   **AA**
  Movie theaters: 2 chain (9 screens)   **A**
Outdoor Recreation Assets
  Federal Protected Area
  Chesapeake and Ohio Canal NHP, 3,095 acres
  State Recreation Area
  Dans Mountain SP, 481 acres

Places Rated Score: 1,168   Places Rated Rank: 233

Dallas, TX
Common Denominators
  Golf courses: 49 private (828 holes), 17 daily fee   **C**
  (279 holes), 20 municipal (333 holes)
  Good restaurants: 8 *, 21 **, 13 ***, 2 ****   **B**
  Movie theaters: 41 chain (252 screens), 11   **A**
  independent (24 screens)
Crowd Pleasers
Aquariums and Zoos: **A**
  Dallas Zoo (332 species, 1,487 specimens)
Family Theme Parks: **C**
  Wet'n Wild (92 days)
Professional Sports: 0.67 game seats per capita   **C**
  Cowboys (NFL Football)
  Mavericks (NBA Basketball)
NCAA Division I: 0.11 game seats per capita   **C**
  Southern Methodist University Mustangs (F, B)
  University of North Texas Mean Green Eagles (F, B)
Outdoor Recreation Assets
State Recreation Areas
  Cedar Hill SRA, 1,811 acres
  Lake Tawakoni SRA, 401 acres
  Ray Roberts Lake SRA, 3,000 acres
MC Access: Dallas-Fort Worth, TX

Places Rated Score: 1,338   Places Rated Rank: 189

Danbury, CT
Common Denominators
  Golf courses: 9 private (126 holes), 2 daily fee (27   **B**
  holes), 2 municipal (36 holes)

	Rating
Good restaurants: 2 *, 3 ***	A
Movie theaters: 4 chain (10 screens), 3 independent (4 screens)	B

Outdoor Recreation Assets
  State Recreation Areas
    Collis P. Huntington SP, 878 acres
    Kettletown SP, 492 acres
    Putnam Memorial SP, 183 acres
    Squantz Pond SP, 172 acres
MC Access: New York–Northern New Jersey–Long Island, NY–NJ–CT
Places Rated Score: 810   Places Rated Rank: 300

Danville, VA
Common Denominators

Golf courses: 5 private (72 holes), 2 daily fee (27 holes),	C
Movie theaters: 2 chain (4 screens), 1 independent (2 screens)	C

Places Rated Score: 200   Places Rated Rank: 343

Davenport–Moline–Rock Island, IA–IL
Common Denominators

Golf courses: 8 private (126 holes), 8 daily fee (108 holes), 8 municipal (135 holes)	AA
Good restaurants: 5 *, 6 **, 2 ***	A
Movie theaters: 6 chain (31 screens)	A

Crowd Pleasers

Pari-mutuel Betting:	A
Quad City Downs (harness, 90 days)	
Professional Sports: 1.77 game seats per capita	A
Q. C. River Bandits (Class A Baseball)	
Quad City Thunder (CBA Basketball)	

Outdoor Recreation Assets
  Federal Protected Area
    Upper Mississippi NWR, 398 acres
Places Rated Score: 1,608   Places Rated Rank: 143

Dayton–Springfield, OH
Common Denominators

Golf courses: 17 private (288 holes), 13 daily fee (198 holes), 12 municipal (198 holes)	A
Good restaurants: 2 *, 8 **, 3 ***, 1 ****	B
Movie theaters: 22 chain (92 screens), 1 independent (1 screen)	A

Crowd Pleasers

Professional Sports: 0.23 game seats per capita	C
Bombers (ECHL Hockey)	
NCAA Division I: 0.25 game seats per capita	B
University of Dayton Flyers (B)	
Wright State University Raiders (B)	

Outdoor Recreation Assets
  State Recreation Areas
    Buck Creek SP, 1,910 acres
    Sycamore SP, 2,295 acres
Places Rated Score: 1,129   Places Rated Rank: 242

Daytona Beach, FL
Common Denominators

Golf courses: 5 private (90 holes), 18 daily fee (297 holes), 3 municipal (54 holes)	AA
Good restaurants: 4 *, 10 **, 1 ***	A
Movie theaters: 14 chain (55 screens), 1 independent (1 screen)	AA

Crowd Pleasers

Pari-mutuel Betting:	AA
Daytona Beach Kennel Club (greyhound, 365 days)	
Volusia Jai-Alai (121 days)	
NCAA Division I: 0.23 game seats per capita	B
Bethune Cookman College Wildcats (F, B)	
Stetson University Hatters (B)	

Outdoor Recreation Assets
  Atlantic Coastline: 49 miles
  Federal Protected Areas
    Canaveral NS, 28,148 acres
    Lake Woodruff NWR, 18,225 acres

  State Recreation Areas
    Blue Spring SP, 2,192 acres
    Bulow Creek SP, 2,198 acres
    De Leon Springs SRA, 401 acres
    Haw Creek SNA, 1,305 acres
    Hontoon Island SP, 1,051 acres
    Spruce Creek SRA, 610 acres
Places Rated Score: 2,477   Places Rated Rank: 47

Decatur, AL
Common Denominators

Golf courses: 2 private (36 holes), 2 daily fee (27 holes), 2 municipal (36 holes)	A
Movie theaters: 3 chain (16 screens)	AA

Crowd Pleasers

Family Theme Parks:	B
Point Mallard Park (107 days)	

Outdoor Recreation Assets
  Federal Protected Areas
    Bankhead NF, 90,050 acres
    Wheeler NWR, 3,489 acres
  State Recreation Area
    Joe Wheeler SP, 400 acres
Places Rated Score: 1,475   Places Rated Rank: 171

Decatur, IL
Common Denominators

Golf courses: 2 private (36 holes), 2 municipal (36 holes)	B
Good restaurants: 1 **	C
Movie theaters: 3 chain (19 screens)	AA

Outdoor Recreation Assets
  State Recreation Area
    Lincoln Trail Homestead SHS, 82 acres
Places Rated Score: 704   Places Rated Rank: 319

Denver, CO
Common Denominators

Golf courses: 26 private (450 holes), 7 daily fee (108 holes), 18 municipal (315 holes)	C
Good restaurants: 4 *, 9 **, 9 ***, 1 ****	B
Movie theaters: 33 chain (186 screens), 3 independent (4 screens)	A

Crowd Pleasers

Aquariums and Zoos:	A
Denver Zoological Gardens (306 species, 1,306 specimens)	
Family Theme Parks:	B
Elitch Gardens (106 days)	
Pari-mutuel Betting:	C
Interstate Kennel Club (greyhound, 78 days)	
Mile High Kennel Club (greyhound, 120 days)	
Professional Sports: 3.49 game seats per capita	AA
Broncos (NFL Football)	
Nuggets (NBA Basketball)	
Rockies (NL Baseball)	
NCAA Division I: 0.02 game seats per capita	C
University of Denver Pioneers (H)	

Outdoor Recreation Assets
  Federal Protected Areas
    Arapaho NF, 2,057 acres
    Pike NF, 243,628 acres
    Roosevelt NF, 160 acres
  State Recreation Areas
    Castlewood Canyon SP, 870 acres
    Cherry Creek SRA, 3,835 acres
MC Access: Denver–Boulder–Greeley, CO
Places Rated Score: 2,293   Places Rated Rank: 61

Des Moines, IA
Common Denominators

Golf courses: 12 private (153 holes), 9 daily fee (126 holes), 4 municipal (72 holes)	A
Good restaurants: 5 *, 8 **, 2 ***	A
Movie theaters: 12 chain (49 screens), 1 independent (1 screen)	AA

Crowd Pleasers

	Rating
Aquariums and Zoos:	B
Blank Park Zoo (92 species, 964 specimens)	
Family Theme Parks:	B
Adventureland Park (100 days)	
Professional Sports: 1.81 game seats per capita	A
Cubs (Triple A Baseball)	
NCAA Division I: 0.33 game seats per capita	A
Drake University Bulldogs (B)	

Outdoor Recreation Assets

State Recreation Areas
Big Creek SP, 1,536 acres
Margo Frankel Woods SP, 136 acres
Walnut Woods SP, 300 acres

Places Rated Score: 2,013   Places Rated Rank: 89

Detroit, MI

Common Denominators

	Rating
Golf courses: 47 private (801 holes), 102 daily fee (1566 holes), 36 municipal (540 holes)	A
Good restaurants: 3 *, 22 **, 9 ***, 1 ****	C
Movie theaters: 51 chain (281 screens), 13 independent (21 screens)	B

Crowd Pleasers

	Rating
Aquariums and Zoos:	A
Belle Isle Zoo and Aquarium (178 species, 1,541 specimens)	
Detroit Zoological Park (266 species, 1,654 specimens)	
Pari-mutuel Betting:	C
Hazel Park (harness, 168 days)	
Ladbroke-Detroit Race Course (thoroughbred, 188 days)	
Northville Downs (harness, 156 days)	
Professional Sports: 1.73 game seats per capita	A
Lions (NFL Football)	
Pistons (NBA Basketball)	
Red Wings (NHL Hockey)	
Tigers (AL Baseball)	
NCAA Division I: 0.01 game seats per capita	C
University of Detroit Titans (B)	

Outdoor Recreation Assets

Lake Huron Coastline: 48 miles
Federal Protected Area
Wyandotte NWR, 304 acres
State Recreation Areas
Bald Mountain SRA, 4,581 acres
Highland SRA, 5,700 acres
Lakeport SP, 566 acres
Ortonville SRA, 3,472 acres
Pontiac Lake SRA, 3,730 acres
Rochester-Utica SRA, 1,125 acres
Seven Lakes SP, 1,426 acres
Sterling SP, 1,035 acres
MC Access: Detroit-Ann Arbor-Flint, MI

Places Rated Score: 2,096   Places Rated Rank: 82

Dothan, AL

Common Denominators

	Rating
Golf courses: 3 private (45 holes), 3 daily fee (45 holes), 2 municipal (36 holes)	AA
Movie theaters: 2 chain (6 screens)	C

Crowd Pleasers

	Rating
Family Theme Parks:	C
Water World (98 days)	

Outdoor Recreation Assets

State Recreation Area
Chattahoochee SP, 596 acres

Places Rated Score: 604   Places Rated Rank: 327

Dover, DE

Common Denominators

	Rating
Golf courses: 3 private (54 holes), 1 daily fee (18 holes)	C
Good restaurants: 2 *, 2 **, 1 ***	AA
Movie theaters: 2 chain (12 screens)	A

Crowd Pleasers

	Rating
Pari-mutuel Betting:	AA

Dover Downs (harness, 100 days)
Harrington Raceway (harness, 41 days)

	Rating
NCAA Division I: 0.36 game seats per capita	A
Delaware State College Hornets (F, B)	

Outdoor Recreation Assets

Delaware Bay Coastline: 30 miles
Federal Protected Area
Bombay Hook NWR, 15,122 acres

Places Rated Score: 2,011   Places Rated Rank: 90

Dubuque, IA

Common Denominators

	Rating
Golf courses: 2 private (27 holes), 1 daily fee (9 holes), 2 municipal (27 holes)	A
Good restaurants: 1 **	C
Movie theaters: 2 chain (14 screens), 2 independent (9 screens)	AA

Crowd Pleasers

	Rating
Pari-mutuel Betting:	AA
Dubuque Greyhound Park (greyhound, 191 days)	

Outdoor Recreation Assets

Federal Protected Area
Upper Mississippi NWR, 476 acres

Places Rated Score: 1,224   Places Rated Rank: 219

Duluth–Superior, MN–WI

Common Denominators

	Rating
Golf courses: 5 private (72 holes), 5 daily fee (45 holes), 11 municipal (135 holes)	AA
Good restaurants: 1 *, 4 **, 1 ***	A
Movie theaters: 5 chain (19 screens), 3 independent (3 screens)	A

Crowd Pleasers

	Rating
Aquariums and Zoos:	C
Lake Superior Zoological Gardens (159 species, 596 specimens)	
NCAA Division I: 0.19 game seats per capita	B
University of Minnesota, Duluth Bulldogs (H)	

Outdoor Recreation Assets

Lake Superior Coastline: 36 miles
Federal Protected Areas
Saint Croix Scenic Riverway, 3,128 acres
Superior NF, 677,520 acres
Voyageurs NP, 120,713 acres
State Recreation Areas
Bear Head Lake SP, 4,384 acres
Pattison SP, 1,374 acres
Soudan Mine SP, 1,300 acres

Places Rated Score: 2,501   Places Rated Rank: 43

Dutchess County, NY

Common Denominators

	Rating
Golf courses: 8 private (90 holes), 7 daily fee (81 holes), 4 municipal (63 holes)	A
Good restaurants: 6 *, 4 **, 5 ***, 1 ****, 1 *****	AA
Movie theaters: 3 chain (20 screens), 3 independent (7 screens)	A

Crowd Pleasers

	Rating
NCAA Division I: 0.15 game seats per capita	B
Marist College Red Foxes (B)	

Outdoor Recreation Assets

Federal Protected Area
Appalachian Trail, 3,856 acres
State Recreation Areas
James Baird SP, 590 acres
Taconic SP, 1,533 acres
MC Access: New York–Northern New Jersey–Long Island, NY–NJ–CT

Places Rated Score: 1,304   Places Rated Rank: 198

Eau Claire, WI

Common Denominators

	Rating
Golf courses: 2 private (36 holes), 5 daily fee (63 holes), 2 municipal (18 holes)	A
Good restaurants: 2 **	B
Movie theaters: 1 chain (6 screens), 2 independent (2 screens)	C

Rating

Outdoor Recreation Assets
State Recreation Area
    Lake Wissota SP, 1,062 acres
Places Rated Score: 610   **Places Rated Rank: 325**

Edmonton, AB
Common Denominators
    Golf courses: 4 private (72 holes), 13 daily fee (180   **A**
    holes), 16 municipal (243 holes)
    Good restaurants: 1 *, 3 **, 5 ***   **B**
    Movie theaters: 20 chain (81 screens), 3   **A**
    independent (4 screens)
Crowd Pleasers
    Aquariums and Zoos: **B**
        Valley Zoo (155 species, 389 specimens)
    Family Theme Parks: **AA**
        West Edmonton Mall (365 days)
    Pari-mutuel Betting: **B**
        Edmonton Northlands (mixed meetings, 191 days)
    Professional Sports: 1.50 game seats per capita   **A**
        Eskimos (CFL Football)
        Oilers (NHL Hockey)
        Trappers (Triple A Baseball)
    CIAU: 0.11 game seats per capita   **C**
        University of Alberta Golden Bears
Outdoor Recreation Assets
    Provincial Recreation Areas
        Hasse Lake PP, 170 acres
        Pembina River PP, 413 acres
        Pigeon Lake PP, 1,095 acres
        Strathcona Science PP, 269 acres
        Wabamum Lake PP, 521 acres
Places Rated Score: 2,018   **Places Rated Rank: 88**

El Paso, TX
Common Denominators
    Golf courses: 4 private (72 holes), 1 daily fee (18   **C**
    holes), 4 municipal (63 holes)
    Good restaurants: 3 *, 6 **   **C**
    Movie theaters: 7 chain (39 screens)   **C**
Crowd Pleasers
    Aquariums and Zoos: **B**
        El Paso Zoo (140 species, 523 specimens)
    Professional Sports: 1.12 game seats per capita   **B**
        Diablos (Class AA Baseball)
    NCAA Division I: 0.61 game seats per capita   **A**
        University of Texas, El Paso Miners (F, B)
Outdoor Recreation Assets
    Federal Protected Area
        Chamizal NM, 55 acres
    State Recreation Area
        Franklin Mountains SP, 23, 744 acres
Places Rated Score: 1,190   **Places Rated Rank: 230**

Elkhart–Goshen, IN
Common Denominators
    Golf courses: 4 private (72 holes), 4 daily fee (63   **AA**
    holes), 2 municipal (36 holes)
    Good restaurants: 1 *, 2 **, 1 ***   **A**
    Movie theaters: 1 chain (1 screen), 5 independent   **C**
    (9 screens)
Places Rated Score: 800   **Places Rated Rank: 306**

Elmira, NY
Common Denominators
    Golf courses: 2 private (36 holes), 3 daily fee (45   **AA**
    holes), 2 municipal (36 holes)
    Good restaurants: 4 **, 1 ****   **AA**
    Movie theaters: 3 chain (14 screens)   **AA**
Crowd Pleasers
    Professional Sports: 3.65 game seats per capita   **AA**
        Pioneers (Class A Baseball)
Outdoor Recreation Assets
    State Recreation Area
        Mark Twain SP, 462 acres
Places Rated Score: 1,615   **Places Rated Rank: 139**

Rating

Enid, OK
Common Denominators
    Golf courses: 1 private (18 holes), 1 daily fee (9   **A**
    holes), 1 municipal (18 holes)
    Good restaurants: 1 *, 1 **   **A**
    Movie theaters: 2 chain (7 screens)   **AA**
Outdoor Recreation Assets
    State Recreation Area
        Museum of the Cherokee Strip SHS, 2 acres
Places Rated Score: 1,000   **Places Rated Rank: 271**

Erie, PA
Common Denominators
    Golf courses: 6 private (90 holes), 8 daily fee (126   **AA**
    holes), 4 municipal (63 holes)
    Good restaurants: 4 **   **B**
    Movie theaters: 6 chain (23 screens), 1   **B**
    independent (1 screen)
Crowd Pleasers
    Aquariums and Zoos: **B**
        Erie Zoological Park (83 species, 270 specimens)
    Professional Sports: 1.67 game seats per capita   **A**
        Panthers (ECHL Hockey)
        Sailors (Class A Baseball)
Outdoor Recreation Assets
    Lake Erie Coastline: 42 miles
    State Recreation Area
        Presque Isle SP, 3,200 acres
Places Rated Score: 1,751   **Places Rated Rank: 115**

✓ Eugene–Springfield, OR
Common Denominators
    Golf courses: 3 private (54 holes), 7 daily fee (99   **B**
    holes), 1 municipal (9 holes)
    Good restaurants: 3 *, 3 **, 1 ***   **A**
    Movie theaters: 6 chain (26 screens), 2   **A**
    independent (3 screens)
Crowd Pleasers
    Professional Sports: 1.72 game seats per capita   **A**
        Emeralds (Class A Baseball)
    NCAA Division I: 1.06 game seats per capita   **AA**
        University of Oregon Ducks (F, B)
Outdoor Recreation Assets
    Pacific Coastline: 30 miles
    Federal Protected Areas
        Siuslaw NF, 245,580 acres
        Umpqua NF, 151,249 acres
        Willamette NF, 1,032,247 acres
    State Recreation Areas
        Carl Washburne Memorial SP, 1,089 acres
        Devil's Elbow SP, 547 acres
        Joaquin Miller Forest Wayside, 112 acres
        Neptune SP, 303 acres
        Willamette River Greenway, 925 acres
Places Rated Score: 3,500   **Places Rated Rank: 8**

Evansville–Henderson, IN–KY
Common Denominators
    Golf courses: 7 private (99 holes), 4 daily fee (54   **B**
    holes), 3 municipal (45 holes)
    Good restaurants: 2 *, 2 **   **C**
    Movie theaters: 1 chain (4 screens), 2 independent   **C**
    (4 screens)
Crowd Pleasers
    Aquariums and Zoos: **B**
        Mesker Park Zoo (203 species, 679 specimens)
    Pari-mutuel Betting: **AA**
        Ellis Park (thoroughbred, 61 days)
        Riverside Downs (mixed meetings, 103 days)
    NCAA Division I: 0.39 game seats per capita   **A**
        University of Evansville Aces (B)
Outdoor Recreation Assets
    State Recreation Area
        John James Audubon SP, 692 acres
Places Rated Score: 1,322   **Places Rated Rank: 192**

	Rating

Fargo–Moorhead, ND–MN
Common Denominators
  Golf courses: 4 private (63 holes), 2 daily fee (18   **A**
    holes), 5 municipal (63 holes)
  Good restaurants: 1 ★, 4 ★★   **A**
  Movie theaters: 5 chain (29 screens), 3   **AA**
    independent (3 screens)
Outdoor Recreation Area
  Buffalo River SP, 1,240 acres
Places Rated Score: 1,003   Places Rated Rank: 268

Fayetteville, NC
Common Denominators
  Golf courses: 6 private (108 holes), 3 daily fee (54   **C**
    holes)
  Good restaurants: 5 ★★   **B**
  Movie theaters: 9 chain (39 screens)   **AA**
Crowd Pleasers
  Professional Sports: 0.81 game seats per capita   **C**
    Generals (Class A Baseball)
Places Rated Score: 800   Places Rated Rank: 306

Fayetteville–Springdale–Rogers, AR
Common Denominators
  Golf courses: 10 private (162 holes), 5 daily fee (81   **B**
    holes)
  Good restaurants: 2 ★, 3 ★★, 3 ★★★   **AA**
  Movie theaters: 6 chain (28 screens), 3   **AA**
    independent (4 screens)
Crowd Pleasers
  NCAA Division I: 1.56 game seats per capita   **AA**
    University of Arkansas Razorbacks (F, B)
Outdoor Recreation Assets
  Federal Protected Areas
    Logan Cave NWR, 124 acres
    Ozark NF, 31,392 acres
    Pea Ridge NMP, 4,279 acres
  State Recreation Areas
    Devil's Den SP, 1,927 acres
    Prairie Grove SP, 130 acres
Places Rated Score: 1,612   Places Rated Rank: 140

Flint, MI
Common Denominators
  Golf courses: 10 private (180 holes), 8 daily fee   **A**
    (126 holes), 5 municipal (72 holes)
  Good restaurants: 2 ★★★   **C**
  Movie theaters: 4 chain (26 screens), 2   **B**
    independent (2 screens)
Crowd Pleasers
  Pari-mutuel Betting: **A**
    Sports Creek Raceway (harness, 125 days)
  Professional Sports: 0.37 game seats per capita   **C**
    Spirits (IHL Hockey)
Outdoor Recreation Assets
  Federal Protected Area
    Manistee NF, 8 acres
MC Access: Detroit–Ann Arbor–Flint, MI
Places Rated Score: 1,080   Places Rated Rank: 262

Florence, AL
Common Denominators
  Golf courses: 4 private (54 holes), 3 daily fee (36   **AA**
    holes), 3 municipal (45 holes)
  Good restaurants: 1 ★, 3 ★★   **A**
  Movie theaters: 3 chain (12 screens)   **A**
Outdoor Recreation Assets
  Federal Protected Area
    Natchez Trace Parkway, 4,175 acres
Places Rated Score: 1,039   Places Rated Rank: 265

Florence, SC
Common Denominators
  Golf courses: 3 private (54 holes), 4 daily fee (72   **AA**
    holes),
  Movie theaters: 4 chain (13 screens)   **A**
Outdoor Recreation Assets
  State Recreation Area

	Rating

    Lynches River SP, 668 acres
Places Rated Score: 707   Places Rated Rank: 315

✓ Fort Collins–Loveland, CO
Common Denominators
  Golf courses: 2 private (36 holes), 2 daily fee (36   **A**
    holes), 4 municipal (63 holes)
  Good restaurants: 4 ★, 2 ★★   **A**
  Movie theaters: 6 chain (17 screens), 1   **A**
    independent (1 screen)
Crowd Pleasers
  Pari-mutuel Betting: **AA**
    Cloverleaf Kennel Club (greyhound, 120 days)
  NCAA Division I: 1.26 game seats per capita   **AA**
    Colorado State University Rams (F, B)
Outdoor Recreation Assets
  Federal Protected Areas
    Rocky Mountain NP, 143,807 acres
    Roosevelt NF, 624,987 acres
  State Recreation Area
    Lory SP, 2,479 acres
Places Rated Score: 3,700   Places Rated Rank: 4

Fort Lauderdale, FL
Common Denominators
  Golf courses: 23 private (414 holes), 23 daily fee   **B**
    (396 holes), 5 municipal (90 holes)
  Good restaurants: 1 ★, 13 ★★, 20 ★★★, 1 ★★★★   **AA**
  Movie theaters: 25 chain (187 screens), 9   **AA**
    independent (22 screens)
Crowd Pleasers
  Pari-mutuel Betting: **A**
    Dania Jai Alai (328 days)
    Gulfstream Park (thoroughbred, 59 days)
    Hollywood Kennel Club (greyhound, 158 days)
    Pompano Park (harness, 156 days)
  Professional Sports: 0.44 game seats per capita   **C**
    Yankees (Class A Baseball)
Outdoor Recreation Assets
  Atlantic Coastline: 25 miles
  State Recreation Area
    Birch SRA, 180 acres
MC Access: Miami–Fort Lauderdale, FL
Places Rated Score: 1,773   Places Rated Rank: 116

Fort Myers–Cape Coral, FL
Common Denominators
  Golf courses: 16 private (279 holes), 18 daily fee   **AA**
    (288 holes), 3 municipal (54 holes)
  Good restaurants: 6 ★, 18 ★★, 4 ★★★   **AA**
  Movie theaters: 6 chain (46 screens), 1   **AA**
    independent (2 screens)
Crowd Pleasers
  Pari-mutuel Betting: **AA**
    Naples–Fort Myers Greyhound Track (greyhound,
    365 days)
  Professional Sports: 1.38 game seats per capita   **A**
    Miracle (Class A Baseball)
Outdoor Recreation Assets
  Gulf Coastline: 38 miles
  Federal Protected Areas
    J. N. Darling NWR, 4,976 acres
    Matlacha Pass NWR, 244 acres
    Pine Island NWR, 404 acres
  State Recreation Areas
    Cayo Cosia SP, 1,629 acres
    Lovers Key SRA, 434 acres
Places Rated Score: 2,358   Places Rated Rank: 54

Fort Pierce–Port St. Lucie, FL
Common Denominators
  Golf courses: 23 private (414 holes), 10 daily fee   **AA**
    (171 holes), 3 municipal (54 holes)
  Good restaurants: 4 ★, 7 ★★, 3 ★★★   **AA**
  Movie theaters: 5 chain (30 screens)   **A**
Crowd Pleasers
  Pari-mutuel Betting: **AA**
    Fort Pierce Jai Alai (202 days)

	Rating
Professional Sports: 1.84 game seats per capita	**A**
Mets (Class A Baseball)	

Outdoor Recreation Assets
Atlantic Coastline: 45 miles
Federal Protected Area
Hobe Sound NWR, 971 acres
State Recreation Areas
Avalon SP, 318 acres
Dickinson SP, 10,328 acres
Places Rated Score: 2,343   Places Rated Rank: 56

Fort Smith, AR–OK
Common Denominators

Golf courses: 2 private (36 holes), 6 daily fee (81 holes), 1 municipal (18 holes)	**A**
Good restaurants: 1 *, 3 **	**B**
Movie theaters: 4 chain (17 screens)	**A**

Crowd Pleasers

Pari-mutuel Betting:	**AA**
Blue Ribbon Downs (thoroughbred, 168 days)	

Outdoor Recreation Assets
Federal Protected Areas
Ouachita NF, 14,888 acres
Ozark NF, 85,266 acres
State Recreation Areas
Lake Fort Smith SP, 126 acres
Tenkiller SP, 1,190 acres
Places Rated Score: 1,640   Places Rated Rank: 134

Fort Walton Beach, FL
Common Denominators

Golf courses: 3 private (45 holes), 12 daily fee (189 holes), 2 municipal (27 holes)	**AA**
Good restaurants: 1 *, 7 **	**AA**
Movie theaters: 3 chain (13 screens), 3 independent (6 screens)	**AA**

Outdoor Recreation Assets
Gulf Coastline: 24 miles
Federal Protected Areas
Choctawhatchee NF, 523 acres
Gulf Islands NS, 3,485 acres
State Recreation Area
Henderson Beach SRA, 209 acres
Places Rated Score: 1,478   Places Rated Rank: 170

Fort Wayne, IN
Common Denominators

Golf courses: 5 private (90 holes), 23 daily fee (360 holes), 1 municipal (18 holes)	**AA**
Good restaurants: 4 **, 1 ****	**B**
Movie theaters: 12 chain (35 screens), 5 independent (6 screens)	**B**

Crowd Pleasers

Aquariums and Zoos:	**B**
Fort Wayne Children's Zoo (185 species, 1,265 specimens)	
Professional Sports: 1.20 game seats per capita	**B**
Fury (CBA Basketball)	
Komets (IHL Hockey)	

Outdoor Recreation Assets
State Recreation Area
Ouabache SP, 1,065 acres
Places Rated Score: 1,203   Places Rated Rank: 225

Fort Worth–Arlington, TX
Common Denominators

Golf courses: 22 private (369 holes), 10 daily fee (162 holes), 12 municipal (198 holes)	**C**
Good restaurants: 6 *, 12 **, 3 ***	**B**
Movie theaters: 23 chain (158 screens), 4 independent (8 screens)	**AA**

Crowd Pleasers

Aquariums and Zoos:	**A**
Fort Worth Zoological Park (725 species, 4,200 specimens)	
Family Theme Parks:	**B**
Six Flags Over Texas (100 days)	

	Rating
Pari-mutuel Betting:	**C**
Trinity Meadows (mixed meetings, 196 days)	
Professional Sports: 2.39 game seats per capita	**AA**
Rangers (AL Baseball)	
NCAA Division I: 0.32 game seats per capita	**A**
Texas Christian University Horned Frogs (F, B)	
University of Texas, Arlington Mavericks (B)	

Outdoor Recreation Assets
State Recreation Areas
Eagle Mountain SRA, 401 acres
Lake Mineral Wells SP, 3,000 acres
MC Access: Dallas–Fort Worth, TX
Places Rated Score: 2,071   Places Rated Rank: 83

✓ Fresno, CA
Common Denominators

Golf courses: 7 private (126 holes), 6 daily fee (99 holes), 4 municipal (72 holes)	**C**
Good restaurants: 3 *, 1 **, 1 ***	**C**
Movie theaters: 9 chain (39 screens), 4 independent (4 screens)	**C**

Crowd Pleasers

Aquariums and Zoos:	**A**
The Fresno Zoo (195 species, 576 specimens)	
NCAA Division I: 0.36 game seats per capita	**A**
California State University, Fresno Bulldogs (F, B)	

Outdoor Recreation Assets
Federal Protected Areas
Devils Postpile NM, 798 acres
Inyo NF, 52,296 acres
Kings Canyon NP, 354,828 acres
Sequoia NF, 130,757 acres
Sierra NF, 1,217,835 acres
Yosemite NP, 66,886 acres
State Recreation Area
Millerton Lake SRA, 3,296 acres
Places Rated Score: 2,664   Places Rated Rank: 32

Gadsden, AL
Common Denominators

Golf courses: 3 private (54 holes), 1 daily fee (18 holes), 3 municipal (54 holes)	**AA**
Movie theaters: 2 chain (11 screens)	**A**

Places Rated Score: 700   Places Rated Rank: 320

Gainesville, FL
Common Denominators

Golf courses: 2 private (36 holes), 2 daily fee (36 holes), 1 municipal (18 holes)	**B**
Good restaurants: 2 **, 2 ***	**A**
Movie theaters: 5 chain (30 screens), 1 independent (1 screen)	**AA**

Crowd Pleasers

Aquariums and Zoos:	**C**
Santa Fe Teaching Zoo (80 species, 240 specimens)	
NCAA Division I: 2.71 game seats per capita	**AA**
University of Florida Gators (F, B)	

Outdoor Recreation Assets
State Recreation Areas
Paynes Prairie State Preserve, 18,400 acres
San Felasco Hammock SNA, 6,034 acres
Places Rated Score: 1,636   Places Rated Rank: 136

Galveston–Texas City, TX
Common Denominators

Golf courses: 5 private (72 holes), 1 daily fee (18 holes), 2 municipal (36 holes)	**C**
Good restaurants: 2 **, 2 ***	**A**
Movie theaters: 2 chain (15 screens), 1 independent (2 screens)	**B**

Crowd Pleasers

Pari-mutuel Betting:	**A**
Gulf Greyhound Park (greyhound, 75 days)	

Outdoor Recreation Assets
Gulf Coastline: 25 miles
MC Access: Houston–Galveston–Brazoria, TX
Places Rated Score: 1,298   Places Rated Rank: 208

Rating

Gary, IN
Common Denominators
Golf courses: 8 private (135 holes), 16 daily fee **A**
(261 holes), 4 municipal (72 holes)
Good restaurants: 2 *, 3 **, 2 *** **C**
Movie theaters: 7 chain (34 screens), 4 **B**
independent (4 screens)
Crowd Pleasers
NCAA Division I: 0.07 game seats per capita **C**
Valparaiso University Crusaders (B)
Outdoor Recreation Assets
Lake Michigan Coastline: 32 miles
Federal Protected Area
Indiana Dunes Lakeshore, 9,097 acres
MC Access: Chicago–Gary–Kenosha, IL–IN–WI
Places Rated Score: 1,218   Places Rated Rank: 220

Glens Falls, NY
Common Denominators
Golf courses: 1 private (18 holes), 10 daily fee (135 **AA**
holes)
Good restaurants: 6 *, 3 **, 2 *** **AA**
Movie theaters: 6 chain (13 screens) **A**
Crowd Pleasers
Family Theme Parks: **C**
The Great Escape (92 days)
Professional Sports: 0.79 game seats per capita **C**
Red Wings (AHL Hockey)
Outdoor Recreation Assets
State Recreation Areas
Lake Lauderdale SP, 117 acres
Luzerne SRA, 728 acres
Rogers Rock SRA, 1,863 acres
Places Rated Score: 1,327   Places Rated Rank: 191

Goldsboro, NC
Common Denominators
Golf courses: 2 private (27 holes), 3 daily fee (54 **A**
holes)
Movie theaters: 3 chain (10 screens) **A**
Outdoor Recreation Assets
State Recreation Areas
Cliffs-Of-the-Neuse, 608 acres
Places Rated Score: 609   Places Rated Rank: 326

Grand Forks, ND–MN
Common Denominators
Golf courses: 3 private (36 holes), 5 daily fee (54 **AA**
holes), 3 municipal (36 holes)
Good restaurants: 2 * **C**
Movie theaters: 3 independent (4 screens) **C**
Crowd Pleasers
NCAA Division I: 0.47 game seats per capita **A**
University of North Dakota Fighting Sioux (H)
Outdoor Recreation Assets
Federal Protected Area
Kelly's Slough NWR, 680 acres
State Recreation Area
Turtle River SP, 784 acres
Places Rated Score: 903   Places Rated Rank: 293

Grand Rapids–Muskegon–Holland, MI
Common Denominators
Golf courses: 17 private (279 holes), 56 daily fee **AA**
(891 holes), 3 municipal (54 holes)
Good restaurants: 5 *, 17 **, 2 *** **A**
Movie theaters: 8 chain (42 screens), 1 **C**
independent (1 screen)
Crowd Pleasers
Aquariums and Zoos: **B**
John Ball Zoological Gardens (167 species, 465
specimens)
Pari-mutuel Betting: **C**
Muskegon Racecourse (harness, 99 days)
Professional Sports: 0.34 game seats per capita **C**
Hoops (CBA Basketball)
Lumberjacks (IHL Hockey)

Rating

Outdoor Recreation Assets
Lake Michigan Coastline: 54 miles
Federal Protected Area
Manistee NF, 12,446 acres
State Recreation Areas
Muskegon SP, 1,165 acres
P. J. Hoffmaster SP, 1,086 acres
Places Rated Score: 1,787   Places Rated Rank: 110

Great Falls, MT
Common Denominators
Golf courses: 1 private (18 holes), 2 municipal (36 **A**
holes)
Good restaurants: 3 ** **AA**
Movie theaters: 3 chain (8 screens) **A**
Crowd Pleasers
Pari-mutuel Betting: **A**
State Fair (thoroughbred, 22 days)
Outdoor Recreation Assets
Federal Protected Areas
Benton Lake NWR, 11,955 acres
Lewis and Clark NF, 178,713 acres
State Recreation Areas
Giant Springs SP, 117 acres
Ulm Pishkun SP, 170 acres
Places Rated Score: 1,857   Places Rated Rank: 105

Greeley, CO
Common Denominators
Golf courses: 2 private (36 holes), 1 daily fee (18 **A**
holes), 2 municipal (36 holes)
Good restaurants: 1 ** **C**
Movie theaters: 5 chain (15 screens) **AA**
Outdoor Recreation Assets
State Recreation Area
Barbour Ponds SRA, 50 acres
MC Access: Denver–Boulder–Greeley, CO
Places Rated Score: 950   Places Rated Rank: 280

Green Bay, WI
Common Denominators
Golf courses: 1 private (18 holes), 10 daily fee (135 **AA**
holes), 1 municipal (18 holes)
Good restaurants: 4 *, 2 ** **B**
Movie theaters: 5 chain (21 screens) **A**
Crowd Pleasers
Professional Sports: 2.37 game seats per capita **AA**
Packers (NFL Football)
NCAA Division I: 0.30 game seats per capita **B**
University of Wisconsin, Green Bay Phoenix (B)
Outdoor Recreation Assets
Lake Michigan Coastline: 21 miles
Places Rated Score: 1,711   Places Rated Rank: 121

Greensboro–Winston-Salem–High Point, NC
Common Denominators
Golf courses: 20 private (342 holes), 34 daily fee **AA**
(540 holes), 13 municipal (216 holes)
Good restaurants: 6 **, 2 *** **C**
Movie theaters: 17 chain (64 screens), 4 **B**
independent (5 screens)
Crowd Pleasers
Aquariums and Zoos: **A**
North Carolina Zoological Park (140 species, 814
specimens)
Family Theme Parks: **C**
Emerald Pointe (98 days)
Professional Sports: 1.36 game seats per capita **A**
Hornets (Class A Baseball)
Monarchs (ECHL Hockey)
Spirits (Class A Baseball)
Thunderbirds (ECHL Hockey)
NCAA Division I: 0.68 game seats per capita **A**
North Carolina A&T State University Aggies (F, B)
University of North Carolina, Greensboro
Spartans (B)
Wake Forest University Demon Deacons (F, B)

Rating

Outdoor Recreation Assets
  Federal Protected Areas
    Guilford Courthouse NMP, 220 acres
    Uwharrie NF, 9,898 acres
  State Recreation Areas
    Boone's Cave, 110 acres
    Hanging Rock, 5,862 acres
Places Rated Score: 1,733   Places Rated Rank: 116

Greenville, NC
Common Denominators
  Golf courses: 3 private (54 holes), 2 daily fee (36   **B**
    holes)
  Movie theaters: 4 chain (11 screens)   **A**
Crowd Pleasers
  NCAA Division I: 2.00 game seats per capita   **AA**
    East Carolina University Pirates (F, B)
Places Rated Score: 900   Places Rated Rank: 295

Greenville–Spartanburg–Anderson, SC
Common Denominators
  Golf courses: 22 private (360 holes), 22 daily fee   **A**
    (369 holes)
  Good restaurants: 2 **, 3 ***   **C**
  Movie theaters: 11 chain (54 screens), 3   **B**
    independent (6 screens)
Crowd Pleasers
  Aquariums and Zoos: **C**
    Greenville Zoo (89 species, 335 specimens)
  Professional Sports: 0.88 game seats per capita
    Braves (Class AA Baseball)
    Phillies (Class A Baseball)
  NCAA Division I: 0.75 game seats per capita   **A**
    Clemson University Tigers (F, B)
    Furman University Paladins (F, B)
Outdoor Recreation Assets
  Federal Protected Areas
    Cowpens NB, 789 acres
    Kings Mountain NMP, 1,416 acres
  State Recreation Areas
    Croft SP, 7,088 acres
    Keowee Toxaway SP, 1,000 acres
    Musgrove Mill SP, 91 acres
    Sadlers Creek SP, 395 acres
    Wildcat Wayside SP, 63 acres
Places Rated Score: 1,163   Places Rated Rank: 235

Hagerstown, MD
Common Denominators
  Golf courses: 1 private (18 holes), 1 daily fee (18   **B**
    holes), 2 municipal (27 holes)
  Good restaurants: 2 *, 1 **   **B**
  Movie theaters: 4 chain (19 screens), 1   **AA**
    independent (1 screen)
Crowd Pleasers
  Professional Sports: 3.36 game seats per capita   **AA**
    Suns (Class AA Baseball)
Outdoor Recreation Assets
  Federal Protected Areas
    Antietam National Cemetary, 11 acres
    Antietam NB, 2,240 acres
    Appalachian Trail, 10 acres
    Catoctin Mountain Park, 75 acres
    Chesapeake and Ohio Canal NHP, 6,376 acres
    Harpers Ferry NHP, 765 acres
  State Recreation Areas
    Gathland SP, 117 acres
    Greenbrier SP, 1,288 acres
MC Access: Washington–Baltimore, DC–MD–VA–WV
Places Rated Score: 1,601   Places Rated Rank: 147

Halifax, NS
Common Denominators
  Golf courses: 3 private (54 holes), 4 daily fee (63   **C**
    holes)
  Good restaurants: 2 *, 2 **, 2 ***   **B**
  Movie theaters: 6 chain (25 screens), 2   **B**
    independent (2 screens)

Rating

Crowd Pleasers
  Aquariums and Zoos: **C**
    Provincial Wildlife Park (98 species, 463
      specimens)
  Professional Sports: 0.58 game seats per capita   **C**
    Citadels (AHL Hockey)
  CIAU: 0.25 game seats per capita   **B**
    Dalhousie University Tigers (B, H)
    St. Mary's University Huskies
Outdoor Recreation Assets
  Atlantic Coastline: 45 miles
  Federal Protected Areas
    Musquodoboit Harbour Outer River Estuary, 2,965
      acres
    Sable Island MBS, 5,807 acres
  Provincial Recreation Areas
    Clam Harbour Beach PP, 974 acres
    Crystal Cresent Beach PP, 452 acres
    Lawrencetown Beach PP, 588 acres
    Lewis Lake PP, 371 acres
    Martinique Beach PP, 151 acres
    Oakfield PP, 133 acres
    Porters Lake PP, 215 acres
    Taylors Head PP, 2,014 acres
Places Rated Score: 1,561   Places Rated Rank: 153

Hamilton, ON
Common Denominators
  Golf courses: 5 private (81 holes), 4 daily fee (72   **B**
    holes), 6 municipal (108 holes)
  Good restaurants: 7 **, 1 ***   **B**
  Movie theaters: 8 chain (39 screens), 6   **B**
    independent (8 screens)
Crowd Pleasers
  Pari-mutuel Betting: **A**
    Flamboro Downs (harness, 215 days)
  Professional Sports: 0.55 game seats per capita   **C**
    Redbirds (Class A Baseball)
    Tiger Cats (CFL Football)
  CIAU: 0.07 game seats per capita   **C**
    McMaster University Marauders (F, B)
Outdoor Recreation Assets
  Lake Ontario Coastline: 15 miles
MC Access: Toronto–Ontario Shore, ON
Places Rated Score: 1,440   Places Rated Rank: 176

Hamilton–Middletown, OH
Common Denominators
  Golf courses: 5 private (81 holes), 4 daily fee (54   **A**
    holes), 6 municipal (108 holes)
  Good restaurants: 2 **   **C**
  Movie theaters: 5 chain (5 screens)   **C**
Crowd Pleasers
  NCAA Division I: 0.80 game seats per capita   **A**
    Miami University Redskins
Outdoor Recreation Assets
  State Recreation Area
    Hueston Woods SP, 990 acres
MC Access: Cincinnati–Hamilton, OH–KY–IN
Places Rated Score: 967   Places Rated Rank: 279

Harrisburg–Lebanon–Carlisle, PA
Common Denominators
  Golf courses: 10 private (162 holes), 16 daily fee   **A**
    (261 holes), 2 municipal (36 holes)
  Good restaurants: 7 **, 2 ***   **B**
  Movie theaters: 13 chain (47 screens), 5   **B**
    independent (5 screens)
Crowd Pleasers
  Aquariums and Zoos: **B**
    Zooamerica Wildlife Park (71 species, 213
      specimens)
  Family Theme Parks: **B**
    Hersheypark (100 days)
  Pari-mutuel Betting: **A**
    Penn National Race Course (thoroughbred, 240
      days)

Rating

Professional Sports: 0.88 game seats per capita   **C**
Bears (AHL Hockey)
Senators (Class AA Baseball)
Outdoor Recreation Assets
Federal Protected Area
Appalachian Trail, 4,606 acres
State Recreation Areas
Colonel Denning SP, 273 acres
Kings Gap SP, 1,443 acres
Pine Grove Furnace SP, 696 acres
Swatara SP, 1,000 acres
Places Rated Score: 1,536   Places Rated Rank: 156

Hartford, CT
Common Denominators
Golf courses: 18 private (288 holes), 23 daily fee   **A**
(351 holes), 8 municipal (126 holes)
Good restaurants: 5 *, 9 **, 7 ***   **B**
Movie theaters: 11 chain (53 screens), 9   **C**
independent (13 screens)
Crowd Pleasers
NCAA Division I: 0.08 game seats per capita   **C**
University of Hartford Hawks (B)
Outdoor Recreation Assets
State Recreation Areas
American Legion SF, 782 acres
Cockaponset SF, 15,652 acres
Day Pond SP, 180 acres
Devil's Hopyard SP, 860 acres
Gay City SP, 1,569 acres
Gillette Castle SP, 184 acres
Haddam Meadows SP, 175 acres
Hurd SP, 884 acres
Mansfield Hollow SP, 2,328 acres
Penwood SP, 787 acres
Peoples SF, 29,544 acres
Salmon River SF, 6,115 acres
Stratton Brook SP, 148 acres
Talcott Mountain SP, 557 acres
Wadsworth Falls SP, 285 acres
Places Rated Score: 986   Places Rated Rank: 277

Hickory–Morgantown, NC
Common Denominators
Golf courses: 7 private (108 holes), 10 daily fee   **AA**
(180 holes)
Good restaurants: 1 *, 2 **   **C**
Movie theaters: 5 chain (16 screens)   **C**
Outdoor Recreation Assets
Federal Protected Areas
Blue Ridge Parkway, 964 acres
Pisgah NF, 97,263 acres
Places Rated Score: 1,954   Places Rated Rank: 97

✓ Honolulu, HI
Common Denominators
Golf courses: 12 private (198 holes), 10 daily fee   **B**
(171 holes), 7 municipal (117 holes)
Movie theaters: 14 chain (52 screens), 1   **B**
independent (2 screens)
Crowd Pleasers
Aquariums and Zoos: **A**
Honolulu Zoo (227 species, 1,051 specimens)
Waikiki Aquarium
Family Theme Parks: **AA**
Waimea Falls Park (365 days)
NCAA Division I: 0.38 game seats per capita   **A**
University of Hawaii, Manoa Rainbow Warriors
(F, B)
Outdoor Recreation Assets
Pacific Coastline: 135 miles
Federal Protected Area
Hawaiian Islands NWR, 1,907 acres
State Recreation Areas
Diamond Head State Monument, 475 acres
Kaena Point SP, 853 acres

Rating

Keaiwa Heiau SRA, 385 acres
Sand Island SRA, 140 acres
Places Rated Score: 2,787   Places Rated Rank: 26

Houma, LA
Common Denominators
Golf courses: 4 private (54 holes), 2 daily fee (18   **C**
holes)
Good restaurants: 2 *   **C**
Movie theaters: 3 chain (10 screens), 1   **B**
independent (2 screens)
Crowd Pleasers
NCAA Division I: 0.53 game seats per capita   **A**
Nicholls State University Colonels (F, B)
Outdoor Recreation Assets
Gulf Coastline: 79 miles
Federal Protected Area
Jean Lafitte NHP, 3 acres
Places Rated Score: 1,490   Places Rated Rank: 167

✓ Houston, TX
Common Denominators
Golf courses: 66 private (1053 holes), 28 daily fee   **C**
(441 holes), 9 municipal (162 holes)
Good restaurants: 10 *, 19 **, 18 ***, 2 ****   **B**
Movie theaters: 54 chain (316 screens), 12   **A**
independent (16 screens)
Crowd Pleasers
Aquariums and Zoos: **A**
Houston Zoological Gardens (661 species, 2,762
specimens)
Family Theme Parks: **A**
Astro World (136 days)
Professional Sports: 1.76 game seats per capita   **A**
Astros (NL Baseball)
Oilers (NFL Football)
Rockets (NBA Basketball)
NCAA Division I: 0.29 game seats per capita   **B**
Prairie View A&M University Panthers (F, B)
Rice University Owls (F, B)
Texas Southern University Tigers (F, B)
University of Houston–University Park Cougars
(F, B)
Outdoor Recreation Assets
Gulf Coastline: 90 miles
Federal Protected Areas
Anahuac NWR, 28,014 acres
Big Thicket NP, 1,472 acres
Sam Houston NF, 47,609 acres
State Recreation Areas
Brazos Bend SP, 4,897 acres
Lake Houston SP, 3,000 acres
MC Access: Houston–Galveston–Brazoria, TX
Places Rated Score: 3,030   Places Rated Rank: 16

Huntington–Ashland, WV-KY-OH
Common Denominators
Golf courses: 4 private (63 holes), 12 daily fee (153   **A**
holes)
Good restaurants: 4 **, 1 ***   **B**
Movie theaters: 3 chain (19 screens)   **B**
Crowd Pleasers
NCAA Division I: 0.84 game seats per capita   **A**
Marshall University Thundering Herd (F, B)
Outdoor Recreation Assets
Federal Protected Area
Wayne NF, 60,690 acres
State Recreation Area
Beech Fork SP, 3,981 acres
Places Rated Score: 1,402   Places Rated Rank: 183

Huntsville, AL
Common Denominators
Golf courses: 4 private (54 holes), 4 daily fee (63   **A**
holes), 6 municipal (108 holes)
Good restaurants: 4 **   **B**
Movie theaters: 3 chain (22 screens)   **B**

	Rating
Crowd Pleasers	
Professional Sports: 2.30 game seats per capita	**AA**
Stars (Class AA Baseball)	
Outdoor Recreation Assets	
Federal Protected Area	
Wheeler NWR, 5,006 acres	
State Recreation Area	
Monte Sano SP, 2,140 acres	
Places Rated Score: 1,116 Places Rated Rank: 248	

Indianapolis, IN

Common Denominators
Golf courses: 26 private (423 holes), 34 daily fee (477 holes), 16 municipal (234 holes) — **A**
Good restaurants: 8 **, 8 *** — **B**
Movie theaters: 31 chain (122 screens), 5 independent (5 screens) — **A**
Crowd Pleasers
Aquariums and Zoos: — **A**
Indianapolis Zoo (371 species, 2,408 specimens)
Professional Sports: 2.15 game seats per capita — **AA**
Colts (NFL Football)
Ice (IHL Hockey)
Indians (Triple A Baseball)
Pacers (NBA Basketball)
NCAA Division I: 0.08 game seats per capita — **C**
Butler University Bulldogs (B)
Outdoor Recreation Assets
State Recreation Area
Mounds SP, 259 acres
Places Rated Score: 1,603   Places Rated Rank: 146

Iowa City, IA

Common Denominators
Golf courses: 1 private (9 holes), 4 daily fee (45 holes), 1 municipal (18 holes) — **AA**
Movie theaters: 4 chain (11 screens) — **A**
Crowd Pleasers
NCAA Division I: 5.07 game seats per capita — **AA**
University of Iowa Hawkeyes (F, B)
Outdoor Recreation Assets
State Recreation Area
Lake Macbride SP, 2,150 acres
Places Rated Score: 1,124   Places Rated Rank: 246

Jackson, MI

Common Denominators
Golf courses: 3 private (45 holes), 16 daily fee (234 holes), 2 municipal (36 holes) — **AA**
Good restaurants: 1 ** — **C**
Movie theaters: 4 chain (21 screens), 1 independent (1 screen) — **AA**
Crowd Pleasers
Pari-mutuel Betting: — **A**
Jackson Raceway (harness, 82 days)
Outdoor Recreation Assets
State Recreation Area
W. J. Hayes SP, 22 acres
Places Rated Score: 1,243   Places Rated Rank: 216

Jackson, MS

Common Denominators
Golf courses: 10 private (171 holes), 4 daily fee (72 holes), 4 municipal (45 holes) — **B**
Good restaurants: 5 **, 2 *** — **B**
Movie theaters: 4 chain (24 screens) — **C**
Crowd Pleasers
Aquariums and Zoos: — **B**
Jackson Zoological Park (131 species, 425 specimens)
Professional Sports: 0.89 game seats per capita — **C**
Generals (Class AA Baseball)
NCAA Division I: 0.81 game seats per capita — **A**
Jackson State University Tigers (F, B)

	Rating
Outdoor Recreation Assets	
Federal Protected Area	
Natchez Trace Parkway, 7,352 acres	
Places Rated Score: 1,203 Places Rated Rank: 225	

✓ Jacksonville, FL

Common Denominators
Golf courses: 28 private (477 holes), 19 daily fee (315 holes), 4 municipal (63 holes) — **A**
Good restaurants: 10 *, 11 **, 2 *** — **A**
Movie theaters: 18 chain (96 screens), 4 independent (10 screens) — **AA**
Crowd Pleasers
Aquariums and Zoos: — **A**
Jacksonville Zoological Park (222 species, 825 specimens)
Pari-mutuel Betting: — **A**
Orange Park Kennel Club (greyhound, 134 days)
St. Johns Greyhound Park (greyhound, 120 days)
Triangle Kennel Club (greyhound, 152 days)
Professional Sports: 0.61 game seats per capita — **C**
Suns (Class AA Baseball)
NCAA Division I: 0.11 game seats per capita — **C**
Jacksonville University Dolphins (B)
Outdoor Recreation Assets
Atlantic Coastline: 80 miles
Federal Protected Areas
Fort Caroline NM, 133 acres
Fort Matanzas NM, 228 acres
Timucuan Ecological and Historic Reserve, 1,984 acres
State Recreation Areas
Big Talbot Island SP, 1,430 acres
Fort Clinch SP, 1,119 acres
Little Talbot Island SP, 2,633 acres
Places Rated Score: 2,642   Places Rated Rank: 33

Jacksonville, NC

Common Denominators
Golf courses: 3 private (54 holes), 2 daily fee (36 holes) — **C**
Good restaurants: 1 * — **C**
Movie theaters: 6 chain (24 screens) — **AA**
Outdoor Recreation Assets
Atlantic Coastline: 30 miles
State Recreation Area
Hammocks Beach, 892 acres
Places Rated Score: 909   Places Rated Rank: 290

Jamestown, NY

Common Denominators
Golf courses: 2 private (36 holes), 11 daily fee (153 holes) — **AA**
Good restaurants: 6 ** — **AA**
Movie theaters: 7 chain (21 screens), 2 independent (2 screens) — **AA**
Crowd Pleasers
Professional Sports: 1.64 game seats per capita — **A**
Expos (Class A Baseball)
Outdoor Recreation Assets
Lake Erie Coastline: 45 miles
State Recreation Area
Long Point SP, 360 acres
Places Rated Score: 1,955   Places Rated Rank: 96

Janesville–Beloit, WI

Common Denominators
Golf courses: 3 private (45 holes), 7 daily fee (81 holes), 3 municipal (45 holes) — **AA**
Good restaurants: 1 ** — **C**
Movie theaters: 3 chain (10 screens) — **B**
Crowd Pleasers
Professional Sports: 1.89 game seats per capita — **A**
Brewers (Class A Baseball)
Places Rated Score: 1,000   Places Rated Rank: 271

	Rating

Johnson City–Kingsport–Bristol, TN–VA
Common Denominators
Golf courses: 5 private (90 holes), 7 daily fee (99 holes), 5 municipal (72 holes) — **B**

Good restaurants: 3 *, 4 **, 2 *** — **B**

Movie theaters: 6 chain (29 screens), 2 independent (3 screens) — **B**
Crowd Pleasers
NCAA Division I: 0.23 game seats per capita — **B**
East Tennessee State University Buccaneers (F, B)
Outdoor Recreation Assets
Federal Protected Areas
Appalachian Trail, 968 acres
Cherokee NF, 193,471 acres
Jefferson NF, 56,188 acres
State Recreation Area
Warriors Path SRA, 870 acres

Places Rated Score: 1,493   Places Rated Rank: 166

Johnstown, PA
Common Denominators
Golf courses: 4 private (54 holes), 14 daily fee (162 holes), 1 municipal (9 holes) — **AA**

Good restaurants: 2 ** — **C**

Movie theaters: 3 independent (6 screens) — **C**
Crowd Pleasers
Professional Sports: 0.67 game seats per capita — **C**
Chiefs (ECHL Hockey)

NCAA Division I: 0.17 game seats per capita — **B**
St. Francis College Red Flash (B)
Outdoor Recreation Assets
Federal Protected Areas
Allegheny Portage Railroad NHS, 329 acres
Johnstown Flood NM, 155 acres
State Recreation Areas
Laurel Hill SP, 3,935 acres
Laurel Ridge SP, 5,582 acres

Places Rated Score: 987   Places Rated Rank: 276

Joplin, MO
Common Denominators
Golf courses: 4 private (63 holes), 1 daily fee (18 holes), 3 municipal (54 holes) — **A**

Good restaurants: 1 *, 2 ** — **B**

Movie theaters: 6 chain (21 screens) — **AA**
Outdoor Recreation Assets
Federal Protected Area
George Washington Carver NM, 210 acres
State Recreation Area
Battle of Carthage SHS, 7 acres

Places Rated Score: 901   Places Rated Rank: 294

Kalamazoo–Battle Creek, MI
Common Denominators
Golf courses: 9 private (153 holes), 21 daily fee (342 holes), 4 municipal (63 holes) — **AA**

Good restaurants: 1 *, 4 **, 1 *** — **B**

Movie theaters: 9 chain (49 screens), 2 independent (3 screens) — **AA**
Crowd Pleasers
Aquariums and Zoos: — **C**
Binder Park Zoo (72 species, 320 specimens)

Professional Sports: 0.46 game seats per capita — **C**
Wings (IHL Hockey)

NCAA Division I: 0.60 game seats per capita — **A**
Western Michigan University Broncos
Outdoor Recreation Assets
Lake Michigan Coastline: 15 miles
State Recreation Area
Van Buren SP, 407 acres

Places Rated Score: 1,664   Places Rated Rank: 128

Kankakee, IL
Common Denominators
Golf courses: 1 private (18 holes), 6 daily fee (108 holes), 1 municipal (18 holes) — **AA**

	Rating

Good restaurants: 1 *, 1 ** — **B**

Movie theaters: 2 chain (8 screens) — **B**

MC Access: Chicago–Gary–Kenosha, IL–IN–WI

Places Rated Score: 920   Places Rated Rank: 283

Kansas City, MO–KS
Common Denominators
Golf courses: 28 private (450 holes), 23 daily fee (369 holes), 17 municipal (279 holes) — **B**

Good restaurants: 11 *, 17 **, 5 ***, 2 **** — **A**

Movie theaters: 28 chain (144 screens), 6 independent (6 screens) — **A**
Crowd Pleasers
Aquariums and Zoos: — **A**
Kansas City Zoological Gardens (168 species, 627 specimens)

Family Theme Parks: — **B**
Worlds of Fun–Oceans of Fun (124 days)

Pari-mutuel Betting: — **B**
Woodlands Horse Racing (thoroughbred, 63 days)
Woodlands Kennel Club (greyhound, 233 days)

Professional Sports: 2.41 game seats per capita — **AA**
Blades (IHL Hockey)
Royals (AL Baseball)

NCAA Division I: 0.07 game seats per capita — **C**
University of Missouri, Kansas City Kangaroos (B)
Outdoor Recreation Assets
State Recreation Areas
Hillsdale SP, 1,475 acres
Watkins Mill SP, 818 acres

Places Rated Score: 2,007   Places Rated Rank: 91

Kenosha, WI
Common Denominators
Golf courses: 1 private (18 holes), 5 daily fee (90 holes), 4 municipal (54 holes) — **AA**

Good restaurants: 1 **, 1 *** — **B**

Movie theaters: 1 chain (5 screens) — **C**
Crowd Pleasers
Pari-mutuel Betting: — **AA**
Dairyland Greyhound Park (greyhound, 347 days)

Professional Sports: 1.60 game seats per capita — **A**
Twins (Class A Baseball)
Outdoor Recreation Assets
State Recreation Area
Bong SRA, 4,515 acres
Lake Michigan Coastline: 12 miles

MC Access: Chicago–Gary–Kenosha, IL–IN–WI

Places Rated Score: 1,679   Places Rated Rank: 127

Killeen–Temple, TX
Common Denominators
Golf courses: 6 private (99 holes), 2 daily fee (36 holes), 2 municipal (27 holes) — **C**

Good restaurants: 1 * — **C**

Movie theaters: 2 chain (11 screens), 4 independent (4 screens) — **C**
Outdoor Recreation Assets
State Recreation Area
Mother Neff SP, 259 acres

Places Rated Score: 301   Places Rated Rank: 339

Kitchener, ON
Common Denominators
Golf courses: 3 private (54 holes), 3 daily fee (45 holes), 3 municipal (54 holes) — **B**

Good restaurants: 4 **, 5 *** — **A**

Movie theaters: 8 chain (18 screens), 1 independent (1 screen) — **C**
Crowd Pleasers
Aquariums and Zoos: — **A**
African Lion Safari (151 species, 1,500 specimens)

Family Theme Parks: — **AA**
Bingeman Park (100 days)
Sportsworld (365 days)

	Rating
CIAU: 0.37 game seats per capita	A
University of Waterloo Warriors	
Wilfrid Laurier University Golden Hawks	

Outdoor Recreation Assets
Provincial Recreation Area
Dumfries Crown Game Preserve, 2,471 acres
MC Access: Toronto-Ontario Shore, ON
Places Rated Score: 1,777   Places Rated Rank: 112

✓ Knoxville, TN
Common Denominators

	Rating
Golf courses: 8 private (144 holes), 14 daily fee (234 holes), 3 municipal (54 holes)	A
Good restaurants: 9 *, 22 **, 3 ***, 1 ****	AA
Movie theaters: 9 chain (59 screens), 3 independent (6 screens)	A

Crowd Pleasers

	Rating
Aquariums and Zoos:	A
Knoxville Zoological Gardens (229 species, 851 specimens)	
Family Theme Parks:	A
Dollywood (191 days)	
Professional Sports: 1.06 game seats per capita	B
Blue Jays (Class AA Baseball)	
Cherokees (ECHL Hockey)	
NCAA Division I: 1.18 game seats per capita	AA
University of Tennessee-Knoxville Volunteers (F, B)	

Outdoor Recreation Assets
Federal Protected Areas
Appalachian Trail, 640 acres
Great Smokey Mountains NP, 225,193 acres
Places Rated Score: 2,932   Places Rated Rank: 18

Kokomo, IN
Common Denominators

	Rating
Golf courses: 1 private (18 holes), 4 daily fee (63 holes), 1 municipal (18 holes)	AA
Good restaurants: 1 *, 1 **	B
Movie theaters: 2 chain (13 screens), 1 independent (1 screen)	AA

Places Rated Score: 1,000   Places Rated Rank: 271

La Crosse, WI-MN
Common Denominators

	Rating
Golf courses: 1 private (9 holes), 7 daily fee (90 holes), 1 municipal (18 holes)	AA
Good restaurants: 2 **, 1 ***	A
Movie theaters: 3 chain (13 screens), 1 independent (1 screen)	AA

Crowd Pleasers

	Rating
Professional Sports: 2.04 game seats per capita	AA
Catbirds (CBA Basketball)	

Outdoor Recreation Assets
Federal Protected Area
Upper Mississippi NWR, 24,779 acres
Places Rated Score: 1,701   Places Rated Rank: 123

Lafayette, IN
Common Denominators

	Rating
Golf courses: 3 private (45 holes), 5 daily fee (81 holes), 1 municipal (18 holes)	AA
Good restaurants: 1 *, 1 **, 1 ***	B
Movie theaters: 4 chain (18 screens)	A

Crowd Pleasers

	Rating
NCAA Division I: 2.91 game seats per capita	AA
Purdue University Boilermakers (F, B)	

Places Rated Score: 1,300   Places Rated Rank: 201

Lafayette, LA
Common Denominators

	Rating
Golf courses: 6 private (90 holes), 2 daily fee (27 holes), 2 municipal (36 holes)	C
Good restaurants: 1 *, 9 **, 3 ***	AA
Movie theaters: 7 chain (30 screens), 1 independent (1 screen)	A

Crowd Pleasers

	Rating
Pari-mutuel Betting:	B
Evangeline Downs (thoroughbred, 82 days)	
NCAA Division I: 0.78 game seats per capita	A
University of Southwestern Louisiana Ragin' Cajuns (F, B)	

Outdoor Recreation Assets
Federal Protected Area
Atchafalaya NWR, 1,472 acres
State Recreation Area
Longfellow-Evangeline SHS, 157 acres
Places Rated Score: 1,307   Places Rated Rank: 196

Lake Charles, LA
Common Denominators

	Rating
Golf courses: 2 private (36 holes), 1 daily fee (18 holes), 2 municipal (36 holes)	B
Good restaurants: 2 **, 2 ***	A
Movie theaters: 3 chain (12 screens), 1 independent (1 screen)	B

Crowd Pleasers

	Rating
Pari-mutuel Betting:	AA
Delta Downs (mixed meetings, 144 days)	
NCAA Division I: 1.05 game seats per capita	AA
McNeese State University Cowboys (F, B)	

Outdoor Recreation Assets
State Recreation Area
Sam Houston Jones SP, 1,087 acres
Places Rated Score: 1,508   Places Rated Rank: 163

Lake County, IL
Common Denominators

	Rating
Golf courses: 24 private (414 holes), 11 daily fee (189 holes), 14 municipal (225 holes)	AA
Good restaurants: 8 *, 6 **, 4 ***	A
Movie theaters: 4 chain (26 screens), 3 independent (3 screens)	C

Crowd Pleasers

	Rating
Family Theme Parks:	A
Six Flags Great America (125 days)	

Outdoor Recreation Assets
Lake Michigan Coastline: 25 miles
State Recreation Area
Illinois Beach SP, 2,978 acres
MC Access: Chicago-Gary-Kenosha, IL-IN-WI
Places Rated Score: 1,639   Places Rated Rank: 135

Lakeland-Winter Haven, FL
Common Denominators

	Rating
Golf courses: 10 private (171 holes), 17 daily fee (279), 4 municipal (63 holes)	AA
Good restaurants: 5 *, 3 **, 2 ***, 1 ****	A
Movie theaters: 10 chain (44 screens)	A

Crowd Pleasers

	Rating
Professional Sports: 3.28 game seats per capita	AA
Red Sox (Class A Baseball)	
Royals (Class A Baseball)	
Tigers (Class A Baseball)	

Outdoor Recreation Assets
State Recreation Area
Lake Kissimmee SP, 5,030 acres
Places Rated Score: 1,458   Places Rated Rank: 173

Lancaster, PA
Common Denominators

	Rating
Golf courses: 6 private (90 holes), 4 daily fee (72 holes), 2 municipal (36 holes)	C
Good restaurants: 3 *, 6 **, 5 ***	AA
Movie theaters: 7 chain (15 screens), 5 independent (5 screens)	C

Crowd Pleasers

	Rating
Family Theme Parks:	B
Dutch Wonderland (116 days)	

Outdoor Recreation Assets
State Recreation Area
Susquehannock SP, 224 acres
Places Rated Score: 802   Places Rated Rank: 304

Rating

Lansing–East Lansing, MI
Common Denominators
Golf courses: 4 private (54 holes), 25 daily fee (369   **AA**
holes), 3 municipal (36 holes)
Good restaurants: 2 *, 2 **   **C**
Movie theaters: 4 chain (31 screens), 4   **B**
independent (6 screens)
Crowd Pleasers
Aquariums and Zoos: **C**
Potter Park Zoo (123 species, 346 specimens)
NCAA Division I: 0.54 game seats per capita   **A**
Michigan State University Spartans
Outdoor Recreation Assets
State Recreation Area
Sleepy Hollow SP, 2,678 acres
Places Rated Score: 1,112   Places Rated Rank: 249

Laredo, TX
Common Denominators
Golf courses: 1 private (18 holes), 1 municipal (18   **C**
holes)
Movie theaters: 2 chain (7 screens)   **C**
Outdoor Recreation Assets
State Recreation Area
Lake Casa Blanca SRA, 371 acres
Places Rated Score: 201   Places Rated Rank: 342

Las Cruces, NM
Common Denominators
Golf courses: 4 private (63 holes), 4 daily fee (63   **A**
holes)
Good restaurants: 2 *, 3 **, 1 ***   **AA**
Movie theaters: 4 chain (14 screens)   **A**
Crowd Pleasers
Pari-mutuel Betting: **AA**
Sunland Park (thoroughbred, 111 days)
NCAA Division I: 1.93 game seats per capita   **AA**
New Mexico State University Aggies (F, B)
Outdoor Recreation Assets
Federal Protected Areas
San Andres NWR, 57,217 acres
White Sands NM, 52,778 acres
Places Rated Score: 2,026   Places Rated Rank: 86

✓ Las Vegas, NV–AZ
Common Denominators
Golf courses: 8 private (135 holes), 21 daily fee   **A**
(342 holes), 6 municipal (99 holes)
Good restaurants: 9 *, 11 **, 6 ***, 3 ****   **A**
Movie theaters: 9 chain (51 screens), 7   **B**
independent (19 screens)
Crowd Pleasers
Family Theme Parks: **A**
Wet'n Wild (165 days)
Professional Sports: 1.42 game seats per capita   **A**
Stars (Triple A Baseball)
Thunder (IHL Hockey)
NCAA Division I: 0.35 game seats per capita   **A**
University of Nevada, Las Vegas Runnin' Rebels
(F, B)
Outdoor Recreation Assets
Federal Protected Areas
Ashe Meadows NWR, 12,849 acres
Death Valley NM, 107,616 acres
Desert NWR, 828,794 acres
Grand Canyon NP, 517,156 acres
Havasu NWR, 12,248 acres
Humboldt NF, 248,321 acres
Kaibab NF, 5,468 acres
Lake Mead NRA, 1,385,836 acres
Toiyabe NF, 1,560,819 acres
State Recreation Areas
Lake Havasu SP, 13,072 acres
Spring Mountain Ranch SP, 17,600 acres
Valley of Fire SP, 34,880 acres
Places Rated Score: 2,642   Places Rated Rank: 33

Rating

Lawrence, KS
Common Denominators
Golf courses: 2 private (36 holes), 2 daily fee (27   **B**
holes)
Good restaurants: 1 ***   **B**
Movie theaters: 4 chain (17 screens), 2   **AA**
independent (2 screens)
Crowd Pleasers
NCAA Division I: 4.79 game seats per capita   **AA**
University of Kansas Jayhawks (F, B)
Outdoor Recreation Area
State Recreation Area
Clinton SP, 1,455 acres
Places Rated Score: 1,225   Places Rated Rank: 217

Lawton, OK
Common Denominators
Golf courses: 3 private (54 holes), 1 municipal (18   **C**
holes)
Good restaurants: 2 **, 1 ***   **A**
Movie theaters: 3 chain (12 screens)   **A**
Outdoor Recreation Assets
Federal Protected Area
Wichita Mountains NWR, 59,019 acres
Places Rated Score: 1,131   Places Rated Rank: 240

Lewiston–Auburn, ME
Common Denominators
Golf courses: 1 private (18 holes), 5 daily fee (72   **AA**
holes)
Good restaurants: 1 **   **C**
Movie theaters: 4 chain (31 screens)   **AA**
Outdoor Recreation Assets
State Recreation Area
Range Ponds SP, 750 acres
Places Rated Score: 912   Places Rated Rank: 287

Lexington, KY
Common Denominators
Golf courses: 11 private (180 holes), 10 daily fee   **A**
(153 holes), 2 municipal (36 holes)
Good restaurants: 4 *, 7 **, 3 ***   **A**
Movie theaters: 11 chain (57 screens), 6   **AA**
independent (7 screens)
Crowd Pleasers
Pari-mutuel Betting: **B**
Keeneland (thoroughbred, 32 days)
The Red Mile (harness, 58 days)
NCAA Division I: 1.55 game seats per capita   **AA**
Eastern Kentucky University Colonels (F, B)
University of Kentucky Wildcats (F, B)
Outdoor Recreation Assets
State Recreation Area
Fort Boonesborough SP, 153 acres
Places Rated Score: 1,601   Places Rated Rank: 147

Lima, OH
Common Denominators
Golf courses: 3 private (45 holes), 9 daily fee (153   **AA**
holes)
Good restaurants: 1 *, 3 **   **A**
Movie theaters: 7 chain (25 screens), 4   **AA**
independent (8 screens)
Outdoor Recreation Assets
State Recreation Area
Lake Loramie SP, 113 acres
Places Rated Score: 1,129   Places Rated Rank: 242

Lincoln, NE
Common Denominators
Golf courses: 3 private (54 holes), 1 daily fee (18   **B**
holes), 3 municipal (54 holes)
Good restaurants: 2 *, 3 **, 1 ***   **A**
Movie theaters: 9 chain (21 screens), 1   **A**
independent (1 screen)

Rating

Crowd Pleasers
  Aquariums and Zoos: **C**
    Folsom Children's Zoo (80 species, 335 specimens)
  Pari-mutuel Betting: **C**
    State Fair Park (thoroughbred, 21 days)
  NCAA Division I: 2.10 game seats per capita   **AA**
    University of Nebraska, Lincoln Cornhuskers (F, B)
Outdoor Recreation Assets
  State Recreation Areas
    Branched Oak SRA, 2,980 acres
    Olive Creek SRA, 602 acres
    Stagecoach SRA, 607 acres
Places Rated Score: 1,486   Places Rated Rank: 168

Little Rock–North Little Rock, AR
Common Denominators
  Golf courses: 14 private (207 holes), 5 daily fee (72 holes), 6 municipal (90 holes)   **B**
  Good restaurants: 6 *, 4 **, 1 ***   **B**
  Movie theaters: 9 chain (53 screens), 1 independent (2 screens)   **A**
Crowd Pleasers
  Aquariums and Zoos: **B**
    Little Rock Zoological Gardens (187 species, 676 specimens)
  Family Theme Parks: **B**
    Wild River Country (100 days)
  Professional Sports: 0.81 game seats per capita   **C**
    Arkansas Travelers (Class AA Baseball)
  NCAA Division I: 0.16 game seats per capita   **B**
    University of Arkansas, Little Rock Trojans (B)
Outdoor Recreation Assets
  Federal Protected Area
    Ouachita NF, 53,463 acres
  State Recreation Areas
    Pinnacle Mountain SP, 1,801 acres
    Toltec Mounds, 182 acres
Places Rated Score: 1,550   Places Rated Rank: 154

London, ON
Common Denominators
  Golf courses: 5 private (90 holes), 4 daily fee (63 holes), 6 municipal (90 holes)   **B**
  Good restaurants: 2 *, 5 **   **B**
  Movie theaters: 6 chain (25 screens), 6 independent (9 screens)   **B**
Crowd Pleasers
  Pari-mutuel Betting: **A**
    Western Fair Raceway (harness, 141 days)
  Professional Sports: 1.06 game seats per capita   **B**
    Tigers (Class AA Baseball)
  CIAU: 0.29 game seats per capita   **B**
    University of Western Ontario Mustangs
Places Rated Score: 1,300   Places Rated Rank: 201

Long Island, NY
Common Denominators
  Golf courses: 61 private (1026 holes), 18 daily fee (261 holes), 27 municipal (441 holes)   **B**
  Good restaurants: 30 *, 90 **, 31 ***   **AA**
  Movie theaters: 38 chain (197 screens), 16 independent (28 screens)   **B**
Crowd Pleasers
  Pari-mutuel Betting: **C**
    Belmont (thoroughbred, 114 days)
  Professional Sports: 0.25 game seats per capita   **C**
    Islanders (NHL Hockey)
  NCAA Division I: 0.01 game seats per capita   **C**
    Hofstra University Flying Dutchmen (B)
Outdoor Recreation Assets
  Atlantic Coastline: 85 miles
  Federal Protected Areas
    Elizabeth A. Morton NWR, 187 acres
    Fire Island Seashore, 6,221 acres

Rating

  Oyster Bay NWR, 3,204 acres
  Seatuck NWR, 183 acres
  Wertheim NWR, 2,398 acres
  State Recreation Areas
    Bayard Cutting Arboretum SP, 690 acres
    Caleb Smith SP, 543 acres
    Cannetoquot River, 3,473 acres
    Caumsett SP, 1,486 acres
    Gilgo SP, 1,223 acres
    Hempstead Lake SP, 727 acres
    Jones Beach SP, 2,413 acres
    Montauk Downs SP, 171 acres
    Napeague SP, 1,364 acres
    Planting Fields Arboretum SP, 409 acres
    Sunken Meadow SP, 1,266 acres
  MC Access: New York–Northern New Jersey–Long Island, NY–NJ–CT
Places Rated Score: 2,277   Places Rated Rank: 64

Longview–Marshall, TX
Common Denominators
  Golf courses: 8 private (99 holes), 4 daily fee (54 holes)   **B**
  Good restaurants: 2 *   **C**
  Movie theaters: 3 chain (10 screens), 2 independent (3 screens)   **B**
Outdoor Recreation Assets
  State Recreation Area
    Caddo Lake SP, 484 acres
Places Rated Score: 502   Places Rated Rank: 334

✓ Los Angeles–Long Beach, CA
Common Denominators
  Golf courses: 34 private (594 holes), 11 daily fee (171 holes), 37 municipal (612 holes)   **C**
  Good restaurants: 29 *, 58 **, 38 ***   **B**
  Movie theaters: 133 chain (541 screens), 37 independent (48 screens)   **B**
Crowd Pleasers
  Aquariums and Zoos: **AA**
    The Los Angeles Zoo (508 species, 1,610 specimens)
  Family Theme Parks: **AA**
    Raging Waters (108 days)
    Six Flags Magic Mountain (184 days)
    Universal Studios Hollywood (363 days)
  Pari-mutuel Betting: **C**
    Hollywood Park Race Track (mixed meetings, 159 days)
    Santa Anita Park (thoroughbred, 92 days)
  Professional Sports: 0.95 game seats per capita   **B**
    Clippers (NBA Basketball)
    Dodgers (NL Baseball)
    Kings (NHL Hockey)
    Lakers (NBA Basketball)
    Raiders (NFL Football)
  NCAA Division I: 0.17 game seats per capita   **B**
    California State University, Long Beach Forty-Niners (B)
    California State University, Northridge Matadors (B)
    Loyola Marymount University Lions (B)
    Pepperdine University Waves (B)
    University of California, Los Angeles Bruins (F, B)
    University of Southern California Trojans (F, B)
Outdoor Recreation Assets
  Pacific Coastline: 55 miles
  Federal Protected Areas
    Angeles NF, 641,960 acres
    Los Padres NF, 8,776 acres
    Santa Monica Mountains NRA, 9,888 acres
  State Recreation Areas
    Castaic Lake SRA, 4,200 acres
    Dockweiler SB, 91 acres
    Placerita Canyon SP, 342 acres
    Will Rogers SHP, 189 acres

Rating

MC Access: Los Angeles–Riverside–Orange County, CA
Places Rated Score: 3,857   Places Rated Rank: 2

Louisville, KY–IN
Common Denominators
Golf courses: 19 private (306 holes), 15 daily fee (189 holes), 10 municipal (153 holes) — **B**
Good restaurants: 2 ★, 7 ★★, 6 ★★★ — **B**
Movie theaters: 10 chain (72 screens), 5 independent (9 screens) — **B**
Crowd Pleasers
Aquariums and Zoos: — **A**
  Louisville Zoological Gardens (412 species, 2,156 specimens)
Pari-mutuel Betting: — **C**
  Churchill Downs (thoroughbred, 79 days)
Professional Sports: 2.70 games seats per capita — **AA**
  Icehawks (ECHL Hockey)
  Redbirds (Triple A Baseball)
NCAA Division I: 0.20 game seats per capita — **B**
  University of Louisville Cardinals (F, B)
Outdoor Recreation Assets
State Recreation Area
  Sawyer SP, 337 acres
Places Rated Score: 1,601   Places Rated Rank: 147

Lubbock, TX
Common Denominators
Golf courses: 4 private (63 holes), 3 daily fee (45 holes), 2 municipal (36 holes) — **B**
Good restaurants: 1 ★, 5 ★★ — **A**
Movie theaters: 7 chain (33 screens) — **AA**
Crowd Pleasers
NCAA Division I: 1.45 game seats per capita — **AA**
  Texas Tech University Red Raiders (F, B)
Outdoor Recreation Assets
State Recreation Area
  Lubbock Lake Landmark SHS, 309 acres
Places Rated Score: 1,303   Places Rated Rank: 199

Lynchburg, VA
Common Denominators
Golf courses: 3 private (45 holes), 7 daily fee (99 holes) — **A**
Good restaurants: 1 ★, 3 ★★, 2 ★★★ — **A**
Movie theaters: 5 chain (30 screens) — **AA**
Crowd Pleasers
Professional Sports: 1.46 game seats per capita — **A**
  Red Sox (Class A Baseball)
NCAA Division I: 0.75 game seats per capita — **A**
  Liberty University Flames (F, B)
Outdoor Recreation Assets
Federal Protected Areas
  Appalachian Trail, 120 acres
  Blue Ridge Parkway, 8,678 acres
  George Washington NF, 57,728 acres
  Jefferson NF, 18,762 acres
Places Rated Score: 2,066   Places Rated Rank: 84

Macon, GA
Common Denominators
Golf courses: 8 private (135 holes), 4 daily fee (63 holes), 2 municipal (36 holes) — **B**
Good restaurants: 1 ★, 3 ★★, 1 ★★★ — **B**
Movie theaters: 7 chain (34 screens) — **AA**
Crowd Pleasers
Professional Sports: 0.71 game seats per capita — **C**
  Braves (Class A Baseball)
NCAA Division I: 0.30 game seats per capita — **A**
  Mercer University Bears (B)
Outdoor Recreation Assets
Federal Protected Areas
  Bond Swamp NWR, 4,544 acres
  Ocmulgee NM, 683 acres
  Oconee NF, 16,476 acres

Rating

Piedmont NWR, 28,305 acres
State Recreation Area
  Jarrell Plantation SHS, 10 acres
Places Rated Score: 1,455   Places Rated Rank: 174

Madison, WI
Common Denominators
Golf courses: 5 private (81 holes), 7 daily fee (99 holes), 4 municipal (63 holes) — **A**
Good restaurants: 2 ★, 6 ★★, 2 ★★★ — **A**
Movie theaters: 11 chain (41 screens), 3 independent (4 screens) — **AA**
Crowd Pleasers
Aquariums and Zoos: — **B**
  Henry Vilas Zoo (174 species, 706 specimens)
Professional Sports: 0.72 game seats per capita — **C**
  Muskies (Class A Baseball)
NCAA Division I: 1.48 game seats per capita — **AA**
  University of Wisconsin, Madison Badgers
Outdoor Recreation Assets
State Recreation Area
  Governor Nelson SP, 422 acres
Places Rated Score: 1,706   Places Rated Rank: 124

Manchester–Nashua, NH
Common Denominators
Golf courses: 3 private (54 holes), 12 daily fee (171 holes), 1 municipal (18 holes) — **A**
Good restaurants: 4 ★, 4 ★★, 3 ★★★ — **A**
Movie theaters: 3 chain (17 screens), 3 independent (8 screens) — **B**
Outdoor Recreation Assets
Federal Protected Area
  Wapack NWR, 1,711 acres
State Recreation Areas
  Greenfield SP, 401 acres
  Miller SP, 489 acres
MC Access: Boston–New Bedford–Nashua, MA–NH
Places Rated Score: 915   Places Rated Rank: 286

Mansfield, OH
Common Denominators
Golf courses: 4 private (63 holes), 8 daily fee (117 holes) — **AA**
Movie theaters: 4 chain (19 screens), 2 independent (2 screens) — **AA**
Outdoor Recreation Assets
State Recreation Area
  Malabar Farm SP, 914 acres
Places Rated Score: 809   Places Rated Rank: 301

McAllen–Edinburg–Mission, TX
Common Denominators
Golf courses: 4 private (63 holes), 3 daily fee (45 holes), 5 municipal (72 holes) — **B**
Good restaurants: 2 ★ — **C**
Movie theaters: 5 chain (28 screens), 3 independent (3 screens) — **B**
Crowd Pleasers
NCAA Division I: 0.12 game seats per capita — **C**
  University of Texas, Pan American Broncs (B)
Outdoor Recreation Assets
Federal Protected Areas
  Lower Rio Grande Valley NWR, 15,002 acres
  Santa Ana NWR, 2,087 acres
State Recreation Area
  Bentsen–Rio Grande Valley SP, 588 acres
Places Rated Score: 688   Places Rated Rank: 321

Medford–Ashland, OR
Common Denominators
Golf courses: 2 private (27 holes), 1 daily fee (18 holes), 1 municipal (9 holes) — **C**
Good restaurants: 1 ★, 3 ★★, 1 ★★★ — **A**
Movie theaters: 3 chain (15 screens) — **A**

Rating

Crowd Pleasers
  Professional Sports: 1.33 game seats per capita   **B**
    Southern O Athletics (Class A Baseball)
Outdoor Recreation Assets
  Federal Protected Areas
    Crater Lake NP, 944 acres
    Klamath NF, 26,334 acres
    Rogue River NF, 411,684 acres
    Umpqua NF, 10,628 acres
Places Rated Score: 2,165   **Places Rated Rank: 74**

Melbourne–Titusville–Palm Bay, FL
Common Denominators
  Golf courses: 7 private (126 holes), 4 daily fee (72   **A**
    holes), 6 municipal (99 holes)
  Good restaurants: 2 *, 4 **, 2 ***   **B**
  Movie theaters: 8 chain (67 screens), 2   **AA**
    independent (3 screens)
Crowd Pleasers
  Pari-mutuel Betting: **AA**
    Sports Palace (greyhound, 365 days)
Outdoor Recreation Assets
  Atlantic Coastline: 72 miles
  Federal Protected Areas
    Canaveral NS, 29,479 acres
    St. Johns NWR, 6,255 acres
  State Recreation Area
    Sebastian Inlet SRA, 121 acres
Places Rated Score: 2,295   **Places Rated Rank: 59**

Memphis, TN–AR–MS
Common Denominators
  Golf courses: 21 private (342 holes), 5 daily fee (90   **C**
    holes), 10 municipal (162 holes)
  Good restaurants: 1 *, 5 **, 5 ***   **C**
  Movie theaters: 14 chain (85 screens), 2   **B**
    independent (2 screens)
Crowd Pleasers
  Aquariums and Zoos: **A**
    Memphis Zoo and Aquarium (416 species, 2,342
      specimens)
  Pari-mutuel Betting: **A**
    Southland Greyhound Park (greyhound, 349 days)
  Professional Sports: 0.67 game seats per capita   **C**
    Chicks (Class AA Baseball)
  NCAA Division I: 0.49 game seats per capita   **A**
    Memphis State University Tigers (F, B)
Outdoor Recreation Assets
  Federal Protected Areas
    Lower Hatchie NWR, 984 acres
    Wapanocca NWR, 5,484 acres
  State Recreation Area
    T. O. Fuller SRA, 384 acres
Places Rated Score: 1,450   **Places Rated Rank: 175**

Merced, CA
Common Denominators
  Golf courses: 2 private (36 holes), 2 daily fee (27   **C**
    holes)
  Good restaurants: 2 **   **C**
  Movie theaters: 2 chain (11 screens), 2   **B**
    independent (3 screens)
Outdoor Recreation Assets
  Federal Protected Areas
    Merced NWR, 2,562 acres
    San Luis NWR, 7,422 acres
  State Recreation Area
    San Luis Reservoir SRA, 26,026 acres
Places Rated Score: 547   **Places Rated Rank: 331**

✓ Miami, FL
Common Denominators
  Golf courses: 10 private (180 holes), 17 daily fee   **C**
    (297 holes), 11 municipal (180 holes)
  Good restaurants: 8 *, 17 **, 12 ***, 3 ****   **A**
  Movie theaters: 22 chain (165 screens), 11   **A**
    independent (15 screens)

Rating

Crowd Pleasers
  Aquariums and Zoos: **A**
    Metrozoo (281 species, 3,080 specimens)
    Miami Seaquarium
  Pari-mutuel Betting: **A**
    Biscayne Kennel Club (greyhound, 158 days)
    Calder Race Course (thoroughbred, 184 days)
    Flagler Kennel Club (greyhound, 159 days)
    Hialeah Park (thoroughbred, 50 days)
    Miami Jai Alai (328 days)
  Professional Sports: 2.94 game seats per capita   **AA**
    Dolphins (NFL Football)
    Heat (NBA Basketball)
    Marlins (NL Baseball)
    South Florida Panthers (NHL Hockey)
  NCAA Division I: 0.28 game seats per capita   **B**
    Florida International University Golden Panthers
      (B)
    University of Miami Hurricanes (F, B)
Outdoor Recreation Assets
  Atlantic Coastline: 84 miles
  Federal Protected Areas
    Big Cypress NP, 12,413 acres
    Biscayne NP, 169,345 acres
    Everglades NP, 415,716 acres
  State Recreation Areas
    Chekika SRA, 636 acres
    Oleta River SRA, 855 acres
MC Access: Miami–Fort Lauderdale, FL
Places Rated Score: 3,904   **Places Rated Rank: 1**

Milwaukee–Waukesha, WI
Common Denominators
  Golf courses: 15 private (252 holes), 23 daily fee   **B**
    (333 holes), 14 municipal (243 holes)
  Good restaurants: 5 *, 18 **, 8 ***, 1 ****   **A**
  Movie theaters: 27 chain (103 screens), 3   **B**
    independent (5 screens)
Crowd Pleasers
  Aquariums and Zoos: **AA**
    Milwaukee County Zoo (380 species, 5,590
      specimens)
  Professional Sports: 4.82 game seats per capita   **AA**
    Admirals (IHL Hockey)
    Brewers (AL Baseball)
    Bucks (NBA Basketball)
    Packers (NFL Football)
  NCAA Division I: 0.03 game seats per capita   **C**
    Marquette University Warriors (B)
    University of Wisconsin, Milwaukee Panthers (B)
Outdoor Recreation Assets
  Lake Michigan Coastline: 49 miles
  State Recreation Area
    Harrington Beach SP, 636 acres
MC Access: Milwaukee–Racine, WI
Places Rated Score: 2,107   **Places Rated Rank: 78**

Minneapolis–St. Paul, MN–WI
Common Denominators
  Golf courses: 30 private (513 holes), 61 daily fee   **A**
    (945 holes), 26 municipal (441 holes)
  Good restaurants: 8 *, 34 **, 11 ***   **A**
  Movie theaters: 35 chain (151 screens), 7   **C**
    independent (10 screens)
Crowd Pleasers
  Aquariums and Zoos: **AA**
    Minnesota Zoological Gardens (387 species,
      2,060 specimens)
    St. Paul's Como Zoo (117 species, 379
      specimens)
  Family Theme Parks: **A**
    Valleyfair! Family Amusement Park (130 days)
  Pari-mutuel Betting: **B**
    Canterbury Downs (thoroughbred, 124 days)
    St. Croix Meadows Greyhound Park (greyhound,
      346 days)

	Rating
Professional Sports: 2.71 game seats per capita	**AA**
North Stars (NHL Hockey)	
Timberwolves (NBA Basketball)	
Twins (AL Baseball)	
Vikings (NFL Football)	
NCAA Division I: 0.20 game seats per capita	**B**
University of Minnesota Gophers	

Outdoor Recreation Assets
  Federal Protected Areas
    Lower St. Croix Scenic River, 5,554 acres
    Minnesota Valley NWR, 4,849 acres
    St. Croix Scenic Riverway, 1,246 acres
    Sherburne NWR, 29,583 acres
  State Recreation Areas
    Afton SP, 1,699 acres
    Interstate SP, 293 acres
    Kinnickinnic SP, 1,242 acres
    Wild River SP, 7,000 acres

Places Rated Score: 2,273   Places Rated Rank: 66

Mobile, AL
Common Denominators

	Rating
Golf courses: 6 private (90 holes), 9 daily fee (162 holes), 8 municipal (144 holes)	**AA**
Good restaurants: 5 *, 8 **, 2 ***	**A**
Movie theaters: 6 chain (38 screens), 1 independent (1 screen)	**B**

Crowd Pleasers

	Rating
Pari-mutuel Betting:	**AA**
Mobile Greyhound Park (greyhound, 350 days)	
NCAA Division I: 0.61 game seats per capita	**A**
University of South Alabama Jaguars (B)	

Outdoor Recreation Assets
  Gulf Coastline: 53 miles
  Federal Protected Areas
    Bon Secour NWR, 3,917 acres
    Grand Bay NWR, 1,410 acres
  State Recreation Area
    Gulf SP, 6,000 acres

Places Rated Score: 2,161   Places Rated Rank: 75

Modesto, CA
Common Denominators

	Rating
Golf courses: 2 private (36 holes), 3 municipal (45 holes)	**C**
Good restaurants: 2 **	**C**
Movie theaters: 3 chain (16 screens)	**C**

Crowd Pleasers

	Rating
Professional Sports: 0.42 game seats per capita	**C**
A's (Class A Baseball)	

Outdoor Recreation Assets
  Federal Protected Area
    San Joaquin River NWR, 777 acres
  State Recreation Area
    Turlock Lake SRA, 409 acres

Places Rated Score: 548   Places Rated Rank: 330

Monmouth–Ocean, NJ
Common Denominators

	Rating
Golf courses: 15 private (252 holes), 10 daily fee (153 holes), 10 municipal (171 holes)	**B**
Good restaurants: 3 *, 10 **, 2 ***	**B**
Movie theaters: 22 chain (82 screens), 1 independent (2 screens)	**B**

Crowd Pleasers

	Rating
Family Theme Parks:	**B**
Six Flags Great Adventure (106 days)	
Pari-mutuel Betting:	**A**
Freehold Raceway (harness, 214 days)	
Monmouth Park (thoroughbred, 73 days)	
NCAA Division I: 0.03 game seats per capita	**C**
Monmouth College Hawks (B)	

Outdoor Recreation Assets
  Atlantic Coastline: 80 miles
  Federal Protected Areas
    Edwin B. Forsythe NWR, 13,015 acres
    Gateway NRA, 1,723 acres

  State Recreation Area
    Island Beach SP, 3,002 acres
  MC Access: New York–Northern New Jersey–Long
    Island, NY–NJ–CT

Places Rated Score: 2,284   Places Rated Rank: 62

Monroe, LA
Common Denominators

	Rating
Golf courses: 3 private (45 holes), 1 daily fee (9 holes), 3 municipal (36 holes)	**B**
Good restaurants: 2 **, 1 ***	**A**
Movie theaters: 2 chain (13 screens)	**A**

Crowd Pleasers

	Rating
NCAA Division I: 1.25 game seats per capita	**AA**
Northeast Louisiana University Indians (F, B)	

Outdoor Recreation Assets
  Federal Protected Area
    D'Arbonne NWR, 7,859 acres

Places Rated Score: 1,300   Places Rated Rank: 201

Montgomery, AL
Common Denominators

	Rating
Golf courses: 12 private (207 holes), 2 daily fee (27 holes), 1 municipal (18 holes)	**C**
Good restaurants: 2 **, 2 ***	**B**
Movie theaters: 6 chain (28 screens)	**A**

Crowd Pleasers

	Rating
Aquariums and Zoos:	**B**
Montgomery Zoo (147 species, 495 specimens)	
NCAA Division I: 0.53 game seats per capita	**A**
Alabama State University Hornets (F, B)	

Places Rated Score: 1,100   Places Rated Rank: 255

Montreal, PQ
Common Denominators

	Rating
Golf courses: 23 private (378 holes), 18 daily fee (297 holes), 22 municipal (342 holes)	**C**
Good restaurants: 6 *, 10 **, 15 ***, 1 ****	**C**
Movie theaters: 31 chain (125 screens), 22 independent (30 screens)	**C**

Crowd Pleasers

	Rating
Aquariums and Zoos:	**A**
Aquarium et Zoo de Montreal (165 species, 3,631 specimens)	
Jardin Zoologique de Montreal (89 species, 605 specimens)	
Pari-mutuel Betting:	**C**
Hippodrome Blue Bonnets (harness, 253 days)	
Professional Sports: 1.72 game seats per capita	**A**
Canadiens (NHL Hockey)	
Expos (NL Baseball)	
CIAU: 0.04 game seats per capita	**C**
Concordia University Stingers	
McGill University Redmen	

Outdoor Recreation Assets
  Federal Protected Areas
    Ile aux Herons MBS, 1,483 acres
    Iles de Contrecoeur NWA, 561 acres
    Iles de la Paix MBS, 2,718 acres
    Iles de la Paix NWA, 299 acres
    Ils St-Ours MBS, 741 acres
    Mount St-Hilaire MBS, 2,347 acres
    Senneville MBS, 741 acres
  Provincial Recreation Areas
    Iles de Boucherville PP, 2,011 acres
    Mount St-Bruno PP, 1,458 acres
    Oka PP, 5,856 acres

Places Rated Score: 1,166   Places Rated Rank: 234

Muncie, IN
Common Denominators

	Rating
Golf courses: 2 private (36 holes), 6 daily fee (99 holes)	**AA**
Good restaurants: 1 *	**C**
Movie theaters: 3 chain (18 screens)	**AA**

Crowd Pleasers

Rating

NCAA Division I: 1.66 game seats per capita   **AA**
Ball State University Cardinals (F, B)
Places Rated Score: 1,300   Places Rated Rank: 201

Myrtle Beach, SC
Common Denominators
Golf courses: 3 private (54 holes), 53 daily fee (891   **AA**
holes)
Good restaurants: 2 *, 4 **, 1 ***   **AA**
Movie theaters: 6 chain (32 screens)   **AA**
Crowd Pleasers
Professional Sports: 1.49 game seats per capita   **A**
Hurricanes (Class A Baseball)
NCAA Division I: 0.12 game seats per capita   **C**
University of South Carolina, Coastal Chanticleers
(B)
Outdoor Recreation Assets
Atlantic Coastline: 75 miles
State Recreation Area
Myrtle Beach SP, 312 acres
Places Rated Score: 2,352   Places Rated Rank: 55

✓ Naples, FL
Common Denominators
Golf courses: 27 private (468 holes), 9 daily fee   **AA**
(162 holes)
Good restaurants: 7 *, 13 **, 11 ***   **AA**
Movie theaters: 3 chain (22 screens), 1   **AA**
independent (1 screen)
Crowd Pleasers
Family Theme Parks: **AA**
Jungle Larry's Zoological Park (363 days)
Outdoor Recreation Assets
Gulf Coastline: 65 miles
Federal Protected Areas
Big Cypress N Preserve, 396,508 acres
Everglades NP, 39,262 acres
Florida Panther NWR, 24,310 acres
State Recreation Area
Delnor-Wiggins Pass SRA, 166 acres
Places Rated Score: 3,600   Places Rated Rank: 7

Nashville, TN
Common Denominators
Golf courses: 20 private (306 holes), 9 daily fee   **B**
(153 holes), 12 municipal (180 holes)
Good restaurants: 5 *, 5 **, 4 ***, 3 ****   **B**
Movie theaters: 27 chain (144 screens), 2   **AA**
independent (3 screens)
Crowd Pleasers
Family Theme Parks: **B**
Opryland (100 days)
Professional Sports: 1.46 game seats per capita   **A**
Knights (ECHL Hockey)
Sounds (Triple A Baseball)
NCAA Division I: 0.71 game seats per capita   **A**
Middle Tennessee State University Blue Raiders
(F, B)
Tennessee State University Tigers (F, B)
Vanderbilt University Commodores (F, B)
Outdoor Recreation Assets
Federal Protected Areas
Natchez Trace Parkway, 2,669 acres
Stones River NB, 350 acres
State Recreation Areas
Bledsoe Creek SP, 164 acres
Radnor Lake SNA, 957 acres
Places Rated Score: 1,617   Places Rated Rank: 138

New Bedford-Fall River-Attleboro, MA
Common Denominators
Golf courses: 11 private (153 holes), 15 daily fee   **A**
(189 holes), 2 municipal (27 holes)
Good restaurants: 1 *, 2 **   **C**
Movie theaters: 10 chain (44 screens), 2   **A**
independent (2 screens)

Rating

Crowd Pleasers
Pari-mutuel Betting: **AA**
Raynham-Taunton Dog Track (greyhound, 365
days)
Outdoor Recreation Assets
Atlantic Coastline: 26 miles
State Recreation Areas
Borderland SP, 1,563 acres
Demarest Lloyd SP, 222 acres
Freetown SF, 5,441 acres
Horseneck Beach State Reservation, 537 acres
Massasoit SP, 1,500 acres
MC Access: Boston-New Bedford-Nashua,
MA-NH
Places Rated Score: 1,460   Places Rated Rank: 172

New Haven-Meriden, CT
Common Denominators
Golf courses: 10 private (171 holes), 6 daily fee (72   **C**
holes), 3 municipal (54 holes)
Good restaurants: 3 *, 7 **, 2 ***   **A**
Movie theaters: 4 chain (27 screens), 1   **C**
independent (1 screen)
Crowd Pleasers
NCAA Division I: 0.76 game seats per capita   **A**
Yale University Elis
Outdoor Recreation Assets
Long Island Sound Coastline: 30 miles
State Recreation Areas
Chatfield Hollow SP, 102 acres
Hammonasset Beach SRA, 919 acres
Sleeping Giant SP, 1,439 acres
West Rock Ridge SP, 293 acres
MC Access: New York-Northern New Jersey-Long
Island, NY-NJ-CT
Places Rated Score: 1,143   Places Rated Rank: 237

New London-Norwich, CT-RI
Common Denominators
Golf courses: 4 private (54 holes), 3 daily fee (36   **B**
holes), 2 municipal (36 holes)
Good restaurants: 2 *, 1 **, 4 ***   **AA**
Movie theaters: 6 chain (20 screens)   **A**
Outdoor Recreation Assets
Long Island Sound Coastline: 35 miles
State Recreation Areas
Bluff Point Coastal Reserve SP, 806 acres
Fort Shantok SP, 170 acres
Haley Farm SP, 198 acres
Harkness Memorial SP, 116 acres
Hopeville Pond SP, 554 acres
Rocky Neck SP, 708 acres
Places Rated Score: 1,281   Places Rated Rank: 210

New Orleans, LA
Common Denominators
Golf courses: 20 private (351 holes), 10 daily fee   **C**
(153 holes), 4 municipal (63 holes)
Good restaurants: 16 *, 20 **, 20 ***, 1 ****   **AA**
Movie theaters: 17 chain (109 screens), 12   **A**
independent (21 screens)
Crowd Pleasers
Aquariums and Zoos: **C**
Audubon Zoo (438 species, 1,830 specimens)
Pari-mutuel Betting: **C**
Fair Grounds (thoroughbred, 65 days)
Jefferson Downs (thoroughbred, 80 days)
Professional Sports: 0.43 game seats per capita   **C**
Saints (NFL Football)
NCAA Division I: 0.39 game seats per capita   **A**
Tulane University of Louisiana Green Wave (F, B)
University of New Orleans Privateers (B)
Outdoor Recreation Assets
Gulf Coastline: 75 miles
Federal Protected Areas
Bayou Sauvage NWR, 18,000 acres

Rating

Bogue Chitto NWR, 23,112 acres
Breton NWR, 9,047 acres
Delta NWR, 45,907 acres
Jean Lafitte NHP, 9,646 acres
State Recreation Areas
Fairview-Riverside SP, 99 acres
Fort Pike S.C.A., 94 acres
St. Bernard SP, 358 acres
Places Rated Score: 2,402   Places Rated Rank: 49

New York, NY
Common Denominators
Golf courses: 49 private (837 holes), 5 daily fee (72   **C**
holes), 20 municipal (360 holes)
Good restaurants: 67 *, 158 **, 84 ***, 11 ****,
2 *****   **AA**
Movie theaters: 115 chain (428 screens), 34   **C**
independent (58 screens)
Crowd Pleasers
Aquariums and Zoos: **AA**
Bronx Zoo (682 species, 4,425 specimens)
Central Park Zoo (108 species, 10,791
specimens)
Staten Island Zoo (196 species, 422 specimens)
Pari-mutuel Betting: **C**
Aqueduct (thoroughbred, 183 days)
Yonkers Raceway (harness, 368 days)
Professional Sports: 1.33 game seats per capita   **B**
Knicks (NBA Basketball)
Mets (NL Baseball)
Rangers (NHL Hockey)
Yankees (AL Baseball)
NCAA Division I: 0.04 game seats per capita   **C**
Columbia University Lions (F, B)
CUNY Brooklyn College Kingsmen (B)
Fordham University Rams (F, B)
Iona College Gaels (B, H)
Long Island University, Brooklyn Blackbirds (B)
Manhattan College Jaspers (B)
St. Francis College Terriers (B)
St. John's University Redmen (B, H)
Wagner College Seahawks (B)
Outdoor Recreation Assets
Atlantic Coastline: 27 miles
Federal Protected Areas
Appalachian Trail, 901 acres
Gateway NRA, 18,652 acres
Statue of Liberty NM, 13 acres
State Recreation Areas
Blauvelt SP, 590 acres
Clay Pit Pond SP, 258 acres
High Tor SP, 565 acres
Rockefeller Preserve SP, 743 acres
Rockwood Hall SP, 170 acres
Tallman Mountain SP, 687 acres
MC Access: New York-Northern New Jersey-Long
Island, NY-NJ-CT
Places Rated Score: 2,125   Places Rated Rank: 77

Newark-Jersey City, NJ
Common Denominators
Golf courses: 32 private (540 holes), 6 daily fee (81   **C**
holes), 14 municipal (234 holes)
Good restaurants: 3 *, 8 **, 8 ***, 2 ****   **C**
Movie theaters: 14 chain (72 screens), 12   **C**
independent (23 screens)
Crowd Pleasers
NCAA Division I: 0.03 game seats per capita   **C**
St. Peter's College Peacocks (B)
Seton Hall University Pirates (B)
Outdoor Recreation Assets
Federal Protected Areas
Great Swamp NWR, 6,992 acres
Morristown NHP, 1,482 acres
Statue of Liberty NM, 45 acres
State Recreation Areas
Great Piece Meadow SP, 793 acres

Rating

Hopatcong SP, 15 acres
MC Access: New York-Northern New Jersey-Long
Island, NY-NJ-CT
Places Rated Score: 720   Places Rated Rank: 314

✓ Norfolk-Virginia Beach-Newport News, VA-NC
Common Denominators
Golf courses: 15 private (261 holes), 16 daily fee   **B**
(279 holes), 11 municipal (180 holes)
Good restaurants: 15 *, 33 **, 6 ***, 1 ****   **AA**
Movie theaters: 24 chain (126 screens), 5   **A**
independent (8 screens)
Crowd Pleasers
Aquariums and Zoos: **B**
Newport News Zoo (101 species, 280 specimens)
Family Theme Parks: **A**
Busch Gardens, The Old Country (165 days)
Ocean Breeze Fun Park (124 days)
Water Country USA (104 days)
Professional Sports: 0.74 game seats per capita   **C**
Admirals (ECHL Hockey)
Peninsula Pilots (Class A Baseball)
Tidewater Tides (Triple A Baseball)
NCAA Division I: 0.16 game seats per capita   **B**
College of William and Mary Tribe (F, B)
Old Dominion University Monarchs (B)
Outdoor Recreation Assets
Atlantic Coastline: 69 miles
Federal Protected Areas
Back Bay NWR, 4,589 acres
Colonial NHP, 8,839 acres
Currituck NWR, 1,820 acres
Great Dismal Swamp NWR, 81,610 acres
Mackay Island NWR, 7,110 acres
Nansemond NWR, 208 acres
Plum Tree Island NWR, 3,276 acres
State Recreation Area
Seashore SP, 2,770 acres
Places Rated Score: 2,764   Places Rated Rank: 29

Northern New Jersey, NJ
Common Denominators
Golf courses: 23 private (342 holes), 13 daily fee   **C**
(198 holes), 7 municipal (117 holes)
Good restaurants: 1 *, 5 **, 2 ***   **C**
Movie theaters: 15 chain (67 screens), 9   **C**
independent (15 screens)
Crowd Pleasers
Aquariums and Zoos: **C**
Bergen County Zoological Park (67 species, 174
specimens)
Family Theme Parks: **C**
Action Park (97 days)
Pari-mutuel Betting: **B**
Meadowlands Racetrack (mixed meetings, 252
days)
Professional Sports: 2.58 game seats per capita   **AA**
Devils (NHL Hockey)
Giants (NFL Football)
Jets (NFL Football)
Nets (NBA Basketball)
NCAA Division I: 0.04 game seats per capita   **C**
Fairleigh Dickinson University Knights (B)
Outdoor Recreation Assets
Federal Protected Areas
Appalachian Trail, 493 acres
Delaware Water Gap NRA, 21,291 acres
State Recreation Areas
Cranberry Lake SP, 199 acres
High Point SP, 14,193 acres
Musconetong SP, 245 acres
Swartswood SP, 1,718 acres
Wawayanda SP, 2,987 acres
MC Access: New York-Northern New Jersey-Long
Island, NY-NJ-CT
Places Rated Score: 1,774   Places Rated Rank: 113

Rating

Oakland, CA
Common Denominators
Golf courses: 17 private (297 holes), 11 daily fee (189 holes), 11 municipal (189 holes) — **C**

Good restaurants: 6 *, 11 **, 7 *** — **C**

Movie theaters: 33 chain (172 screens), 7 independent (14 screens) — **B**

Crowd Pleasers
Aquariums and Zoos: — **B**
Knowland Park–Oakland Zoo (82 species, 361 specimens)

Pari-mutuel Betting: — **C**
Golden Gate Fields (thoroughbred, 110 days)

Professional Sports: 2.35 game seats per capita — **AA**
Athletics (AL Baseball)
Warriors (NBA Basketball)

NCAA Division I: 0.22 game seats per capita — **B**
St. Mary's College of California Gaels (B)
University of California, Berkeley Golden Bears (F, B)

Outdoor Recreation Assets
Federal Protected Area
San Francisco Bay NWR, 10,727 acres
State Recreation Areas
Franks Tract SRA, 3,532 acres
Mount Diablo SP, 20,090 acres
Robert W. Crown Memorial SB, 132 acres

MC Access: San Francisco–Oakland–San Jose, CA

Places Rated Score: 1,659 · Places Rated Rank: 130

Ocala, FL
Common Denominators
Golf courses: 3 private (45 holes), 7 daily fee (117 holes), 3 municipal (45 holes) — **AA**

Good restaurants: 2 **, 1 *** — **B**

Movie theaters: 3 chain (14 screens) — **B**

Crowd Pleasers
Family Theme Parks: — **AA**
Silver Springs and Wild Waters (365 days)

Pari-mutuel Betting: — **B**
Ocala Jai Alai (155 days)

Outdoor Recreation Assets
Federal Protected Area
Ocala NF, 275,404 acres
State Recreation Area
Lake Rousseau SRA, 696 acres

Places Rated Score: 2,788 · Places Rated Rank: 25

Odessa–Midland, TX
Common Denominators
Golf courses: 6 private (99 holes), 1 daily fee (18 holes), 2 municipal (27 holes) — **C**

Good restaurants: 2 *, 5 ** — **A**

Movie theaters: 6 chain (25 screens), 2 independent (4 screens) — **AA**

Crowd Pleasers
Professional Sports: 1.17 game seats per capita — **B**
Angels (Class AA Baseball)

Places Rated Score: 1,000 · Places Rated Rank: 271

Oklahoma City, OK
Common Denominators
Golf courses: 14 private (225 holes), 9 daily fee (144 holes), 13 municipal (216 holes) — **B**

Good restaurants: 4 *, 8 **, 6 *** — **B**

Movie theaters: 18 chain (106 screens), 4 independent (5 screens) — **AA**

Crowd Pleasers
Aquariums and Zoos: — **A**
Oklahoma City Zoo (536 species, 1,999 specimens)

Family Theme Parks: — **B**
Frontier City (108 days)

Pari-mutuel Betting: — **B**
Remington Park (mixed meetings, 159 days)

Professional Sports: 1.44 game seats per capita — **A**
89ers (Triple A Baseball)
Cavalry (CBA Basketball)

Rating

NCAA Division I: 0.50 game seats per capita — **A**
University of Oklahoma Norman Campus Sooners (F, B)

Outdoor Recreation Assets
State Recreation Area
Little River SP, 1,834 acres

Places Rated Score: 2,104 · Places Rated Rank: 80

Olympia, WA
Common Denominators
Golf courses: 1 private (18 holes), 4 daily fee (63 holes) — **B**

Good restaurants: 1 * — **C**

Movie theaters: 2 chain (11 screens) — **C**

Outdoor Recreation Assets
Puget Sound Coastline: 10 miles
Federal Protected Areas
Nisqually NWR, 2,004 acres
Snoqualmie NF, 612 acres
State Recreation Areas
Elbow Lake SP, 320 acres
Tolmie SP, 106 acres

MC Access: Seattle–Tacoma–Bremerton, WA

Places Rated Score: 562 · Places Rated Rank: 329

Omaha, NE–IA
Common Denominators
Golf courses: 13 private (189 holes), 7 daily fee (99 holes), 9 municipal (117 holes) — **B**

Good restaurants: 4 *, 12 **, 8 ***, 1 **** — **AA**

Movie theaters: 19 chain (82 screens), 4 independent (8 screens) — **AA**

Crowd Pleasers
Aquariums and Zoos: — **A**
Henry Doorly Zoo (475 species, 9,338 specimens)

Pari-mutuel Betting: — **AA**
Ak-Sar-Ben (thoroughbred, 77 days)
Bluffs Run (greyhound, 360 days)

Professional Sports: 2.20 game seats per capita — **AA**
Racers (CBA Basketball)
Royals (Triple A Baseball)

NCAA Division I: 0.02 game seats per capita — **C**
Creighton University Bluejays (B)

Outdoor Recreation Assets
Federal Protected Area
De Soto NWR, 4,919 acres
State Recreation Areas
Platte River SP, 418 acres
Two Rivers SRA, 622 acres
Wilson Island SRA, 577 acres

Places Rated Score: 2,229 · Places Rated Rank: 71

✓ Orange County, CA
Common Denominators
Golf courses: 21 private (351 holes), 12 daily fee (216 holes), 8 municipal (144 holes) — **C**

Good restaurants: 14 *, 30 **, 13 ***, 1 **** — **A**

Movie theaters: 50 chain (180 screens), 7 independent (11 screens) — **B**

Crowd Pleasers
Aquariums and Zoos: — **B**
Santa Ana Zoo (87 species, 543 specimens)

Family Theme Parks: — **AA**
Disneyland (365 days)
Knott's Berry Farm (365 days)
Wild Rivers Water Park (96 days)

Pari-mutuel Betting: — **C**
Los Alamitos (mixed meetings, 209 days)

Professional Sports: 2.68 game seats per capita — **AA**
Angels (AL Baseball)
Mighty Ducks (NHL Hockey)
Rams (NFL Football)

NCAA Division I: 0.06 game seats per capita — **C**
California State University, Fullerton Titans (F, B)
University of California, Irvine Anteaters (B)

Outdoor Recreation Assets
Pacific Coastline: 40 miles

Rating

Federal Protected Area
Cleveland NF, 54,343 acres
State Recreation Areas
Crystal Cove SP, 3,940 acres
Doheny SB, 274 acres
Huntington SB, 129 acres
MC Access: Los Angeles–Riverside–Orange County, CA
Places Rated Score: 3,004   Places Rated Rank: 17

Orange County, NY
Common Denominators
Golf courses: 9 private (135 holes), 6 daily fee (72   **B**
holes), 1 municipal (18 holes)
Good restaurants: 5 ★, 4 ★★, 1 ★★★   **A**
Movie theaters: 2 chain (20 screens), 1   **B**
independent (1 screen)
Crowd Pleasers
NCAA Division I: 0.86 game seats per capita   **A**
United States Military Academy Cadets
Outdoor Recreation Assets
Federal Protected Area
Appalachian Trail, 2,597 acres
State Recreation Area
Storm King SP, 1,874 acres
MC Access: New York–Northern New Jersey–Long
Island, NY–NJ–CT
Places Rated Score: 1,259   Places Rated Rank: 213

✓ Orlando, FL
Common Denominators
Golf courses: 33 private (540 holes), 44 daily fee   **AA**
(783 holes), 2 municipal (27 holes)
Good restaurants: 9 ★, 28 ★★, 14 ★★★, 1 ★★★★   **AA**
Movie theaters: 32 chain (184 screens), 2   **AA**
independent (2 screens)
Crowd Pleasers
Aquariums and Zoos: **B**
Central Florida Zoological Park (152 species, 462
specimens)
Family Theme Parks: **AA**
Sea World of Florida (365 days)
Universal Studios Florida (365 days)
Walt Disney World (365 days)
Water Mania (285 days)
Wet'n Wild (300 days)
Pari-mutuel Betting: **A**
Orlando Jai Alai (217 days)
Sanford–Orlando Kennel Club (greyhound, 127
days)
Seminole Greyhound Park (greyhound, 234 days)
Professional Sports: 1.42 game seats per capita   **A**
Astros (Class A Baseball)
Magic (NBA Basketball)
Sun Rays (Class AA Baseball)
NCAA Division I: 0.27 game seats per capita   **B**
University of Central Florida Knights (F, B)
Outdoor Recreation Assets
Federal Protected Areas
Lake Woodruff NWR, 280 acres
Ocala NF, 84,072 acres
State Recreation Areas
Lake Griffin SRA, 255 acres
Lower Wekiva River SNA, 1,878 acres
Tosohatchee SNA, 30,349 acres
Wekiwa Springs SP, 6,396 acres
Places Rated Score: 2,906   Places Rated Rank: 20

Oshawa, ON
Common Denominators
Golf courses: 1 private (18 holes), 2 daily fee (36
holes)   **C**
Movie theaters: 2 chain (14 screens), 1   **C**
independent (1 screen)
Outdoor Recreation Assets
Lake Ontario Coastline: 15 miles
Provincial Recreation Area
Darlington PP, 516 acres

Rating

MC Access: Toronto–Ontario Shore, ON
Places Rated Score: 448   Places Rated Rank: 336

Ottawa–Hull, ON–PQ
Common Denominators
Golf courses: 10 private (162 holes), 9 daily fee   **C**
(144 holes), 5 municipal (81 holes)
Good restaurants: 3 ★, 4 ★★, 2 ★★★   **C**
Movie theaters: 18 chain (62 screens), 7   **B**
independent (8 screens)
Crowd Pleasers
Pari-mutuel Betting: **B**
Hippodrome Connaught (harness, 116 days)
Rideau Carleton Raceway (harness, 105 days)
Professional Sports: 1.45 game seats per capita   **A**
Lynx (Triple A Baseball)
Rough Riders (CFL Football)
Senators (NHL Hockey)
CIAU: 0.19 game seats per capita   **B**
Carleton University Ravens (F, B)
University of Ottawa Gees Gees
Outdoor Recreation Assets
Federal Protected Areas
Beckett Creek MBS, 247 acres
Ile Carillon MBS, 1,236 acres
Provincial Recreation Areas
Carillon PP, 3,501 acres
Fitzroy PP, 457 acres
Rideau River PP, 242 acres
Places Rated Score: 1,117   Places Rated Rank: 247

Owensboro, KY
Common Denominators
Golf courses: 2 private (36 holes), 1 daily fee (9   **A**
holes), 2 municipal (27 holes)
Good restaurants: 2 ★, 1 ★★   **A**
Movie theaters: 3 chain (12 screens)   **AA**
Outdoor Recreation Assets
State Recreation Area
Hawes SP, 297 acres
Places Rated Score: 1,005   Places Rated Rank: 267

Panama City, FL
Common Denominators
Golf courses: 2 private (36 holes), 7 daily fee (117   **AA**
holes)
Good restaurants: 3 ★, 4 ★★   **AA**
Movie theaters: 4 chain (19 screens), 1   **AA**
independent (1 screen)
Crowd Pleasers
Family Theme Parks: **C**
Miracle Strip Amusement Park (92 days)
Outdoor Recreation Assets
Gulf Coastline: 44 miles
State Recreation Area
St. Andrews SRA, 1,268 acres
Places Rated Score: 1,753   Places Rated Rank: 114

Parkersburg–Marietta, WV–OH
Common Denominators
Golf courses: 2 private (36 holes), 6 daily fee (99   **AA**
holes)
Good restaurants: 2 ★★   **B**
Movie theaters: 3 chain (18 screens), 2   **AA**
independent (4 screens)
Outdoor Recreation Assets
Federal Protected Area
Wayne NF, 35,862 acres
State Recreation Area
Muskingum River Parkway SP, 40 acres
Places Rated Score: 1,289   Places Rated Rank: 209

Pensacola, FL
Common Denominators
Golf courses: 4 private (72 holes), 11 daily fee (189   **AA**
holes), 1 municipal (18 holes)

	Rating
Good restaurants: 4 *, 2 **, 1 ***	B
Movie theaters: 5 chain (19 screens), 1 independent (1 screen)	C

Crowd Pleasers

Pari-mutuel Betting:	AA

Pensacola Greyhound Track (greyhound, 365 days)

Outdoor Recreation Assets

Gulf Coastline: 43 miles

Federal Protected Area

Gulf Islands NS, 25,560 acres

State Recreation Areas

Big Lagoon SRA, 698 acres

Perdido Key SRA, 287 acres

Places Rated Score: 1,656   Places Rated Rank: 132

Peoria–Pekin, IL

Common Denominators

Golf courses: 7 private (108 holes), 5 daily fee (81 holes), 7 municipal (126 holes)	AA
Good restaurants: 1 *, 1 **, 2 ***	B
Movie theaters: 9 chain (46 screens), 3 independent (3 screens)	AA

Crowd Pleasers

Aquariums and Zoos:	C

Glen Oak Zoo (117 species, 237 specimens)

Professional Sports: 2.25 game seats per capita	AA

Chiefs (Class A Baseball)

Rivermen (IHL Hockey)

NCAA Division I: 0.30 game seats per capita	A

Bradley University Braves (B)

Outdoor Recreation Assets

State Recreation Areas

Jubilee College SP, 3,185 acres

Places Rated Score: 1,814   Places Rated Rank: 108

Philadelphia, PA–NJ

Common Denominators

Golf courses: 77 private (1278 holes), 59 daily fee (963 holes), 12 municipal (216 holes)	C
Good restaurants: 14 *, 35 **, 32 ***, 1 ****, 1 *****	B
Movie theaters: 72 chain (259 screens), 10 independent (12 screens)	C

Crowd Pleasers

Aquariums and Zoos:	AA

Philadelphia Zoological Garden (494 species, 1,739 specimens)

Pari-mutuel Betting:	C

Garden State Park (mixed meetings, 165 days)

Philadelphia Park (thoroughbred, 278 days)

Professional Sports: 1.56 game seats per capita	A

76ers (NBA Basketball)

Eagles (NFL Football)

Flyers (NHL Hockey)

Phillies (NL Baseball)

NCAA Division I: 0.19 game seats per capita	B

Drexel University Dragons (B)

La Salle University Explorers (B)

St. Joseph's University Hawks (B)

Temple University Owls (F, B)

University of Pennsylvania Quakers (F, B)

Villanova University Wildcats

Outdoor Recreation Assets

Atlantic Coastline: 54 miles

Federal Protected Areas

Edwin B. Forsythe NWR, 2,368 acres

Hopewell Furnace NHS, 320 acres

Supawna Meadows NWR, 2,198 acres

Valley Forge NHP, 2,951 acres

State Recreation Areas

Benjamin Rush SP, 276 acres

Evansburg SP, 3,349 acres

Fort Mott SP, 104 acres

French Creek SP, 875 acres

Neshaminy SP, 330 acres

Rancocas SP, 1,252 acres

Tyler SP, 1,711 acres

MC Access: Philadelphia–Wilmington–Atlantic City, PA–NJ–DE–MD

Places Rated Score: 2,102   Places Rated Rank: 81

✓ Phoenix–Mesa, AZ

Common Denominators

Golf courses: 36 private (639 holes), 56 daily fee (936 holes), 9 municipal (153 holes)	A
Good restaurants: 30 *, 32 **, 12 ***, 4 ****	A
Movie theaters: 41 chain (250 screens), 10 independent (22 screens)	AA

Crowd Pleasers

Aquariums and Zoos:	A

Phoenix Zoo (342 species, 1,264 specimens)

Family Theme Parks:	AA

Island of Big Surf (92 days)

Rawhide (365 days)

Pari-mutuel Betting:	A

Apache Greyhound Park (greyhound, 227 days)

Phoenix Greyhound Park (greyhound, 365 days)

Turf Paradise (thoroughbred, 169 days)

Professional Sports: 1.16 game seats per capita	B

Cardinals (NFL Football)

Firebirds (Triple A Baseball)

Roadrunners (IHL Hockey)

Suns (NBA Basketball)

NCAA Division I: 0.21 game seats per capita	B

Arizona State University Sun Devils (F, B)

Outdoor Recreation Assets

Federal Protected Areas

Casa Grande NM, 472 acres

Coronado NF, 23,312 acres

Tonto NF, 857,724 acres

State Recreation Areas

Boyce Thompson Southwestern Arboretum, 420 acres

Oracle SP, 4,000 acres

Pichaco Peak SP, 3,400 acres

Places Rated Score: 2,877   Places Rated Rank: 21

Pine Bluff, AR

Common Denominators

Golf courses: 2 private (36 holes), 1 daily fee (9 holes), 1 municipal (9 holes)	C
Good restaurants: 1 *	C
Movie theaters: 3 chain (9 screens)	A

Places Rated Score: 500   Places Rated Rank: 335

Pittsburgh, PA

Common Denominators

Golf courses: 52 private (846 holes), 69 daily fee (1044 holes), 5 municipal (72 holes)	B
Good restaurants: 6 *, 12 **, 17 ***	B
Movie theaters: 38 chain (137 screens), 10 independent (22 screens)	B

Crowd Pleasers

Aquariums and Zoos:	A

Pittsburgh Aviary (217 species, 550 specimens)

The Pittsburgh Zoo (398 species, 6,284 specimens)

Pari-mutuel Betting:	C

Ladbroke at The Meadows (harness, 231 days)

Professional Sports: 2.45 game seats per capita	AA

Penguins (NHL Hockey)

Pirates (NL Baseball)

Steelers (NFL Football)

NCAA Division I: 0.18 game seats per capita	C

Duquesne University Dukes (B)

Robert Morris College Colonials (B)

University of Pittsburgh Panthers (F, B)

Outdoor Recreation Assets

Federal Protected Areas

Fort Necessity NB, 894 acres

Friendship Hill NHS, 661 acres

Rating

State Recreation Areas
  Hillman SP, 3,780 acres
  Laurel Mountain SP, 493 acres
  Laurel Ridge SP, 3,603 acres
  Linn Run SP, 565 acres
  Ohiopyle SP, 18,713 acres
  Raccoon Creek SP, 7,324 acres
Places Rated Score: 1,594   **Places Rated Rank: 150**

Pittsfield, MA
Common Denominators
  Golf courses: 4 private (72 holes), 7 daily fee (81   **AA**
    holes)
  Good restaurants: 2 *, 5 **, 4 ***, 1 ****   **AA**
  Movie theaters: 3 independent (3 screens)   **C**
Outdoor Recreation Assets
  State Recreation Areas
    Mt. Greylock SR, 10,327 acres
    October Mountain SF, 15,710 acres
    Pittsfield SF, 9,695 acres
Places Rated Score: 1,200   **Places Rated Rank: 227**

Portland, ME
Common Denominators
  Golf courses: 5 private (90 holes), 9 daily fee (108   **AA**
    holes), 4 municipal (54 holes)
  Good restaurants: 4 *, 5 **, 3 ***   **AA**
  Movie theaters: 1 chain (5 screens), 2 independent   **C**
    (7 screens)
Outdoor Recreation Assets
  Atlantic Coastline: 36 miles
  State Recreation Areas
    Bradbury Mountain SP, 319 acres
    Crescent Beach SP, 243 acres
    Sebago Lake SP, 1,300 acres
    Wolfe's Neck Woods SP, 233 acres
Places Rated Score: 1,280   **Places Rated Rank: 211**

✓ Portland, OR
Common Denominators
  Golf courses: 11 private (198 holes), 25 daily fee   **B**
    (333 holes), 5 municipal (81 holes)
  Good restaurants: 11 *, 16 **, 9 ***   **A**
  Movie theaters: 32 chain (119 screens), 9   **A**
    independent (11 screens)
Crowd Pleasers
  Aquariums and Zoos: **A**
    Metro Washington Park Zoo (192 species, 1,643
      specimens)
  Pari-mutuel Betting: **C**
    Multnomah Kennel Club (greyhound, 67 days)
    New Portland Meadows (thoroughbred, 76 days)
  Professional Sports: 2.13 game seats per capita   **AA**
    Beavers (Triple A Baseball)
    Trail Blazers (NBA Basketball)
  NCAA Division I: 0.01 game seats per capita   **C**
    University of Portland Pilots (B)
Outdoor Recreation Assets
  Federal Protected Areas
    Mt. Hood NF, 614,140 acres
    Siuslaw NF, 25,500 acres
    Willamette NF, 856 acres
  State Recreation Areas
    Benson SP, 272 acres
    Dabney SP, 135 acres
    Guy Talbot SP, 378 acres
    Mary S. Young SP, 133 acres
    Molalla River SP, 567 acres
    Rooster Rock SP, 873 acres
    Sunset Highway Forest Wayside, 338 acres
    Tryon Creek SP, 470 acres
    Willamette Mission SP, 624 acres
    Willamette River Greenway, 617 acres
    Wilson River Highway Forest Wayside, 120 acres
MC Access: Portland–Salem–Vancouver, OR–WA
Places Rated Score: 2,851   **Places Rated Rank: 22**

Rating

Portsmouth–Dover–Rochester, NH
Common Denominators
  Golf courses: 2 private (36 holes), 15 daily fee (207   **AA**
    holes), 1 municipal (9 holes)
  Good restaurants: 2 *, 5 **, 1 ***   **A**
  Movie theaters: 8 chain (31 screens), 7   **AA**
    independent (21 screens)
Crowd Pleasers
  Family Theme Parks: **B**
    Canobie Lake Park (106 days)
  Pari-mutuel Betting: **A**
    Rockingham Park (thoroughbred, 152 days)
    Seabrook Greyhound Park (greyhound, 365 days)
  NCAA Division I: 0.34 game seats per capita   **A**
    University of New Hampshire Wildcats
Outdoor Recreation Assets
  Atlantic Coastline: 26 miles
  State Recreation Areas
    Bear Brook SP, 2,228 acres
    Odiorne Point SP, 339 acres
    Pawtuckaway SP, 5,535 acres
MC Access: Boston–New Bedford–Nashua,
  MA–NH
Places Rated Score: 2,260   **Places Rated Rank: 68**

Providence–Warwick–Cranston, RI
Common Denominators
  Golf courses: 17 private (270 holes), 18 daily fee   **B**
    (243 holes), 3 municipal (45 holes)
  Good restaurants: 1 *, 10 **, 4 ***   **B**
  Movie theaters: 11 chain (39 screens), 10   **C**
    independent (15 screens)
Crowd Pleasers
  Aquariums and Zoos: **B**
    Roger Williams Park Zoo (156 species, 492
      specimens)
  Pari-mutuel Betting: **A**
    Lincoln Greyhound Park (greyhound, 365 days)
  Professional Sports: 0.45 game seats per capita   **C**
    Red Sox (Triple A Baseball)
  NCAA Division I: 0.22 game seats per capita   **B**
    Brown University Bears
    Providence College Friars (B, H)
Outdoor Recreation Assets
  Atlantic Coastline: 22 miles
  Federal Protected Areas
    Ninigret NWR, 407 acres
    Trustom Pond NWR, 642 acres
  State Recreation Areas
    Burlingame SP, 2,100 acres
    Colt SP, 464 acres
    Diamond Hill SP, 373 acres
    East Beach SB, 174 acres
    East Matunuck SB, 102 acres
    Goddard Memorial SP, 489 acres
    Haines Memorial SP, 102 acres
    Lincoln Woods SP, 627 acres
Places Rated Score: 1,530   **Places Rated Rank: 157**

✓ Provo–Orem, UT
Common Denominators
  Golf courses: 2 private (36 holes), 1 daily fee (9   **B**
    holes), 5 municipal (90 holes)
  Good restaurants: 2 *   **C**
  Movie theaters: 4 chain (17 screens), 4   **B**
    independent (5 screens)
Crowd Pleasers
  NCAA Division I: 1.85 game seats per capita   **AA**
    Brigham Young University Cougars (F, B)
Outdoor Recreation Assets
  Federal Protected Areas
    Ashley NF, 3,797 acres
    Manti-La Sal NF, 91,292 acres
    Timpanogos Cave NM, 250 acres
    Uinta NF, 391,324 acres

Rating

State Recreation Area
Utah Lake SP, 308 acres
Places Rated Score: 2,804   Places Rated Rank: 23

Pueblo, CO
Common Denominators
   Golf courses: 1 private (18 holes), 1 daily fee (18   **AA**
   holes), 4 municipal (63 holes)
   Movie theaters: 4 chain (10 screens)   **B**
Crowd Pleasers
   Pari-mutuel Betting: **AA**
     Pueblo Greyhound Park (greyhound, 180 days)
Outdoor Recreation Assets
   Federal Protected Area
     San Isabel NF, 32,761 acres
Places Rated Score: 1,107   Places Rated Rank: 250

Punta Gorda, FL
Common Denominators
   Golf courses: 5 private (81 holes), 7 daily fee (117   **AA**
   holes)
   Good restaurants: 2 *, 2 **   **A**
   Movie theaters: 1 chain (8 screens)   **C**
Crowd Pleasers
   Professional Sports: 3.19 game seats per capita   **AA**
     Rangers (Class A Baseball)
Outdoor Recreation Assets
   Gulf Coastline: 30 miles
   Federal Protected Area
     Island Bay NWR, 20 acres
   State Recreation Area
     Don Pedro Island SRA, 133 acres
Places Rated Score: 1,504   Places Rated Rank: 164

✓ Quebec City, PQ
Common Denominators
   Golf courses: 1 private (18 holes), 10 daily fee (153   **B**
   holes), 2 municipal (36 holes)
   Good restaurants: 6 *, 9 **, 8 ***   **AA**
   Movie theaters: 8 chain (28 screens), 3   **C**
   independent (5 screens)
Crowd Pleasers
   Aquariums and Zoos: **A**
     Aquarium du Quebec
     Jardin Zoologique de Quebec (175 species, 618
       specimens)
   Pari-mutuel Betting: **B**
     Hippodrome de Quebec (harness, 163 days)
   Professional Sports: 0.95 game seats per capita   **B**
     Nordiques (NHL Hockey)
   CIAU: 0.11 game seats per capita   **C**
     Université Laval Rouge et Or (B)
Outdoor Recreation Assets
   Federal Protected Areas
     Cap Tourmente NWA, 5,510 acres
     St-Vallier MBS, 988 acres
   Provincial Recreation Area
     Jacques Cartier PP, 165,705 acres
Places Rated Score: 3,500   Places Rated Rank: 8

Racine, WI
Common Denominators
   Golf courses: 3 private (54 holes), 2 daily fee (36   **A**
   holes), 4 municipal (54 holes)
   Good restaurants: 1 *, 2 **   **B**
   Movie theaters: 3 chain (10 screens)   **C**
Crowd Pleasers
   Aquariums and Zoos: **C**
     Racine Zoo (79 species, 210 specimens)
Outdoor Recreation Assets
   Lake Michigan Coastline: 12 miles
MC Access: Milwaukee–Racine, WI
Places Rated Score: 910   Places Rated Rank: 289

Rating

Raleigh–Durham–Chapel Hill, NC
Common Denominators
   Golf courses: 20 private (333 holes), 25 daily fee   **A**
   (405 holes)
   Good restaurants: 10 *, 4 **, 4 ***   **B**
   Movie theaters: 16 chain (71 screens), 3   **B**
   independent (4 screens)
Crowd Pleasers
   Professional Sports: 1.07 game seats per capita   **B**
     Bulls (Class A Baseball)
     Icecaps (ECHL Hockey)
     Mudcats (Class AA Baseball)
   NCAA Division I: 1.19 game seats per capita   **AA**
     Duke University Blue Devils (F, B)
     North Carolina State University Wolfpack (F, B)
     University of North Carolina Chapel Hill Tarheels
       (F, B)
Outdoor Recreation Assets
   State Recreation Areas
     Eno River, 1,965 acres
     Falls Lake, 1,100 acres
Places Rated Score: 1,322   Places Rated Rank: 192

✓ Rapid City, SD
Common Denominators
   Golf courses: 4 private (45 holes), 1 daily fee (9   **A**
   holes), 2 municipal (27 holes)
   Good restaurants: 3 *, 1 **, 1 ***   **AA**
   Movie theaters: 2 chain (9 screens)   **A**
Crowd Pleasers
   Professional Sports: 3.96 game seats per capita   **AA**
     Thrillers (CBA Basketball)
Outdoor Recreation Assets
   Federal Protected Areas
     Badlands NP, 94,595 acres
     Black Hills NF, 395,121 acres
     Mount Rushmore NM, 1,238 acres
Places Rated Score: 2,781   Places Rated Rank: 27

Reading, PA
Common Denominators
   Golf courses: 5 private (90 holes), 12 daily fee (198   **AA**
   holes)
   Good restaurants: 2 *, 1 **, 2 ***   **B**
   Movie theaters: 5 chain (15 screens), 2   **C**
   independent (3 screens)
Crowd Pleasers
   Professional Sports: 1.45 game seats per capita   **A**
     Phillies (Class AA Baseball)
Outdoor Recreation Assets
   Federal Protected Areas
     Appalachian Trail, 1,321 acres
     Hopewell Furnace NHS, 528 acres
   State Recreation Area
     French Creek SP, 6,470 acres
Places Rated Score: 1,082   Places Rated Rank: 261

Redding, CA
Common Denominators
   Golf courses: 2 private (36 holes), 4 daily fee (45   **B**
   holes)
   Good restaurants: 1 **   **C**
   Movie theaters: 3 chain (16 screens), 1   **A**
   independent (1 screen)
Outdoor Recreation Assets
   Federal Protected Areas
     Lassen NF, 248,007 acres
     Lassen Volcanic NP, 66,862 acres
     Shasta NF, 469,534 acres
     Trinity NF, 30,626 acres
     Whiskeytown–Shasta–Trinity NRA, 42,448 acres
   State Recreation Areas
     Ahjumawi Lava Springs SP, 5,890 acres
     McArthur–Burney Falls Memorial SP, 761 acres
Places Rated Score: 2,392   Places Rated Rank: 53

Rating

Regina, SK
Common Denominators
  Golf courses: 1 private (18 holes), 2 daily fee (27   **AA**
    holes), 10 municipal (135 holes)
  Movie theaters: 4 chain (14 screens)   **B**
Crowd Pleasers
  Pari-mutuel Betting: **A**
    Queensbury Downs (harness, 71 days)
  Professional Sports: 0.57 game seats per capita   **C**
    Roughriders (CFL Football)
  CIAU: 0.12 game seats per capita   **C**
    University of Regina Cougars (B, H)
Outdoor Recreation Assets
  Federal Protected Area
    Wascana Lake MBS, 321 acres
  Provincial Recreation Areas
    Condie Nature Refuge, 719 acres
    Echo Valley PP, 1,594 acres
    McLean PP, 131 acres
    Rowan's Ravine PP, 672 acres
    Valeport PP, 148 acres
    Valley Centre PP, 200 acres
    Wascana Trails PP, 324 acres
    White Butte Trails PP, 1,065 acres
Places Rated Score: 1,106   **Places Rated Rank: 251**

Reno, NV
Common Denominators
  Golf courses: 1 private (18 holes), 4 daily fee (63   **A**
    holes), 5 municipal (81 holes)
  Good restaurants: 1 *, 7 **, 2 ***, 1 ****   **AA**
  Movie theaters: 5 chain (21 screens), 1   **B**
    independent (1 screen)
Crowd Pleasers
  Family Theme Parks: **A**
    Ponderosa Ranch (180 days)
  Professional Sports: 1.02 game seats per capita   **B**
    Silver Sox (Class A Baseball)
  NCAA Division I: 0.52 game seats per capita   **A**
    University of Nevada, Reno Wolf Pack (F, B)
Outdoor Recreation Assets
  Federal Protected Areas
    Anaho Island NWR, 248 acres
    Sheldon NWR, 187,240 acres
    Toiyabe NF, 65,851 acres
  State Recreation Area
    Lake Tahoe SP, 10,552 acres
Places Rated Score: 2,035   **Places Rated Rank: 85**

Richland–Kennewick–Pasco, WA
Common Denominators
  Golf courses: 1 private (18 holes), 2 daily fee (36   **A**
    holes), 2 municipal (36 holes)
  Good restaurants: 2 *, 2 **   **B**
  Movie theaters: 1 independent (1 screen)   **C**
Crowd Pleasers
  Pari-mutuel Betting: **C**
    Sun Downs Race Meet (mixed meetings, 20 days)
  Professional Sports: 1.16 game seats per capita   **B**
    Chinook (CBA Basketball)
Outdoor Recreation Assets
  Federal Protected Area
    Umatilla NWR, 1,466 acres
  State Recreation Areas
    Crow Butte SP, 1,312 acres
    Lyons Ferry SP, 1,150 acres
    Potholes SP, 3,737 acres
Places Rated Score: 921   **Places Rated Rank: 282**

Richmond–Petersburg, VA
Common Denominators
  Golf courses: 13 private (234 holes), 12 daily fee   **C**
    (207 holes), 1 municipal (18 holes)
  Good restaurants: 6 *, 6 **, 3 ***   **B**
  Movie theaters: 15 chain (77 screens), 2   **B**
    independent (2 screens)
Crowd Pleasers

Family Theme Parks: **A**
  Kings Dominion (126 days)
Professional Sports: 1.36 game seats per capita   **A**
  Braves (Triple A Baseball)
  Renegades (ECHL Hockey)
Outdoor Recreation Assets
  Federal Protected Areas
    Petersburg NB, 1,529 acres
    Presquile NWR, 1,329 acres
    Richmond NBP, 764 acres
Places Rated Score: 1,130   **Places Rated Rank: 241**

Riverside–San Bernardino, CA
Common Denominators
  Golf courses: 54 private (891 holes), 65 daily fee   **A**
    (1071 holes), 8 municipal (117 holes)
  Good restaurants: 9 *, 32 **, 10 ***   **B**
  Movie theaters: 38 chain (212 screens), 10   **B**
    independent (15 screens)
Crowd Pleasers
  Aquariums and Zoos: **B**
    The Living Desert (125 species, 850 specimens)
  Family Theme Parks: **A**
    Oasis Waterpark (181 days)
  Professional Sports: 0.21 game seats per capita   **C**
    Angels (Class A Baseball)
    Spirit (Class A Baseball)
Outdoor Recreation Assets
  Federal Protected Areas
    Angeles NF, 10,289 acres
    Cleveland NF, 78,123 acres
    Coachella Valley NWR, 2,589 acres
    Death Valley NM, 82,432 acres
    Joshua Tree NM, 549,669 acres
    San Bernardino NF, 670,100 acres
  State Recreation Areas
    Anza–Borrego Desert SP, 35,177 acres
    Chino Hills SP, 6,775 acres
    Lake Elsinore SRA, 2,976 acres
    Mount San Jacinto SP, 13,718 acres
    Salton Sea SRA, 9,000 acres
    Silverwood Lake SRA, 2,201 acres
MC Access: Los Angeles–Riverside–Orange
County, CA
Places Rated Score: 1,972   **Places Rated Rank: 94**

Roanoke, VA
Common Denominators
  Golf courses: 6 private (99 holes), 5 daily fee (81   **B**
    holes)
  Good restaurants: 1 *, 2 **, 3 ***   **A**
  Movie theaters: 5 chain (22 screens), 1   **A**
    independent (1 screen)
Crowd Pleasers
  Professional Sports: 2.18 game seats per capita   **AA**
    Buccaneers (Class A Baseball)
    Valley Rebels (ECHL Hockey)
Outdoor Recreation Assets
  Federal Protected Areas
    Appalachian Trail, 2,935 acres
    Blue Ridge Parkway, 5,693 acres
    George Washington NF, 13,032 acres
    Jefferson NF, 68,500 acres
Places Rated Score: 2,026   **Places Rated Rank: 86**

Rochester, MN
Common Denominators
  Golf courses: 1 private (18 holes), 2 daily fee (36   **AA**
    holes), 2 municipal (36 holes)
  Good restaurants: 2 **, 2 ***   **AA**
  Movie theaters: 4 chain (19 screens)   **AA**
Places Rated Score: 1,200   **Places Rated Rank: 227**

✓ Rochester, NY
Common Denominators
  Golf courses: 20 private (333 holes), 44 daily fee   **AA**
    (702 holes), 6 municipal (90 holes)

	Rating
Good restaurants: 10 *, 13 **, 10 ***	A
Movie theaters: 12 chain (56 screens), 7 independent (7 screens)	C

Crowd Pleasers

	Rating
Aquariums and Zoos:	B
Seneca Park Zoo (133 species, 367 specimens)	
Family Theme Parks:	A
Darien Lake Theme Park (92 days)	
Raging Rivers Water Park (80 days)	
Seabreeze Amusement Park (80 days)	
Pari-mutuel Betting:	A
Batavia Downs (harness, 126 days)	
Finger Lakes (thoroughbred, 167 days)	
Professional Sports: 1.28 game seats per capita	B
Americans (AHL Hockey)	
Clippers (Class A Baseball)	
Cubs (Class A Baseball)	
Red Wings (Class A Baseball)	

Outdoor Recreation Assets
Lake Ontario Coastline: 90 miles
Federal Protected Area
Iroquois NWR, 10,819 acres
State Recreation Areas
Chimney Bluffs SP, 597 acres
Darien Lakes SP, 1,845 acres
Hamlin Beach SP, 1,224 acres
Lakeside Beach SP, 734 acres
Places Rated Score: 2,737   Places Rated Rank: 31

Rockford, IL
Common Denominators

	Rating
Golf courses: 6 private (99 holes), 4 daily fee (45 holes), 7 municipal (117 holes)	A
Good restaurants: 3 **, 1 ***	B
Movie theaters: 7 chain (36 screens), 1 independent (1 screen)	A

Crowd Pleasers

	Rating
Professional Sports: 1.97 game seats per capita	A
Expos (Class A Baseball)	
Lightning (CBA Basketball)	

Outdoor Recreation Assets
State Recreation Areas
Lowden SP, 208 acres
Rock Cut SP, 3,004 acres
Places Rated Score: 1,128   Places Rated Rank: 245

Rocky Mount, NC
Common Denominators

	Rating
Golf courses: 6 private (90 holes), 1 daily fee (18 holes)	C
Movie theaters: 4 chain (11 screens)	B

Places Rated Score: 300   Places Rated Rank: 340

✓ Sacramento, CA
Common Denominators

	Rating
Golf courses: 9 private (153 holes), 13 daily fee (171 holes), 8 municipal (126 holes)	C
Good restaurants: 8 *, 10 **, 7 ***	B
Movie theaters: 19 chain (75 screens), 7 independent (10 screens)	C

Crowd Pleasers

	Rating
Aquariums and Zoos:	A
Sacramento City Zoo (124 species, 351 specimens)	
Pari-mutuel Betting:	C
Cal-Expo (harness, 60 days)	
Professional Sports: 1.03 game seats per capita	B
Gold Miners (CFL Football)	
Kings (NBA Basketball)	
NCAA Division I: 0.01 game seats per capita	C
California State University, Sacramento Hornets (B)	

Outdoor Recreation Assets
Federal Protected Areas
Eldorado NF, 545,342 acres
Tahoe NF, 274,985 acres
State Recreation Areas
Auburn SRA, 12,000 acres

Burton Creek SP, 1,883 acres
Folsom Lake SRA, 15,400 acres
Lake Valley SRA, 150 acres
Marshall Gold Discovery SHP, 275 acres
MC Access: Sacramento-Yolo, CA
Places Rated Score: 2,802   Places Rated Rank: 24

Saginaw–Bay City–Midland, MI
Common Denominators

	Rating
Golf courses: 6 private (99 holes), 18 daily fee (279 holes), 3 municipal (45 holes)	AA
Good restaurants: 4 *, 6 **, 1 ***	A
Movie theaters: 5 chain (32 screens), 3 independent (5 screens)	A

Crowd Pleasers

	Rating
Family Theme Parks:	A
Deer Acres Storybook Amusement Park (129 days)	
Pari-mutuel Betting:	B
Saginaw Raceway (harness, 88 days)	

Outdoor Recreation Assets
Lake Huron Coastline: 40 miles
Federal Protected Area
Shiawassee NWR, 8,984 acres
Places Rated Score: 1,941   Places Rated Rank: 100

St. Catharines–Niagara, ON
Common Denominators

	Rating
Golf courses: 2 private (36 holes), 6 daily fee (90 holes), 7 municipal (108 holes)	A
Good restaurants: 2 *, 2 **, 2 ***	B
Movie theaters: 8 chain (21 screens), 3 independent (3 screens)	B

Crowd Pleasers

	Rating
Family Theme Parks:	AA
Marineland (348 days)	
Pari-mutuel Betting:	A
Fort Erie (thoroughbred, 101 days)	
Professional Sports: 0.84 game seats per capita	C
Blue Jays (Class A Baseball)	
Pirates (Class A Baseball)	
CIAU: 0.15 game seats per capita	B
Brock University Badgers (B, H)	

Outdoor Recreation Assets
Lake Ontario Coastline: 15 miles
Provincial Recreation Area
Short Hills PP, 1,633 acres
MC Access: Buffalo-St. Catharines-Niagara, NY-ON
Places Rated Score: 1,978   Places Rated Rank: 92

St. Cloud, MN
Common Denominators

	Rating
Golf courses: 2 private (27 holes), 10 daily fee (117 holes), 1 municipal (18 holes)	AA
Good restaurants: 1 *, 1 **	C
Movie theaters: 3 chain (17 screens), 2 independent (3 screens)	AA

Crowd Pleasers

	Rating
NCAA Division I: 0.29 game seats per capita	B
St. Cloud State University Huskies (H)	

Places Rated Score: 1,100   Places Rated Rank: 255

Saint John, NB
Common Denominators

	Rating
Golf courses: 1 private (18 holes), 1 municipal (9 holes)	C
Movie theaters: 2 chain (8 screens), 1 independent (1 screen)	B

Crowd Pleasers

	Rating
Aquariums and Zoos:	C
Cherry Brook Zoo (38 species, 145 specimens)	
Pari-mutuel Betting:	AA
Exhibition Park Raceway (harness, 103 days)	
Professional Sports: 0.47 game seats per capita	C
Flames (AHL Hockey)	

Outdoor Recreation Assets
Bay of Fundy Coastline: 30 miles
Federal Protected Area

Rating

Grand Manan MBS, 618 acres
Provincial Recreation Areas
Herring Cove PP, 1,048 acres
New River Beach PP, 897 acres
The Anchorage PP, 447 acres
Places Rated Score: 1,371   Places Rated Rank: 188

St. John's, NF
Common Denominators
Golf courses: 2 private (36 holes), 1 daily fee (18 holes), 1 municipal (18 holes)	C
Movie theaters: 4 chain (7 screens), 2 independent (2 screens)	C

Crowd Pleasers
Pari-mutuel Betting:	A
Avalon Raceway (harness, 43 days)	
Professional Sports: 0.95 game seats per capita	B
Maple Leafs (AHL Hockey)	
CIAU: 0.05 game seats per capita	C
Memorial University of Newfoundland Sea Hawks (B)	

Outdoor Recreation Assets
Atlantic Coastline: 45 miles
Provincial Recreation Areas
Avalon PWR, 264,397 acres
Baccalieu Island PER, 2,990 acres
Backside Pond PP, 1,389 acres
Bellevue Beach PP, 358 acres
Butter Pot PP, 4,329 acres
Cataracts PP, 425 acres
Chance Cove PP, 5,110 acres
Fitzgerald's Pond PP, 2,009 acres
Gushue's Pond PP, 442 acres
Hawk Hill PER, 324 acres
Holyrood Pond PP, 558 acres
Jack's Pond PP, 1,485 acres
La Manche PP, 3,445 acres
Marine Drive PP, 1,935 acres
Places Rated Score: 1,898   Places Rated Rank: 103

St. Joseph, MO
Common Denominators
Golf courses: 2 private (36 holes), 2 municipal (27 holes)	B
Good restaurants: 3 *, 1 **	A
Movie theaters: 3 chain (9 screens), 1 independent (1 screen)	A

Outdoor Recreation Assets
State Recreation Area
Lewis and Clark SP, 120 acres
Places Rated Score: 801   Places Rated Rank: 305

St. Louis, MO–IL
Common Denominators
Golf courses: 35 private (576 holes), 49 daily fee (684 holes), 12 municipal (144 holes)	B
Good restaurants: 2 *, 17 **, 16 ***, 2 ****, 1 *****	B
Movie theaters: 40 chain (198 screens), 12 independent (16 screens)	B

Crowd Pleasers
Aquariums and Zoos:	AA
Forest Park Zoo (721 species, 4,364 specimens)	
Family Theme Parks:	A
Six Flags Over Mid-America (125 days)	
Pari-mutuel Betting:	C
Fairmount Park (mixed meetings, 239 days)	
Professional Sports: 2.01 game seats per capita	AA
Blues (NHL Hockey)	
Cardinals (NL Baseball)	
NCAA Division I: 0.02 game seats per capita	C
St. Louis University Billikens (B)	

Outdoor Recreation Assets
Federal Protected Area
Jefferson National Expansion NM, 91 acres
State Recreation Areas
Castlewood SP, 1,780 acres
Eldon Hazlett SP, 2,782 acres

Rating

Mastodon SP, 425 acres
Robertsville SP, 1,110 acres
South Shore SP, 833 acres
Places Rated Score: 1,936   Places Rated Rank: 101

Salem, OR
Common Denominators
Golf courses: 2 private (36 holes), 9 daily fee (117 holes)	A
Good restaurants: 2 *, 1 ***	C
Movie theaters: 8 chain (30 screens), 5 independent (5 screens)	AA

Outdoor Recreation Assets
Federal Protected Areas
Ankeny NWR, 2,796 acres
Baskett Slough NWR, 2,492 acres
Mt. Hood NF, 65,915 acres
Siuslaw NF, 1,479 acres
Willamette NF, 135,375 acres
State Recreation Areas
Champoeg SP, 615 acres
North Santiam SP, 120 acres
Willamette Mission SP, 1,062 acres
Willamette River Greenway, 905 acres
MC Access: Portland–Salem–Vancouver, OR–WA
Places Rated Score: 1,784   Places Rated Rank: 111

✓ Salinas, CA
Common Denominators
Golf courses: 8 private (144 holes), 10 daily fee (180 holes), 3 municipal (45 holes)	AA
Good restaurants: 17 *, 14 **, 19 ***, 1 ****	AA
Movie theaters: 10 chain (31 screens), 3 independent (4 screens)	A

Crowd Pleasers
Aquariums and Zoos:	A
Monterey Bay Aquarium	
Professional Sports: 0.57 game seats per capita	C
Spurs (Class A Baseball)	

Outdoor Recreation Assets
Pacific Coastline: 85 miles
Federal Protected Areas
Los Padres NF, 305,072 acres
Pinnacles NM, 1,283 acres
Salinas River NWR, 364 acres
State Recreation Areas
Asilomar Conference and SB, 106 acres
Julia Pfeiffer Burns SP, 3,642 acres
Marina SB, 171 acres
Salinas River SB, 246 acres
Places Rated Score: 3,105   Places Rated Rank: 15

Salt Lake City–Ogden, UT
Common Denominators
Golf courses: 11 private (171 holes), 8 daily fee (108 holes), 20 municipal (324 holes)	B
Good restaurants: 2 *, 12 **, 1 ***	B
Movie theaters: 14 chain (76 screens), 10 independent (11 screens)	B

Crowd Pleasers
Aquariums and Zoos:	A
Utah's Hogle Zoo (300 species, 1,176 specimens)	
Professional Sports: 1.56 game seats per capita	A
Golden Eagles (IHL Hockey)	
Jazz (NBA Basketball)	
NCAA Division I: 0.47 game seats per capita	A
University of Utah Utes (F, B)	
Weber State University Wildcats (F, B)	

Outdoor Recreation Assets
Federal Protected Areas
Cache NF, 67,692 acres
Wasatch NF, 132,677 acres
State Recreation Areas
Jordan River Parkway SP, 440 acres
Saltaire Beach SP, 3,000 acres
Places Rated Score: 2,618   Places Rated Rank: 37

San Angelo, TX
Common Denominators

	Rating
Golf courses: 2 private (36 holes), 1 daily fee (18 holes), 2 municipal (18 holes)	B
Good restaurants: 1 *, 3 **	AA
Movie theaters: 3 chain (13 screens)	AA

Places Rated Score: 1,000   Places Rated Rank: 271

San Antonio, TX
Common Denominators

	Rating
Golf courses: 17 private (279 holes), 3 daily fee (45 holes), 8 municipal (144 holes)	C
Good restaurants: 10 *, 10 **, 6 ***, 1 ****	B
Movie theaters: 17 chain (137 screens), 5 independent (11 screens)	A

Crowd Pleasers

	Rating
Aquariums and Zoos:	AA

San Antonio Zoo and Aquarium (811 species, 3,325 specimens)
Sea World of Texas

	Rating
Family Theme Parks:	B

Schlitterbahn Resorts and Waterpark (108 days)

	Rating
Professional Sports: 1.10 game seats per capita	B

Missions (Class AA Baseball)
Spurs (NBA Basketball)

	Rating
NCAA Division I: 0.03 game seats per capita	C

University of Texas, San Antonio Roadrunners (B)

Outdoor Recreation Assets
  Federal Protected Area
    San Antonio Missions NHP, 250 acres
  State Recreation Area
    Guadalupe River SP, 1,000 acres

Places Rated Score: 1,509   Places Rated Rank: 162

✓ San Diego, CA
Common Denominators

	Rating
Golf courses: 29 private (504 holes), 25 daily fee (423 holes), 6 municipal (108 holes)	C
Good restaurants: 13 *, 42 **, 20 ***	A
Movie theaters: 34 chain (177 screens), 15 independent (23 screens)	B

Crowd Pleasers

	Rating
Aquariums and Zoos:	AA

San Diego Wild Animal Park (440 species, 3,438 specimens)
San Diego Zoo (820 species, 4,034 specimens)
Sea World of San Diego

	Rating
Family Theme Parks:	C

Sengme Oaks Water Park (80 days)

	Rating
Pari-mutuel Betting:	C

Del Mar (thoroughbred, 42 days)

	Rating
Professional Sports: 2.17 game seats per capita	AA

Chargers (NFL Football)
Gulls (IHL Hockey)
Padres (NL Baseball)

	Rating
NCAA Division I: 0.17 game seats per capita	B

San Diego State University Aztecs (F, B)
University of San Diego Toreros (B)

Outdoor Recreation Assets
  Pacific Coastline: 55 miles
  Federal Protected Areas
    Cabrillo NM, 137 acres
    Cleveland NF, 289,263 acres
    Sweetwater Marsh NWR, 316 acres
    Tijuana Slough NWR, 407 acres
  State Recreation Areas
    Border Field SP, 397 acres
    Cardiff SB, 505 acres
    Palomar Mountain SP, 1,909 acres
    San Onofre SB, 3,036 acres
    Silver Strand SB, 363 acres
    Torrey Pines SR, 1,494 acres

Places Rated Score: 3,800   Places Rated Rank: 3

✓ San Francisco, CA
Common Denominators

	Rating
Golf courses: 13 private (234 holes), 8 daily fee (126 holes), 6 municipal (99 holes)	C
Good restaurants: 24 *, 54 **, 22 ***, 8 ****, 1 *****	AA
Movie theaters: 45 chain (124 screens), 24 independent (27 screens)	A

Crowd Pleasers

	Rating
Aquariums and Zoos:	AA

San Francisco Zoological Gardens (343 species, 6,859 specimens)

	Rating
Pari-mutuel Betting:	C

Bay Meadows (thoroughbred, 112 days)

	Rating
Professional Sports: 3.86 game seats per capita	AA

49ers (NFL Football)
Giants (NL Baseball)

	Rating
NCAA Division I: 0.03 game seats per capita	C

University of San Francisco Dons (B)

Outdoor Recreation Assets
  Pacific Coastline: 75 miles
  Federal Protected Areas
    Golden Gate NRA, 28,415 acres
    Muir Woods NM, 523 acres
    Point Reyes Seashore, 64,505 acres
    San Francisco Bay NWR, 1,864 acres
  State Recreation Areas
    Angel Island SP, 730 acres
    Año Nuevo SR, 4,082 acres
    Butano SP, 2,187 acres
    China Camp SP, 1,514 acres
    Half Moon Bay SB, 168 acres
    Montara SB, 780 acres
    Pacifica SB, 21 acres
    Pomponio SB, 421 acres
    Portola SP, 2,507 acres
    San Bruno Mountain SP, 298 acres
    San Gregorio SB, 172 acres

MC Access: San Francisco–Oakland–San Jose, CA
Places Rated Score: 3,697   Places Rated Rank: 5

San Jose, CA
Common Denominators

	Rating
Golf courses: 9 private (153 holes), 5 daily fee (90 holes), 6 municipal (99 holes)	C
Good restaurants: 7 *, 7 **, 5 ***	C
Movie theaters: 23 chain (92 screens), 15 independent (23 screens)	B

Crowd Pleasers

	Rating
Family Theme Parks:	C

Great America (100 days)

	Rating
Professional Sports: 0.23 game seats per capita	C

Giants (Class A Baseball)
Sharks (NHL Hockey)

	Rating
NCAA Division I: 0.50 game seats per capita	A

San Jose State University Spartans (F, B)
Santa Clara University Broncos (B)
Stanford University Cardinals (F, B)

Outdoor Recreation Assets
  Federal Protected Area
    San Francisco Bay NWR, 3,566 acres
  State Recreation Area
    Castle Rock SP, 46 acres

MC Access: San Francisco–Oakland–San Jose, CA
Places Rated Score: 1,430   Places Rated Rank: 177

San Luis Obispo–Atascadero–Paso Robles, CA
Common Denominators

	Rating
Golf courses: 2 private (36 holes), 3 daily fee (54 holes), 2 municipal (27 holes)	B
Good restaurants: 2 *, 10 **, 2 ***	AA
Movie theaters: 4 chain (15 screens), 4 independent (5 screens)	B

Crowd Pleasers

	Rating
Aquariums and Zoos:	C
Charles Paddock Zoo (48 species, 163 specimens)	

Outdoor Recreation Assets
Pacific Coastline: 60 miles
Federal Protected Area
Los Padres NF, 188,944 acres
State Recreation Areas
Montana De Oro SP, 8,227 acres
Pismo SB, 1,055 acres
Places Rated Score: 1,976   Places Rated Rank: 93

✓ Santa Barbara–Santa Maria–Lompoc, CA
Common Denominators

	Rating
Golf courses: 8 private (144 holes), 5 daily fee (72 holes), 1 municipal (18 holes)	C
Good restaurants: 1 *, 9 **, 5 ***	AA
Movie theaters: 10 chain (25 screens), 5 independent (9 screens)	A

Crowd Pleasers

	Rating
Aquariums and Zoos:	B
Santa Barbara Zoological Gardens (142 species, 517 specimens)	
NCAA Division I: 0.16 game seats per capita	B
University of California, Santa Barbara Gauchos (B)	

Outdoor Recreation Assets
Pacific Coastline: 78 miles
Federal Protected Areas
Channel Islands NP, 63,552 acres
Los Padres NF, 629,118 acres
State Recreation Area
Point Sal SB, 84 acres
Places Rated Score: 3,200   Places Rated Rank: 11

Santa Cruz–Watsonville, CA
Common Denominators

	Rating
Golf courses: 6 daily fee (99 holes), 1 municipal (18 holes)	A
Good restaurants: 1 **, 3 ***	A
Movie theaters: 5 chain (9 screens), 5 independent (8 screens)	B

Outdoor Recreation Assets
Pacific Coastline: 40 miles
Federal Protected Area
Ellicott Slough NWR, 126 acres
State Recreation Areas
Big Basin Redwoods SP, 17,213 acres
Sunset SB, 302 acres
The Forest of Nisene Marks SP, 10,121 acres
Wilder Ranch SP, 4,505 acres
MC Access: San Francisco–Oakland–San Jose, CA
Places Rated Score: 2,235   Places Rated Rank: 70

Santa Fe, NM
Common Denominators

	Rating
Golf courses: 1 private (9 holes), 2 daily fee (36 holes), 2 municipal (36 holes)	A
Good restaurants: 7 *, 21 **, 9 ***, 1 ****	AA
Movie theaters: 3 chain (9 screens), 1 independent (1 screen)	B

Crowd Pleasers

	Rating
Pari-mutuel Betting:	A
Downs at Santa Fe (thoroughbred, 47 days)	

Outdoor Recreation Assets
Federal Protected Areas
Bandelier NM, 7,309 acres
Santa Fe NF, 275,035 acres
State Recreation Area
Santa Fe River SP, 5 acres
Places Rated Score: 2,294   Places Rated Rank: 60

Santa Rosa, CA
Common Denominators

	Rating
Golf courses: 1 private (18 holes), 8 daily fee (117 holes), 4 municipal (72 holes)	A

	Rating
Good restaurants: 6 *, 7 **, 2 ***	A
Movie theaters: 5 chain (27 screens), 3 independent (6 screens)	B

Crowd Pleasers

	Rating
Family Theme Parks:	C
Windsor Waterworks and Slides (100 days)	

Outdoor Recreation Assets
Pacific Coastline: 44 miles
Federal Protected Area
San Pablo Bay NWR, 249 acres
State Recreation Areas
Austin Creek SRA, 4,234 acres
Fort Ross SHP, 3,276 acres
Kruse Rhododendron SR, 317 acres
Robert Louis Stevenson SP, 1,538 acres
Sonoma Coast SB, 5,054 acres
Sugarloaf Ridge SP, 2,514 acres
MC Access: San Francisco–Oakland–San Jose, CA
Places Rated Score: 1,587   Places Rated Rank: 151

Sarasota–Bradenton, FL
Common Denominators

	Rating
Golf courses: 22 private (387 holes), 31 daily fee (522 holes), 7 municipal (117 holes)	AA
Good restaurants: 11 *, 20 **, 18 ***, 1 ****	AA
Movie theaters: 12 chain (81 screens)	AA

Crowd Pleasers

	Rating
Pari-mutuel Betting:	A
Sarasota Kennel Club (greyhound, 183 days)	
Professional Sports: 0.97 game seats per capita	B
White Sox (Class A Baseball)	

Outdoor Recreation Assets
Gulf Coastline: 60 miles
Federal Protected Areas
De Soto NM, 25 acres
Passage Key NWR, 36 acres
State Recreation Areas
Lake Manatee SRA, 556 acres
Oscar Scherer SRA, 462 acres
Places Rated Score: 2,478   Places Rated Rank: 46

Saskatoon, SK
Common Denominators

	Rating
Golf courses: 2 private (36 holes), 1 daily fee (18 holes), 8 municipal (108 holes)	AA
Movie theaters: 5 chain (13 screens)	C

Crowd Pleasers

	Rating
Aquariums and Zoos:	C
Forestry Farm Zoo (91 species, 382 specimens)	
Pari-mutuel Betting:	A
Marquis Downs (mixed meetings, 76 days)	
CIAU: 0.21 game seats per capita	B
University of Saskatchewan Huskies	

Outdoor Recreation Assets
Federal Protected Areas
Bradwell NWA, 304 acres
Last Mountain Lake MBS, 11,713 acres
Last Mountain Lake NWA, 38,553 acres
Prairie NWA, 7,448 acres
Stalwart NWA, 3,608 acres
Sutherland MBS, 321 acres
Provincial Recreation Areas
Blackstrap PP, 1,300 acres
Coldwell PP, 259 acres
Elbow Harbour PP, 482 acres
Etter's Beach PP, 363 acres
Otapasoo Trails PP, 321 acres
Pike Lake PP, 1,236 acres
Places Rated Score: 1,143   Places Rated Rank: 237

Savannah, GA
Common Denominators

	Rating
Golf courses: 9 private (153 holes), 4 daily fee (63 holes), 2 municipal (27 holes)	B
Good restaurants: 2 *, 11 **, 3 ***	AA
Movie theaters: 3 chain (19 screens)	B

Rating

Crowd Pleasers
    Professional Sports: 2.13 game seats per capita   **AA**
      Cardinals (Class A Baseball)
Outdoor Recreation Assets
    Atlantic Coastline: 30 miles
    Federal Protected Areas
      Fort Pulaski NM, 5,365 acres
      Savannah Coastal NWR, 11,324 acres
      Wassaw NWR, 10,050 acres
Places Rated Score: 1,713   Places Rated Rank: 120

Scranton–Wilkes-Barre–Hazleton, PA
Common Denominators
    Golf courses: 11 private (180 holes), 15 daily fee   **B**
      (225 holes), 2 municipal (27 holes)
    Good restaurants: 2 **, 1 ***   **C**
    Movie theaters: 8 chain (30 screens), 4   **C**
      independent (7 screens)
Crowd Pleasers
    Pari-mutuel Betting: **B**
      Pocono Downs (harness, 150 days)
Outdoor Recreation Assets
    State Recreation Areas
      Frances Slocum SP, 1,006 acres
      Nescopeck SP, 3,000 acres
Places Rated Score: 660   Places Rated Rank: 322

✓ Seattle–Bellevue–Everett, WA
Common Denominators
    Golf courses: 22 private (342 holes), 17 daily fee   **C**
      (261 holes), 15 municipal (252 holes)
    Good restaurants: 5 *, 24 **, 16 ***, 1 ****   **A**
    Movie theaters: 38 chain (172 screens), 12   **B**
      independent (12 screens)
Crowd Pleasers
    Aquariums and Zoos: **A**
      Woodland Park Zoological Gardens (246 species,
      3,991 specimens)
    Pari-mutuel Betting: **C**
      Longacres Park (thoroughbred, 135 days)
    Professional Sports: 3.01 game seats per capita   **AA**
      Giants (Class A Baseball)
      Mariners (AL Baseball)
      Seahawks (NFL Football)
      Supersonics (NBA Basketball)
    NCAA Division I: 0.20 game seats per capita   **B**
      University of Washington Huskies (F, B)
Outdoor Recreation Assets
    Puget Sound Coastline: 70 miles
    Federal Protected Areas
      Mt. Baker NF, 462,502 acres
      Snoqualmie NF, 516,704 acres
    State Recreation Areas
      Bridle Trails SP, 480 acres
      Dash Point SP, 230 acres
      Everett Jetty SP, 160 acres
      Federation Forest SP, 619 acres
      Flaming Geyser SP, 667 acres
      Fort Ebey SP, 644 acres
      Iron Horse West SP, 448 acres
      Kanaskat–Palmer SP, 320 acres
      Olallie SP, 353 acres
      Squak Mountain SP, 613 acres
MC Access: Seattle–Tacoma–Bremerton, WA
Places Rated Score: 3,620   Places Rated Rank: 6

Sharon, PA
Common Denominators
    Golf courses: 4 private (63 holes), 7 daily fee (108   **AA**
      holes)
    Good restaurants: 3 **   **A**
    Movie theaters: 1 chain (8 screens)   **B**
Outdoor Recreation Assets
    State Recreation Area
      Goddard SP, 1,417 acres
Places Rated Score: 916   Places Rated Rank: 285

Rating

Sheboygan, WI
Common Denominators
    Golf courses: 1 private (18 holes), 7 daily fee (108   **AA**
      holes)
    Good restaurants: 2 **, 1 ***   **AA**
    Movie theaters: 2 chain (10 screens)   **A**
Outdoor Recreation Assets
    Lake Michigan Coastline: 29 miles
    State Recreation Area
      Old Wade House SP, 243 acres
Places Rated Score: 1,407   Places Rated Rank: 182

Sherbrooke, PQ
Common Denominators
    Golf courses: 3 daily fee (45 holes), 2 municipal (27   **A**
      holes)
    Good restaurants: 1 ***   **C**
    Movie theaters: 2 chain (4 screens), 3 independent   **B**
      (5 screens)
Crowd Pleasers
    CIAU: 0.12 game seats per capita   **C**
      Bishop's University Gaiters (F, B)
Outdoor Recreation Assets
    Provincial Recreation Area
      Mount-Orford PP, 14,423 acres
Places Rated Score: 773   Places Rated Rank: 310

Sherman–Denison, TX
Common Denominators
    Golf courses: 1 private (18 holes), 1 daily fee (18   **C**
      holes)
    Movie theaters: 3 chain (16 screens)   **AA**
Places Rated Score: 504   Places Rated Rank: 333

Shreveport–Bossier City, LA
Common Denominators
    Golf courses: 12 private (180 holes), 1 daily fee (9   **C**
      holes), 3 municipal (45 holes)
    Good restaurants: 1 *, 3 **   **C**
    Movie theaters: 5 chain (25 screens)   **B**
Crowd Pleasers
    Family Theme Parks: **C**
      Water Town USA (100 days)
    Pari-mutuel Betting: **A**
      Louisiana Downs (thoroughbred, 140 days)
    Professional Sports: 1.14 game seats per capita   **B**
      Captains (Class AA Baseball)
    NCAA Division I: 0.11 game seats per capita   **C**
      Centenary College Gentlemen (B)
Outdoor Recreation Assets
    Federal Protected Area
      Kisatchee NF, 12,095 acres
    State Recreation Area
      Bickham Dickson SP, 585 acres
Places Rated Score: 1,145   Places Rated Rank: 236

Sioux City, IA–NE
Common Denominators
    Golf courses: 3 private (45 holes), 7 daily fee (72   **AA**
      holes), 1 municipal (18 holes)
    Good restaurants: 2 *, 3 **, 1 ***   **AA**
    Movie theaters: 3 chain (16 screens)   **AA**
Crowd Pleasers
    Pari-mutuel Betting: **B**
      Atokad Park (thoroughbred, 24 days)
Places Rated Score: 1,400   Places Rated Rank: 184

Sioux Falls, SD
Common Denominators
    Golf courses: 4 private (54 holes), 5 daily fee (63   **AA**
      holes), 3 municipal (36 holes)
    Good restaurants: 2 **   **B**
    Movie theaters: 1 chain (7 screens), 2 independent   **B**
      (2 screens)
Crowd Pleasers
    Aquariums and Zoos: **C**
      Great Plains Zoo (69 species, 271 specimens)

Rating

Professional Sports: 1.83 game seats per capita   **A**
Sky Force (CBA Basketball)
Outdoor Recreation Assets
State Recreation Areas
Beaver Creek SNA, 160 acres
Palisades SP, 157 acres
Places Rated Score: 1,210   Places Rated Rank: 222

South Bend, IN
Common Denominators
Golf courses: 4 private (72 holes), 5 daily fee (72   **A**
holes), 3 municipal (54 holes)
Good restaurants: 1 *, 4 **, 1 ***   **A**
Movie theaters: 4 chain (14 screens)   **C**
Crowd Pleasers
Aquariums and Zoos: **C**
Potawatomi Zoo (97 species, 262 specimens)
Professional Sports: 1.40 game seats per capita   **A**
White Sox (Class A Baseball)
NCAA Division I: 1.76 game seats per capita   **AA**
University of Notre Dame Fighting Irish
Outdoor Recreation Assets
State Recreation Areas
Potato Creek SP, 3,840 acres
Places Rated Score: 1,566   Places Rated Rank: 152

Spokane, WA
Common Denominators
Golf courses: 2 private (36 holes), 5 daily fee (81   **A**
holes), 6 municipal (108 holes)
Good restaurants: 4 *, 1 **, 1 ***   **C**
Movie theaters: 9 chain (36 screens)   **A**
Crowd Pleasers
Family Theme Parks: **C**
Splash-Down (92 days)
Pari-mutuel Betting: **B**
Playfair Race Course (thoroughbred, 90 days)
Professional Sports: 1.59 game seats per capita   **A**
Indians (Class A Baseball)
NCAA Division I: 0.30 game seats per capita   **B**
Eastern Washington University Eagles (F, B)
Gonzaga University Zags (B)
Outdoor Recreation Assets
Federal Protected Area
Turnbull NWR, 15,468 acres
State Recreation Area
Mount Spokane SP, 13,821 acres
Places Rated Score: 1,663   Places Rated Rank: 129

Springfield, IL
Common Denominators
Golf courses: 1 private (18 holes), 4 daily fee (63   **A**
holes), 3 municipal (45 holes)
Good restaurants: 3 **, 1 ***   **A**
Movie theaters: 5 chain (20 screens), 2   **AA**
independent (2 screens)
Crowd Pleasers
Aquariums and Zoos: **C**
Henson Robinson Zoo (76 species, 262
specimens)
Professional Sports: 1.83 game seats per capita   **A**
Cardinals (Class A Baseball)
Outdoor Recreation Assets
Federal Protected Area
Lincoln Home NHS, 12 acres
Places Rated Score: 1,400   Places Rated Rank: 184

Springfield, MA
Common Denominators
Golf courses: 11 private (180 holes), 19 daily fee   **AA**
(270 holes), 4 municipal (72 holes)
Good restaurants: 1 *, 6 **, 5 ***   **A**
Movie theaters: 9 chain (35 screens), 4   **B**
independent (6 screens)
Crowd Pleasers
NCAA Division I: 0.20 game seats per capita   **B**
University of Massachusetts Minutemen (F, B)

Rating

Outdoor Recreation Assets
State Recreation Areas
Chicopee Memorial SP, 574 acres
Hampton Ponds SP, 184 acres
Holyoke Range SP, 2,252 acres
Robinson SP, 828 acres
Skinner SP, 390 acres
Places Rated Score: 1,129   Places Rated Rank: 242

Springfield, MO
Common Denominators
Golf courses: 6 private (90 holes), 4 daily fee (63   **B**
holes), 2 municipal (36 holes)
Good restaurants: 3 *, 2 **, 2 ***   **A**
Movie theaters: 7 chain (28 screens), 2   **A**
independent (2 screens)
Crowd Pleasers
Aquariums and Zoos: **B**
Dickerson Park Zoo (111 species, 305 specimens)
NCAA Division I: 0.62 game seats per capita   **A**
Southwest Missouri State University Bears (F, B)
Outdoor Recreation Assets
Federal Protected Areas
Mark Twain NF, 51,312 acres
Wilson's Creek NB, 1,750 acres
Places Rated Score: 1,526   Places Rated Rank: 158

Stamford-Norwalk, CT
Common Denominators
Golf courses: 18 private (306 holes), 2 daily fee (27   **B**
holes), 4 municipal (72 holes)
Good restaurants: 4 *, 5 **, 6 ***   **AA**
Movie theaters: 12 chain (26 screens), 2   **B**
independent (2 screens)
Outdoor Recreation Assets
Long Island Sound Coastline: 19 miles
State Recreation Area
Sherwood Island SP, 234 acres
MC Access: New York-Northern New Jersey-Long
Island, NY-NJ-CT
Places Rated Score: 1,084   Places Rated Rank: 260

State College, PA
Common Denominators
Golf courses: 2 private (27 holes), 5 daily fee (81   **AA**
holes)
Good restaurants: 2 **, 1 ***   **A**
Movie theaters: 3 chain (13 screens)   **A**
Crowd Pleasers
NCAA Division I: 3.82 game seats per capita   **AA**
Pennsylvania State University Nittany Lions (F, B)
Outdoor Recreation Assets
State Recreation Area
Black Moshannon SP, 3,481 acres
Places Rated Score: 1,430   Places Rated Rank: 177

Steubenville-Weirton, OH-WV
Common Denominators
Golf courses: 4 private (54 holes), 6 daily fee (81   **AA**
holes), 1 municipal (9 holes)
Movie theaters: 1 chain (6 screens), 1 independent   **C**
(1 screen)
Crowd Pleasers
Pari-mutuel Betting: **AA**
Mountaineer Park (thoroughbred, 223 days)
Outdoor Recreation Assets
State Recreation Areas
Jefferson Lake SP, 906 acres
Yellow Creek SF, 756 acres
Places Rated Score: 969   Places Rated Rank: 278

Stockton-Lodi, CA
Common Denominators
Golf courses: 8 private (126 holes), 4 municipal (72   **C**
holes)
Good restaurants: 1 **   **C**
Movie theaters: 5 chain (16 screens), 2   **C**
independent (5 screens)

	Rating
Crowd Pleasers	
Aquariums and Zoos:	C
Micke Grove Zoo (96 species, 227 specimens)	
Family Theme Parks:	B
Oakwood Lake Resort (108 days)	
Professional Sports: 0.49 game seats per capita	C
Ports (Class A Baseball)	
NCAA Division I: 0.35 game seats per capita	A
University of the Pacific Tigers (F, B)	

Outdoor Recreation Assets
State Recreation Area
Durham Ferry SRA, 183 acres
Places Rated Score: 1,002   Places Rated Rank: 269

Sudbury, ON
Common Denominators

	Rating
Golf courses: 1 private (18 holes), 1 daily fee (9 holes), 3 municipal (45 holes)	B
Movie theaters: 3 chain (8 screens), 1 independent (1 screen)	C

Crowd Pleasers
CIAU: 0.82 game seats per capita	A

Laurentian University Voyageurs (B, H)
Outdoor Recreation Assets
Federal Protected Area
Fielding MBS, 3,212 acres
Provincial Recreation Areas
Chapleau–Nemegosenda River PP, 20,176 acres
Chutes PP, 267 acres
Fairbank PP, 259 acres
Five Mile Lake PP, 1,127 acres
Halfway Lake PP, 11,688 acres
Ivanhoe Lake PP, 3,926 acres
Killarney Wilderness PP, 119,844 acres
La Cloche PP, 18,404 acres
Mashkinonje PP, 2,323 acres
Missinaibi PP, 108,875 acres
Mississagi River PP, 48,960 acres
The Shoals PP, 26,301 acres
Wakami Lake PP, 21,760 acres
Wanapitei PP, 6,672 acres
Windy Lake PP, 292 acres
Places Rated Score: 1,659   Places Rated Rank: 130

Sumter, SC
Common Denominators

	Rating
Golf courses: 2 private (36 holes), 4 daily fee (72 holes), 1 municipal (9 holes)	AA
Good restaurants: 1 **	C
Movie theaters: 3 chain (11 screens)	A

Outdoor Recreation Assets
State Recreation Area
Woods Bay SP, 924 acres
Places Rated Score: 823   Places Rated Rank: 299

Syracuse, NY
Common Denominators

	Rating
Golf courses: 18 private (297 holes), 45 daily fee (648 holes), 2 municipal (36 holes)	AA
Good restaurants: 4 *, 25 **, 6 ***	AA
Movie theaters: 12 chain (49 screens), 10 independent (12 screens)	B

Crowd Pleasers
Aquariums and Zoos:	B
Burnet Park Zoo (226 species, 997 specimens)	
Pari-mutuel Betting:	C
Syracuse Mile (harness, 7 days)	
Professional Sports: 1.12 game seats per capita	B
Astros (Class A Baseball)	
Chiefs (Triple A Baseball)	
NCAA Division I: 0.61 game seats per capita	A
Colgate University Red Raiders	
Syracuse University Orangemen (F, B)	

Outdoor Recreation Assets
Lake Ontario Coastline: 36 miles
State Recreation Areas
Battle Island SP, 235 acres

Clark Reservation, 326 acres
Fillmore Glen SP, 941 acres
Green Lakes SP, 1,400 acres
Places Rated Score: 2,173   Places Rated Rank: 73

Tacoma, WA
Common Denominators

	Rating
Golf courses: 8 private (126 holes), 9 daily fee (135 holes), 3 municipal (45 holes)	B
Good restaurants: 1 *, 5 **, 3 ***	B
Movie theaters: 6 chain (33 screens), 3 independent (3 screens)	C

Crowd Pleasers
Professional Sports: 0.99 game seats per capita	B
Tigers (Triple A Baseball)	

Outdoor Recreation Assets
Pacific Coastline: 15 miles
Federal Protected Areas
Mount Ranier NP, 206,441 acres
Nisqually NWR, 813 acres
Snoqualmie NF, 124,549 acres
State Recreation Areas
Dash Point SP, 168 acres
Kopachuck SP, 109 acres
MC Access: Seattle–Tacoma–Bremerton, WA
Places Rated Score: 2,498   Places Rated Rank: 45

Tallahassee, FL
Common Denominators

	Rating
Golf courses: 5 private (72 holes), 2 daily fee (36 holes), 3 municipal (36 holes)	B
Good restaurants: 2 *, 3 **, 1 ***	A
Movie theaters: 8 chain (37 screens), 1 independent (1 screen)	AA

Crowd Pleasers
Pari-mutuel Betting:	AA
Golden Crown (190 days)	
NCAA Division I: 2.35 game seats per capita	AA
Florida A&M Rattlers (F, B)	
Florida State University Seminoles (F, B)	

Outdoor Recreation Assets
Federal Protected Area
Appalachicola NF, 104,470 acres
State Recreation Area
Lake Talquin SRA, 22,303 acres
Places Rated Score: 2,542   Places Rated Rank: 40

✓ Tampa–St. Petersburg–Clearwater, FL
Common Denominators

	Rating
Golf courses: 49 private (837 holes), 44 daily fee (765 holes), 6 municipal (108 holes)	B
Good restaurants: 18 *, 26 **, 14 ***, 1 ****	A
Movie theaters: 43 chain (213 screens), 5 independent (5 screens)	A

Crowd Pleasers
Family Theme Parks:	AA
Adventure Island (187 days)	
Busch Gardens, Tampa (365 days)	
Weeki Wachee Spring and Buccaneer Bay (365 days)	
Pari-mutuel Betting:	A
St. Petersburg Kennel Club (greyhound, 180 days)	
Tampa Bay Downs (thoroughbred, 98 days)	
Tampa Jai Alai (328 days)	
Tampa Kennel Club (greyhound, 235 days)	
Professional Sports: 0.90 game seats per capita	B
Blue Jays (Class A Baseball)	
Buccaneers (NFL Football)	
Cardinals (Class A Baseball)	
Phillies (Class A Baseball)	
NCAA Division I: 0.01 game seats per capita	C
University of South Florida Bulls (B)	

Outdoor Recreation Assets
Gulf Coastline: 78 miles
Federal Protected Areas
Chassahowitzka NWR, 6,707 acres
Egmont Key NWR, 328 acres

Rating

State Recreation Areas
Caladesi Island SP, 632 acres
Honeymoon Island SRA, 408 acres
Weedon Island SNA, 602 acres
Places Rated Score: 2,624   Places Rated Rank: 36

Terre Haute, IN
Common Denominators
Golf courses: 3 private (45 holes), 2 daily fee (27   **AA**
holes), 5 municipal (72 holes)
Good restaurants: 1 *   **C**
Movie theaters: 4 chain (10 screens)   **B**
Crowd Pleasers
NCAA Division I: 1.39 game seats per capita   **AA**
Indiana State University Sycamores (F, B)
Places Rated Score: 1,100   Places Rated Rank: 255

Texarkana, TX–Texarkana, AR
Common Denominators
Golf courses: 3 private (45 holes), 1 daily fee (9   **C**
holes
Movie theaters: 1 chain (8 screens)   **B**
Places Rated Score: 300   Places Rated Rank: 340

Thunder Bay, ON
Common Denominators
Golf courses: 2 private (18 holes), 1 daily fee (18   **AA**
holes), 4 municipal (54 holes)
Good restaurants: 1 **   **C**
Movie theaters: 5 chain (19 screens)   **AA**
Crowd Pleasers
Aquariums and Zoos: **C**
Chippewa Park Zoo (27 species, 96 specimens)
CIAU: 0.13 game seats per capita   **C**
Lakehead University Nor'westers (B)
Outdoor Recreation Assets
Lake Superior Coastline: 40 miles
Federal Protected Area
Pukaskwa NP, 464,004 acres
Provincial Recreation Areas
Albert Lake Mesa PP, 321 acres
Arrow Lake PP, 1,063 acres
Arrowhead Peninsula PP, 2,014 acres
Kakabeka Falls PP, 1,038 acres
Kashabowie PP, 5,078 acres
Klotz Lake PP, 294 acres
Lake Nipigon PP, 3,603 acres
Mac Leod PP, 183 acres
Michipicoten Island PP, 90,785 acres
Middle Falls PP, 2,241 acres
Neys PP, 8,513 acres
Rainbow Falls PP, 1,421 acres
Sibley PP, 60,379 acres
Silver Falls PP, 8,058 acres
Wabakimi Wilderness PP, 383,005 acres
White Lake PP, 4,265 acres
Places Rated Score: 1,710   Places Rated Rank: 122

Toledo, OH
Common Denominators
Golf courses: 8 private (144 holes), 11 daily fee   **A**
(180 holes), 5 municipal (72 holes)
Good restaurants: 2 *, 4 **, 1 ***   **C**
Movie theaters: 9 chain (47 screens), 1   **B**
independent (2 screens)
Crowd Pleasers
Aquariums and Zoos: **A**
Toledo Zoological Gardens (463 species, 2,587
specimens)
Pari-mutuel Betting: **B**
Raceway Park (harness, 152 days)
Professional Sports: 1.49 game seats per capita   **A**
Mud Hens (Triple A Baseball)
Storm (ECHL Hockey)
NCAA Division I: 0.76 game seats per capita   **A**
Bowling Green State University Falcons
University of Toledo Rockets (F, B)

Rating

Outdoor Recreation Assets
Lake Huron Coastline: 19 miles
Federal Protected Areas
Cedar Point NWR, 2,445 acres
Ottawa NWR, 2,078 acres
West Sister Island NWR, 477 acres
State Recreation Areas
Crane Creek SP, 852 acres
Goll Woods SNA, 321 acres
Mary Jane Thurston SP, 104 acres
Maumee SF, 3,068 acres
Places Rated Score: 1,956   Places Rated Rank: 95

Topeka, KS
Common Denominators
Golf courses: 3 private (54 holes), 2 daily fee (27   **A**
holes), 3 municipal (45 holes)
Good restaurants: 2 **, 1 ***   **A**
Movie theaters: 5 chain (18 screens)   **A**
Crowd Pleasers
Aquariums and Zoos: **B**
Gage Park Zoo (136 species, 377 specimens)
Places Rated Score: 1,100   Places Rated Rank: 255

Toronto, ON
Common Denominators
Golf courses: 31 private (515 holes), 27 daily fee   **C**
(423 holes), 16 municipal (252 holes)
Good restaurants: 15 *, 37 **, 24 ***, 3 ****   **A**
Movie theaters: 54 chain (244 screens), 22   **B**
independent (30 screens)
Crowd Pleasers
Aquariums and Zoos: **AA**
Metropolitan Toronto Zoo (401 species, 3,141
specimens)
Family Theme Parks: **C**
Canada's Wonderland (100 days)
Pari-mutuel Betting: **C**
Greenwood Race Course (thoroughbred, 203
days)
Orangeville Raceway (harness, 103 days)
Woodbine Race Course (thoroughbred, 135 days)
Professional Sports: 1.21 game seats per capita   **B**
Argonauts (CFL Football)
Blue Jays (AL Baseball)
Maple Leafs (NHL Hockey)
CIAU: 0.05 game seats per capita   **C**
Ryerson Polytechnical Institute Rams (B, H)
University of Toronto Varsity Blues
York University Yeomen
Outdoor Recreation Assets
Lake Ontario Coastline: 45 miles
Federal Protected Area
Wye Marsh NWA, 116 acres
Provincial Recreation Areas
Awenda PP, 7,208 acres
Boyne Valley PP, 1,072 acres
Bronte Creek PP, 1,581 acres
Earl Rowe PP, 771 acres
Forks of the Credit PP, 645 acres
McRae Point PP, 341 acres
Mono Cliffs PP, 1,559 acres
Sibbald Point PP, 558 acres
Springwater PP, 116 acres
Wasaga Beach PP, 3,818 acres
MC Access: Toronto–Ontario Shore, ON
Places Rated Score: 2,157   Places Rated Rank: 76

Trenton, NJ
Common Denominators
Golf courses: 9 private (144 holes), 2 daily fee (36   **B**
holes), 3 municipal (54 holes)
Good restaurants: 2 *, 6 **, 1 ***   **A**
Movie theaters: 6 chain (27 screens), 1   **A**
independent (2 screens)
Crowd Pleasers
NCAA Division I: 1.04 game seats per capita   **AA**

	Rating

Princeton University Tigers
Rider College Broncs (B)
Outdoor Recreation Assets
   State Recreation Area
      Washington Crossing SP, 841 acres
MC Access: New York–Northern New Jersey–Long
Island, NY–NJ–CT
Places Rated Score: 1,278   Places Rated Rank: 212

Trois-Rivieres, PQ
Common Denominators
   Golf courses: 4 daily fee (63 holes), 1 municipal (18   **AA**
   holes)
   Movie theaters: 1 independent (1 screen)   **C**
Crowd Pleasers
   Pari-mutuel Betting: **AA**
      Hippodrome Trois-Rivieres (harness, 99 days)
   CIAU: 0.26 game seats per capita   **B**
      Université du Quebec Les Patriotes (H)
Places Rated Score: 1,100   Places Rated Rank: 255

✓ Tucson, AZ
Common Denominators
   Golf courses: 16 private (279 holes), 12 daily fee   **B**
   (180 holes), 6 municipal (108 holes)
   Good restaurants: 8 *, 19 **, 12 ***, 1 ****, 1 *****   **AA**
   Movie theaters: 13 chain (70 screens)   **A**
Crowd Pleasers
   Aquariums and Zoos: **B**
      Reid Park Zoo (147 species, 994 specimens)
   Family Theme Parks: **AA**
      Old Tucson Studios (363 days)
   Pari-mutuel Betting: **A**
      Tucson Greyhound Park (greyhound, 365 days)
   Professional Sports: 0.77 game seats per capita   **C**
      Toros (Triple A Baseball)
   NCAA Division I: 0.57 game seats per capita   **A**
      University of Arizona Wildcats (F, B)
Outdoor Recreation Assets
   Federal Protected Areas
      Buenos Aires NWR, 21,977 acres
      Cabeza Prieta NWR, 416,211 acres
      Coronado NF, 383,107 acres
      Organ Pipe Cactus NM, 329,316 acres
      Saguaro NM, 81,958 acres
   State Recreation Area
      Catalina SP, 5,511 acres
Places Rated Score: 3,253   Places Rated Rank: 10

Tulsa, OK
Common Denominators
   Golf courses: 10 private (162 holes), 10 daily fee   **B**
   (135 holes), 8 municipal (144 holes)
   Good restaurants: 5 *, 13 **, 3 ***   **A**
   Movie theaters: 12 chain (65 screens), 2   **A**
   independent (3 screens)
Crowd Pleasers
   Aquariums and Zoos: **A**
      Tulsa Zoological Park (283 species, 1,224
      specimens)
   Family Theme Parks: **C**
      Big Splash Water Park (100 days)
   Pari-mutuel Betting: **C**
      Fair Meadows (thoroughbred, 28 days)
      Will Rogers Downs (thoroughbred, 14 days)
   Professional Sports: 1.52 game seats per capita   **A**
      Drillers (Class AA Baseball)
      Zone (CBA Basketball)
   NCAA Division I: 0.31 game seats per capita   **A**
      University of Tulsa Golden Hurricane (F, B)
Outdoor Recreation Assets
   State Recreation Areas
      Keystone SP, 715 acres
      Sequoyah Bay SP, 303 acres
      Walnut Creek SP, 1,429 acres
Places Rated Score: 1,907   Places Rated Rank: 102

Tuscaloosa, AL
Common Denominators
   Golf courses: 5 private (90 holes), 1 daily fee (18   **C**
   holes)
   Good restaurants: 1 *, 3 **   **A**
   Movie theaters: 2 chain (16 screens)   **A**
Crowd Pleasers
   NCAA Division I: 3.21 game seats per capita   **AA**
      University of Alabama Crimson Tide (F, B)
Outdoor Recreation Assets
   Federal Protected Area
      Talladega NF, 10,445 acres
   State Recreation Area
      Lake Lurleen SP, 1,625 acres
Places Rated Score: 1,171   Places Rated Rank: 232

Tyler, TX
Common Denominators
   Golf courses: 5 private (81 holes), 4 daily fee (72   **A**
   holes)
   Good restaurants: 1 *, 2 **   **B**
   Movie theaters: 4 chain (15 screens)   **A**
Outdoor Recreation Assets
   State Recreation Areas
      Tyler SP, 986 acres
Places Rated Score: 808   Places Rated Rank: 302

Utica–Rome, NY
Common Denominators
   Golf courses: 13 private (180 holes), 19 daily fee   **AA**
   (243 holes), 2 municipal (27 holes)
   Good restaurants: 3 *, 6 **, 2 ***   **A**
   Movie theaters: 6 chain (26 screens), 1   **B**
   independent (1 screen)
Crowd Pleasers
   Aquariums and Zoos: **B**
      Utica Zoo (82 species, 223 specimens)
   Pari-mutuel Betting: **A**
      Vernon Downs (harness, 146 days)
   Professional Sports: 1.25 game seats per capita   **B**
      Blue Sox (Class A Baseball)
      Devils (AHL Hockey)
Outdoor Recreation Assets
   Federal Protected Area
      Fort Stanwix NM, 16 acres
   State Recreation Areas
      Delta Lake SP, 400 acres
      Nicks Lake SRA, 320 acres
      Pixley Falls SP, 375 acres
      Verona Beach SP, 1,735 acres
Places Rated Score: 1,618   Places Rated Rank: 137

Vallejo–Fairfield–Napa, CA
Common Denominators
   Golf courses: 5 private (90 holes), 6 daily fee (72   **B**
   holes), 4 municipal (63 holes)
   Good restaurants: 8 *, 9 **, 3 ***, 1 ****   **AA**
   Movie theaters: 7 chain (36 screens), 5   **A**
   independent (13 screens)
Crowd Pleasers
   Aquariums and Zoos: **A**
      Marine World–Africa USA
   Family Theme Parks: **A**
      Marine World Africa USA (141 days)
Outdoor Recreation Assets
   Federal Protected Area
      San Pablo Bay NWR, 248 acres
   State Recreation Areas
      Bothe–Napa Valley SP, 1,779 acres
      Sugarloaf Ridge SP, 139 acres
MC Access: San Francisco–Oakland–San Jose, CA
Places Rated Score: 1,422   Places Rated Rank: 181

✓ Vancouver, BC
Common Denominators
   Golf courses: 8 private (144 holes), 9 daily fee (144   **B**
   holes), 21 municipal (333 holes)

	Rating
Good restaurants: 4 *, 13 **, 19 ***	A
Movie theaters: 20 chain (89 screens), 14 independent (14 screens)	C

Crowd Pleasers
Aquariums and Zoos:	AA

Stanley Park Zoological Gardens (76 species, 265 specimens)
Vancouver Public Aquarium

Pari-mutuel Betting:	B

Cloverdale Raceway (harness, 123 days)
Exhibition Park (thoroughbred, 120 days)

Professional Sports: 0.80 game seats per capita	C

Canadians (Triple A Baseball)
Canucks (NHL Hockey)
Lions (CFL Football)

CIAU: 0.06 game seats per capita	C

Simon Fraser University Clansmen (F, B) N
University of British Columbia Thunderbirds

Outdoor Recreation Assets
Strait of Georgia Coastline: 60 miles
Federal Protected Areas
Alaksen NWA, 741 acres
Reifel MBS, 1,601 acres
Widgeon Valley NWA, 309 acres
Provincial Recreation Areas
Cypress PP, 7,443 acres
Davis Lake PP, 474 acres
Golden Ears PP, 137,378 acres
Mount Judge Howay PP, 15,271 acres
Mount Seymour PP, 8,668 acres
Rolley Lake PP, 284 acres

Places Rated Score: 3,154   Places Rated Rank: 13

Vancouver, WA
Common Denominators
Golf courses: 3 private (54 holes), 2 daily fee (27 holes)	C
Movie theaters: 3 chain (17 screens), 3 independent (8 screens)	A

Outdoor Recreation Assets
Federal Protected Areas
Fort Vancouver NHS, 202 acres
Gifford Pinchot NF, 1,180 acres
Ridgefield NWR, 4,627 acres
Steigerwald Lake NWR, 627 acres
State Recreation Areas
Battle Ground Lake SP, 280 acres
Reed Island SP, 508 acres
MC Access: Portland–Salem–Vancouver, OR–WA
Places Rated Score: 590   Places Rated Rank: 328

✓ Ventura, CA
Common Denominators
Golf courses: 7 private (117 holes), 6 daily fee (108 holes), 5 municipal (90 holes)	B
Good restaurants: 2 *, 3 **, 2 ***	C
Movie theaters: 12 chain (49 screens), 6 independent (9 screens)	B

Outdoor Recreation Assets
Pacific Coastline: 37 miles
Federal Protected Areas
Angeles NF, 1,474 acres
Bitter Creek NWR, 122 acres
Channel Islands NP, 702 acres
Hopper Mountain NWR, 1,871 acres
Los Padres NF, 557,152 acres
Santa Monica Mountains NRA, 6,654 acres
State Recreation Areas
Emma Wood SB, 109 acres
Point Mugu SP, 13,924 acres
MC Access: Los Angeles–Riverside–Orange County, CA
Places Rated Score: 2,630   Places Rated Rank: 35

Victoria, BC
Common Denominators
Golf courses: 2 private (36 holes), 5 daily fee (72 holes), 5 municipal (72 holes)	A

	Rating
Good restaurants: 7 **, 3 ***	AA
Movie theaters: 6 chain (16 screens), 2 independent (2 screens)	C

Crowd Pleasers
Aquariums and Zoos:	A

Crystal Garden (21 species, 180 specimens)
Sealand of the Pacific

Pari-mutuel Betting:	B

Sandown Park (harness, 44 days)

CIAU: 0.04 game seats per capita	C

University of Victoria Vikes (F)

Outdoor Recreation Assets
Strait of Juan de Fuca Coastline: 40 miles
Federal Protected Areas
Esquimalt Lagoon MBS, 321 acres
Shoal Harbour MBS, 371 acres
Victoria Harbour MBS, 4,201 acres
Provincial Recreation Areas
Beaumont Marine PP, 143 acres
Botanical Beach PP, 867 acres
China Beach PP, 151 acres
D'Arcy Island PP, 208 acres
Dionisio Point PP, 351 acres
Discovery Island Marine PP, 151 acres
French Beach PP, 146 acres
Goldstream PP, 813 acres
John Dean PP, 430 acres
Matheson Lake PP, 400 acres
Montague Harbour PP, 240 acres
Mount Maxwell PP, 492 acres
Princess Margaret Marine PP, 1,320 acres
Ruckle PP, 1,201 acres
Sidney Spit Marine PP, 986 acres
Wallace Island Marine PP, 178 acres
Winter Cove PP, 225 acres

Places Rated Score: 1,947   Places Rated Rank: 99

Victoria, TX
Common Denominators
Golf courses: 2 private (36 holes), 1 daily fee (18 holes), 2 municipal (27 holes)	A
Movie theaters: 3 chain (14 screens)	AA

Crowd Pleasers
Aquariums and Zoos:	C

The Texas Zoo (107 species, 252 specimens)
Places Rated Score: 800   Places Rated Rank: 306

Vineland–Millville–Bridgeton, NJ
Common Denominators
Golf courses: 2 daily fee (27 holes)	C
Movie theaters: 3 chain (14 screens)	A

Outdoor Recreation Assets
Atlantic Coastline: 30 miles
MC Access: Philadelphia–Wilmington–Atlantic City, PA–NJ–DE–MD
Places Rated Score: 930   Places Rated Rank: 281

Visalia–Tulare–Porterville, CA
Common Denominators
Golf courses: 2 private (36 holes), 2 daily fee (36 holes), 2 municipal (27 holes)	C
Good restaurants: 2 *, 1 **, 1 ***	C
Movie theaters: 4 chain (9 screens), 3 independent (5 screens)	C

Crowd Pleasers
Professional Sports: 0.44 game seats per capita	C

Oaks (Class A Baseball)

Outdoor Recreation Assets
Federal Protected Areas
Blue Ridge NWR, 897 acres
Inyo NF, 190,798 acres
Kings Canyon NP, 107,017 acres
Pixley NWR, 5,988 acres
Sequoia NF, 698,574 acres
Sequoia NP, 402,299 acres
Places Rated Score: 2,400   Places Rated Rank: 51

Rating   Rating

Waco, TX

Common Denominators

Golf courses: 2 private (36 holes), 3 daily fee (54   **A**
holes), 2 municipal (36 holes)

Good restaurants: 1 *, 3 **   **B**

Movie theaters: 6 chain (21 screens), 1   **AA**
independent (2 screens)

Crowd Pleasers

Aquariums and Zoos: **C**
Central Texas Zoo (145 species, 499 specimens)

NCAA Division   **AA**
Baylor University Bears (F, B)

Places Rates Score 1,400   Places Rated Rank: 184

Washington, DC–MD–VA–WV

Common Denominators

Golf courses: 68 private (1098 holes), daily fee (468   **C**
holes), 17 municipal (279 holes)

Good restaurants: 51 *, 111 **, 53 ***, 5 ****,   **AA**
2 *****

Movie theaters: 87 chain (431 screens), 14   **A**
independent (36 screens)

Crowd Pleasers

Aquariums and Zoos: **AA**
National Zoological Park (531 species, 2,659
specimens)

Pari-mutuel Betting: **B**
Charles Town Races (thoroughbred, 255 days)
Laurel Race Course (thoroughbred, 167 days)
Rosecroft Raceway (harness, 248 days)

Professional Sports: 0.78 game seats per capita   **C**
Bullets (NBA Basketball)
Capitals (NHL Hockey)
Keys (Class A Baseball)
P. W. Cannons (Class A Baseball)
Redskins (NFL Football)

NCAA Division I: 0.15 game seats per capita   **C**
American University Eagles (B)
George Mason University Patriots (B)
George Washington University Colonials (B)
Georgetown University Hoyas (B)
Howard University Bison (F, B)
Mount St. Mary's College Mountaineers (B)
University of Maryland, College Park Terps (F, B)

Outdoor Recreation Assets

Federal Protected Areas
Appalachian Trail, 5,753 acres
Catoctin Mountain Park, 5,695 acres
Chesapeake and Ohio Canal NHP, 4,474 acres
Featherstone NWR, 164 acres
Fort Washington Park, 341 acres
Fredericksburg and Spotsylvania NMP, 5,148
acres
George Washington NF, 6,270 acres
George Washington Parkway, 7,088 acres
Greenbelt Park, 1,175 acres
Harpers Ferry NHP, 1,368 acres
Lincoln NM, 110 acres
Manassas NBP, 4,356 acres
Mason Neck NWR, 1,487 acres
Monocacy NB, 1,014 acres
National Capital Parks, 6,036 acres
National Mall, 146 acres
Piscataway Park, 4,216 acres
Prince William Forest Park, 17,410 acres
Rock Creek Park, 1,754 acres
Shenandoah NP, 13,691 acres
Thomas Stone NHS, 322 acres
Washington Monument, 106 acres
Wolf Trap Farm Park, 130 acres

State Recreation Areas
Caledon NA, 2,579 acres
Calvert Cliffs SP, 1,313 acres
Cedarville SF, 2,706 acres
Gambrill SP, 1,137 acres
Gathland SP, 23 acres

Seneca Creek SP, 6,109 acres
MC Access: Washington–Baltimore, DC–MD–VA–WV

Places Rated Score: 1,857   Places Rated Rank: 105

Waterbury, CT

Common Denominators

Golf courses: 3 private (45 holes), 5 municipal (72   **B**
holes)

Good restaurants: 2 *   **C**

Movie theaters: 2 chain (14 screens)   **B**

Outdoor Recreation Assets

State Recreation Area
Black Rock SP, 443 acres

Places Rated Score: 506   Places Rated Rank: 332

Waterloo–Cedar Falls, IA

Common Denominators

Golf courses: 2 private (36 holes), 2 daily fee (27   **AA**
holes), 5 municipal (81 holes)

Good restaurants: 1 **   **C**

Movie theaters: 6 chain (27 screens)   **AA**

Crowd Pleasers

Pari-mutuel Betting: **AA**
Waterloo Greyhound Park (greyhound, 152 days)

Professional Sports: 3.04 game seats per capita   **AA**
Diamonds (Class A Baseball)

NCAA Division I: 1.54 game seats per capita   **AA**
University of Northern Iowa Panthers (F, B)

Places Rated Score: 2,107   Places Rated Rank: 78

Wausau, WI

Common Denominators

Golf courses: 1 private (18 holes), 4 daily fee (45   **B**
holes)

Good restaurants: 3 *, 3 **   **AA**

Movie theaters: 2 chain (9 screens)   **B**

Places Rated Score: 805   Places Rated Rank: 303

West Palm Beach–Boca Raton, FL

Common Denominators

Golf courses: 97 private (1701 holes), 12 daily fee   **B**
(216 holes), 8 municipal (144 holes)

Good restaurants: 8 *, 14 **, 27 ***, 1 ****, 1 *****   **AA**

Movie theaters: 13 chain (98 screens), 2   **A**
independent (4 screens)

Crowd Pleasers

Aquariums and Zoos: **B**
Dreher Park Zoo (118 species, 467 specimens)

Family Theme Parks: **AA**
Lion Country Safari (365 days)

Pari-mutuel Betting: **AA**
Fronton Jai Alai (318 days)
Palm Beach Kennel Club (greyhound, 365 days)

Professional Sports: 0.32 game seats per capita   **C**
Expos (Class A Baseball)

Outdoor Recreation Assets

Atlantic Coastline: 47 miles

Federal Protected Area
Loxahatchee NWR, 2,550 acres

State Recreation Area
MacArthur Beach SP, 225 acres

Places Rated Score: 2,401   Places Rated Rank: 50

Wheeling, WV–OH

Common Denominators

Golf courses: 3 private (54 holes), 1 daily fee (9   **A**
holes), 3 municipal (54 holes)

Good restaurants: 1 **, 1 ***   **B**

Movie theaters: 1 chain (9 screens), 1 independent   **B**
(1 screen)

Crowd Pleasers

Aquariums and Zoos: **C**
Oglebay Good Children's Zoo (61 species, 213
specimens)

Pari-mutuel Betting: **AA**
Wheeling Downs (greyhound, 310 days)

Rating

Outdoor Recreation Assets
State Recreation Area
Grave Creek Mound SP, 7 acres
Places Rated Score: 1,209 Places Rated Rank: 223

Wichita, KS
Common Denominators
Golf courses: 9 private (144 holes), 7 daily fee (90 holes), 7 municipal (108 holes) **B**
Good restaurants: 1 *, 6 **, 2 *** **B**
Movie theaters: 10 chain (42 screens), 3 independent (3 screens) **A**
Crowd Pleasers
Aquariums and Zoos: **A**
Sedgwick County Zoo (179 species, 1,273 specimens)
Pari-mutuel Betting: **AA**
Wichita Greyhound Park (greyhound, 293 days)
Professional Sports: 0.94 game seats per capita **B**
Wranglers (Class AA Baseball)
NCAA Division I: 0.21 game seats per capita **B**
Wichita State University Shockers (B)
Outdoor Recreation Assets
State Recreation Area
El Dorado SP, 3,800 acres
Places Rated Score: 1,811 Places Rated Rank: 109

Wichita Falls, TX
Common Denominators
Golf courses: 1 private (18 holes), 4 daily fee (54 holes), 2 municipal (36 holes) **AA**
Good restaurants: 1 * **C**
Movie theaters: 3 chain (16 screens) **AA**
Crowd Pleasers
Professional Sports: 1.41 game seats per capita **A**
Texans (CBA Basketball)
Places Rated Score: 1,200 Places Rated Rank: 227

Williamsport, PA
Common Denominators
Golf courses: 1 private (18 holes), 2 municipal (36 holes) **B**
Movie theaters: 2 chain (9 screens), 1 independent (1 screen) **B**
Outdoor Recreation Assets
State Recreation Area
Susquehanna SP, 20 acres
Places Rated Score: 414 Places Rated Rank: 337

Wilmington, NC
Common Denominators
Golf courses: 5 private (90 holes), 4 daily fee (72 holes), 1 municipal (18 holes) **AA**
Good restaurants: 2 *, 8 ** **AA**
Movie theaters: 6 chain (24 screens) **AA**
Crowd Pleasers
Aquariums and Zoos: **A**
North Carolina Aquarium
NCAA Division I: 0.48 game seats per capita **A**
University of North Carolina Wilmington Seahawks (B)
Outdoor Recreation Assets
Atlantic Coastline: 26 miles
Places Rated Score: 1,870 Places Rated Rank: 104

Wilmington-Newark, DE-MD
Common Denominators
Golf courses: 12 private (207 holes), 3 daily fee (54 holes), 2 municipal (36 holes) **C**
Good restaurants: 7 **, 6 *** **A**
Movie theaters: 11 chain (45 screens) **B**
Crowd Pleasers
Aquariums and Zoos: **C**
Brandywine Zoo (56 species, 116 specimens)
Pari-mutuel Betting: **A**
Delaware Park (thoroughbred, 150 days)
NCAA Division I: 0.28 game seats per capita **B**
University of Delaware Blue Hens (F, B)

Rating

Outdoor Recreation Assets
State Recreation Areas
Brandywine Creek SP, 795 acres
Elk Neck SF, 3,035 acres
Fort Delaware SP, 288 acres
Fox Point SP, 171 acres
MC Access: Philadelphia-Wilmington-Atlantic City, PA-NJ-DE-MD
Places Rated Score: 1,688 Places Rated Rank: 125

Windsor, ON
Common Denominators
Golf courses: 3 private (54 holes), 4 daily fee (72 holes), 5 municipal (56 holes) **A**
Good restaurants: 3 *, 8 ** **AA**
Movie theaters: 6 chain (20 screens), 2 independent (4 screens) **A**
Crowd Pleasers
Pari-mutuel Betting: **AA**
Windsor Raceway (harness, 167 days)
CIAU: 0.17 game seats per capita **B**
University of Windsor Lancers
Outdoor Recreation Assets
Federal Protected Areas
Pinafore Park MBS, 988 acres
Point Pelee NP, 3,830 acres
Provincial Recreation Areas
Holiday Beach PP, 227 acres
John E. Pearce PP, 168 acres
Peche Island PP, 378 acres
Port Burwell PP, 561 acres
MC Access: Detroit-Ann Arbor-Flint, MI
Places Rated Score: 1,821 Places Rated Rank: 107

Winnipeg, MB
Common Denominators
Golf courses: 8 private (126 holes), 6 daily fee (81 holes), 3 municipal (54 holes) **C**
Good restaurants: 1 *, 1 *** **C**
Movie theaters: 13 chain (47 screens), 3 independent (5 screens) **B**
Crowd Pleasers
Aquariums and Zoos: **A**
Assiniboine Park Zoo (231 species, 1,062 specimens)
Pari-mutuel Betting: **A**
Assiniboine Downs (mixed meetings, 180 days)
Professional Sports: 1.15 game seats per capita **B**
Blue Bombers (CFL Football)
Jets (NHL Hockey)
CIAU: 0.14 game seats per capita **C**
University of Manitoba Bisons
University of Winnipeg Wesmen (B)
Outdoor Recreation Assets
Federal Protected Areas
Pope NWA, 77 acres
Rockwood NWA, 79 acres
Provincial Recreation Areas
Beaudry PP, 2,170 acres
Birds Hill PP, 8,700 acres
Patricia Beach PP, 153 acres
Places Rated Score: 1,318 Places Rated Rank: 194

Worcester-Fitchburg-Leominster, MA
Common Denominators
Golf courses: 10 private (144 holes), 29 daily fee (378 holes), 4 municipal (54 holes) **AA**
Good restaurants: 4 **, 2 *** **C**
Movie theaters: 8 chain (23 screens), 3 independent (5 screens) **C**
Crowd Pleasers
NCAA Division I: 0.26 game seats per capita **B**
College of the Holy Cross Crusaders
Outdoor Recreation Assets
Federal Protected Area
Oxbow NWR, 711 acres
State Recreation Areas
Ashburnham SF, 2,000 acres

Rating

Buffumville SRA, 400 acres
Douglas SF, 3,752 acres
Federation SF, 586 acres
Hubbardston SF, 800 acres
Lake Dennison SRA, 9,000 acres
Lawton SF, 350 acres
Leominster SF, 4,265 acres
Moore SP, 324 acres
Oakham SF, 390 acres
Otter River SF, 1,220 acres
Petersham SF, 200 acres
Purgatory Chasm SF, 187 acres
Royalston SF, 800 acres
Rutland SP, 1,920 acres
Spencer SF, 1,048 acres
Sutton SF, 135 acres
Templeton SF, 604 acres
Upton SF, 2,660 acres
Wachusett Mountain State Reservation, 1,950 acres
Wells SP, 1,081 acres
MC Access: Boston–New Bedford–Nashua, MA–NH
Places Rated Score: 904   Places Rated Rank: 292

Yakima, WA
Common Denominators
Golf courses: 2 private (36 holes), 4 daily fee (54 holes)   **B**
Good restaurants: 1 *, 1 **, 1 ***   **B**
Movie theaters: 3 chain (12 screens), 3 independent (5 screens)   **A**
Crowd Pleasers
Pari-mutuel Betting: **A**
Yakima Meadows Race Track (mixed meetings, 76 days)
Professional Sports: 2.24 game seats per capita   **AA**
Bears (Class A Baseball)
Sun Kings (CBA Basketball)
Outdoor Recreation Assets
Federal Protected Areas
Gifford Pinchot NF, 37,552 acres
Snoqualmie NF, 466,573 acres
Toppenish NWR, 1,763 acres
State Recreation Area
Yakima Sportsmans SP, 246 acres
Places Rated Score: 2,321   Places Rated Rank: 57

Yolo, CA
Common Denominators
Golf courses: 2 private (36 holes), 1 daily fee (9 holes), 1 municipal (18 holes)   **C**
Good restaurants: 2 *   **C**
Movie theaters: 2 chain (8 screens)   **C**
MC Access: Sacramento–Yolo, CA
Places Rated Score: 370   Places Rated Rank: 338

York, PA
Common Denominators
Golf courses: 5 private (81 holes), 11 daily fee (198 holes)   **A**
Good restaurants: 1 *, 1 **, 3 ***   **B**
Movie theaters: 4 chain (15 screens), 1 independent (1 screen)   **C**
Outdoor Recreation Assets
State Recreation Area
Codorus SP, 3,320 acres
Places Rated Score: 649   Places Rated Rank: 323

Youngstown–Warren, OH
Common Denominators
Golf courses: 7 private (117 holes), 41 daily fee (549 holes), 3 municipal (45 holes)   **AA**
Good restaurants: 3 **, 2 ***   **C**
Movie theaters: 6 chain (24 screens), 3 independent (3 screens)   **C**
Crowd Pleasers
NCAA Division I: 0.25 game seats per capita   **B**
Youngstown State University Penguins (F, B)
Outdoor Recreation Assets
State Recreation Areas
Guilford Lake SP, 92 acres
Kyle Woods SNA, 82 acres
Places Rated Score: 836   Places Rated Rank: 298

Yuba City, CA
Common Denominators
Golf courses: 1 private (18 holes), 3 daily fee (36 holes), 1 municipal (18 holes)   **A**
Movie theaters: 1 chain (8 screens), 2 independent (5 screens)   **A**
Outdoor Recreation Assets
Federal Protected Areas
Plumas NF, 24,086 acres
Sutter NWR, 2,590 acres
Tahoe NF, 20,334 acres
Places Rated Score: 917   Places Rated Rank: 284

Yuma, AZ
Common Denominators
Golf courses: 1 private (18 holes), 3 daily fee (45 holes), 1 municipal (18 holes)   **A**
Good restaurants: 1 *, 2 **   **A**
Movie theaters: 2 chain (4 screens)   **C**
Crowd Pleasers
Pari-mutuel Betting: **AA**
Yuma Greyhound Park (greyhound, 164 days)
Outdoor Recreation Assets
Federal Protected Areas
Cabeza Prieta NWR, 443,800 acres
Kofa NWR, 523,040 acres
Places Rated Score: 2,469   Places Rated Rank: 48

Et Cetera

LOOKING FOR THE BEST SKIING?

Draw a line on a map of North America separating regions with the best conditions for skiing from those with poor conditions or none at all and you'd have a jagged northward arc. It starts in North Carolina's Great Smokey Mountains and extends upward to Atlantic Canada, west to the foothills of the Rockies, then south along the Rocky Mountain cordillera to northern New Mexico and Arizona. Next it would reappear in the

The Fifteen Most Popular Ski Areas

Below are the most-visited resorts in North America, selling more than one-half million day-lift tickets each year.

Resort	Lift Tickets/Year
Vail, CO	1.5 million
Breckenridge, CO	1.0
Keystone, CO	1.0
Mammoth Mountain, CA	1.0
Steamboat Springs, CO	1.0
Killington, VT	.9
Winter Park, CO	.9
Copper Mountain, CO	.8
Blackcomb, BC	.7
Heavenly Valley, NV	.7
Snowmass, CO	.7
Whistler, BC	.6
Mount Bachelor, OR	.5
Mount Ste. Anne, PQ	.5
Squaw Valley, CA	.5

California Sierra Nevada, dropping southwest to end in the San Bernardino National Forest an hour and a half out of Los Angeles.

Although ski areas exist as far south as Alabama and Georgia, the ideal conditions are found north of this imaginary curve in the rolling, rugged terrain and predictable winter weather that everyone except skiers would call bad.

By definition, a ski area is more than a snow-covered hill or mountain. It also has developed trails and lift machinery. Usually, too, there is a lodge for meals and overnight stays. If the area is large and popular, it also

The Top Ski Areas for Vertical Rise

Ski Area	Height
Whistler/Blackcomb Mountains, BC	5,280
Jackson Hole, WY	4,139
Aspen Highlands, CO	3,800
Panorama, BC	3,800
Snowmass at Aspen, CO	3,615
Heavenly Valley, CA	3,600
Steamboat, CO	3,600
Telluride, CO	3,522
Sunshine Village, AB	3,514
Sun Valley, ID	3,400
Beaver Creek, CO	3,340
Aspen, CO	3,267
Lake Louise, AB	3,250
Vail, CO	3,250
Whiteface Mountain, NY	3,216
Killington, VT	3,175
Crystal Mountain, WA	3,100
Mammoth Mountain, CA	3,100
Mt. Bachelor, OR	3,100
Park City, UT	3,100
Snowbird, UT	3,100
Tod Mountain, BC	3,100
Nakiska, AB	3,082

Source: Inter-Ski Services, *The White Book of Ski Areas,* 1992.

The Top Ski Areas for Lift Capacity

Ski Area	Skiers per hour
Squaw Valley, CA	47,370
Mammoth Mountain, CA	46,000
Vail, CO	35,020
Keystone Mountain/The Outback, CO	32,817
Heavenly Valley, CA	31,000
Killington, VT	30,827
Alpental/Ski Acres/Snoqualmie, WA	30,000
Steamboat, CO	29,327
Winter Park, CO	28,310
Copper Mountain, CO	28,250
Mount Snow, VT	26,685
Breckenridge, CO	24,430
Whistler/Blackcomb Mountains, BC	23,850
Sun Valley, ID	23,580
Stratton Mountain, VT	22,120
Alpine Valley, MI	21,330
Sunday River, ME	21,000
Snowmass at Aspen, CO	20,535
Seven Springs, PA	20,400
Afton Alps, MN	20,000
Mount St. Louis–Moonstone, ON	20,000

Source: Inter-Ski Services, *The White Book of Ski Areas,* 1992.

has *aprè-ski*—nighttime entertainment from music to movies to disco—that is as critical as fresh snow and challenging runs to many skiers.

Of the 610 ski areas in North America, half are found in nine states and provinces that border the St. Lawrence River and the Great Lakes—Michigan, Minnesota, New Hampshire, New York, Ontario, Pennsylvania, Quebec, Vermont, and Wisconsin—owing to harsh, long winters and large, outdoors-hungry urban populations.

Vertical Rise . . .

The perpendicular distance from the base to the highest skiable point on a hill or mountain is a ski area's "vertical." British Columbia's 26 ski areas average 1,824 feet, whereas Nebraska's single ski area has a rise of

The Longest Ski Runs

Ski Area	Length
Killington Ski Resort, VT	10.2 miles
Jackson Hole, WY	7
Whistler-Blackcomb Mountains, BC	7
Heavenly Valley, CA	5.5
Taos Ski Valley, NM	5.2
Tod Mountain, BC	5.2
Lake Louise, AB	5
Mission Ridge, WA	5
Sunshine Village, AB	5
Okemo Mountain, VT	4.5
Red Mountain Ski Area, BC	4.5
Vail, CO	4.5
Snowmass at Aspen, CO	4.1
Kimberley Ski Resort, BC	4

Source: Inter-Ski Services, *The White Book of Ski Areas,* 1992.

only 200 feet. Although vertical rise has little to do with the quality of trails, it is a good indication of length of the runs and the mountain's challenge. More than one optimistic ski-area promoter has stretched the distance a bit—some, allegedly, by measuring from the top of the tallest tree on the crest to the surface of the highway below the base lodge.

. . . and Longest Runs . . .

The highest vertical is found at British Columbia's Whistler area, but the longest run is at Killington, in Vermont. The longest run is the lengthiest continuous trail on the mountain, from the top to the runout, which is usually in the base lodge's parking lot.

. . . and Lift Capacities

A ski area's lift capacity is the number of people its lifts can move up the mountain in one hour. Lifts can be elementary rope or cable tows, bars (T-bars, J-bars, pomalifts, or platterpulls), chairs, trams, or gondolas. Whatever the mix of lifts at a ski resort, the total lift capacity is a good indication of how developed the ski area is and often of how efficient the lift lines are. Twenty-one North American ski areas have lift capacities of at least 20,000 skiers per hour. At Squaw Valley and at Mammoth Mountain in the California Sierras, nearly 50,000 skiers per hour can be moved up the mountain.

WHERE ARE THE BEST SPORTS TOWNS?

Ask 100 sports fans to describe the ideal sports town and you'll probably get 100 differing answers. Earlier in this chapter, *Places Rated* looked at major spectator sports from the point of view of easy accessibility and on this basis found the best metro areas to be Elmira, NY; Milwaukee, WI; Rapid City, SD; and San Francisco, CA.

Being able to attend a game easily is not the only thing a fan wants. Rooting for the home team is fun, but rooting for a winning home team is ecstasy. In the lists that follow, *Places Rated* looks at the metro areas with the winningest teams.

Major-League Title Towns

For baseball fans in the mid-1970s, the place to be was Oakland as the A's hauled in three straight World Series championships. In the 1960s, football fans found a warm welcome in frosty Green Bay, where the Packers took five NFL Championships over a seven-year span. No baseball team can really be called a dominant World Series champ for the 1980s. Neither has any football team topped the Packers' record for the 1960s, but Pittsburg Steelers, with four Super Bowl wins, the San Francisco 49ers, with three, and the Washington Redskins, with two, have inspired devotion among fans in the late 1970s and throughout the 1980s.

Basketball lovers, on the other hand, won't ever go far wrong if they back the Boston Celtics, winners of more titles than any other team in NBA history. With all their tradition and mystique—and the renowned parquet floor of the Boston Garden where they play—they have left many opponents bewitched, bothered, and bewildered. Still, in the 1980s the L.A. Lakers didn't do too badly either, with more championships in that decade than any other team.

Our survey of metro areas with major professional championships (in the list just below) looks at the winners in four team sports: baseball, football, basketball, and ice hockey. In the cases of baseball and ice hockey, we include the winners of the World Series (since 1903) and Stanley Cup (since 1894). For football and basketball, we include the Super Bowl and NBA Championship winners. Going back a little more toward the roots, we also list the winning teams from the leagues that preceded the modern NFL (the National Football League, 1933–1969, and American Football League, 1960–1969) and the NBA (the Basketball Association of America, 1947–1949). The NFL and AFL champions of 1966, 1967, and 1968 met in the Super Bowls of 1967, 1968, and 1969, before the formation of the modern NFL; for those years, we name the winners of both the individual league championships and the Super Bowl.

If a team has changed names or towns, we list it with the name it used and in the town it played at the time it won the championship.

Professional Championships in the Metro Areas

Anaheim–Santa Ana, CA
NFL Championship: Los Angeles Rams, 1951

Baltimore, MD
World Series: Orioles, 1966, 1970, 1983
Super Bowl: Colts, 1971
NFL Championship: Colts 1958, 1959, 1968
BAA Championship: Bullets, 1948

Boston, MA
World Series: Somersets, 1903; Red Sox, 1912, 1914, 1915, 1916, 1918
NBA Championship: Celtics, 1957, 1959, 1960, 1961, 1962, 1963, 1964, 1965, 1966, 1968, 1969, 1974, 1976, 1981, 1984, 1986
NHL Stanley Cup: Bruins, 1929, 1939, 1941, 1970, 1972

Buffalo, NY
AFL Championship: Bills, 1964, 1965

Calgary, AB
CFL Grey Cup: Stampede, 1993
NHL Stanley Cup: Flames, 1989

Chicago, IL
World Series: White Sox, 1906, 1917; Cubs, 1907, 1908
NBA Championship: Bulls, 1991, 1992
NFL Championship: Bears, 1933, 1940, 1941, 1943, 1946; Cardinals, 1947; Bears, 1963
NHL Stanley Cup: Black Hawks, 1934, 1938, 1961

Cincinnati, OH–KY–IN
World Series: Reds, 1919, 1940, 1975, 1976, 1990

Cleveland, OH
World Series: Indians, 1920, 1948
NFL Championship: Rams, 1945; Browns, 1950, 1954, 1955, 1964

Dallas, TX
Super Bowl: Cowboys, 1972, 1978, 1993
AFL Championship: Texans, 1962

Detroit, MI
World Series: Tigers, 1935, 1945, 1968, 1984
NBA Championship: Pistons, 1989, 1990
NFL Championship: Lions, 1935, 1952, 1953, 1957
NHL Stanley Cup: Red Wings, 1936, 1937, 1943, 1950, 1952, 1954, 1955

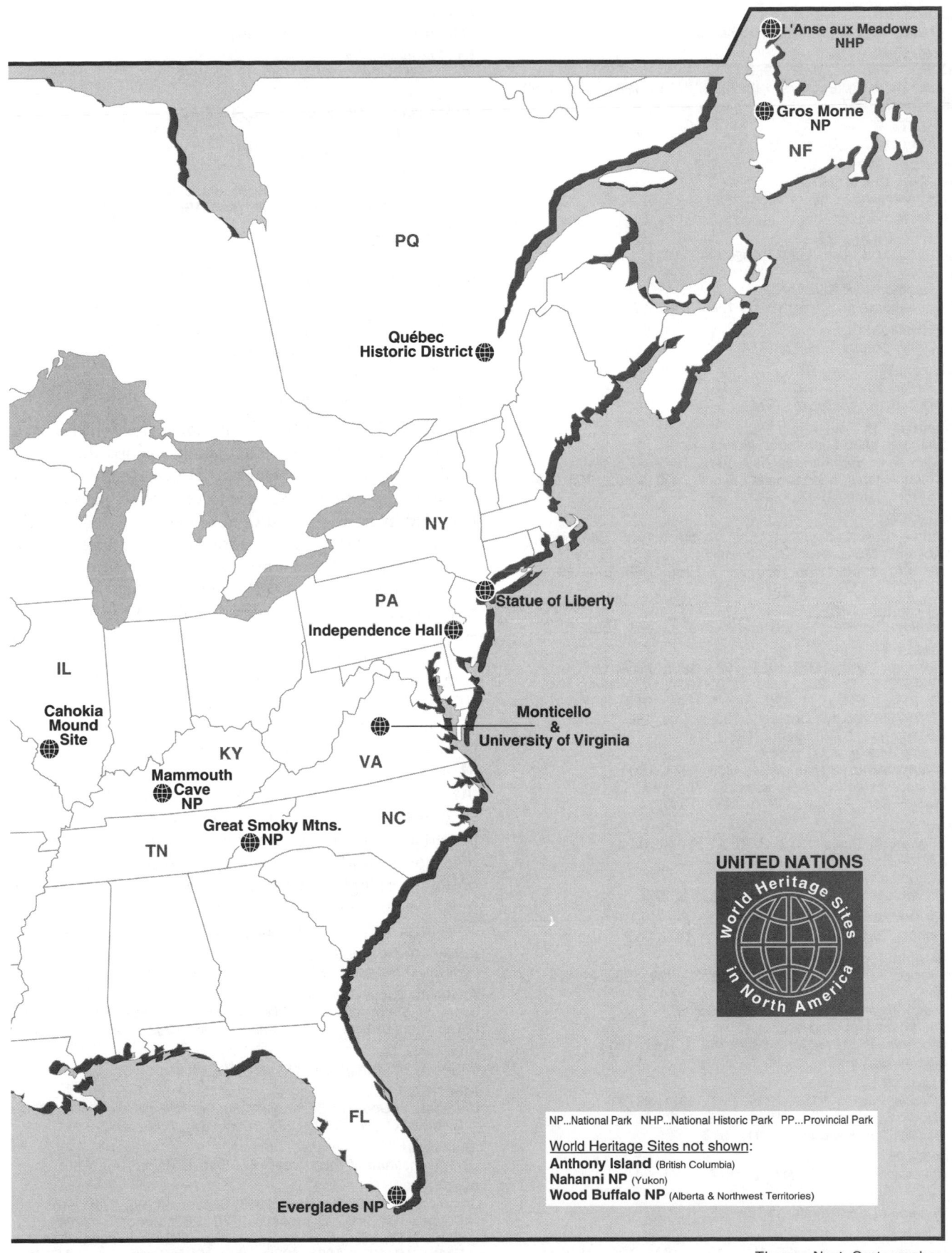

UNITED NATIONS
World Heritage Sites in North America

NP...National Park   NHP...National Historic Park   PP...Provincial Park

<u>World Heritage Sites not shown:</u>
Anthony Island (British Columbia)
Nahanni NP (Yukon)
Wood Buffalo NP (Alberta & Northwest Territories)

Edmonton, AB
NHL Stanley Cup: Oilers, 1987, 1988, 1990

Green Bay, WI
Super Bowl: Packers, 1967, 1968
NFL Championship: Packers, 1936, 1937, 1939, 1944, 1961, 1962, 1965, 1966, 1967

Houston, TX
AFL Championship: Oilers, 1960, 1961

Kansas City, MO
Super Bowl: Chiefs, 1970
AFL Championship: Chiefs, 1966, 1969
World Series: Royals, 1985

Los Angeles–Long Beach, CA
World Series: Dodgers, 1959, 1963, 1965, 1981, 1988
Super Bowl: Raiders, 1984
NFL Championship: Rams, 1951
NBA Championship: Lakers, 1972, 1980, 1982, 1985, 1987, 1988

Miami–Hialeah, FL
Super Bowl: Dolphins, 1973, 1974

Milwaukee, WI
World Series: Braves, 1957
NBA Championship: Bucks, 1971

Minneapolis–St. Paul, MN
NFL Championship: Minnesota Vikings, 1969
BAA Championship: Minneapolis Lakers, 1949
NBA Championship: Minneapolis Lakers, 1950, 1952, 1953, 1954
World Series: Twins, 1987, 1991

Montreal, PQ
NHL Stanley Cup: Canadiens, 1924; Maroons, 1926; Canadiens, 1930, 1931; Maroons, 1935; Canadiens, 1944, 1946, 1953, 1956, 1957, 1958, 1959, 1960, 1965, 1966, 1968, 1969, 1971, 1973, 1976, 1977, 1978, 1979, 1986

Nassau–Suffolk, NY
NHL Stanley Cup: New York Islanders, 1980, 1981, 1982, 1983

New York, NY
World Series: Giants, 1905, 1921, 1922, 1933, 1954; Yankees, 1923, 1927, 1928, 1932, 1936, 1937, 1938, 1939, 1941, 1943, 1947, 1949, 1950, 1951, 1952, 1953, 1956, 1958, 1961, 1962, 1977, 1978; Brooklyn Dodgers, 1955; Mets, 1969, 1986
Super Bowl: Jets, 1969; Giants, 1987, 1991
AFL Championship: Jets, 1968
NFL Championship: Giants, 1934, 1938, 1944, 1956
NBA Championship: Knickerbockers, 1970, 1973
NHL Stanley Cup: Rangers, 1928, 1933, 1940

Oakland, CA
World Series: Athletics, 1972, 1973; A's, 1974, 1989
Super Bowl: Raiders, 1977, 1981
AFL Championship: Raiders, 1967
NBA Championship: Golden State Warriors, 1975

Ottawa–Hull, ON–PQ
NHL Stanley Cup: Senators, 1920, 1921, 1923, 1927

Philadelphia, PA
World Series: Athletics, 1910, 1911, 1913, 1929, 1930; Phillies, 1980
NFL Championship: Eagles, 1948, 1949, 1960
BAA Championship: Warriors, 1947
NBA Championship: Warriors, 1956; 76ers, 1967, 1983
NHL Stanley Cup: Flyers, 1974, 1975

Pittsburgh, PA
World Series: Pirates, 1909, 1925, 1960, 1971, 1979
Super Bowl: Steelers, 1975, 1976, 1979, 1980
NHL Stanley Cup: Penguins, 1991, 1992

Portland, OR
NBA Championship: Trail Blazers, 1977

Rochester, NY
NBA Championship: Royals, 1951

St. Louis, MO–IL
World Series: Cardinals, 1926, 1931, 1934, 1942, 1944, 1946, 1964, 1967, 1982
NBA Championship: Hawks, 1958

San Diego, CA
AFL Championship: Chargers, 1963

San Francisco, CA
Super Bowl: 49ers, 1982, 1985, 1989, 1990

Seattle, WA
NBA Championship: Supersonics, 1979

Syracuse, NY
NBA Championship: Nationals, 1955

Toronto, ON
NHL Stanley Cup: Arenas, 1918; St. Patricks, 1922; Maple Leafs, 1932, 1942, 1945, 1947, 1948, 1949, 1951, 1962, 1963, 1964, 1967
World Series: Blue Jays, 1992

Victoria, BC
NHL Stanley Cup: Cougars, 1925

Washington, DC–MD–VA
World Series: Senators, 1924
Super Bowl: Redskins, 1983, 1988, 1992
NFL Championship: Redskins, 1937, 1942
NBA Championship: Bullets, 1978

Collegiate Title Towns

The 1993–1994 academic year marks the 110th season of American college athletic championships that began all the way back when Harvard University's J. S. Clark captured the first singles title in college tennis in 1883. Founded in 1906, the National Collegiate Athletic Association (NCAA) began sponsoring college athletic championships in 1921, beginning with its first outdoor track meet. It was not until 1981, however, that the association initiated women's championships. Over the years, some 600 colleges and universities have been named national champions in each of the NCAA's three divisions. What follows is a list covering the past decade that shows 67 metro areas with Division I champions.

Many NCAA sports, such as basketball and volleyball, have both men's and women's championships. An M or W after the sport in the list below indicates whether the title was in men's or women's competition. Sports such as baseball, football, ice hockey, and wrestling are played at the championship level by men only, whereas field hockey and softball championships are for women only; accordingly, no M or W designation is given for those sports. Ski teams are coed.

NCAA Division I Championships in the Metro Areas

Albany–Schenectady–Troy, NY
Rensselaer Polytechnic Institute: Ice Hockey, 1985

Anaheim–Santa Ana, CA
California State University, Fullerton: Baseball, 1984; Softball, 1986
University of California, Irvine: Water Polo, 1982

Ann Arbor, MI
University of Michigan: Basketball (M), 1989

Athens, GA
University of Georgia: Baseball, 1990; Football (Division I-A), 1980; Gymnastics (W), 1987, 1989; Tennis (M), 1985, 1987

Atlanta, GA
Georgia Institute of Technology: Football (Division I-A), 1990

Austin, TX
University of Texas: Baseball, 1983; Basketball (W), 1986; Cross Country (W), 1986; Gymnastics (W), 1987; Indoor Track (W), 1986, 1988, 1990; Outdoor Track (W), 1986; Swimming and Diving (M), 1981, 1988, 1989, 1990, 1991; Swimming and Diving (W), 1984, 1985, 1986, 1987, 1988, 1990, 1991; Volleyball (W), 1988

Baltimore, MD
Johns Hopkins University: Lacrosse (M), 1980, 1984, 1985, 1987

Baton Rouge, LA
Louisiana State University: Baseball, 1991; Indoor Track (W), 1987, 1989, 1991; Outdoor Track (M), 1989, 1990; Outdoor Track (W), 1987, 1988, 1989, 1990, 1991, 1992

Bloomington, IN
Indiana University: Basketball (M), 1981, 1987; Soccer (M), 1982, 1983, 1988

Boise City, ID
Boise State University: Football (Division I-AA), 1980

Boston, MA
Harvard University: Ice Hockey, 1989

Boulder–Longmont, CO
University of Colorado: Football (Division I-A), 1990; Skiing, 1982, 1991

Bryan–College Station, TX
Texas A&M University: Softball, 1983, 1987

Burlington, VT
University of Vermont: Skiing, 1980, 1989, 1990, 1992

Charlottesville, VA
University of Virginia: Cross Country (W), 1981, 1982; Soccer (M), 1989, 1991

Chattanooga, TN
University of Tennessee: Basketball (W) 1987

Columbus, OH
Ohio State University: Gymnastics (M), 1985

Dallas, TX
Southern Methodist University: Indoor Track (M), 1983; Outdoor Track (M), 1983, 1986

Denver, CO
University of Denver: Gymnastics (W), 1983

El Paso, TX
University of Texas, El Paso: Cross Country (M), 1980, 1981, 1983; Indoor Track (M), 1980, 1981, 1982; Outdoor Track (M), 1980, 1981, 1982

Eugene–Springfield, OR
University of Oregon: Cross Country (W), 1983, 1987; Outdoor Track (M), 1984; Outdoor Track (W), 1985

Fayetteville, AR
University of Arkansas: Cross Country (M), 1986, 1987, 1991; Indoor Track (M), 1984, 1985, 1986, 1987, 1988, 1989, 1990, 1991, 1992; Outdoor Track (M), 1988, 1992

Fort Worth–Arlington, TX
Texas Christian University: Golf (W), 1983

Gainesville, FL
University of Florida: Golf (W), 1985, 1986; Indoor Track (W), 1992; Swimming and Diving (M), 1983, 1984; Swimming and Diving (W), 1982; Tennis (W), 1992

Grand Forks, ND
University of North Dakota: Ice Hockey, 1980, 1982, 1987

Greensboro–Winston-Salem–High Point, NC
Wake Forest University: Golf (M), 1986

Greenville–Spartanburg, SC
Clemson University: Football (Division I-A), 1981; Soccer, 1984, 1987
Furman University: Football (Division I-AA), 1988

Honolulu, HI
University of Hawaii: Volleyball (W), 1982, 1983, 1987

Houston, TX
University of Houston: Golf (M), 1982, 1984, 1985

Iowa City, IA
University of Iowa: Field Hockey, 1986; Wrestling, 1980, 1981, 1982, 1983, 1984, 1985, 1986, 1991, 1992

Knoxville, TN
University of Tennessee: Basketball (W), 1987, 1989, 1991; Outdoor Track (M), 1991

Lansing–East Lansing, MI
Michigan State University: Ice Hockey, 1986

Las Vegas, NV
University of Nevada: Basketball (M), 1990

Lawrence, KS
Kansas University: Basketball (M), 1988

Lexington–Fayette, KY
University of Kentucky: Cross Country (W), 1988

Lincoln, NE
University of Nebraska: Gymnastics (M), 1980, 1981, 1982, 1983, 1988; Indoor Track (W), 1983, 1984

Los Angeles–Long Beach, CA
California State University, Long Beach: Volleyball (M), 1991; Volleyball (W), 1989
California State University, Northridge: Gymnastics (W), 1982
Pepperdine University: Baseball, 1992; Volleyball (M), 1985, 1986, 1992
University of California, Los Angeles: Golf (M), 1988; Golf (W), 1991; Gymnastics (M), 1984, 1987; Outdoor Track (M), 1987, 1988; Outdoor Track (W), 1982, 1983; Soccer, 1985, 1990; Softball, 1982, 1984, 1985, 1988, 1989, 1990; Swimming and Diving (M), 1982; Tennis (M), 1982, 1984; Volleyball (M), 1981, 1982, 1983, 1984, 1987, 1989; Volleyball (W), 1984, 1990, 1991
University of Southern California: Basketball (W), 1983, 1984; Outdoor Track (W), 1982, 1983; Tennis (M), 1991; Tennis (W), 1983, 1985; Volleyball (W), 1981; Volleyball (M), 1980, 1988, 1990

Louisville, KY–IN
University of Louisville: Basketball (M), 1980, 1986

Madison, WI
University of Wisconsin: Cross Country (M), 1984; Cross Country (W), 1984, 1985; Ice Hockey, 1981, 1983, 1990

Miami–Hialeah, FL
University of Miami: Baseball, 1982, 1985; Football (Division I-A), 1983, 1987, 1989; Golf (W), 1984

Monroe, LA
Northeast Louisiana University: Football (Division I-AA), 1987

New York, NY
Columbia University: Fencing, 1992

Norfolk–Virginia Beach–Newport News, VA
Old Dominion University: Field Hockey, 1982, 1983, 1984, 1988, 1990, 1991; Basketball (W), 1985

Oakland, CA
University of California, Berkeley: Swimming and Diving (M), 1980; Water Polo, 1991

Oklahoma City, OK
University of Oklahoma: Football (Division I-A), 1985; Golf (M), 1989

Philadelphia, PA
Temple University: Lacrosse (W), 1984
Villanova University: Basketball (M), 1985; Cross Country (W), 1989, 1990, 1991

Phoenix, AZ
Arizona State University: Baseball, 1981; Golf (M), 1990; Golf (W), 1990; Gymnastics (M), 1986; Wrestling, 1988

Provo–Orem, UT
Brigham Young University: Football (Division I-A), 1984; Golf (M), 1981

Raleigh–Durham, NC
Duke University: Basketball, 1991, 1992; Soccer, 1986
North Carolina State University: Basketball (M), 1983
University of North Carolina: Basketball (M), 1982, 1993; Field Hockey, 1989; Lacrosse (M), 1981, 1982, 1986, 1991; Soccer (W), 1982, 1983, 1984, 1986, 1987, 1988, 1990, 1991

Salt Lake City–Ogden, UT
University of Utah: Gymnastics (W), 1982, 1983, 1984, 1985, 1986, 1990, 1992; Skiing, 1981, 1983, 1984, 1986, 1987, 1988

San Francisco, CA
University of San Francisco: Soccer (M), 1980

Legalized Gambling by State/Province

State/Province	Lotteries	Horses	Greyhounds	Casinos	Card Rooms	Bingo	Charitable
Alabama			•			•	
Alaska						•	•
Alberta	•	•				•	•
Arizona	•	•	•			•	•
Arkansas		•					•
British Columbia	•	•				•	•
California	•	•			•	•	
Colorado	•	•	•	•		•	•
Connecticut	•	•	•	•		•	•
Delaware	•	•				•	•
District of Columbia	•					•	•
Florida	•	•	•			•	•
Georgia						•	•
Hawaii							
Idaho	•	•	•				
Illinois	•	•		•		•	•
Indiana	•					•	
Iowa	•	•	•	•		•	•
Kansas	•	•	•			•	•
Kentucky	•	•				•	
Louisiana	•	•		•		•	•
Maine	•	•				•	•
Manitoba	•	•		•		•	•
Maryland	•	•		•	•	•	•
Massachusetts	•	•	•			•	•
Michigan	•	•				•	•
Minnesota	•	•				•	•
Mississippi				•		•	•
Missouri	•					•	•
Montana	•	•		•	•	•	•
Nebraska	•					•	•
Nevada				•		•	
New Brunswick	•	•				•	
New Hampshire	•	•	•			•	•
New Jersey	•	•		•		•	•
New Mexico		•				•	•
New York	•	•				•	•
Newfoundland	•	•		•		•	•
North Carolina						•	
North Dakota				•		•	•
Nova Scotia	•	•				•	
Ohio	•	•				•	•
Oklahoma		•				•	
Ontario	•	•		•		•	
Oregon	•	•	•		•	•	•
Pennsylvania	•	•				•	
Prince Edward Island	•	•		•		•	•
Quebec	•	•				•	•
Rhode Island	•	•	•			•	•
Saskatchewan	•	•				•	•
South Carolina						•	
South Dakota	•	•		•	•	•	•
Tennessee							
Texas	•	•	•			•	•
Utah							
Vermont	•	•				•	•
Virginia	•	•				•	•
Washington	•	•			•	•	•
West Virginia	•	•	•			•	•
Wisconsin	•	•				•	•
Wyoming		•				•	•

Source: Gaming and Wagering Magazine, 1993.

San Jose, CA
San Jose State University: Golf (W), 1987, 1989, 1991, 1992
Stanford University: Baseball, 1987, 1988; Basketball (W), 1990, 1992; Gymnastics, 1992; Swimming and Diving (M), 1985, 1986, 1987, 1992; Swimming and Diving (W), 1983, 1989, 1992; Tennis (M), 1980, 1981, 1983, 1986, 1988, 1989, 1990, 1992; Tennis (W), 1982, 1984, 1986, 1987, 1988, 1989, 1990, 1991; Water Polo (M), 1980, 1981
University of Santa Clara: Soccer (M), 1989

Seattle, WA
University of Washington: Football (Division I-A), 1992

South Bend–Mishawaka, IN
University of Notre Dame: Football (Division I-A), 1988

State College, PA
Pennsylvania State University: Fencing, 1990, 1991; Football (Division I-A), 1982, 1986

Stockton, CA
University of the Pacific: Volleyball (W), 1985, 1986

Syracuse, NY
Syracuse University: Lacrosse (M), 1983, 1988, 1989, 1990

Tallahassee, FL
Florida State University: Indoor Track (W), 1985; Outdoor Track (W), 1984

Toledo, OH
Bowling Green University: Ice Hockey, 1984

Trenton, NJ
Princeton University: Lacrosse (W), 1992

Tucson, AZ
University of Arizona: Baseball, 1980, 1986; Golf (M), 1992; Softball (W), 1991

Tulsa, OK
University of Tulsa: Golf (W), 1982, 1988

Tuscaloosa, AL
University of Alabama: Football (Division I-A); Gymnastics (W), 1988, 1991

Washington, DC–MD–VA
George Mason University: Soccer (W), 1985
Georgetown University: Basketball (M), 1984
University of Maryland: Field Hockey, 1987; Lacrosse (W), 1992

Wichita, KS
Wichita State University: Baseball, 1989

Wilmington, DE–NJ–MD
University of Delaware: Lacrosse (W), 1983

Youngstown, OH
Youngstown State University: Football (Division I-AA), 1991

Source: National Collegiate Athletic Association, College Champions, 1993.

In Division I-A Football, the NCAA recognizes as unofficial national champion the team selected each year by the Associated Press poll of sportswriters and the United Press International poll of coaches.

CIAU Championships in the Metro Areas

Canadian college athletes get only three years to play in interuniversity competition. Because there are no athletic scholarships, many football and hockey stars are playing at American universities. Still, rivalry among institutions here goes back to the midnineteenth century; Canadian football predates American football by several years, and ice hockey, the national sport, was invented here.

Calgary, ON
University of Calgary: Football, 1983, 1985, 1988

Edmonton, AB
University of Alberta: Ice Hockey, 1992

Kitchener, ON
Wilfred Laurier University: Football, 1991

London, ON
University of Western Ontario: Football, 1989; Basketball, 1991

Montreal, PQ
Concordia University: Basketball, 1990
McGill University: Football, 1987

St. Catharines–Niagara, ON
Brock University: Basketball, 1992

Saskatoon, SK
University of Saskatchewan: Ice Hockey, 1983; Football, 1990

Toronto, ON
University of Toronto: Ice Hockey, 1984
York University: Ice Hockey, 1985, 1988, 1989

Trois-Rivieres, PQ
Université de Quebec: Ice Hockey, 1987, 1991

Vancouver, BC
University of British Columbia: Football, 1986

Victoria, BC
University, of Victoria: Basketball, 1983, 1984, 1985, 1986

Climate

"The Fortunate people of the planet," John Kenneth Galbraith wrote years ago in *Harper's*, "are those who live by the seasons. There is far more difference between a Vermont farm in the summer and that farm in the winter than there is between San Diego and São Paulo. This means that people who live where the seasons are good and strong have no need to travel; they can stay at home and let change come to them. This simple truth will one day be recognized and then we will see a great reverse migration from Florida to Maine and on into Quebec."

Galbraith's forecast may be too optimistic. Pathways to seasonal sun are well worn; a quick count of Maine and Quebecois license plates in Florida and Texas Gulf parking lots in February proves that. Americans and Canadians say they prefer mild, sunny climates, and when asked where in the continent these climates are, they point to the fast-growing lower half of the Pacific Coast, Florida, and anywhere along the South Atlantic and Gulf Coast Shore. Certainly this area, between 25 degrees and 35 degrees latitude, has been drawing migrants for decades.

But other places north of the Mason-Dixon line and hundreds of miles from ocean beaches benefit from population growth, and many of these enjoy mild climates, too. Some of these places might surprise you.

What has always been surprising is the enormous variety of global climates found right here at home. Northern maritime, mild Mediterranean, southerly mountain, lowland desert, tropical "paradise," desert highland, rugged northern continental, windward slope, leeward slope, humid subtropical—you name it, and you'll meet up with it somewhere in North America.

Climate is a part of your circumstances that can't be bought, built, remodeled, or relocated. A place's climate is there for keeps, and the weather events that make up a place's climate—rain, snow, heat, cold, drought, wind—will have a profound effect on your life.

SIX FACTORS TO KEEP IN MIND

If you can live anywhere you wish and are open to all the variety the continent offers, know that a combination of water, latitude, elevation, prevailing winds, mountain

North American Extremes

Coterminous United States

Geographic center: near Lebanon, Smith County, Kansas
Northernmost point: Lake of the Woods Projection, Minnesota
Southernmost point: Cape Sable, Florida
Easternmost point: West Quoddy Head, Maine
Westernmost point: Cape Alava, Washington
Highest point: Mount Whitney, California: 14,494 feet

United States and Outlying Areas

Geographic center (50 states): Castle Rock, Butte County, South Dakota
Northernmost point: Point Barrow, Alaska
Southernmost point: Orote Point, Guam
Easternmost point: East Point, St. Croix, Virgin Islands
Westernmost point: Kure Island, Hawaii
Highest point: Mount McKinley, Alaska: 20,320 feet

Canada

Geographic center: Arviat, Northwest Territories
Northernmost point: Cape Columbia, Ellesmere Island
Southernmost point: Middle Island, Lake Erie
Easternmost point: Cape Spear, Newfoundland
Westernmost point: Yukon–Alaska border
Highest point: Mount Logan, Yukon: 19,524 feet

Source: U.S. Geological Survey; Canadian National Atlas Information Service.

Inheriting Climates

By the year 2020, greenhouse warming will cause these Canadian metro areas to have the same climates that American metro areas farther south have now.

Toronto, ON	Indianapolis, IN
Sudbury, ON	Cleveland–Lorain–Elyria, OH
Winnipeg, MB	Minneapolis–St. Paul, MN–WI
Edmonton, AB	Cheyenne, WY
Vancouver, BC	San Francisco, CA

Source: Environment Canada, *Climates of Canada.*

ranges, and urban development lies behind any metro area's climate.

Water, particularly an ocean, takes the edge off temperature. It warms up slowly, holds much more heat than does land, and cools more slowly. Places near or surrounded by water tend to be cooler in summer and warmer in winter than others far from water. The hottest it gets in July on the Santa Monica Pier in Los Angeles is 75 degrees Fahrenheit; meanwhile, 15 miles north in the San Fernando Valley, it's 95. If Toronto were to be gathered up and then set down at the same latitude, but hundreds of miles west of its Lake Ontario shore, winter would arrive a month sooner and spring a month later.

Places located in the continent's heartland away from the moderating effects of water experience wide swings of temperature. These continental climates tend to be even more rigorous in the higher *latitudes*. The closer to the poles you get, the more exaggerated the seasonal shifts, because extreme northerly locations see the greatest seasonal variation in the amount and intensity of sunlight. In Fairbanks, Alaska, the average period between the sun's rising and setting during December is just 4 hours. But in late June, the period lengthens to more than 18 hours, and Fairbanks becomes an intensely sunlit spot. Places in the North and far North, then, can experience not only Siberian winters but short, sunbaked summers.

Elevation, or height above sea level, has the same effect as a higher latitude. Each 1,000 feet of elevation lowers the average temperature by 3.3 degrees Fahrenheit. In New Mexico, for example, there are just 3 degrees of difference in annual average temperature between two weather stations at similar elevations, one in the extreme northeast and the other in the extreme southwest. However, at two weather stations just 15 miles apart, but differing in elevation by 4,700 feet, the average annual temperatures differ by 16 degrees.

In the United States, places that combine high altitudes with southerly latitudes get the mild, short winters of the South and the cooler nights and crisp falls of the North. Asheville, NC, in the southern Appalachians, and Sante Fe, NM, in the southern Rockies, have long been known for their mild, four-season climates.

To understand how *prevailing winds* influence climate, look at a pair of metro areas 3,200 miles apart: Portland, OR, and Portland, ME. Each is located at a northerly latitude. Both are situated on ocean coasts. You would naturally suppose the two Portlands would have similar climates.

But Portland, OR, is much milder because of the winds that blow from west to east across the continent. The West Coast is a landfall for air that has moved thousands of miles over water; cities even hundreds of

Windy Metro Areas

	Average Wind Speed
St. John's, NF	15.1 mph
Amarillo, TX	13.6
Rochester, MN	13.1
Casper, WY	13.0
Cheyenne, WY	13.0
Great Falls, MT	13.0
Regina, SK	13.0

Listed above are those metro areas described in the Place Profiles with average annual wind speeds of 13 mph or higher.

Damp Metro Areas

	Relative Humidity
St. John's, NF	83%
Halifax, NS	81
Vancouver, BC	81
Beaumont–Port Arthur, TX	77
Galveston–Texas City, TX	77
Lake Charles, LA	77
Olympia, WA	77
Corpus Christi, TX	76
Eugene–Springfield, OR	76
Gainesville, TX	76
Brownsville–Harlingen–San Benito, TX	75
Houston, TX	75
New Orleans, LA	75
Toronto, ON	75

Dry Metro Areas

	Relative Humidity
Las Vegas NV–AZ	30%
Phoenix–Mesa, AZ	37
Yuma, AZ	38
Tucson, AZ	39
El Paso, TX	42
Albuquerque, NM	44

Listed above are those metro areas described in the Place Profiles with an average annual relative humidity of 75 percent or more or 50 percent or less.

Wet Metro Areas

	Annual Precipitation Days
St. John's, NF	217 days
Quebec City, PQ	175
Syracuse, NY	171
Buffalo–Niagara Falls, NY	169
Erie, PA	164
Olympia, WA	163
Vancouver, BC	163
Montreal, PQ	162
Binghamton, NY	161
Youngstown, OH	160
Seattle–Bellevue–Everett, WA	160

Listed above are those metro areas described in the Place Profiles with 160 or more precipitation days per year. A precipitation day is one on which at least .01 inch of precipitation falls.

miles inland still feel some of the beneficial effects of the Pacific winds. Interior cities in the East feel few consequences of the Atlantic save on those rare occasions when the prevailing wind direction doesn't prevail. Sad to say, this reversal of wind direction often means a storm.

Mountain ranges act as giant barriers that deflect and channel winds, rain, and snow. Mountain people aren't relating folk tales when they tell visitors that the weather on one side of a mountain range is often radically different from that on the other. The windward side of British Columbia's Coast Mountains is a lush coastal rain forest; the leeward side, a dry grass and sagebrush steppe.

Snowy Metro Areas

	Average Annual Snowfall
St. John's, NF	141 in
Quebec City, PQ	135
Syracuse, NY	111
Grand Rapids–Muskegon–Holland, MI	98
Montreal, PQ	93
Buffalo–Niagara Falls, NY	91
Ottawa–Hull, ON–PQ	89
Rochester, NY	88
Erie, PA	85
Binghamton, NY	82

Listed above are those metro areas described in the Place Profiles with average annual snowfalls of 80 inches or more.

Finally, *urban development* makes heat islands within the surrounding countryside. Office buildings, factories, and cars produce enormous amounts of waste heat. Brick, concrete, and asphalt surfaces absorb and store heat during the day; at night the stored heat drifts up into the air, keeping the city from cooling off. At night in winter, Montreal's core can be 30 degrees warmer than the environs. In general, wind speed, visibility, sunshine, and heating needs are less in the center of the city than in nearby country, but temperature, cloudiness, thunderstorm frequency, and air pollution levels are higher.

SCORING: CLIMATE

Temperature affects human comfort and daily range of activities more than any other climate-related variable. Bioclimatologists—scientists who study the connection between weather and health—generally agree that an average temperature of 65 degrees Fahrenheit with 65-percent humidity is ideal for work, play, and general well-being. *Places Rated* uses 65 degrees Fahrenheit as a standard for mildness in the discussions that follow.

Because most people tend to favor mild, sunny climates, *Places Rated* compares the 343 metro areas on the basis of climate mildness, using a combination of temperature and humidity factors. "Mild" does not necessarily mean warm but simply refers to the absence of great variations or extremes of temperature. A mild climate has cool summers and warm winters, with long falls and springs. *Places Rated* defines the mildest climates as those whose mean temperatures remain closest to 65 degrees Fahrenheit for the longest time. Departures from this figure are labeled negative indicators, and are scored as such. Each place's final score indicates its climate mildness.

Cold Metro Areas

Annual Freezing Days

Regina, SK	204 days
Calgary, AB	201
Winnipeg, MB	195
Anchorage, AK	191
Bismarck, ND	186
Duluth–Superior, WI–MN	185
Edmonton, AB	185

Listed above are metro areas described in the Place Profiles with freezing days more than half the year.

Stormy Metro Areas

Thunderstorm Days

Fort Myers–Cape Coral, FL	93
Tampa–St.Petersburg–Clearwater, FL	88
Tallahassee, FL	86
Orlando, FL	81
Mobile, AL	80
Miami, FL	75
Galveston–Texas City, TX	70
Alexandria, LA	69
Houston, TX	69
New Orleans, LA	68

Listed above are metro areas described in the Place Profiles with more than 65 thunderstorm days a year.

Some of the figures presented are referred to as 30-year normals—averages collected over three decades. Each 10 years, the data for the new decade are added into the normal, and the data for the earliest 10 years are dropped. Data are collected and averaged over this period to flatten out irregularities and weather extremes. Atypical events such as a blizzard in San Antonio or a heat wave in Vancouver have little overall effect on a 30-year normal.

Sunny Metro Areas

Percent Possible Sunshine

Yuma, AZ	90%
Redding, CA	88
Phoenix–Mesa, AZ	86
Las Vegas, NV	85
Tucson, AZ	85
El Paso, TX	84
Fresno, CA	79
Reno, NV	79
Sacramento, CA	78
Albuquerque, NM	76

Gray Metro Areas

Percent Possible Sunshine

St. John's, NF	34%
Quebec City, PQ	41
Anchorage, AK	43
Vancouver, BC	43
Halifax, NS	44
Ottawa–Hull, ON–PQ	45
Montreal, PQ	46
Pittsburgh, PA	46
Seattle–Bellevue–Everett, WA	46
Syracuse, NY	46
Grand Rapids–Muskegon–Holland, MI	47
Toronto, ON	47
Portland, OR	48

Listed above are those metro areas described in the Place Profiles with annual sunshine potentials of at least 75 percent or less than 50 percent.

Each metro area is given a base number of 1,000 points, from which points are subtracted according to the following indicators:

1. *Very hot and very cold months.* Ten points are subtracted for each month in which the average temperature is above 70 degrees or below 32. An additional 10 points are subtracted, for a total of 20 points, if the mean temperature is above 80 degrees or below 20.
2. *Seasonal temperature variation.* The difference in degrees Fahrenheit between the summer mean maximum temperature and the winter mean minimum is subtracted from the base score.
3. *Heating- and cooling-degree days.* The total number of these days per year is divided by 50, and the result is subtracted from the score. The base temperature for arriving at heating- and cooling-degree days is 65 degrees, the standard established by the American gas industry. If, for example, the average temperature on a summer day is 66 degrees, 1 degree of cooling is needed, which counts as 1 cooling-degree day. Similarly, if the average temperature on a particular winter day is 55 degrees, 10 degrees of heating are needed, yielding 10 heating-degree days.
4. *Freezing days.* One point is subtracted for each day on which the average temperature is 32 degrees or below.
5. *Zero-degree days.* Five additional points are subtracted for each day the temperature drops to zero or below.
6. *Ninety-degree days.* Since relative humidity has a profound effect on felt heat and daily temperature range, points are subtracted in accord-

ance with each location's mean relative humidity at noon in July, when high temperatures are most likely to occur (see the map on page 392). For each day with a high of at least 90 degrees, 4 points are subtracted if the metro area's July relative humidity is more than 60 percent, 3 points if relative humidity is 51 percent to 60 percent, 2 points if relative humidity is 41 percent to 50 percent, and 1 point if relative humidity is 40 percent or lower.

SCORING EXAMPLES

Phoenix and San Francisco experience dramatically contrasting climate types: desert and marine.

Phoenix, AZ (#181)

If Phoenix's summertime temperatures of 50 years ago were to have persisted to this day, the Arizona capital might be rated much higher than the ranking by *Places Rated*'s standards for climate mildness.

According to climatologists at Arizona State University (ASU), afternoon high temperatures during June, July, and August have remained constant over the years, but low temperatures during those months are now 8 degrees hotter than they were in 1948. These 8 degrees make the difference between formerly bearable warm nights and currently oppressive, hot ones. The change is due to the extraordinary 12-fold increase in population since the end of World War II.

Longtime residents who recall the old desert cowtown days blame the heat on humidity caused by evaporating surface water in swimming pools, fountains, and man-made lakes. Actually, atmospheric moisture hasn't changed much since the late 1940s. According to the ASU scientists, modern Phoenix, with a population of 2.1 million, has classic "urban heat island" features: (1) the ability of concrete and asphalt to absorb and store more radiant energy than natural vegetation and soil, (2) low winds, (3) man-made sources of heat, especially the automobile, and (4) a persistent high-pressure cell that traps air pollution, creating a blanket effect.

There can be no doubt that temperatures in the Valley of the Sun are mild much of the year. Catch a Scottsdale golf tournament on TV in November and you may wish you were there. The biggest comfort liability here, however, is a period from mid-May through September when temperatures rarely drop to 65 degrees at night and usually exceed 100 degrees during the day. More than any other climate factor, it is Phoenix's intense summer heat that influences this metro area's mediocre climate rating.

San Francisco, CA (#1)

Beware of chamber of commerce blandishments about a place's annual average temperature. San Francisco's is 57 degrees. So is St. Louis's. But San Francisco enjoys both a diurnal (24-hour) temperature range of 12 degrees and an annual range (the difference between January's and July's average temperatures) of 12 degrees. St. Louis has a diurnal range of 17 degrees and an annual range of 47.

The temperature swings in these two cities highlight the difference between a marine climate and a continental climate. San Francisco's climate is somewhat cool and remarkably stable year-round. St. Louis's is neither.

In spite of sea fogs and the low stratus associated with them (which appeals to many San Franciscans), this metro area's percent of possible sunshine is greater than that of New York, Boston, and Washington, DC. But more than any other factor, it is San Francisco's infrequent extremes of heat and cold, coupled with a temperature range ideal for human activity and comfort, that produces the top *Places Rated* climate rating.

Rankings: Climate

Six criteria are used to determine a score for climate mildness: (1) very hot and very cold months, (2) seasonal temperature variation, (3) heating- and cooling-degree days, (4) freezing days, (5) zero-degree days, and (6) 90-degree days.

Because the NOAA publication *Local Climatological Data* does not provide specific data for all metro areas in the United States, the scores for some places are calculated from data for the nearest substation (this information appears in the *NOAA Series 20*). Scores derived in this way are enclosed in parentheses. Metro areas that receive tie scores get the same rank and are listed in alphabetical order.

Those metro areas described in the Place Profiles later on in this chapter are shown in boldface type in the list below.

Metro Areas from Best to Worst

Places Rated Rank	Places Rated Score	Places Rated Rank	Places Rated Score	Places Rated Rank	Places Rated Score
1. Oakland, CA	(910)	36. Long Island, NY	(656)	67. Monmouth–Ocean, NJ	(615)
1. **San Francisco, CA**	910	37. **Greenville–Spartanburg–Anderson, SC**	655	67. Riverside–San Bernardino, CA	(615)
3. **San Diego, CA**	903	38. **St. John's, NF**	654	67. Santa Fe, NM	(615)
4. Ventura, CA	(890)	39. **Roanoke, VA**	652		
5. **Los Angeles–Long Beach, CA**	885	40. Bridgeport, CT	648	67. Vineland–Millville–Bridgeton, NJ	(615)
5. Orange County, CA	885	40. Stamford–Norwalk, CT	(648)	72. Reading, PA	(614)
5. San Luis Obispo–Atascadero–Paso Robles, CA	(885)	42. **Raleigh–Durham–Chapel Hill, NC**	647	73. **Birmingham, AL**	612
5. **Santa Barbara–Santa Maria–Lompoc, CA**	885	43. **Charlotte–Gastonia–Rock Hill, NC–SC**	644	74. **Medford–Ashland, OR**	611
9. **Vancouver, BC**	857	44. New Bedford–Fall River–Attleboro, MA	(643)	75. **Amarillo, TX**	609
10. San Jose, CA	(850)	45. Lynchburg, VA	642	75. London, ON	609
11. Victoria, BC	847			77. Yuba City, CA	(608)
12. Salinas, CA	(843)	46. Modesto, CA	(639)	78. Erie, PA	605
12. Santa Cruz–Watsonville, CA	(843)	47. **New York, NY**	638	78. Greenville, NC	(605)
14. Vallejo–Fairfield–Napa, CA	(821)	48. Huntington–Ashland, WV–KY–OH	636	80. **Lubbock, TX**	604
15. Bremerton, WA	(808)	48. Trenton, NJ	(636)		
		50. **Lexington, KY**	635	81. Chico–Paradise, CA	(603)
15. **Seattle–Bellevue–Everett, WA**	808	51. **Miami, FL**	634	81. **Odessa–Midland, TX**	(603)
15. Tacoma, WA	(808)	52. St. Catharines–Niagara, ON	633	83. Fort Pierce–Port St. Lucie, FL	(602)
18. Bellingham, WA	(772)	53. **Norfolk–Virginia Beach–Newport News, VA–NC**	632	83. Windsor, ON	602
19. **Portland, OR**	768	54. **Washington, DC–MD–VA–WV**	631	85. Athens, GA	601
19. Vancouver, WA	(768)	55. **Philadelphia, PA–NJ**	630	85. Newark–Jersey City, NJ	(601)
21. **Eugene–Springfield, OR**	741	55. Rocky Mount, NC	(630)	87. Decatur, AL	(600)
22. Santa Rosa, CA	(732)	57. **Charleston, WV**	627	87. **Huntsville, AL**	600
23. **Galveston–Texas City, TX**	(727)	58. **Greensboro–Winston-Salem–High Point, NC**	626	87. **Nashville, TN**	600
24. Olympia, WA	726	59. Goldsboro, NC	(625)	90. Dover, DE	597
25. Honolulu, HI	717	59. Stockton–Lodi, CA	625	90. Wilmington–Newark, DE–MD	597
26. Salem, OR	716			92. Jamestown, NY	(595)
27. **Atlanta, GA**	696	61. **Boston, MA**	623	93. Oshawa, ON	593
28. **Asheville, NC**	694	61. Hickory–Morgantown, NC	(623)	94. **Boise City, ID**	592
29. Barnstable–Yarmouth, MA	690	63. Charlottesville, VA	(618)	94. El Paso, TX	592
30. Knoxville, TN	670	64. Hamilton, ON	617		
		64. Parkersburg–Marietta, WV–OH	617	96. Cumberland, MD–WV	(591)
31. **Halifax, NS**	669			97. **Tucson, AZ**	589
32. Redding, CA	664	66. Louisville, KY–IN	616	98. **Pittsburgh, PA**	586
32. Richland–Kennewick–Pasco, WA	(664)	67. Atlantic City–Cape May, NJ	615	98. **Providence–Warwick–Cranston, RI**	586
34. **Johnson City–Kingsport–Bristol, TN–VA**	663			100. **Richmond–Petersburg, VA**	585
35. Albuquerque, NM	659			101. Biloxi–Gulfport–Pascagoula, MS	(584)
				101. **Cincinnati, OH–KY–IN**	584

Places Rated Rank	Places Rated Score
103. New Haven–Meriden, CT	(583)
103. New London–Norwich, CT–RI	(583)
105. Melbourne–Titusville–Palm Bay, FL	(582)
106. Joplin, MO	(580)
106. Merced, CA	(580)
108. **Cleveland–Lorain–Elyria, OH**	579
109. **Chattanooga, TN–GA**	576
109. **Sacramento, CA**	576
109. Yolo, CA	(576)
112. **Akron, OH**	**575**
112. Canton–Massillon, OH	(575)
112. Scranton–Wilkes-Barre–Hazleton, PA	575
112. State College, PA	(575)
112. **Toronto, ON**	575
117. **Spokane, WA**	574
118. Fort Lauderdale, FL	(572)
119. **Buffalo–Niagara Falls, NY**	571
120. Sharon, PA	(570)
120. Youngstown–Warren, OH	(570)
122. **Charleston–North Charleston, SC**	569
122. Danbury, CT	(569)
122. Waterbury, CT	(569)
125. Hagerstown, MD	(568)
126. **Baltimore, MD**	567
127. Benton Harbor, MI	(566)
128. Jacksonville, NC	(564)
128. Myrtle Beach, SC	(564)
128. **Wilmington, NC**	564
131. Worcester–Fitchburg–Leominster, MA	562
132. Altoona, PA	(561)
132. **Daytona Beach, FL**	**(561)**
132. Fayetteville, NC	(561)
132. Saint John, NB	561
136. Anniston, AL	(560)
136. **Bakersfield, CA**	560
138. **Allentown–Bethlehem–Easton, PA–NJ**	**559**
138. Central New Jersey, NJ	(559)
138. **Fresno, CA**	559
138. Lancaster, PA	559
138. Northern New Jersey, NJ	(559)
143. Bloomington, IN	(558)
143. **Columbus, OH**	558
143. Mansfield, OH	558
143. Williamsport, PA	558
147. **Indianapolis, IN**	557
147. Terre Haute, IN	(557)
149. **Harrisburg–Lebanon–Carlisle, PA**	(556)
149. **Las Vegas, NV–AZ**	556
151. Oklahoma City, OK	554
152. **Yuma, AZ**	553
153. Florence, SC	(552)
153. Las Cruces, NM	(552)
155. **Binghamton, NY**	550
155. **Evansville–Henderson, IN–KY**	550

Places Rated Rank	Places Rated Score
157. Fayetteville–Springdale–Rogers, AR	(549)
157. **Kansas City, MO–KS**	549
159. **Syracuse, NY**	548
159. Utica–Rome, NY	(548)
161. Johnstown, PA	547
162. Ann Arbor, MI	(546)
162. Florence, AL	(546)
164. Danville, VA	(545)
164. South Bend, IN	(545)
166. Clarksville–Hopkinsville, TN–KY	(544)
166. **Dallas, TX**	544
166. **Dayton–Springfield, OH**	544
166. **Springfield, MO**	544
170. Visalia–Tulare–Porterville, CA	(543)
171. Hamilton–Middletown, OH	(542)
171. **Savannah, GA**	542
171. Steubenville–Weirton, OH–WV	(542)
171. Wheeling, WV–OH	(542)
175. **Columbia, MO**	(541)
175. **Salt Lake City–Ogden, UT**	541
177. Flint, MI	540
177. York, PA	(540)
179. Manchester–Nashua, NH	(538)
180. **St. Louis, MO–IL**	537
181. **Detroit, MI**	536
181. Fort Walton Beach, FL	(536)
181. Panama City, FL	536
181. **Pensacola, FL**	536
181. **Phoenix–Mesa, AZ**	536
181. Rochester, NY	536
187. **Reno, NV**	535
187. **Yakima, WA**	535
189. **Augusta–Aiken, GA–SC**	534
190. Muncie, IN	(530)
190. Sumter, SC	(530)
190. **Tulsa, OK**	530
193. Fort Worth–Arlington, TX	(528)
194. Kalamazoo–Battle Creek, MI	(527)
195. **Colorado Springs, CO**	526
195. **Columbia, SC**	526
195. Gadsden, AL	(526)
198. Champaign–Urbana, IL	(525)
199. Owensboro, KY	(524)
199. Sherman–Denison, TX	(524)
199. **Springfield, IL**	**524**
202. Lima, OH	(522)
203. **Abilene, TX**	521
203. **Denver, CO**	521
203. Elkhart–Goshen, IN	(521)
206. Alexandria, LA	520
207. **Jackson, MS**	(518)
207. **Toledo, OH**	518
209. **Columbus, GA–AL**	(517)
210. **Hartford, CT**	516
211. Kitchener, ON	515
211. Saginaw–Bay City–Midland, MI	(515)
213. **Chicago, IL**	514
213. Lake County, IL	514

Places Rated Rank	Places Rated Score
213. **Memphis, TN–AR–MS**	514
216. **Grand Rapids–Muskegon–Holland, MI**	513
216. Lawrence, KS	(513)
218. Kokomo, IN	(512)
218. **Montreal, PQ**	512
220. Cheyenne, WY	(509)
220. **Fort Wayne, IN**	509
220. Orange County, NY	(509)
220. West Palm Beach–Boca Raton, FL	509
224. **Shreveport–Bossier City, LA**	508
225. Topeka, KS	501
226. Longview–Marshall, TX	(500)
226. Provo–Orem, UT	(500)
226. Tyler, TX	(500)
229. **New Orleans, LA**	498
230. **Little Rock–North Little Rock, AR**	497
230. Pueblo, CO	497
232. Kenosha, WI	(496)
232. Racine, WI	(496)
234. Lafayette, IN	(494)
234. **Wichita, KS**	494
236. **Peoria–Pekin, IL**	491
237. Fort Collins–Loveland, CO	(490)
237. Greeley, CO	(490)
237. Lewiston–Auburn, ME	(490)
240. Dutchess County, NY	(488)
240. **San Angelo, TX**	488
242. Bloomington–Normal, IL	(487)
243. Trois-Rivieres, PQ	485
244. Gary, IN	(483)
244. Kankakee, IL	(483)
244. **Montgomery, AL**	483
244. **Ottawa–Hull, ON–PQ**	483
244. **Portland, ME**	483
249. **Fort Smith, AR–OK**	482
249. Pittsfield, MA	(482)
251. Decatur, IL	(480)
251. Lansing–East Lansing, MI	480
253. Lawton, OK	(479)
254. **Albany–Schenectady–Troy, NY**	476
254. Glens Falls, NY	(476)
256. St. Joseph, MO	(475)
257. Tuscaloosa, AL	(470)
258. Lake Charles, LA	469
258. Portsmouth–Dover–Rochester, NH	(469)
260. Albany, GA	(468)
261. Elmira, NY	(467)
261. Texarkana, TX–Texarkana, AR	(467)
263. Janesville–Beloit, WI	(466)
263. **Rockford, IL**	466
265. Pine Bluff, AR	(463)
266. Enid, OK	(461)
267. **Milwaukee–Waukesha, WI**	460
268. Boulder–Longmont, CO	(459)
269. **Jacksonville, FL**	457
269. Orlando, FL	457

Places Rated Rank	Places Rated Score	Places Rated Rank	Places Rated Score	Places Rated Rank	Places Rated Score
271. Wichita Falls, TX	456	294. Brazoria, TX	(423)	320. Naples, FL	(348)
272. Monroe, LA	(455)				
273. Springfield, MA	(453)	296. Dubuque, IA	419	321. Waterloo–Cedar Falls, IA	(347)
274. Billings, MT	452	297. Jackson, MI	412	322. Fort Myers–Cape Coral, FL	(342)
275. Bangor, ME	(451)	297. Waco, TX	412	323. Dothan, AL	(336)
		299. Great Falls, MT	410	323. Victoria, TX	336
276. Macon, GA	(447)	300. Tallahassee, FL	404	325. Ocala, FL	(333)
277. Des Moines, IA	444				
278. Mobile, AL	442	301. Gainesville, FL	(402)	326. Rochester, MN	308
278. Sheboygan, WI	(442)	302. Casper, WY	401	326. Wausau, WI	(308)
280. Brownsville–Harlingen–San Benito, TX	440	302. Sherbrooke, PQ	401	328. Lakeland–Winter Haven, FL	(307)
		304. Lincoln, NE	398	329. Minneapolis–St. Paul, MN–WI	293
280. Davenport–Moline–Rock Island, IA–IL	440	304. San Antonio, TX	398	330. Chicoutimi–Jonquiere, PQ	287
280. Omaha, NE–IA	440	306. Appleton–Oshkosh–Neenah, WI	(396)	331. Thunder Bay, ON	284
280. Sarasota–Bradenton, FL	440	306. Punta Gorda, FL	(396)	332. Sioux Falls, SD	276
280. Tampa–St. Petersburg–Clearwater, FL	440	308. Edmonton, AB	385	333. Eau Claire, WI	257
285. Austin–San Marcos, TX	435	308. Sioux City, IA–NE	385	334. McAllen–Edinburg–Mission, TX	(238)
		310. Bryan–College Station, TX	(383)	335. Saskatoon, SK	199
286. Cedar Rapids, IA	(434)	310. Burlington, VT	383		
286. Iowa City, IA	(434)	312. Calgary, AB	381	336. Anchorage, AK	195
288. Quebec City, PQ	430	313. Madison, WI	378	336. St. Cloud, MN	(195)
289. Lafayette, LA	(429)	314. Sudbury, ON	375	338. Duluth–Superior, MN–WI	193
290. Baton Rouge, LA	427	315. Rapid City, SD	(373)	339. Regina, SK	174
				340. Winnipeg, MB	171
290. Houma, LA	(427)	316. Green Bay, WI	367		
292. Houston, TX	424	317. Killeen–Temple, TX	(365)	341. Bismarck, ND	149
292. Laredo, TX	(424)	318. Corpus Christi, TX	362	342. Fargo–Moorhead, ND–MN	148
294. Beaumont–Port Arthur, TX	423	319. La Crosse, WI–MN	352	343. Grand Forks, ND–MN	(105)

Place Profiles: Climate

The following pages are brief profiles of 146 weather stations across the continent. The narrative summaries describing climate and terrain at United States and Canadian points are condensed from those that appear in the National Oceanic and Atmospheric Administration's *Local Climatological Data*, and in Environment Canada's *Canadian Climate Program* series, respectively. Canadian climate data have been converted from Celsius and metric measurements to Fahrenheit and English measurements.

These summaries describe each metro area's distinctive climate and terrain features. When terrain is described, it is usually how it influences a place's climate. Few people would deny that terrain is an important element on its own; to many it's as important as climate. Some prefer mountains or seacoast, others rolling hills or flatwoods forest, while still others favor stark desert vistas. Rather than rating terrain, *Places Rated* simply describes it briefly and lets you decide.

The temperature table on the right-hand side of each profile gives you a clear idea of the temperature ranges, averages, and extremes of each place. If you want to know how hot it gets in Albuquerque in July, look at the table in Albuquerque's profile. In July the daily high-temperature (a point reached in midafternoon) average is 93 degrees Fahrenheit. That sounds hot, and it is. But note that the average low temperature (a point reached in the early morning) for the same month is only 65 degrees. July in Albuquerque means hot days and cool nights. This fits New Mexico's largest city's dry, desert location and 5,314-foot elevation.

Rounding out each metro area's climate picture are data for relative humidity, wind speed, amount of snow and rain, number of heating- and cooling-degree days, clear and cloudy days, storms, very hot and cold days, and precipitation days (days on which there is at least .01 inch of precipitation).

A unique graphic in each profile is the circular picture showing the length of the seasons. Seasonal change is best defined by weather conditions, human activities, and growth or dormancy of plant life rather than by the calendar.

In *Places Rated Almanac*, the seasons are defined as follows: Summer begins when the mean monthly temperature rises above 60 degrees Fahrenheit; summer ends when it falls below 60. Winter begins when the average daily low falls below 32 degrees and ends when it rises above that mark. The remaining portions of the year constititue fall and spring. In the seasonal graphs, winter is shown by the black segments, spring and fall appear as gray, and summer is white.

If you look at several of these seasonal graphs you'll see that the length of the seasons varies. Winter is a tiny sliver in Huntsville, AL, and a full half circle in Colorado Springs, CO. Some places have no four-season climates. Places along the Atlantic and Gulf coasts usually have only two—spring and summer. Some, like Honolulu or Miami, have only one—perpetual summer.

A check mark (✓) preceding a metro area's name hightlights it as one of the top 35 places in the country for climate mildness.

Abilene, TX

Terrain: Rolling plains, treeless except for mesquite, broken by low hills to the south and west. Land rises gently to the south and east. Primarily cattle-grazing terrain, with some dry-land cotton and feed.
Climate: Lies roughly midway between the humid climate of East Texas and the semiarid climate to the west and north. Most rain occurs in thunderstorms during April, May, June, September, and October. Severe storms or tornadoes are rare. Summer brings hot days and cool nights, with temperatures dropping to the 60s or 70s most nights. High summer temperatures are usually associated with clear skies, southwesterly winds, and dry air. Low relative humidity, however, makes the climate comfortable. The region receives almost 70% of possible sunshine over the year. Rapid temperature changes occur in winter, as polar air replaces warm, moist tropical air. Temperatures may fall 30 degrees in one hour. Strongest winds come from the north and often bring cold and severe weather.

Pluses: Warm, sunny, and dry.   **Minuses:** Hot summer days; can be dusty.

Places Rated Score: 521   **Places Rated Rank: 203**

Elevation: 1,790 feet

Wind Speed: 12.2 mph

Seasonal Change

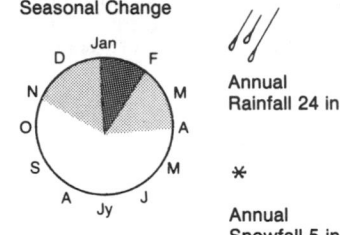

Annual Rainfall 24 in

Annual Snowfall 5 in

Clear 148 days   Partly Cloudy 98 days   Cloudy 119 days

Precipitation Days: 65   Storm Days: 42

Average Temperatures

	Daily High	Daily Low	Relative Humidity
January	56	31	63
February	60	36	64
March	69	43	59
April	78	53	59
May	84	61	65
June	92	69	64
July	95	73	59
August	95	72	60
September	87	65	66
October	78	54	63
November	65	42	63
December	58	34	63

Zero-Degree Days: 0
Freezing Days: 56
90-Degree Days: 89
Heating- and Cooling-Degree Days: 5,076

Akron, OH

Terrain: Rolling, with highest elevations almost 1,300 feet above sea level. Many small lakes provide water for local industry as well as recreation for the densely populated region. The area is mainly industrial; the number of agricultural operations has diminished rapidly in recent years.
Climate: Lake Erie has a considerable effect on area weather, tempering cold air masses during the winter and contributing to brief but heavy snow squalls until the lake freezes over. Snowfall is much heavier north of the weather station near the lake, in the area commonly referred to as the Snow Belt. Spring comes late here. Summers are moderately warm, though humid. September, October, and November are pleasant, but there is considerable morning fog. Average date of last freeze: April 30. First freeze: October 22.

Pluses: Pleasant falls.   **Minuses:** Cold, wet winters with heavy snowfalls; damp and cloudy.

Places Rated Score: 575   **Places Rated Rank: 112**

Elevation: 1,027 feet

Wind Speed: 9.9 mph

Seasonal Change

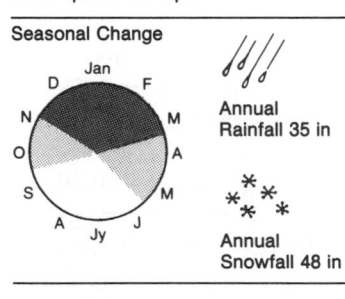

Annual Rainfall 35 in

Annual Snowfall 48 in

Clear 70 days   Partly Cloudy 101 days   Cloudy 194 days

Precipitation Days: 153   Storm Days: 40

Average Temperatures

	Daily High	Daily Low	Relative Humidity
January	33	17	74
February	36	19	72
March	46	28	68
April	59	38	65
May	70	48	66
June	79	57	68
July	82	61	70
August	81	60	73
September	74	53	74
October	63	42	70
November	49	33	72
December	38	23	74

Zero-Degree Days: 5
Freezing Days: 128
90-Degree Days: 7
Heating- and Cooling-Degree Days: 6,858

Albany–Schenectady–Troy, NY

Terrain: On the west bank of the Hudson River 150 miles north of New York City and 8 miles south of the confluence of the Hudson and Mohawk rivers. The point at which the city meets the river is only a few feet above sea level. Eleven miles west, the Helderberg escarpment rises to between 1,400 and 1,800 feet. To the east is a rugged valley floor rising to hills 1,600 to 2,000 feet high. The valley floor on which the city is located is gently rolling.

Climate: Harsh continental but subject to some moderating influences from the Atlantic, to the south. Winters are cold and occasionally severe. Maximum temperatures during cold months often do not rise above 32°F. In the warmer months, temperatures rise quickly during the day to moderate levels, then fall rapidly at night to moderate to cool. Occasional hot spells of a week or so occur during the summer. The growing season is about 160 days, long for a city in this latitude. Average date of last freeze: April 27. First freeze: October 13.

Pluses: Cool summer nights.   **Minuses:** Cold, snowy winters.

Places Rated Score: 476   **Places Rated Rank: 254**

Elevation: 292 feet

Wind Speed: 8.9 mph

Seasonal Change

Annual Rainfall 33 in

Annual Snowfall 71 in

Clear 71 days   Partly Cloudy 111 days   Cloudy 183 days

Precipitation Days: 135   Storm Days: 28

Average Temperatures			
	Daily High	Daily Low	Relative Humidity
January	30	12	70
February	33	14	68
March	43	25	64
April	58	36	61
May	70	45	65
June	78	55	68
July	83	60	68
August	81	58	72
September	73	50	74
October	62	39	72
November	48	31	72
December	35	18	73

Zero-Degree Days: 17
Freezing Days: 155
90-Degree Days: 8
Heating- and Cooling-Degree Days: 7,462

✓ Albuquerque, NM

Terrain: Rests in the Rio Grande Valley 55 miles southwest of Santa Fe, and is surrounded by mountains, most of them to the east. These mountainous areas receive more precipitation than does the city proper. With an annual rainfall of 8 inches, only the most hardy desert flora can grow. However, successful farming—primarily fruit and produce—is carried out in the valley by irrigation.

Climate: Arid continental. No muggy days. Half the moisture falls between July and September in the form of brief but severe thunderstorms. Long drizzles are unknown. These storms do not greatly interfere with outdoor activities, and they have a moderating effect on the heat. The hottest month is July, with temperatures reaching 90°F almost constantly. However, the low humidity and cool nights make the heat much less felt.

Pluses: Sunny and dry, with   **Minuses:** Dust storms.
mild winters.

Places Rated Score: 659   **Places Rated Rank: 35**

Elevation: 5,314 feet

Wind Speed: 9 mph

Seasonal Change

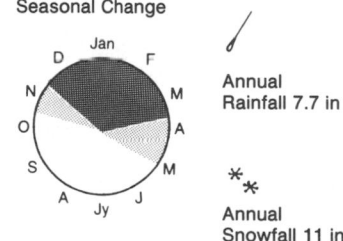

Annual Rainfall 7.7 in

Annual Snowfall 11 in

Clear 172 days   Partly Cloudy 111 days   Cloudy 82 days

Precipitation Days: 59   Storm Days: 43

Average Temperatures			
	Daily High	Daily Low	Relative Humidity
January	47	22	55
February	53	26	49
March	61	32	40
April	71	40	34
May	80	49	33
June	91	58	32
July	93	65	44
August	89	63	48
September	83	55	47
October	72	43	46
November	57	31	51
December	48	23	57

Zero-Degree Days: 1
Freezing Days: 123
90-Degree Days: 61
Heating- and Cooling-Degree Days: 5,608

Allentown–Bethlehem–Easton, PA–NJ

Terrain: Located in the east-central section of the state in the Lehigh River valley. The Blue Mountain lies 12 miles to the north; the South Mountain fringes the southern edge. Other than these rises of up to 2,000 feet, the country is gently rolling with numerous small streams.

Climate: Climate features of the area are modified by the mountain ranges; at times there may be 10 to 15 degrees difference between Allentown and Philadelphia, only 50 miles to the south. Summer maximum temperatures are not excessive; however, humidity is quite high and can cause much discomfort. Winters are comparatively mild, being only infrequently below zero.

Pluses: Mild winters, rarely   **Minuses:** Humid summers.
subfreezing.

Places Rated Score: 559   **Places Rated Rank: 138**

Elevation: 364 feet

Wind Speed: 9.2 mph

Seasonal Change

Annual Rainfall 44 in

Annual Snowfall 32 in

Clear 95 days   Partly Cloudy 111 days   Cloudy 159 days

Precipitation Days: 133   Storm Days: 33

Average Temperatures			
	Daily High	Daily Low	Relative Humidity
January	35	20	69
February	38	21	67
March	48	29	64
April	61	39	63
May	71	49	66
June	80	58	66
July	85	63	68
August	82	62	71
September	75	54	73
October	64	43	71
November	51	34	70
December	39	24	71

Zero-Degree Days: 2
Freezing Days: 155
90-Degree Days: 16
Heating- and Cooling-Degree Days: 6,599

Amarillo, TX

Terrain: Located in the heart of the Panhandle, Amarillo sits on the cap rock, or High Plains, of the Southwest. The area, which includes part of Oklahoma and northern Mexico, has often been called the Dust Bowl. It is a plateau with scrubby growth; cotton and sorghum are the primary crops. Amarillo lies between the Canadian and Red rivers.

Climate: The area is generally dry, but thunderstorms occur between April and September. This, however, can vary greatly from year to year, and droughts are fairly frequent. The area is subject to rapid and great temperature changes, especially in winter, when cold air comes down from the Plains and the Rocky Mountains at high speed. Nearness to paths of moving pressure systems causes strong winds, especially in March and April. Though summer days are hot, the low humidity lessens the felt heat and makes for pleasant mornings and nights.

Pluses: Sunny, dry, and mild, with distinct seasons.

Minuses: Hot; can be dusty.

Places Rated Score: 609

Places Rated Rank: 75

Elevation: 3,604 feet

Wind Speed: 13.7 mph

Seasonal Change

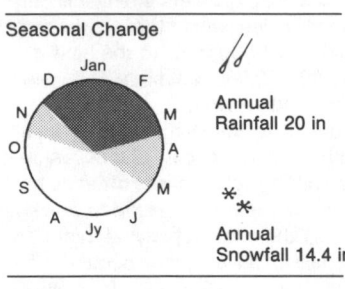

Annual Rainfall 20 in

Annual Snowfall 14.4 in

Clear 163 days | Partly Cloudy 102 days | Cloudy 100 days

Precipitation Days: 67   Storm Days: 48

Average Temperatures			
	Daily High	Daily Low	Relative Humidity
January	49	22	61
February	53	26	61
March	61	32	55
April	71	42	53
May	79	52	59
June	88	62	61
July	91	66	58
August	90	65	62
September	82	57	65
October	73	46	58
November	59	32	60
December	52	25	60

Zero-Degree Days: 2
Freezing Days: 108
90-Degree Days: 63
Heating- and Cooling-Degree Days: 5,616

Anchorage, AK

Terrain: Situated in a broad valley with adjacent narrow bodies of water. Terrain rises gradually to the east with marshes interspersed with glacial moraines, depressions, streams, and knolls. Beyond this area, the Chugach Mountains rise sharply to between 4,000 feet and 5,000 feet, with some peaks 8,000 feet to 10,000 feet high. These mountains block the warm air and the moisture from the Gulf of Alaska. Approximately 100 miles north lies the Alaska Range, which keeps much of the very cold air from the interior. Consequently, when temperatures in the interior are −50°F or −60°F, they will be −15°F to −30°F in Anchorage. The two ranges can also act as a trap, stalling very cold air when winds are light.

Climate: The four seasons are well marked in Anchorage, though in length and other characteristics they differ considerably from the standards of the middle latitudes. The rivers and lakes thaw in mid-April to early May. Snow arrives in October, leaves in mid-April.

Pluses: Well-defined, four-season climate.

Minuses: Rigorous.

Places Rated Score: 195

Places Rated Rank: 336

Elevation: 132 feet

Wind Speed: 6.7 mph

Seasonal Change

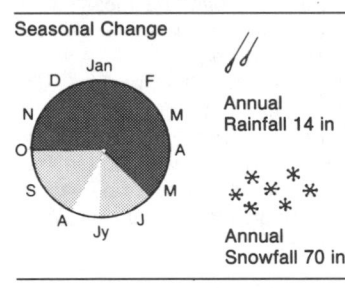

Annual Rainfall 14 in

Annual Snowfall 70 in

Clear 64 days | Partly Cloudy 67 days | Cloudy 234 days

Precipitation Days: 113   Storm Days: 1

Average Temperatures			
	Daily High	Daily Low	Relative Humidity
January	20	6	73
February	26	10	70
March	32	16	63
April	43	28	60
May	54	38	56
June	62	47	62
July	65	51	68
August	63	49	71
September	55	41	72
October	41	28	72
November	28	15	75
December	20	7	76

Zero-Degree Days: 41
Freezing Days: 192
90-Degree Days: 12
Heating- and Cooling-Degree Days: 10,911

✓ Asheville, NC

Terrain: Located on both banks of the French Broad River, near the center of the basin of the same name. Two miles upstream from Asheville, the Swannanoa River joins the French Broad River from the east. The entire valley is called the Asheville Plateau and is flanked on the east and west by mountain ranges. Thirty miles south, the Blue Ridge Mountains form an escarpment, with an average elevation of 2,700 feet. Tallest peaks near Asheville are Mount Mitchell (6,684 feet), 20 miles northeast, and Big Pisgah (5,721 feet), 16 miles southwest.

Climate: Temperate but invigorating. Considerable variation in temperature occurs from day to day throughout the year. The valley has a pronounced effect on wind direction, which is mostly from the northwest. Destructive weather events are rare. However, the French Broad Valley is subject to flooding, with especially high flooding occurring in 12-year cycles.

Pluses: Long spring, beginning early.

Minuses: Drizzly, flood-prone.

Places Rated Score: 694

Places Rated Rank: 28

Elevation: 2,207 feet

Wind Speed: 7.8 mph

Seasonal Change

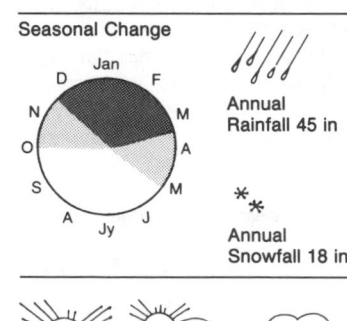

Annual Rainfall 45 in

Annual Snowfall 18 in

Clear 102 days | Partly Cloudy 107 days | Cloudy 156 days

Precipitation Days: 128   Storm Days: 49

Average Temperatures			
	Daily High	Daily Low	Relative Humidity
January	48	26	72
February	51	28	70
March	58	34	69
April	69	43	68
May	76	51	75
June	81	58	77
July	84	62	80
August	84	62	80
September	78	56	81
October	69	43	76
November	59	34	72
December	50	28	73

Zero-Degree Days: 1
Freezing Days: 106
90-Degree Days: 5
Heating- and Cooling-Degree Days: 5,109

✓ Atlanta, GA

Terrain: Located in the foothills of the southern Appalachians in north central Georgia. Terrain is rolling to hilly and slopes downward toward the east, west, and south. Because Atlanta has a mean elevation of 1,000 feet and a location on a plateau with mountains to the north, its exposure to the cold north air is blocked, and its elevation retards the moist hot air from the Gulf of Mexico.

Climate: Abundant rainfall fosters natural vegetation and growth of crops. In summer, afternoon high temperatures equal or exceed 90°F one day in five, but a temperature of 100° F is rare. Atlanta's winters are mild. Cold spells are not unusual, but they rarely disrupt outdoor activities for extended periods. Snow is very light and usually does not stay on the ground long. Ice storms, however, occur about one year in ten and cause heavy damage. Atlanta averages 50 thunderstorms a year, which occur mostly in the spring, sometimes spinning off destructive tornadoes. Average date of last freeze: March 24. First freeze: November 12. Average growing period: 233 days.

Pluses: Mild, sunny, pleasant.   **Minuses:** Hot summers, stormy.
Places Rated Score: 696   **Places Rated Rank: 27**

Elevation: 1,034 feet

Wind Speed: 9.1 mph

Seasonal Change

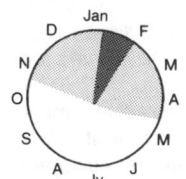

Annual Rainfall 48 in

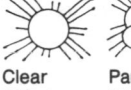

Annual Snowfall 2 in

Clear 108 days   Partly Cloudy 111 days   Cloudy 146 days

Precipitation Days: 116   Storm Days: 50

	Daily High	Daily Low	Relative Humidity
Average Temperatures			
January	51	33	69
February	55	35	65
March	63	42	65
April	73	50	64
May	80	59	68
June	86	66	70
July	88	69	74
August	88	69	75
September	82	64	74
October	73	51	69
November	63	41	68
December	54	35	69

Zero-Degree Days: 0
Freezing Days: 59
90-Degree Days: 19
Heating- and Cooling-Degree Days: 4,684

Atlantic City–Cape May, NJ

Terrain: Located on a sand island south of Absecon Inlet on the southeast coast of New Jersey. Surrounding terrain, composed of tidal marshes and beach sand, is flat and lies slightly above sea level.

Climate: Continental, but the moderating influence of the Atlantic Ocean is apparent throughout the year. Summers are relatively cooler, winters warmer than those of other places at the same latitude. During the warm season, sea breezes in the late morning and afternoon prevent excessive heat. On occasion, sea breezes may lower the temperature between 15 degrees and 20 degrees within a half hour. Temperatures of 90°F or higher are recorded only about three times a year here. Fall is long, lasting until almost mid-November. On the other hand, warming is somewhat delayed in the spring. Ocean temperatures range from an average near 37°F in winter to 72°F in August. Precipitation is moderate and well distributed throughout the year, but great variation is seen from year to year in precipitation during the late summer and early fall (August, September, and October).

Pluses: Moderate temperatures.   **Minuses:** Late springs.
Places Rated Score: 615   **Places Rated Rank: 67**

Elevation: 10 feet

Wind Speed: 10.7 mph

Seasonal Change

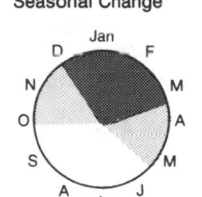

Annual Rainfall 46 in

Annual Snowfall 16 in

Clear 96 days   Partly Cloudy 108 days   Cloudy 161 days

Precipitation Days: 112   Storm Days: 25

	Daily High	Daily Low	Relative Humidity
Average Temperatures			
January	41	23	68
February	42	24	68
March	50	32	66
April	62	40	65
May	71	50	68
June	80	59	69
July	84	65	70
August	83	64	72
September	77	56	73
October	66	45	72
November	55	36	71
December	45	27	68

Zero-Degree Days: 1
Freezing Days: 15
90-Degree Days: 16
Heating- and Cooling-Degree Days: 5,810

Augusta–Aiken, GA–SC

Terrain: Located in eastern Georgia on the Savannah River, which forms part of the boundary between Georgia and South Carolina. The dividing line between the Piedmont Plateau and the Coastal Plain, which is known as the fall line, passes through the Savannah River basin in a northeast-southwest direction near Augusta. The terrain consists of low hills to the western half of the city and swampland immediately to the north and east.

Climate: Warm and mild, with occasional hot spells. In the winter, measurable snow is a rarity and remains on the ground only a short time. In 100 years of weather records, a temperature of zero or colder has never been reached. The growing season averages 241 days, from March 16 to November 16, although frosts have been reported as late as April 21 and as early as October 17. Although Augusta is protected from flooding of the Savannah River by two multipurpose dams, the potential for flooding still exists in some low-lying areas.

Pluses: Very brief winters.   **Minuses:** Can be hot, flood-prone.
Places Rated Score: 534   **Places Rated Rank: 189**

Elevation: 136 feet

Wind Speed: 6.6 mph

Seasonal Change

Annual Rainfall 43 in

Annual Snowfall 1.3 in

Clear 110 days   Partly Cloudy 107 days   Cloudy 148 days

Precipitation Days: 107   Storm Days: 55

	Daily High	Daily Low	Relative Humidity
Average Temperatures			
January	57	33	69
February	60	35	66
March	68	42	66
April	77	50	65
May	84	58	68
June	89	66	69
July	91	70	72
August	91	69	74
September	86	64	73
October	77	50	70
November	68	40	69
December	59	35	69

Zero-Degree Days: 0
Freezing Days: 59
90-Degree Days: 63
Heating- and Cooling-Degree Days: 4,542

Austin–San Marcos, TX

Terrain: Located on the Colorado River where it crosses the Balcones escarpment, which separates the Texas hill country from the blackland prairies of East Texas. Elevations within the city limits vary from 400 feet to 900 feet above sea level. Native trees include cedar, oak, walnut, mesquite, and pecan.

Climate: Subtropical. Although summers are hot, the nights are a bit cooler, with temperatures usually dropping into the 70s. Winters are mild, with below-freezing temperatures on fewer than 25 days; strong northers may bring cold spells, but these rarely last more than a few days. Precipitation is well distributed but heaviest in late spring, with a secondary rainfall peak in September. With summer come heavy thunderstorms; in winter, the rain tends to be slow and steady. Snowfall (1 inch per year) is inconsequential. Prevailing winds are southerly. Destructive weather is infrequent. Freeze-free season: 270 days. Average date of last freeze: March 3. First freeze: November 28.

Pluses: Mild winters.   **Minuses:** Hot.

Places Rated Score: 435   **Places Rated Rank:** 285

Elevation: 570 feet

Wind Speed: 9.4 mph

Seasonal Change

Annual Rainfall 33 in

Annual Snowfall 1 in

Clear 115 days   Partly Cloudy 116 days   Cloudy 134 days

Precipitation Days: 82   Storm Days: 41

Average Temperatures			
	Daily High	Daily Low	Relative Humidity
January	59	39	69
February	64	42	69
March	72	49	67
April	79	58	70
May	85	65	75
June	92	72	73
July	95	74	70
August	95	74	69
September	89	69	71
October	81	59	70
November	69	48	70
December	63	41	70

Zero-Degree Days: 0
Freezing Days: 23
90-Degree Days: 101
Heating- and Cooling-Degree Days: 4,645

Bakersfield, CA

Terrain: Situated in the extreme southern end of the great San Joaquin Valley, the city is partially surrounded by a horseshoe-shaped rim of mountains with an opening at the northwest. The Sierra Nevada to the northeast blocks much of the cold air that flows southward over the country in the winter. This range also catches and stores snow, which is used for irrigation in the valley below. The valley is suited for Mediterranean and specialized forms of agriculture.

Climate: Because of the surrounding topography, there are three different climates within short distances of each other: valley, mountain, and desert. The overall climate, however, is warm and semiarid. Ninety percent of the precipitation falls between October and April, typical of the southern half of California. Thunderstorms and snow are rare in the valley. Summers are hot, cloudless, and dry but occasionally relieved by ocean breezes from the west. Winters are mild. Average growing season: 265 days.

Pluses: Dry; mild winters.   **Minuses:** Hot summers.

Places Rated Score: 560   **Places Rated Rank:** 136

Elevation: 492 feet

Wind Speed: 6.4 mph

Seasonal Change

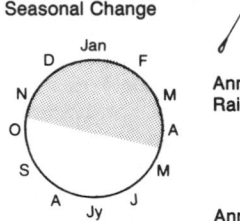

Annual Rainfall 6 in

Annual Snowfall 0 in

Clear 202 days   Partly Cloudy 79 days   Cloudy 84 days

Precipitation Days: 36   Storm Days: 3

Average Temperatures			
	Daily High	Daily Low	Relative Humidity
January	57	39	73
February	64	43	64
March	69	46	58
April	75	50	49
May	84	57	40
June	92	64	37
July	99	70	35
August	96	69	39
September	91	64	43
October	81	55	48
November	67	45	62
December	58	39	72

Zero-Degree Days: 0
Freezing Days: 11
90-Degree Days: 110
Heating- and Cooling-Degree Days: 4,364

Baltimore, MD

Terrain: Baltimore lies in a region about midway between the rigorous climates of the North and the mild ones of the South. It is also adjacent to the modifying influences of Chesapeake Bay and the Atlantic Ocean. Since this region is near the usual path of the low-pressure systems that move across the country, shifts in wind direction are frequent and contribute to the changeable character of the weather. The net effect of the Appalachian Mountains to the west and the ocean to the east is to produce an equable climate compared with other locations farther inland at the same latitude.

Climate: Rainfall is fairly uniform throughout the year but is greatest in late summer and early fall. This is also the time of hurricanes and severe thunderstorms. In summer, Baltimore is influenced by the great high-pressure system known as the Bermuda High. This high brings a constant flow of warm, humid air masses from the Deep South. These air masses, as well as the proximity of water, account for the high humidity here.

Pluses: Mild for its latitude.   **Minuses:** Humid, stormy.

Places Rated Score: 567   **Places Rated Rank:** 126

Elevation: 155 feet

Wind Speed: 9.5 mph

Seasonal Change

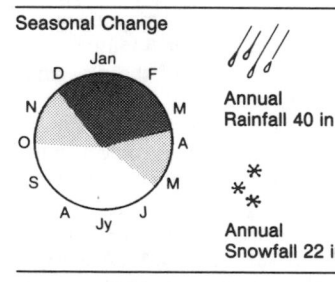

Annual Rainfall 40 in

Annual Snowfall 22 in

Clear 106 days   Partly Cloudy 109 days   Cloudy 150 days

Precipitation Days: 112   Storm Days: 26

Average Temperatures			
	Daily High	Daily Low	Relative Humidity
January	41	24	64
February	44	26	63
March	53	33	61
April	65	43	61
May	74	53	65
June	83	62	66
July	87	67	67
August	86	66	70
September	79	59	70
October	68	46	69
November	56	37	67
December	45	28	66

Zero-Degree Days: 0
Freezing Days: 100
90-Degree Days: 31
Heating- and Cooling-Degree Days: 5,837

Billings, MT

Terrain: Situated on the border between the Great Plains and the Rocky Mountains, and located on the west bank of the Yellowstone River. Billings is the center of a vast, rich agricultural belt; irrigation and sufficient rain during early spring and fall make it possible to raise a variety of crops here.

Climate: Takes on the character of both the Plains and the Rockies but is classified as semiarid. About a third of the yearly total of 14 inches of rain falls during May and June. The winter is usually dry and cold, although heavy snows can occur anytime during the winter months. The heaviest snows come either in spring or fall, when the temperature may take an unexpected drop. Blizzard conditions are expected. Severe cold spells are sometimes relieved by the Chinook, or "drainage," winds moving down Yellowstone Valley and bringing warm Pacific air. Springs: changeable, cloudy, cool. Summers: mild, dry, sunny, with cool to cold nights.

Pluses: Cool summers. **Minuses:** Fairly rugged.

Places Rated Score: 452   **Places Rated Rank: 274**

Elevation: 3,570 feet

Wind Speed: 11.5 mph

Seasonal Change

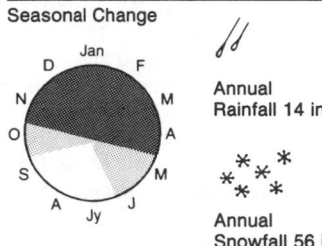

Annual Rainfall 14 in

Annual Snowfall 56 in

Clear 90 days   Partly Cloudy 116 days   Cloudy 159 days

Precipitation Days: 95   Storm Days: 29

Average Temperatures			
	Daily High	Daily Low	Relative Humidity
January	30	12	60
February	38	19	59
March	44	24	57
April	56	33	54
May	66	43	56
June	76	52	55
July	87	58	47
August	84	56	46
September	72	47	51
October	61	38	52
November	44	26	59
December	36	18	60

Zero-Degree Days: 18
Freezing Days: 152
90-Degree Days: 28
Heating- and Cooling-Degree Days: 7,763

Binghamton, NY

Terrain: Binghamton, in south-central New York State, lies in a narrow valley at the confluence of the Susquehanna and Chenango rivers. Within a radius of approximately 5 miles around the city, hills rise to some 1,400 feet to 1,600 feet. In the spring, melting snow and rains sometimes cause flooding along the riverbanks.

Climate: Representative of the humid area of the northeastern United States and decidedly continental in character. Since the area is adjacent to the so-called St. Lawrence Valley storm track and is also subject to intruding arctic air masses that approach from the west and north, the local weather undergoes frequent and rapid changes. Winters are cold but usually not severe. However, moisture-laden winds from the Great Lakes bring much snow. Summers are pleasantly cool and invigorating.

Pluses: Nice summers. **Minuses:** Cloudy, snowy.

Places Rated Score: 550   **Places Rated Rank: 155**

Elevation: 1,590 feet

Wind Speed: 10.3 mph

Seasonal Change

Annual Rainfall 37 in

Annual Snowfall 86 in

Clear 49 days   Partly Cloudy 102 days   Cloudy 214 days

Precipitation Days: 163   Storm Days: 31

Average Temperatures			
	Daily High	Daily Low	Relative Humidity
January	28	14	75
February	30	15	73
March	39	24	71
April	54	35	66
May	65	46	67
June	74	55	70
July	78	59	71
August	76	58	75
September	69	51	77
October	58	41	74
November	44	31	76
December	32	20	78

Zero-Degree Days: 8
Freezing Days: 147
90-Degree Days: 2
Heating- and Cooling-Degree Days: 7,654

Birmingham, AL

Terrain: Hilly and located in a valley between a ridge of hills, extending from the northeast to the west, and the Red Mountain ridge, covering the east to the southwest. This valley is 8 miles long and 2 miles to 4 miles wide. The Red Mountain ridge approaches a height of 600 feet above the valley floor. Rolling terrain extends to the southwest and west. The hills in the Birmingham area, which extend to the northeast and north, are the foothills of the Appalachians and the Cumberland Plateau.

Climate: Ideal solar radiation and cold-air drainage produce extreme temperature inversions and low minimum temperatures. Located 300 miles from the Gulf of Mexico, Birmingham is safe from the direct effects of tropical hurricanes, although it does receive heavy rains from these storms. Birmingham occasionally receives very low temperatures. Average growing season: 239 days.

Pluses: Mild winters. **Minuses:** Humid, rainy.

Places Rated Score: 612   **Places Rated Rank: 73**

Elevation: 630 feet

Wind Speed: 7.4 mph

Seasonal Change

Annual Rainfall 53 in

Annual Snowfall 1 in

Clear 99 days   Partly Cloudy 111 days   Cloudy 155 days

Precipitation Days: 118   Storm Days: 58

Average Temperatures			
	Daily High	Daily Low	Relative Humidity
January	53	33	70
February	57	35	76
March	65	42	66
April	75	50	67
May	82	58	76
June	88	66	76
July	90	70	74
August	90	69	75
September	85	64	74
October	75	50	71
November	64	41	71
December	56	35	71

Zero-Degree Days: 0
Freezing Days: 60
90-Degree Days: 39
Heating- and Cooling-Degree Days: 4,772

Bismarck, ND

Terrain: Located in south-central North Dakota, near the center of the North American landmass, on the east bank of the Missouri River in a shallow basin 7 miles wide and 11 miles long. The closest hills, about 3 miles away, are 200 feet or 300 feet high. West, across the river, the land is hilly and considerably higher.

Climate: Semiarid, typically continental in character, and invigorating. The normal average temperature range from summer to winter is 135 degrees, typical of the northern Great Plains. In summer, readings of 100°F or more may be expected 6 years out of 10. Readings of −30°F in winter are experienced 7 years out of 10. On seven days of the year, the temperature does not rise above zero.

Pluses: Invigorating, variable.

Minuses: Rugged, rigorous; Bismarck has one of the most extreme climates in America.

Places Rated Score: 149   **Places Rated Rank: 341**

Elevation: 1,660 feet

Wind Speed: 10.6 mph

Seasonal Change

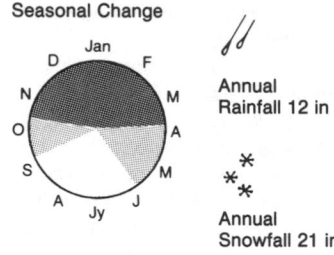

Annual Rainfall 16 in

Annual Snowfall 38 in

Clear 94 days   Partly Cloudy 105 days   Cloudy 166 days

Precipitation Days: 96   Storm Days: 34

Average Temperatures			
	Daily High	Daily Low	Relative Humidity
January	18	−4	71
February	25	4	72
March	36	16	72
April	54	31	65
May	68	42	63
June	77	52	68
July	84	56	65
August	83	54	65
September	71	43	67
October	59	33	65
November	39	18	72
December	26	5	74

Zero-Degree Days: 51
Freezing Days: 186
90-Degree Days: 22
Heating- and Cooling-Degree Days: 9,531

Boise City, ID

Terrain: Cradled in the valley of the Boise River about 8 miles below the mouth of a mountain canyon, where this valley widens. The Boise Mountains rise to a height of 5,000 feet to 6,000 feet within 8 miles. Their slopes are partially mantled with sagebrush and chaparral, changing to stands of fir, spruce, and pine trees higher up.

Climate: Almost a typical upland continental climate in summer but one tempered by periods of cloudy or stormy and mild weather during almost every winter. The cause of this modification in the winter months is the flow of warm, moist Pacific air, called Chinook winds. While this air is considerably moderated by the time it reaches Boise, its effect is nonetheless felt. Summer hot spells rarely last longer than a few days, but temperatures may reach 100°F each year. However, due to the low humidity, the average 5:00 P.M. July temperature of 62°F is comfortable. In general, the climate is dry and temperate, with enough variation to be stimulating.

Pluses: Mild; low humidity.

Minuses: Stormy winters.

Places Rated Score: 592   **Places Rated Rank: 94**

Elevation: 2,868 feet

Wind Speed: 9 mph

Seasonal Change

Annual Rainfall 12 in

Annual Snowfall 21 in

Clear 124 days   Partly Cloudy 90 days   Cloudy 151 days

Precipitation Days: 91   Storm Days: 15

Average Temperatures			
	Daily High	Daily Low	Relative Humidity
January	37	23	76
February	44	28	70
March	52	31	59
April	61	36	53
May	71	44	52
June	80	52	49
July	91	59	38
August	87	57	38
September	78	49	45
October	65	39	53
November	49	31	69
December	39	25	76

Zero-Degree Days: 2
Freezing Days: 124
90-Degree Days: 43
Heating- and Cooling-Degree Days: 6,547

Boston, MA

Terrain: Located in Massachusetts Bay at the mouths of the Mystic and Charles rivers. The western section of Massachusetts Bay is called Boston Bay, and its innermost part is called Boston Harbor, a large, sheltered body of water studded with many small islands, known as the Harbor Islands. Sections of Boston are rolling; two of the more famous hills are Beacon Hill in Boston and Bunker Hill in Charlestown.

Climate: Boston's proximity to the ocean greatly influences its climate—roughly described as damp, changeable, and relatively mild, considering its northern location. Sea breezes from the Atlantic do a great deal to moderate the temperature in both summer and winter. Hot summer afternoons as well as winter cold snaps (which may be severe and aggravated by high winds) are frequently relieved by these breezes. Rain is plentiful and well distributed throughout the year. Boston receives a great amount of snow, although in the city proper and to the south it often falls as sleet with no accumulation.

Pluses: Great variety, frequent changes.

Minuses: Rainy, snowy.

Places Rated Score: 623   **Places Rated Rank: 61**

Elevation: 29 feet

Wind Speed: 12.6 mph

Seasonal Change

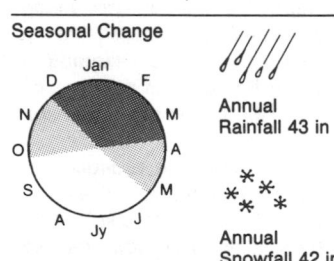

Annual Rainfall 43 in

Annual Snowfall 42 in

Clear 99 days   Partly Cloudy 106 days   Cloudy 160 days

Precipitation Days: 128   Storm Days: 19

Average Temperatures			
	Daily High	Daily Low	Relative Humidity
January	36	23	62
February	38	24	62
March	45	32	63
April	57	41	62
May	67	50	66
June	77	59	66
July	82	65	65
August	80	64	68
September	72	57	70
October	63	47	68
November	52	39	67
December	40	27	64

Zero-Degree Days: 1
Freezing Days: 99
90-Degree Days: 12
Heating- and Cooling-Degree Days: 6,282

Brownsville–Harlingen–San Benito, TX

Terrain: Situated at the extreme southern tip of Texas, on the Mexican border, and on the alluvial soils of the Rio Grande. The only more southerly city in America is Key West, Florida. The Gulf of Mexico is 18 miles to the east, and more than half the land toward the coast consists of tidal marshlands, which have the net effect of "moving" the coast 10 miles nearer to the city.

Climate: Humid subtropical. It's always summer here, accounting for the area's agricultural importance in growing citrus fruits, cotton, and warm-weather vegetables. Part of the climate is man-made; irrigation, used for all the crops, adds considerably to the humidity. Summer temperatures follow a predictable pattern of lower 90s in the day and middle 70s at night. Gulf breezes help temper the summer heat. This is a popular tourist spot in the winter months. The normal daily January minimum temperature is 51°F.

Pluses: Long growing season.   **Minuses:** Hot.

Places Rated Score: 440   **Places Rated Rank: 280**

Elevation: 20 feet

Wind Speed: 11.8 mph

Seasonal Change

Annual Rainfall 25 in

Annual Snowfall 0 in

Clear 96 days   Partly Cloudy 138 days   Cloudy 131 days

Precipitation Days: 73   Storm Days: 24

Average Temperatures			
	Daily High	Daily Low	Relative Humidity
January	70	51	78
February	73	53	75
March	78	60	73
April	83	67	74
May	87	71	76
June	91	75	75
July	93	76	73
August	93	75	74
September	90	73	75
October	84	66	74
November	77	58	74
December	72	53	76

Zero-Degree Days: 0
Freezing Days: 2
90-Degree Days: 102
Heating- and Cooling-Degree Days: 4,524

Buffalo–Niagara Falls, NY

Terrain: The surrounding country is comparatively low and level to the west, and gently rolling to the east and south, rising to pronounced hills within 12 miles to 18 miles, and to 1,000 feet above Lake Erie at a point 35 miles south-southeast of the city. The eastern end of Lake Erie is 9 miles to the west-southwest, and Lake Ontario is 25 miles to the north. The two lakes are connected by the Niagara River and the famous falls of the same name.

Climate: The weather here is varied and changeable. Wide seasonal swings of temperature are tempered somewhat by the surrounding lakes. Spring comes late, primarily because of the ice buildup and cold water on Lake Erie. Summers are mild, with more sun here than anywhere else in the state. Thunderstorms are infrequent. Autumn has long, dry periods and is frost-free until mid-October. Winters are famous for snow: 90 inches are expected each year.

Pluses: Pleasant summers.   **Minuses:** Snowy, cloudy.

Places Rated Score: 571   **Places Rated Rank: 119**

Elevation: 706 feet

Wind Speed: 12.3 mph

Seasonal Change

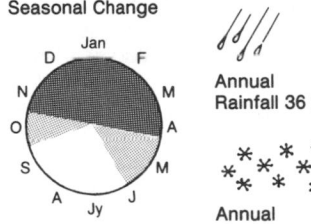

Annual Rainfall 36 in

Annual Snowfall 90 in

Clear 55 days   Partly Cloudy 104 days   Cloudy 206 days

Precipitation Days: 168   Storm Days: 31

Average Temperatures			
	Daily High	Daily Low	Relative Humidity
January	30	17	76
February	31	18	75
March	40	26	73
April	54	36	67
May	66	46	66
June	76	56	67
July	80	61	67
August	78	60	71
September	71	53	72
October	60	43	72
November	47	34	75
December	35	23	77

Zero-Degree Days: 5
Freezing Days: 137
90-Degree Days: 2
Heating- and Cooling-Degree Days: 7,364

Burlington, VT

Terrain: Located on the eastern shore of Lake Champlain at the widest part of that lake. About 35 miles to the west lie the highest peaks of the Adirondacks; the foothills of the Green Mountains begin 10 miles to the east and southeast.

Climate: Burlington's northerly latitude assures the variety and vigor of a true New England climate. Lake Champlain, however, has a tempering effect; during the winter months, temperatures along the lakeshore often run from 5 degrees to 10 degrees warmer than those at the airport 3.5 miles away. The summer, while not long compared with most, is quite pleasant, with only four 90-degree days per year on the average. Fall is cool, extending through October. Winters are cold, with intense cold snaps (usually not lasting long) formed by high-pressure systems moving down from central Canada and Hudson Bay. Because of its location in the path of the St. Lawrence Valley storm track and the effects of the lake, Burlington is one of the cloudiest cities in the United States.

Pluses: Cool summers.   **Minuses:** Long, cold winters.

Places Rated Score: 383   **Places Rated Rank: 310**

Elevation: 340 feet

Wind Speed: 8.8 mph

Seasonal Change

Annual Rainfall 33 in

Annual Snowfall 79 in

Clear 58 days   Partly Cloudy 103 days   Cloudy 204 days

Precipitation Days: 153   Storm Days: 25

Average Temperatures			
	Daily High	Daily Low	Relative Humidity
January	25	8	68
February	27	9	68
March	38	21	66
April	53	33	63
May	66	44	63
June	76	54	66
July	81	59	66
August	78	57	70
September	69	49	74
October	57	39	71
November	44	30	72
December	30	15	72

Zero-Degree Days: 28
Freezing Days: 163
90-Degree Days: 5
Heating- and Cooling-Degree Days: 8,272

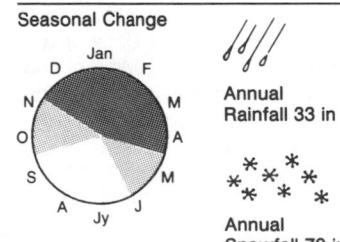

Calgary, AB

Terrain: Sprawling along the valley formed by the Elbow and Bow rivers in a large, treeless tract of undulating prairie grassland. A few miles to the west, the first of the foothills begins rising to meet the eastern slopes of the Rocky Mountains 45 miles away. To the east, generally rolling ground meets flat prairie land.

Climate: Continental, with strong temperature contrasts between day and night as well as summer and winter. Situated on the eastern side of the Rockies, the area rarely enjoys the moderating effects of the Pacific. Embedded in the zone of westerly winds, it has changing seasons marked by northerly air circulations in winter and occasional instances of moist, tropical air from the Gulf of Mexico bringing heavy rainfall in the summer. The higher elevation of the city contributes to longer winters and shorter summers. Location on a valley floor influences the temperature, especially during the winter when the sun is low on the horizon.

Pluses: Moderate summers with cool nights.

Minuses: Long, cold winters.

Places Rated Score: 381

Places Rated Rank: 312

Elevation: 3,445 feet

Wind Speed: 10.1 mph

Seasonal Change

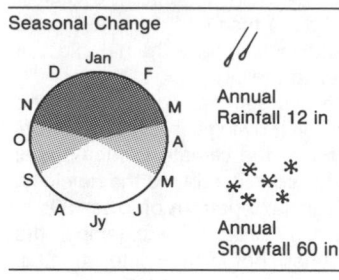

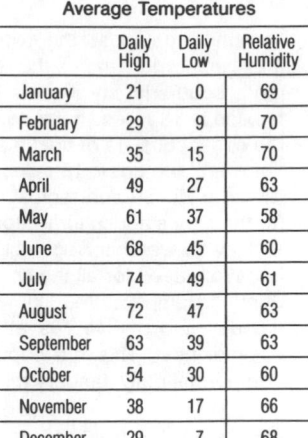

Annual Rainfall 12 in

Annual Snowfall 60 in

Clear 108 days | Partly Cloudy 157 days | Cloudy 100 days

Precipitation Days: 113   Storm Days: 25

Average Temperatures			
	Daily High	Daily Low	Relative Humidity
January	21	0	69
February	29	9	70
March	35	15	70
April	49	27	63
May	61	37	58
June	68	45	60
July	74	49	61
August	72	47	63
September	63	39	63
October	54	30	60
November	38	17	66
December	29	7	68

Zero-Degree Days: 33
Freezing Days: 201
90-Degree Days: 4
Heating- and Cooling-Degree Days: 5,403

Casper, WY

Terrain: Located in the central part of the state in the North Platte River valley. The nearby countryside is rolling and hilly with considerable flat prairie land in all directions except south, where Casper Mountain rises 3,500 feet above the valley floor. The prairie land is used mostly for grazing.

Climate: Rather dry due to the effective moisture barrier of the Cascades, the Sierra Nevada, and the Rocky Mountains, which block most of the moist Pacific winds. Summertime precipitation is almost all in the form of thunderstorms, which generally provide ample moisture for grasslands. Annual snowfall averages 77 inches, but the winter season is not severe, contrary to common belief. The dryness of the air prevents discomfort during both the warm summer months and winter cold snaps. Summer highs average 84°F, winter lows 15°F.

Pluses: Invigorating.

Minuses: Short summers, long winters.

Places Rated Score: 401

Places Rated Rank: 302

Elevation: 5,338 feet

Wind Speed: 13 mph

Seasonal Change

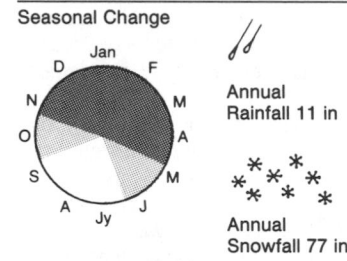

Annual Rainfall 11 in

Annual Snowfall 77 in

Clear 109 days | Partly Cloudy 110 days | Cloudy 146 days

Precipitation Days: 93   Storm Days: 34

Average Temperatures			
	Daily High	Daily Low	Relative Humidity
January	33	12	65
February	37	16	64
March	43	20	60
April	55	29	59
May	66	39	59
June	78	48	54
July	87	55	48
August	85	53	46
September	74	43	49
October	61	33	54
November	44	22	63
December	36	16	65

Zero-Degree Days: 21
Freezing Days: 185
90-Degree Days: 25
Heating- and Cooling-Degree Days: 8,013

Charleston, WV

Terrain: Situated in the western foothills of the Appalachians at the junction of the Kanawha and Elk rivers.

Climate: Characterized by sharp temperature contrasts, both seasonal and day-to-day. May through September is generally warm; November through March moderately cold. April and October are months of rapid transition. Cold spells occur on the average of two or three times each winter, but they seldom last longer than several days. Ample precipitation is well distributed throughout the year, with a maximum in July and a minimum in October. Because of the conditions of terrain and airflow, Charleston experiences 111 fog days per year, more than any other major city in the United States.

Pluses: Changeable climate.

Minuses: Foggy, rainy.

Places Rated Score: 627

Places Rated Rank: 57

Elevation: 951 feet

Wind Speed: 6.5 mph

Seasonal Change

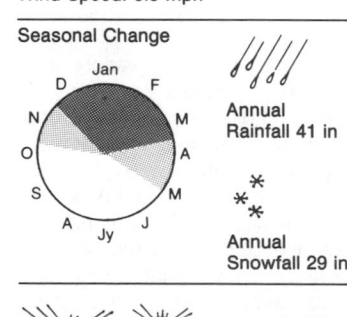

Annual Rainfall 41 in

Annual Snowfall 29 in

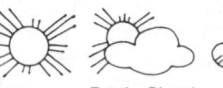

Clear 59 days | Partly Cloudy 116 days | Cloudy 190 days

Precipitation Days: 149   Storm Days: 43

Average Temperatures			
	Daily High	Daily Low	Relative Humidity
January	42	24	70
February	45	26	68
March	55	34	63
April	67	43	61
May	76	52	67
June	83	59	70
July	85	64	75
August	84	63	75
September	79	56	74
October	68	44	71
November	56	35	68
December	46	28	70

Zero-Degree Days: 1
Freezing Days: 101
90-Degree Days: 21
Heating- and Cooling-Degree Days: 4,224

Charleston–North Charleston, SC

Terrain: Before the expansion begun in 1960, Charleston was limited to the peninsula bounded on the west and south by the Ashley River, on the east by the Cooper River, and on the southeast by a spacious harbor that contains historic Fort Sumter. The terrain is generally level and the soil sandy to sandy loam. Because of the low elevation, a portion of the city and nearby coastal islands are vulnerable to tidal flooding.

Climate: Generally temperate, modified considerably by the ocean. Summer is warm and humid, but temperatures over 100°F are infrequent. Most rain—41% of the annual total—occurs then. The fall passes from an Indian summer to the prewinter cold spells that begin in November. From late September to early November, the weather is very pleasant, being cool and sunny. Winters are mild; temperatures of 20°F or less are very unusual. Spring is warm, windy, and changeable. Most storms occur then.

Pluses: Pleasant falls, mild winters.

Minuses: Hot, humid, stormy.

Places Rated Score: 569

Places Rated Rank: 122

Elevation: 48 feet

Wind Speed: 8.8 mph

Seasonal Change

Annual Rainfall 52 in

❄

Annual Snowfall .5 in

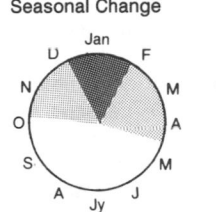

Clear 101 days   Partly Cloudy 113 days   Cloudy 151 days

Precipitation Days: 115   Storm Days: 56

Average Temperatures			
	Daily High	Daily Low	Relative Humidity
January	59	37	70
February	61	38	67
March	68	45	67
April	76	53	67
May	83	61	69
June	87	68	72
July	89	72	75
August	89	71	77
September	85	67	76
October	77	55	72
November	69	45	69
December	61	39	69

Zero-Degree Days: 0
Freezing Days: 36
90-Degree Days: 47
Heating- and Cooling-Degree Days: 4,224

Charlotte–Gastonia–Rock Hill, NC–SC

Terrain: Charlotte is located in the southern Piedmont, an area of rolling country between the mountains to the west and the Coastal Plain to the east. The mountains extend from southwest to northeast, being about 80 miles to 90 miles from the city to the west and north. The ocean is approximately 160 miles to the southeast. The mountains have a moderating effect on winter temperatures, causing appreciable warming of cold air coming from the west and northwest. The ocean is too distant to affect summer weather, but it moderates winter weather.

Climate: Moderate, characterized by cool winters and summers that are quite warm. Winter weather is changeable, alternating between mild and cool spells, with occasional cold periods. Extreme cold is rare. Snow is infrequent, occurring, on the average, once a month from December through March. Summers are long and warm, with afternoon temperatures frequently in the 90s. Nights are cooler, with temperatures dropping into the low 70s even in the warmest months.

Pluses: Moderate, mild winters.   **Minuses:** Long summers.

Places Rated Score: 644

Places Rated Rank: 43

Elevation: 769 feet

Wind Speed: 7.6 mph

Seasonal Change

Annual Rainfall 43 in

❄

Annual Snowfall 6 in

Clear 111 days   Partly Cloudy 103 days   Cloudy 151 days

Precipitation Days: 111   Storm Days: 42

Average Temperatures			
	Daily High	Daily Low	Relative Humidity
January	50	31	67
February	54	32	64
March	62	39	65
April	72	48	62
May	79	57	68
June	85	65	70
July	88	69	72
August	88	68	74
September	82	62	73
October	72	50	70
November	62	40	68
December	53	33	68

Zero-Degree Days: 0
Freezing Days: 71
90-Degree Days: 31
Heating- and Cooling-Degree Days: 4,814

Chattanooga, TN–GA

Terrain: Local topography is complex, with the difference in elevation between minor valleys and ridges being as much as 500 feet. The city is located in the southern portion of the Great Valley of the Tennessee, an area of the Tennessee River between the Cumberland Mountains to the west and the Appalachian Mountains to the east. Most of the city lies south of the river. In winter the Cumberlands have a moderating influence on the local climate, retarding the flow of cold air from the north and west.

Climate: Moderate, characterized by cool winters and summers that are quite warm. Winter weather is changeable and alternates between cool spells and an occasional cold period. Extreme or prolonged cold is rare. Summer temperatures average in the high 80s or low 90s. Most afternoon summer temperatures are modified by brief thundershowers, which cause the mercury to drop 10 degrees to 15 degrees.

Pluses: Mild winters.

Minuses: Can be hot and muggy.

Places Rated Score: 576

Places Rated Rank: 109

Elevation: 665 feet

Wind Speed: 6.2 mph

Seasonal Change

Annual Rainfall 52 in

❄

Annual Snowfall 4.2 in

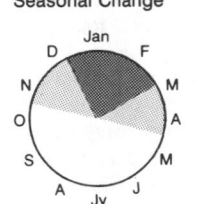

Clear 107 days   Partly Cloudy 106 days   Cloudy 152 days

Precipitation Days: 121   Storm Days: 56

Average Temperatures			
	Daily High	Daily Low	Relative Humidity
January	48	29	72
February	53	31	69
March	61	39	67
April	73	48	66
May	80	56	70
June	86	64	71
July	89	68	73
August	89	67	74
September	83	62	73
October	72	48	71
November	60	38	71
December	51	32	73

Zero-Degree Days: 0
Freezing Days: 75
90-Degree Days: 49
Heating- and Cooling-Degree Days: 5,141

Chicago, IL

Terrain: Sprawls along the southwest shore of Lake Michigan on a plain that, for the most part, is only some tens of feet above the lake. Topography does not significantly affect airflow in or near the city, except that lower frictional drag over Lake Michigan permits winds to be frequently stronger along the lakeshore. Terrain is basically flat.

Climate: Predominantly continental, with warm to hot summers and cold winters. The climate of the city proper is modified by the lake, with summer temperatures near the shore often 10 degrees cooler than elsewhere. Summer hot spells—an uncomfortable combination of high temperature and high humidity—may last for several days, then end abruptly with a shift of winds to the north or northwest. They are often accompanied by thunderstorms. The normal heating season lasts from mid-September to early June. The air-conditioning season lasts from mid-June to early September.

Pluses: Changeable; pleasant falls.

Minuses: Hot summers, cold winters, cloudy.

Places Rated Score: 514 **Places Rated Rank: 213**

Elevation: 623 feet

Wind Speed: 10.4 mph

Seasonal Change

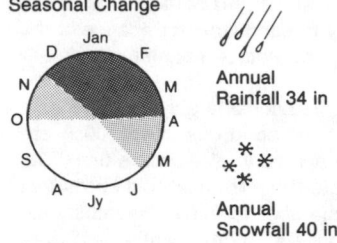

Annual Rainfall 34 in

Annual Snowfall 40 in

Clear 94 days Partly Cloudy 103 days Cloudy 168 days

Precipitation Days: 123   Storm Days: 40

Average Temperatures			
	Daily High	Daily Low	Relative Humidity
January	29	14	72
February	34	18	72
March	44	28	70
April	59	39	66
May	70	48	66
June	79	58	67
July	83	63	69
August	82	62	71
September	76	54	71
October	64	43	69
November	48	31	73
December	35	20	75

Zero-Degree Days: 7
Freezing Days: 119
90-Degree Days: 21
Heating- and Cooling-Degree Days: 7,052

Cincinnati, OH–KY–IN

Terrain: Located on the bank of the Ohio River in extreme southwestern Ohio. It extends over two ranges of hills bisected by the Mill Creek Valley, with hills extending some 400 feet above the valley floor. The city incorporates the lower portion of the Little Miami Valley to the east and extends to within 5 or 6 miles of the Great Miami Valley to the west.

Climate: Basically continental, with a wide range in temperature. Subject to frequent changes in weather due to the passage of numerous cyclonic storms in winter and spring, and thunderstorms during the summer. Fall is very pleasant, with the least rainfall of any season, an abundance of sunshine, and comfortable temperatures. Average freeze-free period: 198 days. Average date of last freeze: April 10. First freeze: October 25.

Pluses: Milder version of continental climate.

Minuses: Summers can be hot; flooding approximately every three years.

Places Rated Score: 584 **Places Rated Rank: 101**

Elevation: 869 feet

Wind Speed: 7.1 mph

Seasonal Change

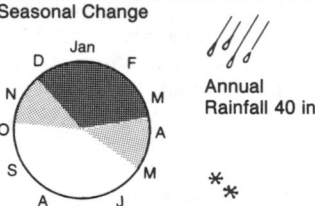

Annual Rainfall 40 in

Annual Snowfall 19 in

Clear 80 days Partly Cloudy 97 days Cloudy 188 days

Precipitation Days: 131   Storm Days: 50

Average Temperatures			
	Daily High	Daily Low	Relative Humidity
January	37	20	73
February	41	23	71
March	52	32	68
April	65	42	65
May	74	52	68
June	82	61	69
July	86	65	71
August	85	63	73
September	79	56	73
October	67	44	69
November	53	34	72
December	42	26	75

Zero-Degree Days: 2
Freezing Days: 98
90-Degree Days: 28
Heating- and Cooling-Degree Days: 6,032

Cleveland–Lorain–Elyria, OH

Terrain: Situated on the south shore of Lake Erie, with a lake frontage of 31 miles. The surrounding terrain is mostly level, except for a ridge of the southeastern edge of the city rising some 500 feet above shore level. A rather deep north-south valley, in which flows the Cuyahoga River, approximately bisects the city. Local topography is of minor importance to the climate.

Climate: In the winter, Cleveland lies in the path of many cold air masses advancing south and east out of Canada, but the low temperatures are somewhat modified by the air having passed over the comparatively warm water of the lake. But this also means considerable winter cloudiness and frequent snows. Spring is generally a brief transition period. Summer heat is moderated somewhat by the lake, since breezes are felt a considerable distance inland. Fall is the most pleasant season, with mild, sunny weather often extending into November or even early December. Average growing season: 195 days.

Pluses: Long, sunny falls.

Minuses: Cloudy, snowy.

Places Rated Score: 579 **Places Rated Rank: 108**

Elevation: 805 feet

Wind Speed: 10.8 mph

Seasonal Change

Annual Rainfall 35 in

Annual Snowfall 52 in

Clear 70 days Partly Cloudy 98 days Cloudy 197 days

Precipitation Days: 156   Storm Days: 36

Average Temperatures			
	Daily High	Daily Low	Relative Humidity
January	33	19	73
February	35	20	73
March	45	28	71
April	58	38	67
May	69	48	68
June	78	57	68
July	82	61	69
August	80	61	73
September	74	54	72
October	63	44	70
November	49	34	71
December	38	25	74

Zero-Degree Days: 5
Freezing Days: 125
90-Degree Days: 8
Heating- and Cooling-Degree Days: 6,767

Colorado Springs, CO

Terrain: At an elevation of more than 6,000 feet, Colorado Springs is located in relatively flat semiarid country on the eastern slope of the Rocky Mountains. Immediately to the west, the mountains rise abruptly to heights ranging from 10,000 feet to 14,000 feet. To the east lies the gently undulating prairie land of eastern Colorado. The land slopes upward to the north, reaching an average height of 8,000 feet within 20 miles, at the top of Palmer Lake Divide.

Climate: The terrain of the area, particularly its wide range of elevations, helps to give Colorado Springs the pleasant plains-and-mountain mixture of climate that has established it as a desirable place to live. Precipitation is generally light, with 80% of it falling between April 1 and September 30. Heavy downpours accompany summer thunderstorms. Temperatures are on the mild side for a city in this latitude and at this elevation.

Pluses: Dry, sunny, variable.   **Minuses:** Long winters.

Places Rated Score: 526   **Places Rated Rank: 195**

Elevation: 6,170 feet

Wind Speed: 10.4 mph

Seasonal Change

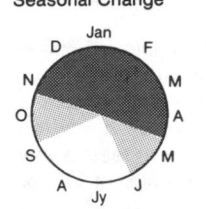

Annual Rainfall 16 in

Annual Snowfall 40 in

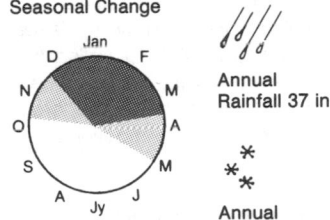

Clear	Partly Cloudy	Cloudy
130 days	119 days	116 days

Precipitation Days: 87   Storm Days: 59

Average Temperatures			
	Daily High	Daily Low	Relative Humidity
January	41	16	52
February	45	20	49
March	49	24	49
April	60	33	47
May	69	43	51
June	80	52	50
July	85	57	53
August	82	56	56
September	75	47	52
October	65	37	47
November	50	25	52
December	44	19	52

Zero-Degree Days: 7
Freezing Days: 162
90-Degree Days: 15
Heating- and Cooling-Degree Days: 6,934

Columbia, MO

Terrain: Columbia, a university town, is located on the broad, gently rolling plains of northern Missouri in the valley of the Missouri River. Its elevation is almost 900 feet, and its location dictates a continental climate.

Climate: With its interior location, Columbia experiences moderately cold winters and warm, often humid summers. Each summer brings some temperatures over 100°F, and winter lows reach zero an average of eight times annually. Yet summer hot spells are relieved by thunderstorms, and winter cold snaps are often interrupted by days that are almost balmy, with temperatures as high as the 50s and 60s. The late spring and early summer months are the rainiest, but by late summer the rain diminishes so that by middle or late August, the moisture in the top 2 feet of soil is often depleted. The last spring freeze is usually on April 9; first autumn frost is October 24.

Pluses: Variable, sunny.   **Minuses:** Tornado-prone.

Places Rated Score: 541   **Places Rated Rank: 175**

Elevation: 887 feet

Wind Speed: 9.8 mph

Seasonal Change

Annual Rainfall 37 in

Annual Snowfall 24 in

Clear	Partly Cloudy	Cloudy
100 days	91 days	174 days

Precipitation Days: 109   Storm Days: 51

Average Temperatures			
	Daily High	Daily Low	Relative Humidity
January	36	19	72
February	42	23	72
March	52	32	69
April	65	44	67
May	75	54	73
June	83	63	72
July	89	67	71
August	87	65	72
September	80	57	73
October	68	46	71
November	53	34	73
December	41	25	74

Zero-Degree Days: 8
Freezing Days: 108
90-Degree Days: 39
Heating- and Cooling-Degree Days: 6,352

Columbia, SC

Terrain: Located on the Congaree River in the center of the state, near the confluence of the Broad and Saluda rivers. The fall line, or division between the Piedmont and the Coastal Plain, is near Columbia. The soil ranges from sand to clay loam. Terrain is rolling, sloping from about 350 feet above sea level in the northern part of the city to about 200 feet at the city's southeastern edge.

Climate: Although the Appalachian chain to the north shields the city from northern cold fronts in the winter, the surrounding gently rolling terrain offers little moderating effect on summer heat. Summers are long and hot, with high temperatures from May to September. Temperatures will surpass 100°F an average of six times a year. Winters are mild; only about a third of the days have freezing temperatures. Snow accumulation is very rare. Spring is changeable and may bring some violent weather. Fall is cool, pleasant, and very sunny. Some grazing crops are grown year-round. Average growing period: 217 days.

Pluses: Cool, sunny falls.   **Minuses:** Long, hot summers.

Places Rated Score: 526   **Places Rated Rank: 195**

Elevation: 225 feet

Wind Speed: 6.9 mph

Seasonal Change

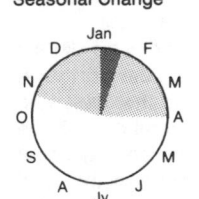
Annual Rainfall 46 in

Annual Snowfall 2 in

Clear	Partly Cloudy	Cloudy
120 days	103 days	142 days

Precipitation Days: 111   Storm Days: 54

Average Temperatures			
	Daily High	Daily Low	Relative Humidity
January	56	33	69
February	60	35	65
March	67	42	66
April	77	51	64
May	84	59	68
June	89	66	69
July	92	70	72
August	91	69	75
September	86	64	74
October	77	50	71
November	67	41	70
December	59	35	69

Zero-Degree Days: 0
Freezing Days: 60
90-Degree Days: 64
Heating- and Cooling-Degree Days: 4,685

Columbus, GA–AL

Terrain: Located on the Chattahoochee River at the western boundary of Georgia, about 225 miles west of the Atlantic and 170 miles north of the Gulf of Mexico. Elevation ranges from between 200 feet to 500 feet. The terrain is basically level, and effects of terrain on climate are therefore negligible.

Climate: Humid and warm, with pronounced maritime effects at some periods and equally pronounced continental effects at others. Rainfall averages an abundant 51 inches a year; the wettest months are March and July, the driest October. Snow is rare but by no means unknown, with each winter usually bringing at least a few flakes. Most days in June, July, and August will see a high of 90°F or higher, with accompanying high humidity. The unpleasant effects of this heat are perhaps balanced by the mild winters, during which temperatures seldom drop below 20°F.

Pluses: Very mild winters.　　**Minuses:** Hot summers; humid.

Places Rated Score: 517　　**Places Rated Rank: 209**

Elevation: 445 feet

Wind Speed: 6.8 mph

Seasonal Change

Annual Rainfall 51 in

Annual Snowfall .5 in

Clear 113 days　Partly Cloudy 103 days　Cloudy 149 days

Precipitation Days: 111　　Storm Days: 58

Average Temperatures			
	Daily High	Daily Low	Relative Humidity
January	57	35	72
February	61	37	69
March	68	44	69
April	77	52	67
May	84	60	68
June	89	68	69
July	91	71	74
August	91	71	74
September	86	66	73
October	77	53	71
November	67	43	71
December	60	37	72

Zero-Degree Days: 0
Freezing Days: 46
90-Degree Days: 74
Heating- and Cooling-Degree Days: 4,521

Columbus, OH

Terrain: Situated in the center of the state and in the drainage area of the Ohio River. Four small rivers—the Scioto, Alum, Big Walnut, and Olentangy—flow through and near the city.

Climate: The city is located in an area of changeable weather. Cold air masses from central and northwest Canada frequently invade the region. Tropical Gulf masses often reach central Ohio during the summer but to a much lesser extent in fall and winter. Columbus's four rivers provide variations in the microclimate of the area, contributing to the formation of shallow ground fog at daybreak in the summer and fall.

Pluses: Changeable climate.　　**Minuses:** Cold spells.

Places Rated Score: 558　　**Places Rated Rank: 143**

Elevation: 833 feet

Wind Speed: 8.7 mph

Seasonal Change

Annual Rainfall 37 in

Annual Snowfall 28 in

Clear 75 days　Partly Cloudy 106 days　Cloudy 184 days

Precipitation Days: 136　　Storm Days: 42

Average Temperatures			
	Daily High	Daily Low	Relative Humidity
January	35	19	72
February	38	22	70
March	49	31	66
April	62	41	64
May	73	50	67
June	81	59	68
July	84	63	70
August	83	62	73
September	77	55	72
October	65	43	69
November	51	34	72
December	39	25	74

Zero-Degree Days: 4
Freezing Days: 122
90-Degree Days: 15
Heating- and Cooling-Degree Days: 6,511

Corpus Christi, TX

Terrain: Located on Corpus Christi Bay, an inlet in the Gulf of Mexico. It is in the southern part of the Texas Gulf coastline, roughly halfway between Galveston to the north and Brownsville to the south. Padre Island National Seashore adjoins the city. Climate and abundant beaches make the area a major resort center.

Climate: Although located on the Gulf, Corpus Christi has a climate midway between humid subtropical conditions to the northeast along the Gulf Coast and the semiarid ones to the west and southwest. Peak rainfall months are May and September, with the winter months being the driest. Tropical storms, which may occur from June through November, add a large portion to the total rainfall. There is little variation in the summer temperature from day to day, which averages in the high 80s or low 90s. But nights are cooler, even pleasant, with temperatures dropping into the low 70s because of sea breezes.

Pluses: Winter vacation spot.　　**Minuses:** Storms.

Places Rated Score: 362　　**Places Rated Rank: 318**

Elevation: 44 feet

Wind Speed: 12 mph

Seasonal Change

Annual Rainfall 29 in

Annual Snowfall 0 in

Clear 104 days　Partly Cloudy 118 days　Cloudy 143 days

Precipitation Days: 77　　Storm Days: 31

Average Temperatures			
	Daily High	Daily Low	Relative Humidity
January	67	46	79
February	70	49	77
March	76	56	74
April	82	64	77
May	87	70	79
June	91	74	78
July	94	76	75
August	94	76	75
September	90	73	76
October	84	64	75
November	75	55	75
December	69	49	75

Zero-Degree Days: 0
Freezing Days: 7
90-Degree Days: 96
Heating- and Cooling-Degree Days: 4,404

Dallas, TX

Terrain: Located in north-central Texas, about 250 miles north of the Gulf of Mexico, near the headwaters of the Trinity River. This hilly area marks the upper boundary of the Coastal Plain. Grasses, live oaks, and coniferous trees compose most of the local vegetation.

Climate: Humid, subtropical, with hot summers. It is also continental, characterized by a wide range in annual temperature. Winters tend to be mild, but northers occur, bringing cold air masses down from the Great Plains and the Rocky Mountains. These cold snaps are not prolonged, however. Much of the rain falls at night; downpours may accompany thunderstorms during April and May. July and August are relatively dry. Hail falls about two or three times a year. Snowfall is slight and doesn't accumulate. Average freeze-free growing period: 249 days.

Pluses: Wide range of weather. **Minuses:** Hot summers.

Places Rated Score: 544 **Places Rated Rank: 166**

Elevation: 596 feet

Wind Speed: 11 mph

Seasonal Change

Annual Rainfall 32 in

Annual Snowfall 3 in

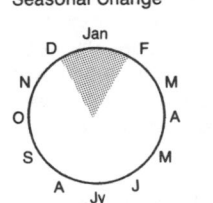

Clear 138 days Partly Cloudy 95 days Cloudy 132 days

Precipitation Days: 79   Storm Days: 46

Average Temperatures			
	Daily High	Daily Low	Relative Humidity
January	54	34	70
February	59	38	69
March	67	45	68
April	77	55	69
May	84	63	74
June	93	71	71
July	98	75	65
August	97	74	65
September	90	68	70
October	80	56	68
November	66	45	69
December	58	37	69

Zero-Degree Days: 0
Freezing Days: 39
90-Degree Days: 88
Heating- and Cooling-Degree Days: 4,969

Davenport–Moline–Rock Island, IA–IL

Terrain: Located on the banks of the Mississippi River. Topography characterized by rolling agricultural prairie. Close to the river there is considerable truck gardening and dairying. Field production of grains and livestock is greater in rolling prairie, away from the large streams.

Climate: Temperate continental, with a wide temperature range throughout the year. Some intensely hot, usually humid periods in summer and severely cold periods in winter. Proximity to major storm tracks brings substantial weather changes, frequently occurring at three- or four-day intervals. Maxima of 90°F or higher have occurred as frequently as 55 days a year (1936), but in 1882 there were none. Readings of zero or below have been made during every winter, ranging from 37 times in 1874–75 to one time during four other winters.

Pluses: Variable climate with average growing season and even precipitation.

Minuses: Unpredictable climate, long winters, hot summer stretches.

Places Rated Score: 440 **Places Rated Rank: 280**

Elevation: 594 feet

Wind Speed: 9.9 mph

Seasonal Change

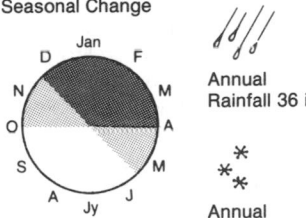

Annual Rainfall 36 in

Annual Snowfall 30 in

Clear 101 days Partly Cloudy 101 days Cloudy 163 days

Precipitation Days: 112   Storm Days: 47

Average Temperatures			
	Daily High	Daily Low	Relative Humidity
January	28	11	70
February	34	16	70
March	45	27	69
April	61	40	66
May	73	50	67
June	82	60	67
July	85	64	71
August	84	62	74
September	76	53	73
October	65	42	68
November	48	30	71
December	34	18	74

Zero-Degree Days: 16
Freezing Days: 136
90-Degree Days: 22
Heating- and Cooling-Degree Days: 7,288

Daytona Beach, FL

Terrain: The land is flat, rising to 15 feet near the ocean and nearly 31 feet at the airport and along a ridge running along the western city limits. Part of Florida's Inland Waterway, the Halifax River, runs through the city.

Climate: Tempered by the effect of land and sea breezes. Temperatures in summer may reach 90°F or above during the late morning or early afternoon, but they will be cut short by the beginning of the sea breeze during midday and late-afternoon convective thundershowers, which lower the temperature to the more comfortable 80s.

Pluses: Mild winters, cooler summer afternoons.

Minuses: Humid; stormy in summer.

Places Rated Score: 561 **Places Rated Rank: 132**

Elevation: 31 feet

Wind Speed: 8.8 mph

Seasonal Change

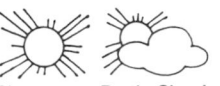

Annual Rainfall 54 in

Annual Snowfall 0 in

Clear 97 days Partly Cloudy 135 days Cloudy 134 days

Precipitation Days: 114   Storm Days: 78

Average Temperatures			
	Daily High	Daily Low	Relative Humidity
January	68	47	73
February	69	48	72
March	75	54	71
April	80	59	69
May	85	65	71
June	88	71	75
July	90	73	77
August	89	73	79
September	87	72	78
October	81	65	75
November	75	56	74
December	70	49	74

Zero-Degree Days: 0
Freezing Days: 6
90-Degree Days: 54
Heating- and Cooling-Degree Days: 900

Dayton–Springfield, OH

Terrain: Situated about 750 feet above sea level, Dayton is 50 to 200 feet below the adjacent rolling country. Located near the center of the Miami River Valley in a nearly flat plain, three rivers converge from the north and join within the city limits flowing south to empty into the Ohio River.

Climate: There is a moderating influence brought by the downward slope of the Miami River. Cold, polar air flowing across the Great Lakes causes cloudiness during the winter, accompanied by frequent snow flurries, which add little to the total snowfall. Extreme temperatures are usually of short duration in either the summer or winter. High relative humidities during much of the year cause some discomfort.

Pluses: Four-season climate.

Minuses: Humid summers.

Places Rated Score: 544

Places Rated Rank: 166

Elevation: 750 feet

Wind Speed: 10.2 mph

Seasonal Change

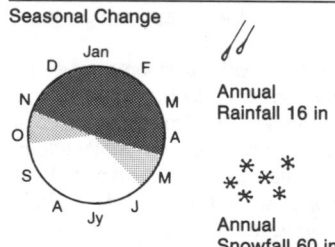

Annual Rainfall 35 in

Annual Snowfall 29 in

Clear 80 days Partly Cloudy 102 days Cloudy 183 days

Precipitation Days: 139   Storm Days: 40

Average Temperatures			
	Daily High	Daily Low	Relative Humidity
January	35	19	74
February	38	21	72
March	49	30	70
April	62	41	66
May	72	51	66
June	82	60	67
July	85	64	69
August	83	63	72
September	77	56	72
October	65	44	70
November	51	34	74
December	39	24	76

Zero-Degree Days: 6
Freezing Days: 150
90-Degree Days: 17
Heating- and Cooling-Degree Days: 2,577

Denver, CO

Terrain: The Mile-High City rests on the eastern slope of the Rocky Mountains. It is far from any source of moisture and is isolated from the Pacific Ocean by three mountain ranges: the Coastal Ranges, the Sierra Nevada, and the Rockies.

Climate: A mild, sunny, semiarid climate, reaching over much of the central Rocky Mountain region. This temperate climate lacks the extremely cold winter mornings of the high elevations and remote mountain valleys, as well as the hot summer afternoons of lower altitudes. There is little humidity or precipitation, and lots of sunshine. During the cold months, invasion of cold air from the north can be abrupt and severe. Yet many of these air masses from Canada are too low to reach Denver and so are deflected off to the east by the mountains. For this reason, Denver often has milder winters than cities of comparable latitude on the Great Plains. Spring is wet, cloudy, and windy. Summers are cool. Fall is the most pleasant season.

Pluses: Sunny, dry, comparatively mild winters.

Minuses: Cold snaps in winter, stormy springs.

Places Rated Score: 521

Places Rated Rank: 203

Elevation: 5,332 feet

Wind Speed: 9.1 mph

Seasonal Change

Annual Rainfall 16 in

Annual Snowfall 60 in

Clear 115 days Partly Cloudy 131 days Cloudy 119 days

Precipitation Days: 88   Storm Days: 41

Average Temperatures			
	Daily High	Daily Low	Relative Humidity
January	43	16	56
February	47	20	56
March	51	25	54
April	61	34	51
May	71	44	54
June	82	52	52
July	88	59	51
August	86	57	52
September	78	48	52
October	67	37	50
November	52	25	58
December	46	19	58

Zero-Degree Days: 10
Freezing Days: 163
90-Degree Days: 32
Heating- and Cooling-Degree Days: 6,641

Des Moines, IA

Terrain: Located close to the center of Iowa, and roughly in the geographic center of the continental United States. The terrain is flat to gently rolling prairie, ideally suited to agriculture. Most of the soil in Iowa is dark, rich, sandy loam with good drainage. The state has the highest rate of agricultural production per acre in the nation.

Climate: Situated in the center of the country far from any large body of water, Des Moines, not surprisingly, has a continental climate, characterized by rather long, cold winters, hot summers, and short springs and falls. Winter cold is often intensified by the winds that sweep over the flat land.

Pluses: Sunny falls.

Minuses: Climate tending toward rigorous.

Places Rated Score: 444

Places Rated Rank: 277

Elevation: 963 feet

Wind Speed: 11.1 mph

Seasonal Change

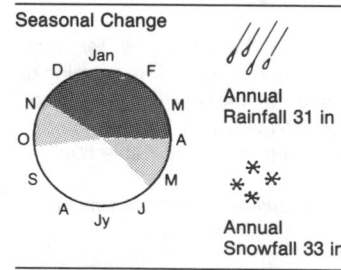

Annual Rainfall 31 in

Annual Snowfall 33 in

Clear 103 days Partly Cloudy 96 days Cloudy 166 days

Precipitation Days: 106   Storm Days: 50

Average Temperatures			
	Daily High	Daily Low	Relative Humidity
January	27	10	71
February	33	16	72
March	44	26	69
April	61	40	66
May	73	52	67
June	82	61	68
July	86	66	70
August	84	64	72
September	76	54	72
October	65	43	67
November	48	30	72
December	34	18	74

Zero-Degree Days: 16
Freezing Days: 137
90-Degree Days: 21
Heating- and Cooling-Degree Days: 7,638

Detroit, MI

Terrain: Detroit is located in the southeastern corner of the state, across the St. Clair River from Windsor, Ontario. Consequently, it is one of the few metro areas that cross international boundaries. Detroit lies on an important waterway that connects Lake Huron to Lake Erie. Nearly flat land slopes up gently from the water's edge northwestward for about 10 miles, then gives way to increasingly rolling terrain. The Irish Hills, about 40 miles northwest, are more than 1,000 feet high.

Climate: The winters, while cold, are modified by the Great Lakes, which warm and moisten the cold arctic air that passes over the northern Plains. As a result, however, the area is quite cloudy, especially in the winter. Summers in the city are warm and sunny. Brief showers usually occur every few days but often fall on only part of the city. Winter storms may bring rain, snow, or both. Freezing rain and sleet are common. Though Detroit is cloudy, its proximity to the Great Lakes helps give it a milder climate than one would expect in a place so far north.

Pluses: Mild for its latitude.
Places Rated Score: 536

Minuses: Cold winters, cloudy.
Places Rated Rank: 181

Elevation: 664 feet

Wind Speed: 10.4 mph

Seasonal Change

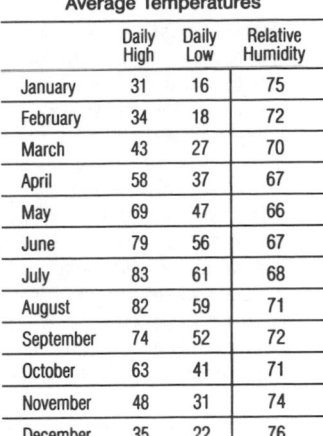

Annual Rainfall 32 in

Annual Snowfall 39 in

Clear 75 days   Partly Cloudy 110 days   Cloudy 180 days

Precipitation Days: 133   Storm Days: 33

Average Temperatures			
	Daily High	Daily Low	Relative Humidity
January	31	16	75
February	34	18	72
March	43	27	70
April	58	37	67
May	69	47	66
June	79	56	67
July	83	61	68
August	82	59	71
September	74	52	72
October	63	41	71
November	48	31	74
December	35	22	76

Zero-Degree Days: 7
Freezing Days: 139
90-Degree Days: 11
Heating- and Cooling-Degree Days: 7,073

Duluth–Superior, MN–WI

Terrain: Located at Lake Superior's western tip, Duluth lies at the base of a range of hills that rise abruptly to between 600 feet and 800 feet above the lake level. Two or 3 miles back from the waterfront, however, the country assumes the character of a slightly rolling plateau. Directly opposite, on the flats occupying the east banks of St. Louis Bay, lies the city of Superior, Wisconsin. These two cities are referred to as the Twin Ports.

Climate: Rugged continental in character. Winters are long and quite cold. Snow comes early and remains on the ground until springtime. While the airport area receives more than 75 inches of snow a year, the city proper receives only about 55 inches. Summers are seldom hot, due to the northerly latitude and proximity of Lake Superior.

Pluses: Cool summers, rugged four-season climate.

Minuses: Cold.

Places Rated Score: 193

Places Rated Rank: 338

Elevation: 1,417 feet

Wind Speed: 11.4 mph

Seasonal Change

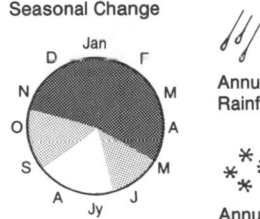

Annual Rainfall 30 in

Annual Snowfall 78 in

Clear 77 days   Partly Cloudy 103 days   Cloudy 185 days

Precipitation Days: 135   Storm Days: 35

Average Temperatures			
	Daily High	Daily Low	Relative Humidity
January	16	−3	73
February	22	2	71
March	32	14	71
April	48	29	66
May	61	39	65
June	71	48	71
July	76	54	72
August	74	53	76
September	64	44	76
October	53	35	72
November	35	21	76
December	22	6	77

Zero-Degree Days: 51
Freezing Days: 187
90-Degree Days: 2
Heating- and Cooling-Degree Days: 9,932

Edmonton, AB

Terrain: The city occupies a rolling plain in central Alberta with an elevation range of plus or minus 100 feet within a 10-mile radius. The land slopes off to the northeast and southeast, except for ridges 20 miles southeast and 20 miles west, which rise 350 feet above the airport elevation. The North Saskatchewan River flows northeast; the Sturgeon, a secondary river, lies 7 miles to the northwest.

Climate: Continental, characterized by two major seasons—summer and winter—with short, rarely orderly transitions of spring and autumn. The occurrence of snow divides the year. The warmer five months rarely have measurable snowfalls. The cooler five receive nearly all their precipitation as snow. The remaining two months, April and October, average half their totals as snow. Winter is characterized by a persistent snow cover that normally begins November 16 and stays through the season until around March 17.

Pluses: Dry, sunny springs; moderate summers with cool nights.

Minuses: Long, cold winters with persistent snow cover.

Places Rated Score: 385

Places Rated Rank: 308

Elevation: 2,201 feet

Wind Speed: 8.8 mph

Seasonal Change

Annual Rainfall 13 in

Annual Snowfall 54 in

Clear 99 days   Partly Cloudy 152 days   Cloudy 114 days

Precipitation Days: 124   Storm Days: 22

Average Temperatures			
	Daily High	Daily Low	Relative Humidity
January	13	−3	76
February	23	6	74
March	31	15	73
April	49	30	61
May	63	42	54
June	69	49	61
July	73	53	66
August	71	51	69
September	62	42	70
October	52	33	65
November	33	18	73
December	21	6	76

Zero-Degree Days: 35
Freezing Days: 185
90-Degree Days: 2
Heating- and Cooling-Degree Days: 5,552

El Paso, TX

Terrain: Located at the extreme western tip of Texas at an elevation of 3,700 feet. Across the Rio Grande to the south lies Ciudad Juárez, Mexico. The Franklin Mountains begin within the city limits and extend northward for about 16 miles. Some of these peaks reach as high as 4,500 feet to 5,000 feet above sea level. The general terrain is composed of mountains and mesas characteristic of western Texas and New Mexico.

Climate: Dry and sunny. Summer temperatures are high but not extreme. The very low relative humidity (39%) lessens the felt heat. The winter is mild, typical of arid areas at low altitudes. Rainfall is scarce year-round and fosters only scrublike desert vegetation. Irrigation is necessary for crops, gardens, and lawns. Winter nights can be cold, but the days are warm, averaging in the 50s. Similarly, summer days are hot but the nights cool, averaging in the 60s.

Pluses: Mild winters, low humidity.

Minuses: Dust storms and sandstorms.

Places Rated Score: 592

Places Rated Rank: 94

Elevation: 3,700 feet

Wind Speed: 9.6 mph

Seasonal Change

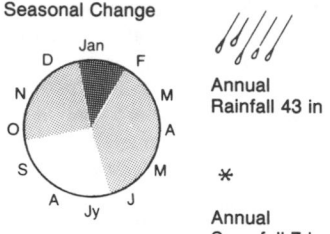

Annual Rainfall 8 in

Annual Snowfall 5 in

Clear 194 days   Partly Cloudy 100 days   Cloudy 71 days

Precipitation Days: 45   Storm Days: 36

Average Temperatures			
	Daily High	Daily Low	Relative Humidity
January	58	30	51
February	63	34	42
March	70	41	34
April	79	49	28
May	87	57	29
June	96	66	32
July	95	70	47
August	93	68	50
September	88	61	52
October	79	49	47
November	66	37	48
December	58	31	52

Zero-Degree Days: 0
Freezing Days: 64
90-Degree Days: 103
Heating- and Cooling-Degree Days: 4,776

✓ Eugene–Springfield, OR

Terrain: Situated at the southern end of the fertile Willamette Valley. This valley is bounded on both sides by mountain ranges: the Cascades to the east and the Coast Ranges to the west. To the north, the valley widens and levels out. Hills of the rolling, wooded Coast Ranges begin about 5 miles west of the airport and rise to between 1,500 feet and 2,000 feet midway between the city and the Pacific, 50 miles to the west. The Cascades, 75 miles east, reach heights of 10,000 feet. These sheltering ranges and the proximity of the ocean contribute heavily to Eugene's extremely mild climate. This is one of the nation's most important agricultural and lumbering areas.

Climate: Very mild maritime climate. Temperature minima below 20°F occur only five times a year. The temperature rarely reaches the mid-90s. Seasonal change is gradual, with intermediate seasons being as long as summer and winter.

Pluses: Mild; gradual change of seasons.

Minuses: Cloudy, damp.

Places Rated Score: 741

Places Rated Rank: 21

Elevation: 373 feet

Wind Speed: 7.6 mph

Seasonal Change

Annual Rainfall 43 in

Annual Snowfall 7 in

Clear 77 days   Partly Cloudy 81 days   Cloudy 207 days

Precipitation Days: 137   Storm Days: 5

Average Temperatures			
	Daily High	Daily Low	Relative Humidity
January	46	34	86
February	51	36	83
March	55	37	78
April	61	39	74
May	67	43	73
June	74	48	70
July	83	51	63
August	81	51	64
September	76	48	66
October	65	42	78
November	53	38	86
December	47	35	89

Zero-Degree Days: 0
Freezing Days: 54
90-Degree Days: 15
Heating- and Cooling-Degree Days: 4,739

Evansville–Henderson, IN–KY

Terrain: Located on the Ohio River near the juncture of Indiana, Illinois, and Kentucky. The country around Evansville ranges from level to rolling. Dress Regional Airport, where weather observations have been made since 1940, is in a shallow valley with low hills to the east and west that run parallel to the valley but slope downward to the south. The open end of this valley slopes down to the south-southwest toward Evansville and the Ohio River.

Climate: Prevailing wind here is from the south, and, although Evansville is 550 miles from the Gulf of Mexico, its weather generally resembles that of its neighbors to the south. Strong cold winds sometimes blow from the north and northwest following cold fronts. As soon as the high-pressure ridge moves by, the wind backs around again from the south. Snowfall varies a great deal from year to year; accumulation is rare. Average growing season: 199 days. Average date of last freeze: April 7. First freeze: October 23.

Pluses: Influenced by Gulf winds.

Minuses: Summers can be hot and humid.

Places Rated Score: 550

Places Rated Rank: 155

Elevation: 388 feet

Wind Speed: 8.3 mph

Seasonal Change

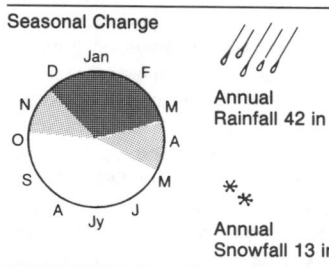

Annual Rainfall 42 in

Annual Snowfall 13 in

Clear 103 days   Partly Cloudy 100 days   Cloudy 162 days

Precipitation Days: 114   Storm Days: 45

Average Temperatures			
	Daily High	Daily Low	Relative Humidity
January	39	22	72
February	44	26	71
March	55	35	70
April	68	45	67
May	77	54	69
June	86	63	68
July	89	67	71
August	87	65	72
September	81	57	73
October	70	45	68
November	55	35	71
December	44	27	74

Zero-Degree Days: 3
Freezing Days: 103
90-Degree Days: 39
Heating- and Cooling-Degree Days: 5,993

Fargo–Moorhead, ND–MN

Terrain: Moorhead, Minnesota, and Fargo, North Dakota, are twin cities in the Red River valley of the north. This river flows between the two cities and is part of the Hudson Bay drainage area. The river has no effect on the climate but does cause occasional, severe spring flooding. Surrounding terrain is flat and open.

Climate: Summers are generally comfortable, with a few days of hot and humid weather; nights are cool. Winter months are cold and dry, with maximum temperatures rising above freezing only six times per month. At night, the temperature drops below zero half the time. With the flat terrain, surface friction has little slowing effect on the wind, contributing to the legendary Dakota blizzards. Strong winds with even, light snowfall cause heavy snowdrifts. Surprisingly, the area averages only 35 inches of snow per year.

Pluses: Pleasant, dry summers.

Minuses: Extremely rigorous; ranks next to last in mildness of the 343 metro areas.

Places Rated Score: 148

Places Rated Rank: 342

Elevation: 899 feet

Wind Speed: 12.7 mph

Seasonal Change

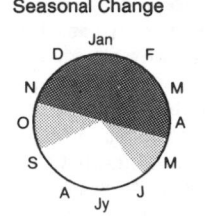

Annual Rainfall 20 in

Annual Snowfall 35 in

Clear 87 days · Partly Cloudy 112 days · Cloudy 166 days

Precipitation Days: 102   Storm Days: 33

Average Temperatures			
	Daily High	Daily Low	Relative Humidity
January	14	−5	73
February	21	2	75
March	33	15	76
April	53	32	68
May	68	43	64
June	77	54	69
July	83	58	70
August	81	56	70
September	70	46	72
October	58	35	70
November	37	19	76
December	21	4	76

Zero-Degree Days: 54
Freezing Days: 181
90-Degree Days: 15
Heating- and Cooling-Degree Days: 9,744

Fort Myers–Cape Coral, FL

Terrain: Located on the south bank of the Caloosahatchee River, about 15 miles from the Gulf of Mexico, Fort Myers sits on land that is level and low, with lush greenery.

Climate: Subtropical, with temperature extremes of both summer and winter checked by the influence of the Gulf. The average annual mean temperature is a warm 74°F, with averages ranging from the low 60s in January to the low 80s in the summer months. Winters are mild, with many bright, warm days and moderately cool nights. Maximum temperatures average in the low 90s from June through the first part of September, with daily highs of 90°F or greater on 80% of the days. Rainfall averages more than 50 inches annually, with two-thirds of this total coming between June and September. Most rain falls as late afternoon or early evening thunderstorms, which in the summer bring welcome relief from the heat and occur almost every day.

Pluses: Mild, sunny winters.

Minuses: Hot, humid, stormy.

Places Rated Score: 342

Places Rated Rank: 322

Elevation: 15 feet

Wind Speed: 8.2 mph

Seasonal Change

Annual Rainfall 54 in

Annual Snowfall 0 in

Clear 103 days · Partly Cloudy 161 days · Cloudy 101 days

Precipitation Days: 112   Storm Days: 93

Average Temperatures			
	Daily High	Daily Low	Relative Humidity
January	74	53	73
February	75	53	72
March	80	58	71
April	85	62	68
May	89	67	69
June	90	72	74
July	91	74	75
August	91	74	75
September	90	74	76
October	85	68	73
November	80	60	73
December	76	54	73

Zero-Degree Days: 0
Freezing Days: 1
90-Degree Days: 106
Heating- and Cooling-Degree Days: 4,168

Fort Smith, AR–OK

Terrain: Located at the confluence of the Poteau and Arkansas rivers. About 20 miles to the northwest are the Cookson Hills, which have an elevation of 1,500 feet. To the northeast are the Boston Mountains (in the Ozark region of Arkansas), 2,700 feet high. To the west, south, and east, the terrain is broken hills separated by creek- and river-bottom land. The bottomlands are very fertile and produce large yields of hay, beans, and spinach. Small wild game is plentiful; lakes and streams have an abundance of game fish.

Climate: Well suited to raising fruits and berries. The climate is generally mild, except during the summer, which can be hot.

Pluses: Mild.

Minuses: Hot summers.

Places Rated Score: 482

Places Rated Rank: 249

Elevation: 463 feet

Wind Speed: 7.6 mph

Seasonal Change

Annual Rainfall 42 in

Annual Snowfall 6 in

Clear 124 days · Partly Cloudy 96 days · Cloudy 145 days

Precipitation Days: 96   Storm Days: 57

Average Temperatures			
	Daily High	Daily Low	Relative Humidity
January	48	27	71
February	54	31	69
March	63	39	66
April	74	49	67
May	81	58	73
June	89	66	73
July	94	71	72
August	93	69	71
September	86	62	72
October	76	49	69
November	62	38	70
December	52	30	72

Zero-Degree Days: 0
Freezing Days: 80
90-Degree Days: 65
Heating- and Cooling-Degree Days: 5,358

Fort Wayne, IN

Terrain: Located at the junction of the St. Mary's, St. Joseph, and Maumee rivers in northeastern Indiana. Terrain is generally level south and east of the city. Southwest and west, the land is somewhat rolling, while to the northwest and north it becomes slightly hilly. The highest point in the area is 40 miles north, near the town of Angola, where the elevation is 1,060 feet above sea level.
Climate: Similar to that of other midwestern cities at the same latitude. Precipitation is well distributed throughout the year, varying from a monthly rate of 2 inches in February to 4 inches in May. Damaging hailstorms may be expected twice a year. Snow usually covers the ground for 30 days each winter, but heavy snowstorms are rare. Average date of last freeze: April 26. First freeze: October 17.

Pluses: Milder version of Great Interior climate.

Minuses: Cold winters, hot summers.

Places Rated Score: 509　　**Places Rated Rank: 220**

Elevation: 828 feet

Wind Speed: 10.3 mph

Seasonal Change

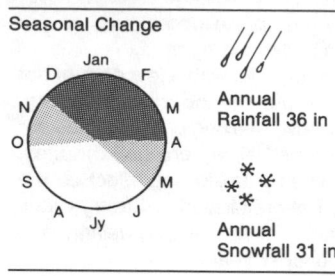

Annual Rainfall 36 in

Annual Snowfall 31 in

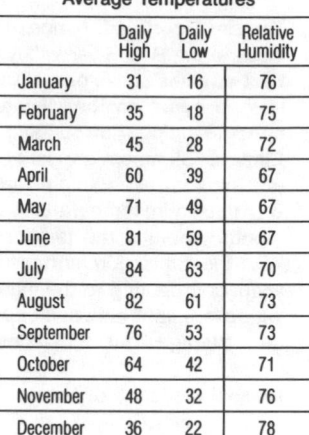

Clear 77 days　Partly Cloudy 105 days　Cloudy 183 days

Precipitation Days: 131　　Storm Days: 41

Average Temperatures			
	Daily High	Daily Low	Relative Humidity
January	31	16	76
February	35	18	75
March	45	28	72
April	60	39	67
May	71	49	67
June	81	59	67
July	84	63	70
August	82	61	73
September	76	53	73
October	64	42	71
November	48	32	76
December	36	22	78

Zero-Degree Days: 10
Freezing Days: 134
90-Degree Days: 14
Heating- and Cooling-Degree Days: 6,957

Fresno, CA

Terrain: Rests in the middle of the San Joaquin Valley, near its eastern edge. The valley runs northwest to southeast and is about 225 miles long, with an average width of about 50 miles. The terrain around Fresno is generally level, with an abrupt upward slope 15 miles eastward to the foothills of the Sierra Nevada. This mountain range lies 50 miles to the east and has elevations from 12,000 feet to 14,000 feet. Forty-five miles to the west lie the foothills of the Coast Ranges.
Climate: Dry and sunny. Winters are mild; summers are hot. Ninety percent of the city's precipitation falls between November and April. Summers are virtually rainless. Because of the great amount of sunshine the valley receives, and the blockage of cooler moist air from the Pacific, daily maximum temperatures in July climb to the upper 90s. But on summer afternoons, the relative humidity is only 5% to 8%; on winter mornings, it is 90%.

Pluses: Sunny; nice springs and falls.

Minuses: Hot summers.

Places Rated Score: 559　　**Places Rated Rank: 138**

Elevation: 327 feet

Wind Speed: 6.3 mph

Seasonal Change

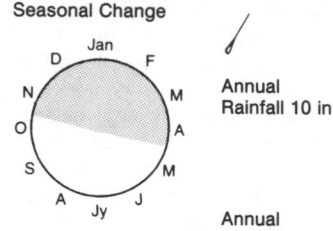

Annual Rainfall 10 in

Annual Snowfall 0 in

Clear 200 days　Partly Cloudy 71 days　Cloudy 94 days

Precipitation Days: 44　　Storm Days: 6

Average Temperatures			
	Daily High	Daily Low	Relative Humidity
January	54	37	79
February	61	40	73
March	67	42	67
April	74	47	58
May	83	53	49
June	91	59	44
July	98	64	42
August	96	62	46
September	90	58	50
October	80	50	56
November	65	41	71
December	54	36	80

Zero-Degree Days: 0
Freezing Days: 29
90-Degree Days: 107
Heating- and Cooling-Degree Days: 4,321

✓ Galveston–Texas City, TX

Terrain: Located on Galveston Island, off the southeast coast of Texas. The island is nearly 3 miles across at its widest point and 29 miles long. It is bounded on the southeast by the Gulf of Mexico and on the northwest by Galveston Bay, which is about 3 miles wide at this point. The island's low-lying terrain makes it especially vulnerable to tidal surges.
Climate: Predominantly marine, with periods of modified continental influence during the colder months, when cold fronts from the northwest sometimes reach the coast. Winters are very mild, with temperatures below 34°F recorded only about four times each winter. Normal daily maximum temperatures range from 60°F in January to 88°F in August, while minima range from 48°F in January to the upper 70s in the summer. The Great Hurricane of 1900, which swept over the island and killed approximately 6,000 people, was the worst natural disaster in American history. It also made inland Houston the major regional city, relegating Galveston to a resort community.

Pluses: Mild maritime climate.　**Minuses:** Hot summer spells.
Places Rated Score: 727　　**Places Rated Rank: 23**

Elevation: 7 feet

Wind Speed: 11 mph

Seasonal Change

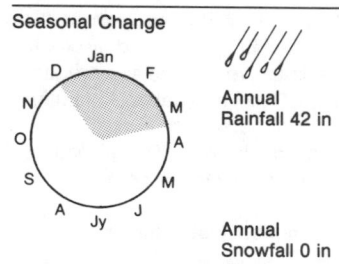

Annual Rainfall 42 in

Annual Snowfall 0 in

Clear 94 days　Partly Cloudy 109 days　Cloudy 162 days

Precipitation Days: 90　　Storm Days: 70

Average Temperatures			
	Daily High	Daily Low	Relative Humidity
January	59	48	81
February	61	50	79
March	66	57	80
April	73	65	81
May	80	72	79
June	85	77	76
July	87	79	76
August	88	79	75
September	85	75	75
October	78	68	73
November	68	58	78
December	62	51	81

Zero-Degree Days: 0
Freezing Days: 4
90-Degree Days: 11
Heating- and Cooling-Degree Days: 4,228

Grand Rapids–Muskegon–Holland, MI

Terrain: Located in the Grand River valley 30 miles east of Lake Michigan. The Grand River, Michigan's largest stream, bisects the city. The valley has tall hills and bluffs rising on all sides, ranging in elevation from 600 feet to 1,000 feet. The area is known for fruit growing, especially peaches and cherries.

Climate: Largely determined by the proximity of Lake Michigan. In spring, the cooling effect of the lake retards the growth of vegetation until the danger of frost is past. In the fall, the warming effect holds off frost until the crops have matured. Summer days are warm and pleasant, with cooler nights. Winters are snowy and cold, but extremely cold temperatures or prolonged cold spells are rare because of the warm lake breeze. Average growing season: 170 days. Average date of last freeze: April 25. First freeze: October 12.

Pluses: Pleasant summers, temperatures moderated by Lake Michigan.

Minuses: Very cloudy, lots of snow.

Places Rated Score: 513

Places Rated Rank: 216

Elevation: 803 feet

Wind Speed: 9.9 mph

Seasonal Change

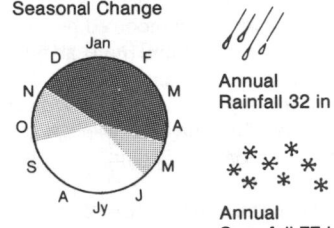

Annual Rainfall 32 in

Annual Snowfall 77 in

Clear 67 days   Partly Cloudy 96 days   Cloudy 202 days

Precipitation Days: 144   Storm Days: 37

Average Temperatures			
	Daily High	Daily Low	Relative Humidity
January	29	15	77
February	32	16	74
March	42	25	72
April	57	36	68
May	69	46	66
June	79	55	68
July	83	60	70
August	81	58	73
September	73	51	75
October	61	40	74
November	46	31	76
December	34	21	79

Zero-Degree Days: 8
Freezing Days: 149
90-Degree Days: 11
Heating- and Cooling-Degree Days: 7,376

Great Falls, MT

Terrain: Located astride the main stem of the Missouri River at its confluence with the Sun River. Except to the north and northeast, the valley is bordered by mountain ranges, which lie about 30 miles away from east to south, 40 miles to the southwest, and 60 miles to 100 miles from west to northwest. Terrain plays an important part in the climate here; the Continental Divide to the west and the Big Belt and Little Belt mountains to the south are major factors in producing the frequent wintertime Chinook winds blowing through this part of the state.

Climate: Semiarid. Summers are cool, sunny, and pleasant. Seventy percent of the annual rainfall occurs between April and September, the growing season. Winters are cold but continually modified by Chinook winds, which bear warm air from the Pacific, causing rapid warming and preventing accumulation of snow.

Pluses: Good, rigorous climate.

Minuses: Long winters.

Places Rated Score: 410

Places Rated Rank: 299

Elevation: 702 feet

Wind Speed: 13.1 mph

Seasonal Change

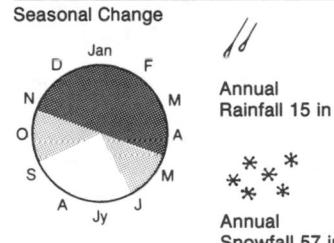

Annual Rainfall 15 in

Annual Snowfall 57 in

Clear 81 days   Partly Cloudy 106 days   Cloudy 178 days

Precipitation Days: 100   Storm Days: 26

Average Temperatures			
	Daily High	Daily Low	Relative Humidity
January	28	9	63
February	37	17	61
March	42	21	59
April	54	31	54
May	65	41	55
June	74	49	55
July	84	54	48
August	82	53	48
September	71	44	53
October	60	36	53
November	44	25	60
December	35	17	63

Zero-Degree Days: 28
Freezing Days: 156
90-Degree Days: 22
Heating- and Cooling-Degree Days: 7,991

Green Bay, WI

Terrain: Located at the mouth of the Fox River, which empties into the southernmost end of Green Bay, a long and narrow bay off Lake Michigan in northeastern Wisconsin. The comparatively small temperature variation and the fact that the majority of precipitation falls during the growing periods contribute to successful dairy farming, as well as large acreages of vegetables, grown mostly for canning. Apple and cherry orchards predominate locally, with potatoes grown widely farther west.

Climate: Continental, modified somewhat by the proximity of Lake Superior to the northwest and Lake Michigan and Green Bay to the east. Summers are pleasant, with cool evenings and nights. Winters tend to be long and cold. Has a moderate amount of snow for a city in this region and latitude.

Pluses: Cool summers.

Minuses: Long winters.

Places Rated Score: 367

Places Rated Rank: 316

Elevation: 702 feet

Wind Speed: 10.2 mph

Seasonal Change

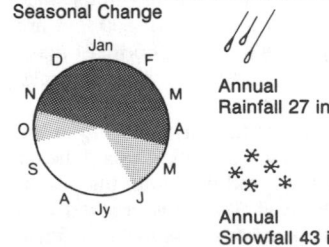

Annual Rainfall 27 in

Annual Snowfall 43 in

Clear 90 days   Partly Cloudy 102 days   Cloudy 173 days

Precipitation Days: 120   Storm Days: 35

Average Temperatures			
	Daily High	Daily Low	Relative Humidity
January	23	5	74
February	27	9	74
March	37	20	73
April	54	34	68
May	67	44	67
June	76	53	69
July	81	58	71
August	79	56	75
September	70	48	76
October	59	38	74
November	42	26	76
December	29	13	77

Zero-Degree Days: 29
Freezing Days: 163
90-Degree Days: 7
Heating- and Cooling-Degree Days: 8,484

Greensboro–Winston-Salem–High Point, NC

Terrain: Located in the northern Piedmont section of North Carolina at the headwaters of the Haw and Deep rivers. Bounded to the west and north by ridges beyond which lie the Brushy and Blue Ridge mountains, respectively.

Climate: Winter temperatures and rainfall are both modified by the mountain barrier. Freezing temperatures occur on more than half the winter days, but zero weather is almost unknown. Light snow may fall, perhaps two snows of an inch or more per year; ice-glazing is more common here than in most of North Carolina—an average of four times a year—but it is seldom severe or long-lasting.

Pluses: Mild, four-season climate; rarely subfreezing.

Minuses: Gray, wet winters.

Places Rated Score: 626

Places Rated Rank: 58

Elevation: 89.7 feet

Wind Speed: 7.6 mph

Seasonal Change

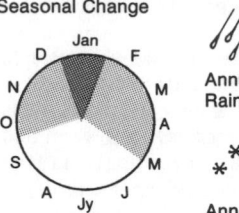

Annual Rainfall 42 in

Annual Snowfall 9 in

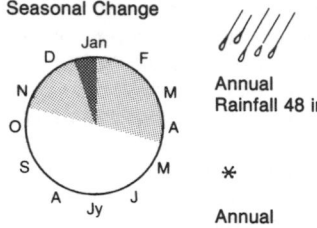

Clear 111 days   Partly Cloudy 106 days   Cloudy 148 days

Precipitation Days: 121   Storm Days: 46

Average Temperatures			
	Daily High	Daily Low	Relative Humidity
January	48	27	68
February	51	29	64
March	59	37	64
April	71	46	63
May	78	55	69
June	84	63	71
July	87	67	74
August	86	66	75
September	80	59	74
October	70	47	71
November	60	37	68
December	50	30	68

Zero-Degree Days: *
Freezing Days: 90
90-Degree Days: 28
Heating- and Cooling-Degree Days: 5,166

Greenville–Spartanburg–Anderson, SC

Terrain: Located on the Piedmont Plateau, on the eastern slope of the southern Appalachian Mountains. It is rolling country with the first ridge of mountains about 20 miles to the northwest. These mountains usually protect the area from the full force of the cold air masses that move southeastward from central Canada during the winter.

Climate: The area's elevation is conducive to cool nights, even during the summer months. The temperature rises to 90°F or above on almost half of the days during the summer but usually falls to 70°F or lower at night. Winters are mild and pleasant, with the temperature falling below freezing during daylight hours only several times annually, though the nights are colder. There are usually two freezing rainstorms and two or three small snowstorms each winter. Rainfall is abundant and well distributed throughout the year. The region is fairly stormy, but tornadoes are infrequent. Average growing season: 225 days.

Pluses: Mildness coupled with variety.

Minuses: Hot summers.

Places Rated Score: 655

Places Rated Rank: 37

Elevation: 971 feet

Wind Speed: 6.8 mph

Seasonal Change

Annual Rainfall 48 in

Annual Snowfall 6 in

Clear 117 days   Partly Cloudy 104 days   Cloudy 144 days

Precipitation Days: 119   Storm Days: 44

Average Temperatures			
	Daily High	Daily Low	Relative Humidity
January	51	31	66
February	55	33	63
March	63	39	64
April	73	48	63
May	80	57	68
June	85	64	70
July	88	68	73
August	88	67	75
September	82	62	74
October	72	49	69
November	62	40	67
December	54	33	67

Zero-Degree Days: 0
Freezing Days: 68
90-Degree Days: 29
Heating- and Cooling-Degree Days: 4,736

✓ Halifax, NS

Terrain: The city lies on the west side of the harbor on a peninsula virtually surrounded by seas: the Gulf of St. Lawrence to the north, the Bay of Fundy to the west, and the Atlantic Ocean to the south and east. The surrounding area is flat to rolling with numerous small lakes, especially to the north and east. Elevations of 500 feet are reached in three areas in the vicinity: 11 miles to the north, 21 miles to the north-northwest in the Devon area, and in the Mt. Uniacke area 25 miles to the northwest.

Climate: Each year there is an average of 122 days with fog at the International Airport. Atlantic and Fundy waters help to keep the air temperature cool in spring and summer and moderate the harshness of winter. The presence of the Gulf Stream is credited with prolonging fall—the season Nova Scotians consider to be the finest of the year. Precipitation is experienced as rain and is spread evenly throughout the year. Atlantic storms produce highly changeable and generally stormy weather; winter storms are especially devastating, packing a variety of weather conditions from hurricane-force winds to heavy precipitation.

Pluses: Cool summers and brilliant falls.

Minuses: Misty, foggy, stormy winters.

Places Rated Score: 669

Places Rated Rank: 31

Elevation: 499 feet

Wind Speed: 10.8 mph

Seasonal Change

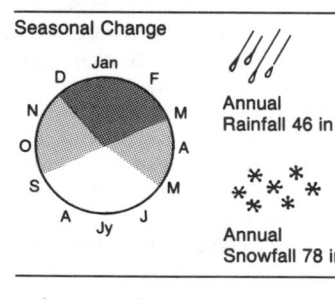

Annual Rainfall 46 in

Annual Snowfall 78 in

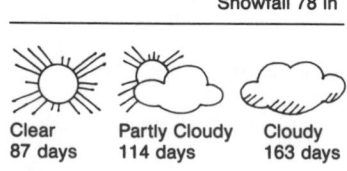

Clear 87 days   Partly Cloudy 114 days   Cloudy 163 days

Precipitation Days: 150   Storm Days: 10

Average Temperatures			
	Daily High	Daily Low	Relative Humidity
January	29	21	82
February	29	21	80
March	37	29	79
April	46	38	78
May	58	49	78
June	69	59	81
July	74	65	83
August	74	65	82
September	66	57	80
October	55	47	80
November	45	38	82
December	34	27	83

Zero-Degree Days: 2
Freezing Days: 146
90-Degree Days: 0
Heating- and Cooling-Degree Days: 4,242

Harrisburg–Lebanon–Carlisle, PA

Terrain: Situated on the east bank of the Susquehanna River in the Great Valley formed by the eastern foothills of the Appalachian chain and about 60 miles southeast of the state's geographic center. It is nestled in a saucerlike depression 8 miles to 10 miles south of the Blue Mountains. This serves as a barrier to severe winter weather experienced 50 miles to 100 miles to the north and west. Although Harrisburg is too far inland (150 miles) to derive full benefits of the coastal climate, it does receive precipitation produced when warm, maritime air from the Atlantic is forced upslope to cross the Blue Ridge Mountains.

Climate: Although the saucer-shaped valley protects the area from generally severe winter weather, it often traps cool air, which causes the accumulation of heavy fog and industrial smoke. Fortunately, the weather is changeable enough so that this trapped air does not remain for long. Average growing season: 201 days.

Pluses: Relatively mild winters, changeable weather.

Minuses: Damp, foggy.

Places Rated Score: 556   **Places Rated Rank: 149**

Elevation: 351 feet

Wind Speed: 7.7 mph

Seasonal Change

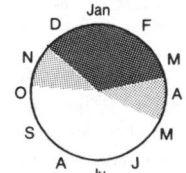

Annual Rainfall 36 in

Annual Snowfall 35 in

Clear 86 days   Partly Cloudy 107 days   Cloudy 172 days

Precipitation Days: 125   Storm Days: 33

Average Temperatures			
	Daily High	Daily Low	Relative Humidity
January	37	22	65
February	40	24	63
March	50	32	62
April	63	42	60
May	73	51	63
June	82	61	65
July	86	65	66
August	84	64	69
September	77	57	71
October	65	45	68
November	52	35	67
December	41	26	66

Zero-Degree Days: 1
Freezing Days: 107
90-Degree Days: 24
Heating- and Cooling-Degree Days: 6,249

Hartford, CT

Terrain: Located on the Connecticut River on a slight rise of ground between north-south mountain ranges whose heights do not exceed 1,200 feet. It is near the state's geographic center, about 30 miles due north of Long Island Sound.

Climate: Varies from the cold continental climate in winter to the warm maritime air of summer. Hartford's latitude places it well within the northern temperate climate zone, with westerly winds bearing the majority of weather systems. The average wintertime polar front, which is the boundary between masses of cold, dry polar air and the warm, moist air of the tropics, is just south of New England. This helps explain the great changeability of the weather in New England, characterized by rapidly shifting winds and temperatures, and frequent storms. Hartford's proximity to the ocean is also significant, since many storms move upward along the Atlantic Coast, frequently producing strong and persistent northeast winds.

Pluses: Changeable, varied, yet relatively mild.

Minuses: Stormy.

Places Rated Score: 516   **Places Rated Rank: 210**

Elevation: 179 feet

Wind Speed: 9 mph

Seasonal Change

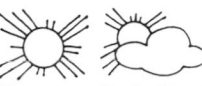

Annual Rainfall 43 in

Annual Snowfall 53 in

Clear 78 days   Partly Cloudy 110 days   Cloudy 177 days

Precipitation Days: 128   Storm Days: 22

Average Temperatures			
	Daily High	Daily Low	Relative Humidity
January	34	17	64
February	36	19	63
March	46	28	61
April	60	38	57
May	71	47	60
June	80	57	64
July	85	62	65
August	83	60	68
September	75	52	70
October	64	41	67
November	51	33	67
December	37	21	67

Zero-Degree Days: 6
Freezing Days: 36
90-Degree Days: 20
Heating- and Cooling-Degree Days: 6,934

✓ Honolulu, HI

Terrain: Oahu, the island on which Honolulu is located, is the third largest of the Hawaiian Islands. The Koolau Range, at an average height of 2,000 feet, parallels the northeast coast. The Waianae Mountains, somewhat higher in elevation, parallel the west coast. Much of the city lies along the coastal plain, leeward (relative to the trade winds) of the Koolaus.

Climate: Mild marine tropical. Honolulu shows the least seasonal temperature change of any American city; the difference between the mean January minimum temperature and the August maximum mean temperature is only about 22 degrees. Honolulu's location just south of the Tropic of Cancer in the Pacific Ocean assures this mildness. It has no snow, fog, or freezing weather, and an average of only nine 90-degree days and seven thunderstorms a year. There are no heating-degree days here. Although it can be uncomfortably warm occasionally, the persistent trade winds give relief.

Pluses: Extremely mild.

Minuses: A bit monotonous.

Places Rated Score: 717   **Places Rated Rank: 25**

Elevation: 15 feet

Wind Speed: 11.8 mph

Seasonal Change

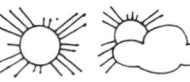

Annual Rainfall 23 in

Annual Snowfall 0 in

Clear 90 days   Partly Cloudy 174 days   Cloudy 101 days

Precipitation Days: 102   Storm Days: 7

Average Temperatures			
	Daily High	Daily Low	Relative Humidity
January	80	65	71
February	80	65	69
March	81	67	65
April	83	69	63
May	85	70	60
June	86	72	59
July	87	73	59
August	88	74	60
September	88	73	60
October	87	72	63
November	84	69	67
December	81	67	70

Zero-Degree Days: 0
Freezing Days: 0
90-Degree Days: 9
Heating- and Cooling-Degree Days: 4,221

Houston, TX

Terrain: Located in the flat Coastal Plain of the state, about 50 miles inland from the Gulf of Mexico and 25 miles from Galveston Bay. The numerous surrounding small streams and bayous, together with the bay, favor the development of both ground and advective fogs. The land is low and flat and, since it receives almost 50 inches of rain a year, is ideal for agriculture—especially fruit farming—and live-stock raising.

Climate: Predominantly marine. Temperatures are modified by winds from the Gulf. Winters are mild. Summer days are hot and humid, though the evenings are relatively cool. Polar air penetrates the area frequently enough to provide some stimulating variety. Although temperatures dip below freezing occasionally, they never remain there long, accounting for a year-round growing season. Destructive windstorms are fairly infrequent, but thunderstorms and hurricanes occur occasionally.

Pluses: Mild winters.   **Minuses:** Hot and humid.

Places Rated Score: 424   **Places Rated Rank: 292**

Elevation: 108 feet

Wind Speed: 6.1 mph

Seasonal Change

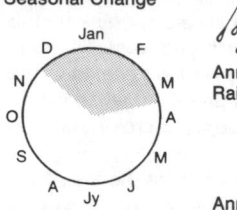

Annual Rainfall 48 in

Annual Snowfall 0 in

Clear 94 days   Partly Cloudy 109 days   Cloudy 162 days

Precipitation Days: 107   Storm Days: 69

Average Temperatures			
	Daily High	Daily Low	Relative Humidity
January	62	41	75
February	66	43	74
March	72	50	73
April	79	58	74
May	85	65	76
June	91	70	76
July	94	73	76
August	93	72	76
September	89	68	77
October	82	58	74
November	72	49	74
December	65	43	74

Zero-Degree Days: 0
Freezing Days: 24
90-Degree Days: 81
Heating- and Cooling-Degree Days: 4,323

Huntsville, AL

Terrain: The city is almost surrounded by the foothills of the Appalachian Mountains. The Tennessee River winds its way westward about 7 miles south of the city, and the broad and fertile Tennessee Valley, with flat to gently rolling terrain, extends to the west.

Climate: Cold air masses from the north predominate during the winter, but at times mild air from the Gulf of Mexico, spreading northward to Huntsville and beyond, may persist for several days. There are very few severely cold days. Temperatures drop below zero on an average of once a year. Springs are variable and can be stormy as cold polar air and warm Gulf air meet. Summers are hot and humid, relieved only by the showers that come about every three days. Falls are dry, cooler, and pleasant. The length of the growing season, 241 days, and high rainfall make the area suitable for truck farming.

Pluses: Mild yet variable winter through spring.   **Minuses:** Hot, humid summers.

Places Rated Score: 600   **Places Rated Rank: 87**

Elevation: 644 feet

Wind Speed: 8 mph

Seasonal Change

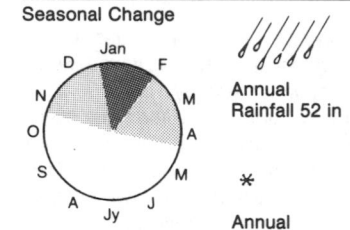

Annual Rainfall 52 in

❄

Annual Snowfall 3 in

Clear 106 days   Partly Cloudy 101 days   Cloudy 158 days

Precipitation Days: 121   Storm Days: 58

Average Temperatures			
	Daily High	Daily Low	Relative Humidity
January	49	31	74
February	54	33	70
March	62	41	68
April	73	50	67
May	80	58	72
June	87	65	72
July	89	69	75
August	89	68	74
September	84	62	75
October	73	49	71
November	62	39	71
December	53	34	72

Zero-Degree Days: 0
Freezing Days: 65
90-Degree Days: 38
Heating- and Cooling-Degree Days: 5,110

Indianapolis, IN

Terrain: Located in the central part of the state on mostly level or slightly rolling terrain. The greater part of the city lies east of the White River, which flows approximately from north to south. From Weir Cook Airport, 7 miles southwest of the city, the terrain slopes gradually downward to the city, then upward again past the city to the east.

Climate: Continental. Rather warm summers, moderately cold winters, and occasional wide variations in temperatures, especially during the cold season. Snowfalls of 3 inches or more occur about three times annually. Periods of muggy weather can occur in summer, although usually air masses from the Gulf of Mexico are soon replaced by cooler air from the northern Plains and Great Lakes. Occasionally, hot dry winds from the Southwest prevail. Late spring and fall are the most pleasant seasons. Precipitation, well distributed throughout the year, is normally adequate for good crops. Several flood-control reservoirs protect most formerly flood-prone areas.

Pluses: Pleasant springs and falls.   **Minuses:** Humid spells in summer, cold winters.

Places Rated Score: 557   **Places Rated Rank: 147**

Elevation: 808 feet

Wind Speed: 9.7 mph

Seasonal Change

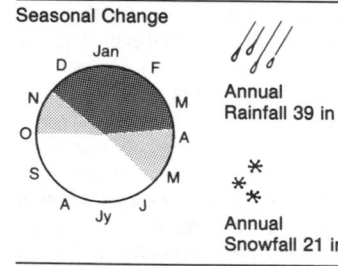

Annual Rainfall 39 in

❄ ❄
❄ ❄

Annual Snowfall 21 in

Clear 90 days   Partly Cloudy 101 days   Cloudy 174 days

Precipitation Days: 122   Storm Days: 45

Average Temperatures			
	Daily High	Daily Low	Relative Humidity
January	34	18	76
February	39	21	74
March	49	31	71
April	63	42	67
May	73	52	69
June	82	61	69
July	85	65	73
August	84	63	76
September	78	55	74
October	66	43	72
November	51	33	75
December	39	24	78

Zero-Degree Days: 7
Freezing Days: 122
90-Degree Days: 15
Heating- and Cooling-Degree Days: 6,551

Jackson, MS

Terrain: Jackson is about 45 miles east of the Mississippi River on the west bank of the Pearl River and about 150 miles north of the Gulf of Mexico. The terrain is gently rolling, with no local topographic features that appreciably influence the weather. Alluvial plains up to 3 miles wide extend along the river near Jackson. Some levees have been built on both sides of the river.

Climate: Significantly humid during most of the year, with one short cold season and one long warm one. In summer, the southerly winds and accompanying warm Gulf air masses predominate, resulting in a warm, humid maritime climate. Summer days are hot and humid, and often so are the nights. In winter, colder northern air occasionally invades the area, causing rapid and sometimes dramatic temperature shifts. Average freeze-free period: 235 days.

Pluses: Long summers.

Minuses: Hot, humid, stormy.

Places Rated Score: 412

Places Rated Rank: 207

Elevation: 331 feet

Wind Speed: 7.6 mph

Seasonal Change

Annual Rainfall 49 in

Annual Snowfall 1 in

Clear 109 days   Partly Cloudy 108 days   Cloudy 148 days

Precipitation Days: 112   Storm Days: 65

Average Temperatures			
	Daily High	Daily Low	Relative Humidity
January	57	35	76
February	61	37	74
March	68	44	72
April	77	53	73
May	84	61	74
June	91	68	74
July	93	71	76
August	92	70	76
September	88	65	76
October	79	51	73
November	68	42	74
December	60	37	76

Zero-Degree Days: 0
Freezing Days: 47
90-Degree Days: 78
Heating- and Cooling-Degree Days: 4,621

Jacksonville, FL

Terrain: Jacksonville, located on the St. Johns River about 16 miles inland from the Atlantic Ocean, is near the northern boundary of the trade winds. The surrounding terrain is level.

Climate: Humid subtropical. The atmosphere is moist, with an average relative humidity of about 75%, ranging from a high of 90% in early morning to about 55% in late afternoon. The average daily sunshine ranges from five and one-half hours in December to nine hours in May. The greatest amount of rain, mostly in the form of local thundershowers, falls during the last summer months, when a measurable amount can be expected every other day.

Pluses: Pleasant winters.

Minuses: Hot, stormy summers.

Places Rated Score: 457

Places Rated Rank: 269

Elevation: 31 feet

Wind Speed: 8.5 mph

Seasonal Change

Annual Rainfall 54 in

Annual Snowfall 0 in

Clear 98 days   Partly Cloudy 128 days   Cloudy 139 days

Precipitation Days: 116   Storm Days: 64

Average Temperatures			
	Daily High	Daily Low	Relative Humidity
January	65	42	72
February	67	43	70
March	73	49	68
April	80	56	67
May	85	63	68
June	89	69	72
July	91	72	73
August	90	72	76
September	87	69	77
October	80	59	75
November	72	49	73
December	66	43	73

Zero-Degree Days: 0
Freezing Days: 12
90-Degree Days: 82
Heating- and Cooling-Degree Days: 3,923

✓ Johnson City–Kingsport–Bristol, TN–VA

Terrain: This tri-city area is located in the extreme upper east Tennessee Valley. Mountain ranges begin about 10 miles to the southeast and 15 miles to the west and north, with many peaks and ridges rising to 4,000 feet, and some to 6,000 feet in the southeast.

Climate: The topography has considerable influence on the weather changes peculiar to this area. Moist, easterly airflow in the lower levels of the atmosphere is more or less blocked on the eastern slopes of the mountains, thus producing an abundance of precipitation in these higher ridges and reaching the tri-city area drier and slightly warmer. Although average annual rainfall is 41 inches in the vicinity, annual amounts of 80 inches have been recorded in mountainous sections to the east and south. Snowfall seldom begins before November and rarely remains on the ground more than a few days. Mountainous regions to the southeast, however, are frequently blanketed for long periods.

Pluses: Mild winters.

Minuses: Can be drizzly.

Places Rated Score: 663

Places Rated Rank: 34

Elevation: 1,525 feet

Wind Speed: 5.6 mph

Seasonal Change

Annual Rainfall 41 in

Annual Snowfall 16 in

Clear 90 days   Partly Cloudy 112 days   Cloudy 163 days

Precipitation Days: 134   Storm Days: 45

Average Temperatures			
	Daily High	Daily Low	Relative Humidity
January	45	26	71
February	48	27	69
March	58	35	66
April	68	44	65
May	76	53	72
June	83	60	74
July	86	64	77
August	85	63	77
September	80	57	75
October	70	45	71
November	57	35	70
December	48	28	72

Zero-Degree Days: 1
Freezing Days: 96
90-Degree Days: 13
Heating- and Cooling-Degree Days: 5,413

Kansas City, MO–KS

Terrain: Kansas City is very near the geographic center of the United States. The surrounding terrain is gently rolling. Its continental climate is modified by a lack of natural obstructions to the free sweep of air currents from all directions.

Climate: Early spring brings a period of frequent and rapid fluctuations of weather, tapering off as spring progresses. Summer days are warm, sometimes hot, but nights are mild with moderate humidity. As with so many locations in America's heartland, fall is the most pleasant season, characterized by many mild sunny days and cool nights. Average date of last freeze: April 7. First freeze: October 26.

Pluses: Sunny; good four-season climate.

Minuses: Variable weather in early spring; winters can be cold, summers hot.

Places Rated Score: 549

Places Rated Rank: 157

Elevation: 1,025 feet

Wind Speed: 10.3 mph

Seasonal Change

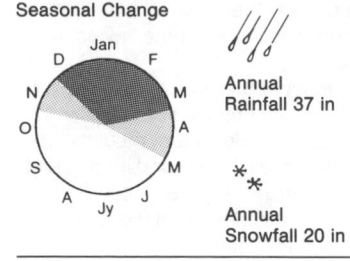

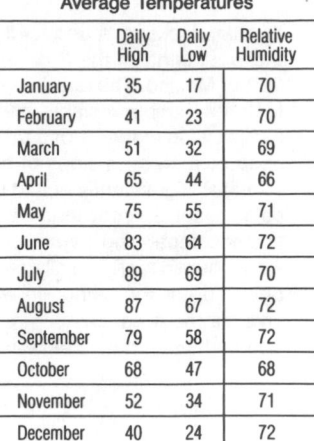

Annual Rainfall 37 in

Annual Snowfall 20 in

Clear 132 days   Partly Cloudy 85 days   Cloudy 148 days

Precipitation Days: 97   Storm Days: 47

Average Temperatures			
	Daily High	Daily Low	Relative Humidity
January	35	17	70
February	41	23	70
March	51	32	69
April	65	44	66
May	75	55	71
June	83	64	72
July	89	69	70
August	87	67	72
September	79	58	72
October	68	47	68
November	52	34	71
December	40	24	72

Zero-Degree Days: 5
Freezing Days: 105
90-Degree Days: 40
Heating- and Cooling-Degree Days: 6,581

✓ Knoxville, TN

Terrain: Located in a broad valley between the Cumberland Mountains to the northwest and the Great Smoky Mountains to the southeast. The Cumberland Mountains serve to retard and weaken the force of the cold winter air moving down from the northern Plains during the colder months, and the Smoky Mountains shelter Knoxville from much of the hot, humid tropical air that moves northward during the summertime.

Climate: Moderate, thanks to the sheltering effects of the two mountain ranges. Though summers are long, the nights are almost always cool, with the average diurnal variation being about 20 degrees. The mean daytime temperature for July is 81°F, but nighttime temperatures are in the mid-70s.

Pluses: Mild mountain climate.

Minuses: Somewhat stormy in summer.

Places Rated Score: 670

Places Rated Rank: 30

Elevation: 980 feet

Wind Speed: 7.3 mph

Seasonal Change

Annual Rainfall 46 in

Annual Snowfall 12 in

Clear 95 days   Partly Cloudy 107 days   Cloudy 163 days

Precipitation Days: 128   Storm Days: 47

Average Temperatures			
	Daily High	Daily Low	Relative Humidity
January	47	30	73
February	51	32	70
March	60	39	67
April	71	48	66
May	78	57	72
June	85	64	73
July	87	68	76
August	87	67	77
September	82	61	76
October	71	48	73
November	59	38	72
December	50	32	73

Zero-Degree Days: 1
Freezing Days: 71
90-Degree Days: 19
Heating- and Cooling-Degree Days: 5,047

La Crosse, WI–MN

Terrain: Situated on the east bank of the Mississippi River at the confluence of the Mississippi, Black, and La Crosse rivers. The town is on a level, sandy plain, but steep-sided hills with narrow valleys are characteristic of most of the surrounding area. The leading field crops are corn, hay, and oats. Dairying is the principal farm activity.

Climate: The location of the city in a natural bowl between the hills results in colder temperatures at night due to air drainage and in valley fogs that often persist through forenoon. The continental climate means frequent variations in temperature. Winters are cold and humid; snows are frequent. Summers are warm and moderately humid. Most of the annual precipitation falls during the main growing season extending from May to September.

Pluses: Five-month growing season with above-average rainfall.

Minuses: Long, cold winters with frequent snow.

Places Rated Score: 352

Places Rated Rank: 319

Elevation: 672 feet

Wind Speed: 8.9 mph

Seasonal Change

Annual Rainfall 29 in

Annual Snowfall 43 in

Clear 95 days   Partly Cloudy 97 days   Cloudy 173 days

Precipitation Days: 109   Storm Days: 40

Average Temperatures			
	Daily High	Daily Low	Relative Humidity
January	23	5	72
February	29	10	72
March	40	22	71
April	58	37	66
May	70	49	67
June	79	58	70
July	84	62	72
August	81	60	76
September	72	51	76
October	61	41	72
November	43	27	75
December	29	14	77

Zero-Degree Days: 26
Freezing Days: 152
90-Degree Days: 16
Heating- and Cooling-Degree Days: 8,112

Las Vegas, NV–AZ

Terrain: Situated near the center of a broad desert valley surrounded by mountains ranging from 2,000 feet to 10,000 feet higher than the valley's floor. These mountains act as effective barriers to moisture-laden storms moving eastward from the Pacific Ocean, so that Las Vegas sees very few overcast or rainy days.

Climate: Summers are typical of a desert climate—low humidity with maximum temperatures in the 100-degree levels. Nearby mountains contribute to relatively cool nights, with minimums between 70°F and 75°F. Springs and falls are ideal; outdoor activities are rarely interrupted by adverse weather conditions. Winters, too, are mild, with daytime averages of 60°F, clear skies, and warm sunshine.

Pluses: Mild year-round climate with especially pleasant springs and falls.

Minuses: High winds, though infrequent, bring dust and sand.

Places Rated Score: 556

Places Rated Rank: 149

Elevation: 2,180 feet

Wind Speed: 9 mph

Seasonal Change

Annual Rainfall 4 in

Annual Snowfall 1.5 in

Clear 216 days
Partly Cloudy 84 days
Cloudy 65 days

Precipitation Days: 24   Storm Days: 15

Average Temperatures			
	Daily High	Daily Low	Relative Humidity
January	56	33	43
February	62	38	38
March	68	42	33
April	77	50	26
May	87	59	23
June	99	69	18
July	105	76	22
August	102	74	26
September	95	66	26
October	82	54	28
November	66	41	37
December	57	34	44

Zero-Degree Days: 0
Freezing Days: 41
90-Degree Days: 131
Heating- and Cooling-Degree Days: 5,547

Lexington, KY

Terrain: Located in the heart of the Kentucky Bluegrass region on a gently rolling plateau with varying elevations of 900 feet to 1,050 feet. The surrounding country is noted for its beauty, fertile soil, excellent grass, stock farms, and burley tobacco. There are no bodies of water nearby that are large enough to have an effect on climate.

Climate: Decidedly continental, temperate, yet subject to sudden large but brief changes in temperature. Precipitation is evenly distributed throughout the winter, spring, and summer, with an average of 12 inches falling in each of these seasons. Snowfall is variable, but the ground does not retain snow for more than a few days at a time. The months of September and October are the most pleasant of the year; they have the least precipitation, the most clear days, and generally comfortable temperatures.

Pluses: Temperate, four-season climate with pleasant falls.

Minuses: Large diurnal temperature range.

Places Rated Score: 635

Places Rated Rank: 50

Elevation: 989 feet

Wind Speed: 9.7 mph

Seasonal Change

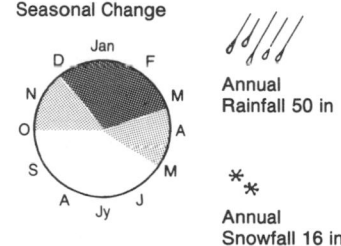

Annual Rainfall 50 in

Annual Snowfall 16 in

Clear 95 days
Partly Cloudy 102 days
Cloudy 168 days

Precipitation Days: 130   Storm Days: 47

Average Temperatures			
	Daily High	Daily Low	Relative Humidity
January	40	23	71
February	44	25	72
March	54	34	68
April	66	44	65
May	75	54	69
June	83	62	70
July	86	66	72
August	85	65	73
September	79	58	74
October	68	46	70
November	54	36	71
December	44	28	74

Zero-Degree Days: 2
Freezing Days: 97
90-Degree Days: 16
Heating- and Cooling-Degree Days: 5,926

Lincoln, NE

Terrain: Lies on rolling prairie in southeastern Nebraska beyond the edge of the tornado and hail belt.

Climate: The majority of winter outbreaks of severely cold air from Canada move over the Lincoln area. However, the centers of some cold air masses move so far to the east that their full effect is not felt here. The Chinook effect often produces rapid rises in temperature during the winter, with a shift of the wind to the west. An average winter brings 26 inches of snow, most of which doesn't melt until spring. The crop season, April through September, receives three-fourths of the yearly precipitation. Nighttime showers occur mostly in the summer. There is much sunshine—Lincoln receives an average of 64% of possible sunlight—with humidity at a comfortable level, except for short periods during the summer.

Pluses: Varied but not too rigorous continental climate.

Minuses: Occasional high winds and high-temperature combinations; long winters.

Places Rated Score: 398

Places Rated Rank: 304

Elevation: 1,189 feet

Wind Speed: 10.5 mph

Seasonal Change

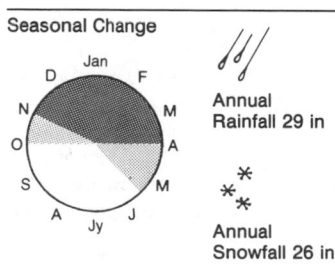

Annual Rainfall 29 in

Annual Snowfall 26 in

Clear 115 days
Partly Cloudy 97 days
Cloudy 153 days

Precipitation Days: 88   Storm Days: 9

Average Temperatures			
	Daily High	Daily Low	Relative Humidity
January	30	9	70
February	38	15	72
March	48	25	70
April	64	39	67
May	74	50	70
June	84	60	68
July	90	66	67
August	87	63	71
September	78	53	70
October	67	41	67
November	50	27	71
December	37	16	73

Zero-Degree Days: 17
Freezing Days: 146
90-Degree Days: 43
Heating- and Cooling-Degree Days: 7,366

Little Rock–North Little Rock, AR

Terrain: Located on the Arkansas River near the geographic center of the state. To the west lie the Ouachita Mountains and to the east the flat lowlands of the Mississippi River valley.

Climate: Modified four-season continental climate. The area is exposed to all North American air-mass types, but the Gulf of Mexico gives the summer season prolonged periods of warm and humid weather. Sixty-two percent of the normal annual precipitation occurs during the growing season, averaging 233 days. Winters are mild, but polar and arctic outbreaks are not uncommon. Glaze and ice storms, though infrequent, can be severe.

Pluses: Negligible snow, long growing season, sufficient precipitation.

Minuses: Long periods of warm, humid days in summer.

Places Rated Score: 497

Places Rated Rank: 230

Elevation: 265 feet

Wind Speed: 8.2 mph

Seasonal Change

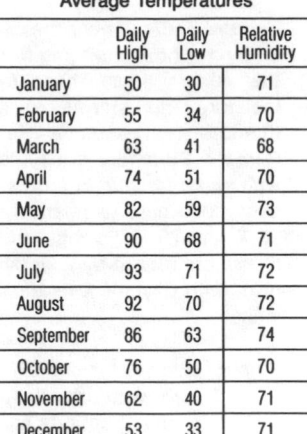

Annual Rainfall 49 in

Annual Snowfall 5 in

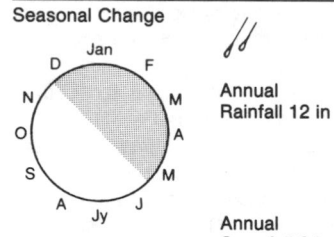

Clear 120 days   Partly Cloudy 100 days   Cloudy 145 days

Precipitation Days: 104   Storm Days: 57

Average Temperatures			
	Daily High	Daily Low	Relative Humidity
January	50	30	71
February	55	34	70
March	63	41	68
April	74	51	70
May	82	59	73
June	90	68	71
July	93	71	72
August	92	70	72
September	86	63	74
October	76	50	70
November	62	40	71
December	53	33	71

Zero-Degree Days: 0
Freezing Days: 63
90-Degree Days: 70
Heating- and Cooling-Degree Days: 5,279

✓ Los Angeles–Long Beach, CA

Terrain: Predominating influences on the climate of Los Angeles are the Pacific Ocean, 3 miles to the west, and the southern California coastal mountain ranges, which line the inland side of the coastal plain of the city and act as buffers to the more extreme conditions of the interior.

Climate: The most characteristic features of this mild, two-season climate are low clouds at night and morning, and sunny afternoons that prevail during the spring and summer and occur often during the remainder of the year. Combined with a sea breeze, the coastal cloudiness is associated with mild temperatures throughout the year. Pronounced differences in temperature, humidity, fog, sunshine, and rain occur over fairly short distances on the coastal plains and adjoining foothills. Temperature ranges are least and humidity is higher close to the coast; precipitation increases with elevation.

Pluses: Positive benefits from Pacific Ocean and surrounding foothills.

Minuses: Frequent haze, fog, and smoke; dry Santa Ana winds.

Places Rated Score: 885

Places Rated Rank: 5

Elevation: 104 feet

Wind Speed: 7.4 mph

Seasonal Change

Annual Rainfall 12 in

Annual Snowfall 0 in

Clear 143 days   Partly Cloudy 115 days   Cloudy 107 days

Precipitation Days: 35   Storm Days: 3

Average Temperatures			
	Daily High	Daily Low	Relative Humidity
January	65	47	65
February	66	49	68
March	65	50	72
April	67	52	72
May	69	56	74
June	72	59	76
July	75	63	77
August	77	64	77
September	76	63	75
October	74	59	72
November	70	52	67
December	66	48	65

Zero-Degree Days: 0
Freezing Days: 0
90-Degree Days: 5
Heating- and Cooling-Degree Days: 2,437

Louisville, KY–IN

Terrain: Located on the south bank of the Ohio River, about 400 miles southwest of Pittsburgh. The eastern part of the city is residential and consists of rolling hills and plateaus. The western, industrial part lies on the river's floodplain. A low range of hills on the Indiana bank provides a partial barrier to icy blasts of winter.

Climate: Continental, but more variable because of its position in midlatitudes, in the belt of westerly winds, not completely shut off from the Gulf of Mexico. Winters are moderately cold. Snows, although seldom heavy, are a usual occurrence from November through March. Summers are quite warm, with high relative humidity and rainstorms of high intensity common during both springs and summers.

Pluses: Well-defined seasons with good precipitation.

Minuses: Humid summers, intense rainfalls.

Places Rated Score: 616

Places Rated Rank: 66

Elevation: 488 feet

Wind Speed: 8.4 mph

Seasonal Change

Annual Rainfall 43 in

Annual Snowfall 17 in

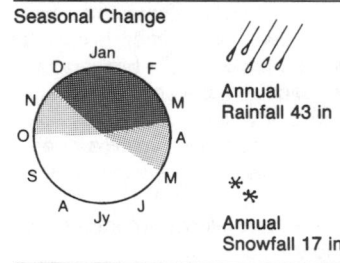

Clear 94 days   Partly Cloudy 103 days   Cloudy 168 days

Precipitation Days: 124   Storm Days: 45

Average Temperatures			
	Daily High	Daily Low	Relative Humidity
January	41	24	70
February	45	27	69
March	55	35	66
April	68	46	64
May	76	55	69
June	84	63	70
July	88	68	72
August	87	66	73
September	81	59	74
October	69	46	70
November	56	37	70
December	45	29	71

Zero-Degree Days: 2
Freezing Days: 92
90-Degree Days: 24
Heating- and Cooling-Degree Days: 5,908

Lubbock, TX

Terrain: Located in a plateau area of northwestern Texas that is often referred to as the South Plains region. It is an essentially level area with numerous small playas, small stream valleys, and low hummocks. There are no appreciable terrain features that affect wind flow across the plateau.

Climate: Semiarid, transitional between desert conditions to the west and humid climates to the east. Normal precipitation is 18 inches per year, with maximum precipitation occurring during May, June, and July, when warm tropical air is carried inland from the Gulf of Mexico. This air mass produces moderate to heavy afternoon and evening convective thunderstorms, sometimes with hail. Dry daytime winds help alleviate summer heat.

Pluses: Generally pleasant climate year-round.

Minuses: During dry spells, high winds cause dusty conditions.

Places Rated Score: 604   **Places Rated Rank: 80**

Elevation: 3,241 feet

Wind Speed: 10.8 mph

Seasonal Change

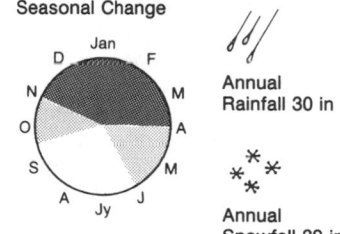

Annual Rainfall 18 in

Annual Snowfall 9.6 in

Clear 164 days   Partly Cloudy 103 days   Cloudy 98 days

Precipitation Days: 60   Storm Days: 45

Average Temperatures			
	Daily High	Daily Low	Relative Humidity
January	53	24	62
February	57	28	62
March	65	35	55
April	75	46	54
May	83	55	60
June	91	64	61
July	92	68	61
August	90	66	64
September	84	59	67
October	75	47	63
November	62	35	60
December	56	27	60

Zero-Degree Days: 0
Freezing Days: 98
90-Degree Days: 77
Heating- and Cooling-Degree Days: 5,192

Madison, WI

Terrain: Madison sits on a narrow isthmus of land between Lakes Mendota (15 square miles) and Monona (5 square miles). Normally these lakes are frozen from December 17 to April 5. Most farming is dairying, with field crops mainly of corn, oats, and alfalfa. The majority of fruits grown are apples, strawberries, and raspberries.

Climate: Continental, typical of interior North America, with a large annual temperature range and frequent short periods of temperature changes. The absolute temperature range is from 107°F to −37°F. Winter temperatures average 20°F and summer ones 68°F. The most common air masses are of polar origin, with occasional outbreaks of arctic air during the winter. Much of the precipitation falls between May and September. Lighter winter precipitation falls over a longer period of time. Average growing season: 175 days.

Pluses: Pleasant summers with moderate growing season; even precipitation.

Minuses: Long, severe winters.

Places Rated Score: 378   **Places Rated Rank: 313**

Elevation: 866 feet

Wind Speed: 9.9 mph

Seasonal Change

Annual Rainfall 30 in

Annual Snowfall 39 in

Clear 94 days   Partly Cloudy 96 days   Cloudy 175 days

Precipitation Days: 117   Storm Days: 40

Average Temperatures			
	Daily High	Daily Low	Relative Humidity
January	25	7	74
February	30	11	73
March	41	22	72
April	58	34	68
May	70	44	68
June	79	54	69
July	83	58	72
August	81	56	75
September	72	48	77
October	61	38	73
November	44	26	76
December	31	14	78

Zero-Degree Days: 25
Freezing Days: 164
90-Degree Days: 12
Heating- and Cooling-Degree Days: 8,190

Medford–Ashland, OR

Terrain: Located in a mountain valley formed by the famous Rogue River and one of its tributaries, Bear Creek. Most of the valley ranges in elevation from 1,300 feet to 1,400 feet above sea level. The valley's outlet to the ocean 80 miles west is the narrow canyon of the Rogue.

Climate: Moderate, with marked seasonal characteristics. Late fall, winter, and early spring are cloudy, damp, and cool. The remainder of the year is warm, dry, and sunny. The rain shadow afforded by the Siskiyous and the Coast ranges results in relatively light rainfall, most of which falls in the wintertime. Snowfalls are very light and seldom remain on the ground more than 24 hours. Winters are mild, with the temperatures just dipping below freezing during December and January. Summer days can reach 90°F, but nights are cool. The climate is ideal for truck and fruit farming, and the area is dotted with orchards.

Pluses: Very mild four-season climate; sunny summers.

Minuses: Half the year is damp and cloudy.

Places Rated Score: 611   **Places Rated Rank: 74**

Elevation: 1,298 feet

Wind Speed: 4.8 mph

Seasonal Change

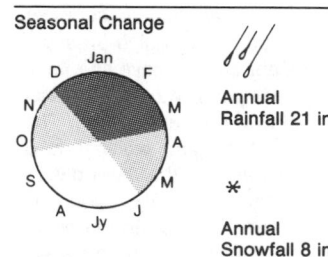

Annual Rainfall 21 in

Annual Snowfall 8 in

Clear 117 days   Partly Cloudy 79 days   Cloudy 169 days

Precipitation Days: 101   Storm Days: 9

Average Temperatures			
	Daily High	Daily Low	Relative Humidity
January	45	30	81
February	53	32	73
March	57	34	68
April	64	37	64
May	72	43	61
June	81	49	56
July	91	54	50
August	89	53	51
September	83	47	55
October	69	40	65
November	53	35	80
December	44	31	84

Zero-Degree Days: 0
Freezing Days: 90
90-Degree Days: 54
Heating- and Cooling-Degree Days: 5,492

Memphis, TN-AR-MS

Terrain: Located on the east bank of the Mississippi River in slightly rolling topography, across from the level alluvial area on the Arkansas side. Major crops are cotton, corn, peaches, apples, and vegetables. The climate is favorable for dairying and for raising cattle and hogs.

Climate: Though not in the normal paths of storms coming from the Gulf of Mexico or from Canada, Memphis is affected by both and therefore has comparatively frequent changes in weather. Extremes in highs and lows are relatively rare; the average annual temperature is in the low 60s and varies from the low 40s in January to the low 80s in July. Average growing season: 230 days.

Pluses: Short winters, long summers, moderate temperature variation.

Minuses: Frequent weather changes, occasional humid periods in summer.

Places Rated Score: 514

Places Rated Rank: 213

Elevation: 284 feet

Wind Speed: 9.2 mph

Seasonal Change

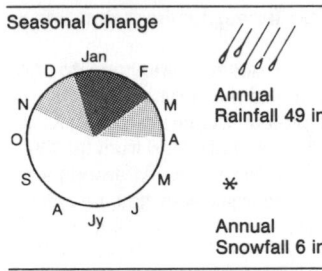

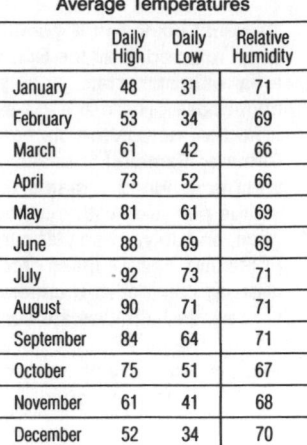

Annual Rainfall 49 in

Annual Snowfall 6 in

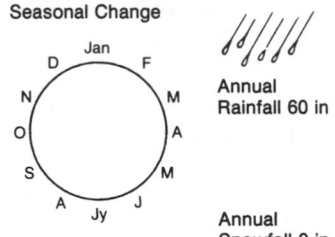

Clear 118 days Partly Cloudy 99 days Cloudy 148 days

Precipitation Days: 106   Storm Days: 53

Average Temperatures			
	Daily High	Daily Low	Relative Humidity
January	48	31	71
February	53	34	69
March	61	42	66
April	73	52	66
May	81	61	69
June	88	69	69
July	92	73	71
August	90	71	71
September	84	64	71
October	75	51	67
November	61	41	68
December	52	34	70

Zero-Degree Days: 0
Freezing Days: 59
90-Degree Days: 64
Heating- and Cooling-Degree Days: 5,256

Miami, FL

Terrain: Located on the lower east coast of Florida. To the east lies Biscayne Bay, and east of it Miami Beach. The surrounding countryside is level and sparsely wooded.

Climate: Essentially subtropical marine, characterized by a long, warm summer with abundant rainfall and a mild, dry winter. The Atlantic Ocean greatly influences the city's small range of daily temperatures and aids the rapid warming of colder air masses that pass to the east of the state. During the early-morning hours, more rainfall occurs at Miami Beach than at the airport (9 miles inland), while during the afternoon the reverse is true. Even more striking is the difference in the annual number of days over 90°F: at Miami Beach, 15 days; at the airport, 60. Freezing temperatures occur occasionally in surrounding farming districts but almost never near the ocean. In 1977, for the first time in Miami's history, traces of snow were reported. Tropical hurricanes affect the area and are most frequent in early fall.

Pluses: Single-season, subtropical climate.

Minuses: Hurricanes, frequent thunderstorms.

Places Rated Score: 634

Places Rated Rank: 51

Elevation: 12 feet

Wind Speed: 9.1 mph

Seasonal Change

Annual Rainfall 60 in

Annual Snowfall 0 in

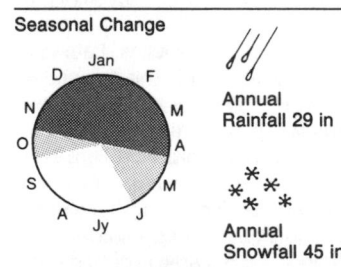

Clear 76 days Partly Cloudy 172 days Cloudy 117 days

Precipitation Days: 129   Storm Days: 75

Average Temperatures			
	Daily High	Daily Low	Relative Humidity
January	75	59	72
February	76	60	70
March	79	64	69
April	82	68	67
May	85	72	70
June	87	75	75
July	89	76	74
August	89	77	76
September	88	76	77
October	84	72	75
November	80	66	73
December	76	61	72

Zero-Degree Days: 0
Freezing Days: 0
90-Degree Days: 30
Heating- and Cooling-Degree Days: 4,244

Milwaukee-Waukesha, WI

Terrain: Milwaukee is situated on the west shore of Lake Michigan, 50 miles north of Chicago.

Climate: Influenced by storms that move eastward across the upper Ohio River valley and the Great Lakes region. Large high-pressure systems moving southeastward out of Canada also have an effect, and it is seldom that two or three days will pass without a distinct change in the weather, particularly during winter and spring. The major influence on the climate is Lake Michigan, which has a particularly marked effect when the temperature of the water differs considerably from that of the air. Generally, the lake cools the shoreline in summer and warms it in winter. Thunderstorms occur less frequently in Milwaukee than in areas to the south and west. Winters are cloudy. Summers are usually clear, receiving an average of 70% of possible sunshine.

Pluses: Lake Michigan has a moderating effect on temperature extremes.

Minuses: Subject to severe winter storm systems.

Places Rated Score: 460

Places Rated Rank: 267

Elevation: 693 feet

Wind Speed: 11.8 mph

Seasonal Change

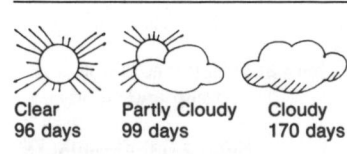

Annual Rainfall 29 in

Annual Snowfall 45 in

Clear 96 days Partly Cloudy 99 days Cloudy 170 days

Precipitation Days: 122   Storm Days: 36

Average Temperatures			
	Daily High	Daily Low	Relative Humidity
January	26	11	72
February	30	16	72
March	39	25	72
April	54	36	70
May	65	45	69
June	75	55	70
July	80	61	72
August	78	60	74
September	71	53	75
October	60	42	72
November	45	30	74
December	32	18	76

Zero-Degree Days: 16
Freezing Days: 146
90-Degree Days: 9
Heating- and Cooling-Degree Days: 7,894

Minneapolis–St. Paul, MN–WI

Terrain: The Twin Cities are located at the confluence of the Mississippi and Minnesota rivers over the heart of an artesian water basin. The topography is flat or gently rolling with numerous lakes that are small, shallow, and ice-covered in winter.

Climate: Predominantly continental (the two cities are near the geographic center of North America). There are wide variations in temperature, ample summer rainfall, and scanty winter precipitation. In general, there exists a tendency toward extremes in almost all climatic features.

Pluses: Changeable weather that many find stimulating and invigorating.

Minuses: Extreme weather features; severe, long winters.

Places Rated Score: 293

Places Rated Rank: 329

Elevation: 838 feet

Wind Speed: 10.5 mph

Seasonal Change

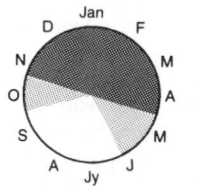

Annual Rainfall 26 in

Annual Snowfall 46 in

Clear 100 days   Partly Cloudy 100 days   Cloudy 165 days

Precipitation Days: 113   Storm Days: 36

Average Temperatures			
	Daily High	Daily Low	Relative Humidity
January	20	2	71
February	26	9	70
March	38	21	69
April	56	36	64
May	69	48	64
June	79	58	67
July	83	63	68
August	81	60	70
September	71	50	72
October	60	39	70
November	41	25	73
December	27	12	74

Zero-Degree Days: 34
Freezing Days: 158
90-Degree Days: 15
Heating- and Cooling-Degree Days: 8,744

Mobile, AL

Terrain: Located at the head of Mobile Bay, approximately 30 miles from the Gulf of Mexico.

Climate: Although Mobile has not had a destructive hurricane since 1926, this seems to be due more to chance than to location. The area is subject to hurricanes from the West Indies and the Gulf of Mexico. The normal annual rainfall is among the highest in the United States. It is evenly distributed throughout the year, with a slight maximum at the height of the summer thunderstorm season (there are thunderstorms every other day during July and August). Most of these storms are showers; long periods of continuous rain are rare. The growing season averages 274 days, enough for citrus fruit to be grown in the area.

Pluses: Mild winters, ample and even precipitation.

Minuses: Summers are hot and muggy with frequent thunderstorms; area prone to hurricanes.

Places Rated Score: 442

Places Rated Rank: 278

Elevation: 221 feet

Wind Speed: 9.2 mph

Seasonal Change

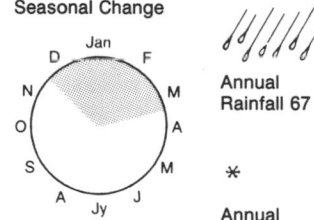

Annual Rainfall 67 in

Annual Snowfall .4 in

Clear 100 days   Partly Cloudy 117 days   Cloudy 148 days

Precipitation Days: 124   Storm Days: 80

Average Temperatures			
	Daily High	Daily Low	Relative Humidity
January	61	41	71
February	64	43	69
March	70	50	70
April	78	58	70
May	85	65	71
June	90	71	71
July	91	73	75
August	91	73	76
September	87	69	74
October	79	58	69
November	69	48	72
December	63	43	73

Zero-Degree Days: 0
Freezing Days: 19
90-Degree Days: 81
Heating- and Cooling-Degree Days: 4,261

Montgomery, AL

Terrain: Located in a gently rolling area of southern Alabama. No local topographic features appreciably influence climate.

Climate: From June through September, humidity and temperature conditions show little daily change. During summer, 100-degree readings are infrequent. From April through September, all precipitation is from local heat thundershowers in the afternoon. Rain is abundant and includes all types and intensities from December through March. During the coldest months (December, January, and February), there are frequent shifts between mild, moist air from the Gulf of Mexico and dry, cool continental air. Hard freezes are infrequent during winter; snow is rare enough to be a curiosity.

Pluses: Mild, two-season climate wih abundant rainfall.

Minuses: Humid summers and falls, lots of cloudy days.

Places Rated Score: 483

Places Rated Rank: 244

Elevation: 202 feet

Wind Speed: 6.8 mph

Seasonal Change

Annual Rainfall 50 in

Annual Snowfall .2 in

Clear 107 days   Partly Cloudy 109 days   Cloudy 149 days

Precipitation Days: 109   Storm Days: 62

Average Temperatures			
	Daily High	Daily Low	Relative Humidity
January	57	36	71
February	61	39	68
March	68	46	68
April	77	53	69
May	84	61	72
June	90	68	72
July	92	72	75
August	91	71	75
September	87	66	73
October	78	53	71
November	67	43	71
December	60	38	71

Zero-Degree Days: 0
Freezing Days: 39
90-Degree Days: 66
Heating- and Cooling-Degree Days: 4,507

Montreal, PQ

Terrain: Located in the St. Lawrence River plain at the confluence of the Ottawa and St. Lawrence rivers. The Laurentians lie to the north, the Appalachians to the south and southeast. Most of Montreal Island is situated between 100 feet and 150 feet above sea level with the exception of Mount Royal, which rises to 750 feet.

Climate: Halfway between the equator and the North Pole, the city has climate influenced by aspects of continental and maritime regimes. There can be severe continental temperature differences between summer and winter, but because of the maritime influence, it is wet more or less uniformly throughout the year. Every Montrealer is familiar with the cold waves of winter, the mild spells of spring, the sultry days of summer, and the gray periods of fall. On average, the first snowflakes appear on November 10, and the first winter "broadside" of 5 inches hits on December 12.

Pluses: Mild springs, changeable.

Minuses: Long, cold winters with heavy snowfalls.

Places Rated Score: 512

Places Rated Rank: 218

Elevation: 118 feet

Wind Speed: 9.7 mph

Seasonal Change

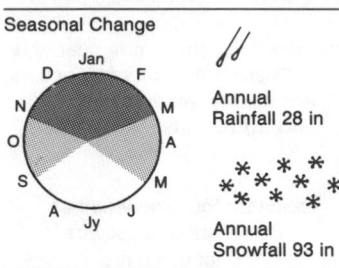

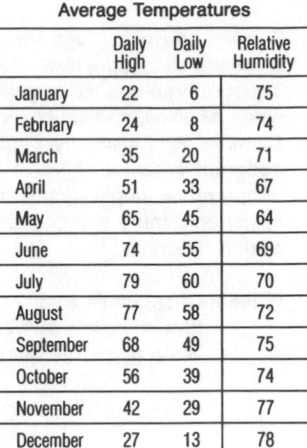

Annual Rainfall 28 in

Annual Snowfall 93 in

Clear 108 days   Partly Cloudy 120 days   Cloudy 137 days

Precipitation Days: 162   Storm Days: 25

Average Temperatures			
	Daily High	Daily Low	Relative Humidity
January	22	6	75
February	24	8	74
March	35	20	71
April	51	33	67
May	65	45	64
June	74	55	69
July	79	60	70
August	77	58	72
September	68	49	75
October	56	39	74
November	42	29	77
December	27	13	78

Zero-Degree Days: 15
Freezing Days: 155
90-Degree Days: 9
Heating- and Cooling-Degree Days: 4,787

Nashville, TN

Terrain: Located on the Cumberland River in the northwestern corner of the Nashville Basin, near the escarpment of the Highland Rim. The rim rises 400 feet above the mean elevation of the basin, forming an amphitheater around the city from the southwest to the southeast.

Climate: Moderate temperatures. Extremes of heat or cold are rare, yet fairly frequent changes give variety. The humidity is moderate compared with other locations east of the Mississippi River and south of the Ohio River. The city is not in the most highly traveled path of general storm systems that cross the country; however, it is in a zone that experiences thunderstorms moderately often. Average growing season: 211 days.

Pluses: Fairly mild four-season climate, long summers.

Minuses: Relatively few clear days.

Places Rated Score: 600

Places Rated Rank: 87

Elevation: 605 feet

Wind Speed: 7.9 mph

Seasonal Change

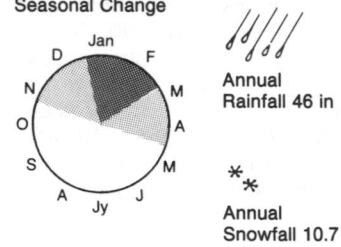

Annual Rainfall 46 in

Annual Snowfall 10.7 in

Clear 103 days   Partly Cloudy 107 days   Cloudy 155 days

Precipitation Days: 119   Storm Days: 55

Average Temperatures			
	Daily High	Daily Low	Relative Humidity
January	46	28	71
February	51	30	69
March	60	38	66
April	71	48	66
May	79	57	71
June	87	65	71
July	90	69	73
August	89	68	74
September	83	61	75
October	72	48	70
November	59	38	71
December	50	31	72

Zero-Degree Days: 1
Freezing Days: 75
90-Degree Days: 37
Heating- and Cooling-Degree Days: 5,390

New Orleans, LA

Terrain: The metropolitan area is surrounded by water: Lake Pontchartrain (610 square miles) to the north; the Mississippi River to the east and south; bayous, lakes, and marshy delta land to the west and south. Elevations in the city vary from a few feet above mean sea level to a few feet below. A massive levee system offers protection from river flooding and tidal surges.

Climate: Best described as humid with surrounding water modifying the temperature and decreasing the range of temperatures. Heavy and frequent rains are typical, and there are daily afternoon thunderstorms from mid-June through September. From December to March, precipitation is likely to be steady rain of two or three days' duration, instead of showers. During winter and spring, cold rain forms fogs that inhibit air and river transportation. The city has been hard hit by three hurricanes since 1900.

Pluses: Tropical climate moderated by water.

Minuses: Hot and humid, heavy rains and fogs, hurricanes.

Places Rated Score: 498

Places Rated Rank: 229

Elevation: 30 feet

Wind Speed: 8.4 mph

Seasonal Change

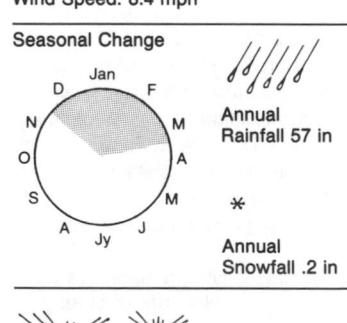

Annual Rainfall 57 in

Annual Snowfall .2 in

Clear 109 days   Partly Cloudy 120 days   Cloudy 136 days

Precipitation Days: 113   Storm Days: 68

Average Temperatures			
	Daily High	Daily Low	Relative Humidity
January	62	43	76
February	65	45	74
March	71	52	72
April	79	59	74
May	85	65	75
June	90	71	77
July	91	74	79
August	90	73	79
September	87	70	77
October	79	59	73
November	70	50	74
December	64	45	76

Zero-Degree Days: 0
Freezing Days: 13
90-Degree Days: 67
Heating- and Cooling-Degree Days: 4,171

New York, NY

Terrain: Located on the Atlantic Coastal Plain at the mouth of the Hudson River. Topography is diversified by numerous waterways; all but one of the city's five boroughs are situated on islands.

Climate: Close to the path of most storm and frontal systems that move across the continent. Therefore, weather conditions affecting the city approach from a westerly direction. New York City can thus experience higher temperatures in summer and lower ones in winter than would otherwise be expected in a coastal area. However, the frequent passage of weather systems often helps reduce the length of warm and cold spells and also keeps periods of air stagnation brief. Although continental influence is dominant, ocean influence is by no means absent. Sea breezes moderate the afternoon heat of summer and delay the advent of winter snows. The Atlantic's influence is also measured in the length of the frost-free season—more than 200 days.

Pluses: Moderating ocean influence, mild summers and falls.

Minuses: Coastal storms bring record snow and rain.

Places Rated Score: 638

Places Rated Rank: 47

Elevation: 87 feet

Wind Speed: 9.4 mph

Seasonal Change

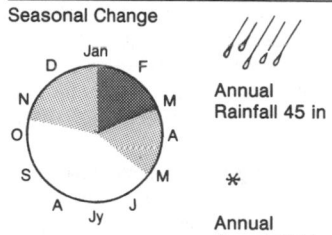

Annual Rainfall 40 in

Annual Snowfall 29 in

Clear 107 days Partly Cloudy 125 days Cloudy 133 days

Precipitation Days: 121 Storm Days: 20

Average Temperatures			
	Daily High	Daily Low	Relative Humidity
January	38	26	64
February	40	27	63
March	49	34	61
April	61	44	59
May	72	53	62
June	80	63	65
July	85	68	65
August	84	67	68
September	76	60	68
October	66	50	66
November	54	41	66
December	42	30	65

Zero-Degree Days: 0
Freezing Days: 81
90-Degree Days: 16
Heating- and Cooling-Degree Days: 5,916

Norfolk–Virginia Beach–Newport News, VA–NC

Terrain: Located on low level land, with Chesapeake Bay immediately to the north, Hampton Roads to the west, and the Atlantic Ocean to the east.

Climate: The metro area is in a favorable geographic position, being north of the track of hurricanes and tropical storms and south of high-latitude storm systems. Winters are mild. Springs and falls are especially pleasant. Summers, though, are warm, humid, and long. A temperature of zero has never been recorded here, although there is occasional snow.

Pluses: Four-season climate suited for year-round outdoor activities.

Minuses: Long, humid summers.

Places Rated Score: 632

Places Rated Rank: 53

Elevation: 30 feet

Wind Speed: 10.6 mph

Seasonal Change

Annual Rainfall 45 in

Annual Snowfall 7 in

Clear 110 days Partly Cloudy 102 days Cloudy 153 days

Precipitation Days: 115 Storm Days: 37

Average Temperatures			
	Daily High	Daily Low	Relative Humidity
January	48	32	67
February	50	32	65
March	58	39	64
April	68	48	62
May	76	57	66
June	83	65	68
July	87	70	71
August	86	70	73
September	80	64	72
October	70	53	71
November	61	43	68
December	52	35	67

Zero-Degree Days: 0
Freezing Days: 54
90-Degree Days: 30
Heating- and Cooling-Degree Days: 4,929

Odessa–Midland, TX

Terrain: Located on the southern extension of the South Plains region of Texas. Topography is level, with only slight and infrequent undulations. Vegetation consists mainly of grasses, and there are very few trees in the area, most of them mesquite.

Climate: Semiarid. Droughts occur with monotonous frequency, resulting in dust storms so severe that suspended dust remains in the air several days after the storm has passed. Though summer afternoon temperatures are frequently above 90°F, low humidity and rapid evaporation have a cooling effect. The climate is generally pleasant, with the most disagreeable weather concentrated in late winter and spring.

Pluses: Short winters; long, pleasant summers and falls.

Minuses: Severe drought conditions, frequent dust storms.

Places Rated Score: 603

Places Rated Rank: 81

Elevation: 2,862 feet

Wind Speed: 10.8 mph

Seasonal Change

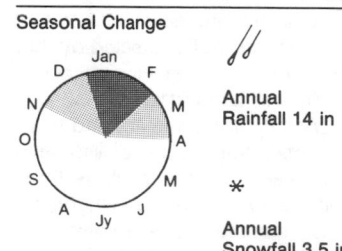

Annual Rainfall 14 in

Annual Snowfall 3.5 in

Clear 167 days Partly Cloudy 97 days Cloudy 101 days

Precipitation Days: 51 Storm Days: 36

Average Temperatures			
	Daily High	Daily Low	Relative Humidity
January	58	30	60
February	62	33	59
March	70	40	51
April	79	49	51
May	86	58	57
June	93	67	60
July	94	69	58
August	93	68	60
September	86	62	66
October	78	51	63
November	66	39	61
December	60	32	59

Zero-Degree Days: 0
Freezing Days: 65
90-Degree Days: 89
Heating- and Cooling-Degree Days: 4,871

Oklahoma City, OK

Terrain: Situated along the North Canadian River at the geographic center of the state. The countryside is rolling, with the nearest hills, the Arbuckles, 80 miles south.

Climate: Although some influence is exerted at times by warm, moist air from the Gulf of Mexico, the climate of the city falls mainly under continental controls characteristic of the Great Plains. The continental effect produces pronounced daily and seasonal temperature changes and considerable variation in seasonal and annual precipitation. Summers are long and usually hot. Winters are comparatively mild and short.

Pluses: Clear days, mild winters.

Minuses: Long, hot summers; tornadoes.

Places Rated Score: 554   **Places Rated Rank: 151**

Elevation: 1,304 feet

Wind Speed: 12.8 mph

Seasonal Change

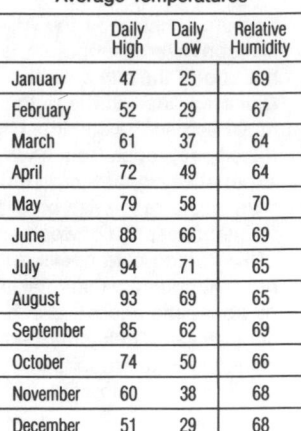

Annual Rainfall 31 in

Annual Snowfall 9 in

Clear 141 days   Partly Cloudy 96 days   Cloudy 128 days

Precipitation Days: 81   Storm Days: 51

Average Temperatures			
	Daily High	Daily Low	Relative Humidity
January	47	25	69
February	52	29	67
March	61	37	64
April	72	49	64
May	79	58	70
June	88	66	69
July	94	71	65
August	93	69	65
September	85	62	69
October	74	50	66
November	60	38	68
December	51	29	68

Zero-Degree Days: 0
Freezing Days: 80
90-Degree Days: 64
Heating- and Cooling-Degree Days: 5,571

Ottawa–Hull, ON–PQ

Terrain: The Ottawa River winds through the city, separating Quebec (Hull) to the north from Ontario and the city of Ottawa to the south, and separating farmland from the Gatineau Hills. The Rideau River flows northward through the city to the Ottawa River. South from the city there is a general rise in elevation from 130 feet at the river valley to an area of generally rolling farmland. On the north side of the Ottawa River the terrain rises sharply in a wooded section of the Gatineau Hills to an elevation of 1,300 feet in the Eardley Escarpment.

Climate: Best described as both stimulating and variable; cold and snowy in winter, warm in summer. There is no pronounced dry season. This is a continental climate with a maritime air from both the Atlantic Ocean and Gulf of Mexico. There are two main seasons with shorter transitional periods of spring and autumn. Good or bad periods usually do not last for more than a few days.

Pluses: Moderate summers; falls are brilliant but short.

Minuses: Cold, snowy winters.

Places Rated Score: 483   **Places Rated Rank: 244**

Elevation: feet

Wind Speed: mph

Seasonal Change

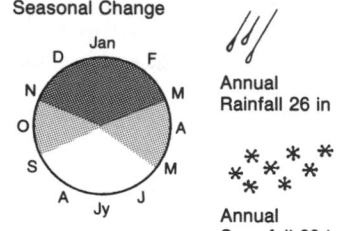

Annual Rainfall 26 in

Annual Snowfall 89 in

Clear 109 days   Partly Cloudy 114 days   Cloudy 142 days

Precipitation Days: 156   Storm Days: 24

Average Temperatures			
	Daily High	Daily Low	Relative Humidity
January	20	6	73
February	23	7	71
March	34	19	69
April	51	33	63
May	65	44	61
June	75	54	66
July	79	59	68
August	76	56	71
September	67	48	74
October	55	38	73
November	41	28	77
December	25	11	77

Zero-Degree Days: 18
Freezing Days: 165
90-Degree Days: 9
Heating- and Cooling-Degree Days: 4,920

✓ Olympia, WA

Terrain: The capital of the state of Washington, Olympia lies at the southernmost end of Puget Sound, some 60 miles south-southwest of Seattle. The Olympic Peninsula, with its fine remnants of the Pacific Northwest rain forests, active glaciers, and alpine meadows, lies to the northwest. The city and vicinity are well protected by the Coast Ranges from the strong south and southwest winds accompanying many Pacific storms during the fall and winter.

Climate: Characterized by warm, generally dry summers and wet, mild winters. Fall rains begin in October and continue with few interruptions until spring. During the rainy season there is little variation in temperature, with days in the 40s and 50s and nights in the 30s, and constant cloud cover. The summer highs are between 60°F and 80°F, with up to 20 days without rain. The summer is marked by clear skies at night and frequent morning fog.

Pluses: Mild winters, dry summers.

Minuses: Cloudy, damp, rainy.

Places Rated Score: 726   **Places Rated Rank: 24**

Elevation: 195 feet

Wind Speed: 6.7 mph

Seasonal Change

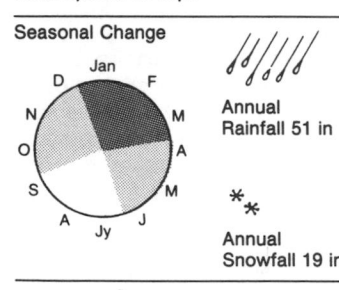

Annual Rainfall 51 in

Annual Snowfall 19 in

Clear 49 days   Partly Cloudy 88 days   Cloudy 228 days

Precipitation Days: 163   Storm Days: 5

Average Temperatures			
	Daily High	Daily Low	Relative Humidity
January	44	31	86
February	49	33	81
March	53	33	77
April	59	36	74
May	66	41	73
June	71	46	73
July	77	49	71
August	76	49	71
September	71	45	74
October	61	39	81
November	50	35	87
December	45	33	88

Zero-Degree Days: 0
Freezing Days: 89
90-Degree Days: 6
Heating- and Cooling-Degree Days: 5,631

Omaha, NE–IA

Terrain: Situated on the west bank of the Missouri River among rolling hills that rise 300 feet above the riverbank.
Climate: Typically continental, with relatively warm summers and cold, dry winters. It is situated midway between two climates, those of the humid East and the dry West, and receives weather conditions characteristic of both. Omaha is also affected by most storms, or "lows," that cross the country. This causes periodic and rapid changes in weather, especially during the winter.

Pluses: Moderate growing season with adequate rainfall.

Minuses: Long, cold winters.

Elevation: 982 feet

Wind Speed: 10.9 mph

Seasonal Change

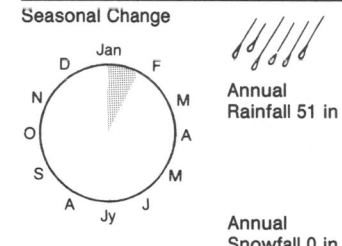

Annual Rainfall 30 in

Annual Snowfall 32 in

Clear 113 days   Partly Cloudy 107 days   Cloudy 145 days

Precipitation Days: 99   Storm Days: 48

Average Temperatures			
	Daily High	Daily Low	Relative Humidity
January	30	10	72
February	37	17	71
March	48	27	68
April	64	40	65
May	75	52	67
June	84	62	69
July	89	67	71
August	86	64	73
September	78	54	73
October	67	42	69
November	50	29	72
December	37	17	74

Zero-Degree Days: 13
Freezing Days: 138
90-Degree Days: 38
Heating- and Cooling-Degree Days: 7,222

Places Rated Score: 440   **Places Rated Rank: 280**

Orlando, FL

Terrain: Located in the central section of the Florida peninsula, almost surrounded by lakes. The countryside is flat, with no natural barriers to exterior weather systems.
Climate: Because of the surrounding water, relative humidity remains high year-round, hovering near 90% at night and dipping to 50% in the afternoon. The rainy season extends from June through September; afternoon thundershowers occur daily. Rain is light during the winter, and snow and sleet are rare. Winter temperatures may drop to freezing at night, but days are usually pleasant, with brilliant sunshine.

Pluses: Mild.

Minuses: Humid year-round; hot summers with daily thundershowers.

Elevation: 106 feet

Wind Speed: 8.7 mph

Seasonal Change

Annual Rainfall 51 in

Annual Snowfall 0 in

Clear 94 days   Partly Cloudy 148 days   Cloudy 123 days

Precipitation Days: 116   Storm Days: 81

Average Temperatures			
	Daily High	Daily Low	Relative Humidity
January	72	49	72
February	73	50	70
March	78	55	69
April	84	60	67
May	88	66	69
June	91	71	73
July	92	73	75
August	92	73	76
September	90	73	76
October	84	65	73
November	78	57	72
December	73	51	73

Zero-Degree Days: 0
Freezing Days: 2
90-Degree Days: 104
Heating- and Cooling-Degree Days: 3,959

Places Rated Score: 457   **Places Rated Rank: 269**

Pensacola, FL

Terrain: Situated on a somewhat hilly, sandy slope bordering Pensacola Bay, separated from the Gulf of Mexico by a long, narrow island that forms a natural breakwater for the harbor. Elevations range from a few feet above sea level to more than 100 feet; most of the city is well above storm tides.
Climate: The Gulf of Mexico, about 6 miles away, moderates the weather throughout the year, tempering the cold northers of winter, and causing cool and refreshing sea breezes during summer days.

Pluses: Mild Gulf winters.

Minuses: Somewhat humid summers; hurricane-prone.

Elevation: 112 feet

Wind Speed: 8.3 mph

Seasonal Change

Annual Rainfall 61 in

Annual Snowfall 0 in

Clear 103 days   Partly Cloudy 117 days   Cloudy 145 days

Precipitation Days: 114   Storm Days: 75

Average Temperatures			
	Daily High	Daily Low	Relative Humidity
January	61	43	72
February	64	45	70
March	69	51	72
April	77	59	71
May	84	66	73
June	89	72	73
July	90	74	76
August	90	74	78
September	87	71	74
October	79	60	70
November	69	50	72
December	63	44	74

Zero-Degree Days: 0
Freezing Days: 16
90-Degree Days: 55
Heating- and Cooling-Degree Days: 4,273

Places Rated Score: 536   **Places Rated Rank: 181**

Peoria–Pekin, IL

Terrain: Located on the Illinois River, with gently rising topography extending to level tableland.

Climate: Typically continental, characterized by changeable weather and a wide range of temperatures. For example, 1936 had 17 days with temperatures of 100° F or higher in July, whereas the early part of that same year had 26 days within a 31-day period when the temperature was zero. The same year had the absolute maximum record of 113° F, set on July 15. June and September are usually the most pleasant months of the year. During October and early November, residents enjoy Indian summer, with its extended period of warm, dry weather.

Pluses: Invigorating continental climate, with especially pleasant falls.

Minuses: Periods of extreme cold and extreme heat.

Places Rated Score: 491

Places Rated Rank: 236

Elevation: 662 feet

Wind Speed: 10.3 mph

Seasonal Change

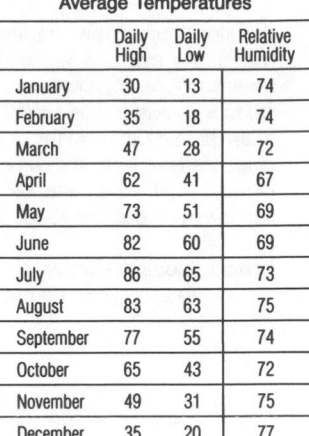

Annual Rainfall 35 in

Annual Snowfall 23 in

Clear 97 days

Partly Cloudy 100 days

Cloudy 168 days

Precipitation Days: 111   Storm Days: 49

Average Temperatures			
	Daily High	Daily Low	Relative Humidity
January	30	13	74
February	35	18	74
March	47	28	72
April	62	41	67
May	73	51	69
June	82	60	69
July	86	65	73
August	83	63	75
September	77	55	74
October	65	43	72
November	49	31	75
December	35	20	77

Zero-Degree Days: 11
Freezing Days: 132
90-Degree Days: 17
Heating- and Cooling-Degree Days: 7,066

Philadelphia, PA–NJ

Terrain: Situated on the Schuylkill and Delaware rivers on the eastern border of Pennsylvania. The Appalachian Mountains to the west and the Atlantic Ocean to the east have a moderating effect on the city's climate.

Climate: Sustained periods of very high or very low temperatures seldom last for more than three or four days. Occasionally during the summer, the area becomes engulfed in marine air, so that high humidity adds to the discomfort of warm temperatures. Precipitation is evenly distributed throughout the year, with maximum amounts during late summer. Snowfall often is considerably higher in the northern suburbs than in the city, where sometimes rain will fall instead. Winters often bring high winds, accompanying cold air after the passage of a deep low-pressure system.

Pluses: Four-season climate moderated by the proximity of the Atlantic Ocean.

Minuses: Humid summer periods; high winter winds accentuate the cold.

Places Rated Score: 630

Places Rated Rank: 55

Elevation: 28 feet

Wind Speed: 9.6 mph

Seasonal Change

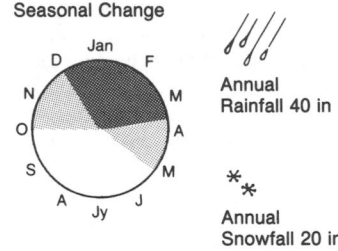

Annual Rainfall 40 in

Annual Snowfall 20 in

Clear 92 days

Partly Cloudy 113 days

Cloudy 160 days

Precipitation Days: 116   Storm Days: 27

Average Temperatures			
	Daily High	Daily Low	Relative Humidity
January	39	24	66
February	41	25	64
March	51	33	62
April	63	43	60
May	73	53	64
June	82	62	65
July	86	67	67
August	85	66	68
September	78	59	70
October	67	47	69
November	55	37	67
December	43	28	67

Zero-Degree Days: 0
Freezing Days: 101
90-Degree Days: 19
Heating- and Cooling-Degree Days: 5,969

Phoenix–Mesa, AZ

Terrain: Located in the center of the Salt River valley, on a broad, oval, nearly flat plain. To the south, west, and north are nearby mountain ranges, and 35 miles to the east are the famous Superstition Mountains, which rise to 5,000 feet.

Climate: Typical desert, with low annual rainfall and low humidity. Daytime temperatures are high throughout the summer. Winters are mild, but nighttime temperatures frequently drop below freezing during December, January, and February. The valley floor is generally free of wind except during the thunderstorm season, in July and August, when local gusts flow from the east. The majority of days are clear and sunny, except for July and August; then, considerable afternoon cloudiness builds up over nearby mountains.

Pluses: Dry, two-season desert climate.

Minuses: Hot summers.

Places Rated Score: 536

Places Rated Rank: 181

Elevation: 1,107 feet

Wind Speed: 6.2 mph

Seasonal Change

Annual Rainfall 7 in

Annual Snowfall 0 in

Clear 214 days

Partly Cloudy 81 days

Cloudy 70 days

Precipitation Days: 34   Storm Days: 23

Average Temperatures			
	Daily High	Daily Low	Relative Humidity
January	65	39	49
February	70	43	43
March	75	47	40
April	83	53	30
May	92	62	24
June	102	71	21
July	105	80	33
August	102	78	37
September	98	71	36
October	88	59	37
November	74	47	43
December	66	40	51

Zero-Degree Days: 0
Freezing Days: 32
90-Degree Days: 164
Heating- and Cooling-Degree Days: 5,060

Pittsburgh, PA

Terrain: Lies at the foothills of the Allegheny Mountains at the confluence of the Allegheny and Monongahela rivers, forming the Ohio. The city is approximately 100 miles south of Lake Erie.
Climate: Humid, continental type, modified only slightly by its nearness to the Atlantic Seaboard and the Great Lakes. The predominant air is of polar origin from Canada and moves in by way of storm tracks, which vary in origin from Hudson Bay to the Rockies. There are frequent inversions of air from the Gulf of Mexico during the summer, resulting in spells of warm, humid weather. Precipitation is well distributed; during the winter, one-fourth of it is snow, and there is a 50% chance of measurable precipitation on any given day.

Pluses: Variable continental climate.

Minuses: Cloudy, wet, cold winters; occasional humid summer days.

Places Rated Score: 586

Places Rated Rank: 98

Elevation: 1,223 feet

Wind Speed: 9.4 mph

Seasonal Change

Annual Rainfall 36 in

Annual Snowfall 45 in

Clear 59 days   Partly Cloudy 102 days   Cloudy 204 days

Precipitation Days: 152   Storm Days: 36

Average Temperatures

	Daily High	Daily Low	Relative Humidity
January	34	19	70
February	37	21	68
March	48	29	66
April	61	39	62
May	71	49	64
June	79	57	66
July	83	61	68
August	81	60	71
September	75	53	71
October	63	42	68
November	50	33	70
December	38	24	72

Zero-Degree Days: 5
Freezing Days: 124
90-Degree Days: 7
Heating- and Cooling-Degree Days: 6,577

Portland, ME

Terrain: Located on a hilly section of the southern coast of Maine, some 45 miles southeast of the White Mountains.
Climate: As a rule, the city has very pleasant summers and falls, cold winters with frequent thaws, and disagreeable springs. Autumn has the greatest number of sunny days. Winters are severe; they begin late but extend deep into what is normally considered springtime, and temperatures well below zero are recorded frequently. Normal monthly precipitation is uniform throughout the year, but heavy snowfalls, sometimes totaling more than 100 inches per year, do occur.

Pluses: Northern marine setting with extremely pleasant summers and falls.

Minuses: Severe winters, with heavy snows, extending well into normal springtime.

Places Rated Score: 483

Places Rated Rank: 244

Elevation: 63 feet

Wind Speed: 8.8 mph

Seasonal Change

Annual Rainfall 41 in

Annual Snowfall 74 in

Clear 107 days   Partly Cloudy 98 days   Cloudy 160 days

Precipitation Days: 127   Storm Days: 18

Average Temperatures

	Daily High	Daily Low	Relative Humidity
January	31	12	68
February	33	13	67
March	41	24	66
April	53	33	64
May	63	42	67
June	73	51	69
July	79	57	70
August	78	56	71
September	70	48	73
October	59	38	72
November	47	30	73
December	35	17	70

Zero-Degree Days: 15
Freezing Days: 160
90-Degree Days: 5
Heating- and Cooling-Degree Days: 7,750

✓ Portland, OR

Terrain: Situated 65 miles inland from the Pacific Ocean and midway between the northerly oriented low Coast Ranges on the west and the higher Cascade Range on the east, each 30 miles distant. The long growing season, with its mild temperatures and ample moisture, favors local nursery and seed industries.
Climate: A rain climate in winter, marked by relatively mild temperatures and cloudy skies. Summers are pleasantly mild with northwesterly winds and very little precipitation. Fall and spring are transitional in nature. Fog occurs frequently in fall and winter. At all times, incursions of marine air are a moderating influence. Extremes in winter and summer come from the continental interior. Destructive winds are infrequent.

Pluses: Short winters; long, pleasant summers; ample precipitation.

Minuses: Daily rains during winter and part of spring; often cloudy.

Places Rated Score: 768

Places Rated Rank: 19

Elevation: 39 feet

Wind Speed: 7.8 mph

Seasonal Change

Annual Rainfall 38 in

Annual Snowfall 7 in

Clear 69 days   Partly Cloudy 68 days   Cloudy 228 days

Precipitation Days: 152   Storm Days: 7

Average Temperatures

	Daily High	Daily Low	Relative Humidity
January	44	34	81
February	50	36	77
March	55	37	73
April	60	41	71
May	67	46	69
June	73	52	67
July	80	56	64
August	79	56	65
September	74	51	68
October	64	45	76
November	52	39	81
December	46	35	83

Zero-Degree Days: 0
Freezing Days: 44
90-Degree Days: 10
Heating- and Cooling-Degree Days: 5,092

Providence–Warwick–Cranston, RI

Terrain: Proximate to Narragansett Bay and the Atlantic Ocean, which produce a moderate marine climate.

Climate: Many major snowstorms change to rain before reaching the area; snow is not uncommon but does not remain for long periods of time. In summer, the area is cooled by refreshing breezes. Fog may be dense at times but is not frequent.

Pluses: Milder winters and summers than inland New England.

Minuses: Foggy; hurricane-prone.

Places Rated Score: 586

Places Rated Rank: 98

Elevation: 24 feet

Wind Speed: 10.7 mph

Seasonal Change

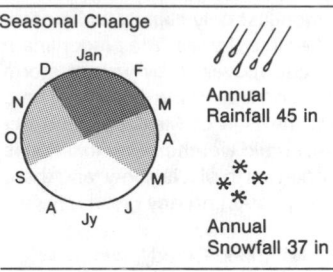

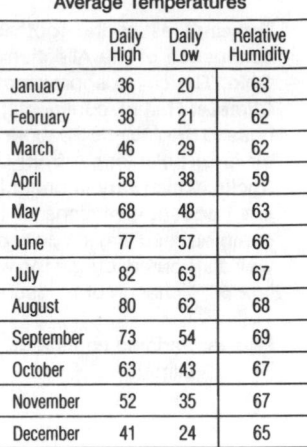

Annual Rainfall 45 in

Annual Snowfall 37 in

Clear 103 days Partly Cloudy 102 days Cloudy 160 days

Precipitation Days: 134   Storm Days: 20

Average Temperatures			
	Daily High	Daily Low	Relative Humidity
January	36	20	63
February	38	21	62
March	46	29	62
April	58	38	59
May	68	48	63
June	77	57	66
July	82	63	67
August	80	62	68
September	73	54	69
October	63	43	67
November	52	35	67
December	41	24	65

Zero-Degree Days: 2
Freezing Days: 151
90-Degree Days: 8
Heating- and Cooling-Degree Days: 6,504

Quebec City, PQ

Terrain: In the vicinity of Quebec City, the relatively narrow St. Lawrence River valley is oriented in a southwest to northeast direction, and is bordered to the north by the Laurentian Mountains and to the south by the Appalachian Mountains. The area immediately surrounding the airport is generally flat and slopes south to the river. From the south shore of the St. Lawrence River, the terrain gradually rises to reach elevations of 900 to 1,800 feet in the Appalachians, 25 miles southeast of the airport. North, the Laurentians rise abruptly to elevations between 900 and 1,800 feet; elevations over 3,000 feet occur some 30 miles northeast.

Climate: The snow season is long, lasting four to five months. Spring arrives suddenly and sometimes not at all. Fall may be as fleeting as spring but almost always is pleasant. Winter's first significant snowfall usually arrives by November 7. Foul weather of any kind seldom lasts for long; most storms leave the area within two days.

Pluses: Moderate summers with pleasant falls.

Minuses: Long, cold winters.

Places Rated Score: 430

Places Rated Rank: 288

Elevation: 239 feet

Wind Speed: 9.9 mph

Seasonal Change

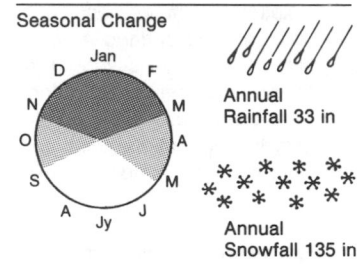

Annual Rainfall 33 in

Annual Snowfall 135 in

Clear 100 days Partly Cloudy 115 days Cloudy 150 days

Precipitation Days: 175   Storm Days: 24

Average Temperatures			
	Daily High	Daily Low	Relative Humidity
January	19	2	75
February	21	4	72
March	32	16	71
April	46	29	67
May	62	41	64
June	72	51	70
July	77	56	72
August	74	53	74
September	64	45	77
October	52	36	75
November	38	26	79
December	23	8	77

Zero-Degree Days: 26
Freezing Days: 180
90-Degree Days: 5
Heating- and Cooling-Degree Days: 5,287

Raleigh–Durham–Chapel Hill, NC

Terrain: Situated in the transition zone between the Coastal Plain and the Piedmont Plateau of North Carolina. The surrounding topography is rolling, with elevations from 200 feet to 500 feet within a 10-mile radius.

Climate: Because it is located between mountains to the west and the Atlantic Coast to the east and south, the metro area enjoys a favorable climate. The mountains form a partial barrier to cold air masses moving eastward from the nation's interior, so that there are very few days in the heart of the winter when the temperature falls below 20°F. Tropical air is present over the eastern and central sections of North Carolina during much of the summer, bringing warm temperatures and high humidity. In midsummer, afternoon temperatures reach 90°F or higher on an average of every fourth day. Rainfall is well distributed throughout the year. July has, on the average, the greatest amount of rainfall, and November the least.

Pluses: Mild four-season climate.

Minuses: Long, humid summers.

Places Rated Score: 647

Places Rated Rank: 42

Elevation: 441 feet

Wind Speed: 7.9 mph

Seasonal Change

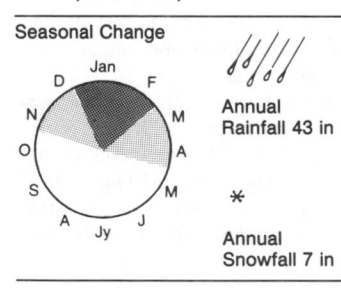

Annual Rainfall 43 in

Annual Snowfall 7 in

Clear 113 days Partly Cloudy 107 days Cloudy 145 days

Precipitation Days: 112   Storm Days: 46

Average Temperatures			
	Daily High	Daily Low	Relative Humidity
January	50	29	67
February	53	30	65
March	61	38	65
April	72	47	63
May	79	55	70
June	85	63	71
July	88	67	74
August	87	67	76
September	82	60	75
October	72	48	71
November	62	38	68
December	53	31	67

Zero-Degree Days: 0
Freezing Days: 82
90-Degree Days: 25
Heating and Cooling-Degree Days: 4,908

Regina, SK

Terrain: The city is situated on the banks of Wascana Creek, which lies in a very shallow basin running southeast to northwest. The surrounding area is a level plain. The land rises slowly to the northeast and peaks at an elevation of about 2,500 feet some 20 miles away. The Qu'Appelle River to the north meanders in an easterly direction in a very deep narrow valley. Draining into the Qu'Appelle, Last Mountain Lake, 50 miles long and 2 to 3 miles wide, lies northwest. Southwest is the Missouri Coteau, a broken escarpment with an average elevation of 2,400 feet. The Dirt Hills, part of the escarpment, rise over 2,700 feet and can be seen to the southwest.

Climate: Regina is Canada's sunniest provincial capital. Being far from influences of oceans or mountains, it has large daily—and extremely large annual—ranges of temperature. High temperature, low humidity, strong winds, and clear skies cause moisture deficits in summer. Winter cold is not only severe but of extremely long duration.

Pluses: Sunny, rigorous, and changeable.

Minuses: Hot, prairie summers; cold, prairie winters.

Places Rated Score: 174　　　　**Places Rated Rank: 339**

Elevation: 1,893 feet

Wind Speed: 12.9 mph

Seasonal Change

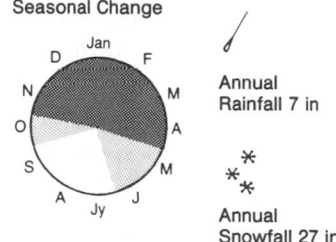

Annual Rainfall 11 in

Annual Snowfall 46 in

Clear 128 days　Partly Cloudy 123 days　Cloudy 114 days

Precipitation Days: 111　　Storm Days: 23

Average Temperatures			
	Daily High	Daily Low	Relative Humidity
January	9	−10	79
February	17	−2	81
March	28	8	81
April	49	27	70
May	65	39	60
June	73	48	63
July	79	53	64
August	77	51	62
September	65	40	66
October	53	29	69
November	32	13	79
December	18	0	81

Zero-Degree Days: 55
Freezing Days: 204
90-Degree Days: 13
Heating- and Cooling-Degree Days: 6,012

Reno, NV

Terrain: Located at the west edge of Truckee Meadows in a semiarid plateau lying in the lee of the Sierra Nevada. To the west, this range rises to elevations of 9,000 feet to 10,000 feet, and hills to the east reach 6,000 feet to 7,000 feet. The Truckee River, flowing from the Sierra Nevada eastward through Reno, drains into Pyramid Lake to the northeast.

Climate: Sunshine is abundant throughout the year. Temperatures are mild, but the daily range may exceed 45 degrees. Even when afternoons reach the upper 90s, a light jacket is needed shortly after sunset. Nights with a minimum temperature over 60°F are rare. Afternoon temperatures are moderate, and only about 10 days a year fail to reach a level above freezing. Humidity is very low during the summer months and moderately low during winter.

Pluses: Mild, sunny climate in alpine setting.

Minuses: Considerable daily temperature variation, little precipitation.

Places Rated Score: 535　　　　**Places Rated Rank: 187**

Elevation: 4,400 feet

Wind Speed: 6.3 mph

Seasonal Change

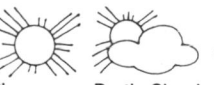

Annual Rainfall 7 in

Annual Snowfall 27 in

Clear 165 days　Partly Cloudy 90 days　Cloudy 110 days

Precipitation Days: 49　　Storm Days: 13

Average Temperatures			
	Daily High	Daily Low	Relative Humidity
January	45	20	65
February	51	24	57
March	56	25	51
April	63	29	47
May	72	37	46
June	82	43	44
July	91	48	41
August	89	45	43
September	81	39	46
October	70	31	50
November	56	24	59
December	46	19	65

Zero-Degree Days: 3
Freezing Days: 189
90-Degree Days: 52
Heating- and Cooling-Degree Days: 6,351

Richmond–Petersburg, VA

Terrain: Located in east-central Virginia at the head of navigation on the James River between Tidewater Virginia and the Piedmont. The Blue Ridge Mountains lie about 90 miles to the west and the Chesapeake Bay 60 miles to the east.

Climate: Water- and mountain-modified continental, with warm, humid summers and generally mild winters. The mountains to the west act as a barrier to outbreaks of cold, continental air in winter; the open waters of the Chesapeake Bay and the Atlantic also contribute to mild winters and to humid summers. Coldest weather usually occurs in late December and in January, with a normal temperature range from 20°F to 50°F. Precipitation is uniformly distributed throughout the year, though dry periods do occur in the autumn, when long periods of pleasant, mild weather are most common.

Pluses: Modified continental climate with long growing season.

Minuses: Humid summers, severe thunderstorms, hurricanes.

Places Rated Score: 585　　　　**Places Rated Rank: 100**

Elevation: 177 feet

Wind Speed: 7.5 mph

Seasonal Change

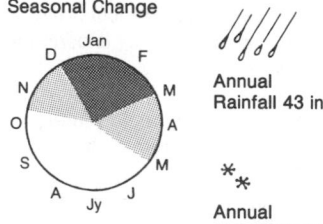

Annual Rainfall 43 in

Annual Snowfall 14 in

Clear 103 days　Partly Cloudy 107 days　Cloudy 155 days

Precipitation Days: 113　　Storm Days: 37

Average Temperatures			
	Daily High	Daily Low	Relative Humidity
January	47	27	69
February	50	28	66
March	59	36	64
April	71	45	61
May	78	54	66
June	85	62	68
July	88	67	71
August	87	66	73
September	81	59	73
October	71	47	71
November	61	37	68
December	50	30	68

Zero-Degree Days: 0
Freezing Days: 85
90-Degree Days: 41
Heating- and Cooling-Degree Days: 5,292

Roanoke, VA

Terrain: Located in the part of the Great Valley that runs from the northernmost part of Virginia southwest to Scott County. The Blue Ridge Mountains are to the west, the Allegheny Mountains to the north.

Climate: Mild. The mountain barrier moderates cold air from the north before it reaches the area. The elevation of the city usually produces cool summer nights. Rainfall is well distributed throughout the year, with an average of 23 inches in the warm season. Snow usually falls each winter, with extremes ranging from a trace to 60 inches.

Pluses: Invigorating, but rare extremes of temperature do occur.

Minuses: Roanoke River liable to flood.

Places Rated Score: 652   **Places Rated Rank: 39**

Elevation: 1,176 feet

Wind Speed: 8.3 mph

Seasonal Change

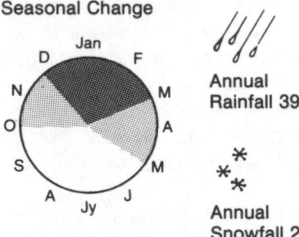

Annual Rainfall 39 in

Annual Snowfall 25 in

Clear 103 days   Partly Cloudy 114 days   Cloudy 148 days

Precipitation Days: 121   Storm Days: 38

Average Temperatures			
	Daily High	Daily Low	Relative Humidity
January	45	26	61
February	48	28	60
March	57	35	59
April	68	44	59
May	76	53	66
June	83	60	67
July	87	65	70
August	86	64	72
September	79	57	73
October	69	45	68
November	57	36	64
December	48	29	63

Zero-Degree Days: 0
Freezing Days: 92
90-Degree Days: 20
Heating- and Cooling-Degree Days: 5,337

Rochester, MN

Terrain: Located in the Zumbro River valley in southeastern Minnesota amid rolling farmland.

Climate: Continental weather pattern with four definite seasons. Winters are cold, but summers are pleasant, with temperatures reaching as high as 90°F on only seven days in an average summer. Thunderstorms (sometimes heavy downpours) occur about once every three days, on the average, during the growing season. These storms often cause high winds. About four times each year, hail will fall. Tornadoes are rare but do occur. Heavy fog occurs 35 times a year on the average.

Pluses: Invigorating four seasons with especially pleasant summers.

Minuses: Cold winters lasting at least five months.

Places Rated Score: 308   **Places Rated Rank: 326**

Elevation: 1,320 feet

Wind Speed: 12.7 mph

Seasonal Change

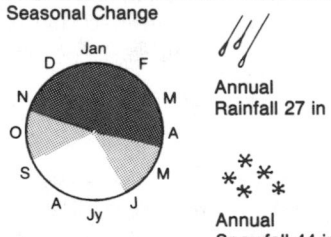

Annual Rainfall 27 in

Annual Snowfall 44 in

Clear 91 days   Partly Cloudy 96 days   Cloudy 178 days

Precipitation Days: 115   Storm Days: 41

Average Temperatures			
	Daily High	Daily Low	Relative Humidity
January	20	2	77
February	26	8	76
March	37	19	76
April	55	34	70
May	68	46	69
June	78	56	70
July	81	60	73
August	79	58	75
September	70	48	76
October	59	38	72
November	41	24	78
December	26	11	80

Zero-Degree Days: 35
Freezing Days: 165
90-Degree Days: 7
Heating- and Cooling-Degree Days: 8,701

Rockford, IL

Terrain: Located northwest of the Chicago area in rolling prairie.

Climate: When winter winds blow from Lake Michigan, cloudiness is often increased, and temperatures are somewhat higher than those to the west around the Mississippi. The lake can also be a moderating influence in summer, sometimes lowering temperatures. Summers are usually hot, however, but oppressive heat seldom prevails for extended periods. Winters are cold, and snow cover is continuous from late December through February.

Pluses: Adequate snow cover for diversified winter sports.

Minuses: Long, cold winters; hot summers.

Places Rated Score: 466   **Places Rated Rank: 263**

Elevation: 743 feet

Wind Speed: 9.9 mph

Seasonal Change

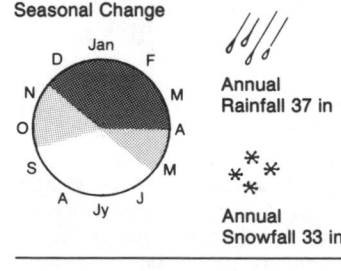

Annual Rainfall 37 in

Annual Snowfall 33 in

Clear 96 days   Partly Cloudy 100 days   Cloudy 169 days

Precipitation Days: 114   Storm Days: 42

Average Temperatures			
	Daily High	Daily Low	Relative Humidity
January	27	10	75
February	32	15	73
March	43	25	71
April	59	37	68
May	71	48	68
June	80	58	68
July	84	62	71
August	82	61	74
September	75	52	74
October	63	41	71
November	46	29	75
December	33	17	78

Zero-Degree Days: 16
Freezing Days: 142
90-Degree Days: 13
Heating- and Cooling-Degree Days: 7,559

Sacramento, CA

Terrain: Located in the heart of a broad, flat valley between California's Coast Ranges and the Sierra Nevada. The land is tabletop-flat and, when irrigated, perfect for growing fruits and vegetables.
Climate: The two mountain ranges shelter the area from many storms and violent weather, thus adding to the mildness of the climate. Occasionally, however, northerly winds, called northers, reach the valley over the Siskiyou Mountains, causing heat waves. Summers are sunny and hot, but low humidity lessens the felt heat. Winters are mild, and snow is rare enough not to be regarded a climatic feature.

Pluses: Sunny, mild.

Minuses: Hot winds from the north on occasion, hot summers.

Places Rated Score: 576   **Places Rated Rank: 109**

Elevation: 25 feet

Wind Speed: 8.3 mph

Seasonal Change

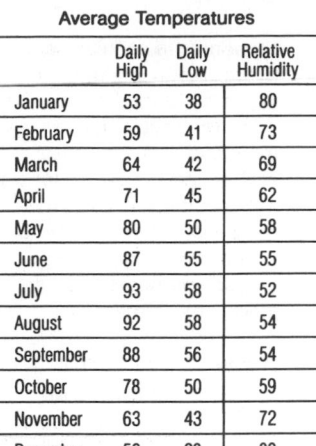

Annual Rainfall 17 in

Annual Snowfall .1 in

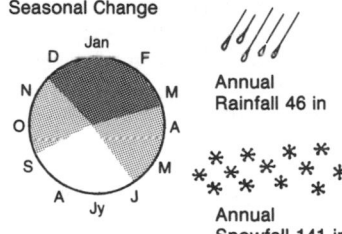

Clear 193 days   Partly Cloudy 72 days   Cloudy 100 days

Precipitation Days: 57   Storm Days: 5

Average Temperatures			
	Daily High	Daily Low	Relative Humidity
January	53	38	80
February	59	41	73
March	64	42	69
April	71	45	62
May	80	50	58
June	87	55	55
July	93	58	52
August	92	58	54
September	88	56	54
October	78	50	59
November	63	43	72
December	53	38	80

Zero-Degree Days: 0
Freezing Days: 17
90-Degree Days: 77
Heating- and Cooling-Degree Days: 4,002

St. John's, NF

Terrain: Rugged, with many small lakes and rivers dominating the surrounding landscape. The Atlantic Ocean lies to the east, Conception Bay is to the west, and Windsor Lake is located to the southwest. The land slopes east to the ocean and, to the west, the terrain plunges in sheer cliffs at Conception Bay. In all but the eastern quadrant, there are many hills within a short distance.
Climate: The marine climate brings more changeable weather, ample precipitation in a variety of forms (sometimes all at once), higher humidity, lower visibility, more clouds, less sunshine, and stronger winds than a continental climate. The open sea keeps winter air temperatures a little higher and summer temperatures slightly lower on the coast than at places inland. The seasons are called character-building and invigorating by proud natives who also boast of Canada's third mildest winters, after Victoria's and Vancouver's.

Pluses: Cool summers; mild winters.

Minuses: Foggy, cloudy, misty.

Places Rated Score: 654   **Places Rated Rank: 38**

Elevation: 459 feet

Wind Speed: 15.1 mph

Seasonal Change

Annual Rainfall 46 in

Annual Snowfall 141 in

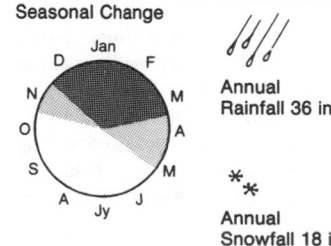

Clear 59 days   Partly Cloudy 110 days   Cloudy 195 days

Precipitation Days: 217   Storm Days: 3

Average Temperatures			
	Daily High	Daily Low	Relative Humidity
January	31	19	84
February	30	18	83
March	34	22	84
April	40	28	84
May	49	34	83
June	60	43	80
July	68	51	81
August	67	52	83
September	60	46	82
October	51	38	83
November	44	32	85
December	35	24	84

Zero-Degree Days: 0
Freezing Days: 176
90-Degree Days: 0
Heating- and Cooling-Degree Days: 4,853

St. Louis, MO–IL

Terrain: Located at the confluence of the Missouri and Mississippi rivers and slightly east of the geographic center of the United States. The surrounding terrain is gently rolling, with occasional high bluffs characteristic of parts of the Mississippi Valley.
Climate: Modified continental. St. Louis is in the enviable position of having a changeable, four-season climate without prolonged periods of extreme cold, heat, or humidity. To the south is the warm, moist air of the Gulf of Mexico and to the north the region of cold polar air masses. Alternating invasions by these influences, and the conflict along the frontal zones where they meet, produce a great variety of weather conditions, but none lasting long enough to become monotonous. Winters are brisk but seldom severe. Snowfall averages less than 20 inches per season. Summers are quite warm, often uncomfortably so when coupled with high humidity. These oppressive spells usually are relieved by storms.

Pluses: Changeable weather, relatively mild winters.

Minuses: Hot, humid summers.

Places Rated Score: 537   **Places Rated Rank: 180**

Elevation: 564 feet

Wind Speed: 9.5 mph

Seasonal Change

Annual Rainfall 36 in

Annual Snowfall 18 in

Clear 105 days   Partly Cloudy 101 days   Cloudy 159 days

Precipitation Days: 108   Storm Days: 45

Average Temperatures			
	Daily High	Daily Low	Relative Humidity
January	38	20	74
February	43	25	73
March	53	33	70
April	67	45	66
May	76	55	69
June	85	64	69
July	89	69	71
August	87	67	72
September	81	59	74
October	69	47	70
November	54	35	73
December	43	26	76

Zero-Degree Days: 3
Freezing Days: 107
90-Degree Days: 37
Heating- and Cooling-Degree Days: 6,225

Salt Lake City–Ogden, UT

Terrain: Spectacular setting. To the east, the Wasatch Mountains rise from heights of 8,000 feet to 12,000 feet; to the southwest, the Oguirrh Mountains climb to 10,000 feet.

Climate: Though by no means mild, it is modified by the surrounding mountains, which deflect stormy weather elsewhere. There are four well-defined seasons, including a long winter. Summers are hot, but the dry air lessens felt heat, and nights are cool. Winters are cold but not severe. Most of the precipitation is snow, with accumulations staying on the ground for most of the winter. Fall is short, with spring longer and sometimes stormy. Nearby Great Salt Lake also helps modify the climate.

Pluses: Scenic setting, good rigorous climate.

Minuses: Cold, snowy winters.

Elevation: 4,227 feet

Wind Speed: 8.7 mph

Seasonal Change

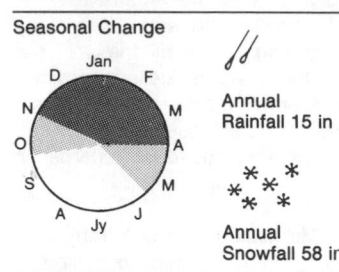

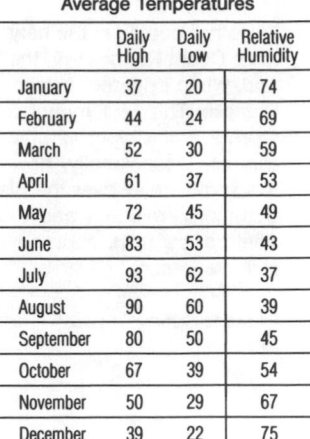

Annual Rainfall 15 in

Annual Snowfall 58 in

Clear 129 days   Partly Cloudy 103 days   Cloudy 133 days

Precipitation Days: 88   Storm Days: 35

Average Temperatures			
	Daily High	Daily Low	Relative Humidity
January	37	20	74
February	44	24	69
March	52	30	59
April	61	37	53
May	72	45	49
June	83	53	43
July	93	62	37
August	90	60	39
September	80	50	45
October	67	39	54
November	50	29	67
December	39	22	75

Zero-Degree Days: 3
Freezing Days: 134
90-Degree Days: 58
Heating- and Cooling-Degree Days: 6,910

Places Rated Score: 541   **Places Rated Rank: 175**

San Angelo, TX

Terrain: Lies on the northern edge of the Edwards Plateau. The land is flat, sometimes slightly rolling, and is classified as semiarid, or steppe, covered with grass, thorny bush, and cacti.

Climate: San Angelo is situated between the humid climate of eastern Texas and the dry High Plains and the Basin and Range region of western Texas. It is hot, though usually dry. However, uncomfortable hot spells with humid air permeate the area occasionally. The wind is brisk, modifying summer heat. Summers are long, winters short and mild.

Pluses: Dry sunny climate, long summers, short winters.

Minuses: Can be dusty; humid hot spells.

Elevation: 1,908 feet

Wind Speed: 10.5 mph

Seasonal Change

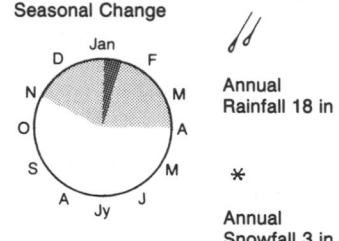

Annual Rainfall 18 in

Annual Snowfall 3 in

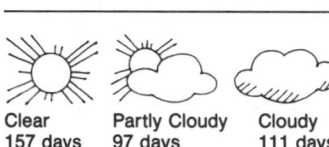

Clear 157 days   Partly Cloudy 97 days   Cloudy 111 days

Precipitation Days: 57   Storm Days: 37

Average Temperatures			
	Daily High	Daily Low	Relative Humidity
January	59	32	64
February	63	36	63
March	72	43	57
April	80	53	59
May	86	62	65
June	93	69	66
July	97	72	61
August	95	71	62
September	88	65	69
October	79	54	68
November	67	42	66
December	61	35	65

Zero-Degree Days: 0
Freezing Days: 52
90-Degree Days: 109
Heating- and Cooling-Degree Days: 4,942

Places Rated Score: 488   **Places Rated Rank: 240**

San Antonio, TX

Terrain: Located between the Edwards Plateau and the Gulf Coastal Plain of south-central Texas. Terrain is rolling. Vegetation consists of grasses and live oak trees, along with mesquite and cacti. Soils are blackland clay and silty loam.

Climate: Two-season, with mild weather during normal winter months and a long, hot summer. Though 140 miles from the Gulf of Mexico, the city feels the influence of its hot moist air. Thunderstorms and rains have occurred in every month of the year, but they are most common during the summer, with most rain falling in May and September. The winds during the winter are from the north, and from the south in the summer. Skies are clear more than 30% of the time, and cloudy about 30%.

Pluses: No winter, attractive terrain.

Minuses: Hot, muggy summers.

Elevation: 794 feet

Wind Speed: 9.3 mph

Seasonal Change

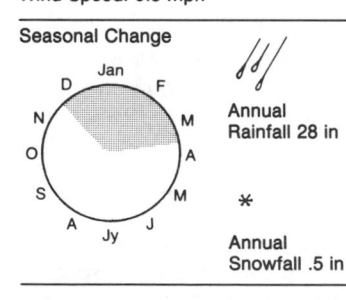

Annual Rainfall 28 in

Annual Snowfall .5 in

Clear 110 days   Partly Cloudy 117 days   Cloudy 138 days

Precipitation Days: 81   Storm Days: 36

Average Temperatures			
	Daily High	Daily Low	Relative Humidity
January	62	39	70
February	66	42	69
March	74	50	66
April	80	59	70
May	86	66	74
June	92	72	72
July	95	74	70
August	95	74	69
September	89	69	71
October	82	59	69
November	71	48	68
December	65	41	69

Zero-Degree Days: 0
Freezing Days: 22
90-Degree Days: 111
Heating- and Cooling-Degree Days: 4,564

Places Rated Score: 398   **Places Rated Rank: 304**

✓ San Diego, CA

Terrain: Located on San Diego Bay in the southwest corner of California near the Mexican border. Its coastal location is backed by coastal foothills and mountains to the east.

Climate: One of the mildest in North America: typically marine, sometimes called Mediterranean. There are no freezing days and an average of only three 90-degree days each year. San Diego has abundant sunshine and mild sea breezes. Only two seasons occur here: a dry, mild summer and a spring that is cooler, with some rain. Storms are practically unknown, though there is considerable fog along the coast, and many low clouds in early morning and evening during the summer.

Pluses: One of the best climates for sun and mildness.

Minuses: Paradise climate lacking variety and seasonal contrasts.

Places Rated Score: 903　　　　**Places Rated Rank: 3**

Elevation: 28 feet

Wind Speed: 6.7 mph

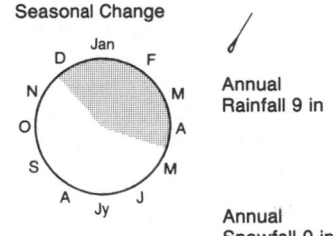

Seasonal Change

Annual Rainfall 9 in

Annual Snowfall 0 in

Clear 150 days　Partly Cloudy 117 days　Cloudy 98 days

Precipitation Days: 41　　Storm Days: 3

Average Temperatures			
	Daily High	Daily Low	Relative Humidity
January	65	48	63
February	66	50	66
March	66	52	67
April	68	55	67
May	69	58	71
June	71	61	74
July	76	65	74
August	78	67	74
September	77	65	73
October	75	60	70
November	70	54	67
December	66	49	65

Zero-Degree Days: 0
Freezing Days: 0
90-Degree Days: 3
Heating- and Cooling-Degree Days: 2,229

✓ San Francisco, CA

Terrain: Unique location—at the northern end of a narrow peninsula that separates San Francisco Bay from the Pacific Ocean and forms the southern shore of the Golden Gate Bridge—causes San Francisco to be known as the "Air-Conditioned City."

Climate: Two-season climate: a cool, pleasant summer and a mild spring. Flowers bloom throughout the year, and warm clothing is needed every month. Sea fogs and associated low stratus clouds are a striking characteristic of the city's climate. On the average, though, the sun shines during 66% of the daylight hours. There are wide contrasts in climate within short distances of the bay; nearby communities of Marin County, to the north across the Golden Gate and sheltered from the prevailing winds by high peaks and ridges of the Coast Ranges, enjoy warmer and sunnier weather than the city.

Pluses: Mild, springlike weather 10 months of the year; ranks first among the 333 metro areas.

Minuses: Invariable climate patterns; fogs and cloudy days.

Places Rated Score: 910　　　　**Places Rated Rank: 1**

Elevation: 155 feet

Wind Speed: 8.7 mph

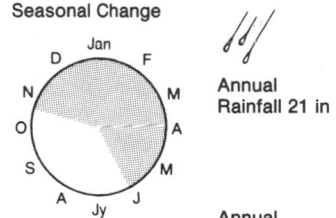

Seasonal Change

Annual Rainfall 21 in

Annual Snowfall 0 in

Clear 162 days　Partly Cloudy 103 days　Cloudy 100 days

Precipitation Days: 67　　Storm Days: 2

Average Temperatures			
	Daily High	Daily Low	Relative Humidity
January	57	44	72
February	61	48	73
March	62	48	71
April	63	49	72
May	65	51	79
June	68	53	81
July	69	55	83
August	70	56	83
September	73	56	77
October	70	54	71
November	63	50	73
December	57	45	72

Zero-Degree Days: 0
Freezing Days: 0
90-Degree Days: 1
Heating- and Cooling-Degree Days: 3,119

✓ Santa Barbara–Santa Maria–Lompoc, CA

Terrain: Located in the Santa Maria valley 150 miles north of Los Angeles and 250 miles south of San Francisco. The valley is flat and fertile, opening onto the Pacific Ocean at its widest point and tapering inland at a distance of 30 miles from the coast. It is bounded by the foothills of the San Rafael Mountains, the Solomon Hills, and the Casmalia Hills.

Climate: Rainfall season, typical of the California coast, is winter. During the rest of the year, particularly from June to October, there is little or no precipitation. Clear, sunshiny afternoons prevail on most days. At night and in the morning, however, the California stratus and fog appear.

Pluses: Year-round mildness moving through gradual transitions.

Minuses: No distinct seasonal changes, night and morning fogs.

Places Rated Score: 885　　　　**Places Rated Rank: 5**

Elevation: 238 feet

Wind Speed: 7 mph

Seasonal Change

Annual Rainfall 12 in

Annual Snowfall 0 in

Clear 177 days　Partly Cloudy 108 days　Cloudy 80 days

Precipitation Days: 45　　Storm Days: 2

Average Temperatures			
	Daily High	Daily Low	Relative Humidity
January	63	41	66
February	64	43	66
March	65	44	69
April	67	47	65
May	68	50	68
June	71	53	75
July	74	57	76
August	75	58	76
September	75	56	73
October	73	51	69
November	69	45	66
December	65	40	67

Zero-Degree Days: 0
Freezing Days: 24
90-Degree Days: 6
Heating- and Cooling-Degree Days: 3,137

Savannah, GA

Terrain: Surrounded by flat land, low and marshy to the north and east, rising to several feet above sea level to the west and south. About half the land to the west and south is clear of trees; the other half is woods, much of which lie in swamp.
Climate: Temperate with a seasonal mean temperature of 51°F in winter, 64°F in spring, 80°F in summer, and 66°F in autumn. Summer temperatures are moderated by thundershowers almost every afternoon. Sunshine is adequate in all seasons; seldom are there more than two or three days in succession without it. The long growing season is accompanied by abundant rain.

Pluses: Mild winters, pleasant autumns.

Minuses: Low, marshy terrain; humid summers.

Elevation: 51 feet

Wind Speed: 8.1 mph

Seasonal Change

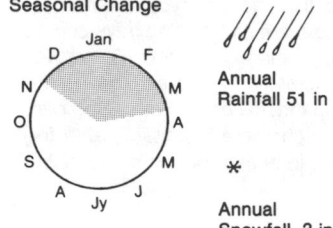

Annual Rainfall 51 in

Annual Snowfall .3 in

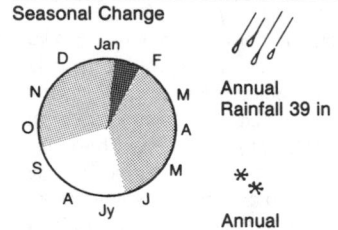

Clear 104 days   Partly Cloudy 113 days   Cloudy 148 days

Precipitation Days: 112   Storm Days: 64

Average Temperatures			
	Daily High	Daily Low	Relative Humidity
January	60	38	68
February	63	40	65
March	70	47	66
April	78	54	65
May	84	62	68
June	89	69	71
July	91	72	73
August	90	71	76
September	86	68	76
October	78	56	70
November	70	46	69
December	63	39	68

Zero-Degree Days: 0
Freezing Days: 35
90-Degree Days: 54
Heating- and Cooling-Degree Days: 4,269

Places Rated Score: 542   **Places Rated Rank: 171**

✓ Seattle–Bellevue–Everett, WA

Terrain: Located on Puget Sound on the northwest Pacific coast of Washington. The Cascade Range and the Olympic Mountains serve as barriers to easterly and northerly weather systems.
Climate: Midlatitude coast climate, characterized by moderate temperatures, a pronounced though not sharply defined rainy season, and considerable cloudiness, particularly during the winter. Occasionally, severe winter storms come in from the north. Summers are very pleasant, and winters are relatively mild, with prevailing temperatures in the 40s. Summer heat and winter cold are modified by the nearness of the ocean.

Pluses: Mild temperatures, especially pleasant summers and autumns.

Minuses: Wet winters, ground fogs, lots of drizzle.

Elevation: 450 feet

Wind Speed: 9.3 mph

Seasonal Change

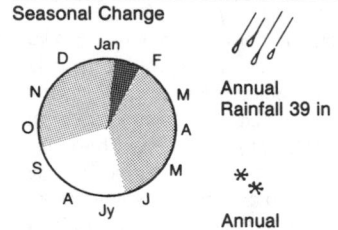

Annual Rainfall 39 in

Annual Snowfall 15 in

Clear 57 days   Partly Cloudy 79 days   Cloudy 229 days

Precipitation Days: 160   Storm Days: 7

Average Temperatures			
	Daily High	Daily Low	Relative Humidity
January	44	34	78
February	49	37	74
March	51	37	72
April	57	41	71
May	64	46	69
June	69	51	68
July	75	54	66
August	74	54	67
September	69	51	72
October	60	45	77
November	50	39	80
December	46	36	81

Zero-Degree Days: 0
Freezing Days: 32
90-Degree Days: 3
Heating- and Cooling-Degree Days: 5,314

Places Rated Score: 808   **Places Rated Rank: 15**

Shreveport–Bossier City, LA

Terrain: Located on the west bank of the Red River opposite Bossier City, in the northwestern section of the state, some 30 miles south of Arkansas and 15 miles east of the Texas state line. Part of the city is situated in the Red River bottomlands and the remainder in the gently rolling hills that begin a mile west of the river.
Climate: Transitional between the humid subtropical climate prevalent to the south and the continental climates of the Great Plains and Middle West to the north. Winter months are normally mild, with cold spells generally of short duration. The typical pattern is a drop in temperature the first day, minimum temperatures the second day, and gradual warming on the third. Summers are hot and humid, relieved only by the thunderstorms that come about eight times per month during that season. April and May are pleasant. Fall, which lasts from late September to December, is delightful for outdoor activities.

Pluses: Mild winters, long falls.

Minuses: Hot, steamy summers; occasional flooding.

Elevation: 259 feet

Wind Speed: 8.8 mph

Seasonal Change

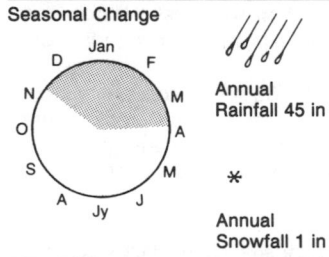

Annual Rainfall 45 in

Annual Snowfall 1 in

Clear 118 days   Partly Cloudy 99 days   Cloudy 148 days

Precipitation Days: 97   Storm Days: 54

Average Temperatures			
	Daily High	Daily Low	Relative Humidity
January	56	36	74
February	61	39	71
March	68	46	70
April	77	55	72
May	84	62	75
June	90	69	75
July	93	73	74
August	93	72	74
September	88	67	74
October	79	55	72
November	67	45	73
December	59	38	74

Zero-Degree Days: 0
Freezing Days: 1
90-Degree Days: 87
Heating- and Cooling-Degree Days: 4,705

Places Rated Score: 508   **Places Rated Rank: 224**

Sioux City, IA–NE

Terrain: Sioux City is located along the Missouri River at a point where Iowa touches both Nebraska and South Dakota. The terrain is rolling, except for the river valleys and bottomlands. The Sioux City business district lies in the river valley, and the residential sections, for the most part, are spread over the hills, which range from 100 feet to 200 feet higher. Corn, small grains, and grazing grasses are products of abundant rainfall here.

Climate: Typically continental and largely determined by the movement and interaction of the large-scale weather systems. Under normal conditions, winters are cold and summers warm, with most rain falling between April and September. Except for an occasional dry year, rain is plentiful. There is considerable fluctuation in temperature and precipitation from season to season and year to year, as elsewhere in the northern Plains. Average growing season: 160 days. The first freeze is in early October and the last in late April.

Pluses: Variable.   **Minuses:** Rugged continental.

Places Rated Score: 385   **Places Rated Rank: 308**

Elevation: 1,103 feet

Wind Speed: 10.9 mph

Seasonal Change

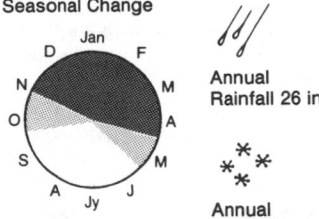

Annual Rainfall 26 in

Annual Snowfall 31 in

Clear 107 days   Partly Cloudy 103 days   Cloudy 155 days

Precipitation Days: 98   Storm Days: 45

Average Temperatures			
	Daily High	Daily Low	Relative Humidity
January	26	6	73
February	33	13	73
March	44	24	71
April	62	38	65
May	73	50	67
June	82	60	70
July	87	65	72
August	84	62	74
September	75	54	72
October	65	40	68
November	47	26	73
December	33	14	76

Zero-Degree Days: 22
Freezing Days: 150
90-Degree Days: 24
Heating- and Cooling-Degree Days: 7,885

Sioux Falls, SD

Terrain: Located in the Big Sioux River valley in the southeastern portion of South Dakota. Surrounding terrain is gently rolling. Within a 100-mile radius of the city, the land slopes upward 300 feet to 400 feet in the north and northwest and downward in the southeast. There is little change in elevation in the other directions.

Climate: Invigorating continental. Cold air masses from the north often move in very rapidly, causing strong, gusty winds for several hours. During late fall and winter, these cold fronts sometimes bring temperature drops of 20 degrees to 30 degrees in a day. Severe cold spells rarely last more than a few days. During a cold winter, frost may penetrate the ground to a depth of 3 feet to 4 feet unless there is heavy snow cover to protect the ground. There are usually one to two very heavy snowstorms each winter. Summer temperatures may climb over 100°F once or twice a year. Thunderstorms are frequent, especially during June and July. Occasional tornadoes and floods.

Pluses: Vigorous four-season climate.   **Minuses:** Extremes in temperature, snowy.

Places Rated Score: 276   **Places Rated Rank: 332**

Elevation: 1,427 feet

Wind Speed: 11.2 mph

Seasonal Change

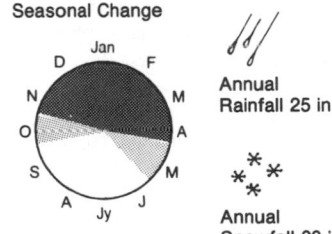

Annual Rainfall 25 in

Annual Snowfall 39 in

Clear 105 days   Partly Cloudy 105 days   Cloudy 155 days

Precipitation Days: 93   Storm Days: 43

Average Temperatures			
	Daily High	Daily Low	Relative Humidity
January	23	2	72
February	29	9	73
March	40	21	73
April	58	35	68
May	71	46	67
June	80	56	68
July	86	62	68
August	84	60	70
September	74	49	71
October	62	37	68
November	44	22	74
December	29	10	76

Zero-Degree Days: 33
Freezing Days: 171
90-Degree Days: 28
Heating- and Cooling-Degree Days: 8,557

Spokane, WA

Terrain: Spokane lies on the eastern edge of the broad Columbia Basin area of Washington, which is bounded by the Cascade Range on the west and the Rocky Mountains to the east. The elevations in eastern Washington vary from less than 400 feet above sea level near Pasco to 5,000 feet in the extreme eastern edge of the state. Spokane is in the upper plateau area, where the long, gradual slope from the Columbia River meets the sharp rise of the Rockies.

Climate: Combines some of the characteristics of the damp coastal climate with the arid interior climate. Most air masses are brought from the west or southwest and lose most of their moisture passing over the Coast and Cascade ranges. Sometimes dry, continental air masses from the east invade the area, bringing high temperatures with low humidity in the summer and subzero temperatures in the winter. Generally, Spokane has a mild, arid climate during summer and a cold, coastal climate during winter.

Pluses: Mild, dry summers.   **Minuses:** Damp winters.

Places Rated Score: 574   **Places Rated Rank: 117**

Elevation: 2,365 feet

Wind Speed: 8.7 mph

Seasonal Change

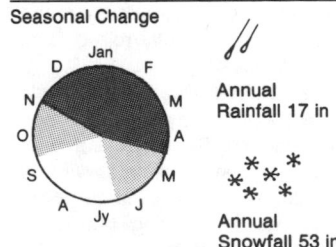

Annual Rainfall 17 in

Annual Snowfall 53 in

Clear 89 days   Partly Cloudy 87 days   Cloudy 189 days

Precipitation Days: 114   Storm Days: 11

Average Temperatures			
	Daily High	Daily Low	Relative Humidity
January	31	20	82
February	39	26	77
March	46	29	68
April	57	35	61
May	66	43	59
June	74	49	56
July	84	55	46
August	82	54	46
September	72	47	53
October	58	37	64
November	41	29	82
December	34	24	85

Zero-Degree Days: 5
Freezing Days: 141
90-Degree Days: 21
Heating- and Cooling-Degree Days: 7,225

Springfield, IL

Terrain: Surrounding country is nearly level. There are no large hills in the area, but rolling terrain is found near the Sangamon River and Spring Creek.

Climate: Typically continental in character, with warm to hot summers and cold winters. Monthly average temperatures range from the upper 20s in January to the upper 70s in July. Considerable variation takes place frequently within each season. Although summer weather is often uncomfortably warm and humid, winters are less severe than those farther to the north, although prairie winds may accentuate the cold. Summers are sunny.

Pluses: Changeable climate.

Minuses: Hot summers, rather cold winters.

Places Rated Score: 524   **Places Rated Rank: 199**

Elevation: 613 feet

Wind Speed: 11.4 mph

Seasonal Change

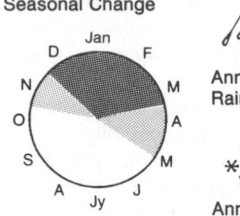

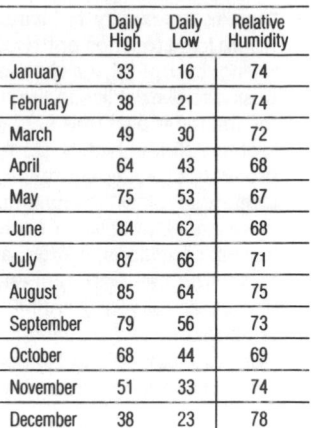

Annual Rainfall 35 in

Annual Snowfall 22 in

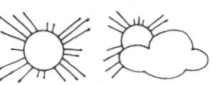

Clear 108 days   Partly Cloudy 92 days   Cloudy 165 days

Precipitation Days: 112   Storm Days: 50

Average Temperatures			
	Daily High	Daily Low	Relative Humidity
January	33	16	74
February	38	21	74
March	49	30	72
April	64	43	68
May	75	53	67
June	84	62	68
July	87	66	71
August	85	64	75
September	79	56	73
October	68	44	69
November	51	33	74
December	38	23	78

Zero-Degree Days: 8
Freezing Days: 119
90-Degree Days: 28
Heating- and Cooling-Degree Days: 6,674

Springfield, MO

Terrain: Located on very gently rolling tableland, almost atop the crest of the Missouri Ozark Plateau. The average elevation of the city proper is just over 1,300 feet above sea level.

Climate: As a result of this advantageous position, the city and surrounding countryside enjoy what is described as a plateau climate. The area possesses the mild and changeable climate often associated with high places in southerly latitudes, with warmer winters and cooler summers than other parts of the state at lower elevations. The city sits astride two major drainage systems: the Missouri River system to the north and the White-Mississippi system to the south.

Pluses: Mild, changeable.

Minuses: Short springs and falls.

Places Rated Score: 544   **Places Rated Rank: 166**

Elevation: 1,270 feet

Wind Speed: 11.2 mph

Seasonal Change

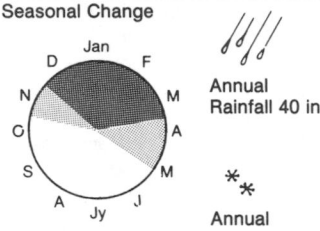

Annual Rainfall 40 in

Annual Snowfall 15 in

Clear 117 days   Partly Cloudy 99 days   Cloudy 149 days

Precipitation Days: 107   Storm Days: 58

Average Temperatures			
	Daily High	Daily Low	Relative Humidity
January	42	21	69
February	47	25	69
March	56	33	67
April	68	44	67
May	77	53	72
June	85	62	73
July	90	66	72
August	89	65	71
September	82	57	73
October	71	46	68
November	56	34	70
December	46	26	71

Zero-Degree Days: 3
Freezing Days: 105
90-Degree Days: 40
Heating- and Cooling-Degree Days: 5,952

Syracuse, NY

Terrain: Located at approximately the geographic center of New York State. Gently rolling terrain stretches northward for about 30 miles to the eastern end of Lake Ontario. Oneida Lake lies about 8 miles northeast of the city. Five miles to the south, hills rise to about 1,500 feet. Immediately to the west, terrain is gently rolling, with elevations 500 feet to 800 feet above sea level.

Climate: Continental and comparatively humid. Nearly all cyclonic systems moving from the interior of the country and passing through the St. Lawrence Valley will affect Syracuse. Seasonal and daily changes are marked and produce an invigorating climate. Winters can be cold and severe; daytime temperatures average 35°F, nighttime lows around 18°F. Autumn, winter, and spring show great changeability. Summer nights generally are cool, but days can be uncomfortable because of the humidity. The area is overcast, and the cloudiest months are December, January, and February.

Pluses: Changeable weather.

Minuses: Snowy, cloudy, rigorous.

Places Rated Score: 548   **Places Rated Rank: 159**

Elevation: 408 feet

Wind Speed: 9.8 mph

Seasonal Change

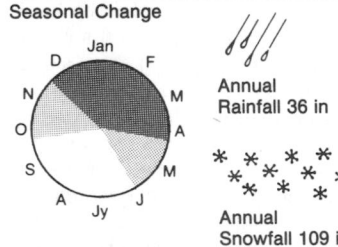

Annual Rainfall 36 in

Annual Snowfall 109 in

Clear 64 days   Partly Cloudy 100 days   Cloudy 201 days

Precipitation Days: 168   Storm Days: 29

Average Temperatures			
	Daily High	Daily Low	Relative Humidity
January	31	15	73
February	32	16	72
March	41	25	69
April	56	36	65
May	68	46	66
June	77	55	68
July	82	60	68
August	80	59	73
September	72	52	75
October	61	42	73
November	48	33	74
December	35	21	76

Zero-Degree Days: 9
Freezing Days: 138
90-Degree Days: 6
Heating- and Cooling-Degree Days: 7,229

Tallahassee, FL

Terrain: Located in flat topography in northwest Florida about 20 miles from the Gulf of Mexico.

Climate: Average year-round temperatures compare with those of southern portions of California, Brazil, China, and Australia. The yearly average of 68°F has varied from 64°F to 71°F. In contrast to the southern part of Florida, there is a more definite march of the four seasons here, with considerable winter rainfall and much less winter sunshine. Summer is the least pleasant time of the year; thunderstorms occur on the average of every other day. High humidities and high temperatures cause discomfort. Maxima of 90°F or higher occur on an average of almost 90 days per year, with readings as high as 95°F on 22 of those days.

Pluses: Warm winters, sufficient rainfall.

Minuses: Long, humid summers; few clear days relative to the rest of the state.

Places Rated Score: 404

Places Rated Rank: 300

Elevation: 68 feet

Wind Speed: 7.0 mph

Seasonal Change

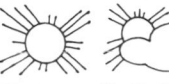

Annual Rainfall 62 in

Annual Snowfall 0 in

Clear 95 days | Partly Cloudy 138 days | Cloudy 132 days

Precipitation Days: 119   Storm Days: 86

Average Temperatures			
	Daily High	Daily Low	Relative Humidity
January	63	40	73
February	66	41	71
March	73	48	71
April	80	54	69
May	86	62	71
June	90	69	74
July	91	72	78
August	91	72	79
September	88	69	76
October	80	56	72
November	72	46	72
December	65	41	73

Zero-Degree Days: 0
Freezing Days: 36
90-Degree Days: 87
Heating- and Cooling-Degree Days: 4,126

Tampa–St. Petersburg–Clearwater, FL

Terrain: Located in flat topography on the Gulf coast of Florida.

Climate: An outstanding feature is the summer thunderstorm season. On the average, there are 88 days of thundershowers per year, occurring mostly in the afternoons in July, August, and September. The resulting temperature drop from 90°F to 70°F produces an agreeable physiologic reaction. Temperature throughout the year is modified by the waters of the Gulf of Mexico and surrounding bays. Snowfall is negligible, and freezing temperatures are rare; during the cooling season, however, night ground fogs occur frequently because of the flat terrain.

Pluses: Mild Gulf climate.

Minuses: Gulf hurricanes, regular summer thundershowers.

Places Rated Score: 440

Places Rated Rank: 280

Elevation: 11 feet

Wind Speed: 8.8 mph

Seasonal Change

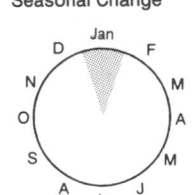

Annual Rainfall 49 in

Annual Snowfall 0 in

Clear 98 days | Partly Cloudy 140 days | Cloudy 127 days

Precipitation Days: 107   Storm Days: 88

Average Temperatures			
	Daily High	Daily Low	Relative Humidity
January	70	50	73
February	71	50	71
March	76	56	71
April	82	61	69
May	87	67	69
June	90	72	74
July	90	74	76
August	90	74	78
September	89	73	77
October	84	65	73
November	77	56	73
December	72	51	73

Zero-Degree Days: 0
Freezing Days: 4
90-Degree Days: 81
Heating- and Cooling-Degree Days: 4,084

Toledo, OH

Terrain: Located on the western end of Lake Erie at the mouth of the Maumee River, on flat ground. The city has excellent harbor facilities, making it a large transportation center for rail, water, and motor freight. Generally rich agricultural land is found in the surrounding area, especially up the Maumee River toward the Indiana state line.

Climate: Nearness to Lake Erie has a moderating effect on temperature, and extremes are seldom recorded. Humidity is high, and there is an excessive amount of cloudiness. In the winter months, the sun shines during only 30% of the daylight hours; December and January, the cloudiest months, sometimes receive as little as 16% of the possible amount of sunshine.

Pluses: Lakefront location moderates extreme temperatures.

Minuses: Humid, cloudy.

Places Rated Score: 518

Places Rated Rank: 207

Elevation: 692 feet

Wind Speed: 9.5 mph

Seasonal Change

Annual Rainfall 32 in

Annual Snowfall 37 in

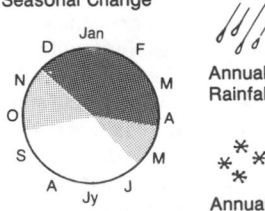

Clear 71 days | Partly Cloudy 110 days | Cloudy 184 days

Precipitation Days: 136   Storm Days: 40

Average Temperatures			
	Daily High	Daily Low	Relative Humidity
January	31	16	75
February	34	18	73
March	45	26	71
April	59	37	68
May	71	47	67
June	80	56	68
July	83	60	71
August	82	58	75
September	75	51	75
October	63	40	72
November	48	31	75
December	36	21	78

Zero-Degree Days: 8
Freezing Days: 145
90-Degree Days: 13
Heating- and Cooling-Degree Days: 7,066

Toronto, ON

Terrain: Located on the northwest shore of Lake Ontario, nestled in a shallow basin with a gentle rise in land to the Niagara escarpment west to northwest.

Climate: One of the most reliable precipitation regimes in the world, with markedly dry or wet spells both uncommon. The four well-marked seasons include cold to cool winters with periods of snow or rain and snow alternating with bright sunshine; the slow return to warmth in spring along with showery weather; periods of heat and humidity in summer with occasional thunderstorms; and increasing cloudiness, more frequent rains, and rapidly dropping temperatures during autumn.

Pluses: Four, reliable, well-marked seasons.

Minuses: Humid summer periods; cold, wet winters.

Places Rated Score: 575

Places Rated Rank: 112

Elevation: 246 feet

Wind Speed: 9.6 mph

Seasonal Change

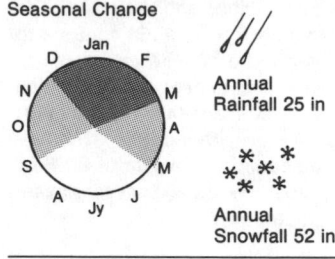

Annual Rainfall 25 in

Annual Snowfall 52 in

Clear 109 days · Partly Cloudy 121 days · Cloudy 134 days

Precipitation Days: 137 · Storm Days: 27

Average Temperatures			
	Daily High	Daily Low	Relative Humidity
January	28	12	80
February	29	13	79
March	38	23	77
April	53	33	70
May	65	43	68
June	75	53	70
July	80	58	69
August	78	56	73
September	70	49	76
October	58	39	77
November	45	31	81
December	33	19	82

Zero-Degree Days: 5
Freezing Days: 155
90-Degree Days: 14
Heating- and Cooling-Degree Days: 4,389

Tucson, AZ

Terrain: Lies at the foot of the Catalina Mountains in a flat to gently rolling valley floor in southern Arizona.

Climate: Desert, characterized by a long, hot season beginning in April and ending in October. Temperature maxima above 90°F are the rule during this period; on 41 days each year, on the average, the temperature reaches 100°F. These high temperatures are modified by low humidity, reducing discomfort. Tucson lies in the zone receiving more sunshine than any other in the United States. Clear skies or very thin, high clouds permit intense surface heating during the day and active radiational cooling at night, a process enhanced by the characteristic atmospheric dryness.

Pluses: Clear, warm, dry.

Minuses: Intense summer heat.

Places Rated Score: 589

Places Rated Rank: 97

Elevation: 2,555 feet

Wind Speed: 8.2 mph

Seasonal Change

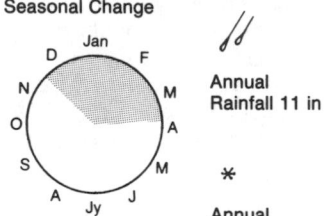

Annual Rainfall 11 in

Annual Snowfall 2 in

Clear 198 days · Partly Cloudy 89 days · Cloudy 78 days

Precipitation Days: 50 · Storm Days: 40

Average Temperatures			
	Daily High	Daily Low	Relative Humidity
January	64	38	48
February	67	40	43
March	72	44	38
April	80	50	29
May	89	58	24
June	99	67	23
July	99	74	43
August	96	72	49
September	94	67	41
October	84	57	39
November	72	45	41
December	65	39	48

Zero-Degree Days: 0
Freezing Days: 21
90-Degree Days: 139
Heating- and Cooling-Degree Days: 4,566

Tulsa, OK

Terrain: Lies along the Arkansas River at an elevation of almost 700 feet above sea level. The surrounding terrain is gently rolling. There are no natural formations—such as mountains or large water surfaces—that influence its climate.

Climate: At a latitude of 30 degrees north, Tulsa is far enough north to escape long periods of heat in summer, yet far enough south to miss the extreme cold of winter. The influence of warm moist air from the Gulf of Mexico is often felt in the high humidity, but the climate is essentially continental, characterized by rapid temperature changes. Generally, the winter months are mild. Temperatures of 100°F or higher are frequently experienced from the latter part of July to early September but are usually accompanied by low humidity and a good southerly breeze. Fall is long, with a great number of pleasant, sunny days and cool, bracing nights.

Pluses: Four-season climate with long summers and pleasant falls.

Minuses: Hot periods during summer months, tornadoes.

Places Rated Score: 530

Places Rated Rank: 190

Elevation: 676 feet

Wind Speed: 10.6 mph

Seasonal Change

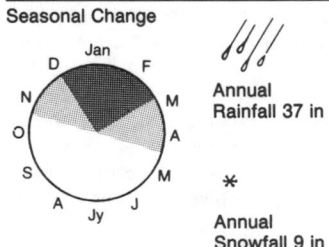

Annual Rainfall 37 in

Annual Snowfall 9 in

Clear 127 days · Partly Cloudy 101 days · Cloudy 137 days

Precipitation Days: 90 · Storm Days: 52

Average Temperatures			
	Daily High	Daily Low	Relative Humidity
January	46	25	69
February	52	30	67
March	61	38	65
April	72	50	65
May	80	59	72
June	88	68	72
July	94	72	68
August	93	70	69
September	85	63	72
October	75	50	68
November	60	38	69
December	50	29	70

Zero-Degree Days: 1
Freezing Days: 85
90-Degree Days: 70
Heating- and Cooling-Degree Days: 5,629

✓ Vancouver, BC

Terrain: The city is located on a narrow peninsula lying between the north arm of the Fraser River on the south, the Strait of Georgia on the west, and Burrard Inlet on the north. The land slopes gradually from south to north; from Burrard Inlet to the top of the ridge of mountains along the north shore the rise becomes very rapid. It is sheltered from the Pacific Ocean by the mass of Vancouver Island, but its proximity to this ocean keeps its climate moderate throughout the year.

Climate: January is normally the most severe month in Vancouver, being slightly colder, snowier, and foggier than December or February. Still the temperatures reflect the climate's overall mild character. Spring arrives by March. July is usually the most pleasant month of the year with moderate temperatures, long periods of sunshine, and only a little rain. The transition to winter occurs from mid-August through September with cooler and longer nights and more moisture in the air, making fog more prevalent. Then the rainy season returns in October.

Pluses: Mild temperatures; especially fine summers and autumns.

Minuses: Wet, foggy winters.

Places Rated Score: 857

Places Rated Rank: 9

Elevation: 10 feet

Wind Speed: 7.4 mph

Seasonal Change

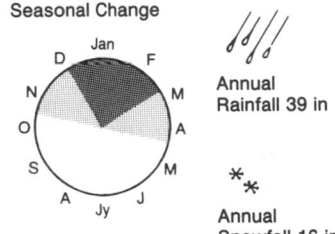

Annual Rainfall 41 in

Annual Snowfall 25 in

Clear 88 days | Partly Cloudy 122 days | Cloudy 156 days

Precipitation Days: 163 Storm Days: 6

Average Temperatures			
	Daily High	Daily Low	Relative Humidity
January	41	32	85
February	46	35	85
March	49	36	80
April	55	40	76
May	62	46	74
June	67	52	75
July	71	55	75
August	71	55	78
September	65	50	82
October	56	44	86
November	48	37	86
December	44	34	87

Zero-Degree Days: 0
Freezing Days: 55
90-Degree Days: 0
Heating- and Cooling-Degree Days: 3,066

Washington, DC-MD-VA-WV

Terrain: Situated at the western edge of the Middle Atlantic Coastal Plain, 50 miles east of the Blue Ridge Mountains and 35 miles west of Chesapeake Bay at the junction of the Potomac and Anacostia rivers.

Climate: Summers are warm and humid, winters mild; generally pleasant weather prevails in the spring and autumn. The coldest weather occurs in late January and early February, and the warmest month is July. There are no pronounced wet and dry seasons. Thunderstorms during the summer often bring sudden and heavy showers and damaging winds, hail, or lightning. In winter, snow accumulations of more than 10 inches are rare.

Pluses: Pleasant springs and autumns, relatively mild winters.

Minuses: Humid summers, heavy thunderstorms.

Places Rated Score: 631

Places Rated Rank: 54

Elevation: 65 feet

Wind Speed: 9.3 mph

Seasonal Change

Annual Rainfall 39 in

Annual Snowfall 16 in

Clear 101 days | Partly Cloudy 106 days | Cloudy 158 days

Precipitation Days: 111 Storm Days: 29

Average Temperatures			
	Daily High	Daily Low	Relative Humidity
January	43	28	62
February	46	29	61
March	55	37	60
April	67	46	59
May	76	56	63
June	84	65	64
July	88	70	65
August	86	69	68
September	80	62	68
October	69	50	66
November	57	40	65
December	47	31	64

Zero-Degree Days: 0
Freezing Days: 75
90-Degree Days: 37
Heating- and Cooling-Degree Days: 5,626

Waterloo-Cedar Falls, IA

Terrain: Situated on the banks of the Cedar River in northeast Iowa, this area is far removed from the moderating influences of any large body of water. The terrain is level to very gently rolling and is ideally suited to agriculture. The flat, open topography has no influence on climate other than the fact that it offers little resistance to winds, which in the winter can greatly enhance the windchill factor.

Climate: Definitely continental in character, with hot summers, cold winters, and short springs and falls. The average annual rainfall is 34 inches, with 71% of this total falling in the April-to-September crop season. As befits its landlocked, northerly location, the temperature range in Waterloo-Cedar Falls is large: January's mean temperature is 16°F, July's 73°F. The lowest and highest temperatures ever recorded here were -34°F and 112°F. Bitterly cold days of zero or below average 31 in number. The mercury hits 90°F or above on an average of 15 days a year, including two 100-degree days.

Pluses: Sunny falls.

Minuses: Hot summers, cold winters.

Places Rated Score: 347

Places Rated Rank: 321

Elevation: 868 feet

Wind Speed: 10.7 mph

Seasonal Change

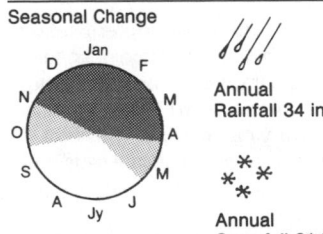

Annual Rainfall 34 in

Annual Snowfall 31 in

Clear 92 days | Partly Cloudy 102 days | Cloudy 171 days

Precipitation Days: 99 Storm Days: 43

Average Temperatures			
	Daily High	Daily Low	Relative Humidity
January	23	5	73
February	30	11	74
March	41	22	74
April	58	36	68
May	71	48	68
June	80	58	69
July	83	62	72
August	82	59	75
September	73	50	74
October	62	39	70
November	45	26	75
December	30	13	77

Zero-Degree Days: 31
Freezing Days: 159
90-Degree Days: 15
Heating- and Cooling-Degree Days: 8,090

Wichita, KS

Terrain: Located in gentle sloping topography. There are no large bodies of water nearby to affect the city's climate.

Climate: Because it lies in the path of alternate masses of warm, moist air moving northward from the Gulf of Mexico and cold, dry air from the polar regions, the city is subject to frequent and often abrupt weather changes. Summers are usually warm and occasionally hot (there are more than 60 days over 90°F during that time). Winters are mild, and snowfalls are light, averaging 16 inches a year.

Pluses: Four-season Great Plains climate with mild winters.

Minuses: Tornadoes, long summers that can be hot.

Elevation: 1,340 feet

Wind Speed: 12.6 mph

Seasonal Change

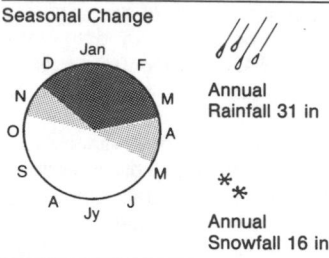

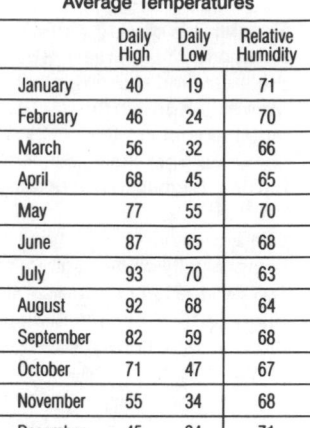

Annual Rainfall 31 in

Annual Snowfall 16 in

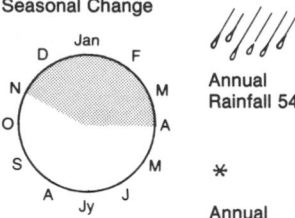

Clear 127 days	Partly Cloudy 97 days	Cloudy 141 days

Precipitation Days: 84   Storm Days: 55

Average Temperatures			
	Daily High	Daily Low	Relative Humidity
January	40	19	71
February	46	24	70
March	56	32	66
April	68	45	65
May	77	55	70
June	87	65	68
July	93	70	63
August	92	68	64
September	82	59	68
October	71	47	67
November	55	34	68
December	45	24	71

Zero-Degree Days: 2
Freezing Days: 114
90-Degree Days: 62
Heating- and Cooling-Degree Days: 6,360

Places Rated Score: 494   **Places Rated Rank: 234**

Wilmington, NC

Terrain: Located in the Tidewater section of southeastern North Carolina, near the Atlantic Ocean. The city proper is built adjacent to the east bank of the Cape Fear River. The surrounding terrain, typical of the state's Coastal Plain, is low-lying (the average elevation is less than 40 feet) and level. There are many rivers, creeks, and lakes nearby, most with considerable swampy growth surrounding them. Large tracts of woods alternate with cultivated fields.

Climate: Wilmington's climate shows a strong maritime influence. Summers are quite warm and humid, but excessive heat is rare. During the colder part of the year, polar air masses reach the coastal areas, causing sharp drops in temperature. However, much of the coldness of these air masses has diminished by the time they reach the Wilmington area. Rainfall is ample and well distributed, with most occurring in summer in the form of thundershowers. In winter, rain may fall steadily for several days. Snowfall is very slight.

Pluses: Warm, moist, mild.

Minuses: Hot and muggy in summertime.

Elevation: 30 feet

Wind Speed: 8.9 mph

Seasonal Change

Annual Rainfall 54 in

Annual Snowfall 1.8 in

Clear 113 days	Partly Cloudy 106 days	Cloudy 146 days

Precipitation Days: 117   Storm Days: 46

Average Temperatures			
	Daily High	Daily Low	Relative Humidity
January	56	35	68
February	58	37	66
March	65	43	67
April	74	52	64
May	81	60	71
June	86	67	72
July	89	71	75
August	89	71	78
September	84	66	76
October	75	54	72
November	67	44	69
December	59	37	68

Zero-Degree Days: 0
Freezing Days: 45
90-Degree Days: 45
Heating- and Cooling-Degree Days: 4,397

Places Rated Score: 564   **Places Rated Rank: 128**

Winnipeg, MB

Terrain: Situated in the broad flat valley of the Red River, which flows north-northeast through the city. The east side of the valley is a nearly level plain comprising extensive swamplands. The west side terminates with an abrupt rise known as the Manitoba escarpment, which is pierced by the broad flat Assiniboine Valley extending to the west.

Climate: Typically continental, the main features are a precipitation regime with an early summer maximum and a wide range of annual, seasonal, day-to-day, and diurnal temperatures. Snowfall is not heavy—it just seems that way. Once the snow arrives it normally stays. Snow has fallen in Manitoba in every month but July. Winter is long, beginning mid-November and lasting at least until the middle of April.

Pluses: Moderate summers with cool nights.

Minuses: Long, cold winters.

Elevation: 784 feet

Wind Speed: 11.6 mph

Seasonal Change

Annual Rainfall 16 in

Annual Snowfall 49 in

Clear 123 days	Partly Cloudy 117 days	Cloudy 125 days

Precipitation Days: 120   Storm Days: 27

Average Temperatures			
	Daily High	Daily Low	Relative Humidity
January	6	−12	79
February	14	−6	80
March	27	8	79
April	48	28	70
May	64	40	61
June	74	51	65
July	79	56	69
August	76	53	69
September	65	43	71
October	53	33	72
November	31	16	80
December	15	−1	81

Zero-Degree Days: 62
Freezing Days: 195
90-Degree Days: 12
Heating- and Cooling-Degree Days: 6,101

Places Rated Score: 171   **Places Rated Rank: 340**

Yakima, WA

Terrain: Located in a small east-west valley in the upper part of the irrigated Yakima Valley in Washington. The local topography is complex, with a number of minor valleys and ridges giving a local elevation as high as 500 feet.

Climate: Relatively mild and dry, with characteristics of both maritime and continental climates, modified by the Cascade and the Rocky Mountain ranges. Summers are dry and hot. Winters are cool with only light snowfall, usually 20 inches to 25 inches per year.

Pluses: Combination of marine and continental climatic features.

Minuses: Cloudy winters, hot summers.

Places Rated Score: 535

Places Rated Rank: 187

Elevation: 1,066 feet

Wind Speed: 7.2 mph

Seasonal Change

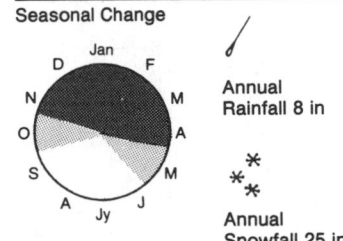

Annual Rainfall 8 in

Annual Snowfall 25 in

Clear 112 days

Partly Cloudy 90 days

Cloudy 163 days

Precipitation Days: 67   Storm Days: 7

	Daily High	Daily Low	Relative Humidity
Average Temperatures			
January	37	20	77
February	46	26	70
March	55	29	59
April	64	35	53
May	73	42	51
June	80	49	51
July	88	53	47
August	86	52	50
September	78	44	55
October	65	35	62
November	48	28	74
December	39	24	80

Zero-Degree Days: 4
Freezing Days: 150
90-Degree Days: 33
Heating- and Cooling-Degree Days: 6,488

Yuma, AZ

Terrain: Yuma is located in the extreme southwest corner of Arizona, near the California and Mexican borders. The land is typical desert-steppe, with dry, sandy, and dusty soil, scant vegetation, and craggy buttes and mountains that take their characteristic texture from wind erosion rather than water erosion. The various mountain ranges that surround Yuma are perhaps the dominant geologic features. They include the Trigo, Chocolate, Castle Dome, Mohawk, and Gila ranges.

Climate: Yuma's climate is definitely a desert product. Home heating is necessary from late October to mid-April. However, outdoor activities can be conducted comfortably during this period from 10:00 A.M. to 5:00 P.M. It is very dry, with many places in the world receiving more rain in a year than has fallen in Yuma in the past 90 years. Yuma is officially the sunniest place in America.

Pluses: America's sunniest spot.

Minuses: Hot, dry, dusty.

Places Rated Score: 553

Places Rated Rank: 152

Elevation: 194 feet

Wind Spood: 7.8 mph

Seasonal Change

Annual Rainfall 2.7 in

Annual Snowfall 0 in

Clear 246 days

Partly Cloudy 68 days

Cloudy 51 days

Precipitation Days: 16   Storm Days: 7

	Daily High	Daily Low	Relative Humidity
Average Temperatures			
January	69	43	43
February	74	46	40
March	79	50	37
April	86	56	33
May	94	63	30
June	103	71	28
July	107	80	36
August	105	80	40
September	101	73	41
October	91	62	39
November	77	50	42
December	69	44	46

Zero-Degree Days: 0
Freezing Days: 2
90-Degree Days: 167
Heating- and Cooling-Degree Days: 5,205

Et Cetera

IT'S NOT THE HEAT, IT'S THE HUMIDITY

Humidity, or the amount of moisture in the air, is an extremely important factor in climatic comfort. As anyone who has experienced a hot, humid summer knows, humidity intensifies heat. A hot day that is also humid is uncomfortable because the body's natural cooling process of evaporation is retarded.

But there is another reason damp air increases felt heat in the summertime. Just as warm air is able to hold more moisture, so damp air is able to hold heat better, and longer. Therefore, in hot, humid climates, heat is retained in the damp air even after the sun goes down, resulting in nights that are almost as hot as the days. In contrast, dry climates offer greater comfort not only during hot summer days but also during the nights, which can be cool and sometimes even chilly.

Excessive humidity can aggravate certain types of arthritis and rheumatism and, combined with low temperatures, can have a harmful effect on those suffering from pulmonary diseases. Very moist air also encourages the growth of a wide variety of bacteria

July Noon Average Relative Humidity

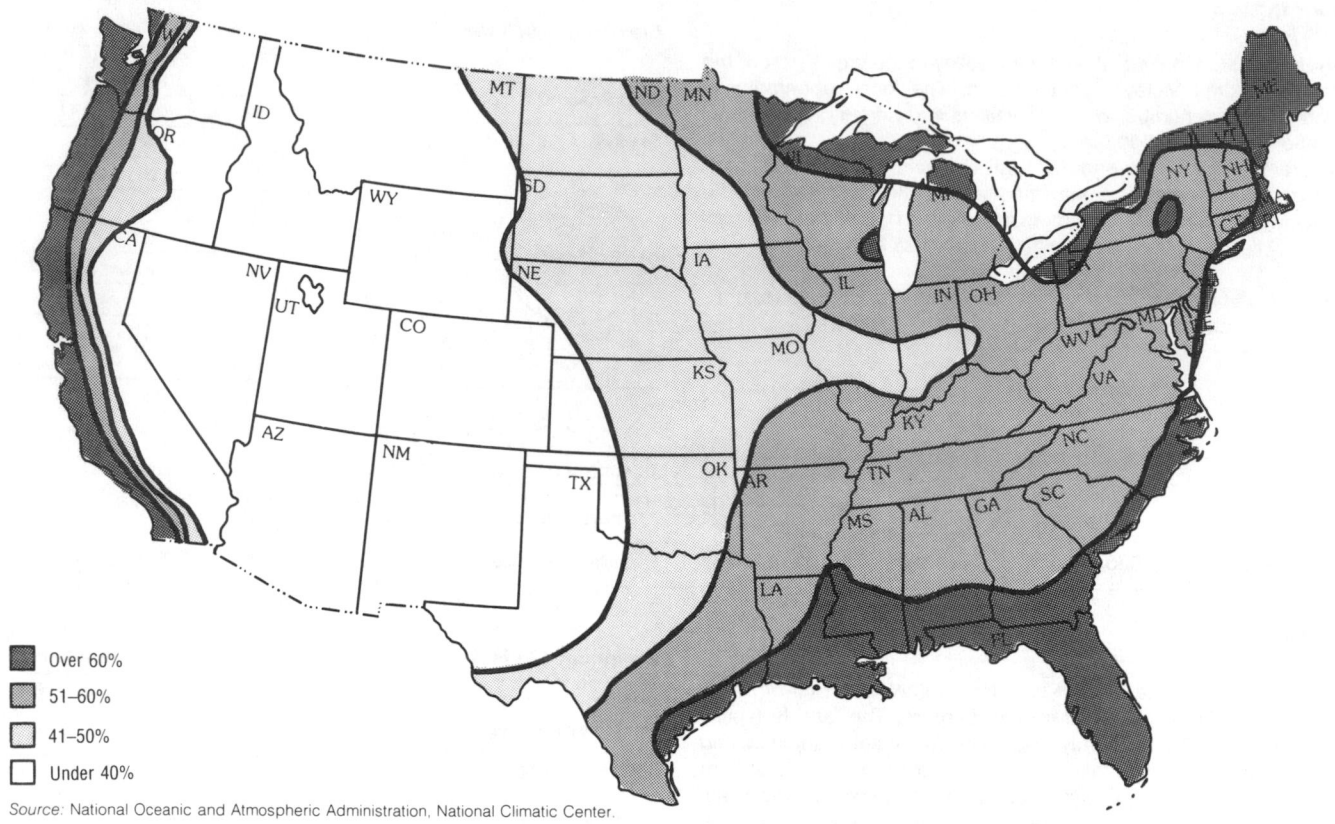

Over 60%
51–60%
41–50%
Under 40%

Source: National Oceanic and Atmospheric Administration, National Climatic Center.

and molds, thus increasing the chances of infection.

Low humidity can also have undesirable consequences. When the humidity falls below 50 percent, most of us experience dry nasal passages and perhaps a dry, tickling throat. In some areas of the Southwest where the relative humidity can drop to 20 percent or below, many people suffer from nosebleeds, flaking skin, and a constant sore throat.

The table "Temperature, Humidity, and Apparent Temperature" examines the relationship between relative humidity and temperature. Relative humidity is the ratio of the amount of water vapor present in the air to the greatest possible amount of water vapor air can hold at that temperature. To find the apparent temperature, locate the air temperature at the left and the relative

humidity along the bottom. The intersection of the horizontal row and figures opposite the temperature with the vertical row above the relative humidity is the apparent temperature. For example, an air temperature of 85 degrees Fahrenheit feels like 89 degrees at 55 percent humidity but like 102 when the humidity is 90 percent.

NATURAL HAZARDS

Perhaps no natural sight was more dramatic on live TV than the eruption of Mount St. Helens in 1980. A blast equal to 10 million tons of TNT blew off the topmost 1,300 feet of the mountain. Fortunately, volcanoes usually give warning. Even more fortunately, the places

Temperature, Humidity, and Apparent Temperature

								Apparent Temperature													
100	99	102	105	108	112	117	123	130	137	143	150										
105	95	97	100	102	105	109	113	118	123	129	135	142	149								
100	91	93	95	97	99	101	104	107	110	115	120	126	132	138	144						
95	87	88	90	91	93	94	96	98	101	104	107	110	114	119	124	130	136				
90	83	84	85	86	87	88	90	91	93	95	96	98	100	102	106	109	113	117	122		
85	78	79	80	81	82	83	84	85	86	87	88	89	90	91	93	95	97	99	102	105	108
80	73	74	75	76	77	77	78	79	79	80	81	81	82	83	85	86	86	87	88	89	91
75	69	69	70	71	72	72	73	73	74	74	75	75	76	76	77	77	78	78	79	79	80
70	64	64	65	65	66	66	67	67	68	68	69	69	70	70	70	70	71	71	71	71	72
	0	5	10	15	20	25	30	35	40	45	50	55	60	65	70	75	80	85	90	95	100

Air Temperature (°F) — left column. **Relative Humidity (%)** — bottom row.

Tornado and Hurricane Risk Areas

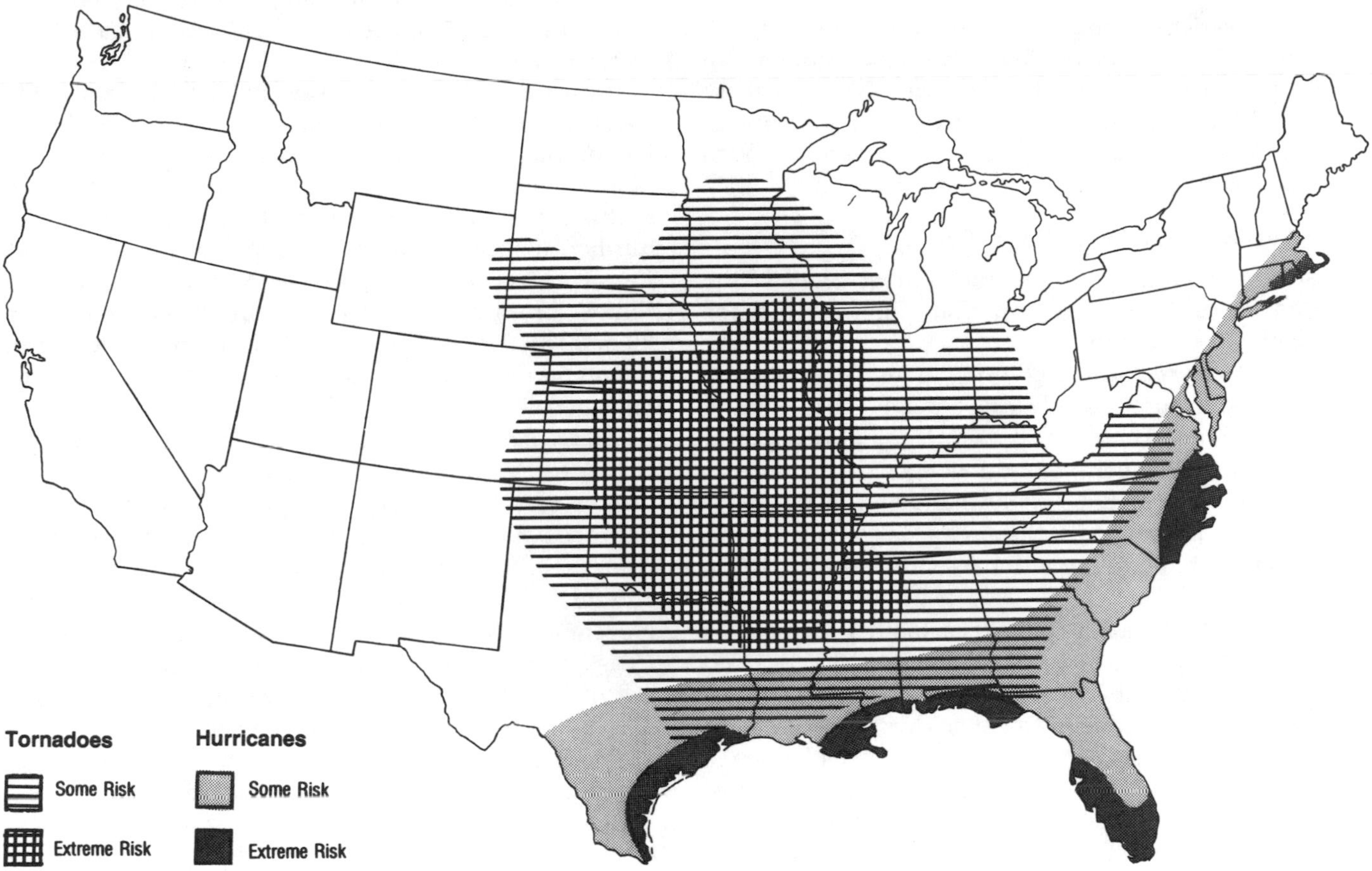

Tornadoes

▦ Some Risk

▦ Extreme Risk

Hurricanes

▦ Some Risk

■ Extreme Risk

Earthquake Hazard Zones

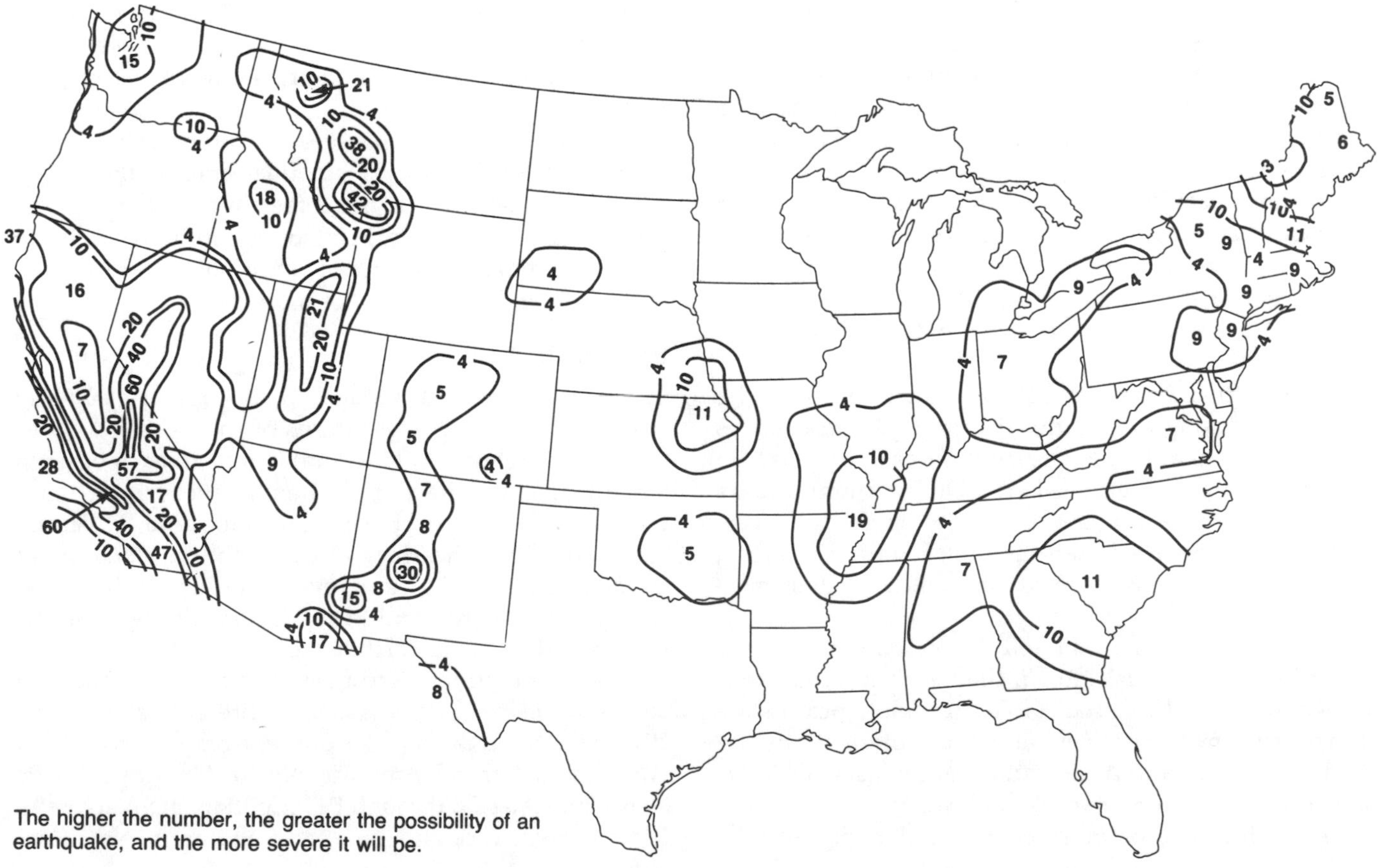

The higher the number, the greater the possibility of an earthquake, and the more severe it will be.

Source: U.S. Geological Survey Open-File Report 76-416, 1976.

where volcanic activity is a potential hazard are very few.

Other violent natural events are more common and, although less cataclysmic than a volcanic eruption, can cause great damage and threaten lives. Many of these natural hazards follow definite geographic patterns in North America, and some metro areas are at much greater risk than others.

The Sun Belt Is Also a Storm Belt

Most severe storms occur in the southern half of the United States. For this reason, you might say that the Sun Belt is also a storm belt.

Thunderstorms and Lightning. Thunderstorms are common and don't usually cause death. But lightning kills 250 North Americans a year. It remains the most common and frequent natural danger. At any given moment there are about 2,000 thunderstorms in progress around the globe; in the time it takes you to read this paragraph, lightning will have struck the earth 700 times.

Florida, the Sunshine State, is actually the country's stormiest state, with three times as much thunder and lightning as any other. California, along with Oregon and Washington, is one of the most storm-free states. In a typical year, coastal California towns will average between two and five thunderstorm episodes. Most American places average between 35 and 50. Fort Myers–Cape Coral, FL, averages 128. (A thunderstorm episode represents the presence of a single storm cell; a metro area like Fort Myers–Cape Coral can register four or five episodes in a single day.)

The Place Profiles earlier in this chapter tell how many thunderstorm days each place can expect in an average year. The southeastern quadrant of the country generally receives more rain and thunderstorms than the rest, although the thunderstorms of the Great Plains are awesome spectacles.

Tornadoes. While they are not nearly as large or long-lived as hurricanes and they release far less total force, tornadoes have more destructive and killing power concentrated in a small area than any other storm known. For absolute ferocity and wind speed, a tornado has no rival.

The hallmark of this vicious inland storm is the violently rotating air column that sweeps and bounces along the ground. Inside, pressure drops to less than 90 percent of normal atmosphere. This vacuum wrecks buildings, sweeps up cars, trains, livestock, and trees, and sucks them up hundreds of feet into a whirling vortex. Wind speeds close to 300 miles per hour have been recorded.

Although no one can tell for certain just where tornadoes might touch down, their season, origin, and direction of travel are predictable. Tornadoes peak in late spring and early summer, and most originate in the central and southern American Great Plains, in Oklahoma, Texas, Arkansas, Kansas, and Missouri.

After forming in intense heat and rising air, the storms proceed northeastward at 25 to 40 miles per hour. Most do not last very long or travel very far. Half travel less than 5 miles, although several have been tracked over 200 miles.

In season, one tornado every five days is reported in Canada, compared to five tornadoes every day in the United States. One third of all tornadoes reported in North America occur in Kansas, Oklahoma, and Texas. Metro areas in Oklahoma, eastern Texas, Arkansas, northern Louisiana and Mississippi, eastern Tennessee, Kansas, Missouri, and parts of Nebraska, Iowa, and Illinois have a high potential for tornado danger. About 70 or 80 hit Canada's populated places in a typical year, mainly in Ontario. Most are too week to cause serious damage.

Hurricanes. Giant tropical cyclonic storms starting up at sea, hurricanes are unmatched for sheer power over a very large area. They last for days, measure hundreds of miles across, and release tremendous energy in the form of high winds, torrential rains, lightning, and tidal surges. They usually occur from June through November and strike the Gulf and southern Atlantic Coast, though they will also strike locations farther north. Like thunderstorms, hurricanes are much less frequent and less severe on the Pacific Coast.

Hurricanes usually originate in the tropical waters of the Atlantic Ocean. Most occur toward summer's end because it takes that long for the water temperature and evaporation rate to rise sufficiently to begin the spiraling, counterclockwise rotation of wind around a low-pressure system. When the winds are less than 39 miles per hour, the cyclone is a tropical depression; when winds speed up to between 39 and 74 miles per hour, the cyclone becomes a tropical storm. And when the winds reach 74 miles per hour, the storm becomes a hurricane.

Often the greatest danger and destruction from hurricanes are not winds but tidal surges that sweep ashore with seas 15 or more feet higher than normal high tides. Although Florida and the southern coasts are most vulnerable to hurricanes, locations as far north as Cape Cod and Maine are not immune.

Earthquake Risks

The cause of an earthquake is the pressure building between two contiguous masses of rock—called plates —that move slowly but inexorably toward each other in slightly different directions. When the pressure becomes too great for the rock substance to hold, it shears suddenly. This shearing, along with the consequent shuddering, swaying, and even shifting of immense masses of underground rock, is experienced on the earth's surface as an earthquake.

Those conditions necessary to cause an earthquake exist only in certain areas. The entire area ringing the Pacific Ocean is earthquake-prone, from western South America to Central America, North America's Pacific states, and Alaska, through the Aleutian chain across to Japan, down through China, and ending in New Zealand. This last area has more earthquakes than any other place in the world.

According to the map "Earthquake Hazard Zones," although much of North America is free from the threat of earthquakes, some areas appear to be resting on powder kegs. (U.S. Geological Survey seismologists warn that the map is still experimental and that its predictions cannot be guaranteed.)

Northeast. There is much disagreement among geologists concerning earthquake risk in the Northeast. A number of theories about seismic trends have been advanced, and attempts have been made to relate these trends to various fault systems. The best known of these systems is the Boston–Ottawa trend, shown on the map as a continuous area from the Atlantic coast of Massachusetts to the St. Lawrence River valley, encompassing the two cities for which it is named. Most people are unaware that Boston suffered a severe earthquake in the 1700s and that it remains earthquake-prone today.

Southeast. One theory about earthquake risk is that possible earthquake epicenters (the points of origin of ground tremors) are not randomly distributed but occur in zones. In the Southeast, these zones run both parallel to and across the Appalachians. The greatest shock recorded east of the Mississippi occurred in Charleston, SC, in 1886. The present hazard in South Carolina and eastern Georgia is as high as in the Boston–Ottawa trend.

Midwest and Rocky Mountains. The zone of greatest hazard in the Mississippi Valley lies around the side of the cataclysmic series of quakes that occurred near New Madrid, Missouri. The biggest city in this zone is Memphis. The risk of seismic activity is greater in the Rocky Mountains region. The three biggest mountain cities—Denver, Albuquerque, and Salt Lake City—all lie within risk zones.

Pacific Northwest. The Puget Sound area near Seattle has experienced two major shocks within the past 30 years, both causing considerable damage. And in 1964, an earthquake in Anchorage registered 8.4 on the Richter scale (a nine-point span on a seismograph used to express the relative magnitude of an earthquake).

California and Nevada. Much more seismic activity (and, therefore, more research and data) is present in California and Nevada than anywhere else in North America. The greatest hazards are found in the San Andreas, Owens Valley, and Garlock fault systems, which are shown on the map as zones numbered as high as 60. All the metro areas in California are affected by these faults, particularly Bakersfield, Los Angeles–Long Beach, Oakland, San Francisco, and San Jose. These places, most of which have mild climates and pleasant terrain, are in real danger.

NORTH AMERICAN WEATHER EXTREMES

No organization validates world records for climate. Data from Environment Canada and from the U.S. Environmental Data Service are current and reliable for North America. These agencies also recognize several world records for temperature, differing forms of precipitation, and other phenomena.

Temperature records are kept at more than 10,000 stations around the world. The theoretical hottest it can ever get has been put at slightly under 140 degrees Fahrenheit, because hot air is lighter and quickly rises above overlying, cooler layers. More than 70 years ago, the highest point a thermometer ever reached in ambient air in the shade was 136 degrees Fahrenheit at El Azizia, Libya, in the northern Sahara.

The current North American heat record, 134 degrees Fahrenheit, was set 80 years ago at Greenland Ranch station in California's Death Valley. Canada's record high temperature, a modest 113 degrees Fahrenheit, hit Midale and Yellow Grass, SK, in 1937.

The theoretical coldest it can get on the earth's surface has been estimated at −130 degrees Fahrenheit, in still air, at 14,000 feet, in the middle of polar night. The new world record is −129 degrees Fahrenheit, measured at 11,000 feet at Vostok, Antarctica, in 1983. The North American record is −81 degrees Fahrenheit, measured at 2,000 feet at Snag, in Canada's Yukon Territory.

World *snowfall* records are entirely North American for a single reason: Among countries that keep meteorological records, Canada and the United States record snow depth while others measure snow in terms of water content. Thus, the world's greatest 24-hour snowfall, 76 inches, occurred at Silver Lake, CO, in mid-April of 1921. The greatest annual snowfall, more than 93 feet total, fell on Ranier Paradise Ranger Station, WA, during the 1971–72 season. The greatest depth of snow on the ground, nearly 38 feet, was measured at Tamarack, CA, on March, 11, 1911. Canadian snowfall records, all set in British Columbia, are nowhere near these amounts.

Records for *rainfall* were generally set at U.S. points and on La Reunion Island east of Madagascar. The gauges set 5,000 feet up on Mt. Waialeale, Kauai Island, Hawaii, record the world's heaviest annual average rains: 460 inches. The North American record outside of Hawaii, 256 inches, was established at Henderson Lake, on Vancouver Island, British Columbia.

The world's heaviest one-hour rainfall, 12 inches, hit Holt, MO, on June 22, 1947. Nine years later, in 1956, an identical amount fell on Kilauea Sugar Plantation, Kauai Island, Hawaii, La Reunion Island, in the path of Indian Ocean tropical storms, regularly gets the world's heaviest short-term rains: 12-hour rain, 53 inches; 24-hour rain, 74 inches; 5-day rain, 152 inches.

Wind is climate's most variable element. The values include *peak wind*, or the greatest 5-second average wind speed during the previous hour, and *fastest mile*, the fastest speed in miles per hour of any wind over a 24-hour observation day. Canada's highest average annual wind (22 mph) is measured at Cape Warwick, on Resolution Island, Northwest Territories. The North American record is 35 mph, measured on top of New

Weather Extremes of the United States & Canada

Thomas Nast, Cartographer

Hampshire's Mt. Washington. Here, too, the world's fastest peak wind (231 mph) and fastest mile (188 mph) were both recorded in the spring of 1934.

Fog, simply put, is a cloud that touches the ground. As a cloud, it is composed of uncountable millions of visible water droplets formed when air is cooled to the saturation point. Cooling occurs when strong nighttime surface radiation cools the air near the ground; when humid and warm air moves across colder land; and when moist air moves up and over higher terrain. Thick fog is reported when visibility is less than half a mile; a day of fog is defined as one on which thick fog occurred once during the day.

The foggiest area in Canada and one of the world's foggiest is Newfoundland's Avalon Peninsula, socked in more than half the year. The two foggiest points in the United States, at opposite ends of the country, are Cape Disappointment at the mouth of the Columbia River in Washington, and Moose Peak Lighthouse, off Maine's northern coast.

Hail is rain collecting into ice lumps as it falls to earth from a convective cloud during a thunderstorm. In North America, the area along the eastern slope of the Rocky Mountains from New Mexico on up to Alberta gets more hail days, more hailstorms, and more and bigger hailstones than any other area on the continent. The heaviest authenticated hailstone (1.67 pounds) fell east of here at Coffeyville, KS, in 1970. Canada's heaviest hailstone (10.23 ounces) fell near Cedoux, SK, in 1973.

Putting It All Together

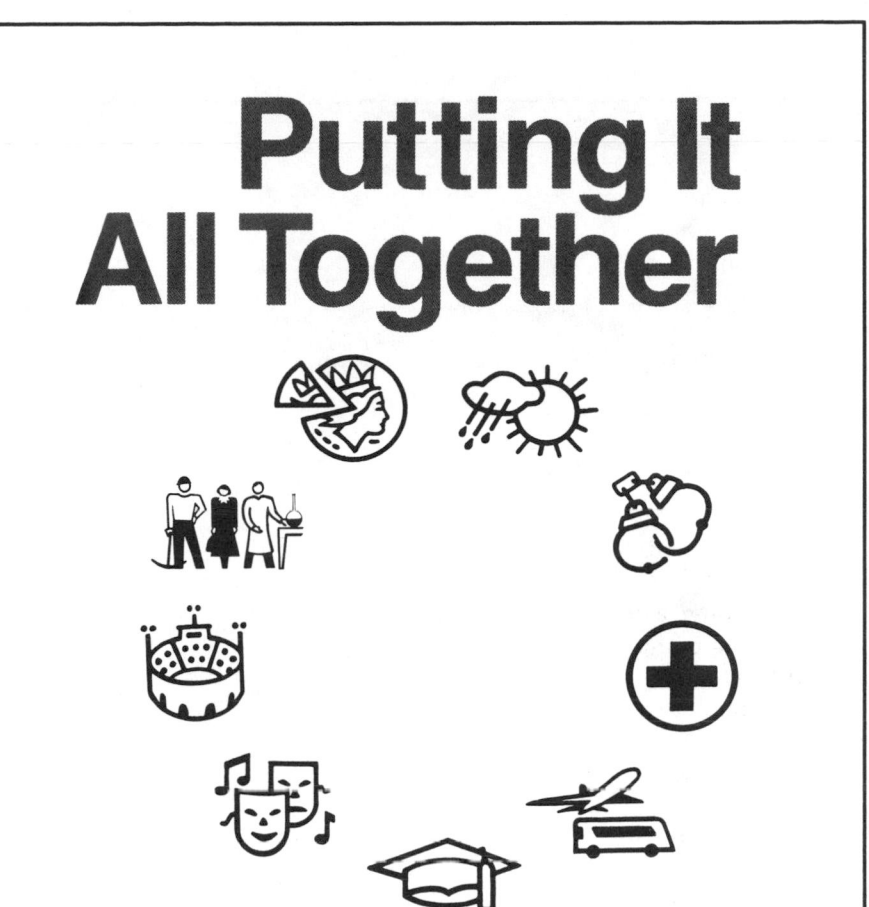

Question: Where will you find a mild climate, inexpensive living, extensive health-care facilities, a low crime rate, a wide range of transportation modes, excellent opportunities for higher education, a wide choice of recreational pursuits, a generous helping of the arts, and a bright job outlook?

Answer: The best place to live. But if you think of the odds of finding these qualities in one place, it sounds too good to be true. Does such a place exist?

To meet all the requirements, this ideal place would have San Francisco's year-round climate, where the weather is moderated by the warm Pacific Ocean and the temperature seldom varies much from a mild 65 degrees. Its composite costs of living might resemble that of Joplin, MO, the lowest in metropolitan North America.

This ideal place must be large enough to match Los Angeles's variety of higher education options, New York's array of cultural attractions, Toronto's public transit system, Chicago's ease of travel to other parts of the continent, and Philadelphia's supply of physicians and health-care facilities.

Yet this place would also need to be small if it were to have a crime rate as low as Johnstown, PA. For quality and variety of man-made and natural recreation amenities, the standard set by Miami would have to be met. Finally, our ideal location would have to present individuals with employment prospects as bright as those of Orange County, CA.

Obviously, this ideal spot is fictional. You can explore the geography long and hard, but you will never find the single metro area that combines all of the "bests" in each of *Places Rated*'s ten categories. Moreover, because one person's long-sought heaven can be another's purgatory, one can argue that there really is no such thing as the ideal metro area.

If you can move anywhere you wish, choosing your destination is still not easy. The best strategy is to focus on your own preferences and needs (the section "Decisions, Decisions" at the front of the book can help you identify what these preferences and needs might be). Having said as much, we can still try to discover which of North America's 343 metro areas come closest to the ideal.

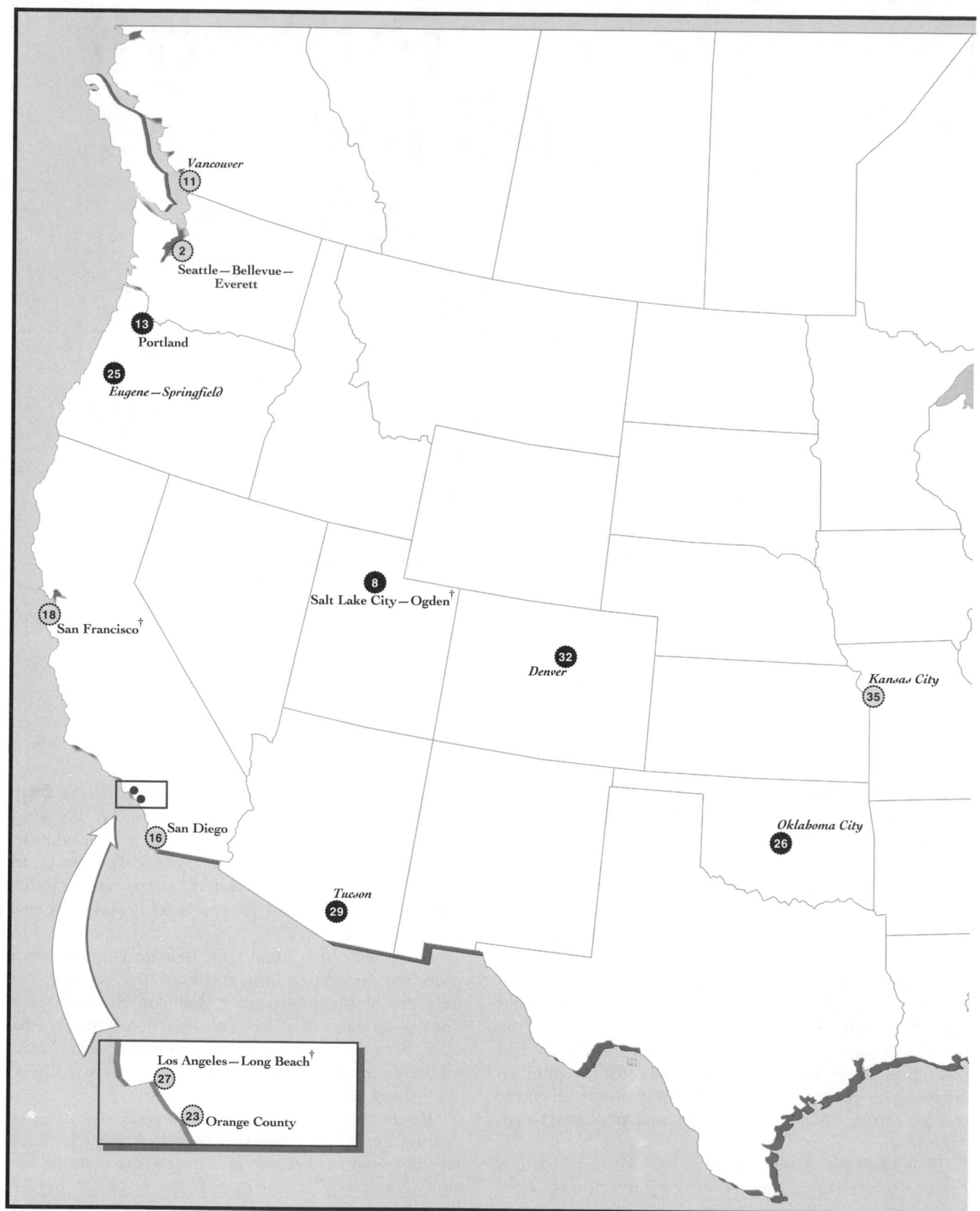

Vancouver
⑪

②
Seattle—Bellevue—
Everett

⑬
Portland

㉕
Eugene—Springfield

⑧
Salt Lake City—Ogden†

⑱
San Francisco†

㉜
Denver

㉟
Kansas City

㉖
Oklahoma City

⑯
San Diego

㉙
Tucson

㉗
Los Angeles—Long Beach†

㉓ Orange County

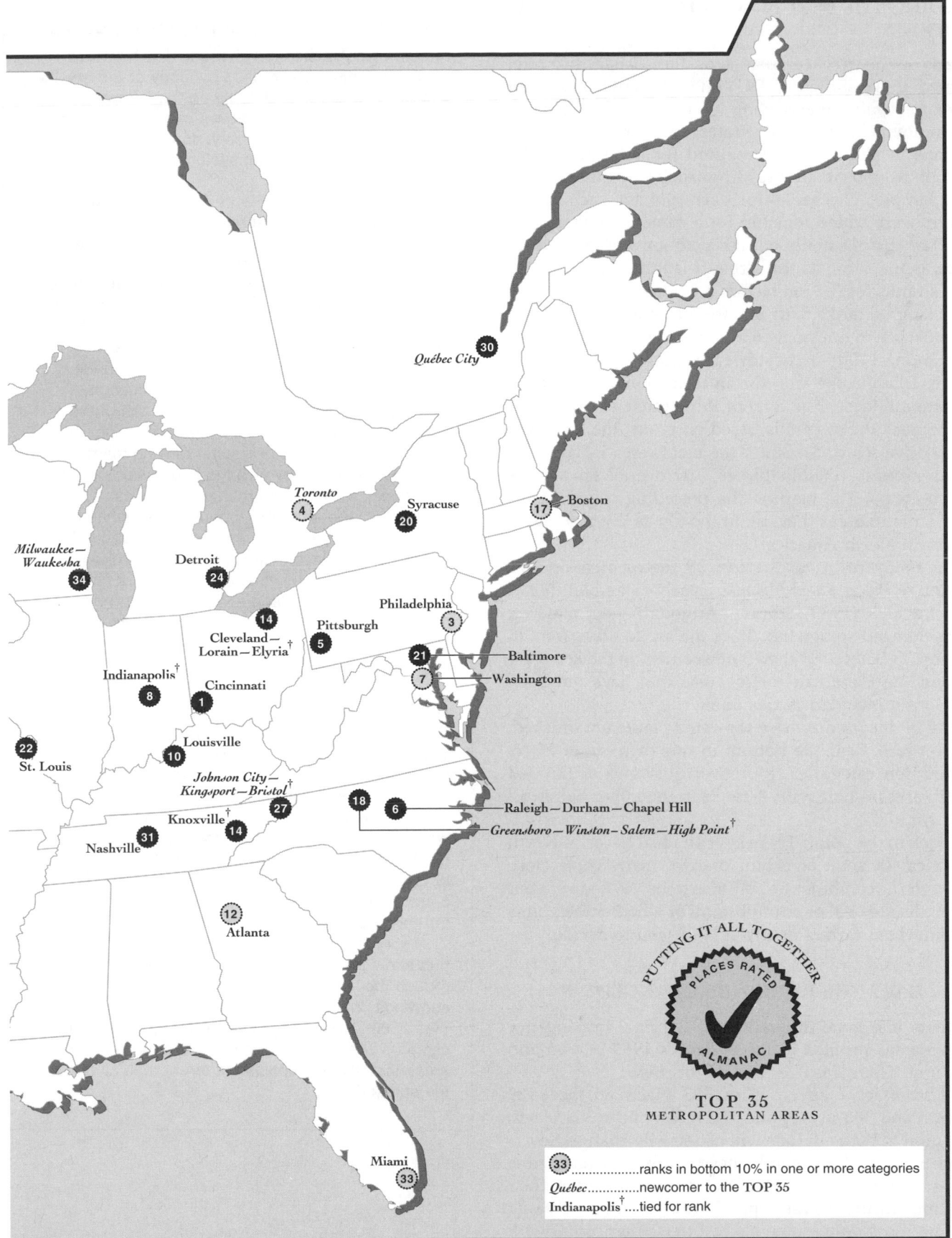

Québec City 30

Toronto 4

Syracuse 20

Boston 17

Milwaukee—
Waukesha 34

Detroit 24

14

Pittsburgh 5

Philadelphia 3

Cleveland—
Lorain—Elyria †

Indianapolis † 8

Cincinnati 1

Baltimore 21

Washington 7

St. Louis 22

Louisville 10

Johnson City—
Kingsport—Bristol † 27

18   6   Raleigh—Durham—Chapel Hill

Knoxville † 14

Greensboro—Winston—Salem—High Point †

Nashville 31

Atlanta 12

Miami 33

PUTTING IT ALL TOGETHER
PLACES RATED
ALMANAC

TOP 35
METROPOLITAN AREAS

33	....................ranks in bottom 10% in one or more categories
Québec	..............newcomer to the TOP 35
Indianapolis †	....tied for rank

Thomas Nast, Cartographer

FINDING THE BEST PLACES TO LIVE IN NORTH AMERICA

Nearly a quarter century ago, the Urban Institute, located in Washington, DC, rated 18 large American cities for livability according to such diverse factors as unemployment rates, crime rates, and per capita contributions to charity. Their method for determining the best all-around city (it was Minneapolis, by the way) was very simple: The ranks for each city for each of the factors were added together for a cumulative score.

Places Rated's method, in this edition and in previous ones, is the same as the Urban Institute's. Each metro area's ranks for the ten factors are totaled. Duluth, MN, for example, ranks 57th in costs of living, 310th in job outlook, 6th in housing, 163d in transportation, 166th in education, 110th in health care, 38th in safety from crime, 165th in the arts, 43d in recreation, and 338th in climate mildness. The total of these ranks equals 1,396.

Because the system is based on ranks, the lower the cumulative score, the better the metro area is judged to be all-around. (Duluth places 71st overall among the metro areas.) The map on the preceding pages locates the 35 metro areas that rise to the top as the best places to live in North America.

In many respects, the top 35 metro areas in this edition of *Places Rated Almanac* closely resembles that of the previous (1989) edition. Although their rankings have changed somewhat, 25 of the metro areas were in the top 35 before. Of the 10 newcomers to the list, 3 are among the Canadian metro areas that have not been previously included in this book.

By no means are these top-rated places untarnished. Fifteen rank near the bottom in one or more of *Places Rated*'s ten categories. Moreover, just one of the 343 metro areas—Louisville—ranks in the upper half in all of them.

Back to the point: There isn't an ideal haven in North America. In spite of a blot or two, many come close through a combination of strengths. Whether their strengths are vital or unimportant, or whether their blots are knockout factors or trivial is for you to decide.

WHY HAVE THE RANKINGS CHANGED?

Readers may note differences in the final rankings for metro areas profiled in *Places Rated*'s 1989 edition and this one. There are five reasons for this:

The interval effect. With 333 places in the 1989 edition and 343 in this one, the ranks of the 309 places common to both editions will necessarily change. Several metro areas, for example, have nearly the same Crime score as they had in the previous edition, yet their rankings in this factor slipped. They aren't necessarily getting more dangerous; it's just that other places with better personal safety ratings have moved them to a lower ranking.

Time series data. Local population figures (for deriving per capita access to public golf courses, for example),

---

If You Read This Chapter First: Some Caveats

Readers who've skipped ahead to see how it all comes out may be surprised by many of the results shown in the cumulative table on the following pages. If you are curious how a metro area receives a rank in a particular category, consult the explanation of the scoring system in the appropriate chapter.

Aside from climate, *Places Rated*'s categories include five scored on facilities (health care, education, recreation, transportation, and the arts) and four scored on indicators (crime, costs of living, housing, and jobs). Generally, smaller metro areas rank better on the indicators (these places typically have lower crime rates and lower costs of living), while larger places score higher on facilities. Because of *Places Rated*'s emphasis on facilities, the larger metro areas perhaps have an edge.

When you review the rankings in each of the chapters, be sure to note the close groupings of scores. With such close results, ranking metro areas from first to 343d may give the impression of greater differences among them than actually exist. Remember, too, that throughout this almanac the unit of comparison is not the incorporated city but the officially defined metropolitan area, typically made up of cities, towns, and other minor civil divisions in New England and Canada, and one or more counties in the rest of the United States.

Consistency Counts

Many high-ranking metro areas have combinations of superior and dismal rankings in *Places Rated*'s ten factors. New York City is the classic example of an uneven performance. It finishes among the top ten in four categories: Transportation, Health Care, The Arts, and options for higher Education. Anyone who knows New York can appreciate these rankings. But what of its miserable showings in Costs of Living (#342), Jobs (#343), and Crime (#342)? High Costs of Living, dangerous streets, and poor prospects for employment growth could, for many people, cancel out this super-city's finer points.

Places Rated decided to seek out metro areas that show steady strength in all the categories, even though they might not have any dramatic first-place showings. We looked for those with ranks no lower than 200th. Even with this forgiving guideline, we came up with just a handful of super solid metro areas that showed consistent strength in all ten of the categories.

prices (for measuring living costs), and household incomes have increased at varying rates since the previous edition was published.

New scoring elements and methods. The scoring in seven chapters has been refined by new data elements, slight changes in scoring methods, or both. For example, state parks have been added to the Recreation chapter for a fuller picture of a metro area's outdoor assets. In the Education chapter, publicly supported colleges and universities carry more weight than previously.

A tenth chapter. In this edition, *Places Rated* reintroduces a chapter on Housing. It details the local supply of single homes, apartments, condominiums, and mobile homes. Together with the Costs of Living chapter, this favors inexpensive or moderate-cost places.

New geography. In January of 1993, the federal government announced the creation of nine new metro areas, plus boundary changes affecting one of every three existing metro areas in the United States. In addition, Canada's 25 metro areas have been included in the *Places Rated* universe for the first time.

Super-Solid Metro Areas

Metro Area (Overall Rank)	Best Rank	Worst Rank
Boise City, ID (59)	Crime (88)	Health Care (195)
Indianapolis, IN (7)	Jobs (30)	Crime (185)
Lexington, KY (36)	Health Care (25)	Crime (200)
Louisville, KY-IN (9)	Climate (66)	Recreation (147)
Salt Lake City-Ogden, UT (7)	Transportation (7)	Housing (190)

An admonition earlier in this book must be voiced again: *Places Rated* is like a snapshot of a moving target. But metro areas are dynamic and won't always sit still for their statistical portraits. With so much in life that's changeable, you'd be wise to supplement this book with your own independent verification. For now, based on fresh facts and figures, what follows is a recap of each place's rankings in ten factors most of us would agree influences liveability in metropolitan North America.

RANKINGS: Putting It All Together

The following table shows the rank of every metro area for each of *Places Rated*'s ten categories. The sum of these—the cumulative score—is also shown, as is the overall rank. Abilene's cumulative score of 2,202, for example, ranks it 315th overall among the 343 metro areas; Akron's cumulative score of 1,253 ranks it 43d. As in golf, the lower the cumulative score, the better. The highest possible score would be 10, meaning a first-place rank in all ten categories.

METRO AREA	Costs of Living	Jobs	Housing	Transportation	Education	Health Care	Crime	The Arts	Recreation	Climate	Cumulative Score	Overall Rank
Abilene, TX	24	330	24	271	266	255	205	306	318	203	2,202	315
Akron, OH	167	126	164	127	44	158	235	62	58	112	1,253	43
Albany, GA	70	319	118	320	292	237	306	232	306	260	2,460	339
Albany-Schenectady-Troy, NY	281	82	271	28	32	103	78	53	180	254	1,362	60
Albuquerque, NM	202	64	238	61	105	87	320	66	39	35	1,217	37
Alexandria, LA	20	327	52	287	327	85	190	300	201	206	1,995	253
Allentown-Bethlehem-Easton, PA-NJ	276	111	275	274	158	134	17	104	221	138	1,708	164
Altoona, PA	81	329	7	232	306	204	5	291	312	132	1,899	222
Amarillo, TX	52	330	67	142	223	91	223	256	254	75	1,713	167
Anchorage, AK	299	125	280	186	157	308	183	169	38	336	2,081	280
Ann Arbor, MI	280	99	259	97	29	32	150	50	169	162	1,327	54
Anniston, AL	6	300	32	250	227	277	206	332	269	136	2,035	267

METRO AREA	Costs of Living	Jobs	Housing	Transportation	Education	Health Care	Crime	The Arts	Recreation	Climate	Cumulative Score	Overall Rank
Appleton-Oshkosh-Neenah, WI	131	159	131	199	188	206	19	181	144	306	1,664	150
Asheville, NC	137	173	169	166	252	54	98	256	116	28	1,449	94
Athens, GA	136	219	195	313	110	246	199	211	199	85	1,913	225
Atlanta, GA	212	4	244	5	25	93	318	26	106	27	1,060	12
Atlantic City-Cape May, NJ	291	59	286	140	125	222	329	92	41	67	1,652	146
Augusta-Aiken, GA-SC	106	70	158	289	209	59	214	237	313	189	1,844	210
Austin-San Marcos, TX	206	39	227	123	22	268	260	95	141	285	1,666	152
Bakersfield, CA	225	74	241	222	200	327	282	282	296	136	2,285	326
Baltimore, MD	267	36	282	9	15	43	314	13	30	126	1,135	21
Bangor, ME	175	172	170	143	178	167	39	208	165	275	1,692	159
Barnstable-Yarmouth, MA	323	167	322	329	301	243	195	119	27	29	2,055	275
Baton-Rouge, LA	115	213	174	212	82	213	340	174	224	290	2,037	268
Beaumont-Port Arthur, TX	42	339	17	261	190	228	291	175	155	294	1,992	251
Bellingham, WA	238	199	268	50	213	255	96	136	11	18	1,484	103
Benton Harbor, MI	165	189	88	189	285	278	295	254	215	127	2,085	281
Billings, MT	121	325	121	66	275	109	65	279	253	274	1,888	220
Biloxi-Gulfport-Pascagoula, MS	44	267	71	296	330	170	153	320	44	101	1,796	194
Binghamton, NY	228	225	207	177	173	237	13	184	252	155	1,851	213
Birmingham, AL	107	174	168	88	111	31	273	139	161	73	1,325	53
Bismarck, ND	111	283	107	165	312	70	20	308	263	341	1,980	248
Bloomington, IN	152	169	178	309	83	280	67	218	160	143	1,759	183
Bloomington-Normal, IL	185	250	153	37	117	274	71	212	195	242	1,736	174
Boise City, ID	118	97	159	95	185	195	88	147	177	94	1,355	59
Boston, MA	329	76	325	4	4	7	221	7	63	61	1,097	17
Boulder-Longmont, CO	273	142	283	170	106	158	125	114	14	268	1,653	147
Brazoria, TX	143	164	112	295	237	342	82	240	263	294	2,172	305
Bremerton, WA	254	238	272	195	249	284	70	171	239	15	1,987	250
Bridgeport, CT	293	177	287	176	195	52	225	87	315	40	1,847	212
Brownsville-Harlingen-San Benito, TX	17	247	10	205	259	333	235	322	52	280	1,960	243
Bryan-College Station, TX	162	122	173	263	65	309	233	302	201	310	2,140	295
Buffalo-Niagara Falls, NY	242	103	183	124	40	93	189	64	72	119	1,229	39
Burlington, VT	294	138	289	55	180	78	134	140	159	310	1,777	188
Calgary, AB	261	69	261	12	92	74	176	46	119	312	1,422	83
Canton-Massillon, OH	103	192	90	302	260	241	114	156	291	112	1,861	214
Casper, WY	41	324	53	249	325	190	154	330	288	302	2,256	323
Cedar Rapids, IA	102	171	108	120	247	168	102	172	196	286	1,672	154
Central New Jersey, NJ	325	41	324	138	33	35	44	16	324	138	1,418	81
Champaign-Urbana, IL	207	181	180	6	63	120	177	161	184	198	1,477	102
Charleston-North Charleston, SC	158	148	224	131	163	103	264	130	19	122	1,407	77
Charleston, WV	63	306	92	76	229	107	59	165	201	57	1,410	78

METRO AREA	Costs of Living	Jobs	Housing	Transportation	Education	Health Care	Crime	The Arts	Recreation	Climate	Cumulative Score	Overall Rank
Charlotte-Gastonia-Rock Hill, NC-SC	183	15	223	44	79	278	319	63	217	43	1,464	100
Charlottesville, VA	256	193	278	128	124	14	72	150	145	63	1,423	84
Chattanooga, TN-GA	47	117	135	215	187	190	245	158	126	109	1,529	114
Cheyenne, WY	112	330	163	149	320	103	63	276	317	220	2,053	274
Chicago, IL	296	50	285	1	3	4	330	4	69	213	1,255	44
Chico-Paradise, CA	239	151	264	228	144	211	138	322	231	81	2,009	259
Chicoutimi-Jonquiere, PQ	229	314	46	279	211	181	42	237	311	330	2,181	307
Cincinnati, OH-KY-IN	203	34	206	46	43	66	131	56	64	101	950	1
Clarksville-Hopkinsville, TN-KY	13	263	48	297	235	337	227	290	266	166	2,142	296
Cleveland-Lorain-Elyria, OH	249	202	221	40	35	34	136	15	42	108	1,082	14
Colorado Springs, CO	200	127	243	211	201	258	164	128	67	195	1,794	191
Columbia, MO	146	233	161	290	108	12	142	205	189	175	1,661	148
Columbia, SC	129	62	208	70	94	158	311	164	142	195	1,533	117
Columbus, GA-AL	68	322	106	272	249	207	173	294	214	209	2,114	286
Columbus, OH	192	19	209	161	28	129	232	52	98	143	1,264	46
Corpus Christi, TX	27	206	77	218	224	211	280	263	297	318	2,121	291
Cumberland, MD-WV	16	310	21	201	245	210	14	334	233	96	1,680	158
Dallas, TX	250	14	256	53	8	136	338	39	189	166	1,449	94
Danbury, CT	305	185	309	273	131	72	10	31	300	122	1,738	176
Danville, VA	21	308	22	270	312	296	8	277	343	164	2,021	262
Davenport-Moline-Rock Island, IA-IL	88	247	34	36	210	232	139	181	143	280	1,590	130
Dayton-Springfield, OH	164	121	160	58	60	78	201	38	242	166	1,288	50
Daytona Beach, FL	182	53	198	98	164	290	286	180	47	132	1,630	139
Decatur, AL	30	258	99	323	284	316	60	286	171	87	1,914	226
Decatur, IL	89	278	19	224	294	195	187	208	319	251	2,064	277
Denver, CO	248	47	254	23	37	43	230	47	61	203	1,193	32
Des Moines, IA	141	200	109	139	185	125	208	151	89	277	1,624	137
Detroit, MI	244	37	188	73	9	25	298	25	82	181	1,162	24
Dothan, AL	26	135	64	338	283	213	228	304	327	323	2,241	320
Dover, DE	193	293	230	339	278	340	121	319	90	90	2,293	329
Dubuque, IA	85	257	56	286	300	185	77	234	219	296	1,995	253
Duluth-Superior, MN-WI	57	310	6	163	166	110	38	165	43	338	1,396	71
Dutchess County, NY	317	237	310	164	216	173	78	109	198	240	2,042	271
Eau Claire, WI	94	179	37	265	199	96	17	271	325	333	1,816	202
Edmonton, AB	252	129	216	34	58	48	277	106	88	308	1,516	109
El Paso, TX	116	68	113	133	119	284	324	273	230	94	1,754	182
Elkhart-Goshen, IN	66	108	124	240	338	296	101	256	306	203	2,038	269
Elmira, NY	168	267	68	183	335	149	84	220	139	261	1,874	216
Enid, OK	2	330	3	331	341	130	203	277	271	266	2,154	300
Erie, PA	159	244	81	84	180	165	53	264	115	78	1,423	84

METRO AREA	Costs of Living	Jobs	Housing	Transportation	Education	Health Care	Crime	The Arts	Recreation	Climate	Cumulative Score	Overall Rank
Eugene-Springfield, OR	178	158	162	33	126	207	130	143	8	21	1,166	25
Evansville-Henderson, IN-KY	55	229	82	248	221	110	146	165	192	155	1,603	135
Fargo-Moorhead, ND-MN	120	287	139	118	141	74	27	193	268	342	1,709	165
Fayetteville, NC	93	307	141	196	236	305	333	205	306	132	2,254	322
Fayetteville-Springdale-Rogers, AR	37	72	102	326	176	217	35	303	140	157	1,565	124
Flint, MI	161	340	42	122	134	195	326	176	262	177	1,935	235
Florence, AL	9	188	43	343	247	229	41	240	265	162	1,767	185
Florence, SC	28	221	98	184	272	155	276	294	315	153	1,996	255
Fort Collins-Loveland, CO	218	117	245	300	138	213	89	198	4	237	1,759	183
Fort Lauderdale, FL	266	20	279	135	142	144	322	55	116	118	1,597	132
Fort Myers-Cape Coral, FL	236	26	267	174	276	284	107	135	54	322	1,881	219
Fort Pierce-Port St. Lucie, FL	246	56	273	321	233	305	257	291	56	83	2,121	291
Fort Smith, AR-OK	11	116	26	310	309	146	104	311	134	249	1,716	168
Fort Walton Beach, FL	170	164	202	315	287	293	62	331	170	181	2,175	306
Fort Wayne, IN	60	54	96	159	179	172	115	248	225	220	1,528	113
Fort Worth-Arlington, TX	198	18	201	126	44	250	328	74	83	193	1,515	108
Fresno, CA	222	77	250	258	100	268	315	254	32	138	1,914	226
Gadsden, AL	3	298	15	319	309	248	198	264	320	195	2,169	304
Gainesville, FL	119	127	170	116	68	18	336	144	136	301	1,535	118
Galveston-Texas City, TX	155	241	142	172	226	96	266	222	208	23	1,751	181
Gary, IN	166	134	114	29	118	141	226	59	220	244	1,451	96
Glens Falls, NY	264	220	246	220	332	248	48	189	191	254	2,212	317
Goldsboro, NC	64	272	91	341	330	336	160	307	326	59	2,286	327
Grand Forks, ND-MN	74	330	58	80	196	141	25	288	293	343	1,828	206
Grand Rapids-Muskegon-Holland, MI	199	33	155	202	91	233	157	122	110	216	1,518	110
Great Falls, MT	113	341	93	117	339	96	128	286	105	299	1,917	229
Greeley, CO	149	218	166	132	146	270	155	179	280	237	1,932	233
Green Bay, WI	144	161	129	147	221	258	43	193	121	316	1,733	173
Greensboro—Winston-Salem—High Point, NC	135	24	197	57	64	207	184	67	116	58	1,109	18
Greenville, NC	96	73	167	278	149	48	164	283	295	78	1,631	140
Greenville-Spartanburg-Anderson, SC	69	31	127	181	93	224	256	90	235	37	1,343	58
Hagerstown, MD	180	150	233	130	256	296	23	137	147	125	1,677	156
Halifax, NS	260	223	187	35	112	15	265	58	153	31	1,339	55
Hamilton, ON	290	175	281	48	81	61	122	44	176	64	1,342	57
Hamilton-Middletown, OH	187	182	192	155	122	320	146	122	279	171	1,876	217
Harrisburg-Lebanon-Carlisle, PA	240	101	194	46	152	148	50	184	156	149	1,420	82
Hartford, CT	320	149	321	54	76	93	173	20	277	210	1,693	160
Hickory-Morgantown, NC	62	83	111	303	264	294	90	233	97	61	1,598	134
Honolulu, HI	340	224	341	72	85	87	116	68	26	25	1,384	66

METRO AREA	Costs of Living	Jobs	Housing	Transportation	Education	Health Care	Crime	The Arts	Recreation	Climate	Cumulative Score	Overall Rank
Houma, LA	19	342	51	330	240	326	81	341	167	290	2,187	311
Houston, TX	208	23	196	91	26	63	311	37	16	292	1,263	45
Huntington-Ashland, WV-KY-OH	22	261	23	242	171	165	33	235	183	48	1,383	65
Huntsville, AL	145	75	204	254	143	258	152	152	248	87	1,718	169
Indianapolis, IN	124	30	165	56	77	62	185	43	146	147	1,035	8
Iowa City, IA	220	232	225	182	101	5	145	204	246	286	1,846	211
Jackson, MI	139	305	33	217	279	333	242	274	216	207	2,245	321
Jackson, MS	94	147	139	153	154	51	247	195	225	297	1,703	162
Jacksonville, FL	177	91	191	81	130	152	339	106	33	269	1,569	126
Jacksonville, NC	76	337	123	337	327	343	94	336	290	128	2,391	338
Jamestown, NY	134	314	30	334	239	312	29	80	96	92	1,661	148
Janesville-Beloit, WI	87	246	39	231	320	289	87	215	271	263	2,048	273
Johnson City-Kingsport-Bristol, TN-VA	15	143	59	257	170	110	30	191	166	34	1,175	27
Johnstown, PA	97	260	4	219	269	250	1	266	276	161	1,803	197
Joplin, MO	1	209	5	311	237	291	75	283	294	106	1,812	200
Kalamazoo-Battle Creek, MI	163	133	75	92	73	190	268	130	128	194	1,446	91
Kankakee, IL	174	281	65	121	218	176	254	127	283	244	1,943	239
Kansas City, MO-KS	157	89	176	49	59	46	305	73	91	157	1,202	35
Kenosha, WI	190	330	156	158	204	284	74	231	127	232	1,986	249
Killeen-Temple, TX	48	319	73	245	274	120	112	340	339	317	2,187	311
Kitchener, ON	285	95	277	15	57	274	69	51	112	211	1,446	91
Knoxville, TN	84	104	150	232	98	155	123	88	18	30	1,082	14
Kokomo, IN	67	293	47	340	281	282	56	218	271	218	2,073	278
La Crosse, WI-MN	125	187	85	86	206	32	26	195	123	319	1,384	66
Lafayette, LA	23	198	57	276	162	267	126	239	196	289	1,904	223
Lafayette, IN	105	197	128	74	71	258	40	149	201	234	1,457	68
Lake Charles, LA	39	290	70	267	232	190	274	315	163	258	2,098	282
Lake County, IL	321	42	320	222	153	139	68	85	135	213	1,698	161
Lakeland-Winter Haven, FL	108	86	148	214	252	296	331	285	173	328	2,221	318
Lancaster, PA	265	100	252	246	207	258	9	224	304	138	2,003	257
Lansing-East Lansing, MI	214	113	151	136	41	229	188	154	249	251	1,726	171
Laredo, TX	58	81	54	266	285	341	300	343	342	292	2,362	336
Las Cruces, NM	148	176	175	243	173	323	181	294	86	153	1,952	241
Las Vegas, NV-AZ	226	12	265	156	116	318	250	115	33	149	1,640	144
Lawrence, KS	100	234	177	243	109	324	177	229	217	216	2,026	265
Lawton, OK	34	337	55	336	258	295	159	337	240	253	2,304	331
Lewiston-Auburn, ME	210	217	237	299	334	164	45	253	287	237	2,283	325
Lexington, KY	128	87	186	180	61	25	200	159	147	50	1,223	36
Lima, OH	91	245	60	291	302	272	251	227	242	202	2,183	308
Lincoln, NE	140	166	132	115	107	127	204	129	168	304	1,592	131

METRO AREA	Costs of Living	Jobs	Housing	Transportation	Education	Health Care	Crime	The Arts	Recreation	Climate	Cumulative Score	Overall Rank
Little Rock-North Little Rock, AR	92	144	133	99	136	38	327	183	154	230	1,536	119
London, ON	283	137	269	77	86	20	146	97	201	75	1,391	70
Long Island, NY	335	52	326	327	16	11	57	9	64	36	1,233	41
Longview-Marshall, TX	36	255	40	251	287	316	207	313	334	226	2,265	324
Los Angeles-Long Beach, CA	334	38	336	114	1	6	337	2	2	5	1,175	27
Louisville, KY-IN	110	110	117	112	72	80	127	102	147	66	1,043	10
Lubbock, TX	78	274	75	148	113	57	229	187	199	80	1,440	90
Lynchburg, VA	79	183	145	206	168	243	52	229	84	45	1,434	87
Macon, GA	86	251	115	216	233	218	211	252	174	276	2,033	266
Madison, WI	251	79	222	71	46	38	98	98	124	313	1,340	56
Manchester-Nashua, NH	310	102	300	227	155	152	55	71	286	179	1,837	207
Mansfield, OH	53	277	28	298	316	319	213	178	301	143	2,126	293
McAllen-Edinburg-Mission, TX	5	84	1	317	202	337	193	325	321	334	2,119	288
Medford-Ashland, OR	219	195	219	79	264	202	105	213	74	74	1,644	145
Melbourne-Titusville-Palm Bay, FL	204	106	238	269	188	303	258	207	59	105	1,937	236
Memphis, TN-AR-MS	147	51	181	78	90	83	307	133	175	213	1,458	97
Merced, CA	231	210	258	281	291	331	129	316	331	106	2,484	342
Miami, FL	262	49	270	102	34	38	343	49	1	51	1,199	33
Milwaukee-Waukesha, WI	247	66	218	42	42	50	156	35	78	267	1,201	34
Minneapolis-St. Paul, MN-WI	257	29	257	62	13	55	146	18	66	329	1,232	40
Mobile, AL	82	178	105	150	161	218	325	222	75	278	1,794	191
Modesto, CA	272	58	291	209	213	250	270	301	330	46	2,240	319
Monmouth-Ocean, NJ	319	78	319	333	89	115	53	27	62	67	1,462	99
Monroe, LA	43	298	69	237	213	152	260	260	201	272	2,005	258
Montgomery, AL	79	234	149	152	88	183	169	249	255	244	1,802	196
Montreal, PQ	275	64	228	13	5	13	210	11	234	218	1,271	48
Muncie, IN	38	275	13	253	139	218	48	246	201	190	1,621	136
Myrtle Beach, SC	169	93	226	236	270	301	304	321	55	128	2,103	284
Naples, FL	306	55	317	316	342	246	249	146	7	320	2,304	331
Nashville, TN	173	40	236	52	70	71	240	75	138	87	1,182	31
New Bedford-Fall River-Attleboro, MA	303	160	301	101	167	320	186	111	172	44	1,865	215
New Haven-Meriden, CT	312	204	313	85	102	53	262	76	237	103	1,747	179
New London-Norwich, CT-RI	311	275	315	210	272	250	57	148	210	103	2,151	299
New Orleans, LA	154	325	193	109	62	35	334	142	49	229	1,632	142
New York, NY	342	343	332	3	2	2	342	1	77	47	1,491	105
Newark-Jersey City, NJ	331	323	327	2	14	9	309	10	314	85	1,724	170

METRO AREA	Costs of Living	Jobs	Housing	Transportation	Education	Health Care	Crime	The Arts	Recreation	Climate	Cumulative Score	Overall Rank
Norfolk-Virginia Beach-Newport News, VA-NC	234	96	255	235	47	272	196	41	29	53	1,458	97
Northern New Jersey, NJ	333	107	331	284	54	27	92	22	113	138	1,501	107
Oakland, CA	332	27	335	87	17	56	296	12	130	1	1,293	51
Ocala, FL	109	98	147	260	296	328	308	305	25	325	2,201	314
Odessa-Midland, TX	98	214	78	232	254	312	271	297	271	81	2,108	285
Oklahoma City, OK	46	207	89	125	39	100	274	60	80	151	1,171	26
Olympia, WA	205	162	231	64	257	186	76	177	329	24	1,711	166
Omaha, NE-IA	126	262	110	151	99	45	161	81	71	280	1,386	68
Orange County, CA	339	1	340	171	11	66	182	19	17	5	1,151	23
Orange County, NY	315	201	303	256	115	195	94	28	213	220	1,940	237
Orlando, FL	215	2	251	103	80	233	317	57	20	269	1,547	121
Oshawa, ON	292	120	276	105	128	309	72	112	336	93	1,843	209
Ottawa-Hull, ON-PQ	287	87	274	8	38	23	132	32	247	244	1,372	63
Owensboro, KY	18	270	40	322	320	222	36	298	267	199	1,993	252
Panama City, FL	114	190	152	306	297	284	219	327	114	181	2,184	309
Parkersburg-Marietta, WV-OH	14	252	36	284	289	282	3	200	209	64	1,633	143
Pensacola, FL	101	205	136	247	191	170	294	154	132	181	1,811	199
Peoria-Pekin, IL	122	269	49	168	217	155	135	172	108	236	1,631	140
Philadelphia, PA-NJ	313	21	297	43	7	3	171	8	81	55	999	3
Phoenix-Mesa, AZ	232	3	253	108	19	106	281	21	21	181	1,225	38
Pine Bluff, AR	8	314	14	324	289	186	284	308	335	265	2,327	334
Pittsburgh, PA	269	109	214	24	24	41	51	36	150	98	1,016	5
Pittsfield, MA	288	265	288	145	333	102	86	137	227	249	2,120	290
Portland, ME	286	80	296	162	165	73	124	126	211	244	1,767	185
Portland, OR	259	28	248	18	51	41	292	88	22	19	1,066	13
Portsmouth-Dover-Rochester, NH	316	43	306	255	137	266	15	81	68	258	1,745	178
Providence-Warwick-Cranston, RI	304	46	299	75	69	144	140	96	157	98	1,428	86
Provo-Orem, UT	138	132	185	259	114	332	32	289	23	226	1,730	172
Pueblo, CO	29	270	35	262	260	124	316	184	250	230	1,960	243
Punta Gorda, FL	195	136	240	318	342	254	22	342	164	306	2,319	333
Quebec City, PQ	241	193	122	39	53	19	116	100	8	288	1,179	30
Racine, WI	195	265	157	113	307	274	163	165	289	232	2,160	301
Raleigh-Durham-Chapel Hill, NC	197	11	263	41	27	28	175	42	192	42	1,018	6
Rapid City, SD	103	318	83	221	319	158	132	244	27	315	1,920	231
Reading, PA	258	226	220	275	203	229	60	221	261	72	2,025	263
Redding, CA	230	168	262	129	243	195	168	334	53	32	1,814	201
Regina, SK	189	301	44	50	175	83	290	69	251	339	1,792	190

METRO AREA	Costs of Living	Jobs	Housing	Transportation	Education	Health Care	Crime	The Arts	Recreation	Climate	Cumulative Score	Overall Rank
Reno, NV	278	115	294	31	169	107	239	244	85	187	1,749	180
Richland-Kennewick-Pasco, WA	132	153	143	26	304	316	144	291	282	32	1,823	205
Richmond-Petersburg, VA	227	61	242	25	193	64	180	77	241	100	1,410	78
Riverside-San Bernardino, CA	297	8	302	107	30	146	321	29	94	67	1,401	72
Roanoke, VA	130	236	179	207	262	29	109	162	86	39	1,439	89
Rochester, MN	216	221	199	178	297	1	23	329	227	326	2,017	261
Rochester, NY	271	48	247	104	55	134	102	65	31	181	1,238	42
Rockford, IL	186	145	120	229	270	158	252	170	245	263	2,038	269
Rocky Mount, NC	61	140	87	226	309	320	177	256	340	55	1,971	246
Sacramento, CA	298	17	307	187	48	181	267	86	24	109	1,524	111
Saginaw-Bay City-Midland, MI	132	240	38	146	193	176	216	213	100	211	1,665	151
St. Catharines-Niagara, ON	270	256	260	22	184	255	93	113	92	52	1,597	132
St. Cloud, MN	171	85	101	157	148	224	118	210	255	336	1,805	198
St. John's, NF	253	288	154	190	150	17	47	189	103	38	1,372	63
Saint John, NB	224	303	97	268	336	130	36	226	188	132	1,997	256
St. Joseph, MO	4	280	12	277	279	233	162	217	305	256	2,025	263
St. Louis, MO-IL	201	45	205	20	21	91	253	23	101	180	1,140	22
Salem, OR	160	119	119	59	205	291	158	153	111	26	1,401	72
Salinas, CA	327	156	334	144	254	263	192	201	15	12	1,898	221
Salt Lake City-Ogden, UT	172	57	190	7	56	120	167	54	37	175	1,035	8
San Angelo, TX	51	310	45	325	249	216	212	280	271	240	2,199	313
San Antonio, TX	150	67	134	32	67	85	310	91	162	304	1,402	74
San Diego, CA	326	7	328	27	12	66	285	33	3	2	1,089	16
San Francisco, CA	343	71	343	21	23	8	288	6	5	1	1,109	18
San Jose, CA	341	35	342	93	20	101	140	17	177	10	1,276	49
San Luis Obispo-Atascadero-Paso Robles, CA	328	112	333	197	140	224	64	240	93	5	1,736	174
Santa Barbara-Santa Maria-Lompoc, CA	337	114	338	100	104	136	137	121	11	5	1,403	75
Santa Cruz-Watsonville, CA	338	92	339	67	132	189	170	78	70	12	1,487	104
Santa Fe, NM	284	155	298	314	297	125	110	110	60	67	1,820	204
Santa Rosa, CA	324	44	330	213	144	130	107	93	151	22	1,558	123
Sarasota-Bradenton, FL	235	22	266	238	276	169	287	125	46	280	1,944	240
Saskatoon, SK	209	293	61	60	103	22	222	45	237	335	1,587	129
Savannah, GA	141	230	182	88	240	203	254	247	120	171	1,876	217
Scranton—Wilkes-Barre—Hazleton, PA	179	184	137	203	95	89	6	120	322	112	1,447	93
Seattle-Bellevue-Everett, WA	302	16	312	15	31	30	240	24	6	15	991	2
Sharon, PA	59	310	8	283	294	263	7	338	285	120	1,967	245

METRO AREA	Costs of Living	Jobs	Housing	Transportation	Education	Health Care	Crime	The Arts	Recreation	Climate	Cumulative Score	Overall Rank
Sheboygan, WI	151	216	103	200	337	305	34	203	182	278	**2,009**	259
Sherbrooke, PQ	237	282	72	68	132	46	90	262	310	302	**1,801**	195
Sherman-Denison, TX	31	212	27	304	307	195	217	322	333	199	**2,147**	298
Shreveport-Bossier City, LA	32	321	86	179	243	80	313	228	236	224	**1,942**	238
Sioux City, IA-NE	40	253	11	204	312	150	194	266	184	308	**1,922**	232
Sioux Falls, SD	90	211	95	82	318	23	46	260	222	332	**1,679**	157
South Bend, IN	32	215	63	90	159	190	191	108	152	164	**1,364**	61
Spokane, WA	75	253	116	19	146	80	171	163	129	117	**1,269**	47
Springfield, IL	127	247	130	63	230	64	196	188	184	199	**1,628**	138
Springfield, MO	77	130	94	185	123	116	113	249	158	166	**1,411**	80
Springfield, MA	295	163	295	154	49	237	230	117	242	273	**2,055**	275
Stamford-Norwalk, CT	330	186	329	111	151	35	100	14	260	40	**1,556**	122
State College, PA	233	226	203	241	74	309	15	225	177	112	**1,816**	202
Steubenville-Weirton, OH-WV	35	330	9	332	324	324	21	274	278	171	**2,098**	282
Stockton-Lodi, CA	277	124	290	198	208	303	301	271	269	59	**2,300**	330
Sudbury, ON	274	291	234	110	219	270	120	199	130	314	**2,161**	303
Sumter, SC	25	296	79	312	320	339	293	316	299	190	**2,469**	340
Syracuse, NY	245	105	200	11	75	139	66	40	73	159	**1,113**	20
Tacoma, WA	243	228	249	47	176	176	289	100	45	15	**1,568**	125
Tallahassee, FL	156	63	189	175	66	204	341	249	40	300	**1,783**	189
Tampa-St. Petersburg-Clearwater, FL	181	6	217	134	36	118	332	30	36	280	**1,370**	62
Terre-Haute, IN	10	304	2	280	182	245	143	202	255	147	**1,770**	187
Texarkana, TX-Texarkana, AR	7	301	20	251	292	176	243	311	340	261	**2,202**	315
Thunder Bay, ON	268	309	212	38	231	173	218	145	122	331	**2,047**	272
Toledo, OH	176	152	144	69	51	74	238	104	95	207	**1,310**	52
Topeka, KS	83	239	84	188	246	128	277	192	255	225	**1,917**	229
Toronto, ON	318	9	316	30	10	21	111	5	76	112	**1,008**	4
Trenton, NJ	314	196	311	140	97	60	234	94	212	48	**1,706**	163
Trois-Rivieres, PQ	211	296	25	334	198	128	83	132	255	243	**1,905**	224
Tucson, AZ	194	32	232	106	50	74	299	84	10	97	**1,178**	29
Tulsa, OK	50	157	126	194	171	176	248	124	102	190	**1,538**	120
Tuscaloosa, AL	64	170	125	173	127	224	272	310	232	257	**1,954**	242
Tyler, TX	72	208	138	308	228	114	246	318	302	226	**2,160**	301
Utica-Rome, NY	223	288	170	167	219	280	11	140	137	159	**1,794**	191
Vallejo-Fairfield-Napa, CA	309	131	318	65	156	183	235	83	181	14	**1,675**	155
Vancouver, BC	322	10	323	17	18	16	283	34	13	9	**1,045**	11
Vancouver, WA	191	90	210	49	329	329	80	216	328	19	**1,841**	208
Ventura, CA	336	25	337	230	95	186	97	61	35	4	**1,406**	76

METRO AREA	Costs of Living	Jobs	Housing	Transportation	Education	Health Care	Crime	The Arts	Recreation	Climate	Cumulative Score	Overall Rank
Victoria, BC	307	139	305	119	183	58	202	103	99	11	1,526	112
Victoria, TX	71	263	74	342	305	99	263	326	306	323	2,372	337
Vineland-Millville-Bridgeton, NJ	213	284	184	293	212	218	259	118	281	67	2,129	294
Visalia-Tulare-Porterville, CA	188	190	211	328	268	330	220	332	51	170	2,288	328
Waco, TX	54	327	50	225	196	237	303	313	184	297	2,186	310
Washington, DC-MD-VA-WV	308	5	314	10	6	10	215	3	105	54	1,030	7
Waterbury, CT	289	284	293	292	282	150	166	270	332	122	2,480	341
Waterloo-Cedar Falls, IA	56	314	18	282	192	141	106	157	78	321	1,666	152
Wausau, WI	99	180	62	301	325	263	12	243	303	326	2,114	286
West Palm Beach-Boca Raton, FL	282	13	292	208	120	173	335	48	50	220	1,741	177
Wheeling, WV-OH	12	286	16	264	242	118	2	159	223	171	1,493	106
Wichita, KS	117	123	104	193	135	110	209	134	109	234	1,468	101
Wichita Falls, TX	45	259	29	288	266	163	302	269	227	271	2,119	288
Williamsport, PA	123	273	66	294	302	136	4	298	337	143	1,976	247
Wilmington, NC	184	146	229	238	224	117	297	266	104	128	1,933	234
Wilmington-Newark, DE-MD	279	60	284	169	87	120	151	72	125	90	1,437	88
Windsor, ON	263	278	215	83	129	195	118	115	107	83	1,586	128
Winnipeg, MB	217	243	100	14	78	66	244	78	194	340	1,574	127
Worcester-Fitchburg-Leominster, MA	301	94	304	137	84	89	27	70	292	131	1,529	114
Yakima, WA	49	242	80	159	316	312	279	235	57	187	1,916	228
Yolo, CA	300	153	308	96	121	233	224	195	338	109	2,077	279
York, PA	255	141	213	305	263	296	31	328	323	177	2,332	335
Youngstown-Warren, OH	73	231	31	191	160	242	85	98	298	120	1,529	114
Yuba City, CA	220	292	235	307	340	302	269	338	284	77	2,664	343
Yuma, AZ	153	203	146	192	312	333	323	281	48	152	2,143	297

Appendix

Metropolitan Complexes (MCs)
& Their Metro Area Components

Boston–New Bedford–Nashua, MA–NH

Boston, MA
Manchester–Nashua, NH
New Bedford–Fall River–Attleboro, MA
Portsmouth–Dover–Rochester, NH
Worcester–Fitchburg–Leominster, MA

Buffalo–St. Catharines–Niagara, NY–ON

Buffalo–Niagara Falls, NY
St. Catharines–Niagara, ON

Chicago–Gary–Kenosha, IL–IN–WI

Chicago, IL
Gary, IN
Kankakee, IL
Kenosha, WI
Lake County, IL

Cincinnati–Hamilton, OH–KY–IN

Cincinnati, OH–KY–IN
Hamilton–Middletown, OH

Cleveland–Akron, OH

Akron, OH
Cleveland–Lorain–Elyria, OH

Dallas–Fort Worth, TX

Dallas, TX
Fort Worth–Arlington, TX

Denver–Boulder–Greeley, CO

Boulder–Longmont, CO
Denver, CO
Greeley, CO

Detroit–Ann Arbor–Flint, MI–ON

Ann Arbor, MI
Detroit, MI
Flint, MI
Windsor, ON

Houston–Galveston–Brazoria, TX

Brazoria, TX
Galveston–Texas City, TX
Houston, TX

Los Angeles–Riverside–Orange County, CA

Los Angeles–Long Beach, CA
Orange County, CA
Riverside–San Bernardino, CA
Ventura, CA

Miami–Fort Lauderdale, FL

Fort Lauderdale, FL
Miami, FL

Milwaukee–Racine, WI

Milwaukee–Waukesha, WI
Racine, WI

New York–Northern New Jersey–Long Island, NY–NJ–CT

Bridgeport, CT
Central New Jersey, NJ
Danbury, CT
Dutchess County, NY
Long Island, NY
Monmouth–Ocean, NJ
New Haven–Meriden, CT
New York, NY
Newark–Jersey City, NJ
Northern New Jersey, NJ
Orange County, NY
Stamford–Norwalk, CT
Trenton, NJ

Philadelphia–Wilmington–Atlantic City, PA–NJ–DE–MD

Atlantic City–Cape May, NJ
Philadelphia, PA–NJ
Vineland–Millville–Bridgeton, NJ
Wilmington–Newark, DE–MD

Portland–Salem–Vancouver, OR–WA

Portland, OR
Salem, OR
Vancouver, WA

Sacramento–Yolo, CA

Sacramento, CA
Yolo, CA

San Francisco–Oakland–San Jose, CA

Oakland, CA
San Francisco, CA
San Jose, CA
Santa Cruz–Watsonville, CA
Santa Rosa, CA
Vallejo–Fairfield–Napa, CA

Seattle–Tacoma–Bremerton, WA

Bremerton, WA
Olympia, WA
Seattle–Bellevue–Everett, WA
Tacoma, WA

Toronto–Ontario Shore, ON

Hamilton, ON
Kitchener, ON
Oshawa, ON
Toronto, ON

Washington–Baltimore, DC–MD–VA–WV

Baltimore, MD
Hagerstown, MD
Washington, DC–MD–VA–WV

Metro Areas by State and Province *

Alabama
Anniston
Birmingham
Columbus (GA–AL)
Decatur
Dothan
Florence
Gadsden
Huntsville
Mobile
Montgomery
Tuscaloosa

Alaska
Anchorage

Alberta
Calgary
Edmonton

Arizona
Las Vegas (NV–AZ)
Phoenix–Mesa
Tucson
Yuma

Arkansas
Fayetteville–Springdale–
 Rogers
Fort Smith (AR–OK)
Little Rock–North Little Rock
Memphis (TN–AR–MS)
Pine Bluff
Texarkana (TX)–Texarkana
 (AR)

British Columbia
Vancouver
Victoria

California
Bakersfield
Chico–Paradise
Fresno
Los Angeles–Long Beach
Merced
Modesto
Oakland
Orange County
Redding
Riverside–San Bernardino
Sacramento
Salinas
San Diego
San Francisco
San Jose
San Luis Obispo–
 Atascadero–Paso Robles
Santa Barbara–Santa
 Maria–Lompoc
Santa Cruz–Watsonville
Santa Rosa
Stockton–Lodi
Vallejo–Fairfield–Napa
Ventura
Visalia–Tulare–Porterville
Yolo
Yuba City

Colorado
Boulder–Longmont

Colorado Springs
Denver
Fort Collins–Loveland
Greeley
Pueblo

Connecticut
Bridgeport
Danbury
Hartford
New Haven–Meriden
New London–Norwich
 (CT–RI)
Stamford–Norwalk
Waterbury

Delaware
Dover
Wilmington–Newark (DE–MD)

District of Columbia
Washington (DC–MD–VA–
 WV)

Florida
Daytona Beach
Fort Lauderdale
Fort Myers–Cape Coral
Fort Pierce–Port St. Lucie
Fort Walton Beach
Gainesville
Jacksonville
Lakeland–Winter Haven
Melbourne–Titusville–Palm
 Bay
Miami
Naples
Ocala
Orlando
Panama City
Pensacola
Punta Gorda
Sarasota–Bradenton
Tallahassee
Tampa–St. Petersburg–
 Clearwater
West Palm Beach–Boca
 Raton

Georgia
Albany
Athens
Atlanta
Augusta–Aiken (GA–SC)
Chattanooga (TN–GA)
Columbus (GA–AL)
Macon
Savannah

Hawaii
Honolulu

Idaho
Boise City

Illinois
Bloomington–Normal
Champaign–Urbana
Chicago
Davenport–Moline–Rock
 Island (IA–IL)

Decatur
Kankakee
Lake County
Peoria–Pekin
Rockford
Springfield
St. Louis (MO–IL)

Indiana
Bloomington
Cincinnati (OH–KY–IN)
Elkhart–Goshen
Evansville–Henderson
 (IN–KY)
Fort Wayne
Gary
Indianapolis
Kokomo
Lafayette
Louisville (KY–IN)
Muncie
South Bend
Terre Haute

Iowa
Cedar Rapids
Davenport–Moline–Rock
 Island (IA–IL)
Des Moines
Dubuque
Iowa City
Omaha (NE–IA)
Sioux City (IA–NE)
Waterloo–Cedar Falls

Kansas
Kansas City (MO–KS)
Lawrence
Topeka
Wichita

Kentucky
Cincinnati (OH–KY–IN)
Clarksville–Hopkinsville
 (TN–KY)
Evansville–Henderson
 (IN–KY)
Huntington–Ashland
 (WV–KY–OH)
Lexington
Louisville (KY–IN)
Owensboro

Louisiana
Alexandria
Baton Rouge
Houma
Lafayette
Lake Charles
Monroe
New Orleans
Shreveport–Bossier City

Maine
Bangor
Lewiston–Auburn
Portland

Manitoba
Winnipeg

Maryland
Baltimore
Cumberland (MD–WV)
Hagerstown
Washington (DC–MD–VA–
 WV)
Wilmington–Newark (DE–MD)

Massachusetts
Barnstable–Yarmouth
Boston
New Bedford–Fall
 River–Attleboro
Pittsfield
Springfield
Worcester–Fitchburg–
 Leominster

Michigan
Ann Arbor
Benton Harbor
Detroit
Flint
Grand Rapids–Muskegon–
 Holland
Jackson
Kalamazoo–Battle Creek
Lansing–East Lansing
Saginaw–Bay City–Midland

Minnesota
Duluth–Superior (MN–WI)
Fargo–Moorhead (ND–MN)
Grand Forks (ND–MN)
La Crosse (WI–MN)
Minneapolis–St. Paul
 (MN–WI)
Rochester
St. Cloud

Mississippi
Biloxi–Gulfport–Pascagoula
Jackson
Memphis (TN–AR–MS)

Missouri
Columbia
Joplin
Kansas City (MO–KS)
Springfield
St. Joseph
St. Louis (MO–IL)

Montana
Billings
Great Falls

Nebraska
Lincoln
Omaha (NE–IA)
Sioux City (IA–NE)

Nevada
Las Vegas (NV–AZ)
Reno

New Brunswick
Saint John

New Hampshire
Manchester–Nashua

Portsmouth–Dover–
   Rochester

New Jersey
Allentown–Bethlehem–
   Easton (PA–NJ)
Atlantic City–Cape May
Central New Jersey
Monmouth–Ocean
Northern New Jersey
Newark–Jersey City
Philadelphia (PA–NJ)
Trenton
Vineland–Millville–Bridgeton

New Mexico
Albuquerque
Las Cruces
Santa Fe

New York
Albany–Schenectady–Troy
Binghamton
Buffalo–Niagara Falls
Dutchess County
Elmira
Glens Falls
Jamestown
Nassau–Suffolk
New York
Orange County
Rochester
Syracuse
Utica–Rome

Newfoundland
St. John's

North Carolina
Asheville
Charlotte–Gastonia–Rock Hill
   (NC–SC)
Fayetteville
Goldsboro
Greensboro–Winston-Salem–
   High Point
Greenville
Hickory–Morgantown
Jacksonville
Norfolk–Virginia Beach–
   Newport News (VA–NC)
Raleigh–Durham–Chapel
   Hill
Rocky Mount
Wilmington

North Dakota
Bismarck
Fargo–Moorhead (ND–MN)
Grand Forks (ND–MN)

Nova Scotia
Halifax

Ohio
Akron

Canton–Massillon
Cleveland–Lorain–Elyria
Columbus
Dayton–Springfield
Hamilton–Middletown
Huntington–Ashland (WV–
   KY–OH)
Lima
Mansfield
Parkersburg–Marietta
   (WV–OH)
Steubenville–Weirton
   (OH–WV)
Toledo
Wheeling (WV–OH)
Youngstown–Warren

Oklahoma
Enid
Fort Smith (AR–OK)
Lawton
Oklahoma City
Tulsa

Ontario
Hamilton
Kitchener
London
Oshawa
Ottawa–Hull (ON–PQ)
St. Catharines–Niagara
Sudbury
Thunder Bay
Toronto
Windsor

Oregon
Eugene–Springfield
Medford–Ashland
Portland
Salem

Pennsylvania
Allentown–Bethlehem–
   Easton (PA–NJ)
Altoona
Erie
Harrisburg–Lebanon–Carlisle
Johnstown
Lancaster
Philadelphia (PA–NJ)
Pittsburgh
Reading
Scranton–Wilkes-Barre–
   Hazleton
Sharon
State College
Williamsport
York

Quebec
Chicoutimi–Jonquiere
Montreal
Ottawa–Hull (ON–PQ)
Quebec City
Sherbrooke

Trois–Rivieres

Rhode Island
New London–Norwich
   (CT–RI)
Providence–Warwick–
   Cranston

Saskatchewan
Regina
Saskatoon

South Carolina
Augusta–Aiken (GA–SC)
Charleston–North
   Charleston
Charlotte–Gastonia–Rock Hill
   (NC–SC)
Columbia
Florence
Greenville–Spartanburg–
   Anderson
Myrtle Beach
Sumter

South Dakota
Rapid City
Sioux Falls

Tennessee
Chattanooga (TN–GA)
Clarksville–Hopkinsville
   (TN–KY)
Johnson City–Kingsport–
   Bristol (TN–VA)
Knoxville
Memphis (TN–AR–MS)
Nashville

Texas
Abilene
Amarillo
Austin–San Marcos
Beaumont–Port Arthur
Brazoria
Brownsville–Harlingen–San
   Benito
Bryan–College Station
Corpus Christi
Dallas
El Paso
Fort Worth–Arlington
Galveston–Texas City
Houston
Killeen–Temple
Laredo
Longview–Marshall
Lubbock
McAllen–Edinburg–Mission
Odessa–Midland
San Angelo
San Antonio
Sherman–Denison
Texarkana, TX–Texarkana,
   AR
Tyler

Victoria
Waco
Wichita Falls

Utah
Provo–Orem
Salt Lake City–Ogden

Vermont
Burlington

Virginia
Charlottesville
Danville
Johnson City–Kingsport–
   Bristol (TN–VA)
Lynchburg
Norfolk–Virginia Beach–
   Newport News (VA–NC)
Richmond–Petersburg
Roanoke
Washington (DC–MD–
   VA–WV)

Washington
Bellingham
Bremerton
Olympia
Richland–Kennewick–Pasco
Seattle–Bellevue–Everett
Spokane
Tacoma
Vancouver
Yakima

West Virginia
Charleston
Cumberland (MD–WV)
Huntington–Ashland
   (WV–KY–OH)
Parkersburg–Marietta
   (WV–OH)
Steubenville–Weirton
   (OH–WV)
Washington (DC–MD–
   VA–WV)
Wheeling (WV–OH)

Wisconsin
Appleton–Oshkosh–Neenah
Duluth–Superior (MN–WI)
Eau Claire
Green Bay
Janesville–Beloit
Kenosha
La Crosse (WI–MN)
Madison
Milwaukee–Waukesha
Minneapolis–St. Paul
   (MN–WI)
Racine
Sheboygan
Wausau

Wyoming
Casper
Cheyenne

Metropolitan Place Finder

The following listing includes cities, towns, and unincorporated areas with populations over 5,000 within metro area boundaries. Whenever these boundaries cross state lines, the state or provincial abbreviation for each place is also included.

Abilene, TX
Abilene, 105,857

Akron, OH
Akron, 223,019
Aurora, 9,192
Barberton, 27,623
Cuyahoga Falls, 48,950
Fairlawn, 5,779
Hudson, 5,159
Kent, 28,835
Macedonia, 7,509
Munroe Falls, 5,359
Norton, 11,475
Portage Lakes, 13,373
Ravenna, 12,069
Stow, 27,702
Streetsboro, 9,932
Tallmadge, 14,870
Twinsburg, 9,606

Albany, GA
Albany, 78,122

Albany-Schenectady-Troy, NY
Albany, 101,082
Amsterdam, 20,714
Ballston, 8,078
Bethlehem, 27,552
Brunswick, 11,093
Clifton Park, 30,117
Cobleskill, 7,270
Coeymans, 8,158
Cohoes, 16,825
Colonie, 76,494
Corinth, 5,935
Duanesburg, 5,474
East Greenbush, 14,076
Glenville, 28,771
Greenfield, 6,338
Guilderland, 28,764
Halfmoon, 13,879
Hoosick, 6,696
Malta, 11,709
Mechanicville, 5,249
Milton, 14,658
Moreau, 13,022
New Scotland, 9,139
Niskayuna, 19,048
North Greenbush, 10,891
Pittstown, 5,468
Rensselaer, 8,255
Rotterdam, 28,395
Sand Lake, 7,642
Saratoga, 5,069
Saratoga Springs, 25,001
Schaghticoke, 7,574

Schenectady, 65,566
Schodack, 11,839
Scotia, 7,359
Stillwater, 7,233
Troy, 54,269
Waterford, 8,695
Watervliet, 11,061
Wilton, 10,623

Albuquerque, NM
Albuquerque, 384,736
Belen, 6,547
Bernalillo, 5,960
Carrales, 5,534
Los Lunas, 6,013
North Valley, 12,507
Paradise Hills, 5,513
Rio Rancho, 32,505
Sandia, 6,742
South Valley, 35,701

Alexandria, LA
Alexandria, 49,188
Pineville, 12,251

Allentown-Bethlehem-Easton, PA-NJ
Allentown, PA, 105,090
Bangor, PA, 5,383
Bethlehem, PA, 87,853
Blairstown, PA, 5,331
Bushkill, PA, 5,512
Catasauqua, PA, 6,662
Easton, PA, 26,276
Emmaus, PA, 11,157
Forks, PA, 5,923
Hackettstown, NJ, 8,120
Hanover, PA, 7,176
Hellertown, PA, 5,662
Jim Thorpe, PA, 5,048
Lehigh, PA, 9,296
Lehighton, PA, 5,914
Lopatcong, NJ, 5,052
Lower Macungie, PA, 16,871
Lower Saucon, PA, 8,448
Mansfield, NJ, 7,154
Moore, PA, 8,418
Nazareth, PA, 5,713
North Whitehall, PA, 10,827
Northampton, PA, 8,717
Palmer, PA, 14,965
Palmerton, PA, 5,394
Phillipsburg, NJ, 15,757
Plainfield, PA, 5,444
Salisbury, PA, 13,401
South Whitehall, PA, 18,261
Upper Macungie, PA, 8,757
Upper Milford, PA, 6,304

Upper Mount Bethel, PA, 5,476
Upper Saucon, PA, 9,775
Washington, NJ, 6,474
Washington, PA, 5,367
Whitehall, PA, 22,779
Wilson, PA, 7,830

Altoona, PA
Allegheny, 7,023
Altoona, 51,881
Antis, 6,176
Frankstown, 7,243
Hollidaysburg, 5,624
Logan, 12,381
Tyrone, 5,743

Amarillo, TX
Amarillo, 157,615
Canyon, 11,365

Anchorage, AK
Anchorage, 226,338

Ann Arbor, MI
Adrian, 22,097
Ann Arbor, 109,592
Brighton, 5,686
Howell, 8,184
Saline, 6,660
Tecumseh, 7,462
Ypsilanti, 24,846

Anniston, AL
Anniston, 26,623
Jacksonville, 10,283
Oxford, 8,333
Piedmont, 5,286
Saks, 11,138

Appleton-Oshkosh-Neenah, WI
Appleton, 65,695
Kaukauna, 11,982
Kimberly, 5,406
Little Chute, 9,207
Menasha, 14,638
Neenah, 23,219
Oshkosh, 55,006

Asheville, NC
Asheville, 61,607
Black Mountain, 5,418

Athens, GA
Athens, 45,734
Gaines School, 11,354

Atlanta, GA
Alpharetta, 13,002

Atlanta, 394,071
Belvedere Park, 18,089
Buford, 8,745
Candler-McAfee, 29,491
Carrollton, 16,029
Cartersville, 12,035
Chamblee, 7,668
Clarkston, 5,385
College Park, 20,457
Conley, 5,528
Conyers, 7,380
Covington, 10,026
Decatur, 17,336
Doraville, 7,626
Douglasville, 11,635
Druid Hills, 12,174
Duluth, 9,029
Dunwoody, 26,302
East Point, 34,402
Fair Oaks, 6,996
Fayetteville, 5,827
Forest Park, 16,925
Gresham Park, 9,000
Griffin, 21,347
Hapeville, 5,483
Kennesaw, 8,936
Lawrenceville, 16,848
Lilburn, 9,301
Lithia Springs, 11,403
Mableton, 25,725
Marietta, 44,129
Monroe, 9,759
Morrow, 5,168
Mountain Park, 11,025
Newnan, 12,497
Norcross, 5,947
North Atlanta, 27,812
North Decatur, 13,936
North Druid Hills, 14,170
Panthersville, 9,874
Peachtree City, 19,027
Powder Springs, 6,893
Redan, 24,376
Riverdale, 9,359
Roswell, 47,923
Sandy Springs, 67,842
Scottdale, 8,636
Smyrna, 30,981
Snellville, 12,084
Stone Mountain, 6,494
Tucker, 25,781
Union City, 8,375
Villa Rica, 6,464
Vinings, 7,417
Winder, 7,373

Atlantic City-Cape May, NJ
Absecon, 7,298

Atlantic City, 37,986
Brigantine, 11,354
Buena Vista, 7,655
Dennis, 5,574
Egg Harbor, 24,544
Galloway, 23,330
Hamilton, 16,012
Hammonton, 12,208
Linwood, 6,866
Lower, 20,820
Margate City, 8,431
Middle, 14,771
Mullica, 5,896
North Wildwood, 5,017
Northfield, 7,305
Ocean City, 15,512
Pleasantville, 16,027
Somers Point, 11,216
Upper, 10,681
Ventnor City, 11,005

Augusta–Aiken, GA–SC
Aiken, SC, 19,872
Augusta, GA, 44,639
Belvedere, SC, 6,133
Evans, GA, 13,713
Martinez, GA, 33,731
North Augusta, SC, 15,344
South Augusta, GA, 55,998
West Augusta, GA, 27,637

Austin–San Marcos, TX
Anderson Mill, 9,299
Austin, 465,622
Brushy Creek, 5,833
Cedar Park, 5,161
Georgetown, 14,842
Jollyville, 15,206
Lockhart, 9,205
Round Rock, 30,923
San Marcos, 28,743
Taylor, 11,472
Wells Branch, 7,094

Bakersfield, CA
Arvin, 9,286
Bakersfield, 174,820
California City, 5,955
Delano, 22,762
Golden Hills, 5,423
Greenacres, 7,379
Lamont, 11,517
McFarland, 7,005
Oildale, 26,553
Ridgecrest, 27,725
Rosamond, 7,430
Shafter, 8,409
Taft, 5,902
Tehachapi, 5,791
Wasco, 12,412

Baltimore, MD
Aberdeen, 13,087
Annapolis, 33,187
Arbutus, 19,750
Arnold, 20,261
Baltimore, 736,014
Bel Air, 8,860
Bel Air North, 14,880
Bel Air South, 26,421
Bowleys Quarters, 5,595
Brooklyn Park, 10,987
Cape St. Claire, 7,878
Carney, 25,578
Catonsville, 35,233
Cockeysville, 18,668
Columbia, 75,883
Crofton, 12,781

Dundalk, 65,800
Edgemere, 9,226
Edgewood, 23,903
Eldersburg, 9,720
Elkridge, 12,953
Ellicott City, 41,396
Essex, 40,872
Fallston, 5,730
Ferndale, 16,355
Garrison, 5,045
Glen Burnie, 37,305
Green Haven, 14,416
Havre de Grace, 8,952
Jessup, 6,537
Joppatowne, 11,084
Lake Shore, 13,269
Lansdowne–Baltimore Highlands,
  15,509
Linthicum, 7,547
Lochearn, 25,240
Londontowne, 6,992
Lutherville–Timonium, 16,442
Maryland City, 6,813
Mays Chapel, 10,132
Middle River, 24,616
Milford Mill, 22,547
Naval Academy, 5,420
North Laurel, 15,008
Odenton, 12,833
Overlea, 12,137
Owings Mills, 9,474
Parkville, 31,617
Parole, 10,054
Pasadena, 10,012
Perry Hall, 22,723
Pikesville, 24,815
Pumphrey, 5,483
Randallstown, 26,277
Reisterstown, 19,314
Riviera Beach, 11,376
Rosedale, 18,703
Rossville, 9,492
Savage–Guilford, 9,669
Severn, 24,499
Severna Park, 25,879
South Gate, 27,564
Towson, 49,445
Westminster, 13,068
White Marsh, 8,183
Woodlawn, 32,907

Bangor, ME
Bangor, 34,692
Brewer, 9,117
Hampden, 5,531
Old Town, 8,426
Orono, 11,235

Barnstable–Yarmouth, MA
Barnstable, 43,154
Bourne, 16,231
Brewster, 9,135
Chatham, 6,654
Dennis, 13,946
Falmouth, 29,220
Harwich, 10,483
Mashpee, 8,856
Orleans, 5,732
Sandwich, 16,999
Yarmouth, 21,861

Baton Rouge, LA
Baker, 13,233
Baton Rouge, 219,531
Brownfields, 5,229
Denham Springs, 8,381
Gardere, 7,209
Merrydale, 10,395

Oak Hills Place, 5,479
Port Allen, 6,277
Shenandoah, 13,429
Village St. George, 6,242
Zachary, 9,036

Beaumont–Port Arthur, TX
Beaumont, 114,323
Bridge City, 8,034
Groves, 16,513
Lumberton, 6,640
Nederland, 16,192
Orange, 19,381
Port Arthur, 58,724
Port Neches, 12,974
Silsbee, 6,368
Vidor, 10,935

Bellingham, WA
Bellingham, 52,179
Ferndale, 5,398
Lynden, 5,709

Benton Harbor, MI
Benton Harbor, 12,818
Benton Heights, 5,465
Fair Plain, 8,051
Niles, 12,456
St. Joseph, 9,214

Billings, MT
Billings, 81,151
Laurel, 5,686

Biloxi–Gulfport–Pascagoula, MS
Bay St. Louis, 8,063
Biloxi, 46,319
D'Iberville, 6,566
Gautier, 10,088
Gulf Hills, 5,004
Gulfport, 40,775
Long Beach, 15,804
Moss Point, 17,837
Ocean Springs, 14,658
Orange Grove, 15,676
Pascagoula, 25,899
Pass Christian, 5,557
St. Martin, 6,349
Waveland, 5,369

Binghamton, NY
Barton, 8,925
Binghamton, 53,008
Candor, 5,310
Chenango, 12,310
Colesville, 5,590
Conklin, 6,265
Dickinson, 5,486
Endicott, 13,531
Fenton, 7,236
Johnson City, 16,890
Kirkwood, 6,096
Maine, 5,576
Owego, 21,279
Union, 59,786
Vestal, 26,733
Windsor, 6,440

Birmingham, AL
Alabaster, 14,732
Bessemer, 33,497
Birmingham, 265,196
Center Point, 22,658
Fairfield, 12,200
Forestdale, 10,395
Fultondale, 6,400
Gardendale, 9,251

Homewood, 22,922
Hoover, 39,788
Hueytown, 15,280
Irondale, 9,454
Leeds, 9,946
Midfield, 5,559
Mountain Brook, 19,810
Pelham, 9,765
Pell City, 8,118
Pinson–Clay–Chalkville, 10,987
Pleasant Grove, 8,458
Tarrant, 8,046
Trussville, 8,266
Vestavia Hills, 19,749

Bismarck, ND
Bismarck, 49,256
Mandan, 15,177

Bloomington, IN
Bloomington, 60,633

Bloomington–Normal, IL
Bloomington, 51,972
Normal, 40,023

Boise City, ID
Boise City, 125,738
Caldwell, 18,400
Garden City, 6,369
Meridian, 9,596
Nampa, 28,365

Boston, MA
Abington, 13,911
Acton, 18,133
Amesbury, 15,106
Andover, 30,112
Arlington, 44,770
Ashland, 12,664
Ayer, 6,917
Bedford, 13,249
Bellingham, 15,201
Belmont, 24,570
Beverly, 38,803
Billerica, 37,299
Boston, 574,625
Boxford, 6,289
Braintree, 33,409
Bridgewater, 22,664
Brockton, 92,247
Brookline, 55,897
Burlington, 23,578
Cambridge, 98,073
Canton, 18,625
Carver, 10,650
Chelmsford, 32,670
Chelsea, 30,245
Cohasset, 6,968
Concord, 17,379
Danvers, 24,186
Dedham, 23,768
Dracut, 26,371
Duxbury, 13,933
East Bridgewater, 11,616
Everett, 35,387
Foxborough, 14,681
Framingham, 65,539
Franklin, 23,333
Georgetown, 6,571
Gloucester, 28,959
Groton, 7,752
Groveland, 5,281
Halifax, 6,674
Hamilton, 7,350
Hanover, 12,088
Hanson, 9,037
Haverhill, 52,817

Hingham, 19,897
Holbrook, 11,122
Holliston, 12,899
Hopkinton, 9,557
Hudson, 17,075
Hull, 10,884
Ipswich, 11,935
Kingston, 9,468
Lakeville, 8,003
Lawrence, 73,601
Lexington, 29,156
Lincoln, 7,644
Littleton, 6,992
Lowell, 108,719
Lynn, 82,588
Lynnfield, 11,236
Malden, 54,081
Manchester, 5,299
Marblehead, 20,167
Marlborough, 32,130
Marshfield, 21,207
Mattapoisett, 5,850
Maynard, 10,538
Medfield, 10,492
Medford, 57,696
Medway, 10,217
Melrose, 27,830
Merrimac, 5,314
Methuen, 40,250
Middleborough, 18,096
Middleton, 5,027
Millis, 7,795
Milton, 25,838
Natick, 30,630
Needham, 27,716
Newbury, 5,755
Newburyport, 16,031
Newton, 82,808
Norfolk, 9,940
North Andover, 22,993
North Reading, 12,063
Norwell, 9,299
Norwood, 28,940
Peabody, 47,409
Pembroke, 14,546
Pepperell, 10,332
Plainville, 7,267
Plymouth, 48,267
Quincy, 86,163
Randolph, 30,850
Reading, 22,534
Revere, 42,424
Rockland, 16,515
Rockport, 7,878
Salem, 38,112
Salisbury, 6,688
Saugus, 25,394
Scituate, 16,699
Sharon, 15,946
Shirley, 6,402
Somerville, 78,175
Stoneham, 22,030
Stoughton, 26,571
Stow, 5,257
Sudbury, 14,467
Swampscott, 13,810
Tewksbury, 28,069
Topsfield, 5,856
Townsend, 8,444
Tyngsborough, 9,143
Wakefield, 24,653
Walpole, 20,458
Waltham, 58,272
Wareham, 18,678
Watertown, 33,481
Wayland, 11,716
Wellesley, 26,648

West Bridgewater, 6,324
Westford, 16,983
Weston, 9,950
Westwood, 12,546
Weymouth, 53,855
Whitman, 13,185
Wilmington, 17,712
Winchester, 20,341
Winthrop, 17,871
Woburn, 35,225
Wrentham, 9,214

Boulder–Longmont, CO
Boulder, 83,312
Broomfield, 16,390
Gunbarrel, 9,388
Lafayette, 14,548
Longmont, 51,555
Louisville, 12,361

Brazoria, TX
Alvin, 19,220
Angleton, 17,140
Clute, 8,910
Freeport, 11,389
Lake Jackson, 22,776
Pearland, 17,234

Bremerton, WA
Bremerton, 38,142
East Port Orchard, 5,409
Parkwood, 6,853
Silverdale, 7,660

Bridgeport, CT
Ansonia, 18,115
Beacon Falls, 5,355
Bridgeport, 141,599
Derby, 12,279
Easton, 6,095
Fairfield, 53,792
Milford, 50,282
Monroe, 17,284
Oxford, 8,958
Seymour, 14,642
Shelton, 35,707
Stratford, 48,899
Trumbull, 31,434

Brownsville–Harlingen–San Benito, TX
Brownsville, 98,962
Harlingen, 48,735
San Benito, 20,125

Bryan–College Station, TX
Bryan, 55,002
College Station, 52,456

Buffalo–Niagara Falls, NY
Alden, 10,372
Amherst, 111,711
Aurora, 13,433
Boston, 7,445
Buffalo, 328,123
Cheektowaga, 99,314
Clarence, 20,041
Collins, 6,020
Concord, 8,387
Depew, 17,673
East Aurora, 6,647
Eden, 7,416
Elma, 10,355
Evans, 17,478
Grand Island, 17,561
Hamburg, 53,735
Kenmore, 17,180
Lackawanna, 20,585

Lancaster, 32,181
Lewiston, 15,453
Lockport, 24,426
Marilla, 5,250
Newfane, 8,996
Newstead, 7,440
Niagara, 9,880
Niagara Falls, 61,840
North Tonawanda, 34,989
Orchard Park, 24,632
Pendleton, 5,010
Porter, 7,110
Royalton, 7,453
Tonawanda, 82,464
West Seneca, 47,830
Wheatfield, 11,125
Williamsville, 5,583
Wilson, 5,761

Burlington, VT
Burlington, 39,536
Colchester, 14,802
Essex, 17,037
Richmond, 5,124
St. Albans, 7,319
Shelburne, 5,967
South Burlington, 13,504
Swanton, 5,679
Williston, 5,226
Winooski, 6,654

Calgary, AB
Airdrie, 12,456
Calgary, 710,677
Cochrane, 5,265

Canton–Massillon, OH
Alliance, 23,304
Canton, 84,161
Louisville, 8,087
Massillon, 31,007
North Canton, 14,748
Perry Heights, 9,055

Casper, WY
Casper, 46,742

Cedar Rapids, IA
Cedar Rapids, 108,751
Marion, 20,403

Central New Jersey, NJ
Bedminster, 7,086
Bernards, 17,199
Bernardsville, 6,597
Bound Brook, 9,487
Branchburg, 10,888
Bridgewater, 32,509
Carteret, 19,025
Clinton, 10,816
Dunellen, 6,528
East Brunswick, 43,548
Edison, 88,680
Franklin, 42,780
Highland Park, 13,279
Hillsborough, 28,808
Jamesburg, 5,294
Lebanon, 5,679
Manville, 10,567
Metuchen, 12,804
Middlesex, 13,055
Milltown, 6,968
Monroe, 22,255
Montgomery, 9,612
New Brunswick, 41,711
North Brunswick, 31,287
North Plainfield, 18,820

Old Bridge, 56,475
Perth Amboy, 41,967
Piscataway, 47,089
Plainsboro, 14,213
Raritan, 15,616
Readington, 13,400
Sayreville, 34,986
Somerville, 11,632
South Amboy, 7,863
South Brunswick, 25,792
South Plainfield, 20,489
South River, 13,692
Spotswood, 7,983
Union, 5,078
Warren, 10,830
Watchung, 5,110
Woodbridge, 93,086

Champaign–Urbana, IL
Champaign, 63,502
Rantoul, 17,212
Urbana, 36,344

Charleston, WV
Charleston, 57,287
Cross Lanes, 10,878
Dunbar, 8,697
Nitro, 6,851
St. Albans, 11,194
South Charleston, 13,645
Teays Valley, 8,436

Charleston–North Charleston, SC
Charleston, 80,414
Goose Creek, 24,692
Hanahan, 13,176
Ladson, 13,494
Moncks Corner, 5,607
Mount Pleasant, 30,108
North Charleston, 72,118
Summerville, 22,519

Charlotte–Gastonia–Rock Hill, NC–SC
Belmont, NC, 8,434
Charlotte, NC, 395,934
Concord, NC, 27,347
Gastonia, NC, 54,732
Kannapolis, NC, 29,696
Lincolnton, 6,847
Matthews, NC, 13,651
Mint Hill, NC, 11,567
Monroe, NC, 16,127
Mount Holly, NC, 7,710
Rock Hill, SC, 41,643
Salisbury, NC, 23,087
South Gastonia, NC, 5,487
York, SC, 6,709

Charlottesville, VA
Charlottesville, 40,341
Commonwealth, 5,538
Rio, 5,133
University Heights, 6,900

Chattanooga, TN–GA
Chattanooga, TN, 152,466
Collegedale, TN, 5,048
East Brainerd, TN, 11,594
East Ridge, TN, 21,101
Fairview, GA, 6,444
Harrison, TN, 7,191
La Fayette, GA, 6,313
Middle Valley, TN, 12,255
Red Bank, TN, 12,322
Signal Mountain, TN, 7,034
Soddy–Daisy, TN, 8,240

Cheyenne, WY
Cheyenne, 50,008

Chicago, IL
Addison, 32,058
Algonquin, 10,194
Alsip, 18,227
Arlington Heights, 75,460
Aurora, 99,581
Barrington, 5,159
Bartlett, 19,350
Batavia, 17,076
Bellwood, 20,241
Bensenville, 17,767
Berkeley, 5,137
Berwyn, 45,426
Bloomingdale, 16,614
Blue Island, 21,203
Bolingbrook, 39,371
Boulder Hill, 8,894
Bridgeview, 14,402
Broadview, 8,713
Brookfield, 18,876
Buffalo Grove, 14,497
Burbank, 27,600
Calumet City, 37,840
Calumet Park, 8,418
Carol Stream, 31,716
Carpentersville, 23,049
Cary, 10,043
Chicago, 2,783,726
Chicago Heights, 33,072
Chicago Ridge, 13,643
Cicero, 67,436
Clarendon Hills, 6,994
Country Club Hills, 15,431
Countryside, 5,716
Crest Hill, 10,643
Crestwood, 10,823
Crete, 6,773
Crystal Lake, 24,512
Darien, 18,341
Des Plaines, 53,223
Dolton, 23,930
Downers Grove, 46,858
Elgin, 76,010
Elk Grove Village, 33,429
Elmhurst, 42,029
Elmwood Park, 23,206
Evanston, 73,233
Evergreen Park, 20,874
Flossmoor, 8,651
Forest Park, 14,918
Frankfort, 7,180
Frankfort Square, 6,227
Franklin Park, 18,485
Geneva, 12,617
Glen Ellyn, 24,944
Glencoe, 8,499
Glendale Heights, 27,973
Glenview, 37,093
Glenwood, 9,289
Goodings Grove, 14,054
Hanover Park, 32,960
Harvard, 5,975
Harvey, 29,771
Harwood Heights, 7,680
Hazel Crest, 13,334
Hickory Hills, 13,021
Hillside, 7,672
Hinsdale, 16,025
Hoffman Estates, 46,561
Homewood, 19,278
Inverness, 6,503
Itasca, 6,947
Joliet, 76,836
Justice, 11,137

La Grange, 15,362
La Grange Park, 12,861
Lake in the Hills, 5,866
Lansing, 28,086
Lemont, 7,348
Lincolnwood, 11,365
Lisle, 19,512
Lockport, 9,401
Lombard, 39,408
Lynwood, 6,535
Lyons, 9,828
Markham, 13,136
Matteson, 11,378
Maywood, 27,139
McHenry, 16,177
Melrose Park, 20,859
Midlothian, 14,372
Mokena, 6,128
Morris, 10,270
Morton Grove, 22,408
Mount Prospect, 53,170
Naperville, 72,931
New Lenox, 9,627
Niles, 28,284
Norridge, 14,459
North Riverside, 6,005
North Aurora, 5,940
Northbrook, 32,308
Northlake, 12,505
Oak Brook, 9,178
Oak Forest, 26,203
Oak Lawn, 56,182
Oak Park, 53,648
Orland Hills, 5,510
Orland Park, 35,720
Palatine, 39,253
Palos Heights, 11,478
Palos Hills, 17,803
Park Forest, 21,347
Park Ridge, 36,175
Plano, 5,104
Prospect Heights, 15,239
Richton Park, 10,523
River Forest, 11,669
River Grove, 9,961
Riverdale, 13,671
Riverside, 8,774
Robbins, 7,498
Rolling Meadows, 22,591
Romeoville, 14,074
Roselle, 20,819
St. Charles, 22,491
Sauk Village, 9,926
Schaumburg, 68,586
Schiller Park, 11,189
Shorewood, 6,264
Skokie, 59,432
South Elgin, 7,474
South Holland, 22,105
Steger, 5,576
Stickney, 5,678
Streamwood, 30,987
Summit, 9,971
Tinley Park, 37,040
University Park, 6,204
Villa Park, 22,253
Warrenville, 11,333
West Chicago, 14,796
Westchester, 17,301
Western Springs, 11,984
Westmont, 21,228
Wheaton, 51,464
Wheeling, 29,911
Willowbrook, 8,598
Wilmette, 26,690
Winfield, 7,096
Winnetka, 12,174

Wonder Lake, 6,664
Wood Dale, 12,425
Woodridge, 26,232
Woodstock, 14,353
Worth, 11,208

Chico-Paradise, CA
Chico, 40,079
Magalia, 8,987
Oroville, 11,960
Oroville East, 8,462
Palermo, 5,260
Paradise, 25,408
South Oroville, 7,463
Thermalito, 5,646

Chicoutimi-Jonquière, PQ
Chicoutimi, 62,670
Jonquière, 57,933
La Baie, 20,995

Cincinnati, OH-KY-IN
Alexandria, KY, 5,592
Bellevue, KY, 6,997
Blue Ash, OH, 11,860
Bridgetown North, OH, 11,748
Burlington, KY, 6,070
Cheviot, OH, 9,616
Cincinnati, OH, 364,040
Covedale, OH, 6,669
Covington, KY, 43,264
Dayton, KY, 6,576
Deer Park, OH, 6,181
Dent, OH, 6,416
Dry Run, OH, 5,389
Edgewood, KY, 8,143
Elsmere, KY, 6,847
Erlanger, KY, 15,979
Finneytown, OH, 13,096
Florence, KY, 18,624
Forest Park, OH, 18,609
Forestville, OH, 9,185
Franklin, OH, 11,026
Groesbeck, OH, 6,684
Harrison, OH, 7,518
Independence, KY, 10,444
Kenwood, OH, 7,469
Landen, OH, 9,263
Lebanon, OH, 10,453
Loveland, OH, 9,960
Mack South, OH, 5,767
Madeira, OH, 9,141
Mason, OH, 11,452
Milford, OH, 5,655
Montgomery, OH, 9,753
Mount Healthy, OH, 7,580
Newport, KY, 18,871
North College Hill, OH, 11,002
Northbrook, OH, 11,471
Northgate, OH, 7,864
Norwood, OH, 23,674
Reading, OH, 12,038
St. Bernard, OH, 5,344
Sharonville, OH, 11,312
Silverton, OH, 5,859
Springboro, OH, 6,590
Springdale, OH, 10,621
Taylor Mill, KY, 5,530
Village of Indian Hill, OH, 5,383
Villa Hills, KY, 7,739
White Oak, OH, 12,430
Wyoming, OH, 8,128

Clarksville-Hopkinsville, TN-KY
Clarksville, TN, 75,494
Hopkinsville, KY, 29,809

Cleveland-Lorain-Elyria, OH
Amherst, 10,332
Ashtabula, 21,633
Avon, 7,337
Avon Lake, 15,066
Bay Village, 17,000
Beachwood, 10,677
Bedford, 14,822
Bedford Heights, 12,131
Berea, 19,051
Brecksville, 11,818
Broadview Heights, 12,219
Brook Park, 22,865
Brooklyn, 11,706
Brunswick, 28,230
Cleveland, 505,616
Cleveland Heights, 54,052
Conneaut, 13,241
East Cleveland, 33,096
Eastlake, 21,161
Edgewood, 5,189
Elyria, 56,746
Euclid, 54,875
Fairview Park, 18,028
Garfield Heights, 31,739
Geneva, 6,597
Highland Heights, 6,249
Independence, 6,500
Kirtland, 5,881
Lakewood, 59,718
Lorain, 71,245
Lyndhurst, 15,982
Maple Heights, 27,089
Mayfield Heights, 19,847
Medina, 19,231
Mentor, 47,358
Mentor-on-the-Lake, 8,271
Middleburg Heights, 14,702
North Madison, 8,699
North Olmsted, 34,204
North Ridgeville, 21,564
North Royalton, 23,197
Oberlin, 8,191
Olmsted Falls, 6,741
Painesville, 15,699
Parma, 87,876
Parma Heights, 21,448
Pepper Pike, 6,185
Richmond Heights, 9,611
Rocky River, 20,410
Seven Hills, 12,339
Shaker Heights, 30,831
Sheffield Lake, 9,825
Solon, 18,548
South Euclid, 23,866
Strongsville, 35,308
University Heights, 14,790
Vermilion, 5,644
Wadsworth, 15,718
Warrensville Heights, 15,745
Westlake, 27,018
Wickliffe, 14,558
Willoughby, 20,510
Willoughby Hills, 8,427
Willowick, 15,269

Colorado Springs, CO
Air Force Academy, 9,062
Black Forest, 8,143
Cimarron Hills, 11,160
Colorado Springs, 281,140
Fountain, 9,984
Security-Widefield, 23,822
Stratmoor, 5,854

Columbia, MO
Columbia, 69,101

Columbia, SC

Cayce, 11,163
Columbia, 98,052
Dentsville, 11,839
Forest Acres, 7,197
Irmo, 11,208
Oak Grove, 7,173
Red Bank, 5,950
St. Andrews, 25,692
Seven Oaks, 15,722
West Columbia, 10,588
Woodfield, 8,862

Columbus, GA–AL

Columbus, GA, 178,681
Phenix City, AL, 24,642

Columbus, OH

Bexley, 13,088
Blacklick Estates, 10,080
Circleville, 11,666
Columbus, 632,270
Delaware, 20,030
Dublin, 16,361
Gahanna, 27,791
Grandview Heights, 7,010
Grove City, 19,661
Heath, 7,231
Hilliard, 11,796
Huber Ridge, 5,255
Lancaster, 34,507
Lincoln Village, 9,958
London, 7,807
Newark, 44,389
Pickerington, 5,645
Reynoldsburg, 25,705
Upper Arlington, 34,128
Westerville, 32,234
Whitehall, 20,572
Worthington, 14,869

Corpus Christi, TX

Aransas Pass, 6,246
Corpus Christi, 257,453
Ingleside, 5,696
Mathis, 5,423
Portland, 12,224
Robstown, 12,849
Sinton, 5,549

Cumberland, MD–WV

Cumberland, MD, 23,706
Frostburg, MD, 8,075
Keyser, WV, 5,870

Dallas, TX

Addison, 8,783
Allen, 18,309
Athens, 10,967
Balch Springs, 17,406
Carrollton, 82,167
Cedar Hill, 19,926
The Colony, 22,113
Commerce, 6,825
Coppell, 16,878
Dallas, 1,006,877
Denton, 66,270
DeSoto, 30,544
Duncanville, 35,748
Ennis, 13,883
Farmers Branch, 24,250
Flower Mound, 15,527
Frisco, 5,873
Garland, 180,635
Grand Prairie, 81,527
Greenville, 23,071
Highland Park, 8,739
Highland Village, 7,027

Irving, 155,037
Kaufman, 5,238
Lancaster, 22,117
Lewisville, 46,400
McKinney, 21,283
Mesquite, 101,484
Midlothian, 5,141
Plano, 128,673
Richardson, 74,861
Rockwall, 10,486
Rowlett, 23,253
Sachse, 5,152
Seagoville, 8,969
Terrell, 12,490
University Park, 22,259
Waxahachie, 18,168
Wylie, 8,662

Danbury, CT

Bethel, 17,597
Brookfield, 14,010
Danbury, 66,113
New Fairfield, 12,462
New Milford, 24,584
Redding, 7,986
Ridgefield, 20,549
Southbury, 15,977

Danville, VA

Danville, 53,056

Davenport–Moline–Rock Island, IA–IL

Bettendorf, IA, 28,132
Davenport, IA, 95,333
East Moline, IL, 20,147
Geneseo, IL, 5,990
Kewanee, IL, 12,969
Milan, IL, 5,831
Moline, IL, 43,202
Rock Island, IL, 40,552
Silvis, IL, 6,926

Dayton–Springfield, OH

Beavercreek, 33,626
Bellbrook, 6,511
Centerville, 21,082
Dayton, 182,044
Drexel, 5,143
Englewood, 11,432
Fairborn, 31,300
Huber Heights, 38,686
Kettering, 60,569
Miamisburg, 17,834
Moraine, 5,989
New Carlisle, 6,049
Northridge, 9,448
Northview, 10,337
Oakwood, 8,957
Overlook–Page Manor, 13,242
Piqua, 20,612
Shiloh, 11,607
Springfield, 70,487
Tipp City, 6,027
Trotwood, 8,816
Troy, 19,478
Union, 5,501
Vandalia, 13,882
West Carrollton City, 14,403
Woodbourne–Hyde Park, 7,837
Xenia, 24,664

Daytona Beach, FL

Daytona Beach, 61,921
De Bary, 7,176
De Land, 16,491
Deltona, 50,828
Edgewater, 15,337

Holly Hill, 11,141
New Smyrna Beach, 16,543
Orange City, 5,347
Ormond Beach, 29,721
Ormond-by-the-Sea, 8,157
Palm Coast, 14,287
Port Orange, 35,317
South Daytona, 12,482

Decatur, AL

Decatur, 48,706
Hartselle, 10,795

Decatur, IL

Decatur, 83,885

Denver, CO

Applewood, 11,069
Arvada, 89,888
Aurora, 222,099
Brighton, 14,186
Broomfield, 8,244
Castle Rock, 8,708
Castlewood, 24,392
Cherry Hills Village, 5,245
Columbine, 24,397
Commerce City, 16,466
Denver, 467,610
Derby, 6,043
Englewood, 29,387
Evergreen, 7,582
Federal Heights, 9,342
Gateway, 7,510
Golden, 13,116
Greenwood Village, 7,589
Highlands Ranch, 10,181
Ken Caryl, 24,391
Lakewood, 126,481
Littleton, 33,577
Northglenn, 27,195
Parker, 5,450
Sherrelwood, 16,636
Southglenn, 43,087
Thornton, 55,031
Welby, 10,218
Westminster, 74,625
Westminster East, 5,197
Wheat Ridge, 29,419

Des Moines, IA

Altoona, 7,191
Ankeny, 18,482
Clive, 7,462
Des Moines, 193,187
Indianola, 11,340
Norwalk, 5,726
Perry, 6,652
Urbandale, 23,500
West Des Moines, 31,695
Windsor Heights, 5,190

Detroit, MI

Allen Park, 31,092
Auburn Hills, 17,076
Berkley, 16,960
Beverly Hills, 10,610
Birmingham, 19,997
Bloomfield Township, 42,137
Canton, 57,047
Center Line, 9,026
Clawson, 13,874
Clinton, 85,866
Dearborn, 89,286
Dearborn Heights, 60,838
Detroit, 1,027,974
East Detroit, 35,283
Ecorse, 12,180
Farmington, 10,132

Farmington Hills, 74,652
Ferndale, 25,084
Flat Rock, 7,290
Fraser, 13,899
Garden City, 31,846
Grosse Ile, 9,781
Grosse Pointe, 5,681
Grosse Pointe Farms, 10,092
Grosse Pointe Park, 12,857
Grosse Pointe Woods, 17,715
Hamtramck, 18,372
Harper Woods, 14,903
Harrison, 24,685
Hazel Park, 20,051
Highland Park, 20,121
Holly, 5,595
Huntington Woods, 6,419
Inkster, 30,772
Lambertville, 7,860
Lapeer, 7,759
Lincoln Park, 41,832
Livonia, 100,850
Madison Heights, 32,196
Marysville, 8,515
Melvindale, 11,216
Milford, 5,511
Monroe, 22,902
Mount Clemens, 18,405
New Baltimore, 5,798
Novi, 32,998
Oak Park, 30,462
Plymouth, 9,560
Plymouth Township, 23,646
Pontiac, 71,166
Port Huron, 33,694
Redford, 54,387
River Rouge, 11,314
Riverview, 13,894
Rochester, 7,130
Rochester Hills, 61,766
Romulus, 22,897
Roseville, 51,412
Royal Oak, 65,410
St. Clair, 5,116
St. Clair Shores, 68,107
Shelby, 48,655
Southfield, 75,728
Southgate, 30,771
South Lyon, 5,857
South Monroe, 5,266
Sterling Heights, 117,810
Taylor, 70,811
Temperance, 6,542
Trenton, 20,586
Troy, 72,884
Utica, 5,081
Walled Lake, 6,278
Warren, 144,864
Waterford, 66,692
Wayne, 19,899
West Bloomfield Township, 54,843
Westland, 84,724
Wixom, 8,550
Woodhaven, 11,631
Wyandotte, 30,938

Dothan, AL

Daleville, 5,117
Dothan, 53,330
Ozark, 12,922

Dover, DE

Dover, 27,630
Smyrna, 5,231

Dubuque, IA

Dubuque, 57,546

Duluth–Superior, MN–WI
Chisholm, MN, 5,290
Duluth, MN, 85,493
Hermantown, MN, 6,761
Hibbing, MN, 18,046
Superior, WI, 27,134
Virginia, MN, 9,410

Dutchess County, NY
Amenia, 5,195
Beacon, 13,243
Beekman, 10,447
Dover, 7,778
East Fishkill, 22,101
Fishkill, 17,655
Hyde Park, 21,230
La Grange, 13,274
Pawling, 5,947
Pleasant Valley, 8,063
Poughkeepsie, 40,143
Red Hook, 9,565
Rhinebeck, 7,558
Wappinger, 26,008

Eau Claire, WI
Altoona, 5,889
Chippewa Falls, 12,727
Eau Claire, 56,880

Edmonton, AB
Beaumont, 5,042
Edmonton, 616,741
Fort Saskatchewan, 12,078
Leduc, 13,970
Morinville, 6,104
St. Albert, 42,146
Spruce Grove, 12,884
Stony Plain, 7,226

El Paso, TX
El Paso, 515,342
Fabens, 5,599
Socorro, 22,995

Elkhart–Goshen, IN
Dunlap, 5,705
Elkhart, 43,627
Goshen, 23,797
Nappanee, 5,510

Elmira, NY
Big Flats, 7,596
Elmira, 33,724
Horseheads, 19,926
Southport, 11,571

Enid, OK
Enid, 45,309

Erie, PA
Corry, 7,216
Edinboro, 7,736
Erie, 108,718
Fairview, 7,839
Harborcreek, 15,108
Millcreek, 46,820
North East, 6,283
Summit, 5,284

Eugene–Springfield, OR
Cottage Grove, 7,402
Eugene, 112,669
Florence, 5,162
North Springfield, 5,451
River Road, 9,443
Santa Clara, 12,834
Springfield, 44,683

Evansville–Henderson, IN–KY
Boonville, IN, 6,724

Evansville, IN, 126,272
Henderson, KY, 25,945
Mount Vernon, IN, 7,217

Fargo–Moorhead, ND–MN
Fargo, ND, 74,111
Moorhead, MN, 32,295
West Fargo, ND, 12,287

Fayetteville, NC
Fayetteville, 75,695
Hope Mills, 8,184
Spring Lake, 7,524

Fayetteville–Springdale–Rogers, AR
Bella Vista, 9,083
Bentonville, 11,257
Fayetteville, 42,099
Rogers, 24,692
Siloam Springs, 8,151
Springdale, 29,034

Flint, MI
Beecher, 14,465
Burton, 27,617
Davison, 5,693
Fenton, 8,444
Flint, 140,761
Flushing, 8,542
Grand Blanc, 7,760

Florence, AL
Florence, 36,426
Muscle Shoals, 9,611
Sheffield, 10,380
Tuscumbia, 8,413

Florence, SC
Florence, 29,813
Lake City, 7,153

Fort Collins–Loveland, CO
Fort Collins, 87,758
Loveland, 37,352

Fort Lauderdale, FL
Broadview Park, 6,109
Broadview–Pompano Park, 5,230
Browardale, 6,257
Coconut Creek, 27,485
Collier Manor–Cresthaven, 7,322
Cooper City, 20,791
Coral Springs, 79,443
Dania, 13,024
Davie, 47,217
Deerfield Beach, 46,325
Fort Lauderdale, 149,377
Hallandale, 30,996
Hollywood, 121,697
Lauderdale Lakes, 27,341
Lauderhill, 49,708
Lighthouse Point, 10,378
Margate, 42,985
Melrose Park, 6,477
Miami Gardens–Utopia–Carver, 7,448
Miramar, 40,663
North Andrews Gardens, 9,002
North Lauderdale, 26,506
Oakland Park, 26,326
Pembroke Pines, 65,452
Pine Island Ridge, 5,244
Plantation, 66,692
Pompano Beach, 72,411
Pompano Beach Highlands, 17,915

Riverland, 5,376
Sunrise, 64,407
Tamarac, 44,822
Washington Park, 6,930
Wilton Manors, 11,804

Fort Myers–Cape Coral, FL
Bonita Springs, 13,600
Cape Coral, 74,991
Cypress Lake, 10,491
Forest Island Park, 5,988
Fort Myers, 45,206
Fort Myers Beach, 9,284
Fort Myers Shores, 5,460
Iona, 9,565
Lehigh Acres, 13,611
McGregor, 6,504
North Fort Myers, 30,027
Page Park–Pine Manor, 5,116
San Carlos Park, 11,785
Sanibel, 5,468
Villas, 9,898
Whiskey Creek, 5,061

Fort Pierce–Port St. Lucie, FL
Fort Pierce, 36,830
Fort Pierce North, 5,833
Fort Pierce South, 5,320
Hobe Sound, 11,507
Jensen Beach, 9,884
Lakewood Park, 7,211
Port St. Lucie, 55,866
Port Salerno, 7,786
Stuart, 11,936

Fort Smith, AR–OK
Fort Smith, AR, 72,798
Sallisaw, OK, 7,122
Van Buren, AR, 14,979

Fort Walton Beach, FL
Crestview, 9,886
Destin, 8,080
Fort Walton Beach, 21,471
Lake Lorraine, 6,779
Niceville, 10,507
Ocean City, 5,422
Wright, 18,945

Fort Wayne, IN
Auburn, 9,379
Bluffton, 9,020
Columbia City, 5,706
Decatur, 8,644
Fort Wayne, 173,072
Garrett, 5,349
Huntington, 16,389
New Haven, 9,320

Fort Worth–Arlington, TX
Arlington, 261,721
Azle, 8,868
Bedford, 43,762
Benbrook, 19,564
Burleson, 16,153
Cleburne, 22,205
Colleyville, 12,724
Crowley, 6,974
Eagle Mountain, 5,847
Euless, 38,149
Everman, 5,672
Forest Hill, 11,482
Fort Worth, 447,619
Grand Prairie, 18,086
Grapevine, 29,199
Haltom City, 32,856
Hurst, 33,574

Keller, 13,683
Mansfield, 14,848
North Richland Hills, 45,895
Rendon, 7,658
Richland Hills, 7,978
River Oaks, 6,580
Saginaw, 8,551
Southlake, 6,823
Watauga, 20,009
Weatherford, 14,804
White Settlement, 15,472

Fresno, CA
Bonadelle Ranchos–Madera Ranchos, 5,705
Chowchilla, 5,930
Clovis, 50,323
Coalinga, 8,212
Fresno, 354,202
Kerman, 5,448
Kingsburg, 7,205
Madera, 29,281
Madera Acres, 5,245
Mendota, 6,821
Orange Cove, 5,604
Parlier, 7,938
Reedley, 15,791
Sanger, 16,839
Selma, 14,757

Gadsden, AL
Attalla, 6,859
Gadsden, 42,523
Rainbow City, 7,673
Southside, 5,436

Gainesville, FL
Gainesville, 84,770

Galveston–Texas City, TX
Bacliff, 5,549
Dickinson, 9,497
Friendswood, 14,979
Galveston, 59,070
Hitchcock, 5,868
La Marque, 14,120
League City, 30,026
Santa Fe, 8,429
Texas City, 40,822

Gary, IN
Cedar Lake, 8,885
Chesterton, 9,124
Crown Point, 17,728
Dyer, 10,923
East Chicago, 33,892
Gary, 116,646
Griffith, 17,916
Hammond, 84,236
Highland, 23,696
Hobart, 21,822
Lake Station, 13,899
Lowell, 6,430
Merrillville, 27,257
Munster, 19,949
Portage, 29,060
Schererville, 19,926
South Haven, 6,112
Valparaiso, 24,414
Whiting, 5,155

Glens Falls, NY
Fort Ann, 6,368
Fort Edward, 6,330
Glens Falls, 15,023
Granville, 5,935
Hudson Falls, 7,651
Kingsbury, 11,851
Queensbury, 22,630

Goldsboro, NC
Goldsboro, 40,709

Grand Forks, ND–MN
Crookston, MN, 8,119
East Grand Forks, MN, 8,658
Grand Forks, ND, 49,425

Grand Rapids–Muskegon–Holland, MI
Allendale, 6,950
Comstock Park, 6,530
Cutlerville, 11,228
East Grand Rapids, 10,807
Forest Hills, 16,690
Grand Haven, 11,951
Grand Rapids, 189,126
Grandville, 15,624
Holland, 30,786
Hudsonville, 6,170
Jenison, 17,882
Kentwood, 37,826
Muskegon, 40,283
Muskegon Heights, 13,176
Northview, 13,712
Norton Shores, 21,755
Walker, 17,279
Wyoming, 63,891
Zeeland, 5,417

Great Falls, MT
Great Falls, 55,097

Greeley, CO
Evans, 5,877
Fort Lupton, 5,159
Greeley, 60,536
Windsor, 5,062

Green Bay, WI
Allouez, 14,431
Ashwaubenon, 16,376
Bellevue Town, 7,541
De Pere, 16,569
Green Bay, 96,466
Howard, 9,874

Greensboro–Winston-Salem–High Point, NC
Archdale, 6,679
Asheboro, 16,362
Burlington, 39,498
Clemmons, 6,020
Graham, 10,426
Greensboro, 183,521
High Point, 68,982
Kernersville, 10,836
Lexington, 16,581
Thomasville, 15,915
Trinity, 5,469
Winston-Salem, 143,485

Greenville, NC
Greenville, 44,972

Greenville–Spartanburg–Anderson, SC
Anderson, 26,184
Berea, 13,535
Clemson, 11,064
Easley, 15,195
Gaffney, 13,145
Gantt, 13,891
Greenville, 58,282
Greer, 10,293
Homeland Park, 6,569
Mauldin, 11,587
Parker, 11,072

Sans Souci, 7,612
Simpsonville, 11,708
Spartanburg, 43,467
Taylors, 19,619
Wade Hampton, 20,014
Welcome, 6,560

Hagerstown, MD
Hagerstown, 35,445
Halfway, 8,873
Long Meadow, 5,594

Halifax, NS
Bedford, 11,618
Dartmouth, 67,798
Halifax, 114,455

Hamilton, ON
Ancaster, 21,988
Burlington, 129,575
Dundas, 21,868
Flamborough, 29,616
Grimsby, 18,520
Hamilton, 318,449
Stoney Creek, 49,968

Hamilton–Middletown, OH
Fairfield, 39,729
Hamilton, 61,368
Middletown, 45,991
Oxford, 18,937
Trenton, 6,189

Harrisburg–Lebanon–Carlisle, PA
Camp Hill, 7,831
Carlisle, 18,419
Derry, 18,408
East Pennsboro, 15,185
Hampden, 20,384
Harrisburg, 52,376
Jackson, 5,732
Lebanon, 24,800
Lower Allen, 15,254
Lower Paxton, 39,162
Lower Swatara, 7,072
Mechanicsburg, 9,452
Middle Paxton, 5,129
Middlesex, 5,780
Middletown, 9,254
Monroe, 5,468
New Cumberland, 7,665
North Lebanon, 9,741
North Londonderry, 5,630
North Middleton, 9,833
Palmyra, 6,910
Silver Spring, 8,369
South Lebanon, 7,491
South Middleton, 10,340
Steelton, 5,152
Susquehanna, 18,636
Swatara, 19,661
Upper Allen, 13,347
West Hanover, 6,125

Hartford, CT
Avon, 14,166
Berlin, 17,131
Bloomfield, 19,405
Bristol, 61,490
Burlington, 7,149
Canton, 8,242
Coventry, 10,360
Cromwell, 12,824
Durham, 5,778
East Haddam, 6,784
East Hampton, 10,882
East Hartford, 51,418

East Windsor, 10,547
Ellington, 11,401
Enfield, 46,858
Farmington, 21,997
Glastonbury, 28,662
Granby, 9,459
Haddam, 6,639
Hartford, 140,619
Harwinton, 5,332
Hebron, 7,339
Lebanon, 6,307
Manchester, 52,572
Mansfield, 21,595
Marlborough, 5,558
Middletown, 44,718
New Britain, 77,217
New Hartford, 6,104
Newington, 29,277
Plainville, 17,393
Plymouth, 12,188
Portland, 8,472
Rocky Hill, 16,921
Simsbury, 21,940
Somers, 9,052
South Windsor, 22,930
Southington, 38,252
Stafford, 11,732
Suffield, 11,726
Tolland, 11,142
Vernon, 30,452
West Hartford, 61,340
Wethersfield, 25,522
Willington, 6,519
Winchester, 11,801
Windham, 22,624
Windsor, 28,506
Windsor Locks, 12,602

Hickory–Morgantown, NC
Conover, 5,465
Hickory, 28,222
Lenoir, 14,192
Morganton, 15,085
Newton, 9,304
St. Stephens, 8,734

Honolulu, HI
Ahuimanu, 8,387
Aiea, 8,906
Aliamanu, 8,835
Ewa Beach, 14,315
Halawa, 13,408
Heeia, 5,010
Hickam Housing, 6,553
Honolulu, 365,272
Kailua, 36,818
Kaneohe, 35,448
Kaneohe Station, 11,662
Laie, 5,577
Maili, 6,059
Makaha, 7,990
Makakilo City, 9,828
Mililani Town, 29,359
Nanakuli, 9,575
Pearl City, 30,993
Schofield Barracks, 19,597
Village Park, 7,407
Wahiawa, 17,386
Waianae, 8,758
Waimalu, 29,967
Waipahu, 31,435
Waipio, 11,812
Waipio Acres, 5,304

Houma, LA
Bayou Cane, 15,876
Cut Off, 5,325
Houma, 30,495

Larose, 5,772
Raceland, 5,564
Thibodaux, 14,035

Houston, TX
Aldine, 11,133
Baytown, 63,826
Bellaire, 13,842
Channelview, 25,564
Cleveland, 7,124
Cloverleaf, 18,230
Conroe, 27,610
Dayton, 5,151
Deer Park, 27,652
First Colony, 18,327
Friendswood, 7,835
Galena Park, 10,033
Highlands, 6,632
Houston, 1,630,524
Humble, 12,060
Jacinto City, 9,343
Katy, 6,453
Kingwood, 37,350
La Porte, 27,910
Liberty, 7,733
Mission Bend, 24,945
Missouri City, 36,219
Pasadena, 119,363
Pecan Grove, 9,502
Richmond, 9,801
Rosenberg, 20,183
Seabrook, 6,685
South Houston, 14,207
Spring, 33,111
Stafford, 8,390
Sugar Land, 24,529
Tomball, 6,370
Town West, 6,166
West University Place, 12,920
The Woodlands, 29,205

Huntington–Ashland, WV–KY–OH
Ashland, KY, 23,622
Flatwoods, KY, 7,799
Huntington, WV, 54,505
Ironton, OH, 12,751
Pea Ridge, WV, 6,535
Westwood, KY, 5,300

Huntsville, AL
Athens, 16,901
Huntsville, 159,450
Madison, 14,862

Indianapolis, IN
Alexandria, 5,709
Anderson, 59,459
Beech Grove, 13,383
Brownsburg, 7,628
Carmel, 25,380
Elwood, 9,490
Fishers, 7,508
Franklin, 12,907
Greenfield, 11,657
Greenwood, 26,265
Indianapolis, 731,327
Lawrence, 26,763
Lebanon, 12,059
Martinsville, 11,677
Mooresville, 5,541
Noblesville, 17,655
Plainfield, 10,433
Shelbyville, 15,336
Speedway, 13,092
Zionsville, 5,281

Iowa City, IA
Coralville, 10,347

Iowa City, 59,738

Jackson, MI

Jackson, 37,446

Jackson, MS

Brandon, 11,077
Canton, 10,062
Clinton, 21,847
Jackson, 195,906
Madison, 7,471
Pearl, 19,588
Ridgeland, 11,714

Jacksonville, FL

Atlantic Beach, 11,636
Bellair–Meadowbrook Terrace, 15,606
Fernandina Beach, 8,765
Fruit Cove, 5,904
Jacksonville, 635,230
Jacksonville Beach, 17,839
Lakeside, 29,137
Middleburg, 6,223
Neptune Beach, 6,816
Orange Park, 9,488
Palm Valley, 9,960
St. Augustine, 11,692
Yulee, 6,915

Jacksonville, NC

Half Moon, 6,306
Jacksonville, 30,013
New River Station, 9,732
Piney Green, 8,999

Jamestown, NY

Busti, 8,050
Dunkirk, 13,989
Ellicott, 9,455
Fredonia, 10,436
Hanover, 7,380
Jamestown, 34,681
Pomfret, 14,224
Westfield, 5,194

Janesville–Beloit, WI

Beloit, 35,573
Janesville, 52,133

Johnson City–Kingsport–Bristol, TN–VA

Abingdon, VA, 7,003
Bloomingdale, TN, 10,953
Bristol, TN, 18,426
Bristol, VA, 23,421
Colonial Heights, TN, 6,716
Elizabethton, TN, 11,931
Erwin, TN, 5,015
Johnson City, TN, 48,341
Kingsport, TN, 36,161

Johnstown, PA

Adams, 6,869
Cambria, 6,357
Conemaugh, 7,737
Jackson, 5,213
Johnstown, 28,134
Richland, 12,777
Somerset, 8,732
Upper Yoder, 5,435
Westmont, 5,789

Joplin, MO

Carthage, 10,747
Joplin, 40,032
Neosho, 9,254
Webb City, 7,449

Kalamazoo–Battle Creek, MI

Albion, 10,066
Battle Creek, 53,540
Eastwood, 6,340
Kalamazoo, 80,277
Marshall, 6,891
Portage, 41,042
South Haven, 5,563
Springfield, 5,582
Westwood, 8,957

Kankakee, IL

Bourbonnais, 13,934
Bradley, 10,792
Kankakee, 27,575

Kansas City, MO–KS

Belton, MO, 18,150
Blue Springs, MO, 40,153
Bonner Springs, KS, 6,410
Excelsior Springs, MO, 10,178
Gladstone, MO, 26,243
Grandview, MO, 24,967
Harrisonville, MO, 7,683
Independence, MO, 112,301
Kansas City, KS, 149,767
Kansas City, MO, 435,146
Lansing, KS, 7,120
Leavenworth, KS, 38,495
Leawood, KS, 19,693
Lee's Summit, MO, 45,985
Lenexa, KS, 34,034
Liberty, MO, 20,459
Merriam, KS, 11,821
Mission, KS, 9,504
Olathe, KS, 63,352
Overland Park, KS, 111,790
Prairie Village, KS, 23,186
Raymore, MO, 5,592
Raytown, MO, 30,601
Richmond, MO, 5,738
Roeland Park, KS, 7,706
Shawnee, KS, 37,993

Kenosha, WI

Kenosha, 80,352
Pleasant Prairie, 11,961

Killeen–Temple, TX

Belton, 12,476
Copperas Cove, 24,079
Gatesville, 11,492
Harker Heights, 12,841
Killeen, 63,535
Temple, 46,109

Kitchener, ON

Cambridge, 92,772
Kitchener, 168,282
Waterloo, 71,181

Knoxville, TN

Alcoa, 6,400
Clinton, 8,972
Eagleton Village, 5,169
Farragut, 12,783
Halls, 6,450
Knoxville, 165,121
Lenoir City, 6,147
Maryville, 19,208
Oak Ridge, 24,743
Powell, 7,534
Sevierville, 7,178
Seymour, 7,104

Kokomo, IN

Kokomo, 44,962

La Crosse, WI–MN

La Crosse, WI, 51,003

Onalaska, WI, 11,284

Lafayette, IN

Frankfort, 14,754
Lafayette, 43,764
West Lafayette, 25,907

Lafayette, LA

Breaux Bridge, 6,515
Carencro, 5,429
Crowley, 13,983
Eunice, 10,930
Lafayette, 94,440
Opelousas, 18,151
Rayne, 8,502
St. Martinville, 7,137

Lake Charles, LA

Lake Charles, 70,580
Moss Bluff, 8,039
Prien, 6,448
Sulphur, 20,125
Westlake, 5,007

Lake County, IL

Antioch, 6,105
Beach Park, 9,513
Buffalo Grove, 21,930
Deerfield, 17,327
Fox Lake, 7,430
Gages Lake, 8,349
Grayslake, 7,388
Gurnee, 13,701
Highland Park, 30,575
Highwood, 5,331
Lake Bluff, 5,513
Lake Forest, 17,836
Lake Zurich, 14,947
Libertyville, 19,174
Lindenhurst, 8,038
Mundelein, 21,215
North Chicago, 34,978
Round Lake Beach, 16,434
Vernon Hills, 15,319
Wauconda, 6,294
Waukegan, 69,392
Winthrop Harbor, 6,240
Zion, 19,775

Lakeland–Winter Haven, FL

Auburndale, 8,858
Bartow, 14,716
Combee Settlement, 5,463
Crystal Lake, 5,300
Cypress Gardens, 9,188
Gibsonia, 5,168
Haines City, 11,683
Inwood, 6,824
Jan Phyl Village, 5,308
Lake Wales, 9,670
Lakeland, 70,576
Lakeland Highlands, 9,972
Winston, 9,118
Winter Haven, 24,725

Lancaster, PA

Brecknock, 5,197
Clay, 5,050
Columbia, 10,701
Earl, 5,515
East Cocalico, 7,809
East Earl, 5,491
East Hempfield, 18,597
East Lampeter, 11,999
Elizabethtown, 9,952
Ephrata, 12,133
Lancaster, 55,551
Lititz, 8,280

Manheim, 28,880
Manor, 14,130
Millersville, 8,099
Mount Joy, 6,398
Penn, 6,760
Providence, 6,071
Rapho, 8,211
Salisbury, 8,527
Upper Leacock, 7,254
Warwick, 11,622
West Cocalico, 5,521
West Donegal, 5,605
West Earl, 6,434
West Hempfield, 12,942
West Lampeter, 9,865

Lansing–East Lansing, MI

Charlotte, 8,083
East Lansing, 50,677
Grand Ledge, 7,579
Haslett, 10,230
Holt, 11,744
Lansing, 127,321
Mason, 6,768
Okemos, 20,216
St. Johns, 7,284
Waverly, 15,614

Laredo, TX

Laredo, 122,899

Las Cruces, NM

Anthony, 5,160
Las Cruces, 62,126
Sunland Park, 8,179

Las Vegas, NV–AZ

Boulder City, AZ, 12,567
Bullhead City, AZ, 21,951
East Las Vegas, NV, 11,087
Enterprise, NV, 6,412
Henderson, NV, 64,942
Kingman, AZ, 12,722
Lake Havasu City, AZ, 24,363
Las Vegas, NV, 258,295
Mohave Valley, AZ, 6,962
New Kingman–Butler, AZ, 11,627
North Las Vegas, NV, 47,707
Pahrump, NV, 7,424
Paradise, NV, 124,682
Spring Valley, NV, 51,726
Sunrise Manor, NV, 95,362
Winchester, NV, 23,365

Lawrence, KS

Lawrence, 65,608

Lawton, OK

Lawton, 80,561

Lewiston–Auburn, ME

Auburn, 25,029
Lewiston, 40,146
Lisbon, 9,346

Lexington, KY

Berea, 9,126
Georgetown, 11,414
Lexington–Fayette, 225,366
Nicholasville, 13,603
Paris, 8,730
Richmond, 21,155
Versailles, 7,269
Winchester, 15,799

Lima, OH

Lima, 45,549
St. Marys, 8,441
Wapakoneta, 9,214

Lincoln, NE
Lincoln, 191,972

Little Rock–North Little Rock, AR
Benton, 18,177
Bryant, 5,269
Cabot, 8,319
Conway, 26,481
Jacksonville, 29,101
Little Rock, 175,795
Maumelle, 6,714
North Little Rock, 61,741
Sherwood, 18,893

London, ON
London, 303,165
St. Thomas, 29,990
Westminster, 6,826

Long Island, NY
Amityville, 9,286
Babylon, 202,889
Bayville, 7,193
Brookhaven, 407,779
Cedarhurst, 5,716
East Hampton, 16,132
East Hills, 6,746
East Rockaway, 10,152
Farmingdale, 8,022
Floral Park, 15,947
Freeport, 39,894
Garden City, 21,686
Glen Cove, 24,149
Great Neck, 8,745
Great Neck Plaza, 5,897
Hempstead, 725,639
Huntington, 191,474
Islip, 299,587
Lake Grove, 9,612
Lawrence, 6,513
Lindenhurst, 26,879
Long Beach, 33,510
Lynbrook, 19,208
Malverne, 9,054
Manorhaven, 5,672
Massapequa Park, 18,044
Mineola, 18,994
New Hyde Park, 9,728
North Hempstead, 211,393
Northport, 7,572
Oyster Bay, 292,657
Patchogue, 11,060
Port Jefferson, 7,455
Riverhead, 23,011
Rockville Centre, 24,727
Sea Cliff, 5,054
Smithtown, 113,406
Southampton, 44,976
Southold, 19,836
Valley Stream, 33,946
Westbury, 13,060
Williston Park, 7,516

Longview–Marshall, TX
Kilgore, 8,258
Longview, 70,311
Marshall, 23,682
White Oak, 5,136

Los Angeles–Long Beach, CA
Agoura Hills, 20,390
Alhambra, 82,106
Alondra Park, 12,215
Altadena, 42,658
Arcadia, 48,290
Artesia, 15,464

Avocado Heights, 14,232
Azusa, 41,333
Baldwin Park, 69,330
Bell, 34,365
Bell Gardens, 42,355
Bellflower, 61,815
Beverly Hills, 31,971
Burbank, 93,643
Carson, 83,995
Cerritos, 53,240
Charter Oak, 8,858
Citrus, 9,481
Claremont, 32,503
Commerce, 12,135
Compton, 90,454
Covina, 43,207
Cudahy, 22,817
Culver City, 38,793
Del Aire, 8,040
Diamond Bar, 53,672
Downey, 91,444
Duarte, 20,688
East Compton, 7,967
East La Mirada, 9,367
East Los Angeles, 126,379
East Pasadena, 5,910
East San Gabriel, 12,736
El Monte, 106,209
El Segundo, 15,223
Florence–Graham, 57,147
Gardena, 49,847
Glendale, 180,038
Glendora, 47,828
Hacienda Heights, 52,354
Hawaiian Gardens, 13,639
Hawthorne, 71,349
Hermosa Beach, 18,219
Huntington Park, 56,065
Inglewood, 109,602
La Canada Flintridge, 19,378
La Crescenta–Montrose, 16,968
La Habra Heights, 6,226
La Mirada, 40,452
La Puente, 36,955
La Verne, 30,897
Ladera Heights, 6,316
Lake Los Angeles, 7,977
Lakewood, 73,557
Lancaster, 97,291
Lawndale, 27,331
Lennox, 22,757
Lomita, 19,382
Long Beach, 429,433
Los Angeles, 3,485,398
Lynwood, 61,945
Manhattan Beach, 32,063
Marina del Rey, 7,431
Maywood, 27,850
Monrovia, 35,761
Montebello, 59,564
Monterey Park, 60,738
Norwalk, 94,279
Palmdale, 68,842
Palos Verdes Estates, 13,512
Paramount, 47,669
Pasadena, 131,591
Pico Rivera, 59,177
Pomona, 131,723
Quartz Hill, 9,626
Rancho Palos Verdes, 41,659
Redondo Beach, 60,167
Rolling Hills Estates, 7,789
Rosemead, 51,638
Rowland Heights, 42,647
San Dimas, 32,397
San Fernando, 22,580
San Gabriel, 37,120

San Marino, 12,959
Santa Clarita, 110,642
Santa Fe Springs, 15,520
Santa Monica, 86,905
Sierra Madre, 10,762
Signal Hill, 8,371
South El Monte, 20,850
South Gate, 86,284
South Pasadena, 23,936
South San Gabriel, 7,700
South San Jose Hills, 17,814
South Whittier, 49,514
Temple City, 31,100
Torrance, 133,107
Valinda, 18,735
View Park–Windsor Hills, 11,769
Vincent, 13,713
Walnut, 29,105
Walnut Park, 14,722
West Athens, 8,859
West Carson, 20,143
West Compton, 5,451
West Covina, 96,086
West Hollywood, 36,118
West Puente Valley, 20,254
West Whittier–Los Nietos, 24,164
Westlake Village, 7,455
Westmont, 31,044
Whittier, 77,671
Willowbrook, 32,772

Louisville, KY–IN
Buechel, KY, 7,081
Charlestown, IN, 5,889
Clarksville, IN, 19,833
Douglass Hills, KY, 5,549
Fairdale, KY, 6,563
Fern Creek, KY, 16,406
Highview, KY, 14,814
Hillview, KY, 6,119
Jeffersontown, KY, 23,221
Jeffersonville, IN, 21,841
Louisville, KY, 269,063
Lyndon, KY, 8,037
Middletown, KY, 5,016
Mount Washington, KY, 5,226
New Albany, IN, 36,322
Newburg, KY, 21,647
Oak Park, IN, 5,630
Okolona, KY, 18,902
Pleasure Ridge Park, KY, 25,131
St. Dennis, KY, 10,326
St. Matthews, KY, 15,800
Scottsburg, IN, 5,334
Sellersburg, IN, 5,745
Shively, KY, 15,535
Valley Station, KY, 22,840

Lubbock, TX
Lubbock, 186,206
Slaton, 6,078

Lynchburg, VA
Bedford, 6,073
Forest, 5,624
Lynchburg, 66,049
Madison Heights, 11,700
Timberlake, 10,314

Macon, GA
Fort Valley, 8,198
Macon, 106,210
Perry, 9,448
Warner Robins, 43,726

Madison, WI
Fitchburg, 15,648
Madison, 191,262

McFarland, 5,232
Middleton, 13,289
Monona, 8,637
Stoughton, 8,786
Sun Prairie, 15,333
Verona, 5,374
Waunakee, 5,897

Manchester–Nashua, NH
Amherst, 9,068
Bedford, 12,563
Goffstown, 14,621
Hollis, 5,705
Hudson, 19,530
Litchfield, 5,516
Manchester, 99,567
Merrimack, 22,156
Milford, 11,795
Nashua, 79,662
Pelham, 9,408
Peterborough, 5,239
Weare, 6,193

Mansfield, OH
Bucyrus, 13,496
Galion, 11,859
Mansfield, 50,627
Shelby, 9,564

McAllen–Edinburg–Mission, TX
Alamo, 8,210
Donna, 12,652
Edinburg, 29,885
Elsa, 5,242
McAllen, 84,021
Mercedes, 12,694
Mission, 28,653
Pharr, 32,921
San Juan, 10,815
Weslaco, 21,877

Medford–Ashland, OR
Ashland, 16,234
Central Point, 7,509
Medford, 46,951
White City, 5,891

Melbourne–Titusville–Palm Bay, FL
Cape Canaveral, 8,014
Cocoa, 17,722
Cocoa Beach, 12,123
Cocoa West, 6,160
Indian Harbour Beach, 6,933
Melbourne, 59,646
Merritt Island, 32,886
Micco, 8,757
Mims, 9,412
Palm Bay, 62,632
Port St. John, 8,933
Rockledge, 16,023
Satellite Beach, 9,889
South Patrick Shores, 10,249
Titusville, 39,394
West Melbourne, 8,399

Memphis, TN–AR–MS
Bartlett, TN, 26,989
Collierville, TN, 14,427
Covington, TN, 7,487
Germantown, TN, 32,893
Horn Lake, MS, 9,069
Memphis, TN, 610,337
Millington, TN, 17,866
Southaven, MS, 17,949
West Memphis, AR, 28,259

Merced, CA
Atwater, 22,282
Livingston, 7,317
Los Banos, 14,519
Merced, 56,216
Winton, 7,559

Miami, FL
Andover, 6,251
Aventura, 14,914
Brownsville, 15,607
Carol City, 53,331
Coral Gables, 40,091
Coral Terrace, 23,255
Cutler, 16,201
Cutler Ridge, 21,268
Florida City, 5,806
Gladeview, 15,637
Glenvar Heights, 14,823
Golden Glades, 25,474
Goulds, 7,284
Hammocks, 10,897
Hialeah, 188,004
Hialeah Gardens, 7,713
Homestead, 26,866
Ives Estates, 13,531
Kendale Lakes, 48,524
Kendall, 87,271
Kendall Lakes West, 6,038
Key Biscayne, 8,854
Lake Lucerne, 9,478
Lakes by the Bay, 5,615
Leisure City, 19,379
Lindgren Acres, 22,290
Miami, 358,548
Miami Beach, 92,639
Miami Lakes, 12,750
Miami Shores, 10,084
Miami Springs, 13,268
Naranja, 5,790
Norland, 22,109
North Bay Village, 5,383
North Miami, 49,998
North Miami Beach, 35,359
Ojus, 15,519
Olympia Heights, 37,792
Opa-locka, 15,283
Opa-locka North, 6,568
Palm Springs North, 5,300
Palmetto Estates, 12,293
Perrine, 15,576
Pinewood, 15,518
Princeton, 7,073
Richmond Heights, 8,583
Scott Lake, 14,588
South Miami, 10,404
South Miami Heights, 30,030
Sunny Isles, 11,772
Sunset, 15,810
Sweetwater, 13,909
Tamiami, 33,845
West Little River, 33,575
West Miami, 5,727
Westchester, 29,883
Westview, 9,668
Westwood Lakes, 11,522

Milwaukee-Waukesha, WI
Brookfield, 35,184
Brown Deer, 12,236
Cedarburg, 9,895
Cudahy, 18,659
Delafield, 5,347
Elm Grove, 6,261
Fox Point, 7,238
Franklin, 21,855
Germantown, 13,658

Glendale, 14,088
Grafton, 9,340
Greendale, 15,128
Greenfield, 33,403
Hales Corners, 7,623
Hartford, 8,179
Hartland, 6,906
Menomonee Falls, 26,840
Mequon, 18,885
Milwaukee, 628,088
Muskego, 16,813
New Berlin, 33,592
Oak Creek, 19,513
Oconomowoc, 10,993
Port Washington, 9,338
St. Francis, 9,245
Shorewood, 14,116
South Milwaukee, 20,958
Sussex, 5,039
Waukesha, 56,958
Wauwatosa, 49,366
West Allis, 63,221
West Bend, 23,916
Whitefish Bay, 14,272

Minneapolis-St. Paul, MN-WI
Andover, MN, 15,216
Anoka, MN, 17,192
Apple Valley, MN, 34,598
Arden Hills, MN, 9,199
Blaine, MN, 38,975
Bloomington, MN, 86,335
Brooklyn Center, MN, 28,887
Brooklyn Park, MN, 56,381
Buffalo, MN, 6,856
Burnsville, MN, 51,288
Cambridge, MN, 5,094
Champlin, MN, 16,849
Chanhassen, MN, 11,732
Chaska, MN, 11,339
Columbia Heights, MN, 18,910
Coon Rapids, MN, 52,978
Corcoran, MN, 5,199
Cottage Grove, MN, 22,935
Crystal, MN, 23,788
Eagan, MN, 47,409
East Bethel, MN, 8,050
Eden Prairie, MN, 39,311
Edina, MN, 46,070
Elk River, MN, 11,143
Falcon Heights, MN, 5,380
Farmington, MN, 5,940
Forest Lake, MN, 5,833
Fridley, MN, 28,335
Golden Valley, MN, 20,971
Ham Lake, MN, 8,924
Hastings, MN, 15,440
Hopkins, MN, 16,534
Hudson, WI, 6,378
Inver Grove Heights, MN, 22,477
Lake Elmo, MN, 5,903
Lakeville, MN, 24,854
Lino Lakes, MN, 8,807
Little Canada, MN, 8,971
Mahtomedi, MN, 5,569
Maple Grove, MN, 38,736
Maplewood, MN, 30,954
Mendota Heights, MN, 9,431
Minneapolis, MN, 368,383
Minnetonka, MN, 48,370
Mound, MN, 9,634
Mounds View, MN, 12,541
New Brighton, MN, 22,207
New Hope, MN, 21,853
New Richmond, WI, 5,106
North St. Paul, MN, 12,376

Oakdale, MN, 18,374
Orono, MN, 7,285
Plymouth, MN, 50,889
Prior Lake, MN, 11,482
Ramsey, MN, 12,408
Richfield, MN, 35,710
River Falls, WI, 10,610
Robbinsdale, MN, 14,396
Rosemount, MN, 8,622
Roseville, MN, 33,485
St. Anthony, MN, 7,727
St. Cloud, MN, 5,246
St. Louis Park, MN, 43,787
St. Paul, MN, 272,235
Savage, MN, 9,906
Shakopee, MN, 11,739
Shoreview, MN, 24,587
Shorewood, MN, 5,917
South St. Paul, MN, 20,197
Spring Lake Park, MN, 6,429
Stillwater, MN, 13,882
Vadnais Heights, MN, 11,041
West St. Paul, MN, 19,248
White Bear Lake, MN, 24,288
Woodbury, MN, 20,075

Mobile, AL
Bay Minette, 7,168
Chickasaw, 6,649
Daphne, 11,290
Fairhope, 8,485
Mobile, 196,278
Prichard, 34,311
Saraland, 11,751
Satsuma, 5,194
Theodore, 6,509
Tillmans Corner, 17,988

Modesto, CA
Ceres, 26,314
Modesto, 164,730
Oakdale, 11,961
Patterson, 8,626
Riverbank, 8,547
Turlock, 42,198

Monmouth-Ocean, NJ
Aberdeen, 17,038
Asbury Park, 16,799
Barnegat, 12,235
Beachwood, 9,324
Belmar, 5,877
Berkeley, 37,319
Brick, 66,473
Colts Neck, 8,559
Dover, 76,371
Eatontown, 13,800
Fair Haven, 5,270
Freehold, 24,710
Hazlet, 21,976
Holmdel, 11,532
Howell, 38,987
Jackson, 33,233
Keansburg, 11,069
Keyport, 7,586
Lacey, 22,141
Lakewood, 45,048
Little Egg Harbor, 13,333
Little Silver, 5,721
Long Branch, 28,658
Manalapan, 26,716
Manasquan, 5,369
Manchester, 35,976
Marlboro, 27,974
Matawan, 9,270
Middletown, 68,183
Millstone, 5,069
Neptune, 28,148

Ocean, 25,058
Oceanport, 6,146
Plumsted, 6,005
Point Pleasant, 18,177
Point Pleasant Beach, 5,112
Red Bank, 10,636
Rumson, 6,701
Spring Lake Heights, 5,341
Stafford, 13,325
Tinton Falls, 12,361
Union Beach, 6,156
Wall, 20,244
West Long Branch, 7,690

Monroe, LA
Brownsville-Bawcomville, 7,397
Claiborne, 8,300
Monroe, 54,909
West Monroe, 14,096

Montgomery, AL
Millbrook, 6,050
Montgomery, 187,106
Prattville, 18,878

Montreal, PQ
Anjou, 37,210
Beaconsfield, 19,616
Beauharnois, 6,449
Beloeil, 18,516
Blainville, 22,679
Bois-des-Filion, 6,337
Boisbriand, 21,124
Bouchervillo, 33,796
Brossard, 64,793
Candiac, 11,064
Carignan, 5,386
Chambly, 15,893
Charlemagne, 5,598
Chateauguay, 39,833
Cote-Saint-Luc, 28,700
Delson, 6,063
Deux-Montagnes, 13,035
Dollard-des-Ormeaux, 46,922
Dorion, 5,920
Dorval, 17,249
Greenfield Park, 17,652
Hampstead, 8,645
Kirkland, 17,495
La Prairie, 14,938
Lachenaie, 15,074
Lachine, 35,266
LaSalle, 73,804
Laval, 314,398
Le Gardeur, 13,814
LeMoyne, 5,412
L'Ile-Perrot, 8,064
Longueuil, 129,874
Lorraine, 8,410
Mascouche, 25,828
Mercier, 8,227
Mirabel, 17,971
Mont-Royal, 18,212
Mont-Saint-Hilaire, 12,341
Montreal, 1,017,666
Montreal-Nord, 85,516
Montreal-Ouest, 5,180
Otterburn Park, 6,046
Outremont, 22,935
Pierrefonds, 48,735
Pincourt, 9,639
Pointe-Claire, 27,647
Repentigny, 49,630
Rosemère, 11,198
Roxboro, 5,879
Saint-Basile-le-Grand, 10,127
Saint-Bruno-de-Montarville, 23,849

Saint-Constant, 18,423
Saint-Eustache, 37,278
Saint-Hubert, 74,027
Saint-Laurent, 72,402
Saint-Léonard, 73,120
Sainte-Anne-des-Plaines, 10,787
Sainte-Catherine, 9,805
Sainte-Julie, 20,632
Sainte-Marthe-sur-le-Lac, 7,410
Sainte-Thérèse, 24,158
Terrebonne, 39,678
Varennes, 14,758
Vaudreuil, 11,187
Verdun, 61,307
Westmount, 20,239

Muncie, IN

Muncie, 71,035

Myrtle Beach, SC

Conway, 9,819
Garden City, 6,305
Myrtle Beach, 24,848
North Myrtle Beach, 8,636
Red Hill, 6,112
Socastee, 10,426

Naples, FL

East Naples, 22,951
Golden Gate, 14,148
Immokalee, 14,120
Marco, 9,493
Naples, 19,505
Naples Park, 8,002
North Naples, 13,422

Nashville, TN

Brentwood, 16,392
Dickson, 8,791
Franklin, 20,098
Gallatin, 18,794
Goodlettsville, 11,219
Green Hill, 6,763
Hendersonville, 32,188
La Vergne, 7,499
Lebanon, 15,208
Mount Juliet, 5,389
Murfreesboro, 44,922
Nashville-Davidson, 488,374
Portland, 5,165
Smyrna, 13,647
Springfield, 11,227

New Bedford-Fall River-Attleboro, MA

Acushnet, 9,554
Attleboro, 38,383
Dartmouth, 27,244
Dighton, 5,631
Easton, 19,807
Fairhaven, 16,132
Fall River, 92,703
Freetown, 8,522
Mansfield, 16,568
New Bedford, 99,922
North Attleboro, 25,038
Norton, 14,265
Raynham, 9,867
Rehoboth, 8,656
Seekonk, 13,046
Somerset, 17,655
Swansea, 15,411
Taunton, 49,832
Westport, 13,852

New Haven-Meriden, CT

Branford, 28,780
Cheshire, 26,461

Clinton, 12,781
East Haven, 26,561
Guilford, 20,192
Hamden, 52,806
Madison, 15,383
Meriden, 60,059
New Haven, 133,986
North Branford, 13,199
North Haven, 22,241
Orange, 12,730
Wallingford, 41,628
West Haven, 54,392
Woodbridge, 7,896

New London-Norwich, CT-RI

East Lyme, 15,810
Griswold, 10,761
Groton, 9,646
Ledyard, 15,110
Montville, 16,500
New London, 28,510
Norwich, 37,082
Old Lyme, 6,383
Old Saybrook, 9,353
Plainfield, 14,740
Preston, 5,029
Waterford, 18,005

New Orleans, LA

Arabi, 8,787
Avondale, 5,813
Belle Chasse, 8,512
Bridge City, 8,327
Chalmette, 31,860
Covington, 7,691
Destrehan, 8,031
Estelle, 14,091
Gretna, 17,208
Harahan, 9,927
Harvey, 21,222
Jefferson, 14,521
Kenner, 72,033
Lacombe, 6,523
Laplace, 24,194
Mandeville, 7,083
Marrero, 36,671
Meraux, 8,849
Metairie, 149,428
New Orleans, 496,938
Reserve, 8,847
River Ridge, 14,800
St. Rose, 6,259
Slidell, 24,124
Terrytown, 23,787
Timberlane, 12,614
Violet, 8,574
Waggaman, 9,405
Westwego, 11,218

New York, NY

Bedford, 16,906
Briarcliff Manor, 7,070
Bronxville, 6,028
Carmel, 28,816
Chestnut Ridge, 7,517
Clarkstown, 79,346
Cortlandt, 37,357
Croton-on-Hudson, 7,018
Dobbs Ferry, 9,940
Eastchester, 30,867
Greenburgh, 83,816
Harrison, 23,308
Hastings-on-Hudson, 8,000
Haverstraw, 32,712
Irvington, 6,348
Kent, 13,183
Larchmont, 6,181

Lewisboro, 11,313
Mamaroneck, 27,706
Mount Kisco, 9,108
Mount Pleasant, 40,590
Mount Vernon, 67,153
New Castle, 16,648
New Rochelle, 67,265
New York, 7,322,564
North Castle, 10,061
North Tarrytown, 8,152
Nyack, 6,558
Orangetown, 46,742
Ossining, 34,124
Patterson, 8,679
Peekskill, 19,536
Pelham, 11,903
Pelham Manor, 5,443
Philipstown, 9,242
Pleasantville, 6,592
Port Chester, 24,728
Putnam Valley, 9,094
Ramapo, 93,861
Rye, 39,524
Rye Brook, 7,765
Scarsdale, 16,987
Somers, 16,216
Southeast, 14,927
Spring Valley, 21,802
Stony Point, 12,814
Suffern, 11,055
Tarrytown, 10,739
Tuckahoe, 6,302
West Haverstraw, 9,183
White Plains, 48,718
Yonkers, 188,082
Yorktown, 33,467

Newark-Jersey City, NJ

Bayonne, 61,444
Belleville, 34,213
Berkeley Heights, 11,980
Bloomfield, 45,061
Boonton, 8,343
Butler, 7,392
Caldwell Borough, 7,549
Cedar Grove, 12,053
Chatham, 9,361
Chester, 5,958
City of Orange, 29,925
Clark, 14,629
Cranford, 22,633
Denville, 13,812
Dover, 15,115
East Hanover, 9,926
East Orange, 73,552
Elizabeth, 110,002
Fairfield, 7,615
Fanwood, 7,115
Florham Park, 8,521
Glen Ridge Borough, 7,076
Guttenberg, 8,268
Hanover, 11,538
Harrison, 13,425
Hillside, 21,044
Hoboken, 33,397
Irvington, 61,018
Jefferson, 17,825
Jersey City, 228,537
Kearny, 34,874
Kenilworth, 7,574
Kinnelon, 8,470
Lincoln Park, 10,978
Linden, 36,701
Livingston, 26,609
Madison, 15,850
Maplewood, 21,652
Millburn, 18,630
Montclair, 37,729

Montville, 15,600
Morris, 19,952
Morris Plains, 5,219
Morristown, 16,189
Mount Olive, 21,282
Mountainside, 6,657
New Providence, 11,439
Newark, 275,221
North Bergen, 48,414
North Caldwell, 6,706
Nutley, 27,099
Parsippany-Troy Hills, 48,478
Passaic, 7,826
Pequannock, 12,844
Plainfield, 46,567
Rahway, 25,325
Randolph, 19,974
Rockaway, 19,572
Roselle, 20,314
Roselle Park, 12,805
Roxbury, 20,429
Scotch Plains, 21,160
Secaucus, 14,061
South Orange Village, 16,390
Springfield, 13,420
Summit, 19,757
Union, 50,024
Union City, 58,012
Verona, 13,597
Washington, 15,592
Weehawken, 12,385
West Caldwell, 10,422
Westfield, 28,870
West New York, 38,125
West Orange, 39,103
Wharton, 5,405

Norfolk-Virginia Beach-Newport News, VA-NC

Chesapeake, VA, 151,976
Gloucester Point, VA, 8,509
Hampton, VA, 133,793
Newport News, VA, 170,045
Norfolk, VA, 261,229
Poquoson, VA, 11,005
Portsmouth, VA, 103,907
Suffolk, VA, 52,141
Virginia Beach, VA, 393,069
Williamsburg, VA, 11,530

Northern New Jersey, NJ

Allendale, 5,900
Andover, 5,438
Bergenfield, 24,458
Bloomingdale, 7,530
Bogota, 7,824
Byram, 8,048
Carlstadt, 5,510
Cliffside Park, 20,393
Clifton, 71,742
Closter, 8,094
Cresskill, 7,558
Dumont, 17,187
East Rutherford, 7,902
Edgewater, 5,001
Elmwood Park, 17,623
Emerson, 6,930
Englewood, 24,850
Englewood Cliffs, 5,634
Fair Lawn, 30,548
Fairview, 10,733
Frankford, 5,114
Franklin Lakes, 9,873
Garfield, 26,727
Glen Rock, 10,883
Hackensack, 37,049
Haledon, 6,951
Hardyston, 5,275

Hasbrouck Heights, 11,488
Hawthorne, 17,084
Hillsdale, 9,750
Hopatcong, 15,586
Leonia, 8,365
Little Falls, 11,294
Little Ferry, 9,989
Lodi, 22,355
Lyndhurst, 18,262
Mahwah, 17,905
Maywood, 9,473
Midland Park, 7,047
Montvale, 6,946
New Milford, 15,990
Newton, 7,521
North Arlington, 13,790
North Haledon, 7,987
Oakland, 11,997
Oradell, 8,024
Palisades Park, 14,536
Paramus, 25,067
Park Ridge, 8,102
Passaic, 58,041
Paterson, 140,891
Pompton Lakes, 10,539
Prospect Park, 5,053
Ramsey, 13,228
Ridgefield, 9,996
Ridgefield Park, 12,454
Ridgewood, 24,152
Ringwood, 12,623
River Edge, 10,603
River Vale, 9,410
Rochelle Park, 5,587
Rutherford, 17,790
Saddle Brook, 13,296
Sparta, 15,157
Teaneck, 37,825
Tenafly, 13,326
Totowa, 10,177
Upper Saddle River, 7,198
Vernon, 21,211
Waldwick, 9,757
Wallington, 10,828
Wanaque, 9,711
Wantage, 9,487
Washington, 9,245
Wayne, 47,025
West Milford, 25,430
West Paterson, 10,982
Westwood, 10,446
Wood-Ridge, 7,506
Woodcliff Lake, 5,303
Wyckoff, 15,372

Oakland, CA

Alameda, 76,459
Alamo, 12,277
Albany, 16,327
Antioch, 62,195
Ashland, 16,590
Berkeley, 102,724
Blackhawk, 6,199
Brentwood, 7,563
Castro Valley, 48,619
Cherryland, 11,088
Clayton, 7,317
Concord, 111,348
Danville, 31,306
Discovery Bay, 5,351
Dublin, 23,229
El Cerrito, 22,869
El Sobrante, 9,852
Emeryville, 5,740
Fairview, 9,045
Fremont, 173,339
Hayward, 111,498
Hercules, 16,829

Lafayette, 23,501
Livermore, 56,741
Martinez, 31,808
Moraga Town, 15,852
Newark, 37,861
Oakland, 372,242
Oakley, 18,374
Orinda, 16,642
Piedmont, 10,602
Pinole, 17,460
Pittsburg, 47,564
Pleasant Hill, 31,585
Pleasanton, 50,553
Richmond, 87,425
Rodeo, 7,589
San Leandro, 68,223
San Lorenzo, 19,987
San Pablo, 25,158
San Ramon, 35,303
Union City, 53,762
Walnut Creek, 60,569
West Pittsburg, 17,453

Ocala, FL

Ocala, 42,045
Silver Springs Shores, 6,421

Odessa-Midland, TX

Midland, 89,443
Odessa, 89,504
West Odessa, 16,568

Oklahoma City, OK

Bethany, 20,075
Choctaw, 8,545
Del City, 23,928
Edmond, 52,315
El Reno, 15,414
Guthrie, 10,518
Midwest City, 52,267
Moore, 40,318
Mustang, 10,434
Norman, 80,071
Oklahoma City, 444,610
Shawnee, 26,017
Tecumseh, 5,750
The Village, 10,353
Warr Acres, 9,288
Yukon, 20,935

Olympia, WA

Lacey, 19,279
Olympia, 33,840
Tanglewilde-Thompson Place, 6,061
Tumwater, 9,976

Omaha, NE-IA

Bellevue, NE, 30,982
Blair, NE, 6,860
Chalco, NE, 7,337
Council Bluffs, IA, 54,315
La Vista, NE, 9,840
Omaha, NE, 335,795
Papillion, NE, 10,372
Plattsmouth, NE, 6,412
Ralston, NE, 6,236

Orange County, CA

Aliso Viejo, 7,612
Anaheim, 266,406
Brea, 32,873
Buena Park, 68,784
Costa Mesa, 96,357
Cypress, 42,655
Dana Point, 31,896
El Toro, 62,685
El Toro Station, 6,869
Fountain Valley, 53,691

Fullerton, 114,144
Garden Grove, 143,050
Huntington Beach, 181,519
Irvine, 110,330
La Habra, 51,266
La Palma, 15,392
Laguna Beach, 23,170
Laguna Hills, 46,731
Laguna Niguel, 44,400
Los Alamitos, 11,676
Mission Viejo, 72,820
Newport Beach, 66,643
Orange, 110,658
Placentia, 41,259
Rancho Santa Margarita, 11,390
Rossmoor, 9,893
San Clemente, 41,100
San Juan Capistrano, 26,183
Santa Ana, 293,742
Seal Beach, 25,098
Stanton, 30,491
Tustin, 50,689
Tustin Foothills, 24,358
Villa Park, 6,299
Westminster, 78,118
Yorba Linda, 52,422

Orange County, NY

Blooming Grove, 16,673
Chester, 9,138
Cornwall, 11,270
Crawford, 6,394
Deerpark, 7,832
Goshen, 11,500
Highlands, 13,667
Kiryas Joel, 7,437
Middletown, 24,160
Monroe, 23,035
Montgomery, 18,501
Mount Hope, 5,971
New Windsor, 22,937
Newburgh, 26,454
Port Jervis, 9,060
Walden, 5,836
Wallkill, 23,016
Warwick, 27,193
Wawayanda, 5,518
Woodbury, 8,236

Orlando, FL

Altamonte Springs, 34,879
Apopka, 13,512
Azalea Park, 8,926
Bay Hill, 5,346
Belle Isle, 5,272
Buena Ventura Lakes, 14,148
Casselberry, 18,911
Clermont, 6,910
Conway, 13,159
Doctor Phillips, 7,963
Eustis, 12,967
Fairview Shores, 13,192
Fern Park, 8,294
Forest City, 10,638
Goldenrod, 12,362
Kissimmee, 30,050
Lady Lake, 8,071
Lake Mary, 5,929
Leesburg, 14,903
Lockhart, 11,636
Longwood, 13,316
Maitland, 9,110
Mount Dora, 7,196
Oak Ridge, 15,388
Ocoee, 12,778
Orlando, 164,693
Orlovista, 5,990
Oviedo, 11,114

Pine Castle, 8,276
Pine Hills, 35,322
St. Cloud, 12,453
Sanford, 32,387
Sky Lake, 6,202
South Apopka, 6,360
Tavares, 7,383
Union Park, 6,890
Wekiva Springs, 23,026
Winter Garden, 9,745
Winter Park, 22,242
Winter Springs, 22,151

Oshawa, ON

Newcastle, 49,479
Oshawa, 129,344
Whitby, 61,281

Ottawa-Hull, ON-PQ

Aylmer, PQ, 32,244
Buckingham, PQ, 10,548
Gatineau, PQ, 92,284
Gloucester, ON, 101,677
Hull, PQ, 60,707
Kanata, ON, 37,344
Masson, PQ, 5,753
Nepean, ON, 107,627
Ottawa, ON, 313,987
Rockland, ON, 6,771
Vanier, PQ, 18,150

Owensboro, KY

Owensboro, 53,549

Panama City, FL

Callaway, 12,253
Lynn Haven, 9,298
Panama City, 34,378
Springfield, 8,715
Upper Grand Lagoon, 7,855

Parkersburg-Marietta, WV-OH

Belpre, OH, 6,796
Marietta, OH, 15,026
Parkersburg, WV, 33,862
Vienna, WV, 10,862

Pensacola, FL

Bellview, 19,386
Brent, 21,624
Ensley, 16,362
Ferry Pass, 26,301
Gonzalez, 7,669
Gulf Breeze, 5,530
Milton, 7,216
Myrtle Grove, 17,402
Pace, 6,277
Pensacola, 58,165
Warrington, 16,040
West Pensacola, 22,107

Peoria-Pekin, IL

Bartonville, 5,643
Chillicothe, 5,959
Creve Coeur, 5,938
East Peoria, 21,378
Morton, 13,799
Pekin, 32,254
Peoria, 113,504
Peoria Heights, 6,887
Washington, 10,099
West Peoria, 5,314

Philadelphia, PA-NJ

Abington, PA, 56,322
Ambler, PA, 6,609
Aston, PA, 15,080
Audubon, NJ, 9,205

Barrington, NJ, 6,774
Bellmawr, NJ, 12,603
Bensalem, PA, 56,788
Berlin, NJ, 5,672
Bordentown, NJ, 7,683
Bristol, PA, 10,405
Brookhaven, PA, 8,567
Buckingham, PA, 9,364
Burlington, NJ, 12,454
Caln, PA, 11,997
Camden, NJ, 87,492
Carneys Point, NJ, 8,443
Cheltenham, PA, 34,923
Cherry Hill, NJ, 69,348
Chester, PA, 41,856
Chesterfield, NJ, 5,152
Cinnaminson, NJ, 14,583
Clayton, NJ, 6,155
Clementon, NJ, 5,601
Clifton Heights, PA, 7,111
Coatesville, PA, 11,038
Collingdale, PA, 9,175
Collingswood, NJ, 15,289
Concord, PA, 6,933
Conshohocken, PA, 8,064
Darby, PA, 11,140
Delran, NJ, 13,178
Deptford, NJ, 24,137
Douglass, PA, 7,048
Downingtown, PA, 7,749
Doylestown, PA, 8,575
East Bradford, PA, 6,440
East Brandywine, PA, 5,179
East Goshen, PA, 15,138
East Greenwich, NJ, 5,258
East Norriton, PA, 13,324
East Pikeland, PA, 5,825
East Whiteland, PA, 8,398
Easttown, PA, 9,570
Edgewater Park, NJ, 8,388
Evesham, NJ, 35,309
Falls, PA, 34,997
Florence, NJ, 10,266
Folcroft, PA, 7,506
Franconia, PA, 7,224
Franklin, NJ, 14,482
Glassboro, NJ, 15,614
Glenolden, PA, 7,260
Gloucester, NJ, 53,797
Gloucester City, NJ, 12,649
Greenwich, NJ, 5,102
Haddon, NJ, 14,837
Haddon Heights, NJ, 7,860
Haddonfield, NJ, 11,628
Hatboro, PA, 7,382
Hatfield, PA, 15,357
Haverford, PA, 49,848
Hilltown, PA, 10,582
Honey Brook, PA, 5,449
Horsham, PA, 21,896
Kennett Square, PA, 5,218
Lansdale, PA, 16,362
Lansdowne, PA, 11,712
Limerick, PA, 6,691
Lindenwold, NJ, 18,734
Logan, NJ, 5,147
Lower Gwynedd, PA, 9,958
Lower Makefield, PA, 25,083
Lower Merion, PA, 58,003
Lower Moreland, PA, 11,768
Lower Pottsgrove, PA, 8,808
Lower Providence, PA, 19,351
Lower Salford, PA, 10,735
Lower Southampton, PA, 19,860
Lumberton, NJ, 6,705
Mantua, NJ, 10,074
Maple Shade, NJ, 19,211
Marple, PA, 23,123

Medford, NJ, 20,526
Media, PA, 5,957
Middletown, PA, 14,130
Milford, PA, 7,360
Monroe, NJ, 26,703
Montgomery, PA, 12,179
Moorestown, NJ, 16,116
Morrisville, PA, 9,765
Mount Holly, NJ, 10,639
Mount Laurel, NJ, 30,270
Nether Providence, PA, 13,229
New Britain, PA, 9,099
New Garden, PA, 5,430
New Hanover, NJ, 5,956
New Hanover, PA, 9,546
Newtown, PA, 11,366
Norristown, PA, 30,749
North Coventry, PA, 7,506
North Hanover, NJ, 9,994
Northampton, PA, 35,406
Norwood, PA, 6,162
Palmyra, NJ, 7,056
Paulsboro, NJ, 6,577
Pemberton, NJ, 31,342
Penns Grove, NJ, 5,228
Pennsauken, NJ, 34,738
Pennsville, NJ, 13,794
Perkasie, PA, 7,878
Philadelphia, PA, 1,585,577
Phoenixville, PA, 15,066
Pine Hill, NJ, 9,854
Pitman, NJ, 9,365
Pittsgrove, NJ, 8,121
Plumstead, PA, 6,289
Plymouth, PA, 15,958
Pottstown, PA, 21,831
Prospect Park, PA, 6,764
Quakertown, PA, 8,982
Radnor, PA, 28,703
Richland, PA, 8,560
Ridley, PA, 31,169
Ridley Park, PA, 7,592
Riverside, NJ, 7,974
Runnemede, NJ, 9,042
Salem, NJ, 6,883
Schuylkill, PA, 5,538
Shamong, NJ, 5,765
Sharon Hill, PA, 5,771
Skippack, PA, 8,790
Solebury, PA, 5,998
Somerdale, NJ, 5,440
Souderton, PA, 5,957
Southampton, NJ, 10,202
Springfield, PA, 5,177
Stratford, NJ, 7,614
Swarthmore, PA, 6,157
Tabernacle, NJ, 7,360
Thornbury, PA, 5,056
Towamencin, PA, 14,167
Tredyffrin, PA, 28,028
Upper Chichester, PA, 15,004
Upper Darby, PA, 81,177
Upper Dublin, PA, 24,028
Upper Gwynedd, PA, 12,197
Upper Makefield, PA, 5,949
Upper Merion, PA, 25,722
Upper Moreland, PA, 25,313
Upper Providence, PA, 9,682
Upper Southampton, PA, 16,076
Uwchlan, PA, 12,999
Voorhees, NJ, 24,559
Warminster, PA, 32,832
Warrington, PA, 12,169
Warwick, PA, 5,915
Washington, NJ, 41,960
Waterford, NJ, 10,940
West Bradford, PA, 10,406
West Brandywine, PA, 5,984

West Caln, PA, 6,143
West Chester, PA, 18,041
West Deptford, NJ, 19,380
West Goshen, PA, 18,082
West Norriton, PA, 15,209
West Whiteland, PA, 12,403
Westampton, NJ, 6,004
Westtown, PA, 9,937
Whitemarsh, PA, 14,863
Whitpain, PA, 15,673
Willingboro, NJ, 36,291
Willistown, PA, 9,380
Winslow, NJ, 30,087
Woodbury, NJ, 10,904
Yeadon, PA, 11,980

Phoenix–Mesa, AZ

Apache Junction, 17,931
Avondale, 16,169
Buckeye, 5,038
Casa Grande, 19,082
Chandler, 90,533
Coolidge, 6,927
El Mirage, 5,001
Eloy, 7,211
Florence, 7,510
Fountain Hills, 10,030
Gilbert, 29,188
Glendale, 148,134
Goodyear, 6,258
Guadalupe, 5,458
Mesa, 288,091
Paradise Valley, 11,671
Peoria, 50,618
Phoenix, 983,403
Scottsdale, 130,069
Sun City, 38,126
Sun City West, 15,997
Sun Lakes, 6,578
Surprise, 7,122
Tempe, 141,865

Pine Bluff, AR

Pine Bluff, 57,140

Pittsburgh, PA

Aliquippa, 13,374
Allegheny, 7,895
Ambridge, 8,133
Arnold, 6,113
Avalon, 5,784
Baden, 5,074
Baldwin, 21,923
Beaver, 5,028
Beaver Falls, 10,687
Bellevue, 9,126
Bethel Park, 33,823
Brentwood, 10,823
Bridgeville, 5,445
Brighton, 7,489
Buffalo, 6,317
Bullskin, 7,323
Butler, 17,625
California, 5,748
Canonsburg, 9,200
Canton, 9,256
Carnegie, 9,278
Carroll, 6,210
Castle Shannon, 9,135
Cecil, 8,948
Center, 10,742
Charleroi, 5,014
Chartiers, 7,603
Chippewa, 6,988
Clairton, 9,656
Connellsville, 9,229
Coraopolis, 6,747
Crafton, 7,188
Cranberry, 14,816

Derry, 15,446
Donora, 5,928
Dormont, 9,772
Dunbar, 7,460
Duquesne, 8,525
East Huntingdon, 7,708
Economy, 9,519
Elizabeth, 14,712
Forest Hills, 7,335
Fox Chapel, 5,319
Franklin Park, 10,109
Georges, 6,525
German, 5,596
Glassport, 5,582
Greensburg, 16,318
Hampton, 15,568
Harrison, 11,763
Hempfield, 42,609
Hopewell, 13,274
Indiana, 6,024
Jeannette, 11,221
Jefferson, 9,533
Kennedy, 7,265
Latrobe, 9,265
Ligonier, 6,979
Lower Burrell, 12,251
McCandless, 28,781
McKees Rocks, 7,691
McKeesport, 26,016
Middlesex, 5,578
Monaca, 6,739
Monessen, 9,901
Moon, 19,631
Mount Lebanon, 33,362
Mount Pleasant, 11,341
Munhall, 13,158
Municipality of Monroeville, 29,169
Municipality of Murrysville, 17,240
New Brighton, 6,854
New Kensington, 15,894
New Sewickley, 6,861
North Braddock, 7,036
North Fayette, 9,537
North Huntingdon, 28,158
North Sewickley, 6,178
North Strabane, 8,157
North Union, 13,910
North Versailles, 12,302
Oakmont, 6,961
O'Hara, 9,096
Penn, 15,945
Penn Hills, 51,479
Peters, 14,467
Pittsburgh, 369,879
Pleasant Hills, 8,884
Plum, 25,609
Redstone, 6,459
Richland, 8,600
Robinson, 10,830
Ross, 33,482
Rostraver, 11,224
Salem, 7,282
Scott, 17,118
Scottdale, 5,184
Sewickley, 6,642
Shaler, 30,533
South Fayette, 10,329
South Huntingdon, 6,352
South Park, 14,292
South Strabane, 7,676
South Union, 10,223
Stowe, 7,681
Swissvale, 10,637
Tarentum, 5,674
Turtle Creek, 6,556
Union, 6,322
Uniontown, 12,034

Rochester, MN

Rochester, 70,745

Rochester, NY

Albion, 8,178
Arcadia, 14,855
Avon, 6,283
Batavia, 16,310
Brighton, 34,455
Brockport, 8,749
Canandaigua, 10,725
Chili, 25,178
Dansville, 5,002
East Rochester, 6,932
Fairport, 5,943
Farmington, 10,381
Gates, 28,583
Geneseo, 9,178
Geneva, 14,143
Greece, 90,106
Hamlin, 9,203
Henrietta, 36,376
Hilton, 5,216
Irondequoit, 52,377
Le Roy, 8,176
Livonia, 6,804
Lyons, 6,315
Macedon, 7,375
Manchester, 9,351
Medina, 6,686
Mendon, 6,845
Newark, 9,849
North Dansville, 5,783
Ogden, 16,912
Ontario, 8,560
Palmyra, 7,690
Parma, 13,873
Penfield, 30,219
Perinton, 43,015
Phelps, 6,749
Pittsford, 24,497
Ridgeway, 7,341
Riga, 5,114
Rochester, 231,636
Shelby, 5,509
Sodus, 8,877
Sweden, 14,181
Victor, 7,191
Walworth, 6,945
Webster, 31,639
Wheatland, 5,093
Williamson, 6,540

Rockford, IL

Belvidere, 15,958
Loves Park, 15,462
Machesney Park, 19,033
Rochelle, 8,769
Rockford, 139,426

Rocky Mount, NC

Rocky Mount, 48,977
Tarboro, 11,037

Sacramento, CA

Arden–Arcade, 92,040
Auburn, 10,592
Cameron Park, 11,897
Carmichael, 48,702
Citrus Heights, 107,439
El Dorado Hills, 6,395
Elk Grove, 17,483
Fair Oaks, 26,867
Florin, 24,330
Folsom, 29,802
Foothill Farms, 17,135
Galt, 8,889
La Riviera, 10,986

Laguna, 9,828
Lincoln, 7,248
Loomis, 5,705
North Auburn, 10,301
North Highlands, 42,105
Orangevale, 26,266
Parkway–South Sacramento,
31,903
Placerville, 8,355
Rancho Cordova, 48,731
Rio Linda, 9,481
Rocklin, 19,033
Rosemont, 22,851
Roseville, 44,685
Sacramento, 369,365
South Lake Tahoe, 21,586

Saginaw–Bay City–Midland, MI

Bay City, 38,936
Bridgeport, 8,569
Buena Vista, 8,196
Carrollton, 6,521
Midland, 37,819
Saginaw, 69,512
Saginaw Township North, 23,018
Saginaw Township South, 13,987
Shields, 6,634

St. Catharines–Niagara, ON

Fort Erie, 26,006
Lincoln, 17,149
Niagara Falls, 75,399
Niagara-on-the-Lake, 12,945
Pelham, 13,328
Port Colborne, 18,766
St. Catharines, 129,300
Thorold, 17,542
Welland, 47,914

St. Cloud, MN

St. Cloud, 43,566
Sauk Rapids, 7,825
Waite Park, 5,020

St. John, NB

Quispamsis, 8,446
St. John, 74,969

St. John's, NF

Conception Bay South, 17,590
Goulds, 6,162
Mount Pearl, 23,689
St. John's, 95,770

St. Joseph, MO

St. Joseph, 71,852

St. Louis, MO–IL

Affton, MO, 21,106
Alton, IL, 32,905
Arnold, MO, 18,828
Ballwin, MO, 21,816
Bellefontaine Neighbors, MO,
10,922
Belleville, IL, 42,785
Berkeley, MO, 12,450
Bethalto, IL, 9,507
Black Jack, MO, 6,128
Breckenridge Hills, MO, 5,404
Brentwood, MO, 8,150
Bridgeton, MO, 17,779
Cahokia, IL, 17,550
Centreville, IL, 7,489
Chesterfield, MO, 37,991
Clayton, MO, 13,874
Collinsville, IL, 22,446
Columbia, IL, 5,524
Concord, MO, 19,859

Crestwood, MO, 11,234
Creve Coeur, MO, 12,304
De Soto, MO, 5,993
Dellwood, MO, 5,245
Des Peres, MO, 8,395
East Alton, IL, 7,063
East St. Louis, IL, 40,944
Edwardsville, IL, 14,579
Ellisville, MO, 7,545
Fairview Heights, IL, 14,351
Ferguson, MO, 22,286
Festus, MO, 8,105
Florissant, MO, 51,206
Glasgow Village, MO, 5,199
Glen Carbon, IL, 7,731
Glendale, MO, 5,945
Godfrey, IL, 5,436
Granite City, IL, 32,862
Hazelwood, MO, 15,324
Highland, IL, 7,525
Jennings, MO, 15,905
Jerseyville, IL, 7,382
Kirkwood, MO, 27,291
Ladue, MO, 8,847
Lake St. Louis, MO, 7,400
Lemay, MO, 18,005
Manchester, MO, 6,542
Maplewood, MO, 9,962
Maryland Heights, MO, 25,407
Mascoutah, IL, 5,511
Mehlville, MO, 27,557
Murphy, MO, 9,342
Northwoods, MO, 5,106
O'Fallon, MO, 16,073
O'Fallon, IL, 18,698
Oakville, MO, 31,750
Olivette, MO, 7,573
Overland, MO, 17,987
Pine Lawn, MO, 5,092
Richmond Heights, MO, 10,448
Rock Hill, MO, 5,217
St. Ann, MO, 14,489
St. Charles, MO, 54,555
St. John, MO, 7,466
St. Louis, MO, 396,685
St. Peters, MO, 45,779
Sappington, MO, 10,917
Shrewsbury, MO, 6,416
Spanish Lake, MO, 20,322
Swansea, IL, 8,201
Town and Country, MO, 9,519
Troy, IL, 6,046
Union, MO, 5,909
University City, MO, 40,087
Washington, MO, 10,704
Washington Park, IL, 7,431
Waterloo, IL, 5,072
Webster Groves, MO, 22,987
Wentzville, MO, 5,088
Wood River, IL, 11,490

Salem, OR

Dallas, 9,422
Four Corners, 12,156
Hayesville, 14,318
Keizer, 21,884
Monmouth, 6,288
Salem, 107,786
Silverton, 5,635
Stayton, 5,011
Woodburn, 13,404

Salinas, CA

Castroville, 5,272
Del Monte Forest, 5,069
Greenfield, 7,464
King City, 7,634
Marina, 26,436

Monterey, 31,954
Pacific Grove, 16,117
Prunedale, 7,393
Salinas, 108,777
Seaside, 38,901
Soledad, 7,146

Salt Lake City–Ogden, UT

Bountiful, 36,659
Canyon Rim, 10,527
Centerville, 11,500
Clearfield, 21,435
Clinton, 7,945
Cottonwood Heights, 28,766
Cottonwood West, 17,476
Draper, 7,257
East Millcreek, 21,184
Farmington, 9,028
Holladay–Cottonwood, 14,095
Kaysville, 13,961
Kearns, 28,374
Layton, 41,784
Little Cottonwood Creek Valley,
5,042
Magna, 17,829
Midvale, 11,886
Millcreek, 32,230
Mount Olympus, 7,413
Murray, 31,282
North Ogden, 11,668
North Salt Lake, 6,474
Ogden, 63,909
Oquirrh, 7,593
Riverdale, 6,419
Riverton, 11,261
Roy, 24,603
Salt Lake City, 159,936
Sandy, 75,058
South Jordan, 12,220
South Ogden, 12,105
South Salt Lake, 10,129
Sunset, 5,128
Taylorsville–Bennion, 52,351
Union, 13,684
Washington Terrace, 8,189
West Jordan, 42,892
West Valley City, 86,976
White City, 6,506
Woods Cross, 5,384

San Angelo, TX

San Angelo, 84,474

San Antonio, TX

Alamo Heights, 6,502
Canyon Lake, 9,975
Converse, 8,887
Floresville, 5,247
Kirby, 8,326
Leon Valley, 9,581
Live Oak, 10,023
New Braunfels, 27,334
San Antonio, 935,933
Schertz, 10,426
Seguin, 18,853
Universal City, 13,057
Windcrest, 5,331

San Diego, CA

Alpine, 9,695
Bonita, 12,542
Bostonia, 13,670
Carlsbad, 63,126
Casa de Oro–Mount Helix, 30,727
Chula Vista, 135,163
Coronado, 26,540
El Cajon, 88,693
Encinitas, 55,386

Dishman, 9,671
Fairwood, 5,807
Opportunity, 22,326
Otis Orchards–East Farms, 5,811
Spokane, 177,196
Veradale, 7,836

Springfield, IL

Chatham, 6,074
Springfield, 105,227

Springfield, MA

Agawam, 27,420
Amherst, 36,712
Belchertown, 11,034
Chicopee, 56,398
East Longmeadow, 13,596
Easthampton, 15,141
Granby, 5,573
Holyoke, 44,556
Longmeadow, 15,011
Ludlow, 18,860
Monson, 7,829
Northampton, 29,754
Palmer, 12,181
South Hadley, 16,913
Southwick, 7,541
Springfield, 160,770
Ware, 9,997
West Springfield, 27,906
Westfield, 38,703
Wilbraham, 12,743

Springfield, MO

Republic, 6,292
Springfield, 140,494

Stamford–Norwalk, CT

Darien, 18,259
Greenwich, 58,527
New Canaan, 17,966
Norwalk, 78,887
Stamford, 111,544
Weston, 8,657
Westport, 24,075
Wilton, 15,999

State College, PA

Bellefonte, 6,358
Benner, 5,085
College, 6,709
Ferguson, 9,368
Patton, 9,971
Spring, 5,344
State College, 38,923

Steubenville–Weirton, OH–WV

Steubenville, OH, 22,125
Toronto, OH, 6,127
Weirton, WV, 22,124

Stockton–Lodi, CA

August, 6,376
Country Club, 9,325
Garden Acres, 8,547
Lathrop, 6,841
Lodi, 51,874
Manteca, 40,773
Ripon, 7,455
Stockton, 210,943
Tracy, 33,558

Sudbury, ON

Nickel Centre, 12,332
Onaping Falls, 5,402
Rayside–Balfour, 15,039
Sudbury, 92,884
Valley East, 21,939
Walden, 9,805

Sumter, SC

Sumter, 41,943

Syracuse, NY

Auburn, 31,258
Baldwinsville, 6,591
Brutus, 5,013
Camillus, 23,625
Cazenovia, 6,514
Cicero, 25,560
Clay, 59,749
De Witt, 25,148
Eaton, 5,362
Elbridge, 6,192
Fulton, 12,929
Geddes, 17,677
Granby, 7,013
Hamilton, 6,221
Hastings, 8,113
LaFayette, 5,105
Lenox, 8,621
Lysander, 16,346
Manlius, 30,656
Marcellus, 6,465
Mexico, 5,050
North Syracuse, 7,363
Oneida, 10,850
Onondaga, 18,396
Oswego, 19,195
Pompey, 5,317
Richland, 5,917
Salina, 35,145
Schroeppel, 8,931
Scriba, 6,472
Skaneateles, 7,526
Solvay, 6,717
Sullivan, 14,622
Syracuse, 163,860
Van Buren, 13,367
Volney, 5,676

Tacoma, WA

Artondale, 7,141
Bonney Lake, 7,494
Edgewood–North Hill, 9,120
Elk Plain, 12,197
Fircrest, 5,258
Fort Lewis, 22,224
Lakewood, 58,412
Midland, 5,587
Parkland, 20,882
Prairie Ridge, 8,278
Puyallup, 23,875
South Hill, 12,963
Spanaway, 15,001
Steilacoom, 5,728
Summit, 6,312
Sumner, 6,281
Tacoma, 176,664
University Place, 27,701
Waller, 6,415

Tallahassee, FL

Quincy, 7,444
Tallahassee, 124,773

Tampa–St. Petersburg–Clearwater, FL

Apollo Beach, 6,025
Bayonet Point, 21,860
Beacon Square, 6,265
Bloomingdale, 13,912
Brandon, 57,985
Brooksville, 7,440
Carrollwood, 7,195
Carrollwood Village, 15,051
Clearwater, 98,784
Dade City, 5,633

Del Rio, 8,248
Dunedin, 34,012
East Lake–Orient Park, 6,171
Egypt Lake, 14,580
Elfers, 12,356
Gibsonton, 7,706
Greater Northdale, 16,318
Gulfport, 11,727
Highpoint, 13,818
Holiday, 19,360
Hudson, 7,344
Jasmine Estates, 17,136
Lake Magdalene, 15,973
Land O' Lakes, 7,892
Largo, 65,674
Lealman, 21,748
Lutz, 10,552
Mango, 8,700
New Port Richey, 14,044
New Port Richey East, 9,683
Oldsmar, 8,361
Palm Harbor, 50,256
Palm River–Clair Mel, 13,691
Pinellas Park, 43,426
Plant City, 22,754
Riverview, 6,478
Ruskin, 6,046
Safety Harbor, 15,124
St. Petersburg, 238,629
St. Petersburg Beach, 9,200
Seffner, 5,371
Seminole, 9,251
South Pasadena, 5,644
Spring Hill, 31,117
Sun City Center, 8,326
Tampa, 280,015
Tarpon Springs, 17,906
Temple Terrace, 16,444
Town 'n' Country, 60,946
Treasure Island, 7,266
University West, 23,760
West Park, 10,347
Zephyrhills, 8,220

Terre Haute, IN

Brazil, 7,640
Clinton, 5,040
Terre Haute, 57,483

Texarkana, TX–Texarkana, AR

New Boston, 5,057
Texarkana, 31,656

Thunder Bay, ON

Thunder Bay, 113,946

Toledo, OH

Bowling Green, 28,176
Maumee, 15,561
Northwood, 5,506
Oregon, 18,334
Perrysburg, 12,551
Rossford, 5,861
Sylvania, 17,301
Toledo, 332,943
Wauseon, 6,322

Topeka, KS

Topeka, 119,883

Toronto, ON

Ajax, 57,350
Aurora, 29,454
Bradford–West Gwillimbury, 17,702
Brampton, 234,445
Caledon, 34,965
East Gwillimbury, 18,367
Etobicoke, 309,993

Georgina, 29,746
Halton Hills, 36,816
Markham, 153,811
Milton, 32,075
Mississauga, 463,388
Newmarket, 45,474
North York, 562,564
Oakville, 114,670
Orangeville, 17,921
Pickering, 68,631
Richmond Hill, 80,142
Scarborough, 524,598
Toronto, 635,395
Vaughan, 111,359
Whitchurch–Stouffville, 18,357
York, 140,525

Trenton, NJ

East Windsor, 22,353
Ewing, 34,185
Hamilton, 86,553
Hightstown, 5,126
Hopewell, 11,590
Lawrence, 25,787
Princeton, 13,198
Trenton, 88,675
Washington, 5,815
West Windsor, 16,021

Trois–Rivieres, PQ

Bécancour, 10,911
Cap-de-la-Madeleine, 33,716
Trois–Rivieres, 49,426
Trois–Rivieres–Ouest, 20,076

Tucson, AZ

Flowing Wells, 14,013
Green Valley, 13,231
Oro Valley, 6,670
South Tucson, 5,093
Tucson, 405,390

Tulsa, OK

Bixby, 9,419
Broken Arrow, 58,441
Claremore, 13,280
Coweta, 6,159
Glenpool, 6,688
Jenks, 7,493
Owasso, 11,063
Sand Springs, 15,015
Sapulpa, 18,074
Tulsa, 367,290
Wagoner, 6,894

Tuscaloosa, AL

Northport, 17,366
Tuscaloosa, 77,759

Tyler, TX

Tyler, 75,450

Utica–Rome, NY

Camden, 5,134
Frankfort, 7,494
German Flatts, 14,345
Herkimer, 10,401
Ilion, 8,888
Kirkland, 10,153
Lee, 7,115
Little Falls, 5,829
Marcy, 8,685
New Hartford, 21,640
Rome, 44,350
Utica, 68,637
Vernon, 5,338
Verona, 6,460
Vienna, 5,564
Westmoreland, 5,737
Whitestown, 18,985

Vallejo–Fairfield–Napa, CA
American Canyon, 7,706
Benicia, 24,437
Dixon, 10,401
Fairfield, 77,211
Napa, 61,842
Suisun City, 22,686
Vacaville, 71,479
Vallejo, 109,199

Vancouver, BC
Burnaby, 158,858
Coquitlam, 84,021
Delta, 88,978
Langley, 66,040
Maple Ridge, 48,422
New Westminster, 43,585
North Vancouver, 75,157
Pitt Meadows, 11,147
Port Coquitlam, 36,773
Port Moody, 17,712
Richmond, 126,624
Surrey, 245,173
Vancouver, 471,844
West Vancouver, 38,783
White Rock, 16,314

Vancouver, WA
Camas, 6,442
Cascade Park East, 6,996
Cascade Park West, 6,656
Ellsworth North, 5,796
Evergreen, 11,249
Five Corners, 6,776
Hazel Dell North, 6,924
Hazel Dell South, 5,796
Lake Shore, 6,268
Minnehaha, 9,661
Orchards North, 6,479
Orchards South, 12,956
Salmon Creek, 11,989
Vancouver, 46,380
Vancouver Mall, 6,938

Ventura, CA
Camarillo, 52,303
El Rio, 6,419
Fillmore, 11,992
Mira Monte, 7,744
Moorpark, 25,494
Ojai, 7,613
Oxnard, 142,216
Port Hueneme, 20,319
Santa Paula, 25,062
Simi Valley, 100,217
Thousand Oaks, 104,352
Ventura, 92,575

Victoria, BC
Central Saanich, 13,684
Colwood, 13,468
Esquimalt, 16,192
North Saanich, 9,645
Oak Bay, 17,815
Saanich, 95,577
Sidney, 10,082
Victoria, 71,228
View Royal, 5,925

Victoria, TX
Victoria, 55,076

Vineland–Millville–Bridgeton, NJ
Bridgeton, 18,942
Commercial, 5,026
Fairfield, 5,699
Maurice River, 6,648

Millville, 25,992
Upper Deerfield, 6,927
Vineland, 54,780

Visalia–Tulare–Porterville, CA
Dinuba, 12,743
Earlimart, 5,881
East Porterville, 5,790
Exeter, 7,276
Farmersville, 6,235
Lindsay, 8,338
Orosi, 5,486
Porterville, 29,563
Tulare, 33,249
Visalia, 75,636
Woodlake, 5,678

Waco, TX
Bellmead, 8,336
Hewitt, 8,983
Robinson, 7,111
Waco, 103,590
Woodway, 8,695

Washington, DC–MD–VA–WV
Adelphi, MD, 13,524
Alexandria, VA, 111,183
Annandale, VA, 50,975
Aquia Harbour, VA, 6,308
Arlington, VA, 170,936
Aspen Hill, MD, 45,494
Bailey's Crossroads, VA, 19,507
Ballenger Creek, MD, 5,546
Belle Haven, VA, 6,427
Beltsville, MD, 14,476
Bethesda, MD, 62,936
Bladensburg, MD, 8,064
Bowie, MD, 37,589
Brunswick, MD, 5,117
Bull Run, VA, 5,525
Burke, VA, 57,734
Burtonsville, MD, 5,853
Cabin John–Brookmont, MD, 5,341
Calverton, MD, 11,961
Camp Springs, MD, 16,392
Centreville, VA, 26,585
Chantilly, VA, 29,337
Chesapeake Ranch Estates, MD, 5,423
Cheverly, MD, 6,023
Chevy Chase, MD, 8,559
Chillum, MD, 31,309
Clinton, MD, 19,987
Cloverly, MD, 7,904
Colesville, MD, 18,819
College Park, MD, 21,927
Coral Hills, MD, 11,032
Countryside, VA, 8,349
Culpeper, VA, 8,581
Dale City, VA, 47,170
Damascus, MD, 9,817
District Heights, MD, 6,704
Dunn Loring, VA, 6,509
East Riverdale, MD, 14,187
Fairfax, VA, 19,622
Fairland, MD, 19,828
Falls Church, VA, 9,578
Forestville, MD, 16,731
Franconia, VA, 19,882
Frederick, MD, 40,148
Fredericksburg, VA, 19,027
Friendly, MD, 9,028
Front Royal, VA, 11,880
Gaithersburg, MD, 39,542
Germantown, MD, 41,145

Glenarden, MD, 5,025
Glenn Dale, MD, 9,689
Great Falls, VA, 6,945
Greater Upper Marlboro, MD, 11,528
Green Valley, MD, 9,424
Greenbelt, MD, 21,096
Groveton, VA, 19,997
Herndon, VA, 16,139
Hillandale, MD, 10,318
Hillcrest Heights, MD, 17,136
Huntington, VA, 7,489
Hyattsville, MD, 13,864
Hybla Valley, VA, 15,491
Idylwood, VA, 14,710
Jefferson, VA, 25,782
Kentland, MD, 7,967
Kettering, MD, 9,901
La Plata, MD, 5,841
Lake Barcroft, VA, 8,686
Lake Ridge, VA, 23,862
Landover, MD, 5,052
Langley Park, MD, 17,475
Lanham–Seabrook, MD, 16,792
Largo, MD, 9,475
Laurel, MD, 19,438
Leesburg, VA, 16,202
Lincolnia, VA, 13,041
Lorton, VA, 15,385
Manassas, VA, 27,957
Manassas Park, VA, 6,734
Mantua, VA, 6,804
Marlow Heights, MD, 5,885
Marlton, MD, 5,523
Martinsburg, WV, 14,073
McLean, VA, 38,168
Merrifield, VA, 8,399
Mitchellville, MD, 12,593
Montclair, VA, 11,399
Montgomery Village, MD, 32,315
Mount Rainier, MD, 7,954
Mount Vernon, VA, 27,485
New Carrollton, MD, 12,002
Newington, VA, 17,965
North Bethesda, MD, 29,656
North Kensington, MD, 8,607
North Potomac, MD, 18,456
North Springfield, VA, 8,996
Oakton, VA, 24,610
Olney, MD, 23,019
Oxon Hill–Glassmanor, MD, 35,794
Palmer Park, MD, 7,019
Pimmit Hills, VA, 6,019
Potomac, MD, 45,634
Redland, MD, 16,145
Reston, VA, 48,556
Riverdale, MD, 5,185
Rockville, MD, 44,835
Rosaryville, MD, 8,976
Rose Hill, VA, 12,675
Rossmoor, MD, 6,182
St. Charles, MD, 28,717
Seat Pleasant, MD, 5,359
Seven Corners, VA, 7,280
Silver Spring, MD, 76,046
South Kensington, MD, 8,777
South Laurel, MD, 18,591
Springfield, VA, 23,706
Sterling, VA, 20,512
Sudley, VA, 7,321
Sugarland Run, VA, 9,357
Suitland–Silver Hill, MD, 35,111
Takoma Park, MD, 16,690
Temple Hills, MD, 6,865
Tysons Corner, VA, 13,124
Vienna, VA, 14,852
Waldorf, MD, 15,058

Walker Mill, MD, 10,920
Washington, DC, 606,900
West Gate, VA, 6,565
West Springfield, VA, 28,126
Wheaton–Glenmont, MD, 53,720
White Oak, MD, 18,671
Wolf Trap, VA, 13,133
Woodbridge, VA, 26,401
Woodlawn, MD, 5,329
Yorkshire, VA, 5,699

Waterbury, CT
Middlebury, 6,078
Naugatuck, 30,683
Prospect, 8,058
Thomaston, 7,311
Waterbury, 112,292
Watertown, 20,859
Wolcott, 14,120
Woodbury, 8,322

Waterloo–Cedar Falls, IA
Cedar Falls, 34,298
Waterloo, 66,467

Wausau, WI
Wausau, 37,060
Weston, 9,714

West Palm Beach–Boca Raton, FL
Belle Glade, 16,177
Boca Del Mar, 17,754
Boca Raton, 61,492
Boynton Beach, 46,194
Century Village, 8,363
Delray Beach, 47,181
Greenacres City, 18,683
Hamptons at Boca Raton, 11,686
Jupiter, 24,986
Kings Point, 12,422
Lake Park, 6,704
Lake Worth, 28,564
Lantana, 8,392
North Palm Beach, 11,343
Pahokee, 6,822
Palm Beach, 9,814
Palm Beach Gardens, 22,965
Palm Springs, 9,763
Riviera Beach, 27,639
Royal Palm Beach, 14,589
Sandalfoot Cove, 14,214
Villages of Oriole, 5,698
Wellington, 20,670
West Palm Beach, 67,643
Westgate–Belvedere Homes, 6,880

Wheeling, WV–OH
Bellaire, OH, 6,028
Martins Ferry, OH, 7,990
Moundsville, WV, 10,753
St. Clairsville, OH, 5,162
Wheeling, WV, 34,700

Wichita, KS
Augusta, 7,876
Derby, 14,699
El Dorado, 11,504
Haysville, 8,364
Newton, 16,700
Park City, 5,050
Wichita, 304,011

Wichita Falls, TX
Burkburnett, 10,145
Iowa Park, 6,072
Wichita Falls, 96,259

Williamsport, PA
Loyalsock, 10,644
Old Lycoming, 5,526
South Williamsport, 6,496
Williamsport, 31,933

Wilmington, NC
Masonboro, 7,010
Seagate, 5,444
Smith Creek, 7,461
Wilmington, 55,530

Wilmington–Newark, DE–MD
Brookside, DE, 15,307
Claymont, DE, 9,800
Edgemoor, DE, 5,853
Elkton, MD, 9,073
Elsmere, DE, 5,935
Newark, DE, 25,098
Pike Creek, DE, 10,163
Stanton, DE, 5,028
Talleyville, DE, 6,346
Wilmington, DE, 71,529
Wilmington Manor, DE, 8,568

Windsor, ON
Essex, 6,759
Tecumseh, 10,495
Windsor, 191,435

Winnipeg, MB
Winnipeg, 616,790

Worcester–Fitchburg–Leominster, MA
Ashburnham, 5,433
Athol, 11,451
Auburn, 15,005
Blackstone, 8,023
Charlton, 9,576
Clinton, 13,222
Douglas, 5,438
Dudley, 9,540
Fitchburg, 41,194
Gardner, 20,125
Grafton, 13,035
Harvard, 12,329
Holden, 14,628
Hopedale, 5,666
Lancaster, 6,661
Leicester, 10,191
Leominster, 38,145
Lunenburg, 9,117
Milford, 25,355
Millbury, 12,228
Northborough, 11,929
Northbridge, 13,371
Oxford, 12,588
Shrewsbury, 24,146
Southborough, 6,628
Southbridge, 17,816
Spencer, 11,645
Sterling, 6,481
Sturbridge, 7,775
Sutton, 6,824
Templeton, 6,438

Uxbridge, 10,415
Webster, 16,196
West Boylston, 6,611
Westborough, 14,133
Westminster, 6,191
Winchendon, 8,805
Worcester, 169,759

Yakima, WA
Grandview, 7,169
Selah, 5,113
Sunnyside, 11,238
Toppenish, 7,419
West Valley, 6,594
Yakima, 54,827

Yolo, CA
Davis, 46,209
West Sacramento, 28,898
Woodland, 39,802

York, PA
Chanceford, 5,026
Dover, 15,668
Fairview, 13,258
Hanover, 14,399
Hellam, 5,123
Jackson, 6,244
Lower Windsor, 7,051
Manchester, 7,517
Newberry, 12,003
North Codorus, 7,565
Penn, 11,658
Red Lion, 6,130

Shrewsbury, 5,898
Spring Garden, 11,207
Springettsbury, 21,564
West Manchester, 14,369
Windsor, 9,424
York, 42,192

Youngstown–Warren, OH
Austintown, 32,371
Boardman, 38,596
Campbell, 10,038
Canfield, 5,409
Cortland, 5,666
East Liverpool, 13,654
East Palestine, 5,168
Girard, 11,304
Howland Center, 6,732
Hubbard, 8,248
Niles, 21,128
Salem, 12,233
Struthers, 12,284
Warren, 50,793
Youngstown, 95,706

Yuba City, CA
Linda, 13,033
Marysville, 12,324
Olivehurst, 9,738
South Yuba City, 8,816
Yuba City, 27,437

Yuma, AZ
Fortuna Foothills, 7,737
Somerton, 5,282
Yuma, 54,923

List of Tables, Maps, and Diagrams

ABOUT THE AUTHORS

David Savageau is one of the featured presenters at the State Department's quarterly seminars on retirement. He is the author of the best-selling *Retirement Places Rated* and principal-in-charge of PreLOCATION, a personal relocation consulting firm.

Richard Boyer is writer-in-residence at Western Carolina University. In addition to co-authoring *Places Rated Almanac,* he is the author of eight novels, including *Billingsgate Shoal,* winner of the Mystery Writers of America's Edgar award for Best Mystery Novel of 1982.

They would appreciate all comments, criticisms, and suggestions for improving the next edition of *Places Rated Almanac.* Write to:

Places Rated Partnership
P.O. Box 1327
Gloucester, MA 01931

New! Places Rated Almanac Interactive Software
It Helps You Find the City That's Best for You!

Introducing a brand-new product that offers unique access to the wealth of information compiled by the *Places Rated Almanac* team—the *Places Rated Almanac Software Companion*.

With this new *Software Companion* you can:

- Create a new ranking of the cities based on the criteria most important to you
- View information at the touch of a button
- Readily compare metro areas
- Print your own specially designed reports

The *Software Companion* comes with the *Places Rated Almanac* in a specially designed Book/Disk set (Price: $34.95, ISBN: 0-671-88395-X). Ask your bookstore for a copy. The *Software Companion* is also available separately by mail (see ordering information below).

Want even more?

Places Rated Almanac Software is an enhanced version of the Software Companion, offering additional information on tourism and real-estate brokerages—and even more ways to personalize and get the most out of the *Places Rated Almanac*. Available for $49.95 by calling Que Software at 1-800-428-5331 or at your local computer software store.

Minimum System Requirements: IBM PC and compatibles; Microsoft Windows Version 3.0 or higher; EGA or VGA display; 2 Mb RAM; 3 Mb available hard disk space.

- -

Mail in this coupon to order the *Places Rated Almanac Software Companion* disk.

YES! Please send me the software indicated below (30-day money-back guarantee if software returned unopened.)

Qty	ISBN#	Product	Price	Total
___	0-671-88393-3	PRA Software Companion 3.5" Disk	$20.00	$____
___	0-671-88394-1	PRA Software Companion 5.25" Disk	$20.00	$____

Subtotal .... $____
Sales Tax (CA, CT, FL, IL, NJ, NY, WA, NY, TN, Canada residents only) .... $____
Shipping (Orders with check or money order are Free Freight. Credit card orders are charged exact UPS shipping amount.) .... $____

Total Due .... $____

Name _____

Street Address _____

City, State, Zip Code _____

Daytime Phone _____

Payment Method: ___ Check or Money Order (Payable to Simon & Schuster Mail Order Dept. ___ Master Card ___ VISA

Card Number _____ Expiration Date _____

Signature _____

Mail to:
Simon & Schuster Mail Order Dept.
200 Old Tappan Rd.
Old Tappan, NJ 07675

- -